Wiley CIAexcel® Exam Review 2019

Wiley CIAexcel® Exam Review 2019

Part 3: Business Knowledge for Internal Auditing

S. Rao Vallabhaneni

Wiley Efficient Learning™

Cover image: © John Wiley & Sons, Inc.
Cover design: © John Wiley & Sons, Inc.

This book is printed on acid-free paper.

Published by John Wiley & Sons, Inc., Hoboken, New Jersey
Published simultaneously in Canada

For general information about our other products and services, please contact our Customer Care Department within the United States at (800) 762-2974, outside the United States at (317) 572-3993 or fax (317) 572-4002.

Wiley publishes in a variety of print and electronic formats and by print-on-demand. Some material included with standard print versions of this book may not be included in e-books or in print-on-demand. If this book refers to media such as a CD or DVD that is not included in the version you purchased, you may download this material at http://booksupport.wiley.com. For more information about Wiley products, visit www.wiley.com.

Library of Congress Cataloging-in-Publication Data:

ISBN 978-1-119-52449-6; ISBN 978-1-119-52445-8 (ePDF); ISBN 978-1-119-52451-9 (ePub)

Printed in the United States of America

V10009243_040919

Contents

Preface

The Certified Internal Auditor (CIA) Examination is a program of the Institute of Internal Auditors (IIA), Inc. The CIA examination certifies a person as a professional internal auditor and is intended to measure the knowledge, skills, and competency required in the field of internal auditing. The Certified Internal Auditor designation is the hallmark of an expert in internal auditing. Wiley's CIA Exam Review Products are developed to help prepare a CIA Exam candidate for the CIA Exam by reflecting the new exam syllabus effective from January 2019 and by reflecting the new International Professional Practices Framework of 2017 (new IPPF of 2017) issued in January 2017 consisting of professional standards. **Note that the IPPF Standards do not apply to Part 3 exam, including the Review Book.**

The new CIA Exam syllabus tests a CIA Exam candidate's knowledge at two cognitive levels—the proficient level and the basic level—as indicated in the IIA's content specifications outlines (www.theiia.org). These cognitive levels suggest allocating more time and effort to prepare for the proficient-level topics and comparatively less time and effort to prepare for the basic-level topics. The scope of the new CIA Exam consists of three parts:

> Part 1: Essentials of Internal Auditing
>
> Part 2: Practice of Internal Auditing
>
> Part 3: Business Knowledge for Internal Auditing

This Review Book covers Part 3 of the CIA Exam effective from January 2019.

For each part of the exam, Wiley has developed a comprehensive suite of review products to study and prepare for the CIA Exam. This suite includes (1) Review Book (Study Guide), (2) Focus Notes, and (3) Web-Based Online Test Bank Software.

1. The **Review Book** provides a thorough presentation of theoretical coverage of the subject matter as required in the exam syllabus.

2. The **Focus Notes** (index cards) provide a quick review of the same subject matter presented in the Review Book but in a condensed manner to reinforce key concepts. Wiley's theme in the Focus Notes is Remember, Reinforce, and Recall key concepts.

3. The **Web-based online test bank software** provides hundreds of sample multiple-choice questions to practice. We suggest repeating the test bank several times for reinforcement before taking the actual exam. The actual CIA Exam questions will be harder than these sample questions. However, practicing the sample questions yields several benefits to

students, such as (1) providing a knowledge base of the subject matter; (2) conditioning students to the exam mode; (3) using sample questions close to the actual exam questions; and (4) above all, building student confidence in taking the real CIA Exam.

Wiley's goal is to provide all the required study materials for CIA Exam study and preparation in one place with one source for either self-study or a group study effort. Visit www.wileyCIA.com for product details and order placement.

We suggest students use a sequential, four-step study approach for each part of the exam:

1. Read the Glossary section at the end of each part's Review Book for a better understanding of key technical terms.

2. Study the theory domains from each part of the Review Book.

3. Practice the multiple-choice questions from the online test bank for each part.

4. Read the Focus Notes for each part for a quick review at any time and especially before taking the actual exam.

Administrative Matters

We encourage the new, prospective CIA Exam candidates to contact the Institute of Internal Auditors directly for exam application forms, exam eligibility requirements, online exam-taking sites and fees, and general information about the exam.

Institute of Internal Auditors

1035 Greenwood Boulevard, Suite 401

Lake Mary, FL, 32746, USA

Phone: +1-407-937-1100, Fax: +1-407-937-1108

Website: www.theiia.org

Acknowledgments

The author is indebted to a number of people and organizations that helped to improve the content and quality of this book. Thanks to the Director of Certifications and the CIA certification team at the Institute of Internal Auditors (IIA), Lake Mary, Florida for providing great assistance during the writing of these books. Special thanks to the IIA for providing previous CIA Exam questions, answers, and explanations, IIA's IPPF *Standards, Implementation Guidance, Code of Ethics, Practice Guides, and CIA's Model Exam* questions. Many thanks also go to Wiley's editorial content management and marketing teams for their capable assistance in completing the CIA Exam Review Products.

Specifically, the author wants to thank the following for using or adapting their materials:

- U.S. Government Accountability Office (GAO), Washington, DC, www.gao.gov

- U.S. Federal Trade Commission (FTC), Washington, DC, www.ftc.gov

- U.S. Securities and Exchange Commission (SEC), Washington, DC, www.sec.gov

- U.S. Federal Reserve System, Washington, DC, www.federalreserve.gov

- U.S. National Institute of Standards and Technology (NIST) publications, Washington, DC, www.nist.gov

- U.S. Computer Emergency Readiness Team (US-CERT) publications, Washington, DC, www.us-cert.gov

- U.S. Office of Management and Budget, Washington, DC, www.omb.gov

- U.S. Federal Financial Institutions Examination Council (FFIEC), IT Examination Handbook, Washington, DC, www.ffiec.gov

- U.S. Department of Justice (DoJ), Criminal Division, Cybersecurity Unit, Washington, DC, www.justice.gov

- U.S. Conference Board, Business Cycle Indicators, Washington, DC, www.conference-board.org

- Open Web Application Security Project (OWASP), Mobile Security and Application Security Risks, 2017, www.owasp.org

- Four Components of an Enterprise Risk Reporting and Management Platform, Analyst Insight, Blue Hill Research, February 2015. www.bluehillresearch.com.

- Audit Processes Add Value and Objectivity to Cyber Risk and Security Programming—Part 1 blog, by Simon Goldstein, October 2018, DoubleCheck Software Company, www.doublechecksoftware.com.

- Cyber Kill Chain Framework by Lockheed Martin Corporation, www.lockheedmartin.com.

CIA Exam Content Syllabus and Specifications

Part 3 of the revised CIA Exam syllabus effective January 2019 is called **Business Knowledge for Internal Auditing** and includes four domains containing several topics. These four domains cover:

1. Business Acumen
2. Information Security
3. Information Technology
4. Financial Management

Each domain is assigned with a relative weight of its importance to each part, expressed as a percentage of study time and effort required (i.e., higher weights require larger amounts of study time and effort). Each topic within a domain will be tested at the cognitive level of Proficient (P) or Basic (B). Here, "proficient" means CIA Exam candidates are required to demonstrate a proficiency in their KSAs. "Basic" means candidates are required to demonstrate a basic comprehension of concepts. Greater amounts of study time and effort are required for topics tested at the proficient level. Note that the combination of higher weight and proficient level requires a greater amount of study time and effort to earn success in the exam than the combination of lower weight and basic level.

The exam duration for Part 3 is 2.0 hours (120 minutes) with 100 multiple-choice questions. The following is a breakdown of domains and topics in Part 3.

Domain 1: Business Acumen (35%)

1. **Organizational Objectives, Behavior, and Performance**

    A Describe the strategic planning process and key activities (e.g., objective setting, globalization and competitive considerations, alignment to the organization's mission and values). (B)

    B Examine common performance measures (e.g., financial, operational, qualitative vs. quantitative methods, productivity, quality, efficiency, economical, and effectiveness). (P)

  C Explain organizational behavior (e.g., individuals in organizations, groups, and how organizations behave) and different performance management techniques (e.g., traits, organizational politics, motivation, job design, rewards, and work schedules). (B)

  D Describe management's effectiveness to lead, monitor, and guide people, build organizational commitment, and demonstrate entrepreneurial ability. (B)

2. Organizational Structure and Business Processes

  A Appraise the risk and control implications of different organizational configuration structures (e.g., centralized vs. decentralized and flat structure vs. traditional structure). (B)

  B Examine the risk and control implications of common business processes (e.g., human resources, procurement, product development, sales, marketing, logistics, and management of outsourced processes). (P)

  C Identify project management techniques (e.g., project plan and scope, time or team or resources, or cost management, and change management). (B)

  D Recognize the various forms and elements of contracts (e.g., formality, consideration, unilateral, or bilateral). (B)

3. Data Analytics

  A Describe data analytics, data types, data governance, and the value of using data analytics in internal auditing. (B)

  B Explain the data analytics process (i.e., define questions, obtain relevant data, clean or normalize data, analyze data, and communicate results). (B)

  C Recognize the application of data analytics methods in internal auditing (e.g., anomaly detection, diagnostic analysis, predictive analysis, network analysis, and text analysis). (B)

Domain 2: Information Security (25%)

1. Information Security

  A Differentiate types of common physical security control (e.g., cards, keys, and biometrics). (B)

  B Differentiate the various forms of user authentication and authorization controls (e.g., password, two-level authentication, biometrics, digital signatures) and identify potential risks. (B)

  C Explain the purpose and use of various information security controls (e.g., encryption, firewalls, and antivirus). (B)

  D Recognize data privacy laws and their potential impact on data security policies and practices. (B)

  E Recognize emerging technology practices and their impact on security (e.g., bring your own device [BYOD], smart devices, and the Internet of Things [IoT]). (B)

  F Recognize existing and emerging cybersecurity risks (e.g., hacking, piracy, tampering, ransomware attacks, and phishing attacks). (B)

  G Describe cybersecurity-related policies and information security–related policies. (B)

Domain 3: Information Technology (20%)

1. Application and System Software

A Recognize core activities in the systems development life cycle and delivery (e.g., requirements definition, design, developing, testing, debugging, deployment, and maintenance) and the importance of change controls throughout the process. (B)

B Explain basic database terms (e.g., data, database, record, object, field, and schema) and the Internet terms (e.g., HTML, HTTP, URL, domain name, browser, click-through, electronic data interchange [EDI], and cookies). (B)

C Identify key characteristics of software systems (e.g., customer relationship management [CRM] systems, enterprise resource planning [ERP] systems, and governance, risk, and compliance [GRC] systems). (B)

2. IT Infrastructure and IT Control Frameworks

A Explain basic information technology (IT) infrastructure and network concepts (e.g., server, mainframe, client-server configuration, gateways, routers, LAN, WAN, and VPN) and identify potential risks. (B)

B Define the operational roles of a network administrator, database administrator, and help desk. (B)

C Recognize the purpose and applications of IT control frameworks (e.g., COBIT, ISO 27000, and ITIL) and basic IT controls. (B)

3. Disaster Recovery

A Explain disaster recovery planning site concepts (e.g., hot site, warm site, and cold site). (B)

B Explain the purpose of systems and data backup. (B)

C Explain the purpose of systems and data recovery procedures. (B)

Domain 4: Financial Management (20%)

1. Financial Accounting and Finance

A Identify concepts and underlying principles of financial accounting (e.g., types of financial statements and terminologies such as bonds, leases, pensions, intangible assets, and research and development). (B)

B Recognize advanced and emerging financial accounting concepts (e.g., consolidation, investments, fair-value partnerships, foreign currency transactions). (B)

C Interpret financial analysis (e.g., horizontal and vertical analysis and ratio analysis (e.g., activity ratios, profitability ratios, liquidity ratios, and leverage ratios). (P)

D Describe revenue cycle, current asset management activities and accounting, and supply-chain management (including inventory valuation and accounts payable). (B)

E Describe capital budgeting, capital structure, basic taxation, and transfer pricing. (B)

2. Managerial Accounting

A   Explain general concepts of managerial accounting (e.g., cost-volume-profit analysis, budgeting, expense allocation, and cost-benefit analysis). (B)

B   Differentiate costing systems (e.g., absorption, variable, fixed, activity-based, and standard). (B)

C   Distinguish various costs (e.g., relevant costs, irrelevant costs, and incremental costs) and their use in decision making. (B)

CIA Exam-Taking Tips

The types of questions a candidate can expect to see in the CIA Exam are fact-based, concept-based, application-based, objective-based, and scenario-based multiple-choice (M/C) questions with four choices of A, B, C, and D or a, b, c, and d. A systematic method in reading, interpreting, and answering the M/C questions can make the difference between a pass or fail in the exam. Moreover, answering the M/C questions requires a good amount of practice and effort.

These tips and techniques will be helpful in answering the CIA Exam questions:

- Stay with your first impression of the correct choice.

- Know the subject area or topic. Don't read too much into the question.

- Remember that questions are independent of specific country, products, practices, vendors, hardware, software, or industry.

- Read the last sentence of the question first followed by all choices and then the body (stem) of the question paragraph containing the last sentence. This is a reversal of normal reading to highlight the key points quickly.

- Read the question twice, read the keywords twice, and watch for tip-off words that denote absolute conditions. Examples of keywords are *most, least, major, minor, all, not,* and *except.* Examples of tip-off words are *always, never,* and *every.*

- Do not project the question into your own organizational environment, practices, policies, procedures, standards, and guidelines. The examination focuses on the IIA's Professional Standards and Publications and on the CIA Exam syllabus (i.e., content specifications). Also, questions require a universal answer and knowledge of best practices.

- Try to eliminate wrong choices as quickly as possible. When you get down to two semifinal choices, take a big-picture approach. For example, if choices A and D are semifinalists, and choice D could be a part of choice A, then select choice A; or if choice D could be a more complete answer, then select choice D.

- Don't spend too much time on one question. If you are not sure of an answer, move on, and go back to it if time permits. The last resort is to guess the answer. There is no penalty for guessing the wrong answer.

Remember that success in any professional certification examination depends on several factors required of any student, such as time management skills, preparation time and effort levels, education and experience levels, memory recall of the subject matter in a timely manner, calm and collected state of mind before or during the exam, and decision-making skills. Good luck on the exam!

Business Acumen (35%)

This domain focuses on several key theoretical topics. It presents a corporation's mission, vision, goals, objectives, business strategy, and strategic planning process. It describes how to measure performance in the right way. It discusses organizational behavior, performance management, organizational structures, and common business processes. It compares and contrasts the roles of managers, leaders, and entrepreneurs. It highlights project management techniques and business contracts. It explores big data and data analytics that can be performed with big data. It explains what is involved in gathering business intelligence for use in formulating a business strategy. This domain highlights major business functions, business development life cycle, business skills, and business controls. All these topics are tested at the basic and proficient cognitive levels in Part 3 of the CIA Exam with a 35% weight given.

With respect to the CIA Exam, cognitive levels are labeled as proficient level and basic level. These cognitive levels suggest that more time and effort should be spent in studying and mastering the subject matter covered in the topics labeled as the proficient level. Comparatively less time and effort should be spent on the topics labeled as the basic level.

1.1 Strategic Planning Process

This section begins with the definition of business acumen, which sets the foundation and tone for the entire domain. A business's strategy, containing mission, vision, strategies, goals, objectives, and plans, is discussed with different types of strategies. Competitive forces, competitive strategies, and competitive analysis are highlighted. This section discusses value chain analysis and business portfolio models (i.e., BCG and GE). An overview of a business's strategic management and strategic planning process is presented. Related strategies and frameworks such as blue-ocean and red-ocean strategies, McKinsey 7-S Framework, and business policy are discussed.

(a) Business Acumen Defined

Business acumen means possessing the essential knowledge, skills, and abilities (KSAs) to succeed in the business field. Simply stated, business acumen means business savvy in terms of increasing revenues, decreasing costs, increasing profits, enhancing the stock market price, and creating a sustainable value to all stakeholders.

Business acumen is a collective term representing several parts, such as:

- Obtaining a deep understanding of a business's mission and vision

- Developing a business's strategies, goals, objectives, and plans

- Developing grand strategy, formulating strategic plans, executing (implementing) strategic plans, and exercising strategic controls

- Understanding the inner workings of core business functions (e.g., marketing, operating, and finance) and noncore business functions (e.g., accounting, human resources, IT, supply chain (procurement and logistics), legal, and public relations).

- Introducing new products and services with a long-lasting and built-in value into existing markets and new markets to increase the size of the market share, revenue, and profits.

- Applying general technology and IT as the major drivers of organizational change with the aim of improving business processes and gaining a competitive advantage.

- Complying with regulatory, legal, and social requirements

- Developing an organization's management reporting structures and systems

- Analyzing and streamlining business policies, procedures, and processes to gain efficiencies and to eliminate waste of resources

- Creating and growing human talent as a strategic asset and possessing the right mix of skill sets containing both soft skills and hard skills

- Analyzing big data for greater insights and better decisions

- Solving business problems and making business decisions

- Conducting business operations and handling all stakeholders in an ethical and legal manner

- Collecting business intelligence to develop better strategies for the company and to outsmart or outperform competitors' strategies

(b) Business Strategy Defined

A corporation's mission, vision, goals, and objectives establish its **business strategies**. The mission/vision and goals/objectives lead a company where it wants to go, and strategies define how it will get there. Strategy shows a big picture of the company and explains how senior management works on developing and executing the big-picture strategy.

Mission/Vision ⟶ Goals/Objectives ⟶ Strategies

(i) Mission and Vision

Mission and vision are the documented reasons for and purposes of the existence of an organization. The mission describes the organization's vision, because the vision is a part of the mission. **Mission** reflects management's values and beliefs. In other words, both mission and vision describe the overall goal of an organization.

Specifically, **vision** is a statement that explains what a company wants to become and what it hopes to achieve. It is an attractive, ideal future that is credible and believable yet not easily and readily attainable. Both mission and vision documents are developed simultaneously.

(ii) Goals

Goals are developed from mission and vision. A **goal** is a statement of general, broad-based, and long-term target, aim, and intent. It is the point toward which management directs its efforts and resources. It is a desired future state that the organization attempts to reach. Goals, which are derived from mission/vision, can be classified as strategic, tactical, operational, and stretch. Goals can be quantitative and qualitative in nature, with qualitative goals most common.

Mission/Vision ⟶ Goals

Goals represent major targets, aims, and intentions of management to make an organization better than before. Goals are of four types: strategic, tactical, operational, and stretch. Operational goals are derived from tactical goals, which, in turn, are derived from strategic goals. Note that stretch goals can be applied to the three primary types of goals (strategic, tactical, and operational). The reason for the varieties of goals is that they all have different purposes and timelines.

Strategic Goals ⟶ Tactical Goals ⟶ Operational Goals

Strategic goals are the starting point for all the other goals and include general, very broad, and high-level measurable results expected of the entire organization. They do not focus on individual divisions, departments, or business units of a company. Strategic goals focus on how to increase market share, how to enter into new markets, how best to position products and services, how to outsmart competitors, how to increase revenues and profits, and how to decrease costs. Strategic plans define how to achieve the strategic goals.

Tactical goals include both specific, broad, and medium-level measurable results in terms of clear outcomes expected of individual divisions, departments, and business units that support the strategic goals. These goals focus on how to get maximum performance from employees, suppliers, vendors, and contractors. Tactical plans define how to achieve the tactical goals.

Operational goals include very specific, very detailed (narrow), and low-level measurable results expected of individual employees and work groups. These goals focus on how to get maximum utilization of resources. Operational plans define how to achieve the operational goals.

Stretch goals expand normal (ordinary) goals to abnormal (extraordinary) goals and require radical thinking in order to achieve major and noteworthy improvements. Stretch goals are highly ambitious, coming from aim-high thinking. Stretch goals are normal goals stretched out, and they are difficult and challenging, not impossible, to achieve. Stretch plans define how to achieve the stretch goals (i.e., extended goals). Note that strategic, tactical, and operational goals can have variations of stretch goals, meaning each goal is further challenged and expanded to get the most out of it.

(iii) Objectives

Objectives are developed from goals. An **objective** is a statement of specific, narrow-based, and short-term target, aim, and intent. It is the expected result or product of a project, usually defined in terms of scope, schedule, and cost. An objective is the quantitative statement of future expectations and an indication of when expectations should be achieved. Objectives flow from goals and specify what needs to be accomplished. Both goals and objectives are developed simultaneously as objectives are derived from goals.

$$\text{Goals} \longrightarrow \text{Objectives}$$

(iv) Strategies

Strategies are developed from goals and objectives, which, in turn, form the basis for developing plans and actions and for producing results. **Strategies** identify general approaches a business should take in order to achieve its mission/vision and goals/objectives. Mission/vision and goals/objectives lead an organization where it wants to go, and strategies define how it will get there. Strategies are developed from goals and objectives.

$$\text{Goals/Objectives} \longrightarrow \text{Strategies}$$

Strategy shows a documented plan of actions with required four resources (men, money, machinery, and materials—4Ms) to achieve an organization's stated goals and objectives. Strategies have time frames of short term (within one year), intermediate term (between one and two years), and long term (three years and up).

(v) Plans, Actions, and Results

A **plan** is a blueprint specifying the resources, schedules, and actions needed to achieve goals. Planning types include strategic, tactical, operational, and contingency plans. The latter plan (contingency plan) is needed to support the former three plans. Planning levels include corporate, business unit, functional, and department. Plans are derived from strategies. Plans are turned into actions, which, in turn, are turned into results.

$$\text{Strategies} \longrightarrow \text{Plans}$$

Actions are systematic and structured steps, tasks, or activities required to achieve the defined plans. Actions are the solid proof that a plan is fully implemented or executed into required operations. Actions produce **results** that management is expecting.

$$\text{Plans} \longrightarrow \text{Actions} \longrightarrow \text{Results}$$

In summary, the correct sequence of elements of a retailer's strategy is:

Mission/Vision ⟶ Goals/Objectives ⟶ Strategies ⟶ Plans/Actions ⟶ Results

(c) Different Types of Strategies

Organizational strategies answer a basic question: What is the basis for developing a strategy internally? Organizational strategies identify general approaches a business should take in order to achieve its stated mission, vision, goals, and objectives. Strategy sets the major directions for the entire organization to follow.

A corporation's strategy is a combination of corporate-level, business unit-level, functional-level, and department-level strategy.

- A *corporate-level strategy* is concerned with the question "What business are we in?" This question is similar to the mission statement's question. Senior managers and executives develop this long-term strategy.

- A *business unit-level strategy* is concerned with the question "How do we compete?" This question is linked to the corporate-level strategy. A business can be divided into business-unit 1, business-unit 2, and business-unit N. These units can be major divisions of a company. The division heads and general managers develop this intermediate-term strategy.

- A *functional-level strategy* is concerned with the question "How do we support our chosen strategy?" This question is linked to both business unit-level and corporate-level strategies. A business is divided into various functions, including marketing, operations, and others. For example, executives in the marketing function develop this intermediate-term strategy.

- A *department-level strategy* is concerned with the question "How do we mobilize our resources to support the chosen strategy?" This question is linked to both functional-level and business unit-level strategy. For example, the marketing function is divided into sales, advertising, and customer service departments. Managers of these departments develop this short-term strategy.

(d) Competitive Forces, Strategies, and Analysis

The essence of formulating a competitive strategy is relating a company to its environment, that is, the industry or industries in which it operates and competes. The major components of competitive strategy include understanding competitive forces, identifying competitive strategies, and performing competitor analysis in a specific industry.

(i) Competitive Forces
Porter's six competitive forces are at work on an industry. These forces include:

1. Threat of new entrants
2. Rivalry among existing firms
3. Pressure from substitute products or services

4. Bargaining power of buyers

5. Bargaining power of suppliers

6. Availability of complementary products and services

All six competitive forces jointly determine the intensity of industry competition and profitability.[1]

1. Threat of new entrants. New entrants to an industry bring new capacity and the desire to gain market share. They often also bring substantial resources. As a result, prices can be low, cost can be high, and profits can be low. A relationship exists between threat of new entrants, barriers to entry, and reaction from existing competitors. For example:

☐ If barriers are high and reaction is high, then the threat of entry is low.

☐ If barriers are low and reaction is low, then the threat of entry is high.

Seven major *barriers to entry* exist, including: economies of scale, product differentiation, capital requirements, switching costs, access to distribution channels, cost disadvantages independent of scale, and government policy.

2. Rivalry among existing firms. Rivalry tactics include price competition, advertising battles, new product introduction, and increased customer service or product/service warranties.

Competitors are mutually dependent in terms of action and reaction, moves and countermoves, or offensive and defensive tactics. Intense rivalry is the result of a number of interacting structural factors, such as numerous or equally balanced competitors, slow industry growth, high fixed costs or storage costs, lack of differentiation or switching costs, capacity increases in large increments, diverse competitors, high strategic stakes, and high exit barriers.

3. Pressure from substitute products or services. In a broad sense, all firms in an industry are competitors with industries producing substitute products. Substitutes limit the potential returns of an industry by placing a ceiling on the prices firms can profitably charge. The more attractive the price–performance alternative offered by substitutes, the stronger or firmer the lid on industry profits. Substitute products that deserve the most attention are those that are subject to trends that improve their price–performance trade-off with the industry's product or that are produced by industries earning high profits.

4. Bargaining power of buyers. Buyers (purchasing agents) compete with the industry by forcing down prices, bargaining for higher quality and larger quantities or for better services, and playing suppliers against each other—all at the expense of industry profits. Buyers acquire full information about product demand, prices, and costs. Informed buyers become empowered buyers.

5. Bargaining power of suppliers. Suppliers can exert bargaining power over participants in an industry by threatening to raise prices or reduce the quality of purchased goods or services. The conditions making suppliers powerful tend to mirror those making buyers powerful.

6. Availability of complementary products and services. This means how buying a product (product 1) from one company impacts the sales of a complementary product (product 2) from the same company or other companies. Customers have a choice of buying product 1 and product 2 either from the same company or from different companies.

The impact is high if product 1 cannot function without product 2. The impact of complementary products can be good or bad for an industry's profitability because the complementary products can belong to the same industry or to different industries.

[1] Michael E. Porter, *Competitive Strategy* (New York: Free Press, 1980).

(ii) Competitive Strategies

Competitive strategy is taking offensive or defensive actions to create a defendable position in an industry, to cope with the six competitive forces in order to achieve a superior return on investment (ROI). It is more important than ever for companies to distinguish themselves through careful strategic positioning in the marketplace.

Competitive Forces ⟶ Competitive Strategies

Porter studied a number of businesses and introduced a framework describing three generic competitive strategies to outperform other firms in an industry. These three strategies include *differentiation, low-cost leadership,* and *focus.* The focus strategy, in which the organization concentrates on a specific market or buyer group, is further divided into a strategy called focused low cost and focused differentiation. Before developing these four basic strategies, managers can evaluate two factors, such as competitive advantage and competitive scope.

Competitive advantage. Managers can determine whether to compete through lower cost or through the ability to offer unique or distinctive products and services that can command a premium price.

Competitive scope. Managers can then determine whether the organization will compete on a broad scope (in many customer segments) or a narrow scope (in a selected customer segment or group of segments). These choices determine the selection of strategies.

   1. Differentiation strategy. The differentiation strategy involves an attempt to distinguish the firm's products or services from others in the industry. An organization may use advertising, distinctive product features, exceptional service, or new technology to achieve a product that is perceived as unique.
   This strategy usually targets customers who are not particularly concerned with price, so it can be quite profitable because customers are loyal and will pay high prices for the product.
   Companies that pursue a differentiation strategy typically need strong marketing abilities, a creative flair, and a reputation for leadership.
   A differentiation strategy can reduce rivalry with competitors and fight off the threat of substitute products because customers are loyal to the company's brand. However, companies must remember that successful differentiation strategies require a number of costly activities, such as product research and design and extensive advertising.
   2. Low-cost leadership strategy. With a low-cost leadership strategy, the organization aggressively seeks efficient facilities, pursues cost reductions, and uses tight cost controls to produce products more efficiently than competitors. A low-cost position means that the company can undercut competitors' prices and still offer comparable quality and earn a reasonable profit. Being a low-cost producer provides a successful strategy to defend against the six competitive forces.
   The low-cost leadership strategy tries to increase market share by emphasizing low cost compared to competitors. This strategy is concerned primarily with stability rather than taking risks or seeking new opportunities for innovation and growth.
   3. Focus strategy. With Porter's third strategy, the focus strategy, the organization concentrates on a specific regional market or buyer group. The company will use either a differentiation or low-cost approach, but only for a narrow target market.

(iii) Competitive Analysis

The objective of a competitive or competitor analysis is to develop a profile of the nature and success of the likely strategy changes, each competitor's response to the strategic moves, and each competitor's probable reaction to the industry changes. A series of what-if questions must be raised and answered during this sensitivity analysis.

Competitive Forces ⟶ Competitive Strategies ⟶ Competitive Analysis

Four diagnostic components to a competitor analysis include:

1. Future goals
2. Current strategy (either explicit or implicit)
3. Assumptions
4. Capabilities (strengths and weaknesses)

Both future goals and assumptions jointly answer the question "What drives the competitor?" Both current strategy and capabilities jointly answer the question "What is the competitor doing and what can it do?"

Future goals should focus on attitude toward risks, financial goals, organizational values or beliefs, organizational structure, incentive systems, accounting systems, leadership styles, composition of the board of directors, and contractual commitments (e.g., debt covenants, licensing, and joint ventures).

Examining assumptions can identify biases or blind spots that may creep into management thinking. Rooting out these blind spots can help the firm identify competitive moves or retaliation methods (i.e., fighting back). Assumptions focus on competitors' relative position in cost, quality, and technology; cultural, regional, or national differences; organizational values; and future demand and industry trends.

A competitor's goals, assumptions, and current strategy will influence the likelihood, timing, nature, and intensity of a competitor's reactions. A competitor's strengths and weaknesses (i.e., strengths, weaknesses, opportunities, and threats [SWOT] analysis) will determine its ability to initiate or react to strategic moves and to deal with industry events that occur.

(e) Value Chain Analysis

(i) Value Defined

Defining the value of a product or service is difficult because different people perceive value very differently. For example, most people equate value of a product to low-cost, friendly service; a pleasant shopping experience; free parking; less driving; more convenience; more time savings; fewer hassles; name brand; high quality; ease of use; and other factors. Value comparison based on cost factor is shown next:

Retailer A is selling a national brand at a price of $1.99 per item.

Retailer B is selling the same national brand at a price of $2.19 per item.

Value to a customer buying this item from Retailer A: $0.20 due to low cost.

Defined in a simple and clear way, value is realized when benefits exceed costs. Within the retail context, value to a retailer or customer is realized when benefits exceed costs, and the difference is value.

Value to retailer = Price received from customer > Costs paid to producers or others
= Benefits − Costs

Value to customer = Benefits received from retailer > Costs paid to retailer
= Benefits − Costs

Note that a retailer receives an initial value for a product when it is purchased from producers (e.g., manufacturers, distributors, or vendors). Then suppliers in the supply chain can add their own value to make the product more functional, and later the same retailer can add its own value to make the product even better to his customers. Customers receive that total value (cumulative value) when they purchase a product from that retailer.

Although a retailer can create or add value anytime during a business process, it is useful and beneficial to add value at the right time and at the right place to seize the right opportunity. A built-in value at the beginning of a process lasts longer and is visible throughout the process than an add-on value later; and it is true with manufacturers, producers, suppliers, and retailers. Most customers can recognize value when they see a product, touch and feel it, and use it.

Example 1: Value is created when fresh apples are not bruised or stained (colored).

Example 2: Value is destroyed when a smartphone catches fire while its battery is charging.

Because a business process consists of a series of several interdependent and interconnected activities with various tasks of different sizes and length, value must be added from the beginning to the end of the process to provide a continuity of and consistency in value for some products. Moreover, value must be built in, not built on for most products; it must be based on forethought, not afterthought; and it must be based on a proactive thinking, not reactive thinking.

Value must be thought through for products and services as a continuum, as shown:

Value to Products ⟶ Product Conception ⟶ Product Commercialization

Value to Services ⟶ Service Initiation ⟶ Service Delivery

(ii) Value Creation

If value given to products and services is so important to customers, how will retailers create or add such value to their products and services? Retailers that create and sustain value to customers will survive; those that do not create or add value to customers will die. There are several places, points, and factors available for retailers to provide value-oriented products and services to customers. Broadly speaking, examples of value-creating places include:

- When a retailer is:
  - Procuring or purchasing a product (merchandise) from a manufacturer, wholesaler, distributor, vendor, dealer, or supplier
  - Receiving a product (merchandise) from a manufacturer, wholesaler, distributor, vendor, dealer, or supplier
  - Placing or displaying the merchandise in a physical store or online store for customers to view and see
  - Selling a product or service, either offline or online

- When a customer is:
  - ☐ Conducting research or making inquiries during a prepurchase phase
  - ☐ Being helped by a retail employee in purchasing a product or service, either offline or online
  - ☐ Purchasing a product or service, either offline or online
  - ☐ Paying for a purchased product or service
  - ☐ Receiving a purchased product or service
  - ☐ Returning a purchased product
  - ☐ Providing feedback after purchasing a product or service (i.e., postpurchase)
  - ☐ Using a product

Note that value creation is a continuous and constant process of improving. Value can be created or destroyed at the level of an individual product, service, employee, store, division, and corporation in the aggregate. All these levels provide an additive value with synergistic and long-lasting effect at the corporation level.

(iii) Value Maximization Goal

Implementing value maximization goals will eventually turn normal organizations into world-class organizations. This is achieved through productive employees, efficient design of business processes, and effective use of quality tools and techniques combined with forward-looking management to create a sustainable and synergistic value for an organization's products and services.

Value-Based Organization = World-Class Organization

Creating new value or adding value to existing value is the major purpose of business corporations. For example, the total value of a manufacturing corporation is the summation of individual values of each product manufactured. Similarly, the total value of a service corporation is the summation of individual values of each service provided.

One way to increase the value of a product or service is by decreasing the cost while keeping the price of a product or service constant. Other ways of increasing the value of a company include breaking the value–cost trade-off with innovative strategies and investing in human capital and technology capital for creating innovative new products and services with sustainable value.

Value creation is the heart of organizational activity at the organization level. Benchmarking provides the metrics by which to understand and judge the value provided by the organization and its resources. Benchmarking focuses on continuous improvements and value creation for stakeholders (i.e., owners, customers, employees, and suppliers), and it can utilize best practices to focus on improving performance. When it comes to valuing or selling a specific brand, division, or a retail company, goodwill is often considered in addition to strategic, operational, and functional advantages. Goodwill is a subjective and qualitative assessment of a company, which is difficult to assess.

(iv) Value Chain Analysis

Michael Porter of Harvard Business School has created a generic value chain concept covering from manufacturing to marketing activities primarily aimed at the manufacturing industry. It includes nine activities divided into five primary activities and four secondary ones, where each activity interacts with other activities and where each activity contributes an incremental value to the total value of a firm or company. Customer consumers are the primary beneficiaries of the value chain; the stockholders and owners are the secondary beneficiaries.[2]

The author of this book adapted and tailored the value chain concept to the retail industry and showed how retailers can add or create value to their customers during customer's shopping journey through retail examples.

Five primary activities include:

1. **Inbound logistics.** The scope of work activities in inbound logistics includes bringing raw materials or ingredients from source to destination (i.e., from suppliers to manufacturers). Inbound logistics balances variables such as delivery speed, cost, and quality. Upstream suppliers (supplier 1, 2, and N) are involved in inbound logistics where they bring raw materials, ingredients, product parts, and product components from various places and deliver them to manufacturers to make finished goods.

2. **Operations.** The scope of work activities in operations includes:

   □ Transforming raw materials into finished goods with just-in-time (JIT) production methods in a manufacturing factory;

   □ Applying total quality management principles to improve quality of products;

   □ Complying with the manufacturing and quality standards issued by the International Organization for Standards (ISO);

   □ Implementing Six Sigma quality concepts to develop and deliver near-perfect products and services;

   □ Implementing statistical process control techniques to reduce variations in processes and products from expected standards or targets and to eliminate defects and errors in manufacturing processes;

   □ Adhering to the generally accepted manufacturing practices, which focus on separating value-added activities from non-value-added activities;

   □ Embracing lean manufacturing practices, which focus on eliminating waste and enhancing the value of a company's products; and

   □ Complying with Underwriters Laboratory guidelines (UL certified logo) to prevent hazards from using unsafe products by children and adults.

3. **Outbound logistics.** The scope of work activities in outbound logistics includes shipping finished goods from manufacturers or producers to wholesalers, distributors, and retailers. Similar to inbound logistics, outbound logistics balances variables such as delivery speed, cost, and quality. Downstream suppliers (supplier 1, 2, and N) are involved in outbound logistics where they bring finished goods from manufacturers or producers to retailers and eventually to customers. Basically, the supply chain members bring products from producers and suppliers and deliver them to consumers and customers; it is a logistics and delivery concept.

4. **Marketing and sales.** The scope of work activities in marketing and sales includes developing strategies and short- and long-term sales plans and budgets; marketing mix, including marketing channels; brand positioning and equity; and developing plans for advertisements and promotions.

---

[2] Michael E. Porter, *Competitive Advantage* [New York: Free Press, 1985].

5. Service. The scope of work activities in service includes postsale service such as addressing product warranties and guarantees; product returns, exchanges, and replacements; product repairs, recalls, and recovery methods. Whether a current customer will repurchase from the same company depends on how well that customer is currently serviced. Service is an important area that is often neglected or forgotten by management at all levels.

Four secondary activities include:

1. Procurement. The scope of work activities in procurement includes:

- Developing short-term and long-term procurement plans and budgets for purchasing various materials and products;
- Negotiating various terms and conditions involved in procuring various types of raw materials and finished products;
- Participating in developing product specifications with manufacturing and design engineers; and
- Placing and receiving raw materials and finished goods.

Procurement is a big-budget item for both manufacturers and retailers, especially for the latter because retailers spend most of their money buying finished goods from manufacturers, wholesalers, distributors, and vendors.

2. Technology development. The scope of work activities in technology development includes formulating short-term and long-term plans and budgets for improving current technology and exploring new technology. It includes computer hardware and software, computer networks, peripheral devices, and mobile devices. Technology is seen as the major driver of many businesses, especially those in retail.

3. Human resource management. The scope of work activities in human resource (HR) management includes hiring, training, and developing talented employees to retain and sustain human talent; providing health benefits to employees and their families; and working with labor unions.

4. Firm infrastructure. The scope of work activities in a firm's infrastructure includes external framework and internal framework. Components of external framework include understanding the economic and political conditions and governmental laws and regulations in a country. Components of internal framework include practicing good corporate governance principles and management strategies in a single firm or company.

(f) Business Portfolio Models

A firm is said to have a sustainable competitive advantage over other firms when it has technical superiority, low-cost production, good customer service/product support, good location, adequate financial resources, continuing product innovations, and overall marketing skills.

Portfolio strategy pertains to the mix of business units and product lines that fit together in a logical way to provide synergy and competitive advantage for the corporation. For example, an individual might wish to diversify in an investment portfolio with some high-risk stocks, some low-risk stocks, some growth stocks, and perhaps a few fixed-income bonds. In much the same way, corporations like to have a balanced mix of business divisions called strategic business units (SBUs). An SBU has a unique business mission, product line, competitors, and markets relative to other SBUs in the corporation. Executives in charge of the entire corporation generally define the grand strategy and then bring together a portfolio of SBUs to carry it out.

Portfolio models can help corporate management to determine how resources should be allocated among the various SBUs, consisting of product lines and/or divisions. The portfolio techniques are more useful at the corporate-level strategy than at the business-level or functional-level strategy. Two widely used portfolio models are the Boston Consulting Group (BCG) matrix and the General Electric (GE) model, which are discussed next.

(i) BCG Matrix Model

The BCG matrix model organizes businesses along two dimensions—business growth rate and market share. **Business growth rate** pertains to how rapidly the entire industry is increasing. **Market share** defines whether a business unit has a larger or smaller share than competitors. The combinations of high and low market share and high and low business growth provide four categories for a corporate portfolio.

The BCG matrix model utilizes a concept of **experience curves,** which are similar in concept to learning curves. The experience curve includes all costs associated with a product and implies that the per-unit cost of a product should fall, due to cumulative experience, as production volume increases. The manufacturer with the largest volume and market share should have the lowest marginal cost. The leader in market share should be able to underprice competitors and discourage entry into the market by potential competitors. As a result, the leader will achieve an acceptable ROI.

The BCG model (growth/market share matrix) is based on the assumption that profitability and cash flows will be closely related to sales volume. Here, **growth** means use of cash, and **market share** means source of cash. Each SBU is classified in terms of its relative market share and the growth rate of the market the SBU is in, and products are classified as stars, cash cows, dogs, or question marks. Relative market share is the market share of a firm relative to that of the largest competitor in the industry.

The following list describes the components of the BCG model:

- **Stars** are SBUs with a high market share of a high-growth market. They require large amounts of cash to sustain growth despite producing high profits.
- **Cash cows** are often market leaders (high market share), but the market they are in is a mature, slow-growth industry (low growth). They have a positive cash flow.
- **Dogs** are poorly performing SBUs that have a low market share of a low-growth market. They are modest cash users and need cash because of their weak competitive position.
- **Question marks (problem children)** are SBUs with a low market share of a new, high-growth market. They require large amounts of cash inflows to finance growth and are weak cash generators because of their poor competitive position. The question mark business is risky: It could become a star, or it could fail.

The desirable sequence of portfolio actions for the BCG model is:

- A star SBU eventually becomes a cash cow as its market growth slows.
- Cash cow SBUs should be used to turn question marks into stars.
- Dog SBUs should either be harvested or divested from the portfolio.
- Question mark SBUs can be nurtured to become future stars.
- Unqualified question mark SBUs should be harvested until they become dogs.

(ii) GE Model

The GE model is an alternative to the BCG model. It incorporates more information about market opportunities (industry attractiveness) and competitive positions (company/business strength) to allocate resources. The GE model emphasizes all the potential sources of business strength and all the factors that influence the long-term attractiveness of a market. All SBUs are classified in terms of business strength (i.e., strong, average, weak) and industry attractiveness (i.e., high, medium, low).

Business strength is made up of market share, quality leadership, technological position, company profitability, company strengths and weaknesses, and company image. The major components of **industry attractiveness** are market size, market share, market growth, industry profitability, and pricing.

Overall strategic choices include either to invest capital to build position, to hold the position by balancing cash generation and selective cash use, or to harvest or divest. The GE model incorporates subjective judgment, and accordingly, it is vulnerable to manipulation. However, it can be made stronger with the use of objective criteria.

(iii) BCG Model versus GE Model

Both the BCG matrix model and the GE model help in competitive analysis and provide a consistency check in formulating a competitive strategy for a particular industry. Either model can be used, based on the manager's preference. However, if a competitor uses the BCG model because of experience curves, then a company can benefit by using the same model.

BCG, GE, and Porter Models Compared

- Both the BCG matrix and the GE model focus on corporate-level strategy accomplished through acquisition or divestment of business.

- Porter's five competitive forces and three competitive strategies focus on business-level strategy accomplished through competitive actions.

- Despite its widespread use in allocating corporate resources and acceptance by managers, the BCG model has been criticized for:

    □ Focusing on market share and market growth as the primary indicators of profitability.

    □ Its assumption that the major source of SBU financing comes from internal means.

    □ Its assumption that the target market has been defined properly along with its interdependencies with other markets.

(g) Strategic Management Process

Strategic management is the set of decisions and actions used to formulate and implement strategies that will provide a competitively superior fit between the organization and its environment so as to achieve organizational goals. Managers ask questions such as: What changes and trends are occurring in the competitive environment? Who are our customers? What products or services should we offer? How can we offer those products and services most efficiently? Answers to these questions help managers make choices about how to position their organization in the environment with respect to rival companies. Superior organizational performance is not a matter of luck. It is determined by the choices that managers make.

Top executives use strategic management to define an overall direction for the organization, which is the firm's grand strategy. The strategic management process is defined as a series of these activities:

Grand Strategy ——→ Strategy Formulation (Planning) ——→ Strategy Implementation
——→ Strategic Control

(i) Grand Strategy

The grand strategy is the general plan of major action by which a firm intends to achieve its long-term goals. Grand strategies can be defined for four general categories: growth, stability, retrenchment, and global operations.

Growth can be promoted internally by investing in expansion or externally by acquiring additional business divisions. Internal growth can include development of new or changed products or expansion of current products into new markets. External growth typically involves *diversification*, which means the acquisition of businesses that are related to current product lines or that take the corporation into new areas. The number of companies choosing to grow through mergers and acquisitions (M&A) is astounding, as organizations strive to acquire the size and resources to compete on a global scale, to invest in new technology, and to control distribution channels and guarantee access to markets.

Stability, sometimes called a *pause strategy*, means that the organization wants to remain the same size or grow slowly and in a controlled fashion. The corporation wants to stay in its current business. After organizations have undergone a turbulent period of rapid growth, executives often focus on a stability strategy to integrate SBUs and to ensure that the organization is working efficiently.

Retrenchment means that the organization goes through a period of forced decline by either shrinking current business units or selling off or liquidating entire businesses. The organization may have experienced a precipitous drop in demand for its products or services, prompting managers to order across-the-board cuts in personnel and expenditures. **Liquidation** means selling off a business unit for the cash value of the assets, thus terminating its existence. **Divestiture** involves the selling off of businesses that no longer seem central to the corporation. Studies show that between 33% and 50% of all acquisitions are later divested. Retrenchment is also called downsizing.

In today's **global operations**, senior executives try to formulate coherent strategies to provide synergy among worldwide operations for the purpose of fulfilling common goals. Each country or region represents a new market with the promise of increased sales and profits. In the international arena, companies face a strategic dilemma between global integration and national responsiveness. Organizations must decide whether they want each global affiliate to act autonomously or whether activities should be standardized and centralized across countries. This choice leads managers to select a basic grand strategy alternative, such as globalization versus multidomestic strategy. Some corporations may seek to achieve both global integration and national responsiveness by using a transnational strategy.

When an organization chooses a strategy of **globalization**, its product design and advertising strategies are standardized throughout the world. This approach is based on the assumption that a single global market exists for many consumer and industrial products. The theory is that people everywhere want to buy the same products and live the same way. A globalization strategy can help an organization reap efficiencies by standardizing product design and manufacturing, using common suppliers, introducing products around the world faster, coordinating prices, and eliminating overlapping facilities. Globalization enables marketing departments alone to save millions of dollars.

When an organization chooses a **multidomestic strategy**, competition in each country is handled independently of industry competition in other countries. Thus, a multinational company is present in many countries, but it encourages marketing, advertising, and product design to be modified and adapted to the specific needs of each country. Many companies reject the idea of a single global market.

A **transnational strategy** seeks to achieve both global integration and national responsiveness. A true transnational strategy is difficult to achieve because one goal requires close global coordination while the other goal requires local flexibility. However, many industries are finding that, although increased competition means they must achieve global efficiency, growing pressure to meet local needs demands national responsiveness.

Although most multinational companies want to achieve some degree of global integration to hold costs down, even global products may require some customization to meet government regulations in various countries or some tailoring to fit consumer preferences. In addition, some products are better suited for standardization than others. Most large multinational corporations with diverse products will attempt to use a partial multidomestic strategy for some product lines and global strategies for others. Coordinating global integration with responsiveness to the heterogeneity of international markets is a difficult balancing act for managers, but it is an increasingly important one in today's global business world.

KEY CONCEPTS TO REMEMBER: Vocabulary Related to Strategic Management

- **Organizational goal.** An organizational goal is a desired state of affairs that the organization attempts to reach. A goal represents a result or an end point toward which organizational efforts are directed. The choice of goals and strategy affects organization design. Top managers give direction to organizations. They set goals and develop the strategies for their organization to attain those goals.

- **Organizational purpose.** Organizations are created and continued in order to accomplish something. This purpose may be referred to as the overall goal or mission. Different parts of the organization establish their own goals and objectives to help meet the overall goal, mission, or purpose of the organization.

    Many types of goals exist in an organization, and each type performs a different function. One major distinction is between the officially stated goals, or mission, of the organization and the operative goals that the organization actually pursues.

- **Mission.** The overall goal for an organization is often called the mission—the organization's reason for existence. The mission describes the organization's vision, its shared values and beliefs, and its reason for being. It can have a powerful impact on an organization. The mission is sometimes called the official goal, which consists of the formally stated definition of business scope and outcomes the organization is trying to achieve. Official goal statements typically define business operations and may focus on values, markets, and customers that distinguish the organization. Whether called a mission statement or an official goal, the organization's general statement of its purpose and philosophy is often written down in a policy manual or annual report.

■ **Operative goals.** Operative goals designate the ends sought through the actual operating procedures of the organization and explain what the organization is actually trying to do. Operative goals describe specific measurable outcomes and are often concerned with the short run. Operative versus official goals represent actual versus stated goals. Operative goals typically pertain to the primary tasks an organization must perform. These goals concern overall performance, boundary activities, maintenance, adaptation, and production activities. Specific goals for each primary task provide direction for the day-to-day decisions and activities within departments.

■ **Purpose of strategy.** A strategy is a plan for interacting with the competitive environment to achieve organizational goals. Some managers think of goals and strategies as interchangeable, but for our purposes, goals define where the organization wants to go and strategies define how it will get there. For example, a goal may be to achieve 15% annual sales growth; strategies to reach that goal might include aggressive advertising to attract new customers, motivating salespeople to increase the average size of customer purchases, and acquiring other businesses that produce similar products.

Strategies can include any number of techniques to achieve the goal. The essence of formulating strategies is choosing whether the organization will perform different activities from its competitors or will execute similar activities more efficiently than its competitors do.

Within the overall grand strategy of an organization, executives define an explicit strategy, which is the plan of action that describes resource allocation and activities for dealing with the environment and attaining the organization's goals. The essence of formulating strategy is choosing how the organization will be different. Managers make decisions about whether the company will perform different activities or will execute similar activities differently than its competitors do. Strategy necessarily changes over time to fit environmental conditions, but to remain competitive, companies develop strategies that focus on core competencies, develop synergy, and create value for customers.

A company's **core competence** is something the organization does especially well in comparison to its competitors. A core competence represents a competitive advantage because the company acquires expertise that competitors do not have. A core competence may be in the area of superior research and development (R&D), expert technological know-how, process efficiency, or exceptional customer service.

When organizational parts interact to produce a joint effect that is greater than the sum of the parts acting alone, synergy occurs. The organization may attain a special advantage with respect to cost, market power, technology, or management skill. When properly managed, synergy can create additional value with existing resources, providing a big boost to the bottom line. Synergy can also be obtained through good relations with suppliers or by strong alliances among companies.

Delivering value to the customer should be at the heart of strategy. Value can be defined as the combination of benefits received and costs paid by the customer. Managers help their companies create value by devising strategies that exploit core competencies and attain synergy.

■ **Levels of strategy.** Another aspect of strategic management concerns the organizational level to which strategic issues apply. Strategic managers normally think in terms of three levels of strategy: corporate, business, and functional.

The question "What business are we in?" concerns corporate-level strategy, which pertains to the organization as a whole and the combination of business units and product lines that make up the corporate entity. Strategic actions at this level usually relate to the acquisition of new businesses; additions or divestments of business units, plants, or product lines; and joint ventures with other corporations in new areas.

(continued)

KEY CONCEPTS TO REMEMBER: Vocabulary Related to Strategic Management (*Continued*)

The question "How do we compete?" concerns business-level strategy, which pertains to each business unit or product line. It focuses on how the business unit competes within its industry for customers. Strategic decisions at the business level concern the amount of advertising, direction and extent of R&D, product changes, new-product development, equipment and facilities, and expansion or contraction of product lines. Many companies are operating e-commerce units as a part of business-level strategy.

The question "How do we support the business-level competitive strategy?" concerns functional-level strategy, which pertains to the major functional departments within the business unit. Functional strategies involve all of the major functions, including finance, R&D, marketing, and manufacturing.

■ **Partnership strategies and business ecosystems.** So far, we have been discussing strategies that are based on how to compete with other companies. An alternative approach to strategy emphasizes collaboration. In some situations, companies can achieve competitive advantages by cooperating with other firms rather than competing. Partnership strategies are becoming increasingly popular as firms in all industries join with other organizations to promote innovation, expand markets, and pursue joint goals. Partnering was once a strategy adopted primarily by small firms that needed greater marketing muscle or international access. Today, however, it has become a way of life for most companies, large and small. The question is no longer whether to collaborate but rather where, how much, and with whom to collaborate. Competition and cooperation often exist at the same time representing business ecosystems. The Internet is both driving and supporting the move toward partnership thinking.

Mutual dependencies and partnerships have become a fact of life, but the degree of collaboration varies. Organizations can choose to build cooperative relationships in many ways, such as through preferred suppliers, strategic business partnering, joint ventures, or M&As. A still higher degree of collaboration is reflected in joint ventures, which are separate entities created with two or more active firms as sponsors. M&As represent the ultimate step in collaborative relationships.

Today's companies embrace both competition and cooperation simultaneously. Few companies can go it alone under a constant onslaught of international competition, changing technology, and new regulations. In this new environment, businesses choose a combination of competitive and partnership strategies that add to their overall sustainable advantage.

Overall effectiveness is difficult to measure in organizations, which are large, diverse, and fragmented. They perform many activities simultaneously and pursue multiple goals. They also generate many outcomes, some intended and some unintended. Managers determine which indicators to measure in order to gauge the effectiveness of their organizations. One study found that many managers have a difficult time with the concept of evaluating effectiveness based on characteristics that are not subject to hard, quantitative measurement. However, top executives at some of today's leading companies are finding new ways to measure effectiveness, using indicators such as "customer delight" and employee satisfaction. A number of approaches to measuring effectiveness look at which measurements the organization managers choose to track. These contingency effectiveness approaches are based on looking at which part of the organization managers consider most important to measure.

■ **Contingency effectiveness approaches.** Contingency approaches to measuring effectiveness focus on different parts of the organization. Traditional approaches include the goal approach, the resource-based approach, and the internal process approach. Organizations bring resources in from the environment, and those resources are transformed into outputs delivered back into the environment. The goal approach to organizational effectiveness is concerned with the output side and whether the organization achieves its goals in terms of desired levels of output. The resource-based approach assesses effectiveness by observing the beginning of the process and evaluating whether the organization effectively obtains resources necessary for high performance. The internal process approach looks at internal activities and assesses effectiveness by indicators of internal health and efficiency.

These traditional approaches all have something to offer, but each one tells only part of the story. A more recent stakeholder approach (also called the constituency approach) acknowledges that each organization has many constituencies that have a stake in its outcomes. The stakeholder approach focuses on the satisfaction of stakeholders as an indicator of the organization's performance.

(ii) Strategy Formulation

The overall strategic management process begins when executives evaluate their current position with respect to mission, goals, and strategies. They then scan the organization's internal and external environments and identify strategic factors that might require change. Internal or external events might indicate a need to redefine the mission or goals or to formulate (plan) a new strategy at the corporate, business, or functional level. The next stage is implementation of the new strategy. The final stage is strategic control to keep strategic plans on track.

Strategy formulation (planning) includes the planning and decision making that lead to the establishment of the firm's goals and the development of a specific strategic plan. Strategy formulation may include assessing the external environment and internal problems and integrating the results into goals and strategy. This contrasts with strategy implementation, which is the use of managerial and organizational tools to direct resources toward accomplishing strategic results. Strategy implementation is the administration and execution of the strategic plan. Managers may use persuasion, new equipment, changes in organization structure, or a reward system to ensure that employees and resources are used to make formulated strategy a reality.

WHAT IS STRATEGIC MANAGEMENT?

Strategic management is strategic formulation (planning) plus strategic implementation plus strategic control.

Formulating (planning) strategy often begins with an assessment of the internal and external factors that will affect the organization's competitive situation. Situation analysis typically includes a search for SWOT (strengths, weaknesses, opportunities, and threats) that affect organizational performance. Situation analysis is important to all companies but is crucial to those considering globalization because of the diverse environments in which they will operate. External information about opportunities and threats may be obtained from a variety of sources, including customers, government reports, professional journals, suppliers, bankers, friends in other organizations, consultants, and association meetings. Many firms hire special scanning organizations to provide them with newspaper readings, Internet research, and analyses of relevant domestic and global trends. Some firms use more subtle techniques to learn about competitors, such as asking potential recruits about their visits to other companies, hiring people away from competitors, debriefing former employees or customers of competitors, taking plant tours posing as innocent visitors, and even buying competitors' trash. In addition, many companies hire competitive intelligence professionals to scope out competitors.

Executives acquire information about internal strengths and weaknesses from a variety of reports, including budgets, financial ratios, profit and loss statements, and surveys of employee attitudes and satisfaction. Managers spend 80% of their time giving and receiving information. Through frequent face-to-face discussions and meetings with people at all levels of the hierarchy, executives build an understanding of the company's internal strengths and weaknesses.

Internal strengths are positive internal characteristics that the organization can exploit to achieve its strategic performance goals. **Internal weaknesses** are internal characteristics that might inhibit or restrict the organization's performance. The information sought typically pertains to specific functions, such as marketing, finance, production, and R&D. Internal analysis also examines overall organization structure, management competence and quality, and HR characteristics. Based on their understanding of these areas, managers can determine their strengths or weaknesses vis-à-vis other companies.

External threats are characteristics of the external environment that may prevent the organization from achieving its strategic goals. **External opportunities** are characteristics of the external environment that have the potential to help the organization achieve or exceed its strategic goals. Executives evaluate the external environment in several sectors of the economy. The task environment sectors are the most relevant to strategic behavior and include the behavior of competitors, customers, suppliers, and the labor supply. The general environment contains those sectors that have an indirect influence on the organization but nevertheless must be understood and incorporated into strategic behavior. The general environment includes technological developments, the economy, legal-political and international events, and sociocultural changes. Additional areas that might reveal opportunities or threats include pressure groups, interest groups, creditors, natural resources, and potentially competitive industries.

(iii) Strategy Implementation

The next step in the strategic management process is **implementation**—how strategy is put into action. Some people argue that strategy implementation is the most difficult and important part of strategic management. No matter how creative the formulated strategy, the organization will not benefit if the strategy is incorrectly implemented. In today's competitive environment, there is an increasing recognition of the need for more dynamic approaches to formulating and implementing strategies. Strategy is not a static, analytical process; it requires vision, intuition, and employee participation. Many organizations are abandoning central planning departments, and strategy is becoming an everyday part of the job for workers at all levels. Strategy implementation involves using several tools—parts of the firm that can be adjusted to put strategy into action. Once a new strategy is selected, it is implemented through changes in leadership, structure, information and control systems, and employees. For strategy to be implemented successfully, all aspects of the organization need to be in concert with the strategy. Implementation involves regularly making difficult decisions about doing things in a way that supports rather than undermines the organization's chosen strategy.

Implementing strategy is more difficult when a company goes global. In the international arena, flexibility and superb communication emerge as mandatory leadership skills. Likewise, structural design must merge successfully with foreign cultures as well as link foreign operations to the home country. Managers must make decisions about how to structure the organization to achieve the desired level of global integration and local responsiveness. Information and control systems must fit the needs of and incentives within local cultures. In Japan or China, for example, financial bonuses for star performance are humiliating to an individual whereas group motivation and reward are acceptable. As in North America, control typically is created through timetables and budgets and by monitoring progress toward desired goals. Finally, the recruitment, training, transfer, promotion, and layoff of international employees create an array of problems not confronted in North America due to labor unions and social cultures. Labor laws, guaranteed jobs, and cultural traditions of keeping unproductive employees on the job provide special problems for strategy implementation.

In summary, strategy implementation is essential for effective strategic management. Managers implement strategy through the tools of leadership, structural design, information and control systems, and employees. Without effective implementation, even the most creative strategy will fail.

(iv) Strategic Control

A formal control system can help keep strategic plans on track. A control system (e.g., reward systems, pay incentives, budgets, information technology [IT] systems, rules, policies, and procedures) should be proactive instead of reactive. Control should not stifle creativity and innovation since there is no trade-off between control and creativity. Feedback is part of control.

The goal of a control system is to detect and correct problems in order to keep plans on target. This means negative results should prompt corrective action at the steps immediately before and after the problem identification. Some examples of corrective actions include updating assumptions, reformulating plans, rewriting policies and procedures, making personnel changes, modifying budget allocations, and improving IT systems.

(v) Tools to Develop Strategies

During the development of an organization's grand strategy, management can use several tools, such as those mentioned next.

- Strengths, weaknesses, opportunities, and threats (SWOT) analysis focuses on a company's internal and external environments. Specifically, it focuses on strategies; competitors; core competencies of products, services, and employees; and government laws. SWOT represents analysis of a situation (i.e., situation analysis).

- Political, economic, social, and technological (PEST) analysis focuses only on the external environment. Specifically, it focuses on political agendas, economic cycles, social trends, and technological factors.

- Market-opportunity matrix analysis focuses only on the external environment. Specifically, it focuses on customers, products, and markets.

- SMART guidelines mean goals and objectives must be Specific (considers exactness), Measurable (consider quantification), Achievable (considers agreeability to all), Realistic (considers resources), and Timely (considers deadlines). Suggests how goals and objectives should be documented and developed. Specifically, SMART guidelines focus on training aspects of managers and executives.

- Fit-gap analysis focuses only on the internal environment. Specifically, it focuses on what fits and what does not fit (gap). It is also known as a gap analysis.

- Strengths, weaknesses, opportunities, and problems (SWOP) analysis focuses on internal environments. Specifically, it focuses on operational aspects of a company to solve day-to-day operational problems.

- Force-field analysis identifies all inhibiting and facilitating forces or positive and negative variables acting on a specific situation at hand, whether those situations are internal or external to an organization. This is a problem-solving tool.

(h) Strategic Planning Process

The output of the strategic planning process is the development of a strategic plan. Its four components include: mission, objectives, strategies, and portfolio plan (see Exhibit 1.1).

EXHIBIT 1.1 Components of the Strategic Planning Process

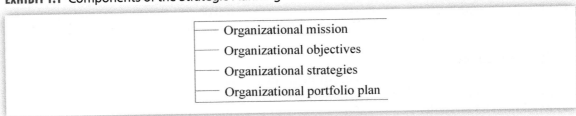

(i) Organizational Mission

Every organization exists to accomplish something, and the mission statement is a reflection of this. The mission statement of an organization should be a long-term vision of what the organization is trying to become, the unique aim that differentiates the organization from similar ones. The mission statement raises questions such as: "What is our business?" and "What should it be?" In developing a statement of mission, management must take into account three key elements: the organization's history, its distinctive competencies, and its environment.

The organization's environment dictates the opportunities, constraints, and threats that must be identified before a mission statement is developed.

When completed, an effective mission statement focuses on markets rather than products and is achievable, motivating, and specific. A key feature of mission statements has been their external rather than internal focus. This means that a mission statement should focus on the broad class of needs that the organization is seeking to satisfy (external focus), not on the physical product or service that the organization is offering at present (internal focus). As Peter Drucker, a prominent management consultant and author, puts it, the question "What is our business?" can be answered only by looking at the business from the outside, from the point of view of customer and market.

WHAT IS OUR BUSINESS?

- A business is defined by the want the customer satisfies when he or she buys a product or service.
- Satisfying the customer is the mission and purpose of every business.

A mission statement should be realistic and achievable and should not lead the organization into unrealistic ventures far beyond its competencies. A mission statement is a guide to all employees and provides a shared sense of purpose that offers a strong motivation to achieve the organization's objectives.

A mission statement must be specific to provide direction to management when it is choosing between alternative courses of action. For example, a mission to provide the highest-quality products at the lowest possible cost sounds good, but it is not specific enough to be useful. Specific quantitative goals are easier to measure.

(ii) Organizational Objectives

An organization's mission is converted into specific, measurable, and action-oriented commitments and objectives. These objectives, in turn, provide direction, establish priorities, and facilitate management control. When these objectives are accomplished, the organization's mission is also accomplished. Peter Drucker recommends at least eight areas for establishing objectives, including:

1. Market standing

2. Innovations

3. Productivity

4. Physical and financial resources

5. Profitability

6. Manager performance and responsibility

7. Worker performance and attitude

8. Social responsibility

(iii) Organizational Strategies

Organizational strategy involves identifying the general approaches a business should take in order to achieve its objectives. It sets the major directions for the organization to follow. Specific steps include understanding and managing the current customer and current products and identifying new customers and new products. *Mission and objectives lead an organization where it wants to go. Strategies help an organization to get there.*

Marketing writers describe organizational strategy in terms of a product/market matrix. The matrix is shown in Exhibit 1.2.

EXHIBIT 1.2 Product/Market Matrix

	Current Products	New Products
Current customers	Market penetration	Product development
New customers	Market development	Diversification

A **market penetration strategy** focuses on improving the position of the current product with an organization's current customers. It involves designing a marketing plan to encourage customers to purchase more of a product. It can also include a production plan to produce more efficiently than what is being produced at present. A **market development strategy** would seek to find new customers for current products. With a **product development strategy,** new products are developed to direct to current customers. A **diversification strategy** seeks new products for new customers.

(iv) Organizational Portfolio Plan

An organization can be thought of as a portfolio of businesses (i.e., combination of product lines and divisions, and service lines and divisions). It is understandable that some product lines will be more profitable than others. Management must decide which product lines or divisions to build, maintain, add, and eliminate.

(i) Related Strategies and Frameworks

Some related strategies and frameworks addressed include a discussion about blue-ocean and red-ocean strategies, McKinsey 7-S Framework, and business policy.

(i) Blue-Ocean and Red-Ocean Strategies

Authors Kim and Mauborgne first discussed the concept of **blue-ocean strategy,** where its scope encompasses all the industries not in existence today—the unknown market space that is untainted by competition (*Harvard Business Review,* October 2004). In a blue-ocean strategy, demand is created rather than fought over. There is ample opportunity for both profits and growth created by the blue-ocean strategy because it deals with new and uncontested market space that makes competition irrelevant.

In contrast, the **red-ocean strategy** works within the established market spaces that are slowly and steadily shrinking. It deals with old and highly contested market space where competition is relevant, vigorous, and overcrowded. One firm tries to steal a share of demand from other firms, instead of creating its own demand. Exhibit 1.3 presents the differences between the red-ocean and blue-ocean strategies.

EXHIBIT 1.3 Comparison of Red-Ocean Strategy with Blue-Ocean Strategy

Red-Ocean Strategy	Blue-Ocean Strategy
Compete in existing market space	Create uncontested market space
Beat the competition	Make the competition irrelevant
Exploit existing demand	Create and capture new demand
Make the value–cost trade-off	Break the value–cost trade-off
Align whole system of company activities with its strategic choice of differentiation or low cost separately	Align whole system of company activities in pursuit of differentiation and low cost simultaneously

It is interesting to note that both the blue- and red-ocean strategies have always coexisted and always will, and the one who separates them and breaks out of the old mold will win big. Practical reality, therefore, requires that corporate management understand the strategic logic of both types of oceans before diving into them.

(ii) McKinsey 7-S Framework

A management consulting firm McKinsey & Company has developed a 7-S framework as criteria for an organization's success. This framework includes seven elements: structure, strategy, skills, staff, style, systems, and shared values.

Structure is the way in which tasks and people are specialized and divided and authority is distributed. It consists of the basic grouping of activities and reporting relationships into organizational subunits and includes the mechanisms by which activities of members of the organization are coordinated. There are four basic structural forms—functional, divisional, matrix, and network, with the functional form being the most common of all.

Strategy is the way in which competitive advantage is achieved. It includes taking actions to gain a sustainable advantage over the competition, adopting a low-cost strategy, and differentiating products or services.

Skills include the distinctive competencies that reside in the organization. They can be distinctive competencies of people, management practices, systems, and/or technology.

Staff includes employees, their backgrounds, and competencies. It consists of the organization's approaches to recruitment, selection, and socialization and focuses on how people are developed; how recruits are trained, socialized, and integrated; and how employee careers are managed.

Style deals with the leadership style of top management and the overall operating style of the organization. Style impacts the norms employees follow and how they work and interact with each other and with customers.

Systems include the formal and informal processes and procedures used to manage the organization, including management control systems; performance measurement and reward systems; planning, budgeting, and resource allocation systems; information systems; and distribution systems.

Shared values are the core set of values that are widely shared in the organization and serve as guiding principles of what is important. These values have great meaning to employees because they help focus attention and provide a broader sense of purpose. Shared values are one of the most important elements of an organization's culture.

In order to manage the change process and seek improvements needed, organizations are classifying these seven elements into two groups: hard S's and soft S's. Hard S's include strategy, structure, and systems, which are easier to change than the soft S's, and the change process can begin with hard S's. Soft S's include staffing, skills, style, and shared values, which are harder to change directly and take longer to do. Both hard S's and soft S's are equally important to an organization.

(iii) Business Policy

Business goals and objectives (ends) are derived from a company's mission and vision statements. Business strategy (means) is designed to achieve such goals and objectives. Business policy, along with budgets, is a part of strategy execution and implementation in that the policy supports the strategy. Business policies are explicit statements of management's intentions to support a business strategy.

$$\text{Mission/Vision} \longrightarrow \text{Goals/Objectives} \longrightarrow \text{Business Strategy}$$

$$\text{Business Strategy} \longrightarrow \text{Business Policy}$$

Business policies can be established either at high level (e.g., ethical behavior and pollution control) or low level (e.g., a policy requiring or not requiring a receipt for customer product returns; a policy of requiring signed contracts prior to acquisition of assets or start of projects; and a policy on employee compensation, benefits, and training).

Similar to business strategy, business policy can be both proactive (intended and deliberate as in the case of hiring employees with diverse backgrounds) and reactive (adaptive as in the case of handling a major issue or crisis such as a nationwide product recall).

Moreover, business strategy precedes business policy, whereas business ethics succeeds business policy. Also, note that business ethics precedes social responsibility because the latter is derived from the former. The policy statements are expressed in several ways such as in the form of detailed rules, procedures, standards, and guidelines so employees can follow them during their job execution.

The following shows the linkages between business policy, strategy, ethics, and social responsibility and the linkages between policies, rules, procedures, standards, and guidelines.

Business Strategy ⟶ Business Policy ⟶ Business Ethics ⟶ Social Responsibility

Policies ⟶ Rules and Procedures

Policies ⟶ Standards and Guidelines

Example 1: An example of an ethical behavior policy is that no employee is allowed to take or give gifts to any customer, supplier, and contractor for doing business except for receiving small, nominal gifts not more than $25.

Example 2: An example of a pollution control policy is that no manufacturing division is allowed to dump its toxic substances (waste) discharged from factories into drinking water lakes, ponds, or oceans. All factories are required to comply with the U.S. Environmental Protection Agency's (EPA's) rules and standards.

Example 3: A retailer's policy in the area of customer product returns states that customers can return their purchased products for cash, credit, exchange, or a store credit within 15 days from the date of purchase only after showing a valid sales receipt, provided that the product is in working condition.

Example 4: A retailer's policy in the area of customer product returns states that customers can return their purchased products for cash, credit, exchange, or a store credit within 30 days from the date of purchase without showing a valid sales receipt, provided that the product is in working condition.

Example 5: An example of a rule is that employees should not take more than 45 minutes for lunch, except with supervisory permission.

Example 6: An example of a procedure for handling a customer's claim filed for a car damage consists of 11 steps performed as follows:

Steps 1 through 5 can be performed in the sequential order

Steps 6 and Step 7 can be performed in the parallel order

Steps 8 through 11 can be performed in the sequential order

Example 7: An example of a standard is to allow two hours to open a new customer's auto claim case file. Allow one hour to complete an already opened and being worked on auto claim case file (i.e., work-in-process case).

Example 8: An example of a guideline is to allow a 5% discount when a customer wants to purchase a one-half case of six bottles and a 10% discount on a full case of 12 bottles. No discount is allowed on three bottles or on individual bottles.

1.2 Performance Measurement Systems

Topics such as performance indicators, design of performance measurement systems, specific performance measures (e.g., productivity, effectiveness, efficiency, and economy), cycle times, business velocities, key performance indicators, balanced scorecard system, benchmark studies, metrics, dashboards, and data visualization tools are discussed in this section.

(a) Performance Indicators

In work settings, employees accomplish job-related activities and tasks that are measured by their supervisors. These accomplishments become a part of the employee's performance record, which is used during the employee appraisal review. It is a fact of business life that an organization's performance is an aggregation of each employee's performance. Strategic, financial, regulatory, legal, and organizational reasons drive the measurement of an organization's performance.

SELECTION CRITERIA FOR PERFORMANCE INDICATORS

The type of performance indicators utilized should be credible, meaningful, and significant to the business. For better management of the measurement process, only a few performance indicators should be assessed.

Leading organizations, in both the public and the private sector, are using various performance indicators to measure, track, and report organization performance levels for improvement as part of their value chain. These include scorecards (balanced, strategy, stakeholder, KPI, functional, and dashboard scorecards), metrics, cycle times, and standards (including national, international, organization, industry, and professional standards). For example, some U.S. organizations compare their performance to that of the U.S. Malcolm Baldrige Criteria for Performance Excellence Results, which is an example of a national standard.

Performance indicators such as scorecards, metrics, cycle times, and standards are part of an organization's value chain. The value chain should be enhanced by increasing value-added activities and by eliminating non-value-added activities to provide permanent value to internal and external customers as well as to the organization as a whole.

Selecting the right type of performance indicators (stretch goals) is as important as initiating the performance measurement program, if not more important. Incorrect selection leads to unusable results. The selected indicators should be: simple to understand, easy to implement and measure, and able to interpret results without much difficulty. Performance indicators should be selected from various generic sources, such as an organization's:

- Strategic and business plans
- Functional and operational goals and objectives
- Internal and external benchmark reports
- Employee performance targets that employees commit to
- Quality, process, and operations improvement plans
- Teachings from "lessons learned" files
- Industry white papers; list of critical success factors
- Internal/external audit reports
- Publicly available databases on best practices and benchmarks

(b) Design of Performance Measurement Systems

Performance measures should be accurately defined, analyzed, and documented so that all interested parties are informed about them. Performance standards should bring meaning to measurements. Employees who are being measured should feel that standards and specific performance measures are fair and achievable. Self-measurement may create confidence and trust and permit fast feedback and correction from employees. But it can also lead to distortions, concealment, and delays in reporting.

One design objective is that performance standards must be simple, meaningful, comparable, reproducible, and traceable, given similar business conditions. Care should be taken to compare items that are alike in terms of units of measurements (pounds, grams, liters, or gallons), time frames (hours or days), quantity (volume in units or tons), and quality (meeting the requirements).

During the design of performance measurements, the design team should take both human factors and technical factors into account. From a human factor viewpoint, the performance measures must not be so loose that they present no challenge or so tight that they cannot be attainable. Ideally, both subordinates and superiors must participate in identifying and developing the performance metrics. From a technical factor viewpoint, employees should be given proper tools, training, and equipment to do their job. Otherwise frustration will result. Above all, performance measures should be based on objective measurement instead of subjective measurement to minimize human bias and suspicion of the reported measurements.

Periodically, the performance measurements should be reviewed and updated to ensure their continued applicability to the situations at hand. Evaluations of performance measures should concentrate on significant exceptions or deviations from the standards. Therefore, exception reporting is preferred. Significant variances (deviations) require analysis and correction of standards or procedures.

The standards should match the objectives of the operation or function being reviewed. In developing standards, it is better for the auditor to work with the client than alone, with standards later validated by subject matter experts (SMEs) or industry experts for authentication. Usually the standards can be found in standard operating procedures, job descriptions, organizational policies and directives, product design specifications, operating budgets, trade sources, organization's contracts, applicable laws and regulations, generally accepted business practices, generally accepted accounting principles, and generally accepted auditing standards.

(c) Specific Performance Measures

Performance is the organization's ability to attain its goals by using resources in an efficient and effective manner. In this section, topics such as productivity, effectiveness, efficiency, and economy are discussed, compared, and contrasted.

(i) Productivity Defined

Productivity is the organization's output of goods and services divided by its inputs. This means productivity can be improved by either increasing the amount of output using the same level of inputs or reducing the number of inputs required to produce the output.

Two approaches for measuring productivity are total factor productivity and partial productivity. **Total factor productivity** is the ratio of total outputs to the inputs from labor, capital, materials, and energy. **Partial productivity** is the ratio of total outputs to a major category of inputs (e.g., labor, capital, or material). Productivity measurement is used to indicate whether there is a need for any improvement in the first place. It is often a part of the improvement process itself and is used to gauge whether improvement efforts are making any progress.[3] Measurement alone has a dramatic impact on productivity since the effects of feedback are so powerful. Measurement helps diagnose productivity needs and can be used to focus improvement resources on the most-needed operations. Monitoring of performance, feedback, and regular consideration of performance peaks and valleys as indicated by measurement data are powerful stimuli for change.

Productivity measurement strategies must be simple and practical and must be continually reevaluated. From a classical viewpoint, productivity is defined as a ratio such that the output of an effort under investigation is divided by the inputs (e.g., labor and energy) required to produce the output. Examples of productivity measurement metrics are:

- Number of customers helped divided by the number of customer service representatives
- Number of pages typed divided by the number of hours of clerical time

(ii) Components of Productivity Measurement

Four components of productivity measurement exist: inputs, processes, interim outputs, and final outputs. From these four components, all measures of productivity are built (see Exhibit 1.4).

EXHIBIT 1.4 Components of Productivity Measurement

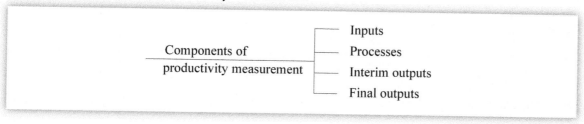

Inputs represent the amount of resources consumed in the production of outputs such as clerical time, budget, and labor hours. **Processes** transform inputs to final outputs through **interim outputs. Final outputs** represent some unit of production or results, such as number of contracts negotiated and amount of profit per completed contract. Both outputs and inputs must be measurable and quantifiable.

(iii) Criteria for Productivity Improvement

In addition to accuracy, four other criteria must be considered as part of the continuous process of productivity improvement: quality, mission and goals, rewards and incentives, and employee involvement (see Exhibit 1.5).

---

[3] Robert O. Brinkerhoff and Dennis E. Dressler, *Productivity Measurement: A Guide for Managers and Evaluators.* Applied Social Research Methods Series, Volume 19 (Newbury Park, CA: Sage Publications), 1990.

EXHIBIT 1.5 Factors of Productivity Improvement

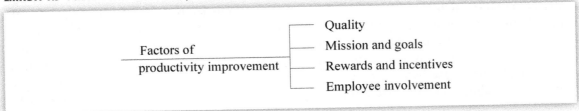

1. **Quality.** A measure that assesses only quantity of outputs can lead to reduced productivity in the long run. Both quality and quantity must be defined and measured.

2. **Mission and goals.** The measure must be related to an organization's mission and strategic goals. Measures directed to products and services that are not consistent with mission and goals threaten productivity.

3. **Rewards and incentives.** Measures must be integrated with performance incentives, reward systems, and practices. Measures that have no important contingencies will not work to improve productivity. Rewards include both intrinsic rewards and extrinsic rewards.

4. **Employee involvement.** Employees must participate in the definition and construction of productivity measures. Lack of employee involvement can result in lack of commitment and buy-in, the output results from the measures are not likely to be received favorably by employees or to have any positive impact on future productivity. Empowering employees can encourage employee involvement.

COMMON KINDS OF CRITERIA FOR MEASUREMENT OF OUTPUTS

- Accuracy
- Timeliness
- Quantity
- Customer satisfaction
- Completeness
- Cost performance

(iv) Guidelines for Productivity Measurement

Productivity measurement occurs within a dynamic and complex organization. This means that the organization's culture, the values and experience of employees, and the political context all will have a greater impact on the measurement process. The ideal organization is the one that institutionalizes a productivity measurement system as a way of doing business.

Brinkerhoff and Dressler[4] provide the following guidelines for successful productivity and performance measurement:

- Handle productivity measurement as a change strategy in the organization. It requires carefully laid out groundwork and the expectation of barriers and resistance.

---

[4] Ibid.

- Create a vision for productivity improvement through productivity measurement. Management should expect to provide strong leadership by showing a can-do attitude in the face of skepticism and barriers. The vision needs to be sold by finding win-win examples in productivity measurements improvement.

- Involve and get buy-in from senior management. Productivity efforts require massive changes in the corporate culture, policies, and procedures. These changes will need more than onetime approval of senior management.

- Aim initial efforts at targets with a high probability for success. A careful survey of the organization is required to seek out a high potential win situation.

- Be alert to, and account for, the political ramification of measurements. The introduction of productivity measurement procedures into the current organizational context may be viewed as disruptive of the power balance. Any change in resources threatens some power bases and offers others the opportunity for new power.

- Grow the productivity measurement effort from the ground up. This means that lower-level employees should be viewed as valued partners in productivity improvement efforts. They must clearly agree that any output measurers are those that they have control over. They must be given a reason to know and appreciate how productive they are. Productivity measurement systems imposed from above are likely to involve the traditional labor argument over who is responsible for productivity.

- Build ongoing communication networks and procedures. Because productivity improvement is a process in change management, the no-surprises rule is critical. It is good to involve employees from all levels of the organization. Ongoing communication includes posting results, updating newsletters, and sending internal memos.

- Provide the necessary training and support to implement and sustain productivity improvement efforts. Analytical skills are required to look at processes and see opportunities. Productivity requires an ability to quantify and measure in simple ways. Productivity demands interpretive skills so that gathered data can be put to good use. Productivity change requires the abilities to communicate, solve problems, and coach people concerning new products and processes.

  Implementation of productivity measures requires training in basic productivity and quality concepts. Helping team leaders and supervisors conduct productivity meetings is vital to productivity improvement.

  Employees also need training in using data in decision making. People must be able to spot productivity trends. They must be able to take measurement data and determine the causes of both productivity gains and declines. Employees must be trained to use statistical process control techniques.

  Supervisors and managers need training in coaching and feedback skills. Managers who catch their subordinates in the act of doing things right will find the right behaviors repeated. Early and ongoing positive feedback can make the difference between success and failure.

- Evaluate the productivity measurement system and diffuse the process across the organization. All systems must be open for inspection and evaluation. The only effective way to evaluate productivity measurement efforts is to have clearly defined goals and benchmarks. With those in place, productivity improvement efforts can be objectively evaluated. Evaluation provides the fuel for revising productivity measurement systems. Evaluation will feed directly into finding those areas where productivity can be improved.

Evaluation of productivity measurement results must support a reward system for those responsible for creating those outcome results. Both public recognition and financial recognition should be in place. The culture of the organization usually prescribes the type of reward. Information about productivity progress must be made highly visible through charts and graphs of productivity growth.

The success of the initial pilot project is very important to spread or institutionalize the process throughout the organization. Keeping internal curiosity high but reporting the challenges and opportunities presented in the process helps all employees, especially those who are not part of the pilot project. It is good to use personnel from the pilot as mentors or coaches in other areas of the organization. Their experience and success can be quite contagious. It also makes the system a peer-to-peer effort. Relying solely on management expertise may slow the process of producer-level mentoring and hinder success in measuring and raising productivity.

The traditional performance and productivity measurements, such as time schedules, on-time delivery, and cost savings, continue to be valid. However, new concepts, such as benchmarking, continuous process improvement, concurrent engineering, quality circles, self-managed teams, statistical process control, and total quality management, should be practiced and should complement the traditional measurements.

(v) Improving Productivity

When an organization decides that it is important to improve productivity, there are three places to look: technological productivity, worker productivity, and managerial productivity. **Increased technological productivity** refers to the use of more efficient machines, robots, computers, and other technologies to increase outputs. **Increased worker productivity** means having workers produce more outputs in the same time period. This includes employees working harder, improving work processes, acquiring more knowledge, more resources, improved task or workplace design, and motivating employees. **Increased managerial productivity** simply means that managers do a better job of running the business. Often the real reason for productivity problems is due to poor management.

(vi) Effectiveness, Efficiency, Economy, and Economics

Effectiveness is the degree to which an organization achieves a stated goal or objective. **Efficiency** is the use of minimal resources—raw materials, money, and people—to provide a desired volume of output. Efficiency measures how well a task or activity is performed relative to existing standards. **Economy** means whether an organization is acquiring the appropriate type, quality, and amount of resources at an appropriate cost. **Economics** deals with the allocation and utilization of scarce resources (e.g., men, money, materials, and machinery; 4Ms) to produce goods and provide services. These 4Es and 4Ms are connected with the common term **resources**.

Effectiveness and efficiency are related to productivity measurement. Effective production is the process that produces the desired results. Efficient production means achieving the desired results with a minimum of inputs. Efficiency and effectiveness must go hand in hand in productive organizations. Organizations can temporarily survive without perfect efficiency; they usually die if they are ineffective. Productivity is defined as the number of goods produced per hour, productivity does not measure the number of dollars spent in producing those goods.

MANAGEMENT APPROACHES TO IMPROVE EFFICIENCY

Management approaches to improve efficiency include:

- Restructuring outmoded business functions and operations
- Implementing BPI methods
- Deploying technology improvement methods
- Implementing a strategic approach to spending using spend analysis

A return-on-value metric can be computed as annualized savings in operating costs divided by annual total operating costs. The resulting fraction is multiplied by 100 to yield a percentage. Here, **value** refers to savings. The goal is to increase the return-on-value metric every year.

Note that economy and efficiency are directly related with "resources" being the common factor. At the same time, economy and efficiency are indirectly related to effectiveness, where the latter is achieving the stated objectives. For example, an employee can be efficient at work (i.e., increased production with fewer resources) but may not be effective due to misdirected nature of that employee's work (i.e., did not achieve the stated objective).

(d) Cycle Times and Business Velocities

Cycle time is the maximum time that a product or service is allowed to spend at a workstation, machine, or office desk. In a manufacturing company, the scope of cycle time starts from raw materials and ends up with finished goods shipping to customers. It includes all the transformation (processing) stages, inspection steps, and transportation stages. Similarly, in a service company, the scope of process analysis starts, for example, with claims application and ends up with making payment to the claimant. The goal of process analysis is to facilitate change for improvement. Doing this requires looking not only at the individual processes where problems exist but also at the upstream and downstream processes that are related to the process in question. Process improvements can be made by rearranging equipment layout, plant layout, inspection points, and testing stages with the help of motion, material, time, and material handling studies. In this effort, both product processes and service processes should be examined for waste, delays, and improvement.

Business processes, whether manufacturing or service, go through cycles from initiation to completion of defined tasks and activities. Each process has a beginning point and an ending point, and consumes resources (e.g., time, money, people talent, materials, machinery, and energy) to accomplish the defined tasks and activities. The goal is to consume as few of these resources as possible and complete these tasks and activities as efficiently and effectively as possible. Industrial engineers, also called efficiency experts, can help in establishing and measuring cycle times. Cycle time measures focus on the time dimension, expressed as hours or days.

EXAMPLES OF CYCLE TIMES

- Cycle times can be used in retail merchandising operations to determine metrics such as time to order, time to receive, time to display, time to replenish, and time to sell.
- Cycle times can be used in marketing to develop and introducing new products (time to market), improve existing products, and deliver new products to the markets.
- Cycle times can be used in HR to determine metrics such as time to hire, hire to retire, time to train, and time to promote.

Out of all the resources mentioned, time is a limited and critical resource because lost time cannot be gained. Organizations that can beat the time clock are clear winners in the highly competitive global business environment. The goal is to become the best in the best-in-class group using shorter cycle times. The shorter the cycle time, the better it is, because more work can be accomplished in less time. Cycle times measure the elapsed time between two or more successive events, the time taken to reach from point A to point B and back, or the time taken to complete a task from the beginning to the end.

If cycle times are found to be unacceptable (i.e., too long), management should do the following to make them acceptable (i.e., shorter):

- Streamline the upstream and downstream work processes through work-study, process-flow, flowcharting, and process-mapping analyses.
- Simplify the work processes by eliminating or decreasing non-value-added activities, deleting duplicate tasks, and removing unnecessary hand-offs.
- Standardize the work processes by issuing new policies, procedures, and tools for organization-wide use.
- Institutionalize standardized work processes across the entire organization in phases (i.e., phased roll-outs).

The sequence of steps needed to reduce the cycle time in the value chain is:

$$\text{Streamline} \longrightarrow \text{Simplify} \longrightarrow \text{Standardize} \longrightarrow \text{Institutionalize}$$

Velocity refers to speed and rate of turnover of something tangible, such as inventory and money currency. As mentioned, cycle time is the time taken to complete a task from the beginning to the end. "Time" is the common element between velocity and cycle time. Let us look at the velocity concept in two business settings: manufacturing industries and service industries.

BUSINESS VELOCITIES

For Manufacturing Industries

Sales Velocity $\longrightarrow$ Inventory Velocity $\longrightarrow$ Production Velocity $\longrightarrow$ Finance velocity
Human capital velocity
Systems velocity

For Service Industries

Sales Velocity $\longrightarrow$ Service Velocity $\longrightarrow$ Finance velocity
Human capital velocity
Systems velocity

For manufacturing industries, as sales are increasing (sales velocity), inventory is depleted quickly (inventory velocity), and it should be filled with increased production (production velocity). Money needs to be invested to support the increased production in terms of buying raw materials, parts, and components and paying the workforce (finance velocity). More employees may need to be hired to meet the increased production levels (human capital velocity). All these velocities in aggregate may require developing new systems or modifying existing ones, whether manual or automated (systems velocity). The same logic applies to pure service industries except that they have no inventories to sell.

When sales velocity is increasing (i.e., more sales), production velocity should also be increasing (i.e., more production) in synchronization with sales velocity. However, longer cycle times for specific internal tasks and operations within production departments can delay production of the required quantities of goods, thus preventing the organization from meeting the sales velocity demand. This delay requires optimizing the cycle times for all internal tasks and operations within production departments prior to handling the production velocity. Cycle times should not become a bottleneck to achieving any type of velocity.

In summary, velocities and cycle times are solidly linked in that shorter cycle times increase any type of business velocity, which, in turn, can increase revenues, decrease costs, and increase profits. For example, sales velocity, in part, cannot be increased if time-to-market cycle time for introducing new products is taking longer.

(e) Key Performance Indicators

Key performance indicators (KPIs) state what is most important to management to operate a company. It means that achieving a KPI is a success and its absence is a failure. KPIs are a type of metrics that show whether a business activity or function is achieving its stated objectives, established milestones, or performance targets. KPIs are warning mechanisms or red flags because they can signal or alert when an actual outcome deviates much from the targeted or expected outcome. Because KPIs should represent key measurements, they should be few in number. They must be reliable, valid, appropriate, and meaningful to be of any use. Dashboards are often used to show the periodic progress of KPIs requiring management attention. Some companies combine KPIs with metrics due to their similarity in function and focus. Therefore, both management and employees should focus on a few significant KPIs.

Some KPIs or red flags in an IT function are listed next.

- Computer system reports indicate unauthorized disclosures of customer information and/or lapses of security practices in protecting customer privacy information.

- Computer system reports are not timely or are incomplete, inconsistent, or inaccurate.

- Computer system reports lack relevance and are too detailed for use as an effective decision-making tool.

- Computer systems do not have a fully tested and ready business continuity plan.

- Computer system problems are attributed to integration of systems when old computer systems of an old company are merged with a new company's new computer systems. These problems include system failures and unreliable systems as they do not keep pace with new technologies.

- Computer systems are exposed to fraudulent activities due to lack of built-in preventive and detective controls.

- Computer systems are not audited frequently or have many unresolved control deficiencies.

Some KPIs in a production plant safety operation are listed next.

Number of:

- Safety inspections conducted in a month, quarter, and year

- Factory equipment tested and calibrated in a month, quarter, and year

- Factory operations observed for safety conditions in a month, quarter, and year
- Safety accidents investigated and reported in a month, quarter, and year
- Accidents reduced from month to month, quarter to quarter, and year to year

Amount of:

- Machine downtime reduced resulting from reduced accidents in a month, quarter, and year
- Worker compensation insurance premiums reduced resulting from reduced accidents

Some KPIs in the board room operations are listed next.

- Percentage of bad directors*
- Percentage of independent directors
- Percentage of qualified directors
- Percentage of female directors
- Percentage of minority directors
- Percentage of re-nominated directors
- Percentage of directors with excessive job length
- Percentage of shadow directors
- Percentage of directors with personal reputation at risk

---

*Bad directors are unprofessional at work with negative attitude, they are outdated in knowledge and skills, and they stick to their own agenda which is at odds with the company's agenda. Moreover, they are not team players, they are incompetent and inadequate for the job, they are a big distraction in the board room with their constant focus on trivial matters, and they bring down the productivity and performance of the entire board. Hence, they should be replaced.

Internal auditors need to be aware that some employees may manipulate and distort KPIs to survive and may distort performance results to receive larger bonuses and promotions. Therefore, auditors should compare KPIs with industry norms as well as with the same company data from period to period. Also, auditors should be careful in analyzing both KPIs that look too good and KPIs that do not meet standards.

(f) Balanced Scorecard System

Most businesses have traditionally relied on organizational performance based almost solely on financial or accounting-based data (e.g., ROI and earnings per share [EPS]) and manufacturing data (e.g., factory productivity, direct labor efficiency, and machine utilization). Unfortunately, many of these indicators are inaccurate and stress quantity over quality. They reward the wrong behavior; lack predictive power; do not capture key business changes until it is too late; reflect functions, not cross-functional processes; and gave inadequate amount of considerations to difficult-to-quantify resources such as intellectual capital. Most measures are focused on cost, not so much on quality.

Robert Kaplan and David Norton of Harvard Business School coined the term "balanced scorecard" in response to the limitations of traditional financial and accounting measures.[5] They recommend that key performance measures should be aligned with the organization's strategies

---

[5] Robert Kaplan and David Norton, *The Strategy-Focused Organization* (Boston: Harvard Business School Press, 2001).

and action plans. They suggest translating the strategy into measures that uniquely communicate the organization's vision. Setting targets for each measure provides the basis for strategy deployment, feedback, and review.

A good balanced scorecard system contains both leading and lagging indicators and both financial and nonfinancial measures. For example, a customer survey (performance drivers) about recent transactions might be a leading indicator for customer retention (a lagging indicator); employee satisfaction might be a leading indicator for employee turnover (a lagging indicator); and so on. These measures and indicators should also establish cause-and-effect relationships across the four perspectives. The cause-and-effect linkages describe the path by which improvements in the capabilities of intangible assets (people) get translated into tangible customer satisfaction and financial outcomes.

Balanced scorecards provide a graphical presentation on strategy maps and a logical and comprehensive way to describe strategy. They communicate clearly the organization's desired outcomes and describe how these outcomes can be achieved. Both business units and their employees will understand the strategy and identify how they can contribute by becoming aligned to the strategy.

Measures should include both financial and nonfinancial ones. Financial measures include ROI, residual income, EPS, profit, cost, and sales. Nonfinancial measures include customer measures, internal business process measures, innovation and learning measures, and manufacturing measures. Customer measures include satisfaction, perception, and loyalty. Internal business process measures include efficiency, quality, and time. Innovation and learning measures include R&D investment, R&D pipeline, skills and training for employees, and time to market a product or service. Manufacturing measures include factory productivity, direct labor efficiency, and machine utilization.

The balanced scorecard system is a comprehensive management control system that balances traditional financial measures with nonfinancial measures (e.g., customer service, internal business processes, and the organization's capacity for innovation and learning). This system helps managers focus on key performance measures and communicate them clearly throughout the organization.

Kaplan and Norton divided the strategy-balanced scorecard into four perspectives:

1. The **financial perspective** focuses on matters from the shareholders' perspective. It measures the ultimate results that the business provides to its shareholders, including profitability, revenue growth (net income), ROI, economic value added, residual income, costs, risks, and shareholder value. Financial measures are lagging measures (lag indicators); they report on outcomes, the consequences of past actions. They tell what has happened. The financial perspective looks back.

2. The **internal business process perspective** focuses on strategic priorities for various business processes, which create customer and shareholder satisfaction. It focuses attention on the performance of the key internal processes that drive the business, including such measures as quality levels, efficiency, productivity, cycle time, and production and operating statistics such as order fulfillment or cost per order. Internal process measures are leading measures (lead indicators); they predict what will happen. The internal process theme reflects the organization's value chain. The internal process (operations) perspective looks from the inside out.

3. The **customer perspective** is aimed at creating value and differentiation from the customers' perspective. It focuses on customer needs and satisfaction as well as market share, including service levels, satisfaction ratings, loyalty, perception, and repeat business. The customer perspective looks from the outside in.

4. The **innovation and learning perspective** sets priorities to create a climate that supports organizational change, innovation, and growth. It directs attention to the basis of future success—the organization's people and infrastructure. Key measures might include intellectual assets, employee satisfaction and retention, market innovation (new product introductions), employee training and skills development, R&D investment, R&D pipeline, and time to market a product or service. The innovation and learning perspective looks ahead.

WHICH SCORECARD PERSPECTIVE IS WHICH?

- The financial perspective looks back.
- The internal process perspective looks from inside out.
- The customer perspective looks from outside in.
- The innovation and learning perspective looks ahead.

(g) Business Process Analysis

The scope of business process analysis includes two topics: business process reengineering (BPR) and business process improvement (BPI).

(i) Business Process Reengineering

In an effort to increase revenues and market growth, organizations are conducting business process reviews. The idea behind business process reviews, whether for a production process or a service process, is to streamline operations and eliminate waste. The result is increased efficiencies, which can lead to greater effectiveness. A proven technique is BPR, which requires big thinking and making major, radical changes in business processes. Workflow analysis is a part of BPR.

BPR is one approach for redesigning the way work is done to support the organization's mission and reduce costs. BPR starts with a high-level assessment of the organization's mission, strategic goals, and customer needs. Basic questions are asked, such as: Does our mission need to be redefined? Are our strategic goals aligned with our mission? Who are our customers? An organization may find that it is operating on questionable assumptions, particularly in terms of the wants and needs of its customers. Only after the organization rethinks *what* it should be doing does it go on to decide *how* best to do it.

Within the framework of this basic assessment of mission and goals, reengineering focuses on the organization's business processes: the steps and procedures that govern how resources are used to create products and services that meet the needs of particular customers or markets. As a structured ordering of work steps across time and place, a business process can be decomposed into specific activities and can be measured, modeled, and improved. It can also be completely redesigned or eliminated altogether. Reengineering identifies, analyzes, and redesigns an organization's core business processes with the aim of achieving dramatic improvements in critical performance measures, such as cost, quality, service, and speed.

BUSINESS PROCESS REENGINEERING AND BUSINESS PROCESS IMPROVEMENT

BPR and BPI are used to improve efficiency, reduce costs, and improve customer service. IT is an enabler of BPR and BPI, not a substitute for them.

Reengineering recognizes that an organization's business processes are usually fragmented into subprocesses and tasks that are carried out by several specialized functional areas within the organization. Often no one is responsible for the overall performance of the entire process. Reengineering maintains that optimizing the performance of subprocesses can result in some benefits but cannot yield dramatic improvements if the processes themselves are fundamentally inefficient and outmoded. For that reason, reengineering focuses on redesigning processes as a whole in order to achieve the greatest possible benefits to the organization and its customers. This drive for realizing dramatic improvements by fundamentally rethinking how the organization's work should be done distinguishes reengineering from BPI efforts that focus on functional or incremental improvement.

Reengineering is not a panacea. There are occasions when functional or incremental improvements are the method of choice, as when a process is basically sound or when the organization is not prepared to undergo dramatic change. When there is a need to achieve order-of-magnitude improvements, reengineering is the method of choice.

(ii) Business Process Improvement

BPI should be continuous, not discrete, and it tends to be more of an incremental change that may affect only a single task or segment of the organization. The concept of fundamental or radical change is the basis of the major difference between BPR and BPI. Quite often BPI initiatives limit their focus to a single existing organizational unit. This in itself breaks one of the tenets of BPR, which is that BPR must focus on redesigning a fundamental business process, not existing departments or organizational units. While BPR seeks to define what the processes should be, BPI focuses more on how to improve an existing process or service.

Through BPI, organizations can achieve significant incremental improvements in service delivery and other business factors (e.g., increase in employee productivity). The expected outcomes of BPI are not as dramatic as those associated with BPR initiatives, but the process is also not as traumatic as occurs when achieving the radical changes seen with BPR. In many cases, incremental changes may be achieved in situations lacking the support necessary for more radical changes. Exhibit 1.6 shows the key differences between BPR and BPI.

EXHIBIT 1.6 BPR versus BPI

Element	BPR	BPI
Degree of change	Radical (e.g., 80%)	Incremental (e.g., 10–30%)
Scope	Entire process	Single area, function/unit
Time	Years	Months
Driver	Business	Technology
Focus	Redefine process	Automate/eliminate function
Work structure	Unified	Fragmented
Orientation	Outcome	Function

BUSINESS PROCESS REENGINEERING VERSUS BUSINESS PROCESS IMPROVEMENT

- BPR focuses on achieving dramatic improvements.
- BPI focuses on achieving incremental improvements.

(h) Benchmarking Studies

(i) Benchmarking Defined

Benchmarking is the selection of best practices implemented by other organizations. **Best practices** are the best ways to perform a business process. Organizational change and improvement are the major elements of benchmarking. Benchmarks are the result of a study of organizational processes and performance through internal comparisons (i.e., between and among a company's business units and divisions) and external comparisons (i.e., between two or more outside organizations). The first-level, basic processes that define a company's operations are listed next.

- Understanding markets and customers
- Designing products and services
- Marketing and selling those products and services
- Producing what customers need and want
- Delivering products and services
- Providing service to customers

Supporting these basic processes, management and support processes maximize the value with the use of human resources, IT, and financial/physical resources.

The best way to practice benchmarking is to:

- Analyze business processes (inventory major business processes, conduct documentary research, and attend conferences to understand new developments).
- Plan the benchmark study (define scope, request site visits, and develop a methodology for capturing the new data).
- Conduct the benchmark study (analyze best practices and identify performance gaps).
- Implement the benchmark results (incorporate best practices into business processes and reevaluate the business processes).

(ii) Types of Benchmarking

Two types of benchmarking exist: business process benchmarking and computer system benchmarking. Business process benchmarking deals with BPI and BPR to reduce costs and to improve quality and customer service. Computer system benchmarking focuses on computer hardware/software acquisition, computer system design, computer capacity planning, and system performance. Each type of benchmarking has its own place and time.

Business benchmarking is an external focus on internal activities, functions, or operations in order to achieve continuous improvement.[6] The objective is to understand existing processes and

---

[6] C. J. McNair and Kathleen Leibfried, *Benchmarking* (New York: Harper Business, 1992).

activities and then to identify an external point of reference, or standards, by which that activity can be measured or judged. A benchmark can be established at any level of the organization in any functional area, whether manufacturing or service industries. The ultimate goal is to attain a competitive edge by being better than the best.

Value creation is the heart of organizational activity, whether in a profit or a nonprofit entity. Benchmarking provides the metrics by which to understand and judge the value provided by the organization and its resources. Benchmarking focuses on continuous improvements and value creation for stakeholders (i.e., owners, customers, employees, and suppliers), utilizing the best practices to focus improvement efforts.

Benchmarking targets the critical success factors for a specific organization. It considers the mission of an organization, its resources, products, markets, management skills, and others. It requires an identification of customer(s), whether internal or external to the organization. Benchmarking is an early warning system of impending problems and is not a onetime measurement. Benchmarking can focus on improving organization structures, analyzing managerial roles, improving production processes, and developing strategic issues.

Benchmarking can be done by using published materials, insights gained at trade association meetings, and conversations with industry experts, customers, suppliers, academics, and others.

(iii) The Right Time for Business Process Benchmarking

Benchmarking should be undertaken when triggers are present. These triggers can arise internally or externally in response to information needs from some other major project or issue or problem in the company. *Examples of these triggers* include quality programs, cost reduction programs, new management, new ventures, and competitive moves. Benchmarking should be done as needed, without any preconceived notions.

(iv) Reasons for Business Process Benchmarking

A company should benchmark for three reasons:

1. It wants to attain world-class competitive capability.
2. It wants to prosper in a global economy.
3. It simply wishes to survive (desperation).

A company can benchmark in six distinct ways:

1. Internal benchmarking
2. Competitive benchmarking
3. Industry benchmarking
4. Best-in-class benchmarking
5. Process benchmarking
6. Strategic benchmarking

Internal benchmarking is the analysis of existing practices within various departments or divisions of the organization, looking for best performance as well as identifying baseline activities and drivers. Drivers are the causes of work: the triggers that set in motion a series of actions or activities that will respond to the requests or demands by the stockholders.

In doing internal benchmarking, management is looking downward, examining itself first before looking for outside information. Significant improvements are often made during the internal analysis stage of the benchmarking process. Value-added activities are identified, and non-value-adding steps are removed from the process. Internal benchmarking is the first step because it provides the framework for comparing existing internal practices to external benchmark data. Internal benchmarking focuses on specific value chains or sequences of driver-activity combinations.

Competitive benchmarking looks outward to identify how other direct competitors are performing. Knowing the strengths and weaknesses of competitors provides good input for strategic and corrective actions.

Industry benchmarking extends beyond the one-to-one comparison of competitive benchmarking to look for trends. It is still limited in the number of innovations and new ideas it can uncover because every company is following every other company in the industry. At best, industry benchmarking can help establish the performance baseline or can give an incremental gain. It gives a short-run solution and a quick fix to an existing problem. However, it does not support quantum leaps or breakthroughs in performance since the comparison is limited to one industry.

Best-in-class benchmarking looks across multiple industries in search of new, innovative practices, no matter what their source. Best-in-class benchmarking is the ultimate goal of the benchmarking process. It supports quantum leaps in performance and gives a long-run competitive advantage.

Process benchmarking centers on key work processes, such as distribution, order entry, or employee training. This type of benchmarking identifies the most effective practices in companies that perform similar functions, no matter in what industry.

Strategic benchmarking examines how companies compete and seeks the winning strategies that have led to competitive advantage and market success.

WHICH BENCHMARKING DOES WHAT?

- Internal benchmarking looks downward and inward.
- Competitive benchmarking looks outward.
- Industry benchmarking looks for trends. It provides a short-run solution and a quick fix to a problem.
- Best-in-class benchmarking looks for the best all around. It provides a quantum jump in improvement.
- Process benchmarking is specific.
- Strategic benchmarking is broad with big impact.

(i) Metrics

Metrics are performance measurements that provide a baseline where progress can be compared and assessed. They provide an accurate yardstick against which an employee's and individual department's progress can be evaluated. Metrics may or may not have warning mechanisms, signals, and alerts as KPIs do. Some companies could combine the metrics with KPIs due to their similarity in function and focus. For example, quality metrics can be developed for the cost of quality measurement to help managers monitor quality, as listed next.

- The total cost of quality (COQ) as percentage of revenue by year
- The cost of conformance as percentage of total COQ
- The cost of nonconformance as percentage of total COQ

Prior to measuring metrics performance, metrics criteria must be established consisting of the following.

- Align with the organization's goals and objectives
- Drive organizational efficiency and effectiveness either directly or indirectly
- Be applicable and linkable to the organization's mission, vision, and value
- Be actionable, accountable, and implementable in practice
- Be practical in terms of cost effectiveness, cost acceptance, cost reduction, and operationally economical and efficient
- Be reliable, stable, predictable, and measurable
- Be valid, accurate, and appropriate for its purpose
- Be reproducible given the same circumstances, which is a sign of metric design strength
- Be repeatable to ensure consistency in metric outcomes and results
- Be traceable from the origination to the destination in both directions (i.e., forward tracing and backward tracing)
- Above all, metrics must be significant in size and scope, few in number for manageability, meaningful, and useful to decision makers

(j) Presentation Methods

Performance measurement outcomes and results can be presented to management using at least three methods such as traditional reports, dashboards, and data visualization tools. The latter two methods are further discussed next.

(i) Dashboards

Dashboards in general and specifically business data dashboards are a collection of performance indicators showing an object's or a device's status and quality levels in colors. Dashboards are used to present vital data in order to develop a strategy or plan. They provide a concise and visual summary of overall performance. Data dashboards are presented in several forms, including numerical, graphical, and interactive formats (exhibits, slides, audios, and videos). They use drill-down and drag-and-drop features. An example is showing an automobile's performance in terms of its speed, revolutions per minute, oil pressure, and temperature.

Dashboards are of two types: static and interactive (basic and advanced). Static dashboards show traditional reports that are mainly focused on financial information (e.g., sales, revenues, costs, and profits). Basic interactive dashboards show information about customers' buying habits and cross-sales to them. Advanced interactive dashboards can have built-in simulation models to do what-if type of analyses (i.e., sensitivity analysis).

Today, most organizations present only structured data on dashboards. Better insights and rewards can be achieved if dashboards show structured data, unstructured, and semistructured data to provide big-picture perspectives of businesses.

Data filters can be built into dashboards so data can be sliced from different perspectives or drilled down to a more detailed level using parameters, such as:

- Transaction date, month, quarter, or year
- Cost data by contract
- Revenue or profit data by a retail store
- Sales data by a market region
- Quarterly performance by a business segment

Data filters provide the ability to explore data at multiple levels and to customize user-driven data analysis. Data filters show only the requested data and ignore the rest of the data not requested.

(ii) Data Visualization tools

Data visualization tools are data presentation methods and include various reporting and information dissemination methods to report data results to management for their actions and decisions. These methods include charts and graphs (e.g., tabular, column, bar, pie, line, layer, Pareto, and radar charts; as well as dashboards, histograms, and scatter diagrams).

1.3 Organizational Behavior

This section discusses topics such as organizational theory, group dynamics and group development; management structures and organization systems (i.e., closed or open system); and organizational effectiveness and decline.

(a) Organizational Theory

(i) Theories of Organization

Basically, two theories of organization exist: the traditional view and the modern view. The traditional view has closed-system thinking while the modern view incorporates open-system thinking (see Exhibit 1.7).

EXHIBIT 1.7 Theories of Organization

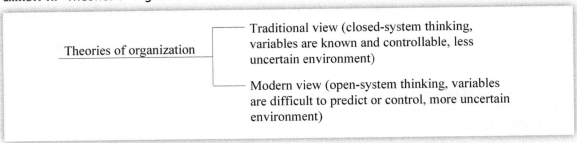

The **traditional view** assumes that the surrounding environment is fairly predictable and that uncertainty within the organization can be eliminated through proper planning and strict control. The primary goal is economic efficiency. All goal-directed variables are known and controllable.

The **modern view** assumes that both the organization and its surrounding environments are filled with variables that are difficult to predict or control. The organization interacts continuously with an uncertain environment. The primary goal is survival in an environment of uncertainty and surprise. The modern view deals with more variables that cannot be controlled or predicted.

Next we explore the evolution of traditional organization theory and its challenges followed by system characteristics.

(A) Traditional View of Organizations

Henri Fayol and Frederick Taylor treated organizing as a subfield of management. They believed that close supervision, obedience, orders, and rules were the norm. Four traditional principles of organization emerged:

1. A well-defined hierarchy of authority (to ensure the coordinated pursuit of organizational goals)

2. Unity of command (each individual answered to only one superior)

3. Authority equal to responsibility (Authority is the right to get subordinates to accomplish objectives, and responsibility is the obligation to accomplish those objectives. Individuals should be accountable for getting something done only when they were given formal authority to get it done.)

4. Downward delegation of authority but not of responsibility (The obligation for getting something done remains with the superior although the authority and responsibility were passed along to subordinates.)

Later Max Weber called bureaucracy efficient because of these four characteristics: division of labor, hierarchy of authority, a framework of rules, and impersonality (hiring and promoting people on the basis of what they know, not who they know). Bureaucracy is a matter of degree, and a moderate degree of bureaucratization can enhance organizational efficiency while extreme cases can hinder efficiency. However, trying to eliminate bureaucracy is impractical.

The traditionalists' rigid recommendations for organizing and managing were challenged by Weber since they did not work in all situations. Experience has proved that organizing was more than just strict obedience to authority and that bureaucracy has become the epitome of inefficiency. In addition, bottom-up authority and environmental complexity and uncertainty also challenged the traditional thinking about organizations.

Authority. Is authority top-down or bottom-up? Traditionalists believed that authority was tied to property ownership and therefore naturally flowed from the top of the organization to the bottom. Chester Barnard questioned the traditional assumption about the automatic downward flow of authority. Instead, he proposed a more democratic *acceptance theory of authority* in which a leader's authority is determined by subordinates' willingness to comply with it.

Acceptance Theory of Authority. The acceptance theory of authority opened the door for upward communication and the informal organization that is based on friendship rather than work rules. Subordinates are viewed as active controllers of authority, not mere passive recipients.

Barnard believed that a subordinate recognizes a communication from a superior as being authoritative and decides to comply with it only when

1. The message is understood,

2. The subordinate believes it is consistent with the organization's purpose,

3. It serves the subordinate's interest, and

4. The subordinate is able to comply.

Uncertainty. Charles Perrow observed that the increasing complexity of markets, variability of products, increasing number of branch plants, and changes in technology all required more adaptive organizations, not rigid structure. Plans usually have to be made on the basis of incomplete or imperfect information, and, consequently, things do not always work out according to plan.

(B) Modern View of Organizations

Proponents of open-systems views realize that system-to-system interactions are often as important as the systems themselves. Here the "system" includes social, political, legal, and economic systems. A highly organized and vigorously interactive world needs realistically dynamic models, which is a characteristic of open-system thinking.

CLOSED SYSTEMS VERSUS OPEN SYSTEMS

- Traditional closed-system thinking emphasizes rigid organization structure. It largely ignores environmental influences. Closed-system thinking does not have permeable boundaries. It assumes that all organizations are systems with common characteristics.

- Modern open-system thinking emphasizes the need for flexibility and adaptability in organization structure. It fosters a more realistic view of the interaction between an organization and its environment. Open systems have permeable boundaries. All modern organizations are open systems.

Four characteristics that emphasize the adaptive and dynamic nature of all modern open systems are: interaction with the environment, synergy, dynamic equilibrium, and equifinality.

Since open systems are not self-sufficient, they depend on the environment for survival (i.e., on **interaction with the environment**). An open system adds up to more than the sum of its parts (i.e., **synergy**). A successful business is more than the factors of production: labor, land, and capital.

In open systems, dynamic equilibrium is the process of maintaining the internal balance necessary for survival by importing needed resources from the environment (i.e., **dynamic equilibrium**). **Equifinality** means reaching the same result by different means. It indicates that there is more than one way to get the job done.

Another way of looking at open systems is in relation to subsystems. If a system is made up of subsystems, *three organizational subsystems would include technical, boundary spanning, and managerial*. The technical subsystem (production function) physically transforms raw materials into finished goods and services. Boundary-spanning subsystems facilitate the organization's interaction with its general environment. Most boundary-spanning jobs (interface functions) are easily identified by their titles. The managerial subsystem controls and directs the other subsystems in the organization.

KEY CONCEPTS TO REMEMBER: Open Systems

- Technical subsystems are the very core of the organization.
- Boundary-spanning subsystems are directed outward toward the general environment.
- The managerial subsystem serves as a bridge between the other two subsystems.

Many traditional theories of organizing exist, including bureaucracy, administrative theory, scientific management theory, and human relations theory. The latter topic is discussed briefly.

(ii) Human Relations Theory

Many management philosophers rejected the individualism, which was emphasized in the theories of bureaucracy, administrative theory, and scientific management. These philosophers deplored competition between individuals in the organization and supported the idea of a cooperative group ethic. Emphasis was placed on the relations between people who are members of groups.

Mary Parker Follett and George Elton Mayo were two prominent philosophers associated with the **human relations movement**. Follett proposed the idea that individual freedom must be subordinated to the interest of the group. She was concerned with the individual but thought that the individual finds his or her creative self only by relating to others in groups. Follett thought that all authority rested on the consent of those who are directed. Therefore, she proposed that demands should arise from the situation rather than from the superior. Follett proposed that superiors should give reasons for their orders to subordinates. Participative management style is most likely to produce subordinates with management skills.

Mayo was very concerned with groups in the organization. He attempted to employ scientific methods to study the behavior of groups. He is most famous for his experiments at the Hawthorne Electric Plant in 1928, which in part investigated the influence of the degree of illumination on the productivity of workers. According to the Hawthorne studies, worker behavior is a complex system of forces that include personalities of the workers, nature of their jobs, and formal measurement and reward practices of the organization.

Closely related to the human relations movement is the **behavioral science** approach. Both of these approaches deal with the individual and his or her interaction in groups. However, the behavioral science approach arose because of the discontent with the methodology of researchers such as Mayo. Behavioral scientists deplored the small amount of data gathered by human relations advocates and the unsystematic examination of the data gathered.

Also, behavioral scientists thought that human relations writers overemphasized group behavior at the expense of individual behavior. Finally, behaviorists rejected the overriding concern with cooperation, when conflict may result in such benefits as innovation. It is easy to see that behavioral scientists emphasize the scientific method in investigating the individual and groups so that conclusions can be objective.

Behavioral scientists use three primary methods to study individuals and groups so that management can learn better ways of handling people: the case study, the sample survey, and the experiment. These three methods are inductive approaches since they involve studying a small number of persons or one organization and generalizing the results to other persons and organizations.

There are two primary criticisms of the behavioral science approach. First, behavioral science is not as precise a science as physics or chemistry because people are not as predictable as the nature of the universe. Second, behavioral science conclusions are useful, but since people and the environment in each organization are different, the application of findings may produce different results in different settings.

Douglas McGregor outlined a set of highly optimistic assumptions about human nature. He recommended **Theory Y**, which is a set of assumptions for his optimistic perspective about people. This is in contrast with the traditional view of people by managers (Theory X). McGregor criticized Theory X for being pessimistic, stifling, and outdated. Exhibit 1.8 shows the comparison between Theory X and Theory Y assumptions about people from the manager's perspective.

EXHIBIT 1.8 McGregor Theory X/Y Assumptions

Theory X Assumptions	Theory Y Assumptions
Most people are lazy, dislike or avoid work.	Work is a natural activity, and people are creative, energetic, and imaginative.
Most people must be coerced and threatened, and are unwilling to take responsibility.	The average person is willing to take responsibility.
Most people prefer to be directed.	People are capable of self-direction and self-control.
Most people are interested only in job security.	People are committed to do a good job if they are rewarded adequately.

Senior management believes employees will volunteer to serve on committees because they: (1) want to play a greater role in the operation of their company, (2) want to receive more from their jobs than just a paycheck, and (3) have interests that extend beyond the boundaries of their specific jobs and will welcome the opportunity to pursue those interests. The motivational strategy that senior management has adopted is McGregor's Theory Y.

William Ouchi discovered a type of organization that exhibited a style of management that effectively combines the traits of typical American and Japanese companies. He called these hybrid companies **Theory Z organizations**. These companies focus on the employee in areas such as:

- Long-term employment
- Relatively slow evaluation and promotion

- Cross-functional career paths
- Participative decision making
- Individual responsibility
- Concern for the employee
- Emphasis on employee self-control

Theory Z is an organizational culture based on a participative decision-making process.

Theory T and **Theory T+** are complementary theories based on these Southeast Asian assumptions:

- Work is a necessity but not a goal itself.
- People should find their rightful place in peace and harmony with their environment.
- Absolute objectives exist only with God.
- In the world, persons in authority positions represent God, so their objectives should be followed.
- People behave as members of a family and/or group.
- Those who do not are rejected by the general society.

(iii) Contingency Design Theory

Organizing is the structuring of a coordinated system of authority relationships and task responsibilities. It spells out who does what and who reports to whom. Organizational structure can translate strategy into an ongoing productive operation (see Exhibit 1.9).

EXHIBIT 1.9 Strategy and Structure

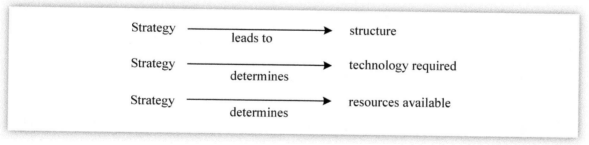

Contingency design is an extension of the modern open-system view that permits the custom tailoring of organizations to meet unique external and internal situational demands. This design is based on the assumption that there is no single best way to structure an organization. It is the process of determining the degree of environmental uncertainty and adapting the organization and its subunits to the situation. *Contingency design is fitting the organization's strategy to its internal and external environment.*

Two popular contingency models that validate the contingency approach by systematically matching structural characteristics with environmental demand include the Burns and Stalker model and the Lawrence and Lorsch model.

(A) Burns and Stalker model

Behavioral scientists Tom Burns and G. M. Stalker proposed a typology for categorizing organizations by structural design. They distinguished between mechanistic and organic organizations (see Exhibit 1.10).

EXHIBIT 1.10 Structural Design of Organizations

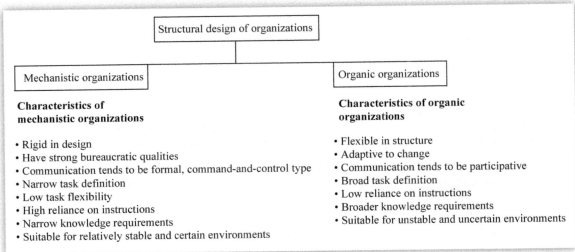

(B) Lawrence and Lorsch Model

Paul Lawrence and Jay Lorsch documented the relationships between two opposing structural forces (differentiation and integration) and environmental complexity.

Differentiation resulting from a division of labor and technical specialization is the tendency among specialists to think and act in restricted ways. Differentiation tends to fragment and disperse the organization.

Integration, in opposition to differentiation, is the collaboration among specialists that is needed to achieve a common purpose. Integration is a unifying and coordinating force and is partially achieved through hierarchical control, standard policies and procedures, departmentalization, cross-functional teams and committees, better human relations, and liaison individuals and groups.

According to Lawrence and Lorsch, every organization requires an appropriate dynamic equilibrium (an open-system theme) between differentiation and integration. *They demonstrated that in successful firms, both differentiation and integration increased as environmental complexity increased.* These findings are equally applicable to the overall organization, departments, or divisions. They also found that the more differentiated an organization, the more difficult it is to achieve integration. These findings suggest that organizational failure in the face of environmental complexity probably results from a combination of high differentiation and inadequate integration. Under these conditions, specialists work at cross-purposes and become involved in counterproductive conflicts.

Contingency design models conclude that there is no single best organization design and that the more uncertain the environment, the more flexible and adaptable the organization structure must be.

KEY CONCEPTS TO REMEMBER: Various Theories of Management

- Bureaucratic organization is characterized by division of labor, hierarchy (top-down) authority, a framework of rules, impersonality, formal policies and procedures, and a competency level for hiring and promotions. Bureaucracies focus on organizational tasks rather than people and emphasize productivity of human behavior and task results. Bureaucracies tend to be stable in the long run. Division of work deals with specialization of labor to achieve organizational objectives.

- The classical view of an early theory of management includes the universality concept. Esprit de corps, one of Fayol's 14 universal principles of management, emphasizes teamwork, communications, and harmonious effort among individuals. An example is "employees of a small retail outlet are highly motivated and genuinely concerned about the store's prosperity."

- The universal process is based on the belief that a single management process can be applied in all organizations. It believes that good managers are interchangeable among organizations. It uses a rigid, inflexible organizational structure regardless of the external environment.

- The operational approach, also known as scientific management or operations research, is concerned with technical, quantitative, and objective means of achieving efficiency in production operations. The manager is production oriented, and his or her primary interest is in improving efficiency and reducing waste. Standardization of work is a goal of the scientific school of management.

- Behavioral approaches to management primarily focus on people. They imply that it is in management's best interest to be concerned about employees' well-being. The behavioral approach to management most likely to have resulted from the prospect of unionization.

- Operations management is a management process that designs, operates, and controls production systems. The focus of productive systems is to transform physical resources and human talent into needed goods and services. The operations management theory or approach views organizations as productive systems consisting of inputs, a transformation process, and outputs.

- In general systems theory, the term "subsystem" is used to describe the relationship of each system component to the next higher component. In the opinion of general systems theorists, all organizations are identified as being open. The systems approach to management views the organization as a system of interconnected and interdependent parts. It believes that the whole is greater than the sum of its parts. The systems approach to management is demonstrated by a chief executive officer (CEO) who stresses the importance of the interdependencies among the various components of the organization.

- The contingency management approach is practiced by a member of an organization who assigns responsibility and delegates authority based on the task to be performed and the individual available for assignment. Contingency management theory uses multivariate analysis to determine how a grouping of variables react together to produce an outcome.

- According to contemporary management thought, managers should be given training in a course linking key staffing issues with organizational strategy and structure. Such a course should include HR planning, selection, training, and performance appraisal.

- The principle of equity is concerned with fairness and justice.

- Under the scalar chain principle (chain of command), there is a chain of direct authority relationship from superior to subordinate. The scalar principle of management is violated when an employee goes over a supervisor's head and receives special permission from the departmental manager to, for example, take an extra week of vacation.

- The unity of command principle is violated when an employee answers to several bosses.

- Unity of direction requires the focus of all efforts aimed toward accomplishing the same, common goal, that is, all employees move in the same direction.

(b) Group Dynamics

(i) How Groups Think and Make Decisions

(A) Overview

Today, groups or committees make many decisions in organizations. There is a link between communication concepts and the subject of group decision making. Since messages are transmitted between members of the group, the effectiveness of this communication process will have a greater impact on the quality of the group's decisions.

Groups offer an excellent vehicle for performing many of the steps in the decision-making process.[7] They are a source of both breadth and depth of input for information gathering. If the group is composed of individuals with diverse backgrounds, the alternatives generated should be more extensive and the analysis more critical. When the final solution is agreed on, there are more people in a group decision to support and implement it. These pluses, however, can be more than offset by the minuses—time consumed by group decisions, the internal conflicts they create, and the pressures they generate toward conformity.

KEY CONCEPTS TO REMEMBER: The Group Decision—Strengths and Weaknesses

- **Strengths or assets.** Breadth of information, diversity of information, acceptance of solution, and legitimacy of process
- **Weaknesses or liabilities.** Time consuming, conformity, domination of discussion, ambiguous responsibility, and loss of personal accountability

(B) Group Behaviors

Group psychology studies have revealed that various groups produced contradictory behavior. Sometimes people did better at their tasks when there were other people around and sometimes they did worse.

Groupthink, groupshift, and group polarization are the three by-products of group decision making, all of which have the potential to affect the group's ability to evaluate alternatives objectively and arrive at quality decision solutions (see Exhibit 1.11).

EXHIBIT 1.11 Types of Group Behavior

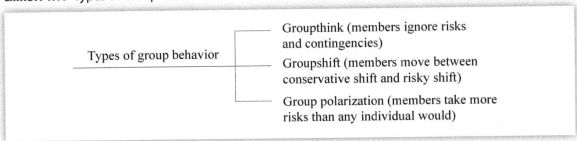

Types of group behavior
- Groupthink (members ignore risks and contingencies)
- Groupshift (members move between conservative shift and risky shift)
- Group polarization (members take more risks than any individual would)

Groupthink is related to norms and describes situations in which group pressures for conformity deter the group from critically appraising unusual, minority, or unpopular views. Groupthink is a

---

[7] Stephen P. Robins, *Organizational Behavior* (Englewood Cliffs, NJ: Prentice Hall, Inc.), 1993.

disease that attacks many groups and can dramatically hinder their performance. Individuals who hold a minority position that is different from that of the dominant majority are under pressure to suppress, withhold, or modify their true feelings and beliefs. Opposition is viewed as disloyal and is discouraged. Groupthink can ignore risks and contingencies. The group leader must remain impartial and play the devil's advocate to come up with new challenges and alternatives.

Groupshift indicates that in discussing a given set of alternatives and arriving at a solution, group members tend to exaggerate the initial position that they hold. Groups move between conservative shift and risky shift. The fact that it is a group decision frees any single member from accountability for the group's final choice. Greater risk can be taken because even if the decision fails, no one member can be held fully responsible.

Group polarization can occur when a group decides to take more risks than any individual would have judged reasonable. Groups tend to make more extreme decisions than individuals who are part of the group. Group polarization and groupthink are two extremes on a risk measurement scale (see Exhibit 1.12).

EXHIBIT 1.12 Groupthink and Group Polarization

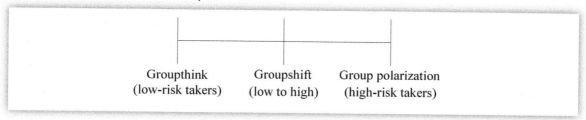

Groupthink   Groupshift   Group polarization
(low-risk takers)   (low to high)   (high-risk takers)

(ii) Factors Affecting Group Decisions

Many factors affect group decisions, including ownership, nature, and structure of the problem; and nature, maturity level, size, and climate of the group (see Exhibit 1.13).

EXHIBIT 1.13 Factors Affecting Group Decisions

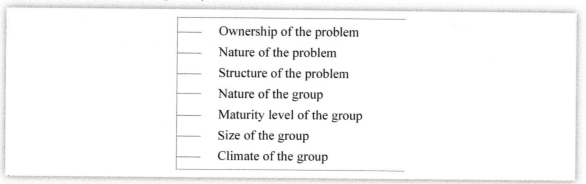

— Ownership of the problem
— Nature of the problem
— Structure of the problem
— Nature of the group
— Maturity level of the group
— Size of the group
— Climate of the group

(A) Ownership of the Problem

One of the selection criteria for a problem-solving method focuses on whether the problem is one that is "owned" by an individual or by a group. Individual ownership means that one person has the major interest in the solution of a problem; in effect, the group then works for that person. Group ownership means that several individuals or departments have an investment in the solution of a particular problem. Synectics is a good technique to use to solve problems owned either by individuals or by groups.

(B) Nature of the Problem

Not all problems can or should be solved by a group of people. One or two people might straighten out a problem if they have enough information and if they can take actions to remedy the problem by themselves. But if the problem is uncertain—that is, if not enough is known about it or the strategies for achieving a solution, or if implementation of the solution requires the acceptance, investment, or action of many people—then the best approach is to work with a group.

(C) Structure of the Problem

Another dimension to decision making is the structure of the problem. Structure has to do with the routineness of the decision required. How much is known or understood about the problem? If a problem is structured, if it is well understood, and if there are routine ways of dealing with it, the group can usually move quickly from the problem identification stages to the generation of solutions. But if a problem is unstructured or if it is not well understood, the group will need to spend a good deal of time identifying the problem before moving on to subsequent stages.

(D) Nature of the Group

Basically, group membership should reflect the level of the problem. For example, if the problem is a departmental one, then members of the department should be asked to resolve it. Participants should also be considered with regard to their potential functions within the group. Ideally, the membership should include people who are knowledgeable about various aspects of the problem: technical, political, organizational, environmental, personal, and so on. In addition, since any final solution needs to be accepted by those who will implement it, the people who actually will carry out the solution should be present in the group. The presence of knowledgeable people improves the quality of the decision; implementers improve the acceptance of it.

(E) Maturity Level of the Group

Knowledge of the maturity of the group helps to gain a clear understanding of its dynamics. "Group maturity" refers to the length of time a group has worked together and the kinds of dynamics that usually accompany old or new relationships. Chris Argyris,[8] a management theorist, suggests that, over time, a group develops from an immature, passive state to a mature, self-directive state. Dependency of members on the group leader, passivity of individuals, a scarcity of overt verbal or nonverbal behaviors, inner-directed responses, short time perspective, and erratic, shallow interests characterize the behavior of the immature, passive group. The mature group, however, characteristically displays independence of the members from the leader, activity of group members, many overt verbal or nonverbal behaviors, outer-directed responses, long-range time perspective, and a deep, strong interest among members concerning the direction of the group.

Many problem-solving groups will exist for only short periods of time, and group maturity will most likely be minimal. In another setting, however, the group may be an ongoing problem-solving group that is very mature.

(F) Size of the Group

The size of the group should be decided after considering organizational role, group functions, and group maturity. Although the size should reflect all of these factors, the optimum number of participants for problem-solving technique is between 6 and 10 persons. A group of this size allows for involvement and idea generation in a workable situation.

---

[8] Chris Argyris, "Teaching Smart People How to Learn," in *Harvard Business Review* May–June 1991.

(G) Climate of the Group

The climate of the group is also important for decision making. Certain behaviors are clues to the climate in the group. Members in a supportive group will offer positive reinforcement, stroking, smiling, head nodding, direct eye contact, forward body movement, and so on. Members in a hostile or nonsupportive environment will discount ideas and people, sigh deeply, frown, avoid eye contact, and behave passively. Passive behaviors in this situation are those that deny the problem.

(H) Criteria and Determinants of Group Effectiveness

A group is defined as two or more freely interacting individuals who share a common identity and purpose. Individuals join groups for various reasons to satisfy their personal and professional goals. Two kinds of groups exist: informal and formal groups. An informal group is a collection of individuals seeking friendship while a formal group is a collection of individuals doing productive work. Individuals can be subjected to ostracism, which is rejection from a group.

Two criteria for group effectiveness include attractiveness and cohesiveness. Attractiveness has the outside-looking-in view, while the cohesiveness has the inside-looking-out view. Cohesive group members tend to stick together as they focus on "we" instead of "I." An individual's perception and frames of reference have a lot to do with how groups can be attractive or cohesive.

Factors that can enhance a group's attractiveness and cohesiveness include cooperative relationships among members, a high degree of interaction among group members, a relatively small-size group, and similarities among group members.

Factors that can detract from a group's attractiveness and cohesiveness include unreasonable demands on the individual, disagreement over work rules and procedures, unpleasant experience with some group members, and destructive competition or conflict.

(c) Group Development

Effectiveness and efficiency increase as the group matures. Similarly, immature groups are ineffective and inefficient. A significant benefit of group maturity is that a person's individuality strengthens. Also, members of mature groups tend to be emotionally mature.

Kreitner[9] suggests six stages of group development:

1. Orientation
2. Conflict and challenge
3. Cohesion
4. Delusion
5. Disillusion
6. Acceptance

During stages 1 through 3, group members attempt to overcome the obstacles of uncertainty over and authority, while during stages 4 through 6, they overcome the obstacles of uncertainty over interpersonal relations. An understanding of group development stages will improve an employee's time management skills.

---

[9] Robert Kreitner, *Management*, 9th ed. (Boston: Houghton Mifflin Company, 2004).

Stage 1: Orientation. Group members give the impression to managers and leaders that they want permanent control expressed through their wants and needs.

Stage 2: Conflict and change. Group members struggle for control by suggesting alternative courses of action and strive to clarify and reconcile their roles. Many groups do not continue past this stage because they get bogged down due to emotionalism and political infighting. An "I" feeling is dominant at this stage for power and authority.

Stage 3: Cohesion. A "we" feeling becomes apparent at this stage as everyone becomes truly involved in the project and any differences over power and authority are resolved.

Stage 4: Delusion. Issues and problems are dismissed or treated lightly. Group members work in group participation and promote harmony at all costs.

Stage 5: Disillusion. Disillusion sets in as unlimited goodwill wears off and disenchantment grows. Some members will prevail by showing their strengths while others hold back. Tardiness and absenteeism are the norm, which is symptomatic of diminishing cohesiveness and commitment.

Stage 6: Acceptance. Some group members move from conflict to cohesion and act as group catalysts as their expectations are more realistic. Power and authority structure is accepted. Consequently, the group members tend to be highly effective and efficient.

(d) Management Structures and Organization Systems

In this section, we review two organization systems—closed system and open system—and two management structures—mechanistic and organic. A relationship between management structures and organization systems is established.

A closed system is independent of its external environment; it is autonomous, enclosed, and sealed off from the external environment. It focuses on internal systems only. Its external environment is simple, stable, and predictable. The major issue for management is to run the business efficiently with centralized decision making and authority. A closed system represents a bureaucratic organization.

An open system is dependent on its environment to survive; it both consumes resources and exports resources to the external environment. It transforms inputs into outputs. It must continuously change and adapt to the external environment. Open systems are complex, unstable, and unpredictable, and internal efficiency is a minor issue for management. Open systems represent modern organizations.

A mechanistic management structure is characterized by rules, procedures, and a clear hierarchy of authority. Organizations are formalized and centralized, and the external environment is stable.

An organic management structure is characterized by a fluid (looser) and free-flowing nature, which is adaptive to changes in the external environment with few or no written rules and regulations and operates without a clear hierarchy of authority. Organizations are informal and decentralized, and responsibility flows down to lower levels. An organic management structure encourages teamwork and problem solving by letting employees work directly with each other.

> **MANAGEMENT STRUCTURES AND ORGANIZATION SYSTEMS**
>
> ■ A mechanistic management structure resembles a closed system of an organization.
>
> ■ An organic management structure resembles an open system of an organization.

(e) Organizational Effectiveness and Decline

The next items are highlights of organizational effectiveness and organizational decline:

- Effectiveness is a measure of whether organizational objectives are accomplished or not.

- Efficiency is the relationship between outputs and inputs.

- The effectiveness criteria are prescribed by society in the form of explicit expectations, regulations, and laws and by stockholders in the form of profits, ROI, and growth.

- Organizational effectiveness has a time dimension to it (i.e., near, intermediate, and distant future).

- Organizational decline results from management complacency (usually the primary culprit), unsteady economic growth, resource shortages, competition, and weak demand for products and services. It typically involves a reduction in the size or scope of the organization.

Ways to prevent organizational decline are listed next.

- Organize the company into definable ventures that have explicit goals.

- Concentrate on the toughest competitors and the most difficult customers.

- Define each job so that it is closely tied to a venture.

- Promote individual diversity to take risks and experiment with new ideas.

- Strengthen the participative management process.

- Emphasize more effective information flow, both downward and upward.

1.4 Performance Management Techniques

This section defines motivation, presents motivation theories and motivation strategies (e.g., job design, rewards, participative management, work schedules, and hard-sell and soft-sell tactics), and discusses organizational politics.

(a) Motivation Defined

All employees, whether they are doing routine tasks or not, need to increase their motivation levels to excel in their day-to-day jobs. **Motivation** refers to the psychological process that gives a purpose and direction to human behavior. Motivation theories are generalizations about the "why" and "how" of purposeful behavior. The goal is to move individual employees toward achieving organizational objectives, including job performance. Job performance is defined as follows:

$$\text{Job Performance} = \text{Ability} \times \text{Motivation}$$

Both ability (skills and competence) and motivation (willingness to work hard) are necessary for effective and efficient job performance. Ability and skills are acquired through education, training, and on-the-job experience. The individual's motivational factors such as needs, satisfaction, expectations, and goals are affected by challenging work, rewards, and participation. Motivational factors are both inborn and learned.

(b) Motivation Theories

Four popular motivation theories exist: Maslow's needs hierarchy theory, Herzberg's two-factor theory, expectancy theory, and goal-setting theory (see Exhibit 1.14).

EXHIBIT 1.14 Motivation Theories

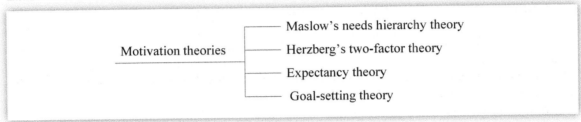

(i) Maslow's Needs Hierarchy Theory

Maslow's theory focuses on five needs structured as a hierarchy, from bottom to top, and includes physiological, safety, love, esteem, and self-actualization needs. Individuals proceed up the hierarchy of needs, one level at a time. Higher needs emerge as lower needs are met. A fulfilled need does not motivate an individual. Needs are related to motivation in that unsatisfied needs motivate behavior. Maslow's esteem needs are most closely associated with Herzberg's concept of job enrichment.

A major deficiency of Maslow's theory was which higher-order needs come into play after the lower ones are satisfied and in which order they come into play cannot be predicted. If anything, it seems that most people are simultaneously motivated by several of the same-level needs. Another criticism is that individual perception is secondary. Maslow's needs theory failed under actual testing.

(ii) Herzberg's Two-Factor Theory

Herzberg's theory was based on employee satisfaction in that a satisfied worker is motivated from within to work harder and a dissatisfied employee is not self-motivated. Herzberg's two factors are satisfiers and dissatisfiers. Dissatisfaction is associated with complaints about the job context or factors in the immediate work environment. Exhibit 1.15 presents some factors labeled as satisfiers and dissatisfiers.

EXHIBIT 1.15 Satisfiers versus Dissatisfiers

Dissatisfiers	Satisfiers
Company policy and administration	Achievement
Supervision	Recognition
Relationship with supervisor, peers, and subordinates	Work itself
Work conditions	Responsibility
Salary	Advancement
Personal life	Growth
Status	
Security	

The elimination of dissatisfaction is not the same as truly motivating an employee. Herzberg is convinced that money is a weak motivational tool because, at best, it can only eliminate dissatisfaction. To satisfy and motivate employees, an additional element is required: meaningful, interesting, and challenging work. Some critics argued that his theory was weak on an empirical basis, and the individual's perception was secondary. Others argued that one person's dissatisfier may be another's satisfier. Herzberg's biggest contribution is the motivating potential for enriched work.

(iii) Expectancy Theory

Individual perception, although secondary in the Maslow and Herzberg models, is central to expectancy theory. Expectancy theory is based on the assumption that motivational strength is determined by perceived probabilities of success. The term "expectancy" refers to the subjective probability (or expectation) that one thing will lead to another. The focus of this model is as follows: One's motivational strength increases as one's perceived effort–performance and performance–reward probabilities increase. This theory has received empirical support from researchers and is based on common sense since *Effort* $\longrightarrow$ *Performance* $\longrightarrow$ *Reward*. Employees tend to work harder when they believe they have a good chance of getting personally meaningful rewards.

(iv) Goal-Setting Theory

Goal setting is the process of improving individual or group job performance with clear objectives and high standards. Management by objectives (MBO) is an example of goal-setting theory.

Management by Objectives. Organizational goals can be better achieved if the goals of superiors and subordinates are integrated with organizational goals. All levels of management should be involved in setting the objectives of the organization in working toward the common goals.

The essence of MBO is close consultation between superior and subordinate in the setting of and agreement on goals. They must agree on the goals to be achieved. Feedback is necessary during the period of working toward the goals and after the goals are accomplished. A key requirement is unity of command. Unity of command requires subordinates to be evaluated by a single superior—the manager.

MBO characteristics are listed next.

- Organizational common goals and measures of the achievement of those goals are fully complied with.

- If necessary, the organizational structure is changed. That is, the chain of command and the unity of command may have to be changed.

- Each superior confers with each subordinate on the subject of the subordinate's goals.

- The superior and subordinate must agree on the subordinate's goals and the criteria for achieving the goals.

- The subordinate must be given feedback on achievement of the goals based on the criteria established.

- The performance of the subordinate must be reviewed.
- The performance of the organization must be reviewed periodically.

When implementing MBO, these problems/barriers can be encountered:

- Unity of command must be achieved.
- Managers must change to a democratic style of leadership.
- Accomplishment of goals that are nonquantifiable may be difficult to measure.

See Exhibit 1.16 for advantages and disadvantages of MBO.

EXHIBIT 1.16 Advantages and Disadvantages of MBO

Advantages	Disadvantages
Improves communications between superiors and subordinates	Opposition by managers for employee participation
Performance evaluation relatively easier due to established criteria	Suboptimization can occur
	Difficulty in reaching agreement on goals
Room for innovation and creativity	Learning is on trial-and-error basis
Results in fewer or no surprises to managers	Imposition of external factors (e.g., economy) on employee goals without full control over them

WHICH MOTIVATION THEORY IS WHICH?

- Maslow's theory is built around the hierarchy of human needs.
- Herzberg's theory is concerned with job performance and job satisfaction and focuses on maintenance and motivational factors.
- Expectancy theory is based on concept that people's expectations of rewards are derived from their unique personal motive structure, beliefs, and perceptions.
- Goal-setting theory (MBO) is based on improving individual or group job performance.

(c) Motivation Strategies

Motivation strategies are derived from the motivational theories. Five strategies are listed next (see Exhibit 1.17):

1. Motivation through job design
2. Motivation through rewards
3. Motivation through employee participation
4. Motivation through work schedules and services
5. Motivation through hard-sell and soft-sell tactics

EXHIBIT 1.17 Motivation Strategies

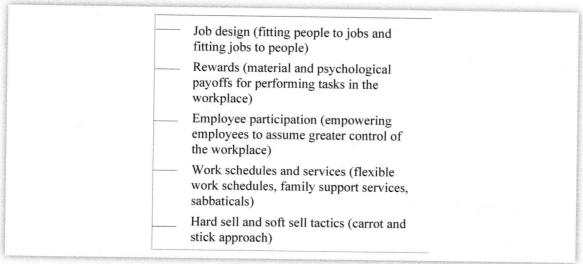

Job design (fitting people to jobs and fitting jobs to people)

Rewards (material and psychological payoffs for performing tasks in the workplace)

Employee participation (empowering employees to assume greater control of the workplace)

Work schedules and services (flexible work schedules, family support services, sabbaticals)

Hard sell and soft sell tactics (carrot and stick approach)

(i) Motivation through Job Design

Motivation through job design deals with two specific strategies: fitting people to jobs and fitting jobs to people. Three proven alternatives in fitting people to jobs include realistic job previews, job rotation, and limited exposure.

Job previews deal with audiovisual previews about the job and written descriptions in booklet form. Surveys have shown that those who were given realistic job previews tended to have lower initial expectations, greater organizational commitment and job satisfaction, and a lower turnover rate. However, the impact of realistic job previews on job performance was mixed.

Job rotation involves periodically moving people from one specialized job to another. It permits employees to rotate among several job positions. Job rotation provides for the continual development of managerial skills.

Limited exposure deals with limiting the individual's exposure to tedious and highly fragmented jobs. This technique is called "earned time off," which involves establishing a challenging yet fair daily performance standard and letting employees go home when the standard is reached.

The strategy of fitting jobs to people includes job enlargement and job enrichment. **Job enlargement** is the process of combining two or more specialized tasks in a workflow sequence into a single job. **Job enrichment** is redesigning a job to increase its motivating potential. It increases the challenge of work by reversing the trend toward greater specialization. Unlike job enlargement, which merely combines equally simple tasks, job enrichment builds more complexity and depth into jobs by introducing planning, decision making, and responsibility normally carried out at higher levels. Job enrichment may motivate employees because it addresses the work itself instead of trying to change the workers to fit the jobs.

JOB ENRICHMENT VERSUS JOB ENLARGEMENT

- Job enrichment adds depth to a job.
- Job enlargement adds width to a job.

Exhibit 1.18 presents a comparison of characteristics between job enrichment and job enlargement.

EXHIBIT 1.18 Comparison of Job Enrichment and Job Enlargement

Characteristics of Job Enrichment	Characteristics of Job Enlargement
Jobs are loaded vertically. It allows employees to participate in planning and controlling. It promotes employee discretion and judgment. It gives a feeling of personal responsibility.	Jobs are loaded horizontally. It combines two or more specialized tasks but does not increase the planning or decision-making aspects of the job.

(ii) Motivation through Rewards

Every employee expects to be rewarded in some way for work performed. Rewards may include material and psychological payoffs for performing tasks in the workplace. Managers have found that job performance and satisfaction can be improved by properly administered rewards. Two types of rewards exist: (1) extrinsic rewards, which are payoffs granted to the individual by other people (e.g., money, employee benefits, promotions, recognition [employee of the month], status symbols, and praise) and (2) intrinsic rewards, which are self-granted and internally experienced payoffs (e.g., sense of accomplishment, self-esteem, and self-actualization). An intrinsic reward is an internally generated benefit or satisfaction resulting from good work performed. See Exhibit 1.19 for the types of rewards.

EXHIBIT 1.19 Types of Rewards

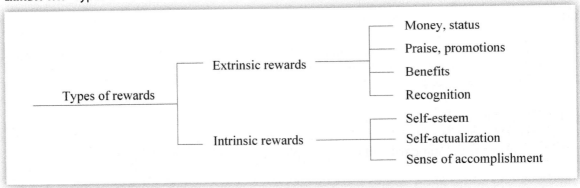

EXAMPLE

A positive motivational effect will take place when a director of internal auditing decides to fill a supervisory vacancy by promoting a senior auditor rather than recruiting an outsider for the position.

(iii) Motivation through Employee Participation

Participative management is defined as the process of empowering employees to assume greater control of the workplace. Employees may participate in setting goals, making decisions, solving problems, and designing and implementing organizational changes. Employee participation will not work if individual values and attitudes are not in tune with it. Organizational factors, such as job design and corporate culture, can also help or hinder the process.

Environmental factors, such as technological change and competition, also affect the participation process.

Two team-oriented approaches to employee participation include quality control circles and self-managed teams. *Quality control circles* are small groups of voluntary, problem-solving employees who meet regularly to discuss quality improvement and ways to reduce costs. To be successful, the quality control circles should be introduced in an evolutionary manner rather than by management order.

Self-managed teams (or autonomous work groups) take on traditional managerial tasks as part of their normal work routine. Advocates say self-managed teams foster creativity, motivation, and productivity. The manager's role will be more of a facilitator than an order giver, and supervision tends to be minimal. Hiring, training, and job design need to be skillfully interlocked with self-managed teams, thus driving up front-end costs. Traditional authoritarian supervisors view self-managed teams as a threat to their authority, job security, and power.

QUALITY CONTROL CIRCLE VERSUS SELF-MANAGED TEAMS

- Quality control circles foster employee participation within the confines of the existing power structure.
- Self-managed teams create a whole new decentralized power structure.

(iv) Motivation through Work Schedules and Services

Approaches such as flexible work schedules, family support services, and sabbaticals are aimed at enhancing employee motivation and increasing job performance. While employees liked flexible work schedules, employers did not like them because of greater administrative expense, supervisory resistance, and inadequate coverage of jobs. Alternative approaches were invented, such as compressed workweeks (40 hours in fewer than five days), permanent part-time jobs (workweeks with fewer than 40 hours), and job sharing (complementary scheduling that allows two or more part-timers to share a single full-time job).

(v) Motivation through Hard-Sell and Soft-Sell Tactics

If an employee has no motivation other than salary, then that employee's quality of work and quantity of work will simply and slowly deteriorate over a period of time. Something more is needed here. When motivating employees, managers can use general motivational strategies such as hard-sell or soft-sell tactics based on an employee's personality type. The carrot (soft sell) and stick (hard sell) approach is another name for hard-sell and soft-sell tactics.

> **Example 1:** Hard-sell tactics use outnumbering (outmaneuvering, outsmarting, and overpowering), pressure (pushy and aggressive behavior), tough (mean and hard-nosed), and rank-pulling (threats and intimidations) approaches, which can make an employee uncooperative and unfriendly. The outcome from using the hard-sell approach is a lose-lose situation. If the hard-sell approach does not work for some reason, then switch to the soft-sell approach.

> **Example 2:** Soft-sell tactics use logical reasoning, emotional appeals, convincing, negotiating, nonthreatening, advice, and praise approaches, which can make an employee listen and cooperate. The outcome from using the soft-sell approach is a win-win situation. If the soft-sell approach does not work for some reason, then switch to the hard-sell approach.

(d) Organizational Politics

Organizational politics (OP) focuses on self-interest in response to opposition at the workplace. Many employees feel that freedom from office politics is important to their job satisfaction. Positive aspects of OP include exchanging favors, forcing coalitions, and seeking sponsors at upper levels of the organization. Negative aspects of OP include whistle-blowing, revolutionary coalitions, threats, and sabotage.

WHAT IS APPLE POLISHING?

Apple polishing is a political strategy prompted by a desire to favorably influence those who control one's career. Its major purpose is to make the supervisor look good.

Why do employees and employers promote OP? Employees resort to OP when they are unwilling to trust their career solely to competence, hard work, or luck. An organization's climate or culture placing unreasonable barriers to individual or group success promotes OP.

Research on OP has indicated that:

1. The larger the organization and the higher the levels of management, the greater the perceived amount of political activity.
2. People in staff positions were viewed as more political than those in line positions.
3. Marketing people were viewed as more political than those in production.
4. "Reorganization changes" prompted more political activity than any other types of change.

Examples of positive impact resulting from OP include gaining visibility for ideas, improving coordination and communication, developing teams and groups, advancing one's career, and increasing esprit de corps. Examples of negative impact resulting from OP include distraction from organizational goals, misuse of resources, and organizational conflict.

Tactics that are common expressions of OP in the workplace include posturing (one-upmanship), empire building, making the superior look good (apple polishing), political favors, creating power and loyalty cliques, reciprocating, engaging in destructive competition, and sabotaging (as a last resort).

Remedies to OP include creating openness and trust, measuring employee performance rather than personalities, integrating individual and organizational goals, implementing job rotation techniques, and practicing better work scheduling and timely career planning.

Rules for winning at OP include:

1. Finding out what the supervisor expects.
2. Finding out how the grapevine works.
3. Finding a mentor.
4. Fighting over major issues only.
5. Not hiring family members or close friends.

1.5 Managers, Leaders, and Entrepreneurs

This section defines the roles and responsibilities of managers, leaders, and entrepreneurs (MLEs). It also presents skills, traits, tools, and theories applicable to MLEs. In addition, this section compares managers, leaders, and entrepreneurs.

(a) Management Defined

Management is defined as the attainment of an organization's strategies, goals, and objectives in an effective, efficient, economical, and productive manner. To this end, management is carried out through people by utilizing resources. Managers make things happen through hiring employees and deploying resources to accomplish their goals and objectives.

Managers get their power from the organizational structure (i.e., administrative power). This power comes from the manager's job title or position status in the organization. Managers need the administrative power to provide stability, discipline, and continuity within the organization and to fulfill their roles and responsibilities. Managers share some common qualities with leaders in the areas of problem solving, decision making, and change implementation. Note that an organization has many managers and many more supervisors.

(b) Management Functions

Management achieves its strategies, goals and objectives through four functions of planning, organizing, directing (leading), and controlling an organization's resources. Managers use a multitude of management skills (e.g. conceptual, human, and technical) and a variety of management styles (e.g., directive, analytic, intuitive, and behavioral) to perform these functions. The correct sequence of management functions is shown next:

Planning ⟶ Organizing ⟶ Directing ⟶ Controlling

(i) Planning

Planning defines where the organization wants to be in the future and how to get there. It describes action steps, detailed tasks, timelines for each task, and resources needed for each task. A lack of planning—or poor planning—can hurt an organization's overall performance.

Plans are developed from strategies. Four types of plans include strategic, tactical, operational plans, and contingency plans. Tactical plans are derived or translated from the strategic plans, and operational plans are derived or translated from the tactical plans, in that order. Contingency plans are developed for all the other three types of plans because they also need backup plans.

The time horizon for a *strategic plan* is long term (between three and five years or more) as it deals with the broadest and complex issues that will have a dramatic impact, both positively and negatively, on the success and survival of an entire organization.

The time horizon for a *tactical plan* is middle term or intermediate term (between one and two years) as it deals with a specific business and its product lines by translating strategic plans.

The time horizon for an *operational plan* is short term (less than a year) as it deals with a specific department and its functions by translating tactical plans.

The time horizon for a *contingency plan* (backup plan) is short term and long term to address all time frames and all planning types.

These four types of plans are connected with each other in the correct sequence with their timelines, as follows:

Mission/Vision ⟶ Goals/ Objectives ⟶ Strategies ⟶ Plans

Planning Types = Strategic Plans ⟶ Tactical Plans ⟶ Operational Plans ⟶ Contingency Plans
        (Long Term)   (Middle Term)   (Short Term)   (Short and Long Term)

Planning levels include corporate level (higher level), business unit level (middle level), and functional and departmental level (lower level). These levels are developed by managers at various levels of the company. The lower levels support the higher levels, meaning that the functional level supports the business unit and corporate levels and that the business unit level supports the corporate level. For example,

- Strategic plans are developed at the corporate level and the business unit level.
- Tactical plans are developed at the business unit level and the functional level.
- Operational plans are developed at the functional level and the department level.
- Contingency plans are needed if the original plan does not work out for some reason.

    Example 1: The strategic plan for the KPX Company, a consumer product manufacturing company, is to produce and sell the green dishwashing liquid brand 146 in all retail stores in two years.

    Example 2: The tactical plan for the KPX Company, a consumer product manufacturing company, is to locate the supplier sources in the world, to reformulate the green dishwashing liquid brand 146, and to fully test the product within one year.

    Example 3: The operational plan for the KPX Company, a consumer product manufacturing company, is to obtain commitments (including slotting fees) from retailers that they will carry and sell the green dishwashing liquid brand 146 in all retail stores in six months after the product is made in factories.

    Example 4: The contingency plan for the KPX Company, a consumer product manufacturing company, is to develop alternate, backup plans if the original plan does not work out for some reason. A total of three separate contingency plans are needed—one for each of the strategic, tactical, and operational plans.

The planning process consists of six stages or steps:

1. Analyzing external environment
2. Assessing internal resources
3. Establishing goals and objectives
4. Developing action plans
5. Implementing action plans
6. Monitoring outcomes

The planning tools include budgets and performance goals, resulting from the translation of plans.

(ii) Organizing

The organizing function typically follows the planning function and reflects how the organization tries to accomplish the strategic plan. Organizing involves the assignment of tasks, the grouping of tasks into jobs and departments, the assignment of authority, and the allocation of resources across the organization. Organizing is important because it follows from strategy in that strategy defines what to do and organizing defines how to do it. The organization structure is a tool that managers use to allocate resources for getting things accomplished.

Five design approaches to organizing a business function include:

1. Establishing authority, responsibility, accountability, and delegation
2. Developing organization charts
3. Establishing span of control or span of management
4. Organizing line and staff functions
5. Organizing departments

(iii) Directing

Directing (leading) is the use of influence to motivate employees to achieve organizational goals and objectives. Directing involves creating a shared culture and values, communicating goals to employees throughout the organization, and infusing employees with the desire to perform at a higher level. Directing involves motivating entire departments and divisions as well as those individuals working immediately with the manager.

(iv) Controlling

Controlling is the fourth and final function of management. Controlling helps measure whether a department or company is meeting its established plans and performance standards. Controlling is monitoring employees' activities, determining whether the organization is on target toward its goals, and making corrections as necessary. Managers must ensure that the organization is moving toward its goals. New trends toward empowerment and trust of employees have led many companies to place less emphasis on top-down controls (i.e., a form of management-imposed controls, such as punishments and disciplinary actions) and more emphasis on bottom-up controls in terms of training employees to monitor and correct themselves (i.e., a form of self-control).

IT is also helping managers provide needed organizational control without strict top-down constraints. Companies can use computer programs to put *more* constraints (e.g., policies, procedures, and rules) on employees if managers believe the situation demands it.

Traditional controlling tools include operating budgets, capital budgets, analyzing financial statements for profitability and liquidity ratios, and adapting total quality management principles. Note that budgets can act as both planning and controlling tools.

(c) Managers' Styles

The quality of a decision is a direct reflection of how the decision maker processes information. Managers approach decision making and problem solving in very different ways, depending on the availability of information. Their approaches, perceptions, and recommendations vary because their minds work differently. Researchers have identified four management styles: directive, analytic, behavioral, and intuitive. One is not superior to the others.

The **directive style** focuses on "more telling and less doing" instead of "less telling and more doing." This style comes across as a command-and-control style, representing an autocratic management style. Most employees get turned off with this style.

Analytic-style managers tend to be logical, precise, and objective. They prefer routine assignments that require attention to detail and systematic implementation. The manager uses deductive reasoning. The analytic style is good to use in model-building exercises and forecasting involving projections.

The **behavioral style** takes into account an employee's emotions and feelings that people go through. This style considers what people are saying, what they mean, and why they are saying it, requiring a participative management approach. Most employees favor this style.

The **intuitive-style** manager is creative, is comfortable in handling a dynamic and nonroutine environment, follows hunches, and is mostly subjective. This manager likes to address broad issues and use inductive reasoning and sees things in complex patterns rather than as logically ordered bits and pieces. The intuitive style is good to use in brainstorming sessions and where traditional assumptions need to be challenged.

In practice, many managers use a combination of directive, analytic, behavioral, and intuitive styles.

(d) Managers' Skills

Management skills can be broadly classified as conceptual, human, and technical. These skills are not exhibited equally across management levels. They vary with the nature of the job, the level of decision making, and the type of interaction with people.

Conceptual skill is the cognitive ability to see the organization as a whole and the relationship among its parts. It involves the manager's thinking, information processing, and planning. It requires the ability to think strategically—to take the broad, long-term view. Conceptual skills are needed by all managers but are especially important for managers at the top. Many of the responsibilities of top managers, such as decision making, resource allocation, and innovation, require a broad view.

Human skill is the manager's ability to work with and through other people and to work effectively as a group member. It includes the ability to motivate, facilitate, coordinate, lead, communicate, and resolve conflicts. As globalization, workforce diversity, uncertainty, and competition for highly skilled knowledge workers increase, human skills (i.e., interpersonal and people skills) become even more crucial. Here, focus is on emotional needs of employees instead of the physical needs related to the job.

Technical skill is the understanding of and proficiency in the performance of specific tasks. It includes mastery of the methods, techniques, and equipment involved in specific functions, such as engineering, manufacturing, or finance. These skills are particularly important at lower organizational levels. Many managers get promoted to their first management job by having excellent technical skills. However, technical skills become less important than human and conceptual skills as managers move up the hierarchy.

The next table lists the importance of these skills for three management levels in highest to lowest order of importance.

Management Levels	Management Skills
Supervisors	Technical, Human, Conceptual
Managers	Technical, Human, Conceptual
Executives	Human, Conceptual, Technical

(e) Managerial Roles

Henry Mintzberg[10] studied what managers do by focusing on the key roles they play. He criticized the traditional, functional approach as unrealistic and believed that it does not tell what managers actually do. Mintzberg believed that the functional approach portrays the management process as far more systematic and rational and less complex than it really is.

In his view, the average manager is not the reflective planner and precise "orchestra leader" that the functional approach suggests. Mintzberg used a method called "structured observation," which included recording the activities and correspondence of few selected top-level executives. He then isolated 10 roles he believed are common to all managers. These 10 roles have been grouped into three major categories: interpersonal, informational, and decisional roles.

(i) Interpersonal Roles

Because of their formal authority and superior status, managers engage in a good deal of interpersonal contact, especially with subordinates and peers. The three interpersonal roles that managers play are:

1. **Figurehead.** As a symbol of legal authority, performing certain ceremonial duties (e.g., signing documents and receiving visitors)

2. **Leader.** Motivating subordinates to get the job done properly

3. **Liaison.** Serving as a link in a horizontal and vertical chain of communication

(ii) Informational Roles

Every manager is a clearinghouse for information relating to the task at hand. Informational roles are important because information is the heart of organizational decision making. The three typical informational roles of managers are:

1. **Nerve center.** Serving as a focal point for nonroutine information; receiving all types of information

2. **Disseminator.** Transmitting selected information to subordinates

3. **Spokesperson.** Transmitting selected information to outsiders

---

[10] Henry Mintzberg, "Managerial Work: Analysis from Observation," *Management Science* (October 1971).

(iii) Decisional Roles

In their decision roles, managers balance conflicting interests and make choices. Through decisional roles, strategies are formulated and put into action. Managers play four decisional roles:

1. **Entrepreneur.** Designing and initiating changes within the organization
2. **Disturbance handler.** Taking corrective action in nonroutine situations
3. **Resource allocator.** Deciding exactly who should get what resources
4. **Negotiator.** Participating in negotiating sessions with other parties (e.g., vendors and unions) to make sure the organization's interests are adequately represented

(f) Managers' Tools

Managers can deploy several tools to motivate and control employees' behavior with the ultimate goal of increasing their work-related productivity and performance. The use of each tool depends on the business situation, the manager's goals, and employee's performance at a point in time. Five examples of these tools include

1. Management by objectives
2. Management by example
3. Management by exception
4. Management by walking about
5. Management by technology

(i) Management by Objectives

MBO is an example of goal-setting and motivational theory, where it is a process of improving an individual's or a group's job performance with clearly established objectives and high standards. MBO is also called management by results, management by standards, or management by authority because an employee's actual performance (results) is compared with the standards or objectives set for that employee. All this work is accomplished because of a manager's job authority.

An organization's goals can be better achieved if the goals of superiors and subordinates are integrated with those of the organization. All levels of management should be involved in setting objectives for their employees that align with the organization's objectives; that is, all should work toward common goals.

The essence of MBO is a formal agreement between the superior and subordinate in the setting of goals for the upcoming year (i.e., a meeting of minds or a mental contract). They must agree in advance on the goals to be achieved. Feedback mechanisms are necessary during the goal-setting process and after the goals are accomplished (quarterly meetings). A key requirement of MBO is unity of command, meaning that a subordinate's performance is to be evaluated by only a single superior—the manager.

(ii) Management by Example

Management by example is the ultimate test for all managers and leaders because it is leading or showing by example, meaning it is doing walk the talk. It means practicing what is preached, putting the words into actions, and putting the plans to implementation. This is where most managers and leaders fall short because management by example is not an easy thing to live by. It requires setting the right tone at the top of the management hierarchy. Employees expect their managers to behave as management by example.

(iii) Management by Exception

Management by exception operates when what actually occurs deviates from the established norms and standards. Only transactions with exceptions—not all transactions—are listed and reported to management for review. Management by exception recognizes that managers have limited time and that their time should not be wasted by requiring them to review and take actions on every business transaction that comes across their desk. This requirement is a waste of resources.

To reduce the unnecessary workload, managers need to establish tolerance or threshold levels for major types of transactions, and business rules need to be defined and programmed into computer systems. Any transaction that goes beyond the threshold level will be flagged and reported to management.

Examples of business rules follow:

- Notify the manager only when actual revenues fall by 5%.
- Notify the manager only when actual expenses go up by 10%.
- Notify the manager only when actual profits fall by 3%.

Management by exception is also called management by reports, meaning a manager notices the exceptions by reviewing some printed or online reports.

(iv) Management by Walking About

The principle of management by walking about (walking around or wandering around) (MBWA) means that managers walk around their business facilities (offices, stores, and warehouses) to talk to employees to find out their problems firsthand and to teach them about company's direction and management values. MBWA should be practiced regularly so that employees do not think that management is spying on them. The idea is to build trust between management and employees. MBWA is also called open-book management thinking, meaning that employees have the right to be informed about the company's plans and activities because they have a big stake in the company's well-being.

> **Fact:** The Hewlett-Packard (HP) Company is well known to practice the MBWA principle, which was implemented by many corporations in the United States.

> **Example:** Examples of informal communications include MBWA and the grapevine.

MBWA means higher-level employees (e.g., executives and senior managers) talk directly with the lower-level employees (e.g., hourly workers at factory, office, or warehouse) to learn about problems and issues confronting them as well as to share their key ideas and values. These meetings are informal and unannounced. The idea behind MBWA is practicing an open-book management principle, meaning that business matters are kept open on purpose for employees to see with their own eyes. The goal of open-book management is to build trust between management and employees.

(v) Management by Technology

Here, the term "technology" means use of IT (e.g., computers, networks, and mobile devices), manufacturing technology (e.g., computer-aided design and manufacturing), service technology (e.g., customer relationship management system), retail technology (e.g., sensors, tags, electronic commerce, and mobile commerce), and management technology (e.g., decision support systems and data dashboards). All these technologies use the Internet, computers, and mobile devices regardless of the location and who uses them.

Virtual technology with collaborative software is facilitating the vast growth of virtual managers, virtual leaders, virtual employees, virtual teams, and virtual organizations where employees, managers, leaders, suppliers, vendors, and business partners work together in a cooperating and coordinating manner in seamless and borderless global work environments to achieve common business goals and objectives very efficiently and effectively.

(g) Management Staffing Levels

Managers use conceptual, human, and technical skills to perform the four management functions of planning, organizing, leading, and controlling in all organizations. But not all managers' jobs are the same. Managers are responsible for different departments, work at different levels in the hierarchy, and meet different requirements for achieving high performance. Two management types that describe the need for staffing levels include vertical differences and horizontal differences.

Vertical Differences. An important determinant of the manager's job is hierarchical level. Three levels in the hierarchy include top managers, middle managers, and front-line (first-line) managers. Top managers are responsible for setting organizational goals, defining strategies for achieving them, monitoring and interpreting the external environment, and making decisions that affect the entire organization. They share a long-term vision for the organization, shape corporate culture, and nurture an entrepreneurial spirit that can help the company keep pace with rapid change. Middle managers are responsible for implementing the overall strategies and policies defined by top managers. They are concerned with the near future and are expected to establish good relationships with peers around the organization, encourage teamwork, and resolve conflicts. First-line managers are directly responsible for the production of goods and services. They include titles such as supervisor, line manager, section chief, and office managers. Their primary concern is the application of rules and procedures to achieve efficient production, provide technical assistance, and motivate subordinates. The time horizon in which they work is short, with the emphasis on accomplishing day-to-day goals.

Horizontal Differences. The other major difference in management jobs occurs horizontally across the organization. These jobs include functional managers and general managers. Functional mangers are responsible for departments that perform a single functional task and have employees with similar training and skills. Line managers are responsible for the manufacturing (operations) and marketing departments that make or sell the product or service. Staff managers are in charge of departments such as finance and HR that support the line managers. General managers are responsible for several departments that perform different functions. Project managers also have general management responsibility, because they coordinate people across several departments to accomplish a specific project.

(h) Organizational Commitment

The hallmark of any organization is the strong and sincere commitment to excellence of senior management (i.e., directors, executives, and officers). To achieve this excellence, management needs to consider various facilitating and inhibiting forces or factors that could change the expected outcomes of excellence. Facilitating factors increase the chances of achieving the organizational excellence; inhibiting factors decrease such chances. Senior management's goal must be to encourage the facilitating factors and discourage the inhibiting factors to achieve excellence. Here, only strong commitment to excellence will succeed, not weak or mediocre commitment. This level of commitment is also needed when building organizational commitment from all levels of management and nonmanagement. Commitment goes both ways, which means that commitment flows from management to employees and flows from employees to management. Management is the catalyst, change agent, goal-setter, inspirer, enabler, and motivator whereas employees are supporters and achievers of management's goals. Note that employees support management only when they see clear benefits coming to them (i.e., financial and nonfinancial benefits). Exhibit 1.20 presents facilitating and inhibiting factors to achieve organizational excellence and commitment.

EXHIBIT 1.20 Facilitating and Inhibiting Factors to Achieve Organizational Excellence and Commitment

Factor or Force	Facilitators	Inhibitors
Organizational design	Well-structured business functions and job duties	Ill-structured business functions and job duties
Organizational development	Well-planned and executed training and growth programs	Ill-planned and poorly executed training and growth programs
Organizational change	Well managed, encourages change	Ill managed, discourages change
Incentives to managers and employees	Fair and achievable	Unfair and not achievable
Budget	Well funded	Ill funded
Human talent	Up-to-date knowledge, skills, and abilities (KSAs)	Outdated KSAs
Technology	Leader	Follower
Employees	Empowered	Not empowered
Business strategy	Well formulated and executed	Ill formulated and poorly executed
Organizational harmony	Synchronized and united (i.e., everybody is singing the same song). Goal congruence is in place.	Unsynchronized and divided (i.e., everybody is pulling in different directions). Goal congruence is not in place.

Often, management undertakes new initiatives or projects to increase an organization's efficiency and effectiveness in terms of increasing productivity, performance, sales, revenues, profits, stock market price, and market share and decreasing costs and operating expenses. However, the organizational commitment could be in jeopardy due to organizational politics (i.e., turf building and protecting) and organizational conflicts (i.e., favor one and disfavor others) which, in turn, could derail the organizational harmony. These politics and conflicts are often at play to defund one project and fund another project of interest and to favor one functional department manager to become a project sponsor and disfavor other functional department managers. These politics and conflicts are dysfunctional when unchecked; when they are combined with lack of innovation and bad (toxic) culture, they could lead to an organization's decline.

The following is a list of issues or problems that should be addressed, which could decide whether organizational excellence and building organizational commitment is possible:

- Commitment by all levels of management and all types of employees must be solid, genuine, trustworthy, and honest. The commitment cannot be a lip service and it cannot come across as a token gesture, flaky, or fake.

- Commitment can quickly become weak or can fail if business strategy is flawed.

- Commitment must be driven by top-level management and supported by lower-level management and employees. Input from all levels of management and all types of employees is a requirement.

- Incentives to managers and employees are poorly defined and structured. Ill-defined incentives are very hard to motivate managers and employees in order to reach the expected performance levels.

- Many new projects fail due to sudden budget cuts, reprioritization of projects, project sponsor leaving the company or changing job responsibilities, lack of a project sponsor. Forging alliances with other businesses is becoming very difficult.

- Organizational commitment must be continuous and relentless regardless of budget cuts and changes in job responsibilities unless otherwise overruled by changes in laws, rules, and regulations.

(i) Leadership Defined

Leadership occurs when a leader mobilizes an organization's resources to fulfill its mission and vision. Leaders have inherent power (personal and charismatic power) and built-in qualities, such as motivating, inspiring, innovative, imaginative, and visionary. Leadership power promotes creativity and change in the organization. Leaders share some common qualities with entrepreneurs in the areas of innovation, creativity, imagination, and vision. Note that there are few leaders and many managers in an organization. Leaders use depth charts to develop succession plans for executives, officers, and senior managers.

(j) Leadership Theories

Over the past several decades, leadership theories have been slowly evolving due to constant research conducted on this mysterious topic. This evolution will continue until all the old mysteries and new mysteries are fully uncovered. The evolution of leadership theories can be presented in five ways.

1. Trait leadership theory

2. Behavioral styles leadership theory

3. Situational leadership theory

4. Transformational leadership theory

5. Miscellaneous leadership theories

(i) Trait Leadership Theory
It was assumed that leaders are born, not made. Later, this assumption was changed to accept that leadership traits are not completely inborn but can also be acquired through learning and experience.

Although hundreds of physical, mental, and personality traits were said to be the key determinants of successful leadership, researchers reached agreement on only five traits:

1. Intelligence
2. Scholarship
3. Dependability in exercising responsibilities
4. Activity and social participation
5. Socioeconomic status

Trait profiles do provide a useful framework for examining what it takes to be a good leader. Managers from across the United States were surveyed to determine the traits they admired in superior leaders. Results indicated that honesty (top of the scale), competent, forward looking, inspiring, and intelligent (bottom of the scale) were the most widely admired.

(ii) Behavioral Styles Leadership Theory

Researchers began turning their attention to patterns of leader behavior instead of concentrating on the personal traits of successful leaders. In other words, attention turned from who the leader was to how the leader actually behaved. Subordinates preferred managers who had a democratic style to those with an authoritarian style or a laissez-faire (hands-off) style. Exhibit 1.21 presents strengths and weaknesses of behavioral styles leadership theory.

EXHIBIT 1.21 Strengths and Weaknesses of Behavioral Styles Leadership Theory

Strengths of Behavioral Styles Theory	Weaknesses of Behavioral Styles Theory
Authoritarian style stresses prompt, orderly, and predictable performance.	Authoritarian approach tends to stifle individual initiative.
Democratic style enhances personal commitment through participation.	Democratic process is time consuming. This style does not always stimulate better performance. Some employees prefer to be told what to do rather than to participate in decision making.
Laissez-faire permits self-starters to do things as they see fit without leader interference.	Laissez-faire groups may drift aimlessly in the absence of direction from leader.

Two popular models that have received a great deal of attention are the Ohio State Model and the Leadership Grid by Robert R. Blake and Jane Srygley Mouton.[11]

Ohio State Model. A team of Ohio State University researchers defined two independent dimensions of leader behavior.

> **Dimension 1: Initiating structure** (*x*-axis from low to high). This dimension represents the leader's efforts to get things organized and get the job done.

---

[11] Robert R. Blake and Jane Srygley Mouton, "Management by Grid Principles of Situationalism," *Group & Organization Studies*, December 1981.

Dimension 2: Consideration (*y*-axis from low to high). This dimension is the degree of trust, friendship, respect, and warmth that the leader extends to subordinates.

The researchers drew a matrix from these two dimensions. High-structure, high-consideration was generally hailed as the best all-around style.

Leadership Grid Blake and Mouton[12] remain convinced that there is one best style of leadership, which they described in a grid with two axes.

1. Horizontal (*x*) axis shows concern for production involving a desire to achieve greater output, cost effectiveness, and profits
2. Vertical (*y*) axis shows concern for people involving promoting friendship, helping coworkers get the job done, and attending to things that matter to people, such as pay and working conditions

By scaling each axis from 1 to 9, the grid consists of these five leadership styles:

1. **9, 1 style.** Primary concern for production; people secondary
2. **1, 9 style.** Primary concern for people; production secondary
3. **1, 1 style.** Minimal concern for either production or people
4. **5, 5 style.** Moderate concern for both production and people to maintain the status quo
5. **9, 9 style.** High concern for both production and people as evidenced by personal commitment, mutual trust, and teamwork

Most managers prefer the 9,9 style, regardless of the situation at hand, since this style correlates positively with better results, better mental and physical health, and effective conflict resolution.

(iii) Situational Leadership Theory

Situational theory or contingency thinking is based on the assumption that successful leadership occurs when the leader's style matches the situation. It stresses the need for flexibility and rejects the notion of a universally applicable style.

BEHAVIORAL STYLES LEADERSHIP THEORY VERSUS SITUATIONAL LEADERSHIP THEORY

- Behavioral style theorists believe that there is one best style of leadership.
- Situational theorists are convinced that no one best style of leadership exists.

Different approaches to situational leadership include Fred Fiedler's contingency theory, the path-goal theory, and the Vroom-Yetton-Jago decision-making model, as shown in Exhibit 1.22.

---

[12] Robert R. Blake and Jane Srygley Mouton, "A Comparative Analysis of Situationalism and 9,9 Management by Principle." *Organizational Dynamics*, Spring 1982.

EXHIBIT 1.22 Situational Leadership Approaches

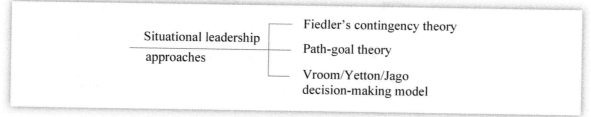

Fiedler's contingency theory, which has been thoroughly tested, is based on two interrelated factors. The performance of a leader depends on two interrelated factors: (1) the degree to which the situation gives the leader control and influence to accomplish the job and (2) the leader's basic motivation: whether to accomplish the task or having close supportive relations with others (the task-motivated leader has a concern for production and the relationship-motivated leader has a concern for people).

WAYS TO ENHANCE WORKER MOTIVATION

Worker motivation can be increased by increasing the number and kinds of personal payoffs for achieving work goals. Other ways to increase worker motivation involve making paths to these payoffs easier to travel by clarifying the paths, reducing roadblocks and pitfalls, and increasing the opportunities for personal satisfaction en route.

Fiedler and his colleagues summed up their findings by noting that "everything points to the conclusion that there is no such thing as an ideal leader." Instead, *there are leaders, and there are situations*. The challenge to a manager is to analyze a leader's basic motivation and then match that leader with a suitable situation to form a product in combination. Fiedler believed that it is more efficient to move leaders to a suitable situation than to tamper with their personalities by trying to get task-motivated leaders to become relationship-motivated ones, or vice versa.

The **path-goal theory**, which is a derivative of expectancy motivation theory, emphasizes that leaders should motivate their followers by providing clear goals and meaningful incentives for reaching them. *Motivation is seen as essential to effective leadership.*

Path-goal proponents believe that managers need to rely contingently on four different leadership styles since personal characteristics of subordinates, environmental pressures, and work demands on subordinates will all vary from situation to situation. These four leadership styles include: directive (tell people what to do), supportive (treat subordinates as equals), participative (consult with subordinates), and achievement-oriented (set challenging goals). For example, a directive situational leadership style would be appropriate for a subordinate who possesses very low task maturity for a particular assignment.

PATH-GOAL THEORY VERSUS FIEDLER THEORY

- Path-goals theorists assume that managers can and do shift situationally from style to style.
- Fiedler theorists assume that managers cannot and do not change their basic leadership styles.

The Vroom-Yetton-Jago decision-making model. Vroom helped develop the expectancy theory of motivation based on the assumption that motivational strength is determined by perceived probabilities of success. The term "expectancy" refers to the subjective probabilities (or expectancy) that one thing will lead to another. Researchers Vroom, Yetton, and Jago (the Vroom model) portray leadership as a decision-making process with five distinct decision-making styles, each of which requires a different degree of participation from subordinates. The Vroom model qualifies as a situational-leadership theory because it prescribes different decision styles for varying situations managers typically encounter.

Of these five decision-making styles, two are autocratic, two are consultative, and one is group directed (see Exhibit 1.23). In addition, the Vroom model gives managers the tools for matching styles with various individual and group situations.

EXHIBIT 1.23 Five Decision-Making Styles

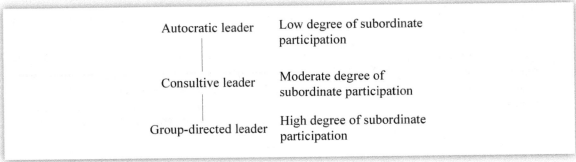

(iv) Transformational Leadership Theory

Transformational leaders are characterized as visionaries who challenge people to achieve exceptionally high levels of morality, motivation, and performance. Transformational leaders are masters of change, have charisma, rely on referent power, and can envision a better future, effectively communicate that vision, and get others to willingly make it a reality.

There is a distinction between a transactional leader and a transformational one. Transactional leaders monitor people so they do the expected, according to plan (i.e., maintain status quo). In contrast, transformational leaders inspire people to do the unexpected, above and beyond the plan (fostering creative and productive growth).

TRANSACTIONAL LEADERS VERSUS TRANSFORMATIONAL LEADERS

- Transactional leaders can best handle stable situations.
- Transformational leaders can best handle rapidly changing situations.
- Transformational theory combines the behavioral style leadership theory and situational leadership theory. Charismatic behavior is blended with the traditional behavior.
- Laboratory and field research evidence positively supports the transformational leadership pattern.
- Followers of transformational leaders tend to perform better and to report greater satisfaction than followers of transactional leaders.

(v) Miscellaneous Leadership Theories

At least six other theories of leadership are available in light of globalization, electronic commerce, the Internet, employee diversity and empowerment, and virtual organizations. They include the following:

1. The **level 5 leader** has no ego as he or she reaches the highest level in the management hierarchy in terms of knowledge, skills, and abilities. This leader gives credit for successes to subordinates while taking responsibility for failures.

2. The **interactive leader** is one who uses consensual and collaborative process in problem solving and decision making by including subordinates. This leader's power is derived from relationship building and caring attitudes instead of positional power. Female leaders are found to be better than male leaders as interactive leaders because they can motivate, communicate, and listen better.

3. The **virtual leader** is one who is open-minded, flexible, and exhibits positive attitudes that focus on solution instead of problems. This leader is good at communicating, coaching, building relationships, and caring skills.

4. The **servant leader** is one who operates on two levels: (1) to fulfill subordinates' needs and goals and (2) to achieve the organization's mission. This leader gives away power, ideas, information, recognition, and credit to subordinates and connects the subordinate's motives to the organization's mission. The servant leadership position is upside down, meaning that the leader serves the subordinates working for him or her and the organization that the leader works for. The servant leader is at the bottom and others are at the top.

5. The **Zen Principles of leadership** tap into the creative and innovative side of a leader. The seven Zen principles include:

    a. Communicating in a plain, simple, clear, concise, and natural manner.

    b. Staying positive and achieving a balance in solving problems, despite differences, ambiguities, imperfections, and irregularities.

    c. Spending more time in guiding, mentoring, coaching, and delegating and less time in telling, micromanaging, and directing.

    d. More trusting and less doubting and behaving honestly and openly.

    e. Managing change very carefully while respecting the organizational culture.

    f. Striving for innovation by breaking away from the tradition to achieve a competitive edge.

    g. Motivating more and asserting less authority. (The last principle includes creating harmony at workplace, listening with an open mind, and establishing stretch goals.)

6. **Dual-hat leadership,** commonly practiced in the military sector, applies to situations where an incoming executive or officer is given two job responsibilities (dual-hat leadership) in two different organizations, functions, or departments simultaneously. This military practice can be applied to nonmilitary sectors during a transition period where one executive leaves the organization and another executive assumes responsibilities for the two functions simultaneously until a new executive is hired to replace the executive who left the organization. Advantages of this leadership approach include: (1) more in-depth coordination and collaboration; (2) faster decision making; and (3) more efficient

use of resources. Disadvantages of this leadership approach include: (1) concerns about unfair prioritization of requests for support services between the two functions at the same time; (2) broader span of control (i.e., increased breadth, depth, and magnitude of issues to deal with); (3) increased tension between the two functions for routine resource prioritization, allocation, and sharing; and (4) conflict-of-interest situations where the leader favors one function and disfavors other functions.

(k) Leadership Categories

There are two categories of leaders: (1) good and bad leaders and (2) formal and informal leaders. Effective leadership is associated with both better performance and more ethical performance. According to Chester Schriesheim, James Tolliver, and Orlando Behling,[13] leadership is "a social influence process in which the leader seeks the voluntary participation of subordinates in an effort to reach organizational objectives."

Exhibit 1.24 provides a comparison between formal and informal leadership.

EXHIBIT 1.24 Comparison of Formal Leadership with Informal Leadership

Formal Leadership	Informal Leadership
Formal leadership is the process of influencing relevant others to pursue official organizational objectives.	Informal leadership is the process of influencing others to pursue unofficial objectives that may or may not serve the organization's interests
Formal leaders have a measure of legitimate power because of their formal authority.	Informal leaders lack formal authority.
Formal leaders rely on an expedient combination of reward, coercive, referent, and expert power.	Informal leaders rely on an expedient combination of reward, coercive, referent, and expert power.
Formal leaders can be an asset or a liability to the organization (asset when they work for the organization; liability when they work against the organization).	Informal leaders can be an asset or a liability to the organization (asset when they work for the organization; liability when they work against the organization).

(l) Leaders' Powers

Power is needed in all organizations. Power must be used because managers need to influence those they depend on, such as employees. It is powerlessness, not power, that undermines organizational effectiveness. Power is the ability to manage all types of resources to accomplish something of value to the organization. These resources could be human, material, and informational in content.

Power affects organizational members in three areas: decision making, behavior, and situations. Another dimension to power is how people distinguish between "power over" (ability to dominate), "power to" (ability to act freely), and "power from" (ability to resist the demands of others).

[13] Chester Schriesheim, James Tolliver, and Orlando Behling, "Influence Tactics Used by Subordinates" *Journal of Applied Psychology*, June 1990.

Here, one needs to differentiate between authority and power.

- Authority is the right to direct the activities of others. It is an officially sanctioned privilege that may or may not get results.
- Power is the demonstrated ability to get results.
- One may alternatively possess authority but have no power, possess no authority yet have power, or possess both authority and power.
- A manager who gets subordinates to work hard on an important project has both authority and power.

Experts on power say that power is neutral. It is a tool that can be used in a positive or negative manner. Power exercised for power's sake can be quite dangerous to all parties affected. Leaders exhibit five bases of power:

1. **Reward power** is gaining compliance through rewards.
2. **Coercive power** is gaining compliance through fear or threat of punishment.
3. **Legitimate power** is compliance based on one's formal position and parallels formal authority (job title). It can be eroded by frequent abuse or overuse.
4. **Referent power** is compliance based on charisma, personal identification, or attraction and has no relation to job title. A *charismatic leader* is one who has the ability to motivate subordinates to transcend their expected performance. A charismatic leader is also a *visionary leader* who speaks to the hearts of subordinates, letting them to be a part of his or her vision and their vision combined.
5. **Expert power** is compliance based on the ability to dispense valued information and is guided by the knowledge or skills possessed by a person (e.g., unique or special skills in computer technology, space technology, nuclear science, business strategy, or bioengineering fields).

(m) Leaders' Intelligences

Leaders need to possess certain type of intelligence to be successful in all business circumstances they face. Four types of intelligence are briefly presented next: cognitive, emotional, social, and contextual.

Cognitive intelligence is based on a person's intelligent quotient (IQ), which is determined in part genetically by birth and in part by education, income, and life environment. The IQ measures cognitive abilities of a person, such as memory, attention, and speed, which are shown as positive predictors of job performance, school performance, and income. Employers use the IQ test scores to hire, train, develop, and promote employees.

Emotional intelligence is based on qualities such as self-awareness, self-regulation, motivation, empathy, and social skill. Although it is determined in part genetically, it can be learned or improved by training, coaching, practice, and effort. Specifically, it involves an awareness of others' feelings and a sensitivity to one's own emotions and the ability to control them. Emotional intelligence requires the ability to monitor a person's behavior and adjust that behavior according to assessment of the social context and circumstances.

Social intelligence focuses more on being able to "read" other people's minds and their intentions, which is different from emotional intelligence. Three components of social intelligence are social perceptions (i.e., the ability to "see" the world around a person keenly), behavioral flexibility (i.e., the ability to modify one's own behavior in response to what that person perceives socially), and social savviness (i.e., the possession of tacit knowledge). Social intelligence requires the ability to monitor a person's behavior and adjust that behavior according to assessment of the social context and circumstances.

Contextual intelligence refers to the ability of a person to adjust to a specific context or circumstance at hand. This requires flexibility and adaptability to adjust to new contexts and situations without much delay and deliberation. This type of intelligence is highly required in a fluid and rapidly changing business environment. Leaders wear different hats at different times.

(n) Leaders' Tools

Leaders have several tools and techniques at their disposal to train, develop, and improve the performance of subordinates as well as themselves. The four tools include job rotation, coaching, delegation, mentoring (job shadowing). These tools have a similar purpose of learning and growing personally and professionally with the advice and experience of others. The goal of leaders' using these tools is to motivate employees in terms of getting them inspired and excited to make them ready for future leaders.

One of the responsibilities of a leader is to develop future leaders—to get them ready for other similar or different jobs as needed or make them a part of succession plans. Six tools are available for leaders to develop future leaders:

1. Formal training and development programs

2. Mentoring

3. Coaching

4. Job rotation

5. Delegation

6. Assistant to or deputy positions

(i) Formal Training and Development Programs

Management development (MD) is a broad term encompassing elements such as upgrading the knowledge, skills, and abilities (KSAs) required for a manager or a professional to apply them in either the current job or a future job.

Managerial talent consists of a complex group first-line supervisors, middle-level managers, and higher-level executives. For this reason, different types of MD programs cater to the needs of each level in the management hierarchy. For example, as the level goes up in the hierarchy, there should be a strong focus on soft skills and general business knowledge and less focus on hard skills, and vice versa.

MD programs can be conducted either inside or outside the company. The reasons for conducting the program outside the company are that it brings new viewpoints, different perspectives, and broad exposure to outside experts. The reasons for conducting the program inside the company are that customized courses can be developed in less time and at a reduced cost, the course content is controlled, teamwork is facilitated, and the company culture is known.

Five related concepts in MD programs include mentoring, coaching, job rotation, delegation, and assistant to or deputy position, all with the similar purpose of learning and growing personally and professionally with the advice and experience of others.

(ii) Mentoring

Mentoring is advising, coaching, and nurturing a protégé to enhance his or her career development. The mentor can be anywhere in the same organization as the protégé or may work in another organization or another industry. The mentor (or sponsor) could be the same or different gender as the protégé. Sometimes a protégé may have more than one mentor to learn the unwritten rules to make it to the top.

Mentoring is not a form of direct training in the pure meaning because the mentor provides a limited amount of guidance and time to a protégé with infrequent meetings set in advance.

Mentoring is of two types: regular mentoring and reverse mentoring.

Regular mentoring is a relationship in which experienced managers help employees in the earlier stages of their careers. Such a relationship provides an environment for conveying technical, interpersonal, and organizational skills from more experienced to less experienced persons. Not only does the inexperienced employee benefit, but the mentor may enjoy the challenge of sharing wisdom and knowledge.

In *reverse mentoring*, older employees learn from younger ones because the latter group has some special skills that the former group does not have. This approach will keep the older employees more productive with special skills and thus more useful to the company.

> Regular Mentoring = Less Experienced Person Learns from More Experienced Person
>
> Reverse Mentoring = Older, Less Experienced Person Learns from Younger, More Experienced Person

However, mentoring has problems. Young minority managers frequently report difficulty in finding mentors. Also, men generally show less willingness than women to be mentors. Further, mentors who are dissatisfied with their jobs and those who teach a narrow or distorted view of events may not help a young manager's development. Fortunately, many managers have a series of advisors or mentors during their careers and may find advantages in learning from the different mentors. For example, the unique qualities of individual mentors may help less experienced managers identify key behaviors in management success and failure. Further, those being mentored find previous mentors to be useful sources for networking.

> **Fact 1:** Research has shown that mentoring can break the glass ceiling facing women and minorities.
>
> **Fact 2:** Research has shown that women who have women mentors have done well in enhancing their careers.

Fact 3: Research has shown that African American women who have at least one mentor are more likely to get promoted.

Fact 4: Research has shown that African American women who have more than one mentor are most likely to get promoted.

Although coaching and mentoring concepts sound good in theory, there are some practical problems in selecting and pairing the right mentor and the right protégé, in the amount of attention given by the mentor to the protégé, in the temperament of both parties, and in personality conflicts between the two parties.

When the mentoring option is not available to employees or is not working out, then job rotation, coaching, and delegation practices can help an employee to learn management and leadership skills.

In **job shadowing**, the protégé closely follows and watches the mentor's actions and goes wherever the mentor goes. The purpose is to learn how the mentor deals with people, communicates and behaves with other people, makes decisions, and so on. This direct, interactive, and visible learning experience is powerful and strong in that it stays with the protégé for a long time to come. Note that job shadowing is a part of mentoring.

(iii) Coaching

Coaching is a method of instruction where the desired outcome is to obtain a certain level of knowledge or skills. This thought-provoking and creative process inspires employees to maximize their personal and professional potential.

Coaching is a form of direct training that a supervisor or manager provides in the form of work assistance to an employee (i.e., teaching while working). Note that coaching is a part of mentoring because the coach is much like a mentor. Coaching is different from mentoring because it is more intense than mentoring and provides a more detailed learning task.

(iv) Job Rotation

Job rotation provides rotational opportunities for employees to move from job to job to provide them with variety of tasks and mental stimulation. In this method, new or current employees get training to broaden their work experience and to increase their overall knowledge, skills, and abilities.

Job rotation is a form of cross-functional training in preparing an employee for future jobs. It provides a well-rounded experience in other jobs, so an employee can take on a new job or take on more responsibilities in the current job. Note that job rotation programs are based on a manager creating the employee's career plans, so employees can reach their career goals. For example, an employee doing job A now is sent to job B, then to job C, and comes back to job A.

Job A $\longrightarrow$ Job B $\longrightarrow$ Job C $\longrightarrow$ Job A

(v) Delegation

Delegation is a higher-level management right to transfer authority and responsibility to a lower-level management, where the latter group develops managerial skills, such as problem solving and decision making, and learns how to take more responsibility and accountability for achieving results. Delegation involves developing and empowering lower-level management. Although managers are encouraged to delegate, they often find it difficult to do so.

Delegation is a process of assigning various degrees of authority to subordinates. It is not an all-or-nothing proposition. Authority may be passed along to subordinates; ultimate responsibility cannot be passed along because it stays with the manager who delegates. Thus, delegation is the sharing of authority, not the abdication of responsibility.

Delegation is a form of functional training for an employee to take on more responsibilities than the current job provides. It provides the employee additional managing skills in problem solving and decision making. Experts say that it is good to for managers to delegate those activities they know the best.

Advantages to Delegation

- Managers can free more of their time for planning and motivating.
- Subordinates will be better trained and developed as future managers (e.g., can work on a task force or committee to solve problems and to develop new policies and procedures).

Barriers to Delegation

- Lack of confidence and trust in subordinates
- Vague job definition
- Fear of competition from subordinates
- Poor example set by superiors who do not delegate
- Reluctance in taking the risks involved in depending on others

(vi) Assistant to or Deputy Positions

Assistant to or deputy positions (second-tier) job titles are created for high-potential individuals to provide direct, hands-on work experience in performing day-to-day activities and functions. Individuals in second-tier jobs help individuals in first-tier jobs (C-level executives or department heads), and the former can step right into the job when the latter is not available for some reason.

(o) Leadership Styles

A leader's traits are the person's distinguishing personal characteristics, such as intelligence, values, and appearance. Research has revealed that (1) leaders who had achieved a level of greatness and higher rates of success were called great man, and (2) a strong relationship exists between personal traits and a leader's success. Three types of leadership styles or approaches exist: autocratic leader, democratic leader, and hybrid leader.

The **autocratic leader** is one who tends to centralize authority and rely on legitimate, reward, and coercive power to influence subordinates. Group members with autocratic leaders performed very high so long as the leader was present to supervise them. However, group members were displeased with the close, autocratic style of leadership and negative feelings (hostility) associated with this type of leader.

The **democratic leader** is one who delegates authority to others, encourages participation, and relies on expert and referent power to influence subordinates. The performance of groups who were assigned democratic leaders was good with positive feelings. In addition, group members performed well even when the leader was absent and left the group on its own. The participative techniques and majority-rule decision making used by democratic leaders trained and involved group members such that they performed well with or without the leader present. These characteristics of democratic leadership explain why the empowerment of lower-level employees (front-line employees) is a popular trend in companies today.

The **hybrid leader** is one who exercises both autocratic leader and democratic leader styles, depending on the situation. Most leaders have favored styles that they tend to use most often. However, while switching from autocratic to democratic or vice versa is not easy, leaders may adjust their styles depending on the situation

In conclusion, leadership styles could be a continuum reflecting different amounts of employee participation. Thus, one leader might be autocratic (superior-centered), another democratic (subordinate-centered), and a third a mix of the two styles (hybrid leader). It is the "behavior" of the leader rather than the "style" of the leader that determines leadership effectiveness.

(p) Leaders' Personality Factors

In common usage, people think of personality in terms of traits or relatively stable characteristics of a person. Researchers have investigated whether any traits stand up to scientific scrutiny. Although investigators have examined thousands of traits over the years, their findings have been distilled into five general dimensions that describe personality. These often are called the "Big Five" personality factors. Each factor may contain a wide range of specific traits. The **Big Five personality factors** describe an individual's openness to experience, conscientiousness, extraversion, agreeableness, and emotional stability (neuroticism).

1. **Openness to experience.** The degree to which a person has a broad range of interests and is imaginative, creative, artistically sensitive, and willing to consider new ideas.

2. **Conscientiousness.** The degree to which a person is focused on a few goals, thus behaving in ways that are responsible, dependable, persistent, and achievement oriented.

3. **Extraversion.** The degree to which a person is sociable, talkative, assertive, and comfortable with interpersonal relationships.

4. **Agreeableness.** The degree to which a person is able to get along with others by being good-natured, cooperative, forgiving, understanding, and trusting.

5. **Emotional stability.** The degree to which a person is calm, enthusiastic, and secure rather than tense, nervous, depressed, moody, or insecure.

However, despite growing use of personality tests in employment situations, there is little evidence that they are a valid predictor of job success. In addition, the Big Five dimensions have been criticized because they are difficult to measure precisely. Because each dimension is made up of a number of specific traits, a person might score high on some traits but low on others. For example, considering the dimension of conscientiousness, a person might score high on a trait such as dependability but score low on achievement orientation. Furthermore, research on the Big Five has mostly been limited to the United States, so there are dangers in applying the theory globally and especially cross-culturally. Next, each factor is divided into few, specific traits, as shown in Exhibit 1.25.

EXHIBIT 1.25 Personality Factors and Personality Traits

Personality Factors	Personality Traits
Openness to experience	Possesses creative and imaginative skills with new and unusual ideas; likes art and adventure; prefers novelty in and variety of things; and enjoys varieties of activities and experiences in life and work.
Conscientiousness	Exhibits self-discipline character; shows as a well-planner and organizer with tasks to be done; and comes across as dependable and believable.
Extraversion	Presents positive emotions, energy, assertiveness, and talkativeness.
Agreeableness	Shows trusting relationships and helpful nature with good-tempered manners.
Emotional stability	Exhibits calmness, security, and confidence.

(q) Leaders' Personality Traps

Leaders should avoid the next cognitive traps rooted either in their own personality zone or in their organizational culture. Note that these traps are equally applicable to supervisors, managers, and entrepreneurs.

The **mirror-imaging trap** is a leader's false assumption that followers and others think exactly like him- or herself. With this trap, leaders are unwilling to examine or analyze other viewpoints, variations, or alternatives of the subject matter at hand. This is similar to saying "My way or the highway." Here, the real issue is that the leader is blindly committing to a set of common assumptions and beliefs and not challenging those assumptions, which leads to failures and disappointments. One way to avoid the mirror-imaging trap is to have a peer review by people from a different background, which will provide a good safeguard of checks and balances. The mirror-imaging trap is also called the bandwagon effect or blind spot bias and is the major cause of numerous common sense failures.

In the **target fixation trap,** individuals get fixated on one hypothesis, rely only on evidence that is consistent with their preconceptions, and ignore other relevant views. In a way, they lose sight of the big-picture perspectives and push for a quick closure. One way to avoid this trap is to have an open mind and broad views. This trap is based on the person's confirmation bias.

The **analogy trap** arises when a leader is unaware of differences between his or her own context and that of others. This is a case of inappropriate or incorrect use of analogies. The net result is that important knowledge and information is missing because the leader fails to admit ignorance from (1) insufficient study of data and information; or from the inability to (2) differentiate between old facts and new facts and failure to reconcile them; (3) accept conflicting facts to avoid discomfort; and (4) separate relevant information from irrelevant information.

The **projection trap** (halo and horn error) occurs when a leader is conducting an employee's performance appraisals. The halo error occurs when a leader projects one positive performance feature or incident onto the rest, resulting in an overall higher rating of that employee's performance. The horn error occurs when a leader projects one negative performance feature or incident onto the rest, resulting in an overall lower rating of that employee's performance. Both halo and horn errors are based on a recent behavior bias.

In the **stereotyping trap,** leaders strive to maintain the status quo (no changes) and fail to invite creativity and innovation (requiring changes). This trap results from a personal bias of the leader and leads to lost growth opportunities.

In the **stovepiping trap,** the leader acknowledges only one source of information or knowledge base as the official source and disregards other sources of information or knowledge bases as unofficial sources. This trap is similar to a silo trap or legacy trap, which reflects a functional specialization.

A **decision trap** occurs when ill-defined and unstructured problems are solved and when wrong problems and only symptoms are addressed. Current decisions, in part, are made (1) to undo previously made wrong decisions, (2) to fix satisficing decisions (i.e., not really a good decision but good enough at that time, and (3) to correct nonoptimizing decisions (i.e., not maximizing or not balancing all the resources). Satisficing decisions are suboptimal and dysfunctional in nature, meaning that the benefits to a business unit are less than the costs to the entire organization.

A **measurement trap** stems from quantifying or counting the wrong items of importance. Mainly, this trap results from using incorrect, untimely, and incomplete data and results from inappropriate application of quantitative methods to process and analyze data. Using underskilled, untrained, and unqualified employees to analyze and interpret data results (outputs) and the inability of management to separate irrelevant data from relevant data are also measurement traps. This trap also results from using the wrong metrics to measure performance. Note that measurement traps can lead to decision traps.

An **organizational culture trap** can make someone unwilling to challenge the views and perspectives of SMEs and senior-level managers. Other examples of cultural traps include:

- Assuming that small things in one culture are small things in every culture (reflecting a stereotyping trap). In reality, they work differently and in the opposite manner. For example, adhering to time schedules and waiting in lines is well accepted in some cultures and is not followed at all in other cultures.

- Assuming that all cultures in all countries follow the same way as one culture in one country. (This a reflection of mirror-imaging trap.)

- Knowing that American businesspeople may push for quicker decisions during negotiations whereas Japanese businesspeople may push for building consensus and trust first followed by faster decisions. (This a reflection of cultural diversity effect.)

Other examples of organizational culture traps include the not-invented-here syndrome, and the this-is-how-we-do-things-here syndrome: This is the idea that senior managers know best, and that an employee golden suggestion system (i.e., a suggestion box at the workplace) does not work because it is a waste of time and effort.

One way to avoid the organizational culture trap is to read as many books as possible covering organizational and international cultures in order to gain a better working knowledge of various cultures. Another way is to receive cultural, diversity, and sensitivity training.

(r) Leaders' Personal Biases

Leaders should be keenly aware of personal, built-in biases that could harm people due to inappropriate actions taken and damage business investments due to prejudiced decisions made. These biases could negatively influence a leader's job performance. Note that these biases are equally applicable to supervisors, managers, and entrepreneurs. Several biases are listed next.

Confirmation bias is the tendency to seek out only that information that supports a person's preconceptions or misconceptions. This bias could lead to lost or missed opportunities in growth.

Anchoring bias is the tendency to develop an estimate of something of value based on a person's preferences, which could be a completely wrong base to use due to lack of objectivity and clarity. Examples of these estimates could be demand and supply numbers for products and services, quotes, bids, prices, costs, profits, and time lines. This bias could lead to loss of revenues, profits, customers, market share, and suppliers.

Hindsight bias is the tendency to assess one's previous decisions or actions as more or less efficient and effective than they were. Here, there is no use of digging into the past, which is similar to a sunk cost concept or spilled beans saying.

The **bandwagon effect** is the tendency to do or behave blindly that others do or believe. This suggests a lack of confidence in a person's abilities.

The **halo effect** is the tendency to project unverified capabilities of a person (employee) based on an observed event. This reflects a leader's blind spot and could result in loss of employees during the employee performance appraisal process.

The **framing effect** is the tendency to react to how information is presented or packaged to others, despite its facts. This bias results from knee-jerk reactions leading to hasty decisions. Problems could be ill-defined with framing errors or effects. Consequently, incorrect problems could be solved, leading to decision traps.

The snowball effect is the tendency for one judgment-related mistake and decision-making error to increase, thus becoming an endless chain of mistakes and errors. It is a cascading effect of mistakes and errors leading to magnified negative results.

Availability bias results from a fallacy in thinking that what is available today or what happened today will be repeated tomorrow. This bias results from the belief that nothing changes between then and now (i.e., status quo is maintained).

The **overconfidence bias** results from unchecked assumptions, not verifying or confirming the actual facts and figures with other affected or interested parties. It is a person thinking that something she or he does, or did, is correct, and believing absolutely that it was the best decision. This bias leads to validation errors.

Optimism bias results from assuming that everything—every outcome, everyone, and every task or event—is good. The overconfidence bias often occurs alongside the optimism bias. One way to reduce optimism bias is to validate inputs, questions, assumptions, processes, and outcomes with SMEs or authorities in the field.

A **blind spot bias** results from not seeing all angles or viewpoints to a problem or situation and using a one-track mind.

The **status quo bias** results when people do not like changes and prefer to keep things the same as before (i.e., status quo). Lost or missed growth opportunities not goods are the major risks here.

The **cultural diversity effect** is the tendency to misunderstand or misinterpret the scope and nature of other cultures in the world. One culture assumes that it is the best culture there is and that the other cultures are not good in terms of (1) different in interacting with people, (2) different in thinking patterns and mind-sets, and (3) different in attitudes toward people, life, and the world. Hence, people do not recognize, respect, and appreciate existing cultural diversity.

(s) Leaders' Handling of Issues and Crises Situations

Both private and public sector organizations face unexpected issues and crises situations at times. Issues can be one-time or recurring events, and the issues can be soft or hard. Either type of issue needs management's immediate attention and corrective action to bring business operations back to normal. Issues often develop over time, very slowly, and, surprisingly, unnoticed.

> **Example 1:** An example of a soft issue is reputation risk resulting from unhappy customers posting unpleasant comments about a company's products or services on social media platforms and websites.

> **Example 2:** An example of a hard issue is reports of bribery and corruption charges and unethical practices against a company's management.

It is up to management to decide what is a soft issue or a hard issue because management needs to determine an issue's visibility level (low, average, or high) and impact level (low, moderate, and high) and act accordingly. Usually issues with high visibility and high impact deserve high attention of management.

Issues and crises are related to each other. When does an issue become a crisis situation? When issues are not handled properly and in a timely manner the first time they occur or when they are completely neglected, they become severe crises situations later because many crises are embedded in or erupt from issues. Sometimes a crisis situation can occur abruptly all by itself.

> Issues ⟶ Crises
>
> Ignored Issues ⟶ Severe Crises

Examples of issues (first) becoming crises (later) are listed next.

- Management's bribery and corruption charges and other unethical and illegal practices.

- A stockholder files a lawsuit against company management and it becomes a class action lawsuit when joined by other stockholders to show their disapproval of and dissatisfaction with the way the company is being run and decisions are made.

- Management of a fast food chain restaurant ignored its employee strikes in one location for a minimum wage increase. Later, it became a severe crisis situation when employees in many other locations in the country joined the minimum wage momentum.

- Data losses and data breaches (millions of customers' credit and debit card data were lost) occurred due to computer hacking at a major department store resulted in the firing of the CEO and the chief information officer.

(t) Entrepreneurship Defined

Entrepreneurship is defined as an economic enterprise founded by an ambitious person who is characterized as a risk taker, idea generator and implementer, opportunity grabber, change agent, and a value creator. Entrepreneurs have different mind-sets and bigger missions and visions than managers and leaders to take advantage of uncertainty (risk). Note that there are very few entrepreneurs, few leaders, and many managers

(u) Entrepreneurs' Roles and Skills

Entrepreneurs are one-of-a-kind, unique individuals (a rare breed) with unparalleled mission and vision to achieve something new on their own better than others. They want to discover products and services that are better than current products and services. They want to explore something new and exciting that did not exist before (e.g., a new product or a new service).

Entrepreneurs wear many hats and play diverse roles, such as leaders, innovators, decision makers, problem solvers, creators, discoverers, explorers, dreamers, thinkers, doers, and above all trend setters.

Entrepreneurship skills are innate skills, meaning that some people are born with them (although some specific skills, such as presentation and writing skills, can be learned through training and development programs or from others through observation).

Characteristics of Entrepreneurs

- They want to become the owners of their own destiny, not depend on others.
- They are leaders, not followers.
- They want to be self-employed, not employed by others.
- They want to pay others, not be paid by others.
- They like to give orders and instructions to others, not to take orders and instructions from others.
- They defy and break the ground rules.
- They challenge the status quo.
- They do not easily accept no for an answer.
- They question silo thinking (narrow thinking).
- They expect and accept failures and use the failures as stepping-stones to success.
- They are economic machines in terms of increasing a country's gross domestic product (GDP) and employment levels and improving the standards of living for the country's citizens

Fact: Founders such as Steve Jobs of Apple, Jeff Bezos of Amazon.com, Bill Hewlett and Dave Packard of HP Corporation, Bill Gates of Microsoft, and Warren Buffett of Berkshire Hathaway are examples of entrepreneurs.

(v) Types of Entrepreneurships

Several types of entrepreneurship businesses exist. One needs to choose a business that suits in terms of what to achieve and how to achieve it. Some examples of these businesses include:

- Startups or small businesses
- Licenses or franchises
- Joint ventures or cooperatives
- Strategic alliances or acquisitions

Note that the type of business selected depends on the entrepreneur's financial resources and previous work experience. For example, entrepreneurs with limited financial resources can launch small businesses; entrepreneurs with significant financial resources can launch startups, licenses, franchises, or joint ventures.

(i) Startups or Small Businesses

The scope and size of startups or small businesses can vary significantly in terms of number of employees (1 to 100), the level of technology (low tech to high tech), the type of work performed (making products or providing services), and the type of legal structure required (proprietorship, partnership, or corporation).

Startups and small business owners can apply to the U.S. Small Business Administration (www.sba.gov) and to commercial banks for business loans to obtain the initial capital (one-time capital as investment) and working capital (ongoing capital to pay bills).

A small business or a startup owner needs to develop a business plan to monitor his or her own business progress and to get a loan from a bank because banks ask for business plans before granting loans to owners.

At a minimum, the components of a business plan should include a:

- Business strategy showing mission, vision, goals, and strategies describing the major reason for the business to exist and what it wants to accomplish in the short term and the long term
- Operations plan (includes manufacturing plan and service plan) describing the types of products to make or the types of services to be delivered to customers
- Marketing plan describing the major markets in which the products and services will be sold, marketing channels (wholesalers, distributors, or retailers), pricing strategies (low or high prices), and selling strategies (direct, online, or store)
- Financial plan containing pro forma or projected income statement, balance sheet, and cash flow statements
- People plan containing the type of employees to be hired (skilled or nonskilled and experienced or inexperienced) and how they will be trained and developed

Fact: Hollywood actor Ashton Kutcher invested in several high-tech startup firms, such as Skype and Foursquare.

Example 1: A licensed cosmetologist opens a new salon (a small business) in a shopping center to provide haircuts and manicure, and pedicure services.

Example 2: Examples of startups and small businesses include flower shops, salons, dry cleaners, laundries, pizza stores, gas stations, product assembly factories, package delivery services, food delivery services, consulting services, home improvement contracting services, and Internet services.

(ii) Licenses or Franchises

A license or franchise grants the right to provide a product or service or use a property, and fees are paid for such use. Licensing or franchising arrangements come in several forms to meet various specific needs.

Licensing occurs when a firm gives a legal permission to another firm to produce or package its product.

- A licensing agreement is an arrangement in which one firm permits another to use its intellectual property (IP) in exchange for compensation, typically a royalty.

- A licensing program consists of proprietary information, such as patent rights or expertise that is licensed by the owner (licenser) to another party (licensee). Compensation paid to the licenser usually includes license issuance fees, milestone payments, and/or royalties.

- Licensing occurs when a multinational enterprise sells a foreign company the right to use technology or information.

- Licensing is an arrangement in which a local firm in the host country produces goods in accordance with another firm's (the licensing firm's) specifications; as the goods are sold, the local firm can retain part of the earnings.

Franchising is a form of licensing in which an organization (owner, franchisor) provides its domestic or foreign franchisees with a complete assortment of products and services.

- It is a business arrangement by which the owner of a product or service allows others to purchase the right to distribute the product or service with help from the owner.

- It is an agreement by which a firm provides specialized sales or service strategy, support assistance, and possibly an initial investment in the franchise in exchange for periodic fees.

- It is a form of licensing that grants a wholesaler, distributor, or retailer exclusive rights to sell a product or a service in a specified area.

  Example: Popular name brands such as McDonald's, Pizza Hut, Subway, Kentucky Fried Chicken, and Dunkin Donuts have various licensing and franchising agreements and operations inside and outside of the United States.

(iii) Joint Ventures or Cooperatives

There are various forms, sizes, and locations for joint ventures. Joint ventures are formed when two or more individuals or companies come together to establish business operations either in domestic or foreign markets. They are unincorporated business organizations that usually exist for a limited time period. These ventures capitalize on each other's resources, strengths, knowledge, skills, and expertise in fulfilling their mission. They share efforts, profits, assets, liabilities, risks, and duties. Joint ventures are also known as cooperatives and strategic alliances.

A joint venture differs from a proprietorship because the former is formed between two or more companies or individuals whereas the latter is formed with a single individual. Also, the life of a proprietorship is longer than a joint venture. Nonetheless, the law of partnerships generally governs a joint venture.

> **Example 1:** An example of a joint venture is a manufacturing or service operation in a domestic or a foreign country to produce goods or provide services.

> **Example 2:** An example of a joint venture is involving a major research conducted by two or more corporations with researchers participating from different countries.

> **Example 3:** An example of a joint venture is the exploitation of natural resources, such as minerals, coal, iron, copper, water, gold, and oil and gas.

> **Example 4:** An example of a joint venture is a securities underwriting syndicate formed to acquire a certain tract of real estate land for subdivision and resale.

(iv) Strategic Alliances or Acquisitions

A **strategic alliance** is formed when two or more domestic or foreign companies band together to achieve mutual economic benefits. Strategic alliances are similar to joint ventures and cooperatives. They occur when one company in one country work in collaboration with one or more companies in other countries to share rights, responsibilities, revenues, expenses, and profits as defined in a written agreement. Some common types of strategic alliances are research collaborations, licensing programs, and copromotion deals. Strategic acquisitions occur when one company merges with another company to achieve business synergy.

> **Example 1:** An example of a domestic U.S. strategic alliance occurs when a food retailer establishes a strategic alliance with a gas company such that customers who purchase $50 worth of groceries will get a 5-cent discount per gallon at the gas station.

> **Example 2:** A strong local pizza store acquires a weaker local pizza store to capitalize on the brand name of the stronger store.

(w) Comparisons between Managers, Leaders, and Entrepreneurs

People may have more leadership qualities than management qualities, or vice versa, but ideally they should develop a balance of both qualities. Examples of leadership qualities include visionary, inspiring, creative, innovative, imaginative, and change agent. Examples of management qualities include possessing problem-solving skills, decision-making skills, analytical skills, authority, and stability.

One major difference between management and leadership qualities relates to the source of power and the level of a follower's compliance with it. **Power** is the ability to influence the behavior of others. Management power comes from position power (e.g., legitimate, reward, and coercive power) while leadership power comes from personal power (e.g., expert and referent power). An effective manager must have leadership qualities.

Entrepreneurs are characterized as risk takers, idea generators and in[...] grabbers and exploiters, change agents and innovators, go-getters, and [...]enters, opportunity different mind-sets, are a different breed, and have a bigger mission ar[...]reators. They have and leaders to take advantage of uncertainty (risk). Both large and sm[...]n than managers established firms can be entrepreneurial. All managers and leaders sh[...]s and new and entrepreneurs. [...]k and act like

(i) Leaders versus Managers

Much has been written in recent years about the leadership role of mana[...] leaders are both important to organizations. Effective managers have to be le[...] there are distinctive qualities associated with management and leadership th[...]ers and strengths for the organization; some of the leader's qualities include being vi[...]cause innovative, and imaginative. Some manager's qualities include possessing prob[...]rent decision-making skills, analytical skills, authoritative, and stabilizing. Manageme[...]g, reflect two different sets of qualities and skills that frequently overlap within a s[...], A person might have more of one set of qualities than the other, but ideally a ma[...] a balance of both manager and leader qualities.

One of the major differences between manager and leader qualities relates to [...] power and the level of compliance it engenders within followers. **Power** is the poten[...] influence the behavior of others. Management power comes from the individual's po[...] organization (i.e., administrative power). Because managers' power comes from org[...] structure, it promotes stability, order, and problem solving within the structure. 1[...] power, in contrast, comes from personal sources that are not as invested in the org[...] such as personal interests, goals, and values. Leadership power promotes vision, creat[...] change in the organization.

KEY CONCEPTS TO REMEMBER: Managers versus Leaders versus Entrepreneurs

- All leaders are managers, but all managers are not leaders.

- All entrepreneurs are managers and leaders, but all managers and leaders are not entrepreneurs.

- Most managers and leaders work for an organization that someone already established whereas all entrepreneurs work for their own organization that they created.

- The difference between managers, leaders, and entrepreneurs lies in their personalities, ambitions, and risk appetites (i.e., risk profiles).

- All managers, leaders, and entrepreneurs—in fact, all people—can be classified by their risk appetite levels such as risk taking, risk neutral, risk averse, and risk divert (i.e., moving the risk into other directions). The risk appetite is the level of risk that an individual or organization is willing to accept or live with.

- Entrepreneurs are positively identified as risk takers due to their bold and adventurous business projects and social programs that they undertake.

- In the business world, there are many many supervisors in number, many managers, few leaders, and very few entrepreneurs. This is listed here for comparative purposes only.

Entrepreneurs are characterized as risk takers, idea generators and implementers, opportunity grabbers and exploiters, change agents and innovators, go-getters, and value creators. They have different mind-sets, are a different breed, and have a bigger mission and vision than managers and leaders to take advantage of uncertainty (risk). Both large and small firms and new and established firms can be entrepreneurial. All managers and leaders should think and act like entrepreneurs.

(i) Leaders versus Managers

Much has been written in recent years about the leadership role of managers. Managers and leaders are both important to organizations. Effective managers have to be leaders, too, because there are distinctive qualities associated with management and leadership that provide different strengths for the organization; some of the leader's qualities include being visionary, inspiring, innovative, and imaginative. Some manager's qualities include possessing problem-solving skills, decision-making skills, analytical skills, authoritative, and stabilizing. Management and leadership reflect two different sets of qualities and skills that frequently overlap within a single individual. A person might have more of one set of qualities than the other, but ideally a manager develops a balance of both manager and leader qualities.

One of the major differences between manager and leader qualities relates to the source of power and the level of compliance it engenders within followers. **Power** is the potential ability to influence the behavior of others. Management power comes from the individual's position in the organization (i.e., administrative power). Because managers' power comes from organizational structure, it promotes stability, order, and problem solving within the structure. Leadership power, in contrast, comes from personal sources that are not as invested in the organization, such as personal interests, goals, and values. Leadership power promotes vision, creativity, and change in the organization.

KEY CONCEPTS TO REMEMBER: Managers versus Leaders versus Entrepreneurs

- All leaders are managers, but all managers are not leaders.

- All entrepreneurs are managers and leaders, but all managers and leaders are not entrepreneurs.

- Most managers and leaders work for an organization that someone already established whereas all entrepreneurs work for their own organization that they created.

- The difference between managers, leaders, and entrepreneurs lies in their personalities, ambitions, and risk appetites (i.e., risk profiles).

- All managers, leaders, and entrepreneurs—in fact, all people—can be classified by their risk appetite levels such as risk taking, risk neutral, risk averse, and risk divert (i.e., moving the risk into other directions). The risk appetite is the level of risk that an individual or organization is willing to accept or live with.

- Entrepreneurs are positively identified as risk takers due to their bold and adventurous business projects and social programs that they undertake.

- In the business world, there are many many supervisors in number, many managers, few leaders, and very few entrepreneurs. This is listed here for comparative purposes only.

1.6 Risk and Control Implications of Different Organizational Structures

In this section, organizations are defined and classified; organizational charts are explained; organizational structures are defined; contingency design alternatives are discussed; types of departmentalization are presented; traditional organizational structures are revisited; and the evolution of organizational structures is discussed.

(a) Organization Defined

(i) What Is an Organization?

Organization and management theorist Chester Barnard defines an organization as "a system of consciously coordinated activities or forces of two or more persons." In other words, when people gather together and formally agree to combine their efforts for a common purpose or goal, an organization is the result.

The purpose of the management process is to achieve organizational objectives in an effective and efficient manner. According to Edgar Schein, a prominent organizational psychologist, all organizations share four characteristics (see Exhibit 1.26).

EXHIBIT 1.26 Common Characteristics of Organizations

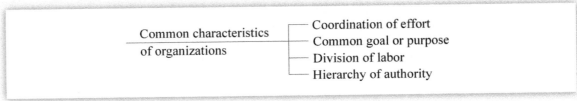

Coordination of effort is based on the idea that two heads are sometimes better than one. Individuals who join together and coordinate their mental and/or physical efforts can accomplish great things. There is a synergy in that coordination of effort multiplies individual contributions.

A **common goal or purpose** gives organization members a rallying point. Coordination of effort is enhanced when employees join together to strive for something of mutual interest.

Division of labor breaks complex tasks into specialized jobs so those employees become more proficient by repeatedly doing the same specialized task.

A **hierarchy of authority** is needed to see that the intended goals are carried out effectively and efficiently through outcomes and results. Authority is the right to direct the actions of others. People who promote flatter organizational structure (fewer levels of management) do not favor the traditional hierarchy of authority. However, some people encourage hierarchy of authority, as shown in Exhibit 1.27.

EXHIBIT 1.27 Proponents of Flatter Organizations and of Hierarchy of Authority

Proponents of Flatter Organizations	Proponents of Hierarchy of Authority
Fewer levels of management is present	Hierarchy is the most efficient, the hardiest, and the most natural structure.
Hierarchy connotes bureaucracy.	
Managerial hierarchy kills initiative and crushes creativity.	Hierarchy can release energy and creativity, rationalize productivity, and improve morale.
Communications are accelerated.	

(ii) Classifying Organizations

Organizations can be classified according to their intended purposes. Four categories exist, although some large and complex organizations have overlapping categories. The primary goals of these four types of organizations are described next.

1. **Business organizations.** These organizations must make a profit to survive. The focus is on satisfying the demand for products and services and earning profits.

2. **Nonprofit service organizations.** Here the focus is on service, not profits. Specific service is the goal as long as the organization is solvent. These organizations have greater pressure to operate more efficiently in light of limited funds available. Such organizations serve a specific segment of society.

3. **Mutual-benefit organizations.** For these organizations (e.g., a labor union or other association), the focus is on serving members' needs. Individuals join together to press for their own self-interest. Such organizations have greater pressure to operate effectively and efficiently to survive. Examples include professional associations, such as the Institute of Internal Auditors, and unions.

4. **Commonweal organizations.** Here the focus is on offering standardized public services without attempting to earn a profit. Such organizations (e.g., fire and police departments and public schools) serve all segments of society. Their great size makes them unwieldy and difficult to manage.

(iii) Organization Charts

An **organization chart** is a visual display of an organization's structural skeleton. Such charts show how departments are tied together along the principal lines of authority. They show reporting relationships, not lines of communication. Organization charts are tools of management to deploy human resources (HR) and are common in both for-profit and nonprofit organizations.

Every organization chart has two dimensions—vertical hierarchy and horizontal hierarchy—and two types—formal and informal, as shown in Exhibit 1.28.

EXHIBIT 1.28 Organization Charts

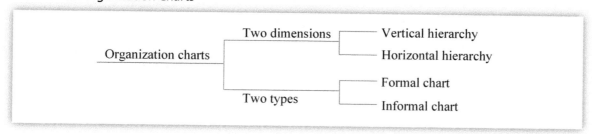

A typical organization chart, displaying the managerial pyramid, will have two dimensions: horizontal and vertical. These dimensions represent the division of labor and chain of command respectively.

The **vertical hierarchy** establishes the chain of command, or who reports to whom. It does not show responsibilities, cannot show informal organization, and cannot show all lines of communication. A person with a lower job rank may be shown at a higher level on the chart (e.g., administrative secretary or assistant).

The **horizontal hierarchy** establishes the division of labor and specialization, such as marketing, production, and finance. Generally, specialization is achieved at the expense of coordination when designing organizations. A workable balance between specialization and coordination can be achieved through contingency design. The horizontal hierarchy does not show responsibilities, cannot show informal organization, cannot show all lines of communication, and does not show reporting channels or hierarchy of authority. A person with a lower job rank may be shown at a higher level on the chart (e.g., administrative secretary or assistant). Networking is accomplished through the horizontal hierarchy where the interaction of persons of equal status takes place for the purpose of professional or moral support.

The **formal chart** is the documented, official map of the company's departments with appointed leaders who get things done through power granted by their superiors. Formal charts include job titles and are used to fill employee positions and management staffing levels.

Informal charts are not documented and are composed of natural leaders who get things done through power granted by peers. Informal charts do not include job titles as they do not exist physically; they exist only in mind.

KEY CONCEPTS TO REMEMBER: Organization Charts

- Job title does not necessarily indicate everything about a person's level of authority.
- Formal organization charts show nominal power.
- Informal organization charts show real power.
- Even supervisors need to use the informal power network to get things done.

Formal organization charts serve as guidelines, but they may not always keep track of changes in power relationships. One of the reasons why natural leaders evolve is that modern organizations are complex; they require the close cooperation of many people doing jobs that formal organization charts cannot accommodate. *There is at least one person available in every company with people skills and technical skills together that make him or her a natural leader. There may be more than one informal leader; there is only one formal leader in each area of the company.*

Natural leadership is intangible. It can cause factions, but it can also build a positive team spirit. Formal leaders should be tuned in to informal power to get things done. Formal leaders have the nominal power, and most subordinates obey it. But a formal leader's job is made easier if he or she can influence the informal employee leadership network and win its support. This may even lay the foundation for establishing real rapport and motivating employees.

Management consultant Gareth Morgan made an interesting observation about organization charts.[14] He said that organization charts are useful tools, but they can also be extremely limiting because they entrench the idea that an organization is a structure that can be engineered and reengineered to produce appropriate results. A new organization chart is often seen as a solution to an organization's problems. But, more often than not, it can leave the basic problems unchanged. Morgan says, for example, that when a large bureaucracy is reshaped or downsized, the result is a smaller bureaucracy. When the current bureaucracy is moved to matrix structure, the result is bureaucratic management in another form. Morgan's main concern is that this restructuring

---

[14] Gareth Morgan, *Imaginization: The Art of Creative Management* (Newbury Park, CA: Sage Publications, 1993).

does not create an organization that can flow and self-organize along with the changes faced. The same old organization is reshaped with similar problems and weaknesses.

Organization charts, clearly defined systems, flow diagrams, and other engineered blueprints have provided effective models for systematizing organizational activity. They still do for routine, predictable tasks. However, they do not in nonroutine, unpredictable task environments.

As IT takes us into a world where old structures and forms of organization dissolve and become almost invisible, the old approach no longer works. Through the use of telephone, efaxes, electronic mail, computers, and video conferencing, employees and their organizations are becoming disconnected physically. They can act as if they are completely connected while remaining far apart. Employees can transcend traditional barriers of space and time, continually creating and re-creating themselves through changing networks of interconnection based on real-time communication. As one network comes into being, others dissolve. Organizations do not have to be organizations anymore.

Nowadays, mechanistic thinking breaks down, and managers have to find fresh images for understanding and shaping what they are doing. Morgan suggests designing organizations as if they were spider plants or dandelion seeds blowing in the wind. He proposes that the management of change is the process of imagination, which invites creativity.

(b) Organizational Structures Defined

Organizational structures are defined as the design of how an organization's business functions and operations are arranged into departments, groups, or divisions (e.g., physical stores, online stores, outlet stores, and catalog stores for a retailer); how individual departments are organized; how jobs and tasks are divided and assigned to employees and departments; who reports to whom with pyramid structure showing management hierarchy and span of control; and how employees and managers interact with each other in performing their day-to-day work through communication, coordination, and collaboration.

The mission statement of an organization, in large part, dictates its organizational structure. The other part dictating the organizational structure is the legal structure: whether the organization is legally registered as a corporation, partnership, or proprietorship. For example:

- A public corporation is less risky than a private corporation.

- A regular corporation is less risky than a proprietorship or partnership.

- A limited liability corporation is less risky than a regular corporation.

- A proprietorship is riskier than a partnership or corporation because all the risks, profits, and losses go to the proprietor or owner.

- A partnership's risk falls between that of a corporation (low risk) and a proprietorship (high risk).

(c) Contingency Design Alternatives

Contingency design requires managers to select from a number of situationally appropriate alternatives instead of blindly following fixed principles of organization. Design alternatives include span of control, centralization and decentralization, and line and staff organizations.

(i) Span of Control
(A) Narrow and Wide

The number of people who report directly to a manager represent that manager's span of control or span of management. The optimal size of a span of control in a work area is dependent on four things:

1. The department's function
2. Organizational levels
3. Changes in the nature of the work
4. The clarity of instructions given employees

The optimal span of control is not dependent on the total number of employees in the department or company.

NARROW SPAN OF CONTROL VERSUS WIDE SPAN OF CONTROL

- A **narrow span of control** means few people to oversee, which in turn creates many hierarchical levels (tall organizations), which in turn requires many managers. The number of subordinates supervised is small. Workers are geographically dispersed.

- A **wide span of control** means many people to oversee, which in turn creates few hierarchical levels (flat organizations), which in turn requires few managers. Jobs are similar, procedures are standardized, all workers are in the same work area, and tasks are simple and repetitive. An upper limit of the number of employees supervised must exist.

Obviously, a balance between too little and too much supervision is required. The ideal span of control ranges from four subordinates at the top of the organization to 12 at the lowest level. The reason for the difference is that top-level managers are supervising people and lower-level managers are responsible for supervising specific tasks.

(B) Tall and Flat

A tall organization has many levels of hierarchy and a narrow span of control. A flat organization structure is one with relatively few levels of hierarchy and is characterized by a wide span of management control. A tall organization is riskier than a flat organization due to coordination and cooperation problems and turf wars between too many managers working in a function (see Exhibit 1.29).

EXHIBIT 1.29 Characteristics of Tall and Flat Organization Structures

Characteristics of Tall Organization Structure	Characteristics of Flat Organization Structure
Tasks are highly complex and varied.	Tasks require little direction and control of subordinates.
Work areas are geographically dispersed.	Work areas are geographically dispersed.
Subordinates perform distinctly different tasks.	
Employees are good at problem resolution due to discipline imposed by the hierarchy.	Employees must be able to work with little or no supervision.
Information flows slowly from top to bottom.	Employees make timely and efficient decisions.
	Information flows quickly from top to bottom.

In summary:

- A management's hierarchical levels can be many or few.

- A span of control can be narrow or wide.

- A span of control or span of management refers to the number of employees a supervisor or manager can oversee. Wider span means more employees and narrow span means fewer employees to manage or oversee. Thus, a span of control can be narrow or wide.

- **Organizational structure** refers to the number of hierarchical levels in management. A tall structure means many levels, and a flat structure means fewer levels.

- A tall organizational structure has many levels of hierarchy and a narrow span of control. It is characteristic of traditional organizations.

- A flat organizational structure has fewer levels of hierarchy and a wide span of control. It is characteristic of agile organizations.

Exhibit 1.30 summarizes the combination of organizational structures, hierarchical levels, and span of control.

EXHIBIT 1.30 Summary of Organizational Structures, Hierarchical Levels, and Span of Control

Organizational Structures	Hierarchical Levels	Span of Control
Tall (traditional)	Many	Few (narrow)
Flat (agile)	Few	Many (wide)

(ii) Centralized and Decentralized Organizations

Two methods of organizing organizations exist: centralized and decentralized. In a **centralized organization,** decisions are made at the higher levels of management. Decisions in a decentralized organization are made at the lower levels. Authority is delegated to lower levels of the organization.

CENTRALIZATION AND DECENTRALIZATION

The extent of an organization's centralization or decentralization is determined by the span of control, the number of levels in the hierarchy, and the degree of coordination and specialization.

Centralization is typically used in those organizations that emphasize coordination of decisions that must be applied uniformly to a set of known or common problems.

Companies that allow managers (e.g., business unit managers or division managers) a great deal of autonomy are described as utilizing decentralized management. Management considers the factors shown in Exhibit 1.31 in determining whether a centralized or decentralized design should be adopted.

EXHIBIT 1.31 Factors to Consider for Centralization and Decentralization

Factors	Decentralization	Centralization
Number and kind of decisions	Many unique decisions	Generic or uniform decisions
Organization culture	Less formal	More formal
Value of uniform procedures and rules	Rapidly changing products and industries	Slowly changing products and industries
Lower-level manager skills	Must be generalists	Do not require as much training
Firm size and growth rate	Larger organizations and/or rapid growth rate	Smaller organizations and/or less rapid growth rate
Strategy	Emphasis on new product development through company research	Emphasis on production of standard products in large volume

(A) Two Approaches to Achieve Decentralization

Functional decentralization occurs when related activities or functions are grouped within an organization. For instance, all functions relating to marketing are grouped under one head. The main advantage of functional decentralization is that it allows specialists to work in areas where they contribute the most to the firm. This is very important in industries that survive mainly because of technical expertise.

However, once the specialist can make decisions independently, coordination with other areas, such as production, may suffer. Another problem is that when one group is created, it is difficult to measure the performance of the individual specialists. As the firm grows, this problem also will grow.

Divisional decentralization is the creation of units whose managers are in charge of producing and marketing a certain product, a group of related products, or activities for a geographic region. A division thus created will involve many if not all of the functions in which the entire organization is engaged. Divisional decentralization results in many semi-independent units equivalent to small organizations within the larger parent.

The main advantage of divisional decentralization is that it enables decision making that is closer to the activities of the organization in contrast to decision making that arises from a central office far away. A second advantage is that responsibility can be assigned easily to the manager of a division so that his or her contribution to the company can be evaluated. A third advantage of divisional decentralization is that greater unity of command is achieved. The primary disadvantage is that this method can lead to suboptimization of resources (i.e., resources are not properly and fully utilized).

Divisional decentralization can create a feeling of autonomy in division managers that results in dysfunctional competition between them. As a result, the entire firm will suffer. Some managers will emphasize short-term gains to promote their careers to the detriment of the long-term interests of the organization.

(B) Advantages and Disadvantages of Decentralization

The advantages of decentralization arise from the greater autonomy assumed by lower-level management and workers. Top management is free to concentrate on more important problems, such as long-range planning, because lower-level management is handling many details on its own. The general speed of business activity is increased since lower-level management does not have to wait for upper-level approval. Probably the greatest advantage of decentralization is that it allows managers the freedom to think boldly and creatively, stimulates a sense of personal freedom, raises morale, and provides an excellent training ground for future top executives.

This greater autonomy also gives rise to the disadvantages of decentralization. With each unit making its own decisions, activities are likely to be duplicated. Normally, it is cheaper to perform some activities centrally (e.g., finance, accounting). Managers of autonomous units may possibly ignore the advice of specialists. Decentralization can lead to suboptimization of resources. In the interest of the whole organization, top management should install some controls to attempt to correct some of the disadvantages of decentralization.

(iii) Line and Staff Organizations

Line and staff organization structure is designed to maximize the unity of command principle by giving only the managers the authority to make decisions affecting those in the chain of command. There is no crossover between line and staff organization structure since each structure has its own chain of command.

Line managers have the authority to make decisions and give orders to all subordinates in their chain of command. Staff authority is generally limited to subordinates within the department. There is a natural conflict between these two parties (i.e., between line managers and staff managers) due to power differences and different backgrounds.

One important source of conflict is the fact that line employees have formal authority while staff employees have informal power. Line managers tend to emphasize decisiveness, results, costs, and implementation, whereas staff members advise and prefer completeness, controls, adherence to policies and procedures, and systematic analysis to solve organizational problems. The staff function supports the line function but does not control it.

(d) Types of Departmentalization

Two common forms of integration are through the hierarchical chain of command and departmentalization. Some integration is needed to offset the negative effects of differentiation. It is through departmentalization that related jobs, activities, or processes are grouped into major organizational subunits, such as departments, divisions, groups, or units. Four basic types of departmentalization include: (1) functional departments, (2) product-service departments, (3) geographic location departments, and (4) customer classification departments

(i) Functional Departments

In both for-profit and nonprofit organizations, functional departments categorize jobs according to the activity performed. Manufacturing, marketing, and finance are some examples of functional departments, and the structure is popular because it permits those with similar technical expertise to work in a coordinated subunit. The structure becomes unpopular when departmental concerns tend to override more important organizational concerns. Functional departments can encourage differentiation at the expense of integration. A small, single, standard product line may be organized as a functional department, such as manufacturing, accounting, and sales. Unbroken organizational and reporting lines are indications of functional departmentalization.

> **CHARACTERISTICS OF ORGANIZATION STRUCTURES**
>
> - Functional departments, product-service departments, geographic location departments, and customer classification departments are the pure forms of organization structures. In practice, a combination of these structures is found.
>
> - Product-service, geographic location, and customer classification departments can create costly duplication of personnel and facilities. Functional departments do not create duplication of personnel and facilities.

(ii) Product-Service Department

In the product-service department category, a product or service, rather than a functional category of work, is the unifying theme. Ideally, those working in a product-service department have a broad business orientation rather than a narrow functional orientation. One weakness of the product-service approach is that inefficient and costly duplication of effort may take place. A product departmentalization strategy may be good for a firm making multiple products. An example would be a computer manufacturer that organizes into mainframe computers, personal computers, mobile technology, and cloud technology groups.

(iii) Geographic Location Departments

In this organization structure, geographic location dictates the structure and format of the organization and emphasizes the concept that managers should be closer to the action. Advantages include knowledge of the local business and customers. Disadvantages include long lines of communication and the fact that the force behind the geographical lines is global competition. *"Think globally and act locally"* is the catchphrase for companies operating in a global market.

(iv) Customer Classification Departments

Customers have different needs and are of different types (e.g., business versus residential, retail versus wholesale, industrial versus commercial). The rationale behind organizing the company into customer classifications is to better service the distinctly different needs of each customer type.

(e) Traditional Organizational Structures

Organizations with traditional organizational structures are primarily organized by function or department, and the organizational structures are in the shape of pyramids. The traditional structures are inefficient due to their silo design and are less adaptable than the modern structures due to their inflexibility. In general, they are slow to respond and react to changes taking place around them in both internal and external environments.

Traditional organizational structures have a tall management hierarchy with too many job levels/layers and a narrow span of control, meaning a supervisor can manage fewer employees. They have strict job descriptions and job titles combined with well-defined boundaries built around functions, departments, and jobs. Employees' skills are limited, can become stagnant, and are not easy to transfer to other functions or departments. Two common forms of traditional organizational structures include organizing by function and organizing by department.

(i) Organizing by Function

Most retail businesses are organized according to functions, such as marketing, merchandising, operations (stores, warehouses, and distribution centers), loss prevention, human resources, accounting and finance, and IT. These functions, in turn, are classified as line functions or staff functions. Managers of a line function have a major role and responsibility in meeting the organization's primary goals of producing goods, providing services, and marketing such goods and services. Managers of a staff function have a secondary role of supporting the managers of the line function.

Line and staff structure is designed to maximize the unity of command principle by giving only managers the authority to make decisions affecting those in the chain of command. There is no cross-over between the line and staff structures since each structure has its own chain of command.

Line managers have the authority to make decisions and give orders to all subordinates in their chain of command. Staff authority is generally limited to subordinates within the department. There is a natural conflict between these two parties (i.e., line managers and staff managers) due to power differences and different backgrounds.

One important source of conflict is the fact that line employees have formal authority and power while staff employees have informal authority and power. Line managers tend to emphasize decisiveness, results, costs, and implementation, whereas staff members advise and prefer completeness, controls, adherence to policies and procedures, and systematic analysis to solve organizational problems. The staff function supports the line function but does not control it.

The managers of a staff function have a supporting role and responsibility of working with managers of a line function. An HR manager in the HR function supports a marketing manager in recruiting marketing staff. A budget manager in the accounting/finance function supports an operations manager in developing a production or service budget. In other words, staff managers act as advisors or coordinators to line managers.

(ii) Organizing by Department

A business function can contain few or several departments, and each department can contain many employees. For example, the marketing function can be divided into sales, advertising, public relations, and customer service departments. These departments can be organized using either the traditional or the innovative method. Each of these departments will have internal customers (employees within the department) and external customers (employees in other departments of the company and people outside the company, such as customers, suppliers, vendors, and contractors).

A **silo or legacy department** is a product of traditional design and uses a rigid, vertical hierarchy of management with tightly bounded structures with solid walls built around the department. It has a tall organizational structure with a narrow span of control. It is not at all responsive to customer requests, queries, problems, and issues. Employees working in siloed departments are not empowered at all and receive little or no training (or somewhat ad hoc training) in customer service and organizational excellence, where the latter results from the former.

Unfortunately, most departments today are still operating as silo or legacy departments using traditional methods, which may not work well in ever-changing modern businesses. The time has come to change the silo department structure to something better, such as borderless department or, even better, to agile departments using innovative methods.

A **borderless or seamless department** is a product of innovative design and uses a flexible, horizontal hierarchy of management with loosely bounded structures with built-in soft walls around the department. This department has a flat organizational structure with a wide span of control. It is somewhat responsive to customer requests, queries, problems, and issues. Employees working in borderless departments are reasonably empowered and frequently receive training in customer service and organizational excellence.

Silo/Legacy Department ⟶ Borderless/Seamless Department

An agile or lean department is a product of innovative design and uses a flexible organizational structure and diagonal communication channels combined with little/no walls built around the department. and loosely designed job descriptions. It has a flat organizational structure with a very wide span of control (i.e., too few job levels and too many employees to manage to become a lean department). It provides a rapid response to customer requests, queries, problems, and issues. Employees working in agile departments are fully empowered, self-organized, and self-managed, as they work in teams and receive continuous training in customer service and organizational excellence.

As organizations become more customer-focused, they will need to transform their silo departments into borderless departments as an intermediate step and finally transform into agile departments. The evolution of a silo department into an agile department is shown next.

Silo/Legacy Department ⟶ Borderless/Seamless Department ⟶ Agile/Lean Department

(f) Evolution of Organizational Structures

Organizational structures are evolving as they are challenging and reshaping the traditional pyramid-type organizational structures. These evolving organizational structures not only improve the quality of life in the workplace but also improve the practice of management. Seven types of organizational structures are available based on evolution in business:

1. Matrix organizations
2. Hourglass organizations
3. Cluster organizations
4. Network organizations
5. Porous organizations
6. Ambidextrous organizations
7. Agile organizations

Each organization type is discussed next.

(i) Matrix Organizations

In a matrix organization, employees working in departments with vertical (down) and horizontal (across) lines of authority are grouped together to accomplish a specific objective. This design is suitable to a project environment where the project manager is responsible for completing a project without formal line authority. Under these conditions, project managers tend to use negotiation skills, persuasive ability, technical competence, and the exchange of favors to complete a project in order to compensate for their lack of formal authority (see Exhibit 1.32).

EXHIBIT 1.32 Advantages and Disadvantages of Matrix Organizations

Advantages	Disadvantages
Efficient use of resources	Power struggles
Project integration	Conflict
Improved information flow	Slow reaction time
Flexibility	Difficulty in controlling and monitoring tasks and people
Discipline	Overhead
Improved motivation and commitment	Stress due to dual reporting

The matrix organization structure will likely have unity of command problems unless there is frequent and comprehensive communication between the various functional managers and project managers.

For example, a large internal auditing department employs specialists in areas such as computer auditing (IT auditing) and statistical sampling. All specialists report directly to the assistant manager for technical services. When needed on a specific audit, they report to the audit supervisor responsible for the assignment. The matrix form of organizational structure exists in relation to the specialists.

(ii) Hourglass Organizations

The hourglass organization consists of three layers, with the middle layer distinctly pinched. The first layer is strategic management, whose members formulate a vision for the organization and make sure it becomes a reality. The second layer is a shrunken middle management, whose members carry out a coordinating function for diverse lower-level activities. These middle managers wear different hats all the time (i.e., they handle accounting problems one day, product design issues the other day, and marketing dilemmas the next day).

HOURGLASS ORGANIZATION VERSUS TRADITIONAL PYRAMID ORGANIZATION

- Middle managers in the hourglass organization structure are business generalists. They deal with complex interfunctional problems.

- Middle managers in the traditional pyramid organization structure are business specialists. They deal with narrow and yet complex infrastructural problems.

At the bottom of the hourglass is a broad layer of technical employees who act as their own supervisors much of the time. Consequently, the distinction between supervisors and rank-and-file employees is blurred. Employees at this operating level complain about a real lack of promotional opportunities. Management should try to keep them motivated with challenging work assignments, lateral transfers, skill training opportunities, and pay-for-performance schemes.

(iii) Cluster Organizations

Teams are the primary structural unit in cluster organizations. Employees are multiskilled and move from team to team as projects dictate. Flexible work assignments are the norm. This structure promotes innovation and responsiveness. Pay for knowledge is a common practice. Motivation will be high, but so will stress levels. On the downside, job security is an issue due to constantly changing projects. Employees need to attend training programs in team building and communications.

(iv) Network Organizations

Network organizations do not produce what they sell. Hence, their only function is administrative oversight. An independent contractor handles business operations for each organizational function (production, marketing). In other words, network organizations buy a product with their own label on it and then hire other companies to distribute and sell the product.

Network organizations are hollow or virtual corporations built on relationships; employees spend much of their time communicating via computers, emails, text messages, telephones, and efaxes. Advantages are lean and mean, well-run, efficient operations. Drawbacks include national security issues when operating in key industries, friction and vertical polarization (because employees are either executives or clerical workers with big pay differentials), and high turnover among nonmanagerial employees due to the fast pace of the work. Both executives and clerical employees need to attend training programs in negotiation skills, conflict management, effective communication, and handling stress.

KEY CONCEPTS TO REMEMBER: Evolving Organizational Structures

- The hourglass organization is a three-layer structure (strategic layer, middle layer, and operating layer) with a constricted middle layer.
- The cluster organization is a collaborative structure in which teams are the primary unit.
- In the network organization, the only function is coordination between subcontracted production and marketing operations.

(v) Porous Organizations

Porous organizations have a fluid and open network structure consisting of boundaryless, nontraditional, and virtual organizations that are interconnected, representing volunteer members from the public sector, private sector, and academia. Globally, they work together as a virtual team in the digital age to address and respond to disasters (e.g., earthquakes, hurricanes, fires, floods, and cyclones) and other crisis situations occurring worldwide.

Since members are volunteers, they can enter and leave porous organizations easily. These members communicate and coordinate with each other through emails, blog postings, text messages, telephone conversations, video conferences, and voicemails.

Porous networks are more open than others to new ideas and technologies and are more likely to identify useful developments and connections or synergies. In addition, porous network organizations, which are virtual organizations, may have an adaptive advantage over traditional structures (e.g., functional, departmental, and divisional structures) in that they are better able to sense changes (trends and shifts) in the external world and are able to quickly respond and react to such changes. Nongovernmental organizations (NGOs) and international charitable organizations such as UNICEF and Red Cross are examples of porous organizations.

(vi) Ambidextrous Organizations

Ambidextrous organizations, in general, are efficient in operations and adaptable to changes using exploration and exploitation methods. These organizations must achieve a balance between exploration and exploitation methods; they cannot pursue one method at the expense of the other. Each method is discussed next.

Exploration methods include R&D efforts and brainstorming sessions to discover new ideas, representing risk-taking experiments. A risk is that these exploration methods may not be successful. Entrepreneurs and innovators by nature focus on the exploration methods.

> **Example:** Retailers who are innovators and entrepreneurs utilize exploration methods. Jeff Bezos of Amazon.com and Steve Jobs of Apple, Inc. are examples of innovators. For example, Amazon pioneered in retail technologies such as drones, robots, and artificial intelligence (AI) and Apple pioneered in smartphones and smart tablets. Similarly, most retailers (e.g., Walmart, Target, Zappos, Lowe's, and Warby Parker) successfully applied exploration methods in developing omnichannel strategies (i.e., integrated channels). These retailers are efficient because they embrace change and produce radical and significant outcomes.

Exploitation methods include revisiting, restrategizing, replanning, redesigning, and reimplementing existing ideas to find better approaches. Basically, these methods are a kind of tweaking existing methods to make them little better with incremental benefits. Essentially, management has a status quo thinking and attitude. A risk is that exploitation methods can result in small outcomes and may not reach the levels of significant outcomes.

> **Example:** Most retailers with brick-and-mortar stores, such as Sears and K-Mart, are taking on exploitation methods and have been unable to see much success with their status quo thinking, which has resulted in the closing of several stores for Sears, K-Mart, Toys R Us, and other retailers.

(vii) Agile Organizations

An agile or lean organization has the ability to rapidly adapt to changing market conditions (e.g., changes in demand and supply factors for products and services) and competitive environments (e.g., competitors' aggressive plans and actions) in an efficient and effective manner. The agile organization assumes that change is constant and normal and is built into its life. This organization acknowledges the threats facing it and takes advantage of opportunities waiting to be seized.

Threats $\longrightarrow$ Opportunities

Some agile organizations practice holacracy, a distribution of management power, which is claimed to increase agility, efficiency, innovation, transparency, responsibility, and accountability. It is a system of distributed, not centralized, authority. Distributed authority means lower-level employees and managers can make their own decisions without too much dependence on higher-level managers. Agility in operations (i.e., lean operations) and passion for the customer are the two major prerequisites to a successful holacracy practice. However, criticisms against the holacracy include its one-size-fits-all approach and administrative burden with rigorous rules and procedures. Employees working in agile operations have no job descriptions and no job titles; instead, they have roles, work circles, and teams, which are called holarchy, a type of hierarchy.

Agile/lean organizations have a flat organizational structure and a wider span of control, meaning that a supervisor can manage many employees. An agile organization is an innovative one because its employees can customer-related problems through a team-based structure, empowering employees, and sharing information. Here, "empowering employees" does not mean that they abdicate responsibility; instead, it means giving employees power, authority, delegation, and decision making. However, there could be an imbalance between power and authority.

At this time, it is good to compare the agile organization structure with the traditional organization structure (sometimes called bureaucratic organization). See Exhibit 1.33.

EXHIBIT 1.33 Comparison Between Agile Organizations and Traditional Organizations

Comparative Item	**Agile Organizations**	**Traditional Organizations**
Organizational structure	Flexible	Fixed
Hierarchy and span of control	Flat (few levels), wide (many employees)	Tall (many levels), narrow (few employees)
Management authority	Distributed	Centralized
Decision making	Dynamic	Static
Speed of decisions	Fast	Slow
Employees' roles	Fluid	Rigid
Employees' expertise	Wide-area expertise	Narrow-area expertise with SMEs
Human communication channels	Diagonal, vertical, and horizontal	Vertical only

Example: Zappos, an online shoe retailer, implements the holacracy philosophy. It has no formal job descriptions or job titles for its employees and it operates with a flat organizational structure. Employees work in a team environment and can perform any job given to them. Employees get constant training and retraining to make customers fully satisfied.

Example: Retailers such as Amazon, Zappos, Walmart, Target, Home Depot, Lowe's, Warby Parker, and Kroger are known to be agile organizations because they are able to adapt quickly to changing retail market conditions and are innovative and customer-oriented.

In summary:

- Traditional pyramid organizational structures are inefficient due to their silo design and less adaptable to changes due to their inflexibility.

- Matrix organizations work as a team to solve a common problem and to find a solution.

- Hourglass organizations represent three diverse layers of employees (strategic layer, middle layer, and operating layer) with a constricted middle layer.

- Cluster organizations consist of employees moving from team to team because they are multiskilled and multitalented. These organizations are collaborative structures in which teams are the primary unit.

- Network organizations provide administrative oversight only. The only function is coordination between subcontracted production, marketing operations, and sales activities. They are also called learning organizations and boundaryless organizations.

- Porous organizations represent volunteer members from boundaryless global companies and are best suited to sense trends and shifts and react and respond to them.

- Ambidextrous organizations, in general, are efficient in operations and adaptable to changes using exploration and exploitation methods. They are also, in part, innovative organizations due to the use of exploration methods.

- Agile organizations are lean and innovative organizations with the ability to adapt quickly to changing conditions.

1.7 Risk and Control Implications of Common Business Processes

In this section, risk and control implications of common business processes are discussed, including human resources (HR) management; procurement and supply chain management; new product development process; marketing and sales management; logistics and distribution management; and outsourced business processes.

(a) Human Resources Management

This section presents HR planning process, employee recruiting and selection methods, the preemployment screening process, employee training and development methods, the employee performance appraisal process, and employee termination and resignation procedures.

(i) Human Resource Planning Process

HR planning is a part of an organization's strategic planning. The HR planning process is a systematic approach of matching the internal and external supply of people with job openings anticipated over a specified period of time. Specifically, it includes three major elements:

1. Forecasting HR requirements

2. Forecasting HR availability

3. Comparing the HR requirements with the HR availability

In **forecasting the HR requirements**, the demand for employees is matched against the supply of employees. If they are equal, no action is necessary. Several methods exist to forecast the HR requirements, including zero-based forecasting, bottom-up approach, simulation models, and relating sales volume to the number of employees needed.

In **forecasting the HR availability**, the number of employees with the required skills and at the required locations is determined. The needed employees may be found internally, externally, or in combination. If a shortage is forecasted, needed employees may come from developing creative recruiting methods, increasing compensation incentives to employees, conducting special training programs, and using different selection standards, such as lowering employment requirements in terms of hiring an inexperienced employee and providing on-the-job training to that employee.

In **comparing the HR requirements with the HR availability**, surplus workers may exist. This surplus can be handled through various reduction methods, such as restricted hiring, reduced work hours, encouraging early retirements, buyouts, mandatory layoffs (furloughs), or even downsizing (restructuring and rightsizing) the department or the company.

The outcome of the HR planning process can be either a surplus or a shortage of workers. HR management needs to address both of these outcomes.

Surplus of Workers = HR Availability > HR Requirements

Shortage of Workers = HR Requirements > HR Availability

(ii) Employee Recruiting and Selection Methods

Recruitment is the process of attracting qualified individuals on a timely basis and in sufficient numbers to fill the required jobs, based on job descriptions and job specifications. Risks can exist in hiring due to judgment errors, such as yes-hire error and no-hire error.

- Yes-hire error exists when an unqualified or less qualified job candidate is accepted. This means selecting a wrong job applicant.

- No-hire error exists when a qualified job candidate is rejected. This means rejecting a right job applicant.

Two factors affect the job recruiting: external factors and internal factors. **External factors** consist of labor market considerations (e.g., demand and supply) and legal considerations, such as nondiscriminatory practices (e.g., gender, race, and ethnicity). **Internal factors** consist of promotion policies (e.g., promotion from within).

(iii) Pre-Employment Screening Process

The pre-employment screening process starts after a job candidate completes an employment application, submits a resume, takes the required selection tests, and undergoes an employment interview. At this point, the candidate is being considered for the job and requires further meetings and interviews prior to hiring.

Two types of pre-employment screening include background investigations and reference checks, where the latter supplements the former.

The focus of background investigations is to determine the accuracy of information submitted or to determine whether the required information was not submitted. Background investigations involve collecting data from various sources, such as previous employers, business associates, credit bureaus, government agencies, academic institutions, and the applicant's mode of living and the nature of character. Some sensitive jobs require fingerprinting and security clearances.

Reference checks from outsiders verify the accuracy of information provided by applicants. A problem with reference checks is that they do not tell the whole truth about applicants. Another problem is that previous employers are reluctant to reveal information about applicants due to privacy reasons.

Risks can exist when conducting pre-employment screening work due to judgment errors, such as yes-negligent error and no-negligent error. Yes-negligent error results when a current employer was negligent in conducting a thorough background investigation of a job applicant. No-negligent error results when a current employer was not negligent in conducting a thorough background investigation of a job applicant.

HR management needs to be concerned about four legal liabilities when hiring, which provide additional justification for conducting a thorough background investigation of the job applicant. Management's judgment error is the major reason for the legal liabilities.

1. **Negligent hiring** is the liability of current employers when they fail to conduct a reasonable investigation of a job applicant's background and then hires a potentially dangerous person who can damage company property and/or harm employees and others. The definition of reasonable investigation depends on the nature of the job. Due diligence is required in conducting background investigations. The hiring organization must be able to foresee the harm resulting from a dangerous employee being hired.

2. **Negligent referral** is the liability of former employers when they fail to warn a potential employer about a severe problem with a past employee.

3. **Negligent retention** is the liability of current employers if they keep on the payroll an employee whose records indicate strong potential for wrongdoing and if they fail to take necessary steps to defuse a possibly violent situation.

4. **Negligent promotion** is the liability of current employers when an incompetent and unqualified employee was promoted at the expense of competent and qualified employees.

NEGLIGENT HIRING VERSUS REFERRAL VERSUS RETENTION VERSUS PROMOTION

Negligent hiring is a legal liability for the current employer.

Negligent referral is a legal liability for the former employer.

Negligent retention results from negligent hiring, which is a legal liability for the current employer.

Negligent promotion is a legal liability for the current employer.

(iv) Employee Training and Development Methods

Training and development requirements of employees (i.e., nonsupervisors and nonmanagers) are different from those of supervisors and managers. Similarly, the training and development needs of general managers, senior managers, executives, and leaders are very different from those of supervisors and managers.

(v) Employee Performance Appraisal Process

Just as corporations want to grow in sales and market share to increase profits and stakeholder value, employees need to grow personally and professionally to reach their career goals and make a positive contribution to the company they work for and to help the company reach its goals. The goal congruence concept is at play here.

Although neither employees nor supervisors like to give and receive performance appraisal evaluations, such evaluations are a very important part of employee career growth plans. They can be used in justifying employee termination and promotion decisions and can help in identifying employee training and development needs.

(A) Characteristics of an Effective Performance Appraisal System

Characteristics of an effective performance appraisal system include job-related criteria, performance expectations, standardization, trained appraisers, continuous open communications, periodic performance reviews, and due process to appeal appraisal results.

Results from the employee performance appraisal process can be put to several good uses, such as input into HR planning, recruitment, and selection; training and development; career planning and development; compensation programs; employee relations; succession planning; promotion or demotion; and assessment of employee potential in the company.

(B) Factors Affecting Employee Performance Appraisals

Both external factors and internal factors can affect a company's process of employee appraisals.

Two external factors include government legislation requiring that nondiscriminatory practices be followed and labor union preferences for seniority, not performance, as the basis for promotions.

One major internal factor that affects performance appraisals is the organization's culture, where nontrusting culture does not encourage high performance.

The employee performance appraisal process is divided into a series of steps, including identifying specific performance appraisal goals, establishing performance criteria and communicating them to employees (e.g., traits, behaviors, competencies, goal achievement, and improvement potential), examining employees' work performed, appraising employees' performance, and discussing appraisal results with employees.

Individuals responsible for conducting employee performance appraisals include the employee him- or herself, immediate supervisor, senior managers, subordinates, peers and team members, and internal and external customers. In this **360-degree feedback** evaluation method, the biggest risk is confidentiality, whether the evaluation is done internally or externally.

A **720-degree review** focuses on the big picture at the company level for all of its employees, not on the individual employee level. The review is all about senior managers and their performance. The participants in the review include senior managers, subordinates, customers, and investors because senior managers deal more with external parties, such as customers and investors.

Performance appraisal methods include these: 360-degree feedback, 720-degree review, graphic rating scales method, ranking and comparison method, critical incident method, written essay method, goal-setting exercises, work standard method, multirater appraisals, weighted checklists, forced distribution method, behaviorally anchored rating scales (BARS) method, and results-based system.

Problems and risks associated with the performance appraisal process include appraiser discomfort, lack of objectivity, halo/horn error, leniency/strictness effect, central tendency error, recent behavior bias, personal bias (stereotyping), manipulating the evaluation, and employee anxiety.

HALO ERROR VERSUS HORN ERROR

A **halo error** occurs when a manager projects one positive performance feature or incident onto the rest, resulting in a higher rating.

A **horn error** occurs when a manager projects one negative performance feature or incident onto the rest, resulting in a lower rating.

(vi) Employee Termination and Resignation Procedures

Termination is the most severe penalty requiring careful consideration on the part of the employer. Termination of nonmanagerial and nonprofessional employees is handled differently from the termination of higher-level executives and middle-/lower-level managers and professionals.

For example, termination procedures for nonmanagerial and nonprofessional employees (e.g., truck drivers and waiters) are dictated by whether these employees belong to a union or not.

Usually, executive jobs are protected under a contract, if there is one. Executives have no formal appeal rights, because the termination could be due to valid business reasons (e.g., economic downturn, reorganization and downsizing, and decline in performance and productivity). However, if executives are involved in illegal activities, such as management fraud, insider trading, or sexual harassment suits, they can be terminated. Terminated executives can be costly to replace, and terminated executives can make negative statements about the company to the press in order to damage its reputation.

Middle- and lower-level managers and professionals are most vulnerable to termination, unless they belong to a union, because their employment depends on the wills and whims of their immediate supervisor.

Based on the performance appraisal process, some employees could be fired or terminated. It is expensive to fire an employee, especially when there is a judgment error associated with it. There are two types of firing errors:

1. **Yes-fire error** exists when the employer decides to fire an employee who does not deserve firing.

2. **No-fire error** exists when the employer does not fire an employee who deserves firing.

Resignations occur on a voluntary basis by employees or are forced by the employer. When an employee resigns voluntarily, the employer must determine the reasons for leaving through the use of exit interview (before an employee departs) and a postexit questionnaire (after an employee departed).

(A) Exit Interviews and Attitude Surveys

Exit interviews, which are face-to-face meetings, can identify the reasons for leaving, which can be used to change the HR planning process, modify training and development programs, and determine other areas needing improvement. A major problem with face-to-face exit interviews is that departing employees may not tell the interviewer the real reasons for leaving due to their sensitivity.

Postexit questionnaires are sent to former employees several weeks after they leave the company to determine the real reasons they left, which can negate the problems with the exit interviews. Departed employees may respond freely to the questionnaire because they are not in front of the interviewer.

The best way to manage employee relations is to conduct a periodic **attitude survey** of current employees to determine their feelings, issues, and concerns related to their jobs and to seek their ideas for improvement. The scope of the survey can include nature of the work, supervisor relations, work environment (tools and materials), flexibility in the work schedules, opportunities for job advancement, training and development opportunities, pay and benefits, and workplace safety and security concerns. Survey results can help the employer to correct identified gaps on a proactive basis before the problems get out of hand. If gaps go uncorrected, employees may leave the company.

Note: Exit interviews and postexit questionnaires are reactionary in nature and not timely. Employee attitude surveys are proactive in nature and timely. However, all these methods focus on the same thing: obtaining employee feedback.

(b) Procurement and Supply Chain Management

This section discusses two separate and yet interrelated topics: procurement management and supply chain management.

(i) Procurement Management

Procurement management is purchasing management where a company's purchasing agents or buyers acquire materials (e.g., raw materials, ingredients, tools, parts, components, subassemblies, packaging materials, and other production supplies) from outside product suppliers to manufacture products. The purchasing agents also award contracts for acquiring services (e.g., building and equipment maintenance, welding, and painting) from outside service vendors. The procurement function is risky in several ways due to huge amounts of money involved in purchasing needed materials and due to the attitude of buyers with potential conflict-of-interest situations and motivation (honesty and integrity) and dismotivation (dishonesty and no integrity) levels, all leading to fraud and collusion with suppliers.

(ii) A Primer on Bid-Rigging: A Major Risk in Procurement Management

Bid-rigging is a fraud scheme involving procurement bids from vendors. It is an agreement among competitors and vendors as to who will be the final winning bidder (seller). Bid rigging occurs when a purchaser (buyer) solicits bids to purchase goods or services from sellers. The bidders agree in advance who will submit the winning bid. The purchaser, who depends on competition between the bidders to generate the lowest competitive price, receives instead a "lowest bid" that is higher than the competitive market would bear.

There are five basic schemes involved in most bid-rigging conspiracies:

1. Bid Suppression: In this type of scheme, one or more competitors agree not to bid, or withdraw a previously submitted bid, so that a designated bidder will win. In return, the non-bidder may receive a subcontract or payoff.

2. Complementary Bidding: In this scheme, co-conspirators (competitors) submit token bids which are intentionally high or which intentionally fail to meet all of the bid requirements in order to lose a contract. It is also called a courtesy bidding and it is the most commonly and frequently used form of bid-rigging.

3. Bid Rotation: In bid rotation, all co-conspirators submit bids, but by agreement, take turns being the low bidder on a series of contracts.

4. Customer or Market Allocation: In this scheme, co-conspirators agree to divide up customers or geographic areas. The result is that the co-conspirators will not bid or will submit only complementary bids when a solicitation for bids is made by a customer or in

an area not assigned to them. This scheme is most commonly found in the service sector and may involve quoted prices for services as opposed to bids.

5. Subcontracting arrangements are often part of a bid-rigging scheme. Competitors who agree not to bid or to submit a losing bid frequently receive subcontracts or supply contracts in exchange from the successful low bidder. In some schemes, a low bidder will agree to withdraw its bid in favor of the next low bidder, in exchange for a lucrative subcontract that divides the illegally obtained higher profits between them.

All bid-rigging schemes have one thing in common: an agreement among some or all of the bidders which predetermines the winning bidder and limits or eliminates competition among the conspiring vendors.

The laws of both agency and contracts apply to procurement because purchasers (buyers) enter into contracts with suppliers, vendors, and contractors as an agent and employee. The common law recognizes the laws of both agency and contract as valid legal instruments.

Law of Agency = Company (Principal) $\longrightarrow$ Buyer (Agent)

Law of Contracts = Company (Principal) $\longrightarrow$ Employee (Agent)

There are two basic approaches to purchasing: traditional purchasing and reverse purchasing. The latter is preferred by buyers over the former because the buyer has a better control on purchases.

In traditional purchasing, the supplier approaches the purchaser (buyer) to sell materials or products. The supplier establishes prices, terms, and conditions. The buyer takes a reactive, mild, and short-term approach, which does not gain the buyer a competitive advantage in the supply chain.

Traditional Purchasing = Supplier $\longrightarrow$ Buyer

In reverse purchasing, the buyer approaches the supplier to buy materials or products. The buyer establishes prices, terms, and conditions. The buyer takes a proactive, aggressive, and long-term approach to achieve a competitive advantage in the supply chain (e.g., reduced supplier inefficiencies, reduced inventory levels, improved accuracy in demand forecasting, and increased cost savings). Reverse purchasing is also known as reverse marketing and supplier development because suppliers themselves are improved by a collaborative and participative approach with buyers.

Reverse Purchasing = Buyer $\longrightarrow$ Supplier

(A) Sourcing Options in Procurement

A buyer (purchasing agent) in a manufacturing company has several choices to source raw materials, parts, and components that go into a finished product. A buyer in a retail company purchases finished products from a manufacturing company to sell in retail stores. It is important to understand how a manufacturer sources its materials to determine the risks it faces. A manufacturer's risks can automatically and ultimately become a retailer's risks.

In retail purchasing and procurement, sourcing of finished goods (merchandise) is everything because without merchandise there are no sales to customers. A caution is required here: Excessive purchase of merchandise from several and similar sources can increase total inventory count and decrease the ROI and the gross margin return on inventory (GMROI) metrics. Sourcing can be domestic or global.

Usually, retail buyers acquire white market goods such as consumer goods, convenience goods, capital goods, private goods, and public goods that are legal goods and that contribute to sales revenues for a retailer and gross domestic product for a country. Consumer goods and convenience goods are further divided into (1) durable and nondurable goods and (2) soft and hard goods based on their useful life (either short or long life). However, retail buyers should be aware of risks in acquiring questionable goods, such as counterfeit (fake) goods, and gray market and black market goods either intentionally or unintentionally.

RISKS IN BUYING QUESTIONABLE GOODS

- Counterfeit goods (fake goods) are illegal as they imitate the appearance of well-known brand-name products and are sold to mislead or confuse consumers. It includes knockoff goods and pirated goods.

- Grey market goods are illegal and unauthorized products sold outside of normal distribution channels. Grey market goods are sold in black markets.

- Gray market goods are legal or illegal and unauthorized products that are parallel imported from one country to another country. They are legal or illegal based on where the goods are made and sold.

- Black market goods are illegal products and are unofficially sold in an informal economy.

- White market goods are legal products and are officially sold in a formal and local economy.

- Any products sold in the United States that violate the rights of a U.S. intellectual property owner are illegal in the United States. The products could be legal in other countries based on their IP laws until the IP owner is aware of the IP rights violation.

EXAMPLES OF SOURCING OPTIONS

In-sourcing is keeping core products or services in-house or buying the same merchandise from the same supplier as before.

Outsourcing is acquiring noncore products or services from external sources.

Sole sourcing (solo sourcing) or single sourcing (mono-sourcing) is using only one supplier for an inventory item, which could be risky because no backup supplier is available. Sole sourcing also can occur with unique items for which second suppliers cannot be found.

Multiple sourcing is more common in the supply chain environment today where there are several suppliers for each item in the chain. However, too many suppliers are not good due to problems in communication and coordination, which is in conflict with the goal of reducing the base of suppliers. A few strong and stable suppliers with long-term commitments are better than many weak and unstable suppliers with short-term commitments.

Cross-sourcing (or cosourcing or dual sourcing) is a compromise between single-sourcing and multiple-sourcing options where one supplier is used for one item and another supplier is used for a similar item. Natural competition, incentives, and backups are created between these two suppliers to win a greater share of procurement dollars.

Offshoring is moving a business function or process to a foreign country but retaining control of it in the home country.

Near-shoring is choosing an outsource provider located either in the home country or in a nearby foreign country.

Back-sourcing is the return of a business activity to the original firm in the home country.

Local sourcing is using only suppliers within a country to supply all or most of items, thus saving transportation costs, customs duties, and import taxes required in global sourcing.

Next-shoring means finding the best source, whether it is in-sourcing, outsourcing, offshoring, or near-shoring, only after carefully considering various decision factors, such as technology, efficiency, cost, raw material availability, skilled labor availability, and political conditions. The next-shoring location could be a new offshoring or near-shoring location or the original in-sourcing location (i.e., back-sourcing).

Global sourcing is using suppliers from foreign countries because certain items (e.g., unique and rare) are only found in those countries.

Combo sourcing occurs when a domestic source is combined with a foreign source to procure unique and rare items and when two or more sources are combined, as in insourcing and outsourcing.

Crowd-sourcing is open sourcing, meaning anybody from anywhere in the world can bid and supply the requested materials. It brings the best talents and capabilities out in the market.

Cosourcing is having two suppliers for an inventory item where one supplier works as a backup for the other. Care should be taken not to unwittingly turn cosourcing into multiple sourcing or crowd-sourcing.

Reshoring or next-shoring results from changing the previous outsourcing decision to offshoring or near-shoring due to changing market conditions in the world of manufacturing.

(B) In-Source Analysis versus Outsource Analysis

Manufacturing companies usually perform a make-or-buy analysis when deciding to manufacture a part or component inside the company or to buy it from outside companies. Costs for each choice (make or buy) are developed and compared to determine which choice is less expensive.

Purchasing or procurement management in a retail company can perform similar analysis to determine whether to in-source a product (i.e., buy from the same supplier as before) or outsource a product (i.e., buy from a different supplier now). Costs for each choice (in-source or outsource) are developed and compared to determine which choice is less expensive.

A PRIMER ON VARIOUS TYPES AND TOOLS OF BUYING

Types of Buying

Speculative buying occurs when purchasing materials in excess of current and future known requirements with the intention of profiting on up and down price movements. Speculative buying is risky; financial losses can occur when actual prices significantly deviate from speculative prices.

Forward buying, also known as bridge buying, occurs when a buyer purchases higher quantities of products than the current needs during a manufacturer's announced off-invoice allowances to take advantage of lower prices and special payment discounts consisting of coupons and credits.

Routine buying is purchasing small items and office supplies (e.g., pencils, pens, paper clips, rubber bands, copier/printer paper, and writing pads) through supplier websites.

Discount buying, also called opportunity buying, occurs when a buyer purchases end-of-season goods, customer-returned goods, slightly imperfect goods (seconds), closeouts, and excess inventory from a manufacturer at significant discounts and sell them to end customers at lower prices.

(continued)

A PRIMER ON VARIOUS TYPES AND TOOLS OF BUYING *(Continued)*

Consignment buying is a method of procurement in which a supplier or vendor maintains an inventory on a retailer's (purchaser's) premises. The purchaser's obligation to pay for the goods begins when goods are drawn from the consigned stock for use or to sell. In the beginning, suppliers assume greater risk because they own the title to goods until they are sold and, at this point, retailers have no risk because they have no title to and no ownership of goods. Retailers assume risk when they acquire ownership of goods to sell. Suppliers with a low-reputation and a low selling power encourage consignment buying practices because retailers pay to the suppliers only for goods sold and can return the unsold goods to suppliers.

Before a product is sold   After a product is sold
(Supplier owns the goods and risks)   →   (Retailer owns the goods and risks)

Informal buying, also called memorandum buying, means buying without contracts. The retailer takes the title to goods on delivery and is responsible for damaged goods. Suppliers with poor reputation and low selling power encourage informal purchasing because retailers pay to suppliers only for goods sold and can return the unsold goods to suppliers.

Stockless purchasing is an arrangement where a supplier holds inventory until the buyer places orders and the buyer releases specific items. It is also called vendor-managed inventories and is similar to a just-in-time (JIT) purchasing philosophy used in manufacturing. Examples include blanket orders, open-ended orders, and system contracts.

Staple purchasing is buying basic merchandise items that have a continuous demand for day-to-day consumption, such as milk, bread, eggs, salt, sugar, fruits, vegetables, and soups.

A **systems contract** is a contract generated by the purchasing department that authorizes designated employees of the buying firm to place orders directly with the supplier. A release system is developed for specific materials during a given contract period.

Tools of Buying

A **purchase order** is a legal document binding a buyer and a seller that describes the product items and quantities a buyer wants to purchase from a seller, the prices to be paid, the shipping costs to be incurred, and the payment terms to be accepted. A purchase order can be a discrete order (a separate order is issued for each item to be procured) or a firm release order (a group of items to be procured over a specified period of time based on flexible/floating demand forecasts).

A **blanket order** is a commitment to a supplier for certain goods over a predetermined period (one year) at predetermined prices or at prices to be determined.

Purchase cards (P-cards) are a special type of charge cards used to buy products and services without requiring paperwork and advance approvals, as they are based on dollar limits established for each P-card owner. These P-cards track and report all transactions incurred by transaction type, by the amount of purchase, and by the card owner. P-cards are efficient and save time because the card owner does not have to fill out paperwork needed in traditional purchasing and ensures card owner accountability. Each retail buyer and store buyer should be given a P-card to buy merchandise as needed.

Progress payments are specified in a procurement contract to be made to a supplier at specific times, based on a supplier's progress in completing the job.

Spend analysis is a tool that provides retail merchandise and manufacturing buyers with knowledge about how much is being spent for what goods and services, who the buyers are, and who the suppliers are. This tool provides buyers with opportunities to leverage buying, save money, and improve financial performance. Spend analysis has some elements of open-to-buy analysis for retailers.

(iii) Supply Chain Management

This subsection defines supply chain, explains how to manage the supply base, defines the value chain, presents supply chain risks, and suggests best practices to reduce such risks.

(A) Supply Chain Defined

A **supply chain** is a series of partnering firms providing value-added activities and value-delivery chain in logistics from raw materials to finished goods purchased by a final consumer/customer. It is a system of organizations, people, activities, information flows, and resources involved in moving a product or service from a supplier or producer to a consumer or customer. The goal is to keep a relatively narrow breadth of supply chain (i.e., few key suppliers) with long-term financial and quality commitments between purchasers (buyers), suppliers, manufacturers (producers), distributors, retailers, and customers (consumers). The supply chain can be domestic and/or global in nature as the suppliers are available from several countries. The players and partners in a supply chain are shown next.

$$\text{Supply Chain} = \text{Purchasers} \longrightarrow \text{Suppliers} \longrightarrow \text{Manufacturers} \longrightarrow \text{Distributors} \longrightarrow \text{Retailers} \longrightarrow \text{Customers}$$

Here, the supply chain runs from purchasers (a company's buying agents) to consumers (end customers). Suppliers and vendors (upstream suppliers) provide or bring raw materials into a manufacturing facility to produce products. Distributors and wholesalers (downstream suppliers) bring manufactured or finished products from the same manufacturing facility and deliver them to retailers.

(B) Managing the Supply Base

Managing the supply base requires several strategic approaches such as integrating suppliers, early involvement of suppliers, supplier reduction practices, supplier performance levels, and supplier certification requirements. The purpose of managing the supply base is to manage quality, quantity, delivery, service, and price of a product.

Integrating suppliers means reducing or balancing the number of suppliers available so that they become part of the buyer/purchaser operation to lower inventories, to increase response time and quality, and to decrease total cost. Here, the focus is on the supplier mix which is a supplier composition dealing with the number of suppliers (i.e., 100 or 1,000), size of suppliers (i.e., large or small), location of suppliers (i.e., domestic or foreign), type of suppliers (i.e., intermediary or final), and nature of suppliers (i.e., strategic or operational).

Early involvement of suppliers in the procurement and product design process reduces cost, improves quality, and shortens product development cycle time. This is achieved through supplier review of product specifications and production standards. Other benefits include a supplier buy-in.

Supplier reduction practices include deciding who will be single-sourcing, second-sourcing, or last-sourcing vendors.

Supplier performance levels are measured in terms of quality, delivery, service, and cost/price, as follows:

- **Quality measures** may include incoming defect rate, product variability, number of customer complaints, use of statistical process control, documented process capabilities, and supplier's quality philosophy.

- **Delivery measures** include on-time delivery, percentage and availability of product within quoted lead time, and quantity accuracy.

- **Service measures** include invoice accuracy and length of time required to settle claims, availability of a supply plan, and availability of engineering support.

- **Cost/price measures** include product cost, price reductions, transportation cost, willingness to participate in price reviews, and minimum buy requirements.

Supplier certification requirements is a process conducted by the purchasing organization so that shipments go directly into use, inventories, or production. The goal of certification is to reduce or eliminate a purchaser's inspection of goods coming from a supplier. Certification involves evaluating the supplier's quality systems, approving the supplier's processes, and monitoring incoming product quality. The advantages of supplier certification are increased product quality, reduced inspection costs, and reduced process variation.

Two important concepts in the supply chain and logistics include pull supply chain and push supply chain.

Pull supply chain means customers are driving the demand (pull) in that they place the orders at the retail stores, online, or by phone to pull the products out of the logistics system into their hands.

Push supply chain means historical sales are driving the demand (push) in that purchasing management or retail store management initiates the orders to push the products from the logistics system into the customers' hands.

Two types of suppliers exist in a supply chain management: upstream suppliers and downstream suppliers.

Upstream and downstream suppliers are partners in a supply chain operation consisting of many suppliers (S-1 to S-N), whether local or global forming a solid business chain. The chain is presented as follows:

Upstream Suppliers 1, 2, and 3 $\longrightarrow$ Manufacturer $\longrightarrow$ Downstream Suppliers 4, 5, and 6 $\longrightarrow$ Retailers $\longrightarrow$ Customers

Here, suppliers 1, 2, and 3 are called upstream suppliers because they transport and deliver raw materials, ingredients, parts, and components to a manufacturer to make a full or partial product. Suppliers 4, 5, and 6 are called downstream suppliers because they transport and deliver a fully completed product from a manufacturer to a retailer, where it is eventually sold to customers. Note that a supply chain can contain only one manufacturer or multiple manufacturers.

All partners in a supply chain are affected by the **bullwhip effect** (also known as the Forrester effect), which refers to a rippling and magnifying effect on inventory due to changes in product demand between producers and suppliers. This means that a small change in demand at the first downstream supplier (DS-1) creates a big change in demand at the first upstream supplier 1 (US-1) and demand at the producer, as shown next.

US-1 $\longrightarrow$ US-N $\longrightarrow$ Producer $\longleftarrow$ DS-N $\longleftarrow$ DS-1

The bullwhip effect results in unnecessary over orders, overproduction, overstorage, over-buildup of inventory, and excessive inventory costs and investments due to an excess of caution exhibited by all levels in the supply chain. In other words, the bullwhip effect is a result of a just-in-case exaggeration of demand incorrectly assumed by all partners in the supply chain, thus reflecting chaos and uncertainty.

(C) Value Chain Defined

The real challenge in the supply chain is to ensure that value is added at every step to achieve customer satisfaction. Both purchasers (buyers) and suppliers (sellers) play a large role in achieving the customer value chain. The correct sequence of partners in the customer value chain is buyers (purchasers), suppliers (vendors), producers (manufacturers), distributors (wholesalers), retailers, and end customers (consumers).

$$\text{Value Chain} = \text{Purchasers} \longrightarrow \text{Suppliers} \longrightarrow \text{Manufacturers} \longrightarrow \text{Distributors} \longrightarrow \text{Retailers} \longrightarrow \text{Customers}$$

The value chain of a manufacturing company includes all activities and departments from idea creation to idea commercialization. This includes suppliers, producers, retailers, and R&D to postsale customer service. Discontinuing a product or department does not take away any value to a customer unless the product or department was providing the value before.

The value chain is improved when delays, defects, waste, and inventories are eliminated in business processes. The goal of the value chain is to make such processes lean, flexible, stable, and predictable. Doing this requires elimination of sources of inefficiency, rigidity, and variability and use of IT to integrate business subprocesses.

Several partners in the value chain can add value to a product or service. Assume that there are two suppliers, one producer, and one retailer in the value chain. Also assume that there is a little or no need for the cost of capital invested. The next equations explain how these partners can all add value to a product.

Value added by Supplier 1 = Supplier 1 price − Supplier 1 cost

Value added by Supplier 2 = Supplier 2 price − Supplier 2 cost − Supplier 1 price

Value added by producer = Producer price − Producer cost − Supplier 2 price

Value added by retailer = Retailer price − Retailer cost − Producer price

Total value added to a product is the summation of value added by all partners involved in the value chain. The value of a firm is the summation of all value added for all products that a firm produces. The same logic applies to services.

Value analysis is the organized study of an item's function as it relates to value and cost. The value of an item is defined as the function of the item divided by the cost of the item. The goal of value analysis is to make improvements in a product while the product is being produced and after deciding that a new product is a success.

There are valued-added and non-value-added tasks in any function due to tasks that were neither changed nor challenged. The goal is to identify those tasks or activities that are not adding value to a function, product, or process. Value engineering techniques can be implemented to identify non-value-added activities and streamline business processes in order to improve their efficiency and effectiveness.

Assembling tasks, whether subassembly or final assembly, and process times are value-added activities of a manufactured product while other activities are non-value-added activities. Examples of non-value-added activities from a customer's viewpoint include inspection, move, reporting, governmental compliance, storage, wait, and queue time.

VALUE-ADDED AND NON-VALUE-ADDED ACTIVITIES

Enhance or increase value-added activities, such as production pure process time; ingredients mix time; part fabricating time; part plating, soldering, and painting time; part subassembly time; part final assembly time; customer order processing time; customer order ship time; internal/external customer access points to manufacturing systems; and manufacturing management decision points and control points.

Eliminate or decrease non-value-added activities, such as material storage, handling, and movement steps; inspection steps; rework steps; waiting time; product recall time; product warranty time; and delays at interdepartmental and interdivisional boundaries and at intradepartmental workstations.

Handling these activities requires having the right resources available at the right place and at the right time so that delays and waste in manufacturing operations are decreased.

(D) Supply Chain Risks

Supply chain risks include any threat event that can affect manufacturing and logistics of goods. The goal is to ensure timely production, transportation, and delivery of safe, salable, and quality-based goods to customers. Supply chain risks can arise during manufacturing, logistics, and outsourcing operations and can affect customers' safety.

A risk assessment exercise should be undertaken with the supply chain describing several risk scenarios explaining upstream and downstream impacts in the supply chain. Risk management asks whether a company possesses risk-mature or risk-immature capabilities. Research has shown that companies with risk-mature capabilities perform better than those with risk-immature capabilities in terms of carrying less inventory in the pipeline; managing with shorter lead times for raw materials and finished goods; earning a larger increase in operating income; and creating faster cash-to-cash cycle times.

Specific examples of supply chain risks include:

- Poor manufacturing practices that do not conform with generally accepted manufacturing practices.
- Poor warehousing and distribution center practices and processes.
- Violation of IP rights such as copyrights, trademarks, service marks, and patents.
- Tampering and manipulating good products with bad parts and components during factory assembly or delivery in-transit.
- Insertion of counterfeit products.
- Insertion of malware (viruses and worms) and ransomware software.

- Theft of goods during transportation and delivery.

- Insertion of dangerous and inferior-quality parts and components in finished goods.

Best practices for a procurement or purchasing management to reduce supply chain risks include:

- Conduct a detailed risk assessment exercise and due diligence review on a potential supply chain vendor's (provider's) legal history, financial solvency, tax history, and corporate reputation in the marketplace.

- Encourage that a provider's legal counsel review contracts and agreements to ensure protection of IP, manufacturing production and service processes, or other sensitive material.

- Understand that vetting a foreign provider is more difficult than vetting a domestic provider due to physical distance, time zones, and foreign laws and policies.

- Request an advance notice of changes in a provider's ownership or product development and marketing strategies.

- Request all providers to establish and maintain visitor logs to their manufacturing, warehouse, and distribution facilities.

- Identify and review a provider's processes and procedures to verify the quality of its products or third-party products, including inspections of incoming and outgoing materials.

- Determine how providers clean or wipe sensitive information from their electronic equipment and computer devices prior to their disposal or retirement in order to prevent data leakage or data loss.

- Deploy a defense-in-breadth strategy, which focuses on installing horizontal, multiple layers of security protections (security controls) to provide a strong security mechanism. This preventive control concept centers on people, technology, operations, and access policies and procedures. Multiple layers of security controls need to be built into computer systems, networks, mobile devices, data at the source, data in transit, and data in storage. Defense in breadth increases protection and reduces risk in supply chain management as there are several partnering firms (breadth of firms) in the chain.

- Conduct onsite audits of provider's product development, manufacturing facilities, and physical and cybersecurity standards.

- Establish regular communication channels and maintain a collaborative relationship with all providers.

(c) New Product Development Process

This subsection discusses the new product development process with its required steps to be followed, causes of new product failures, and how to develop a new product policy.

(A) New Product Steps

A company that can bring out new products faster than its competition enjoys many advantages and benefits. To increase speed in introducing new products, many companies are bypassing time-consuming regional tests in favor of national programs. The goal is to develop a new product right the first time. Yet the rate of new product failures is high (33–90%), and the investment is high too. An opportunity cost is involved due to other possible alternative uses of funds spent on product failures and the time spent in unprofitable product development. Marketing writers estimate that the primary reason for new product failure is the selling company's inability to match its offerings to customer needs. This inability to satisfy customer needs can be attributed:

1. Inadequacy of up-front marketing intelligence efforts.

2. Failure of the company to stick close to what it does best.

3. Inability to provide better value than competing products and technologies.

Developing products that generate a maximum dollar profit with a minimum amount of risk is asking for the best of both worlds—an ideal solution. A more practical, systematic approach is needed to formalize the process for new product planning. New product policy guidelines should be a prerequisite for proper product planning. These guidelines should consist of procedures for various steps shown in sequence (see Exhibit 1.34).

EXHIBIT 1.34 Sequences of Steps in the New Product Development Process

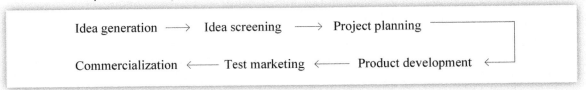

(B) Causes of New Product Failures

Many of the reasons for new product failure relate to execution and control problems—mostly management-oriented problems. A brief list of some of the more important causes of new product failures is presented next.

- Faulty estimates of new product potential
- Unexpected reactions from competitors
- Poor timing in the introduction of the product
- Rapid change in the market (economy) after the product introduction was approved
- Inadequate quality control
- Faulty estimates in production costs
- Inadequate expenditures on initial promotion programs
- Faulty market testing
- Improper channel of distribution

To properly address the causes of new product failures, it is important to consider both marketing research and technical research combined with relevant information for decision-making purposes. For example, to calculate a ROI, one needs to know the pricing strategy to be used and the investment outlay. Similarly, to use the payback method, which is the rate of investment outlay to annual cash flow, one needs to estimate the magnitude of the product investment outlay and the annual cash flow. The basic information required in the investment outlay includes estimates of such things as production equipment, R&D costs, and marketing expenditures; the annual cash flow requires a forecast of quantity demanded in units and unit prices.

(C) New Product Policy

Developing a new product policy is complicated since new products are the lifeblood of successful business firms. Thus, the critical product policy question is not whether to develop new products but in what direction to move. Marketing management needs to develop criteria (standards/norms) for success that new products must meet if they are to be considered candidates for launching. Possible areas for standards development include profits, costs, use of plant capacity, and market share.

There are at least 10 different ways a product can be presented as new:

1. A product performs an entirely new function.

2. A product offers improved performance of an existing function.

3. A product is a new application of an existing product.

4. A product offers additional functions.

5. An existing product is offered to a new market.

6. A product is able to reach more buyers that through lower cost.

7. A product is upgraded (defined as an existing product integrated into another existing product).

8. A product is downgraded.

9. A product is restyled.

10. A growth vector matrix to indicate the direction in which the organization is moving with respect to its current products and markets (see Exhibit 1.35).

EXHIBIT 1.35 Matrix of Current/New Markets and Current/New Products

	Current Products	**New Products**
Current Markets	Market penetration	Product development
New Markets	Market development	Diversification

Market penetration denotes a growth direction through the increase in market share for current product markets. **Market development** refers to finding new customers for current products. **Product development** refers to creating new products to replace existing ones. **Diversification** refers to developing new products and cultivating new markets.

The 10 steps in the development of a new product policy are listed next.

1. Prepare a long-range industry forecast for existing product lines.

2. Prepare a long-range profit plan for the company, using existing product lines.

3. Review the long-range profit plan.

4. Determine what role new products will play in the company's future.

5. Prepare an inventory of company capabilities.

6. Determine market areas for new products.

7. Prepare a statement of new product objectives.

8. Prepare a long-range profit plan, incorporating new products.

9. Assign new product responsibility.

10. Provide for evaluation of new product performance.

(d) Marketing and Sales Management

This subsection discusses marketing functions, such as marketing mix; customer management; customer service; price management; product life cycles (including product management and product audit); digital marketing; marketing of services; and marketing analysis. Sales functions, such as lead management cycle, the sales process, and selling methods, are presented.

(i) Marketing Mix

A **mix** is a combination of more than one element of something of importance. Five types of marketing mix can exist for retail and manufacturing companies, including customer, product, service, channel, and communication mix. Note that retailers should analyze the customer mix first because it drives the other types of mixes and its results can be applied in designing the other types of mixes. The rationale is that without a customer, there is no product to sell or no service to provide.

Customer Mix $\longrightarrow$ Product Mix, Service Mix, Channel Mix, and Communication Mix

Customer Mix. Customer mix defines the composition and profile of a company's current customers. The customer mix concept is similar to the product mix concept, where the latter refers to a group of products that are closely related to each other in terms of their use, customer user groups, and price ranges.

A company can group its current customers based on their sales volume in a given year into four categories, such as loyal customers (highly valued customers), major customers (prime and high-end customers), average customers (middle-of-the-road customers), and below-average customers (minor and low-end customers).

The business purpose of developing a customer mix is to group, track, monitor, and grow the customer base depending on their relative value to the company in terms of the sales volume and contribution margin (sales dollars minus variable costs) they provide to the company. This means loyal customers are treated and valued very dearly and better than minor customers. Note that each company may define, classify, and group its customers differently based on its specific business purpose.

Loyal Customers $\longrightarrow$ Minor Customers
(Most Valued)   (Least Valued)

Loyal Customers	Highly committed and highly valued loyal customers who will repeatedly purchase a company's products or services. Marketing management allocates more resources to nurturing, valuing, and growing loyal customers because they make a very big impact, very highly deserved special attention, and very high-risk to ignore. Note that loyalty and profitability are closely linked because the financial rewards of loyalty run deep.
Major Customers	Prime and high-end customers are the next most valued customers after loyal customers. Consequently, more resources are spent on increasing the major customer group and converting them into loyal customers because they make a big impact, highly deserved personal attention, and high-risk to ignore.
Average Customers	Average customers are valued less than major customers. Companies are searching for ways to move this group into the major customer group because they make a moderate impact, reasonably deserved attention, and medium risk to ignore.
Below-Average Customers	Below-average customers provide no value to some companies and hence are completely ignored because they are not at all committed to a company's products or services.
	They switch companies very easily when: a company's prices are higher and its competitor's prices are lower; a company's customer service is poor; and a competitor's sales discounts are larger (coupons, rebates, and promotions). Marketing management will not spend any money on this type of customer group to convert them into average customers because it is not worth it. These customers make a very low impact, very highly undeserved attention, and very low-risk to ignore.

Product Mix. Product mix represents the seller's view of the marketing tools available for influencing buyers. It includes the 4 Ps (product, price, promotion, and place):

1. **Product** includes variables such as product variety, quality, design, features, brand name, packaging, sizes, services, warranties, and returns.

2. **Price** includes variables such as list price, discounts, allowances, payment periods, and credit terms.

3. **Promotion** includes variables such as sales promotion, advertising, personal selling, direct sales, public relations, and direct marketing.

4. **Place** includes variables such as channels, coverage, assortments, locations, inventory, and transport.

A company can change only few variables in the short run, such as price, sales force size, and advertising expenses. A firm can develop new products and modify its distribution channels only in the long run.

Service Mix. A company's service mix groups customers into residential, commercial (e.g., institutional, business, and professional groups), seasonal, or nonseasonal customers. The major determinant of this type of category is the amount of service revenues and contribution margins provided to the company.

Channel Mix. Channel mix groups marketing channels of distribution into major (primary), intermediary, and minor (secondary) channels. Channels can also be classified as wholesalers (e.g.,

Costco and Sam's Club), distributors, retailers (Walmart), or resellers. A channel mix determines the availability of products to customers at different locations. A typical channel mix and its flow is:

Manufacturers ⟶ Wholesalers ⟶ Distributors ⟶ Retailers or Resellers

Communication Mix. A marketing communication mix should represent the voice of the company and its brands in building relationships with consumers, combined with the voice of the customer. Marketing communications, such as advertising and celebrity endorsements, contribute to building brand equity through the memories and images they create in consumers' minds, which, in turn, drives sales, margins, and profits. Marketers use tools such as email, text, or apps to communicate with customers.

Marketing Communications ⟶ Voice of the Company + Voice of the Customer ⟶ Brand Equity

The marketing communications mix consists of eight major modes of communications:

1. Advertising
2. Sales promotion
3. Events and experiences
4. Public relations and publicity
5. Direct marketing
6. Interactive marketing
7. Word-of-mouth marketing
8. Personal selling

Advertisement mix is a nonpersonal communication to a target market from a sponsor using mass communications channels. Communications mix includes traditional communications (e.g., newspaper, radio, television [TV], and billboards) and digital communications (e.g., the Internet, social media platforms, and mobile devices).

(ii) Customer Management

This subsection examines a customer's life cycle with a retailer, how a retailer should treat a customer as a king, and how a retailer should get a well-rounded and full view (360-degree) of a customer by collecting data from multiple channels to win, sell, and serve the customer better and forever.

(A) Customer Life Cycle

Customers go through a life cycle of events or experiences with a specific retailer during their shopping or purchase journey. This includes how customers start with a retailer, buy from the same retailer, stay with that retailer, or leave that retailer based on good (positive) or bad (negative) shopping experiences with that retailer. Of course, all customers want a positive and pleasant shopping experience with a retailer. A customer's good or bad shopping experience depends on how a retailer handles the touch points between the customer and the retailer. It means that properly handled touch points lead to happy points and poorly handled touch points lead to hassle points or pain points.

This shopping journey or experience must be closely and carefully managed to make the customer king and to keep the customer satisfied and retained for life. This is because customers have greater mobility, meaning they are free to shop at any retailer, anywhere, and anytime. Here, customer mobility means customer switching to other retailers.

Although it is difficult to design and implement customer-volume data and customer-purchase data, all retailers must measure and monitor such data to determine trends because customers are the heart and soul of a retailer. This measuring and monitoring system must integrate customers' data from multiple channels and provide a full view of a customer to serve the customer better. Due to customer mobility, retailers need to develop a customer database showing an aggregate of the number of new customers acquired and the number of existing customers retained. The difference between acquired and retained customers is the number of customers who defected.

Customer purchase data can help a retailer's customer service associates most in retrieving a customer's previous purchase data to verify and validate certain purchases in processing the customer's product returns. This is a good feature of customer service function.

Customers defected = Customers acquired − Customers retained

The four phases of a customer life cycle include:

Phase 1: Customer acquisition

Phase 2: Customer retention

Phase 3: Customer defection

Phase 4: Customer reacquisition

Each phase is discussed next.

Phase 1: Customer Acquisition. Acquiring a new customer is a difficult task for any retailer because reaching new consumers and turning them into new customers is based on guesswork, which is not a scientific approach. (It is a trial-and-error approach.) Activities such as customer research and discovery are part of the customer acquisition phase of finding and winning over new customers. Retailers often lure new customers with heavy advertising and promotional activities, such as coupons, discounts, rebates, instant savings, free shipping, flexible return policies, and special sale events, all of which create value to customers. Increasing the customer acquisition rate or penetration rate is a strategic move with long-term benefits of increased revenues and profits. Value is created for the customer in this phase.

Phase 2: Customer Retention. Acquiring new customers is a difficult task, but retaining existing customers is even more difficult. To retain customers, a retailer must care for and fully engage them during their shopping journey. Losing a current customer, whether large or small, is much riskier than acquiring a new customer because the retailer has already spent time, money, and effort in supporting and keeping current customers. With customer retention, the retailer is hoping for repeated purchases from retained customers. Retained customers are customers who are satisfied with the value received, resulting in assured future sales revenues. Value is increased for customers in this phase.

Positive activities such as customer nurturing and pampering are part of the customer retention phase. Other positive activities, such as customer relationship management and loyalty programs combined with customized, personalized, direct, or one-to-one marketing programs can retain customers. Mutual values hold loyal customers and progressive retailers together.

A related measure of customer retention is customer referral rate, meaning that a happy retained customer is sure to refer to a friend or family members.

Another way to retain current customers is to obtain their feedback or ask them to write product reviews right after purchase transactions are completed or to conduct periodic surveys with such customers. Negative results from such feedback and surveys need to be compiled, and action plans must be established to correct the negative results.

Phase 3: Customer Defection. A defected customer is a dissatisfied customer, resulting in a loss of sales revenue for the retailer. A defected customer is a lost customer. Somehow, the value of a retailer's products, services, policies, practices, and customer services is destroyed. Activities such as customer examination and analysis are part of the customer defection phase with the goal of finding reasons and causes of customer defection.

A customer defection means a loss of customer to a retailer. Unfortunately, retailers do not know or are not aware of how and when they lost existing customers. This is because customers can leave retailers quickly and silently at will and eventually switch to competing retailers. Customers who are not satisfied with a retailer are sure to defect eventually because they are not receiving a value from the retailer. Value is destroyed for the customer in this phase.

A defected customer from one retailer is a new source of customer acquisition for a competing retailer.

Retailers are very much concerned about customer defection rates. If these rates continue to grow, the retailers will not be left with any customers, which is a dangerous situation for any retailer to be in. This implies that "no customers mean no retailers," a situation that has really occurred with many retailers. For example, Sports Authority and Toys R Us closed all of their stores and filed for bankruptcy due to a slow and steady loss of customers.

Defection rates pinpoint problems and weaknesses in a retailer's marketing policies, procedures, and practices, problems that must be corrected without delays. Here, the retailer's goal is to stop or reduce the defection rate to an acceptable level. In addition, root causes of defection must be identified and addressed in a timely manner.

Customer Engagement, Customer Retention, and Customer Defection. A direct and proven relationship exists between customer engagement, customer retention, and customer defection. Customer engagement means a store associate making a new or existing customer happy by assisting her, asking the right questions, suggesting new products, searching and locating a product, and explaining good things and bad things about a product, all with great sincerity and honesty. Whether a customer purchases a product or not depends on how a customer is attended to and engaged with. Paying careful attention to customers is a basic requirement of a store associate. Note that a customer can be engaged in several ways, such as in-person, a live chat on the website, phone, email, efaxes, text, or a combination. Simply stated, more attention and full engagement lead to customer retention; less attention and no engagement lead to customer defection.

Customer Retention = More Attention and Full Engagement

Customer Defection = Less Attention and No Engagement

Phase 4: Customer Reacquisition. Customer reacquisition means trying to reacquire a lost or defected customer, which may not be possible or practical based on cost-benefit analysis. It could cost many times more to reacquire a lost customer than the initial acquisition or retention cost of a customer because the customer has already made up her mind to leave the retailer for her own good reasons. Reacquisition efforts are based on the number of lost or defected customers. Customer win-back efforts take place in the customer reacquisition phase to re-create value. Value is enhanced for the customer in this phase.

Some retailers try to reacquire customers with incentives such as cash bonuses, low prices, increased bonus points, gift cards, vacation trips, prizes, instant savings, coupons, rebates, and one-time special offers to lure the lost customers to comeback. This approach to value re-creation may or may not work.

Companies trying to reacquire the lost customers include retail, telephone, cable and satellite, TV, Internet service providers, utility, and insurance firms. This is possible if these companies have the contact information on lost customers in their customer databases.

EXAMPLE: CALCULATION OF CUSTOMER ACQUISITION, RETENTION, AND DEFECTION RATES

The marketing department of BXK Retailers has been consistently gathering data on customer volumes for many years from multiple retail channels. BXK is experiencing declines in sales revenues from the last two years, and senior management wants to know the reasons for such declines. The following data is available from the marketing department.

Customers at the beginning of a month	1.2 million
New customers added during the month	0.3 million
(Total acquired customers = Beginning customers + New customers)	1.5 million
Customers at the end of the month (Retained customers)	1.4 million
Customers defected during the month (Acquired customers – Retained customers)	0.1 million

What are the customer acquisition, retention, and defection rates for the BXK Retailers?

Customer acquisition rate = (New customers/Beginning customers) × 100 = (0.3/1.2) × 100 = 25.0%

Customer retention rate = (Ending customers/Total customers) × 100 = (1.4/1.5) × 100 = 93.3%

Customer defection rate = (Defected customers/Total customers) × 100 = (0.1/1.5) × 100 = 6.7%

Four major takeaway points include (1) how changing consumer behavior affects a retailer's sales and profits, (2) how value creation and value enhancements differentiate retailers, (3) how retailers must change their value creation and re-creation processes as consumers' mindsets and preferences change, and (4) why retailers need to understand consumer psychology and how to handle customer management processes to succeed and survive in the changing retail marketplace.

(B) Customer Service

This section focuses on two areas: consumer behavior before deciding to purchase a product and consumer experience after deciding to buy a product. Lessons learned from these two areas could be different. A customer service audit is suggested. A comparison is shown between consumer behavior and customer service.

Most manufacturing, retail, and other service-oriented companies are big providers and implementers of customer service activities. Other names for the customer service function include customer support, technical support, customer credit services, and customer care center. What companies do or do not do in the customer service function can greatly affect their current and future sales, and that could tarnish their image and reputation very quickly in the marketplace. This is especially true when unhappy customers post bad experiences with customer service on social media platforms. Yet some retail company management does not seem to be serious about customer service issues when they staff their customer service departments. For example, location of the customer service department (i.e., front end or back end of a store) and its staffing levels are crucial as they signify importance to customers.

(C) Consumers Purchasing Behaviors

Buyers or consumers go through an explicit or implicit decision-making process in their mind prior to purchasing the desired product or service because they have a specific need or want to satisfy either for themselves or for their family. Consumers have too many choices to choose from, which makes identifying and selecting products and services a confusing and difficult task.

Note that buyers who are greatly influenced by either friends or family, combined with personal beliefs and opinions, may not make a purchase decision until they learn, feel, hear, see, and touch a product themselves. The buying process can be divided into three phases, as follows:

1. Pre-Purchase
2. Purchase
3. Post-Purchase

In a way, the buyer's decision-making process is a mental, psychological exercise in deciding whether to buy or not to buy a specific product or service brand; if the buyer decides what to buy, the issues then are where to buy, when to buy, and how much to pay.

Pre-Purchase Phase. Only the buyer is involved in this phase's activities, which include identifying the specific need or want and researching for relevant information about a specific product or service using sources such as consumer reports, marketer websites, friends and families, and trade journals. After completing the information search, the buyer starts with several alternatives for consideration, eliminates undesirable alternatives, and selects only one alternative to proceed further. An explicit outcome at the end of this phase is a go/no-go decision; go is to proceed with the next phase (purchase), and no-go is not to buy any product or service at this time (i.e., no purchase). The buyer may be taking a wait-and-see approach, hoping to get new information on a product or service, better pricing and timing, and quality products and services later.

> Go Decision = Purchase
>
> No-Go Decision = No Purchase

Purchase Phase. Only the buyer is involved in this phase's activities, which include proceeding with the selected alternative and purchasing the product or service within the time and budget limits. Some buyers may wait for special promotions and discounts to pay a low price.

Post-Purchase Phase. Both buyers and sellers are involved in this phase's activities. A self-question to the product or service sellers is whether the buyer is fully satisfied with the performance of the purchased item because dissatisfied buyers may not purchase the item again in the future, resulting in lost customers.

- Unhappy buyers can voice dissatisfaction through word of mouth or social media networks, resulting in a loss of reputation to sellers.

- Satisfied buyers can become a loyal or disloyal consumer (i.e., exhibits stay or switch behavior), meaning they buy the same product or service repeatedly (i.e., become loyal). If they have a doubt about the previous purchase, they may exhibit switching behavior between product brands (i.e., become disloyal). Some reasons for buyer doubt about previous purchases may include the price paid and the value received from the use of the purchased product or service.

(D) Consumer Buying Experiences

A consumer's buying experience can be divided into three phases, as follows:

1. Pre-transaction services

2. Transaction services

3. Post-transaction services

Pre-Transaction Services. Briefly, the tasks involved in the pre-transaction services phase are inquiring about a product's availability, pricing information, product return policy, and store hours and directions. At this point, the customer has a good intention to buy a product.

Transaction Services. Briefly, the tasks involved in the transaction services phase consist of a store associate helping a customer in locating and discussing about a product, the associate's personal selling methods and approaches used (whether it is a hard sell or soft sell), and the customer completing the sales transaction to his or her satisfaction.

This is a crucial phase because customers have two choices once they are in the store:

- Buy the product that they intended to buy.

- Walk away from the store and not buy the product.

The outcome of these two choices, in part, depends on the associate's product knowledge and methods used in convincing customers to make a buying decision. Most customers notice a lack of sales assistance in a store or when the associate's product knowledge is incomplete or incorrect; both are bad situations.

Post-Transaction Services. Briefly, the tasks involved in the post-transaction services phase consist of handling customer complaints, merchandise returns and repairs, merchandise warranties and guarantees, and product delivery problems in terms of delayed shipping and shipping wrong products with wrong prices charged. This last product delivery problem is especially true with online retailers.

Whether customers return to the same store depends on how their previous product return was handled, their overall experience with the last purchase (pleasant or unpleasant), and the quality and competency of store employees (no product knowledge, new employee, untrained employee, and poor interpersonal skills). Unhappy customers do not come back; happy ones do.

(E) Customer Service Audit

The customer service audit must be performed by someone working in a different department from the customer service department in order to maintain independence and objectivity. To make it completely independent, an outside consultant could perform this audit. The focus of a customer service audit is to determine whether

- Customers are satisfied with the overall quality of a company's products and services. If not, what are their major suggestions for improvement of quality?

- Customers' questions, issues, problems, complaints, and concerns are properly addressed and resolved timely.

- Actual experiences of customers meet or exceed their expectations; assess whether any gaps exist. Determine how these gaps can be removed.

- Customers are convinced to stay with the company or decided leave the company. If they decided to leave, what factors might have contributed to their decision?

(F) Comparison between Consumer Behavior and Customer Service

Exhibit 1.36 compares outcomes between a consumer's purchase behaviors (consumer behavior) and a company's customer service offering (customer service). A consumer becomes a customer after he or she purchases a product from a manufacturer or retailer.

EXHIBIT 1.36 Comparison of Outcomes between Consumer Behavior and a Company's Customer Service

Item of Comparison	Consumer Behavior Outcomes	Customer Service Outcomes
Pre-purchase phase	Purchase/ no-purchase decision	
Purchase phase	Consumer purchases a product	
Post-purchase phase	Satisfied or dissatisfied consumer	
Pre-transaction phase		Intent to buy a product
Transaction phase		Either buys or does not buy a product
Post-transaction phase		Happy or unhappy customer

(iii) Price Management

Pricing decisions that integrate the firm's costs with its marketing strategy, business conditions, competition, consumer demand, product variables, channels of distribution, and general resources can determine the success or failure of a business. Pricing of products or services is the cornerstone of the marketing function. If the price is too high, buyers may purchase competitive brands leading to a loss of sales and profits. If the price is too low, profitability may suffer despite increases in sales.

Effective pricing should consider these factors: demand influences, supply influences, and competitive and regulatory influences (see Exhibit 1.37).

EXHIBIT 1.37 Effective Price Considerations

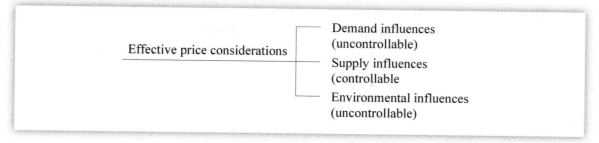

(A) Demand Influences

From a demand perspective, three primary considerations are demographic factors, psychological factors, and price elasticity. Demographic factors include: number, location, and economic strength of potential buyers; type of consumer (i.e., resellers or final); and expected quantity of purchases by type of consumer. These demographic factors help determine market potential and are useful for estimating expected sales at various price levels.

The heart of psychological factors focuses on how consumers perceive various prices or price changes. It is difficult to predict how much potential buyers will be willing to pay for the product and whether they use price as an indicator of product quality. The best way to find out answers to these questions is to conduct marketing research. Although not conclusive, many research studies have found that persons who choose high-priced product categories see the consequences of a poor choice as being undesirable. They believe that quality is related to price and see themselves as good judges of product quality. In general, the reverse is true for persons who select low-priced items in the same product categories.

Both demographic and psychological factors affect price elasticity. Price elasticity (e) is a measure of consumers' price sensitivity, which is estimated by dividing relative changes in the quantity (Q) sold by the relative changes in price (P). This is expressed as

$$e = (\Delta Q/Q) \div (\Delta P/P) = \text{Change in quantity}/Q \div (\text{Change in price}/P)$$

Price elasticity can be estimated from historical data or from price/quantity data across different sales districts and by sampling a group of consumers from the target market and surveying them concerning various price/quantity relationships. However, surveying consumers can be expensive and time consuming.

(B) Supply Influences

Supply influences can be understood in terms of pricing objectives, costs, and nature of the product. To be effective, pricing objectives need to be derived from corporate objectives via marketing objectives as shown in Exhibit 1.38.

EXHIBIT 1.38 Pricing Objectives

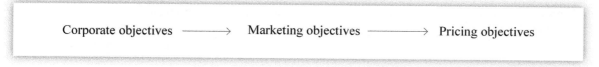

Marketing research has found that the most common pricing objectives are pricing to achieve a target ROI, stabilization of price and margin, pricing to achieve a target market share, and pricing to meet or prevent competition.

ADDITIONAL PRICING OBJECTIVES

- Target ROI and market share.
- Maximize short-run and long-run profits.
- Grow and stabilize market.
- Desensitize customers to price.
- Maintain price-leadership arrangement.
- Discourage new low-price entrants.
- Speed exit of marginal firms.

Marketing managers focus on multiple objectives when making pricing decisions. This situation becomes even more important considering that managers do not have perfect information about cost, revenue, and market.

Every profit-oriented organization must make a profit after covering production, marketing, and administrative costs. Cost-oriented pricing is the most common approach in practice, and there are at least three basic variations: markup pricing, cost-plus pricing, and rate-of-return pricing. This is shown in Exhibit 1.39.

EXHIBIT 1.39 Variations of Cost-Oriented Pricing Methods

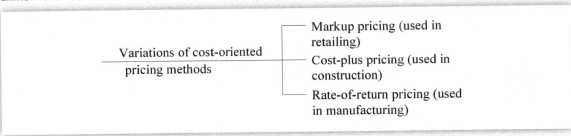

Markup pricing is used in the retail industry, where a percentage is added to the retailer's invoice price to determine the final selling price. In **cost-plus pricing**, the costs of producing a product or completing a project are totaled and a profit amount or percentage is added on. It is used in job-oriented and nonroutine and difficult-to-cost advance situations, such as military installations. In **rate-of-return or target pricing**, price is determined by adding a desired rate of ROI to total costs. Generally, a breakeven analysis is performed for expected production and sales levels, and a rate of return is added on. This is shown in Exhibit 1.40.

EXHIBIT 1.40 Advantages and Disadvantages of the Cost-Oriented Approach to Pricing

Advantages	Disadvantages
Simple to calculate	Gives little or no consideration to demand factors
Simple to understand	Price determined by a markup or cost-plus method has no necessary
Simple to explain	relationship to what people will be willing to pay for the product
Simple to trace	Places little emphasis on estimating sales volume in rate-of-return
Provides objective evidence	pricing
Yields a good pricing decision	Fails to reflect competition adequately, because costs and markups are different for each producer

Three important product characteristics that can affect pricing are perishability, distinctiveness, and stage in the product life cycle. Goods that are very perishable in a physical sense (e.g., food, flowers) must be priced to promote sales without costly delays. Perishable items also include high-fashion and seasonal products since their demand is based on time. One of the primary marketing objectives of any firm is to make its product distinctive in the minds of buyers and charge higher prices. Homogeneous goods, such as bulk wheat and whole milk, are perfect substitutes for each other; most consumer goods are heterogeneous goods.

The price of a product often depends on the stage of the life cycle that a product is in and is explained in terms of price skimming and price penetration (see Exhibit 1.41).

EXHIBIT 1.41 Pricing Policies

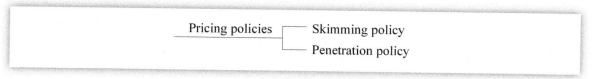

A **skimming policy** is one in which the seller charges a relatively high price on a new product. The price may be lowered later as competition moves in. This pricing strategy is good for monopoly companies and where the demand for the product is price inelastic.

A **penetration policy** is one in which the seller charges a relatively low price on a new product to discourage competition. This pricing strategy is good where competitors can move in rapidly and where demand for the product is price elastic. Regardless of what pricing strategy is used when a new product is introduced, the price may have to be altered later to accommodate changes in market forces.

(C) Competitive and Regulatory Influences

Competitive and government regulations are two uncontrollable variables that have environmental influence on pricing. Many factors help determine whether the firm's selling price should be at, below, or above competition. **Competitive factors** include:

- Number, size, location, and cost structure of competitors
- Conditions of entry into the industry
- Degree of vertical integration of competition
- Number of products sold by competitors
- Historical reaction of competitors to price changes

KEY CONCEPTS TO REMEMBER: Competition and Pricing

- **Pricing a product at competition** is called going-rate pricing, which is the average price charged by the industry and is widely used for homogeneous products.

- **Pricing a product below competition** can be found in sealed-bid pricing, where a firm is bidding directly against competitors for project contracts. It is an intentional move to obtain the job contract.

- **Pricing a product above competition** is used when a firm has a superior product or because a firm is the industry price leader.

Governmental regulation includes both state and federal government. The scope of state regulation includes pricing by public utility companies while the scope of federal regulation covers price fixing, deceptive pricing, price discrimination, and promotional pricing.

(D) Price Equation

Price is a monetary amount charged to a customer who is buying a retailer's products or services. To most customers, price of a product or service is a major issue and concern before purchase because customers are price sensitive, meaning sales will be lower when the prices are higher and vice versa. Establishing a product's price is not an art or a science; instead, it is a combination of art and science due to several constraints working on it. Major constraints include pricing policies and practices of competitors and price controls by government regulations.

A question might arise whether a customer should consider "product first" or "price first" when shopping online or offline. The answer is "product first" for the following reasons. Focusing on "price first" can cloud a customer's purchase decision and raise doubts about the value of the product because most people equate price to value. The rationale is that the customer needs to buy a particular product to fulfill a specific need, so the product should come first.

Similar to most customers, most retailers are also concerned about prices because they determine whether a retailer is going to make a profit or incur a loss at the end of an accounting period where profit is an incentive for retailers to invest in their specific businesses. In other words, profit is the ROI and is a balancing act. The basic price equation is:

$$Price = Costs + Profits$$

Costs are of two types: (1) direct costs of merchandise and materials and employees' wages, salaries, and benefits; and (2) indirect costs of rent, advertisements, supplies, utilities, insurance, taxes, and others. A targeted or expected percentage of profit (called a markup) is added to the cost amount to arrive at the price of a product. Profits are the remaining amounts after the cost amount is subtracted from the price amount.

> **Example:** It costs $2.65 for a retailer to buy a product# 265 from a manufacturer or supplier. If the targeted or expected markup is 10%, what is the price of the product# 265?

$$Price = Costs + Profits$$

$$Price = (\$2.65) + (\$2.65 \times 0.10) = \$2.65 + \$0.265 = \$2.915 = \$2.92 \text{ (rounded)} = \$2.99 \text{ (adjusted to reflect odd-pricing practice)}$$

The price of the product# 265 is $2.99.

(E) Factors Affecting Profits

Let us look at the various factors affecting profits where some factors decrease profits while others increase profits. Note that factors that can decrease profits are the opposite of factors that can increase profits.

Factors that can decrease profits include:

- Lower prices for products and services (initial lower prices and no markups later)
- Increased direct costs and indirect costs

- Increased price markdowns
- Frequent sales with progressive and deep discounting of prices
- Increased employee theft of merchandise
- Increased customer theft of merchandise
- Increased loss of or damage to merchandise
- Increased amounts of customer returns of merchandise that cannot be resold
- Increased misplacing or miscounting of merchandise
- Increased and unauthorized overriding of prices by a cashier at the point-of-sale (POS) terminal
- Incorrect price scanning of products by a cashier at the POS terminal due to pricing errors resulting from mismatched prices with products
- Increased billing errors in products ordered and shipped with incorrect prices
- Increased quantity of free samples and product giveaways to customers and others
- Increased unavailability of products for customers to purchase

Factors that can increase profits include:

- Higher prices for products and services (initial higher prices and markups later)
- Decreased direct costs and indirect costs
- Decreased price markdowns
- Infrequent sales with less progressive discounting of prices
- Decreased employee theft of merchandise
- Decreased customer theft of merchandise
- Decreased loss of or damage to merchandise
- Decreased amounts of customer returns of merchandise that can be resold
- Decreased misplacing or miscounting of merchandise
- Decreased and authorized overriding of prices by a cashier at the POS terminal
- Decreased price scanning of products by a cashier at the POS terminal due to no pricing errors resulting from mismatched prices with products
- Decreased billing errors in products ordered and shipped with incorrect prices
- Decreased quantity of free samples and product giveaways to customers and others
- Decreased unavailability of products for customers to purchase

(F) Pricing Strategies

Price is a dollar amount charged by a retailer for the sales of its products and services to customers. Pricing strategies include setting a base price for a product or service and making adjustments to the base price over time. These adjustments include markups and markdowns.

There is no right way to set prices since multiple factors are involved, including: government price regulations; production cost, marketing cost, and other costs; consumer psychology; company's profit and market share goals; product demand and supply conditions; consumers' personal income levels; competitors' prices; and prices of substitute or complementary products. Pricing decisions are very complex and uncertain, to say the least. Hence, retailers should develop a systematic strategy and structured approach to establishing, adapting, and changing prices.

The pricing continuum is as follows:

Very Low Price ⟶ Floor Price ⟶ Ceiling Price ⟶ Very High Price

(No Profits)   (Base price   (Base price   (No Sales)
               + Small profit)   + Large profit)

(G) Pricing Methods

Seven popular methods exist to establish prices, including markup pricing, cost-plus pricing, target-return pricing, perceived-value pricing, value pricing, going-rate pricing, and auction-type pricing.

The **markup pricing method** adds a percentage of profit (markup) to the retailer's invoice price (cost to the retailer) to determine the final selling price. This method is popular, easy to determine, and fairer to both buyers and sellers. Wholesalers, dealers, and retailers will add their own markup to the manufacturer's markup price, thereby increasing the manufacturer's markup price significantly. Frequently, some retailers take markdowns to lower prices and to increase sales.

> **Example:** If a retailer's invoice price is $15 for an item and if the required profit is 10%, then the markup price is $16.50. That is, ($15 + ($15 × 10%)) = $16.50.

The **cost-plus pricing method,** although it is similar in approach to the markup pricing method, is used in industries other than the retail industry. Here, the costs of producing a product or completing a project are totaled and a profit amount or percentage is added on. This method is used in job-oriented projects, such as in the construction business, and nonroutine situations that are difficult to "cost" in advance, such as in military installations.

> **Example:** If a project's total cost is $100,000 and if the required profit is 20%, then the cost-plus price is $120,000. That is, ($100,000 + ($100,000 × 20%)) = $120,000.

The **target-return pricing method** adds a required rate of ROI to total costs to determine the target price. This method ignores external factors, such as competitors' prices, because it is based on internal factors such as costs and profits.

$$\text{Target Cost} + \text{Target Profit} = \text{Target Price}$$

> **Example:** If the target cost for an item is $20 and if the required rate of return is 10% (target profit), then the target price is $22 for the item. That is, ($20 + ($20 × 10%)) = $22.

The perceived-value pricing method is based on what the customer, not the company, thinks about the value of a product. Organizations use advertising and sales force to communicate and enhance perceived value in buyers' minds. The goal is to deliver more value to a customer than the competitor and to demonstrate this value to prospective buyers. Market research methods such as focus groups, surveys, judgments, and experimentation are used to determine the value of a product to customers.

Example: Most customers who buy high-end fashion products from Chanel and other retailers believe that they are buying high-value products worthy of high prices.

The value pricing method purposefully charges a low price for a high-quality product with cost savings realized from reengineering the production processes and becoming a low-cost producer without sacrificing quality. The cost savings are passed on to value-conscious customers through programs such as everyday low pricing (e.g., Walmart), high-low pricing, extreme everyday low pricing, and double guarantee pricing (Aldi food store).

Example: Walmart and Aldi food stores are known for value pricing methods; Walmart offers everyday low prices and Aldi offers double guaranteed prices.

The going-rate pricing method focuses on meeting or beating competitors' prices. Some companies adopt the follow-the-leader strategy, where they change the price when competitors change their price, not when the company's demand or cost structure changes. This is also referred to as "we will match or beat the price." This method is appropriate when costs are difficult to estimate and when competition is uncertain.

Example: Few retailers do not offer any price match (i.e., a retailer deciding not to compete can make it hard for him to survive in the long run); most offer 100 percent match (matching the competition); and very few offer more than 100% match of a competitor's price (beating the competition).

The auction-type pricing method uses the Internet as the primary medium to transact between buyers and sellers. The items that are auctioned include excess inventories and used goods of all kinds. Bids are exchanged between various members, such as one seller and many buyers, one buyer and many sellers, and one buyer and many suppliers (as in procurement of supplies). In general, online auctions give greater overall satisfaction to buyers and sellers due to a large number of bidders, greater economic stakes, and less visibility in pricing.

Example: Procurement officers at some retail companies purchase small-dollar items (e.g., toothpicks, pens, and pencils) or some unique products from auction houses (e.g., artistic or antique type items).

A PRIMER ON PRICING ISSUES AND RISKS

This primer discusses seven issues and risks dealing with price fixing, price discrimination, loss leader pricing, predatory pricing, drip pricing, price discounts, and conditional pricing.

Price Fixing

Price fixing is illegal in the United States because it restricts competition and the result is often higher prices. Price fixing occurs when competitors agree to raise prices, lower prices, stabilize prices, or change other competitive terms, such as shipping fees. Customers expect that retail prices are established based on supply and demand factors and that retailers set their own prices independently, not based on collusive agreements. The agreement can be written, verbal, or inferred from conduct (i.e., practice or intent).

Price fixing relates not only to prices of products but also to other related items that affect the final cost to customers, such as shipping fees, warranties, discount programs, and financing rates.

(continued)

A PRIMER ON PRICING ISSUES AND RISKS (*Continued*)

Example: A collusive agreement between two or more retailers operating in the same retail channel who are in direct competition with each other and who decide to charge higher prices to end customers is called horizontal price fixing. It can occur between Retailer A and Retailer B and is illegal.

Example: A collusive agreement between two or more parties operating in different retail channels who are not in direct competition with each other and who decide to charge higher prices to end customers is called vertical price fixing. It can occur between a retailer and a vendor (supplier) and is illegal.

In summary,

- Horizontal price fixing occurs between two or more competing retailers because they are in the same hierarchical level in the marketplace. It is illegal.

- Vertical price fixing occurs between a retailer and a manufacturer and between a wholesaler and a retailer because they are in the different hierarchical position in the marketplace and they agreed together to maintain the same prices or increase prices. It is called price maintenance and is illegal.

Price Discrimination

Price discrimination occurs when a seller (retailer) charges customers (buyers) different prices for the same commodity or product. This discrimination also applies to advertising and promotional allowances. Generally, price discriminations are legal, particularly if the price differences reflect the different costs of dealing with different buyers or are the result of a seller's attempts to meet a competitor's offering. If the price discriminations do not reflect these issues, they are illegal. Here, the price differences are justified by different costs incurred to manufacture, sell, or deliver, or the price concessions were given in good faith to meet a competitor's price (i.e., price matching). In the United States, the Robinson-Patman Act prohibits price discrimination.

Price discrimination rules include the following:

- When two retailers buy the same product from the same supplier and pay the same prices, there is no price discrimination.

- When two retailers buy the same product from the same supplier and pay different prices, there is price discrimination except when the different prices are cost justified based on cost differences or cost savings.

Example: When retailers offer price matching of 50%, 100%, or 115% to customers in order to compete with other retailers, then the price matching practice is legal. Coupon-based prices and volume-based discount prices are legal.

The following practices are illegal under the Robinson-Patman Act:

- Below-cost sales prices by a retailer that charges higher prices in different locations with a secret plan of recoupment.

- Price differences in the sale of identical products that cannot be justified on the basis of cost savings or cost differences to meet a competitor's prices.

- Allowances given for advertisements and promotions that are not equally and practically available to all customers on proportionately equal terms.

Loss Leader Pricing

Loss leader pricing is a retail pricing practice where a primary product is priced at near or below cost to bring more customers into retail stores, whether they are physical or online stores. Retailers hope that when customers come to their stores to buy the primary product, they will also purchase secondary products, such as accessories, derivative products, or complementary products related to the primary product, thus bringing additional sales revenues. Here, primary products are sold at lower prices and secondary products are sold at higher prices because they are connected together to make them complete and wholesome. Offering loss-leading prices is legal. Selling eggs at low prices on or before Easter and selling turkeys at low prices on or before Thanksgiving are examples of loss-leader pricing.

Predatory Pricing

Predatory pricing is a controversial and confusing topic in pricing where retailers charge lower prices to customers to drive competitors out of the marketplace. The U.S. Supreme Court has been skeptical about claims by the Federal Trade Commission (FTC) of predatory pricing practices, stating that they are illegal and unsustainable and that they destroy healthy competition. However, the Supreme Court did not agree with the FTC, stating that these pricing practices are temporary and unsustainable, and hence legal. Reduced prices for items in a clearance sale are legal and are not a predatory pricing practice.

Predatory pricing works as follows:

Today $\longrightarrow$ Below-cost, low prices to drive competitors out of the market

Tomorrow $\longrightarrow$ Above-cost, high prices after competitors leave the market

A list of various pricing scenarios follows.

- Customers are harmed only if below-cost pricing allows a dominant retailer to knock its rivals out of the market and then later raise prices to above-market levels for a substantial time.

- A retailer's independent decision (not a collusive decision) to reduce prices to a level below its own costs does not necessarily injure competition and, in fact, may simply reflect vigorous competition. This is good for a free market system.

- Cases of a large retailer using low prices to drive smaller retailers out of the market in hopes of raising prices after smaller retailers leave the market are rare because smaller retailers simply do not go away. This strategy can be successful only if long-term profits from higher prices make up for short-run losses from lower prices.

End-of-season sales where products are priced at very low prices to get rid of old, obsolete, and excess merchandise do not come under predatory pricing guidelines. Also, frequently advertised "clearance items" are excepts to the predatory pricing practices.

Drip Pricing

Drip pricing means back-end prices are different from front-end prices and vice versa, and it is illegal. In drip pricing, additional charges are added to a customer's final prices without disclosing them to the customer at the beginning. Drip pricing can be found in the hospitality industry, such as hotel reservations and vacation resorts, and in consumer financing, such as home mortgage loans and short-term loans. Legal liabilities exist with deceptive and discriminatory price practices in violation of the FTC's Robinson-Patman Act.

Price Discounts

The sky is the limit when comes to designing various innovative ways of offering price discounts among vendors, retailers, and customers. Price discounts are frequently used to attract customers and to turn them into buyers. Price discounts go two ways: from vendors to retailers and from retailers to customers, as follows:

Price Discounts = Vendors $\longrightarrow$ Retailers = Value to Retailers

Price Discounts = Retailers $\longrightarrow$ Customers = Value to Customers

Next, we elaborate the price discounts.

Discounts given to retailers include trade discounts (e.g., 10%), quantity discounts (volume discounts), seasonal discounts (off-season low prices), cash discounts (2/10, net 30 days), and allowances given to retailers for spending on advertisement and sales promotions.

(*continued*)

A PRIMER ON PRICING ISSUES AND RISKS (*Continued*)

Discounts given to customers include instant savings (today's savings); mail-in rebates (tomorrow's savings); current/future coupons; current/future rebates; buy one get one free (BOGO); volume discounts; 10%, 20% or 30% off list prices; clearance sale prices; fixed discounts (10% off on $30 purchase); sales events; loss leader pricing; current/future discounts; flash/special sales; buy 2 get the third one free; and buy 1 and get the second one at 50% off.

One of the best ways to reduce the cost of merchandise (cost of sales) for a retailer is to receive various forms of price discounts from the providers of the merchandise (e.g., manufacturers, vendors, suppliers, wholesalers, distributors, agents, and brokers). After receiving those price discounts from the merchandise providers, the retailer can pass on some of the discounts to end consumers and customers. Some retailers have greater flexibility than others in offering various forms of price discounts to end consumers and customers; and this is where retailers are differentiated in increasing sales using various forms of price discounts.

Legality of Price Discounts

Price discounts are legal only when they are properly designed, represented, and advertised. Otherwise, they can be illegal. A list of retailers using deceptive pricing practices with price discounts follows.

Example: Los Angeles prosecutors have initiated lawsuits against J. C. Penney, Sears, Kohl's, and Macy's, accusing the retailers of misleading customers into believing they were buying products at more significant markdowns than they actually did. To avoid potential litigation, retailers that advertise "sale prices" in comparison with "regular prices" in California should ensure that the products were actually offered for purchase at those regular prices within the preceding three months.

Example: Kate Spade, Macy's, and Bloomingdale's in California were accused of falsely advertising original prices and sales prices and for intentionally duping customers by way of their pricing practices.

Example: Nike and Burberry were accused of using misleading price tags at their outlet stores.

Example: Nike was accused of misrepresenting and misleading the amount of price discounts by advertising false suggested retail prices (SRPs) to mean the same as manufacturer's suggested retail price (MSRP), which caused confusion among customers. The terms "SRP" and "MSRP" are not the same.

Example: Zara, a fashion retailer, was accused of using deceptive pricing practices using a classic bait-and-switch scheme where customers overpaid for garments they purchased.

Conditional Pricing

Conditional pricing practices occur when a seller establishes its product prices based on factors such as volume (quantity) of products purchased, the set of products purchased, or the buyer's share of purchases from the seller. The broad range of these practices include incremental discounts, quantity (volume) discounts, bundling and tying of multiple products, bundled discounts, market-share discounts (i.e., loyalty discounts based on loyalty pricing), and exclusive dealing (i.e., agreement not to deal in the goods of another seller). Note that these practices are implemented by companies having a large market share as well as companies with a small market share.

In summary:

- Price fixing is illegal.
- Price discrimination can be legal or illegal depending on the cost structure or cost justification.
- Loss leader pricing is legal.
- Predatory pricing is not illegal, as it is not sustainable.
- Drip pricing is illegal.
- Price discounts can be legal or illegal based on their true intent.
- Conditional pricing can be legal or illegal based on their true intent.

(iv) Product Management and Product Life Cycles
This subsection discusses product management, the product life cycle concept, and product audit.

(A) Product Management
Product strategy is a part of the marketing mix (i.e., product, price, place, and promotion). Other parts include promotion strategy, distribution strategy, and pricing strategy.

There are many decision areas in product management, including product definition, product classification, product mix and product line, and packaging and branding (see Exhibit 1.42).

EXHIBIT 1.42 Decision Areas in Product Management

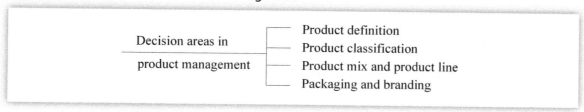

Product Definition. The way in which the product variable is defined can have important implications for a firm's survival, profitability, and long-run growth. See Exhibit 1.43 for how a product can be viewed.

EXHIBIT 1.43 Views of a Product

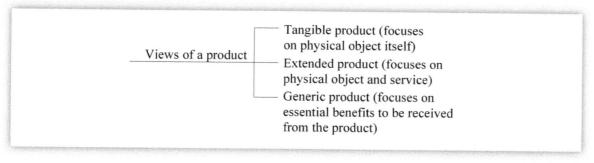

A classic example of an improper definition can be found in railroad passenger service, which defines itself as being in the railroad business instead of in the transportation business. A reasonable definition of **product** is that it is the sum of the physical, psychological, and sociological satisfaction the buyer derives from purchase, ownership, and consumption.

Product Classification. Product classification is an analytical device to assist in planning marketing strategy and programs. A basic assumption underlying such classifications is that products with common attributes can be marketed in a similar manner. In general, products are classified according to two basic criteria: end use or market and degree of processing or physical transformation required.

Examples of product classification are agricultural products and raw materials, industrial goods, and consumer goods. The market for industrial products has certain attributes that distinguish it from the consumer goods market. For certain products, there are a limited number of buyers, known as a **vertical market** (which means that it is narrow), because customers are restricted to a few industries, and it is deep, in that a large percentage of the producers in the market use the product. Some products, such as office supplies, have a **horizontal market**, which means that the goods are purchased by all types of firms in many different industries.

Product Mix and Product Line. The product mix is the composite of products offered for sale by the firm's product line. It refers to a group of products that are closely related in terms of use, customer groups, price ranges, and channels of distribution. There are three primary dimensions of a firm's product mix, as shown in Exhibit 1.44.

EXHIBIT 1.44 Dimensions of a Product Mix

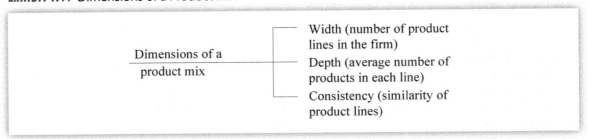

Width of the product mix refers to the number of product lines the firm handles. **Depth** of the product mix refers to the average number of products in each line. **Consistency** of the product mix refers to the similarity of product lines. Product line plans take into account consumer evaluation of the company's products (strengths and weaknesses) and objective and accurate information on sales, profits, and market share (actual and anticipated levels).

Packaging and Branding. Distinctive or unique packaging is one method of differentiating relatively homogeneous products, such as toothpaste or soap. The packaging design should focus on the size of the product, how easy it is to open, how strong the packaging should be in protecting the product, the attractiveness of the packaging, and costs.

Many companies use branding strategies to increase the strength of the product image. Factors to be considered include: product quality, whereby products do what they do very well; consistent advertising, in which brands tell their story often and well; and brand personality, where the brand stands for something unique (e.g., Xerox and Kodak). A good brand name can evoke feelings of trust, confidence, security, and strength. Markov analysis can be used to determine the extent to which customers switch brands.

Markov analysis is useful in studying the evolution of certain systems over repeated trials. This analysis has been used, for example, to describe the probability that a machine, functioning in one period, will function or break down in another period and to identify changes in the customer's account receivables collection experience.

(B) Product Life Cycle Concepts

A firm's product strategy must consider the fact that products have a life cycle—phases or stages that a product will go through in its lifetime. This product life cycle (PLC) varies according to industry, product, technology, and market. In general, product growth follows an S-shaped curve (although it is shown in Exhibit 1.45 as linear) due to innovation, diffusion of a new product, and changes in the product and the market. A typical product goes through four phases: introduction, growth, maturation, and decline. Some products skip a phase, such as introduction or maturity, while some products are revitalized after decline and thereby do not go through the S-shaped pattern. Each phase is described briefly next.

EXHIBIT 1.45 Phases/Stages of a Product Life Cycle

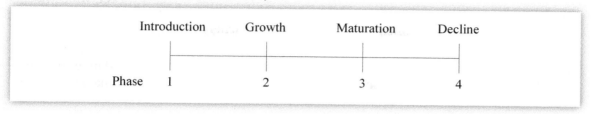

Introduction phase (phase 1) incurs high production and marketing costs. Profits are low or nonexistent. This phase is flat due to difficulties of overcoming buyer inertia and stimulating trials of the new product.

Profits increase and are possibly correlated with sales during the **growth stage** (phase 2) as the market begins trying and adopting the product. As the product **matures** (phase 3), profits do not keep pace with sales because of competition. Penetration of the product's potential buyers is eventually reached, causing the rapid growth to stop and level off. Price concessions, increasing product quality, and expanding advertising will be planned to maintain market share.

At some point, sales will **decline** (phase 4), and the seller must decide whether to drop the product, alter it, seek new uses for the product, seek new markets, or continue with more of the same. Growth will eventually taper off as new substitute products appear in the market. The advice for the decline phase is not to invest in slow or negative growth or unfavorable markets but instead to pull the cash out.

Due to changing conditions, the marketing mix has to be changed in line with PLC changes. The PLC concept can help in forecasting, pricing, advertising, and product plans. The difficult part of the PLC concept is estimating the exact time periods for these four phases, as it is hard to know when a phase begins and ends. The fact that the duration of each phase varies from product to product diminishes the usefulness of the PLC concept as a marketing planning tool.

(C) Product Audit

The **product audit** is a marketing management technique whereby the company's current product offerings need to be reviewed to ascertain whether each product should be continued as is, improved, modified, or discontinued. The product manager, who is responsible for the product, should ensure that the product audit is performed at regular intervals as a matter of marketing policy. One of the major purposes of the product audit is to detect "sick" products for possible discontinuation. Some critical factors to be considered in this area are:

- **Sales trends.** How have sales moved over time? Why have sales declined?
- **Profit contribution.** What has been the profit contribution of this product to the company?
- **PLC.** Has the product reached a level of maturity and saturation in the market? Has the product outgrown its usefulness? The product discontinuation issue is a hard one because it involves consideration of negative impact on employees, keeping consumers supplied with replacement parts, disposing of inventory, and providing repair and maintenance services.

One objective of the product audit is to determine whether to modify or improve the product or to leave things as they are (status quo). Modifying the product requires changes in product features, design, packaging, promotion, price, and channels of distribution. Product improvement suggestions often come from advertising agencies, consultants, sales staff, consumers, and intermediaries, and involve many functions, such as engineering, manufacturing, marketing, and accounting. Market research is advised when a product improvement is planned because it is not always clear as to how consumers will react to improvements or changes.

KEY CONCEPTS TO REMEMBER: Elements of Product Strategy

- An audit of the firm's actual and potential resources includes financial strength, access to raw materials, plant and equipment, operating personnel, management, engineering and technical skills, and patents and licenses.

- Approaches to current markets include: more of the same products; variations of present products in terms of grades, sizes, and packages; new products to replace or supplement current lines; and product deletions.

- Approaches to new or potential markets include geographical expansion of domestic sales, new socioeconomic or ethnic groups, overseas markets, new uses of present products, complementary goods, and mergers and acquisitions.

- The state of competition includes new entries into the industry, product limitations, and competitive mergers or acquisitions.

(v) Digital Marketing

Digital marketing is other than traditional marketing (e.g., newspapers, magazines, billboards, radio, and TV). The scope of digital marketing includes the Internet; social media websites and platforms; digital phones, tablets, notebook computers, and other devices; and mobile apps.

Many traditional elements of marketing easily translate into Internet marketing, such as price, product, place, and promotion. For example, consider the following with respect to "promotion" tactics:

Traditional Marketing	Digital Marketing
Broadcast advertising	Banner advertising
Direct mail	Email/inbox mail
Press releases	Website pressroom
Promotions	Online events/Chat rooms/Alerts/Notifications
Networking	Social media websites/platforms/blogs
Word of mouth	Viral marketing/Apps

Like traditional marketing, successful online and Internet marketing requires persistence and commitment to a long-term strategy. Unfortunately, even with innovative technology, Internet marketing cannot be done with the click of a mouse. If the goal of the marketing is to build stronger relationships between the customer and the brand, the power of a web-based plan should not be ignored.

Companies are realizing that they must approach web-based techniques and strategies as they would with any traditional marketing activity. Fundamental questions must still be answered:

- Who are our customers?
- What is the competition doing?

- What are the channel dynamics?

- Which marketing mix strategies are most effective?

- Are our business models realistic?

- How and when we will make a return on sales and return on investment?

(vi) Marketing of Services
(A) Service Characteristics

The service sector of the U.S. economy has grown to such an extent that it captures about 50 cents of the consumer's every dollar. The definition of what constitutes a service remains unclear. These common variables comprise the marketing mix of both products and services:

- Product or service itself

- Price

- Distribution system

- Promotion

- Marketing research

Yet services possess certain distinguishing characteristics and have unique problems that result in marketing mix decisions that are substantially different from those found in communication with the marketing of goods. *These characteristics include intangibility, inseparability, fluctuating demand, a highly differentiated marketing system, and a client relationship.* Each of these characteristics is discussed next.

- **Intangibility** arises when a service firm is selling an idea or experience, not a product. It is often difficult to illustrate, demonstrate, or display the service in use. Examples include airline or hotel service.

- **Inseparability** arises when a service cannot be separated from the person of the seller. In other words, the service must be created and marketed simultaneously. An example is an insurance agent who is selling a policy.

- **Fluctuating demand** occurs when services fluctuate by season (tourism), days (airlines), or time of day (movie theaters). One example of stimulating demand or unused capacity is when downtown hotels (or those that are used predominantly by business travelers) offer significant discounts for a weekend stay.

- **Highly differentiated marketing systems** offer different service approaches for different services. For example, a different approach is required to market banking or financial services than to market computer services or airline services.

- **Client relationships** exist between the buyer and the seller, as opposed to customer relationships. Examples include physician–patient and banker–investor relationships. The buyer follows the suggestions provided by the seller.

(B) Service Quality

Poor quality of service and nonperformance are two major reasons for switching to the competition, and high price is a minor reason. Service quality is measured against performance, which can be very difficult to ascertain. In general, problems in the determination of good service quality are attributable to differences in expectations, perceptions, and experiences regarding the encounter between service providers and service users.

It is easier and cheaper to keep an existing customer than to find a new one. Product quality can be measured against accepted standards, which are tangible, while service quality is measured against expected performance, which is intangible.

Service quality is the gap between expected service and perceived service. Determinants of service quality, which can help marketing managers avoid losing customers, are listed next.

- **Reliability** involves dependability and consistency of performance.
- **Responsiveness** concerns the willingness or readiness of employees to provide service.
- **Competence** means possession of the necessary skills and knowledge to perform the service.
- **Access** involves approachability and ease of contact.
- **Courtesy** involves politeness, respect, consideration, and friendliness of contact personnel.
- **Communication** means keeping customers informed in language they can understand. It also means listening to customers.
- **Credibility** involves trustworthiness, believability, and honesty.
- **Security** is the freedom from danger, risk, or doubt.
- **Understanding the customer** involves making the effort to understand the customer's needs.
- **Tangibles** include the physical evidence of the service.

(C) Overcoming Obstacles in Service Marketing

In view of the size and importance of the service economy, considerable innovation and ingenuity are needed to make high-quality services available at convenient locations for consumers. The actual services offered by service providers often fall behind the opportunities available due to five obstacles:

1. Limited view of marketing
2. Lack of competition
3. Lack of creative management
4. Concept of "no obsolescence"
5. Lack of innovation in the distribution of services

(vii) Marketing Analysis

Marketing analysis focuses on two topics: market opportunity matrix analysis and market basket analysis.

(A) Market Opportunity Matrix Analysis

The market opportunity matrix analysis identifies two dimensions (level of attractiveness and probability of success) to develop a market matrix. This matrix can be used when introducing new products into new markets in order to study their success levels. This matrix focuses on external assessment of factors such as markets, products and services, customers, and competitors.

Three values (such as high, medium, or low) can be assigned to the level of attractiveness. Similarly, three values (such as high, medium, or low) can be assigned to the probability of success. A product's success can be determined with the following formula. (See Exhibit 1.46.)

Product's Success = Level of Attractiveness × Probability of Success

Examples of marketing variables to consider for this analysis include target products, target markets, target customers, target customers, target market share, and target financial results. This matrix provides a high-level, summary-type assessment of each product for market screening purposes (i.e., market feasibility analysis). Later, the same marketing results can be used to proceed further with low-level, detailed financial analysis (i.e., financial feasibility analysis).

Step 1. Market Feasibility Analysis = First-Level Impact Analysis

Step 2. Financial Feasibility Analysis = Second-Level Impact Analysis

The scope and nature of financial feasibility analysis can include calculating financial metrics such as return on sales, ROI, and gross/net profits.

EXHIBIT 1.46 Formula for a Product's Success

Marketing Variables	A = Level of Attractiveness (H,M,L)	B = Probability of Success (H,M,L)	C = Outcome (C = A × B) Product's Success
Target Product 1	L	L	LL
Target Product 2	L	M	LM
Target Product 3	H	M	HM
Target Product 4	H	H	HH

Decision Rule 1: First select all the products and services with HH outcomes, deserving high priority.

Decision Rule 2: Next select all the products and services with HM outcomes when resources are available.

Decision Rule 3: Next select all the products and services with LM outcomes only when resources are still available.

Decision Rule 4: Do not select any product or service with LL outcomes because they will not be successful.

(B) Market Basket Analysis

Market basket analysis is a marketing management tool to study and understand the purchase behavior of consumers. Also called affinity analysis, it is similar in concept and approach to the consumer price index (CPI) study of determining the price changes in a basket of consumer goods.

Affinity analysis or market basket analysis finds intrinsic relationships between products that a customer is currently purchasing or has purchased in the past. The output of this analysis can be used to promote cross-selling or up-selling opportunities, to design discount plans and loyalty programs, and to offer special coupons and rebates in order to make customers excited and interested in buying more of the same items that they have been buying.

Market basket analysis is mainly targeted at current customers who are actively purchasing some type of goods. For example, this market analysis can be used to reveal

- What products customers are buying.
- Why customers are buying what they are buying.
- What complementary or substitute products customers are buying. How frequently customers are buying such products? (e.g., eggs and cheese are complementary while cow milk and almond milk are substitutes).
- What group of products customers are buying (e.g., eggs, cheese, and bacon to make omelets).

The best place to collect this type of customer data applicable to market basket analysis is the POS registers and online customer ordering systems.

A hypothetical application of market basket analysis is shown next.

Time Period	Products Purchased	Interrelationships
1	B, J, K	No causal relationship
3	P, M, R, D	Unclear relationship
6	V, T	Very useful relationship

There could be four sales recommendations from the market basket analysis:

1. Cross-selling (a common practice)
2. Up-selling (a common practice)
3. Lateral selling (a common practice)
4. Down-selling (an uncommon practice)

Example 1: Cross-selling occurs, for example, when Amazon.com makes purchase recommendations to a customer during product selection. The computer system displays a message "Customers who bought book V also bought book T." This recommendation is possible only due to Amazon's use of affinity analysis software and/or because previous customers must have ordered this combination of books.

Example 2: Up-selling occurs when an airline premier and frequent traveler purchases a coach ticket for some reason. The airline's computer system recommends an upgrade to either first class or business class with a small incremental price increase.

Example 3: Up-selling also occurs when a computer system recommends to a customer who is making a weekend hotel reservation for a family suite A to upgrade to suite B with better amenities and a better view at a small incremental price.

Example 4: Lateral selling occurs when a computer recommends buying bed pillows of the same brand to a customer ordering only bed sheets of the same brand. A generous discount might be offered to customers to make this dual purchase decision.

Example 5: Down-selling occurs when a customer is buying a normal item at regular price with a low profit margin and the computer system recommends buying a similar item at a low price with a high profit margin.

(viii) Lead Management Cycle

World-class sales management focuses on two major things: lead management cycle and managing the sales process, because the former feeds the latter.

Lead management is the process of rapidly and effectively creating, nurturing, distributing, and analyzing leads. The ultimate goal is to increase the likelihood that a lead will convert to a qualified sale opportunity and then to a new, satisfied customer.

To implement a lead management strategy, marketing and sales functions must work closely together. The key focus here is on the quality, not the quantity, of leads. Marketing and sales management should focus on the conversion rates of leads to sales (i.e., percentage of leads resulted in closed sales), not so much on the number of raw leads generated.

For best results, a lead management system must bring together the right people, processes, and information at various stages in the lead management cycle:

- Identify hot leads and automatically route to direct sales or channel partners.
- Actively engage the remaining leads (i.e., not-so-hot leads) and nurture them through the pipeline to eventual sale.
- Track all leads to closure and evaluate the return on sales and ROI of marketing campaigns.
- Integrate the external channels, including value-added resellers, other resellers, and strategic partners.
- Integrate off-line qualification resources such as call centers.

Business organizations should do the following to manage the lead management cycle:

- Plan and generate leads.
- Qualify leads.
- Distribute leads.
- Nurture leads.
- Measure and evaluate leads.

(ix) The Sales Process

The sales process to sell a complicated product or service (i.e., rich in features and functions) consists of eight basic steps or stages.

1. Prospecting
2. Pre-approach and planning
3. Approaching the client/customer
4. Identifying the client needs

5. Presenting the product/service to the client

6. Handling buyer objections

7. Gaining commitment from the buyer

8. Following up and keeping promises

(x) Selling Methods

Selling methods are changing very rapidly due to the Internet-based electronic commerce and mobile commerce technologies. The traditional methods of in-person selling are fading away fast, and new methods of selling are being invented daily to make the entire selling process quick and impersonal.

Salespeople use either the traditional selling method or the professional selling method, where the latter method is better. Professional selling methods are still needed to sell engineering-based products, which need product knowledge to explain complicated features and functions to prospective clients or customers.

Traditional Selling Method. In the *traditional selling method*, little time is spent on the early stages of the sales process (i.e., approaching the client/customer and identifying client needs) and no time is spent on the beginning stages of prospecting and pre-approach and planning. Because prospective buyers are not usually convinced that they really need the product, gaining buyer commitment is difficult, tedious, and time consuming.

In the traditional selling method, little time is spent on:

- Approaching the client/customer
- Identifying the client needs

No time is spent on:

- Prospecting
- Pre-approach and planning

Professional Selling Method. In the *professional selling method*, a great deal of time is spent in the early stages of the sales process (i.e., prospecting, pre-approach and planning, approaching the client/customer, and identifying client needs), so that commitment is gained as a very natural or logical, next step. Essentially, customers are convinced that the product will solve their problems or meet their needs, because early in the sales process proper care has been taken to establish that need and link it to the benefits of the product.

In the professional selling method, more time is spent on:

- Prospecting
- Pre-approach and planning
- Approaching the client/customer
- Identifying the client needs

Less time is spent on:

- Presenting the product/service to the client
- Handling buyer objections
- Gaining commitment from the buyer
- Following up and keeping promises

(e) Logistics and Distribution Management

This subsection defines and discusses logistics management, inventory management, and distribution systems.

(i) Logistics Management Defined

Logistics management is moving finished goods from where they were produced (manufacturers and producers) to where they will be consumed (consumers and customers) using various transportation methods, such as trucks, trains, air cargos, and sea cargos. In a way, logistics management supports supply chain management.

$$\text{Logistics Management} = \text{Producers} \longrightarrow \text{Consumers}$$

Two important concepts in the supply chain and logistics include pull supply chain and push supply chain.

In the **pull supply chain,** customers are driving the demand (pull) in that they place the orders at the retail stores, online, or by phone to pull the products out of the logistics system into customers' hands.

In the **push supply chain,** historical sales drive the demand (push) in that purchasing management or store management initiates orders to push products from the logistics system into customers' hands.

- Customers' demand drives the pull supply chain.
- Historical sales drive the push supply chain.

Forward logistics and reverse logistics are two diverse concepts in logistics. Merchandise returns use the reverse logistics approach, meaning the supply chain works backward.

In **forward logistics**, raw materials and finished products are moved from upstream suppliers to manufacturers to suppliers and eventually to downstream customers for purchase and consumption.

In **reverse logistics**, already sold finished products are moved from downstream customers to stores to distribution centers to upstream suppliers and eventually to manufacturers for returns, repairs, rework, redesign, remanufacturing, refurbishing, and recycling. These returns could also include recalls of defective products. Later, these repaired products are resold to customers or others to recover some of the original price. Both types of logistics are shown next:

Forward Logistics: Upstream Suppliers ⟶ Manufacturers ⟶ Downstream Customers

Reverse Logistics: Downstream Customers ⟶ Upstream Suppliers ⟶ Manufacturers

(ii) Inventory Management Defined

Both manufacturing and retail companies invest huge amounts of money (millions and billions of dollars) in making, holding, and storing inventory (i.e., finished products, parts, components, raw materials, and ingredients) before it is sold to customers. Therefore, a large portion of a production operations manager's job consists of inventory management. Inventory management is risky due to outdated, obsolete, stolen, misplaced, damaged, and miscounted items. Therefore, inventory assets should be managed similar to any other assets (i.e., cash, buildings, and machinery) to ensure that inventory is tracked and protected until it is sold to customers.

Inventory is the goods the organization keeps on hand for ready to use (raw materials) or already used (finished goods) in the production process. When inventory levels can be kept at an absolute minimum, operations management is considered excellent. When inventory levels are kept above the minimum levels without a business justification, operations management is considered inefficient and ineffective.

A production process deals with transforming resources (inputs such as raw materials, labor, energy, and machines) into products and services (outputs). The transformation of raw materials, labor, and overhead results in finished goods. A company keeps these finished gods in inventory as sellable goods until they are sold to customers.

Raw Materials + Labor + Overhead = Finished Goods ⟶ Sellable Goods ⟶ Sales to Customers

Here, **overhead** means those costs incurred other than the raw materials cost and labor cost. Overhead costs include utility costs (gas, electric, and water), rent and taxes on the facilities, management salaries, and other costs not directly related to production of goods.

(iii) Distribution Systems Defined

Inventory in a distribution system can be managed through the use of independent demand models, such as continuous and periodic review models. Examples of these models include single order point, double order point, periodic review system, and sales replacement system, which are described below.

The primary **advantage** of distribution models is that they allow the various levels in the distribution chain to manage their inventories autonomously. The primary **disadvantage** of these models is that they ignore the other stages in the supply chain, leading to stock-outs and back orders. Excess shipping costs can be incurred since no one is coordinating the movement of materials within the system. Also, the demand for replenishment occurs without any regard for what is currently being produced or planned to be produced. Under these situations, the need for an item incurs extra setup costs, lost productivity, and excess transportation costs.

(A) Single Order Point System

The single order point system basically ignores the fact that the order takes place in a chain and assumes that each element in the distribution system is independent of all other components. This independent behavior can cause large swings caused by a phenomenon called lumpy demand at the next level down in the distribution chain. Lumpy demand comes from the lack of communication and coordination among the factory, warehouse(s), distributors, and retailers.

(B) Double Order Point System

The double order point system considers two levels down in the distribution system, hence the name "double." For example, if a distributor is quoted a lead time from the factory warehouse of two weeks and it takes the factory warehouse three weeks to have stock replenished, the reorder point is set based on the demand for a five-week period. This system does not produce lumpy demand, as does the single order point system. An advantage is that it reduces the risk of stock-outs. Increasing the safety stock is its disadvantage.

(C) Periodic Review System

In a periodic review system, orders are placed on a predetermined time schedule. The advantage is that order times can be staggered throughout the chain to smooth demand at each point in the distribution chain. This reduces peaks and valleys caused by several customers ordering at the same time.

(D) Sales Replacement System

In the sales replacement system, the supplier ships only what the customer used or sold during the period. The objective is to maintain a stable inventory level in the system. This method requires having enough inventory to cover the potential demand during the replenishment cycle. In essence, the sales replacement system is a periodic review model with variable order quantities.

(E) Distribution Requirements Planning

Distribution requirements planning (DRP) is an application of the time-phasing logic of material requirements planning (MRP) applied to the distribution system. The purpose of DRP is to forecast the demand by distribution center to determine the master production scheduling needs. DRP uses forecasts and known order patterns from customers in the distribution chain to develop the demand on the master schedule.

DISTRIBUTION REQUIREMENT PLANNING VERSUS ORDER POINT–BASED DISTRIBUTION SYSTEM

- The DRP anticipates future needs throughout the distribution chain and plans deliveries accordingly.
- The order point–based distribution system does not anticipate future needs. It simply reacts to the current needs.

(F) Inventory Distribution Methods

The functions of warehouse distribution, production, and purchasing are closely interrelated and constantly interacting with each other in a manufacturing firm. The decision problems considered during inventory distribution strategy are:

- When, what, and how much to ship to a warehouse.
- When, what, and how much to produce at the factory, with what size workforce.
- When, what, and how much to purchase as inputs to the factory warehouse system.

(G) Warehouse Inventory Control

In a distribution system, warehouses usually stand between a factory and final customers or other warehouses, as shown in Exhibit 1.47.

EXHIBIT 1.47 Warehouse Inventory Control

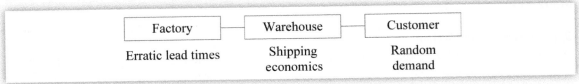

On the sales side, warehouses face a demand from customers that usually is subject to random demand fluctuations and usually requires fast service. On the supply side, warehouses usually face significant and sometimes erratic lead time for receiving shipments of products from factories.

Payments to carriers for making shipments to the warehouse are frequently of major importance in designing the warehouse ordering and distribution system. Economies usually can be achieved by increasing the size of shipment up to some upper limit, such as a full truckload or carload. Efforts to economize on shipping costs by increasing the size of shipments increase the time between shipments and hence decrease the speed of service.

(H) Types of Warehouse Shipments

Warehouses usually stock a very large number of products—the larger the shipment size, the more products are involved, and the greater are the problems of controlling the inventories of different products jointly. These are some of the considerations involved in decisions to order shipment to warehouses. Two basic types of shipments can take place: periodic shipments and trigger shipments (see Exhibit 1.48).

EXHIBIT 1.48 Types of Warehouse Shipments

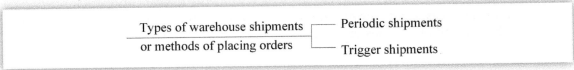

Periodic Shipments. The periodic system of placing orders has the virtue of automatically synchronizing the decisions on many products. Under this system of operation, warehouse shipping decisions can be handled in two steps. First, the product can be considered in the aggregate, and next the shipping costs for different sizes of shipping lot can be weighed against the cost of holding inventory associated with each size lot. On this basis, the optimum shipping lot can be determined. By using the forecasted aggregate shipping rate, the decision period can be determined.

The shipment received at the beginning of a period is associated with the period because that shipment must carry the warehouse through the period. However, because the lead time Tl is required to obtain the shipment, the order for the tth period must be initiated a length of time Tl before the beginning of the tth period. When the time arrives for placing an order, the inventory records for the products involved are brought up to date. The position of inventories on hand and on order is then known. Orders can then be placed for the amount of each product to be included in the shipment on the basis of expected product sales, initial inventory position at the time of ordering, and expected final inventory position at the end of the period.

In calculating the distribution of forecast errors, the forecast span is $(Tl + Td)$, where Td is the length of the decision period, which is equal to the interval between the receipt of shipments.

When decisions on the timing of a shipment are made in advance, any random fluctuations in aggregate sales tend to cause shipment sizes to vary randomly. This may be quite satisfactory in situations where shipments of less than a truckload or carload are being made and variations in the size of the shipment can be accommodated readily. If the fluctuations in the size of the shipment exceed the available capacity, a supplementary shipment may be required or the aggregate inventory buffer may be changed.

Trigger Shipments. A warehouse may aggregate its products and decide on the optimal size of shipment but allow timing to be triggered by sales. Because the timing of shipments is irregular, orders for individual products cannot depend on a simple constant lead time. Instead, *the lead time for any single product is a random variable that depends partly on orders placed for other products.* When the total orders for all products have reached the total desired for a shipping lot, the orders will be placed for a shipment. Under this system, the lead time for any one product is a random variable that depends on the random sales of other products. The outcome for an individual product depends on the correlation between its sales and the aggregate sales.

Advantages and Disadvantages. The trigger system is more responsive to fluctuations in sales than the periodic system is. A further advantage is that shipment size is predetermined rather than random; hence problems of overburdening carrier capacity are minimized. However, the costs of administering the continuous review of inventory position for a trigger system are usually somewhat higher than under the periodic system.

Cost of Alternative Shipping Carriers. In estimating the cost of alternative shipping carriers, the cost of having valuable inventory tied up while the vehicle is in transit should be considered. While this cost usually is not large, taking it into account will systematically lower the costs of using faster rather than slower carriers. Another economy associated with fast shipments that may be overlooked is the fact that time in transit is one component of lead time. *Shortening the lead time allows a reduction in inventory buffers and hence a decrease in inventory holding costs.*

A warehouse may be put under a financial constraint in response to the working capital needs of the company; the warehouse also may be constrained by the production-smoothing requirements of the factory; and the warehouse itself may have certain constraints on its capacity to receive shipment or its storage space. Some constraints may be equality constraints on the exact amount of inventory that should be held, and some may be inequality restraints that establish upper or lower limits. Briefly stated, if an inequality restraint is not violated when the corresponding variable is set to zero, then the constraint can be ignored. If it is violated, then the solution is carried through as if an exact constraint applied.

In estimating the costs of stock-outs at the warehouse, the least costly alternative should be used. If the warehouse is out of stock on a product, it may disappoint a customer, or it may initiate a rush order from another warehouse or from the factory. In the latter cases, the cost of depletion may well be the cost of making a special rush shipment, taking into account communication and expediting costs. Although few warehouses keep adequate records on stock-outs and failures to render customer service, these data could be useful in estimating depletion costs as well as costs associated with customer service.

When estimating the cost of holding inventory, the cost of obsolescence should be considered. The indirect costs of having very large inventories in a warehouse may be increased because of product damage resulting from high stacking. Also, increased handling costs from crowded aisles and poor housekeeping and access may show up as overtime payments.

A single warehouse may utilize several different decision systems on different types of products or products from different suppliers according to particular needs. For example, fast-moving products might be segregated from slow-moving products, and a different decision system may be used for each.

(f) Outsourced Business Processes

This subsection discusses the scope, reasons, risks, and benefits from outsourcing. It focuses on how to conduct due diligence reviews in selecting outsourced service providers and how to write the required contractual provisions. It defines vendor governance, service levels required of outsourced vendors, including performance metrics. In addition, it provides guidance on how to manage third-party outsourced organizations.

(i) Outsourced Services Defined

An **outsourced service provider** broadly includes all entities or firms that have entered into a contractual relationship with a user organization (i.e., the company engaging the service provider) to provide business functions or operational activities. Examples of these functions or activities include accounting, internal audit, human resources, sales and marketing, procurement, tax and legal services, risk and insurance management, and IT. Outsourcing a business function does not mean abdication of management's responsibility. Instead, it means management is searching for the best alternative in an effective and efficient manner and knowing that management is always responsible for and accountable for all business functions, whether they are outsourced or not.

The ability to contract for business or technology services typically enables an organization to offer its customers enhanced services without the various expenses involved in owning the required technology or maintaining the human capital required to deploy and operate it. In many situations, outsourcing offers the organization a cost-effective alternative to in-house capabilities. Outsourcing, however, does not reduce the fundamental risks associated with IT or the business lines that use it. Risks, such as loss of funds, loss of competitive advantage, damaged reputation, improper disclosure of information, and regulatory action, remain. Because the functions are performed by an organization outside the financial institution, for example, the risks may be realized in a different manner than if the functions were inside the organization resulting in the need for controls designed to monitor such risks.

(ii) Scope of Outsourcing

Outsourcing means an organization goes "outside" for the knowledge and experience required to do a specific job. In simpler terms, it means subcontracting or farming out for business functions, systems, and services. The scope of outsourcing includes human resources, tax, legal, help-desk services, technical support, telecommunications and network, facilities (computer center) management, disaster recovery services, education and training, ongoing hardware maintenance, data center design and construction, equipment relocation services, systems integration, application development and maintenance, and other services. The scope is broad and could include all or part of any function, service, process, or system operation.

(iii) In-Source Analysis versus Outsource Analysis

Manufacturing companies usually perform a make-or-buy analysis when deciding to manufacture a part or component inside the company or to buy it from the outside companies. Costs for each choice (make or buy) are developed and compared to determine which choice is less costly.

Similarly, purchasing or procurement management in a retail company can perform in-source or outsource analysis to determine whether to in-source a product (i.e., buying from the same supplier as before) or outsource a product (i.e., buying from a different supplier now). Costs for each choice (in-source or outsource) are developed and compared to determine which choice is less costly.

Examples of IT operations frequently outsourced by financial organizations include: the origination, processing, and settlement of payments and financial transactions; information processing related to customer account creation and maintenance; other information and transaction processing activities that support critical banking functions, such as loan processing, deposit processing, fiduciary and trading activities; security monitoring and testing; system development and maintenance; network operations; help desk operations; and call centers.

(iv) Decision Criteria in Outsourcing

From a strategic viewpoint, user organizations should outsource only noncore functions and keep core functions in-house. Core functions are those that closely relate to and are vital to achieving a user organization's mission, vision, strategy, success, and growth. Note that core functions for each user organization could be different. For example, core functions for a manufacturing company are operations (i.e., production, supply chain, logistics, and inventory), marketing, and finance.

User organizations often outsource their business functions in five cases:

1. Senior management is managing too many internal functions with little time available.

2. Skills and competency levels of internal employees are scarce.

3. Internal operating costs for managing business function are slowly increasing year after year.

4. External vendors possess unique and specialized skills that internal employees do not have.

5. Senior management can improve core functions better because more time can be allocated to them.

Deciding on a wrong function to outsource has several negative consequences, including

- Changing business outcomes
- Creating unknown problems
- Increased operating costs
- Noncompliance with laws, rules, and regulations
- Delaying services to customers

In summary, deciding what function to outsource is more critical than deciding when to outsource (time and conditions), where to outsource (domestic, foreign, local, and regional vendors), and whom to outsource to (known, unknown, old, or new vendors).

(v) Reasons for Outsourcing

Management may choose to outsource business operations and functions for various reasons. These include:

- Gaining operational or financial efficiencies
- Increasing management focus on core business functions
- Refocusing limited internal resources on core functions
- Obtaining specialized expertise
- Increasing availability of services
- Accelerating delivery of products or services through new delivery channels
- Increasing ability to acquire and support current technology and avoid obsolescence
- Conserving capital for other business ventures

Outsourcing of business or technology-related services may improve quality, reduce costs, strengthen controls, and achieve any of the objectives listed previously. Ultimately, the decision to outsource should fit into the organization's overall strategic plan and corporate objectives.

Before considering the outsourcing of significant functions, an organization's directors and senior management should ensure such actions are consistent with their strategic plans and should evaluate proposals against well-developed acceptance criteria. The degree of oversight and review of outsourced activities will depend on the criticality of the service, process, or system to the organization's operation as well as quality of service and quality of protection.

(vi) Risks from the Use of Service Providers

Organizations should have a comprehensive outsourcing risk management process to govern their business or technology service provider relationships. The process should include risk assessment, selection of service providers, contract review, and monitoring of service providers. Outsourced relationships should be subject to the same risk management, security, privacy, and other policies that would be expected if the organization were conducting the activities in-house.

The use of service providers and third parties to perform operational functions present various risks to user organizations. Some risks are inherent to the outsourced activity itself, whereas others are introduced with the involvement of a service provider. If service providers are not managed effectively, their use may expose user organizations to risks that can result in regulatory action, financial loss, litigation cases, and loss of reputation.

User organizations should consider these seven risks before entering into and while managing outsourcing arrangements:

1. **Operational risks** arise when a service provider exposes a user organization to losses due to inadequate or failed internal processes or systems or from external events/threats and human error.
2. **Compliance risks** arise when the service, products, or activities of a service provider fail to comply with applicable laws, rules, and regulations (LRRs).
3. **Concentration risks** arise when outsourced services or products are provided by a limited number of service providers or are concentrated in limited geographic locations (i.e., regional or local).
4. **Reputational risks** arise when actions or poor performance of a service provider causes the public to form a negative opinion about a user organization.

5. **Legal risks** arise when a service provider exposes a user organization to legal expenses and possible lawsuits.

6. **Country risks** arise when a user organization engages a foreign-based service provider, exposing the user organization to possible economic, social, and political conditions and events/threats from the country where the service provider is located. A few additional requirements apply to the foreign-based service providers: (1) complying with the U.S. laws and regulations, (2) receiving home-country permission to conduct on-site operational reviews by host-country staff; and (3) home-country staff accessing host-country computer systems and vice versa.

7. **Technology risks** arise when a service provider's computer technology platforms do not fit well with the user organization's computer technology platforms; business computer application systems lack adequate security protections; security controls over network equipment and mobile devices are weak; and computer backup and contingency plans are not tested.

According to Neo Advisory at www.neogroup.com, offshore outsourcing comes with risk, including cultural compatibility, legal framework, technical infrastructure, geopolitical risks, and security and privacy risks. Security concerns over the IT outsourced vendors include these:

■ Business continuity and disaster recovery, which includes risk assessments, restoration process, testing of backup systems, audits, ongoing monitoring, managing the alternate site, key resources, and post disaster communication

■ Information protection, which includes vulnerability assessment and penetration studies (technical and nontechnical), data access, data audits, data security, data transmission, data storage, and virus management

■ Data backup and recovery, which includes scheduled backups, data recovery, nonstorage of production code and data in an offshore location, and disposal of sensitive data

■ Insurance coverage, which includes protection over buildings, equipment, personnel, and electronic information

■ Intellectual property rights protection, which includes agreements, country laws, data security, physical security, legal obligations, compliance to international security and data privacy standards, logging and auditing, employee contract, and security management training.

■ Network security, which includes dedicated infrastructure, network security, and network device security.

■ Personnel security, which includes background checks, reference checks, integrity checks, nondisclosure and confidentiality agreements, Internet usage, suppliers' access to hardware, usage of mobile commuting, and housekeeping.

■ Physical security, which includes access control, limited access, camera surveillance, and fire safety.

(vii) Due Diligence and Selection of Service Providers

A user organization should conduct an evaluation of and perform the necessary due diligence review for a prospective service provider prior to engaging the service provider. The depth and formality of this review will vary depending on: (1) the scope, complexity, location, and importance of the planned outsourcing arrangement; (2) the user organization's familiarity with prospective service providers; and (3) reputation and industry standing of the service provider. Throughout the due diligence review process, a user organization's financial team, technical consultants, operational experts, legal analysts, external consultants, and business staff must be engaged in the review and approval process.

Three major areas of due diligence review of a prospective service provider include:

1. Business background, reputation, and strategy
2. Financial performance and condition
3. Operations and internal controls

Business background, reputation, and strategy looks into seven areas of a service provider:

1. Its status in the industry, corporate history and qualifications, and accomplishments
2. Its reputation of management
3. Whether it conducts background checks when hiring employees
4. The qualifications and competencies of people to perform the service
5. Compatibility of the business model of the two companies
6. Required licenses and certifications for service staff
7. Any pending legal or regulatory compliance issues, including number of legal cases filed, complaints registered, and cases resolved and pending; the amount of fines and penalties assessed, announced, and protested; and the amount of fines paid and not paid.

Financial performance and condition looks into four areas:

1. Most recent financial statements and annual reports with regard to outstanding commitments, such as debt and other obligations, capital strength, liquidity, and operating results
2. Sustainability record in terms of number of years in service business and the percentage annual growth of market share
3. Adequacy of insurance coverage
4. Financial condition of any contractors and subcontractors employed

Operations and internal controls look into seven areas:

1. Compliance with applicable laws and regulations
2. Adequacy of operating standards, policies, procedures, and internal controls
3. Employee training programs and hiring controls, such as background checks
4. Business record retention and maintenance procedures
5. Security controls over data, equipment, and devices
6. Whether computer systems development and maintenance work is in-sourced (less risk) or outsourced (more risk)
7. Whether business continuity, resumption, and contingency plans are developed and tested (i.e., tested is less risky and not tested is more risky)

(viii) Contract Provisions and Considerations

User organizations should understand the service contract and legal issues associated with proposed outsourcing arrangements. The terms of service agreement with defined service levels should be included in the written contract developed and approved by the legal counsel prior to signing and execution. Internal auditors can review and evaluate the terms and conditions of the contract, including provisions for the breach of contract, remedies, and consequential actions. Specific topics in the written contract can include these:

- Scope of work, rights and responsibilities of each party, time frames, insurance coverage, compliance with laws and regulations, and the ability to subcontract service providers (domestic or foreign) after verifying their financial condition. Foreign-based service providers need to comply with U.S. laws as well as the laws in their own countries. Legal advice is required regarding the enforcement and ramifications of foreign contractual arrangements.

- Costs, fees, commissions, and compensation for services.

- Right to audit with access to audit reports from the servicer, including the frequency of the audit reports and on-site inspections by the auditors or others.

- Establishment and monitoring of performance standards for products, services, processes, people, and technology.

- Protecting user organizations' confidential and sensitive information with proper security and privacy controls.

- Ownership and license issues, such as who owns the data generated by service providers, what data from a user organization service providers can use, whether a software escrow agreement is available for purchasing software from service providers.

- Indemnification of user organizations for any claims filed against the user organization resulting from the service provider's gross negligence.

- Dispute resolution in terms of speed and satisfaction.

- Limits on liability established by service providers to make sure those limits are in line with the assumed risks.

- Customer complaints in terms of tracking and resolution.

- Business resumption and contingency plan of the service provider in terms of its responsibility to back up data; to develop, maintain, and test the contingency plans; and to submit the test results to the user organization.

- Default and termination conditions, including:
  - Defining what constitutes a default;
  - Acceptable remedies and opportunities for curing default;
  - Contract termination and notification procedures;
  - Preservation and timely return of user organization's data, records, and materials;
  - Remedies for not meeting performance standards with damages paid;
  - Conditions when to transfer services to another service provider as a backup provision; and
  - Required notices to user organizations about changes in control and ownership; merger or acquisition plans; violations of laws, rules, and regulations; business failures and closures; and insolvency and bankruptcy of a service provider.

(ix) Benefits of Outsourcing

Organizations turn to outsourcing to improve performance (system and people) and to reduce operating costs. On the positive side, outsourcing offers solutions when there is a shortage of in-house skills, when a high-risk and high-overhead project needs to be managed, and when there is an unacceptable lead time to complete a project using company personnel.

The benefits from outsourcing usually focus on performance improvements and/or cost reduction. Another benefit is that it allows internal management to devote its time and resources more to the core business and the company's future. Outsourcing prevents hiring additional employees to meet temporary needs. However, outsourcing does not mean surrendering control and internal management responsibility of subcontracted functions and projects to outside vendors.

Some of the organization's IT employees could work for the outsourcing vendor. The key point here is to monitor the performance of the outsourced vendor during the contract period. Selection of an outsourcing vendor is no different from selecting other types of vendors. Selection factors such as proximity of the vendor, attitude of the vendor's personnel, vendor's reputation and knowledge, and the vendor's financial condition and management's integrity are important to consider.

The fixed-price-type service contract is best for the user organization because the price is known in advance. However, the fixed-price contract may not be feasible in all situations, especially when cost variables are uncertain and vendors may overbid because of perceived risk and because they have never done this kind of work before. An alternative is the incentive contract where (1) attainable targets are communicated to the contractor and (2) incentive arrangements are designed to motivate contractor efforts that might not otherwise be emphasized and discourage contractor inefficiency and waste. Another type of contract is the share-in-savings arrangement, which includes not only sharing in costs and savings but also providing training and education to the supplier.

The contract should spell out vendor performance-level guarantees, the remedies for nonperformance, and the right to audit clause. Contractual risks can be addressed or mitigated through terms and conditions, vendor certifications, evaluation factors for award, and risk mitigation requirements included in the statement of work.

From the economics point of view, the outsourcing approach provides an option to buy IT or business services from outsiders rather than from the organization's IT or other departments. Users can perform make-or-buy analysis to see which approach would be more cost effective.

(x) Vendor Governance

Vendor governance requires a vendor to establish written policies, procedures, standards, and guidelines regarding how to deal with its customers or clients in a professional and businesslike manner. It also requires establishing an oversight mechanism and implementing best practices in the industry. Customer (user) organizations should consider these five criteria when selecting potential hardware, software, consulting, or contracting vendors:

1. Experience in producing or delivering high-quality security products and services on time and all the time

2. Track record in responding to security flaws in vendor products, project management skills, and cost and budget controls

3. Methods to handle software and hardware maintenance, end user support, and maintenance agreements

4. Vendor's long-term financial, operational, technical, and strategic viability

5. Adherence to rules of engagement during contractual agreements, procurement processes, and product/service testing

(xi) Service-Level Agreements

Contractual agreements in procurement processes for outsourced vendors should include a service-level agreement (SLA). For example, the SLA represents the understanding between the cloud subscriber and cloud provider about the expected level of service to be delivered and, in the event that the provider fails to deliver the service at the level specified, the compensation available to the cloud subscriber. The overall scope of the service contract or service agreement includes the SLA, licensing of services, criteria for acceptable use, service suspension and termination, liabilities, guarantees, privacy policy, and modifications to the terms of service.

SLAs are focused approaches for computer center management to improve the quality of computing services to system users. The computer center management must define a set of user service levels or service objectives that describe application systems, transaction volume, processing windows, online system response times, and batch job turnaround times. Without well-defined service levels to monitor against actual performance determined in the resource utilization function, a computer system's capacity limit is difficult to identify.

Without SLAs, the computer center management will consider computer capacity at its limit when users begin to complain about computer performance. By monitoring performance against SLAs, computer center management can identify upcoming problems in meeting service objectives. In order to achieve these goals, computer center management needs to develop service-level objectives for internal use.

(xii) Areas Needing Service-Level Objectives

Some examples of IT areas requiring service-level objectives are:

- System capacity during peak hours in terms of average central processing unit (CPU) usage, average demand paging rate, and maximum channel activity

- Number of online users, of online transactions per minute, and of batch jobs per hour

- Online system average response time in seconds by application

- Percentage of time the online system is available

- Turnaround time for test and production batch jobs processed under each job class by application

For each of these objectives, a range of minimum and maximum numbers should be identified. The rationale behind developing service-level objectives internally first is that they provide a basis for negotiating SLAs with the user community.

(xiii) Performance Metrics for Service Levels

After developing service-level objectives internally, IT management is ready to negotiate with each business user to develop formal SLAs in terms of performance metrics. Some examples of these metrics include:

- Number of complaints received from system users for each application system

- Average response times for each online application system

- Turnaround times for each batch job by application system
- System availability time (system uptime) by each application system
- Accuracy limits in terms of number of errors by cause for each application system
- Number of job reruns by each application system
- Number of transactions to be processed during peak hours in each application system
- Number of production problems by application system per week
- Computer-report delivery times by application system
- A plan for reporting service-level problems
- Action priorities if services cannot be delivered
- Scheduled meetings to discuss service levels between end users and computer center management
- Number of job reruns and time lost due to job reruns
- Number of abnormal terminations by application program per operating shift

It is important to remember that these SLAs are not static. They require periodic adjustment and refinement, such as at least once a year or preferably when renegotiating the agreement with customers (users).

(xiv) Third-Party Organizations

Third parties include external organizations such as business partnerships, joint ventures, licensing agreements, outsourcing arrangements, and supply chain exchanges (with acquirers, integrators, and suppliers). Note that there could be more than one supplier in an outsourcing arrangement or supply chain exchange. External organizations operate external systems to provide the needed software products and support services to internal user organizations.

The growing dependence on external service providers and new relationships being forged with those providers present new and difficult challenges for organizations, especially in the area of information system security. These challenges include:

- Defining the types of external services provided to the organization
- Describing how the external services are protected in accordance with the security requirements of the organization
- Obtaining the necessary assurances that the risk to organizational operations and assets, individuals, and other organizations arising from the use of the external services is acceptable

The assurance or confidence that the risk from using external services is at an acceptable level depends on the trust that the organization places in the external service provider. This leads to three security issues that must be addressed:

- Level of trust
- Level of control
- Chain of trust

In some cases, the **level of trust** is based on the amount of direct control the organization is able to exert on the external service provider with regard to employment of security controls necessary for the protection of the service and the evidence brought forth as to the effectiveness of those controls.

The **level of control** is usually established by the terms and conditions of the contract or SLA with the external service provider and can range from extensive (e.g., negotiating a contract or agreement that specifies detailed security control requirements for the provider) to very limited (e.g., using a standard contract or SLA to obtain commodity services, such as commercial tele-communications services).

In other cases, the level of trust is based on factors that convince the user organization that the requisite security controls have been employed and that a determination of control effectiveness exists. For example, a separately authorized external information system service provided to an organization through a well-established line of business relationship may provide a degree of trust in the external service within the tolerable risk range of management.

Ultimately, the responsibility for adequately mitigating unacceptable risks arising from the use of external information system services remains with the user organization's management. Organizations require that an appropriate **chain of trust** be established with external service providers when dealing with the many issues associated with information system security. A chain of trust requires that the organization establish and retain a level of confidence that each participating service provider in the potentially complex consumer-provider relationship provides adequate protection for the services rendered to the organization.

The chain of trust can be complicated due to the number of entities participating in the consumer-provider relationship and the type of relationship between the parties (i.e., long or short supply chain). External service providers may also in turn outsource the services to other external entities, making the chain of trust even more complicated and difficult to manage. Depending on the nature of the service, it may be unwise for an organization to place significant trust in the service provider, not due to any inherent untrustworthiness on the provider's part but due to the intrinsic level of risk in the service.

Where a significant level of trust cannot be established in the external services and/or service providers, the user organization (1) employs compensating security controls, (2) accepts a greater degree of risk, (3) does not obtain the service, or (4) performs business operations with reduced levels of functionality or no functionality at all.

The chain of trust is related to the level of confidence, level of trust, level of control, and degree of trust in that order.

Chain of Trust = Level of Confidence $\longrightarrow$ Level of Trust $\longrightarrow$ Level of Control $\longrightarrow$ Degree of Trust

(xv) Managing Third-Party Organizations

Managing third-party organizations and their systems is a difficult and complicated task because they are not under the direct control of the user organizations. Managing requires four steps:

1. Needs assessment (i.e., initial risk assessment and security requirements).

2. Service contract (i.e., request for information (RFI), request for proposal (RFP), or request for quotation (RFQ)), statement of work, contract negotiations, SLA agreement,

and due diligence). Before finalizing a service contract, a due diligence review should be performed, and these documents should be prepared: an RFP, a statement of work, and an SLA (in that order).

3. Security appraisal (i.e., system vulnerabilities, software patches and upgrades, security incidents, software disposal/decommissioning, and change management).

4. Third-party audit (i.e., review of operational systems of external service providers).

1.8 Project Management and Change Management

This section describes two major topics: project management techniques (e.g., program evaluation and review technique (PERT) and critical path method (CPM)) and change management methods.

(a) Project Management Techniques

In order for projects to be successfully implemented, they must be well managed. Many organizations apply a variety of project management techniques to optimize project success and enhance the likelihood of meeting project-specific as well as organization-wide goals. These techniques include monitoring project performance, establishing incentives to meet project goals, and developing a project management team with the right people and the right skills. All these techniques can help avert cost overruns, schedule delays, and performance problems common to many organizations.

It is important to develop performance measures and link project outcomes to business unit and strategic goals and objectives. The key is monitoring project performance and establishing incentives for accountability and using cross-functional teams to involve those with the technical and operational expertise necessary to plan and manage the project.

Typically, a **project plan** is used to manage and control project implementation. It includes performance measurement baselines for schedule and cost, major milestones, and target dates and risks associated with the project. By tracking cost, schedule, and technical performance, a project team is aware of potential problem areas and is able to determine any impact of the deviation and decide if corrective action is needed. Regular review of the status of cost, schedule, and technical performance goals by individuals outside the project team allows for an independent assessment of the project and verification that the project is meeting stated goals.

Major projects should include **multidisciplinary teams**, consisting of individuals from different functional areas and led by a project manager, to plan and manage projects. Typically, a core project team is established early in the life cycle of a project, and additional individuals with particular technical or operational expertise are added during appropriate phases of the project. The team must not only possess technical and operational expertise, but it must also be composed of the "right" people. The selection of the team members is critical—they must be knowledgeable, willing to trade off leadership roles, and able to plan work and set goals in a team setting. The successful team will have a high spirit, trust, and enthusiasm. A sense of ownership and the drive of the team committed to a project are key factors in the successful completion of a project. This integrated and comprehensive approach improves communication between upper management and project managers and among the various stakeholders in the project. It also increases the likelihood that potential problems will be identified and resolved quickly, thus increasing the chances that the project will remain on schedule and within budget.

(i) Why Project Management?

Management needs to know what parts of the project or program are most likely to cause serious delays. This knowledge will lead to management actions that will achieve the project or program objectives and deadlines.

When is project management preferred? The project management approach is the preferred method for dealing with projects defined once. The task is very complex and involves interdependence between a number of departments. The task has great significance to the organization. Onetime tasks can be accomplished with a minimum interruption of routine business.

Managers need to coordinate diverse activities toward a common goal. Management must devise plans that will tell with reasonable accuracy how the efforts of the people representing these functions should be directed toward the project's completion. In order to devise such plans and implement them, management must be able to collect pertinent information to:

- Form a basis for prediction and planning
- Evaluate alternative plans for accomplishing the objective
- Check progress against current plans and objectives
- Form a basis for obtaining the facts so that decisions can be made and the job can be done

A single master plan for a project should include planning, scheduling, and controlling functions. The plan should point directly to the difficult and significant activities—the problem of achieving the objective. For example, the plan should form the basis of a system for management by exception. It should indicate the exceptions (red flags). Under such a system, management need act only when deviations from the plan occur.

A reporting system should be designed for middle to senior management to use. The monthly progress report calls for specific reestimates only for those events on critical paths and subcritical events. The report should accomplish these tasks:

- Preparing a master schedule for a project
- Revising schedules to meet changing conditions in the most economical way
- Keeping senior management and the operating department management advised of project progress and changes

Plans should be separated from scheduling. **Planning** is the act of stating what activities must occur in a project and in what order these activities must take place. **Scheduling** follows planning and is defined as the act of producing project timetables in consideration of the plan and costs. **Controlling** is ensuring that plans are accomplished. The correct sequence is

$$\text{Planning} \longrightarrow \text{Scheduling} \longrightarrow \text{Controlling}$$

Project structure is a characteristic of all projects that provides for all work being performed in some well-defined order. For example: In R&D and product planning, specifications must be determined before drawings can be made. In advertising, artwork must be made before layouts can be done. Exhibit 1.49 shows factors responsible for a successful performance of a project as well as symptoms of project management failures.

EXHIBIT 1.49 Successful Factors and Symptoms of Project Management Failures

Factors Responsible for Successful Project Performance	Symptoms of Project Management Failures
Organization of the project	High costs
Authority of the project manager	Schedule overruns
Scheduling and planning techniques used	Poor-quality product
Project manager's good relationship with senior management	Failure to meet project objectives
	Customer or user dissatisfaction with end result
Use of resources, including slack time	

(ii) Project Management's Basic Guidelines

Basic guidelines for project management are listed next.

1. **Define the objective(s) of the project.** This includes defining management's intent in undertaking the project, outlining the scope of the project, and describing the end results of the project including its effects on the organization.

2. **Establish a project organization.** This includes appointment of one experienced manager to run the project full time, organization of the project management function in terms of responsibilities, assignment of manpower to the project team, and maintenance of a balance of power between the functional department managers and the project manager.

3. **Install project controls.** This includes controls over time, cost, and quality.

(iii) Project Organization

Project organization is where the reporting relationships and the work location rest predominantly with the project manager. Three common types of project organization include the traditional structure, the matrix organization, and the hybrid form (see Exhibit 1.50).

EXHIBIT 1.50 Types of Project Organization

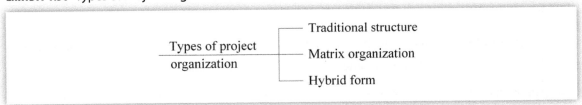

In a **traditional structure**, the basic interrelationship is with the functional manager. A hierarchy of reporting relationships is followed. In a **matrix organization**, most of the personnel are directly responsible to the project manager for work assignments but remain physically located with their functional manager. Other forms of organization include combining a large project team with several small functional teams or basic functional teams with a small project task force.

Matrix team members must learn new ways of relating and working together to solve cross-functional problems and to attain synergy. According to Dr. Jack Baugh,[15] the matrix management structure must be used when there is:

---

[15] *WINGS: Project Leaders Guide*, Volumes 1 and 2 (King of Prussia, PA: AGS Management Systems, 1986). Original citation by Dr. Jack Baugh of Hughes Aircraft Company.

1. A rapid technological advancement, a need for timely decisions

2. A vast quantity of data to be analyzed

3. An increased volume of new products and services to be introduced

4. A need for simultaneous dual decision making

5. A strong constraint on financial and/or human resources

Baugh also cited reasons for using a matrix management structure. According to Baugh, such a structure:

1. Provides a flexible adaptive system

2. Provides timely, balanced decision making

3. Permits rapid management response to a changing market and technology

4. Trains managers for ambiguity, complexity, and executive positions

5. Helps in synergizing and motivating human resources

The **hybrid form** is the best possible option since it can achieve technical excellence and, at the same time, meet cost and schedule deadlines.

Project authority is a measure of the degree of control the project manager has over all the activities necessary to complete the project successfully. Delays can be reduced if the project manager can make decisions without having to wait for the approval of someone higher up. This type of delay is often the cause of schedule and cost overruns.

The authority of the project manager is seldom spelled out in formal directives or policies. The traditional forms of management—one person, one boss—is simply not adequate for completing projects.

A natural conflict can exist between the project manager and the functional manager. It is the influence rather than the authority that matters. What counts is the priority assigned to the project and the experience and personal characteristics of the project manager. *There may not be any relation between the formal authority of the project manager and the actual success of the project.*

KEY CONCEPTS TO REMEMBER: Most Common Reasons for Project Management Failures

- The basis for a project is not sound.

- The wrong person is appointed as the project manager.

- Company management fails to provide enough support.

- Task definitions are inadequate.

- Management monitoring techniques are not appropriate.

- Project termination is not planned properly (i.e., to reduce adverse effects on the employee's progress in the company after the project is completed).

- Redefinitions of the project's scope are unclear.

- Large-scale design changes are occurring.

- Additional funding is not approved.

(iv) Problems in Project Management

Project managers face unusual problems in trying to direct and harmonize the diverse forces at work in the project situation. Their main difficulties arise from three sources: organizational uncertainties, unusual decision pressures, and inadequate senior management support (see Exhibit 1.51).

EXHIBIT 1.51 Nature of Project Problems

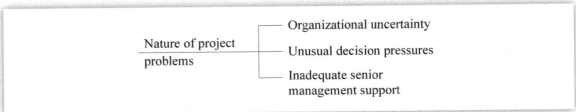

(A) Organizational Uncertainty

In a situation of organizational uncertainty, the working relationships between the project manager and the functional department managers have not been clearly defined by senior management. Uncertainties arise with respect to handling delays, cost overruns, work assignments, and design changes. Unless the project manager is skillful in handling these situations, senior management may resolve them in the interest of functional departments, at the expense of the project as a whole.

(B) Unusual Decision Pressures

When uncertainties are added to the situation, the project manager has to make decisions based on limited data and with little or no analysis. The project manager must move fast, even if it means making an intuitive decision that might expose him or her to senior management criticism. *Decisions to sacrifice time for cost, cost for quality, or quality for time are common in most projects.* These trade-offs are clear indications that the project manager needs support from senior management.

(C) Inadequate Senior Management Support

Senior management seldom can give the project manager as much guidance and support as his or her line counterpart gets. Delays in initial approval of the project by senior management, inability to resolve conflicts between the project manager and the functional department managers, and delays in allocating resources are the most common issues on which the project manager needs more attention from senior management. Otherwise, project performance can be hampered.

(v) Project Scheduling Techniques

The six project scheduling techniques discussed in this section are listed next.

1. Program evaluation and review techniques (PERT)

2. Critical path methods (CPMs)

3. Line-of-balance (LOB) method

4. Graphical evaluation and review technique (GERT)

5. Work breakdown structure (WBS)

6. Gantt chart

(See Exhibit 1.52.)

EXHIBIT 1.52 Project Scheduling Techniques

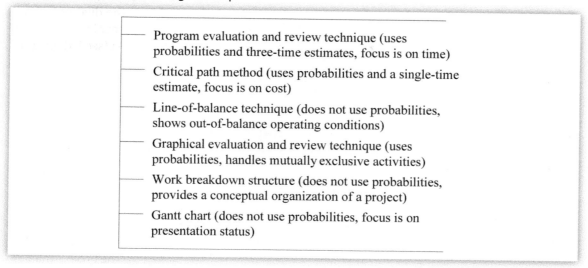

— Program evaluation and review technique (uses probabilities and three-time estimates, focus is on time)

— Critical path method (uses probabilities and a single-time estimate, focus is on cost)

— Line-of-balance technique (does not use probabilities, shows out-of-balance operating conditions)

— Graphical evaluation and review technique (uses probabilities, handles mutually exclusive activities)

— Work breakdown structure (does not use probabilities, provides a conceptual organization of a project)

— Gantt chart (does not use probabilities, focus is on presentation status)

(A) Program Evaluation and Review Techniques

Project management frequently uses network diagrams to plan projects, evaluate alternatives, and control large and complex projects toward completion. PERT requires extremely careful plans from the very outset of a project. These careful plans allow management to allocate resources to important areas before they become critical. Doing so will alert a manager to trouble areas or bottlenecks before they become major problems and sources of project overruns. PERT also helps to allocate resources but has no influence on the excellence of the end product.

PERT improves communication upward to the manager and the customer (client). PERT lets the supervisor believe that the project manager is doing a superior job, regardless of how well the project manager is actually performing.

PERT Features. Features of PERT are listed next.

- PERT manages one-of-a-kind programs as opposed to repetitive tasks. It develops a network diagram that identifies the sequence of events and their relationships to one another along with estimated start and completion times.

SENSITIVITY ANALYSIS AND PERT

Sensitivity analysis can be performed on the PERT network. This analysis provides the ability to check the feasibility of current schedules and to permit management to experiment with or evaluate the effects of proposed changes.

- Uncertainties involved in programs can be handled where no standard cost and time data are available.

- PERT includes a network comprised of events and activities. An event represents a specified program accomplishment at a particular instant in time. An activity represents the time and resources necessary to progress from one event to the next.

- Events and activities must be sequenced on the network under a highly logical set of two ground rules, which allow the determination of critical and subcritical paths. The ground rules are: (1) No successor event can be considered completed until all of its predecessor events have been completed; and

(continued)

SENSITIVITY ANALYSIS AND PERT (*Continued*)

(2) no looping is allowed (i.e., no successor event can have an activity dependency that leads back to a predecessor event).

- Time estimates are made for each activity of the network on a three-way basis: optimistic, most likely, and pessimistic. The three time estimates are required as a gauge of the "measure of uncertainty" of the activity and represent the probabilistic nature of many tasks. The three estimates are then reduced to a single expected time and a statistical variance.

- Interrelationships of activities are depicted in a network of directed arcs (arcs with arrows, which denote the sequence of the activities they represent). The **nodes**, called events, represent instants in time when certain activities have been completed and others can then be started. All inward-directed activities at a node must be completed before any outward-directed activity of that node can be started. A **path** is defined as an unbroken chain of activities from the origin node to some other node. The origin node is the beginning of the project. An **event** is said to have occurred when all activities on all paths directed into the node representing that event have been completed.

PERT Assumptions. An assumption of PERT is that all activities are started as soon as possible. This assumption may not hold true when scarce resources must be allocated to individual activities.

PERT Applications. The development of a critical path network is accomplished by establishing the major milestones that must be reached. Construction of the network diagram requires identification and recording of the project's internal time dependencies—dependencies that might otherwise go unnoticed until a deadline slips by or impacts other activities. A new activity can be added by identifying its successor and predecessor.

An ordered sequence of events to be achieved would constitute a valid model of the program. The network provides a detailed, systematized plan and time schedule before the project begins. As the project progresses, the time estimates can be refined. A top-down approach is taken when developing the network. The total project is fully planned, and all components of the plan are included.

APPLICATIONS OF PERT AND CPM

- Construction and maintenance of chemical plant facilities, highways, dams, buildings, railroads, and irrigation systems

- Planning of retooling programs for high-volume products in plants, such as automotive and appliance plants

- Introduction of a new product

- Installation of a computer system

- Acquisition of a company

Critical path scheduling helps coordinate the timing of activities on paper and helps avert costly emergencies. The network diagram must be developed in as much detail as possible so that discrepancies, omissions, and work coordination problems can be resolved inexpensively, at least to the extent that they can be foreseen.

Project diagrams of large projects can be constructed by sections. Within each section, the task is accomplished one arrow at a time by asking and answering these questions for each job:

- What immediately preceded this job?
- What immediately succeeds (follows) this job?
- What can be concurrent with this job?

If the maximum time available for a job equals its duration, the job is called critical. A delay in a critical job will cause a comparable delay in the project completion time. A project contains at least one contiguous path of critical jobs through the project diagram from beginning to end. Such a path is called a critical path.

MEANING OF THE CRITICAL PATH

Typically only about 10% to 15% of the jobs in a large project are critical. The primary purpose of determining the critical path is to identify those activities that must be finished as scheduled if the new program or project is to be completed on time. The critical path of those activities cannot be delayed without jeopardizing the entire program or project.

If the maximum time available for a job exceeds its duration, the job is called a **floater**. Some floaters can be displaced in time or delayed to a certain extent without interfering with other jobs or the completion of the project. Others, if displaced, will start a chain reaction of displacements downstream in the project.

The technological ordering is impossible if a cycle error exists in the job data (i.e., job a preceded b, b precedes c, and c precedes a). The time required to traverse each arrow path is the sum of the times associated with all jobs on the path. The critical path is the longest path in time from start to finish; it indicates the minimum time necessary to complete the entire project.

In order to accurately portray all predecessor relationships, dummy jobs often must be added to the project graph. The critical path is the bottleneck route; only by finding ways to shorten jobs along the critical path can the overall project time be reduced. The time required to perform noncritical jobs is irrelevant from the viewpoint of total project time.

PERT Approach. The status of a project at any time is a function of several variables, such as resources, performance, and time. Resources are in the form of dollars or what "dollars" represent—manpower, materials, energy, and methods of production; and technical performance of systems, subsystems, and components. An optimum schedule is the one that properly balances resources, performance, and time.

Information concerning the inherent difficulties and variability in the activity being estimated are reflected in the three numbers: The optimistic, pessimistic, and most likely elapsed time estimates should be obtained for each activity. The purpose of the analysis is to estimate, for each network event, the expected times (mean or average) and expected calendar time of occurrence.

When PERT is used on a project, the three time estimates are combined to determine the expected duration and the variance for each activity.

- **Optimistic**—An estimate of the minimum time an activity will take. This is based on everything going right the first time. It can be obtained under unusual, good-luck situations.

- **Most likely**—An estimate of the normal time an activity will take, a result that would occur most often if the activity could be repeated a number of times under similar circumstances.

- **Pessimistic**—An estimate of the maximum time an activity will take, a result that can occur only if unusually bad luck is experienced.

The expected times determine the critical path. The variances for the activities on this path are summed to obtain the duration variance for the project. A probability distribution for the project completion time can be constructed from this information. However, the variances of activities that do not lie on the critical path are not considered when developing the project variance, and this fact can lead to serious errors in the estimate of project duration.

An estimate of the length of an activity is uncertain. A stochastic model can be used to reflect this uncertainty. This model measures the possible variation in activity duration. It may take the form of a distribution showing the various probabilities that an activity will be completed in its various possible completion times. Alternatively, it may be nondistribution, such as range or standard deviation.

$$\text{Expected time} = 1/6\ (a + 4m + b)$$

where

a = Optimistic time

m = Most likely time

b = Pessimistic time

The expected activity times derived from a three-estimate, PERT-type calculation provide a more accurate estimate and allow the activity time variance to be calculated and included in estimates of project duration.

APPLICATION OF PERT

Example

A company is planning a multiphase construction project. The time estimates for a particular phase of the project are:

Optimistic: 2 months

Most likely: 4 months

Pessimistic: 9 months

Question: Using PERT, what is the expected completion time for this particular phase?

Answer: The expected completion time would be 4.5 months, as shown next.

Expected time = $1/6\ (a + 4m + b) = 1/6\ (2 + 4 \times 4 + 9) = 27/6 = 4.5$.

The latest calendar time at which an event must be accomplished so as not to cause a slippage in meeting a calendar time for accomplishing the objective event is referred to as the latest time (denoted TL). The difference between the latest and expected times, TL – TE, is defined as slack.

Slack can be taken as a measure of scheduling flexibility that is present in a workflow plan, and the slack for an event also represents the time interval in which it might reasonably be scheduled. Slack exists in a system as a consequence of multiple path junctures that arise when two or more activities contribute to a third.

WHAT IS SLACK TIME?

Slack time is free time associated with each activity. It represents unused resources that can be diverted to the critical path. Noncritical paths have slack time while critical paths have no slack time.

Slack is extra time available for all events and activities not on the critical path. A negative slack condition can prevail when a calculated end date does not achieve a program date objective established earlier.

The manager must determine valid means of shortening lead times along the critical path by applying new resources or additional funds, which are obtained from those activities that can afford it because of their slack condition. "Safety factor" is another name for "slack." Alternatively, the manager can reevaluate the sequencing of activities along the critical path. If necessary, those activities that were formerly connected in a series can be organized on a parallel or concurrent basis, with the associated trade-off risks involved. Or the manager may choose to change the scope of work of a critical path alternative in order to achieve a given schedule objective.

When some events have **zero slack**, it is an indication that the expected and latest times for these events are identical. If the zero-slack events are joined together, they will form a path that will extend from the present to the final event. This path can be looked on as the critical path. Should any event on the critical path slip beyond its expected date of accomplishment, then the final event can be expected to slip a similar amount. The paths having the greatest slack can be examined for possible performance or resource trade-offs.

When jobs or operations follow one after another, there is no slack. The criteria for defining a subcritical event is related to the amount of slack involved in the event. Those events having as much as five weeks slack are considered subcritical.

PERT analysis permits a quantitative evaluation of conceivable alternatives. Each job in the project is represented by an arrow, which depicts the existence of the job and the direction of time flows from the tail to the head of the arrow. The arrows are then connected to show graphically the sequence in which the jobs in the project must be performed. The junctions where arrows meet are called events. These are points in time when certain jobs are completed and others must begin.

The difference between a job's early start and its late start (or between early finish and late finish) is called total slack (TS). Total slack represents the maximum amount of time a job may be delayed beyond its early start without necessarily delaying the project's completion time.

 KEY CONCEPTS TO REMEMBER: Pert Time Dimensions

ES = Earliest start time for a particular activity

EF = Earliest finish time for a particular activity

(continued)

> **KEY CONCEPTS TO REMEMBER: Pert Time Dimensions (*Continued*)**
>
> $EF = ES + t$, where t is expected activity time for the activity
>
> LS = Latest start time for a particular activity
>
> LF = Latest finish time for a particular activity
>
> $LS = LF - t$, where t is expected activity time for the activity
>
> Total slack time $(TS) = LS - ES$ or $LF - EF$
>
> Free slack time $(FS) = EF - ES$

The manager examines the work demand and indicates if sufficient resources are available to accomplish all jobs by their early finish. If resources are insufficient, activities are rescheduled within their late finish, using project priority and available slack. Later, the manager is asked for additional resources or for a decision to delay an activity beyond its late finish.

Critical jobs are those on the longest path throughout the project. That is, critical jobs directly affect the total project time.

If the target date (T) equals the early finish date for the whole project (F), then all critical jobs will have zero total slack. There will be at least one path going from start to finish that includes critical jobs only—that is, the critical path. There could be two or more critical paths in the network, but only one at a time.

If T is greater (later) than F, then the critical jobs will have total slack equal to T − F. This is a minimum value; since the critical path includes only critical jobs, it includes those with the smallest TS. All noncritical jobs will have greater total slack.

Another kind of slack is **free slack** (FS). It is the amount a job can be delayed without delaying the early start of any other job. A job with positive total slack may or may not also have free slack, but the latter never exceeds the former. For purposes of computation, the free slack of a job is defined as the difference between the job's EF time and the earliest of the ES times of all its immediate successors.

When a job has zero total slack, its scheduled start time is automatically fixed (i.e., ES + LS); to delay the calculated start time is to delay the whole project. Jobs with positive total slack, however, allow the scheduler some discretion in establishing their start times. This flexibility can usefully be applied to smoothing work schedules.

Peak load may be relieved by shifting jobs on the peak days to their late starts. Slack allows this kind of juggling without affecting project time.

Possible Data Errors in PERT

- The estimated job time may be in error.
- The predecessor relationship may contain cycle errors (job a is a predecessor for b, b is a predecessor for c, and c is a predecessor for a).
- The list of prerequisites for a job may include more than the immediate prerequisites (e.g., job a is a predecessor of b, b is a predecessor of c, and a and b both are predecessors of c).

- Some predecessor relationships may be overlooked.

- Some predecessor relationships listed may be spurious.

- The errors in the PERT-calculated project's mean and standard deviation will tend to be large if many noncritical paths each have a duration approximately equal to the duration of the critical path. However, the more slack time there is in each of the noncritical paths, the smaller will be the error.

One way to minimize errors and omissions is to continually back-check the data and challenge the assumptions. Exhibit 1.53 presents advantages and limitations of PERT.

EXHIBIT 1.53 Advantages and Limitations of PERT

Advantages of PERT	Limitations of PERT
Greatly improved control over complex development work and production programs.	Little interconnection between the different activities pursued.
Ability to distill large amounts of data in brief, orderly fashion.	Requires constant updating and reanalysis of schedules and activities.
Requires a great deal of planning to create a valid network.	Requires greater amount of detail work.
Represents the meaning of the management-by-exception principle.	Does not contain quantity information; only time information is available.
People in different locations can relate their efforts to the total task requirements of a large program.	
"Downstream" savings are achieved by earlier and more positive action on the part of management in early project stages.	

The next list provides issues that should be considered during PERT implementation.

- The people and organization of a project are more important considerations than the use of a particular planning and control technique.

- Consideration should be given to managerial issues, such as project organization, personalities of project members, and operating schemes.

- There is a big difference between the criteria of success for the task to be accomplished and the criteria of success for the management system.

- The project manager is a miniature general manager. However, he or she usually lacks commensurate authority and depends on various management techniques to carry out his or her job.

- The project management approach is the preferred method to deal with onetime defined projects.

- A person making time estimates must have thorough understanding of the work to be done.

- Precise knowledge of task sequencing is required or planned in the performance of activities.

APPLICATION OF PERT

Example 1

The network in Exhibit 1.54 describes the interrelationships of several activities necessary to complete a project. The arrows represent the activities. The numbers above the arrows indicate the number of weeks required to complete each activity.

EXHIBIT 1.54 PERT Network

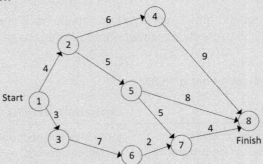

Question: What is the shortest time to complete the project?

Answer: The longest path from node (1) to node (8) is path 1–2–4–8. Since all other paths are shorter in duration than path 1–2–4–8, the activities along those paths can be completed before the activities along path 1–2–4–8. Therefore, the amount of time to complete the activities along path 1–2–4–8, which is 19 weeks (4 + 6 + 9), is the shortest time to complete the project.

Question: What is the critical path for the project?

Answer: The critical path is the sequence of activities that constrains the total completion time of the project. The entire project cannot be completed until all the activities on the critical path (the longest path) are completed.

Path 1–2–4–8, which takes 19 weeks, is the critical path. Activities along each of the other three paths can be completed (each requires less than 19 weeks) before the activities along 1–2–4–8 can. The other three paths are: 1–2–5–8 (requires 4 + 5 + 8 = 17 weeks), 1–2–5–7–8 (requires 4 + 5 + 5 + 4 = 18 weeks), and 1–3–6–7–8 (requires 3 + 7 + 2 + 4 = 16 weeks).

Example 2

During an operational audit, an internal auditing team discovers the following document, titled Project Analysis.

Activity	Time in Weeks	Preceding Activity
A	3	—
B	3	A
C	7	A
D	4	A
E	2	B
F	4	B
G	1	C, E
H	5	D

Using the Project Analysis document, the audit supervisor prepares the PERT diagram shown in Exhibit 1.55.

EXHIBIT 1.55 PERT Project Analysis

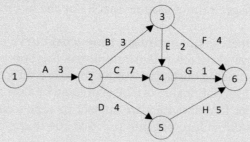

Question: What is the earliest completion time that is indicated by the project analysis?

Answer: There are three paths.

Path 1: A–B–F = 3 + 3 + 4 = 10 weeks

Path 2: A–C–G = 3 + 7 + 1 = 11 weeks

Path 3: A–D–H = 3 + 4 + 5 = 12 weeks

Path 3 has the earliest completion time of 12 weeks since it has the longest time to complete.

Question: What is the earliest time by which Node 4 would be reached?

Answer: There are two paths by which Node 4 can be reached.

Path A: A–C = 3 + 7 = 10 weeks

Path B: A–B–E = 3 + 3 + 2 = 8 weeks

Path A has the earliest time of 10 weeks to reach Node 4 since it has the longest time.

PERT Cost. Once the network has been established, based on the project WBS, costs can be estimated. If the breakdown has been made satisfactorily, it will serve as both an estimating and actual cost accumulation vehicle. PERT cost adds the consideration of resource costs to the schedule produced by the PERT procedure. *The basic PERT handles the problem of time uncertainty while PERT cost addresses cost uncertainty.* Cost uncertainty as it relates to time can be handled by different cost estimates for three time differences. The ultimate objective is not only to improve planning and control but also to assess possibilities for trading off time and cost (i.e., adding or subtracting from one at the expense of the other).

There is an optimum time–cost point for any activity or job as indicated by the U shape of the curve drawn between total direct cost (on *y*-axis) versus time (on *x*-axis). It is assumed that total costs will increase with any effort to accelerate or delay the job away from this point in the case where resource application varies. Crashing the project involves shortening the critical path or paths by operating on those activities that have the lowest time–cost slopes.

At least three approaches are available to develop the cost estimates:

1. A singe cost estimate of expected cost
2. Three cost estimates
3. Optimum time–cost curves

A **single cost estimate** of expected cost is based on the summation of the individual cost elements. The three-cost estimate approach determines the expected cost. The advantage of the **three-cost estimate** over the single-cost estimate is that the result is subject to probability analysis. With this expected cost, the manager cannot assume that he or she has the optimum time–cost mix.

The third approach to estimate is the **optimum time–cost curve concept**. This is differential costing with time as the variability factor. The intention of this approach is to optimize time and costs by using optimum estimated costs. It assumes there is a direct relationship between time and costs on any activity. This relationship can be expressed by a continuous curve. This method is also based on the concept that activities are subject to time–cost trade-offs. The optimum time–cost curve method is difficult to put into practice due to the need to develop continuous time–cost curves.

(B) Critical Path Method

The CPM is a powerful but basically simple technique for analyzing, planning, and scheduling large, complex projects. In essence, the tool provides a means of determining which jobs or activities, of the many that comprise a project, are critical in their effect on total project time and how best to schedule all jobs in the project in order to meet a target date at minimum cost. CPM is an extension of PERT.

Characteristics of Project for Analysis by CPM

- The project consists of a well-defined collection of jobs or activities that, when completed, mark the end of the project.
- The jobs may be started and stopped independently of each other, within a given sequence.
- The jobs are ordered in a technological sequence (e.g., the foundation of a house must be constructed before the walls are erected).

CPM focuses attention on those jobs that are critical to the project time. It provides an easy way to determine the effects of shortening various jobs in the project. It also enables the project manager to evaluate the costs of a crash program.

NORMAL TIME AND CRASH TIME

Time estimates for both normal and crash options are used in the CPM method. Crash time is the time required by the path if maximum effort and resources are diverted to the task along this path. A balance can be obtained when a project manager knows what the normal time and the crash time would be.

It is a costly practice to crash all jobs in a project in order to reduce total project time. If some way is found to shorten one or more of the critical jobs, then not only will the whole project time be shortened, but the critical path itself may shift and some previously noncritical jobs may become critical. It is physically possible to shorten the time required by critical jobs by: assigning more people to the jobs; working overtime; and using different equipment, materials, and technology.

When CPM is used in a project to develop a crashing strategy, two or more paths through the network may have nearly the same length. If the activity duration is allowed to vary, a decrease in the length of the critical path may not result in an equivalent decrease in the project duration because of the variance inherent in the parallel or alternate paths. These variations of activity times can even allow the alternate path to become a critical path. Thus, simply allowing the activity times to vary slightly from their estimates in order to make the length of the paths different can cause serious errors in a CPM crashing strategy and lead to wasted resources and cost overruns.

Characteristics of CPM Networks

- CPM networks attempt to build the entire project on paper at a very early stage of the project—even when the scope is not defined, vaguely defined, or incorrectly defined. In a way, CPM is to project management what modeling or simulation is to economic studies, production problems, plant design, and transportation problems.

- CPM provides a graphic view of the entire project with completion dates, support activities, and costs affixed to every stage of the project.

VALUE OF THE CRITICAL PATH TECHNIQUES

Critical path techniques are as valuable on short- and middle-range planning jobs as they are on major and extremely complex projects.

- CPM's single time estimate fails to consider the effects of variability in path-completion times on the crashing strategy.

- The CPM chart is an excellent tool for communicating scope as well as details of the job to other persons directly and indirectly concerned with the development and completion of the job's various phases.

- The CPM chart serves as a permanent record and reminder of the substance of this communication to all management levels.

- The CPM chart shows the timing of management decisions.

- CPM enables the manager to measure progress (or lack of it) against plans and to take appropriate action quickly when needed. The underlying simplicity of CPM and its ability to focus attention on crucial problem areas of large projects make it an ideal tool for the senior manager.

CPM versus PERT. CPM and PERT methods are essentially similar in general approach and have much in common. However, important differences in implementation details exist. The two methods were independently derived and based on different concepts. Both techniques define the duration of a project and the relationships among the project's component activities. An important feature of the PERT approach is its statistical treatment of the uncertainty in activity time estimates, which involves the collection of three separate time estimates and the calculation of probability estimates of meeting specified schedule dates.

CPM differs from PERT in two areas:

1. The use of only one time estimate for each activity (and thus no statistical treatment of uncertainty)

2. The inclusion, as an integral part of the overall scheme, of a procedure for time/cost trade-off to minimize the sum of direct and indirect project costs

Common Features of PERT and CPM

- They both use a network diagram for project representation. On the diagram, circles represent activities and arrows indicating precedence.
- They both calculate early and late start and finish times and slack time.

Exhibit 1.56 provides a comparison of CPM and PERT.

EXHIBIT 1.56 Comparison of CPM and PERT

CPM	PERT
CPM uses a single deterministic time estimate to emphasize minimum project costs while minimizing consideration of time restraints.	PERT uses three time estimates to define a probabilistic distribution of activity times that emphasizes minimum project duration while minimizing consideration of cost restraints.
It is the choice of cost-conscious managers.	It tends to be used by time-conscious managers.

Although these two techniques are based on different assumptions, they are related to each other because of the obvious relationship between time and cost. The ideal network technique would combine the concepts of CPM's crashing strategy with PERT's probability distribution of activity times to derive the optimum project duration and cost.

(C) Line-of-Balance Technique

Line of balance (LOB) is a basic tool of project management and was an early forerunner of PERT and CPM. LOB was not as popular as PERT and CPM are. The most successful project management techniques involve methods such as CPM and PERT, which combine simplicity and clarity. These are managerial tools involving planning, scheduling, and control. CPM and PERT require complicated mathematical models while LOB does not.

SCOPE OF THE LOB TECHNIQUE

- LOB can be performed manually and can be used on large production jobs, maintenance jobs, R&D jobs, and construction jobs.
- Little training is required to use the LOB technique.
- Complex, large-scale LOB problems may require a computer to solve.

LOB is a dynamic managerial tool that can show, at a glance, what is wrong with the progress of a project. It can also point to future bottlenecks. The tool is easy to develop and maintain, manually or by computer, and requires no equations or models. It forces the manager to make a plan for the program's completion, and it presents graphical information that sometimes is overlooked in a large volume of data. It does not attempt to optimize operations, but it is a sound basic tool.

The main purpose of the LOB method is to prepare a progress study on critical operations at given times during the actual progress of the job. Each operation is checked against some target; that is, we find where each operation is with respect to where it ought to be. Operations that fall short of target are pointed out for further analysis. LOB uses the principles of management by exception. *LOB allows the manager to pay special attention only to those activities that are both critical and do not conform to the schedule.*

The LOB technique involves four steps:

1. Develop an objective chart or delivery schedule.
2. Prepare a program chart or plan of operation.
3. Develop a progress chart including the LOB.
4. Perform the analysis.

The **objective chart** presents the cumulative delivery schedule of finished goods or services for the entire project in a graphical form. The LOB is graphically derived from the objective chart. It can also be calculated analytically, manually, or by computer.

The **program chart** is best constructed by working backward, starting with the delivery of the finished product as lead time zero. It shows the schedule of each of the critical operations with completion dates and the source and/or responsibility for each operation.

The **progress chart** is a flow process with all critical operations performed from receipt of raw materials to completion.

The objective chart and the program chart are constructed only once. Progress charts must be developed from scratch each time the project is analyzed. Progress charts therefore are good only for a specified date. The core of LOB is **performing analysis** of the progress chart. The analysis pinpoints out-of-balance operations. *It is customary to draw the objective chart, the program chart, and the progress chart on one sheet to get a big, quick picture of the entire project.*

LOB and PERT/CPM are complementary, although each can be used effectively by itself. The distinction between them is that PERT is primarily a planning and evaluation tool for one unit–type projects, such as R&D with one completion date. PERT's major objective is to identify critical operations, but it can also be used as a control tool by pinpointing deviations from actual performance and rescheduling accordingly.

LOB monitors a project involving many units to be shipped at certain intervals. LOB can also be used in large projects with one completion date. LOB deals both with operations and components and inventories. PERT deals with only one unit and its critical operations. PERT in general requires a computer while LOB is essentially a graphic, manual tool.

LOB and PERT are related to each other. LOB can complement PERT in this way: Once the critical path has been identified, it can be used as part of the program or the production plan of LOB. Other thinking is that these two techniques can be integrated into a single management planning and control system that can be employed from planning stages through production and delivery for a given quantity of items.

Major assumptions of LOB include: The production method is independent of quantities, critical operations do not change with time, and lead time is constant or known with certainty. These assumptions can be related, making the LOB method more complex than PERT and CPM.

Reasons for LOB's low popularity include:

- Lack of awareness of the technique and its potential applicability and advantages
- Management skepticism, which is common to all managerial techniques
- The lack of a canned computer program for LOB
- Lack of a sound delivery forecast, which is necessary and which is difficult to obtain, considering the difficulty of obtaining market demand and supply forecast
- Requires deterministic lead times (i.e., a single estimate) when, in fact, a range is better

---

PERT VERSUS CPM VERSUS LOB

- PERT considers the time domain only.
- CPM considers cost information only.
- LOB considers quantity information only.
- PERT is good for production prototype construction, assembly, and test of final production equipment that is still high on the learning curve.
- PERT can be applied to smaller projects, single projects, large projects, and multiple projects.
- PERT, CPM, and LOB can be integrated to get maximum benefits.

(D) Graphical Evaluation and Review Technique

The GERT system permits the modeling of a wide variety of situations not possible with traditional PERT/CPM models. Simulation programs can be used to implement GERT, since it uses stochastic networks (i.e., networks in which certain arcs, representing activities, have designated probabilities of occurrence). GERT allows the performance of alternative, mutually exclusive activities, which are not allowed in the PERT/CPM method. In GERT, activity performance times can be expressed as probability distributions. Heuristic sequencing rules are used to give good resource-feasible schedules.

(E) Work Breakdown Structure

The WBS was first intended to be the common link between schedules and costs in PERT cost application. Later it became an important tool for conceptual organization of any project. The WBS provides the necessary logic and formalization of task statements. It prepares the work packages, which usually represent the lowest division of the end items.

(F) Gantt Chart

The Gantt chart is a bar chart that is essentially a column chart on its side and is used for the same purpose. The horizontal bar chart is a tool that allows a manager to evaluate whether existing resources can handle work demand or whether activities should be postponed. The Gantt chart is used for milestone scheduling where each milestone has a start and completion date. A milestone represents a major activity or task to be accomplished (e.g., a design phase in a computer system development project).

The Gantt chart is a graphical illustration of a scheduling technique. The structure of the chart shows output plotted against units of time. It does not include cost information. It highlights activities over the life of a project and contrasts actual times with projected times. It gives a quick picture of a project's progress in regard to the status of actual time lines and projected time lines. Exhibit 1.57 presents advantages and disadvantages of PERT and Gantt charts.

EXHIBIT 1.57 Advantages and Disadvantages of PERT and Gantt Charts

Advantages	
PERT	**Gantt chart**
A good planning aid.	A good planning tool.
Interdependencies between activities can be shown.	A graphical scheduling technique that is simple to develop, use, and understand.
Network diagram is flexible to change.	Useful for large projects.
Activity times are probabilistic.	Shows a sequence of steps or tasks.
A good scheduling tool for large, nonroutine projects.	Actual completion times can be compared with planned times.
A good tool in predicting resource needs, problem areas, and impact of delays on project completion.	

Disadvantages	
PERT	**Gantt chart**
Difficult to apply to repetitive assembly line operations where scheduling is dependent on pace of machines.	Interrelationships among activities not shown on chart.
Large and complex projects are difficult to draw manually.	Inflexible to change.
Requires computer hardware and software to draw a complex network.	Activity times are deterministic.
Requires training to use the computer program.	Difficult to show very complex situations.
	Cannot be used as procedure documenting tool.
	Does not show critical path in chain of activities.

WHAT ARE SOPHISTICATED TECHNIQUES FOR PROJECT MANAGEMENT?

- PERT, GERT, and CPM techniques are more sophisticated scheduling methods due, in part, to the consideration of probabilities.
- LOB, WBS, Gantt charts, bar charts, and milestones are less sophisticated scheduling methods due, in part, to not considering the probabilities.
- GERT handles alternate, mutually exclusive activities, while PERT/CPM cannot.

If PERT is used, there may be a lower probability of a cost/schedule overrun because of its sophistication as a scheduling method compared to less sophisticated methods such as Gantt charts, milestone scheduling, line of balance, and bar charts. If there is a slack time, there is no need to use sophisticated and tight scheduling methods, such as PERT.

(vi) Project Controlling Methods

In any project, at least four major types of controls will be applied: time control, cost control, quality control, and earned value management (EVM) control. Sometimes other types of controls are also used (e.g., logs, checklists, and status reports).

Time Control. Project network scheduling begins with the construction of a diagram that reflects the interdependencies and time requirements of the individual tasks that make up a project. Work plans must be prepared in advance of the project. Once the overall schedule is established, weekly or biweekly review meetings should be held to check progress against schedule. Control must be rigorous, especially at the start, so that immediate corrective action is taken for missed commitments.

Cost Control. Periodic reports showing the budget, the actual cost, and variances are good starts for cost controls. It is necessary to break the comprehensive cost summary reports into work packages or major tasks and focus on major problems and opportunities. The cost reports should be distributed to technical and functional managers.

Quality Control. Quality control comprises three elements: defining performance criteria, expressing the project objective in terms of quality standards, and monitoring progress toward these standards. Examples of performance criteria include market penetration of a product line and processing time for customer inquiries. Both quantitative and qualitative measures need to be defined

EVM Control. EVM control provides a standard means of objectively measuring work accomplished based on the budgeted value of that work—it is what you got for what it cost. EVM is a project management technique that integrates cost, schedule, and technical performance measures to monitor and control project resources and compile results into one set of metrics so that effective comparisons can be made. It also helps evaluate and control project risk by measuring project progress in monetary terms. It provides the project manager with a more complete picture of the health of the entire project, not just certain segments of the project.

EVM incorporates three vital aspects of effective project/program management: scoping, costing, and scheduling. EVM is a technique aimed at comparing resource planning to schedules and to technical, cost, and schedule requirements.

The EVM technique serves two distinct purposes: It encourages the effective use of internal cost and schedule management systems, and it affords the organization the ability to rely on timely data produced by those systems for determining product-oriented contracts status. In order to perform an EVM analysis, you need to start with a solid baseline schedule that accurately reflects how much work is planned for each time period. After this baseline is determined and captured, work becomes earned in hours and dollars as work is performed. This earned work is then compared to the initial resource allocation estimates in order to determine if the project or investment has utilized its resources meaningfully and cost efficiently.

EXAMPLE OF APPLICATION OF EVM TECHNIQUE

Schedule and Cost Variances

The percentage complete estimate method allows the project manager in charge of the work package to make a monthly or quarterly estimate of the percentage of completed work. These estimates are expressed as cumulative values against 100% of the milestone value. The earned value is then calculated by applying that percentage to the total budget for that work package.

Project A is authorized with a budget of $1,000,000 over a four-quarter, one-year time period. The planned value for the first quarter called for an accomplishment of 30%, or $300,000 ($0.30 \times \$1,000,000$) in the value of the work scheduled. Actual costs are amounted to $250,000. The earned value estimate is based on 20% of work completed, or $200,000 (i.e., $0.20 \times \$1,000,000$).

$$\text{Schedule variance} = \text{Earned value} - \text{Planned value} = \$200,000 - \$300,000 = -\$100,000$$
(i.e., a negative amount means the project is behind schedule)

$$\text{Cost variance} = \text{Earned value} - \text{Actual costs} = \$200,000 - \$250,000 = -\$50,000$$
(i.e., a negative amount means the project is experiencing a cost overrun)

Schedule and Cost Performance Indices

$$\text{Schedule performance index (SPI)} = \text{Earned value/Planned value} = \$200,000/\$300,000 = 0.67$$

$$\text{Cost performance index (CPI)} = \text{Earned value/Actual costs} = \$200,000/\$250,000 = 0.80$$

A project with SPI and CPI of 1.0 is good, less than 1.0 is not good, and the largest negative value should be given a top priority to work on first.

Forecast of Final Project Costs

A range of final cost requirements can be forecast for project A using the SPI and CPI indices as follows:

Low-end forecast is:

$$\text{Total budget value/SPI} = \$1,000,000/0.67 = \$1,492,537 = \$1.5 \text{ million (approximately)}$$

High-end forecast is:

$$\text{Total budget value/(SPI} \times \text{CPI)} = \$1,000,000/(0.67 \times 0.80) = \$1,000,000/0.536 = \$1,865,672$$
$$= \$1.9 \text{ million (approximately)}$$

A range of final cost projection between a minimum of $1.5 million and a maximum of $1.9 million is needed to complete project A.

EVM is most effective when implemented using a bottom-up approach. Such an approach dictates that information is planned and managed in small increments that can be quickly and accurately cumulated to view and manage the project as a whole. Examining small, manageable chunks is a more efficient way to identify problems and root causes, and allows the project manager to assess the health and risks of a project more accurately. Generally, small milestones are easier to plan for (their scope can be defined more specifically) and can be measured more objectively than large ones. Project managers should ensure that milestones (or submilestones) are as small and specific as possible in terms of scheduling. It is good to limit milestone duration to a single fiscal year (or less) instead of multiyear milestones.

Other Types of Project Controls. Since a project can have a number of people working on it for a long time, monitoring and control become essential management tools. Formal control techniques include: change-management policy, procedures, and forms; logs; checklists; and status reports. Phone conversations and face-to-face communications are some examples of informal control techniques. Where possible, formal control techniques should be practiced, since they provide some evidence as to what has been said and when to resolve a question or dispute.

(vii) Project Governance Mechanisms

Project governance mechanisms include establishing a project steering committee and a project oversight board and conducting a project management audit.

The **project steering committee** is a high-level committee to integrate several functions of the organization. The **project oversight board** is similar to the steering committee except that it is focused on a specific project at hand. The board:

1. Reviews the project request and scope.

2. Assesses the project impact.

3. Approves the project funding.

4. Challenges the costs, schedules, and benefits.

5. Monitors the project progress.

6. Reviews project deliverables.

7. Solves project-related problems.

Regarding the project scope, the board determines what is in scope and what is out of scope so that scope creep does not happen. Any changes in project scope are controlled by change management procedures.

(viii) Project Management Audit

The scope of a project management audit consists of: reviewing project planning, organizing, staffing, and directing activities; controlling tasks for effectiveness and efficiency; and determining whether project objectives and goals are achieved.

The major objective of the project management process, which is part of the software assurance process, is to establish the organizational structure of the project and assign responsibilities. The process uses the system requirements documentation and information about the purpose and criticality of the software, required deliverables, and available time and other resources to plan and manage the software development and maintenance processes. The project management process begins before software development starts and ends when its objectives have been met. The process overlaps and often repeats other software assurance processes. It establishes/approves standards, implements monitoring and reporting practices, develops high-level policy for quality, and cites laws and regulations for compliance. An audit program is suggested next.

A. Review the next 10 activities performed by the project manager in the project planning area.

1. Set objectives or goals; determine the desired outcome for the project:

    a. Analyze and document the system and software requirements; define the relationships between the system and software activities.

    b. Determine management requirements and constraints (resource and schedule limitations)

    c. Define success criteria; always includes delivery of software that satisfies the requirements, on time and within budget.

2. Plan for corrective action.

3. Develop project strategies—decide on major organizational goals (e.g., quality), and develop a general program of action for reaching those goals.

4. Develop policies for the project—make standing decision on important recurring matters to provide a guide for decision making.

5. Determine possible courses of action—develop and analyze different ways to conduct the project; anticipate possible adverse events and project areas; state assumptions; develop contingency plans; predict results, possible courses of action.

6. Make planning decisions—evaluate and select a course of action from among alternatives. This includes:

  a. Choosing the most appropriate course of action for meeting project goals and objectives.

  b. Making trade-off decisions involving costs, schedule, quality, design strategies, and risks.

  c. Selecting methods, tools, and techniques (both technical and managerial) by which the output and final product will be developed and assured and the project will be managed.

7. Set procedures and rules for the project—establish methods, guides, and limits for accomplishing the project activities.

8. Select scheduling process appropriate for development and maintenance methods.

9. Prepare budgets—allocate estimated costs (based on project size, schedule, staff) to project functions, activities, and tasks, and determine necessary resources.

10. Document, distribute, and update project plans.

B. Review the next six activities performed by the project manager in the project organizing area.

  1. Identify and group required tasks—tasks are grouped into logical entities (e.g., analysis tasks, design tasks, coding tasks, test tasks) and are mapped into organizational entities.

  2. Select and establish organizational structures—define how the project will be organized (e.g., line, staff, or matrix organization) using contractual requirements and principles of independent verification and validation.

  3. Create organizational positions—specify job titles and position descriptions.

  4. Define responsibilities and authorities—decide who will have the responsibility of completing tasks and who has the authority to make decisions related to the project.

  5. Establish position qualifications—identify the qualities personnel must have to work on the project (e.g., experience, education, programming languages, tool usage).

  6. Document organizational structures—document lines of authority, tasks, and responsibilities in the project plan.

C. Review the next eight activities performed by the project manager in the project staffing area.

1. Fill organizational positions—fill the jobs established during organizational planning with qualified personnel.

2. Assimilate newly assigned personnel—familiarize newly assigned personnel with any project procedures, facilities, equipment, tools, or plans.

3. Educate and train personnel as necessary.

4. Provide for general development of project staff members.

5. Evaluate and appraise personnel.

6. Compensate project personnel (e.g., salary, bonus).

7. Terminate project assignments—reassign or terminate personnel at the end of a project.

8. Document staffing decisions—document staffing plans, training policies adopted.

D. Review the next seven activities performed by the project manager in a project leading area.

1. Provide leadership—the project manager provides direction to project members by interpreting plans and requirements.

2. Delegate project authority.

3. Build project teams.

4. Coordinate and communicate project activities between in-house and contractor personnel.

5. Resolve project conflicts.

6. Manage changes after considering the inputs, outputs, costs/benefits.

7. Document directing decisions taken.

E. Review the next five activities performed by the project manager in the project controlling area.

1. Develop standards of performance—select or approve standards to be used for the software development and maintenance activities.

2. Establish monitoring and reporting systems, such as milestones, deliverables, and schedules.

3. Analyze results by comparing achievements with standards, goals, and plans.

4. Apply corrective action to bring requirements, plans, and actual project status into conformance.

5. Document the controlling methods used.

(b) Change Management Methods

(i) Agents of Change

Organizations must change to survive in a competitive environment. This requires everyone in the organization to believe in and accept the change. Ideally, managers need to be architects or agents of change rather than victims of change. When introducing changes, managers often are surprised that things do not turn out as planned. This is because the change process is not carried out properly. The change itself is not the problem. When managers are acting as agents of change, their company will be much more responsive, flexible, and competitive. In addition to managers, internal auditors can act as change agents due to their nature of work. Auditors facilitate change through their recommendations to management. Each recommendation auditors make requires some change in existing policies, procedures, and practices or creation of new ones.

(ii) How to Change

A corporation can change in a number of ways. These include:

- Reengineering business policies, processes, jobs, and procedures; outsourcing nonstrategic activities.
- Partnering with major suppliers and customers.
- Implementing total quality management programs.
- Redesigning the organizational structure to fit the business strategy.
- Renovating physical plants and facilities.
- Installing computer-based systems and technologies.
- Understanding its own products, services, markets, and customers and those of competitors.
- Installing performance measurement methods and reward systems.

PROMOTERS VERSUS RESISTORS OF CHANGE

People at the top of the organization usually promote change because they have clear vision and better goals to achieve.

People at the bottom of the organization usually resist change the least because they know how bad things really are at their level.

People at the middle of the organization usually resist change the most because they know neither top management goals nor how bad things really are at the bottom. They are in a confused stage since they know neither the top nor the bottom.

(iii) Types of Organizational Change

Organization psychologists David Nadler and Michael Tushman developed an instructive typology of organizational change describing four types of changes (see Exhibit 1.58).[16]

EXHIBIT 1.58 Typology of Organizational Change

	Incremental	Strategic
Anticipatory	Tuning 1	Reorientation 3
Reactive	Adaptation 2	Re-creation 4

---

[16] Originally noted by Nadler and Tushman and later cited by Robert Kreitner, *Management*, 9th ed. (Boston: Houghton Mifflin Company, 2004).

As the exhibit shows, **anticipatory changes** are any systematically planned changes intended to take advantage of expected situations (e.g., following demographics). **Reactive changes** are those necessitated by unexpected environmental events (e.g., responding to competitor's action). **Incremental changes** involve subsystem adjustments needed to keep the organization on its chosen path (e.g., adding a third shift in a manufacturing plant). **Strategic changes** alter the overall shape or direction of the organization (e.g., switch from building houses to apartments by a construction contractor).

The four specific types of organizational change that result from the previous exhibit are tuning, adaptation, reorientation, and re-creation (see Exhibit 1.59).

EXHIBIT 1.59 Specific Types of Organizational Change

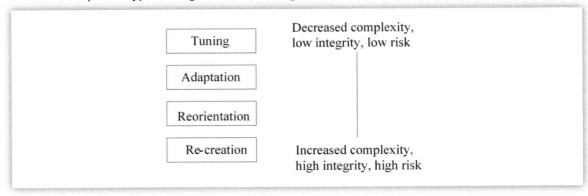

In this exhibit, **tuning** is the most common form of organizational change covering preventive maintenance and continuous improvement. The major thrust of tuning is to actively anticipate and avoid problems rather than passively waiting for things to go wrong before taking action. *Managers should seek change, not just expect change.*

Adaptation, like tuning, involves incremental changes. The difference is that the changes are in reaction to external problems, events, or pressures. The **reorientation** change is anticipatory and strategic in scope. It is also called frame bending because the organization is significantly redirected while continuing its original mission. **Re-creation** is a type of change that is reactive and strategic in scope. It is also called frame breaking because the new organization is completely different from the organization of the past.

(iv) Resistance to Change
Organizational change comes in all forms, sizes, and shapes and with various degrees of impacts and consequences for employees. Some of the most common reasons for resistance to change are listed next.

- Surprise
- Inertia
- Misunderstanding
- Emotional side effects
- Lack of trust
- Fear of failure

- Personality conflicts
- Lack of tact
- Threat to job status or security
- Breakup of work groups

Management faces the challenge of foreseeing and neutralizing resistance to change, as the resistance is both rational and irrational.

Management theorists have offered at least six options to overcome resistance to change:

1. Education and communication
2. Participation and involvement
3. Facilitation and support
4. Negotiation and agreement
5. Manipulation and co-optation
6. Explicit and implicit coercion

Situational appropriateness is the key to success.

- **Education and communication.** This option promotes prevention rather than cure. The idea here is to help employees understand the true need for a change as well as the logic behind it. Various media may be used, including face-to-face discussions, formal group presentations, and special reports or publications. *Advantages*: Once persuaded, employees will help with the implementation of the change. *Drawbacks*: Education and communication can be time consuming if many employees are involved.

- **Participation and involvement.** Personal involvement through participation tends to defuse rational and irrational fears about a workplace change. Involvement in the design and implementation of a change makes one become an owner of the change process and its success. *Advantages*: Participation and involvement lead to commitment from employees. *Drawbacks*: Participation and involvement can be time consuming if participators design an inappropriate change.

- **Facilitation and support.** Support from management in the form of special training, job stress counseling, and compensatory time off can be helpful when fear and anxiety are responsible for resistance to change. *Advantages*: No other approach works as well with adjustment problems. *Drawbacks*: Facilitation and support can be time consuming and expensive and still can fail.

- **Negotiation and agreement.** Management can neutralize resistance to change by exchanging something of value for cooperation. *Advantages*: Negotiation and agreement are relatively easy ways to avoid major resistance. *Drawbacks*: Negotiation and agreement can be too expensive in many cases if others are alerted to negotiate for compliance.

- **Manipulation and co-optation.** Manipulation occurs when managers selectively withhold or dispense information and consciously arrange events to increase the chance that a change will be successful. Co-optation normally involves token participation of employees, and the impact of their input is negligible. *Advantages*: It can be a relatively quick and inexpensive solution to resistance problems. *Drawbacks*: The process can lead to future problems if people feel manipulated.

- **Explicit and implicit coercion.** Managers who cannot or will not invest the time required for the other strategies can force employees to go along with a change by threatening them with termination, loss of pay raises or promotions, transfer, and so forth. *Advantages*: Coercion is speedy and can overcome any kind of resistance. *Drawbacks*: This process can be risky if it leaves employees mad at the initiators.

(v) Factors to Consider during the Change Process

Internal auditors should consider the following factors during their audit work:

- A real paradigm shift is needed for changes to take place. Excuses like "It is company policy" and "We have no resources" no longer work. Forward-looking people are needed.

- Motivating stakeholders (employees, customers, and suppliers) can have a multiplier effect on the change initiative. Stakeholder involvement in problem solving and knowledge sharing is vital.

- The active performance measures are not always obvious. They should be made explicit.

- During the change implementation process, expect setbacks and roadblocks. Address them on a case-by-case basis.

- Communicating honestly is important. Act straightforward with all stakeholders.

- Use the grapevine to a project's advantage; do not let the project be abused by it.

- Empower employees so they feel that they have real influence over standards of production, quality, and service. Empowering people brings significant changes in employees' behavior. However, managers who do the empowering must also change. Empowerment means that employees have the correct knowledge and appropriate tools to do things well, not just have the authority to do the job.

- Identify the barriers to change. If possible, dismantle them; at the least, deal with them.

- Today's change projects require border crossing of departments, divisions, suppliers, and customers. Borderless projects should be encouraged since border-bound projects like to maintain their own turf.

- A goal-focused and results-oriented performance measurement system is needed to institutionalize the changes since performance measures are a primary strategy deployment tool. Do not settle for a single measurement; instead, opt for a set of measures.

- Understand and consider the cultural differences at the workplace. Do not discount them.

(vi) Organizational Development

Organizational development (OD) is a systematic approach to planned change programs intended to help employees and organizations function more effectively. OD combines the knowledge from various disciplines, such as behavioral science, psychology, sociology, education, and management. OD is a process of fundamental change in an organization's culture. For OD programs to be effective, not only must they be tailored to unique situations, but they also must meet the seven common objectives in order to develop trust. *Problem-solving skills, communication, and cooperation are required for success.*

1. Deepen the sense of organizational purpose and align individuals with that purpose.

2. Strengthen interpersonal trust, communication, cooperation, and support.

3. Encourage a problem-solving rather than a problem-avoiding approach to organizational problems.

4. Develop a satisfying work experience capable of building enthusiasm.

5. Supplement formal authority with authority based on personal knowledge and skill.

6. Increase personal responsibility for planning and implementing.

7. Encourage personal willingness to change.

Organization development brings out pros and cons.

> **Pros:** General management lacks a systematic approach and is often subject to haphazard, bits-and-pieces management style. OD gives managers a vehicle for systematically introducing change by applying a broad selection of management techniques as a unified and consistent package. This approach leads to greater personal, group, and organizational effectiveness.

> **Cons:** The seven common objectives listed above are not new. They have been addressed by one or another management techniques.

(A) OD Process
Social psychologist Kurt Lewin recommended that change agents unfreeze, change, and then refreeze social systems related to three major phases or components of OD.[17]

Unfreezing phase ⟶ Change phase ⟶ Refreezing phase

Unfreezing involves neutralizing resistance by preparing employees for change. Change involves implementing the change strategy. Refreezing involves systematically following up a change program for permanent results.

(B) Unfreezing Phase
The objective of the unfreezing phase is to assess the situation and suggest an appropriate change strategy. The scope of work includes making announcements, holding meetings, and launching a promotional campaign in the organization's newsletter and on bulletin boards. The goal is to deliver a clear message to employees about the change. Management needs to avoid creating unrealistic expectations such as miracles.

During the unfreezing phase, management may choose to diagnose the situation by using several approaches, such as:

- Reviewing records (personnel or financial) for signs of excessive absenteeism, cost over-runs, budget variances.

- Interviewing employees with specific questions about their job and the organization.

- Mailing survey questionnaires for opinions and suggestions.

- Observing employees at work, since people tend to say one thing and do another.

---

[17] Ibid.

After the data are collected and compiled, it is good to compare the results with past results to see how things have changed. This would help in mapping a future course of action.

(C) Change Phase

The objective of the change phase is to implement the change strategy through enhanced collaboration and cooperation. In this phase of intervention, the wheels of change are set in motion. "Intervention" here means that a systematic attempt will be made to correct an organizational deficiency uncovered through diagnosis.

Six popular OD interventions designed to increase effectiveness are listed next.

1. Life and career planning
2. Skill development
3. Role analysis
4. Team building
5. Survey feedback
6. Grid OD

These six interventions are grouped into three categories: individual, group, and entire organization targets, as shown in Exhibit 1.60.

EXHIBIT 1.60 Organization Development Interventions

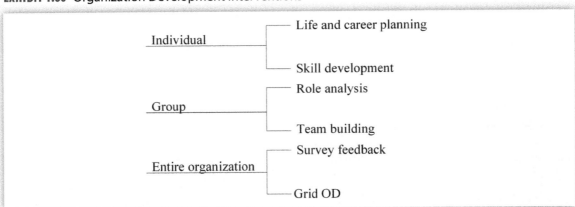

Individual Interventions. The overall objective of *life and career planning* is to get individuals to define their personal goals for growth and development and to plan ways to achieve them. Here an assumption is made that organizational growth and development is a function of individual growth and development. The overall objective of *skill development* is to place emphasis on learning how to do a job in terms of delegation, problem solving, conflict resolution, and leading. Skill development deals with content rather than process.

Group Interventions. The overall objective of *role analysis* is to define a prescribed way of behaving. A systematic clarification of interdependent task and job behavior is made. The overall objective of *team building* is to emphasize interactive group processes, the "how" of effective group behavior. This intervention is the most widely used HR development technique.

Entire Organization Interventions. The overall objective of *survey feedback* is to inform employees where they stand in relation to others on important organizational issues so that constructive problem solving can take place. Effective feedback should be relevant, understandable, descriptive, verifiable, controllable, comparative, and inspiring. The overall objective of *grid OD* is to present a package covering several OD interventions arranged in an orderly and coherent fashion. OD grid is based on Blake and Mouton's leadership grid, a popular OD approach.

(D) Refreezing Phase

The objective of the refreezing phase is to address unanticipated problems and side effects and to maintain positive changes. The effectiveness of change strategy is also evaluated. The scope includes follow-up and monitoring to ensure lasting change.

Maintaining Positive Changes. The goal is to induce employees to behave differently and positively. This calls for more cooperation, more collaboration, and more productivity among employees. Some of ways to maintain positive changes include top management support, peer group support, and a formal reward and punishment system, all of which lead to a supportive climate for change on the job.

Evaluating the OD Program. An objective evaluation of results is desired even though it is difficult, time consuming, and expensive. According to a statistical analysis conducted by Neuman, Edwards, and Raju:[18]

- Combined interventions were more effective at improving employee attitudes and satisfaction than were single-technique interventions.

- Team building was the most effective OD intervention for improving attitudes and satisfaction.

- OD interventions tend to have a stronger influence on attitudes than on satisfaction.

- The empirical linkages between OD interventions and productivity are not strong.

1.9 Business Contracts

This section discusses three major topics: law of agency, law of sale, and law of contracts. Regarding contracts, it recognizes the various forms and elements of contracts, including requirements of a contract (e.g., formality and consideration), classification of contracts (e.g., unilateral and bilateral), and damages resulting from a contract (e.g., compensatory and consequential). In addition, this section presents several topics related to contracts, such as product reviews and warranties, ultra vires and intra vires legal actions, and contractual issues with IP assets.

(a) Law of Agency

The law of agency or agency law deals with business duties, relationships, and obligations between a principal and his or her agents. Agency law establishes the ground rules (boundaries) about what a principal or agent can and cannot do to fulfill duties, responsibilities, and obligations. Usually, agents can be one or more individuals whereas the principal can be only one person.

---

[18] Neuman, Edwards, and Raju, "Organizational Development Interventions: A Meta-Analysis of Their Effects on Satisfaction and Other Attitudes." *Personnel Psychology* (September 1989).

Company (principal) ⟶ Buyer (agent)

Company (principal) ⟶ Salesperson (agent)

Company (principal) ⟶ Employee (agent)

Company (principal) ⟶ Consultant/Contractor (agent)

Shareholder (principal) ⟶ Manager (agent)

Both the law of agency and the law of contracts apply to procurement because purchasers (buyers) enter into contracts with suppliers, vendors, and contractors as an agent and employee.

Law of Agency = Company (Principal) ⟶ Buyer (Agent)

Law of Contracts = Company (Principal) ⟶ Employee (Agent)

Three types of authority can exist between the principal and the agent: actual authority, apparent authority, and ratified authority. Both principal and agent have their own duties to perform.

Actual authority, whether explicit or implicit, occurs when the principal gives the authority to the agent with consensus agreement. The principal is bound to this authority and cannot deny it.

Apparent authority (also called agency by estoppel) occurs based on the principal's words or conduct, and the principal cannot deny it if third parties relied on it. Apparent authority is based on impressions of the third parties.

Ratified authority occurs when the principal accepts the liability from third parties even if the agent acted without authority.

Duties of a principal require duty to compensate an agent, duty to reimburse the agent, duty to indemnify the agent, and duty to cooperate with the agent.

Duties of an agent require duty of performance to a principal, duty of notification to the principal, and duty of accountability to the principal. In addition, an agent should not involve in self-dealing, usurp an opportunity, compete with the principal, or misuse confidential information, and should not maintain a dual-agency relationship (i.e., one agent reporting to two principals at the same time).

(b) Law of Sale

The sale of personal property is a large part of commercial activity. Article 2 of the **Uniform Commercial Code** (the Code, or UCC) governs such sales in all states except Louisiana. The Code has its own contract law. Common law governs all general contracts outside the scope of the UCC's contract law.

A sale consists in the passing of title to goods from seller to buyer for a price. A contract for sale includes both a present sale of goods and a contract to sell goods at a future time. The Code essentially defines goods and products as tangible personal property. Personal property is any property other than an interest in real property (land and any attachments to it such as buildings).

Example 1: Examples of personal property covered by the UCC transactions include the purchase of a TV set, an automobile, or a textbook because they represent a sale of goods.

Example 2: The Code does *not* apply to employment contracts, service contracts, insurance contracts, contracts involving real property, and contracts for the sale of intangible assets (e.g., trademarks, patents, and copyrights). These transactions continue to be governed by general contract law.

(c) Law of Contracts

Every business enterprise, whether large or small, will enter into contracts with its employees, its suppliers of goods and services, and its customers in order to conduct its business operations. Thus, contract law is an important subject for business managers. Contract law is also basic to other fields of law, such as agency, partnerships, corporations, sale of personal property, commercial paper, and secured transactions. Note that contracts are primarily governed by state common law.

Law of contracts or general contract laws can be applied to business contracts where they are governed by state common law. A contract is a binding agreement between two or more parties that the courts will enforce. It is a promise or a set of promises for the breach of which the law gives a remedy, cure, relief, or the performance of which the law in some way recognizes a duty. A promise manifests or demonstrates the intention to act or to refrain from acting in a specified manner.

Those promises that meet all of the essential requirements of a binding contract are contractual and will be enforced. All other promises are not contractual, and usually no legal remedy is available for a breach of or a failure to properly perform these promises. The remedies provided for breach of contract include compensatory damages, equitable remedies, reliance damage, and restitution. Thus, a promise may be contractual (and therefore binding) or noncontractual. In other words, all contracts are promises, but not all promises are contracts.

When properly executed, business contracts can turn into purchase orders, invoices, and payments between the contracting parties.

Business Contracts $\longrightarrow$ Purchase Orders $\longrightarrow$ Invoices $\longrightarrow$ Payments

(i) Definition of a Contract
Contracts are legal documents that describe terms and conditions under which two or more willing parties agree to commit, honor, and discharge their respective duties and obligations to each other as defined in the contract (i.e., work products and deliverables). It describes penalties for breach of contract and remedies for damages.

(ii) Requirements of a Contract
In most cases, an oral contract is binding and enforceable. However, in a limited number of instances, contracts must be in writing. Moreover, for a contract to be valid, there must be an absence of invalidating conduct, such as duress, undue influence, misrepresentation, or mistake. It is always a good practice for a contract to be in writing because it avoids miscommunications and misunderstandings.

The parties can be principals or qualified agents. The parties cannot engage in any fraudulent activities. The use of force or coercion to reach an agreement is not acceptable in signing a contract because both parties must enter into the agreement on their own free will. Both parties must indicate a willingness to enter into the agreement and be bound by its terms.

A promise meeting all of these requirements is contractual and legally binding. However, if any requirement is unmet, the promise is noncontractual.

The five basic requirements of a contract include:

1. Mutual assent (agreement by offer and acceptance).

2. Consideration (either express or implied mutual obligation).

3. Legality of object and subject matter (must be for a legitimate purpose, not for criminal and illegal purposes, or not against the public policy). If the purpose is illegal, the resulting contract is null and void.

4. Capacity (only competent parties can have the full capacity to contract; adjudicated incompetents have no capacity to contract; and minors, incompetent persons, and intoxicated persons have limited capacity to contract).

5. Formality (i.e., in writing).

Mutual Assent. The parties to a contract must manifest by words or conduct that they have agreed to enter into a contract. The usual method of showing mutual assent is by offer and acceptance. An offer is a proposal or expression by one person that he or she is willing to do something for certain terms. A contract does not exist until the offer is formally accepted, either verbally or in written form. The offer and acceptance have to match. If they match, there is an agreement leading up to a contract. If they do not, it is more like a negotiation, to which someone responds with a counteroffer rather than an acceptance, which continues until both parties reach an agreement or a meeting of the minds.

Consideration. Each party to a contract must intentionally exchange a legal benefit or incur a legal detriment as in inducement to the other party to make a return exchange. Consideration is a form of mutual obligation. In the business world, mutual promises in a contract of sale, whether express or implied, are generally sufficient consideration.

Legality of Object and Subject Matter. The purpose of a contract must not be criminal, illegal, or otherwise against public policy. If the purpose is illegal, the resulting contract is null and void. The performance of a party in regard to the contract must not be an unlawful act if the agreement is to be enforceable. However, if the primary purpose of a contract is legal, but some terms contained within the agreement are not, then the contract may or may not be itself be illegal, depending on the seriousness of the illegal terms and the degree to which the legal and illegal terms can be separated.

Capacity. The parties to a contract must have contractual capacity. Certain persons, such as adjudicated incompetents, have no legal capacity to contract, while others, such as minors, adjudicated incompetents, and intoxicated persons, have limited capacity to contract. All others have full contractual capacity. The parties can be principals or qualified agents. The parties cannot engage in any fraudulent activities. The use of force or coercion to reach an agreement is not acceptable in signing a contract because both parties must enter into the agreement on their own free will. Both parties must indicate a willingness to enter into the agreement and be bound by its terms.

Formality. In addition, though in a limited number of instances a contract must be evidenced in writing to be enforceable (i.e., formality), in most cases an oral contract is binding and enforceable. Moreover, there must be an absence of invalidating conduct, such as duress, undue influence, misrepresentation, or mistake. A promise meeting all of these requirements is contractual and legally binding. However, if any requirement is unmet, the promise is noncontractual.

(iii) Classification of Contracts

Contracts can be classified based on several characteristics, such as method of formation, content, and legal effect. The standard classifications are express or implied contracts; bilateral or unilateral contracts; valid, void, voidable, or unenforceable contracts; and executed or executory contracts. These classifications are not mutually exclusive. For example, a contract may be express, bilateral, valid, executory, and informal.

Express and Implied Contracts. A contract formed by conduct, is an implied or, more precisely, an implied-in-fact contract. In contrast, a contract in which the parties manifest assent in words is an express contract. Both are contracts, equally enforceable. The difference between them is merely the manner in which the parties manifest their assent.

Bilateral and Unilateral Contracts. When each party is both a promisor (a person making a promise) and a promisee (the person to whom a promise is made), the contract is called a bilateral contract. A unilateral contract is one where only one of the parties makes a promise.

Insurance contracts are considered unilateral because only the insurance company (insurer) makes a promise under the contract. The insurer promises to pay a benefit upon the occurrence of a certain event, such as an auto accident, death, or disability. Applicants do not make any promise; they can even elect to stop paying premiums if they desire. The insurer will, however, have the right to cancel the policy if premiums are not paid.

Valid, Void, Voidable, and Unenforceable Contracts. A **valid contract** is one that meets all of the requirements of a binding contract. It is an enforceable promise or an agreement. A **void contract** is an agreement that does not meet all of the requirements of a binding contract. It has no legal effect, and it is merely a promise or agreement. An example is an agreement entered by a person whom the courts have declared incompetent. A contract that is neither void nor voidable may nonetheless be unenforceable. An **unenforceable contract** is a contract for the breach of which the law provides no remedy. After the statutory time period has passed, a contract is referred to as unenforceable rather than void or voidable.

Executed and Executory Contracts. A contract that has been fully carried out and completed by all of the parties to it is an executed contract. By comparison, the term "executory contract" applies to contracts that are still partially or entirely unperformed by one or more of the parties.

Aleatory Contracts. Insurance contracts are considered to be *aleatory* because the outcome is affected by chance and may be unequal. It is possible that there is an element of chance for both parties involved in the contract, and the dollar values exchanged may not be equal.

Conditional Contracts. Insurance contracts are *conditional contracts*; the payment of benefits by the insurance company is conditioned upon the insured or owner paying the premium.

Doctrine of Promissory Estoppel. In certain circumstances, the courts enforce noncontractual promises under the doctrine of promissory estoppel in order to avoid injustice. A noncontractual promise is enforceable when it is made under circumstances that should lead the promisor to reasonably expect that the promisee, in reliance on the promise, would be induced by it to take definite and substantial action or to forbear, and the promisee does take such action or does forbear.

Quasi Contracts. Quasi (meaning "as if") contracts are not contracts at all. A quasi contract is based neither on an express nor on an implied-in-fact contract. Rather, a quasi contract is a contract implied in law, which is an obligation imposed by law to avoid injustice. Quasi contracts sometimes are used to provide a remedy when the parties enter into a void, an unenforceable, or a voidable contract that is avoided. In such a case, the law of quasi contracts will determine what recovery is permitted for any performance rendered by the parties under the invalid, unenforceable, or invalidated agreements.

(iv) Damages Resulting from Business Contracts

Courts award various damages, mostly monetary in nature, to an injured claimant (plaintiff) from suffering caused by another party (defendant) that breached any contractual terms and conditions. These awards are paid to an individual or organization for loss or injury. The rules for awarding damages vary with the type of claim filed (breach of contract claim vs. tort claim) and location and the type of jurisdiction (i.e., state or federal). Damages are of four major types: compensatory, consequential, liquidating, and punitive damages.

A **compensatory damage** is a direct (normal) and actual damage paid to compensate the claimant (victim) for loss suffered as a result of another party's breach of duty. Compensatory damages paid by the party that breached the contract are called expectation damages in the contract law involving business contracts. The goal is to make the victim whole and satisfied.

A **consequential damage** is an indirect and special damage awarded due to loss of product or service, loss of profits, or loss of operating revenue if the court decides that such damages are reasonable, foreseeable, or expected of the parties at the time of contract formation. Note that the U.S. Supreme Court has held that consequential damages are not available in the federal courts.

A **liquidating damage** clause in a contract will be not enforced if it amounts to a penalty (i.e., penal damages). The clause will be enforced only if it involves a genuine attempt to quantify a loss in advance and is a good-faith estimate of economic loss. Courts have ruled that excessive liquidating damages are equal to penal damages.

A **punitive damage** is a noncompensatory damage that may be awarded to a plaintiff in order to deter a defendant. Punitive damages are awarded that are over and above compensatory damages and are subjected to the limitations imposed by the due process of law. Punitive damages may be awarded in the case of fraud and product liability cases.

CALCULATION OF COMPENSATORY AND CONSEQUENTIAL DAMAGES

Example

John (the seller) and Tom (the buyer) entered into a contract for the sale and purchase of Item K for $12,000. Later, John finds out that Tom wants to resell the item to Gary, a reseller, for a 10% profit after the purchase. John breaches the contract and sells the item directly to Gary instead of to Tom. The market price of Item K at the time of breach is $13,000. Now Tom sues John for breach of the contract. How much Tom can expect in compensatory damages and consequential damages, if anything?

Compensatory damage = Market price − Contract price = $13,000 − $12,000 = $1,000

Consequential damage = Profit percentage of the contract price = 10% of $12,000 = $1,200

(d) Other Topics Related to Contracts

This section discusses several miscellaneous topics, such as product reviews by consumers, ultra vires and intra vires legal actions, letter of intent, customers agree not to sue a company, product warranties, and contractual issues with IP assets.

(i) Product Reviews by Consumers

Regarding product reviews, before the U.S. Congress passed the Consumer Review Fairness Act of 2016, a company might sue customers who wrote honest but negative reviews about a company's product or service or claim they had to pay much more than the advertised price for the product. This act made such actions illegal.

The Consumer Review Fairness Act says businesses cannot use contracts that prevent customers from writing a truthful comment or penalize customers for writing negative reviews. If a business, including an online business, uses contract terms or conditions that limit a customer's right to comment, it is breaking the law.

An ethical question that can be raised with product reviews by customers is whether a seller (company) can buy post-sale feedback from a buyer (customer). The seller could pay the buyer in several ways, such as a gift card, cash card, reward points, vacation, travel trip, or discounts on future purchases. Another ethical question is whether product reviews are written by real customers (good and bad reviews), paid or unpaid ghost customers (good reviews only), a seller's employees (good reviews only), a competitor's employees (bad reviews only), or a bot software (good and bad reviews).

(ii) Ultra Vires and Intra Vires Legal Actions

Sometimes, lower-level managers may take business-related actions with or without the explicit authority and power given to them by upper-level managers. Examples of these actions could be dealing with outside contractors, suppliers, vendors, consultants, other businesses, and government authorities. The law views the validity of these actions differently, as follows:

- Actions taken without proper authority are called ultra vires (i.e., beyond the power). These actions can be construed by law as invalid actions.

- Actions taken with proper authority are called intra vires (i.e., within the power). These actions can be construed by law as valid actions.

(iii) Letter of Intent

A letter of intent drawn between two or more parties could be a binding contract depending on how it is written. This means that if the letter is very detailed and specific with names, dates, action plans, and locations, it could be binding. If the letter is general and vague, then it is not binding.

(iv) Customers Agree Not to Sue a Company

A contract requiring customers not to sue a company during their lifetime for any reason in exchange for a gift card, a small cash amount, or other token rewards is illegal and unenforceable.

(v) Product Warranties

A retail or manufacturing company must adhere to the Magnuson-Mass Warranty Act of 1974, which governs consumer product warranties. The act requires manufacturers and sellers of consumer products to provide consumers with detailed information about warranty coverage. In addition, it affects both the rights of consumers and the obligations of warrantors under written warranties.

Two types of warranties exist: product warranty and service contract.

(A) Product Warranty

When a customer makes a major purchase of a product, the manufacturer or retailer (seller) makes an important promise to stand behind the product. It's called a warranty. Although not required by law, written warranties come with most major purchases. U.S. federal law requires that warranties be available for customers to read before they buy, even when the customers are shopping by catalog or on the Internet. Three essential elements of warranties include type (i.e., limited or full), time (i.e., 30 days or 90 days), and coverage (i.e., what parts and repairs covered, personal use versus business use, and what damages are covered). For example, consequential damage of spoiled food resulting from a freezer breakdown at a home and the time and expense incurred in getting damage repaired are not usually covered by warranties.

(B) Service Contract

When a customer buys a car, an appliance, or an electronic device, a service contract is called an extended warranty. But there is an important difference: A normal warranty cost is included in the price of a product whereas a service contract cost is not part of the product price. Instead, the service cost is an extra or add-on cost that might not be worth the price. Some service contracts duplicate the warranty coverage that the manufacturer provides; some cover only part of the product; and some make it nearly impossible to get repairs when a customer needs them.

(C) Express Warranty

Express warranty is a type of guarantee given by a manufacturer or retailer for a specific product purchased by a customer. The express warranty document describes the terms and conditions of the warranty in a clear and complete manner so customers know what is included in or excluded from the warranty. The cost of an express warranty is included in the price of a product.

(D) Implied Warranty

An implied warranty is created by state law, and all states have these warranties. Almost every purchase a customer makes is covered by an implied warranty. The most common type of implied warranty—a warranty of merchantability—means that a seller promises that the product will do what it is supposed to do (e.g., a car will run and a toaster will toast). Here, the seller assures customers that the product a customer buys meet all standards for the ordinary purposes for which such product was designed and used in the manner described in the product manual.

Another type of implied warranty is the warranty of fitness for a particular purpose. This applies when a customer buys a product on the seller's advice that it is suitable for a particular use. For example, a seller who suggests that a customer buy a certain sleeping bag for zero-degree weather warrants that the sleeping bag will be suitable for zero degrees.

If a customer's purchase does not come with a written warranty, it is still covered by implied warranties unless the product is marked and sold "as is," or the seller otherwise indicates in writing that no warranty is given. The cost of an implied warranty is included in the price of a product.

(E) Exclusive Warranty

A seller or servicer can make an exclusive warranty to a customer for a high-priced product, a custom-made product, or a special service work. It is so exclusive that no other customers would get the same type of warranty. Exclusive warranties can be expensive because they are for special products or services. The cost of an exclusive warranty is included in the price of a product.

(F) Quasi Warranty

A quasi warranty is not a full and complete warranty. It may lack the full strength and coverage of a regular warranty. "Quasi" means partial or limited, perhaps with lower warranty cost. The cost of a quasi warranty is included in the price of a product.

(G) Oral Warranty

If a salesperson makes a promise orally, such as that the company will provide free repairs, get it in writing. Otherwise, a customer may not be able to get the warranty service that was promised. The cost of an oral warranty is not included in the price of a product because the warranty never became official.

(H) Extended Warranty

A seller offers an extended warranty to a customer when the customer is buying a car, an appliance, or an electronic device. This extended warranty is called a service contract. Both service contracts and warranties provide repair or maintenance for a specific time. The cost of an extended warranty is not included in the price of a product because it is a separate cost item.

(vi) Contractual Issues with IP Assets

This section defines intellectual property (IP) assets, risks and best practices in IP assets, software escrow arrangements, source code vulnerabilities, software licensing practices, software piracy, copyright laws, penalties in contracts, and acceptance testing of contracts.

(A) Intellectual Property Assets

Intellectual property (IP) assets consists of copyrights, trademarks, service marks, patents, trade secrets, and know-how (i.e., talent, skill, knowledge, expertise, technology, management, engineering, design, development, and implementation). The amount of IP assets has a direct relationship to the level of innovation in a country. This means, the larger the IP asset pool, the greater the levels of innovation. Computer software is copyrightable and it is a part of IP assets and so it must be protected.

Major IP risks include:

- Softlifting (copying), stealing, and selling of IP software and data by insiders (employees) and outsiders (hackers). Softlifting can occur when employees silently and illegally copy a company's licensed computer software using "bring your own device" (BYOD) for whatever reason.

- Employee turnover making employee accountability a difficult task

- Lack of employee training and awareness about IP assets and their value

- Inadequate policies on employee hiring and termination practices, including job previews and exit interviews addressing IP policies

- Lack of purchase of IP liability insurance to protect against infringement claims such as mitigation damages and legal expenses

- Source code vulnerability in terms of not having a solid software escrow arrangement and not having a clear access to source code

Software escrow arrangement represents something (e.g., a paper document, a digital document, software source code, a lockbox key, or an encryption key) that is delivered to a third person to be given to the grantee only upon the fulfillment of a condition or a contract.

Source code vulnerability means the source code can become an entry point into computers, similar to mobile devices, which can be a target for hackers to launch attacks. This is a risk, not the major risk.

Source code vulnerability does not apply to internally developed software because the developing company owns and keeps the source code in its possession. No need to obtain the source code from outside developers. Source code vulnerability is not possessing or not accessing source code (i.e., a computer program) which is vital to running, operating, and maintaining a computer system.

Source code vulnerability applies to commercially developed software, off-the shelf software, and open-source software, and other outside sources. The outside developer owns the source code and does not give the code to its customers so a vulnerability exists to his customers. The buying customer needs to obtain a copy of the source code to run and maintain his computer systems in case the commercial developer goes out of business.

- Infringement claims and costs from violating IP laws (i.e., lawsuits, court fines, and penalties). Infringement claims address costs incurred when the rights of the IP asset owners are ignored or violated (e.g., patents and trade secrets

- Not conducting a software piracy audit periodically to assess the level and severity of piracy in a company

Best Practices in IP include:

- **Purchasing an IP liability insurance policy** is a good risk strategy because this policy can cover litigation expenses and infringement costs and protect the IP assets.

- **Conducting a due diligence review of IP assets** such as a source code review is a good business practice and should be conducted at the beginning a contract and on an ongoing basis. This may include vetting a third-parry source code before signing a contract, before loading the code, before hosting the software, and before paying any bills to the third-party.

- **Updating employee hiring and terminating programs** is a good company policy so employees are aware of the rules and restrictions placed on the IP assets at the time of hiring and at the time of termination through exit interviews and cancellation of access rights to IP assets. A confidentiality agreement and a conflict-of-interest document needs to be signed by every employee.

- **Limiting employee access to IP assets** is the best security strategy based on an employee's job duties and need-to-know principle. Here, use of a Digital Rights Management (DRM) software is good so it can restrict access to IP asset files.

- **Training employees in IP laws, rules, and regulations**

Laws Protecting IP Assets. Major laws protecting IP assets include the following:

Computer Software Copyright Act. Computer Software Copyright Act includes computer programs in the list of tangible writings protected by copyright law. The creator (owner) of a copyrightable software program obtains automatic copyright protection. This choice can protect computer software from infringement claims.

Digital Millennium Copyright Act. The Digital Millennium Copyright Act (DMCA) criminalizes production and dissemination of technology, devices, or services that are used to circumvent measures that control access to copyrighted works and criminalizes the act of circumventing an access control, even when there is no infringement of copyright itself. The DMCA also heightens the penalties for copyright infringement on the Internet. DMCA implements treaties of the World Intellectual Property Organization (WIPO). This choice can protect computer software from infringement claims.

Invisible digital watermarking. Watermarking is a type of marking that embeds copyright information about the copyright owner. Digital watermarking is the process of irreversibly embedding information into a digital signal. Watermarking can be visible (i.e., information is shown in a picture, video, text, or logo) and invisible (i.e., information is hidden). Invisible digital watermarking protects copyright materials which are intended to prevent or deter unauthorized copying of digital media. Invisible watermarking can protect computer software from infringement claims.

(B) Software Licensing Practices

Several variations exist in software licensing practices. The next list indicates how software is licensed for personal computers (PCs), local area networks (LANs), and workstations:

- Major characteristics of the application, whether it is a single-user or multiple-user application

- Major classification of software agreements, such as single-user program or multiple-user software

- Multiuser software is further subdivided into site licenses, per-server licenses, per-PC licenses, and number-of-users licenses.

- Maximum number of concurrent users. Regardless of the machine in use, a LAN software license can be bought only for the number of employees who would use the software simultaneously. Either a LAN operating system or a utility program can monitor concurrent access to the software on a network.

- Floating licenses. In a client-server environment, often a single copy of a software program is bought, and a client license is obtained for each workstation. In this arrangement, the specified number of licenses is bought and only required workstations can use it. It does not matter who uses the workstations as long as the number of users does not exceed the number contracted for. Floating licenses are distributed by the server when a license request is received from a client.

Requirements for a successful and complete software contract negotiation include:

- The basis for the license per CPU machine
- Specifying most-favored-customer status generally through price concessions
- Arbitration clauses where disputes are submitted for binding arbitration
- Cancellation clauses with time periods and charges required
- Software fixes, upgrades, and future options
- Responsibility for the independent or subcontractors hired and provided by the vendor

- Responsibility for inherent defects in the software or hardware
- Insurance requirements on the software product or the hardware device
- Software and hardware maintenance requirements
- Notification of unauthorized use or possession of vendor software
- Document and software reproduction rights and limitations
- Computer virus damage, detection, and prevention requirements
- Access to source code and its modifications
- Global use of software and hardware

Legal and contractual issues when end users directly acquire or use software from third parties or software publishers include:

- The end user licensing agreement is a legal contract between a buyer or acquirer (end user) and a seller (third parties or software publishers). It spells out the terms and conditions for using the software. The agreement might say that only the buyer can install the software on the buyer's computer for personal use, that the buyer agrees to third-party monitoring of the software, or that the buyer allows access to parts of the buyer's computer.

- The licensing agreement can affect the buyer's online security, privacy, flexibility, and freedom. Specifically, the buyer should be concerned about agreements that allow the software publisher or third parties to:
  - □ Monitor the buyer's Internet activity.
  - □ Collect the buyer's personal information.
  - □ Use or share the buyer's computing resources or information.
  - □ Hold the buyer accountable for the software agreements governing third-party software components.

- Most agreements limit the buyer's ability to sue the third party or the publisher for any damages cause by using the software.

- The use of free software or peer-to-peer (P2P) file-sharing software can be risky because it might require the buyer to exchange some personal information in order to use the software.

- Cascading end user licensing agreements can be very risky due to several unknown and intermediate firms involved in the production and distribution of the final software that the buyer is acquiring or using. There could be a primary software vendor, an upstream third-party software vendor, or a downstream third-party software vendor; each vendor may force the buyer to accept its own licensing agreements. The primary software vendor might not fully know about the use of upstream or downstream vendors' software components that went into the final software and the terms and conditions required of these third-party software licensing agreements.

(C) Software Piracy

The vast majority of the software involved in software piracy legal cases is off-the-shelf, PC software, such as word processing, spreadsheets, graphics, and databases. The issue is illegal use, copying, and distribution of software both inside and outside the organization. Here "illegal" means that a user has not paid for the software.

Software piracy policies are needed to protect the organization from legal suits by owners. The policy should include:

- Prohibiting illegal copy and use of software.
- Developing a software inventory management system that includes a list of popular application programs. This list can be compared to the organization's purchase orders, original software diskettes, or original documentation manual.
- Periodically checking PC hard disks for illegally copied software.
- Making illegal copying of software grounds for employee dismissal.
- Requiring all employees to sign a statement that they will not use illegal software at work and not use the illegal software taken from home to work.
- Prohibiting copying of internally developed software.
- Prohibiting pirated externally developed software from being brought into the organization.
- Monitoring all sensitive computer programs against illegal copying.

(D) Copyright Laws

Copyright laws protect software. The act of illegally (not paying for) copying, duplicating, or using the software is called software piracy. Internet piracy involves illegally gaining access to and using the Internet. Many companies on the Internet receive customer fees for research, services, information (e.g., sports and market analysis), and products. When unauthorized people use such services illegally, Internet firms lose revenues. Both software piracy and Internet piracy are increasing.

Copyright laws give protection to authors for almost anything they create that can be expressed in tangible form. Under the law, only authors or copyright owners may make copies unless permission is granted to others. When authors sell the copyright, the new owner takes over all the rights and privileges of authors.

Computer programs are copyrightable. Source code, microcode, and object code can be copyrighted. Blank forms can be copyrighted if they convey some information by their organization and have considerable originality. Similarly, computer terminal screens can be copyrighted if they are part of a computer program, and vice versa. However, procedures, concepts, and principles cannot be copyrighted.

One computer program is said to be an **infringement** on another when the alleged infringing product and the copyrighted product contain many similar design features and functions. Although the structure, sequence, and organization of a computer program are protected by copyright, the physical order of the subroutines and their calling sequences are not protected.

Input formats are copyrightable in some courts but not in others. Statistical formulas are not copyrightable when they are used in an input format. Even innocent or unintentional infringers may be liable for using a copyrighted material without the written permission of the owner.

Legal penalties for copyright infringement may include injunction, punitive damages, and possible criminal prosecution. However, penalties do not include payment of actual damages as well as any profits. Attorneys' fees and costs may be awarded.

Fair use is a defense against a charge of copyright infringement. Fair use depends on the:

- Amount of material and economic impact of the material that was "taken."
- Nature of the copyrighted work.
- Nature and purpose of the use (i.e., whether it is commercial or not).

When a teacher copies substantial portions of a text for students, it is not a fair use. If what is copied is a small portion of the text, it would come under fair use. *Selling illegal copies of software for profit would not be fair use, whereas making one backup copy for archival purposes would be fair use.*

When consultants, software developers, and employees are doing work for an organization, the organization becomes the owner of the work products. In order for an organization to claim product ownership, the work should be a part of an employee's job description.

(E) Penalties in Contracts

If the customer/client refuses to pay due to nonperformance by a vendor/contractor, can the contractor "electronically repossess" the software that he or she developed/maintained for or supplied to the customer? The question is: Who is right?

Even where it is clear that the client wrongfully refused to pay for the contractor's work, electronic repossession of software is not always justified. The contractor/developer's claim for payments due does not automatically include a right to repossess or disable the software, especially without going to the court. One exception is when the contractor is the owner or has a personal property interest in the software product. Disabling of computer software could interrupt business operations and customer services.

Even where the vendor has an arguable right to "repossess" or disable the software, the manner in which the repossession is executed may itself be wrongful. If a contractor/developer must access the customer/client's computer in order to remove or disable the software, this may constitute a violation of federal and/or state computer crime statutes.

If a contractor disables the client's software, the client can sue the contractor for trespass, intentional interference with contractual relations, and breach of contract.

Automatic disabling mechanisms, such as time/logic bombs; drop-dead devices; Trojan horses; access keys; and unauthorized program code inserted into the computer system to be activated by the system date on the computer; by turning up a counter; or by occurrence of some specific event or condition are all illegal.

Software-disabling mechanisms by vendor/contractor require advance notice to the client (i.e., clients must be notified prior to entering into a software agreement).

Courts do not appreciate the idea that business operations are at the mercy of, or slaves to, a computer. The courts would prohibit the vendor from activating the drop-dead device if prior notice is not given to the customer. However, courts would allow a vendor to activate a drop-dead device where notice of the device was included in the contract. In either case, such contractual protection will not protect the vendor/contractor if the vendor itself is in default (i.e., nonperformance).

(F) Acceptance Testing of Contracts

The next list provides guidelines for acceptance testing of software contracts.

- A well-drafted contract will not guarantee the quality of software development and maintenance work, but it can provide the developer a strong incentive to do the job right, and it can give the client some legal protection in the event there is a problem.

- Every software acquisition or development contract should include one element: the right to conduct an acceptance test. Successful completion of an acceptance test should be a condition that must be met before final payment is made to the contractor or vendor. If the software does not perform properly, the final payment should be withheld until the contractor/vendor corrects the problem, refunds the amounts previously paid, fixes the software without pay, or provides some other remedy.

- Defining what constitutes acceptance testing is a major question and concern. Here the buyer or the client needs to evaluate both the performance and the reliability of the software. It is important that the specifications contained in the contract be clear, thorough, and complete since the test results are measured against these specifications.

The contract should define the obligations of each party during the acceptance test. The contract should specify, for example:

- Whether the test is done by the client, vendor, third party, or in combination.
- Who supplies or prepares the test data.
- Who corrects software problems during the test.
- How long postinstallation support is provided.
- What happens if the software fails or is defective or inoperable. The fallback plan must be specified.
- How the software acceptance is to be communicated.
- When the warranty begins.

When the software does not work as expected, the customer can:

- Return the software.
- Cancel the contract.
- Obtain a refund of all or partial sums paid.
- Accept the defective software at a reduced price.

1.10 Big Data and Data Analytics

This section discusses five major topics: big data, data counting methods, data analytics, data mining, and big-data audit.

(a) Big Data

Simply stated, the term "big data" means vast amounts of data collected from a variety of sources. It is big in terms of many data volumes, several datasets, and many data types. Data volumes are related to data files stored in databases and mass storage devices (e.g., redundant array of independent disks [RAIDs]). Datasets include several data elements, such as customer name and account number. Data types mean alphabetic, numeric, alphanumeric, and special characters. The term "big data" is subjective, depending on the size and complexity of an organization. New and actionable insights can be deduced from the big data. Here, data analytics are the major topic and focus in data analysis and extraction methods, as shown in the next table:

Big Data ⟶	Data Analysis and Extraction Methods ⟶	New Knowledge
Structured data	Data analytics	New information
Unstructured data	Statistical analyses	Actionable insights and inferences
Semistructured data	Data mining methods	Meaningful actions
Sanitized data	Simulation techniques	New results and decisions
Data patterns and trends	Forecasting methods	New value uncovered/created

(i) Data Life Cycle

Similar to a PLC, data has its own life cycle showing how data is discovered, created, generated, deployed, and used from beginning to the end.

$$\text{Data Life Cycle} = \text{Discover} + \text{Deploy}$$

Here, "Discover" focuses on tasks such as prepare, explore, and model, and "Deploy" focuses on tasks such as implement, act, and evaluate.

Another way of viewing the data life cycle is to see how data turns into results and decisions. This is shown next.

$$\text{Data} \longrightarrow \text{Analytics} \longrightarrow \text{Insights} \longrightarrow \text{Results} \longrightarrow \text{Decisions}$$

Data is subjected to analysis to yield new insights, results, and decisions. Here, the term "data" refers to collecting or generating data in a form that can be processed. "Analytics" means cleansing, normalizing, aggregating, extracting, and analyzing the data. "Results" means improving decisions, actions, and outcomes to realize new benefits. "Decisions" means (1) acquiring new customers, suppliers, and vendors; (2) increasing sales, revenues, and profits; (3) decreasing costs; (4) signing new business contracts; (5) developing new business partners and strategic alliances; and (6) above all, gaining a competitive edge.

Big data does not necessarily mean a good data; it could be bad data. Consequences are:

Good Data ⟶ Good Results, Outcomes, and Decisions

Bad Data ⟶ Bad Results, Outcomes, and Decisions

What makes data good data or bad data is related to data quality, data security, and data privacy. Data owners and data stewards within an organization manage and control the data quality, security, and privacy.

(ii) Data Owners and Stewards

Big data needs owners and stewards to manage and control the data assets on an ongoing basis to reduce risks facing data.

A **data owner** is a person or department responsible for safeguarding or securing data with security controls, classifying data (sensitive or not sensitive), and defining data access rules (grant or deny).

A **data steward** or **data custodian** is a person or department delegated the responsibility for managing a specific set of data resources (e.g., data volumes, files, and elements). This person defines, specifies, and standardizes the data assets of an organization within and across all functional areas. There can be several data owners and data custodians protecting data assets. Data owners and stewards establish acceptable use policies and access rules because data usage rules stem from data usage policies.

Acceptable use policies require that a system user, an end user, or an administrator (e.g., system, security, and network administrator) agrees to comply with such policies prior to accessing computer systems, internal networks, and external networks (the Internet). Acceptable use is based on authorized access.

For example, in a cloud computing environment, subscribers ensure that all subscriber personnel read and understand the provider's acceptable use policy and negotiate an agreement for resolution of agreed-on policy violations in advance with the provider. The agreement also includes a process for resolving disputes over possible policy violations.

Two concepts related to acceptable use policies and access rules are *rules of behavior* and *rules of engagement*.

Access rules are clear action statements dealing with expected user behavior in a computer system. Access rules reflect security policies and practices, business rules, information ethics, system functions and features, and individual roles and responsibilities, which collectively form access restrictions.

Rules of behavior are conditions established and implemented concerning use of, security in, and acceptable level of risk of the system. Rules will clearly delineate responsibilities and expected behavior of all individuals with access to the system. The organization establishes and makes readily available to all information system users a set of rules that describes their responsibilities and expected behavior with regard to information system usage. Rules of behavior are established to control the behavior of employees on computer systems.

Rules of engagement are detailed guidelines and constraints regarding the execution of information security testing. These rules are established before the start of a security test. The rules give the test team authority to conduct the defined activities without the need for additional permissions. Rules of engagement are established to control the behavior of contractors, vendors, and suppliers during their work for an organization.

(iii) Data Analytics Process

A structured and standard methodology is needed for performing data analysis to yield consistent results and insights. A five-step analytical procedure is suggested here:

1. Define the question and hypothesis.

2. Obtain relevant data from known data sources.

3. Clean and normalize the selected data.

4. Conduct data analysis.

5. Communicate analytical results and outcomes.

Step 1: Define the Question and Hypothesis

This step requires formulating a basic question and its associated hypothesis that can be tested by data analysis. For example, a retailer might put a question as follows: How does the merchandise return policy affect current and future sales? The corresponding hypothesis might look like this: A rigid return policy with a shorter period could decrease sales while a flexible return policy with a longer period could increase sales.

Step 2: Obtain Relevant Data from Known Data Sources

This step requires identifying relevant data needed from all data sources to test the hypothesis. For example, retailers can look at their past sales and past return policies and can gather similar information from other retailers to study.

Step 3: Clean and Normalize the Selected Data

Before data mining software tools are applied, the target raw datasets must be cleaned and normalized to remove missing, erroneous, or inappropriate data. **Data cleansing methods** purify data or filter inappropriate data and include log management functions, such as log filtering, log correlations, and log analysis. One reason to perform data cleansing is due to data mingling. In data mingling, data related to some event, incident, or activity is mixed with data unrelated to that event, incident, or activity, thus making these two data types often indistinguishable. Data mingling can be attributed to inadequate labeling and limited memory storage. The comingling of data will make the task of an auditor, analyst, or investigator more challenging because it is difficult to know which data caused an event or incident. Thus, data mingling problems make the data unclean.

Data normalization methods convert clean data into a standardized format and label it consistently. One of the most common uses of normalization is storing computer transaction dates and times (system clocks) in a single format (e.g., synchronizing time stamps of 12-hour format or 24-hour format with different time zones in a country or continent). Converting data to consistent formats and labels makes data analysis and reporting much easier.

Data wrangling software also cleans and normalizes raw data because it refines and reshapes raw data into actionable and usable data.

In summary, the data cleansing and data normalizations actions are performed in a preprocessing prior to data mining step as shown:

Preprocessing	→	Data Mining	→	Postprocessing
Raw data		Software tools		Insights and decisions
Data cleansing		Data analytics		Results and reports
Data normalization				

Step 4: Conduct Data Analysis

After raw data is cleansed and normalized, the data analyst can analyze the data to test different hypotheses by developing different data models to identify retail sales patterns and to show how they are correlated with the merchandise return policy. For example, a retailer found out that a rigid return policy (e.g., 15 days are allowed to return merchandise after purchase) decreased sales while a flexible return policy (e.g., 30 days are allowed to return merchandise after purchase) increased sales. This is because customers want a longer period to determine whether to keep or return a product based on how it works. So, customers want to buy from a retailer with a flexible return policy, resulting in increased sales, and customers do not want to buy from a retailer with a rigid return policy, resulting in decreased sales. The same thing can be said about shipping terms for merchandise where free shipping increases sales and no free shipping decreases sales.

Step 5: Communicate Analytical Results and Outcomes

The last step is to convert the discovered data analytical results and outcomes into the retailer's strategy and put it into operational use. The retailer changed its merchandise return policy to a flexible policy of 30 days. These results can be communicated to management through the use of data visualization tools, such as charts, graphs, tables, or exhibits.

(iv) Data Analysis and Internal Auditors

Data analysis can help internal auditors meet their auditing objectives, such as detecting changes or vulnerabilities in business processes that could expose an organization undue and unplanned risks. The data sources can be fully manual, semiautomated or semimanual, and fully automated. A specific audit objective in analyzing data is to identify fraud, errors, inefficiencies, or noncompliance.[19]

Examples of analytical tests to find patterns and trends in data include:

- Calculation of basic statistical parameters (e.g., averages, standard deviations, variance, highest and lowest values [ranges], excessively high values or low values, and control totals) to identify outlying transactions.

- Numeric digit testing using Benford's law of first-digit test to identify statistically unlikely occurrences of specific digits in naturally occurring datasets. Benford's law gives the expected frequencies of the first digits in tabulated data and finds that the first digits are not all equally likely. There is a biased skewness in favor of the lower digits. This means that the digit 1 has a higher likelihood of occurring as the first digit than the digit 9.

- Data match testing of names, addresses, and account numbers in disparate systems and locations.

- Data duplicate testing of payments, payroll, customer claims, or expense reports line items.

- Data gap testing to identify missing numbers in sequential data.

- Date checking tests where time stamps are used to identify transaction posting times or data entry times to determine their appropriateness and correctness.

(v) Data Mapping and Data Matching Tools

Data mapping involves laying out a clear data path containing related data elements of interest to achieve an end goal of identifying data relationships.

---

[19] *IPPF—Practice Guide, GTAG-16, Data Analysis Technologies* (Altamonte Springs, FL: Institute of Internal Auditors, August 2011). www.theiia.org.

Data matching is a computer matching technique that can prevent improper payments and detect fraudulent activities by comparing data from several, related computer systems. Here data from several different data files (i.e., internal and external) are matched to verify the eligibility prior to payment; improper payments are stopped when they happen. Hence, data matching is both a preventive and a detective control. The goal is to identify data inconsistencies across several computer data files.

Applications of data mapping and matching tools in government include stop payments of:

- Social Security benefits to dead people
- Maternity benefits to a male employee
- Overtime hours to a terminated employee
- Weekly wages to an imposter employee
- Invoices of a phony vendor

(vi) Why Use Big Data?

Traditionally, organizations relied heavily on internal data for decision-making purposes but soon found out that these internal sources are too limited to grow their businesses. Later, organizations realized that they can discover and explore vast amounts of external data that allow them to gain additional insights to grow their businesses. This so-called big data came from internal and external sources. Other names given for big data are data mart, data mall, data highway, data lakes, data hounds, data bazaar, data stash, and data tsunami.

Big Data = Internal Data + External Data = New Opportunities

Big Data $\longrightarrow$ Big Decisions

Big Data $\longrightarrow$ New Insights $\longrightarrow$ New Strategies $\longrightarrow$ New Decisions $\longrightarrow$ New Actions

Big Data = New Data Asset = New Strategic Asset

Big Data $\longrightarrow$ Assurance Procedures and Consulting Services

For internal auditors, utilizing big data can reveal new insights, which, in turn, will allow them to make new recommendations to management that will result in new improvements for the organization, resulting in an additional or incremental value.

(vii) Nature and Types of Big Data

Big data can be structured and well organized or it can be unstructured and very disorganized. Whether data is organized or disorganized is attributed to its source. However, valid and useful data can be found in both structured data and unstructured data; the only question is how much and where. In comparison, one can say internal data is structured data and external data is unstructured data. Big data can also come in a semistructured format from external sources. It has been said that more than 80% of business data is unstructured data.

Big Data = Structured Data + Unstructured Data + Semi-structured Data

Internal Data = Structured Data

External Data = Unstructured Data + Semi-structured Data

Structured data consists of internal data sources with fixed-form format; data warehouses; traditional and fixed data structures; database files (e.g., relational or hierarchical); flat data files; interconnected computer systems and data sources; data that is easy to manage and control; validated data; data that uses a standard data structure; data owners and data stewards are known; and data that uses incompatible data file formats.

Unstructured data consists of external data sources with free-form format; nontraditional data structures; nonfixed data structures; disconnected computer systems and data sources; data that is not easy to manage and control; nonvalidated data; data that does not use a standard data structure; data whose owners and stewards are unknown; and data that uses incompatible data file formats.

Semistructured data consists of external data sources with fixed-form format: Extensible Markup Language (XML), Hypertext Markup Language (HTML), and Extended Hypertext Markup Language (XHTML). XML is a metalanguage with a flexible text format designed to describe data for electronic publishing. The web browser interprets the XML, and the XML takes over the HTML for creating dynamic web documents. HTML is a markup language that is a subset of standard generalized markup language (SGML). It is used to create hypertext and hypermedia documents on the web that incorporate text, graphics, sound, video, and hyperlinks. HTML is a mechanism used to create dynamic web pages on the Internet. XHTML is a unifying standard that brings the benefits of XML to HTML. XHTML is the new web standard and should be used for all new web pages to achieve maximum portability across platforms and browsers.

(viii) Sources of Big Data

When comparing different sources of data, internal data sources provide structured data and external data sources provide unstructured and semistructured data.

Structured data sources include internal source documents, such as sales orders and invoices; purchase requests and orders (procurement records); operating expenses; production and service records; materials and labor records; finished goods inventory records; payments to employees and vendors (employee payroll and vendor invoices); charge card transactions; cash receipts; payments from customers (receivable receipts); operating budget and capital budget records; contracts; and customer merchandise returns.

Unstructured data sources include external sources, such as public online, search engine, private online, and research websites; public libraries; governmental agency websites, social media websites, website blogs, online chats, publicly posted videos and audios, electronic mail, office memos, reports, and notes; white papers and research studies; spreadsheet data; text messages (short messaging service [SMS] and multimedia messaging service (MMS)); and human language, audio, and video. Specifically, unstructured data consists of multimedia files, image files, sound files, and unstructured text files.

Semistructured data sources include web documents and web pages.

Another way of classifying big data is by where it is found, such as government data (more reliable), proprietary data (a company's internal data, which is more reliable), open source data (i.e., Internet-based, which is not reliable), research data (more reliable), industry data (more reliable), and anonymous data (less reliable).

In summary:

- Structured data is found in data tables, data records, and computer flat files.
- Unstructured data is found in human languages, audio, and video.

- Semistructured data is found in XML and HTML web languages.
- Raw data is found in customer orders and POS terminals.
- Complex data is found in databases (e.g., relational or hierarchical) and legacy systems.
- Social media data is found in blogs, tweets, and posts.
- Machine-generated data is found in electronic sensors, retail merchandise (RFID) tags, mobile devices, and the Internet of Things (IoT) technologies.

(ix) Characteristics of Big Data

According to the IIA's *Global Technology Audit Guide*, big data can have seven dimensions, characteristics, or attributes, which are discussed next.[20]

(A) Seven Vs of Big Data

1. **Volume** is the amount of data being created; it is vast compared to traditional data sources.

2. **Variety** of data comes from all types of formats. This can include data generated within an organization as well as data created from external sources, including publicly available data.

3. **Velocity** means data is being generated extremely quickly and continuously.

4. **Veracity** means data must be able to be verified based on both accuracy and context.

5. **Variability** means big data is extremely variable and always changing.

6. **Visualization** means translating vast amounts of data into readily presentable graphics and charts that are easy to understand and are critical to end user satisfaction where these graphs and charts may highlight additional insights. Data visualization software tools are available to bring out these insights in the form of pictures, graphs, exhibits, tables, and storyboards because raw analytic results from big data are often hard to read and interpret. *Datafication*, the process of putting information in an easily searchable and analyzable format, is a prerequisite to data visualization. Examples of datafication efforts include turning paper documents into electronic health and medical records to allow searches, electronically indexing paper documents to allow searches, and electronically indexing websites to allow searches. The idea is that when data is put in a searchable and analyzable format, it can be presented easily.

7. **Value** means organizations, societies, and consumers can all benefit from big data. Value is generated when new insights are translated into actions that create positive outcomes.

In summary, business insight (value of data) and speed (velocity of data) are the main business drivers of investment in big data. Variety of data continues to outweigh volume and velocity as the technical drivers behind big data investment.

(B) Virtual Data Tsunami

According to the United States Government Accountability Office, big data is a "virtual data tsunami." It is a twenty-first-century development consisting of volume, variety, and velocity characteristics that allow management performing new analytics, improving cognitive computing systems, and building advanced machine-learning technologies.[21]

---

[20] IIA's Global Technology Audit Guide, *Understanding and Auditing Big Data* (2017). www.theiia.org

[21] *Data and Analytics Innovation*, GAO-16-659SP (Washington, DC: GAO, September 2016). www.gao.gov.

New analytics are tools for examining large amounts of varied data to uncover subtle or hidden patterns, correlations, and other insights, such as market trends and customer purchasing preferences.

The term **"cognitive computing systems"** refers to computing systems that perform human cognitive functions like memory, recall, judgment, inference, and learning.

Advanced machine learning technology is an artificial intelligence (AI) discipline that allows computers to handle new situations via analysis, self-training, observation, and experience, all with minimal "supervision" by humans.

(C) Return on Data

The real value of big data does not come from a mere collection of data from several sources. Instead, the real value comes from data usage and application, which can lead to major insights and better decisions. Because big data (data asset or strategic asset) is put to so many good uses and with so many benefits, a return on data (ROD) metric can be calculated for value-measuring purposes. ROD indicates how data assets of an organization are utilized effectively and efficiently (i.e., 10% or 40%). ROD is calculated as follows:

$$ROD = (\text{Dollar benefits from big data}) / (\text{Dollar investment in big data}) \times 100$$

(D) Technologies in Big Data

Big data requires deployment of new technologies that are different from traditional technologies used to simply process day-to-day business transactional, financial, and operational data. New technologies require new software (either developed in house or acquired from outside), new hardware, and new employees with new technical skills. The reason for deploying new technologies to process and handle big data is that big data comes from disparate and disconnected systems from inside and outside of an organization. A proof of concept is required to illustrate the value of deploying a new technology and to obtain management commitment, support, and funding.

Examples of technologies used in big data are listed next.

- Company's online websites
- Company's databases, data warehouses, and data marts
- Data mining software tools to identify patterns and trends in big data
- Data visualization software
- Data dashboard software
- Search engine websites (e.g., Google, Yahoo, and Bing)
- Mobile website operating systems (Apple's iOS and Google's Android)
- Text messaging services (e.g., SMS and MMS)
- Electronic mail services (e.g., individual or group)
- Mobile device technologies (e.g., smartphones and digital tablets)
- Social media websites (e.g., Facebook and Twitter)
- Government websites (e.g., U.S. Bureau of Labor Statistics, U.S. Bureau of Economic Analysis, U.S. Department of Labor, and U.S. Census Bureau)

- General research websites (e.g., Pew Research Center, Forrester, Aberdeen, and Gartner)
- Cloud-based data storage
- Active data backup storage
- Inactive data archived storage
- Advanced technologies (e.g., sensors and cameras used in retail, RFID tags, tags on products in manufacturing and retail, the IoT, machine learning, AI, cognitive computing systems that learn by themselves, augmented reality, virtual reality, and robots)

(E) Risks in Big Data

Like other types of internal data, such as financial data or operational data, big data is not immune to risk. In fact, risks in big data are magnified due to its combination of internal sources and external sources and when the big data is compared to internal sources alone. General risks in big data are data quality, data security, data privacy, and data governance.

Examples of specific risks in big data are listed next.

- Discovering wrong data and bad data leading to wrong and bad decisions
- Digging deeper into data, thus creating an "analysis paralysis" situation leading to a situation of being analytics rich but information poor
- Proceeding with invalid data patterns and trends, assuming that they are valid patterns and trends, thus wasting resources
- Lack of data governance standards leading to poor-quality data and information
- Lack of data quality standards leading to wrong decisions
- Lack of information quality standards leading to bad decisions
- Lack of data security and privacy control guidelines leading to data breaches
- Inability to apply the right technology to big data, thus wasting resources and missing opportunities

(x) Other Topics Related to Big Data

Next we focus on several topics related to big data, including data governance standards, data reliability standards, data quality standards, information quality standards, data security policies and controls, and data insurance policies all due to their relative importance to management.

(A) Data Governance Standards

Data governance standards address several oversight-related issues, such as data ownership and usage policies; data classification and declassification schemes; data cleansing, separation, and normalization; data security policies and controls; and data backup, retention and recovery methods. Data governance standards include data access, data separation, data integrity, data regulations, data cleansing and disposition, and data recovery.

(B) Data Reliability Standards

Data reliability, especially as it relates to computer-processed data, means that data are reasonable complete, accurate, consistent) and valid. **Complete** refers to the extent that relevant data records are present and that the data fields in each record are populated appropriately. **Accurate** refers to the extent that recorded data reflect the actual underlying information, **Consistent**, a subcategory of accurate, refers to the need to obtain and use data that are clear and well defined enough to yield similar results in similar analyses. For example, if data is entered at multiple sites, inconsistent interpretation of data entry rules can lead to data that, taken as a whole, is unreliable. **Valid** refers to whether the data actually represents what is being measured. So, analysts must consider risks associated with the possibility of using insufficiently reliable data.

(C) Data Quality Standards

Data is a collection of facts and figures, and it is raw. Data is transformed into information in the course of data processing activities. The perception of quality depends on the purpose for which data or information is to be used. For information to be useful, it should be available where, when, and in the form it is needed, and with costs equal to or less than the benefits to be derived from it. The concept of *information economics* dealing with information costs and information benefits should be used here.

For data or information to be of any use to management, it should possess certain data quality dimensions and information quality elements and standards, which are described next.

Achieving a **data excellence goal** must be the top priority of a business data analyst who collects, compiles, interprets, and presents data results to business managers and executives. The data excellence goal needs to be applied to regular business data as well as statistical data, whether it is generated internally or externally.

Achieving the goal of data excellence is not a one-time task; instead, it must be an ongoing task where the data is continuously and constantly monitored and improved in all seven dimensions of quality: relevance, accuracy, credibility, timeliness, accessibility, interpretability, and coherence.

1. The **relevance** of a data reflects its ability to satisfy the needs of users. This depends on its utility in adding to the users' knowledge with regard to the topics of greatest importance to them. The evaluation of relevance is subjective and varies according to users' needs. The basic question here is: Is the data what the user expects?

2. **Accuracy** represents the level at which the data or information correctly describes the phenomenon it has been developed to measure. It is normally expressed in terms of the error in the statistical data, which can, in turn, be broken down into different components. The basic question here is: Is the data reliable?

3. The **credibility** of data or information refers to the confidence level that users have in the analyst or entity producing the data or statistic. It is normally based on the reputation of the producer as demonstrated over time, which, in turn, relates to factors such as the objectivity, technical independence, professionalism, and transparency shown by the producer during the course of analytical activities. Its basic question is: Is the data producer trustworthy?

4. The **timeliness** of a data refers to the time it takes to disseminate the data with regard to the reference period, requiring a timetable for releasing data and measuring performance. The timelines of data have a significance impact on its relevance, meaning data that is presented late may not be relevant. In addition, there is a clear trade-off between data timeliness and accuracy. The basic question here is: Does the user receive the data in time and on schedule?

5. The **accessibility** of data reflects the ease with which it can be identified and utilized by a user. Accessibility therefore depends on the means with which the data is made available

to the user, either on paper medium or electronic medium; the search procedures required, whether they are too long and convoluted; the user's ability to make use of the data in meeting needs; the existence of barriers to access (approvals, cost, and time); and the availability of user support services (hourly, daily, or weekly). The basic question here is: Is the data reachable?

6. **Interpretability** reflects the ease with which users can understand the basic characteristics of the data and thereby evaluate its utility for their own needs. Some fundamental factors of interpretability include the adequacy of data provided within the coverage limits, the comparability of data over time, the methods used to collect and generate data, and the accuracy of data. The basic question here is: Is the data understandable?

7. **Coherence** relates to the degree to which particular data is logically connected and mutually consistent with other related data. Coherence implies that the same term should not be used without explanation for different data items, different terms should not be used without explanation for the same data item, and variations in methodology that might affect data values should not be made without explanation. The use of standard concepts, definitions, and classifications increases the coherence of the data or information supplied by various sources, while changes in methodology can impede the comparability of the same parameter over time. The basic question here is: Is the data consistent and reconcilable with other data?

(xi) Information Quality Standards

Information quality is composed of three elements: utility, integrity, and objectivity. Quality will be ensured and established by management at levels appropriate to the nature and timeliness of the information to be disseminated.

$$\text{Information Quality} = \text{Utility} + \text{Integrity} + \text{Objectivity}$$

Utility means that disseminated information is useful to its intended users. "Useful" means that the content of the information is helpful, beneficial, or serviceable to its intended users or that the information supports the usefulness of other disseminated information by making it more accessible or easier to read, see, understand, obtain, or use. Where the usefulness of information will be enhanced by greater transparency, care is taken that sufficient background and detail is available to maximize the usefulness of the information.

Integrity refers to security, which is the protection of information from unauthorized access or revision, to ensure that the information is not compromised through corruption or falsification. Integrity also means information is safeguarded from improper access, modification, or destruction, to a degree commensurate with the risk and magnitude of harm that could result from the loss, misuse, or unauthorized access to or modification of such information.

Objectivity consists of two distinct elements: presentation and substance. The presentation element includes whether disseminated information is presented in an accurate, clear, complete, and unbiased manner and in a proper context. The substance element involves a focus on ensuring accurate, reliable, and unbiased information. In a scientific, financial, or statistical context, the original and supporting data will be generated, and the analytic results will be developed, using sound statistical and research methods.

Two standards or concepts related to information quality include reproducibility and transparency. **Reproducibility** means that the information is capable of being substantially reproduced, subject to an acceptable degree of imprecision. For information judged to have more (less) important impacts, the degree of imprecision that is tolerated is reduced (increased).

Transparency is at the heart of the reproducibility standard in that transparency provides information in sufficient background and detail to maximize the usefulness of such information. The level of such background and detail is commensurate with the importance of the particular information, balanced against the resources required (i.e., cost, time, people, hardware, software, tools, and techniques), and is appropriate to the nature and timeliness of the information to be disseminated.

In summary:

- Data quality dimensions include relevance, accuracy, credibility, timeliness, accessibility, interpretability, and coherence.

- Information quality elements and standards include utility, integrity, objectivity, reproducibility, and transparency.

(xii) Data Security Policies and Controls

Data security policies and controls address various issues, such as rules of behavior, rules of enforcement, access rules, acceptable use policies, rules of engagement, and access agreements for employees and nonemployees (e.g., vendors, consultants, contractors, and third parties). Here, the common issues include: (1) controlling an individual's behavior, whether this individual is internal or external to an organization; (2) describing consequences for noncompliance with rules; and (3) making these rules official through issuing policy documents. The goal is to reduce the potential damage to computer systems and property and to minimize harm to people.

(xiii) Data Insurance Policies

Unfortunately, several organizations in the public and private sectors have experienced data security breaches and cyberattacks (e.g., ransomware) by hackers. The average total cost of a data security breach has been estimated at $4 million, and only 15% of organizations have purchased commercial insurance to protect against data security breaches and cyberattacks.

Because data is a strategic asset and a valuable commodity, it should be protected with an insurance policy covering data security breaches, cyberattacks, data losses, data stealing, and protection of customers' personal data.

(b) Data Counting Methods

Raw data has value in providing actionable insights and inferences that can be turned into meaningful actions in terms of new decisions and results in achieving a competitive advantage. After raw data under consideration is sanitized or cleaned and before data mining techniques are applied to big data, such data must be organized and counted for its intended purposes. According to the Stevens' power law developed by Stanley Stevens, four types of scales can be used to define how data or things can be coded, scaled, ordered, measured, ranked, arranged, grouped, organized, or otherwise counted. These four data scales are the nominal, ordinal, interval, and ratio scales. Moreover, organized data can be converted into indices, quartiles, percentiles, and outliers, which have several applications in business. Each type of data scale is discussed next.

(i) Nominal Scales

Nominal scales are easy to understand, are nonnumeric, and are mutually exclusive (i.e., no overlap) as they are used to label, name, or code variables such as data or things. They have no inherent order to data values. Nominal scales can be expressed in a dichotomous manner, such as male or female, yes or no, true or false, or accept or reject. Here, either "true" or "false" can be labeled as "1" or "2," indicating that there is no order to the data values.

> **Example:** A human resources department can determine the number of female employees and the number of male employees in a company's workforce. These gender numbers can be tracked over a time period to see if one gender is increasing or decreasing in number over the other gender.

(ii) Ordinal Scales

Ordinal scales are nonnumeric, have inherent order to data values, and the difference between each value is unknown. A disadvantage of ordinal ranking is that it does not show quantities.

> **Examples:** The marketing department can conduct customer surveys to determine the number of customers who are very unsatisfied (1) or very satisfied (5) or very unhappy (1) or very happy (5). Here the scale is from 1 through 5, implying an order to data values. Ordinal scales are also used to rank first, second, or third place in student grades, games, sports, and competitive awards.

(iii) Interval Scales

Interval scales are numeric values with an order and a space (gap) values where the difference between each value is known. Statistical analysis (e.g., computing mean, mode, median, standard deviation, and variance) can be conducted with interval scale data.

> **Example:** Interval scales are used to measure temperature either in Celsius (C) or Fahrenheit (F) degrees. Because temperatures do not have a true zero value, ratios cannot be computed.

(iv) Ratio Scales

Ratio scales are the ultimate goal of data because they are numeric; they show the order of values and data relationships; the difference between data units is known; and they have "true zero" values. Hence, they are good for applying descriptive statistics (e.g., computing mode, median, quartiles, and outliers) and inferential statistics (e.g., testing hypotheses, deriving estimates, and drawing inferences). Ratio variables can be subject to basic mathematical calculations, such as adding, subtracting, multiplying, and dividing. Height and weight measurements can be done with ratios. In addition, ratios can be used to measure length, mass, energy, and statistical data.

> **Examples:** Popular ratios in business include ROI, return on sales, return on assets (ROA), and return on equity. Popular ratios in economic statistics shown as indices are the CPI, producer price index, and wholesale price index.

(A) Indices, Quartiles, Percentiles, and Outliers

Indices are index numbers that compare two specific measurements in two time periods, such as current period and base period, and the result is expressed as a ratio. A simple index number represents an individual product. The CPI data and the population census data are the two most watched, measured, and monitored economic statistics in any country. For example, the CPI is computed as follows:

$$CPI = (\text{Current price / Base price}) \times 100$$

$$\text{Current price per item} = (\text{Base-year price}) \times (\text{Current CPI / Base CPI})$$

Examples: Several indices are given as examples next.

- The annual percentage change in a CPI is used as a measure of inflation. CPI is a price index at the retail store level.

- The index of industrial production represents an aggregate of a quantity index.

- A composite index number or an aggregate index number represents a group of products.

- The producer price index represents price changes to acquire raw materials, intermediate materials, and finished goods. Here, the producer can be a farmer or manufacturer or simply a processor.

- The wholesale price index represents the price index for finished goods at the wholesale level.

Quartiles are three data points that divide the data into four equal groups where each group consists of a quarter of the data.

- The first quartile (lowest quartile) is defined as the middle number between the smallest number and the median of the data. It is called the 25th percentile because it splits off the lowest 25% of data from the highest 75% of data.

- The second quartile is defined as the median of the data. It is called the 50th percentile because it cuts the data in half.

- The third quartile (upper quartile) is defined as the middle value between the median and the highest value of the data. It is called the 75th percentile because it splits off the highest 25% of data from the lowest 75% of data.

- The interquartile range (IQR) shows extreme values (outliers) that can skew the data. It is a relatively robust statistic compared to the traditional range and standard deviation. The IQR helps to establish boundaries with lower fence (bounds) and upper fence levels. Any data falling outside these defined bounds is considered an outlier.

  Example: Quartiles are used to express wages, salaries, income levels, tax payments, and student grades (i.e., grade point average). A median salary of $100,000 for a highly technical employee can be said to fall in the second quartile.

Percentiles simply divide the data into 100 pieces; they are not dependent on the distribution of the data. Percentiles are a measure of data dispersion similar to standard deviation and range. Usually percentiles are expressed as 25, 50, 75, 90, or 95. When we say 70th percentile, we mean 70% of data is below the mean and 30% of data is above the mean. Quartiles use percentiles, but they are not the same. Quartile 1 means the 25th percentile; quartile 2 means the 50th percentile (median).

Outliers are data points that are outside of the expected point estimates or range estimates. They can be abnormal data points that should be looked at for further analysis to determine causes or origins.

  Example: If a monthly utility bill for natural gas usage is expected to fall within a range of $100 and $150 based on historical data, an actual gas bill of $400 for a month can be called as an outlier.

In summary:

- Nominal, ordinal, interval, and ratio scales all count the frequency of occurrence of data or things.

- Nominal scales are qualitative variables with no inherent order to data or things.

- Ordinal, interval, and ratio scales have an inherent order to data or things.

- Nominal variables are used to name, code, or label data or things.

- A nominal variable is a qualitative variable where data attributes have no inherent order.

- An ordinal variable is a qualitative variable where data attributes are ordered and the difference between adjacent attributes is unknown or unequal.

- An interval variable is a quantitative variable where data attributes are ordered but for which the numerical difference between adjacent attributes is interpreted as known or equal.

- Interval variables provide the order of values plus the ability to quantify the difference between variables. They do not have true zero values.

- A ratio variable is a quantitative variable where data attributes are ordered, spaced equally, and with a true zero point.

- Ratio variables provide the order of values plus interval values plus the ability to calculate ratios. They do have true zero values.

- Indices, quartiles, percentiles, outliers, and interquartile rages are examples of descriptive statistics.

(c) Data Analytics

Data analytics involve applying quantitative and qualitative tools and techniques to big data in order to gain new insights and new opportunities. Several types of data analytics exist, including these:

- Predictive analytics
- Embedded data analytics
- Fraud data analytics
- Streaming data analytics
- Social media data analytics
- Web-based data analytics
- Text-based data analytics
- Open-source data analytics
- Data modeling analytics
- Visual analytics
- Descriptive analytics
- Prescriptive analytics
- Cognitive analytics

- User behavior analytics
- Customer analytics
- Benford's law of first-digit test

(i) Predictive Analytics

Predictive analytics are the process of estimating future outcomes based on the analysis of past data and/or current data. They describe what could happen.

For example, the U.S. Department of Health and Human Services has applied the following analytic techniques to identify improper payments and fraudulent activities perpetrated by healthcare providers (bad actors) in its Centers for Medicare & Medicaid Services:

- A rules-based technique filters fraudulent claims and associated behaviors with rules. It identifies providers that bill using a Medicare identification number that was previously stolen and used improperly.

- An anomaly-based technique detects individual and aggregated abnormal patients versus a peer group. It identifies providers that bill for more services in a single day than the number of services that 99% of similar providers bill in a single day.

- A predictive-based technique assesses the known fraud cases. It identifies providers that have characteristics similar to those of known bad actors.

- A network-based technique discovers knowledge using associative link analysis. It identifies providers that are linked to known bad actors through addresses or phone numbers.

For example, retail industry can use these predictive analytics:

- Estimating what customers will buy what products and from what markets
- Store customer foot traffic analysis through sensors and cameras
- Customer orders online
- Actual sales transactions
- Customer merchandise returns
- Online shopping cart abandonment
- Customer financial chargebacks
- New store location
- Cross-store merchandise locator
- Endless aisles of inventory
- Estimating customer retention rates and defection rates

These predictive analytics can be applied to any industry:

- Identifying new revenue opportunities by products or by markets
- Forecasting workforce requirements by type and skill
- Identifying the factors leading to employee satisfaction and productivity

- Identifying factors for customers' filing a fraudulent claim
- Discovering the underlying reasons for employees' attrition rates
- Predicting what type of customers will default on a loan payment or credit card payment
- Predicting employee turnover rates
- Predicting equipment breakdowns before they disrupt operations

(ii) Embedded Data Analytics

Many organizations use embedded data analytics, such as data visualization tools, reporting routines and methods, and data dashboards, in their business-oriented application systems. The embedded analytics provide a real value to end users of such systems. Embedded analytics are a part of predictive analytics as they predict future events and outcomes. In contrast, traditional data analytics present past events and outcomes.

(iii) Forensic Data Analytics

The focus of fraud-related forensic data analytics is on fraud prevention, detection, and response (correction). Forensic data analytics use tools such as data visualization, text mining, web-scraping tools, data dashboards, statistical analysis (e.g., discovery sampling), link analysis, and social media. These tools are in addition to the older, traditional tools of inspecting, tracing, observing, counting, reconciling, comparing, and contrasting. Usually business rules, such as a dollar amount of claims or frequency of claims, are used to detect fraud.

(iv) Streaming Data Analytics

Streaming data analytics are performed in real time and in memory where they collect data from electronic sensors to produce time-series data. The use of streaming analytics increases as machine-generated data sources increase. Temporal analysis, which is based on the concept of time and which is a part of streaming data analytics, helps to understand different scenarios that are based on changing times. For example, the selling, activating, or redeeming thousands of gift cards within a short period of time (e.g., three to four hours) in a retail store can be an indication of fraud or a sudden surge of activity is an application of streaming data analytics. This unusual activity in gift cards is a red flag.

Data stream processing presents current events as they are occurring. In contrast, traditional data analytics present past events and embedded data analytics predict future events.

Traditional Data Analytics ⟶ Show Past Events

Streaming Data Analytics ⟶ Show Current Events

Embedded Data Analytics ⟶ Show Future Events

(v) Social Media Data Analytics

Social media analytics take thousands and thousands of data items from online posts, followers, fans, page views, reviews, comments, pins, and mentions in various social media websites to evaluate marketing campaigns, advertisements, and promotions and to conclude what marketing efforts worked and what did not work.

(vi) Web-Based Data Analytics

Web scraping is a web-based data extraction and data mining approach. For example, it can search Twitter, a social media network, and look for keywords relating to fraud. Web mining is a data mining technique for discovering and extracting information from web documents. Web mining explores both web content and web usage.

(vii) Text-Based Data Analytics

Text analytics focus on prescriptive analytics and descriptive analytics where they concentrate on written materials and mobile text messages using SMS and MMS. Text analytics also include information from web call-center notes, comment fields posted on social media platforms, traditional reports, customer inquiries, web chats, and regular books. Text-based data are unstructured data and are useful to mine for fraud-related words on various data sources.

(viii) Open-Source Data Analytics

Open-source analytical tools and techniques are available, including open-source software, interoperable systems, and data-sharing facilities at low or no cost. The open-source algorithms can be consolidated in a central location to allow ease of access across several organizations to identify fraud, waste, and abuse. Moreover, the use of open-source tools could lessen the challenge of developing licensing agreements for proprietary software tools. Open-source data libraries can help in audits, inspections, and investigations.

(ix) Data Modeling Analytics

Data modeling analytics involve building data models, using simulation models, and testing them with what-if questions to see their answers in the form of changing outputs (outcomes) when inputs to the model changes.

(x) Visual Analytics

Visual analytics use data visualization tools, such as line, bar, scatter, bubble, and pie charts, to present relationships among big data in an easy-to-understand format. Senior managers prefer visual analytics, similar to data dashboards.

(xi) Descriptive Analytics

Descriptive analytics describe what already happened and include content analysis and context analysis.

Content analysis is a set of procedures for transforming unstructured written material into a format for analysis. It is a methodology for structuring and analyzing unstructured written material in documents and reports. For example, two or more documents can be analyzed to discover fraud-related content using specific words, symbols, names, events, outcomes, and addresses.

> **Example:** Using text-data analytics, governmental agencies are looking at social media platforms for specific words or comments to: identify terrorist activities; discover fraudulent activities in social security benefit payments and other social assistance programs to citizens, and pinpoint fraud, waste, and abuse in healthcare payments.

Context analysis is useful because data can be contextual, meaning some data is related to a specific context (in context). Hence, a pool of data must be separated between in-context data and out-of-context data to analyze data trends and patterns. Examples of in-context data involve insurance companies analyzing claims data during natural disasters; and retail companies analyzing sales data during holiday shopping seasons, during special weeklong promotions (e.g., blast sales, flash sales, or tent sales), and during a season (in-context) and outside of the season (out of context) if the focus is on seasonal sales.

(xii) Prescriptive Analytics

Prescriptive analytics help management decide what should happen and thrive on big data. When faced with a number of potential decisions, prescriptive analytics analyze for the best possible outcome.

Examples:

- Optimal allocation of a company's stock market portfolio after considering expected returns and dividends

- Airline companies determining ticket prices after considering travel variables, such as customer demand, travel timings, travel locations, and holidays (for example, ticket prices are higher during holidays)

(xiii) Cognitive Analytics

Cognitive analytics use artificial intelligence (AI) technology as it applies to cybersecurity, health-care, transportation, and finance areas. The AI group of technologies such as machine learning and natural language processors can provide clear insights into problems with greater confidence, speed, and accuracy. For example, the AI technology can be used in cybersecurity in performing threat-hunting and threat-defending exercises, in healthcare in diagnosing a patient's health risks, in transportation in predicting airline delays, and in finance in estimating the reasons for late bill payments from customers and business partners and how to improve and speed up accounts receivable collection frequency.

(xiv) User Behavior Analytics

User behavior analytics studies an online user's (shopper's) behavior to show that user's activity trails such as the number of browser-clicks made, the types of website navigation paths visited, the variety of product purchases made, and the number of online advertisements viewed. All this user activity data is used to compute the click-to-conversion time metric, which indicates the amount of effort and time a user put in before a product was purchased online. Performing user behavior analytics is a part of electronic commerce improvement program.

(xv) Customer Analytics

Customer analytics, which is a part of customer relationship management (CRM) analytics, looks at a customer's online transactions to study customer demographics, online shopping patterns, and the Internet usage activity so predictive analytics can be applied to determine potential sales and profits from customers. In addition, marketing management can capture a customer's profile (e.g., age, gender, location, income, occupation, education, and shopping habits and interests) without a direct contact with the customer. Conducting customer analytics is a part of electronic commerce improvement program.

(xvi) Benford's Law of First-Digit Test

As part of fraud investigations, internal auditors can apply Benford's law of first-digit test to detect unusual data patterns arising from human errors, data manipulations, or fraudulent transactions. If the first digit in a financial account number or business transaction number is 1, chances are that it is a naturally occurring number (i.e., fraud-free). If the first digit is 9, good chances are that it might be purposefully assigned number (i.e., fraudulent) to perpetrate fraud. The law looks to see whether the first digit is 1 or 9 because the digit 1 occurs 30% of the time and the digit 9 occurs only 5% of the time. In general, lower numbers (1 to 5) are usually freer of fraud than higher numbers (6 to 9), which are known to be fraudulent on the scale of 1 to 9. The following conditions apply:

The number is fraud-free if digits 1, 2, 3, 4, and 5 are present. They occur in combination 78% of the time.

It is fraudulent if digits 6, 7, 8, and 9 are present. They occur in combination 22% of the time.

If actual first-digit analysis indicates that digits 6 through 9 occur more often than their expected frequency, it is an indication of fraud or other irregularities, and further investigation as to their causes is required.

(d) Data Mining

(i) Data Mining Defined

Data mining is the application of database technologies and advanced data analytics to uncover hidden patterns, trends, correlations, outliers, anomalies, and subtle relationships in data and to infer rules that allow for the prediction of future results and outcomes. Data mining analyzes data for relationships that have not been discovered previously and other insights not suggested by a priori hypotheses or explicit assumptions. For example, data insights might apply to retail marketers in identifying trends in terms of customer buying preferences and customer shopping behaviors.[22]

Today, mining can be performed on many types of data, including structured, unstructured, textual, Web, multimedia, and semistructured data (e.g., XML and HTML). Data mining overlaps with a wide range of analytical activities, including data profiling, databases, data warehouses, data marts, virtual databases, online analytical processing (OLAP), structured query language (SQL), statistical analyses, data modeling, and predictive data analytics.

Both private sector and public sector organizations are increasingly using data mining applications to achieve their purposes.

(ii) Data Mining in Private Sector

Private sector organizations are using data mining applications to explore new business opportunities with the sole goal of growing their business. A list of major purposes includes:

- Improving service or performance in increasing sales, revenues, and profits (major purpose)
- Detecting fraud, waste, and abuse
- Analyzing intelligence and detecting terrorist activities
- Analyzing scientific and research information
- Detecting criminal activities and patterns

A minor purpose of data mining is to improve employee, customer, and vendor safety.

Broadly speaking, private sector applications of data mining include customer relationship management, market research, retail, supply chain, medical analysis and diagnostics, financial analysis, and fraud detection.

(iii) Data Mining in Public Sector

Public sector organizations are using data mining applications for a variety of purposes ranging from improving service or performance to analyzing and detecting terrorists' patterns and activities. A list of major purposes includes:

- Improving service or performance levels to citizens (major purpose)
- Detecting fraud, waste, and abuse, such as improper payments
- Analyzing scientific and research information for new drugs and new medical treatments

---

[22] Adapted from *Data Mining: Federal Efforts Cover a Wide Range of Uses* (May 2004), GAO-04-548, www.gao.gov.

- Managing human resources for promotions, pay scales, pay grades, contractor security clearances, and employee background checks
- Detecting criminal activities or patterns, such as identity theft cases

A minor purpose is analyzing intelligence and detecting terrorist activities using Internet sources.

Broadly speaking, public sector applications of data mining focus on detecting financial fraud and abuse in procurement card and credit card programs and analyzing intelligence and detecting terrorist activities.

(iv) Privacy Concerns over Data Mining

A number of privacy concerns about mined or analyzed personal data exist, including worries about these issues:

- The quality and accuracy of the mined data
- The use of the data for other than the original purpose for which the data were collected without consent of the individual
- The protection of the data against unauthorized access, modification, or disclosure
- The right of individuals to know about the collection of personal information, how to access that information, and how to request a correction of inaccurate information

(v) Technologies in Data Mining

Seven technical topics presented in this section include databases, virtual databases, data warehouses, data marts, OLAP, SQL, and advanced technologies such as AI and machine learning.

(A) Databases

A database contains files with facts and figures on various types of information, such as sales, costs, and personnel. These files are collectively called the firm's database. A database is a collection of related data about an organization, intended for sharing of this data by multiple users. A database management system (DBMS) is comprised of software, hardware, and procedures. The DBMS acts as a software controller enabling different application systems to access large numbers of distinct data records stored on direct access storage devices (e.g., disks).

The DBMS handles complex data structures and should be compatible with the operating system environment. Unauthorized access to data elements is a major concern in a database system due to concentration of data. The DBMS provides a user interface with the application system through increased accessibility and flexibility by means of data views.

A data model describes relationships between the data elements and is used as a tool to represent the conceptual organization of data. A relationship within a data model can be one to one (e.g., between patient and bed in a hospital environment; at any given time, one bed is assigned to one patient), one to many (e.g., between hospital room and patients; one hospital room accommodates more than one patient), and many to many (e.g., between patient and surgeon; one surgeon may attend to many patients and a patient may be attended by more than one surgeon).

The primary purpose of any data model is to provide a formal means of representing information and of manipulating the representation. A good data model can help describe and model the application effectively. A DBMS uses one or more data models, such as relational, hierarchical, network, object, or distributed.

(B) Virtual Databases

A virtual database is created when data from multiple database sources is integrated to provide a total perspective on a specific topic. It is virtual in that such database does not exist physically but is created on demand. For example, an auditor comparing performance of a multiplant organization can use virtual database technology to view key operating and financial ratios of plants side by side.

(C) Data Warehouses

Data warehouses have several definitions and purposes. The purpose of a data warehouse is information retrieval and data analysis. It stores precomputed, historical, descriptive, and numerical data. It involves a process of extracting and transferring operational data into informational data and loading it into a central data store, or warehouse. Once loaded, users can access the warehouse through query and analysis tools. The data warehouse can be housed on a computer different from the production computer.

A data warehouse is a storage facility where data from heterogeneous databases are brought together so that users can make queries against the warehouse instead of against several databases. The warehouse is like a big database. Redundant and inconsistent data are removed from the databases, and subsets of data are selected from them prior to placing them in a data warehouse done automatically or manually, or a combination. Usually, data warehouses contain summary data, correlated data, or data that is otherwise massaged.

Data integrity and security issues are as applicable to warehouses as they are to databases. An issue is: What happens to the warehouse when the individual databases are updated?

Data modeling is an essential task for building a data warehouse along with access methods, index strategies, and using query languages. For example, if the data model is relational, then an SQL-based language is used. If the data model is object-oriented, an object-based language may be appropriate.

Metadata management is another critical technology for data warehousing. Metadata includes mapping between the data sources (databases) and the warehouse. Another issue is whether the warehouse can be centralized or distributed.

(D) Data Marts

A data mart is a subset of a data warehouse (i.e., a mini-data warehouse). It brings the data from transaction processing systems to functional departments (i.e., finance, manufacturing, and human resources) or business units or divisions. Data marts are scaled-down data warehouses. Data marts place targeted business information into the hands of more decision makers.

(E) Online Analytical Processing

OLAP programs are available to store and deliver data warehouse information from multidimensional databases. These programs allow users to explore corporate data from a number of different perspectives, such as product, geography, time, and salesperson.

OLAP servers and desktop tools support high-speed analysis of data involving complex relationships, such as combinations of a company's products, regions, channels of distribution, reporting units, and time periods. Access to data in multidimensional databases can be very quick because the data is stored in structures optimized for speed, and the databases avoid using SQL and index processing techniques. In other words, multidimensional databases have greater retrieval speed and longer update times.

Consumer goods companies (e.g., retail) use OLAP to analyze the millions of consumer purchase records and transactions captured by electronic scanners at the checkout stand. This data is used to spot trends in purchases and to relate sales volume to store promotions (coupons) and store conditions (displays). The data in OLAP is generally aggregated, giving information such as total or average sales in dollars or units. Users can examine the OLAP's hierarchical data in the time dimension, such as sales by year, by quarter, by month, by week, or by day.

(F) Structured Query Language

The primary components of an SQL database are schemas, tables, views, parser, optimizer, executor, access rights checker, and access rights grantor or revoker. A schema describes the structure of related tables and views. Tables, which consist of rows and columns, hold the actual data in the database. Each row is a set of columns; each column is a single data element. Views are derived tables and may be composed of a subset of a table or the result of table operations (e.g., a join of different tables). A parser is a program that breaks input into smaller chunks so that a program can act on the information.

SQL is a standard query language for a DBMS; SQL also is used to query and update the data managed by the DBMS. The SQL standard, which is used by most commercial DBMSs, includes specific requirements for enforcing discretionary access controls.

(vi) Advanced Technologies

Advanced technologies such as AI, machine learning, expert systems, neural networks, and text mining are part of overall umbrella of AI where they are used in answering questions from retail shopping customers and recognizing human voice or speech with pay-by-phone systems.

Neural networks learn by training. They can be used or reused in reviewing credit card transactions to detect anomalies and fraudulent activities. Text-mining tools are used to scan unstructured documents, such as emails, web pages, and audio/video files, and to scan structured data found in databases or data warehouses.

Summary of Technologies Used in Data Mining with Their Purposes

- A database contains raw data collected from daily business transactions.
- A data warehouse contains massaged, cleansed, and normalized data.
- End users query many points with heterogeneous databases.
- End users query only a single point with homogeneous data warehouses.
- A data warehouse provides summary data for the entire business.
- A data mart provides detailed data for a specific function of a business (a mini-data warehouse).
- Data mining is an end user tool to select information from a data warehouse.
- Data mining is an auditing tool to detect fraud, intrusion incidents, and security problems in a data warehouse.
- Advanced technologies, including AI, machine learning, expert systems, neural networks, and text mining, are used to perform sophisticated analysis.

(vii) Applications in Data Mining

Data mining is the process of asking (posing) a series of questions (queries) against a database or data warehouse containing large amounts of data to extract some meaningful, relevant, and useful information to perform management analysis. A data warehouse or data mart itself does not attempt to extract information from the data it contains. A data mining tool is needed to extract data.

Data mining applications are best suited to data-intense organizations with millions of customers' data collected in their databases or data warehouses. Examples of data-intense organizations include retailers, market research firms, governmental agencies, online order takers, casinos, travel agencies, vacation cruise line firms, hotels, rental car companies, and airline companies. There is no end to the data mining applications; the imagination of the person requesting the data analysis work is the only limit.

Data mining applications software is available from a number of vendors. Off-the-shelf software generally makes these applications easier to use and less expensive than custom-built software.

Data mining is data analysis, data fishing, data snooping, and data drilling in order to get to the bottom of the vast amounts of data (big data) collected by organizations during their business operations. Another name for data mining is data analytics.

WHAT IS WEB MINING?

Web mining is a data mining technique for discovering and extracting information from web documents. Web mining explores both web content and web usage.

To analyze data, find relationships between data elements, and draw meaningful conclusions that can be incorporated into its decision-making process, management uses various quantitative techniques, such as regression analysis, factor analysis, cluster analysis, sampling, and other statistical methods. The ultimate goal of data mining is to improve business operations and increase profits.

Data mining can be applied to databases as well as to data warehouses and data marts. A warehouse structures the data in such a way so as to facilitate query processing. Data mining is a set of automated tools that convert the data in the warehouse into some useful information. It selects and reports information deemed significant from a data warehouse or database.

Before data mining software tools are applied, the target data (raw datasets) must be cleansed (sanitized) and normalized to remove missing, erroneous, or inappropriate data. Here, data mining tools can discover data relationships and data clusters (i.e., groupings of similar data items). Data mining also uncovers patterns and trends in data.

There are several types of data mining applications, including data classifications, data sequencing, data dependencies, and deviation analysis. Data records can be grouped into clusters or classes so that patterns in the data can be found. Data sequencing can be determined from the data. Data dependencies, such as relationships or associations between the data items, can be detected. Deviation analysis can be performed on data. Fuzzy logic, neural networks, and set theory are some techniques used in data mining tools.

Data mining techniques can also be used for intrusion and fraud detection and to audit the databases. Data mining tools can be used to detect abnormal patterns in data, which can provide clues to fraud. A security problem can be created when a user poses queries and infers sensitive hypotheses. That is, the inference problem occurs via a data mining tool. A data mining tool can be applied to see if sensitive information can be deduced from unclassified information legitimately obtained. If so, then there is an inference problem. An inference controller can be built and placed between the data mining tool and the database to detect user motives and prevent inference problems from occurring. Since data mining tools are computationally intensive, parallel processing computers are used to carry out the data mining activities.

Harrah's Casino and Hotel in Las Vegas, an entertainment company, is a big user of data mining applications. Interested customers (guests) are given an electronic card before gambling. This card collects data on guests' gambling actions in terms of what games they play, how much time they spend on each type of game, what games they lose or win, how many times they visit the casino in a year, how many days they stay in the hotel for each visit, whether they come alone or with family, and their personal income. For example, if a guest's personal income is very high, this application recommends that the guest play high-stakes games with very attractive incentives and rewards. Different incentive and reward programs are available for guests with more typical personal income. This application is a win-win situation in that the casino makes additional profit on the guest and the guest enjoys extra perks (royal treatment) that he or she would not have received otherwise.

Other examples of application of data mining are listed next.

- Market segmentation, where data mining identifies the common characteristics of customers who buy the same products
- Customer defection, where data mining predicts which customers are likely to leave the company
- Fraud detection, where data mining identifies which transactions are most likely to be fraudulent
- Direct marketing, where data mining identifies which prospects are the target for mailing
- Market basket analysis, where data mining identifies what products or services are commonly purchased together
- Trend analysis, where data mining reveals the difference between a typical customer this month versus last month.

(e) Big-Data Audit

In addition to asking traditional questions about data quality, data security, data sources, and data privacy during a big-data audit, internal auditors should ask intense and deep questions about data models, use of IP assets, audit resources, and audit team structure. These questions are consistent with rating the big data as a high-risk audit area and due to the popular saying "Garbage in, garbage out," especially in relation to data sources and data models. Questions to ask about data sources and data models are listed next.

Data Sources

- Are data sources known, unknown, valid, invalid, questionable, reputable, illegitimate, unethical, clean, or dirty sources?
- Are data timelines recent or old? (Recent data is more relevant than the old data.)

- Are data sanitized to remove erroneous (bad), inappropriate, and irrelevant data?
- Are the selected data elements for data extraction from databases, data warehouses, or data marts suitable in achieving the business objective of data mining applications?

Data Models

- Has a pilot model been developed on a small-scale size prior to launching a final model on a full-scale size? (Pilot models require fewer resources than final models.)
- Does the model-building process follow a structured approach with clear phases, such as model development, model testing, model implementation, and model termination?

Model development focuses on data collection and preparation (garbage in, garbage out) and validation of data sources to identify missing, biased, or incomplete data; out-of-range numeric data; or out-of-time frame data (data quality). Model development assures model quality and data quality.

Model testing focuses on validating the model's processing logic and rules and interpretation of test results to ensure that the model's results are the expected results. Model testing assures model validation.

Model implementation focuses on placing the tested pilot model on a full-scale basis and operationalizing and institutionalizing it. Model implementation produces model results, outputs, and outcomes.

Model termination focuses on whether the current model is appropriate to process current or old data. Data currency changes as business conditions change. The nature of current business problems to be solved can change since the model was developed. New data requires new models, and old models can be terminated or retired.

(i) Use of Intellectual Property Assets

Big data can come from two sources: private and public, where public data is free and private data is not. Private data or software may be owned by someone or some organization with associated IP rights (i.e., copyrights, trademarks, service marks, and patents) that should be respected and paid for where applicable. Internal auditors should determine whether such IP rights are protected, acknowledged, and paid for with written permission obtained from the IP owners. Here the goal is to protect the rights of the IP asset owners, thus reducing reputation risk. Many times, "acceptable use" of IP assets is permitted by asset owners without written permission as long as users properly acknowledge and credit that use.

In general, the nature of IP rights could be of three types: unlimited data rights, limited data rights, and restricted software rights.

1. **Unlimited data rights.** A company is given the rights to use, modify, reproduce, display, release, or disclose technical data or computer software in whole or in part, in any manner, and for any purpose, whatsoever, and to have or authorize others to do so.

2. **Limited data rights.** A company is permitted to use, modify, reproduce, release, perform, display, or disclose technical data, in whole or in part, within the company. The company must obtain the express permission of the party providing the technical data to release or disclose it outside the company.

3. **Restricted software rights.** A company is given the rights to use computer software with only one computer at one time and to make the minimum number of copies of the computer software required for archive, backup, or modification purposes. The company may modify restricted rights software, subject to restrictions, and release or disclose restricted rights software outside the company in limited situations.

(ii) Audit Resources

Conducting a big-data audit is technical in nature. As such, it requires a mix of technical skills and competencies from internal and external sources. Internal audit management must ensure that the internal audit resources are in-sourced (audit staff), cosourced (nonaudit internal staff), or outsourced (external talent) with SMEs, consultants, and contractors for a successful completion of the audit project work. Nonaudit staff can include marketing, operations, and other internal staff.

Audit Resources = In-Sourced Audit Staff + Cosourced Nonaudit Staff + Outsourced Staff

(A) Audit Team

Internal audit management must ensure that the data analytics team, consisting of legal staff, IT staff, and a statistical analyst, selects the data analytics tools (i.e., software and hardware). For example, (1) legal staff can advise the data analytics team about legal requirements to protect privacy of data or access to the external data; (2) IT staff can help in developing data analytic tools and to avoid duplicative software and hardware purchases; and (3) a statistician can help educate the team about the merits and applications of each type of statistical method.

(B) Audit Applications

Imagination is the only limit to audit applications of big data, data analytics, and data mining. Examples of audit applications are listed next.

- The Office of Inspector General (OIG) of the U.S. Housing and Urban Development (HUD) developed an analytical methodology using data visualization tools to track default rates as early indicators of trends in the housing mortgage market.

- The OIG of HUD tracked how hurricane storm surges (e.g., Sandy) affected the HUD public housing assets.

- The OIG of the U.S. Department of Defense identified a vendor charging nearly $1 million to ship two flat washers costing 20 cents each. The vendor was convicted of conspiracy, sentenced to prison time, and ordered to pay restitution.

- The OIG of the U.S. Department of Health and Human Services in partnership with the Centers for Medicare & Medicaid Services used link analysis, a part of data analytics, to discover overpayment or improper payment fraud to healthcare providers linked with known bad actors (bad providers) through addresses or phone numbers.

- The OIGs of several federal government agencies detected credit card fraud using data mining tools.

- Internal auditors can use statistical analyses, such as regression, factor, cluster, link, and correlation analysis, to detect fraudulent transactions.

- Internal auditors can use data analytics and data mining software tools to assess the overall control environment after identifying systemic breakdowns in controls.

- Internal auditors can use data analytics techniques and data mining software tools to assess data integrity and security controls over databases, data warehouses, and data marts.

- Internal auditors can use big-data analytics as a part of their analytical reviews conducted during audit planning and engagement work.

1.11 Business Intelligence

This section defines business intelligence (BI), discusses how the BI is collected, presents applications of BI data, and discusses data visualization tools.

(a) Business Intelligence Defined

Business intelligence (BI) is collecting and analyzing internal data and external data to provide new insights that were not apparent before. Business specialists, not technology specialists, must gather the BI information because the business specialists know their vital information needs and wants and are the end users and beneficiaries of the BI efforts. These new insights are then incorporated into new strategies and built into new decisions, resulting in new results. Although most businesses collect BI information in the past, the need for increasing efforts to explore new BI information is growing due to heavy global competition, to exploit new business opportunities, and to gain a competitive advantage in the marketplace. Simply stated, gathering BI can lead to new business development opportunities and growth in current business and its absence can lead to business downturns slowly and business declines eventually.

(b) Traditional Ways of Collecting BI Data

In the past, organizations collected BI information in several discrete ways, including by department or function, by manager or executive, and by business unit or division—all independent ways with no collaboration, coordination, or integration. Ad hoc analysis emerged. These isolated or siloed efforts are useful in local decisions, not in corporate decisions. An organization's resources are wasted due to duplication of efforts, inconsistent results, and wrong decisions.

Traditionally, stand-alone spreadsheet software and/or end user– developed specific application software were used in collecting and analyzing BI information. For example, spreadsheets are used in financial budgeting, project costing, product costing, payroll, word processing, basic analytical calculations and comparisons (e.g., ratios and data ordering), and others. The IT staff was helping and guiding end users in introducing and developing specific software products to meet their specific, local needs. However, these spreadsheet software products had limited capabilities and problems, such as lack of: data governance; data standardization; data sanitization (data cleansing and normalizing); data integrity, security, and privacy; user-friendly interfaces; verified controls; documentation regarding formulas used and assumptions made; and tracing of results (outputs) to original data sources. Consequently, noticeable errors were made during data entry and data processing operations, which were not detected or corrected. The use of copy-and-paste feature in spreadsheets increased errors due to its magnification effect. Moreover, the data sources in the spreadsheet could not be trusted, verified, controlled, and traced.

In summary, problems in using stand-alone spreadsheets can arise: (1) through improper usage of spreadsheet software; (2) due to inadequate planning, design, and documentation of spreadsheet application; and (3) due to human errors. The consequences of these problems and errors are significant as the outputs of spreadsheet are used in decision making.

(c) Modern Ways of Collecting BI Data

Today, several sources of BI information exist, including government, open-source (Internet-based), proprietary (i.e., a company's internal data), research, industry, simulated, and anonymous data. Information from all these sources is called big data, and software companies have developed several tools, called business analytics, to utilize such big data. Big data and business analytics are the backbone of the today's BI efforts where core business users and the IT staff work together in developing new analytical software tools to derive maximum value from the big data.

Today, the term "business analytics" is a well-accepted, easily recognized, and a comprehensive term for all types of businesses (e.g., proprietorships, partnerships, or corporations), although software vendors have introduced several new terms, such as collaborative analytics, agile analytics, guided analytics, advanced analytics, and self-service analytics. The trend in business analytics is moving toward self-service analytics where end users perform their own analytics using big data, collaborate and coordinate with others, and share their results with others. Efficiencies are gained with self-service analytics through better utilization of resources such as unified software investment, time savings, knowledge sharing, and better decisions.

(d) Technologies Supporting Self-Service Analytics

Self-service analytics are user-driven in a business function or department, not analyst-driven in an IT function or department. End users are encouraged and empowered to do their own self-service analytical tasks and share the results with others. End users need to switch from the use of individual spreadsheets to the use of unified business analytics software. Intuitive and user-friendly data queries are built into the self-service analytics software. In this regard, several emerging technologies, described next, support the scope, nature, and size of self-service analytics.

- Cloud technology with massive cloud-based data warehouses where big data are located and stored
- Embedded analytics where the analytical software is build directly into business applications software that end users work with daily in providing a seamless user experience
- Machine learning algorithms that iteratively and interactively learn from data through repetitive processes and guide end users to the next operations
- Natural language processors with search capabilities that can understand an end user's regular spoken words or languages in locating the required data or information
- Dashboard software with drill-down and drag-and-drop features that can bring new insights and better clarity in business results
- Data visualization software tools that can present the requested data analytical results in a clear and concise manner through charts, graphs, tables, maps, and exhibits

(e) Applications of BI Data

Today, applying BI information to business decision making is no longer a theoretical exercise; it is a reality. All applications start with a "question" and a "hypothesis" that can be tested by data analysis.

For example, a retail company could ask: Is the bad cold weather affecting consumer shopping? The corresponding hypothesis could be: Long-lasting cold temperatures are reducing the number of shoppers coming into stores.

Several applications of business analytics include statistical modeling; simulation of equipment breakdowns; data clustering analysis in marketing; data correlation analysis in cost estimations; forecasting of sales, inventory, cash, and profits; relationships between multiple variables using regression analysis; resource optimization techniques in transportation and manufacturing; and data mining to understand customer preferences and buying habits.

According to Accenture, several companies are already benefitting from the use and application of business analytics using the BI information.[23]

- CVS Health used government health data to provide consumers with personalized recommendations for preventive healthcare services such as vaccinations and health screening tests.

- Starbucks used demographic data on the number of local smartphone users (potential customers) to determine whether mobile applications (apps) discounts will be most impactful.

- Best Buy used government data to innovate a market segmentation strategy where each customer represents a different consumer segment with specific buying habits. Best Buy used these data-driven profiles to restructure its offline (in-store) and online buying experiences.

- The Kellogg Company, which is in the food manufacturing business, used government data to improve operations and spur product innovation. Consequently, it increased revenues, decreased costs, and better met its customer needs.

- Walmart is using machine learning technology to improve customer experience inside its retail stores, detecting unhappy customers with facial recognition software. It is also using a combination of government data and machine learning to optimize its truck delivery routes.

(f) Data Visualization Tools

Data visualization software tools help in data presentation and include several reporting and information dissemination methods to report data results to management for action and decisions. These methods include various charts and graphs, such as column, bar, Gantt, pie, part-to-whole, line, area, layer, radar, and tabular charts; box plot, histograms; Pareto charts; bullet charts, scatter diagrams; dashboards; pivot tables; contingency tables; responsibility assignment matrixes (RACI diagrams); spaghetti plot, maps, decision tables, and decision trees.[24]

The basic purpose of a chart or graph is to give a visual comparison between two or more things. For example, changes in budget from one year to the next may be represented in a graph. One significant reason for visualizing a comparison is to reinforce its comprehension. Charts and graphs are used to dramatize a statement, a fact, a point of view, or an idea. They are data presentation tools and visual aids assisting in the quick comprehension of simple and complex data, statistics, or problems. A chart should explain itself in silence; it should be completely understood without the assistance of a caption. The caption must act only as reinforcement to its comprehension.

Column Chart

The column chart is most commonly used for demonstrating a comparison between two or more things. The column chart is vertical.

---

[23] *Accenture's Report on Government Data for Business Innovation in the 21st Century* (December 2017), www.accenture.com

[24] Partially adapted from Visual Analysis Best Practices by Tableau at www.tableau.com.

Bar Chart

The bar chart is essentially a column chart on its side, and is used for the same purpose. The bar chart is horizontal. It is a tool that allows a manager to evaluate whether existing resources can handle work demand or whether activities should be postponed. The bar chart looks like a Gantt chart.

Gantt Chart

A Gantt chart is a graphical illustration of a scheduling technique. The structure of the chart shows output plotted against units of time. It does not include cost information. It highlights activities over the life of a project and contrasts actual times with projected times using a horizontal (bar) chart. It gives a quick picture of a project's progress in terms of actual time lines and projected time lines. The Gantt chart looks like a bar chart.

The Gantt chart is used for milestone scheduling where each milestone has start and completion dates. A milestone represents a major activity or task to be accomplished (e.g., design phase in a computer system development project).

Pie Chart

The pie chart is used to represent a 100% total of two or more items. It is not recommended to use in part-to-whole analysis, but it can be used in drawing maps, such as a website's traffic. Pie charts look like Pareto charts, but they are not the same.

Part-to-Whole Chart

The part-to-whole chart shows the percentage of a part in relation to its whole. For example, a retailer's marketing department can conduct the part-to-whole demographic analysis to show how customers' age groups are distributed in each market region, such as South, North, East, and West.

Line Chart

The line chart is exceptionally impressive when comparing several things but could present a visual problem if the comparisons are too many or too close in relation to one another. *Advantages*: It is simple to draw. *Disadvantages*: If the lines are close to each other, it is difficult to distinguish some of the plotted points.

Area Chart

An area chart uses the same data as the line chart but presents it in an area format, which is easy to visualize.

Layer Chart

The layer chart is linear in appearance but has a different representation. It depicts the accumulation of individual facts stacked one over the other to create the overall total. This chart is more complex than the others, since it illustrates much more. In addition to showing the comparison of layers that add up to the total, this type of chart also shows how each group of layers relates to subsequent groups. Layer charts require more work to prepare than the other charts. There is more arithmetic involved, and a good deal of concentration is required to draw layer charts.

Radar Chart

The radar chart is a visual method to show in graphic form the size of gaps in a number of areas, such as current performance versus ideal (expected) performance and current budget versus previous budget.

Tabular Chart

The tabular chart is used to represent items of interest. It requires a fair amount of study in order to grasp the full meaning of the figures. This is because it takes longer to digest the meaning of an itemization of compiled figures than if the same figures are presented graphically.

Box Plot

A box plot is a part of data distribution analysis to show how quantitative values are distributed across a full range of quantitative values. An example of the box plot application is distribution of patient treatment length in time for each type of treatment category, such as most urgent, less urgent, and nonurgent services. Here, the key indicator, such as number of minutes per patient, is shown in a box format in terms of quartiles, percentiles, low values, middle values, and high values. The two dimensions are time on the y-axis and treatment category on the x-axis.

Histogram

A histogram is an alternative to a box plot showing data distributions with a different perspective. An example of the histogram application is distribution of patient treatment length in time for each type of treatment category, such as most urgent, less urgent, and nonurgent services. The histogram can reveal peak and nonpeak treatment times. Here, the number of patients in each category is displayed on the y-axis and the time in minutes on the x-axis.

From a statistics viewpoint, a histogram is a graphic summary of variations in a dataset. It shows data patterns that are difficult to notice in a simple table of numbers. A histogram is a vertical bar chart providing a frequency distribution of measured data. It looks like a normal Bell curve.

Pareto Charts

Pareto charts can be drawn to separate the vital few items from the trivial many items. They are based on the 80/20 rule, that is, 20% of items contribute to 80% of problems. These charts are problem-solving tools. A Pareto chart looks like a pie chart, but they are not the same.

Bullet Charts

Bullet charts are good to compare two variables, such as sales dollars and salesperson. Actual sales data and target (quota) sales data can be compared for each salesperson to visualize which salesperson meets the assigned target sales quota (i.e., above or below the quota). Here, two charts are combined with a bar chart showing actual sales dollars on the horizontal x-axis and a vertical reference line (quota line) on the vertical y-axis.

Scatter Diagram

A scatter diagram or scatter plot is used to determine whether a relationship exists between an independent variable (vertical, y-axis) and a dependent variable (horizontal, x-axis) as shown in a graph. It detects correlation or trends between two measured factors or variables of interest, such as product price (y-axis) and sales quantity (x-axis) and sales quantity (y-axis) and net profit or gross profit (x-axis). Note that a correlation, whether it is positive or negative, does not guarantee a true relationship; it only suggests a potential relationship.

Dashboards

Dashboards are presented in several forms, including numerical, graphical, and interactive formats. They use drill-down and drag-and-drop features. In general, data dashboards are a collection of performance indicators showing an object's or a device's status and quality levels in colors. They provide a concise and visual summary of overall performance. An example is showing an automobile's performance in terms of its speed, revolutions per minute, oil pressure, and temperature.

A data dashboard is a color-coded visual presentation of vital data used in developing a strategy or a plan. Data can be presented in several ways, such as tables, figures, charts, graphs, maps, exhibits, slides, audios, and videos. Data can also be presented at different times, such as on demand or as scheduled. A dashboard can be created using a drag-and-drop facility available on mobile devices and desktop/laptop computers.

Dashboards are of two types: static (basic) and interactive (advanced). Static dashboards show traditional reports that are mainly financial focused (e.g., sales, revenues, costs, and profits). Basic interactive dashboards show information about customers' buying habits and cross-sales to them. Advanced interactive dashboards can have built-in simulation models to do what-if type of analyses (i.e., sensitivity analysis).

Today, some organizations present only structured data on their dashboards. Better insights and rewards can be achieved if they show structured data, unstructured, and semistructured data on their dashboards because it gives them a big-picture perspective of their business.

Data filters can be built into dashboards so data can be sliced from different perspectives or drilled down to a more detailed level using various parameters, such as: transaction date, month, quarter, or year; cost data by contract; revenue or profit data by a retail store; sales data by a market region; or quarterly performance by a business segment. Data filters provide the ability to explore data at multiple levels and to customize user-driven data analysis. Data filters show only the requested data and ignore the rest of the data not requested.

Pivot Table

A pivot table (or pivot chart) is a second, revised table in rows and columns containing reformatted data using the raw data from the first, original table in rows and columns.

First Table ⟶ Original Table

Second Table ⟶ Pivot Table

The basic data values are the same between the original table and the pivot table. However, the pivot table contains sorted, rearranged, and summarized data, providing better insights. For example, a retail marketing manager can create a pivot table showing which salesperson has the highest sales dollars in a given month or quarter from the original sales data tables. Exhibit 1.61 compares the first, original table with the second, pivot table.

EXHIBIT 1.61 Comparison between the First and the Second Pivot Table

First, Original Table	Second, Pivot Table
Presents discrete raw data in columns and rows found in spreadsheets	Presents summarized data after sorting, counting, grouping, averaging, and summarizing data in columns and rows. Spreadsheets, data visualization programs, or business intelligence software can be used to create pivot tables.
Cannot answer the question "How many product units were sold in each market region for each ship date?"	Can answer the question "How many product units were sold in each market region for each ship date?"
	Can be used in data mining applications.
	Descriptive statistics can be applied to compute standard deviation and variance.
	Simplifies complex data found in OLAP servers using data query tools.

Contingency Table

A contingency table is a type of table presented in a matrix format displaying frequency distribution, showing their statistical probabilities. Contingency tables (cross-tabulations) are used in business intelligence, market research, and customer surveys where interrelations and interactions between two or more variables can be studied to obtain greater insights of data. Due to its statistical focus, a contingency table shows a measure of association between variables. For example, a table can be put together showing how male and female customers prefer to purchase Product A and Product B from a retailer.

Responsibility Assignment Matrix

A responsibility assignment matrix (or RACI diagram) deals with four items: responsible (the "R"), accountable ("A"), consulted ("C"), and informed ("I"). Typically, a task is associated with one or more roles using the RACI diagram. Simply stated, the RACI diagram connects people to their assigned jobs, duties, tasks, activities, or projects so they can complete them.

The RACI diagram describes and clarifies participation by several individuals assuming various roles in completing the assigned tasks or deliverables required in a project, process, or facility. It can be applied either in one business function or department or across functions or departments.

Spaghetti Plot

A spaghetti plot (chart, diagram, or map) is a workflow system to visualize data flows through a system where flows appear as noodles. This plot is used to: track product routing and material movement through a factory; reduce inefficiencies in an office, factory, or warehouse workflow system; and show the effects of medical drugs on test patients during a new drug trial, among others. The results of a spaghetti plot can be useful in streamlining or simplifying workflow to save resources, such as time, money, materials, and energy.

Maps

Maps are used to show geographical data, such as a location (city or country) and an activity. They are often paired with pie, line, or bar charts. An example of application of maps is a distribution of website traffic by country for the number of blogs visited.

Decision Table

A decision table documents rules used to select one or more actions based on one or more conditions. These conditions and their corresponding actions can be presented either in matrix or tabular form. Decision rules are used in decision tables where a sentence in the table is called a "rule." Each rule shows conditions that must be considered, their relationships to each other, and the decision instructions (actions).

A decision table is a tabular means of analyzing decision alternatives (courses of actions) and states of nature (outcomes). The alternatives are listed on the left side, the states of nature are listed across the top, and the payoffs (i.e., conditional values) are listed in the body of the decision table.

Decision Tree

A decision tree is a graphical representation of possible alternative decisions, events, or states of nature resulting from each decision with its associated probabilities and outcomes of the events or states of nature. The decision problem displays the sequential nature of the decision-making situation. The decision tree has nodes, branches, and circles to represent junction boxes, connectors between the nodes, and states-of-nature nodes, respectively.

The decision tree approach is suitable for multiple sequential decisions, where later decisions are based on the outcome of prior ones. The approach includes decision alternatives, states of nature with their respective probabilities, and payoff amounts for each combination of decision alternatives and states of nature.

The expected monetary value (EMV) is computed by working backward (i.e., by starting at the right of the tree and working back to decision nodes on the left of the tree). The decision node leading to the state-of-nature node with the highest EMV will be chosen. Decision trees are used in evaluating capacity planning and capital investment decisions.

Which Data Visualization Tool Is Used for What and When?

- Line charts, area charts, and bar charts show trends and patterns over a time period where the "time" dimension is put on the x-axis and the "amount" dimension is put on the y-axis to measure a relationship between time and amount.

- A bar chart is good for comparison and ranking of the measured values.

- A combo chart is a combination of a line chart and a bar chart to identify trends.

- A scatter plot is good for identifying relationships between the measured values.

- The part-to-whole chart shows the percentage of a part in relation to its whole (e.g., Part A is 20%, Part B 30%, and Part C is 50%).

- The pie chart should not be used in conducting part-to-whole analysis due to difficulty in visualizing the parts. However, a bar chart can be used in maps for a better visualization.

- Maps show geographical data, such as a location (city or country) and an activity. Maps are often best used when paired with another chart, such as a pie, line, or bar chart.

- It is good to put the most important data on the x-axis or y-axis and to put the least important data on color, size, or shape attributes.

1.12 Business Functions

The manufacturing industry and the service industry are the two major industries in any nation's economy after excluding the agriculture and defense industries. The retail industry possesses elements of both manufacturing and service where the retailer becomes a manufacturer when it manufactures and sells its own store brands (private labels) to customers. Examples of store brands include Kirkland Signature brand for Costco, the up&up brand for Target, and the Great Value brand for Walmart.

This section focuses on the manufacturing industry and service industry, including the retail industry. Regardless of the industry, three common **core business functions** (primary functions) include: (1) the operations function (i.e., manufacturing operations to produce goods or service operations to render services to customers), (2) the marketing function (marketing and sales) to market and sell those goods and services, and (3) the finance function (accounting and finance) to invest money in those goods or services and to receive revenue and profits from making and selling those goods and services. These three core functions drive a company's mission and vision and generate revenues, incur costs, and make profits. Further, the sales function can be considered a subset of the marketing function whereas accounting function can be considered as a subset of finance function. For example, (1) marketing management develops the marketing strategy and sales management executes that strategy; and (2) finance management raises money and accounting management tracks how that money was spent. Note that marketing and sales are the two sides of a coin similar to accounting and finance.

Many **noncore business functions** (support functions) exist; they help the core functions to succeed and include human resources management, quality management, IT, engineering, R&D, legal, internal audit, public relations, and other functions. These support functions do not bring any sales, revenues, and profits but facilitate them.

Manufacturing operations, service operations, marketing and sales function and quality management function are further discussed next.

(a) Manufacturing Operations

Manufacturing (production) strategies include increasing productivity, decreasing costs, and improving quality by adding value to inputs (raw materials) through the transformation process and producing quality outputs (products or goods). This strategy fits with the concept that consumers purchase their products from the company that offers them the most value for their money. The manufacturing strategy should fit with the overall business strategy, such as less time to market new products, cost minimization, improved quality, and greater market share. Several topics discussed in the manufacturing operations include workflow analysis; bottleneck management; theory of constraints; production process flows; inventory management techniques and concepts; inventory types and costs; just-in-time systems, and production scheduling and control systems.

(i) Workflow Analysis

Workflow analysis looks at the overall flow of work to find ways to improve this flow. It can reveal value-added and non-value-added activities (e.g., waste and delays) and identify interdependence among departments. The outcome would be eliminating the non-value-added activities and waste and improving efficiency and effectiveness. Assembling tasks, whether subassembly or final assembly, and process time are value-added activities of a manufactured product, while other activities are non-value-added activities. Examples of non-value-added activities from a customer's viewpoint include inspection time, move time, reporting time, governmental compliance time, storage time, wait time, and queue time.

Analyzing and updating workflow systems would make organizations undergo huge managerial and cultural changes, help employees apply business rules, enable process reengineering, provide parallel processing of documents, eliminate information float or overload, and ensure that established policies and procedures are followed. Workflow software allows business processes to be redesigned and streamlined and automatically routes work from employee to employee.

Interdependence means the extent to which departments depend on each other for resources or materials to accomplish their tasks. Low interdependence means that departments can do their work independent of each other and have little need for interaction, consultation, or exchange of materials. High interdependence means departments must constantly exchange resources and materials.

Three types of interdependence influence organization structure: pooled, sequential, and reciprocal. Pooled interdependence is the lowest form of interdependence among departments. Work does not flow between units. Each department is part of the organization and contributes to the common good of the organization, but it works independently. When interdependence is of serial form, with parts or documents produced in one department becoming inputs to another department, sequential interdependence exists. Here departments exchange resources and depend on others to perform well. Management requirements for sequential interdependence are more demanding than for pooled interdependence. These requirements include coordination, communication, integrators, and task forces. The highest level of interdependence is reciprocal interdependence. This exists when the output of operation A is the input to operation B, and the output of operation B is the input back again to operation A. The outputs of departments influence those departments in reciprocal fashion. Management requirements for complex reciprocal interdependence include greater planning, coordination, communication, permanent teams, and frequent adjustments in work and its associated plans.

(ii) Bottleneck Management

A **bottleneck** is a constraint in a facility, function, department, or resource whose capacity is less than the demand placed on it. For example, a bottleneck machine or work center exists where jobs are processed at a slower rate than they are demanded. Another example is where the demand for a company's product exceeds the company's ability to produce the product.

Bottlenecks influence both product profitability and product price. The contribution margin per bottleneck hour or the value of each bottleneck hour should be analyzed. This measure is better than the normal contribution margin per unit. The contribution margin per hour of bottleneck can be used to adjust the product price to better reflect the value of the product's use of a bottleneck. Products that use a large number of bottleneck hours per unit require a higher contribution margin than products that use few bottleneck hours per unit.

(iii) Theory of Constraints

The theory of constraints (TOC) is a manufacturing strategy that attempts to remove the influence of bottlenecks on a process. According to Dr. Eliyahu M. Goldratt, TOC consists of three separate but interrelated areas: logistics, performance measurement, and logical thinking. Logistics include drum-buffer-rope scheduling, buffer management, and VAT analysis. Performance measurement includes throughput, inventory and operating expense, and the five focusing steps. Logical thinking process tools are important in identifying the root problems (current reality tree), identifying and expanding win-win solutions (evaporating cloud and future reality tree), and developing implementation plans (prerequisite tree and transition tree).

Drum-buffer-rope scheduling is the generalized process used to manage resources to maximize throughput. The drum is the rate or pace of production set by the system's constraint. The buffers establish the protection against uncertainty so that the system can maximize throughput. The rope is a communication process from the constraint to the gating operation that checks or limits material released into the system to support the constraint.

Buffer management is a process in which all expediting in a factory shop is driven by what is scheduled to be in the buffers (constraint, shipping, and assembly buffers). By expediting this material into the buffers, the system helps avoid idleness at the constraint and missed customer due dates. In addition, the causes of items missing from the buffer are identified, and the frequency of occurrence is used to prioritize improvement activities.

VAT analysis is a procedure for determining the general flow of parts and products from raw materials to finished products (the logical product structure). A "V" logical product structure starts with one or a few raw materials, and the product expands into a number of different products as it flows through divergent points in its routings. The shape of an "A" logical product structure is dominated by converging points. Many raw materials are fabricated and assembled into a few finished products. A "T" logical product structure consists of numerous similar finished products assembled from common assemblies, subassemblies, and parts. Once the general parts flow is determined, the system control points (gating operations, convergent points, divergent points, constraints, and shipping points) can be identified and managed.

The **five focusing steps** is a process to continuously improve organizational profit by evaluating the production system and the marketing mix to determine how to make the most profit using the system constraint. The steps consist of:

1. Identifying the constraint to the system.

2. Deciding how to exploit the constraint to the system.

3. Subordinating all nonconstraints to the system.

4. Elevating the constraint to the system.

5. Returning to Step 1 if the constraint is broken in any previous step, while not allowing inertia to set in.

(iv) Production Process Flows

Three operational process flow measures include flow time, inventory, and throughput. They are interrelated in that defining targets on any two of them defines a target for the third.[25]

Inventory = Throughput × Flow time

The basic managerial levers for process improvement are:

Decrease in flow time

Increase in throughput

Decrease in inventory and waiting time

Control process variability

Manage process flows and costs

(A) Levers for Managing Flow Time

Levers for managing flow time include decreasing the work content of a critical path by shortening the length of every critical path in these ways:

1. Reduce the work content of an activity on the critical path.

   ☐ Eliminate non-value-adding aspects of the activity (i.e., work smarter).

   ☐ Increase the speed at which the activity is done (i.e., work faster) by acquiring faster equipment and/or by increasing incentives to work faster.

   ☐ Reduce the number of repeat activities (i.e., do it right the first time).

---

[25] Anupindi et al., *Managing Business Process Flows*, 2nd ed. (Upper Saddle River, NJ: Pearson/Prentice Hall, 2006), pp. 313–315.

2. Work in parallel.

- ☐ Move work from a critical path to a noncritical path (i.e., perform work in parallel rather than in sequence).
- ☐ Move work from a critical path to the "outer loop" (i.e., either preprocessing or post-processing).

3. Modify the product mix.

- ☐ Change the product mix to produce products with smaller work content with respect to the specified activity.

(B) Levers for Managing (Increasing) Process Throughput

Levers for managing (increasing) throughput of a process are listed next.

1. Decrease resource idleness.

- ☐ Synchronize flows within the process to reduce starvation and set appropriate size of buffers to reduce blockage.

2. Increase net availability of resources to increase effective capacity.

- ☐ Improve maintenance policies.
- ☐ Perform preventive maintenance outside periods of scheduled availability.
- ☐ Institute effective problem-solving measures that reduce frequency and duration of breakdowns.
- ☐ Institute motivational programs and incentives to reduce employee absenteeism and increasing employee morale.

3. Reduce setup waste.

- ☐ Reduce the frequency of setups, and reduce the time required for a single setup.

4. Increase theoretical capacity.

- ☐ Decrease unit load on the bottleneck resource pool (e.g., work faster, work smarter, do it right the first time, change production mix, subcontract or outsource, and invest in flexible resources).
- ☐ Increase the load batch of resources in the bottleneck resource pool (i.e., increase the scale of resources).
- ☐ Increase the number of units in the bottleneck resource pool (i.e., increase scale of process).
- ☐ Increase the scheduled availability of the bottleneck resource pool (i.e., work longer).
- ☐ Modify the production mix.

(C) Levers for Reducing Inventory and Waiting Time

Levers for reducing inventory and waiting time are listed next.

1. Reduce cycle inventory (i.e., reduce batch size).

- ☐ Reduce setup or order cost per batch or reduce forward buying.

2. Reduce safety inventory.

- ☐ Reduce demand variability through improved forecasting.

- ☐ Reduce replenishment lead time and its variability.
- ☐ Pool safety inventory for multiple locations or products through either physical or virtual centralization of specialization or some combination thereof.
- ☐ Exploit product substitution.
- ☐ Use common components.
- ☐ Postpone product differentiation closer to the point of demand.

3. Manage safety capacity.

- ☐ Increase safety capacity.
- ☐ Decrease variability in arrivals and service patterns.
- ☐ Pool available safety capacity.

4. Synchronize flows.

- ☐ Manage capacity to synchronize with demand.
- ☐ Manage demand to synchronize with available capacity.
- ☐ Synchronize flows within the process.

5. Manage customers' psychological perceptions.

- ☐ Reduce the cost of waiting in a line by managing customers' perceptions.

(D) Levers for Controlling Process Variability

Levers for controlling process variability are listed next.

1. Measure, prioritize, and analyze variability.

- ☐ Check key performance measures over time.

2. Utilize feedback control to limit abnormal variability.

- ☐ Set control limits of acceptable variability in key performance measures.
- ☐ Monitor actual performance and correct any abnormal variability.

3. Decrease normal process variability.

- ☐ Design for processing (i.e., simplify, standardize, and mistake-proof).

4. Immunize product performance.

- ☐ Utilize robust design to minimize process variability.

(E) Levers for Managing Process Flows and Costs

Levers for managing process flows and costs are listed next.

1. Manage flows in a plant.

- ☐ Process structure with cellular layout.
- ☐ Information and material flow using demand pull system.
- ☐ Level production with batch size reduction.
- ☐ Quality at source with defect prevention and decentralized control.
- ☐ Supplier management with partnerships and incentives.

□ Supply consistency through maintenance of safety capacity.

□ Employee involvement and empowerment.

2. Manage flows in a supply chain.

□ Reduce information and material flow times using technology and efficient logistics.

□ Reduce fixed costs of ordering and quantity discounts.

□ Share information on customer demand and product availability.

□ Coordinate forecasts between affected parties.

□ Stabilize prices.

3. Improve processes.

□ Utilize continuous improvement and reengineering.

□ Utilize increased visibility, incentives, plan-do-check-act (PDCA) cycle, and benchmarking.

(v) Inventory Management Techniques and Concepts

From the viewpoint of inventory management, demand is of two types: independent demand and dependent demand. Independent demand inventory systems are based on the premise that the demand or usage of a particular item is independent of the demand or usage of other items. Examples include finished goods; spare parts; material, repair, and operating (MRO) supplies; and resale inventories.

(A) Independent Demand Inventory Systems

Independent demand inventory systems are "pull" systems in that materials are pulled from the previous operation as they are needed to replace materials that have been used. For example, finished goods are replaced as they are sold. These types of inventory systems answer the question of when to place the replenishment order and how much to order at one time. Reorder point models and fixed/variable order quantity models (e.g., economic order quantity [EOQ]) are examples of independent demand inventory systems as they review inventory either continuously or periodically.

(B) Dependent Demand Inventory Systems

Dependent demand inventory systems are based on the premise that the demand or usage of a particular item is dependent on the demand or usage of other items. Examples include raw materials, work-in-process (WIP) inventories, and component parts.

(C) Inventory Levels and Profit Levels

A company manages its inventory by using various methods and approaches (e.g., EOQ). Inventory consists of raw materials, work in process, and finished goods. Efficient inventory management is needed to support sales, which is necessary for profits. Benefits such as high turnover rate, low write-offs, and low lost sales can be attributed to efficient inventory management. These benefits, in turn, contribute to a high profit margin, a higher total asset turnover, a higher rate of ROI, and a strong stock price. Inventory management is a major concern for product-based organizations (e.g., manufacturing and retail), since 20% to 40% of their total assets is inventory. For that reason, poor inventory control will hurt the profitability of the organization.

(vi) Inventory Types and Costs

This section presents several topics: types of inventory, costs of inventory, investments in inventory, management views on inventory, inventory ordering and reordering techniques, ABC inventory analysis with inventory counts, inventory management methods, inventory costing methods, and inventory estimation methods.

(A) Types of Inventory

Inventory represents the single largest investment in assets for most manufacturers, wholesalers, and retailers. These are the six primary types of inventory:

1. Raw materials inventory (basic and bulk items)
2. WIP inventory (semifinished inventory)
3. Finished goods inventory
4. MRO supplies inventory
5. In-transit inventory
6. Cross-docked inventory.

Raw materials inventory includes the basic inputs to the organization's production process. This inventory is cheapest, because the organization has not yet invested labor and other efforts and costs in it. Examples of raw materials inventory (ingredients) for a baking shop include eggs, flour, sugar, butter, oil, and food flavoring agents, such as vanilla extract and fennel seeds.

WIP inventory includes the materials moving through the various stages of the production process that are not yet fully converted to finished products. A WIP inventory for an automobile manufacturing plant includes engines, wheels, tire assemblies, and dashboards waiting to be installed.

Finished goods inventory includes products that have passed through the entire production process but have yet to be sold. Finished goods are the fully completed products that are available for future or current shipment and to fill future customer orders. Finished goods are highly visible inventory and expensive, because the organization has already invested in raw materials, labor, and other costs (overhead costs) to make the finished product. Note that finished goods levels change as production levels go and up down and as sales levels go and up down. New cars parked in the storage lot of an automobile factory or at a car dealership are examples of finished goods inventory.

MRO supplies inventory includes the items used to support production and other factory operations (miscellaneous supplies). These items are not physically part of a finished product but are critical for the continuous operation of a plant, equipment, or office. Examples of MRO supplies inventory include office supplies, spare parts, tools, cleaning clothes and liquids, paper towels, and computers.

In-transit inventory is in transit to a customer or is located throughout distribution channels. Most consumable goods inventory is either on trucks or on grocery store shelves. In fact, grocery stores provide shelf space for products but do not own any inventory. The supplying company or distributor owns the inventory and receives payment when a consumer buys a product. In-transit inventory is carried to distributors and retailers using trucks, trains, air cargos, sea cargoes, and other transportation methods.

Cross-docked inventory refers to products that are unloaded from an inbound truck coming from a manufacturer at one dock of a retailer's warehouse and are reloaded onto an outbound truck at a different dock of the same warehouse within a short time. The outbound truck is going to retail stores based on the stock keeping unit code on a product's package. In other words, products are coming from a manufacturer and immediately going to retail stores without being stored in the warehouse.

A cross-docking approach to inventory can optimize materials handling and movement costs in a warehouse because these in-transit products do not require storage as they are shipped from a manufacturer to a retailer as outbound deliveries. This expedited approach ships goods to customers as quickly as possible.

Benefits to the cross-docking inventory approach include:

- No delays from the manufacturer to the retailer, which helps improve customer satisfaction.
- No storage space required, which leaves more space for other products to store.
- No labor costs involved as there is no need for picking, sorting, and storing of cross-docked products in the warehouse.

However, there are some risks associated with the cross-docked inventory approach: Warehouse employees or truck drivers can steal the products during the dock changeover without any accountability, and these products cannot be tracked and monitored in the same way as other products. Products suitable to the cross-docking approach are perishable items (e.g., fruits and vegetables), high-quality products that do not require incoming inspection; products that are pretagged and preticketed with bar codes and RFID tags; staple products with constant demand that are consumed quickly; prepicked and prepackaged customer orders coming from other manufacturers or warehouses; and sales promotional products that are ready and waiting for sale at retail stores.

(B) Costs of Inventory

Inventory is not cheap, and various costs are associated with inventories due to their direct relationships with production activities. The cost structure, consisting of variable costs and fixed costs, affects the amount and type of investment needed. Four types of inventory-related costs are carrying or holding costs, ordering costs, stock-out costs, and quality costs.

1. **Carrying costs**

   Carrying (or holding) costs are the costs associated with carrying a given level of inventory. These costs rise in direct proportion to the average inventory carried or held. The components of carrying costs include:

   a. The costs of capital tied up in inventory

   b. The opportunity cost associated with not being able to use the capital for other investment

   c. Warehouse storage and handling costs

   d. Insurance premiums

   e. Property taxes

   f. Depreciation

   g. Pilferage, spoilage, spillage costs

   h. Property damage costs

   i. Obsolescence costs due to deterioration from wear and tear

The holding of inventory may create other costs. Examples include duties, tooling costs, exchange rate differentials, packaging costs, transportation and logistics costs, and administrative costs.

Carrying costs vary with the level of inventory, which makes these costs variable. Fixed costs are not included as part of inventory carrying costs, because inventory levels typically have no effect on a fixed cost, at least in the short run. For most industries, inventory carrying costs typically range from 15% to 25% of the value of the total inventory.

EXAMPLE

Carrying cost of inventories is calculated as follows:

Inventory carrying cost = Average inventory in units × Unit price × Carrying cost per year

If a company averages 1,000 units in inventory, for which the unit price is $1.00 per unit and the annual carrying cost is 25%, the total inventory carrying cost per year for that level of inventory is $250 (i.e., (1,000 × $1 × 0.25) = $250).

---

2. Ordering costs

Ordering costs are the costs associated with placing an order and are fixed regardless of the average size of inventory. The components of ordering costs include the cost of placing orders and production setup and shipping and handling costs.

Ordering costs are a composite of the costs associated with the release of a material order. These costs may include the cost of generating and sending a material release, transportation costs, and any other cost connected with acquiring a good. If a firm produces an item or good itself, the ordering cost will also include machine setup costs. Examples of inventory ordering costs include salaries of the buyers and their staff; cost of paper, postage, telephone, and transportation; and receiving costs of materials.

EXAMPLE

Ordering cost of inventories is calculated as follows:

Total ordering costs = Fixed costs associated with ordering inventories
× Number of orders per year

If a company incurs $20 for fixed costs associated with ordering inventories and if it places 15 orders per year, the total ordering costs are $300 (i.e., $20 × 15 = $300).

HOLDING COSTS VERSUS ORDERING COSTS

Holding costs are the costs associated with carrying a given level of inventory; these costs are dependent on the size of the inventory. They include interest cost for the capital tied up in inventory, opportunity cost associated with not being able to use the money for investment, insurance fees, taxes, pilferage and damage, as well as other warehouse overhead costs.

Ordering costs are the costs associated with placing an order and include salaries of the purchasers, paper, postage, telephone, transportation, and receiving costs.

3. Stock-out costs

Stock-out costs are costs of running short of inventory and require safety stock as a cushion. This means that safety stock reduces a stock-out situation. However, safety stock increases carrying and investment costs and decreases stock-out costs. The components of stock-out costs include the loss of sales, the loss of customer goodwill, and problems or delays in production schedules. Stock-outs or out-of-stock situations have an opportunity cost due to inability to meet customer demand and from consequent loss of sales revenue and profits. Stock-outs at a retailer can cause a rippling effect in the entire supply chain, called a bullwhip effect.

WHAT IS THE BULLWHIP EFFECT?

The bullwhip effect, also known as the Forrester effect, refers to a rippling and magnifying effect on inventory levels due to changes in product demand levels between producers and suppliers. This means that a small change in demand at the first downstream supplier (DS-1) creates a big change in the demand at the first upstream supplier 1 (US-1) and generates a huge demand at the producer, as shown below.

US-1 ⟶ US-N ⟶ Producer ⟵ DS-N ⟵ DS-1

The bullwhip effect results in unnecessary over-orders, overproduction, overstorage, over-buildup of inventory, and excessive inventory costs and investments due to an excess of caution exhibited by all levels in the supply chain. In other words, the bullwhip effect is a result of a just-in-case exaggeration of demand incorrectly assumed by all partners in the supply chain, thus reflecting chaos and uncertainty. In a way, the bullwhip effect represents uncontrolled and uncoordinated activities in the inventory channel as well as in the supply chain.

---

4. Quality costs

Quality costs include any costs associated with nonconforming goods produced. The total cost of inventory ownership is more than simply the ordering and carrying costs because it should include the cost of poor quality. Quantifying the cost of poor quality is difficult, but it can help identify the causes of quality-related problems. Examples of quality costs due to producing and shipping defective inventory include field-site failure costs, rework costs, losses due to poor product yields, inspection time and costs, lost production, and product warranty and recall costs.

(C) Investment in Inventory

The investment in the finished goods inventory is hiding in working stock and safety stock. The amount of this investment depends on the actual level of inventory carried. The relevant question is how many units of each inventory item the retail firm should hold in its stock. A relevant metric here is gross margin return on inventory investment (GMROII) or gross margin return on inventory (GMROI), where higher numbers are preferred. This is calculated as:

$$\text{GMROII} = \text{GMROI} = (\text{Gross margin amount}) / (\text{Average inventory at cost}) \times 100$$

Two types of stock concepts must be understood: working stock and safety stock. The actual level of finished goods inventories carried will equal the sum of the working stock and safety stock.

Working stock is needed to meet normal, expected production and sales demand levels. Producing more goods than are currently needed increases the firm's carrying costs and exposes it to the risk of obsolescence if demand should fall. Remember that demand for sales is uncertain. Working stock is a basic stock or cycle stock where inventory levels go up and down due to sales activity and inventory ordering and reordering activities.

Safety stock is needed to guard against changes in sales rates or delays in production and shipping activities that could result in a stock-out situation. Safety stock is additional stock beyond the working stock and meets when demand is greater than expected. The additional costs of holding safety stock must be balanced against the costs of sales lost due to inventory shortages. Safety stock will not affect reorder quantities as it is the inventory level at the time of reordering minus the expected usage while the new goods are in transit.

Another name for safety stock is buffer stock; it provides a safety cushion for working stock to prevent stock-outs when demand exceeds the sales forecast.

The goal is to minimize both the cost of holding safety stock and the cost of stock-outs. Production bottlenecks lead to stock-outs. Factors to be considered in controlling stock-outs include time needed for delivery, rate of inventory usage, and safety stock.

SAFETY STOCK VERSUS STOCK-OUTS

Safety stock is the amount of extra stock that is kept to protect against stock-outs. Running out of an inventory item is called a stock-out situation. Safety stock is the inventory level at the time of reordering minus the expected usage while the new goods are in transit.

Economic order quantity is not relevant to stock-outs. Production bottlenecks lead to stock-outs. Factors to be considered in controlling stock-outs include time needed for delivery, rate of inventory usage, and safety stock.

(D) Management Views on Inventory

There have been serious debates whether inventory is an asset or a liability of a company. Since inventories need to be available prior to sales, an increase in production to meet increased sales requires an increase in notes payable (a liability account). Since assets (inventories) are increasing, liability (notes payable) must also increase at the same time. This means that inventory is both an asset and a liability at the same time.

From an accounting point of view, inventory is an asset of a company because the company makes money by selling the inventory to customers. A company's marketing department also views inventory as an asset. Owners and investors may see the inventory as a liability.

There are conflicting views about the status of inventories within the management team of a manufacturing or retail company due to different goals they have. Examples of these conflicting objectives include:

- Sales managers prefer large inventories so they can sell more when needed.
- Production managers prefer large production runs to gain production efficiencies.

- Warehouse managers prefer minimum inventory to optimize storage space.

- Purchasing agents prefer large lot purchases to save money on total purchases due to volume discounts.

- Finance managers prefer low inventories and small production runs to reduce inventory funding.

- Chief executives want more production, more sales, more profits, and higher market stock prices.

(E) Inventory Ordering and Reordering Techniques

In this section, we discuss optimal order quantities and how to calculate reorder points.

Inventory managers face two decision rules in the management of inventories: how much to order and when to order that will result in the lowest possible total inventory cost. The how-much-to-order decision rule can be satisfied with the use of an EOQ. This decision rule involves selecting an order quantity that draws a compromise between (1) keeping smaller inventories and ordering frequently (results in high ordering costs) and (2) keeping large inventories and ordering infrequently (results in high holding costs). The when-to-order decision rule can be satisfied with the use of a reorder point.

Optimal Order Quantity. How many units should be ordered or produced at a given time is a major question faced by the inventory manager. Either too much or too little inventory is not good. An optimum inventory level is designed and is found through the use of the EOQ model. EOQ provides the optimal, or least-cost, quantity of inventory that should be ordered. If a company's cost of ordering per order increases while carrying costs per order remain the same, the optimal order size as specified by the EOQ model would increase.

EOQ cost characteristics are listed next.

- The point at which the total cost curve is minimized represents the EOQ, and this, in turn, determines the optimal average inventory level. Here, total cost is the sum of ordering and carrying costs.

- Some costs rise with larger inventories whereas other costs decline.

- The average investment in inventories depends on how frequently orders are placed.

- Ordering costs decline with larger orders and inventories due to reduced order frequency.

If Q is the order quantity, then the how-much-to-order decision involves finding the value of Q that will minimize the sum of holding and ordering costs.

$$Q = \text{EOQ} = \sqrt{\frac{2D\,Co}{Ch}}$$

Where

D = annual sales demand in units

Co = cost of placing one order

Ch = cost of holding (or carrying) one unit in inventory for the year

Note that the data needed to calculate EOQ includes: the volume of product sales, the purchase price of the products, the fixed cost of ordering products, and carrying costs. It does not include the volume of products in inventory, inventory delivery times, delays in transportation, or quality of materials.

Due to the square root sign, a given increase in sales will result in a less-than-proportionate increase in inventories, and the inventory turnover ratio will thus increase as sales grow.

EXAMPLE: CALCULATION OF OPTIMUM ORDER SIZE

A retail firm expects to sell 1,000 units of product 576 during the coming year. Ordering costs are $100 per order, and carrying costs (holding costs) are $2 per unit per year. Using the EOQ model, what is the optimum order size?

The optimum order size is 316, as shown below. The answer is to find the square root of (2 × $100 × 1,000) / $2. This is the square root of 100,000, or 316.

Reorder Points. Another major problem facing the inventory manager is at what point inventory should be ordered or produced. The point at which stock on hand must be replenished is called the "reorder point." It is also the inventory level at which an order should be placed. The formula is

$$\text{Reorder point} = \text{Lead time} \times \text{Usage rate}$$

Where lead time = time lag required for production and shipping of inventory

Usage rate = usage quantity per unit of time (Note: the time period should be the same in both lead time and usage rate—days, weeks, or months.)

EXAMPLE: CALCULATION OF REORDER POINT

A retailer's usage rate (sales) for product 576 is 25 units per week. If the lead time for the same product is four weeks from suppliers, what is the reorder point for product 576?

$$\text{Reorder point} = \text{Lead time} \times \text{Usage rate}$$

$$\text{Reorder point} = 4 \times 25 = 100 \text{ units}$$

This means that the retailer will reorder product 576 when its current inventory level is 100 units.

A complication in the calculation of the reorder point arises when we introduce a concept of goods in transit. This situation occurs when a new order must be placed before the previous order is received. Goods in transit are goods that have been ordered but have not been received. A goods-in-transit situation exists if the normal delivery lead time is longer than the time between orders. The formula for a reorder point when goods in transit is considered is:

$$\text{Reorder point} = (\text{Lead time} \times \text{Usage rate}) - (\text{Goods in transit})$$

EOQ Assumptions. There are two major assumptions of EOQ. First, the demand for an item is constant. Since the constant demand assumption is not realistic, managers would have to be satisfied with the near-minimum-cost order quantity instead of a minimum-total-cost order quantity. Second, the entire quantity ordered arrives at one point in time. Again, this may not be realistic because some vendors will deliver partial shipments. Managers usually add a judgmental value-based order quantity to the EOQ suggested order quantity to accommodate unrealistic assumptions of constant demand rate by the EOQ model.

Specific assumptions of the EOQ model are listed next.

- Sales can be forecasted perfectly. This is unrealistic.
- Sales are evenly distributed throughout the year. This is not realistic. What about seasonal or cyclical demands?
- Orders are received without delay. This is also unrealistic.
- Fixed costs, carrying costs, and purchase prices are all fixed and independent of the ordering procedures. This is not possible either.

EOQ Cost Characteristics

- The point at which the total cost curve is minimized represents the EOQ, and this, in turn, determines the optimal average inventory level. Here, total cost is the sum of ordering and carrying costs.
- Some costs rise with larger inventories whereas other costs decline.
- The average investment in inventories depends on how frequently orders are placed.
- Ordering costs decline with larger orders and inventories due to reduced order frequency.

Sensitivity Analysis and EOQ. It is good to know how much the recommended order quantity would change if the estimated ordering and holding costs had been different. Depending on whether the total annual cost increased, decreased, or remains the same, we can tell whether the EOQ model is sensitive or insensitive to variations in the cost estimates.

Effects of Inflation on Inventory Management.
There is no evidence that inflation either raises or lowers the optimal level of inventory of firms in the aggregate. Inflation should be considered, however, since it will raise an individual firm's optimal inventory holdings if the rate of inflation is above average, and vice versa.

Decision rules and consequences of inflation are listed next.

- For moderate inflation, it is safe to ignore inflation and the benefit is not worth the effort.
- For relatively constant inflation, subtract the expected annual rate of inflation from the carrying cost percentage (Ch) in the EOQ model and recalculate the EOQ. Since the carrying cost will be smaller, the recalculated EOQ and the average inventory will increase.

- For higher inflation, the higher the rate of inflation, the higher the interest rates will be. This will cause the carrying cost to increase and thus lower the EOQ and average inventories.

(F) ABC Inventory Control System

ABC is a method of classifying inventory based on usage and value. Expensive, frequently used, high stock-out cost items with long lead times are most frequently reviewed in an ABC inventory control system. Inexpensive and infrequently used items are reviewed less frequently.

ABC inventory analysis is a method of classifying on-hand inventory based on usage and value. It applies the Pareto principle (20% critical few and 80% trivial many) to inventory. Expensive, frequently used, high stock-out cost items with long lead times (A items) are most frequently reviewed. Inexpensive and infrequently used items (B and C items) are reviewed less frequently. To classify the inventory based on annual dollar volume, the annual demand of each item is multiplied with its cost per unit.

Class A items (i.e., approximately 20% of stock items) have a high annual dollar volume representing approximately 80% of the total dollar usage.

Class B and C items (i.e., together approximately 80% of stock items) have a medium annual dollar volume for Class B items and a low annual dollar volume for Class C items, together representing approximately 20% of the total dollar usage.

Example: Retailers often develop and monitor a never-out list of products that must be available at all times because they are the best sellers with high sales volume and high margins. Hence, these products are separately planned and controlled from the rest of the products and qualify as A items in the ABC analysis of inventory system.

Example: A retail firm uses an ABC inventory control system. About 10% of inventory items are classified into group A. Another 20% are in group B. The remainder items are in group C. Which classification is most likely to hold the greatest number of days of supply?

a. Group C

b. Group B

c. Group A

d. All groups are likely to have an equal number of days of supply

Choice **a** is the correct answer. Group C items are low-dollar-value items and receive less management attention. Extensive use of models and records is not cost effective. It is cheaper to order large quantities infrequently. Group A items are high-dollar value, and management would try to keep investment in such items low. Therefore, by definition, choices b, c, and d are incorrect.

Inventory Counts. Cycle counting is a continuing reconciliation and audit of inventory items with inventory records. It is an alternative to the annual physical inventory exercise and uses the inventory classifications developed through ABC analysis. With cycle counting procedures, stock items are counted, records are verified, inaccuracies are documented, and corrective actions are taken to ensure integrity of the inventory system. Cycle counting focuses on tracing inventory from book to floor and from floor to book and reconciling the differences and making the necessary adjustments. The frequency of cycle counting depends on the type of inventory item. The cycle counting policy might be as follows:

- "A" stock items may be counted once a month.
- "B" stock items may be counted once every three months.
- "C" stock items may be counted once every six months.

The number of stock items of each classification to be counted each working day can be computed as follows:

- Stock quantity for class A divided by the cycle counting policy days gives the number of items to be counted per working day.
- Stock quantity for class B divided by the cycle counting policy days gives the number of items to be counted per working day.
- Stock quantity for class C divided by the cycle counting policy days gives the number of items to be counted per working day.
- Add the number of items to be counted per working day for A, B, and C classes.

(G) Inventory Management Methods

At least six inventory management methods exist for a retailer, including manufacturer-managed inventory, retailer-managed inventory, vendor-managed inventory, consignment-based inventory, just-in-time (JIT) inventory, and buyback inventory. Each method is discussed next.

1. **Manufacturer-managed inventory** is the inventory located in a manufacturer's factory, warehouse, or distribution center. A manufacturer participates in vendor-managed inventory, consignment-based inventory, and JIT inventory practices. The manufacturer forecasts a retailer's sales demand or the forecast is given to the manufacturer, who creates production plans based on the forecasts to supply the retailer. Some manufacturers sell their finished goods directly to wholesalers who, in turn, sell them to retailers. Sometimes manufacturers sell their finished goods directly to retailers, depending on the product. Inventory risks solely rest with manufacturers due to their ownership of inventory. Manufacturers could experience stock-out situations due to little or no safety stock, resulting in back orders.

2. **Retailer-managed inventory** is the inventory located at a retailer's stores, warehouses, distribution centers, and fulfillment centers. When retailers need new inventory, they place the order and receive the inventory from manufacturers, wholesalers, suppliers, or distributors, depending on the product. Retailers could experience stock-out situations if the inventory order-and-delivery cycle is delayed for some reason and if there is little or no safety stock, resulting in back orders. Inventory risks solely rest with retailers due to their ownership of inventory. Retailers take out insurance policies to cover any losses due to fire and theft.

3. **Vendor-managed inventory** is a partnership arrangement between a retailer and major suppliers where suppliers monitor sales and inventory levels of their products in all stores and automatically replenish low inventories to prevent stock-out situations without much involvement of the retailer's procurement staff.

It is an inventory practice where a supplier or vendor manages the inventory at a retailer's store or warehouse. The vendor works in the store to track inventory sales and stock balances and to place replenishment orders based on the retailer's previous or blanket order instructions. Any unused or unsold inventory goes back to the supplier. Advantages of this practice to retailers are that (1) they do not need to order and track the inventory because the vendor takes care of it; (2) stock-out situations are minimized; (3) overall inventory levels in the supply chain are reduced; and (4) the size of the bullwhip effect is decreased. Inventory risks solely rest with vendors due to their ownership of inventory. Chances of stock-out situations are smaller because some safety stock is held. It may or may not result in back orders. Walmart, the Home Depot, and other big-box retailers use vendor-managed inventory.

4. **Consignment-based inventory** is the inventory located at a retailer's store or warehouse and is not owned by the retailer. Instead, it is owned by a manufacturer (first party) and held by a second party, such as a distributor or supplier. Unused or unsold inventory is returned to the second party. The ownership risk solely rests with the manufacturer until the inventory is sold by the retailer. When the retailer sells the inventory, it becomes an accounts receivable item for the manufacturer and an accounts payable item for the retailer. Chances of stock-out situations are smaller because some safety stock is held. It may or may not result in back orders.

5. **JIT inventory** means that retailers receive inventory only when they need it, not before or not after. Hence the name "just-in-time inventory." JIT inventory avoids early inventory purchase costs and reduces storage costs, thus increases the ROI and ROA. Because there is no safety stock because the retailer operates with lower levels of inventory on hand, the retailer could face stock-out situations if the inventory delivery is delayed for some reason. This stock-out situation results in back orders. Therefore, it is good to have a backup supplier to cover emergencies when a single-source supplier cannot deliver. Inventory risks solely rest with the manufacturer or supplier due to their ownership of inventory. Toyota Motor Corporation invented the JIT management philosophy and perfected it. Now Toyota sends new orders to suppliers for automobile parts or components to make new cars only when it receives new car orders from car dealers or customers.

6. **Buyback inventory** is a contractual arrangement between a retailer and a supplier where the supplier buys back all unsold or slow-moving inventory from the retailer. Here, there are no risks to the retailer because the retailer never bought the inventory to begin with; the supplier faces all the risks from unsold merchandise. The supplier could be a manufacturer, vendor, wholesaler, dealer, agent, distributor, or broker. Of course, not all retail products qualify for buyback arrangements; only certain products, such as fashion items, music CDs, movie CDs, and books are eligible for buyback agreements. For example, fashion items could be outdated (i.e., go out of style) where many customers are not interested in buying them anymore and textbooks could be old versions, which are not being used for any course.

In addition, buyback inventory is mostly applicable to brand-new products introduced into the marketplace for retailers to out to determine customer response and feedback. Sometimes these new products could be competing products, such as fruit yogurt, where there are already several competing products in the market either from the same supplier or from different supplier.

In summary:

- Inventory risks solely rest with manufacturers due to their ownership of inventory in manufacturer-managed inventory situations. Manufacturers could experience stock-out situations.

- Inventory risks solely rest with retailers due to their ownership of inventory in retailer-managed inventory situations. Retailers could experience stock-out situations.

- Inventory risks solely rest with vendors due to their ownership of inventory in vendor-managed inventory situations. Chances of stock-out situations are smaller.

- Inventory risks solely rests with manufacturers due to their ownership of inventory until inventory is sold by retailers in consignment-based inventory situations. Chances of stock-out situations are smaller.

- Inventory risks solely rest with manufacturers or suppliers due to their ownership of inventory in the JIT inventory situation. Retailers could face stock-out situations if the inventory delivery is delayed.

- Inventory risks solely rest with suppliers and retailers bear no risks with buyback inventory because retailers never bought this inventory to begin with. Suppliers face all risks from unsold merchandise.

(H) Inventory Costing Methods

Manufacturing companies have four types of inventory: raw materials, work in process, finished goods, and supplies. Inventory is the largest current asset of a manufacturing company balance sheet. In contrast, retail companies have two types of inventory: finished goods purchased from manufacturers and operating supplies represent the largest current asset of a retailer's balance sheet. A major objective of accounting for inventories for manufacturers or retailers is the proper determination of income through the process of matching appropriate costs against revenues at the end of each accounting period. Doing this requires calculating what costs are to be included in the cost of goods sold (cost of sales) item and what costs are to be assigned to the inventory on-hand item at the end of an accounting period.

Five inventory costing methods are used based on differing inventory flow assumptions:

1. **Specific identification method,** where the cost of the specific items sold is included in the cost of goods sold, while the costs of the specific items on hand are included in the inventory. This method is used for valuing jewelry, fur coats, automobiles, and high-priced furniture. *Advantage*: Accuracy where cost flow matches the physical flow of the goods. *Disadvantage*: It requires detailed recordkeeping and elaborate manual and/or computer systems.

2. **Average cost method,** where the items in inventory are priced on the basis of the average cost of all similar goods available during the period. The weighted-average method or moving-average technique is used for calculating the ending inventory and the cost of goods sold. *Advantage*: It is simple to apply and it is objective. *Disadvantage*: The inventory is priced on the basis of average prices paid, which is not realistic.

EXAMPLE: APPLICATION OF AVERAGE COST METHOD

MPS Retailer has purchased the following quantities of men's belts in three batches of merchandise during the month of January.

January 10	20 belts	$10 each
January 15	25 belts	$8 each
January 20	10 belts	$7 each

Assume that a total of 50 belts are sold in January. What are the cost of goods sold for January and valuation of ending inventory in January under the average cost method?

$$\text{Average cost of all purchases} = (20 \times \$10) + (25 \times \$8) + (10 \times \$7) = (\$200 + \$200 + \$70) / 55 = \$8.55$$

$$\text{Cost of goods sold for January} = (50 \times \$8.55) = \$428$$

$$\text{Valuation of ending inventory} = (5 \times \$8.55) = \$43$$

3. **First-in, first-out (FIFO) method,** where goods are used in the order in which they are purchased; the first goods purchased are the first used. FIFO assumes that the oldest products are sold first. The inventory remaining must represent the most recent purchase with current costs. Cost flow matches the physical flow of the goods, similar to the specific identification method. Ending inventory contains the newest inventory with current costs.

Advantage: The ending inventory is close to current cost and provides a reasonable approximation of replacement cost on the balance sheet when price changes have not occurred since the most recent purchases.

Disadvantage: Current costs are not matched against current revenues on the income statement. The oldest costs are charged against the more current revenue, which can lead to distortions in gross profit and net income. This creates transitory or inventory profits (i.e., paper profits).

EXAMPLE: APPLICATION OF FIFO METHOD

MPS Retailer has purchased the following quantities of men's belts in three batches of merchandise during the month of January.

January 10	20 belts	$10 each
January 15	25 belts	$8 each
January 20	10 belts	$7 each

Assume that a total of 50 belts are sold in January. What are the cost of goods sold for January and valuation of ending inventory in January under the FIFO method?

$$\text{Cost of goods sold for January} = (20 \times \$10) + (25 \times \$8) + (5 \times \$7) = (\$200 + \$200 + \$35) = \$435$$

$$\text{Valuation of ending inventory} = (5 \times \$7) = \$35$$

4. **Last-in, first-out (LIFO) method,** where the cost of the last goods purchased are matched against revenue. LIFO assumes that the newest products are sold first. The ending inventory would be priced at the oldest unit cost. LIFO is the most commonly used method. The LIFO method matches the cost of the last goods purchased against revenue, and the ending inventory is costed at the oldest units remaining in the inventory. In other words, in LIFO, the inventory with current costs becomes part of the cost of goods sold for the current period, and this cost of goods sold is matched against revenues and sales for that current period. Ending inventory contains the oldest inventory with oldest costs.

Advantages:

- □ During periods of inflation, current costs are matched against current revenues and inventory profits are thereby reduced. Inventory profits occur when the inventory costs matched against sales are less than the inventory replacement cost. The cost of goods sold is understated and profit is considered overstated.

- □ Lower tax payments. The tax law requires that if a firm uses LIFO for tax purposes, it must also use LIFO for financial accounting and reporting purposes.

- □ Improved cash flow due to lower tax payments, which could be invested for a return unavailable to those using FIFO.

Disadvantages:

- □ Lower profits reported under inflationary times. The company's stock could fall.

- □ Inventory is understated on the balance sheet because the oldest costs remain in ending inventory. This understatement of inventory makes the firm's working capital position appear worse than it really is.

- □ LIFO does not approximate the physical flow of the items.

- □ LIFO falls short of measuring current cost (replacement cost) income, though not as far as FIFO.

- □ Manipulation of income at the end of the year could occur by simply altering a firm's pattern of purchases.

EXAMPLE: APPLICATION OF LIFO METHOD

MPS Retailer has purchased the following quantities of men's belts in three batches of merchandise during the month of January.

January 10	20 belts	$10 each
January 15	25 belts	$8 each
January 20	10 belts	$7 each

Assume that a total of 50 belts are sold in January. What are the cost of goods sold for January and valuation of ending inventory in January under the LIFO method?

Cost of goods sold for January $= (10 \times \$7) + (25 \times \$8) + (15 \times \$10) = (\$70 + \$200 + \$150) = \$420$

Valuation of ending inventory $= (5 \times \$10) = \$50$

5. Next-in, first-out (NIFO) method is not currently acceptable for purposes of inventory valuation. NIFO uses replacement cost. When measuring current cost income, the cost of goods sold does not include the most recently incurred costs; rather, the cost that will be incurred to replace the goods that have been sold.

(I) Other Methods of Costing Inventory

Generally, **historical cost** is used to cost the period-ending inventories and cost of goods sold. In certain circumstances, though, departure from cost is justified. Two other methods of costing inventory include net realizable value and lower of cost or market.

With **net realizable value,** damaged, obsolete, or shopworn goods should never be carried at an amount greater than net realizable value. Net realizable value is equal to the estimated selling price of an item minus all costs to complete and dispose of the item.

The **lower of cost or market method** involves writing down the inventory to reflect loss if its value declines below its historical cost. A departure from the historical cost principle is required when the future utility of the item is not as great as its original cost. When the purchase price of an item falls, it is assumed that its selling price has fallen or will fall. The loss of the future utility of the item should be charged against the revenues of the period in which the loss occurred. "Market" in this context generally means the replacement cost of the item.

However, **market cost is limited by a floor and ceiling cost**. Market cannot exceed net realizable value, which is the estimated selling price minus the cost of completion and disposal (ceiling). Market also cannot be less than net realizable value minus a normal profit margin (floor). Lower of cost or market can be applied to each inventory item, each inventory class, or to total inventory.

(J) Inventory Estimation Methods

A retail organization may estimate its inventory to compare with physical inventories to determine whether shortages exist, to determine the amount of inventory destroyed in a fire or stolen, or to obtain an inventory cost figure to use in monthly or quarterly (interim) financial statements. There are two methods of estimating the cost of ending inventory:

1. **Gross margin method,** which establishes a relationship between gross margin and sales; prior-period gross margin rates are used to estimate the current inventory cost. The gross margin method is based on the assumption that the relationship between gross margin and sales has been fairly stable. Gross margin rates from prior periods are used to calculate estimated gross margin. The estimated gross margin is deducted from sales to determine estimated cost of goods sold. Estimated cost of goods sold is then deducted from cost of goods available for sale to determine estimated inventory cost.

2. **Retail inventory method,** which establishes a relationship between prices and costs. The cost/price ratio is used to estimate the current inventory cost.

The retail inventory method is used by organizations that mark their inventory with selling prices. These prices are converted to cost using a cost/price (cost-to-retail) ratio. The cost/price ratio is simply what proportion cost is to each sales dollar. This ratio is applied to ending inventory stated at retail prices to estimate the cost of ending inventory.

The proper treatment of net additional markups and markdowns in the cost-to-retail ratio calculation is to include the net additional markups in the ratio and to exclude net markdowns. This approach approximates the lower-of-average-cost-or-market valuation.

(vii) Just-in-Time Systems
(A) JIT Strategy

JIT is a production strategy to continuously improve productivity and quality. It is based on the belief that small could be better, not "more" is better. An effective JIT strategy encompasses the entire PLC from the acquisition of raw materials to delivery of the end product to the final customer. *The scope includes topics such as JIT purchasing, processing, inventory, and transportation.* Each topic is discussed next.

JIT is based on these management principles:

- Eliminate waste.

- Produce to demand and one at a time.

- Think long term.

- Develop, motivate, trust, and respect people.

- Achieve continuous improvement.

JIT is made possible when the focus is quality at the source, and the tools used are statistical process control, fail-safe, and problem-solving methods. "Quality at the source" means producing perfect parts every time and all the time. The major benefits of JIT strategy are improved productivity, quality, service, and flexibility; and reduced costs, inventory investment, lead times, lot sizes, and physical space.

(B) JIT Purchasing

JIT purchasing requires a partnership between a supplier and a customer, which is a major departure from traditional purchasing. JIT supplier relations call for long-term partnerships with single-source suppliers that provide certified quality materials while continuously reducing costs. The JIT supplier's manufacturing processes must be under statistical process control, and its capability should be certified by the customer. Statistical process control charts serve as the documentation to ensure that the process stayed in control during the time the parts were made.

JUST-IN-TIME PURCHASING

Under JIT purchasing, competitive bidding may not occur prior to selecting a supplier because sole-sourcing, single-sourcing, or dual-sourcing approaches are utilized. The supplier is selected based on quality, commitment to excellence, and performance, not cost.

A JIT supplier is expected to support the production flow with frequent, small-lot shipments that can be used immediately by the customer. Usually, no inspection is required at the receiving side of the materials.

A JIT supplier will have to become a JIT producer with the idea of pushing costs out of the supply chain, not passing costs down to the next supplier. Since JIT suppliers are considered partners, customers must notify JIT suppliers of plant disruptions, temporary shutdowns, or anticipated engineering changes so that suppliers can make adjustments to production schedules and inventory plans. Doing this requires sharing of information and open communications.

> **TRADITIONAL PURCHASING PRACTICES VERSUS JIT PURCHASING PRACTICES**
>
> - Traditional purchasing practices call for infrequent, large-lot shipments.
>
> - JIT purchasing practices call for frequent, small-lot shipments.
>
> - Traditional purchasing practices call for inspection, since they focus on continuous checking by the customer. These practices are reactive due to their after-the-fact focus.
>
> - JIT purchasing practices call for no inspection, since they focus on continuous improvement by the supplier. JIT is proactive due to its before-the-fact focus.

(C) JIT Production Processing

JIT production processing requires setup reduction, focused factory, group technology, uniform scheduling and mixed model scheduling, and the pull system. The objective here is to produce many varieties of products in small quantities on short notice. Manufacturing flexibility is the hallmark of the JIT production processing strategy.

Setup Reduction. Traditional production systems require large lot sizes due to excessive setup or changeover time. JIT suggests reduced setup time so that lot sizes are reduced or evolve to lot size of 1 with the first piece made right every time. The goal is to accomplish any setup in single minutes (i.e., in less than 10 minutes). Setup reduction requires eliminating equipment downtime and machine adjustments as much as possible combined with good housekeeping in the manufacturing plant.

With reduction in setup time comes many other benefits, such as:

- Increased quality due to closer tie-in between the machine operator and the setup.

- Increased productivity and profitability due to elimination of many non-value-added activities associated with moving, storing, inspecting, and reworking.

- Reduced manufacturing lead time resulting in lower inventories and associated physical space requirements.

- Reduced scrap, lowering unit costs.

Focused Factory. Focused factory is a concept where the plant layout is dedicated to a single product family that maximizes overall productivity and quality while minimizing space and resource requirements. It is intended to physically link all the involved manufacturing operations together to minimize the distance between them, minimize the complexity, maximize task integration, and enhance interaction between workers. This approach eliminates waste and increases communications.

Group Technology. While focused factory is a macro approach, group technology is a micro approach in which equipment is laid out to produce a family of parts, one at a time, by physically linking all possible operations in the process. It can be viewed as self-contained, integrated parts factories within the focused factory.

Group technology uses a cell concept, where the shape of the cell is a U or C. The starting and ending points are near each other to save walking time. The idea is that a single worker performs every operation, in the proper sequence, to make one finished unit at a time. All operations are close together as much as possible with little or no staging space between workstations. A worker in a group technology cell not only performs every operation in the process but also sees how they relate to one another. This improves productivity and quality.

GROUP TECHNOLOGY VERSUS TRADITIONAL TECHNOLOGY

- Group technology is a low-volume, high-mix work center for an entire family of similar parts.
- Traditional technology is a high-volume, single-part work center.

Uniform and Mixed Model Scheduling. Uniform scheduling calls for smaller lot sizes, essentially making every part every day. It is a variable flow management concept instead of trying to coordinate "lumps" of production. It provides level loading for manufacturing operations, building the same product mix every day during a given month. Levels may change from month to month, and hence the term "variable" flow. Under uniform scheduling, the interval between like units is called "cycle time." The shorter the cycle time, the faster the parts will be made.

Mixed model scheduling is employed to produce the same parts every hour. Yet production levels will change from month to month to meet customer demand.

Pull System. Conventional scheduling systems push orders through the production shop, making it difficult to synchronize the diverse activities required to produce the end products. This method results in either excess inventory or insufficient inventory.

Like uniform scheduling, the pull system is based on the variable flow manufacturing principle to make parts repetitively in a low-volume production. The pull system links every process in the plant using simple signaling cards to synchronize production with changing customer demands. It uses a production signal to authorize the machine center to produce parts that have been taken from the storage area next to it. It uses a withdrawal signal as a permission to consume.

PUSH SYSTEM VERSUS PULL SYSTEM

- The push system is based on a fixed-flow manufacturing principle.
- The pull system is based on a variable-flow manufacturing principle.
- The traditional (push) production system has a contingency (i.e., safety stock) mentality.
- The JIT (pull) production system has a no-contingencies (i.e., no safety stock) mentality.

The pull system uses standard lot sizes and employs standard-size containers to enhance visual control on the factory floor. This sets the stage for a "precision" mentality. The pull system ensures that the right parts will be in the right place at the right time with a minimal investment in inventory. The pull system provides better production control for less cost.

(D) JIT Inventory

A misconception about JIT is that it is just a program to reduce inventory. Fortunately, JIT does more than that. JIT purchasing is called "stockless inventory"; the customer has no inventory to stock, as it is used up in the production right after it was received. The major goal is to reduce or eliminate work-in-process inventory so that all raw materials are consumed in the production process.

(E) JIT Transportation

While JIT purchasing is the starting point of a JIT cycle, JIT transportation is the execution part of the JIT cycle. JIT transportation is the physical linkage between the inside and the outside processes. It is a process that starts at a supplier location and ends at a customer location. It requires the analysis of all transport events and elimination of the non-value-added events. The basic value-added events include:

1. Move load to dock at a supplier location.
2. Load carrier.
3. Move load to customer location.
4. Return empty trailer to terminal.
5. Unload by the customer.
6. Move load to assigned customer location.

Similar to the JIT supplier–customer partnership, JIT transportation requires that all three parties—supplier, carrier, and customer—work together more closely than ever before. With frequent, small quantities moved each time, the traffic at both the supplier and the customer plants will increase, creating a demand for rapid load and unload capabilities.

To support JIT flow of production, frequent deliveries will be required. This means receiving parts at a specific customer location on specific days at specific times during those days.

Reusable containers and small delivery windows are new approaches. Reusable containers save money when compared with expendable containers. Small delivery windows means rapid loading and unloading, which can be enhanced by using point-of-use doors, driver self-unloading, and innovative equipment, such as portable ramps and end-loading trailers.

(F) JIT Partnerships

JIT partnerships are needed between suppliers and purchasers of raw materials, parts, and components to remove waste and to drive down costs for mutual benefit. Long-term partnerships are better than short-term ones, so a few suppliers can invest money to improve quality.

(G) JIT Quality

JIT quality is realized as JIT forces down inventory levels, meaning fewer bad units are produced, which, in turn, means fewer units must be reworked, thus improving quality. As JIT shrinks queues and lead times, it creates an early warning system for quality problems and production errors. As JIT quality is increased, there is less need for safety stock (inventory buffers) to protect against unreliable quality levels and unpredictable customer demand levels.

(H) JIT Scheduling

JIT scheduling improves the ability to meet customer order due dates, reduces inventory with smaller lot sizes, and reduces work in process. Two techniques include level schedules and kanban. A **level schedule** means each day's production quantity meets the demand for that day, using frequent small batches. A **kanban** system moves parts through production via a "pull" from a signal. Kanban uses a card system giving authorization for the next container of material to be produced.

(I) JIT Layout

An efficient JIT layout reduces waste in the form of minimizing the movement of materials on a factory floor or paper in an office because these movements do not add value. The benefits of a JIT facility include distance reduction, increased operational flexibility, employees working closer to each other, and reduced space and inventory.

(J) JIT and Lean Operations

This subsection presents interactions between lean operations, JIT, TPS, MRP, and EOQ.

Lean operations mean identifying customer value by analyzing all the activities required to produce a product and then optimizing the entire process to increase value from the customers' perspective. The highlights of lean operations include understanding what the customer wants and ensuring that customer input and feedback are obtained to increase value to that customer. Lean operations adopt a philosophy of minimizing waste by striving for perfection through continuous learning, creativity, and teamwork, which can be equally applied to manufacturing and service industries.

Both JIT and the Toyota production system (TPS) have an internal focus on jobs, employees, work practices, materials, and training. Lean operations have an external focus on the customer. Lean operations need both JIT and TPS techniques and more.

Materials requirements planning (MRP) is suitable for managing raw materials, components, and subassemblies, which have dependent demands that may be calculated from the forecasts and scheduled production of finished goods. In other words, the order for component inventory is placed based on the demand and production needs of other items that use these components.

NORMAL INVENTORY DEDUCTION METHOD VERSUS BACKFLUSH INVENTORY DEDUCTION METHOD

- In a normal inventory deduction method, the amount of component parts used in an assembly operation is deducted from its inventory records based on a planned or scheduled production count of end products. MRP system uses this method by exploding the bill of materials list for planning purposes.

- In a backflush inventory deduction method, the amount of component parts used in an assembly operation is deducted from its inventory records based on an actual count of end assemblies produced. This method works backward from end products to raw materials or component parts and uses the bill of materials list for explosion into individual items.

Benefits of MRP include reduced investment in inventory, improved workflow, reduced shortage of raw materials and components, and reliable delivery schedules.

DETERMINISTIC INVENTORY VERSUS PROBABILITY INVENTORY

- Deterministic inventory models assume that the rate of demand for the item is constant (e.g., EOQ).

- Probabilistic inventory models assume that the rate of demand for the item fluctuates and can be described only in terms of probabilities.

In addition to considering dependent demand in the determination of net requirements for components, an MRP system also determines when the net requirements are needed by using the time-phasing concept. This concept works by starting with the time that the finished product must be completed and working backward to determine when an order for each component must be placed based on lead times.

The approach to determining net requirements whenever a dependent demand situation exists is:

Net component requirement = Gross component requirement − Scheduled receipts
− Number of components in inventory

Where Gross component requirement = Quantity of component needed to support production at the next higher level of assembly

---

EOQ VERSUS MRP

- The EOQ model focuses on finished goods inventories, which have an independent demand from customers or from forecasts.

- The demand for raw materials and components in the MRP model is directly dependent on the demand for the finished goods in the inventory system.

(viii) Production Scheduling and Control Systems

This section discusses three types of production scheduling and control systems: JIT production systems, traditional production systems, and kanban production and inventory systems.

(A) Just-in-Time Production Systems

JIT represents a management philosophy whose objective is to eliminate all sources of waste, including unnecessary inventory. The basic principle of JIT is to produce the right products in the right quantity at the right time in the right place. JIT's primary goal is to minimize production inventory levels while providing needed raw materials, parts, and components just before they are used. To facilitate this goal, JIT purchasing places the orders such that delivery immediately precedes usage.

With JIT, products are manufactured or assembled only when they are needed. This means that the number of parts produced or purchased at any one time should be just enough to produce one unit of the finished product. Therefore, inventories are better managed to the extent that they are not needed or at least are minimized.

JIT AND RISK

JIT requires fundamental changes in traditional production systems. These changes encompass production layout, material flows, setup times, employee attitudes, and work culture. A risk of JIT is the critical dependency on a few vendors.

JIT requires a commitment to continuously improve activities and the quality of products while eliminating all non-value-added activities and work-in-process inventory. Lead times, waiting time for materials or other delays, and inspection are grouped as non-value-added activities.

Production flow in a JIT system is demand-pulled through the plant by the downstream workstations ordering subassemblies and parts from upstream workstations. These pull orders are controlled by a kanban system, which is a system of cards and empty bins. Kanban is explained later in the section.

JIT can be viewed as an intermediate step toward more advanced manufacturing technologies, such as computer-integrated manufacturing. Producing one unit of a finished product at a time allows the implementation of strict quality control standards. The worker under JIT is fully responsible for ensuring that the subassemblies that are received or produced are error free. If errors are detected, production stops and errors are immediately corrected. *Therefore, the JIT system relies on employee involvement in production operations, quality control, and productivity improvements.*

KEY CONCEPTS TO REMEMBER: Benefits of JIT

- Increased inventory turnover measured as sales divided by inventory. Increased inventory turnover is an indication of increased productivity.
- Increased production rates due to little or no waiting time and increased productivity.
- Lower storage space due to lower inventory levels required.
- Lower spoilage costs due to high-quality products.
- Lower material handling costs since the materials are delivered directly to the assembly floor.
- Reduced production lead times due to shorter setup times and better coordination with suppliers.
- Reduced indirect labor since most or all non-value-added activities are removed.
- Reduced warranty claim costs due to better-quality products.

The total quality control system developed by W. Edwards Deming is an integral part of the JIT philosophy. Frederick Taylor's principles of scientific management influenced the development of the JIT system. Reduction of waste, zero inventories, quality circles, and the use of computer robotics are seen as management tools to increase efficiency and output—a theme familiar to scientific management and JIT production systems.

Raw material and WIP inventories are reduced significantly, thereby decreasing carrying costs and floor space requirements. JIT production systems are most appropriate in repetitive assembly type manufacturing, such as automobiles or appliances.

The JIT system requires the setting of daily production targets, so that feedback on worker performance is timely. Workers are given more responsibility for building perfect quality into the product and producing the desired quantity. Detailed variance reports are no longer needed in JIT systems because defects become fewer and fewer.

JIT promotes work simplification procedures and relies on few suppliers to deliver raw materials and parts on time. Competitive bids are not common. Close ties tend to develop between two parties (customers and suppliers) as they work closely together to improve quality and to implement the JIT philosophy. JIT requires mutual trust between vendor and customer. The customer places greater reliance on the vendor to perform and deliver as expected.

(B) Traditional Production Systems

Traditional production systems practice a "push" production system concept where each worker produces a subassembly at his or her own pace and passes the output to the next worker until the final product is completed. A WIP inventory is commonly maintained at each workstation. Plant workers are controlled by work standards and motivated by a piece-rate incentive system. This approach leads to producing quantity rather than quality products. Workers have little or no incentive to correct errors or problems.

Workers are encouraged to make good-quality products, not punished for the production of poor-quality work. Under a traditional production system, quality control is the responsibility of a quality control inspector, not the production worker. This quality control inspection is not done quickly enough to trace production problems. Inspection is not done continuously; it is often done for the finished goods only.

Work standards or standards of performance are established by using either imposition or participation techniques, where the latter approach is more motivating for the worker than is the former. A performance report is issued periodically. A variance investigation occurs when significant discrepancies exist between the standard and the actual output. Investigation could reveal that either the worker is inefficient or the standard is not set properly. Exhibit 1.62 shows a comparison between traditional production systems and JIT production systems.

EXHIBIT 1.62 Characteristics of Traditional Production Systems and JIT Production Systems

Characteristics of Traditional Production Systems	Characteristics of JIT Production Systems
Quality is seen as a hit-or-miss event, and there is no explicit commitment to continuous improvement and production of quality products.	Quality is a planned event, and there is an explicit commitment to continuous improvement and production of quality products.
The system is evolutionary.	The system is revolutionary since long-held beliefs are discarded.
More WIP is maintained.	Little or no WIP is maintained.
There is no reliance on employee involvement and participation in decision making.	Systems rely on high employee involvement and participation in decision making.
The quality control inspector is responsible for the quality of the product.	The production worker is responsible for ensuring the quality of the product.
The push system begins with the first worker on the assembly line dictating the flow of work.	The pull system begins with the last worker on the assembly line dictating the flow of work.
Workers are compensated based on a piece-rate incentive system.	Workers are compensated based on a group incentive system.
Inventory investment is increased.	Inventory investment is decreased.
Need for detailed variance reports is great due to many defects. Reports are more useful as problem detectors.	There is little or no need for detailed variance reports due to fewer defects. Reports are less useful as problem detectors.
Long production runs and long setup times are typical.	Short production runs and short setup times are common.

(C) Kanban Production and Inventory Systems

Working under a pull system, production procedures and work instructions are communicated by a system of signals sent among workers through the use of a series of cards called "kanbans." The JIT production system and kanban inventory system work together. In kanban, the last workstation is informed of the day's production needs; all other workstations respond to the kanban cards and containers (i.e., all other workstations are pulled in).

KEY CONCEPTS TO REMEMBER: Benefits of the Kanban Inventory System

- Paperwork-free system
- Product made to order
- Diminished need to take physical inventory for income determination purposes
- Lower finished goods inventory amounts
- Simple procedures for taking physical inventory, when needed
- Lower WIP inventory amounts
- Zero or fewer defective products

After the kanban system informs the final assembly production needs, each workstation then "orders" products or parts from the preceding workstation. This chain moves back to the point of purchasing raw materials. One condition is that a workstation cannot produce unless an order has been placed.

Two kinds of kanban cards are used for posting and tracking inventory activity and to communicate among workers at the workstation: move cards and production cards (see Exhibit 1.63).

EXHIBIT 1.63 Kanban Card Types

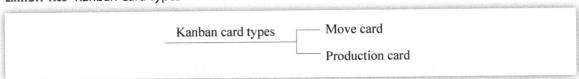

The **move card** allows the worker to take one standard container of a specific part from one work center to another. The **production card** tells another production work center to produce the number of parts that will fit a standardized container. There is only one card with each container at any point in time.

The number of Kanban containers needed to operate in a JIT production environment is calculated as follows:

Number of Kandan containers needed = (Demand during production lead time in units plus the required safety stock in units)/container size in units.

MRP is a widely used computerized system that operates under the push principle, while kanban represents the pull system. The newer version of MRP is MRP II, which takes the bill of materials for the products to be produced and calculates all subassembly and raw materials needed by time and quantity. Then the workstations are informed as to the number of units to be produced. This method is equated to the push system where the work is pushed through the plant.

TRADITIONAL PRODUCTION SYSTEMS VERSUS MRP VERSUS JIT VERSUS KANBAN SYSTEMS

- A traditional manufacturing system practices a push production system.
- MRP systems operate under the push production system.
- A JIT manufacturing system practices a pull production system.
- A kanban manufacturing system practices a pull production system since it responds to the JIT production plan.

(b) Service Operations

In this section, service strategy is defined and five service management principles are explained.

(i) Service Strategy

Service strategy is to provide an excellent service to current customers, acquire new customers, and prevent customer defection of existing customers.

(ii) Service Management Principles

Service strategy focuses on customers and on satisfying their needs, which will result in a loyal customer base. Winning customers in the marketplace means competing on several dimensions. Customers base their purchase decisions on many variables, including price, convenience, reputation, and safety. The importance of a particular variable to a firm's success depends on the competitive marketplace and the preferences of individual customers. There can be at least five principles of service management, including:

> **Principle 1: Streamline internal service processes to improve their efficiency and effectiveness**
>
> This principle requires analyzing value-added activities and non-value-added activities within current processes and eliminating most or all non-value-added activities. It also requires adding new value-added activities to increase overall value. Implement total quality management principles, quality tools, poka-yoke (a Japanese term for mistake-proofing), fishbone diagrams, root cause analysis, and Kaizen (continuous improvement)

> **Principle 2: Create a true and sustainable value for customers and clients**
>
> The value creation process must not be a one-time and temporary exercise; instead, it must be a continuous and permanent process. Potential or existing customers or clients must be able to notice the value and suggest ways to improve the value process so all parties can benefit. By involving customers in the product/service design, development, testing, and implementation work can help in value creation.

Principle 3: Deliver the promised services on time and within budget

This principle requires stopping all the delays and obstacles in delivering services to customers or clients. It requires innovative ideas and approaches to see how fast the service can be delivered to the promised customer or client. Delivery cost is not the primary concern here; instead, customer satisfaction should be. Errors in the delivery cycle should be eliminated or reduced to a minimum. Customer surveys and follow-up are needed by implementing poka-yoke technique and other remedial actions.

Principle 4: Correct problems in the delivered services to increase customer satisfaction

Customers or clients do not like a rework of their original product because the company promised to deliver the original product with built-in quality. Rework cost is not the primary concern here; instead, customer satisfaction until the problem is corrected should be.

Principle 5: Convert one-time customers into repeat and loyal customers

It has been said that it is easier and cheaper to keep an existing customer than to find a new one. Retaining customers or clients is not an easy task for any service firm as it requires constant monitoring of what went wrong or what went right during the entire-value creation cycle and fixing the wrong things in a timely manner so customers notice it explicitly and become repeat and loyal customers.

Service organizations should treat repeat and loyal customers by paying special attention to them in the form of incentives, discounts, and rewards. It is challenging to manage customers' expectations, perceptions, and experiences between a service provider and a service receiver. A gap can exist between expected service quality performance and perceived service quality performance.

(c) Marketing and Sales Function

Marketing and sales functions go together as they are complementary and supportive of each other. If marketing is considered a front-end operation (planning), then, sales is considered as the back-end operation (implementation) to complete the marketing and sales cycle. Topics discussed include marketing and sales strategy, marketing channels management, brand management, service marketing, marketing administration, and types of marketing programs.

(i) Marketing and Sales Strategy

World-class marketing and sales management have a clear sales and marketing strategy. They strive to satisfy customers with the products and services that customers need and want, meet or beat the competition, and increase revenues, cash flows, and profits for the company. They also integrate marketing and sales functions for maximum synergy, efficiency, and effectiveness.

The combined marketing and sales strategy involves deploying major financial and human capital resources to develop a superior, distinctive, and difficult-to-imitate competitive advantage that the company can claim as its own based on superior product design and technology, superior distribution system, superior cost structure, and superior brand reputation. This combined strategy should contain important elements such as target markets, product positioning, product/service features and functions, flexible pricing, distribution channels, promotion programs (i.e., marketing mix), and above all customer service.

In other words, this combined strategy focuses on markets, products, services, customers, and competitors. It is a functional strategy, similar to a financial or manufacturing strategy. Marketing management and senior management of a company must ask the following fundamental questions and must seek and receive honest answers for each question.

- What business are we in?

- Is our business model realistic?

- What are we selling? Is it a product, service, or both?

- What is our product or service profiles, including their good or bad reputation?

- What are our strengths and weaknesses from our viewpoint and from the viewpoint of our customers, competitors, and the government? What are the gaps between these viewpoints?

- Who are our customers, including their profiles, preferences, strengths, and weaknesses?

- Who are our major and minor competitors, including their strengths and weaknesses?

- What is our competition doing? Are we better or worse than our major competitors?

- Which marketing mix strategies are most effective to us?

- How and when we will measure and make a satisfactory return on sales, return on investment, return on assets, and return on equity?

Because marketing function and sales function are the two sides of a coin with one mission and one vision, they go hand in hand and should work toward accomplishing their company's goal first then accomplishing their individual functional goals. Company goals precede functional goals, meaning the company is first and the function is next, which is an example of the goal congruence concept.

Management experts say that marketing managers and executives should be leaders in developing marketing strategy while sales managers and executives are followers in executing and implementing that strategy. Sometimes marketing and sales functions can be in conflict with each other due to miscommunications, cross-communications, misunderstandings, turf-building practices, organizational politics, and differences in management's operating styles and philosophies, all leading to marketing blunders, missteps, and lies, which should be avoided at all costs and at all times.

Linkages between Sales and Marketing. Although the heads of the marketing and sales functions work for the same department and report to the same chief marketing officer, they often have conflicting and diverse roles and responsibilities due to the nature of their jobs. The chief marketing officer and the chief executive officer should do the following to fulfill the defined roles and responsibilities of marketing and sales management to provide a stronger linkage between these two functions:

- Pay close attention to the voice of the customer (i.e., shopper-customer). Sales and marketing managers should carefully listen to and deeply understand external customers' needs, wants, and expectations and provide products and services that truly meet those needs, wants, and expectations. Examples of other external customers include manufacturers (producers), suppliers, vendors, investors, lenders, regulators, and union members. The same thing applies to understanding the needs of internal customers (i.e., managers and nonmanagers in departments or functions within a retail organization). The voice of the shopper-customer can be listened through or heard from customers' feedback through surveys, focus groups, and emails; comments, likes, and reviews posted to social media platforms; and complaints and compliments received during a consumer's purchase decision-making process (i.e., during pre-purchase, purchase, and post-purchase activities).

- Understand that marketing management finds the sales leads and that the sales management converts those leads into real sales and supports both existing and new customers. Automate the lead management process as much as possible to increase efficiency and effectiveness.

- Understand that sales leads are the "touch points" between marketing and sales functions.

- Understand that sales management focuses on short-term results while marketing management focuses on long-term results. Both functions must coexist in harmony and consistency.

- Salespeople should increase face-to-face time with their customers and spend not so much time on phone calls, emails, voice mails, efaxes, and websites. The key is to increase the number of touch points between salespeople and customers as they establish a solid business relationship.

- Salespeople should increase the selling time and decrease the nonselling time with customers because the former is a value-added activity whereas the latter is a non-value-added activity.

- Sales management should remove customer "pain points" and "hassle points" experienced when dealing with a company and focus on increasing both up-selling and cross-selling activities with customers.

- Building a one-to-one business relationship with the customer is an example of a guided selling process.

- Marketing should develop product usage scenarios, and sales staff should receive training on product usage.

- Marketing and sales must work together to develop sales campaigns for pushing a product.

- Marketing should develop "proof points" to convince potential customers and these should be given to sales staff. These proof points include customer success stories, press releases, customer testimonials, product demonstrations, and focused presentations.

- Implement sales force automation technologies to increase the overall effectiveness of salespeople by reducing the sales cycle time, by completing all sales calls on time, and by speeding the resolution of customer inquiries. This requires that customer data be available to the entire sales staff in real time.

- In summary, the marketing function feeds the sales function with new sales leads and prospects. The sales function, in turn, feeds the marketing function with new business opportunities. These business relationships establish a solid linkage, and this cycle continues between the marketing function and the sales function.

Marketing $\longrightarrow$ Sales $\longrightarrow$ Marketing $\longrightarrow$ Sales

(ii) Marketing Channels Management

It takes a considerable amount of time, money, and effort to set up marketing channels of sales and distribution. Because of this heavy commitment of resources, once decisions are made about channels of sales and distribution, they are not easy to retract. Yet these decisions are very critical to the success of the firm. Decisions based on inaccurate or incomplete information can be very costly. Channels of sales and distribution for consumer and industrial goods provide the user with time, place, and possession value (utility). *Thus, an efficient channel is one that delivers the product when and where it is wanted at a minimum total cost. Marketing intermediaries exist to bring about product exchanges between buyers and sellers in a reasonably efficient manner.*

Marketing Intermediaries. The primary role of intermediaries is to bring supply and demand together in an efficient and orderly manner. Since it would be very difficult for each consumer to deal with each manufacturer directly for products, considering product complexity and the distance between sellers and buyers, the need for intermediaries becomes apparent. Marketing intermediaries can perform product exchange functions more cheaply and more efficiently than manufacturers can. Also, competition among intermediaries will result in lower costs to consumers. There are many types of marketing intermediaries, many of which are specialized by function and industry. Major types of marketing intermediaries include middlemen, merchant middlemen, agents, wholesalers, retailers, brokers, sales agents, distributors, jobbers, and facilitating agents.

Channels of Distribution. A channel of distribution is the integration of intermediaries through which a seller markets products to users or consumers. Agents, wholesalers, and retailers are called intermediaries or middlemen. Channels with one or more intermediaries are referred to indirect channels.

Degree of Control Desired. The degree of control desired by the seller is proportional to the directness of the channel. When the market is concentrated in a limited geographic area, with many small buyers, the seller selling directly can influence the buyer significantly with his or her own policies and procedures. Seller control is somewhat diluted when indirect channels are used and control is more indirect rather than direct. Indirect control can be exercised through sharing promotional expenditures, providing sales training, and sharing the computer-based application system for quick response.

Total Distribution Cost. A total cost concept is suggested for the channels of distribution to avoid suboptimization. The concept states that a channel of distribution should be viewed as a total system composed of interdependent subsystems, with the objective to optimize total system performance. Cost minimization is a part of total system performance. Major distribution cost factors to be minimized include these:

- Order processing and transportation costs
- Cost of lost business (an opportunity cost due to inability to meet customer demand)
- Inventory carrying cost including storage space charges, cost of capital invested, taxes, insurance, obsolescence, and deterioration
- Packaging and materials handling costs

Other factors that must be considered include level of customer service desired, sales volume, profit levels, and the marketing mix desired.

Channel Flexibility. Channel flexibility involves forecasting and/or adapting the channels of distribution in relation to changing buyer habits and population moves, such as inner cities to suburbs or north to south relocation. Changing from individual stores to shopping centers and malls is also a consideration. Under changing conditions, establishing a new channel of distribution is not that easy and takes time, money, and effort.

Selecting Intermediaries. The two basic methods of selecting intermediaries (middlemen) are pushing and pulling. Pushing a product through the channel means using normal promotional effort—personal skills and advertising—to help sell the whole marketing mix to possible channel members. This is a common approach with the producer working through a team to get the product to the user. By contrast, pulling means getting consumers to ask intermediaries for the product. This involves distributing samples and coupons to final consumers. If the promotion works, the intermediaries are forced to carry the product to satisfy customer needs.

PUSH VERSUS PULL

- Pushing a product through the channel means using normal promotional effort—personal skills and advertising.
- Pulling a product means getting consumers to ask intermediaries for the product.

(A) Managing Channels of Distribution

From a management point of view, entire channels of distribution should be treated as a social system since each party plays a defined role and each has certain expectations of the other. The interaction with each other is very critical for all parties involved, and the behavioral implications of channel parties are many.

The channels of distribution do not manage themselves. Someone needs to manage or exert primary leadership in each channel. Although there are exceptions, channels controlled by the manufacturer seems to dominate. Even though the question of managing channels of distribution is obvious, the answer is not, as indicated by the following arguments:

- Some marketers believe the brand manufacturer or owner should be the channel leader. This is because the owner has the most to lose if the system fails, has the most technical expertise, and has greater resources than others.

- Some marketers believe the retailer should be the channel captain or leader, since the retailer is the closest link to the consumer and therefore can better judge consumer needs and wants.

- Some marketers argue that wholesalers should seek to gain channel control.

- Some marketers suggest that the locus of control should be at the level where competition is greatest.

- Some marketers believe that the most powerful member, whether it is a manufacturer, wholesaler, or retailer, should assume channel leadership.

(B) Retail Channels

Retail Channels Defined. A retail channel is a place, an avenue, or a mechanism where customers can research and purchase merchandise of their choice. Varieties of channels are available to customers, including physical stores (in-store and offline), pure-play online stores (online only), a retailer's online stores (web stores), social media platforms (social sites), cloud networks, mobile commerce (mobile devices), online catalog stores, call centers (product advisors and technical support), electronic mail, text (SMS/MMS), wearable commerce, shop-from-home commerce, make-at-home commerce, electronic commerce (business to business and business to customer), kiosks, and smart vending machines.

Psychologists have determined that most customers prefer to touch and feel products in a store before making the final purchase decision. Despite the various channel choices available, most customers prefer physical store experience, followed by online shopping experience, and followed by mobile channel experience. Note that these channel choices may change due to a retailer's technology implementation levels, consumer disposable income levels, consumer buying preferences, customers' computer savviness, population changes (demographics), and above all changing consumer mind-sets.

Strategic Move Defined. Moving from a single channel to an omnichannel presents many benefits to retailers and customers alike. Major benefits include increased sales revenues to retailers and pleasant shopping experience to customers. Unfortunately, not all retailers have reached the omnichannel (an integrated channel) stage, because doing so requires heavy investment and management foresight. A retailer using a single channel today is similar to a customer buying a black-and-white TV set today; both have no future.

Channel Evolution. Channel evolution started with a single channel (physical store), moved to multiple channels (physical store and online store) and cross-channels (moving from an online store to a manufacturer's or supplier's website), and finally stayed with omnichannel. It has been reported that most customers visit all channels (i.e., channel hopping) during a holiday season to find the right product at the right price.

Single Channel ⟶ Multiple Channels ⟶ Cross-Channels ⟶ Omnichannel

Single channel means using only one channel, whether offline or online, to make a purchase. This is a channel with limited capabilities due to limited products and prices. Retailers operating with a single channel cannot survive in the long term due to the limited scope and options of the channel.

> **Example:** A customer visits a nearby retailer's physical store to inquire about a specific product's availability and price. The customer learned that the product is available and the price is reasonable. Later or at the same time, the customer buys the product from the same retailer. This example describes a single-channel scenario because there is only one place—the physical store—to purchase.

Multiple channels mean using more than one channel of the same retailer or channels of other retailers to make a purchase.

> **Example:** A customer first visits a nearby retailer's physical store to inquire about a specific product's availability and its price. This is a single channel of a retailer's physical store. Later the customer checks the same retailer's website for the same product and its price. This is a single channel of the same retailer's online store. Later, the customer visits the websites of two other retailers and call centers to check and compare the same product and its prices. This is an example of multiple channels because the customer visited more than one siloed channel operating separately, such as physical store, websites, and call centers.

Cross-channels mean using any combination of channels, such as a retailer's physical store, pure-play online store (online only), retailer's online store, call center, catalog store, mobile site, manufacturer's website, and supplier's website, to make a purchase. What matters is the type, number, and variety of channels visited to make the final purchase. Visiting the same channel more than one time counts as only one channel.

> **Example:** A customer first visits a nearby retailer's physical store him to look at a product, places an order on his mobile device, schedules a delivery date to his home on his mobile

device, and checks the order status on the retailer's website. This example describes a cross-channel scenario.

Omnichannel means using only one channel that will reach several channels and integrates them into one seamless channel. This method provides a seamless brand experience delivered across all points of brand websites, interactions, and relationships. This is the best and ideal channel because it eliminates problems and delays in visiting several stores and websites. In other words, only one uniform resource locator (URL) is used in one shopping session for all websites instead of several URLs for several websites, knowing that one URL is required for to visit one website.

In summary, all individual retail channel strategies are converging into omnichannel strategies to provide a seamless and hassle-free shopping experience to customers during their product ordering, payment, and shipping (delivery) stages.

> **Example:** Amazon's use of a one-click buy button strategy is an example of implementing an omnichannel strategy (meaning it uses one URL, instead of several URLs). It means customers need not enter their basic information for each order and need not visit several websites (URLs) to place an order, make a payment, change or cancel an order, or receive email order notifications and confirmations. In a one-click strategy, all these actions or steps are done in the background and in one seamless Amazon's website.

(iii) Brand Management

In this section, topics such as the brand image, brand types, brand assets, and brand equity are discussed.

(A) Brand Image

Product and service brands are strategic and economic assets of a company, similar to physical assets, such as buildings and equipment. These strategic and economic assets generate sales revenues when they are sold to customers. Because of their revenue-generating ability, a company's brand images should be developed, protected, and sustained.

Business organizations must build a strong brand image by:

- Crafting the brand identity in the form of describing the customer value proposition and understanding the views of a customer about a company.
- Analyzing all the touch points that a customer comes in contact with in regard to the company's products, services, and functions. The touch points, whether direct or indirect, revolve around topics, issues, products, and services.
- Removing all unnecessary hand-offs and delays at the touch points.
- Obtaining continuous feedback from customers so the brand continues to evolve and to anticipate customer needs.
- Ensuring that a brand's image is properly communicated to social media platforms and protecting its image when inappropriate negative comments are posted on the social media.

(B) Brand Types

There are two types of brands: national brands and private brands. Manufacturing companies create **national brands,** which are sold in almost every retail store. Some retailers and dealers create their own **private brands,** which are known as local, store, own, dealer, and generic brands (private labels). Retailers become manufacturers when they create their own private brands. Private brands offer cost savings to customers over national brands when the product's features and quality levels are the same between the two brands. Retail sales worldwide can be approximated to 80/20 rule (Pareto principle) meaning that 80% of total retail sales come from national brands and 20% of total sales come from private brands.

Examples of national brands: Tide detergent, Dove soaps and shampoos, Palmolive dishwashing liquid, Charmin toilet tissues and paper towels, Levi's jeans, and Colgate/Crest toothbrushes and toothpastes.

Examples of private brands: up&up brand for Target Company, Great Value brand for Wal-Mart, HDX brand for the Home Depot, Geek Squad computer services for Best Buy, Kirkland Signature brand for Costco wholesaler, and 365 brand for Whole Foods Market.

Other Brands. Terry O'Reilly, the host of *Under the Influence* radio program broadcast on National Public Radio, presents the following list of other types of brands.

Enviable brands include Water Displacement-40 (WD-40) spray, Heinz Ketchup, Kraft's Macaroni & Cheese dinner, Canada Dry Ginger Ale, Car-Freshners, Converse Sneakers, and Mr. Potato Head.

21st-century brands include iRobot Roomba vacuum cleaners, smartphones, digital tablets, app stores, e-readers (Kindle), Facebook, YouTube, Twitter, Instagram, Netflix, e-cigarettes, wearables (GoogleGlass and smartwatches), the IoT, and reality TV shows.

Billion-dollar brands include Kraft's Oreo cookies and various Procter & Gamble products, such as Tide detergent, Gillette Fusion blades, Pampers, Crest toothpaste, Charmin, Head & Shoulder shampoo. Billion-dollar fashion brands include Chanel, Ralph Lauren, Louis Vuitton, and Georgio Armani.

The world's oldest brands include Faber pencil and eraser, Stella Artois beer, Molson beer, the Hudson's Bay Company (a retailer in Canada), A & W Root beer, Tabasco sauce, and Chevrolet Suburban automobile.

Limited edition or special-edition products include Chevrolet Camaro Special Hot Wheels Edition, Dolce & Gabbana's Animalier Bronzer cosmetics, Warhol's Campbell soup cans with Warhol-inspired artwork, vodka-based liquor called Oddka, and Jack Daniel's Sinatra Select whiskey.

Strange brands are those that are unexpected: Pizza Hut Cologne, Burger King Flame Body spray, Marine Corps Devil Dog Cologne, Marine Corps Hot Sauce, Zippo's Fragrance for Him and Her, Coty's Vespa Fragrance for Him and Her, and Play-Doh Cologne.

Zombie brands are brands that were once popular, disappeared, and then came back later. These brands include Brim Coffee, Sony Walkman, Aqua Velva Aftershave, Brylcreem Original Men's Hair Cream, Salon Selectives Shampoo, and Eastern Airlines.

Mocking brands are brands that imitate or copy competing brands, resulting in actions, reactions, counteractions, reprisals, and retaliations between the parties involved. Examples of mocking brand examples include Miller High Life beer mocking Anheuser Busch during Super Bowl TV commercials; Jaguar car mocking Mercedes cars, then Mercedes mocking Jaguars; Samsung phone and tablet mocking the Apple phone and tablet, then Apple mocking Samsung right back; and Apple mocking Microsoft and Microsoft eventually retaliating.

(C) Brand Assets and Brand Equity

The term "assets" and "equity" are accounting terms used in financial statements, such as a retailer's balance sheet where "assets" mean cash and inventory and "equity" mean owner's investment in a company. In contrast, the terms "brand assets" and "brand equity" are marketing terms used by marketing departments to signal their internal value to retailers; these values are not shown on the retailer's financial statements. Inventory or merchandise assets were purchased, acquired, and paid for through a normal course of business transactions with external parties. Brand assets were developed and improved internally. Accounting standards require that assets must be acquired with external proof of buying and selling between two or more parties in an objective manner. Brand assets do not meet this standard of objectivity, as they are acquired subjectively and developed internally.

Brand loyalty increases brand assets, meaning loyal customers can create and sustain a brand's assets due to their continued commitment and loyalty through buying that branded product repeatedly. Branded assets are very valuable to the companies that own them because they generate sustainable revenues and profits during their product lives. Brand equity is built around and through the loyal customers. Examples of valuable branded assets include the Tide detergent brand for the P&G and the 365 brand for Whole Foods.

Brand Assets. Brand assets include strategic, operational, and technical assets. Some brands are in a strong position in one or all three types of assets. Some brands may have higher tangible assets (using modern, advanced, and efficient equipment, machinery, buildings, manufacturing plants, retail stores, warehouses, and distribution centers); some brands may have higher intangible assets (e.g., IP assets such as copyrights, product trademarks, service trademarks, and patents); and other brands may a combination of tangible and intangible assts. A brand's good name, strong reputation, and goodwill are part of its intangible assets.

Brand assets include brand-building elements and brand-defensive elements. When combined, these elements provide real value to targeted customers. Brand assets grow as brand awareness grows; assets include a brand's name and image with its visibility, associations, and loyalty factors. A SWOT analysis should be performed along with fit-gap analysis to get a big-picture perspective about a brand.

Brand Equity. Brand equity drives sales in many ways through brand awareness, brand image, brand responses, and brand relationships. Brand equity is closely related to the number of customers who are devoted to a brand. Some brands have a higher degree of awareness, acceptability, and preference than others. Brand awareness drives a brand's equity, which, in turn, consists of brand loyalty and brand associations. A set of assets (i.e., strengths) and liabilities (i.e., weaknesses) is linked to a brand where the goal is to increase the former and decrease the latter. In addition to brand names, logos and slogans lead to building a brand's equity. Although brand equity is not shown in a company's financial statements, similar to human equity, it is reflected in the acquisition price of a company as a premium the brand commands in the market (represented as goodwill).

(iv) Service Marketing

The global economy, especially the U.S. economy, is becoming more service-oriented than before. Some manufacturing organizations are strictly product-oriented whereas some service organizations are purely service-oriented. Yet there are some manufacturing and service organizations that are both product- and service-oriented. The major issue in service marketing is controlling service employees' costs (i.e., wages and salaries, employee benefits, and employee travel-related costs). The challenging goal is to reduce overall service costs while improving service quality and responding to customers.

In view of the size and importance of service economy, considerable innovation and ingenuity are needed to make high-quality services available at convenient locations for consumers. The actual services offered by service providers often fall behind the opportunities available due to these obstacles: a limited view of marketing, a lack of competition, a lack of creative management, a concept of "no obsolescence," and a lack of innovation in the distribution of services.

A service gap can exist when a customer's expected service is different from the actual service.

> Service Gap = Expected Service − Actual Service

The goal of the service marketing management is to remove or minimize service gaps in the service chain as much and as soon as possible and to make customers happy. In addition, the "moments of failure" should be minimized to make customers satisfied or delighted.

(v) Marketing Administration

The scope of marketing administration includes several topics, such as sales contract management, market research, advertising and promotion, data mining, and marketing budgets.

(A) Sales Contract Management

A **contract** is a formal and legal document between two parties (buyer and seller), and it is binding on both parties in a court of law. Marketing and sales management handle various sales contracts with their customers involving huge amounts of money. Sales contracts increase revenues, which affects both the top line (i.e., revenues) and the bottom line of the income statement (i.e., profits). The Uniform Commercial Code applies to sales contracts because it deals with the sale of goods, and the sales staff sells goods to customers.

Both sales and supply contracts require a systematic approach to reduce the overall contract cycle time, which runs from contract initiation to contract execution. Because the contract amounts are large, the contract time frames are long, and the contracting parties are several; hence, violation of any contractual terms and conditions can lead to legal, financial, and reputation risks.

(B) Market Research

One of the major uses of market research is to segment markets. Market segmentation is a powerful and well-developed marketing tool. A properly segmented market can improve marketing, distribution (logistics), and manufacturing efficiency and can generate additional profits and/or market share. Market segmentation research, especially baseline segmentation research, must be carefully planned and executed. A mis-segmented market is often worse than a market that is not segmented. Foreign firms often enter a domestic market by segmenting the market, uncovering an underserved niche market, and then concentrating their marketing and financial resources on that niche market.

Another use of market research is using focus groups to understand consumer buying experiences in using the current products and to obtain their insights about new products and services that a company is planning to introduce.

(C) Advertising and Promotion

Just as markets are segmented, advertising is also segmented according to TV spot commercials, print ads, radio ads, outdoor (billboards) ads, company website banner ads, emails, and direct mail. Advertisers and advertising researchers have not reached consensus on the best way to test advertising or measure its effectiveness.

Most advertising testing is done with TV spot commercials because they are the most expensive forms of advertising to produce. Print ads are also frequently tested, though not as often. Occasionally radio ads, outdoor (billboards) ads, and even website banner ads are tested too. Direct mail is tested, but by small-batch mailings where the evaluation is based on direct response measures. Website banner ads that have a click-through response feature can also be tested.

In order to test an ad, one has to create a stimulus to expose to respondents. The validity and accuracy of their responses is only as good as the stimulus. Clearly, the most valid stimulus is the ad in its final, finished form. For simple print ads, this is not much of a problem. For expensive TV spot commercials, however, testing the ad only after it has been produced largely defeats the purpose of doing ad testing.

In order, from roughest to most finished form, the following are the recommended types of stimuli to test TV spot commercials: storyboards (hand-drawn ideas), roughs (prototypes), and finished ads (what consumers see). It is rare that ad testing is done with finished ads first due to heavy costs involved.

Traditional Advertising. Big retailers spend huge amounts of money for product advertisements and promotions with the hope of increasing sales revenues and profits, expressed as a certain percentage of the total marketing budget.

The scope of traditional advertising includes print ads in newspapers and magazines; outdoor ads (billboards, street and park benches, bicycles, motor vehicles, door-to-door flyers and leaving flyers in public places, such as libraries and restaurants); radio ads; TV ads with spot commercials; press releases; direct mailing of coupon and rebate books, flyers, and sample products to potential customers; and most of all, word-of-mouth from customers, friends, and family.

According to a survey by Influence Central (www.influence-central.com), the value of using traditional media and advertisement is on the decline. It says that seeing a TV advertisement impacts the decision to buy in just 1.9% of consumers; while 2.2% of consumers decide to buy a product after seeing an article or mention of it in a newspaper or magazine. This survey also said more than 80% of consumers use social media and digital advertisements for product advice and marketing promotions, resulting in a big impact.

> **Example:** Beauty retailers such as Kiehl's and Urban Decay do not use expensive traditional media, as they operate with a very low budget for traditional advertisements and promotions. However, these retailers are successful due to word-of-mouth advertising from their customers.

Digital Advertising. The scope of digital advertising includes the Internet; a retailer's website banner ads and press room; mobile sites; mobile apps; social media platforms and blogs; mobile devices (e.g., digital phones, tablets, and notebook computers); emails; text messages; efaxes; webinars; online chat rooms; mobile alerts and notifications; viral advertising and marketing; user-generated content; user recommendations; and blogger recommendations.

There is a direct relationship between user reviews, comments, and recommendations posted in a social media about a product and customer conversion rates and who posted them. In general, an increased number of reviews leads to higher conversion rates and vice versa. Reviews, testimonials, endorsements, and recommendations posted by famous bloggers have a bigger positive impact on conversion rates than reviews and recommendations posted by normal users.

> **Example 1:** Sephora, a beauty retailer, claims to get five times more user reviews, comments, and recommendations than its competitors. Consequently, it increased its customer conversion rates significantly.

> **Example 2:** Famous bloggers, especially in fashion and beauty retail, can exercise tremendous influence on millions of subscribers to social media platforms, such as YouTube and Instagram. Millions of these subscribers (customers and followers) trust these famous bloggers. These famous bloggers have a big positive impact on a brand's name and a company's sales.

Traditional Advertising versus Digital Advertising. Many elements of traditional marketing easily translate into digital marketing, such as price, product, place, and promotion. However, there are clear and major differences between traditional advertising and digital advertising regarding cost, speed, reach, and communication channels, as shown next.

Traditional advertising	Expensive, slow, and does not reach all the intended audience at the right time and at the right place. It uses a one-to-many communication channel. This is especially true with print media, such as newspapers and magazines as well as radio and TV.
Digital advertising	Inexpensive, fast, reaches all the intended audience very quickly. It uses a one-to-one communication channel. This is especially true with social media because there is a direct communication line to the customer.

Viral Advertising. Viral advertisements and viral videos are examples of new advertising methods using the Internet as the communication media. The word "viral" here refers to a computer virus that infects and spreads other computers at a great speed. Viral advertising has the same effect as computer virus in terms of speed, benefit, and damage to some.

Viral videos are short films lasting 90 seconds or longer, made with low cost and large-scale reach with fast delivery in mind. The number of video views in a time period (e.g., zero to thousands to millions of views per hour or per day) is a measure of a viral video's success or failure. Marketing management can use viral advertising to introduce a new product or improvements to existing products. Individuals can also upload videos to the Internet for fun and revenge. The video is not viral until it spreads.

There are no ground rules in terms of who can post (upload) what types of videos and under what conditions. Some videos are good in message and meaning while others are bad in content and taste. Similarly, some videos are viewed by millions while others have no viewers. Viral advertising or marketing campaigns deal with messages forward to a friend, incentivized viral, stealth, and buzz or word of mouth.

Digital Promotions. Digital promotions include digital coupons and digital gift cards. The old days of cutting and clipping coupons from various sources is over with the introduction of paperless digital coupons. The same is true with digital gift cards due to their convenience. Digital coupons are very popular among deal hunters, bargain hunters, and cost-conscious shoppers; there is nothing wrong in saving money.

Most retailers undertake extensive promotional campaigns to entice current and new customers to come into their online and offline stores for purchase with sales coupons and gift cards with staggered expiration dates based on the amount of purchase. The goal of these promotions is to increase sales through increased conversion rates.

> **Example 1:** Target, a mass merchandise retailer, is enjoying the highest total average daily visits. This success is due, in part, to its price-matching policy. Target also added vendor-issued coupons (manufacturers' coupons) to its Cartwheel app, which is very popular with customers due to its personalized recommendations, interactive store maps to locate saved items, and proximity-based messages.

> **Example 2:** Safeway, a food supermarket retailer, increased its coupon distribution due, in part, to its rewards program, which personalizes deals based on a customer's purchase history. This means that the higher the purchase amounts, the greater the amount of rewards, which is a good motivation and incentive.

> **Example 3:** Walgreens, a pharmacy retailer, enables its customers to redeem paperless (digital) coupons from the retailer and manufacturers for both online and offline purchases. Walgreens combines the digital coupons with a customer's rewards card.

> **Example 4:** Lord & Taylor, a division of the Hudson's Bay Company, has introduced mobile couponing to provide relevant coupons to customers at any point in time. Customers with its app receive push notifications when they come within 500 meters of a store. The app combines a location technology with mobile coupons.

> **Example 5:** The Home Depot, Sephora, Starbucks, Dunkin Donuts, and Cheesecake Factory are ranked at the top of the digital gifting experience list.

Product Placement and Advertising. Celebrity endorsements, movies, and public media (e.g., magazines, TV programs, newspapers, and radio announcements) show, present, discuss, and promote brand-name products as silent salespeople. For example, advertising agencies, representing the owners of brand-name products (advertisers), will pay an agreed amount to movie producers or studio owners for showing or mentioning their products in movies. Just as celebrities have agents, brand-name products have product agents. It is a documented fact that sales for these products increase after they are shown or mentioned in movies. Note that it is still worth the gamble for the advertisers to get their products out in front of a captive and captivated audience as it is a risk-reward balancing act. There is always a risk that product placement may not work.

> **Example 1:** Brand-name products placed or mentioned in movies and public media include fashion clothes, expensive cars, luxury watches, home furniture, home appliances, sunglasses, shoes, handbags, alcohol, restaurants, and others.

Whether a particular product placement in a specific public media is a success or failure depends on how that product ad is created and communicated to its intended audiences and how that ad was received by such audiences. Some ads can be good or bad. Product placement in advertisements is based on the cross-promotions concept, meaning one party is helping another party in terms of creating new sales, revenues, and profits. In the end, it is a win-win outcome for both parties.

Example 2: Brand-name products that were successful due to their placement in movies include Ray-Ban sunglasses worn by Tom Cruise in the movie *Risky Business*; Reese's Pieces in the movie *E.T. the Extra-Terrestrial*; Taco Bell restaurant after its mention in the movie *Demolition Man*; Budweiser beer receiving an award for Overall Product Placement in Hollywood in 2014; BMW, which replaced James Bond's usual Aston Martin, and Heineken beer, which replaced his usual vodka martini, in James Bond movies.[26]

Truth in Advertising and Trust in Advertising. Truth in advertising leads to trust in advertising as they are linked to each other; the former comes first and establishes the latter. Note that truth in advertising deals with legal matters (legal factors) whereas trust in advertising deals with human matters (people factors).

Truth in Advertising. The FTC defines and enforces "truth in advertising" laws to protect consumers from fraud and deception from misleading and confusing advertisements. Federal law says that any ads that target consumers, whether they are on the Internet, radio or television, or anywhere else, must be truthful, not misleading, and, when appropriate, backed by scientific evidence. Ads can appear anywhere, such as newspapers, magazines, the Internet, electronic mail, regular mail, billboards, or buses. The FTC focuses on advertising claims that can affect consumers' health or their pocketbooks in the areas of food, over-the-counter drugs, dietary supplements, alcohol, tobacco, high-tech products, and the Internet.

When the FTC finds a case of fraud perpetrated on consumers, it files actions in federal district court for immediate and permanent orders to stop scams, prevent fraudsters from perpetrating scams in the future, freeze their assets, and get compensation for victims.

Example 1: Wrigley, a major U.S. chewing gum maker, was ordered to pay $7 million in 2010 to compensate consumers and pay court costs due to misleading advertisement about its Eclipse gum containing a new ingredient that can kill germs that cause bad breath. Eclipse ads incorrectly said that products of Wrigley's competitors merely masked bad breadth.

Example 2: Kellogg, a major U.S. food manufacturer, was ordered to discontinue all Rice Krispies advertising that claimed the cereal could boost a child's immune system, which the courts found dubious. Prior to this, Kellogg was barred from claiming that Frosted Mini-Wheats boosted kids' attentiveness by 20%.

Example 3: General Mills Company, a major U.S. food manufacturer, was limiting its customers' legal options for suing the company. In 2015, it posted an alert on its website stating that customers would give up their right to sue the company if they download a coupon or if they post "liked" the company on Facebook. This means that any such customer who had a dispute with the company and who filed a complaint against it would be treated and negotiated with informally via emails, not formally and legally. The company removed this statement from its website after customers complained. A lesson the company learned was never underestimate the power of customers and always be legal and ethical.

Trust in Advertising. Trust between people, products, and companies can be created and lost. It can take a very long time to earn trust, a very short time to lose it, and may never be restored.

---

[26] Terry O'Reilly, *Under the Influence* radio program, National Public Radio.

According to Terry O'Reilly, trust in marketing transactions is based on relationships between sellers and buyers of goods and services. His radio program cites the following examples.[27]

Example 1: The most trusted industry in the United States was technology, followed by tourism, retail, consumer products, and telecommunications. The advertising industry was near the bottom of the list.

Example 2: In a study done by the Advertising Standards Council, most people believe in ads placed in newspapers as number one, billboards as number two, followed by radio, magazines, and television in that order. Ads on the Internet were at the bottom of the list.

Example 3: Chris Zanes, the founder of Zanes Cycle Company in Connecticut, built his business of selling and repairing bicycles purely based on trust and relationships between his company and his customers. He allows customers to take test rides on their bikes without charging them and without asking for any identification. In fact, when customers offer to leave their driver's licenses, they were politely refused. Five thousand bikes are taken for a test rides every year, and only five bikes are lost due to theft annually. Zanes believes that he is in the trust and relationship business, not in the bike business, and that his customers will return that trust by becoming loyal, lifelong customers and by referring family and friends over and over again.

Marketing and the Laws. Marketers must respect the promotion laws (dealing with sweepstakes, games of chance, and skill contests), trademark laws, copyright laws, and advertising laws (dealing with free offers, discount offers, television ads, radio and print ads, solicitation letters and efaxes, telemarketing calls, email and direct mail offers, viral marketing campaigns, and website offers). Various federal, state, and local laws and regulations govern these areas. Both the FTC and the Federal Communications Commission actively enforce federal laws and regulations.

(D) Data Mining

Data mining is the process of asking (posing) a series of questions (queries) against a database or data warehouse containing large amounts of data to extract some meaningful and relevant information to perform management analysis.

Data mining applications are best suited to data-intense organizations with data from millions of customers in their databases or data warehouses. Examples of data-intense organizations include retailers, market research firms, governmental agencies, online order takers, casinos, travel agencies, vacation cruise line firms, hotels, rental car companies, and airline companies. There is no end to the data mining applications; they are only limited by the imagination of the person requesting the data analysis work.

Data mining applications software is available from several vendors such as HP, IBM, Microsoft, Oracle, SAS, and many others. This off-the-shelf software is relatively easier to use and less expensive than custom-built software.

Data mining is data analysis, data fishing, data snooping, and data drilling in order to get to the bottom of the vast amounts of data (big data) collected by organizations during their business operations. Another name for data mining is data analytics.

---

[27] Ibid.

Management uses various quantitative techniques, such as regression analysis, factor analysis, cluster analysis, sampling, and other statistical methods, to analyze data, find relationships between data elements, and draw meaningful conclusions that can be incorporated into its decision-making process. The ultimate goal is improving business operations and increasing profits.

(E) Marketing Budgets

Holding a current market share or growing the market share requires financial resources in the form of a marketing budget, which is based on the strategic market plan and the marketing-mix strategy.

Three kinds of marketing budgets exist: percentage of sales, customer mix, and bottom-up. A top-down budget is not recommended as it is a budget imposed by top management onto marketing management without considering specific marketing tasks. The bottom-up budget is a self-control budget after considering the specific marketing tasks.

The **percentage-of-sales budget** is based on previous years' data and experience levels, adjusted higher for the growth strategy and lower for the harvest strategy (i.e., no growth strategy). This kind of budget is simple to develop, but its accuracy is low.

The **customer-mix budget** includes the cost of acquiring new and retaining current customers. This kind of budget is logical to develop, but the cost data is difficult to obtain. This budget amount can be expressed as a percentage of sales for comparative purposes.

A **bottom-up budget** requires specifying each marketing task required and determining the amount needed to accomplish that task. It is good to divide the budget into as personnel expenses and nonpersonnel expenses to facilitate comparison between time periods and to provide better control. This budget amount can also be expressed as a percentage of sales for comparative purposes.

(vi) Types of Marketing Programs

Several types of marketing programs are discussed in this section, including personalized, relationship, alliance, cause, loyalty, and event marketing.

(A) Personalized Marketing

Personalized marketing, a new approach in retail marketing, means a retailer is paying attention to or taking care of each and every customer very sincerely and seriously to ensure that customer's specific needs and wants are fulfilled to satisfaction. It is an example of one-to-one marketing, and it is a tall order to fulfill due to the huge customer base involved and the variety of customer needs that must be addressed. Because of the large number of customers, an automated approach can help in this area.

An automated approach is mainly facilitated by beacon (sensor) technology with a Wi-Fi communication network installed in a retail store linked to a customer's mobile devices. Interested customers agree to access terms and conditions and register a mobile connection to the retailer's beacon technology system. When registered customers enter a store equipped with such technology and walk around, the system sends push alerts and notifications to their mobile devices that they are carrying with them. The system offers special discounts and coupons on the mobile devices to encourage customers to make additional purchases.

Personalized marketing is also called location-based marketing, direct marketing, and targeted marketing because the personalization acts follows wherever customers go with their mobile devices in a retailer's facility and all the marketing promotions are targeted at those customers one at a time. Location-based marketing deploys location-based technology and uses mobile-proximity technology. Personalized marketing is a new trend in retail business; it benefits customers most directly.

Personalized Marketing = Beacon Technology + Location-Based Marketing

Today, more than ever, customers expect retailers to provide personalized marketing programs, not mass marketing programs. Customers want retailers to deal with them based on one customer at a time with customized approaches, as if they are the only customer for that retailer. Customers want retailers to treat them as special, royal, and loyal. For example, luxury shoppers need or expect a personalized service or experience from retailers because they buy high-priced items.

Regarding personalization, there is a gap between what retailers believe they are delivering and what customers are actually receiving or experiencing. A survey reported that 93% of retailers believe that personalization is their strategic focus yet only 25% of customers say they actually received a consistent and personalized experience across all retail channels. This is because customers want to receive a consistent, focused, and personalized experience from all retail channels, including receiving personalized advertisement messages, product offers and recommendations, product promotions, and price incentives, as shown next.

Personalization Gap = Personalization Expected − Personalization Received

Note that the personalization gap increases when a customer's expectations increase and when that customer's disappointments increase and vice versa.

(B) Relationship Marketing

Relationship marketing is treating and pampering loyal customers, prime customers, and major customers differently from regular or average customers. These loyal customers are treated with special care and attention because they bring continued and assured sales and profits to a retailer. Relationship marketing requires creating mutual value that is sustainable because both loyal customers and retailers receive benefits and values. This can happen only when a retailer's sales associates keep in contact with loyal customers periodically, announcing new products, ordering products, shipping orders, and following up, including dealing with product returns. In a way, the sales associate's role is that of a personal assistant. This type of relationship marketing is known by many names, such as a targeted, direct, smart, one-to-one, and personalized marketing. Such marketing can turn regular customers into loyal customers.

A customer relationship management (CRM) computer application system operating on a desktop or laptop computer or on smartphones and tablets enables associates to fulfill the role of personal sales assistant.

There is a difference between personalized marketing and relationship marketing, as explained next.

- Personalized marketing can be applied to any type of customers: regular, average, major, and loyal customers. Personalized marketing contains some aspects of relationship marketing.

- Relationship marketing can be applied to only one type of customer—loyal customers. It would be expensive and time-consuming to maintain that kind of relationship with all customers. Relationship marketing contains some aspects of personalized marketing.

(C) Alliance Marketing

Alliance marketing is a type of partnership between two or more for-profit companies operating in different and unrelated businesses. Marketing partnerships are established in the form of strategic alliances between retailers and nonretailers for a mutual benefit in terms of increased cross-sales, increased customer base, and increased customer traffic, all resulting in increased revenues, margins, and profits. In short, strategic alliances are business collaborations and partnerships with a common purpose and goal. Partnership marketing is a form of affinity marketing. It is a new trend in retail business that results in win-win outcomes for all parties.

In general, a strategic alliance arrangement occurs when a large and highly established company with proven products, markets, and distribution channels wishes to invest its money in a small and emerging company in the areas of new R&D activities that could help the large company grow. Another variation of a strategic alliance arrangement is establishing a business partnership between two firms for mutual benefit and to reach a win-win outcome. It requires honest commitment, trust, and a common direction for the future. This business arrangement is not a legal partnership but a strategic alliance or strategic partnership.

(D) Cause Marketing

Cause marketing is a type of partnership between for-profit corporations and not-for-profit organizations for mutual benefit. For-profit corporations commit to support the not-for-profit organizations in terms of raising funds for the latter using the formers' reputation and goodwill. It is a win-win situation for both entities because the partnership satisfies individual goals and needs of both entities. Cause marketing is not a philanthropic activity for the for-profit corporation because it does not explicitly donate money to the needy not-for-profit organization.

Cause marketing is good for for-profit corporations because giving something back to society is a part of their corporate social responsibility. Moreover, cause marketing gives great visibility and lasting goodwill to sponsoring for-profit corporations. The partnership arrangement can cause for-profit corporations' revenues and profits to increase.

Cause marketing is good for not-for-profit organizations because it enables these organizations to fulfill their mission of serving society and its citizens. Without the partnership arrangement with the for-profit corporation, the not-for-profit would not have the funds to fulfill its mission. The partnership arrangement can cause not-for-profit organizations' financial resources to increase.

The **mutual benefit** is shown below:

    Cause Marketing = Funds to Not-for-Profit Organizations

    Cause Marketing = Goodwill to For-Profit Corporations

Surveys have shown that 70% of customers prefer to do business with companies that commit to good causes and that 90% of customers would switch from one product brand to another if it was associated with a good cause.

(E) Loyalty Marketing

Retailers of all sizes and locations implement loyalty programs with incentives and rewards to retain existing customers for life and to turn regular customers into loyal customers, all to achieve customer sustainability goals. The airline industry initiated loyalty programs through frequent flyer mileage rewards. Later, the retail industry adopted loyalty programs for customers.

Innovation is required in creating and executing loyalty programs because knowing what it takes to get customers excited is the crux of loyalty programs. The sky is the limit when it comes to creating innovative ways of attracting, pampering, and protecting loyal customers because they bring predictable and consistent sales revenues, margins, and profits to a retailer. Loyal customers are few in number compared to regular customers, but they are stronger financially with a greater buying power than other types of customers. Loyal customers have a big impact in increasing a retailer's revenues, margins, and profits. Loyal customers also are called prime, preferred, and honored customers.

Loyal Customers ⟶ Prime Customers

Loyal Customers ⟶ Preferred Customers

Loyal Customers ⟶ Honored Customers

Loyalty or reward cards can give loyal customers a variety of incentives to buy from a retailer. These incentives include points, miles, coupons, rebates, special offers and deals, and even free merchandise just for shopping with that retailer. Customers feel that they are getting repeat values from repeat purchases, and retailers feel that they are getting repeat values through repeat sales. This is a win-win situation for both the customer and the retailer. Note that brand loyalty is related to brand assets, meaning loyal customers can create and sustain a brand's assets due to their continued commitment and loyalty through buying that branded product repeatedly.

There is an inverse relationship between the loyalty scores customers give to retailers and customer churn rates (customer turnover or defection). This means that the higher the loyalty scores are, the lower the customer churn rates would be. One way to keep loyalty scores high is to make customers delighted with each purchase they make and to seek out continued feedback from customers to identify gaps in their unmet needs.

Various survey results indicated the following:

- 62% of retailers have increased their budgets for the loyalty programs.
- 35% of middle-class shoppers said they do not want to join a fee-based loyalty program because generic point-based rewards (free programs) are good enough for them.
- Most popular loyalty programs are found in food supermarkets (food retailers).
- Most millennials are willing to join a fee-based rewards program at their favorite retailer. They said rewards in fee-based programs are better than the no-fee rewards.

According to a special report by Boston Retail Partners in 2015, customer experience and engagement is ranked as the first priority for retailers and the customer loyalty program is ranked as the second priority. Here, the idea is that if the customer experience is superior and customer engagement is exciting, then regular customers would automatically join a loyalty program. The report also indicates that most retailers offer traditional coupons and discounts; only few retailers are giving personalized offers to customers.

Because loyalty programs focus on one-to-one marketing concept, it requires retailers to take care of one customer at a time with specialized and personalized approaches. This approach requires customer identification and recognition methods so that retailers can customize the customer experience and engagement tasks.

(F) Event Marketing

Event marketing is a type of marketing program where a corporation supports and sponsors various local, regional, and national programs in various areas, such as social, educational, sports, music, cultural, art, and healthcare events; research programs for chronic diseases; fundraising for good causes, such as disaster relief; and other philanthropic and charitable activities. Event marketing represents good corporate citizenship with goodwill and a positive reputation in the eyes of general public in a specific community. Moreover, event marketing reflects a smart advertising strategy with high visibility and a big positive impact on the corporation.

(d) Quality Management Function

This section discusses several topics: drivers of quality, employee empowerment, quality definition, cost of quality (COQ), Six Sigma program, quality metrics, quality tools, statistical process control techniques, quality loss function (QLF), and inspection.

(i) Drivers of Quality

Drivers of quality include customers; suppliers; vendors; employees; products; services; organizational culture and ethics; organizational policies, procedures, and standards; and total organizational focus and commitment. Note that these drivers can either increase or decrease quality, depending on which direction they move, up or down.

(ii) Employee Empowerment

Employee empowerment means involving employees in every step of a production or service process to solicit their input. It is based on the idea that employees who are close to the action would better know the shortcomings of a system, machine, or process than those who are not. Quality circles are part of employee empowerment in managing quality.

Empowerment happens when higher-level employees (e.g., executives and senior managers) decide to distribute and share their power and authority—not their responsibility and accountability—with lower-level employees to make decisions in a timely manner. The reason for empowerment is to put the power where the real action is taking place in the organization—with lower-level employees—so there are no delays in producing products and delivering services to customers. Note that employee empowerment is not a blank check for employees to do anything they want without checking with their supervisors or managers. Empowerment puts upper limits on what employees can do on their own. Exhibit 1.64 compares critical items before and after empowerment.

EXHIBIT 1.64 A Comparison between Before Empowerment and After Empowerment

Comparative Items	Before Empowerment	After Empowerment
Power	Concentrated in few and hoarded by few	Distributed to and shared by many
Decision-making approach	Command and control	Participative
Response to customers	Slow	Fast

(iii) Quality Defined

Quality has many definitions because it is viewed from many perspectives. Six criteria are presented next.

1. **Judgment-based criteria** are synonymous with superiority or excellence, which is abstract, subjective, and difficult to quantify.

2. **Product-based criteria** assume that higher levels or amounts of product characteristics are equivalent to higher quality and that quality has a direct relationship with price.

3. According to **user-based criteria**, quality is fitness for intended use or how well a product performs its intended function. It is basically dictated by user wants and needs.

4. **Value-based criteria** focus on the relationship of usefulness or satisfaction of a product or service to price. This means a customer can purchase a generic product at a lower price if it performs the same way as the brand-name product.

5. **Manufacturing-based criteria** refer to conformance to specifications (e.g., engineering or manufacturing) that are important to customers. Taguchi, a Japanese statistician, opposes the manufacturing-based definition of quality due to built-in defects to be produced at a higher cost.

6. **Customer-driven quality criteria** refers to meeting customer needs or exceeding customer expectations. This definition is simple and powerful; hence, most companies use it.

A Japanese professor, Noriaki Kano, suggested three classes of customer requirements in understanding customer needs in the marketplace: dissatisfiers, satisfiers, and delighters. Customers are **dissatisfied** when the features that they assumed or expected are not present in a product. Customers are **satisfied** when the features that they wanted are present in a product, although those features are not expected. Customers are **delighted** when the features that they did not assume or expect are present in a product because the features exceed their expectations.

(iv) Cost of Quality

The COQ means the price of nonconformance to standards, policies, or procedures. COQ is the cost of doing things wrong, which results in poor quality of products or services. COQ is really the cost of poor quality.

Four categories of COQ are discussed next.

1. **Prevention costs** are associated with reducing the potential for producing defective products or rendering poor-quality services in the first place. Examples include quality improvement programs, employee training and education, investment in equipment and facilities, operator inspection costs, supplier ratings, supplier reviews, supplier certification, product design reviews, pilot projects, prototype tests, vendor surveys, quality-related design costs, purchase-order technical data reviews, and quality department review costs.

2. **Appraisal costs** are associated with evaluating products, processes, parts, or services. Examples include material testing, product testing, production line inspection, quality checks, purchasing appraisal costs, qualifications of supplier product, equipment calibration, receiving and shipping inspection costs, production tests, and product quality audits.

3. **Internal failure costs** are associated with producing defective products or rendering poor-quality services before delivering them to customers. Examples include repair, redesign, reinspection, rework, retesting, sorting, scrap, waste, machine downtime, employee fatigue, and employee carelessness.

4. **External failure costs** are associated with correcting defective products or poor-quality services after delivering them to customers. Examples include product returns, product warranty charges, product recalls, liability suits resulting from damage to customers, field service staff training costs, lost customer goodwill, and poor reputation to a firm.

A $1.00 investment in a prevention category will reduce many dollars of internal and external failure costs, which in turn will improve overall product or service quality many times over.

Quality costs can be reported as an index—the ratio of the current value to a base-period value—and expressed as a percentage or as a fraction. The **quality cost index** increases the understanding of the underlying cost data. Some common measurement bases include direct labor cost, manufacturing cost, sales dollars, and units of production.

(v) Six Sigma Program
This subsection defines Six Sigma, explains how to design for Six Sigma, and focuses on the key Six Sigma players.

(A) Six Sigma Defined
Six Sigma is a statistical concept to describe accuracy and quality levels in a process, product, or service that can lead to a competitive advantage in the marketplace. The word "sigma" is associated with the statistical term "standard deviation," which is the distance from the mean (average).

Six Sigma is a strategy, discipline, system, program, and tool to achieve quality improvement continuously, to solve problems, to improve functions and features of a product or service, to reduce cost and time, and to increase customer satisfaction.

MEANING OF DIFFERENT SIGMA LEVELS

- Three Sigma means 66,800 defects in a million parts produced.
- Four Sigma means 6,210 defects in a million parts produced.
- Five Sigma means 230 defects in a million parts produced.
- Six Sigma means 3.4 defects in a million parts produced.
- The goal of reaching Six Sigma from Three Sigma is a challenging one as reaching the goal is a nonlinear process.

Six Sigma follows an improvement model called DMAIC (define, measure, analyze, improve, and control stage). *D* defines the project's purpose, scope, and outputs, *M* measures the process and collects data, *A* analyzes the data to ensure repeatability and reproducibility, *I* improves or redesigns the existing process, and *C* controls the new or modified process for increased performance.

Implementing a Six Sigma program requires a strong commitment from employees and management in terms of time, training, and expertise.

Six Sigma redefines quality performance as **defects per million opportunities (dpmo).** It is calculated as:

$$dpmo = (\text{Defects per Unit}) \times 1,000,000 / \text{Opportunities for Error}$$

where

Defects per Unit = Number of Defects Discovered/Number of Units Produced

> **EXAMPLES OF TOOLS AND TECHNIQUES USED IN THE DMAIC MODEL**
>
> Define stage: brainstorming, cause-and-effect diagram, and process mapping
>
> Measure stage: cause-and-effect diagram and process mapping
>
> Analyze stage: regression and correlation analysis and process mapping
>
> Improve stage: brainstorming, simulation, design of experiments, and process mapping
>
> Control stage: mistake-proofing (poka-yoke), statistical process control, and control charts

(B) Design for Six Sigma

Design for Six Sigma (DFSS) is a proactive approach to prevent problems from occurring in the first place and/or in resolving problems after they occur. The focus is on functional and quality improvement at the early design stage. An approach to DFSS is established in terms of **DCOV** model, which stands for define, characterize, optimize, and verify.

> **EXAMPLES OF TOOLS AND TECHNIQUES USED IN THE DCOV MODEL**
>
> Define stage: Kano model, quality function deployment, and regression and conjoint analysis
>
> Characterize stage: design of experiments and TRIZ (a problem-solving tool)
>
> Optimize stage: design of experiments, simulation, mistake-proofing, and control charts
>
> Verify stage: design walkthroughs and reviews and product tests

DFSS is similar to other design concepts, such as design for manufacturability (e.g., lean production and standard parts), design for low cost (e.g., overhead costs, supply chain costs, and quality costs), design for faster production (e.g., flexible manufacturing and concurrent engineering), design for faster marketing (e.g., time to market, quality function deployment, and voice of the customer), design for safety and ergonomics (e.g., safe products and human factors), design for a better environment (e.g., pollution control and recycling), and design for serviceability (e.g., postsales activities, such as ease of repair and maintenance).

(C) Six Sigma Players

Several Six Sigma players exist in the planning and implementation of the Six Sigma program in an organization, including White Belts (at the bottom), Green Belts, Yellow Belts, Black Belts, Master Black Belts, Project Champions, and Senior Champions (at the top of the Six Sigma hierarchy). All of these players assume defined roles and responsibilities and need specific training of varying lengths to make the Six Sigma program a success.

White Belts are hourly employees who need basic training in Six Sigma goals, tools, and techniques to help Green Belts and Black Belts on their projects.

Green Belts are salaried employees who have a dual responsibility in implementing Six Sigma in their function and in carrying out their regular duties in that function. They gather and analyze data in support of a Black Belt project and receive a simplified version of Black Belt training.

Yellow Belts are seasoned salaried employees who are familiar with quality improvement processes.

Black Belts are salaried employees who have a full-time responsibility in implementing Six Sigma projects. They require hard skills and receive extensive training in statistics and problem-solving and decision-making tools and techniques, as they train Green Belts. Black Belts are very important to Six Sigma's success.

Master Black Belts are also salaried employees who have a full-time responsibility in implementing Six Sigma projects. They require soft skills, need some knowledge in statistics, and need more knowledge in problem-solving and decision-making tools and techniques, as they train Black Belts and Green Belts.

Senior Champions are sponsors and executives in a specific business function. They manage several **Project Champions** at the business unit level, who in turn manage specific projects. Senior Champions develop plans, set priorities, allocate resources, and organize projects. Project Champions deploy plans, manage projects that cut across the business functions, and provide managerial and technical guidance to Master Black Belts and Black Belts. All champions require soft skills.

WHICH SIX SIGMA PLAYER DOES WHAT?

White Belts help Green Belts and Black Belts.

Green Belts help Black Belts.

Black Belts help Master Black Belts.

Master Black Belts help Project Champions.

Project Champions help Senior Champions.

Senior Champions decide *what* gets done. Project Champions, Master Black Belts, and Black Belts decide *how* to get it done.

(vi) Quality Metrics

Return on quality (ROQ) is similar to ROI in terms of measurement, requiring the same attention as ROI. Quality improvement initiatives have a direct financial impact, which cannot be ignored.

ROQ is similar to cost of quality (COQ) in terms of measurement except that COQ takes an internal perspective, such as costs and defects, and ROQ takes an external perspective, such as revenues and customer satisfaction.

The **COQ** means the price of nonconformance to standards, policies, or procedures.

Critical to quality (CTQ) is a quality measurement technique that dictates a product's output specifications in terms of a customer's needs, wants, and expectations, whether the customer is internal or external to an organization. CTQ focuses on customer requirements, design and test parameters, mistake-proofing, quality robustness, and control charts.

COMPARISON AMONG COQ, ROQ, AND CTQ

COQ takes an internal perspective.

ROQ takes an external perspective.

CTQ takes both internal and external customer perspectives.

ROQ measures expected revenue gains against expected costs associated with quality improvement initiatives. ROQ is computed as net present value (NPV) of benefits resulting from quality improvement initiatives divided by NPV of costs associated with quality improvement initiatives minus 1.0.

Return on quality (ROQ), expressed as a percentage, is computed as:

ROQ = [(Net present value of quality benefits)/(Net present value of quality costs)] − 1.00

The result is multiplied by 100 to get the percentage.

All benefits and costs are multiplied with the corresponding present value factors to result in NPV of benefits and costs respectively.

(vii) Quality Tools

Several quality tools exist that can be used to analyze processes, prioritize problems, report the results, and evaluate the results of a corrective action plan. There are seven quality control tools and seven quality management tools.

(A) Seven Quality Control Tools

1. Check sheets are used for collecting data in a logical and systematic manner.

2. A **histogram** is a frequency distribution diagram in which bars represent the frequencies of occurrences of the different variables being plotted.

3. A **scatter diagram** is a plot of the values of one variable against those of another variable to determine the relationship between them. These diagrams are used during analysis to understand cause-and-effect relationships between two variables. Scatter diagrams are also called correlation diagrams.

4. A **Pareto diagram** is a special use of the bar graph in which the bars are arranged in descending order of magnitude. The purpose of Pareto analysis, using Pareto diagrams, is to identify the major problems in a product or process or, more generally, to identify the most significant causes for a given effect. This allows a developer to prioritize problems and decide which problem area to work on first.

5. A **flowcharting** tool can be used to document every phase of a company's operation, for example, from order taking to shipping in a manufacturing company. It is an effective way to break down a process or pinpoint a problem. Flowcharting can be done at both the summary level and the detailed level serving different user needs.

6. One form of a **cause-and-effect (C&E) diagram** is used for process analysis when a series of events or steps in a process creates a problem and the it major cause of the problem is not clear. Each process or subprocess is examined for possible causes; after the causes from each step in the process are discovered, significant root causes of the problem are selected, verified,

and corrected. C&E diagrams are also called fishbone or Ishikawa diagrams; they were invented as problem-solving tools.

Stratification helps the C&E diagram because it is a procedure used to describe the systematic subdivision of population or process data to obtain a detailed understanding of the structure of the population or process. It is not to be confused with a stratified sampling method. Stratification can be used to break down a problem to discover its root causes and can establish appropriate corrective actions, called countermeasures.

7. A **control chart** assesses a process variation. The control chart displays sequential process measurements relative to the overall process average and control limits. The upper and lower control limits establish the boundaries of normal variation for the process being measured.

(B) Seven Quality Management Tools

1. An **affinity diagram** is a data-reduction tool that organizes a large number of qualitative inputs into a smaller number of major categories. These diagrams are useful in analyzing defect data and other quality problems and are useful in conjunction with cause-and-effect diagrams or interrelationship digraphs.

2. A **tree diagram** can be used to show the relationships of a production process by breaking the process down from a few larger steps into many smaller steps. The greater the detail of steps, the more simplified they are. Quality improvement actions can progress from the rightmost side of the tree to the leftmost.

3. A **process decision program chart** is a preventive control tool that prevents problems from occurring in the first place and mitigates the impact of problems that do occur. In this way, it is a contingency planning tool. The objective of the tool is to determine the impact of the "failures" or problems on the project schedule.

4. A **matrix diagram** is developed to analyze the correlations between two groups of ideas with the use of a decision table. This diagram allows one to systematically analyze correlations. Quality function deployment is an extension of the matrix diagram.

5. An **interrelationship digraph** is used to organize disparate ideas. Arrows are drawn between related ideas. An idea that has arrows leaving it but none entering is a root idea. More attention is given to the root ideas for system improvement. The digraph is often used in conjunction with affinity diagrams.

6. **Prioritization matrices** are used to help decision makers determine the order of importance of activities being considered in a decision. Key issues and choices are identified for further improvement. These matrices combine the use of tree diagrams and matrix diagrams.

7. **Activity network diagrams** are project management tools to determine which activities must be performed, when they must be performed, and in what sequence. These diagrams are similar to program evaluation and review technique (PERT) and critical path method (CPM), the popular tools in project management. Unlike PERT and CPM, activity network diagrams are simple to construct and require less training to use.

(viii) Statistical Process Control Techniques

Management's goal is to reduce causes of process variation and to increase process capabilities to meet customer expectations.

Process Variation. Variation is present in every process as a result of a combination of four variables:

1. Operator variation (due to physical and emotional conditions)
2. Equipment variation (due to wear and tear)

3. Materials variation (due to thickness, moisture content, and old and new materials)

4. Environmental variation (due to changes in temperature, light, and humidity)

Variation is either expected or unexpected, and it results from common, special, or structural causes.

Variation affects proper functioning of a process in that process output deviates from the established target. **Common causes** of variation affect the standard deviation of a process and are caused by factors internal to a process. These causes, which are present in all processes, are also called **chance** (random) **causes.** Chance causes are small in magnitude and are difficult to identify. Examples of common random causes include worker availability, number and complexity of orders, job schedules, equipment testing, work-center schedules, changes in raw materials, truck schedules, and worker performance.

Special causes affect the standard deviation of a process and are factors external to a process. Special causes, also known as assignable causes, are large in magnitude and are not so difficult to identify. They may or may not be present in a process. Examples of special (assignable) causes include equipment breakdowns, operator changes, new raw materials, new products, new competition, and new customers.

Structural causes affect the standard deviation of a process; they are factors both internal and external to a process. They may or may not be present in a process; they are a blend of common and special causes. Examples of structural causes include sudden sales/production volume increase due to a new product or a new customer, seasonal sales, and a sudden increase in profits.

A **control chart** is a statistical tool that distinguishes between natural (common) and unnatural (special) variations. The control chart method is used to measure variations in quality. The control chart is a picture of the process over time. It shows whether a process is in a stable state and is used to improve the process quality.

Natural variation is the result of random causes. Management intervention is required to achieve quality improvement or a quality system. It has been stated that 80% to 85% of quality problems are due to management or the quality system and that 15% to 20% of problems are due to operators or workers. Supervisors, operators, and technicians can correct the unnatural variation. Control charts can be drawn for variables and attributes.

The control chart method for variables is a means of visualizing the variations that occur in the central tendency and dispersion of a set of observations. It measures the quality of a particular characteristic, such as length, time, or temperature.

A **variable chart** is an excellent technique for achieving quality improvement. True process capability can be achieved only after substantial quality improvements have been made. Once true process capability is obtained, effective specifications can be determined. The sequence of events taking place with the control chart is shown next.

Variable chart → Quality improvement
→ Process capability
→ Specifications

To improve the process continuously, **variable control charts** can be used to overcome the limitations of attribute control charts. Continuous process improvement is the highest level of quality consciousness. Control charts based on variable data reduce unit-to-unit variation, even within specification limits. Variable data consist of measurements such as weight, length, width, height, time, and temperature. Variable data contain more information than attribute data. Variable control charts can decrease the difference between customer needs and process performance.

The **attribute chart** refers to those quality characteristics that conform or do not conform to specifications (specs). It is used where measurements are not possible, such as for color, missing parts, scratches, or damage. Quality characteristics for a product can be translated into a **go/no-go decision**.

GO/NO-GO DECISION FOR PRODUCT QUALITY

Go conforms to specifications.

No-go does not conform to specifications.

Two types of **attribute control charts** exist: charts for nonconforming units and charts for nonconformities. A **nonconforming unit** is a product or service containing at least one nonconformity. A **nonconformity** is a departure of a quality characteristic from its intended level that is not meeting a required specification.

Two types of statistical errors in quality can occur, leading to incorrect decisions: **Type I error** is called producer's risk (alpha risk), which is the probability that a conforming (good-quality) product will be rejected as a poor-quality product and not sold to customers. This product meets the established acceptable quality level. This error results in an incorrect decision to reject something when it is acceptable. **Type II error** is called consumer's risk (beta risk), which is the probability that a nonconforming (poor-quality) product will be accepted as a good-quality product and sold to customers. This error results in an incorrect decision to accept something when it is unacceptable. Type II error occurs when statistical quality data fails to result in the scrapping or reworking of a defective product.

Stable and unstable processes are defined as follows. When only chance causes of variation are present in a process, the process is considered to be in a state of statistical control (i.e., the process is stable and predictable). When a process is in control (stable), there is a natural pattern of variation, and only chance causes of variation are present. Small variations in operator performance, equipment performance, materials, and environmental characteristics are expected and are considered part of a stable process. Further improvements in the process can be achieved only by changing the input factors (i.e., operator, equipment, materials, and environment). These changes require action by management through quality improvement ideas.

When an assignable cause of variation is present in a process, the process is considered to be out of statistical control (i.e., the process is unstable and unpredictable). When an observed measurement falls outside its control limits, the process is said to be out of control (unstable). This means that an assignable cause of variation is present. The unnatural, unstable variation makes it impossible to predict future variation. The assignable causes must be found and corrected before a natural, stable process can continue.

Process Capability. **Process capability** is the ability of a production process to manufacture a product within customers' desired expectations. The **process capability index (PCI)**, which indicates whether a process is capable of meeting customer expectations, must be equal to or greater than 1.00 to meet customer expectations. A PCI of less than 1.00 means that the process does not meet customer expectations.

The PCI is computed in several ways:

$$PCI = (UL - LL)/(6 \times \text{standard deviation of a process})$$

where UL = Upper specification limit

LL = Lower specification limit

The upper specification limit means that some data points will be above the central line in a control chart. The lower specification limit means that some data points will be below the central line in a control chart.

Capability ratio (Cp) is specification tolerance width divided by process capability. Specification tolerance width refers to variability of a parameter permitted above or below a nominal value. Cp is a widely used PCI.

(ix) Quality Loss Function

Taguchi believes that variation in a production process can be reduced by designing products that perform in a consistent manner, even under conditions of varying or adverse use. He emphasizes proactive steps at the design stage instead of late, reactive steps at the production stage.

Taguchi believes in pushing a process upstream to focus on product and process design, which is called **offline quality control**. This is contrary to **online quality control**, where traditional quality control activities take place downstream with the focus on final inspection procedures, sampling methods, and statistical process control techniques. Offline quality control methods reduce costs and defects.

Taguchi uses quality engineering and statistical experimental design methods to reduce all process and product variations from the target value with the goal of producing a perfect product. He views **quality engineering** as composed of three elements: system design, parameter design, and tolerance design.

Taguchi developed three related concepts using statistical experimental design: quality robustness, quality loss function (QLF), and target-oriented quality. The QLF measures quality in monetary units that reflect both short- and long-term losses.

Quality robustness means products are consistently produced despite adverse manufacturing and environmental conditions. The goal is to remove the effects of adverse conditions rather than removing the causes, which is more expensive to do. It is assumed that small variations in materials and process do not destroy the overall product quality.

A **QLF** identifies all costs associated with poor quality and shows how these costs increase as the product moves away from the target value. Examples of costs included in the QLF are customer dissatisfaction costs, warranty costs, service costs, internal inspection costs, equipment or product repair costs, scrap costs, and overall costs to society due to bad reputation and loss of goodwill. The QLF concept can be equally applied to products and services.

Target-oriented quality is a philosophy of continuous improvement, where the goal is to bring the product exactly on target, instead of falling within the tolerance limits, which are is too simplistic and costly to customers. Traditionally, products are manufactured using conformance-oriented specifications with tolerance limits allowed. Taguchi opposes conformance to specification limits due to the built-in tolerance range, which allows defective products to be produced. He advocates manufacturing a perfect product at the desired specifications, with no tolerance limits and at a relatively low cost.

The QLF is computed as:

$$L = D^2 \times C$$

> where L = Loss to society
> D^2 = Distance from the target value
> C = Cost of the deviation at the specification limit

The smaller the loss, the more desirable the product. However, the farther the product is from the target value, the greater the loss. QLF is zero when a product is produced at the target value and rises exponentially as the product is produced to meet the tolerance limits.

(x) Inspection and Quality at the Source

Inspection is a means of ensuring that an operation or a process is producing at the expected quality level. The best processes have little variation from the standard level. Three basic issues relating to inspection (audit) are what to inspect, when to inspect, and where to inspect. The audit can take place at several places and several times:

- At supplier's plant while the supplier is producing goods, such as raw materials, ingredients, parts, or components
- At company facility upon receipt of goods from the supplier
- During the company's production processes, either in-house or outside
- Before delivery to the customer

Source inspection means individual employees are checking their own work with proper training and empowerment before they pass their work to the next employee, who is considered an internal customer. Inspectors may be using a checklist, a sampling plan, and controls such as fail-safe devices (poka-yoke) for mistake-proofing.

Inspection rules help inspectors to prioritize where inspection should be performed. The **inspection priority index** is computed as:

Inspection priority index = Cost of inspection/Cost of failure

If the index is less than 1.0, that item should be inspected first; if the index is greater than 1.0, that item should be inspected last.

Two other inspection methods include **in-process inspection,** where all work is inspected at each stage of the production process, and the **$N = 2$ technique,** where the first and last pieces in a supplier's shipment lot are checked to see whether they meet the specifications. If they do, then the entire shipment lot is accepted. The $N = 2$ technique is an alternative to **acceptance sampling**, where a lot is accepted if two or fewer defects are found and rejected if more than two defects are found.

Quality at the source is a defect- or error-prevention technique with greater visibility of immediate results and with a decentralized control where the first and local action is taking place at the source. The source could be: (1) where raw materials, ingredients, parts, and components are inspected as they are received, used, or stored; (2) where purchased parts and components are fabricated; or (3) where fabricated parts and components are assembled into a finished product with other items. It is always better to detect defects and errors at the beginning rather than at the end of a process. Quality at the source, which means finding defects or errors and taking immediate corrective action, requires employee training and empowerment.

1.13 Business Development Life Cycle

Business cycles and the causes of those cycles are discussed in this section. In addition, how business cycles affect consumer durable and nondurable goods is explained. Growth concepts between a company and a nation are compared. Four business cycle indicators—leading, coincident, lagging, and composite indicators—are presented. Key economic indicators are highlighted, and how a business forecasts its demand variables (i.e., sales and inventory) is explained.

(a) Business Cycles

Any nation (country) seeks economic growth, full employment, and price-level stability. However, achieving full employment and price-level stability is not steady or certain. In the United States, both unemployment and inflation have threatened or interrupted the long-term trend of economic growth.

The term "business cycle" refers to the recurrent ups and downs in the level of economic activity that extend over time. Economists suggest four phases of the business cycle: peak, recession, trough, and recovery (see Exhibit 1.65). The duration and strength of each phase is variable. Some economists prefer to talk about business fluctuations rather than cycles because cycles imply regularity while fluctuations do not.

EXHIBIT 1.65 Business Cycle Phases

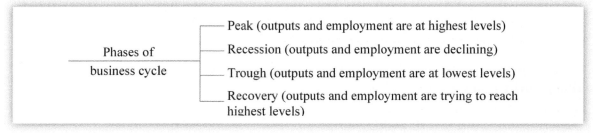

1. **Peak.** The economy is at full employment, and the national output is close to capacity. Price levels are likely to rise.

2. **Recession.** Both output and employment decline, but prices tend to be relatively inflexible in a downward direction. Depression sets in when the recession is severe and prolonged, and prices fall. In an economy experiencing a recession with low inflation, the central bank could stimulate the economy by purchasing securities in the secondary market, which will increase money supply.

3. **Trough.** Both output and employment bottom out at their lowest levels.

4. **Recovery.** Both output and employment expand toward full employment. As recovery intensifies, price levels may begin to rise prior to the realization of full employment and capacity production.

(b) Causes behind Business Cycles

Economists offer many theories for the four phases of the business cycle and the cycle's impact on business activity. Examples are listed next.

- Innovations (e.g., computers, drugs, synthetic fibers, automobiles) have greater impact on investment and consumer spending and therefore on output, employment, and the price level. This innovation is not regular and continuous.

- Political and random events, such as wars, have a major impact on increasing employment and inflation. A slump follows when peace returns.

- The government's monetary policy has a major impact on business activity. When a government creates too much money, inflation results. When a government restricts money supply, lower output and unemployment result.

- The level of total government expenditures has a major impact on the levels of output and employment.

KEY CONCEPTS TO REMEMBER: Total Expenditures

- When total expenditure is low, output, employment, and incomes will be low. Less production will be profitable to the business.

- When total expenditure is high, output, employment, and incomes will be high. More production will be profitable to the business.
  - Many businesses, such as retail, automobile, construction, and agriculture, are subject to seasonal variations (e.g., pre-Christmas, pre-Easter).
  - Business activity is also subject to secular trends. The secular trend of an economy is its expansion or contraction over a long period of time (i.e., 25 or more years). Both seasonal variations and secular trends are due to noncyclical fluctuations.

(c) Durable and Nondurable Goods

It is important to note that various individuals and various segments of the economy are affected in different ways and in different degrees by business cycles. For example, consumer durable and consumer nondurable goods industries are affected in different ways, as explained next.

- **Consumer durable goods.** Those industries producing heavy capital goods and consumer durables (e.g., household appliances, automobiles), called hard goods industries, are highly sensitive to the business cycle. Both production and employment will decline during recession and increase during recovery.

  The reason for the sensitivity of the consumer durable industry to the business cycle is that consumers and producers alike can postpone the purchase of hard goods.

Producers do not invest in capital goods during a recession; they postpone investment until the economy gets better. Consumers also postpone the purchase of hard goods during a recession and extend the life of hard goods by repairing old appliances and automobiles rather than buying new models. Producers cut output and employment instead of lowering prices due to producers concentration in the industry. Price cuts could be modest, even if they occur.

- **Consumer nondurables.** Output and employment in nondurable consumer goods industries are less sensitive to the business cycle. This is because food and clothes, which are examples of the consumer nondurable industry, are necessities of life. These are called soft good industries. Because soft good industries are highly competitive and low concentration, they will cut prices instead of production and employment. Production decline would be modest, even if it occurs.

Financial managers need to develop financial forecasts and capital investment plans according to the phase of the business cycle the firm is going through and the type of industry to which the firm belongs (i.e., consumer durables or consumer nondurables).

(d) Growth Concepts

Another interesting concept is to compare the growth of a firm (company) with that of a nation's economy. Four growth concepts emerge: supernormal, normal, zero, and negative growth (see Exhibit 1.66). Each growth concept is briefly explained next.

EXHIBIT 1.66   Industry Growth Concepts

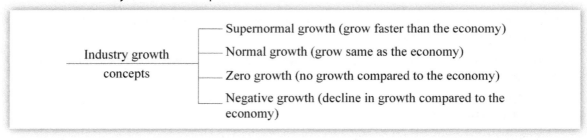

1. **Supernormal growth** is the part of a firm's life cycle in which its growth is much faster than that of the economy as a whole.

2. **Normal growth** is growth that is expected to continue into the foreseeable future at about the same rate as that of the economy as a whole. The growth rate of a firm is equal to the nominal gross national product (GNP), which is real GNP plus inflation.

3. **Zero growth** indicates that a firm experiences a 0% growth compared to the economy as a whole.

4. **Negative growth** indicates that a firm is experiencing a decline in growth compared to the economy as a whole.

(e) Business Cycle Indicators

Four types of business cycle indicators are used in economic forecasting of a country: leading indicators, coincident indicators, lagging indicators, and composite economic index. They all deal with timing of certain events taking place in an economy. Specifically, they signal peaks (highs) and troughs (lows) in the business cycle. A nation's economic growth rate can go up and down as these indicators move up and down (upward and downward swings).

(i) Leading Indicators

Leading indicators change in advance of other variables. These are the least likely to be accurate. However, they are the most useful for business planning, because they provide information for action.

For example, capital goods purchases are a leading indicator for recession. The CPI is often used in planning for inflation and wages because it is a leading economic indicator.

The index of leading indicators is broadly representative of the economy as its components are drawn from six separate groups of cyclical indicators:

1. Labor force, employment, and unemployment

2. Sales, orders, and deliveries

3. Fixed capital investment

4. Prices

5. Personal income and consumer attitudes

6. Money, credit, interest rates, and stock prices

The leading index is useful primarily during times of uncertainty.

According to the U.S. Conference Board (www.conference-board.org), examples of leading indicators include:

- Average weekly hours for production workers in manufacturing, where an increase in these hours results in an increase in GNP

- Average workweek of production workers in manufacturing

- Average weekly initial claims for state unemployment insurance

- New orders for consumer goods and materials, adjusted for inflation

- Supplier or vendor performance levels (e.g., companies receiving slower and missed deliveries from suppliers)

- Manufacturers' new orders for nonmilitary capital goods purchases, adjusted for inflation, and excluding aircraft

- New building permits issued and permits issued for new private housing units

- Index of stock prices of 500 common stocks

- Money supply (M2 adjusted for inflation)

- Interest rate spread on 10-year Treasury bonds minus federal funds

- Institute of Supply Management issues a purchasing managers' index (PMI) for purchasing of materials going into manufacturing production

- Index of consumer expectations for business conditions

- Consumer price index (CPI)

- Producer price index (PPI), where PMI is used, in part, to calculate the PPI
- Leading credit index
- PMI's new orders index

Diffusion indexes are highly correlated with growth rates expressed by leading indicators. That is, a low diffusion index is associated with low growth rates, and a high diffusion index is associated with high growth rates. When a diffusion index is 40%, it means that 60% of the leading indicators have fallen.

(ii) Coincident Indicators

Coincident indicators change at the same time as other variables change. Examples include inflation, unemployment, and consumer confidence. The coincident economic index is used primarily as a tool for dating the business cycle (i.e., determining turning points such as cyclical peaks and troughs). Manufacturing and trade sales volume will determine whether a business cycle is turning into peaks or troughs.

Examples of coincident indicators from the U.S. Conference Board (www.conference-board.org) include:

- Manufacturing and trade sales volume
- Employees on nonagricultural payroll
- Industrial production (i.e., durable goods and nondurable goods)
- Personal income minus transfer payments, where the latter includes government benefits paid to citizens such as Social Security, disability, annuities, welfare, and retirement

(iii) Lagging Indicators

Lagging indicators change after the other variables change. These are more accurate than the other indicators, but the information is much less useful for decision making. For example, unemployment figures are lagging indicators of recession.

Examples of lagging indicators from the U.S. Conference Board (www.conference-board.org) include:

- Average duration of unemployment in weeks and months
- Inventories to sales ratio for manufacturing and trade business
- Change in labor cost per unit of output in manufacturing
- Average prime interest rates from the central bank (lender bank) to borrower banks
- Commercial and industrial loan volume
- A ratio of consumer installment credit outstanding to personal income
- Change in CPI for services

(iv) Composite Economic Index

The composite economic index is one integrated index based on three individual indicators: leading, coincident, and lagging indicators. The composite economic indexes are the key elements in an analytic system designed to signal peaks and troughs in the business cycle. Composite indexes are constructed to summarize and reveal common turning points and patterns in economic data in a clearer and more convincing manner than any individual component (i.e., leading, coincident, and lagging), primarily because they smooth out some of the volatility of individual components.

(f) Key Economic Indicators

Businesses use macroeconomic forecasts in making investment and production decisions. When they foresee an economic downturn, businesses may reduce their inventories. When prices are expected to rise quickly, businesses buy goods in advance and add to equipment and plant. These decisions are based on these key economic indicators: gross domestic product (GDP) gross national product (GNP), net national product (NNP), consumer price index (CPI), producer price index (PPI), balance of payments (BOP), and balance of trade (BOT).

(i) Gross Domestic Product

GDP is the total market value of final goods and services produced by a country in a given year. It measures total output of a country. The two main variables that contribute to increases in a nation's real GDP are labor productivity and total worker hours. GDP is computed as follows:

$$GDP = Consumption + Investment + Government\ purchases + Net\ exports$$

Where Consumption = Purchases by consumers

Investment = Purchases by private sector firms

Government purchases = Purchases by all levels of government

Net exports = Net purchases by foreign sectors (i.e., net exports are equal to domestic exports minus domestic imports).

Economic growth is the sustained increase in real GDP over a long period of time. Real GDP takes price changes into account; nominal GDP takes current prices into account.

Real GDP per hour is a general indicator of hourly productivity. Real GDP per capita is an indicator of overall wealth in a country. Real GDP results from after adjusting for or incorporating the inflation. It is the usual measure of living standards across time periods in a country and between countries. Usually increases in productivity signal a potential for increases in a country's standard of living.

The GDP deflator is the most appropriate inflation index to use when a company is attempting to estimate the inflation rate on all goods and services over a recent time period. This deflator is a measure of the average price level in a country's economy. Exports and imports, as well as all components of nominal and real GDP, enter the calculations for GDP deflators.

Sharp swings in quarterly GDP deflators are often caused by changes in prices for oil, apparel, and computers as well as by annual wage increases for government employees and occasionally by drought or other disasters affecting crops and commodities.

GDP deflator is calculated as follows:

$$GDP\ deflator = [(Nominal\ GDP)\ /\ Real\ GDP)] \times 100$$

EXAMPLE

Real GDP in year 2018 is $50,000, which is the base year with an index of 100. Nominal GDP in year 2018 is $60,000. What is the GDP deflator for 2019, and what percentage did prices increase between the two years?

$$\text{GDP deflator for 2019} = (\$60,000) / (\$50,000) \times 100 = 112$$

$$\text{Price increase} = (112 - 100) / 100 = 0.12 = 12\%$$

(ii) Gross National Product

GNP is GDP plus total income earned worldwide by U.S. firms and residents. The sale of final goods is included in the GNP; the sale of intermediate goods is excluded from the GNP. *GNP is all inclusive and better than GDP due to its comprehensiveness.*

$$\text{GNP} = \text{GDP} + \text{Worldwide income earned}$$

The GNP price deflator is a measure of the change in prices for all final goods and services produced in the economy. This inflation index can be used to estimate the inflation rate on all goods and services over a recent time period.

KEY CONCEPTS TO REMEMBER: GNP

- The GNP is a measure of quantity, not quality. Hence, it measures national economic performance, market-oriented activity, and the size of national output, not improvements in product quality.

- GNP will rise with an increase in government purchases of services (i.e., government spending).

- GNP will fall following an increase in imports.

- An increase in the average hours worked per week of production workers would provide a leading indicator of a future increase in GNP.

(iii) Net National Product

NNP equals GNP minus depreciation. NNP is composed of the total market value of all final goods and services produced in the economy in one year minus the capital consumption allowance (i.e., depreciation).

$$\text{NNP} = \text{GNP} - \text{Depreciation}$$

Depreciation is a reduction in the accounting value (not the real value) of capital assets (e.g., buildings, machinery, and equipment) over a time period of one year due to physical wear and tear and technological obsolescence.

Economic growth is defined and measured in two ways: (1) as the increase in real GNP or NNP, which occurs over a specific period of time, or (2) as the increase in real GNP or NNP per capita, which occurs over a range of time period.

(iv) Consumer Price Index

CPI measures the cost of a fixed basket of goods chosen to represent the consumption pattern of a typical consumer. It is a statistic used to measure price changes in a market basket of selected items.

The CPI is one factor in setting the cost of living index (COLI) and cost of living adjustments (COLA) in a country. Critics of CPI argue that it overstates increases in the cost of living due to the constant composition of the market basket of items whose prices are measured. The chain-weighted index is a method for calculating changes in prices that uses an average of base years from neighboring years.

$$CPI \longrightarrow COLI \longrightarrow COLA$$

WHAT IS INCLUDED IN THE CPI CALCULATION?

Eight categories of the CPI include food and beverages, housing, apparel, transportation, medical care, recreation, education and communication, and other goods and services (e.g., haircuts, college tuition, and bank fees).

Taxes directly associated with the prices of specific goods and services, such as sales and excise taxes, are also included. The CPI includes various governmental charged user fees, such as water and sewage charges, auto registration fees, and vehicle tolls. Taxes not directly associated with the purchase of consumer goods and services, such as income taxes and Social Security taxes, are excluded. In addition, the CPI does not include investment items, such as stocks, bonds, real estate, and life insurance, because they relate to savings, not daily living expenses.

Only urban residents (consumers) are included in the CPI calculation. Excluded from the population are rural residents outside metropolitan areas, all farm residents, the military personnel, and individuals in institutions.

EXAMPLE

Assume that in 2015 a business analyst is making $40,000 per year and five years later his income increases to $90,000. The CPI increases from 100 to 250 during this period. What is the real income in 2015 prices for the later years?

The real income (in 2015 prices) for the later years is as follows:

Inflation rate = (250 − 100) / 250 = 150 / 250 = 0.60 = 60%

Real income = Nominal income − Inflation rate = 100% − 60% = 40%

Therefore, real income in 2015 prices is:

$90,000 × 0.40 = $36,000

(v) Producer Price Index

Producer price index (PPI) measures the price of a basket of commodities at the point of their first commercial sale by producers or manufacturers to consumers. Actually, PPI measures changes in net unit revenues received by U.S. producers. Taxes received by the government are not included. PPI includes sales promotions and rebates offered by manufacturers but does not include car dealer rebates offered to customers. The PPI attempts to capture actual transaction prices, not list prices. Purchasing managers' index (PMI) is a composite index based on data from a monthly report on producers' or manufacturers' prices. PMI is an input into the calculation of PPI.

CPI VERSUS PPI

CPI reflects price changes occurring from a purchaser's or consumer's perspective whereas PPI measures price changes occurring from a seller's or manufacturer's perspective. The difference between CPI and PPI is due to processing, distribution, shipping, and selling costs and producer's and distributor's costs and profits. PPI does not include retailer's costs and profits.

(vi) Balance of Payments

Balance of payments (BOP) deals with an accounting of money inflows and money outflows in a year for a country.

$$\text{Money inflows} = \text{Price of exports} + \text{Other factors}$$

$$\text{Money outflows} = \text{Price of imports} + \text{Other factors}$$

$$\text{BOP} = \text{Money inflows} - \text{Money outflows} \pm \text{Other factors}$$

Examples of other factors influencing the BOP are tourism, military expenditures, foreign investment, financial aid given to other countries, and financial aid received from other countries.

(vii) Balance of Trade

Balance of trade (BOT) is the simple ratio of a country's exports to imports. Note that GNP decreases as imports increases.

$$\text{BOT} = \text{Exports/Imports}$$

(g) Business Forecasting

Business conditions relate to business cycles. Decisions such as ordering inventory, borrowing money, increasing staff, and spending capital are dependent on the current and predicted business cycle. For example, decision making in preparation for a recession, such as cost reduction and cost containment, is especially different and difficult. Also, during a recession, defaults on loans can increase due to bankruptcies and unemployment.

Timing is everything when it comes to making good cycle-sensitive decisions. Managers need to make appropriate cutbacks prior to the beginning of a recession. Similarly, managers cannot get caught short during a period of rapid expansion. Economic forecasting is a necessity for predicting business cycles and swings. Trend analysis, economic surveys, opinions, and simulation techniques are useful to managers trying to stay abreast of the latest economic developments.

APPLICATIONS OF BUSINESS FORECASTING

The following is a list of applications of business forecasting, mainly to develop future estimates of important business factors or variables of interest to management.

- Sales in physical units, sales in dollars, sales by region, sales by quarter, and sales per year

- Operating costs, product costs, service costs, overhead costs, and payroll costs

- Cash flows (inflows and outflows), cash needs, debt needs, and dividend needs (i.e., dividend payout ratio)

- Earnings per share, dividends per share, and stock market price for share, and a company's market share

- Operating budget needs and capital budget needs

- Impact of changes in interest rates, inflation rates, employment rates, and wage rates on earnings and profits

- Simulation of factory equipment breakdowns and key parts replacement times

- Performing sensitivity analysis (what-if analysis) to solve business problems in finance, manufacturing, and marketing

Businesses use economic forecasts in making investment and production decisions. When they foresee an economic downturn, they may reduce inventories. When prices are expected to rise quickly, they buy goods in advance and add to equipment and plant.

Statistical models are most successful when past circumstances can be used to predict future events. Economic models use historical data to develop predictive models. Current input to the model provides meaningful results only if the important factors retain the same proportional significance. During the energy crisis of the early 1970s, most economic models performed very poorly because key relationships had changed. Predictive models improved once new historical patterns emerged.

The opposite of forecasting economic events is measuring economic events. This historical information is important in evaluating and providing information for predicting the future. The business cycle is the up-and-down movement of an economy's ability to generate wealth. Historical economic data show a clear pattern of alternating recessions and expansions. In between there have been peaks and troughs of varying magnitude and duration. Business cycles have a predictable structure but variable timing.

The simplest form of forecasting is the projection of past trends called extrapolation. Model building activities are examples of analytical techniques. A model breaks down a major problem into parts or subproblems and solves the parts sequentially. Some examples of applications of forecasting models in managerial accounting are pricing, costs, revenue, and inventory decisions.

For example, when forecasting purchases of inventory for a firm, factors such as knowledge of the behavior of business cycles, econometrics, and information on the seasonal variations in demand are important.

Models require a set of predetermined procedures. If there are no well-ordered and fully developed procedures, there is no need to model. That is, no procedure, no model. For example, a onetime crisis situation cannot be modeled due to lack of a preset procedure.

A key concept in all forecasting models dealing with probabilities is expected value. Expected value equals the sum of the products of the possible payoffs and their probabilities.

(i) Time-Series Analysis

Time-series analysis is the process by which a set of data measured over time is analyzed. Decision makers need to understand how to analyze past data if they expect to incorporate past information into future decisions. Although the factors that affect the future are uncertain, the past often offers a good indication of what the future will hold. The key is to know how to extract the meaningful information from all the available past data.

All time series contain at least one of four time-series components: long-term trend, seasonal, cyclical, and random or irregular components. Time-series analysis involves breaking down data measured over time into one or more of these components. Time-series analysis is similar to regression analysis in that both techniques help to explain the variability in data as much as possible. The four components of time-series analysis help explain that variability (see Exhibit 1.67). The purpose of time-series analysis is to use these components to explain the total variability in past data. The problem is how best to separate each component from the others so that each can be analyzed clearly.

EXHIBIT 1.67 Components of Time Series

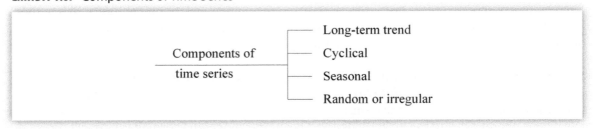

(A) Long-Term Trend

The trend component is the long-term increase (growth) or decrease (decline) in a variable being measured over time. An example is annual sales over the past 10 to 15 years. Because long-term forecasting is becoming increasingly important due to severe global competition, the trend component in time-series analysis is important to all organizations.

Long-term growth patterns have a wide variety of shapes, such as the first-degree, exponential, and Gompertz curves. The easiest method to fit trend lines to a series of data is to graph the data and draw the trend line freehand. Another way of fitting a trend line to a set of data is to use the least square regression method.

(B) Cyclical Component

In addition to the seasonal component, data can contain certain cyclical effects. Cyclical effects in a time series are represented by fluctuations around a long-term trend. These fluctuations are thought to be caused by pulsations in factors such as interest rates, money supply, consumer demand, market conditions, and government policies. Cyclical fluctuations repeat themselves in a general pattern in the long term but occur with differing frequencies and intensities. Thus, they can be isolated but not totally predicted. Firms affected by cyclical fluctuations are those vulnerable to unexpected changes in the economy. The effect is different each time the fluctuation occurs.

Cyclical variations in time-series data do not repeat themselves in a regular pattern as do seasonal factors, but they cannot be considered random variations in the data either.

Organizations hardest hit by the cyclical component are those connected with items purchased with discretionary income (e.g., big-ticket items, such as home appliances and automobiles). Because consumers can postpone purchasing these items, organizations that produce them are most affected by economic downturns.

The cyclical component is isolated by first removing the long-term trend and seasonal factors from the time-series data. Then statistical normal values are calculated by multiplying the trend value by the seasonal index values. Finally, the cyclical component, which also contains the irregular component, is determined for each time period.

(C) Seasonal Component

The seasonal component represents those changes in a time series that occur at the same time every year. An example is peak sales occurring once in the spring and once in the fall.

Some organizations (e.g., toy stores, food processors, lumber mills) are affected not only by long-term trends but also by seasonal variations. The demand for products or services is highly dependent on the time of year. Organizations that face seasonal variations are interested in knowing how well or poorly they are doing relative to the normal seasonal variation. The question is whether the increase or decrease is more or less than expected, or whether it occurs at more or less than the average rate.

A seasonal index known as the ratio to moving average can be calculated to measure seasonal variation in a time series. A 12-month moving average is used here. Seasonal variation affects the overall planning process, especially in labor requests, inventory levels, training needs, and periodic maintenance work.

Some prefer to eliminate irregular components in the data by taking the normalized average of the ratio to moving averages. A requirement prior to separating the irregular components from the data is to make sure that the ratio to moving averages is stable from year to year. Another assumption to be made prior to eliminating irregular components is that the irregular fluctuations are caused by purely random circumstances.

(D) Random or Irregular Component

The **random or irregular component** is the one that cannot be attributed to any of the three components already discussed (long-term trend, seasonal, and cyclical components) (see Exhibit 1.68). Random fluctuations can be caused by many factors, such as economic failures, weather, political events.

FIGURE 1.68 Types of Irregular Fluctuations

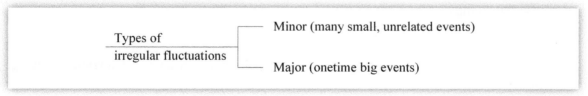

Minor irregularities show up as sawtooth-like patterns around the long-term trend. Individually they are not significant, but collectively they can be significant and can cause problems or many organizations.

LARGE VERSUS SMALL IRREGULAR VARIATIONS

■ Large irregular variations cause greater problems.

■ Small irregular variations cause lesser problems.

Major irregularities are significant one-time, unpredictable changes in the time series due to such extended and uncontrolled factors as war, oil embargoes, summer droughts, or severe winter storms.

Almost all industries and organizations are affected by irregular components. Agriculture, insurance, and mining companies will be more interested in this component. Minor irregularities can be smoothed out by using a moving average method. The goal is to eliminate as much as possible the irregular influences so that the true seasonal and cyclical components can be recognized and used. *A random component is unwanted. Buying insurance coverage is one way to mitigate risks resulting from major irregular fluctuations.*

(ii) Time-Series Models

The scope of time-series models includes the naive (intuitive) approach, moving averages, exponential smoothing, and trend projection. The **naive approach** assumes that demand in the next period will be equal to demand in the most recent period. The **moving-averages** method uses an average of the most recent periods of data to forecast the next period. The **exponential smoothing** method uses a weighted-moving-average technique in which data points are weighted by an exponential function. The **trend projection** method fits a trend line to a series of historical data points and then projects the line into the future.

The following formulas are related to time-series models:

$$\text{Moving average} = (\text{Sum of demand in previous n periods}) \, / \, n$$

$$\text{New forecast using exponential smoothing} = (\text{Last period's forecast}) + \text{alpha} (\text{Last period's actual demand} - \text{Last period's forecast})$$

where alpha = a weight (smoothing constant) with a value between 0 and 1 (The value of alpha can be high if more weight is given to recent data and can be low if more weight is given to past data.)

$$\text{Trend line using the least-squares method} = y = a + b \, x$$

where y = intercept (height)
b = slope (angle of the line)

Examples: Business applications of time-series forecasting methods include these types of forecasting: sales (demand), profit, cash, bank interest rates, foreign currency exchange rates, and inventory.

Time-series analysis use past data points to project future data points and have four components: trends (upward or downward data movement), seasonality (data patterns that repeats itself periodically in weeks and months), cycles (data patterns that occur every several years that tied into the business cycles), and random variation (no data patterns shown as bumps or blips in the data caused by chance and unusual conditions; hence cannot be predicted).

(iii) Regression Analysis

Regression analysis is a statistical technique used to measure the extent to which a change in the value of one variable, the independent variable, tends to be accompanied by a change in the value of another variable, the dependent variable.

Most measures of associations are nondirectional; that is, when calculated, it is not necessary to indicate which variable is hypothesized to influence the other. Measures of association show to what degree, on a 0 to 1 scale, two variables are linked.

DEFINITION OF KEY TERMS: Regression Analysis

- Analysis of covariance. A method of analyzing the differences in the means of two or more groups of cases while taking account of variation in one or more interval ratio variables.

- **Analysis of variance.** A method for analyzing the differences in the means of two or more groups of cases.

- **Asymmetric measure of association.** A measure of association that makes a distinction between independent and dependent variables.

- **Auxiliary variable.** Another name for "independent variable."

- **Correlation.** A synonym for "association." Correlation is one of several measures of association. Correlation means the interdependence between two sets of numbers or a relation between two quantities, such that when one changes, the other changes. Simultaneous increasing or decreasing of quantities is called positive correlation; when one quantity increases while the other decreases, it is called negative correlation.

- **Dependent variable.** A variable that may, it is believed, be predicted by or caused by one or more other variables called independent variables. It will show the effect.

- **Discriminant analysis.** A tool for discriminating between effective and ineffective policies or procedures. It is based on subjective assessment (not on statistics) and discrete values.

- **Explanatory variable.** Another name for "independent variable."

- **Independent variable.** A variable that may, it is believed, predict or cause fluctuation in a dependent variable.

- **Primary variable.** Another name for "dependent variable."

- **Regression.** The line of average relationship between the dependent (or primary) variable and the independent (or auxiliary) variable.

- **Regression analysis.** A method for determining the association between a dependent variable and one or more independent variables.

- **Regression coefficient.** A measure of change in a primary variable associated with a unit change in the auxiliary variable. An asymmetric measure of association; a statistic computed as part of a regression analysis.

- **Regression estimate.** An estimate of a population parameter for one variable that is obtained by substituting the known total for another variable into a regression equation calculated on the basis of the sample values of the two variables. Note that ratio estimates are special kinds of regression estimates.

- **Symmetric measure of association.** A measure of association that does not make a distinction between independent and dependent variables.

Managers often need to determine the relationships between two or more variables prior to making a decision, for predicting and planning purposes, or when analyzing a problem. When two variables are involved, simple linear regression and correlation analysis are the statistical tools most often applied for decision making. They provide a basis for analyzing two variables and their relationship to each other.

When more than two variables are involved, multiple regression analysis will be useful. Where only one independent variable is involved in the analysis, the technique is known as simple regression analysis; where two or more independent variables are involved, the technique is called multiple regression analysis (see Exhibit 1.69).

EXHIBIT 1.69   Simple Regression and Multiple Regression

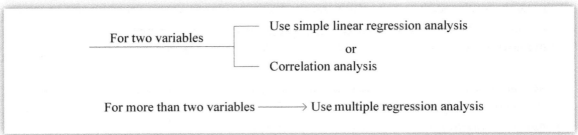

The basic diagram, or scatter plot, can be used to depict potential relationships between a dependent variable Y (e.g., sales) and an independent variable X (e.g., advertising). The scatter plot provides a visual feel for the relationship between variables (qualitative measurement). A dependent variable is the variable whose variation is of interest. An independent variable (or explanatory variable) is a variable used to explain variation in the dependent variable. Three possible relationships can emerge from scatter plots: linear, curvilinear, and no relationship (see Exhibit 1.70).

EXHIBIT 1.70   Scatter Plot Relationships

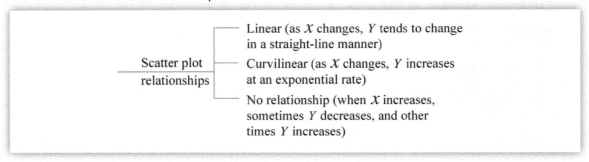

1. **Linear relationship.** As X changes, Y tends to change in a straight line or nearly straight-line manner. The change can be positive (Y increases as X increases) or negative (Y decreases as X increases).

2. **Curvilinear relationship.** As X increases, Y increases at an exponential rate (e.g., as production increases, overtime is increasing at an exponential rate). As X increases, Y increases at a diminishing rate (e.g., when advertising is allowed to grow too large, diminishing returns will occur for sales).

3. **No relationship.** When X increases, sometimes Y decreases; other times, Y increases.

In addition to qualitative measurement (i.e., visual feel), quantitative measurement using the correlation coefficient is needed to measure the strength between two variables. The correlation coefficient can range from a perfect positive correlation (+1.0) to a perfect negative correlation (−1.0). If two variables have no linear relationship, the correlation between them is 0. Consequently, the more the correlation differs from 0, the stronger the linear relationship between the two variables. The sign of the correlation coefficient indicates the direction of the relationship but does not aid in determining its strength.

EXAMPLE

Given four values of correlation coefficient −0.15, −0.75, 0.19, and 0.35, which value indicates the weakest linear association between two variables?

Answer: The value −0.15 has the weakest linear association because it is farther from −1.0 than the other choices.

USES OF REGRESSION ANALYSIS

Two basic uses of regression analysis are as a descriptive tool and as a predictive tool. Some examples of using the descriptive tool are listed next.

- To describe the relationship between a loan's term (number of months) and its dollar value in a bank. A positive linear relationship might exist between time and amount in which smaller loans would tend to be associated with shorter lending periods whereas larger loans would be for longer periods.

- To explain the meaning of economy as viewed by economists.

- To describe the factors that influence the demand for products as presented by market researchers.

Some examples of using the predictive tool are listed next.

- To predict manufacturing production levels

- To forecast annual tax revenues

- To predict inventory levels

Determining whether the linear relationship between sales and advertising is significant requires us to test whether the sample data support or refute the hypothesis that the population correlation coefficient is 0. A t-statistic is used to test the hypothesis that the population coefficient is 0.

The correlation does not imply cause and effect, since two seemingly unconnected variables often are highly correlated. When a correlation exists between two seemingly unrelated variables, the correlation is spurious at best. Even in the case of sales and advertising, one might be tempted to say that a cause and effect exist, but in reality there is no guarantee of a cause-and-effect (C&E) situation.

(A) Simple Linear Regression Analysis

When the relationship between the dependent variable and the independent variable is a straight line (linear), the technique used for prediction and estimation is called the simple linear regression model. Exhibit 1.71 shows simple linear regression where the plotted data represents the heights of boys of various ages. The straight line represents the relationship between height (the dependent variable) and age (the independent variable) as disclosed by regression analysis. If the change in the dependent variable associated with a change in the independent variable does not occur at a constant rate, the relationship can be represented by a curved line and is referred to as curvilinear.

EXHIBIT 1.71 Simple Linear Regression

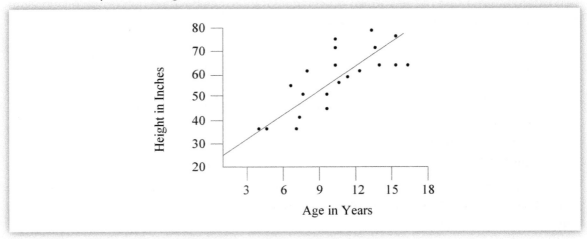

The simple linear regression model is represented by the next equation:

$$Yi = ß0 + ß1Xi + ei$$

where Yi = value of the dependent variable

$ß0$ = Y-intercept (a regression coefficient defining the true population model)

$ß1$ = slope of the regression line (a regression coefficient defining the true population model)

Xi = value of the independent variable

ei = error term or residual (a random component)

The random component is the difference between the actual Y value and the value of Y predicted by the model, and i could be positive or negative, depending on whether a single value of Y for a given X falls above or below the regression line. These ei values will have a mean of 0 and a standard deviation called the standard error of the estimate. If this standard error is too large, the regression model may not be very useful for prediction.

Here the regression model connects the averages of dependent variable Y for each level of independent variable X. The regression line, a straight line, is determined by two values, $ß0$ and $ß1$.

SIMPLE REGRESSION ANALYSIS

In simple regression analysis, the correlation coefficient measures the strength of the linear relationship between any two variables (X and Y); the analysis of variance "F" test indicates whether the regression model explains a significant proportion of variation in the dependent variable.

Managers would like to estimate the true linear relationship between dependent and independent variables by determining the regression model using sample data. A scatter plot can be drawn with the sample data to estimate the population regression line. The least squares criterion is used to select the best line since many possible regression lines exist for a sample of data. According to the least squares criterion, the best regression line is the one that minimizes the sum of squared distances between the observed (X,Y) points and the regression line. *The residual is the difference between the true regression line and the actual Y value.*

(B) Assumptions of the Simple Linear Regression Model

Assumptions of the simple linear regression model are listed next.

- Individual values of the dependent variable, Y, are statistically independent of one another.

- For a given X value, there can exist many values of Y. Further, the distribution of possible Y values for any X value is normal.

- The distribution of possible Y values has equal variances for all values of X.

- The mean average of the dependent variable, Y can be connected by a straight line. The result is called the population regression model.

Some major considerations in using regression analysis as a predictive tool are listed next.

- Conclusions and inferences made from a regression line apply only over the range of data contained in the sample used to develop the regression line. The applicable range of data is called the relevant range of data. Any predictions beyond the relevant range of data lead to overpredictions. Thus, the range of data in the sample should cover the range of data in the population. Only then will a true relationship between the dependent variable and the independent variable emerge.

- A significant linear relationship existing between two variables does not imply that one variable causes the other. Although there may be a C&E relationship, managers should not infer the presence of such a relationship based only on regression and/or correlation analysis. Other factors, such as judgment, experience, and knowledge of the specific area of interest, should also be considered.

- A C&E relationship between two variables is not necessary for regression analysis to be used for prediction. It is important to make sure that the regression model accurately reflects the relationship between the two variables and that the relationship remains stable.

- A high coefficient of determination (R^2) does not guarantee that the regression model will be a good predictor. The R^2 applies only to the sample data—measuring the fit of the regression line to the sample data—not to any other data.

The least squares regression line minimizes the sum of squared residuals. This value is called the sum of squares error (SSE). It represents the amount of variation in the dependent variable that is not explained by the least squares regression line; the amount of variation in the dependent variable that is explained by the regression line is called the sum of squares regression (SSR).

$$SSR = TSS - SSE$$

where TSS = total sum of squares explaining the amount of total variation in the dependent variable

The percentage of the total variable in the dependent variable that is explained by the independent variable is called the coefficient of determination (R^2). R^2 can be a value between 0 and 1.0. R^2 indicates how well the linear regression line fits the data points (X,Y). *The better the fit, the closer R^2 will be to 1.0.*

INTERPRETATION OF COEFFICIENT OF DETERMINATION (R^2)

- R^2 is 1.0 when there is a perfect linear relationship between two variables.

- R^2 will be close to zero when there is a weak linear relationship or no linear relationship at all.

When R^2 is 1.0, it corresponds to a situation in which the least squares regression line would pass through each of the points in the scatter plot. The least squares criterion ensures that R^2 will be maximized. R^2 applies only to the sample data used to develop the model.

APPLICATION OF REGRESSION ANALYSIS

XYZ Company derived the following cost relationship from a regression analysis of its monthly manufacturing overhead cost:

$$C = \$80,000 + \$12\,M$$

where C = monthly manufacturing overhead cost

M = machine hours

The standard error of estimate of the regression is $6,000. The standard time required to manufacture a case of the company's single product is four machine hours. XYZ applies manufacturing overhead to production on the basis of machine hours, and its normal annual production is 50,000 cases.

Question: What is the estimated variable manufacturing overhead cost for a month in which scheduled production is 5,000 cases?

Answer: In the cost equation C = $80,000 + $12M, $80,000 is the fixed cost component and $12M is the variable cost component. That is, $12 × 5,000 cases × 4 machine hours per case = $240,000.

Question: What is the predetermined fixed manufacturing overhead rate?

Answer: Since $80,000 is the fixed component per month, we need to multiply this by 12 to obtain one-year fixed cost. The predetermined overhead rate per machine hour is ($80,000 × 12) / (50,000 × 4) = $4.80.

The linear regression equation, Y = 15.8 + 1.1(x), was used to prepare the next data table.

Actual X	Predicted Y	Actual Y	Residual
0	15.8	10	−5.8
1	16.9	18	1.1
2	18.0	27	9.0
3	19.1	21	1.9
4	20.2	14	−6.2

Question: What do you conclude from the data table?

Answer: The best description of the data is that the relationship is not linear. A linear equation was used with a nonlinear relationship. If the relationship was linear, the results of actual Y would have been higher than or equal to 15.8; it is not. Two values (10 and 14) are less than 15.8, indicating a non-linear relationship.

(C) Multiple Regression Analysis

Regression analysis is used for prediction and description to determine the relationship between two or more variables. The multiple regression analysis technique analyzes the relationship between three or more variables and is an extension of simple regression analysis. *In simple regression analysis, there is only one independent variable. In multiple regression analysis, there is more than one independent variable.* Exhibit 1.72 presents a comparison between simple regression and multiple regression analysis.

EXHIBIT 1.72 Comparison between Simple Regression and Multiple Regression

Characteristics of Simple Regression	**Characteristics of Multiple Regression**
Sales is a dependent variable, and advertising expenditures are an independent variable.	House price is a dependent variable. Square footage of house, age of house, number of bedrooms, and number of bathrooms are examples of independent variables.
The model is an equation for a straight line in a two-dimensional space.	The model forms a hyperplane through multidimensional space.
Each regression coefficient represents a slope and involves a matrix algebra.	Each regression coefficient represents a slope and involves a matrix algebra.
A graph or calculator can be used to solve the problem. Use of computer is optional.	Computers must be used to solve the problem.
The correlation coefficient is calculated.	The correlation matrix is calculated.

From a theoretical viewpoint, the sample size required to compute a regression model must be at least one greater than the number of independent variables; that is, for a model with four independent variables, the absolute minimum number of case samples required is five. Otherwise, the model will produce meaningless values. From a practical standpoint, the sample size should be at least four times the number of independent variables.

SIMPLE REGRESSION VERSUS MULTIPLE REGRESSION

■ When there are two variables (one dependent and one independent), we call it a bivariate or simple regression.

■ When there are more than two variables (one dependent and more than one independent), we call it a multivariate or multiple regression.

■ The multivariate model offers a better fit than the bivariate model.

(D) Assumptions of the Multiple Regression Model

The next list provides assumptions about the multiple regression model.

- The errors are normally distributed.

- The mean of the error terms is zero.

- The error terms have a constant variance for all combined values of the independent variables.

In multiple regression analysis, additional independent variables are added to the regression model to explain some of the yet-unexplained variation in the dependent variable. Adding appropriate additional variables would reduce the standard error of the estimate where the value of the latter is too large for the regression model to be useful for prediction.

The correlation matrix is useful for determining which independent variables are likely to help explain variation in the dependent variable. A value of ± 1.0 indicates that changes in the independent variable are linearly related to changes in the dependent variable.

Similar to simple regression, multiple regression uses R^2, the multiple coefficient determination, and is determined as shown in the following example:

EXAMPLE

If R^2 is 0.75, then 75% of the variation in the dependent variable can be explained by all independent variables in the multiple regression model.

When highly correlated independent variables are included in the regression model, a condition of overlapping called **multicollinearity** can exist. Specifically, when two independent variables are correlated with each other, adding redundant information to the model, multicollinearity does exist in practice. The best practical advice is to drop the independent variable(s) that is (are) the main cause of the multicollinearity problems from the model.

Multicollinearity influences the regression model negatively—the regression coefficient sign is the opposite of the expected sign. The independent variable causing multicollinearity is not necessary to the functioning of the model and hence can be removed without any loss. It is highly correlated with other independent variables and has low correlation with the dependent variable.

(E) Symptoms of Multicollinearity in Regression

Symptoms of multicollinearity in regression analysis are listed next.

- Incorrect signs on the coefficients

- Values of the previous coefficients change when a new variable is added to the model

- A previously significant variable changes to insignificant when a new variable is added to the model

- An increase in the standard error of the estimate when a variable is added to the model

Not all independent variables contribute to the explanation of the variation in a dependent variable. Some variables are significant but not all are. *The significance of each independent variable can be tested using a "t" test. The test is calculated by dividing the regression coefficient by the standard deviation of the regression coefficients.*

"F" TEST VERSUS "t" TEST

■ The "F" test is used to explain the significance of just one independent variable.

■ The "t" test is used to explain the significance of each independent variable. Multicollinearity affects the "t" test.

The regression model used for prediction should contain significant independent variables only. If insignificant variables exist, they should be removed and the regression model rerun before it is used for prediction purposes. Any coefficient with an unexpected sign indicates a problem condition. An unexpected sign implies unreasonable relationships between variables.

Developing a multiple regression model is an art. Judgment is required when selecting the best set of independent variables for the model that are less in conflict and contribute to the best predictor.

(F) Dummy Variables in Regression Models

When an independent variable in a regression model is a nominal or ordinal variable, it is called a qualitative variable. For example, in a model for predicting individual income, each manager may assign different values for a potential qualitative variable—for example, sex (male or female)—affecting the regression analysis.

In order to assign unique numerical values for these qualitative variables, dummy variables are added to the regression model. Rules for dummy variables include:

■ If the qualitative variable has two possible categories (e.g., male or female), one dummy variable is added.

■ For more than two possible categories, one less than the number of possible categories is added (i.e., for five categories, only four dummy variables).

Not following these rules can introduce unwanted multicollinearity and the fact that least squares regression estimates cannot be obtained if the number of dummy variables equals the number of possible categories. Dummy variables take on values of 0 and 1, and they represent the qualitative variables in the regression analysis.

(G) Regression Methods

Basically, there are two methods for developing a regression model: ordinary regression and stepwise regression (see Exhibit 1.73).

EXHIBIT 1.73 Regression Methods

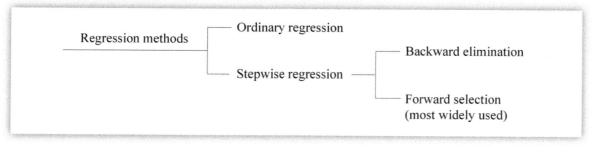

In the **ordinary regression method,** all independent variables are brought into the model at one step. The **stepwise regression method** develops the least squares regression equation in steps, through either backward elimination or forward selection.

Backward Elimination. The backward elimination stepwise method begins by developing an ordinary regression model using all independent variables. All insignificant independent variables are eliminated in a stepwise fashion. The only independent variables left are the ones that have coefficients that are significantly different from zero. The advantage of this method is that the manager has the opportunity to look at all the independent variables in the model before removing variables that are not significant.

Forward Selection. The forward selection procedure works in the opposite direction from the backward elimination procedure. It begins by selecting a single independent variable that is highly significant—the one highly correlated with the dependent variable. In the next step, a second independent variable is selected based on its ability to explain the remaining unexplained variation in the dependent variable.

The forward selection procedure prevents multicollinearity from occurring. It does this by dropping an insignificant variable that is causing the overlap from occurring. The forward selection procedure is widely used in decision-making applications and is generally recognized as a useful regression method. Because the selection process is automatic by the computer, managers need to use judgment to make sure the regression model is usable and meaningful.

(H) Econometrics

The application of statistical methods to economic data is called **econometrics**. Econometrics analyzes the relationships between two or more economic variables and uses multiple regression analysis.

EXAMPLE

Recent events caused the time-series forecasting model used by an electric utility company to become too unpredictable for practical use. An econometric model is developed to predict the demand for electricity (i.e., usage volume and sales revenue) based on factors such as class of service (residential or commercial), population growth (increasing or decreasing), and unemployment in the area of service (increasing or decreasing). Since there are three independent variables (i.e., service, growth, and unemployment), multiple regression analysis is used instead of the time-series model.

(iv) Sensitivity Analysis

Sensitivity analysis ("what-if" analysis) is an evaluation of how certain changes in inputs results in what changes in outputs of a model or system. It also deals with what changes in assumptions produce what changes in outcomes. (see Exhibit 1.74).

EXHIBIT 1.74 Scope of Sensitivity Analysis

	Lead to	
Changes in inputs	⟶	Changes in outputs
Changes in assumptions	Lead to ⟶	Changes in outcomes

The primary reason that sensitivity analysis is important to managers is that real-world problems exist in a dynamic environment. Change is inevitable. Prices of raw materials change as demand fluctuates, and changes in the labor market cause changes in production costs. Sensitivity analysis provides managers with the information needed to respond to such changes without rebuilding the model. Moreover, sensitivity analysis promotes the management-by-exception theory, meaning it focuses on abnormal things, not on normal things. For example, bank management can use the sensitivity analysis technique to determine the effects of policy changes on the optimal mix for its portfolio of earning assets.

Computer simulation techniques can be used to perform sensitivity analysis. The ability to ask what-if questions is one of the biggest advantages of computer simulation. In a way, what-if analysis deals with a Q&A session, meaning it asks a question and gets an answer. Sensitivity analysis, scenario analysis, and simulation techniques are used to measure a standalone risk. The next sections present sensitivity analysis for manufacturing applications, linear programming applications, financial applications, network applications, and inventory applications.

(A) Manufacturing Applications

The linking of production process improvement to financial results is critical to a successful computer-integrated manufacturing implementation. Management has established priorities to decrease process variability, shorten feedback time, and reduce support functions. A process model was developed with these parameters: facilities and equipment cost, theoretical materials consumption, actual materials consumption, and supplies cost. Sensitivity analysis was used to study the behavior of those parameters.

Sensitivity analysis was applied to the process model to compare the cash flows associated with various plan alternatives. Testing the model for changes in several parameters indicated that the model is sensitive to process inefficiency, product yields, volume variation, and price variations. Conversely, the model is relatively insensitive to change in labor costs.

The relationships between increased labor efficiency and gross profit can be studied using sensitivity analysis in a manufacturing plant environment.

Sensitivity analysis is the study of how changes in the coefficient of a linear program affect the optimal solution. The optimal solution is a feasible solution that maximizes or minimizes the value of the objective function. The objective function is used to measure the profit or cost of a particular solution.

(B) Linear Programming Applications

Sensitivity analysis associated with the optimal solution provides valuable supplementary information for decision makers. In the linear programming case, sensitivity analysis can be used to answer questions such as:

- How will a change in the coefficient of the objective function affect the optimal solution?
- How will a change in the right-hand side value for a constraint affect the optimal solution?

However, there is one prerequisite prior to making these changes: The optimal solution to the original linear programming problem needs to be in place. The changes are applied to the optimal solution. For this reason, sensitivity analysis is often called postoptimality analysis. For example, in a production environment, sensitivity analysis can help determine how much each additional labor hour is worth and how many hours can be added before diminishing returns set in.

(C) Financial Applications

Integer linear programming techniques have been used successfully to solve capital budgeting problems. Only the integer variables are permitted to ensure the values of 0 or 1. The variables could be either all integers or mixed integers. Fractional values of the decision variable are not allowed. The firm's goal is to select the most profitable projects and budgets for the capital expenditures. The outcome is usually project acceptance (a value of 1) or rejection (a value of 0).

Another advantage of using an integer linear programming technique in capital budgeting is its ability to handle multiple-choice constraints, such as when multiple projects are under consideration and only one project can be selected in the end.

Sensitivity analysis is more critical for integer linear programming problems than that for linear programming problems because a small change in one of the coefficients in the constraints can cause a large change in the value of the optimal solution. An example would be that one additional dollar in the budget can lead to a $20 increase in the return.

(D) Network Applications

Sensitivity analysis can be performed on the network. It provides the ability to check the feasibility of current schedules and to permit management to experiment with or evaluate the effects of proposed changes.

(E) Inventory Applications

It is good to know how much the recommended order quantity would change if the estimated ordering and holding costs had been different. Depending on whether the total annual cost increased, decreased, or remained the same, we can tell whether the EOQ model is sensitive or insensitive to variations in the cost estimates.

(v) Simulation Models

The primary objective of simulation models is to describe the behavior of a real system. A model is designed and developed, and a study is conducted to understand the behavior of the simulation model. The characteristics that are learned from the model are then used to make inferences about the real system. Later the model is modified (asking what-if questions) to improve the system's performance. The behavior of the model in response to the what-if questions is studied to determine how well the real system will respond to the proposed modifications. Thus, the simulation model will help the decision maker by predicting what can be expected in practice. A key requisite is that the logic of the model should be as close to the actual operations as possible. In most cases, a computer is used for simulation models.

Computer simulation should not be viewed as an optimization technique but as a way to improve the behavior or performance of the system. Model parameters are adjusted to improve system performance. When good parameter settings have been found for the model, these settings can be used to improve the performance of the real system.

The three steps involved in a computer simulation model are listed next.

1. A computer simulation model that behaves like or simulates the real-world system is developed.

2. A series of computer runs or experiments is performed to learn about the behavior of the simulation model.

3. The model design is changed to determine if the modifications improve system performance. What-if questions are asked of the model in this step. Thus, the simulation model helps managers predict the future.

Usually, a simulation exercise is conducted on a computer using a computer simulator. The simulator run by the computer program performs mathematical calculations and keeps track of the simulation results. Examples of calculations in a retail store environment include:

- Number of customers serviced at a retail store during the 20 hours of simulated operations.
- The average profit per hour per store
- Number of lost customers at a store per hour
- Average dollar loss per hour per store due to lost customers

(A) Simulation Applications in Forecasting

Some simulation applications in forecasting are listed next.

- To perform a role-play to reflect reality in a person being trained
- To study the performance of a waiting line system
- To simulate traffic flow through a busy street intersection to determine the number of traffic signals required to improve traffic flow
- To simulate airplane flight conditions for training pilots
- To simulate the behavior of an inventory system to determine the best order quantity and reorder point
- To model a dry-run evacuation in an office due to fire in a high-risk building
- To create mock disasters to provide experience in dealing with crisis situations, such as product tampering, power outages, and floods
- To train auditors by providing financial statements and operating data to conduct a financial audit or an operational audit, respectively

(B) Simulation Procedures and Approaches

Computer simulation is performed using the two basic procedures—heuristic and probabilistic—as shown in Exhibit 1.75.

EXHIBIT 1.75 Simulation Procedures

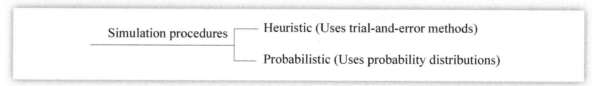

Simulation procedures —— Heuristic (Uses trial-and-error methods)

Probabilistic (Uses probability distributions)

Heuristic procedures do not require probabilistic components. A variety of deterministic values are generated for the decision variables, and the best of the feasible solutions is selected.

When **probabilistic distributions** are involved, it is called the Monte Carlo simulation. Model inputs, such as the number of customer arrivals in a service center, are generated from probability distributions. These models are based on probabilities and time intervals of outcomes. When probabilities are involved, it is called a stochastic model.

Two approaches exist to the logic and record keeping of a simulation model: fixed time period and next event. In the fixed-time-period approach, each time period is of equal length, and the state of the system is updated at either the beginning or the end of each time period. The time between system updates is fixed.

In the next-event approach, the time between arrivals and the time to complete service is randomly generated for a customer. The state of the system is updated each time a customer either arrives or completes service. The time between system updates is variable. Exhibit 1.76 presents advantages and disadvantages of simulation models.

EXHIBIT 1.76 Advantages and Disadvantages of Simulation Models

Advantages	Disadvantages
The models solve complex problems where analytical procedures cannot be used.	There is a high cost of model development for design and programming.
The models provide convenient experimental laboratories. What-if questions can be asked of the models.	The models do not guarantee an optimal solution to a problem. Decision variables are selected that have a good chance of being near the optimal solution. Also, the models do not try all values of the decision variables because doing so would be costly.
The danger of obtaining bad solutions to a problem is slight, and the consequences have no effect on the organization.	
The models can be run long enough to reach a steady state that will enable managers to identify the apparent best decisions.	Simulation may not be able to replicate all situations or complexities that may arise in a real-world case.
Learning is active for participants.	Participants may tend to generalize from the models. Doing so can create a false sense of confidence concerning their ability to cope with reality.
Mistakes are made in a risk-free environment.	
Time spans can be compressed for key problems.	
The models provide immediate feedback concerning proper and improper actions or decisions. Corrective action is timely.	

ANALYTICAL PROCEDURES VERSUS COMPUTER SIMULATION

- Analytical procedures are best used to solve simple problems.
- Computer simulation is best used to solve complex problems.

The sequence of model activities is

Model validation ⟶ Model implementation

Model validation is a step in the simulation procedure.

(C) Simulation Model Validation

Validation involves verifying that the simulation model accurately describes the real-world system it is designed to simulate. The purpose of model validation is to make sure that it is a reasonable reflection of the real world. These methods will help to validate the model:

- The simulation results can be compared with the current and past behavior of the real system. The model is run with an actual set of past observations, and the output is compared directly with the behavior of the actual system.

- The model is reviewed by experts who evaluate the reasonableness of the simulation model and the simulation results.

- The assumptions made during model construction need to be revisited, clarified, expanded, and adjusted as needed.

- The model is peer reviewed or desk-checked by programming staff to detect errors. *Improper programming of the model can lead to inaccurate results.*

- The simulated distributions for the probabilistic components can be compared with the corresponding probability distributions in the real system.

- It is good to collect the data on the system after it has reached a stable or steady-state condition. Management is interested in what happens during "normal" business hours of operation. The steady-state condition of the model is synonymous with the normal hours of operation.

(D) Simulation Model Implementation

Model implementation includes various steps, such as searching for errors, exceptions, gaps between actual and expected, overlaps or duplications between procedures, and root causes of poor implementation.

1.14 Business Skills

This section presents business skills needed for supervisors, managers, executives, leaders, and entrepreneurs. Possessing the right skills can help solve the right business problems, make the right decisions at the right time, properly deal with people, and implement the required controls fully to reduce risks, decrease costs, and increase profits, Lack of business skills in supervisors, managers, executives, leaders, and entrepreneurs can make them inefficient, ineffective, incompetent, inadequate, and incomplete for the job. This section focuses on nine specific skills:

1. Team-building skills
2. Problem-solving and decision-making skills
3. Communication skills
4. Negotiating skills
5. Conflict management skills
6. Team-managing skills
7. Diversity management skills
8. Public-servicing skills
9. Organizational skills

(a) Team-Building Skills

(i) Role of Worker as Individual or Team Member

Every worker has a dual role: as an individual and as a member of a group. A group is defined by functional qualities, not physical properties.[28] A group consists of a minimum of two or more people who interact with, communicate with, and influence each other for a period of time. To comprise a group, a collection of people must share more than circumstances. They must share perceptions and goals. Group members must be aware of, interact with, and exert influence on each other. To communicate with each other, they must both send and receive messages. And they must be engaged in these processes for more than a few moments.

Why do people join groups? Formal or otherwise, there are two common reasons why people join groups: goal attainment and needs gratification. By working together, people can accomplish goals that might be difficult or impossible for solitary individuals to achieve. Additionally, group participation addresses many social needs, such as access to approval, a sense of belonging, friendship, and love.

(A) Individuals in the Group Context

People do not inevitably lose their individuality in groups, although groups may help lessen self-awareness and produce a state of deindividuation. In fact, group membership can heighten certain aspects of the individual experience. Three important effects of the group on the individual are identity, deviance, and social impact (see Exhibit 1.77).

EXHIBIT 1.77 Effects of the Group on the Individual

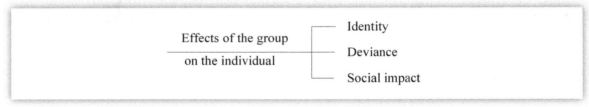

1. **Identity.** Belonging to a group is a form of social categorization: The group becomes one aspect of social identity (e.g., a member of IIA). Reference groups are particularly important in defining not only identity but also aspirations. A reference group is a social network people consult for social comparison. When groups come into contact with each other, individuals may compare their own group favorably to the alternatives available.

2. **Deviance.** Group goals sometimes can override or conflict with the personal goals of individual members. When a member breaks with the group's norms to satisfy personal needs, he or she becomes a deviant. Members of a group are important in validating each other's beliefs. A deviant threatens that validation by defecting and reducing consensus. Ultimately the deviant will most likely be pushed out of the group, thus restoring group consensus with one fewer member.

3. **Social impact.** Social impact theory explains social influence. According to this theory, the degree to which a targeted individual is influenced depends on three factors: the strength of the source of influence, the immediacy of the influence, and the number of sources. Group membership can be seen as having social impact on an individual. Taken factor by factor, a group will have greater influence on each member if it is strong, if the group's influence is immediate, and if the group is large in number.

---

[28] Ann L. Weber, *Social Psychology* (New York: HarperCollins Publishers, Inc.), 1992.

(B) Group Structures

Groups have tasks, such as solving problems and making decisions (task agenda) and meeting the emotional needs and social roles of the group's members (social agenda). Groups meet these two agendas through several key processes and structures: norms, roles, and cohesiveness (see Exhibit 1.78).

EXHIBIT 1.78 Group Processes and Structures

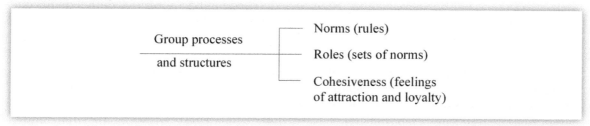

Norms are rules or guidelines for accepted and expected behavior. Some norms are explicit; members know what they are and can explain them to newcomers. Others are implicit or subtle, occasionally taken for granted until a deviation occurs. Most groups have a norm for how decisions are made. For example, a group of coworkers in a small business may agree that important contracts are to be voted on by all members, with a simple majority of more than half ruling. The coworker who tries to play dictator will be violating norms and may be treated as a deviant until the group restores consensus or pushes the deviant out.

Roles are sets of norms defining appropriate behaviors. Groups usually involve roles; some are broad (leaders and followers), while others are more specific. Roles differentiate members' functions and contributions within the group. Roles may be organized according to individual talents. Roles can be a source of reward as well as a source of problems within a group. Group membership offers personal benefits, and group participation achieves goals that solitary individuals may not.

Roles may differ not only in function but also in value to the group. Values are abstract ideas that shape an individual's thinking and behavior. Roles associated with greater prestige or respect are said to have higher-status position or rank. Status affects the way members of the group communicate and work with each other. For example, high-status members, such as bosses and managers, may initiate communication with lower-status members, but not vice versa. A manager can interrupt a subordinate worker to ask a question, but a subordinate worker is not free to enter a manager's office and ask questions without permission. Status can be a reward for specific members, but it carries a cost, since differences in status can be a source of resentment or competition among members.

Two kinds of role conflict commonly occur: person–role conflict and interrole conflict. Person–role conflict is where a person finds his or her group role difficult to perform. For example, a committee member may be required to criticize other members' work but might feel uncomfortable having to do this.

Interrole conflict is where members in different groups compete with each other. For example, a church member may feel conflicted when her company schedules a workshop on a date with church significance. To be a good church member, she should skip the workshop; to be a good employee, she must violate church standards. Interrole conflict can be a familiar—if not minor—problem.

When a person's responsibilities within a group are unclear or unstable, the individual suffers the difficulty of role ambiguity. Roles are likely to be ambiguous when a member first joins a group or when task performance changes. Role ambiguity will occur when office tasks and factory tasks are automated.

Cohesiveness is a feeling of attraction and loyalty that motivates members to stay in the group. Members of cohesive groups like each other more and support common goals more strongly than members of less cohesive groups. High cohesiveness can be a source of both benefits and liabilities. Members of highly cohesive groups enjoy their membership and interaction more but are also prone to make mistakes by giving group feeling a higher priority than other group goals.

Anything that makes a group more valuable to its members increases cohesiveness. Competition within the group can reduce cohesiveness, since members fear threats from each other. Another barrier to fellowship is disliking or special preferences among members. When members are drawn to and away from each other, subgroups form, which break down organizational unity. Preferential differences in members' feelings are more likely to develop in large groups, and thus group size is negatively related to cohesiveness; the larger the organization, the harder it is to maintain attraction, loyalty, and fairness evenly among all members.

(ii) Methods Used in Team Building

After a team has been created, there are distinct stages through which it develops. New teams are different from mature teams. Recall a time when you were a member of a new team, such as a fraternity or sorority pledge class, a committee, or a small team formed to do a class assignment. Over time, the team changed. In the beginning, team members had to get to know one another, establish roles and norms, divide the labor, and clarify the team's task. In this way, members became parts of a smoothly operating team. The challenge for leaders is to understand the stage of the team's development and take action that will help the group improve its functioning.

Research findings suggest that team development is not random but evolves over definitive stages. One useful model for describing these stages contains five phases:

1. Forming
2. Storming
3. Norming
4. Performing
5. Adjourning

The **forming** stage of development is a period of orientation and getting acquainted. Members break the ice and test one another for friendship possibilities and task orientation. Team members find which behaviors are acceptable to others. Uncertainty is high during this stage, and members usually accept whatever power or authority is offered by either formal or informal leaders. Members are dependent on the team until they find out what the ground rules are and what is expected of them. During this initial stage, members are concerned about such things as "What is expected of me?" "What is acceptable?" and "Will I fit in?" During the forming stage, the team leader should provide time for members to get acquainted with one another and encourage them to engage in informal social discussions.

During the **storming** stage, individual personalities emerge. People become more assertive in clarifying their roles and what is expected of them. Conflict and disagreement mark this stage.

People may disagree over their perceptions of the team's mission. Members may jockey for positions, and coalitions or subgroups based on common interests may form. One subgroup may disagree with another over the total team's goals or how to achieve them. The team is not yet cohesive and may be characterized by a general lack of unity. Unless teams can move beyond this stage, they may get bogged down and never achieve high performance. During the storming stage, the team leader should encourage participation by each team member. Members should propose ideas, disagree with one another, and work through the uncertainties and conflicting perceptions about team tasks and goals.

During the **norming** stage, conflict is resolved, and team harmony and unity emerge. Consensus develops on who has the power, who is the leader, and members' roles. Members come to accept and understand one another. Differences are resolved, and members develop a sense of team cohesion. This stage typically is of short duration. During the norming stage, the team leader should emphasize oneness within the team and help clarify team norms and values.

During the **performing** stage, the major emphasis is on problem solving and accomplishing the assigned task. Members are committed to the team's mission. They are coordinated with each other and handle disagreements in a mature way. They confront and resolve problems in the interest of task accomplishment. They interact frequently and direct discussion and influence toward achieving team goals. During this stage, the leader should concentrate on managing high task performance. Both socioemotional and task specialists should contribute to the group.

The **adjourning** stage occurs in committees, task forces, and teams that have a limited task to perform and are disbanded afterward. During this stage, the emphasis is on wrapping up and gearing down. Task performance is no longer a top priority. Members may feel heightened emotionality, strong cohesiveness, and depression or even regret over the team's disbandment. They may feel happy about mission accomplishment and sad about the loss of friendship and associations. At this point, the leader may wish to signify the team's disbanding with a ritual or ceremony, perhaps giving out plaques and awards to signify closure and completeness.

The five stages of team development typically occur in sequence. In teams that are under time pressure or that will exist for only a short period of time, the stages may occur quite rapidly. The stages may also be accelerated for virtual teams. For example, bringing people together for a couple of days of team building can help virtual teams move rapidly through the forming and storming stages.

(iii) Assessing Team Performance

Another important aspect of the team process is cohesiveness. **Team cohesiveness** is defined as the extent to which members are attracted to the team and motivated to remain in it. Members of highly cohesive teams are committed to team activities, attend meetings, and are happy when the team succeeds. Members of less cohesive teams are less concerned about the team's welfare. High cohesiveness is normally considered an attractive feature of teams.

Characteristics of team structure and context influence cohesiveness. The first characteristic is **team interaction**. The greater the contact among team members and the more time spent together, the more cohesive the team. Through frequent interactions, members get to know one another and become more devoted to the team. The second is the concept of **shared goals**. If team members agree on goals, they will be more cohesive. Agreeing on purpose and direction binds the team together. The third characteristic is **personal attraction to the team**, meaning that members have similar attitudes and values and enjoy being together.

Two factors in the team's context also influence group cohesiveness. The first is the presence of competition. When a team is in moderate competition with other teams, its cohesiveness increases as it strives to win. Finally, team success and the favorable evaluation of the team by outsiders add to cohesiveness. When a team succeeds in its task and others in the organization recognize the success, members feel good, and their commitment to the team will be high.

The outcome of team cohesiveness can fall into two categories: morale and productivity. As a general rule, morale is higher in cohesive teams because of increased communication among members, a friendly team climate, maintenance of membership because of commitment to the team, loyalty, and member participation in team decisions and activities. High cohesiveness has almost uniformly good effects on the satisfaction and morale of team members.

With respect to team productivity, research findings are mixed, but cohesiveness may have several effects. First, in a cohesive team, members' productivity tends to be more uniform. Productivity differences among members are small because the team exerts pressure toward conformity. Noncohesive teams do not have this control over member behavior and therefore tend to have wider variation in member productivity.

With respect to the productivity of the team as a whole, research findings suggest that cohesive teams have the potential to be productive, but the degree of productivity depends on the relationship between management and the working team. Thus, team cohesiveness does not necessarily lead to higher team productivity. One study surveyed more than 200 work teams and correlated job performance with their cohesiveness. Highly cohesive teams were more productive when team members felt management support and less productive when they sensed management hostility and negativism. Management hostility led to team norms and goals of low performance, and the highly cohesive teams performed poorly, in accordance with their norms and goals.

HOW MANY TEAMS ARE THERE?

In most organizations, employees work in teams to achieve goals. Many types of teams can exist within organizations. The easiest way to classify teams is in terms of those created as part of the organization's formal structure and those created to increase employee participation. Examples include formal teams, vertical teams, horizontal teams, virtual teams, global teams, special-purpose teams, problem-solving teams, self-directed teams, self-managing teams, multidisciplinary teams, dream teams, and X-teams.

Formal teams are created by the organization as part of the formal organization structure. Two common types of formal teams are vertical and horizontal, which typically represent vertical and horizontal structural relationships.

A **vertical team** is composed of a manager and his or her subordinates in the formal chain of command. Sometimes called a functional team or a command team, the vertical team may in some cases include three or four levels of hierarchy within a functional department. Typically, the vertical team includes a single department in an organization. The third-shift nursing team on the second floor of St. Luke's Hospital is a vertical team that includes nurses and a supervisor. A financial analysis department, a quality control department, an accounting department, and a HR department are all command teams. Each is created by the organization to attain specific goals through members' joint activities and interactions.

A **horizontal team** is composed of employees from about the same hierarchical level but from different areas of expertise. A horizontal team is drawn from several departments, is given a specific task, and may be disbanded after the task is completed. The two most common types of horizontal teams are task forces and committees.

As part of the horizontal structure of the organization, task forces and committees offer several advantages:

- They allow organization members to exchange information.
- They generate suggestions for coordinating the organizational units that are represented.
- They develop new ideas and solutions for existing organizational problems.
- They assist in the development of new organizational practices and policies.

A **virtual team** is made up of geographically or organizationally dispersed members who are linked primarily through advanced information and telecommunications technologies. Although some virtual teams may be made up of only organizational members, virtual teams often include contingent workers, members of partner organizations, customers, suppliers, consultants, or other outsiders. Team members use email, voice mail, videoconferencing, Internet and intranet technologies, and various types of collaboration software to perform their work, although they may also sometimes meet face to face.

Virtual teams are highly flexible and dynamic. Some are temporary cross-functional teams pulled together to work on specific projects or problems while others are long-term or permanent self-directed teams.

Team leadership typically is shared or altered, depending on the area of expertise needed at each stage of the project. In addition, team membership in virtual teams may change fairly quickly, depending on the tasks to be performed. One of the primary advantages of virtual teams is the ability to rapidly assemble the most appropriate group of people to complete a complex project, solve a particular problem, or exploit a specific strategic opportunity. The success of virtual teams depends on several factors, including selecting the right members, building trust, sharing information, and effectively using technology. For example, VeriFone Company uses virtual teams in every aspect of its business.

Global teams are cross-border work teams made up of members of different nationalities whose activities span multiple countries. Generally, global teams fall into two categories: intercultural teams, whose members come from different countries or cultures and meet face to face; and virtual global teams, whose members remain in separate locations around the world and conduct their work electronically.

Global teams can present enormous challenges for team leaders who have to bridge gaps of time, distance, and culture. In some cases, members speak different languages; use different technologies; and have different beliefs about authority, time orientation, decision making, and so forth. Culture differences can significantly affect teamwork and relationships. Organizations using global teams invest the time and resources to adequately educate employees. They have to make sure all team members appreciate and understand cultural differences, are focused on goals, and understand their responsibilities to the team. For a global team to be effective, all team members must be willing to deviate somewhat from their own values and norms and establish new norms for the team. As with virtual teams, carefully selecting team members, building trust, and sharing information are critical to success.

Special-purpose teams, sometimes called project teams, are created outside the formal organization structure to undertake a project of special importance or creativity. Special-purpose teams focus on a specific purpose and expect to disband once the specific project is completed.

Problem-solving teams typically consist of 5 to 12 hourly employees from the same department who voluntarily meet to discuss ways of improving quality, efficiency, and the work environment. Recommendations are proposed to management for approval. Problem-solving teams usually are the first step in a company's move toward greater employee participation. The most widely known application is quality circles, initiated by Japanese companies, in which employees focus on ways to improve quality in the production process.

(*continued*)

HOW MANY TEAMS ARE THERE? (*Continued*)

Self-directed teams. Employee involvement through teams is designed to increase the participation of low-level workers in decision making and the conduct of their jobs, with the goal of improving performance. Employee involvement started out simply with techniques such as information sharing with employees or asking employees for suggestions about improving the work. Gradually, companies moved toward greater autonomy for employees, which led first to problem-solving teams and then to self-directed teams.

As a company matures, problem-solving teams gradually can evolve into self-directed teams, which represents a fundamental change in how employee work is organized. Self-directed teams enable employees to feel challenged, find their work meaningful, and develop a strong sense of identity with the company. Self-directed teams typically consist of 5 to 20 multiskilled workers who rotate jobs to produce an entire product or service or at least one complete aspect or portion of a product or service (e.g., engine assembly, insurance claim processing). The central idea is that the teams themselves, rather than managers or supervisors, take responsibility for their work, make decisions, monitor their own performance, and alter their work behavior as needed to solve problems, meet goals, and adapt to changing conditions. Characteristics of these self-directed teams, which are permanent teams, are listed next.

- The team includes employees with several skills and functions, and the combined skills are sufficient to perform a major organizational task. A team may include members from the foundry, machining, grinding, fabrication, and sales departments, with members cross-trained to perform one another's jobs. The team eliminates barriers among departments, enabling excellent coordination to produce a product or service.

- The team is given access to resources, such as information, equipment, machinery, and supplies, needed to perform the complete task.

- The team is empowered with decision-making authority, which means that members have the freedom to select new members, solve problems, spend money, monitor results, and plan for the future.

In a self-directed team, team members take over managerial duties, such as scheduling or ordering materials. They work with minimum supervision, perhaps electing one of their own as supervisor, who may change each year. The most effective self-directed teams are those that are fully empowered. In addition to having increased responsibility and discretion, empowered teams are those that: have a strong belief in their team's capabilities; find value and meaning in their work; and recognize the impact the team's work has on customers, other stakeholders, and organizational success. Managers create the conditions that determine whether self-directed teams are empowered by giving teams true power and freedom, complete information, knowledge and skills, and appropriate rewards.

The scope of **self-managing teams** includes not only the normal work routine but also some traditional managerial tasks. Employees are assigned to self-managed teams. Team members get rotated for cross-training purposes. The manager's role becomes more of a facilitator than a traditional supervisor role.

Teamwork is the key strategy to improving productivity, because all improvements involve people implementing change in a system. A system is a combination of social and technical systems. Management researchers say that better social systems, even at the expense of the technical systems, yield better results. The optimal social system is the self-managing team concept. It consists of a series of work teams consisting of 5 to 10 members who rotate jobs and produce an entire product or service with minimal supervision. The team assumes all responsibilities and makes all decisions regarding their product or service.

Self-managing teams have been extremely effective, because they challenge all workers to actively and mentally participate rather than blindly execute policies. This results in continuous productivity and quality improvements and, ultimately, success. Meaningful participation by workers always will have a positive impact on productivity. Empowering workers to do those things that enable them to work smarter is a powerful tool in increasing productivity.

Venture teams (V-teams) are groups of employees working together focusing exclusively on the development of a new product or acquisition of a new business.

Training teams (T-teams) are groups of employees participating in the basic skills training and development sessions away from the workplace.

A **focus group** is a team representation of individuals, either inside or outside of a firm, who are solicited to share their opinions (likes and dislikes) about a specific product, service, or process for its improvement under the direction of a trained moderator. Focus groups are used for several purposes in functions such as marketing, operations, and finance.

Complex and mission-critical projects often require **multidisciplinary teams,** consisting of individuals from different functional areas and led by a project manager, to plan and manage projects. Typically, a core project team is established early in the life cycle of a project, and additional individuals with particular technical or operational expertise are added during appropriate phases of the project. The team must not only possess technical and operational expertise, but it must also be composed of the "right" people. The selection of the team members is critical—they must be knowledgeable, willing to trade off leadership roles, and able to plan work and set goals in a team setting. The successful team will have a high spirit, trust, and enthusiasm. Key factors in the successful completion of a project are a sense of ownership and the drive of the team. This integrated and comprehensive approach improves communication between upper management and project managers and among the various stakeholders in the project. It also increases the likelihood that potential problems will be identified and resolved quickly, thus increasing the chances that the project will remain on schedule and within budget.

A **dream team** is an ideal team consisting of unique members from inside and outside an organization where a member's skills, experiences, attitudes, and work-related goals and ethics perfectly match with those of other members of a project, the project manager, and the project sponsor. The goal-congruence principle is at play here.

The scope and nature of **X-teams** is different from the traditional teams (e.g., vertical teams, horizontal teams, and self-directed teams); X-teams have both inward and outward focus while traditional teams have inward focus only. Outward focus means reaching out to the external stakeholders; inward focus is on the internal stakeholders to obtain relevant information for a project. X-teams focus on both inward and outward sides and works with external and internal stakeholders.

Another difference is that X-teams are composed of multiple groups of individuals, such as core and noncore members, whereas traditional teams have only one type of individuals, such as team members with a team leader. Another notable difference is that X-teams operate in a dynamic and unpredictable environment whereas traditional teams operate in a stable and predictable environment within an organization.

An excellent application of X-teams is in a new-product development project where team members need to work with several external parties, such as product consultants, materials, suppliers, and hardware/software vendors, and several internal parties, such as the staff of the manufacturing department, marketing department, R&D, design engineering, and quality department. The purpose is to solicit and receive pertinent information about the planning, designing, producing, and marketing of the new product. The goal is to involve all affected parties in the team for open discussion, idea generation, idea sharing, and knowledge sharing on a proactive basis so that problems and obstacles can be estimated or assessed earlier and prevented quicker from occurring with careful planning at the outset. Traditional teams do not have this kind of broad focus. In other words, X-teams exist for multiple purposes whereas most traditional teams exist for a single purpose.

(b) Problem-Solving and Decision-Making Skills

This section describes problem-solving and decision-making topics to show how the right problems can be solved with the right kind of decisions.

(i) Problem-Solving Skills

(A) What Is a Problem?

In this section, we first discuss the theory behind problem solving followed by its application to internal auditing. A problem exists when there is a gap between "what is" and "what should be." Individuals recognize a problem when they feel frustrated, frightened, angry, or anxious about a situation. Organizations recognize problems when: outputs and productivity are low; quality of products and services is poor; people are not cooperating, sharing information, or communicating; or there is a dysfunctional degree of conflict among people in various departments. When the gap between "what is" and "what should be" causes anxiety and inefficiency, something needs to be done to solve the problem (see Exhibit 1.79).

EXHIBIT 1.79 General Definition of a Problem

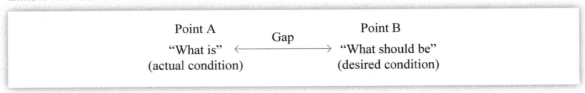

A **problem** is the gap between where one is and where one wants to be. Problem solving is the process of closing the gap between the actual situation and the desired situation. Problems do not solve themselves—people solve problems. In a way, audit reports are problem-solving tools. The deficiency findings contained in audit reports describe and compare the actual condition (what is) with the desired condition (what should be), thus creating a gap. The auditor's recommendations are aimed at closing this gap. Audit work is then a type of problem solving. Audit findings are the result of comparing "what should be" with "what is" and analyzing the impact (see Exhibit 1.80).

EXHIBIT 1.80 Audit Definition of a Problem

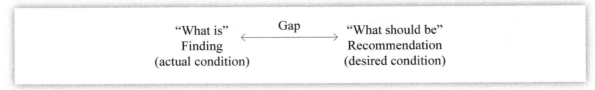

If internal auditing reports are problem-solving tools, then internal auditors are problem solvers since the audit work is done by auditors, who then prepare the audit report. The management principle behind the problem solving is Theory Y in that both managers and auditors will take responsibility for and are interested in solving organizational problems. Effective written and oral communication skills are prerequisites to effective problem-solving skills.

(B) Problem-Solving Process

Problem solving is a systematic process of bringing the actual situation or condition closer to the desired condition. Although there are many ways to handle problems, problem-solving is a four-step sequence: (1) identifying the problem, (2) generating alternative solutions, (3) selecting a solution, and (4) implementing and evaluating the solution.[29] These four steps are depicted in Exhibit 1.81 with a possible recycling from Steps 3 and 4 to Steps 1 and 2.

EXHIBIT 1.81 Steps in the Problem-Solving Process

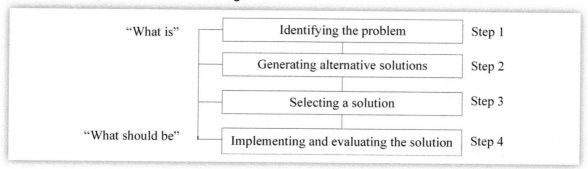

Step 1: Identifying the Problem. The scope of this step includes awareness of a problem, problem diagnosis and identification, and criteria for solution. Identifying the problem is a major, crucial work. It can consist of initial awareness that something is not right. The problem-solving cycle begins with some identified need. If there is no need, the cycle is unnecessary. Problems could be defined with framing errors or effects. Consequently, incorrect problems could be solved leading to decision traps. Moreover, ill-defined and unstructured problems can waste resources (e.g., time, money, and effort). Symptoms should be separated from problems because symptoms will be repeated.

Some examples of problem indications are listed next.

■ A production manager finds a gap between actual weekly production and the desired level of production.

■ A plant department manager finds a gap between actual attendance levels and desired attendance levels.

■ A marketing manager finds a gap between the actual market share for a product and the desired market share.

■ A financial manager finds a gap between the actual earnings for a quarter and the desired earnings.

■ An audit manager finds a gap between the actual report issuance time and the desired report issuance time.

The adage "A fully developed problem is half solved" is truly applicable here. Problem identification is a two-dimensional process. The first dimension deals with the degree or condition of the problem, and the second one addresses the structure of the problem. Each dimension is discussed briefly.

It is necessary to understand the degree or intensity of a problem in order to plan the appropriate timing and strategies for its solutions. There are three issues involved here: stable, dynamic, and critical.

---

[29] Robert Kreitner, *Management*, 9th ed. (Boston: Houghton Mifflin Company, 2004).

A **stable issue** is one in which there is a little or no controversy. The decision maker requires little input and can usually solve the problem in a task-oriented fashion. A **dynamic issue** is one around which there is a good deal of controversy and the decision maker turns to a group for input. Leadership is process-oriented. A **critical issue** is immersed in controversy and requires resolution by senior management. Leadership is most effective in resolving critical issues when it is task as well as process oriented.

The Structure of the problem has to do with the routineness of the decision required. Questions to ask include: How much is known or understood about the problem? Is this a new problem? Do mechanisms exist within the organization to deal with this problem?

Two types of problems exist: structured and unstructured problems. Structured problems have only one unknown and have routine programs available to respond; unstructured problems have at least two unknowns and no routine programs available to respond. As an organization faces the same unstructured problem repeatedly, it gradually develops mechanisms to respond to the problem, which then becomes structured.

After being aware of the problem, it is good to obtain valid information about the problem in order to identify what it is. Problem identification is a description of present conditions, symptoms, and underlying causes. The outcome should be a written statement identifying the root problem.

Defining the criteria for a solution addresses what the desired condition should be. This condition should be measurable and specific. True agreement on the criteria that a solution must meet is important to help avoid conflict at a later time in the problem-solving cycle.

STUMBLING BLOCKS FOR PROBLEM FINDERS

- *Defining the problem according to a possible solution* means ruling out alternative solutions in the way one states a problem

- *Focusing on narrow, low-priority areas* means ignoring organization goals and objectives

- *Diagnosing problems in terms of their symptoms* means inability to differentiate between short-run and long-run handling of symptoms. Treating symptoms rather than underlying causes is acceptable in the short run but is not acceptable in the long run since symptoms tend to reappear. The real cause(s) of the problem should be discovered. Causes are variables, whether they are controllable or uncontrollable. The problem can be solved or the gap can disappear by focusing on adding or removing these variables.

Step 2: Generating Alternative Solutions. During this step, the problem solver needs to identify the possible methods and means to get from what is to what should be. The information collection effort includes researching new ideas and methods and resources for achieving the goals. Generating alternative solutions is time consuming and demanding mental work.

People have a tendency to settle for the first answer or alternative without really developing several answers or alternatives from which to choose. Developing several alternatives requires a combination of careful and thorough analysis, intuition, creativity, and a sense of humor. Several techniques using individual and group creativity are available to develop alternatives. These include brainstorming, synectics, and others, which are discussed later in the section.

Step 3: Selecting a Solution. In this step, the various alternatives are evaluated against the established criteria for the solutions. In this way, the solution that best fits the criteria can be selected. Each alternative must be compared to others. Since "best" is a relative term, the alternative solutions must be evaluated to provide a reasonable balance of effectiveness and efficiency, considering the constraints and intangibles, if any.

If during this step the problem solver cannot establish a satisfactory solution, it may be necessary to return to Step 1 in order to redefine the problem or to repeat Step 2 in order to generate more realistic alternatives and solution criteria.

As part of the decision-making process, alternative solutions should be screened for the most appealing balance of effectiveness and efficiency in view of relevant constraints and intangibles. Russell Ackoff, a specialist in managerial problem solving, contends that three things can be done about problems: They can be resolved, solved, or dissolved (see Exhibit 1.82).

EXHIBIT 1.82 How Are Problems Handled?

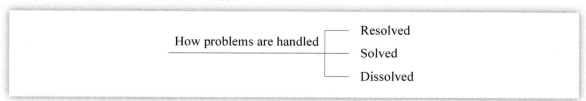

Resolving the problem includes selecting a course of action that is good enough to meet the minimum constraints. Here the problem solver satisfices rather than optimizes. Optimizing or maximizing is selecting the best possible solution. When a problem is resolved by selecting a course of action that meets the minimum constraints, a manager is said to be satisficing. The manager uses a minimal amount of information to make a quick, good-enough, and not the best, decision. Satisficing has been criticized as a shortsighted and passive technique emphasizing survival instead of growth. Idealizing involves dreaming that no problem exists or changing the current situation so that the problem no longer exists.

SATISFICING VERSUS OPTIMIZING VERSUS IDEALIZING

- *Satisficing* is settling for a solution that is good enough.
- *Optimizing* is systematically searching for a solution with the best combination of resources and benefits.
- *Idealizing* is changing the nature of a problem's situation.

Solving the problem is when one selects the best possible solution with the best combination of benefits. A **problem is dissolved** when the situation in which it occurs is changed so that the problem no longer exists. Problem dissolvers are said to idealize because they actually change the nature of the system in which a problem resides.

RESOLVING VERSUS SOLVING VERSUS DISSOLVING

- Resolving the problem requires a qualitative, subjective approach.
- Solving the problem requires scientific observations and quantitative measurements.
- Dissolving the problem requires a combination of quantitative and qualitative tools.

Step 4: Implementing and Evaluating the Solution. Once a solution has been chosen, implementation must be planned in detail. This step includes deciding who will do what and when. It requires implementation plans, checkpoints, schedules, and resources. Implementation of the action plan should move the situation from what is to what should be.

PROBLEM-SOLVING STRATEGY CHECKLIST

- Look for a pattern.
- Account for all possibilities.
- Act it out.
- Make a model or diagram.
- Work backward.
- Reason hypothetically.
- Restate the problem or change the problem representation (take an observer's point of view).
- Identify given, wanted, needed information.

At this point, both product and process evaluation are important. The outcomes must be measured against the desired criteria to determine if the goal has been reached and the problem solved. If people are still uncomfortable with the way things are, it may be necessary to start again at Step 1.

(C) Impediments to Problem Solving

Business problems are solved either by individuals or by groups. The most neglected area of problem solving is human resources, the people who participate in the problem-solving group. The group leader can encourage new ideas and creativity in group members by following these guidelines.

- Practice effective listening because people think much more rapidly than they speak. Effective listening is the best way to gather information. Try not to be distracted.

- Practice "stroking," a concept borrowed from transactional analysis. A stroke is a unit of recognition. Provide recognition to people and ideas. Positive stroking makes people more important and secure and invites more ideas and creativity.

- Discourage "discounting" (i.e., not paying attention), another concept borrowed from transactional analysis. When discounting is high, group members will feel reluctant to respond to questions and will be constantly ready to attack or retreat. This is not a healthy climate for successful problem solving, and it encourages dysfunctional behavior and uncooperative attitudes among the members of the group.

- Keep the group members informed about progress and what is expected of them.

Psychology researchers frequently cite these reasons for people making mistakes in solving problems: lack of understanding of concepts, reasoning errors, failure to note details, and insufficient computation skills.[30] Researchers have identified these common traits that good problem solvers possess:

- Good estimation and analysis skills
- Ability to perceive similarities and differences
- Reflective and creative thinking
- Ability to visualize relationships
- Strong understanding of concepts and terms
- Ability to disregard irrelevant data
- Capability to switch methods easily, but not impulsively
- Ability to generalize on the basis of a few examples
- Ability to interpret quantitative data
- Strong self-esteem

A problem-solving attitude, an inquiring and questioning mind, can be developed. It does not occur by accepting from others truths and conclusions that the learner ought to establish by him- or herself. The attitude is produced by continued experience in solving real problems, one consequence of which is that the learner comes to expect new problems and to look for them. Auditors have the same agenda in mind. The ability to discriminate among possible alternatives is a valuable life skill. Problem-solving skills are not a single, uniform capability. *Problems of different kinds may require substantially different problem-solving skills.*

Problem-solving expertise consists of skill in identifying obstacles that can be easily circumvented and of ingenuity in dealing with particular obstacles. The identification of problem obstacles is generally given too little priority because people are solution oriented. We spend too little time in exploring the problem situation.

IDEA GETTING VERSUS IDEA EVALUATION

- Reaching a final solution depends on both idea getting (generating alternatives) and idea evaluation (choosing the best alternative). Sometimes we do not achieve a satisfactory solution because we put too little effort into considering alternatives or we make a poor selection from those alternatives evaluated. Often the obstacle to successful problem solving is the tendency to evaluate and select an alternative before better ideas have been generated.

- Unless idea getting is stressed and idea evaluation is temporarily suppressed, the presence of available alternatives can impede the possible consideration of other, more viable alternatives.

---

[30] *Problem Solving–Volume 2* (Columbus, OH: Ohio Department of Education, State Board of Education, 1980).

(D) Problem Solving and Creativity

The reorganization of experience into new configurations is called creativity. The best argument in favor of creativity is that environmental changes make creativity essential for long-term survival. Stagnation can lead to organizational failure or demise. Creativity is not easy to get or to manage, as it requires hiring intelligent people and motivating them to deliver to the fullest extent of their skills.

A creative act is one that is original, valuable, and suggests that the person performing the act has unusual mental abilities.[31] A creative act is a problem-solving act; in particular, it is the solution of an ill-defined problem. Four cognitive processes especially important for creativity include problem finding, idea generation, planning, and preparation.

The discovery of a new problem not suggested by anyone else is important in any field. Three procedures that can help people to find problems are bug listing, searching for counterexamples, and searching for alternative interpretations.

Sometimes, when we are trying to solve an ill-defined problem, we are blocked by difficulty in generating ideas for solution. Brainstorming and discovering analogies may help us out of this difficulty. Planning is important in creative activities, as it is in any form of problem solving. Good writing and good art depend on good planning.

Internal auditors need to use creative skills during audit planning, the preliminary survey, and development of the audit program. Identification of audit objectives is important in the audit planning phase. Development of a good approach to conduct the preliminary survey requires creativity. Deciding what audit procedures need to be performed requires creativity during audit program development. Both new audits and repeat audits benefit from applying creative skills.

(E) Reasons Why Individuals Solve Problems Differently

Different people have different problem-solving skills. Five factors (see Exhibit 1.83) are key to a person's problem-solving capabilities:

1. Value system
2. Information filtration
3. Interpretation
4. Internal representation
5. External representation

EXHIBIT 1.83 Factors Contributing to Different Problem-Solving Skills

—— Value system
—— Information filtration
—— Interpretation
—— Internal representation
—— External representation

---

[31] John R. Hayes, *The Complete Problem Solver*, 2nd ed. (Mahwah, NJ: Lawrence Erlbaum Associates, 1989).

Value System. Individuals make decisions and solve problems differently because people have different value systems. If two people make different choices in the same situation, it does not mean that one of them is wrong; it may just be that they have different values. This means that we cannot tell how good people's decision-making processes are by the choices they make. However, training in formal decision-making methods and problem-solving skills would help. No matter what people's values are, if they use good decision-making methods, they should tend to agree with themselves when they make the same decision again.

Information Filtration. Some people can filter relevant information from the irrelevant. It is a skill that can be acquired through reasoning and practice. Problem solving is simpler for people who can think simply and clearly in their minds. Also, a multiple-level organization structure is most likely to produce information filtration. Information is subject to distortion or filtration as it moves through many channels of communication. The greater the level of communication, the greater the information filtration.

Even when two people present the same problem, they may not represent it in the same way. A person who is very good at filtering out irrelevant details may produce a very sparse representation. Another person who is not good at filtering out irrelevant details may produce a complex and ornate representation.

Interpretation. Forming an interpretation is a very active process in which a person adds and subtracts information and interprets information in the original situation. Pictures can be used during the process of interpretation.

Internal Representation. Internal representation deals with analogies and schemas in our minds. When we encounter a problem, we recognize that we have seen a similar problem before. This is called analogy.

INTERNAL REPRESENTATION OF A PROBLEM

Examples of internal representation of a problem include imaging, inferencing, decision making, and retrieving of knowledge from memory in an effort to understand the problem.

Our skill in problem solving depends in a very important way on our store of problem schemas. Each problem schema we know gives us a very valuable advantage in solving a whole class of problems—an advantage that may consist in knowing what to pay attention to, or how to represent the problem, or how to search for a solution, or all three. *Clearly, the more schemas we know, the better prepared we are as problem solvers.*

Different people may create different internal representations of the same problem. There are more differences between representations, though, than just the amount of detail they contain. One person may represent a problem in visual imagery, another in sentences, and a third in auditory images. If two people represent a problem in visual images, they may not use the same images. For example, people frequently use both auditory and visual imagery in solving arithmetic problems. While doing problems in their heads, people use visual images of the digits of the answer and of marks indicating borrowing or cancellation.

External Representation. In many cases, an external representation is very helpful for solving problems. Drawing a sketch, jotting down lists, writing out equations, and making diagrams can help us to remember information and to notice new relationships in the problem. Some relationships in problems are easier to discover when diagrams are used. For example, a matrix representation is useful in solving control identification problems (e.g., matching controls to control objectives).

External representations are very helpful in solving complex problems, but they are not useful without an internal representation of the problem. An internal representation is essential for intelligent problem solving since it is the medium in which people think—the same way the words are the medium for speech. Sometimes an internal representation is sufficient for solving simple problems. However, external representation alone is not useful. Both representations are needed for most cases.

(F) Prospective and Retrospective Methods

Often management asks auditors to deal with forward-looking, future-oriented problems or questions. Collectively they are referred to as **prospective methods** to distinguish them from approaches designed to answer questions about what is happening now or what has happened in the past—that is, **retrospective methods**. An auditor's problem-solving skill set should contain both of these methods. Conducting a repeat audit of accounts payable is an example of a retrospective method. Performing a due diligence review is an example of a prospective method of problem solving.

TYPES OF PROSPECTIVE METHODS

Four types of methods exist: actual, empirical, logical, and judgmental.

1. Actual types include experimental test and demonstration programs.

2. Empirical types include simulation and forecasting.

3. Logical types include front-end analysis, risk assessment, systems analysis, scenario building, and anticipatory analysis.

4. Judgmental types include Delphi techniques and expert opinion.

Basically, two types of forward-looking situations exist: anticipate the future or improve the future. In both situations, auditors would critique others' analyses or would do their own analyses. Future needs, costs, and consequences are analyzed when anticipating the future issues. Courses of action that have the best potential for success are analyzed to improve the future. These types of questions are most appropriate in acquisition and divestiture audits.

The type of questions being addressed dictates the need for a systematic method of analysis. Where the questions are controversial, far-reaching, and sensitive, more systematic methods of analysis may be called for. Simple questions need simple methods. Some advantages of using systematic methods include the full range of existing information can be brought to bear on the question and high-quality standards of evidence and analysis can be used in documenting the basis for answers about the future. Exhibit 1.84 compares retrospective methods with prospective methods.

EXHIBIT 1.84 Comparison of Retrospective Methods with Prospective Methods of Problem Solving

Retrospective Methods	Prospective Methods
Require less judgment due to the lower level of uncertainty involved	Require more judgment due to the higher degree of uncertainty involved
Decreased need for alternatives and options	Increased need for alternatives and options
Source of questions: existing criteria, issues, and policies	Sources of questions: ideas and assumptions about problems, probable causes, possible solutions
Primary sources of information: documents, administrative data, interviews, observations, surveys	Primary sources of information: prior research, theory, pilot tests, experimental tests of proposed approaches, expert opinions
Primary types of analysis: qualitative and quantitative approaches to empirical data, information syntheses in relation to criteria and issues	Primary types of analysis: simulations, forecasting, and information syntheses in relation to conceptual and operational assumptions of proposed solutions; Delphi techniques; analyses of likely effects

(G) Tools and Techniques for Problem Solving

Many tools and techniques are available for the problem solver to solve problems. They include brainstorming, synectics, nominal group technique, force-field approach, systems analysis, and others (see Exhibit 1.85).[32] Differences exist among the problem-solving methods, and all of them do not work equally well in all situations. In any given situation, one or two methods might have a greater probability of leading to the desired outcomes.

EXHIBIT 1.85 Tools and Techniques for Problem Solving

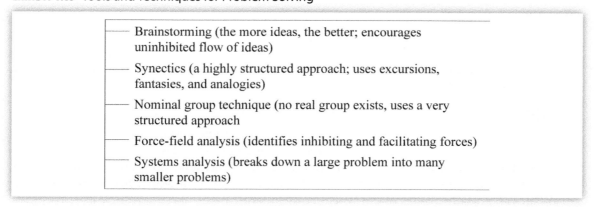

- Brainstorming (the more ideas, the better; encourages uninhibited flow of ideas)
- Synectics (a highly structured approach; uses excursions, fantasies, and analogies)
- Nominal group technique (no real group exists, uses a very structured approach
- Force-field analysis (identifies inhibiting and facilitating forces)
- Systems analysis (breaks down a large problem into many smaller problems)

(H) Brainstorming

The purpose of the brainstorming technique is to generate a great number of ideas; that is, its purpose is idea generation. The key is to let group members feel free to express whatever ideas come to mind without fear of judgment or criticism. Uninhibited flow of ideas is permitted; negative thinking is not permitted. Recording all ideas and deferring judgment until the later phases of the analysis is the hallmark of brainstorming. See Exhibit 1.86 for advantages and disadvantages of the brainstorming technique.

---

[32] Francis L. Ulschak, Leslie Nathanson, and Peter G. Gillan, *Small Group Problem Solving* (Reading, MA: Addison-Wesley, 1981).

EXHIBIT 1.86 Advantages and Disadvantages of the Brainstorming Technique

Advantages	Disadvantages
Rapid generation of ideas	Focuses on idea generation, not on specific solutions
Identification of many factors of a particular topic	
Expression of a cross section of views from various disciplines	Does not work well where problems are not open-ended

The brainstorming technique is most effective when the presence of an expert is not necessary, the high level of creativity is seen as a bonus rather than an irritant, and a large quantity of ideas is needed.

MISCONCEPTIONS ABOUT BRAINSTORMING

There are two misconceptions about brainstorming: (1) there is a total lack of control and direction in a brainstorming session, and (2) brainstorming does not involve judgment or evaluation of ideas; all ideas are seen as equally effective and productive.

There are four rules for effective brainstorming sessions.

1. **Postpone evaluation of ideas of others as well as one's own.** This rule is the most critical, because the best way to reduce effective idea generation is to make premature evaluations and/or judgments.

2. **"Freewheeling" is welcome and invited.** "Freewheeling" means that any idea is permitted, no matter how outlandish or fanciful. One person's flight of fantasy may be the trigger for another's generation of a very workable idea.

3. **Many ideas are wanted.** The greater the number of ideas, the greater the possibility that quality ideas will emerge.

4. **Encourage hitchhiking. Hitchhiking** is the art of combining and improving on ideas; in other words, building on another's suggestion. Frequently, a group will develop a cue for members to use when they want to hitchhike—for example, snapping a finger. Hitchhiking is a by-product of brainstorming.

(I) Synectics

Synectics is a technique for creating an environment that encourages creative approaches to problem solving. It is a highly structured approach for an individual who needs a group to help solve a problem. It involves the use of nontraditional activities, such as excursions and fantasies and analogies. Synectics is good for idea generation and team building. See Exhibit 1.87 for advantages and disadvantages of the synectics technique.

EXHIBIT 1.87 Advantages and Disadvantages of the Synectics Technique

Advantages	Disadvantages
The method works exceptionally well when people feel in a rut or blocked with a problem.	Participants may have difficulty with excursions; some may be reluctant to fantasize.
The process is fun—there is a lot of energy flowing.	The process works best with small groups of six to eight members.
It generates a great number of new perspectives on a problem.	The process works better for individual problems than for group problems.
In addition to structure, there is plenty of room for flexibility.	Although the process sounds easy, it requires much preparation.
Participants feel very involved in the process.	

Excursions and fantasies are deliberate moves to get participants away from consciously thinking about the problem. In synectics, the excursion is used to involve the subconscious mind to work on the problem and find clues to possible solutions. Excursions are productive with regard to developing possible solutions, and they also serve to energize the group members.

Analogies are an important source of ideas when searching for problem solutions. A checklist is prepared for each type of analogy, including personal, direct, symbolic, fantasy, and attribute. The user works through the checklist and tries to find analogies of each type. Personal analogy is where the problem solver puts him- or herself directly into the problem situation. Direct analogy involves searching for a setting where the same function is accomplished.

Symbolic analogy is associated with symbols, notations, figures, and pictures. Fantasy analogy includes magic and science fiction. In an attribute analogy system, the checklist would list attributes of an object—its name, form, function, color, and material. After listing the attributes, analogies are attached to each one by screening for useful insights. Analogies and symbols are also called free association, where unconventional thinking is encouraged.

(J) Nominal Group Technique

The nominal group technique (NGT) is an idea-generating, consensus-building tool. *No real group exists—it is a group in name only.* A strength of this process is that it permits a problem to become focused in a short period of time. It uses a very structured approach and is an excellent technique to use when the group members are drawn from various levels of the organizational hierarchy or when they are in conflict with one another. The technique gives everyone an opportunity to express ideas without being interrupted by others in the group. See Exhibit 1.88 for advantages and disadvantages of NGT.

EXHIBIT 1.88 Advantages and Disadvantages of the Nominal Group Technique

Advantages	Disadvantages
NGT can be used with groups of varying backgrounds, cultures, education, or work roles who share a common problem or goal.	The technique calls for a trained leader or group facilitator.
The technique can be used in groups where participants do not have previous training in group process or communication skills.	It can deal with only one question at a time. NGT is inappropriate to use in a group that does not already have interactive problem-solving and team-building skills.
The highly structured process is a quick way of bringing people together to approach a common task.	
NGT promotes the generation of many ideas about an issue.	
NGT allows for maximum and equal participation of all group members, encouraging input from many areas of expertise.	
The NGT process is easy to run.	

Social psychology researchers have found that individuals working in groups generate more ideas than when they work alone. Furthermore, nominal groups—groups in name only, where people are brought together but not allowed to communicate—have been found to be more effective for idea generation than interacting groups, where people meet to discuss, brainstorm, and exchange information. Such interacting groups tend to inhibit creative thinking. However, for purposes of attitude change, team building, and consensus generation, interacting groups have been found superior.

> **BRAINSTORMING VERSUS SYNETICS VERSUS NOMINAL GROUP TECHNIQUE**
>
> ■ If the goal is idea generation, use brainstorming or synectics, since each facilitates more diverse or creative thinking.
>
> ■ If the goal is for a group of relative strangers to meet in order to reach group consensus concerning common issues, use the NGT since it is a structured process of consensus building.

The unique NGT process combines a silent time for idea generation with the social reinforcement of an interactive group setting. This structured process forces equality of participation among members in generating and sharing information about the issue. NGT groups may consist of five to eight participants.

(K) Force-Field Analysis

Force-field analysis involves the identification of a problem and the factors or forces contributing to making it a problem, and steps for generating solutions. Two main sets of forces are identified: inhibiting forces—those that resist the resolution of the problem; and facilitating forces—those that push the problem toward resolution. Once the forces acting on a problem are identified, actions can be taken to decrease the major resisting forces, increase the major facilitating forces, or both. This process, then, is basically an analysis of the forces acting to keep the problem a problem. See Exhibit 1.89 for advantages and disadvantages of force-field analysis.

EXHIBIT 1.89 Advantages and Disadvantages of Force-Field Analysis

Advantages	Disadvantages
The outcome of the force-field analysis process is a detailed action plan with evaluation criteria built in.	The group may get lost in arguments about what the problem really is, what forces are the most important, which action steps to begin with, and the like.
It is an excellent process for a group to use in dealing with group problems.	
It is an effective tool to define problems, analyze problems, and develop solutions into workable action plans.	Problems that are not easily and clearly defined many be difficult for this process.
Group size is not a critical factor, and force-field analysis can be used as a team-building process.	The team leader needs to be a good listener and should be able to help the team weight and rank alternatives.

Force-field analysis calls for the definition of current conditions and desired conditions. Once a clear image of these conditions is established, effective intervention strategies can be devised to move from the present to the desired condition. As a problem-solving process, force-field analysis involves identifying and analyzing problems, developing strategies for change, and clarifying specific steps to be taken to confront the problem. It is an excellent analytical tool. The outcome will be a detailed action plan outlining when, to whom, and how the problem will be addressed. The force-field approach is useful for viewing a problem that involves the entire group, and it may be combined with other problem-solving methods in order to establish a long-term plan of action.

(L) Systems Analysis

Systems analysis breaks down a large problem into many smaller problems. It is an excellent technique if the desired outcome of the problem-solving session is a detailed understanding of a problem. The technique offers a structure for analyzing a problem and various alternative solutions. However, it does not structure the roles of participants. The major strength of this process is that it offers a method of reviewing the total context of a problem. The phrase "systems analysis" does not mean analysis of computer-based information systems. The scope is broader than that—manual, automated, or both. See Exhibit 1.90 for advantages and disadvantages of systems analysis.

EXHIBIT 1.90 Advantages and Disadvantages of Systems Analysis

Advantages	Disadvantages
The problem is fully analyzed, touching on important questions and areas of concern.	There may be a tendency for the group to get bogged down in the process.
Several alternatives are developed, leaving abundant options for choice.	
It can be combined with other problem-solving methods.	

This method requires the problem solver to look beyond the unit of the problem to the environment for various possible solutions. It focuses on three attributes: open systems, multiple reasons and causes, and the entire picture.

The first attribute of systems theory assumes that a system is open; it interacts with its environment and can be represented by three models: hierarchical, input-output, and entities model. In the hierarchical model, systems are seen within a structure of subsystems. This framework may be useful in identifying the context in which the group finds itself. An input-output model may be useful in identifying the inputs that are needed and how they are to be transformed toward the desired outputs. The entities model may be used to form tentative hypotheses about how group members may interact.

The second attribute of systems theory looks at multiple reasons or causes for things; it keeps the problem solver from having tunnel vision concerning the nature of the problem. The systems approach moves away from linear causation, which assumes that the effects of a situation are based on single causes. Realizing that problems often have more than one cause helps the problem solver to attack the problem from several fronts.

The third attribute of the system model examines the entire picture rather than only one part or element. Remember the classic elephant story—different views of the elephant by six blind people.

Tools and Techniques for Problem Solving

Many tools and techniques are available for the problem solver to handle problems. They include brainstorming, synectics, nominal group technique, force-field approach, systems analysis, and others. Differences exist among the problem-solving methods, and all of them do not work equally well in all situations. In any given situation, one or two methods might have a greater probability of leading to the desired outcomes. Specific tools and techniques for problem solving include the following.

Imagineering. Imagineering involves the visualization of a complex process, procedure, or operation with all waste eliminated. The imagineer assumes the role of dreamer, realist, and critic. The steps in imagineering consist of taking an action, comparing the results with the person's imagined "perfect" situation, and making mental correction for the next time. This approach will eventually improve the situation and bring it to the desired level. Imagineering is similar to value analysis.

Value analysis. Value analysis is a systematic study of a business process or product with a view to improving the process or product and reducing cost. Creative skills are required while doing value analysis. Its goal is to ensure that the right activities are performed in the right way the first time. Industrial engineering techniques, such as work measurement and simplification methods, can be used to achieve the goals.

Leapfrogging. Leapfrogging is taking a big step forward in thinking up idealistic solutions to a problem. For example, leapfrogging can be applied to value analyzing comparable products to identify their best features and design. These ideas are then combined into a hybrid product that, in turn, can bring new superior products to enter a new market.

Blasting, creating, and refining. Blasting, creating, and refining are used when a completely new way of thinking or speculation is required or when answering a question, such as "What else will do the job?" Blasting is good when the group members are free to speculate and come up with totally new ideas that were never heard of or thought about before. Creativity comes into full play.

Attribute listing. Attribute listing emphasizes the detailed observation of each particular characteristic or quality of an item or situation. Attempts are then made to profitably change the characteristic or to relate it to a different item.

Edisonian. Edisonian, named after Thomas Edison, involves trial-and-error experimentation. This method requires a tedious and persistent search for the solution.

Investigative questions. The scope includes asking six investigative (journalism) questions: who, what, when, where, why, and how—to better understand the root causes of issues and problems.

Cause and effect diagrams. Cause and effect (C&E) diagrams (also called Ishikawa or fishbone diagrams) can be used to identify possible causes for a problem. The problem solver looks for the root causes by asking the "why" five or six times to move from broad (possible) causes to specific (root) causes. The idea is that by repeating the same question "why," the true source of a problem is discovered. This process will help identify the real problem. Then the problem solver chooses the most likely cause for further review. Brainstorming can be used in developing the C&E diagrams.

Pareto charts. Pareto charts can be drawn to separate the vital few from the trivial many. They are based on the 80/20 rule; that is, 20% of items contribute to 80% of problems.

Psychodramatic approaches. These approaches involve role-playing and role-reversal behavior. In psychodrama, the attempt is made to bring into focus all elements of an individual's problem; in sociodrama, the emphasis is on shared problems of group members.

Checklists. Checklists focus one's attention on a logical list of diverse categories to which the problem could conceivably relate.

General semantics. These include approaches that help the individual to discover multiple meanings or relationships in words and expressions.

Morphological analysis. This is a system involving the methodical interrelating of all elements of a problem in order to discover new approaches to a solution.

Panel consensus technique. This technique is a way to process a large number of ideas, circumventing organizational restraints to idea creation, using extensive participation and emphasizing methods for selecting good ideas.

Delphi technique. This technique is a method used to avoid groupthink. Group members do not meet face-to-face to make decisions. Rather, each group member independently and anonymously writes down suggestions and submits comments, which are then centrally compiled. The compiled results are then distributed to the group members who, independently and anonymously, write additional comments. These comments are again centrally compiled and the process is repeated until consensus is obtained. The Delphi technique is a group decision-making method.

Work measurement. This industrial engineering program applies some of the general principles of creative problem solving to the simplification of operations or procedures.

Storyboards. Storyboarding is a group problem-solving technique to create a picture of relevant information. A storyboard can be created for each group that is making decisions. A positive outcome of storyboarding is that it takes less time than interviewing, and many employees can get involved in problem solving, not just the managers.

Humor. In addition to being a powerful tool to relieve tension and hostility, humor is a problem-solving tool. When correctly executed, it opens the mind to seeking creative solutions to a problem. Humor can be in the form of detached jokes, quips, games, puns, and anecdotes. Humor gives perspective and solves problems. Stepping back and viewing a problem with a certain level of detachment restores perspective. A sense of humor sends messages of self-confidence, security, and control of the situation. However, humor should not be sarcastic or scornful.

Operations research. Operations research is a management science discipline attempting to find optimal solutions to business problems using mathematical techniques, such as simulation, linear programming, statistics, and computers.

Intuitive approach. The intuitive approach is based on hunches (gut feelings). It does not use a scientific approach and uses subjective estimates or probabilities, which are difficult to replicate.

T-analysis. T-analysis is a tabular presentation of strengths on one side and weaknesses on the other side of the letter "T." The goal is to address the weaknesses (problems).

Closure. Closure is a perceptual process that allows a person to solve a complex problem with incomplete information. It is the last step in problem solving.

TRIZ. TRIZ (a Russian acronym) is a theory of solving inventive problems. It supports the idea that unsolved problems are the result of contradicting goals (constraints) and nonproductive thinking. It suggests breaking out of a nonproductive thinking mold by reframing the contradicting and competing goals in such a way that the contradictions disappear.

Stratification. Stratification is a procedure used to describe the systematic subdivision of population or process data to obtain a detailed understanding of the structure of the population or process. It is not to be confused with a stratified sampling method. Stratification can be used to break down a problem to discover its root causes and can establish appropriate corrective actions, called counter-measures. *Failure to perform meaningful stratification can result in the establishment of inappropriate countermeasures, which can then result in process or product deterioration in quality.*

(M) Considerations of Problem Solving: Traits and Behaviors

All auditors should be familiar with certain traits and behaviors during problem solving. While certain problem-solving behaviors, such as conjecturing, predicting, and drawing conclusions, can be learned and taught, other behaviors and problem-solving traits, such as self-reliance, risk taking, creative thinking, and interacting, are examples of affective-related behaviors that are fostered through individual encouragement.[33]

An auditor needs to focus on the traits and behaviors listed next.

Traits

- **Curious.** Eager to investigate, to learn new approaches and techniques, to understand how a problem is solved.

- **Keen.** Interested in problems, quick to respond to individual challenges.

- **Interactive.** Participates freely with others, seeking and sharing ideas.

- **Creative.** Responds to problem situations in new or unusual ways; not confined in problem approaches or ways of thinking.

- **Receptive.** Willing to listen to and consider ideas of others.

- **Intuitive.** Able to act on hunches or educated guesses.

- **Retentive.** Draws on and applies previously acquired information in new situations.

- **Self-confident.** Believes that skills and abilities are adequate to meet the challenge of new problems.

- **Relishes challenges.** Desires and enjoys pitting abilities against problems.

- **Critical.** Evaluates ideas and explanations carefully; looks for exceptions to generalizations.

- **Organized.** Approaches problems systematically, investigates problem ideas in an orderly, sequential manner; keeps a record of successful and unsuccessful attempts.

- **Tolerant.** Listens to ideas and problem approaches that are not personal choices; willing to bide time in making and seeing suggestions acted on; respects problem-solving efforts and achievement of others.

- **Resourceful.** Able to overcome obstacles in more than one way.

- **Flexible.** Capable of changing or expanding thinking to incorporate new or different ideas from others.

- **Self-directed.** Motivated from within to pursue and continue with challenges.

- **Introspective.** Considers own thinking processes in problem solving; reflects on how new knowledge or discoveries integrate with previous information or thinking.

- **Risk taker.** Unafraid to be wrong in ideas or to be unsuccessful in efforts to solve a problem; willing to present ideas about a problem to others for evaluation.

Behaviors

- **Questions.** Expands on problem-solving discussion by asking about other cases; how the situation varies by changing givens; pursues matters that need clarification in own or others' thinking.

- **Notes details.** Considers all information that may affect the outcome of a problem; alert to recognizing relationships among variable quantities.

---

[33] *Problem Solving–Volume 2* (Columbus, OH: Ohio Department of Education, State Board of Education, 1980).

- **Discriminates.** Perceives similarities and differences among objects or relationships that are important to the problem; distinguishes relevant information from irrelevant problem material.

- **Recognizes patterns.** Detects similarities that characterize a set of information; able to predict missing elements.

- **Anticipates.** Examines alternatives using cause and effect reasoning without carrying action to conclusion; capable of meeting problems before they arise.

- **Predicts.** Foresees or foretells the outcomes of or results to a problem based on previous background, experience, or reasoning.

- **Generalizes.** Extends the results of a particular problem or set of data to a larger and more general situation.

- **Visualizes.** Forms mental images of problem variables to perceive interrelationships among them.

- **Infers.** Examines problem information carefully to derive hypotheses and draw conclusions.

- **Speculates.** Reflects on and reasons about problem components, interrelationships, and implications; forms educated conjectures from available evidence.

- **Concentrates.** Summons all of his or her skills and resources to attack a problem; overcomes extraneous influences and distractions.

- **Synthesizes.** Integrates individually acquired skills and information into a larger understanding of the processes and components of problem solving.

- **Draws conclusions.** Able to bring thinking to a decision to direct problem-solving actions; able to summarize the results of problems or implications.

- **Deliberates.** Recognizes the appropriate times to consider carefully the information of a problem before acting, the implications of a result before generalizing, the alternatives before choosing.

- **Perseveres.** Persists with a problem despite lack of success, discouragement, or opposition to his or her ideas; reluctant to give up on a problem.

- **Makes refined judgments.** Able to adjust thinking or statements based on additional information; able to improve the work of others by noting subtleties, distinctions, exceptions, or special cases.

- **Uses divergent thinking.** Able to perceive more than one implication or consequence to a problem action; able to consider unique or unusual approaches or outcomes to a problem; able to expand thinking throughout a problem rather than narrowing it.

(N) Problem Solving and the Internal Auditor

Internal auditors solve problems for their company when they engage in an audit work, but do not make decisions for the company management because it is the management who makes decisions. An example of a problem-solving skill required of internal auditors is that of determining which audit procedures are most appropriate for a given situation. Because internal auditing involves examining evidence and reaching conclusions based on that evidence, auditors must understand and be adept in the use of inductive reasoning. In addition, internal auditors must be able to evaluate a specific audit situation and deduce, for example, what evidence should be gathered to reach a valid audit conclusion.

It is true that auditors should not challenge or second-guess the management's decisions in problem-solving, strategic planning, capital expenditures, advertising budgets, marketing initiatives, manufacturing plant capacity expansions, mergers and acquisitions, and other strategic matters. Instead, auditors can ask and evaluate management about their rationale, justification, constraints, and assumptions went into the decision-making process. From a company's business viewpoint, internal auditors are problem solvers, not decision makers. On the other hand, an audit director is the sole and final decision maker when managing the internal audit department.

(ii) Decision-Making Skills

In this section, we first discuss the theory behind decision making, followed by its application to internal auditing. Decision making is a process of choosing among alternative courses of action. The correct sequence of the decision-making process is shown in Exhibit 1.91.

EXHIBIT 1.91 Steps in the Decision-Making Process

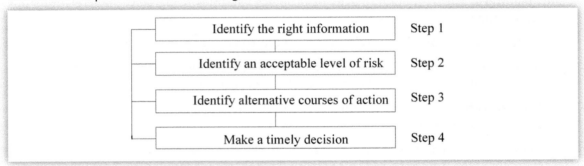

Note the difference between the problem-solving and decision-making steps. Identify an acceptable level of risk (Step 2) does not enter into the problem-solving process. Risk is unique to decision making and is an integral part of it. Decision making reduces or increases the risk, depending on the quality of the decision making and the level of uncertainty.

The process of management is fundamentally a process of decision making. The functions of management (planning, organizing, directing, and controlling) all involve the process of initiating, selecting, and evaluating courses of action. Therefore, decision making is at the center of management functions. The manager makes decisions in establishing objectives: planning, organizing, motivating, and control decisions.

Professor Igor Ansoff classifies the organizational decisions into three categories: strategic, administrative, and operating (see Exhibit 1.92).[34]

EXHIBIT 1.92 Decision Categories

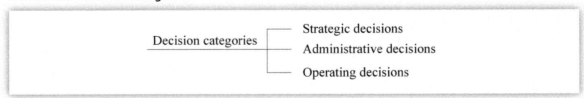

Strategic decisions are primarily concerned with a firm's external problems rather than its internal problems. Examples include product mix and markets to sell.

---

[34] Igor H. Ansoff, *Corporate Strategy* (New York: McGraw-Hill, 1965).

Administrative decisions are concerned with structuring the firm's resources to create maximum performance potential.

Administrative decisions are further divided into organizational structure and resource acquisition and development. Organizational structure involves structuring of authority and responsibility relationships, workflows, information flows, distribution channels, and location of facilities. Resource acquisition and development involves the development of raw material sources, personnel training, personnel development, financing, acquisition of facilities, and equipment.

Operating decisions are primarily concerned with maximizing the profitability of current operations. They include pricing, establishing market strategy, setting production schedules and inventory levels, and deciding on the relative expenditures in support of R&D, marketing, and operations.

Basically, a decision must be made when the organization faces a problem, when it is dissatisfied with existing conditions, or when it is given a choice. There is no unified agreed-on structure for decision theory because each decision maker has a different value system. Staff and line people perform a significant amount of work in discovering problems, defining the problems, and preparing the alternatives for decisions. The actual decision is only the conclusion of a decision-making process. The intelligence phase in the decision-making process includes finding the problem.

The three-step sequence of setting objectives is listed next.

1. Broad objectives are established at the senior managerial levels.
2. Strategies and department goals are developed from the broad objectives. The department goals provide a framework for decision making at lower managerial levels.
3. The manager needs to balance multiple objectives, conflicting objectives, and the hierarchy of objectives.

As the term indicates, "multiple objectives" means that the manager is focusing on two or more objectives at the same time. Examples include market growth, diversification, profit/sales maximization, employee attitudes, social responsibility, and employee development. The latter three objectives are difficult to quantify.

Conflicting objectives arise when two objectives are at odds with each other. For example, social responsibility, such as pollution control projects, may adversely affect profit margins.

Hierarchy of objectives means that objectives of organizational units must be consistent with the objectives of higher organizational units. This means there are objectives within objectives. If the cascade of organizational objectives is not consistent, suboptimization results. Suboptimization occurs, for example, where a departmental level maximizes its own objectives but, in doing so, subverts the overall objectives of the organization. Examples include dichotomies where the sales manager prefers large inventories; the production manager prefers large production runs; the warehouse manager prefers minimum inventory; the purchasing agent prefers large lot purchases; and the financing manager prefers low inventories, low production runs, and so on.

(A) Many Facets of Decision Making

Managers and leaders make a variety of decisions. The type of decision made depends on the level of that manager in the organization hierarchy. To accommodate this variety of decisions, many facets of decision making exist, as depicted in Exhibit 1.93.

EXHIBIT 1.93 Many Facets of Decision Making

— Sequential versus nonsequential
— Static versus dynamic
— Structured versus unstructured
— Programmed versus nonprogrammed
— Routine versus nonroutine

Sequential/Nonsequential Decision Making. Sequential decision making is the process of successively solving interrelated subproblems that make up a large complex problem. It uses the principle of divide and conquer. Decision C cannot be made until decisions A and B are made. Most senior management decisions are nonsequential in nature for strategic issues; lower-level management mostly makes sequential decisions.

DECISION RULES

Decision rules are behind the programmed decisions procedures. Decision rules require that there is a standard approach to resolve recurring problems and that the problems need to be solved only once.

There are no decision rules behind nonprogrammed decision making. Every situation is different, unique, and complex, requiring innovative and creative problem-solving approaches.

Static/Dynamic Decision Making. Static decisions are one-time events leading to one-shot decisions. Dynamic decision making emphasizes that management's decisions are not usually one-time events but are successive over a time frame. Future management decisions are influenced to some degree by past decisions.

Structured/Unstructured Decision Making. Structured decisions have formal rules while unstructured decisions have no rules. Examples of structured decisions include production scheduling, inventory reordering, and MRP. These models have a rigid structure to the decision processes and are programmed to perform routinely without much human involvement. Examples of unstructured decision models include decision support and executive support systems. All decision models are rational within their own limits and boundaries. Structured decisions can mean programmed decision making; unstructured decisions can mean nonprogrammed decision making.

Programmed/Nonprogrammed Decision Making. Programmed decisions are those that are repetitive and routine, requiring definite procedures. Examples of programmed decisions are employee hiring, billing, supply order, consumer loan, and pricing decisions. In contrast, nonprogrammed decisions are unstructured and novel; there are no set patterns for handling them. Higher levels of management are associated with the unstructured, nonprogrammed decisions.

Nonprogrammed decisions are complex, important situations, often under new and unfamiliar circumstances. These decisions are made much less frequently than are programmed decisions. Examples of nonprogrammed decisions include building a new manufacturing plant or warehouse and merger and acquisition decisions. There is no cut-and-dried method for handling nonprogrammed decisions because the problem has not arisen before, or because its precise nature and structure are not clear, or because it is so important that it deserves a custom-tailored approach. See Exhibit 1.94 for a hierarchy of management decision making.

EXHIBIT 1.94 Hierarchy of Management Decision Making

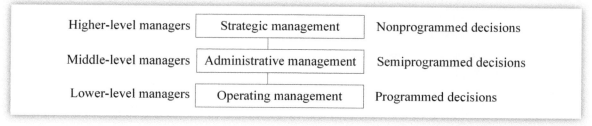

Senior-level managers make nonprogrammed (nonroutine) decisions for strategic management purposes. Programmed (routine) decisions address lower-level and highly repetitive tasks, as they are fully programmed. Clerks and computers are involved in routine programmed decisions, such as production scheduling and machine loading. Programmed decisions serve the needs of operating management. However, there is an overlap with semiprogrammed decisions in the sense that such decisions are made by both higher-level managers and middle-level managers.

The Institute of Management Accountant's research study identified nine models to describe nonroutine decision-making environments and labeled them semiprogrammed decisions.[35] The nine decision models are listed next.

1. New product decision

2. Distribution channels decision

3. Acquisition decision

4. Divestment (product abandonment) decision

5. Capital expenditure decision

6. Make-or-buy decision

7. Lease-or-buy decision

8. Pricing decision

9. Manpower planning decision

Routine/Nonroutine Decision Making. Routine decisions involve structured and programmed tasks. Nonroutine decisions involve unstructured and nonprogrammed tasks. Higher levels of management deal with nonroutine decision making while lower-level management handles routine decisions. Exhibit 1.95 depicts who makes what decisions.

---

[35] *World-Class Accounting for World-Class Manufacturing* (Montvale, NJ: Institute of Management Accountants, 1990).

EXHIBIT 1.95 Who Makes What Decisions?

Type of Decision	Lower-Level Management	Higher-Level Management
Sequential decisions	x	
Nonsequential decisions		x
Structured decisions	x	
Unstructured decisions		x
Programmed decisions	x	
Nonprogrammed decisions		x
Routine decisions	x	
Nonroutine decisions		x

(B) Decision-Making Models

Models are predetermined procedures that specify the step-by-step actions to be taken in a particular situation. Two types of decision models exist: normative and empirical models. Normative models prescribe the decision-making process—*what should be*. These models do not describe actual management practice in decision making. Instead, they describe how a decision procedure should be followed.

Empirical decision models do not describe how a decision maker should go about making a decision. Instead, they describe the actual decision processes followed by a decision maker—*what is*. A decision process is any interrelated set of activities leading to a "decision"—a commitment of resources. Reconciliation is needed between the normative and descriptive results in order to develop theories and hypotheses about how managers make use of information. *When there is no set of procedures for a decision process, then by definition there is no model for it. Examples include crisis handling and leadership.*

Normative models are programmed decisions. They help lower-level operating management implement programs, such as production scheduling or inventory control. Empirical models are nonprogrammed decisions. They help middle to senior management in making strategic decisions, such as pricing and new product introduction.

NORMATIVE MODEL VERSUS EMPIRICAL MODELS

- Normative models are prescriptive in nature, address what and how it should be, and are programmed.
- Empirical models are descriptive in nature, address what is, and are nonprogrammed.

(C) Types of Data Used in Decision Making

Decision making is a process that incorporates the estimating and predicting of the outcome of future events. When specific events are known with certainty, the decision maker does not use probabilities in the evaluation of alternatives. When specific events are uncertain, the decision maker uses probabilities in the evaluation of alternatives. The decision maker often uses the most likely outcome stated in deterministic format rather than incorporating all outcomes in a probabilistic (stochastic) format.

A decision maker uses two types of data: deterministic data and probabilistic data. Deterministic data are known and not subject to any error or distribution of error. They are based on historical data; their environment is stable and predictable. Decision results will be certain with a single unique payoff. There is only a single outcome for each possible action.

The decision maker uses probabilistic data to evaluate decisions under situations of risk and uncertainty. An estimation of distribution of possible outcomes can be made, not an assured or a predictable outcome. The environment is characterized as unstable and unpredictable since each event is assigned a probability of occurrence. Probabilistic data allows for better risk evaluation since sensitivity analysis can be performed on each action to measure the material impact of the various events.

An estimated payoff table or decision tree can be developed for analysis. A drawback of using probabilistic data is the availability and integrity of data to determine multiple courses of action because probabilistic data are not known.

DETERMINISTIC DATA VERSUS PROBABILISTIC DATA

- Deterministic data are known, and the environment is stable and predictable.
- Probabilistic data are not known, and the environment is unstable and unpredictable.

Decision making is a frequent and important human activity and is especially a managerial activity. Decisions are not all of one kind. The procedure for making one decision, such as buying a home, is entirely different from making another decision, such as taking a CIA examination.

Decision making is related to risk levels. With respect to risk, individuals act differently and can be grouped into three categories: risk takers, risk neutral, and risk averters. When contrasted with a risk-taking entrepreneur, a professional manager (or an auditor) is likely to be more cautious as a risk taker (i.e., either risk neutral or risk averter). Another factor is that risks are related to returns. The higher the risk, the greater the return, and vice versa. Also, controls are related to risks. The higher the risk, the greater the need for controls, and vice versa. Controls reduce or eliminate risks and exposures.

Four general types of decisions exist that require different decision procedures: decisions under certainty, decisions under risk, decisions under uncertainty, and decisions under conflict or competition (see Exhibit 1.96).

EXHIBIT 1.96 Types of Decisions

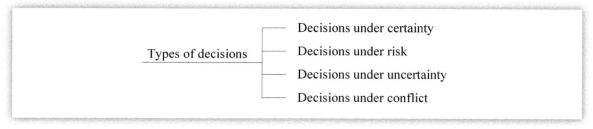

Decision Making under Certainty. In decision making under certainty, a decision maker is operating in an environment where all of the facts surrounding a decision are known exactly, and each alternative is associated with only one possible outcome. The environment is known as certainty.

Five different methods exist that are useful for making decisions under certainty. The first four methods are optimization methods—that is, they attempt to identify the very best alternative available. The fifth method, satisficing, simply looks for the first satisfactory alternative (see Exhibit 1.97).

EXHIBIT 1.97 Optimization Methods

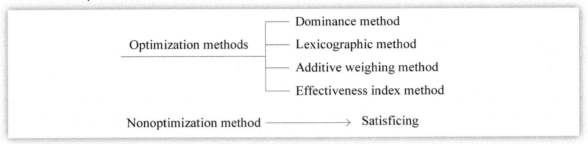

The **dominance method** is the simplest of the decision procedures. To use it in making decisions, it is necessary to find the dominance relations among the alternatives. One alternative dominates another if both of the following are satisfied:

1. It is at least as good as the other on all properties, and

2. It is better on at least one property.

Any alternative that is dominated by another is dropped from consideration since it will never be judged the best alternative by any reasonable decision procedure. Any alternative that dominates all the others is chosen as best.

VALUE SYSTEM IN DECISION-MAKING CHOICES

- If two people make different choices in the same situation, it does not mean that one of them is wrong; it may just be that they have different values. Therefore, the correct choice in any decision-making situation depends on the decision maker's individual value system.

- Generating alternatives, examining their properties, and choosing among the alternatives are all activities that may add considerable cost to the decision-making process.

The advantage of the dominance method is that people can agree about which alternatives are dominant. This method is easy to apply, and its results are reliable. Its disadvantages are that it is not a powerful decision-making method because it usually does not eliminate very many of the alternatives. Examples of applications of decision making under certainty are linear programming, transportation problems, inventory models, and break-even analysis.

The **lexicographic method** is so named because of its resemblance to the procedure for ordering the definitions of words in the dictionary. In this method, first look at the most important definitions of interest. If two alternatives have the same value on this property, then decide on the basis of the second most important property, and so on. It is necessary to specify the order of importance of the properties of the alternatives.

To make a decision by this method, consider the most important property first. If one alternative is better than the other alternatives on the most important property, then that alternative is the one chosen. If two or more alternatives are tied on the most important property, then drop the other alternatives from consideration and consider the next most important property in order to break ties. If any ties remain unbroken, then consider the third property, and so on. Changing the order of importance of the properties in the lexicographic method does not always change the alternative chosen as best.

The lexicographic method is most appropriate when one of the properties outweighs all of the others in importance. The method's major strengths under these circumstances are that it is quick and easy to apply. This method is least appropriate when the properties are roughly equal in importance. Under these circumstances, the method may lead us to choose an alternative that has a slight advantage in the most important property, even though that advantage is outweighed by big disadvantages in other properties. This situation occurs because the lexicographic method typically ignores all but the most important property.

The **additive weighing method** takes all of the properties into account but does not give them equal weight. The more important properties receive heavy weights and the less important ones receive lighter weights. To use this method, numbers for both weights and values of the properties must be available.

To make a decision by the additive weighing method, multiply numerical values of the properties by the weights of the properties for each alternative. Then choose the alternative with the largest sum as "best." This method takes all of the properties into account in making the decision but does not take the interactions of the properties into account. Therefore, this method can lead to inappropriate decisions by ignoring these interactions, just as the lexicographic method can lead to inappropriate decisions by ignoring the less important properties. The major drawback of this method is that it is time consuming and obtaining the numbers for the weights and values of the properties is difficult.

USE OF DECISION-MAKING METHODS

Decision methods such as lexicography and additive weighing are useful because they allow people to substitute reliable objective procedures for unreliable subjective ones.

The **effectiveness index method** takes into account the interactions that the additive weighing method ignores. This method is used when the interactions are especially strong or because errors in decisions are very costly, or both. The method requires an extensive analysis of the situation under consideration, and designing and implementing such a method is very expensive and time consuming.

Satisficing is a nonoptimizing approach to decision making under certainty. The satisficing method requires the decision maker to identify the worst value he or she is willing to accept for each of the attributes. The decision maker then considers all of the alternatives in order, rejecting any alternatives that fall below the minimal values of the attributes and accepting the first alternative that meets all of the minimal values.

The satisficing method is particularly useful when we have to choose among a very large number of alternatives and it is not necessary to find the best. This method is less costly since it does not examine all of the alternatives and may not yield a decision at all if the decision-making standards are very high.

KEY CONCEPTS TO REMEMBER: Decision Making under Certainty

- All optimizing methods are designed to find the best available alternative and are suitable for idealized situations. They examine all alternatives available.

- The nonoptimizing method is not designed to identify the best alternative. Rather, it is designed to find the first satisfactory alternative that is more suitable to real-world situations. Only some alternatives are examined.

Decision Making under Risk. When a decision maker is faced with a decision and the probabilities of various outcomes are known, the situation is said to be decision making under risk (see Exhibit 1.98). Gambling decisions are typical of decisions under risk. An essential feature of decisions under risk is that we can calculate a probability for the effect of the chance event. Tossing a fair coin, rotating a roulette wheel, and rolling a die are examples of decisions under risk. Examples of decision making under risk can be found in queuing theory, statistical quality control, acceptance sampling, and PERT. Decision trees are used to assist the decision maker under conditions of risk.

EXHIBIT 1.98 Perfect Certainty versus Risk versus Perfect Uncertainty

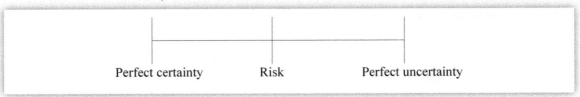

Risk is a condition faced by managers when they have to make a decision based on incomplete but reliable information. Uncertain conditions exist when little or no reliable information is available. Certainty conditions exist when complete, reliable information is available.

One widely recommended technique for making risky decisions is to choose the action that has the greatest expected value. The expected value of an action is the average payoff value we can expect if we repeat the action many times.

EXAMPLE OF EXPECTED VALUE

Game 1. Win $2.00 whether the coin comes up heads or tails when a fair coin is tossed.

Game 2. Win $10.00 if the coin comes up heads and lose $5.00 if it comes up tails.

Expected value = Average payoff = Probability of a head (PH) × Payoff for heads (VH)
+ Probability of a tail (PT) × Payoff for tails (VT)

$$EV = PH \times VH + PT \times VT$$

Here PH and PT have equal chances, that is, 1/2.

$$EV \text{ (for game 2)} = 1/2\,(10.00) + 1/2\,(-5.00) = 5.00 - 2.50 = 2.50$$

$$EV \text{ (for game 1)} = 1/2\,(2.00) + 1/2\,(2.00) = 1.00 + 1.00 = 2.00$$

Since the expected value of game 2 is greater than the expected value of game 1, we should choose game 2 in order to maximize our expected value. Whether we choose to play game 1 or 2 depends on whether we are risk averse or not. Game 1 is a no-lose game while game 2 is not.

Decision Making under Uncertainty. Like decisions under risk, decisions under uncertainty involve a chance factor. The unique feature of decisions under uncertainty is that we cannot calculate a probability for the effect of the chance event. This is a situation in which a decision must be made on the basis of little or no reliable factual information. When considering pricing of competitors, actions of regulatory agencies, and strikes of suppliers, the decision maker is addressing the problem of uncertainty.

Multiple outcomes are possible. The first task is to establish subjective probabilities of occurrence for the multiple outcomes. Under conditions of uncertainty, the rational, economic decision maker will use expected monetary value as the decision criteria. The expected monetary value of an act is the sum of the conditional profit (loss) of each event times the probability of each event occurring.

There are four strategies for making decisions under uncertainty: the mini-max strategy, the maxi-max strategy, the Hurwicz strategy, and the mini-max regret strategy (see Exhibit 1.99).

EXHIBIT 1.99 Strategies for Making Decisions under Uncertainty

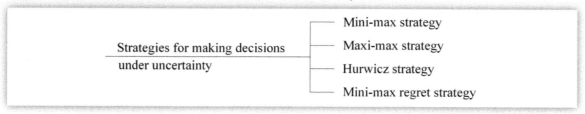

The **mini-max strategy** is a very conservative, pessimistic strategy that assumes that whatever action we choose, nature is against us and will cause the worst possible outcome. The values of the worst outcomes are the row minima. This strategy calls for choosing the action that gives us the best (largest) of these minima. That is, it chooses the action whose worst possible outcomes are not as bad as the worst possible outcomes of the other actions.

The best examples of applications for uncertainty are in problems of the military, war, and various types of athletic competition, product development, product pricing, collective bargaining, arbitration, foreign policy decisions, contract bidding, and oligopolistic and monopolistic market conditions.

A nice property of the mini-max strategy is that it guarantees an outcome that is no worse than the minimum value for the action. The outcome may be better than the minimum, but it will certainly be no worse. However, this strategy, which focuses on preventing disaster, has the unfortunate property of possibly eliminating the best outcomes from consideration.

The **maxi-max strategy** is an optimistic strategy that assumes that nature will cooperate with us to provide the best possible outcome for the action we choose—the row maxima. This strategy chooses the action that yields the best of the possible outcomes. However, it does not defend the decision maker against the possibility of occurring the worst possible outcome, as does the mini-max strategy. Decision makers who are attracted to large gains would most likely use the maxi-max decision rule.

APPROACHES TO DECISION PROBLEMS

Whatever strategy we decide to use in approaching decision problems, it is wise to make a habit of determining if any of the alternatives is dominant and could therefore be eliminated.

The **Hurwicz strategy** is a compromise between the very pessimistic mini-max strategy and the very optimistic maxi-max strategy. A value between 0 and 1 is chosen for the coefficient of optimism, A, keeping in mind that low values of A are an indication of pessimism and high values of A are an indication of optimism. The goal is to find both the row minima and the row maxima and choose the activity that yields the maximum of the computed quantities. When A is zero, the Hurwicz strategy is the same as the mini-max strategy; when A is 1, the Hurwicz strategy is the same as the maxi-max strategy.

MINI-MAX STRATEGY VERSUS MAXI-MAX STRATEGY

- The mini-max strategy is a pessimistic strategy and finds the row minima. It gives a conservative feel when playing a game against nature but not when playing against a human opponent. This is because we know our opponents.

- The maxi-max strategy is an optimistic strategy and finds the row maxima.

The **mini-max regret strategy** is good for situations where the expected values concept fails. Why does the expected value technique fail? Expected values are averages of values. They are appropriate when we are trying to balance values that are close together, for example the chance of losing $2.00 versus the chance of winning $4.00. Averages are much less appropriate when we balance values that are very different, such as the cost of a modest insurance premium versus the risk of being impoverished by a serious car accident.

The mini-max regret decision criteria choose the strategy that minimizes the maximum opportunity cost. To measure regret, take the difference between the value of the outcome actually obtained and the maximum value that could have been obtained if a different alternative had been chosen.

Decision Making under Conflict. Decision making under conflict is referred to as game theory. The mini-max strategy is used for analyzing decisions under conflict or competition. There are two types of games under conflict: zero-sum games and non-zero-sum games.

Game theory is used when the states of nature of the decision maker are the strategies of the opponent (i.e., the other player or the other decision maker). When one opponent gains at the loss of the other, it is called a **zero-sum game** involving a complete conflict of interest. Games with less than complete conflict of interest are called **non-zero-sum games**. In non-zero-sum games, the gains of one competitor are not completely at the expense of the other competitors.

The majority of business competitive actions involve non-zero-sum games. Non-zero-sum games require that the payoffs be given for each player since the payoff of one player can no longer be deducted from the payoff of the other, as in zero-sum games. The **prisoner's dilemma** is a type of business game situation where one firm is concerned about the actions of its rivals. The outcome of the prisoner's dilemma game cannot be predicted conclusively. An example of payoff table is shown in Exhibit 1.100.

EXHIBIT 1.100 Payoff Table

| | States of Nature | | | | |
	1	2	3	4	Expected Profit
A					
B					
C					

States of nature are uncontrollable future events that can affect the outcomes of a decision. The best examples of applications of zero-sum games are in problems of the military, war, and various types of athletic competition. The best examples of applications of non-zero-sum games are in product development, product pricing, collective bargaining, arbitration, foreign policy decisions, contract bidding, and oligopolistic and monopolistic market conditions.

The simplest type of gain is the two-person zero-sum game. The players, X and Y, are equal in intelligence and ability. The term "zero sum" is used because the sum of gains exactly equals the sum of losses. The sum of player X's gains (or losses) and player Y's losses (or gains) is zero. Such a game, in which the sum of gains and losses added up over all players is zero, is called a zero-sum game.

EXAMPLE OF UTILITY FOR ALTERNATIVES

Assume a linear utility for money and a risk-neutral decision maker. From the next payoff table, we can conclude that the utility for alternative A is

	State of Nature		
	S1	**S2**	**Expected Profit**
Alternative A	100	200	$160
Alternative B	140	40	$ 80

a. $300.

b. High.

c. Exactly twice that of B.

d. Approximately twice that of B.

The correct answer is **c**. The utility function for money would be linear, and the decision maker's behavior would be consistent with the maximization of expected profit. A risk-neutral decision maker will select the alternative with the highest profit, that is, alternative A, which is exactly twice that of B (160 / 80 = 2). Choice a is incorrect. Utility is measured in utils, not in dollars. It does not compare the two alternatives. Choice b is incorrect. This requires a judgment about the utility function of the decision maker, which is unknown. Choice d is incorrect. The linearity assumption leads to exact statements, not approximations.

(D) Pure Strategy and Mixed Strategy

A pure strategy exists if there is one strategy for player X and one strategy for player Y that will be played each time. The payoff, which is obtained when each player pays the pure strategy, is called a **saddle point**. The saddle point represents an equilibrium condition that is optimum for both competitors.

The **Wald criterion**, which is a variant of decision making under uncertainty, is a useful technique to determine if a pure strategy exists. A saddle point can be recognized because it is both the smallest numerical value in its row and largest numerical value in its column. Not all two-person zero-sum games have a saddle point. When a saddle point is present, complex calculations to determine optimum strategies and game values are unnecessary.

When a pure strategy does not exist, a fundamental theorem of game theory states that the optimum can be found by using a mixed strategy. In a mixed strategy, each competitor randomly selects the strategy to employ according to a previously determined probability of usage for each strategy. Using a mixed strategy involves making a selection each time period by tossing a coin, selecting a number from a table of random numbers, or using some probabilistic process.

There is a simple test to determine whether a pure or mixed strategy is best. If the maximum of the row minima (the maxi-min) equals the minimum of the column maxima (the mini-max), then a pure strategy is best. Otherwise, use the mixed strategy.

KEY CONCEPTS TO REMEMBER: Which Decision Criterion Is What?

Mini-max criteria	$\longrightarrow$	Minimizing the maximum losses
Maxi-max criteria	$\longrightarrow$	Maximizing the maximum profits
Maxi-min criteria	$\longrightarrow$	Maximizing the minimum profits
Mini-min criteria	$\longrightarrow$	Minimizing the minimum losses or maximum profits (not worth pursuing)
Mini-max regret criteria	$\longrightarrow$	Minimizing the maximum opportunity cost

(E) Decision Making versus Problem Solving

Decision making and problem solving are not the same; they have two different time dimensions. The basic difference is that decision making is future oriented and problem solving is past oriented. Decision making deals with risk while problem solving does not.

Decision Making $\longrightarrow$ Future Oriented

Problem Solving $\longrightarrow$ Past Oriented

Decision making is the probability of success. Examples of decision-making situations include investing in a new product line, buying new equipment, and selecting an employee for a key position. Examples of problem-solving situations include handling a tardy employee, correcting a poor-quality production, and working with a slow-paying customer.

Exhibit 1.101 presents an overview of differences between decision making and problem solving.

EXHIBIT 1.101 Differences between Decision Making and Problem Solving

Decision Making	Problem Solving
Decision making is concerned with future consequences; it changes the environment and the situation.	Problem solving is concerned with looking back; this is the way it should be and it no longer is.
A decision is made to create a change and therefore generates a new set of circumstances.	A problem is solved now so that decision making is not needed later. This is because the problem-solving approach has restored the process where it should be.
Decision making focuses on making things happen in the future.	
A decision has a risk and an uncertainty, but it also creates an opportunity.	Problem solving can be excessive because it creates a fear of change.
	A change should be seen as an opportunity to go forward, not to go back to the past.

Source: Peter F. Drucker, *The Frontiers of Management* (New York: Harper & Row; 1986).

Although the element of risk is different between decisions and problems, they are intertwined in that a decision is needed to fix a problem. Although decisions are made to solve problems, some bad decisions create more problems, causing a circular effect. Problems come first and decisions come next. Note that current decisions are made to fix past problems, to detect and solve current problems, and to prevent future problems from occurring. Also note that future management decisions are influenced to some degree by past decisions.

(F) Decision Making and the Internal Auditor: Applications

In order for auditors to reach decisions, they must understand how the various pieces of information are combined. For example, the issues of materiality, conflicting evidence, and determining whether sufficient evidence has been gathered all influence the auditor's decision-making process.

The internal auditor will be making decisions under various circumstances. When the auditor must make an important decision in a hurry and that decision is based on incomplete information, the decision-making process would be called satisficing, not maximizing, minimizing, or rationalizing. Satisficing is a non-optimization decision-making method. The auditor presents several audit situations that require a decision.

(G) Tools and Techniques for Decision Making

- **Differential analysis.** Differential analysis is a technique to compare differences in revenues or costs of two or more alternatives.

- **Decision table.** A decision table is a tool that documents rules used to select one or more actions based on one or more conditions. These conditions and their corresponding actions can be presented either in a matrix or tabular form.

- **Flowcharts.** Flowcharts help a decision maker in analyzing a large, complex problem. Flowcharts and decision trees both show flow or sequencing. Unlike the flowchart, a decision tree shows outcome probabilities.

- **Discriminant analysis.** Discriminant analysis is a qualitative, subjective tool to differentiate between effective and ineffective procedures or actions.

- **Management science.** Operations research, or management science, provides management an approach that focuses on decision making and reliance on formal mathematical models.

- **Decision trees.** A decision tree is a graphical representation of possible decisions, events, or states of nature resulting from each decision with its associated probabilities, and the outcomes of the events or states of nature. The decision problem displays the sequential nature of the decision-making situation. The decision tree has nodes, branches, and circles to represent junction boxes, connectors between the nodes, and states-of-nature nodes, respectively.

- **Payoff table.** A payoff table is a tabular representation of the payoffs for a decision problem. It shows losses and gains for each outcome of the decision alternatives.

- **Cost-benefit analysis.** Cost-benefit analysis is a decision procedure in which we compare the expected costs and benefits of alternative actions. We choose the action for which the expected value of the benefits minus the expected value of the costs is greatest. The expected value is the desirability of alternative multiplied by the probability of success. The likelihood of an occurrence that is derived mathematically from reliable historical data is called objective probabilities. However, subjective probabilities do not have mathematical reliability since they are derived from intuition and "gut feel" of the decision maker.

- **Success-failure analysis.** Success-failure analysis is a qualitative approach to brainstorm conditions for both success and failure. A T-column can be used with headings such as "What will guarantee success" and "What will guarantee failure."

- **Devil's advocate techniques.** In the devil's advocate technique, the decision maker focuses on failures and identifies ways an action or an alternative can be less than successful.

- **Reality check.** The reality check decision is tested in the pseudo-real-world conditions. A T-column is used with possible headings "Our expectations" and "Our concerns" to facilitate the analysis.

- **Risk analysis.** Risk analysis is the analysis of possible risks to be encountered and the means to handle them that can be performed. A T-column can be used with possible headings "Anticipated risks" and "Actions to overcome risks."

- **Activity analysis.** All current activities can be labeled as either value-added or non-value-added using a T-account diagram. The goal is to eliminate or reduce non-value-added activities since they are adding little or no value to the process at hand. Decisions affecting costs incurred for non-value-added activities can then be challenged or revisited by performing a detailed analysis of all tasks and activities with the purpose of eliminating or reducing them. A T-column can be used with possible headings "Value-added activities" and "Non-value-added activities" to facilitate the activity analysis.

(c) Communication Skills

Topics such as communication chain, factors in the communication process, formal and informal communications, elements of effective communication, presentation of information, barriers to communication, and organizational dynamics are discussed in this section.

(i) Communication Chain

One thing that is common to all four functions of management—planning, organizing, directing, and controlling—is communication. Surveys have shown that 80% of a manager's time is spent on communication and 20% is spent on other activities. Communication can be either formal or informal. It involves two or more people and includes written and oral where people are transferring information and understanding that information from one person to another. The effectiveness of organizational communication can be increased with clear verbal and written messages with little or no noise. Nonverbal communications (body language and messages sent through actions, not words) and listening skills (the art of receiving messages) are also important. Research describes communication as a chain made up of identifiable links—sender, encoding, medium, decoding, receiver, and feedback. The communication chain is only as strong as its weakest link.

(A) Sender

The sender is an individual or a group of people whose goal is to convey or transmit the message to a receiver in the best possible media and in the fastest way.

(B) Encoding

The objective of encoding is to translate internal thought patterns into a language or code that the intended receiver of the message will be able to understand. Words (written or oral), numbers, gestures, or other symbols are used in encoding. The purpose of the message affects the medium of encoding. For example, if a manager were proposing a new employee benefit plan, which is a sensitive program, a meeting with emotional appeal and gestures would have a bigger impact than a normal written (cold) report. A meeting conveys personal interest and empathy, unlike a report.

(C) Medium

Many types of media exist to send and receive a message, including face-to-face communications, telephone calls, regular meetings and electronic meetings (video-conferencing), emails, text messages, memos, letters, reports, efaxes, bulletin boards, newsletters, and others. Each media type varies in richness from high rich to low rich. **Media richness** is described as the capacity of a given medium to convey information properly and promote learning. *The goal is to match media richness with the situation. Otherwise, mismatching occurs, which can lead to confusion and embarrassment.*

Examples of high-rich media include face-to-face conversation, telephone, or video-conferencing, since they provide multiple information cues (e.g., message content, tone of voice, facial expressions), facilitate immediate feedback, and are personal in focus. High-rich media is good for discussing nonroutine issues and problems.

Examples of low-rich or lean media include bulletin boards, reports, memos, email, text messages, and letters. These media provide a single cue, do not facilitate immediate feedback, and are impersonal. Low-rich media is good for discussing routine problems.

(D) Decoding

Decoding is the translation of the transmitted message from the sender's language and terminology to the receiver's language and terminology. Effective decoding requires that these messages be the same between the sender and the receiver. The receiver's willingness to receive the message is a primary criterion for successful decoding.

(E) Receiver

The **receiver** is an individual or a group of people whose goal is to acknowledge and receive the intended message sent by a sender. The receiver will take an action based on the message received.

(F) Feedback

The communication process is not complete until the receiver acknowledges the message (via verbal or nonverbal feedback) to the sender. Without feedback, the sender is not sure whether the receiver has received the message. Feedback affects follow-up: If the receiver does not understand the message, follow-up meetings should be scheduled.

(ii) Factors in the Communication Process

Two factors in the communication process include noise and perception.

(A) Noise

Noise is not part of the chainlike communication process. It is any interference with the normal flow of understanding of a message from one person to another. Examples of noise include misperception, illegible print, speech impairment, and garbled computer data transmission. Understanding has an inverse relationship with noise—the higher the noise, the less the understanding. For effective communication to take place between and among people, we all need to identify the sources of noise and reduce it. Greater amounts of noise in communication not only waste resources (time and money) but also create frustration between the sender and the receiver.

(B) Perception

Perception is a process of giving meaning to one's environment and is a vital link in the communication process. It consists of three subprocesses: selectivity, organization, and interpretation. Selectivity is sensory screening and a sorting-out process. Organization is mentally creating meaningful patterns from disorganized thoughts. Interpretation is how people understand a message, which is often different for different people.

(iii) Formal and informal Communications

Formal communication channels are those that flow within and outside the chain of command. They include downward, upward, horizontal, and diagonal communication.

Downward communication refers to the messages and information sent from a higher level to a lower level in the management hierarchy (e.g., goals, strategies, mission, vision, directives, policies, procedures, and performance feedback).

Upward communication refers to the messages and information transmitted from a lower level to a higher level in the management hierarchy (e.g., grievances and disputes, routine progress and performance reports, suggestions for improvement, and problems reporting and exceptions reporting).

Horizontal communication refers to the lateral or diagonal exchange of messages and information among peers or coworkers, occurring within or across departments (e.g., intradepartmental problem-solving requests, interdepartmental coordination on joint projects, and use of task forces and committees). Horizontal communication is important in learning organizations with teams solving problems.

Diagonal communication refers to the exchange of messages and reports from a lower-level employee in one department to a higher-level employee in another department. This communication occurs only when the manager of the lower-level employee is fully informed and gives the employee permission to initiate such communication. Diagonal communication also occurs when a higher-level employee requests special studies and projects from a lower-level because the latter has the necessary skills and knowledge to conduct such activities. Diagonal communication can take place in both directions between lower-level employees and higher-level employees and vice versa. Note that this type of communication violates the chain-of-command management principle because the subordinate is receiving orders from two superiors and reporting to two supervisors.

Informal communication channels exist that do not consider the organization's formal or official hierarchy of authority and chain of command. Examples include MBWA and the grapevine. In MBWA, higher-level employees (e.g., executives and senior managers) talk directly with lower-level employees (e.g., hourly workers at factory, office, or warehouse) to learn about problems and issues confronting them as well as to share their key ideas and values. These meetings are informal and unannounced.

The **grapevine** is the unofficial and informal communication system. It sometimes conflicts with the formal system; at other times, it complements and reinforces the formal system. The grapevine will remain in organizations as long as people are working in a group environment. It has both positive and negative sides. On the positive side, grapevine communication can help management learn how employees truly feel about policies, procedures, and programs—a type of feedback mechanism. A negative consequence of grapevines is rumors. Other places for spreading rumors are around the water cooler and in hallways, break rooms, and cafeterias.

(iv) Elements of Effective Communication

Research has shown that the three essential elements of effective communication are genuineness, respect, and empathy. The person who has mastered the skills of communication but lacks genuineness, respect, and empathy will find her professional expertise irrelevant or even harmful. **Genuineness** means being what one really is without a front or facade. Genuineness is essential to all vital relationships, especially auditor–auditee relationships. It is being honest and open with others and open about one's feelings, needs, and ideas. **Respect** and acceptance mean having a positive regard for others. Respect recognizes the sanctity of the other's privacy, supports the other person's self-direction, and respects his or her individuality. **Acceptance** is an attitude of neutrality toward another person. Every person is in the need of acceptance. Acceptance and respect may or may not be accompanied by warmth, and they do not mean blindly agreeing and cold submission. Once you accept and respect a person, that person tends to be more at ease around you. **Empathy** is simply putting oneself in someone else's shoes. It is the ability to understand another person in the same way as that person understands him or herself. It refers to the ability to really see and hear another person and understand the person from her perspective. One needs to be careful with empathy because it can be perceived as excessive if a person identifies very closely with another. There must be a balance between detached and attached involvement.

When an internal auditor practices the three elements of communication skills (i.e., genuineness, respect, and empathy), it is easier to agree to disagree with the audit client about audit findings, values, and other issues. The goal is to solve real problems on a win-win basis (i.e., both parties win).

APATHY VERSUS EMPATHY VERSUS SYMPATHY

- Apathy is a lack of feeling or a lack of interest or concern (e.g., "I don't care").
- Empathy involves experiencing the feelings of another person without losing one's own identity (e.g., "Looks like you are feeling down").
- Sympathy is defined as feelings for another person (e.g., "I feel just dreadful for you").

(v) Presentation of Information

Information can be improperly analyzed and incorrectly interpreted. The causes of poor business decisions can be attributed not only to a lack of information but also to the failure to properly interpret information. Proper interpretation of information depends largely on the reliability of the source (i.e., internal versus external source or single versus multiple sources), the manner in which the information is presented, and the personal perception of the person receiving or giving the information. For example, surveys and census data are firsthand information (mostly reliable), and hearsay is secondhand information (mostly unreliable).

The manner in which information is presented can significantly affect its use. Most information that has been assembled from statistics, data, and facts has been "massaged" (assembled in a manner applicable to a particular problem at hand). This is because if 10 people created charts from the same set of statistics, we would have 10 different charts. Each person would massage the information in a different way—yet all the different charts could be correct.

Proper and accurate interpretation also depends on our own abilities of perception. One should always keep the original question or problem in mind and pay close attention to details. It is good to view all information with a bit of healthy skepticism because information is not an exact science. *The return on an investment in information is knowledge.*

(vi) Barriers to Communication

It is false to assume that if people can talk, they can communicate. Talking is different from communicating. Many barriers exist between all people, which make communications much more difficult than most people seem to realize. The auditor needs to know all the barriers that exist that can block effective communication. The negative effects of roadblocks to communication include diminishing of self-respect in others, triggering defensiveness, resistance, and resentment. Negative effects can also lead to dependency, withdrawal, and feelings of defeat or of inadequacy.

(vii) Organizational Dynamics

Organizational dynamics is a combination of individual dynamics, group dynamics, and work-related dynamics.

(A) Individual Dynamics

Individual dynamics deal with how an individual's needs and wants are satisfied at the workplace. Managers should understand Maslow's hierarchy of needs, which help to explain the actions of employees at the workplace.

(B) Group Dynamics

Group dynamics deal with how group members interact with each other at the workplace and how managers resolve group problems. Each member of the group plays an expected role, and the group has its own biases, values, and beliefs. Another dimension affecting group dynamics is conflicts among departments or functions within an organization, including organizational politics.

(C) Work-Related Dynamics

The environment—physical, social, and cultural—is part of the situational context of human behavior at the workplace. We are affected not only by our relationships with others but by the places and spaces in which we interact. Environmental psychology is the science of transactions between human behavior and the environment.

(d) Negotiating Skills

Negotiation is a decision-making process among different parties with different preferences. Negotiation is gaining the favor of people from whom we want things such as money, justice, status, and recognition.

Two common types of negotiation include two parties (buyer and seller) and three parties (buyer, seller, and agent). Traditionally, negotiation takes a win-lose attitude, which is based on power, position, and competition. Here, one person's success is achieved at the expense of the success (loss) of others. It takes something away from the other party. A win-win attitude is based on high principles and cooperativeness among parties. Here, one person's success is not achieved at the expense of the success of others. With a win-win attitude, every party gets something, meaning each party wins something.

Four outcomes are possible in a negotiation process involving two parties, as follows:

First Party	Second Party
Win	Win
Win	Lose
Lose	Win
Lose	Lose

Of course, each party's goal is to win the negotiation. Successful collaborative negotiations depend on finding out what the other side really wants and showing them a way to get it, while still getting what you want. It is the definition of a win-win situation. Managers should practice successful collaborative negotiations to reach win-win situations.

Dos of Negotiations

- Do use phrases such as "I don't know," or "I don't understand it," which can result in negotiating leverage.
- Do approach others and ask for help. Doing so tends to set the climate for a mutually beneficial relationship. At the very least, you will cause the other side to make an investment that ultimately accrues to your advantage

Don'ts of Negotiations

- Don't be too quick to "understand" or prove your intellect at the outset of an encounter. Learn to ask questions, even when you think you might know the answers.
- Never give an ultimatum at the beginning of a negotiation. An ultimatum must come at the end of a negotiation, if at all.
- Do not use "hard" ultimatums, such as "Take it or leave it" or "It is this way or else!" These attitudes are self-defeating. Use "soft" ultimatums, such as "Your position is valid, but this is all I can do at the moment. Help me."
- Never leave the other side without alternatives. Always allow others to make some kind of choice.
- Don't reduce the other side's stress unless you receive what you are shooting for.
- Don't be abrasive, because how you say something will often determine the response you get.
- Avoid using absolutes when responding to people. Learn to preface your replies with phrases such as "What I think I may have heard you say . . ." This "lubricant demeanor" will soften your words, consecrate your actions, and minimize the friction.
- Avoid publicly embarrassing the people with whom you deal. Never ridicule anyone in front of others. Even when you are right, shun all opportunities to humiliate people, especially in public.
- Never forget the power of your attitude.
- Never judge the actions and motives of others.

(i) Added-Value Negotiating and Best Alternative to a Negotiated Agreement

Two related topics in negotiation are added-value negotiating and best alternative to a negotiated agreement. Each is discussed next.

(A) Added-Value Negotiating

Added-value negotiating (AVN) is a value-added process (win-win) involving development of multiple deals with multiple outcomes as opposed to traditional (win-lose) negotiating, which is based on a single outcome with a single winner.

AVN is based on openness, flexibility, and a mutual search for the successful exchange of value. AVN allows one to build strong relationships with people over time. It bridges the gap between win-win theory and practice.

AVN is comprised of five steps:

1. **Clarify interests.** Both parties jointly identify subjective and objective interests so that a common goal is found.

2. **Identify options.** A variety of choices are developed to create value for both parties.

3. **Design alternative deals.** Multiple win-win offers are designed to promote creative agreement.

4. **Select a deal.** Each party selects a mutually acceptable deal after testing the various deals for value, balance, and fit.

5. **Perfect the deal.** Unresolved details are openly discussed and agreements are put in writing, which strengthens the relationship for future negotiations.

(B) BATNA

The members of the Harvard Negotiation project discovered a new concept in negotiations known as the best alternative to a negotiated agreement (BATNA) to establish a standard (i.e., bottom line) against which any proposed agreement should be measured. BATNA describes the anchor point for both sellers and buyers when negotiations do not produce the desired outcome(s) for each negotiating party in terms of a settlement amount.

Each negotiating party's BATNA is a decision point in terms of accepting or rejecting the offer by the other party. The difference between the seller's BATNA and the buyer's BATNA is known as the bargaining zone, which becomes the only basis for further negotiation due to overlapping range of acceptable outcomes. Negotiation is either useless or unnecessary outside the bargaining zone because it is not a common ground for both parties. Agreement is possible within the bargaining zone and not possible outside the zone. Therefore, estimating one party's BATNA is essential in protecting the negotiating parties from accepting offers that are unfavorable and from rejecting offers that are favorable.

EXAMPLE OF CALCULATING THE BARGAINING ZONE GIVEN THE SELLER'S AND BUYER'S BATNA

An item's original price was $400, current appraised value is estimated at $500, its owner is making a final offer to sell the item at $600, and a buyer's final offer to buy the same item is $350. The seller's BATNA is $400, and the buyer's BATNA is $500. What is the bargaining zone in amount and range?

The bargaining zone amount is Buyer's BATNA minus Seller's BATNA = $500 − $400 = $100.

The bargaining zone range is $400 to $500.

A realistic BATNA can protect against four decision-making traps: framing error, escalation of commitment, overconfidence, and negotiating without a standard.

- Framing error deals with how information is presented (i.e., positively or negatively), which can lead to bias in behavior and decision making.

- Escalation of commitment is like the throwing good money after bad dilemma in that managers continue to fund losing projects to save face.

- A positive relationship exists between overconfidence and task difficulty. Managers exhibit extra courage needed to handle difficult situations, which leads to unreasonable risks.

Careful analysis of situations and critical thinking about decision alternatives can help managers avoid the overconfidence trap.

- Negotiating parties usually move aimlessly in the dark due to a lack of negotiating standards, which results in accepting unfavorable terms and rejecting favorable terms. A negotiating standard such as BATNA helps in making better decisions because a seller's BATNA becomes the standard for accepting or rejecting offers.

(e) Conflict Management Skills

(i) Conflict Defined

Social scientists say that conflict is inevitable between people, and without conflict there is no major personal change or social progress. Conflict is based on scarcity of power, availability of resources, social position, and difference in value structure between individuals or groups involved in the situation.

Conflict is the medium by which problems are recognized and solved. Conflict is closely related to change and interpersonal dealings. It refers to all kinds of opposition or antagonistic interaction.

Conflict management involves accepting or even encouraging constructive conflict as necessary. The key point is to minimize the destructive form of conflict. Despite its drawbacks of creating friction, conflict has some benefits. It can spur technological development, encourage personal and intellectual growth, and help renew business organizations.

> **Example:** A manager creates a constructive conflict on purpose by introducing a work-related healthy competition among employees to get the best out of them. A reward is given to the employee who handled the competition best.

Because human behavior varies with people and is difficult to predict, there are a variety of types of conflict, such as disruptive and destructive conflict, realistic and unrealistic conflict, and functional and dysfunctional conflict.

(ii) Disruptive Conflict and Destructive Conflict

To be human is to experience conflict. This conflict arises due to differences in personal values, opinions, desires, habits, and needs of people. It is impossible for people to rise completely above selfishness, betrayals, misrepresentations, anger, and strain. The best way to depict conflict is on a scale of disruptive and destructive dimensions (see Exhibit 1.102).

EXHIBIT 1.102 Scale of Disruptive and Destructive Dimensions

Conflict at best is disruptive; at worst it is destructive. Once conflict erupts, it is difficult to control. Disruptive conflict is temporary and not harmful, caused by few employees due to their personal grudges. Destructive conflict has a tendency to expand until it consumes all the things and all people it touches.

(iii) Realistic Conflict and Unrealistic Conflict

When two or more people are together for any length of time, some conflict will be generated. That is inevitable. Social scientists make an important distinction between two types of conflict: realistic conflict and unrealistic conflict.

Realistic conflict, which is based on rationality, arises from opposing needs, goals, means, values, or interests. Realistic conflict can be resolved by focusing on the emotions first followed by substantive issues and using collaborative problem-solving methods.

Unrealistic conflict, which is based on irrationality, arises from ignorance, error, tradition, prejudice, dysfunctional organizational structure, win-lose types of competition, hostility, or the need for tension release. Unrealistic conflict creates unwarranted tension between people and can cause unnecessary destruction. It should be handled very carefully; it can be prevented to some extent.

(iv) Functional Conflict and Dysfunctional Conflict

Conflict can be divided into two types, functional and dysfunctional conflict; the former is better than the latter.

The benefits of functional conflict are increased effort and improved performance, enhanced creativity, and personal development and growth. It is like expressing anger in a constructive manner, without actually showing the anger. Functional conflict is always encouraged.

The signs and symptoms of dysfunctional conflict include indecision, resistance to change, destructive emotional outbursts, apathy, and increased political maneuvering. The goal of management is to resolve or neutralize the dysfunctional conflict, which is always discouraged.

(v) Personal Conflict Prevention and Control Methods

Although it is impossible to totally eradicate conflict, personal conflict prevention and control methods can avert much needless strife (unrealistic conflict). Both individuals and organizations need to develop prevention and control methods. Robert Bolton[36] recommends five methods to reduce the amount of conflict, as follows.

1. **Reduce roadblocks.** Use fewer roadblocks to diminish the amount of conflict. Ordering (dominating), threatening, judging, name-calling, and other roadblocks are conflict-promoting interactions, so do not use them.

2. **Improve listening skills.** Listen to others when they have a strong need or a problem. Doing so helps other people dissipate "negative" emotions.

3. **Improve assertion skills.** Enable people to get their needs met with minimal strife. One can prevent the buildup of emotions that so often cause conflict. Both listening skills and assertion skills help to clear up two major sources of conflict: errors and lack of information.

4. **Improve awareness skills.** Know what behaviors are likely to start a needless conflict between people. Possessing awareness skills can eliminate many types of confrontations. Certain words, looks, or actions tend to trigger specific people into conflict. These behaviors may be rooted in early childhood experiences. Some people can sense that a storm is brewing.

---

[36] Robert Bolton, *People Skills* (New York: Simon & Schuster, 1979).

5. **Achieve a win-win result with collaborative problem-solving methods.** In collaborative problem solving, once people discover they have conflicting needs, they join together to find a common solution acceptable to both. It entails redefining the problem, discovering alternatives, and focusing on overlapping interests. In this process, neither person capitulates to or dominates the other. Because no one loses, no one gives up or gives in. Because all parties benefit, this is often called a win-win way of dealing with conflicting needs.

(f) Team-Managing Skills

Selecting individuals (employees) to become team members is the most important and difficult task for supervisors, managers, and leaders alike. The selection is based on an individual's job skills, experience, and attitudes. The selection is a difficult task because it is the team members that can make or break the team since the success of the team entirely depends on the success of each member. Selecting the wrong team members will make the entire team wrong. Managers and leaders need to establish and manage teams successfully because a team consists of individuals with different personalities, behaviors, and goals. Understanding team dynamics is very critical in terms of team members' good and bad interactions. Team-managing skills include planning, organizing, directing, and controlling skills to guide team members and to evaluate their performance.

Team's Overall Performance = Sum of Team Member's Performance

(g) Diversity Management Skills

Treating all employees in the workplace fairly and equally without showing prejudice, bias, and discrimination is the hallmark of possessing diversity management skills.

Today, most organizations hire a mix of employees of different genders; different skill sets; different skin colors, nationalities, and ethnicities; different languages with varied communication tones and sounds; and different attitudes, behaviors, and cultures—today's workplace is indeed very diverse and complex.

This complex workplace requires that all employees, supervisors, managers, and leaders are open-minded and have high levels of tolerance and acceptance to ambiguity and diversity. Obtaining sensitivity training (T-group training) and role-playing games are suggested to each and every employee in order to treat other employees fairly and equally. T-groups also consist of employees participating in organizational development training programs conducted away from the primary workplace.

(h) Public Servicing Skills

As a part of social responsibility, the scope of public servicing skills is large. It includes such things as (1) making monetary donations to charities and other legal and eligible religious organizations; (2) sponsoring and/or participating in various public and social events such as community services and fundraising programs; (3) helping disabled and chronic unhealthy citizens; and (4) providing educational assistance to underprivileged students. Society at large expects business corporations to provide these types of public services. Not all managers and leaders have the right amounts of public servicing skills.

(i) Organizational Skills

The scope of organizational skills applies to both supervisors and managers and includes knowing how to: perform job analysis; develop job or position descriptions; to coordinate a person's work with others' work and vice versa; make presentations to a group of people; conduct interviews; manage budget and time: set priorities among competing tasks. It also involves learning how to draw organizational charts, not playing organizational politics, and understanding how to conduct employee performance appraisals and evaluations.

Skills such as work planning, work organizing, and work completion ideas (e.g., preparing a to-do list with a timeline can help in this area), combined with time management skills (i.e., not exceeding time allocations for specific tasks) can improve the overall organizational skills of supervisors and managers.

1.15 Business Controls

Control strategies should be linked to business strategies in that an organization's controls and control environment should facilitate the achievement of business goals and objectives. To this end, business controls are established to achieve business objectives of reducing risks, decreasing costs, and increasing profits.

(a) Hard Controls and Soft Controls

An organization's control environment consists of developing and implementing business controls, which can be classified as hard controls and soft controls.

Hard controls are formal, tangible, objective, and much easier to measure and evaluate than the soft controls. Examples of hard controls include strategies, plans, policies, procedures, budgets, forecasts, dual controls, written approvals, reconciliations, authorization levels, verifications, and segregation of duties. Tools to evaluate hard controls include big data, data analytics, data mining, flowcharts, system narratives, testing, and counting. By definition, hard controls are strong controls in terms of their effectiveness and validation.

Soft controls are informal, intangible, subjective, and much harder to measure and evaluate than the hard controls. Examples of soft controls include an organization's legal and ethical climate, integrity, honesty, values, culture, vision, people's behaviors and attitudes, commitment to competence, tone at the top, voice of the top, management philosophy and operating style, level of understanding and commitment, and communication. Tools to evaluate soft controls include self-assessments, questionnaires, interviews, workshops, focus groups, and role playing. By definition, soft controls are weak controls in terms of their effectiveness and validation.

(b) Hard Skills and Soft Skills

Skills of an individual can be labeled as two types: hard skills and soft skills.

Hard skills are mostly quantitative in nature and include analytical, technical, functional, problem-solving, decision-making, managing, application, integration, and negotiation skills.

Soft skills are mostly qualitative in nature and include people (interpersonal), motivation, leadership, communications, presentation, coordination, comprehension, project management, implementation, time management, creative, and critical thinking skills.

(c) Controls and Skills

Managers and executives need to possess certain type of skills to exercise and implement specific controls over employees and nonemployees as well as over tasks and activities. This means skills should match with controls and vice versa. A link exists between controls and skills, as described next.

- Problem-solving and decision-making skills, which are hard skills, are needed to exercise and implement hard controls, such as strategies, plans, policies, and procedures.

- Leadership skills and people skills, which are soft skills, are needed to exercise and implement soft controls, such as integrity, honesty, legal and ethical values, and culture.

- Soft skills, such as leadership skills containing team-building skills, motivation skills, and conflict management skills, are needed to exercise and implement soft controls, such as management philosophy, management operating style, tone at the top, voice of the top, and management commitment.

In summary, higher-level managers and executives need more depth in soft skills and soft controls and less depth in hard skills and hard controls. Lower-level managers and executives need more depth in hard skills and hard controls and less depth in soft skills and soft controls.

(d) Controls and Risks

Countermeasures (controls) are established to reduce risks. The relationship between controls and risks is described next.

Business events, transactions, activities, and business owners create risks.

High-risk activities need strong controls to contain risks.

Medium-risk activities need medium controls to contain risks.

Low-risk activities need light controls to contain risks.

Strong controls discourage excessive risk-taking approaches.

Strong controls encourage risk-inhibiting approaches.

Business strategies, plans, policies, and procedures are designed into controls (i.e., built-in controls are better than built-on).

Business controls are built into daily procedures and practices.

Controls mitigate risks to an acceptable level of risk tolerance.

A risk and control map can help managers and auditors to document the relationship between risks and controls. Possible outcomes from the risk and control mapping are listed next.

Some high risks are undercontrolled (open to fraud, threats, and vulnerabilities).

Some low risks are overcontrolled (waste of resources, delays in operations).

Some risks are not controlled at all (open to fraud, threats, and exposures).

Some controls are not needed (waste of resources, delays in operations).

Some controls do not address any risks (waste of resources, open to threats).

Some weak controls are overdesigned (waste of resources, delays in operations).

Some strong controls are underdesigned (open to fraud, threats, and vulnerabilities).

Some simple controls are overcomplicated (waste of resources, delays in operations).

Some complex controls are oversimplified (open to fraud, threats, and vulnerabilities).

Some controls and risks have no relationship (mismatch of design and function).

(e) Types of Controls

Three types of controls are discussed: business control systems, management control systems, and corporate control systems.

(i) Business Control Systems
(A) Control Requirements

The auditor needs to understand the control requirements of an application system or a business operation before assessing control strengths and weaknesses. In other words, there should be a basis or baseline in place (i.e., standards, guidelines, and benchmarks) prior to control measurement and assessment. In the absence of a baseline of standards, the auditee will question and not accept the auditor's findings, conclusions, and recommendations.

(B) Combination Controls

Rarely does a single control suffice to meet control objectives. Rather, a combination of controls or complementary controls is needed to make up a whole and to provide a synergistic effect. An example of a combination of controls is a situation where fire-resistant materials are used in the computer center (a preventive control) to prevent a fire while smoke and fire detectors are used to detect smoke and fire (a detective control) and fire extinguishers are used to put out the fire (a corrective control). Here a single preventive control would not be sufficient. All three controls are needed to be effective.

(C) Complementary Controls

Complementary controls (hand-in-hand controls) have an important place in both the manual and the automated control environment. Complementary controls are different from compensating controls in that, with compensating controls, weak controls in one area or function are balanced by strong controls in other areas or functions, and vice versa. A function or an area need not be weak to use complementary controls. Complementary controls can enhance the effectiveness of two or more controls when applied to a function, program, or operation. These individual, complementary controls are effective as stand-alones and are maximized when combined or integrated with each other. In other words, complementary controls have a synergistic effect.

Controls in these areas can complement each other: administrative, physical security, personnel security, technical security, electromagnetic emanations security from equipment, operations, applications, procedural, environmental (heat, humidity, air-conditioning), and telecommunications security controls.

(D) Compensating Controls

Normally the auditor will find more control-related problems in first-time audits of an area. Generally, the more frequently an area is audited, the lower the probability of many control weaknesses. Therefore, auditors need both audit instinct and business judgment to determine the nature of efficient and effective operations. During the control evaluation process, auditors should consider the availability of compensating controls as a way to mitigate or minimize the impact of inadequate or incomplete controls. In essence, the concept of compensating controls deals with balancing weak internal controls in one area with strong internal controls in other areas of the organization. Here the word "area" can include a section within an end user department or IT department.

An example of a weak control is a situation where data control employees in the IT department are not reconciling data-input control totals to data-output control totals in an application system. This control weakness in the IT department can be compensated for by strong controls in the user department where end users reconcile their own control totals with those produced by the application system. Sometimes automated compensating controls and procedures are needed to shorten lengthy manual controls and procedures (e.g., replacing a manual report balancing system with an automated report balancing system).

(E) Contradictory Controls

Sometimes two or more controls are in conflict with each other. Installation of one control does not fit well with the other controls due to incompatibility. This means that implementation of one control can affect another, related control(s) negatively. Some examples follow.

- Installation of a new software patch can undo or break another related existing software patch either in the same system or other related systems. This incompatibility can be due to errors in the current patch(es) or previous patch(es) or because the new patches and the previous patches were not fully tested by the software vendor or by the user organization.

- Telecommuting work and organization's software piracy policies could be in conflict with each other if a noncompliant telecommuter implements such policies improperly and in an unauthorized manner when purchasing and loading unauthorized software on home/work personal computers.

(F) Control Assessment

During an assessment of control strengths and weaknesses, auditors might run into situations where a business function, system, or manual/automated procedure is overcontrolled or under-controlled. This means that there may be too many controls in one area and not enough controls in other areas. Also, there may be duplication or overlapping of controls between two or more areas. Under these conditions, auditors should recommend the elimination of some user controls, some IT controls, some manual controls, some automated controls, or a combination of them. The same may be true of situations where a system or operation is oversecured or undersecured, and where an application system is overdesigned or underdesigned. This assessment requires differentiating between relevant and irrelevant information, considering compensating controls, considering interrelationships of controls, and judging materiality and significance of audit findings taken separately and as a whole.

(G) Cost-Benefit Analysis

A cost-benefit analysis is advised during the process of designing each type of control into an application system during its development and maintenance as well as during its operation (i.e., built-in controls). Ideally, costs should never exceed the benefits to be derived from installing controls. However, costs should not always be the sole determining factor because it may be difficult or impractical to quantify benefits such as timeliness, improved quality and relevance of data and information, and improved customer service and system response time. When controls are properly planned, designed, developed, tested, implemented, and followed, they should meet one or more of these 12 attributes:

1. Practical
2. Reliable
3. Simple
4. Complete
5. Operational
6. Usable
7. Appropriate
8. Cost-effective
9. Timely
10. Meaningful
11. Reasonable
12. Consistent

(H) Costs versus Controls versus Convenience

Costs of controls vary with their implementation time and the complexity of the system or operation. Control implementation time is important to realize benefits from installing appropriate controls. For example, it costs significantly more to correct a design problem in the implementation phase of an application system under development than it does to address it in the early planning and design phases.

There are **trade-offs** among costs, controls, and convenience factors. The same is true among usability, maintainability, auditability, controllability, and securability attributes of systems.

(I) Controls by Dimension

Control can be viewed through three different dimensions of timing: pre-control (proactive control), concurrent control (ongoing control), and post-control (reactive control).

Pre-control (e.g., policy) anticipates problems and is proactive in nature. Concurrent control is exercised through supervision and monitoring. Post-control identifies deviations from standards or budgets and calls for corrective action, and is similar to feedback control. Pre-control and feed-forward control are interrelated since they deal with future-directed actions. Forecasting, budgeting, and real-time computer systems are examples of feed-forward controls. Pre-control is the most preferred action; the least preferred action is post-control. The difference in these controls is when a corrective action is taken—the sooner the better.

A feedback control is used to evaluate past activity in order to improve future performance. It measures actual performance against a standard to ensure that a desired result is achieved. Feedback controls have been criticized because corrective action takes place after the fact (reactive).

Feedback controls can allow costs to build up due to their back-end position. An example is HR managers holding exit interviews with employees who have resigned to go to work for competitors. Management tabulates the interviewee's responses and uses the information to identify problems with training, compensation, working conditions, or other factors that have caused increased turnover. Other examples include customer surveys, increased finished goods inspections, increased WIP inspections, variance analysis, postaction controls, monitoring product returns, and evaluating customer complaints.

Feed-forward controls attempt to anticipate problems and effect timely solutions (proactive); hence they are important to management. An example is when a key auditee employee will not be available for a few weeks for audit work due to illness, and the audit supervisor reschedules the audit work to be done in this auditable area. Other examples include: defect prevention by quality control inspection of raw materials and WIP, quality control training programs, budgeting, forecasting inventory needs, and advance notice of a purchase.

(J) Controls by Function

Controls prevent adverse effects of risks. Controls can be classified according to the function they are intended to perform. Among the different types of control functions are directive, preventive, detective, corrective, manual, and computer controls.

Directive controls ensure the occurrence of a desirable event. Specific examples of directive controls include requiring all members of the internal auditing department to be Certified Internal Auditors and providing management with assurance of the realization of specified minimum gross margins on sales. Other examples include policies, directives, guidance, and circulars.

Preventive controls are needed to avoid the occurrence of an unwanted event. Examples of such controls include segregation of duties, use of checklists, use of systems development methodology, competent staff, use of passwords, authorization procedures, and documentation. Segregation of duties means duties are divided among different people to reduce the risk of error or inappropriate actions. For example, it includes dividing the responsibilities for authorizing transactions, recording them, and handling the related asset. A manager authorizing credit sales would not be responsible for maintaining accounts receivable records or handling cash receipts. Similarly, salespersons would not have the ability to modify product price files or commission rates. Segregation of duties calls for a separation of the functional responsibilities of custodianship, record keeping, operations, and authorization. Other examples include separating threats from assets to minimize risks and separating resource allocation from resource use to prevent resource misuse.

Detective controls are needed to discover the occurrence of an unwanted event. The installation of detective controls is necessary to provide feedback on the effectiveness of preventive controls. Examples of detective controls include reviews and comparisons, bank reconciliations, account reconciliations, and physical counts.

Corrective controls are needed to correct after an unwanted event has occurred. They fix both detected and reported errors. Examples of corrective controls include correction procedures, documentation, and control and exception reports.

Manual controls include budgets, forecasts, policies, and procedures; reporting; physical controls over equipment, inventories, securities, cash, and other assets that are periodically counted and compared with amounts shown on control records (i.e., official book records).

Computer controls include general controls and application controls. General controls include controls over data center operations, system software, access security, and application system development and maintenance. Application controls are designed to control application processing, helping to ensure the completeness and accuracy of transaction processing, authorization, and validity. Many application controls depend on computerized edit checks. These edit checks consist of format, existence, reasonableness, and other checks on the data, and they are built into each application during its development. When these checks are designed properly, they can help provide control over the data being entered into the computer system. Computer controls are performed to check accuracy, completeness, and authorization of transactions.

(K) Controls by Objectives

Data objectives such as data completeness, data accuracy, data authorization, data consistency, and data timeliness are examples of controls by objectives.

Data completeness refers to the presence or absence of information. All required data elements must be present for a transaction or record to be complete. Examples include all numeric places should be filled and a check cannot be issued unless all fields have a valid value. Examples of data completeness controls include use of prenumbered forms, obtaining transaction authorization, and system logging of transactions.

Data accuracy asks whether data values have been entered into the system correctly and whether they have been distorted during processing. The sources of the data in terms of where they came from and incorruptibility of data are also important here. This means that the received data are unchanged (no additions, changes, and deletions from the original order, without repetition and omission) with positive assurance and an acceptable degree of confidence. Examples include checking for numeric ranges, spelling errors, data duplication, and data omission. Examples of data accuracy controls include use of batch and hash totals, check digits, balance controls, and system-assigned numbers to documents.

Data authorization looks at whether transactions are authorized by appropriate personnel for proper accountability. The person who is approving the transactions is also important here. Moreover, the authorization function should be tailored or responsive to the requirements of the application system. Examples of data authorization controls include management approvals, two-person controls, and management overrides.

Data consistency asks whether policies, procedures, and standards have been uniformly applied. This refers to the relation between intra-data elements and intra- and inter-records and files. Examples include a requestor's name cannot equal an approver's name, and an approver's name cannot equal a signatory's name in a check-approval scenario. The causes of data inconsistencies can be due to invalid, untimely, incomplete, and inaccurate data.

Data timeliness means that data are not stale for intended use and that they are current. Management needs to understand the need for establishing controls to ensure data integrity. This understanding makes the system more effective and useful. Examples of data timeliness controls include use of electronic mail and text messages to send urgent messages instead of phone and use of efaxes to send urgent letters instead of regular mail.

(ii) Management Control Systems

Topics such as control systems, closed control systems, open control systems, broader management controls, and specific management controls are discussed in this section.

(A) Control Systems Defined

All control systems contain two variables: an input variable (reference value) and an output variable (controlled value). Control systems are of two types: closed and open. The main difference is that closed systems have a feedback mechanism while open systems do not have a feedback mechanism. Hence, closed systems are much stronger, more effective, and more complete than open systems. In a feedback mechanism, actual output of a system is fed back to the input end (reference value) for comparison with the desired output (controlled value).

Most business control systems (e.g., paying vendor bills by check; the feedback mechanism is when the check clears a bank) and engineering control systems (e.g., a thermostat to control a room's temperature where the thermostat is the feedback mechanism) are examples of closed control systems due to their feedback mechanisms. Here, closed control systems provide a feedback to indicate whether: a control has worked or not worked operationally; a control is effective or ineffective in achieving objectives; an error or a deviation has occurred or not occurred; and errors and deviations were corrected or not corrected. There is no improvement in management's plans and actions without timely feedback.

(B) Closed Control Systems

Closed control systems contain six elements to operate: a process element, a measurement element, a comparison element, an error element, a control element, and a correction element. Note that the measurement element, comparison element, and error element are the basic functions of a feedback mechanism. Each element with its purpose is described next.

1. The **process element** transforms inputs to outputs.

2. The **measurement element** observes output and sends error signals to the comparison element to decide if there are errors or deviations (feedback).

3. The **comparison element** is a person or device comparing inputs to measured output and sends error signals.

4. The **error element** sends error or deviation signals from input to the control element.

5. The **control element** decides what actions to take when it receives error or deviation signals.

6. The **correction element** makes changes in the process to remove errors and deviations.

(C) Open Control Systems

Open control systems contain three elements to operate: a process element, a control element, and a correction element. What is missing in an open control system is the measurement element, comparison element, and error element, which are the basic functions of a feedback mechanism. An example of an open control system is an electric fireplace to heat a room where the room temperature cannot be regulated due to lack of a thermostat, which acts as a feedback mechanism.

(D) Broader Management Controls

Management controls, in the broadest sense, include the plan of organization, methods, and procedures adopted by management to ensure that its goals and objectives are met. Management controls, also known as internal controls, include accounting and administrative controls.

Management control systems must be integrated with ongoing management practices and, where appropriate and effective, with other management initiatives, such as productivity improvement, quality improvement, BPI, reengineering, and performance measures and standards. Examples of management practices include periodic staff meetings, quarterly management reviews, budget planning and execution, and variance analysis.

Management control systems must be effective and efficient—balancing the costs of control mechanisms and processes with the benefits the systems are intended to provide or control. They should identify who is accountable and provide accountability for all activities.

Traditional Management Controls. Management controls include the process for planning, organizing, directing, and controlling the entity's operations. They include the management control systems for measuring, reporting, and monitoring operations. Specifically, they include automated and manual systems, policies and procedures, and other ongoing management activities that help ensure risks are managed and controlled. Internal auditing is an important part of management control.

Managerial control can be divided into feed-forward and feedback controls. A feed-forward control is a proactive control, such as defect prevention, inspection, training, and budgeting. A feedback control is used to evaluate past activity to improve future performance. It measures actual performance against a standard to ensure that a defined result is achieved. Examples of feedback controls include surveys and variance analysis.

Contemporary Management Controls. Many new management controls have evolved over the years, including economic value added (EVA), market value added (MVA), activity-based costing (ABC), open-book management, and the balanced scorecard system.

EVA is a financial control technique that is defined as a company's net (after-tax) operating profit minus the cost of capital invested in the company's tangible assets. It captures all the things a company can do to add value from its activities, such as running the business more efficiently, satisfying customers, and rewarding shareholders. Each job, department, or process in the organization is measured by the value added.

MVA measures the stock market's estimate of the value of a company's past and projected capital investment projects. For example, when a company's market value (the value of all outstanding stock plus the company's debt) is greater than all the capital invested in it from shareholders, bondholders, and retained earnings, the company has a positive MVA, an indication that it has created wealth. A positive MVA usually goes hand in hand with a high EVA measurement.

ABC attempts to identify all the various activities needed to provide a product or service and allocate costs accordingly. Because ABC allocates costs across business processes, it provides a more accurate picture of the cost of various products and services. In addition, it enables managers to evaluate whether more costs go to activities that add value or to activities that do not add value. Managers can then focus on reducing costs associated with non-value-added activities.

Open-book management allows employees to see for themselves—through charts, computer printouts, meetings, and reports—the financial condition of the company. It also shows individual employees how their job fits into the big picture and affects the financial future of the organization. Finally, it ties employee rewards to the company's overall success. The goal of open-book management is to get every employee thinking like a business owner rather than like a hired hand—what money is coming in and where it is going. Open-book management helps employees appreciate why efficiency is important to the organization's success. It turns the traditional control on its head.

The **balanced scorecard system** is a comprehensive management control system that balances traditional financial measures with measures of customer service, internal business processes, and the organization's capacity for learning and growth. The financial perspective reflects a concern that the organization's activities contribute to improving short- and long-term financial performance (e.g., net income and ROI). Customer service indicators measure such things as how customers view the organization as well as customer retention and satisfaction. Internal business process indicators focus on production and operating statistics, such as order fulfillment or cost per order. The learning and growth indicator focuses on how well resources and human capital are being managed for the company's future. Metrics may include employee retention and the introduction of new products.

(E) Specific Management Controls

Management controls are a part of closed control systems because management always wants feedback on its plans and actions. Management controls can be divided in several ways, such as positive controls, negative controls, feed-forward controls, concurrent controls, feedback controls, proactive controls, ongoing controls, reactive controls, pre-controls, current controls, and post-controls.

Positive controls will increase the motivation levels of employees in making them sincere, honest, efficient (productive), and effective (achieving goals) in their work (e.g., bonuses, promotions, and wage increases).

Negative controls will decrease the motivation levels of employees in making them sincere, honest, efficient (productive), and effective (achieving goals) in their work (e.g., punishments, demotions, and wage decreases).

Feed-forward and feedback controls are based on actions. A feed-forward control is a proactive control, such as error prevention, inspection of incoming materials and products, employee training and development, and operating and capital budgeting. A feedback control is a reactive control used to detect errors and to evaluate past activity to improve future performance. It measures actual performance against a standard to ensure that a defined result is achieved. Examples of feedback controls include surveys from customers, employees, and suppliers and variance analysis from budgets.

Management controls can also be viewed through three different dimensions of timing: pre-control (proactive control), concurrent control (ongoing control), and post-control (reactive control).

Feed-Forward Controls ⟶ Proactive Controls ⟶ Pre-Controls ⟶ Preventive Controls

Concurrent Controls ⟶ Ongoing Controls ⟶ Current Controls ⟶ Detective Controls

Feedback Controls ⟶ Reactive Controls ⟶ Post-Controls ⟶ Corrective Controls

(iii) Corporate Control Systems
(A) Definition of Controls

Control strategies should be linked to business strategies in that controls and the control environment in an organization should facilitate the achievement of business goals and objectives. **Control** is any positive and negative action taken by management that would result in accomplishment of the organization's goals, objectives, and mission. Controls should not lead to compulsion or become a constraint on employees. Controls should be natural and should be embedded in the organizational functions and operations. More so, controls should be accepted by the employees using or affected by them. Use and implementation of controls should be inviting, not inhibiting.

Controls should be seen as beneficial from the employee's personal and professional viewpoints. Ideally, controls should facilitate the achievement of employee and organizational goals and objectives. In other words, any control that does not help or promote in achieving the goals and objectives should not be implemented.

Controls should be effective and efficient. Controls should not cost more than the benefits derived. Controls reduce risks, but they cannot completely eliminate all risks due to their high-cost nature. Note that current controls address current risks only; as new risks always emerge, new controls are needed in a timely manner to address new risks; otherwise, new control-related problems can occur.

(B) Classification of Controls

Controls can be classified into five major categories: management (previously discussed), accounting, administrative, operational, and internal controls. The reason for classifying controls in different ways is that different controls work best in different departments or functions.

Accounting controls are defined in professional standards published by accounting authorities. They help ensure there is full accountability for physical and financial assets and that all financial transactions are recorded and reported in a timely and accurate fashion (i.e., bookkeeping and record keeping). Accounting controls provide checks and balances over people, tasks, and activities to prevent errors, fraud, and collusion.

Administrative controls help ensure resources are safeguarded against waste, loss, fraud, abuse, and misappropriation and support the accomplishment of organization's goals and objectives. Administrative controls provide an oversight role.

Operational controls are the day-to-day procedures and mechanisms used to control operational activities. The goal is to ensure that they are carried out effectively and efficiently. They also address computer security methods focusing on mechanisms primarily implemented and executed by people and computer systems. These controls are put in place to improve the security of a particular computer system or group of systems. They often require technical or specialized expertise and often rely on management controls and technical controls.

Internal controls are processes within an organization designed to provide reasonable assurance regarding the achievement of five primary objectives:

1. The reliability and integrity of information
2. Compliance with policies, plans, procedures, laws, regulations, and contracts
3. The safeguarding of assets
4. The economical and efficient use of resources
5. The accomplishment of established objectives and goals for operations and programs

1.16 Sample Practice Questions

In the actual CIA Exam for Part 3, 100 multiple-choice (M/C) test questions appear. This book contains 100 M/C sample practice questions divided into syllabus-based domains using the approximate domain weight given in the exam. These questions are added at the end of each applicable domain of this book with the sole purpose of showing the flavor and structure of the exam questions and of creating a self-quiz experience. The answers and explanations for these questions are shown in a separate section at the end of this book just before the Glossary section. This separate section is titled "Sample Practice Questions, Answers, and Explanations." If CIA Exam candidates need to practice more sample questions to obtain a higher level of confidence, Wiley offers a separate online test bank software product with hundreds of similar, sample practice questions.

1. Which of the following is very useful in developing succession plans for executives and senior management of a corporation?
   a. Depth charts
   b. Organization charts
   c. Responsibility charts
   d. Accountability charts

2. In addition to the four basic requirements of a contract, which of the following must also occur in order to have a valid contract?
   a. The agreement always must be in writing.
   b. There must be evidence of undue influence.
   c. There must be an absence of an invalidating contract.
   d. A legal remedy need not be available for there to be a breach.

3. Some economic indicators lead the economy into a recovery or recession, and some lag it. An example of a lag variable would be:
   a. Chronic unemployment.
   b. Orders for consumer and producer goods.
   c. Housing starts.
   d. Consumer expectations.

4. The relationship between organizational structure and technology suggests that in an organization using mass production technology (e.g., automobile manufacturing), the best structure would be:
   a. Organic, emphasizing loose controls and flexibility.
   b. Matrix, in which individuals report to both product and functional area managers.
   c. Mechanistic, that is, highly formalized, with tight controls.

   d. Integrated, emphasizing cooperation among departments.

5. Routine tasks, which have few exceptions and problems that are easy to analyze, are conducive to:
   a. Formalized structure, where procedure manuals and job descriptions are common.
   b. Decentralized decision making, where decisions are pushed downward in the organization.
   c. Organic structures that emphasize adaptability and flexibility to changing circumstances.
   d. High degrees of job satisfaction on the part of employees performing them.

6. Which of the following theories predicts that employee behavior depends on the belief that good performance will be rewarded by continued employment?
   a. Equity theory: Employees compare their job inputs and outcomes with those of others and then react to eliminate inequities.
   b. Expectation theory: The strength of a tendency to act in a certain way depends on the strength of an expectation that an act will be followed by a given outcome.
   c. Goal-setting theory: Specific and difficult goals lead to higher performance.
   d. Reinforcement theory: Behavior is a function of its consequences.

7. Which of the following has a flat organizational structure compared to others?
   a. Organization A with 11 hierarchical levels
   b. Organization B with three hierarchical levels
   c. Organization C with eight hierarchical levels
   d. Organization D with six hierarchical levels

8. The **most** fundamental flaw of cost-plus pricing is that it:

a. Fails to account for competition.

b. Ignores demand.

c. Ignores industry-wide standard markup policies.

d. Places too much emphasis on competition.

9. "Selling price = Unit cost + Desired profit" represents which of the following pricing approaches?

a. Profit maximization

b. Demand-based pricing

c. Target return pricing

d. Standard markup

10. Choosing vendors based solely on which of the following factors is detrimental to the long-term success of a buying firm?

a. Quality

b. Service

c. Price

d. Delivery

11. Supplier audits are an important first step in:

a. Supplier certification.

b. Supplier relationships.

c. Supplier partnerships.

d. Strategic partnerships.

12. Customers in which of the following phases of the product life cycle are called laggards?

a. Introduction

b. Growth

c. Maturity

d. Decline

13. Few competitors exist in which phase of the product life cycle?

a. Introduction

b. Growth

c. Maturity

d. Decline

14. Regarding the theory of constraints in operations, which of the following does **not** describe a bottleneck situation appropriately?

a. A machine exists where jobs are processed at a slower rate than they are demanded.

b. A work center exists where jobs are processed at a slower rate than they are demanded.

c. An employee's skill levels are more than needed for a specific job but less than needed for any general job.

d. The demand for a company's product exceeds its ability to produce that product.

15. Regarding production process flows, which of the following is **not** a part of the levers for managing throughput of a process?

a. Decrease resource idleness.

b. Increase effective capacity.

c. Reduce setup resources.

d. Decrease theoretical capacity.

16. Which of the following inventory items would be the **most** frequently reviewed in an ABC inventory control system?

a. Expensive, frequently used, high stock-out cost items with short lead times

b. Expensive, frequently used, low stock-out cost items with long lead times

c. Inexpensive, frequently used, high stock-out cost items with long lead times

d. Expensive, frequently used, high stock-out cost items with long lead times

17. What are the three factors a manager should consider in controlling stock-outs?

a. Holding costs, quality costs, and physical inventories Incorrect. These are inventory-related terms, but none will controls stock-outs.

b. Economic order quantity, annual demand, and quality costs

c. Time needed for delivery, rate of inventory usage, and safety stock

d. Economic order quantity, production bottlenecks, and safety stock

18. Reordering of specific items from vendors should be based on:
    a. Computations on the basis of economic order quantities.
    b. Demand forecasting based on early orders for the items.
    c. Market demographics.
    d. Vendor quantity discounts and warehouse space.

19. A risk associated with just-in-time (JIT) production is the:
    a. Increased potential for early obsolescence of inventories of finished goods.
    b. High cost of material handling equipment.
    c. Potential for significant costs associated with reworking defective components.
    d. Critical dependency on a few vendors.

20. With regard to inventory management, an increase in the frequency of ordering will normally:
    a. Reduce the total ordering costs.
    b. Have no impact on total ordering costs.
    c. Reduce total carrying costs.
    d. Have no impact of total carrying costs.

21. In which of the following phases of business development life cycle will both outputs and employment be declining?
    a. Peak
    b. Recession
    c. Trough
    d. Recovery

22. Which of the following scope items for an outsourced vendor takes on a significant dimension in a supply chain environment?
    a. Liabilities and guarantees
    b. Well-defined service levels
    c. Licensing of services and products
    d. Changes to terms and conditions of services

23. When managing a third-party organization such as an outsourcing vendor, which of the following is **not** applicable?
    a. Due diligence review
    b. Rules of engagement
    c. Rules of behavior
    d. Contractual agreement

24. Where does the information about opportunities and threats come from for a company?
    a. An analysis of the organization's internal environment
    b. A department-by-department study of the organization
    c. A scan of the external environments
    d. An analysis of employee grievances

25. The auditor has recognized that a problem exists because the organizational unit has been too narrow in its definition of goals. The goals of the unit focus on profits, but the overall organizational goals are much broader. The auditor also recognizes that the auditee will resist any recommendations about adopting broader goals. The **best** course of action would be to:
    a. Avoid conflict and present only those goals that are consistent with the auditee's views since all others will be ignored.
    b. Identify the broader organizational goals and present a set of recommendations that attempts to meet both organizational and auditee goals.
    c. Subtly mix the suggested solution with the problem definition so that the auditee will identify the solution apparently independently of the auditor.
    d. Only report the conditions found and leave the rest of the analysis to the auditees.

26. Which of the following problem-solving tools is an idea-generating and consensus-building technique?
    a. Brainstorming
    b. Synectics
    c. Systems analysis
    d. Nominal group technique

27. Job performance is **best** defined as follows:

a. Job performance = Motivation × Ability

b. Job performance = Needs × Skills

c. Job performance = Satisfaction × Job experience

d. Job performance = Goals × Training

28. Which of the following is a critical challenge in implementing the employee empowerment principle?

a. Pushing authority downward closer to front-line employees

b. Expecting accountability from all employees

c. Delegating employees with restrictive rules to achieve objectives

d. Developing clear and complete job descriptions for employees

29. In light of rapidly changing technologies and increasing competition and to provide the ability to affect quality initiatives, which of the following human resources policies and practices is **not** enough?

a. Hiring competent employees

b. Providing one-time training for employees

c. Encouraging continuing education for employees

d. Conducting periodic performance evaluations for employees

30. From a human resources policies and practices viewpoint, which of the following sends a strong message to all interested parties?

a. Expected levels of integrity

b. Expected levels of disciplinary actions

c. Expected levels of ethical behavior

d. Expected levels of competence and trust

31. Commitment falls under which of the following types of a leader's power?

a. Reward power

b. Coercive power

c. Expert power

d. Referent power

32. Which of the following defines the process of evaluating an individual's contribution as a basis for making objective personnel decisions?

a. Performance appraisal

b. Environmental factors

c. Facilitation skills

d. Training and development

33. Negotiation, manipulation, coercion, employee education, and increased communication are all ways in which managers can:

a. Improve employee morale.

b. Overcome resistance to change.

c. Maintain control of information.

d. Demonstrate their power to both their supervisors and subordinates.

34. The adoption of a new idea or behavior by an organization is known as organizational

a. Development.

b. Change.

c. Structure.

d. Intervention.

35. In project management, which of the following outcomes of the schedule performance index (SPI) analysis should be worked on first?

a. A negative SPI of 1.0.

b. A positive SPI of 1.0.

c. A negative SPI of 2.0.

d. A positive SPI of 2.0.

Information Security (25%)

This domain focuses on key theoretical topics. It presents a discussion of physical security controls, such as cards, keys, and biometrics. It explains what the authentication and authorization controls are with their benefits, including a discussion about alternatives to passwords. It delves into information security controls, such as encryption, firewalls, antivirus, and defense-in-depth strategies to mitigate major risks. It discusses data privacy issues and compares them to security issues, including the European Union's General Data Protection Regulation (GDPR). It highlights emerging technology practices, such as mobile technology; artificial intelligence (AI) and machine language; blockchain (bitcoin) and beacon technology; three-dimensional (3D) technology and wearable technology; Internet of Things (IoT), Network of Things (NoT), and Location of Things (LoT); augmented and virtual reality (VR) technology; robotic technology; and retail technologies. It explains cybersecurity risks, controls, and policies, such as hacking, identity theft, data breaches, piracy, tampering, ransomware (bitcoins), Internet theft, data integrity attacks, and phishing, vishing, and smishing attacks with their associated risks and controls. In addition, this domain presents offender's and defender's strategies, cyber-resiliency techniques; digital forensics; cybersecurity risk management program; cybermetrics; and cybersecurity audits. All these topics are tested at the basic cognitive levels in Part 3 of the CIA Exam with a 25% weight given.

With respect to the CIA Exam, cognitive levels are labeled as proficient level and basic level. These cognitive levels suggest that more time and effort should be spent in studying and mastering the subject matter covered in the topics labeled as the proficient level. Comparatively, less time and effort should be spent on the topics labeled basic level.

2.1 Physical Security Controls

The scope of the review of physical security controls includes access controls (e.g., keys, cards, and biometrics), access restrictions (i.e., limited access to known people), camera surveillance with closed circuit television (CCTV), and fire safety. Specifically, it requires a review of physical access to storerooms, cash vaults, research laboratories, manufacturing plants and factories, computer centers, preventive maintenance procedures, and environmental controls. Physical access controls include limiting unauthorized access using electronic cards and biometrics access devices (e.g., thumbprint, eye retina scans, facial recognition, voice recognition, and electronic signature verification), fire prevention techniques, security guards, and electric power supply and conditioning.

(a) Primary Functions of a Physical Protection System

The primary functions of a physical protection system (PPS) include detection, delay, and response. Detection includes exterior/interior intrusion sensors, alarm assessment, alarm communication and display, and entry control systems. Delay includes access delay. Response includes protective/response force (first responders and security guards) and response force communications. The correct sequence of the primary functions of a PPS:

$$\text{Detection} \longrightarrow \text{Delay} \longrightarrow \text{Response}$$

A **detection** measure senses an act of aggression, assesses the validity of the detection, and communicates the appropriate information to a response force (e.g., a security guard). To be effective, a detection system must provide all three of these capabilities—detection, delay, and response. Detection measures may include access-control elements that assess the validity of identification credentials. These control elements may provide a programmed response (admission or denial), or they may replay information to a response force. Security guards serve as detection elements, detecting intrusion and controlling access. Equipment (alarms and sensors), entry control, and response force are elements of detection.

Entry control refers to allowing entry to authorized personnel and detecting attempted entry of unauthorized personnel and material. The measures of effectiveness of entry control are throughput (i.e., number of authorized personnel allowed access per unit time), false acceptance rate (i.e., rate at which false identities or credentials are allowed entry), and false rejection rate (i.e., frequency of denying access to authorized personnel). Once an alarm is initiated and reported, assessment of the situation begins. The assessment includes whether the alarm is a valid alarm or a nuisance (false) alarm and details about the cause of the alarm (i.e., what, who, where, and how many). The probability of detection will decrease as assessment time increases, and detection is not complete without assessment.

Delay is the slowing down of adversary progress. Delay can be accomplished by human response forces (employees and security guards), physical barriers, locks, and activated devices. Delay before detection is a deterrent and is of little or no value because it does not provide additional time to respond to the adversary. Detection must occur before delay. Detection is most effective at the perimeter and delay is more effective at the target.

Response consists of the actions taken by the response force to prevent adversary success. Here, response actions include interruption to stop the adversary's progress, communication to the response force, and deployment of the response force to the adversary's location. Response effectiveness is measured as the time between receipt of a communication of adversary action and the interruption of that action. The effectiveness measure of deployment is the probability of deployment to the adversary location and the time required to deploy the response force. Another response action used in nonindustrial and high-security applications is neutralization, which is a one-on-one confrontation between the response force and the adversary.

(b) Secondary Functions of a Physical Protection System

The secondary functions of a PPS include deterrence, defense, and defeat in that order:

Deterrence ⟶ Defense ⟶ Defeat

Deterrence. A potential aggressor who perceives a risk of being caught may be deterred from attacking an asset. The effectiveness of deterrence varies with the aggressor's sophistication, the asset's attractiveness, and the aggressor's objective. Although deterrence is not considered a direct design objective, it may be a result of the design. The deterrence is not proved to be effectively working all the time.

Defense. Defensive measures protect an asset from aggression by delaying or preventing an aggressor's movement toward the asset or by shielding the asset from attacks. Defensive measures include: delaying aggressors from gaining access by using tools in a forced entry (these measures include barriers along with a response force); preventing an aggressor's movement toward an asset (these measures provide barriers to movement and obscure lines of sight to assets); and protecting the asset from the effects of tools and attacks.

Defensive measures may be active or passive. Active defensive measures are manually or automatically activated responses to acts of aggression. Passive defensive measures do not depend on detection or responses. They include such measures as blast-resistant building components and fences. Security guards (response/protective force) may also be considered defensive measures.

Defeat. Most protective systems depend on response personnel to defeat an aggressor. Although defeat is not a design objective, defensive and detection systems must be designed to accommodate (or at least not interfere with) response force activities.

(c) Physical Security Threats and Risks

Five threats and risks exist in physical security, including interruptions in providing computer services, physical damage, unauthorized disclosure of information, loss of control over system integrity, and physical theft.

1. **Interruptions in providing computer services**

   An external threat may interrupt the scheduled operation of a system. The magnitude of the losses depends on the duration and timing of the service interruption and the characteristics of the operations end users perform.

2. **Physical damage**

   If a system's hardware is damaged or destroyed, it usually has to be repaired or replaced. Data may be destroyed as an act of sabotage by a physical attack on data storage media (e.g., rendering the data unreadable or only partly readable). If data stored by a system for operational use is destroyed or corrupted, it must be restored from backup copies or from the original sources before the system can be used. The magnitude of loss from physical damage depends on the cost to repair or replace the damaged hardware and data as well as costs arising from service interruptions.

3. **Unauthorized disclosure of information**

   The physical characteristics of the facility housing a computer system may permit an intruder to gain access to media both external to system hardware (such as universal serial bus (USB) flash drives, CD disks, and printouts) and within system components (e.g., hard drive disks, solid-state disks, optical disks, and other types of disks), transmission lines, or display screens. All may result in loss or disclosure of sensitive information.

4. **Loss of control over system integrity**

    If an intruder gains access to the central processing unit (CPU), it is usually possible to reboot the system and bypass logical access controls. This can lead to information disclosure, fraud, replacement of systems and application software, introduction of a Trojan horse, and more. Moreover, if such access is gained, it may be very difficult to determine what has been modified, lost, or corrupted.

5. **Physical theft**

    System hardware may be stolen. The magnitude of the loss is determined by the costs to replace the stolen hardware and to restore data stored on stolen media. Theft may also result in service interruptions.

(d) Physical Security System Integration

A physical security system integrates people, policies, procedures, standards, hardware, software, equipment, facilities, and controls to protect assets against potential threats and vulnerabilities.

An asset's value is determined by considering three things: (1) the criticality of the asset for the user, (2) how easily the asset can be replaced, and (3) some measure of its relative value. Note that relative value differs for each asset. For some assets, relative value is measured in terms of monetary cost. The likelihood of the threat is assessed for each applicable aggressor (criminal, vandal, perpetrator, or adversary) category by considering the asset's value to the aggressor, the history of or potential for aggressors attempting to compromise the asset, and the vulnerability of the asset based on existing or planned protective measures.

Threats must be described in specific terms to help determine asset vulnerabilities or to establish protective measures. This description should include the tactics that aggressors will use to compromise the asset (i.e., tools and techniques).

The level of protection applies to the design of a protective system against a specified threat and is based on the asset's value. The level increases as the asset's value increases.

Vulnerabilities are gaps in asset protection. Gaps are identified by considering the tactics associated with the threat and the levels of protection that are associated with those tactics. Vulnerabilities may involve inadequacies in intrusion-detection systems and physical and logical barriers. Where vulnerabilities have been identified, protective measures must be identified to mitigate them.

(i) Physical Protection System

The PPS focuses on protecting specific assets against well-defined threats to a targeted level of protection. Protection systems integrate physical protective measures and security procedures to protect assets against threats. In designing and implementing PPSs, it is important to blend technology factors and human factors.

The characteristics or functions of integrated protection systems include deterrence, defense, defeat, detection, delay, and response. A PPS must accomplish its objectives by either deterrence or a combination of detection, delay, and response. The last three primary functions—detection, delay, and response—must be performed in this order and within a length of time that is less than the time required for the adversary to complete his or her task.

The order is important because there must be awareness that there is an attack (detection) and a slowing of adversary progress to the targets (delay), thus allowing the response or protective force enough time to interrupt or stop the adversary (response). The total time for detection, delay, and response must be less than the adversary's actual time to attack a critical asset.[1]

(ii) Physical Security Countermeasures

Deterrence is the preferred method to deal with attacks against property, whether criminal or not. If attacks are not deterred, access to selected areas or properties should be denied. If attacks are not denied, attacks that occur should be detected. If attacks are not detected in time, they should be delayed to allow time for response by authorities.

Physical security controls or countermeasures (e.g., locks and keys) are the first line of defense against potential risks and exposures and are mostly hardware related. People (employees) are the last line of defense by questioning strangers and others unfamiliar to them.

Physical security protective measures can be divided into three types: preventive measures, corrective measures, and detective measures.[2] **Preventive measures** reduce the likelihood of a deliberate attack, reduce impact, introduce delays, reduce vulnerabilities, or cause an attack to be unsuccessful. Examples of preventive measures include physical deterrents, such as fences, lighting, physical barriers, access controls, locks, visitor controls, and window grilles, and psychological deterrents, such as CCTV cameras, employee screening, employee supervision, and visible security officers (protective/response force).

Corrective measures reduce the effect of an attack and restore the facility to normal operation. The corrective action should be in line with the identified threats. Examples of corrective measures include procedures for monitoring the protection system, assessing the information produced by alarms, and dispatching an appropriate response either through protective force or law enforcement authorities, or a combination.

Detective measures help discover attacks and activate appropriate preventive or corrective measures. Examples of detective measures include intrusion detection systems (IDSs), identification badges, access controls, visual surveillance through CCTV, searching equipment by metal detectors, and investigation by protective force. Note that access controls such as doors, keys, and locks are both preventive and detective measures.

(iii) Design and Measurement of PPS

The design goals of a PPS must be based on sound engineering principles of protection in depth, minimum consequences of component failure, and balanced protection. The design process must be based on performance criteria, not on feature criteria. The feature-based criterion focuses on external factors and uses checklists to determine whether a feature is present or absent. This criterion does not look at internal factors. The performance-based criterion looks at measures and procedures and is more inclusive, as it is internal.

---

[1] Mary Lynn Garcia, *The Design and Evaluation of Physical Protection Systems* (Burlington, MA: Butterworth-Heinemann, 2001).

[2] David G. Patterson III, *Implementing Physical Protection Systems* (Alexandria, VA: ASIS International, 2004).

The performance measures for the detection function are listed next.

- Probability of detection
- Time for alarm communication and assessment
- Frequency of nuisance alarms

The performance measure for the delay function is time to defeat obstacles.

The performance measures for the response function are listed next.

- Probability of accurate communication going to response force
- Time taken for accurate communication to response force
- Probability of response force deployment to adversary location
- Time to deploy
- Response force effectiveness

Analytical techniques to analyze a complex PPS system can include identifying system deficiencies, evaluating improvements, performing trade-off analysis of cost versus performance, and making comparisons.

(e) Memory Cards, Smart Cards, Hardware Tokens, Physical Tokens, and Biometrics

This section[3] highlights the importance of memory cards, smart cards, hardware tokens, physical tokens, and biometrics in improving the overall physical security posture of an organization.

(i) Memory Cards

Memory cards are data storage devices. These cards allow storage of information used for personal authentication, access authorization, card integrity, and applications. The cards do not process information but serve as a repository of information. The data can be written to a magnetic stripe, bar code, or optically stored on the integrated circuit chip. When a smart card is used as a repository of information without requiring the cardholder to input a personal identification number (PIN) or present a biometric reference sample, the smart card is used as a memory card. This method is often used for touch-and-go access and does not provide a high level of assurance since wireless transmissions can be intercepted easily.

If a user presents a memory card to a reader and enters valid PIN using a keypad or keyboard, then two-factor authentication is employed. If the access control application determines that the PIN is valid and corresponds to the memory card presented, then the user is allowed access privileges based on something the user has (a memory card) and something that the user knows (a PIN).

(ii) Smart Cards

A **smart card** has one or more integrated chip circuits and can also store data using memory chips. The difference between a smart card and a memory card is that a smart card processes data like a simple computer. Communications with a smart card can be via contact or contactless (proximity) interfaces. At an access control point, the smart card is presented to the reader.

---

[3] Developed by the Defense Information Security Agency for the U.S. Department of Defense, "Access Controls in Support of Information Systems Security," December 26, 2008.

Many applications require cardholders to enter a valid PIN to enable smart card and cardholder authentication and subsequent establishment of a secure communication channel. This type of access represents two-factor authentication comprised of something a user has (a smart card) and something the user knows (a PIN).

(iii) Hardware Tokens

Hardware tokens (also called hard tokens or eTokens) are hardware devices with computing capability integrated into them. As with biometrics systems, these devices can be integrated into either physical or logical access control solutions, depending on the technology implemented on the token. For example, validation of the possession of a valid token can be used for access when low assurance is adequate for physical access; storing a user's private key on a token increases overall assurance because the adversary now needs an additional item (the token) to breach the system.

These hardware token devices include smart cards and USB cryptographic tokens. Use of hardware tokens, which contain tamper protections such as zeroization of contents and tamper detection switches, is essential. Entering a PIN with a hardware token represents a two-factor authentication: something a person has (a token) and something a person knows (a PIN). USB key-chain tokens that generate a passcode simply by pushing a button on the devices represent single-factor authentication, something the user has. Tokens come in various shapes, sizes, and technologies and can perform various functions. Not all cryptographic modules are in separate hardware tokens. Some are implemented in software, called software modules. Many applications and operating systems have software modules, which unfortunately do not provide as high a degree of security as hardware.

(iv) Physical Tokens

Physical tokens consist of keys and unique documents, such as hand-carried orders. Access control methods used for single-factor personal authentication include simple physical keys, three-plane (complex) physical keys, and hand-carried orders. These physical tokens are authorized for the protection of non-mission-critical, unclassified, and nonsensitive assets. Like public key infrastructure (PKI), physical tokens represent something the user has. Unlike PKI, they provide a low level of assurance and are suitable for use only when protecting information technology (IT) assets with a low risk and low confidentiality level.

Simple physical keys provide minimal protection and assurance, as they are highly susceptible to copying or theft, and locks controlled by simple keys are relatively easy to compromise.

A three-plane key is one of the more secure key systems since the keys themselves are more complicated to copy, blank key stocks are not readily available to adversaries and are more difficult to counterfeit, and the locks controlled by three-plane keys are more difficult to compromise.

(v) Biometrics

Biometrics is becoming a popular physical security measure with unique features that often cannot be defeated or compromised. The term "biometrics" usually refers to technologies for measuring and analyzing human body characteristics, such as voice and facial pattern recognition (e.g., voice print, facial image, and eye retina or iris image) and hand measurements (e.g., fingerprints, handwriting, hand geometry, wrist veins, and thumb impressions). Unfortunately, equipment used in biometrics can lead to two types of errors: Type I and Type II. In practice, it is generally necessary to adjust the equipment for a compromise between false rejections of correct individuals (Type I error) and false acceptances of imposters (Type II error). The goal is to obtain low numbers for both types of errors. An equal error rate (cross-over error rate) occurs when false rejection rates and false acceptance rates are equal. Biometrics can act as a strong security control mechanism in a multifactor authentication process.

(f) Internal Physical Security Systems

This section discusses security guards and dogs, keys and combination locks, door control devices, motion detectors, and mantraps and turnstiles.

(i) Security Guards and Dogs

Physical protection measures, physical barriers, and intrusion detectors ultimately depend on human intervention. Security guards, whether they are assigned fixed posts or roving patrols, can help in this area. A guard may be assigned to a fixed post, such as a lobby, entrance door, truck dock, entrance gate, or security control desk. The guard's post orders may include:

- Checking entrant credentials and use of the sign-in log
- Issuing and recovering visitor badges
- Monitoring intrusion and fire alarm systems and dispatching personnel to respond to alarms
- Controlling movement of materials into and out of the building and enforcing property pass systems
- Enforcing rules and regulations established for the building
- Accepting registered mail

To make optimum use of guards, post orders must be complete and clear and guards must be properly trained. For example, if guards are to control the movement of tapes, disks, and other computer media, they must be able to recognize them and understand what they are. If guards must receive visitors, prepare badges, and telephone for escorts, they cannot be expected to check employee credentials vigorously at the same time. Color-coded badges are better than the non-color-coded badges to identify certain type of visitors. Computer security planners who intend to make use of a specific guard post to support the computer security program should review the guard's post orders and workload with the building security director to be sure expectations can be met.

Security guards may be roving patrol guards with specific routes or general areas that they may cover on foot or in a vehicle. Duties may include these functions:

- Verifying that doors, windows, and other openings are properly locked during designated periods
- Observing, correcting, and reporting safety hazards, such as immediate fire hazards, equipment or machinery left on, stumble hazards, fire doors propped open
- Verifying the condition of fire extinguishers, hose lines, and automatic sprinkler systems
- Checking that files, safes, and restricted areas are properly secured
- Being alert to suspicious persons or activity, unusual odors, leaks, or other abnormal conditions

If roving guards are to be effective, they must be under some kind of control. This means either that the guards report to a control point at regular intervals either in person or by telephone or that they are provided with portable two-way radios (i.e., walkie-talkies). In the latter case, guards can be dispatched to the scene immediately should an emergency arise. As with fixed post guards, computer security planners must ensure that roving guards have the necessary orders and training to properly protect the computer facility.

For example, if a roving guard smells smoke in an unattended computer room, what should she do beyond giving the alarm? Can she turn off electric power? If so, does she know where the disconnect switch is located? Similar questions about air conditioning problems, plumbing leaks, and other computer-related emergencies during unattended hours should be analyzed carefully. Appropriate orders must be formulated, and guards must be trained to carry them out. Firms should have contracts with companies that specialize in security dogs for investigation purposes.

(ii) Keys and Combination Locks
The objective of entrance door controls is to screen entrants, deny entrance where appropriate, and control the flow of materials into and out of the building.

Screening can be done in two ways: by a guard's personal recognition of the entrant or acceptance of credentials or by the entrant's possession of a suitable device to unlock a door. Screening by a guard is by far the most positive method when applied conscientiously but costs more than use of electronic or mechanical devices. Electronic or mechanical devices can accomplish entrant screening. Authorized entrants may use a key (conventional or electronic), enter the combination of a push-button lock, or be screened by a device that compares an entrant characteristic (hand geometry, fingerprint, or voice characteristics) with stored information about authorized entrants.

Access control that depends on a key lock or screening device rather than a guard has several shortcomings. Keys or combinations can fall into the wrong hands. An intruder may enter immediately behind an authorized entrance (often referred to as tailgating or piggybacking). Skilled intruders may defeat locks. Although these shortcomings can be managed (careful key control, security-conscious employees, burglar-alarmed doors, etc.), computer security planners should be aware of these problems and not fall into the trap of accepting blanket statements like "This door is always locked" or "This key cannot be duplicated."

Each entrance door should be capable of resisting forced or covert entry up to the level of effort likely to be applied. This type of entry requires careful consideration of door hardware and its installation. Where appropriate, heavy-duty lock sets, reinforced strike plates and door frames, tamper-resistant hinges, and break-resistant glass in vision panels can be used. In addition to utilizing reinforced doors, companies can also connect critical doors to a perimeter alarm system to signal a security guard when a door is opened. This can be done for electric strike-equipped doors in such a way that an alarm is not sounded when normal entry is made but forced entry will cause an alarm.

(iii) Door Control Devices
At least five door control devices exist: conventional keys and lock sets, pick-resistant lock sets, electronic key systems, electronic combination locks, and mechanical push-button combination locks.

1. **Conventional keys and lock sets** have low cost per cylinder, and almost any door can be equipped. However, keys are easily duplicated, and locks can be picked. A key holder can enter at any time. There is no control over entrance and exit of materials.

2. **Pick-resistant lock sets** cost about two or three times more than conventional locks, keys are much more difficult to duplicate, and locks are much harder to pick. Other characteristics are the same as conventional locks.

3. **Electronic key systems** use specially encoded cards to actuate an electronic door strike. Depending on features and installation, both keys and cards can be expensive. Simple systems perform as pick-resistant lock sets. Higher-cost systems can include the ability to lock out specified cards, limit access to specified times, log all entrances and exits, and control a group of doors such that access to each door in the group can be specified for each card.

4. **Electronic combination locks** typically have electronic push buttons into which users key the combination to actuate an electric strike. Costs and features are generally similar to electronic key systems except users need not carry a card. Some allow users to use a special code when under duress, which will open the door but at the same time sound a remote alarm.

5. **Mechanical push-button combination locks** retract the bolt and allow users to open the door after they press the correct combination. These locks do not offer the special features described for electronic locks, but their cost is much lower.

(iv) Motion Detectors

There exist several technological means of determining access to or occupancy of critical areas during periods when the areas should be vacant. Two popular systems are light beams and CCTV systems.

> **NOTE**
>
> CCTV systems are best used only to determine of an area's status after there has been an alert from some other, more positive intrusion detector.

There are at least four distinct technologies for detecting the presence of an intruder.

1. **Photoelectric systems** are passive systems that detect a change in an area's light level due to added sources of light. Since these systems are sensitive to the ambient light level, they may be used only in windowless areas or areas in which the windows have been covered.

2. **Motion-detection systems** are based on the Doppler effect. When the source of a sound or electromagnetic signal, or a reflector of such a signal, moves toward or away from a receiver, the frequency or pitch of the signal received will be higher or lower, respectively. If a body moves within a room that has a source of wave energy and a receiver, the motion can be detected from the change in frequency of received waveforms. The receiver picks up the source frequency strongly but also detects a slightly different frequency at a much lesser strength.

3. **Acoustical-seismic detection systems (audio)** employ microphone-type devices to detect sounds that exceed the ambient noise level of the area under protection. A nuisance alarm is possible due to sounds from rain, thunder, aircraft, construction, and others. Seismic (vibration) systems utilize the same principle as audio detection systems except that highly sensitive and specialized microphones are attached directly to objects such as safes, filing cabinets, windows, walls, and ceilings.

4. **Proximity detection systems** detect the approach or presence of an object or an individual. In principle, a proximity system employs an electrical field that, when upset by a foreign body, causes an alarm. The field may be set up around a cabinet, or it may simply surround a wire. The field could be electromagnetic or electrostatic.

   Proximity systems are designed to be supplemental and are not effective as primary systems because they are susceptible to nuisance alarms caused by electric supply fluctuations and by the presence of items placed near them. Animals and birds can trigger alarms if systems are too sensitive. Therefore, proximity systems should be backed up by other security systems.

(v) Mantraps and Turnstiles

Both mantraps and turnstiles are examples of physical security access controls.

Mantraps can provide an additional security at the entrance to high-risk areas. The outermost door may be opened inward with the use of access control cards. However, the inner door may be opened inward only, and the outer door may be opened outward only by security personnel from inside a room. Thus, an intruder who got past the outer door with the use of false identification would be trapped in front of the inner door. For highly sensitive areas, mantraps require a biometric measure, such as fingerprints combined with the weight of the person entering the facility.

Turnstiles decrease the everyday piggybacking or tailgating by forcing people to go through a turnstile one person at a time. Turnstiles cannot be outer-wall perimeter devices unless they are enclosed to maintain environmental continuity within the building (i.e., heat and air conditioning).

Optical turnstiles communicate to users via visual/audible annunciation. Detection, scanning, and control electronics located within the bollards ensure that only one individual per valid access card presented is granted access, thus preventing tailgating. Any attempt to enter without a valid card trips an alarm replay output that can trigger any number of responses to prevent further access. These responses include alerting security personnel, switching CCTV cameras, and locking down interior doors and elevators. In addition to preventing tailgating, optical turnstiles can track employee time, attendance, and location and resolve issues regarding employee security, safety, theft, and accountability.

(g) Perimeter Security Systems

This section discusses various perimeter security systems, such as physical intrusion detection sensors and alarms; physical and cyberaccess to equipment; physical perimeter access; manual override control; and intraperimeter communications.

(i) Physical Intrusion Detection Sensors and Alarms

Intrusion detection devices, commonly referred to as burglar alarms, are used to detect and signal unauthorized or attempted entry. Doors, windows, and other movable coverings of openings in perimeter barriers must be equipped with magnetic contacts or vibration-detecting devices. All alarm-system circuits must be supervised to detect any interruption in electric power or tampering. Intrusion alarms must have emergency power or another direct current (DC) power source. Auxiliary power must provide for longer periods of operation (e.g., 120 hours) for intrusion alarms.

An IDS must be fail-safe, have a backup power source, must resist and detect tampering, and must be linked to security guard force. The basic triggers for operation of IDS include breaking an electrical circuit, interrupting a light beam, or detecting sound, vibration, and a change in capacitance due to penetration of an electrostatic field.

Alarms are to be placed in the secure mode position by a member of the staff after the workforce leaves. A primary and an alternate staff member should be designated in writing to activate the alarm system at the close of business. Personnel at all remote monitoring locations must have an up-to-date list of persons authorized to arm systems and place them in the open mode at the beginning of the workday. The security office monitoring the alarms should have the names of the primary and alternate contact points to notify during nonbusiness hours if an alarm signal is received. All alarm systems must be properly maintained and tested as recommended by the manufacturer or installer.

The perimeter of buildings must be checked for other possible entry points, such as windows, transformer vaults, air conditioning louvers, roof hatches, and the like. Each point that represents a potential intruder route should be appropriately secured physically or added to the perimeter alarm system. For example, exposed windows can be glazed with break-resistant glass or plastic. Louvers can be protected with heavy-gauge screens.

The most common causes of false alarms are user negligence, poor installation/servicing, and faulty equipment. The basic parts of an alarm system include a sensor or triggering device, a circuit that carries messages to the signaling equipment, and a signaling system or device (annunciator).

There are two types of alarm systems: electromechanical and volumetric. Electromechanical alarms include metallic foil, magnetic switches, wire lacing, and pressure mats. Volumetric alarms include vibration, microwave, ultrasonic, passive infrared, photoelectric, and capacitance.

The electromechanical type of IDS is in widest use today. It consists of a continuous electrical circuit so balanced that a change or break in the circuit will set off an alarm. Examples of systems that use a continuous electrical circuit are listed next.

- Foil strips on a window that will break if the window is broken
- Magnetic or contact switches on doors
- Mercury switches on opening that tilt
- Vibration detectors to detect breaking through walls
- Screens and traps that consist of fine wires embedded in breakable dowels or in the walls, ceilings, and floors

Any tampering with the mechanical parts of the system or breaking or grounding of the electrical circuitry will cause an alarm in the central station.

The various kinds of devices used in perimeter protection are listed next.

- **Window foil** is a metallic tape affixed to windows and glass doors. When the glass is broken, the foil breaks, an open circuit results, and an alarm is sounded. A hairline crack or scratch will activate the system causing an alarm.

- **Wire lacing and screening** uses fine wires laced across door panels, floors, walls, and ceilings. Forced entry into the protected area will break a strand of the laced wire, causing an alarm.

- **Taut wire** is used to detect intrusion into a protected area. A fine strand of wire is strung under tension across internal openings, such as air ducts and utilities tunnels. Any changes in the tension of the wire will cause an alarm.

- **Intrusion switches,** magnetic or mechanical, are frequently used to protect doors, windows, skylights, and other accessible openings. Switches may be surface-mounted or recessed.

In summary, entry into a building is best controlled through either surveillance or high-integrity access controls at desired points of entry and by either surveillance or alarm systems around the remainder of the building perimeter.

The various kinds of sensors and alarms are listed next.

- **Video motion detectors** activate when movement is picked up by a video camera.

- **Duress sensor** is used to call for assistance, and it consists of a hand- or foot-operated switch (usually found in bank teller areas).

- **Microwave sensors** are radio/radar frequency transceivers that detect motion by interruption of a linear signal.

- **Photoelectric (beam) sensors** operate by an interruption of a light beam that causes an alarm. Beam sensors operate on infrared and microwave principles.

- **Passive ultrasonic sensors** detect the sounds of forced entry throughout walls, ceilings, and doors.

- **Penetration sensors** detect entry through doors, windows, walls, or any other openings into the protected area.

- **Passive infrared sensors** detect body heat.

- **Ultrasonic motion sensors** detect by frequency shift (sound waves) the motion of an intruder inside the protected area.

- **Vibration sensors** detect forced entry through metal barriers placed over windows and ventilators or attempts to drill, saw, or cut through walls, ceilings, floors, or doors.

- **Closed-circuit sensors** activate when an electrical circuit is broken by, for example, cutting a wire inside a wall or window.

- **Pressure mat sensors** activate when weight is applied, such as when an intruder steps on a pressurized mat concealed under a rug.

- **Contact sensors** activate when an electrical circuit is broken by, for example, the separation of a magnet installed on a door or window.

(ii) Physical Access and Cyber Access

Physical access to cyber equipment circumvents all cybersecurity controls. Physical access to computer systems should have the same level of security as cyber access. Often computer components, such as CPUs and keyboards, are locked in cabinetry while pointing devices (e.g., mice or mouse), limited keyboards, and monitors for operator functions are available.

Higher-security facilities require at least two-factor authentication for cyber access. Methods can include biometrics, passwords, and security tokens/certificates. Some authentication can be tightly coupled with physical security (e.g., proximity monitors and keycard access to buildings) and control access and logoff to cybersystems.

(iii) Physical Perimeter Access

Perimeter security includes, but is not limited to, fences, walls, fully enclosed buildings, entrance gates or doors, vehicle barriers, lighting, landscaping, surveillance systems, alarm systems, and security guards. Physical security may also include site entry and exit logging as well as room or area logging, possibly through a keycard access system.

Lack of perimeter identification can lead to physical intrusions. Lack of notification of unauthorized physical access (e.g., monitoring and alarms) can allow unknown breached perimeters. The ability to detect perimeter intrusions is the key to preventing physical attacks. Individuals with access to critical components could compromise the entire system, whether due to a skillful or a blind attack.

(iv) Manual Override Control

In industrial control systems, manual override controls include circuit breaker hand switches, valve levers, and end-device panels. Physical security of manual override controls is commonly overlooked, resulting in the potential for exploit and system damage. Physical access to manual override controls should be heavily restricted to authorized personnel only. Unauthorized access to manual override controls poses the risk for system damage or intrusion and therefore must be secured.

(v) Intraperimeter Communications

Mechanisms within the perimeter may rely on intraperimeter communication to ensure secure operation. The communication medium may consist of physical, electrical (fly-by-wire), or wireless connections. Security concerns often overlook intraperimeter communications. Access to the intraperimeter communication medium constitutes access to the function or device itself with the potential for exploit and damage. The communication path must be physically secured to the same level as the components.

The length and complexity of the communication channel to be protected should be minimized. The communication channel and access ports should also be hidden from view, out of reach, and/or behind layers of perimeter security if possible. A conduit may be placed around the communication medium to provide additional resistance to tampering. Wireless communication should not be detectable or accessible outside the perimeter.

(vi) Summary of Entry Control Guidelines

The entry control perimeter should be under visual control at all times during working hours to prevent entry by unauthorized personnel. Security guards or monitored video surveillance systems should be in place.

A list of entry control guidelines is presented next.

- Limit the number of entrances to the computer facility to a minimum. There should be coordination of this measure with those responsible for fire protection and building security. Doors should be of sufficient strength to resist forced entry.

- Install a screening device at every entrance, be it a guard, a badge reader, an electronic lock, a TV camera manned by a guard in another location, or a physical lock. Maintain entry logs wherever possible. Monitor closely all items moving into or out of the facility, whether expected or not (e.g., scheduled deliveries).

- If there is an extensive perimeter requiring protection, consider use of exterior lighting, TV cameras, roving patrols, and intrusion detection devices. However, such protection requires coordination with building security staff.

- Secure all openings through which an intruder could gain entrance or receive material.

- Control the use of badges to permit entry. Badges should not be issued in such quantity that guards cannot verify badge holders. When people leave the employ of the facility, whatever the reason, all keys and badges issued to them must be retrieved. Visitors should be issued temporary badges that differ in appearance from employee badges.

- In case of any unusual diversions, such as power outages, bomb threats, or false fire alarms, make a thorough search of the facility to prevent or uncover loss or destructive activity that might have taken place. Entry logs or other records of facility activity should be consulted; they might reveal any unusual occurrence that could serve as a clue to the perpetrator's identity.

- Provide adequate protection of remote terminals, data libraries, and trash areas (to prevent dumpster-diving attacks) that are both within and outside the confines of the computer facility. **Dumpster diving** refers to going through a company's trash and garbage containers to find valuable proprietary and confidential information that was discarded carelessly and using that information against the company for personal and/or financial gain.

(vii) Summary of Storage and Handling Protection Guidelines

Protection of sensitive and classified assets must include classified storage, proper security marking, transportation, destruction, and incident handling. Classified information (e.g., top secret or secret) must be guarded and/or alarmed 24/7. Intrusion alarms must be implemented and monitored with response times appropriate to the classification of the materials protected. To gain access at the access control perimeter of facilities or workplaces processing classified information, a two-factor authentication is required. This requirement can be met using visual monitoring by an attendant or through use of an automated entry system. Either automated or manual classified access logs should also be maintained to ensure accountability.

A list of storage and handling protection guidelines is presented next.

- Devise fire protection plans with data storage media in mind. Consider the risks that fire-fighting imposes on stored data. Tape and disk library vaults (safes) can be certified to have a particular protection rating and design that keeps contents safe from steam and water damage as well as from heat and flame. These ratings should be considered in evaluating and selecting storage facilities.

- Include protective measures in planning for disaster response. Disaster recovery procedures should be periodically tested and exercised. Arrangements should be made for the removal to a place of safekeeping storage media, computer printouts, records of disclosure, and source material before a disaster. If potential threats of looting and pilfering exist, security guards should be posted; if data is vulnerable to water damage, protective plastic covers should be available.

- To ensure that protection of data is adequately maintained, conduct frequent unscheduled security inspections. Check for unlocked doors, doors propped open, locks that do not latch, and fire and intrusion alarms that have been turned off because they are too easily activated.

In summary, physical security measures are the first line of defense against the risks that stem from uncertainties in the environment and the unpredictability of human behavior. Frequently, they are the simplest safeguards to implement and can be put into practice with the least delay. Naturally, not all physical security measures are required at any one installation; rather, a judicious selection should be made that provides a realistic overall coverage for the lowest expenditure.

2.2 Authentication and Authorization Controls

This section is divided into five subsections: identification and authentication; identity management and privilege management; integrating identification and authentication methods; alternatives to passwords; and single point of failure.

(a) Identification and Authentication

Identification purpose, application authentication techniques for system users, application authentication techniques for devices, identity management and privilege management, and integrating identification and authentication methods are discussed in this section.

(i) Identification Purpose

Identification refers to establishing the identity of a user, process, or device prior to authentication. It is the means by which a user provides a claimed identity to the system. **Authentication** is verifying the identity of a user, process, or device, often as a prerequisite to allowing access to system resources. It is the means of establishing the validity of this claim. **Authorization** is the process of defining and maintaining the allowed actions. **Accountability** is making individuals responsible for their actions and inactions equally, and it supports the identification, authentication, and audit requirements, nonrepudiation, deterrence, fault isolation, intrusion prevention and detection, and after-action recovery and legal action. Accountability should be reflected in audit trails. Access rules support accountability.

Identification and authentication (I&A) establishes the basis for accountability, and the combination of all three enables the enforcement of identity-based access control (IBAC). The correct sequence of actions taking place in an access control mechanism is as follows:

$$\text{Identification} \longrightarrow \text{Authentication} \longrightarrow \text{Authorization} \longrightarrow \text{Accountability}$$

Note that identification comes before authentication, authorization comes after authentication, and accountability comes after authorization.

The user's identity can be authenticated using the following basic I&A mechanisms:

- Knowledge-based I&A techniques (e.g., what you know, using password, user ID, username, or PIN)

- Token-based I&A techniques (e.g., what you have, using memory card, smart card, personal identification verification [PIV] card, hardware token, noncryptographic key, and digital certificate)

- Physical location–based I&A techniques (e.g., where you are, using global positioning system [GPS] and wireless sensor network)

- Biometrics-based I&A techniques (e.g., what you are, using fingerprints for, iris recognition for, and what you are using the dynamic biometrics, such as handwriting and voice recognition, for)

Biometrics is the science and technology of measuring and statistically analyzing biological data. In IT, the term usually refers to technologies for measuring and analyzing human body characteristics, such as voice and facial pattern recognitions, eye retina scans, and hand measurements (e.g., fingerprints, handwriting, hand geometry, wrist veins, and thumb prints). Unfortunately, equipment used in biometrics can lead to two types of errors: Type I and Type II. In practice, it is generally necessary to adjust the equipment for a compromise between false rejection of correct individuals (Type I error) and false acceptance of imposters (Type II error). The goal is to obtain low numbers for both types of errors. Equal error rate (crossover error rate) occurs when the false rejection rates and the false acceptance rates are equal. Biometrics provide the strongest security control in a multifactor authentication process.

WEAK AND STRONG AUTHENTICATION METHODS

Weak authentication methods include user IDs, PINs, and reusable (static and simple) passwords.

Strong authentication methods include dynamic passwords (i.e., one-time passwords using challenge-response protocols), hardware tokens, passphrases, encrypted time stamps, smart cards, location-based authentication, memory cards, multiple factors of authentication, biometrics, and PKI systems, such as digital signatures and digital certificates.

The principal forms of authentication include static, dynamic, and multiple factors.

- **Static authentication** reuses a specific authenticator (e.g., static password) where an attacker cannot obtain this authenticator. The strength of the authentication process is highly dependent on the difficulty of guessing or decrypting the authentication value.

- **Dynamic authentication** uses cryptography to create one-per-session authenticator, and it changes with each authentication session between a claimant and verifier.

- **Multiple-factor authentication** requires two or more types of authentication techniques. It can include both static and dynamic authentication mechanisms. One example is the user of a password along with a smart card token.

Authorization mechanisms fall into several major categories, such as local, network, single sign-on, reduced sign-on, single log-in and single log-out, as follows:

- **Local authorization** is performed for each application and computer to which a user requires access. The local operating system and applications are employed to set up and maintain the authorizations for that computer or application.

- **Network authorization** is performed at a central authorization server, providing access to a user's account from one or more workstations on the network and giving access to a single user account or multiple accounts. Security tokens (e.g., memory cards, flash memory, USB tokens, and smart cards) are used to allow access first to a computer and then to a network.

- **Single sign-on (SSO)** system employs a central authorization server to enable a user to authenticate once and then access all the resources that the user is authorized to use. SSO achieves access to multiple applications, computers, workstations, and domains operating with a variety of authentication mechanisms (e.g., a Kerberos implementation used within a heterogeneous network). The central server establishes and maintains the authorizations at each application, computer, workstation, or domain that the user is allowed to access.

- **Reduced sign-on (RSO)** system is a technology that allows a user to authenticate once and then access many, but not all, of the resources that the user is authorized to use.

- **Single log-in** is similar to single sign-on. It eliminates the need for authorization at each resource and for individual authentications to each resource.

- **Single log-out** is closing all open programs, files, functions, sessions, and screens with one system command so no computer resource is vulnerable to attackers.

(ii) Application Authentication Techniques for System Users

Organizational users include employees and outsiders, such as contractors. Users must uniquely be identified and authenticated for all accesses. Unique identification of individuals in group accounts (e.g., shared privilege accounts) may need to be considered for detailed accountability of activity. Authentication of system user identities is accomplished through the use of passwords, tokens, biometrics, or, in the case of multifactor authentication, some combination thereof.

Access to systems is defined as either local or network. Local access is any access to an organizational information system by a user (or process acting on behalf of a user) where such access is obtained by direct connection without the use of a network. Network access is any access to an organizational information system by a user (or process acting on behalf of a user) where such access is obtained through a network connection. Remote access is a type of network access that involves communication through an external network (e.g., the Internet). Internal networks include local area networks (LANs), wide area networks (WANs), and virtual private networks (VPNs) that are under the control of the organization. For a VPN, the VPN is considered an internal network if the organization establishes the VPN connection between organization-controlled endpoints in a manner that does not require the organization to depend on any external networks across which the VPN transits to protect the confidentiality and integrity of information transmitted.

Specific controls for system users are listed next.

- The system should use multifactor authentication for network access to privileged and nonprivileged accounts.

- The system should use multifactor authentication for local access to privileged and nonprivileged accounts.

- The organization should allow the use of group authenticators only when used in conjunction with an individual/unique authenticator and should require individuals to be authenticated with an individual authenticator prior to using a group authenticator.

- The system should use multifactor authentication for network access to privileged and nonprivileged accounts where one of the factors is provided by a device separate from the information system being accessed.

- The system should use replay-resistant authentication mechanisms for network access to privileged and nonprivileged accounts. An authentication process resists replay attacks if it is impractical to achieve a successful authentication by recording and replaying a previous authentication message. Techniques used to address this include protocols that use nonces or challenges (e.g., Transport Layer Security [TLS]), and time-synchronous or challenge-response one-time authentication.

- The organization should conduct a risk assessment to determine the risks of identifying and authenticating nonorganizational users. Factors such as scalability, practicality, and security must be considered simultaneously to balance ease of use with protection.

(iii) Application Authentication Techniques for Devices

An information system should uniquely identify and authenticate specific types of devices before establishing a connection. Devices include mobile devices (e.g., USB memory sticks, external hard disk drives, notebook/laptop computers, cellular/mobile telephones, digital cameras, audio and recording devices) and mobile ID devices (used to acquire fingerprint, face, and iris images in personal ID verification programs). These devices can use either shared known information (e.g., Media Access Control [MAC] or Transmission Control Protocol/Internet Protocol [TCP/IP] addresses) for identification or authentication solution (e.g., IEEE 802.1x and Extensible Authentication Protocol, remote authentication dial-in user service [RADIUS] server with EAP-Transport Layer Security authentication, or Kerberos) to identify and authenticate devices on LANs, WANs, and wireless networks. The required strength of the device authentication mechanism is determined by the security categorization of the information system.

General controls over devices are listed next.

- The information system should authenticate devices before establishing LAN, WAN, and wireless network connections using bidirectional authentication between devices that is cryptographically based.

- Usage restrictions and operational guidance include proper configuration management, device identification and authentication, implementation of mandatory protective software (e.g., malicious code detection and firewall), scanning devices for malicious code, updating virus protection software, scanning for critical software updates and patches, conducting primary operating system integrity checks, and disabling unnecessary hardware (e.g., wireless and infrared).

- Guidance for employees who are traveling includes providing computers with sanitized hard drives, limited applications, and additional hardening with stringent configuration settings. Security measures for employees who have returned from travel include examining the device for signs of physical tampering and purging or reimaging the hard disk drive.

- Regarding dynamic address allocation for devices, the organization should standardize Dynamic Host Control Protocol (DHCP) lease information and the time assigned to devices and audit lease information when assigned to a device. DHCP-enabled clients typically obtain **leases** for Internet Protocol (IP) addresses from DHCP servers.

- Using the RADIUS protocol, a remote client can exchange authentication, access control, accounting, and device configuration information with a RADIUS server. The RADIUS server can authenticate a user or a device from its database or user I&A parameters.

- Using the Terminal Access Controller Access-Control System + (TACACS+) protocol enables a network resource to offload the user administration to a central server.

Specific controls over mobile devices are listed next.

- Smart card authentication (i.e., proof by possession)
- Password authentication (i.e., proof by knowledge)
- Fingerprint authentication (i.e., proof by property)

Specific controls over mobile ID devices are listed next.

- The data encryption algorithm should use Advanced Encryption System-256 (AES-256) for transmission and should provide for the encryption and decryption of bidirectional traffic.
- Data at rest should use encryption for all data residing on the device either as a temporary file or a part of the database.
- Data storage cards should use encryption for all of the device data, files, or databases written to storage medium.
- Biometric operator authentication should be achieved by a two-factor authentication, one of which should be a biometric.
- A password of minimum length with alphabetical, numerical, and/or special characters should be used for biometric operator authentication.

WHAT ARE USER AUTHENTICATORS AND DEVICE AUTHENTICATORS?

User authenticators include passwords, passphrases, passcodes, tokens, biometrics, and public key infrastructure (PKI) certificates, such as electronic signatures and digital certificates, and key cards.

Device authenticators include passwords and PKI certificates, such as electronic signatures and digital certificates.

- The device should provide the capability for biometric operator reauthentication after a designated length of time. The device should be reauthenticated itself after a designated amount of idle time or result in a device shutoff.
- The device should provide the capability to lock the device or render it inoperable, erase selected files, and/or erase all files on it based on failed security protocols.
- The device should provide the capability to establish a maximum limit of failed authentication attempts before the handheld device clears all application data or requires unlock only by a security administrator.
- After a biometric operator's authentication and authorization is established, the device's identification should be verified by matching against a list of specified devices (i.e., blacklists or lost/stolen lists). A matched device should not be authorized to communicate with the central system.
- To provide greater protection, all devices should be updated whenever policies change or software is updated.
- When inserting a protected (encrypted) memory card into the mobile device's expansion slot, the device should be able to detect an encrypted card and prompt the biometric

operator for the card's authentication code. Access to information would be granted only when the correct authentication code has been provided.

■ The data authentication algorithm should use the Rivest, Shamir, Adelman-2048 (RSA-2048) key size. The secure hash function for the signature should use Secure Hash Algorithm (SHA-256) key size.

(b) Identity Management and Privilege Management

Tasks in identity management and privilege management occur first; tasks in authentication and authorization occur later.

Identity management is the comprehensive management and administration of user permissions, privileges, and profiles. It provides a single point of administration for managing the life cycle of accounts and profiles. **Identity** is the distinguishing character or personality of an individual based on a set of physical and behavioral characteristics by which that individual is uniquely recognized.

Access control ensures that only authorized access to resources occurs. It helps protect confidentiality, integrity, and availability and supports the principles of legitimate use, least privilege, and separation of duties. Access control simplifies the task of maintaining enterprise network security by reducing the number of paths that attackers might use to penetrate system or network defenses. Identity and access management ensures that adequate safeguards are in place to secure authentication, authorization, and other identity and access management functions.

In the past, users typically subscribed to each system or resource separately, as needed for their job functions, by undertaking multiple systems and user registration processes. This resulted in users having to manage multiple security credentials (i.e., certificates, usernames, and passwords). This arrangement is tedious, expensive, time consuming, unattractive, and frustrating for users, as it scales poorly as the number of resources increases.

In light of these problems, a single solution is needed that allows user management processes to be efficiently and effectively leveraged and reused across trust domains, thereby facilitating interoperability between various information systems. This solution is accomplished through an access life cycle consisting of these five phases:

1. **Provisioning (vetting)** is a procedure for enabling end users to access and use system services. It involves creating for each user an account in a directory service and populating the account with the user-specific information needed by each service. It asks a question: What can you access?

2. **Permissioning** is the authorization given to users that enables them to access specific resources on the network, such as data files, applications, printers, and scanner. User permissions also designate the type of access, such as read only (view) or update only (read/write). It asks a question: What can you access?

3. **Credentialing** involves a certification authority issuing a certificate after validating an applicant who is requesting the access. It asks a question: How do I know it is you?

4. **Analyzing** is reviewing current accounts, old accounts, and expired accounts for correctness and appropriateness against their access rights and permissions.

5. **Revoking** includes canceling user accounts, expired accounts, and illegal accounts and decertifying users who are no longer valid, appropriate, or correct.

In addition, identity binding and identity proofing are required. **Identity binding** is tying the vetted claimed identity according to the credential-issuing authority, perhaps through biometrics. **Identity proofing** is the process by which a credential-issuing authority validates sufficient information (e.g., source documents, credentials, personal identification cards, and photo IDs) and validates them to uniquely recognize an individual.

Major benefits of identity and access management include providing SSO, RSO, and single logout capabilities to end users for accessing multiple online systems and services. This will eliminate the need for registering end user identity information in multiple systems and services. This type of management is supported by several basic security technologies, including cryptographic trust model, identity management standards and middleware, and a metadata model for securely exchanging information about users.

Although the SSO system is designed for user convenience, cost savings, and efficiency, it can be subjected to a single point of failure due to concentration of risks in one place and at one time. Thus, if the SSO system is compromised, all the connected multiple systems can be compromised too.

Privilege management creates, manages, and stores the attributes and policies needed to establish criteria that can be used to decide whether an authenticated entity's request for access to some resource should be granted. Enterprise-level privilege management fits under the umbrella of enterprise-level access control. At the enterprise level, access management encompasses all the practices, policies, procedures, data, metadata, and technical and administrative mechanisms used to manage access to the resources of an organization. Access management includes access control, privilege management, and identity management, as shown:

Access Management = Access Control + Privilege Management + Identity Management

Access control ensures that resources are made available only to authorized users, programs, processes, or systems by reference to rules of access that are defined by attributes and policies. In privilege management, resources can be both computer-based objects (e.g., files and Web pages) and physical objects (e.g., buildings and vault safes). The entities requesting access to resources can be users (people) and processes running on a computer, application, or system. Identity management deals with identification and authentication, authorization, decision, and enforcement processes.

(c) Integrating Identification and Authentication Methods

Four factors exist to identify and authenticate a person or device to a computer system prior to permitting an access to that system. Four-factor authentication methods have been proven stronger and better than single-factor authentication methods, shown next.

One-Factor Authentication (1FA) Method. Any one of the following can represent a 1FA method, which is not strong and secure.

- Something you have (e.g., photo ID, memory card, smart card, PIV card with PIN for swiping into a reader with photo, decal mounted onto a motorized vehicle, transponder mounted on a motorized vehicle used for operating an automated entry point, visitor badge without name and photo, physical key, digital certificate, hardware token, and mobile ID device).

- Something you know (e.g., password or PIN; shared or unshared combination, such as electronic safe, cipher lock, PIN pad combination, and digital certificate).

- Something you are (e.g., photo ID, PIV card with PIN or photo, fingerprint identification [one to many], fingerprint verification [one to one], hand geometry [one to many], iris scan [one to many], colleague [peers and coworkers] recognition, and user [peers or security guards] recognition). Colleague and user recognitions are considered attended access.

- Somewhere you are (e.g., geodetic location, such as a building, city, state, or country using a GPS) for employees traveling to and from the company's remote location or to and from vendor/customer location.

Two-Factor Authentication (2FA) Methods. Any one of the following can represent a 2FA method. Note that there are many combinations due to use of several authentication devices.

- Combination of something you have and something you know (e.g., digital certificate where a digital signature is used with a PIN to unlock the private key; cryptographic hardware token with one-time password device and PIN; and PIV card with PIN or password for after-hours entry without after-hours attendant).

- Combination of something you have and something you are (e.g., verified digital or optical photo ID with driver's license and personal identity card with photo or attended/unattended access, hardware token with biometrics).

- Combination of something you know (e.g., user ID, PIN, and passwords) and something you are (e.g., biometric sample).

- Combination of something you have, something you know, and something you are (e.g., personal identity card with attended access and PIN). This combination is an attended or two-person access control method using the card and the PIN and is not the strongest 2FA because of the attendant.

- Combination of something you have (1), something you have (2), which is the same as in (1), and (3) something you know (e.g., PIV card and digital certificate). This combination illustrates that multiple instances of the same factor (i.e., something you have two times is counted as 1FA) results in 2FA. That is, 1FA is something you have and 2FA is something you know. However, this implementation represents a higher level of assurance than other instances of 2FA. Two-factor authentication methods are better than one-factor methods.

Three-Factor Authentication (3FA) Methods. The combination of something you have (i.e., PKI keys or a hardware token), something you know (i.e., PIN or password), and something you are (i.e., comparing the cardholder to the biometric image stored on the biometric database and/or on the access card) represents the strongest 3FA. A hardware token can be used in support of this level of assurance in logical access control. Three-factor authentication methods are better than one-factor and two-factor methods.

Four-Factor Authentication (4FA) Methods. The combination of something you have (i.e., card, key, or mobile ID device), something you know (i.e., PIN or password), something you are (i.e., fingerprint or signature), and something about where you are (i.e., building or company/remote location, or vendor/customer location) represents the strongest and highest form of all authentication methods.

(d) Alternatives to Passwords

This section first presents major problems associated with passwords in terms of their use and misuse and the resulting negative consequences of poor security controls. Various alternatives to passwords are discussed to improve and strengthen the overall posture of security controls.

(i) Problems with Passwords

Passwords provide a basic entry point into an organization's websites, computer systems, networks, data files, cloud services, and more. In a way, passwords are the keys to the front door of a house. This means that if passwords are compromised somehow, then all the computer systems and networks are compromised and the entry points become death points.

Although passwords are so easy to select, use, and manage for users, they become a nightmare for the IT staff to control (i.e., protecting the password files with encryption and enforcing the password rules and policies) and a gold mine for hackers to attack (i.e., can easily break into password files to steal them using password cracking programs and when the password files are not encrypted). Data breaches and other cyberattacks are primarily known to occur due to use of weak passwords (e.g., Target Corporation), which is a great opportunity for hackers to attack (i.e., it is like picking a low-hanging fruit).

Despite their importance, passwords are the most neglected topic by management due to their multidimensional scope, such as technological and behavioral aspects. Some specific aspects include:

- Some users share their passwords with others for the sake of speed and convenience, which is risky due to lack of accountability of knowing who did what and when.

- When asked to change a password, some people reuse the same password and the password system lets them do it, which is bad.

- Some users use the same password across multiple websites and computer systems for ease of use and convenience. This is clearly evidenced due to the explosive growth of websites and computer systems users must access daily to do their work. Naturally, users will be tempted to take a shortcut in accessing so many websites and computer networks.

- When users are selecting a password, their focus is on simplicity and convenience, not on security and protection.

- Passwords pose a real problem with no clear solution.

(ii) Specific Alternatives to Passwords

Because passwords alone do not provide a strong security control, something else is required. Therefore, management must plan to either fortify the weak passwords with additional security mechanisms or replace passwords entirely with better and stronger security mechanisms.

When a user enters her username (user ID) and a password into a computer system, this entry represents a 1FA, which is a very weak security control due to weak selection and management of passwords and is subjected to attacks. Here, the combination of a user ID/username and a password is counted as one factor as they are linked together. More than 1FA or multifactor authentication (MFA) is needed to make security controls stronger and better. Simply stated, 2FA is stronger than 1FA; 3FA is much stronger than 2FA; and so on.

Similarly, a hacker's work factor (i.e., cost, time, and effort) to break into computer systems and steal passwords is increased when the system requires the user to present higher levels of authentication factors (i.e., 3FA is harder to break into than 2FA; 1FA is much easier to break into than 4FA). Alternative methods to a password method are needed to make the passwords much stronger or simply to eliminate the use of passwords entirely (i.e., removing the barrier or bottleneck). Next is a list of several alternative methods to the basic password method.

(A) Passwords and Personal Identification Numbers

A combination of username (user ID) and password has been a long practice and is counted as 1FA. When this 1FA is combined with a PIN, it becomes a 2FA, which is much stronger than 1FA. Retail merchants and other online sellers require their customers presenting credit cards or debit cards with built-in security chip (smart chip) to enter a PIN.

User ID and Password + Personal Identification Number

(Weak 1FA)   (Strong 2FA)

(B) Passwords and Security Questions Based Authentication

Before login or sign-in, some computer systems and websites require users to answer personal security questions based on previously saved questions and answers. These questions are in addition to traditional practices of entering user ID and password. The types of questions are personal in nature, such as the model of your first car. When the user answers the randomly posed questions later, the system will give permission to proceed further. If not, the user is declined access to the system. The idea behind these questions is that no hacker would know the answers to these questions because they are too personal in nature, even though hackers could steal the user ID and password.

User ID and Password + Personal Security Questions

(Weak 1FA)   (Strong 2FA)

(C) Passwords and Secure Verification Code

When new customers open a new bank account or create a new account with online retailers and other sellers, and even to reset lost or forgotten passwords, the bank or retailer sends a secure verification code through electronic mail (email) or short message service (SMS) text message to enter into the new account along with the username and password. This secure code establishes the authenticity of the new customer. However, this secure code sent through email or SMS is subject to man-in-the-middle (MitM) attacks through impersonation. MitM attacks represent data-in-transit attacks.

User ID and Password + Secure Verification Code

(Weak 1FA)   (Strong 2FA)

(D) Authenticator Apps

Authenticator applications (apps) can provide a strong 2FA because they use encryption to protect data (e.g., Google's Authenticator).

(E) Passwords and Security Keys or Hardware Tokens

Use of a security key (e.g., Yubikey) or hardware token (i.e., eToken) can act as a strong 2FA. This security key is known to fight against spoofing and phishing attacks.

User ID and Password + Security Key or Hardware Token

(Weak 1FA)   (Strong 2FA)

(F) Selfie Authentication Apps

Retail merchants with the help of commercial charge card companies (e.g., MasterCard) require customers to send selfie picture through a mobile device. After matching the new selfie picture to an old stored selfie picture, the purchase transaction is approved and completed. The selfie photo acts as a master password to open the customer's password wallet.

User ID and Password + User Selfie Picture

(Weak 1FA)   (Strong 2FA)

(G) Password-less Authentication Apps

Password-less apps use a fingerprint and Touch ID button, say on the Apple's iPhone or iPad, to authenticate a user. No password is required. The encryption inside the iPhone device protects and verifies the user's identity. This device is not subject to MitM attacks because the encryption keys are not transmitted anywhere else; instead, they stay inside the phone.

(H) Device-Based Authentication

A device-based authentication is stronger and better than a phone number-based authentication. IBM introduced a security product called FIDO (fast identity online) as a shift toward password-less authentication. Users can choose bring-your-own authentication (BYOA) from a range of PINs to biometrics after entering their private keys. Online fraud and phishing attacks can be reduced with the use of FIDO. A push notification feature on the FIDO connects a user's identity to a user's device rather than to a user's phone number. When the authentication system suspects a fraud situation, it requires the user to submit additional credentials, such as a user location (i.e., geolocation feature on the device).

(I) One-Time Passwords and Biometrics-Based Authentication

For highly sensitive computer systems and confidential data transactions and when the access request is a remote location from a foreign country, a stronger authentication is required, such as a combination of a one-time password with challenge-response mechanism and biometrics (e.g., fingerprint, iris, and thumbprint scans, voice and facial recognition, and digital signatures).

One-Time Password + Biometrics

(Strong 1FA)   (Strong 2FA)

(J) Full-Size Biometric-Based Authentication

A full-size and full-scope biometric-based authentication measure is the best alternative to passwords only. When biometrics are used, users still need to present a regular user ID and password at the login time. Biometrics provide stronger and better security measures with high-quality and consistent results because hackers or imposters cannot cheat or break into the biometrics system in the same way they can break into passwords. Fingerprint scans, iris scans, and voice recognition methods are more popular than the facial recognition method. Although biometric measures are known to be secure, strong, and reliable, sometimes they are subject to operational problems of not recognizing a user due to changes in physiological characteristics (e.g., changes in hand geometry, eyes, voice, and face).

User ID and Password + Biometrics

(Weak 1FA)   (Very Strong 2FA)

(e) Single Point of Failure

This section discusses causes of single points of failure along with solutions to eliminate such failures.

(i) Causes of Single Points of Failure

A single point of failure is a security risk due to concentration of risk in one place, system, or process or with one person. No single point of vulnerability means no single point of failure. A system with a single point of failure is a very risky one since it is like putting all eggs in one basket, and this situation should be avoided if possible. If attacks on these systems are successful, then the entire system is compromised. Multiple levels of passwords, multiple layers of controls, timely network changes, and proper security administration would provide multiple defenses which, in turn, prevent single points of failure because the risk is spread out and minimized.

Single point of failure can occur in the following areas:

- **Placement of web server.** A web server provides a single point of failure when it is placed before an organization's firewall or router that provides IP filtering.

- **Centralized identity management.** A major drawback of the centralized identity management architecture is that the identity providers may act as a single point of failure. Should all of an organization's identity providers suffer a denial of service (DoS) attack, it will not be possible for providers to accept any requests.

- **Universal description, discovery, and integration (UDDI) registry in Web services.** One of the primary goals of a distributed system is the ability to recover when a node in the system fails. Through dynamic discovery and binding, Web services can be designed to recover if a single service fails, whether the failure is accidental or intentional. UDDI supports listing multiple uniform resource identifiers (URIs) for each Web service. When one instance of a Web service has failed, requesters can use an alternate URI. Using UDDI to support failover causes the UDDI registry to become a single point of failure. To remedy this, UDDI supports replication. Through replication, UDDI registries can support multiple nodes, where each node is an instance of the UDDI registry. This way, backup nodes can be used when an individual node is faced with a DoS attack.

- **Single sign-on systems.** If an SSO system did not work, the entire system would be compromised. There is a trade-off between security and convenience in the SSO system.

- **Firewalls.** If a firewall failed, the entire system would be compromised.

- **System administrators.** If the system administrator is ineffective or if no backup person is available, customer service can be limited.

- **Kerberos.** If a Kerberos did not function, the entire system would be compromised

- **Cabling, topology, and power failures.** If a cable is broken, the entire system could be disconnected.

- **Equipment, data, facilities, systems, and programs without redundancy.** Duplication and backup protects essential technology assets.

- **Dial-up network phones.** If a toll-free phone number does not work in a dial-up network system, no calls can go through. Some people still use dial-ups.

Compensating **controls,** such as backup personnel; backup systems, programs, and data files; alternate facilities; fallback procedures; and/or redundancy features, are required to ensure that damage or loss resulting from a single point of failure is minimized.

(ii) Solutions to Eliminate Single Points of Failure

A single point of failure is eliminated through **defense-in-depth** strategy, which is the best practice strategy, and is based on two security engineering principles: (1) implement layered security and (2) design and operate an IT system to limit damage and to be resilient in response. Other related strategies include defense in breadth, defense in technology, defense in time, defense in density, and defense in intensity.

The defense-in-depth strategy recommends a balance between the protection capability, cost, performance, and operational considerations. This strategy is based on the paradigm of Protect, Detect, and React. This means that in addition to incorporating protection mechanisms, organizations need to expect attacks and include attack detection tools and procedures that allow them to react to and recover from the attacks. An important principle of the defense-in-depth strategy is that achieving information assurance requires a balanced focus on three primary elements: *people, technology,* and *operations.*

People. The people element focuses on policies and procedures, training and awareness, allocation of resources, system security administration, physical security, personnel security, and facilities countermeasures. The major theme in this area is to hire good people, train and reward them well, and penalize unauthorized behavior.

Technology. To ensure that the right technologies are procured and deployed, an organization should establish effective policy and processes for technology acquisition. These should include security policy, information assurance principles, system level architecture and standards, criteria for needed technology products, acquisition of products that have been validated by a reputable third party, configuration guidance, and processes for assessing the risk of the integrated systems. The major theme in this area is installation of evaluated products and solutions in support of a layered defense strategy.

Operations. The operations leg focuses on all the activities required to sustain an organization's security posture on a day-to-day basis. These include:

1. Maintaining visible and up-to-date system security policy.

2. Certifying and accrediting changes to the IT baseline acknowledging that a risk accepted by one is a risk shared by many.

3. Managing the security posture by installing security patches and virus updates, and maintaining access control lists (ACLs).

4. Providing key management services.

5. Performing system security assessments using vulnerability scanners and red teams to assess the continued security readiness.

6. Monitoring and reacting to current threats.

7. Reacting to attack sensing, warning, and response.

8. Implementing recovery and reconstitution procedures.

The major theme is this area is enforcing security policy, responding quickly to intrusions, and restricting critical services.

2.3 Information Security Controls

This section is divided into four subsections: information security objectives, system security controls, information protection methods, and encryption and cryptography.

(a) Information Security Objectives

Security objectives, security controls, and security impact analysis are presented in this section.

(i) Security Objectives

There are five security objectives: confidentiality, integrity, availability, accountability, and assurance. However, information systems literature focuses primarily on three security objectives or attributes: confidentiality, integrity, and availability. These three objectives form the three legs of the **CIA triad**. Another definition of security, according to the International Organization for Standardization and the International Electrotechnical Commission (ISO/IEC) 13335 Standard, is that it encompasses all aspects related to defining, achieving, and maintaining confidentiality, integrity, availability, accountability, authenticity, and reliability.

1. **Confidentiality.** Confidentiality of data and information is the requirement that private or confidential information not be disclosed to unauthorized individuals. Confidentiality protection in regard to data concerns data in storage, during processing, and while in transit. Confidentiality is the preservation of authorized restrictions on information access and disclosure, including means for protecting personal privacy and proprietary information. Thus, confidentiality is related to privacy.

2. **Integrity.** Integrity of system and data is required as protection against intentional or accidental attempts to violate either data integrity—the property that data have not been altered in an unauthorized manner while in storage, during processing, or while in transit, or system integrity—the quality that a system has when performing the intended function in an unimpaired manner, free from unauthorized manipulation. In other words, integrity is lack of improper modification, alteration, or destruction.

3. **Availability.** Availability of system and data is a requirement intended to ensure that systems work promptly and service is not denied to authorized users. This objective protects against intentional or accidental attempts to either perform unauthorized deletion of data or otherwise cause a denial of service/data and attempts to use system or data for unauthorized purposes. Availability means that data are continually and reliably accessible and usable in a timely manner, including the ability to share.

4. **Accountability.** Accountability is the requirement that actions of an entity may be traced uniquely to that entity. Accountability (i.e., taking responsibility for one's own actions and inactions) is dependent on confidentiality and integrity. If confidentiality or integrity is lost, accountability is threatened. Note that availability and accountability share the same concerns and controls. Accountability is often an organizational policy requirement and directly supports nonrepudiation, deterrence, fault isolation, intrusion detection and prevention, and after-action recovery and legal action (e.g., audits, investigations, and courts). Here accountability is at the individual level. It is the ability to associate actors

with their acts and to include nonrepudiation (i.e., ensuring that actors are unable to deny—repudiate—an action).

5. **Assurance.** Assurance is the basis for confidence that the security measures, both technical and operational, work as intended to protect the system and the data it processes. Assurance verifies that the other four security objectives—confidentiality, integrity, availability, and accountability—have been adequately met by a specific implementation. Something is "adequately met" when (a) required functionality is present and performs correctly, (b) there is sufficient protection against unintentional errors (by users or software), and (c) there is sufficient resistance to intentional penetration or bypass. Assurance addresses the question of the amount of uncertainty one should have in software system.

When designing an information system, a system architect or system designer should establish an assurance level as a target. This target is achieved by both defining and meeting the functionality requirements in each of the other four security concepts and doing so with sufficient quality. Assurance highlights the fact that for an information system to be secure, it must not only provide the intended functionality but it also must ensure that undesired actions do not occur. Assurance is essential; without it, the other security objectives are not met. However, assurance is a continuum; the amount of assurance needed varies between information systems.

Another view of an information system is that it must be dependable at all times. "Dependable" is a qualitative, umbrella term. Dependability is an integrating concept that encompasses six attributes or properties:

1. Confidentiality

2. Integrity

3. Availability

4. Reliability

5. Safety

6. Maintainability

Although properties such as reliability (i.e., continuity of correct service), safety (i.e., absence of catastrophic consequences on the user and the environment), and maintainability (i.e., the ability to undergo modifications and repairs) may not directly result in secure software, they all contribute to keeping the security up-to-date and showing that the software is secure.

(ii) Security Controls

Access controls fortify the CIA triad by identifying, authenticating, and authorizing users to access systems and data. Poor access controls and inadequate disaster recovery plans can prevent an organization from reasonably ensuring the objectives or goals of the CIA triad.

The interdependencies between the CIA triad and security controls are listed next.

Confidentiality (i.e., sensitivity, criticality, secrecy, nondisclosure, and privacy) is dependent on integrity, in that if the integrity of the system is lost, then there is no longer a reasonable expectation that the confidentiality mechanisms are still valid. Thus, confidentiality is tied to integrity. Implementing the safeguards (controls) suggested in Exhibit 2.1 can help toward achieving the confidentiality objective.

EXHIBIT 2.1 Controls to Achieve the Confidentiality Objective

Security Objective	Security Controls
Confidentiality	Use encryption techniques during data/program storage and transmission; use digital signature verification techniques; develop data classification schemes; require all employees to sign nondisclosure statements to ensure transaction privacy; implement accountability principles by logging and journaling system activity; implement security policies, procedures, and standards; implement system user identification, authentication, and authorization techniques; implement a reference monitor concept in the design of an operating system; implement layers of controls to prevent impersonation and tailgating; implement logical and physical access controls; establish employee security awareness and training programs; establish document and file disposition controls; establish security labels and tags to storage media and data files to reflect their sensitivity; install audit trails and journals to provide transaction monitoring capability; and audit the adequacy of confidentiality safeguards.

Integrity (i.e., accuracy, authenticity, nonrepudiation, accountability, and completeness) is dependent on confidentiality, in that if the confidentiality of certain information is lost (e.g., due to the use of the superuser password), then the integrity mechanisms are likely to be bypassed. Implementing the safeguards (controls) suggested in Exhibit 2.2 can help toward achieving the integrity objective.

EXHIBIT 2.2 Controls to Achieve the Integrity Objective

Security Objective	Security Controls
Integrity	Implement system/user identification, authentication, and authorization techniques; implement logical and physical access controls; use encryption techniques during data/program storage and transmission; use digital signature verification techniques; implement intrusion detection and response programs; install data editing and validation routines for data input, process, and output; install antivirus software; implement security policies, procedures, and standards; implement layers of controls to prevent impersonation and tailgating; establish data reconciliation controls; implement a reference monitor concept in the design of an operating system; use disk repair utility programs for personal computers (PCs); make system and data backups; establish employee security awareness and training programs; implement variance detection techniques in sensitive transaction processing; install audit trails and journaling to provide transaction monitoring capability; audit the adequacy of integrity safeguards.

Availability (i.e., usability and timeliness) is dependent on confidentiality and integrity, in that if confidentiality is lost for certain information (e.g., superuser password), the mechanisms implementing these objectives are easily bypassable; and if system integrity is lost, then confidence in the validity of the mechanisms implementing these objectives is also lost. Implementing the safeguards (controls) suggested in Exhibit 2.3 can help toward achieving the availability objective.

EXHIBIT 2.3 Controls to Achieve the Availability Objective

Security Objective	Security Controls
Availability	Establish software configuration controls; implement disaster recovery and contingency plans; purchase insurance coverage; implement logical and physical access controls; implement user/system authorization mechanisms; implement intrusion detection and response programs; implement records management programs; install asset management system for tracking software and hardware inventory; implement logical and physical access controls; make system and data backups; use loosely coupled parallel processor architecture for fail-safe operation; implement incident logging and reporting; install fault-tolerant hardware and software for continuous operation; require extra power supplies and cooling fans; establish employee security awareness and training programs; conduct computer capacity planning; implement redundancy and recovery features; and audit the adequacy of availability safeguards.

(iii) Security Impact Analysis

In an information system, an **impact** is the magnitude of harm that can be expected to result from the consequences of unauthorized disclosure, unauthorized modification, unauthorized destruction, or loss of information or loss of information system availability.

Impact levels are categorized as high, moderate, or low in regard to the intensity of a potential impact that may occur if the information system is jeopardized or compromised.

- A **high-impact system** is an information system in which at least one security objective (i.e., confidentiality, integrity, or availability) is assigned a potential impact value of high.

- A **moderate-impact system** is an information system in which at least one security objective (i.e., confidentiality, integrity, or availability) is assigned a potential impact value of moderate and no security objective is assigned a potential impact value of high.

- A **low-impact system** is an information system in which all three security objectives (i.e., confidentiality, integrity, and availability) are assigned a potential impact value of low.

- A **potential impact** considers all three levels of impact regarding the loss of confidentiality, integrity, or availability. It could be expected to have a

  a. Limited adverse effect (low);

  b. Serious adverse effect (moderate); or

  c. Severe or catastrophic adverse effect (high) on organizational operations, systems, assets, individuals, or other organizations.

Security management analyzes changes to the information system to determine potential security impacts prior to change implementation. **Security impact analysis** (SIA) is conducted by internal employees with information security responsibilities (e.g., system administrators, security officers, security managers, and security engineers). Individuals conducting SIA must have the appropriate skills and technical expertise to analyze the changes (e.g., system upgrades and modifications) to information systems and the associated security ramifications.

The scope of SIA includes:

1. Reviewing information system documentation, such as the security plan, to understand how specific security controls are implemented within the system and how the changes might affect the controls.

2. Assessing risk to understand the impact of the changes and to determine if additional security controls are required.

3. Relating the amount of analysis to the impact level (i.e., a system with high impact requires more analysis).

In addition, security management analyzes new software in a separate test environment before installation in an operational environment, looking for security impacts due to flaws, weaknesses, incompatibility, or intentional malice.

After the information system is changed, security management checks the security functions to verify that they are implemented correctly, operating as intended, and producing the desired outcome with regard to meeting the security requirements for the system.

KEY CONCEPTS TO REMEMBER: Security

To provide reasonable security mechanisms over computer systems and networks:

- Implement access controls, firewalls, routers, sensors, hardware and software guards, and demilitarized zones (DMZs) to protect computer systems and networks from attacks.

- Build security into a system now, do not add it on later because doing so is too late, costly, and risky. Building it in requires the integration of security principles, standards, policies, procedures, controls, safeguards, and mechanisms into all phases or processes of a system development life cycle (i.e., from beginning to the end).

- Keep security as simple as possible. Complexity leads to problems in design, development, and implementation, thus making a system unusable, unstable, unmanageable, and uncontrollable and even vulnerable to threats.

- Avoid single-point-of-failure situations, which are security risks due to concentration of risk in one place, system, process, or with one person. Besides placement of Web services and domain name system (DNS) servers and password synchronization problems, other causes leading to these situations include these:

  - Primary telecommunication services without backups
  - Centralized identity management
  - Central certification authority
  - Single-sign-on systems
  - Firewalls
  - Kerberos
  - Converged networks with voice and data
  - Cloud storage services and system administrators

(Continued)

KEY CONCEPTS TO REMEMBER: Security (*Continued*)

- Fix security problems and issues correctly and timely as soon as possible.

- Practice separation of duties, whether manual or electronic.

- Require mandatory vacations for all employees.

- Practice rotation of job duties.

- Practice the principle of least privilege with secure defaults and fail securely in a known, safe, and secure state. The efficiency and effectiveness of access control policy and its implementation depends on the system state and secure state in which the system is in at any point in time and the use of fail-safe defaults. A **secure state** is a condition in which no subject can access any object in an unauthorized manner.

- Implement system hardening techniques to make computer systems and networks more robust. To do so:

  - Remove all nonessential and unnecessary computer programs and their associated utility programs to prevent or eliminate backdoor or trapdoor attacks.

  - Implement security engineering principles (which are fully discussed in the application development section of this domain).

- Implement secure coding principles. To do so:

  - Minimize attack surface.

  - Establish secure defaults.

  - Implement the principle of least privilege.

  - Deploy the defense-in-depth principle.

  - Fail securely in a known system state.

  - Avoid security by obscurity.

  - Keep security simple.

  - Minimize programming errors that lead to software vulnerabilities.

  - Implement secure coding standards.

- Connect to a secure network (e.g., the Internet)

- Enable and configure a firewall and router. Install and use antivirus and anti-spyware software on computer systems and networks.

- Remove unnecessary software from computers and networks.

- Disable nonessential services from computers and networks (e.g., file sharing and print sharing).

- Modify unnecessary default features and options in software.

- Operate under the principle of least privilege to restrict access to computer systems and networks.

- Secure Web browsers by disabling mobile code (e.g., Active X, Java, JavaScript, VB, VBScript, Flash, and cookies).

- Apply software patches and fixes and enable future automated updates.

- Use caution and implement good security practices when opening email attachments from unknown parties, connecting to untrusted links, and providing sensitive information to unknown parties.

- Create strong passwords with passphrases.

- Balance the costs, risks, and benefits equation: Do not spend $10 on controls to protect an asset, information, or a risk costing $1. Costs should not exceed benefits.

- Note the trade-off that exists in security: Pay now or pay later.

(b) System Security Controls

This section discusses access controls, access control principles, access rights and permissions, access control policies, firewalls, and demilitarized zones (DMZs).

Access is the ability to make use of any information system's resource. Subjects (e.g., an individual, process, or device) access objects (e.g., programs, files, records, tables, processes, domains, devices, directories, and Web pages) on a computer system or network. A **subject** is an activity entity that causes information to flow among objects or changes to the system state, and an **object** is a passive entity that contains or receives information.

(i) Access Controls

Access controls are used for a number of purposes:

- To identify and authenticate users to prevent unauthorized access
- To enforce the principle of least privilege to ensure that authorized access was necessary and appropriate
- To establish sufficient boundary protection mechanisms
- To apply encryption to protect sensitive data on networks and portable devices
- To log, audit, and monitor security-relevant events

Access control is the process of granting or denying specific access requests. Access controls are of two types: physical and logical. Examples of physical access controls are listed next.

- Physical and electronic keys
- Visitor logs
- Physical and electronic locks
- Human security guards
- Gates and guns
- Security cameras
- Smart cards and PINs
- Access codes
- Dual control activity
- Employee rotation of duties and vacations
- Biometrics
- Motion detectors with sensors and alarms
- Physical tokens

Examples of logical access controls are listed next.

- Passwords (e.g., repeat or reuse passwords, one-time passwords, and challenge-response passwords)

- Passphrases
- Passcodes
- Personal identification numbers (PINs)
- Firewalls
- Routers
- Sensors (Intrusion detection and prevention systems)
- Hardware guards and software guards
- Demilitarized zones (DMZs)
- Memory cards and smart cards
- Hardware tokens, software tokens, and e-Tokens

(ii) Access Control Principles

Access control principles include need to know, least privilege (e.g., need to withhold and access safety), and separation of duties, as follows.

The **need-to-know principle** is a legitimate requirement of a prospective recipient of data to know, access, or possess any specific and sensitive information represented by these data to perform official tasks or services. The data custodian of the classified or sensitive unclassified information, not the prospective recipient, determines the need to know.

The **least privilege principle** states that every user and process should have the least set of privileges (i.e., restrictive set of privileges) needed to perform the task at hand. The implementation of this principle has the effect of limiting damage that can result from system errors, accidents, unauthorized use, or malicious events. This principle addresses the need for minimal interactions between privileged programs and the need to prevent improper uses of such privileges.

The least privilege principle is also related to **need-to-withhold concept**, which is the necessity to limit access to some confidential information when broad access is given to all the information. The least privilege principle is same as the need-to-know concept and is related to **access safety**, where safety includes a mechanism for preventing leakage of privileges through either constraints or confinements.

Safety is achieved from separation of duties enforced by access control policy systems.

The **separation of duties principle** is of two types: static and dynamic. In general, the purpose of separation of duty (SOD) is to ensure that failures of omission or commission with an organization are caused only by collusion among individuals, making such failures riskier and less likely. It also minimizes chances of collusion by assigning individuals of different skills or divergent interest to separated tasks; thus, SOD is enacted whenever conflict of interest may otherwise arise in assignment of tasks within an organization.

(A) Static Separation of Duty

As a security mechanism, static separation of duty (SSOD) addresses two separate but related problems: static exclusivity and assurance principle.

- **Static exclusivity** is the condition for which it is considered dangerous for any user to gain authorization for conflicting sets of capabilities (e.g., a cashier and a cashier supervisor). The motivations for exclusivity relations include, but are not limited to, reducing the likelihood of fraud or preventing the loss of user objectivity.

- The **assurance principle** is the potential for collusion where the greater the number of individuals who are involved in the execution of a sensitive business function, such as purchasing an item or executing a trade, the less likely any one user will commit fraud or that any few users will collude in committing fraud.

SOD constraints may require that two roles be mutually exclusive, because no user should have the privileges of both roles. Popular SSOD policies are RBAC and RuBAC, defined later in this chapter.

(B) Dynamic Separation of Duty

Separation of duties can be enforced dynamically (i.e., at access time), and the decision to grant access refers to the past access history (e.g., a cashier and an accountant are the same person who plays only one role at a time).

One type of dynamic separation of duty (DSOD) is a *two-person rule*, which states that the first user to execute a two-person operation can be any authorized user, whereas the second user can be any authorized user different from the first. Another type of DSOD is a *history-based separation of duty*, which states that the same subject (role) cannot access the same object for variable number of times. Popular DSOD policies are the workflow and Chinese wall policies.

(iii) Access Rights and Permissions

Access control policies should deal with access rights in terms of file permissions, program permissions, and data permissions.

- File permissions deal with the right to create, read, edit, or delete a file on server or other places.

- Program permissions deal with the right to read, append, write, copy, change, or execute a program on an application server or other places.

- Data permissions deal with the right to view (read only), read, write, retrieve, delete, or update data in a database or file directory.

A problem with incorrect or inappropriate design of access rights and permission is authorization creep, where an authorized employee continues to maintain access rights for previously held positions within an organization. This can lead to misuse of privileges due to human error. Another problem is escalation of privileges, which can lead to exploits due to system flaws and security weaknesses.

(iv) Access Control Polices

Access control is exercised through procedures and controls to limit or detect access to critical information resources. This control can be accomplished through software, biometrics devices, or physical access to a controlled area. Access control policy is the set of rules that define the conditions under which an access may take place.

Access control *policies* are high-level requirements that specify how access is managed and who may access information under what circumstances. Policies are the set of rules that define the conditions under which an access may take place. A security policy is the statement of required protection for information objects. For instance, policies may pertain to resource usage within or across organizational units or may be based on need-to-know, need-to-withhold, competence, authority, obligation, or conflict-of-interest factors.

Access control *decisions* are usually based on access control policies, such as discretionary access control or mandatory access control. The function of access control decision is to grant or deny requests for access.

At a high level, access control policies are enforced through a mechanism that translates a user's access request, often in terms of a structure that a system provides. An ACL is a familiar example of an access control mechanism. The access control mechanisms use logical, physical, and administrative controls.

Specific access control policies are listed next.

- A **discretionary access control (DAC) policy** leaves a certain amount of access control to the discretion of the object's owner or anyone else authorized to control the object's access. DAC is known as surrogate access control. DAC is generally used to limit a user's access to a file; the owner of the file controls other users' accesses to the file. Only those users specified by the owner may have some combination of read, write, execute, and other permissions to the file. A DAC policy tends to be very flexible and is widely used in the private and public sectors. This policy is often referred to as identity-based controls. It applies the need-to-know principle and uses ACLs, but not capability lists, for implementation. DAC also uses a combination of access mechanisms for individual owners, groups, and other categories. Four basic models for DAC control exist: hierarchical, concept of ownership, laissez-faire, and centralized. DAC is a means of optionally restricting access to objects (programs and files) based on the identity of subjects (users and devices), the groups to which they belong, or both of these criteria. Access controls are discretionary in the sense that a subject with a particular access right can pass that access to any other subject. The user has control and ownership of access privileges over the items that he or she creates.

- The **nondiscretionary access control (NDAC) policy** includes all access control policies other than the DAC policy. The NDAC policy has rules that are not established at the discretion of the user. This policy establishes access controls that can be changed only through administrative action, not by users. NDAC policies may be employed in addition to DAC policies.

WHAT ARE GENERIC ACCESS CONTROL POLICIES?

- Discretionary access control
- Mandatory access control
- Role-based access control
- Workflow access control + Chinese wall access policy
- High-latency access control

- A **mandatory access control (MAC) policy** is a means of restricting access to system resources based on the sensitivity (as represented by a security label) of the information contained in the system resource and the formal authorization (i.e., security clearance) of users to access information of such sensitivity. Users cannot change the privileges; system administrators can. MAC is often referred to as rule-based controls. It applies the marking (label) principle and uses security clearances for implementation. MAC policy establishes coverage over all subjects and objects under its control to ensure that each user receives only that information to which the user has authorized access based on classification of the information and on user clearance and formal access authorization. The information system assigns appropriate security attributes (e.g., labels/security domains/types) to subjects and objects and uses these attributes as the basis for MAC decisions.

- The **role-based access control (RBAC) policy** supports higher-level organizational policies and access control mechanisms, and RBACs are natural to the way the enterprises typically conduct their business. RBAC policy establishes coverage over all users and resources to ensure that access rights are grouped by role name and that access to resources is restricted to users who have been authorized to assume the associated role.

In the RBAC method, the role of a requester is the key determinant for access. The RBAC method better supports the implementation of *least privilege and separation of duties* but, like the IBAC method, does not measure well. In the commercial world, RBAC is the de facto access control implementation at the enterprise level because it is what most solutions support. In fact, a role-based implementation security policy is the only logical choice for an organization that experiences a large turnover of personnel. RBAC is the privilege to use computer information in some manner based on an individual's role (i.e., teller or doctor).

- The **IBAC policy** is a mechanism based only on the identity of the subject and object. An IBAC decision grants or denies a request based on the presence of an entity on an ACL. This means that IBAC requires an authenticated identity before granting any access. IBAC and DAC are considered equivalent.

- The **rule-based access control (RuBAC) policy** is a security policy based on global rules imposed for all subjects. These rules usually rely on a comparison of the sensitivity of the objects being accessed and the possession of corresponding attributes by the subjects requesting access. It is a mechanism for MAC policy where rules cannot be changed by users. It allows users to access systems and information based on predetermined and preconfigured rules. These controls can be combined with role-based controls such that the role of a user is one of the attributes in rule setting. The RuBAC provides for flexibility in administering security policies; however, it does not provide access assignments and constraints directly related among subjects, operations, and objects as other access control mechanisms do. RuBAC relies on security labels, where labels are attached to all objects (e.g., files, directories, and devices) and sometimes to subjects (i.e., roles). In RuBAC, access to a resource is granted on the basis of an entity's authorizations rather than an entity's identity.

- A **workflow policy** separates the various activities of a given organizational processes into a set of well-defined tasks. Hence, typically, a workflow (often synonymous with a process) is specified as a set of tasks and a set of dependencies among the tasks, and the sequencing of these tasks is important. The various tasks in a workflow are usually carried out by several users in accordance with organizational rules relevant to the process represented by the workflow. The representation of a business process using a workflow involves a number of organizational rules or policies. The goal of the workflow policy is to maintain consistency between the internal data and external users' expectations of that data. The workflow management system is the basis for workflow policy access control system because this management system schedules and synchronizes various tasks within the workflow.

- The **Chinese wall policy** states that once a person accesses one side of the wall, he or she cannot access the other side of the wall, thereby avoiding conflicts of interest in access. It addresses the conflict-of-interest issues related to consulting activities within banking and other financial disciplines. Like the workflow policy, the Chinese wall policy is application-specific in that it applies to a narrow set of activities that are tied to specific business transactions (e.g., giving out proprietary or insider information to outsiders). The stated objective of this policy is to prevent illicit flows of information that can result in conflicts of interest. The Chinese wall policy is often combined with MAC policy.

- In **history-based access control policies** (e.g., workflow and Chinese wall), previous access events are used as one of the decision factors for the next access authorization; the policies require sophisticated historical system-state control for tracking and maintaining of historical events.

- The **attribute-based access control (ABAC) policy** is an approach in which access is mediated based on attributes associated with subjects (requesters) and the objects to be accessed. Each object and subject has a set of associated attributes, such as location, time of creation, and access rights. ABAC deals with subjects, objects, targets, initiators, resources, or the environment. It uses rule sets to define the combination of attributes under which an access may take place.

- The **authority-based access control (AuBAC) policy** focuses on ABACs that can enable a RuBAC policy to be implemented based on the most current information available about a user at the time of an access attempt. In other words, AuBAC = ABAC + RuBAC.

- The **high-latency-based transaction policy** deals with provisions, prerequisites, and obligations. It can prevent identity theft, such as stealing credit/debit card, Social Security, driver's license, bank account, bank routing, and other identification numbers.

- The **extensible markup language-based (XML-based) access control policy** combined with the extensible access control markup language (XACML) framework provides a general-purpose language for specifying distributed access control policies. In XML terms, it defines a core schema with a namespace that can be used to express access control and authorization policies for XML objects. The XACML specification describes building blocks from which a RBAC solution is constructed. XACML has the potential to address the concerns of privilege management in terms of policy, legal, and compliance requirements. Since XACML is based on a language, it does not deal with access control processes and policy enforcements. XACML has two components: a policy enforcement point and a policy decision point. XACML uses policy combining and overriding algorithms when the policies overlap or conflict. The XML limitation, similar to RuBAC, is in the expressive power of higher-order logic, such as the expressions of historical-based constraints and domain constraints.

SUMMARY OF SPECIFIC ACCESS CONTROL POLICIES AND TECHNIQUES

- Three primary access control policies are DAC, MAC, and RBAC.

- DAC was developed originally to implement controlled sharing and to enforce the need-to-know principle. This is done with the maximum efficiency of system data and resource administration while retaining protection effectiveness.

- Both DAC and MAC policies are not well suited for private and public sectors processing unclassified but sensitive information. In these environments, security objectives often support higher-level organizational policies derived from existing policies, laws, ethics, regulations, or generally accepted practices. Such environments usually need to control individuals' actions, beyond the individuals' ability to access information, according to how that information is labeled, based on its sensitivity.

- Both DAC and MAC support lower-level organizational policies and access control mechanisms.

- RBAC is an improvement on DAC and MAC, but it ties users to roles and privileges toward objects.

- DAC policy implements the need-to-know principle.

- RBAC policy better supports the implementation of least privilege and separation of duties.

- DAC and IBAC policies are considered equivalent.

- MAC and RuBAC policies are considered equivalent.

- High-latency-based transaction policy deals with provisions, prerequisites, and obligations.

- ACLs, but not capability lists, are used to implement DAC, IBAC, and RuBAC policies.

- RBAC is a composite policy because it is a variant of both IBAC and RuBAC.

- RuBAC and RBAC policies can be combined so that rules can either replace or complement roles.

- Three basic access control policies are RBAC, ABAC, and IBAC. Whatever access control can be defined with IBAC or RBAC can also be defined with ABAC. In addition, the ABAC method can provide more complex access control than can be accomplished with IBAC or RBAC. However, this complexity comes with additional administrative and managerial burdens. With the ABAC method, the policies to be supported must be known in order to assess the trade-off between capability and complexity.

- International access control policy standards do not use the U.S.-based MAC or DAC policies; instead, they use IBAC or RuBAC policies.

- The structured query language (SQL) database incorporates many aspects of RBAC and RuBAC policies.

- Nondiscretionary access control (NDAC) policies include RBAC, RuBAC, ABAC, UDAC, MAC (most-mentioned NDAC), and temporal constraints, where the latter covers workflow policy and Chinese wall policy.

- The ABAC or RBAC policy is used to implement separation of domains.

- AuBAC = ABAC + RuBAC.

- RBAC and RuBAC policies are used to achieve static separations of duty.

- Workflow and Chinese wall policies are used to achieve dynamic separations of duty.

- Workflow policy is applied to organize tasks based on process rules.

- The Chinese wall policy addresses the conflict-of-interest issues arising in specific workplaces.

- Temporal constraints are related to history-based access control policies, such as workflow and Chinese wall policies.

- Note that although a person may be free to read sensitive information under the Chinese wall policy, he or she may be restricted from reading such information under a MAC policy.

- RBAC, not ABAC, implements privilege management capabilities.

- No access control policy is better or worse than any other; each has its own place and should be adopted according to its suitability for a particular set of requirements and circumstances after its strengths and weaknesses are analyzed.

Exhibit 2.4 highlights the connection between the security objectives and access control policies.

EXHIBIT 2.4 Linking Security Objectives to Access Control Policies

Security Objective	Access Control Policy
Confidentiality	MAC, RBAC, and Chinese wall
Integrity	Workflow
Availability	None

(v) Firewalls and Demilitarized Zones

Firewalls and DMZs provide boundary controls to protect from external bad actors (hackers) entering into an organization's internal computer networks and systems. Together, firewalls and DMZs provide stronger system security mechanisms.

(A) Firewalls

A **firewall** is a network connectivity device that mediates all traffic between two computer networks and protects one of them or some part thereof against unauthorized access. Generally, the protected network is a private, internal network. A firewall may permit messages or files to be transferred to a high-security workstation within the internal network without permitting such transfer in the opposite direction.

Many enterprise networks employ firewalls to restrict connectivity to and from the internal networks used to service more sensitive functions, such as accounting or personnel. By employing firewalls to control connectivity to these areas, an organization can prevent unauthorized access to its systems and resources. Inclusion of a proper firewall provides an additional layer of security. Organizations often need to use firewalls to meet security requirements from regulatory mandates.

Enclave boundary protection takes the form of firewalls and VPNs. While these technologies offer perimeter and access controls, authorized internal and external (remote) users can attempt probing, misuse, and malicious activities within an enclave. Firewalls do not monitor authorized users' actions, nor do they address internal (insider) threats. Firewalls also must allow some degree of access, which may open the door for external vulnerability probing and the potential for attacks.

Configuration management activities can be extended to firewalls using a firewall rule set, which is a table of instructions that the firewall uses for determining how network packets or data packets should be routed between firewall's interfaces.

Firewall Technology. Firewall technologies include packet filtering, stateful inspection, application firewalls, application-proxy gateways, dedicated proxy servers, and personal firewalls or personal firewall appliances, as discussed next.

Packet Filtering. The most basic feature of a firewall is the packet filter (also known as stateless inspection firewall), operating at the network layer. A packet filter does not keep track of the state of each flow of traffic that passes though the firewall; this means, for example, that it cannot associate multiple requests within a single session to each other. Characteristics of packet filters are listed next.

- Packet filters are not concerned about the content of packets.

- Rule sets govern the access control functionality of packet filters.

- Packet-filtering capabilities are built into most operating systems and devices capable of routing; the most common example of a pure packet filtering device is a network router that employs ACLs.

Stateless packet filters are generally vulnerable to attacks and exploits that take advantage of problems within the TCP/IP specification and protocol stack.

Stateful Inspection. Stateful inspection improves on the functions of packet filters by tracking the state of connections and blocking packets that deviate from the expected state. This is accomplished by incorporating greater awareness of the transport layer. As with packet filtering, stateful inspection intercepts packets at the network layer and inspects them to see if they are permitted by an existing firewall rule. Unlike packet filtering, stateful inspection keeps track of each connection in a state table. While the details of state table entries vary by firewall product, they typically include source IP address, destination IP address, port numbers, and connection state information.

Application Firewalls. A newer trend in stateful inspection is the addition of a stateful protocol analysis capability, referred to by some vendors as deep packet inspection. Stateful protocol analysis improves on standard stateful inspection by adding basic intrusion detection technology—an inspection engine that analyzes protocols at the application layer to compare vendor-developed profiles of benign protocol activity against observed events to identify deviations. This allows a firewall to allow or deny access based on how an application is running over the network.

Application-Proxy Gateways. An **application-proxy gateway** is a feature of advanced firewalls that combines lower-layer access control with upper-layer functionality. These firewalls contain a proxy agent that acts as an intermediary between two hosts that wish to communicate with each other and never allows a direct connection between them. Each successful connection attempt actually results in the creation of two separate connections—one between the client and the proxy server, and another between the proxy server and the true destination. The proxy is meant to be transparent to the two hosts—from their perspectives, there is a direct connection. Because external hosts communicate only with the proxy agent, internal IP addresses are not visible to the outside world. The proxy agent interfaces directly with the firewall rule set to determine whether a given instance of network traffic should be allowed to transit the firewall.

In addition to the rule set, some proxy agents have the ability to require authentication of each individual network user. This authentication can take many forms, including user ID and password, hardware or software token, source address, and biometrics.

Dedicated Proxy Servers. Dedicated proxy servers differ from application-proxy gateways in that while dedicated proxy servers retain proxy control of traffic, they usually have much more limited firewalling capabilities. They have a close relationship to application-proxy gateway firewalls. Many dedicated proxy servers are application-specific, and some actually perform analysis and validation of common application protocols, such as Hypertext Transfer Protocol (HTTP). Because these servers have limited firewalling capabilities, such as simply blocking traffic based on its source or destination, typically they are deployed behind traditional firewall platforms. A main firewall could accept inbound traffic, determine which application is being targeted, and hand off traffic to the appropriate proxy server (e.g., email proxy). This server would perform filtering or logging operations on the traffic and then forward it to internal systems. A proxy server could also accept outbound traffic directly from internal systems, filter or log the traffic, and pass it to the firewall for outbound delivery. An example of this is an HTTP proxy deployed behind the firewall—users would need to connect to this proxy en route to connecting to external Web servers. Dedicated proxy servers generally are used to decrease firewall workload and conduct specialized filtering and logging that might be difficult to perform on the firewall itself.

Personal Firewalls or Personal Firewall Appliances. Securing PCs at home or at remote locations is as important as securing them at the office; many employees telecommute or work at home and use an organization's data. Personal firewalls usually do not offer protection to other systems or resources. They do not provide controls over network traffic that is traversing a computer network because they protect only the computer system on which they are installed.

Personal firewall appliances are similar to traditional firewalls in that they are designed to protect small networks, such as those that might be found in a home office. These appliances run on specialized hardware and integrate some other forms of network infrastructure components in addition to the firewall itself. These components include broadband modem WAN routing, LAN routing with dynamic routing support, network hub, network switch, DHCP, simple network management protocol (SNMP) agent, and application-proxy agents.

Although both personal firewalls and personal firewall appliances address connectivity concerns associated with telecommuters or branch offices, most organizations are employing them on their intranets, practicing a layered defense strategy.

Limitations of Firewalls. Firewalls can work effectively only on traffic that they can inspect. Regardless of the firewall technology chosen, a firewall that cannot understand the traffic flowing through it will not handle that traffic properly—for example, allowing traffic that should be blocked. Many network protocols use cryptography to hide the contents of the traffic (e.g., IPsec, TLS, Secure Shell [SSH], and Secure Real-time Transport Protocol [SRTP]). Firewalls also cannot read application data that is encrypted, such as email that is encrypted using the Secure/Multipurpose Internet Mail Extensions (S/MIME) or Open Pretty Good Privacy (OpenPGP) protocols or files that are manually encrypted. Another limitation of some firewalls is understanding traffic that is tunneled, even if it is not encrypted. For example, IPv6 traffic can be tunneled in IPv4 in many different ways. The content may still be unencrypted, but if the firewall does not understand the particular tunneling mechanism used, it cannot interpret the traffic.

Firewall Management. Managing the firewall solution involves maintaining firewall architecture, policies, software, and other components of the solution chosen to be deployed, as described next.

- Test and apply patches to firewall devices.
- Update policy rules as new threats are identified and requirements change, such as when new applications or hosts are implemented within the network. Policy rules should also be reviewed periodically to ensure they remain in compliance with security policy.
- Monitor the performance of firewall components to ensure that potential resource issues are identified and addressed before components become overwhelmed.
- Monitor logs and alerts continuously to identify threats, successful and unsuccessful, that are made to the system.
- Perform periodic testing to verify that firewall rules are functioning as expected.

- Regularly back up the firewall policies and rule sets.

- Conduct penetration testing to assess the overall security of the network environment. This testing can be used to verify that a firewall rule set is performing as intended by generating network traffic and monitoring how it is handled by the firewall in comparison with its expected response. Employ penetration testing in addition to, rather than instead of, a conventional audit program.

(B) Demilitarized Zones

A DMZ is an interface on a routing firewall that is similar to the interfaces found on the firewall's protected side. Traffic moving between the DMZ and other interfaces on the protected side of the firewall still goes through the firewall and can have firewall protection policies applied.

A DMZ is a separate network subnet designed to expose specific services to a larger, untrusted network. The subnets are used in large corporations or organizations to safely expose functions to the Internet, such as Web or database applications. DMZs also are used internal to networks to facilitate secure data transfer from a high-security network zone to a zone with lower security. A DMZ uses explicit access control and contains computer hosts that provide network services to both low-security and high-security network zones. DMZ networks are usually implemented with a firewall or other traffic routing network device. They can be split into several sub-DMZ networks with specific functional groupings for the computers, such as Web servers, timeservers, or file transfer protocol (FTP) repositories. Having multiple DMZs protects the information resources from attacks using virtual LAN hopping and trust exploitation, thus providing another layer to the defense-in-depth strategy.

A possible architecture is to use firewalls with the ability to establish a DMZ between two networks. The use of a DMZ-capable firewall allows the creation of an intermediate network. Creating a DMZ requires that the firewall offer three or more interfaces rather than the typical public and private interfaces. If a patch management server, a Web server, an authentication server, a system log (syslog) server, a remote access server, a DNS server, an antivirus server, or a VPN server is to be used for a network, it should be located directly on the DMZ. Limitations of DMZ include that it cannot work by itself and needs to work with a firewall or router.

(c) Information Protection Methods

In this section, topics such data and information, threats and vulnerabilities, threat events, threat sources, information protection methods, privacy management, and compliance with privacy laws and information protection laws and regulations are discussed.

(i) Data and Information

Data is a collection of facts and figures, and it is usually expressed as numbers. Information is data that is:

- Computed using mathematical equations and formulas.

- Aggregated or summarized in a designated way.

- Combined with several data items in different ways.

- Compared and contrasted in some manner.

- Analyzed and reported in some manner.

- Arranged or sorted either in ascending or descending order.

- Otherwise manipulated or massaged in different ways.

In other words, data is raw data, and information is processed data. Data by itself is meaningful to some whereas information is meaningful to many, because information is derived from data. Most people use the terms "data" and "information" interchangeably and loosely.

A simple example will suffice here: Raw data is when an employee's number of hours worked in a week is 40 and the hourly wage rate is $15. Information is when this employee's payroll check shows the weekly gross earned amount of $600 and weekly gross earned amount for 10 employees is $6,000.

Information, data, software, copyrights, trade secrets,, trademarks, and patents are a big part of an organization's intangible (vital) assets, similar to tangible (physical) assets, such as computers, terminals, workstations, scanners, plotters, printers, network-related equipment (e.g., cables, wires, and devices), mobile devices (e.g., regular phones, smartphones, digital pads and tablets), and portable storage devices (e.g., disks, flash drives, thumb drives, pen drives, tapes, and paper). These intangible assets, especially data and information, are vital assets, so they must be protected at all times because an organization's management depends on them in day-to-day, short-term, and long-term decision-making processes. Note that tangible assets either contain or store these intangible assets.

Possible risks for data and information include destruction, loss, damage, or stealing credit and debit card information and Social Security numbers, and disclosure to unauthorized parties, which leads to privacy issues and legal disputes.

Specifically, these vital assets are easily and constantly exposed to greater risks from insiders (current, disgruntled, and previous employees) and outsiders (e.g., attackers, hackers, adversaries, suppliers, vendors, customers, contractors, and business partners) for personal and financial gain, including intelligence-gathering purposes for competitive reasons.

Data and information are spread out everywhere in an organization and in all organizations. Because of this, most people want these assets since they have intrinsic and extrinsic value. These vital assets, such as data and information, are the major targets of insiders and outsiders alike. For example, insiders (managers and executives) want them for decision making and to run business operations. Outsiders (e.g., attackers, adversaries, competitors, consultants, contractors, suppliers, and vendors) want them for personal gain, financial benefit, competitive advantage, grudge, revenge, and even fun. Therefore, data and information must be protected at all times and with whatever means necessary.

If data and information are so vital, how well are organizations protecting them? The answer is not so well because threat sources are constantly changing, vulnerabilities are increasing rapidly, security controls are not adequate or appropriate, and attackers are getting more sophisticated in their attack methods.

(ii) Threats and Vulnerabilities

A **threat** is any circumstance or event with a potential to adversely impact an organization's operations (e.g., mission, functions, image or reputation), assets, information, or individuals through an information system via unauthorized access, destruction, disclosure, modification of information, and/or even DoS. Also, a potential for a threat source can exploit a particular system's vulnerability. These threats, whether cyber or not and whether local or global, have far-reaching negative effects with increasing speed and spread of attacking. The presence of a threat event does not mean that it will necessarily cause actual harm or loss. To become a risk, a threat must take advantage of vulnerabilities in system security features and controls.

A **vulnerability** is a fault, weakness, bug, or a security hole in a system's functions and operations, security procedures, and design and implementation of internal controls that could be exploited or triggered by a threat source.

A relationship exists among vulnerabilities, threats, risks, and controls, as follows:

Vulnerabilities ⟶ Threats ⟶ Risks ⟶ Controls

Lack of adequate and/or inappropriate controls often increases the vulnerabilities in a system. Therefore, one needs to focus on vulnerabilities first, threats next. Note that controls reduce risks.

(iii) Threat Events
All organizations face many threat events. Organizations that may be targeted include, among others:

- Business corporations
- Governmental agencies, including defense
- Industrial control systems
- Electric power grid systems
- Railroad computer systems
- Gas utility systems
- Water purification and pumping station computer systems
- Oil refinery computer systems
- Personal computer systems

(iv) Threat Sources
Many threat sources exist, such as:

- Malware and malicious code (e.g., viruses, worms, logic bombs, time bombs, and Trojan horses)
- Mobile code on mobile devices (e.g., mobile botnets, mobile applications, exploitation of mobile commerce, exploitation of social media networks, and social engineering)
- Web browser–based attacks (e.g., browser session hijacking, applets, flash, Active X, Java, plug-ins, cookies, JavaScript, and VBScript)
- Eavesdropping (e.g., packet snarfing)
- Masquerading (i.e., impersonating, spoofing, and mimicking)

(v) Information Protection Methods
Several protection methods are available to protect valuable data and information. A number of these are described next.

- **Deploy a defense-in-depth strategy.** Securing data/information and computer systems against the full spectrum of threats requires the use of multiple, overlapping protection approaches addressing the people, technology, and operational aspects of IT. This is due to the highly interactive nature of the various systems and networks and the fact that any single system cannot be adequately secured unless all interconnecting systems are also secured.

  By using multiple, overlapping protection approaches, the failure or circumvention of any individual protection approach will not leave the system unprotected. Through user training and awareness, well-crafted policies and procedures, and redundancy of protection mechanisms, layered protections enable effective protection of IT assets for the purpose of achieving its objectives. The concept of layered protections is called security in depth.

  The defense-in-depth strategy recommends two information assurance principles: defense in multiple places and layered defenses.

  □ **Defense in multiple places.** Given that adversaries can attack a target from multiple points using either insiders or outsiders, an organization needs to deploy protection mechanisms at multiple locations to resist all classes of attacks. As a minimum, these defensive focus areas should include defending:

    □ The networks and infrastructure by (a) protecting the local and wide area communications networks from denial-of-service (DOS) attacks and (b) providing confidentiality and integrity protection for data transmitted over these networks by using encryption and traffic flow security measures to resist passive monitoring.

    □ The enclave (envelope) boundaries by deploying firewalls and intrusion detection mechanisms to resist active network attacks.

    □ The computing environment by providing access controls on hosts and servers to resist insider, close-in, and distribution attacks.

  □ **Layered defenses.** Adversaries are quick to find exploitable vulnerabilities. An effective countermeasure is to deploy multiple defense mechanisms between the adversary and the target. Each of these mechanisms must present unique obstacles to the adversary. Further, each mechanism should include both protection and detection measures. These help to increase risk of detection for the adversary while reducing chances of success or by making successful penetrations unaffordable. Deploying nested firewalls, each coupled with intrusion detection, at outer and inner network boundaries is an example of a layered defense. The inner firewalls may support more granular access control and data filtering.

- **Deploy a defense-in-breadth strategy.** This strategy includes a planned, systematic set of multidisciplinary activities that seek to identify, manage, and reduce risk of exploitable vulnerabilities at every stage of the system, network, or subcomponent life cycle (system, network, or product design and development; manufacturing; packaging; assembly; system integration; distribution; operations; maintenance; and retirement). This strategy deals with scope-of-protection coverage of a system. It is also called supply chain protection control. It supports an agile defense strategy and is the same concept as security in depth.

- **Deploy a defense-in-technology strategy.** This strategy deals with a diversity of information technologies used in the implementation of a system. Complex technologies can create complex security problems.

- **Deploy a defense-in-time strategy.** This strategy deals with applying controls at the right time and at the right geographic location. It considers global systems operating at different time zones.

- **Deploy a defense-in-density strategy.** This strategy requires stronger security controls for high-risk and high-complex systems.

- **Deploy a defense-in-intensity strategy.** This strategy deals with a range of controls and protection mechanisms designed into high-visibility and high-impact systems.

WHICH SECURITY DEFENSIVE STRATEGY DEALS WITH WHAT?

- The defense-in-depth strategy deals with controls placed at multiple levels and at multiple places in a given system.

- The defense-in-breadth strategy deals with supply-chain protection and agile defense strategy.

- The defense-in-technology strategy deals with a diversity of information technologies used in the implementation of a system.

- The defense-in-time strategy deals with applying controls at the right time and at the right geographic location.

- The defense-in-density strategy deals with controls for high-risk and high-complex systems.

- The defense-in-intensity strategy deals with controls for high-visibility and high-impact systems.

- **Deploy agile defenses combined with the concept of information system resilience.** Agile (robust) defense assumes that a small percentage of threats from cyberattacks will be successful by compromising information systems through the supply-chain by defeating the initial security controls implemented by organizations. The supply-chain also exploits previously unidentified vulnerabilities for which protections are not in place. In this scenario, adversaries are operating inside the defensive parameters established by organizations and may have substantial or complete control of systems.

    Information system resilience is the ability to quickly adapt and recover from any known or unknown changes to the system environment through holistic implementation of risk management, contingency mechanisms, and continuity planning.

    Agile defense deploys the concept of information system resilience—that is, the ability of systems to operate while under attack, even in a degraded or debilitated state, and to rapidly recover operational capabilities for essential functions after a successful attack. The concept of system resilience can be applied not only to cyberattacks but also to environmental disruptions and human errors of omission or commission. The agile defense and system resilience concepts should be combined with defense-in-depth and defense-in-breadth strategies to provide a stronger protection against attacks.

- **Install several lines of defenses. Lines of defenses** are security mechanisms for limiting and controlling access to and use of computer system resources. They exercise a directing or restraining influence over the behavior of individuals and the content of computer systems. They can be grouped into four categories—first, second, last, and multiple—depending on their action priorities. A first line of defense is always preferred over the second, or the last. If the first line of defense is not available for any reason, the second line of defense should work. These lines of defenses form a core part of defense-in-depth strategy or security-in-depth strategy. If the second line of defense is not available or does not work, then the last line of defense must work. The term "multiple defenses" here denotes more than one control, device, policy, layer, factor, mode, or level acting in concert to provide greater synergy, strength, and security to a system.

Multiuser, multiplatform, remote access, resource-sharing, and data-sharing computer systems require different and stronger controls than single-user, single-platform, and local access systems. For a multiuser environment, a minimum security requirement should be provided as a reasonable first line of defense against an unauthorized user's attempt to gain access to the system or against an authorized user's inadvertent attempt to gain access to information for which he or she has not been granted access.

Examples follow for each of these four lines of defenses.

First Line of Defense

- Network infrastructure between the Internet and a public Web server
- Policies and procedures against people's bad behavior
- Internal controls, especially preventive controls, against bad business practices
- Passwords and user identification codes against unauthorized access and use of computer system resources
- Firewalls and software/hardware guards against network compromises (e.g., attacks by outsiders)
- Border routers
- Separation of duties against errors, omissions, irregularities (e.g., fraud and theft), and system compromises
- Identification and authentication techniques against unauthorized access (e.g., impostors and impersonators)
- Training, awareness, and education against weak technical and procedural safeguards
- Physical security controls (e.g., keys and locks, and access control systems) against unauthorized entry and exit and to prevent access to computer hardware and servers
- Network monitoring against spoofing attacks
- Quality assurance against poor quality, inconsistency, or poor integrity
- Vigilant and diligent system/security administrators against system tampering, fraud, abuse, and intrusions
- Fault tolerant (e.g., disk-mirroring and Redundant Arrays of Independent Disks [RAID] technology) and redundancy (duplicate equipment) techniques against data loss and DoS attacks
- Security containers to place objects
- Entrapment techniques against attacks by outsiders using fake data and systems (decoys and honeypot systems)

- Program change controls against unauthorized program changes

- Dial-back technique against unauthorized access

- Limited unsuccessful attempts prior to login connectivity

- Perimeter barriers, such as gates, fences, and human security guards, against property damage, intrusion, or unauthorized entry and exit

- Integrity verification software against poor-quality data

- System isolation techniques against virus and other attacks

- Sprinkler systems, water detectors, waterproof covers, and temperature regulators

- Minimum security requirements against an unauthorized user's attempt to gain access to the system or against an authorized user's inadvertent attempts to gain access to information for which he or she has not been granted access in a multiuser and multi-platform environment

- Split knowledge procedures against compromise of system integrity and system components

- Employee security and employment policies, procedures, and practices (screening and clearance procedures and education, experience, and background verification procedures before hiring; access agreements and employment contracts after hiring; return of company property [e.g., keys, ID cards, and building passes]) and disconnection of system access after termination of employment

- Third-party security provider policies, procedures, and practices defining roles, responsibilities, and sanctions for contractors, consultants, outsourcers, service bureaus, and other organizations providing IT products and services

- Network-based computing environment consisting of LANs, Integrated Services Digital Networks, and WANs

Second Line of Defense

- Audit trails and logs against unauthorized actions (e.g., additions, changes, and deletions)

- Monitoring of systems and employees against unauthorized actions (e.g., monitoring employees through keyboard strokes)

- Attack-detection software against harmful attacks

- Penetration testing (e.g., blue team or red team testing) against circumventing the security features of a computer system

- Exterior protection, such as walls and ceilings, against unauthorized entry

- Automated alarms and sensors to detect abnormal events

Last Line of Defense

- Software testing against design and programming defects

- Property insurance against disasters (natural and man-made)

- Insurance bonding coverage against dishonest employees and contractors

- Backup files to recover from lost data

- Host-based computing environment consisting of workstations and servers

- Configuration management practices against improper release of a system prior to its distribution and use

- Quality control checks and integrity control checks and inspection tests against poor quality

- Contingency planning against unforeseen events and conditions

- Security assessments to determine the overall effectiveness of the security controls in an information system.

- Employee vigilance against anything that has escaped the first and/or second line of defense mechanisms

Multiple Lines of Defense

- Employ multilayered controls, where controls are layered, as in defense-in-depth and defense-in-breadth strategies.

- Use multifactor authentication systems, where two factors or three factors are used to authenticate a person, system, process, or device.

- Employ multilevel testing, where several types of testing are conducted for cryptographic modules.

- Use multilayer system security services, where operating system security service layers are working together with distributed system security service layers and user application system security service layers. Each layer can depend on capabilities supported by lower layers.

- Use multilevel security policies, where a subject is permitted to access an object only if the subject's security level is higher than or equal to the object's security classification level.

- Employ a multilevel security mode, where the mode handles multiple information classification levels at a number of different security levels simultaneously

- Use multilayered switches, where they can look deeper than a single switch within a network packet and make informed decisions based on the data found there to facilitate better routing and traffic management tasks.

- Use multihomed firewalls, which can create several independent DMZs—one interfacing the Internet (public network), one interfacing the DMZ segments, and another one interfacing the internal company network. These firewalls work with more than one network interface card.

- **Implement traditional backup methods** to protect data files, computer programs, and computer systems with full, incremental, differential, and hybrid backups (e.g., a full backup on the weekend and a differential backup each evening). These backup methods are good for disks and tapes rotation. Remember that no backup means no recovery from disasters and damages to organization's assets.

- **Implement a zero-day backup method**, which is similar to a traditional or full backup, which archives all selected files and marks each as having been backed up. This method is the fastest restore operation because it contains the most recent files. A disadvantage is that it takes the longest time to perform the backup.

- **Deploy advanced backup methods** on large storage media using disk arrays (e.g., redundant array of independent disk, redundant array of independent disks (RAID) technology), which are a cluster of disks used to back up data onto multiple disk drives at the same time, to provide data protection, data availability, and data reliability.

- **Defend against attack-in-depth strategies** and zero-day attacks. Malicious code attackers use an attack-in-depth strategy to carry out their goals. Single-point solutions will not stop all of their attacks because a single countermeasure cannot be depended on to mitigate all security issues. In addition, a single-point solution can become a single point of failure (or compromise) that can provide extended access due to preexisting trust established among interconnected resources.

The attack-in-depth strategy can create advanced persistent threats where an adversary with sophisticated expertise and significant resources can create opportunities to achieve its objectives by using multiple attack vectors, such as cyber, physical, logical, and deception. Mitigate advanced persistent threats with agile defenses combined with boundary protection controls. Agile defense employs the concept of information system resilience.

Multiple countermeasures against the attack-in-depth strategy include agile defenses, boundary protection controls (e.g., firewalls, routers, and software/hardware guards), and the defense-in-depth and defense-in-breadth strategies because they can disseminate risks over an aggregate of security mitigation techniques.

- **Protect Web browsers** from attacks by: (1) disabling mobile code on Web sites that you are not familiar with or do not trust; (2) disabling options to always set cookies; and (3) setting the security levels for trusted Web sites (i.e., those that you most often visit and trust) to the second highest level. Note that at the highest security level, some Web sites may not function properly.

- **Implement strong password methods** such as passphrases, encrypted passwords, and dynamic passwords with challenge-response protocols to protect password-based attacks, including brute-force password attacks.

Password management may seem simple, but it is not simple when doing business on the Internet. One should not think that some passwords are less important than others; all passwords are important to hackers. Some hackers can piece together password-related information stored online and shared on social media networks. Another risk is that some commercial websites give customers the ability to store billing and shipping addresses along with their credit/debit card information. Bank account numbers, Social Security numbers, user IDs, and passwords could be stolen. This could lead to identity theft, which involves stealing personal information (mostly financial) and using it illegally. It is a form of phishing attack.

Three common mistakes many users make with passwords and remedies for them are listed next.

Mistake 1: Using a weak password, such as common phrases, dictionary terms, name, and birthday.

Remedy 1: Use a passphrase that is long; is not a common phrase; and includes numbers, lowercase and uppercase letters, and special characters (e.g., punctuation, a dollar sign, or a pound sign).

Mistake 2: Using the same password for every account.

Remedy 2: Use a different password for each website with password manager software, which is an encrypted database.

Mistake 3: Exposing passwords to others, such as logging in from a public computer, keeping a note with passwords written on it where it can be found, or sharing passwords with others.

Remedy 3: Avoid the use of public computers and public access networks, if possible. If there is a need to use them, do not send or receive private, sensitive, or confidential information, and change your password afterward. Store passwords in an encrypted file or password manager and avoid sharing passwords.

- **Install software patches, updates, hot fixes, and service packs** for operating system software and applications in a timely manner to close security holes and to avoid potential vulnerabilities. The goal is to implement a robust software patch management process in order to reduce vulnerabilities in an information system. As patches greatly impact the secure configuration of an information system, the patch management process should be integrated into configuration management at a number of points, as follows.

    □ Perform security impact analysis of patches.

    □ Test and approve patches as part of the configuration change control process.

    □ Update baseline configurations to include current patch level.

    □ Assess patches to ensure they were implemented properly.

    □ Monitor systems/components for current patch status.

- **Understand zero-day exploits and zero-day incidents (attacks).** Zero-day exploits (i.e., actual code that can use a security vulnerability to carry out an attack) are used or shared by attackers before the software vendor fixes those exploits. A **zero-day attack** or threat is a computer threat that tries to exploit computer application vulnerabilities that are unknown to others, undisclosed to the software vendor, or for which no security fix is available. Sophisticated attackers play this timing game on user organizations. Most organizations are helpless in the face of zero-day attacks.

- **Protect data on storage media** with sanitization methods, such as overwriting (i.e., clearing), degaussing (i.e., purging), and physical destruction (i.e., disintegration, pulverization, melting, incineration, shredding, sanding, and acid solutions). Overwriting, not erasing, is an effective method for clearing data from magnetic media because the deleted data cannot be retrieved later on. The same thing cannot be said for the erasing. Note that destruction is a strong form of sanitization; disposal in a waste container is a weak form of sanitization. The goal is to ensure that there is no residual data on the storage media because attackers can target it for personal gain. Remember that residual data is residual risk for the user organization.

- **Sanitize computer memory**, both volatile memory and nonvolatile memory, to prevent memory leakage to attackers. The contents of volatile memory found in random access memory chips can be sanitized by removing the electrical power from the chip; the chip requires power to maintain its content. The contents of nonvolatile memory as found in programmable read-only memory (PROM) flash memory is permanent until reprogrammed; it can be sanitized using ultraviolet light, overwriting, and physical destruction.

- **Protect data at rest** with cryptographic mechanisms, which are discussed in the encryption section of this domain. The scope of data at rest, in storage, or on a hard drive includes protecting the confidentiality, integrity, and availability of data residing on servers, workstations, computers, storage/disk arrays (e.g., RAID), network-attached storage appliances, disk drives, tape drives, and removable media, such as flash drives, thumb drives, and pen drives.

- **Protect data in transit** with cryptographic mechanisms, which are discussed in the encryption section of this domain. The scope of data in transit or in flight or data on the wire includes protecting the confidentiality, integrity, and availability of data as it is transferred across the storage network, the LAN, and the WAN.

- **Protect from dumpster-diving activities** (i.e., physical scavenging) by shredding sensitive or confidential documents instead of disposing them in recycling bins (which are high risk).

- **Protect from industrial espionage activities** (i.e., electronic scavenging) by sanitizing (e.g., degaussing and overwriting) the electronic storage media.

- **Protect from hardware-based and software-based key logger attacks**, which are spyware attacks. Hardware devices usually slip inline between the keyboard cable and computer; they are difficult to install because doing so requires physical access to the cable and computer. Software key loggers capture keyboard events and record the keystroke data before it is sent to the intended application for processing. As a remedy, install anti-spyware software.

- **Protect configuration data** by creating a gold disk (master disk) that contains a baseline configuration data about an operating system so that the system's software, ports, system services, and login credentials are run in a safe and efficient manner, using the gold disk. This master disk contains all the necessary information about configuration in one place, instead of several places. Ensure that the gold disk does not contain guest accounts and unnecessary user accounts and that it contains only the least amount of privileges. Because of this approach, the gold disk increases the organization's security posture and lowers the attack surface. Even with a gold disk, however, misconfiguration is possible. This security risk leading to a security breach should be managed well. Misconfiguration means that initial configuration settings are established incorrectly and inappropriately or implemented ineffectively and that changes to configuration data are made incorrectly. Misconfiguration leads to vulnerability. Configuration management is fully discussed in the application development section of this domain.

- **Implement fault-tolerance mechanisms**, such as fail-stop processors and redundancy mechanisms with fault detection, error recovery, and failure recovery abilities. Refer to the business continuity section of this domain for full details.

- **Control superusers, special privileged users, privileged programs, guest accounts, and temporary accounts**. A superuser is a user who is authorized to modify and control IT processes, devices, networks, and files. Special privileged users are given permissions to access files, programs, and data beyond normal users, thus creating a security risk. Privileged programs are those programs that, if unchecked, could cause damage to computer files (e.g., some utility programs).

- **Install antivirus software** to control viruses and other forms of malware, and keep it up-to-date with current signatures.

- **Implement stackguarding technology** to prevent buffer overflow exploits, which, in turn, lead to worm attacks.

- **Install spam-filtering software**, Web content filtering software, Bayesian spam filters, whitelists, and blacklists to control spamming attacks.

- **Implement antispoofing methods** to prevent the unauthorized use of legitimate identification and authentication data.

- **Install anti-spyware software** to detect both malware and nonmalware forms of spyware attacks, such as browser session hijacking, cookies, Web bugs, and bots.

- **Install antijam methods** to control jamming attempts. These methods ensure that transmitted information can be received despite deliberate jamming attempts. Jamming is an attack in which a device is used to emit electromagnetic energy on a wireless network's frequency to make it unstable.

- **Install web content filtering software to control web bugs.** A web bug is a tiny image of a malicious code, invisible to a user, placed on web pages, websites, or web browsers to enable third parties to track use of web servers and collect information about the user, including IP address, host computer name, browser type and version, operating system name and version, and cookies. Web content filtering software is a program that prevents access to undesirable websites, typically by comparing a requested website address to a list of known bad websites. In general, content filtering is the process of monitoring communications, such as emails and web pages, analyzing them for suspicious content, and preventing the delivery of suspicious content to users.

- **Implement the Kerberos authentication protocol** to provide authentication and authorization of users and systems on the network. This protocol uses symmetric cryptography. Implement digital signatures, digitized signatures, electronic signatures, and digital certificates to provide a strong form of authentication. See the encryption section of this domain for more details.

- **Keep the PC's browser settings and email configurations current** and accurate to control Internet-based attacks.

- **Protect from social engineering and pretexting attacks**, which are nontechnical methods, through system user training and education, by implementing good computing practices, by advising system users and administrators to be more vigilant, and by using electronic tokens with dynamic authenticators.

- **Implement biometric measures** with their unique features that often cannot be defeated or compromised. Biometrics usually refers to technologies for measuring and analyzing human body characteristics, such as voice and facial pattern recognitions (e.g., voice print, facial image, and eye retina or iris image) and hand measurements (e.g., fingerprints, handwriting, hand geometry, wrist veins, and thumb prints). Unfortunately, equipment used in biometrics can lead to two types of errors: Type I and Type II. In practice, it is generally necessary to adjust the equipment for a compromise between false rejection of correct individuals (Type I error) and false acceptance of imposters (Type II error). The goal is to obtain low numbers for both types of errors. Equal error rate (crossover error rate) occurs when the false rejection rates and the false acceptance rates are equal. Biometrics can act as a strong security control mechanism in a multi-factor authentication process.

- Eliminate or reduce single points of failure because they are very risky.

(d) Encryption and Cryptography

This section discusses foundational concepts; methods, types, modes, and alternatives to encryption; basic types of cryptographic key systems; basic uses of cryptography; digital signatures, digitized signatures, electronic signatures, and digital certificates; cryptographic methods to protect data at rest and data in transit; and alternatives to cryptography.

(i) Foundational Concepts
Cryptography is the science of transforming data so that it is interpretable only by authorized persons, and it involves encryption and decryption methods in transforming such data. **Encryption** is disguising plaintext results in ciphertext (i.e., encrypted data). **Decryption** is the process of

transforming ciphertext back into plaintext (i.e., unencrypted data). This means that the original process is encryption and the reverse process is decryption. Cryptography and encryption are related in that encryption technologies are used in the cryptographic transformation of plaintext data into ciphertext data to conceal the data's original meaning to prevent it from being known or used. When interception, theft, or destruction is a likely threat to information, encryption provides an additional layer of protection.

The relationship among cryptology, cryptography, and cryptanalysis is as follows:

Cryptology = Cryptography + Cryptanalysis

Cryptology is the field that encompasses both cryptography and cryptanalysis. It is the science that deals with hidden, disguised, or encrypted communications and encompasses communications security and communication intelligence.

Cryptography relies on two basic components: an algorithm and a key. **Algorithms** are complex mathematical formulas, and **keys** are strings of bits used in conjunction with algorithms to make the required transformations. For two parties to communicate, they must use the same algorithm(s) that are designed to work together. In most cases, algorithms are documented, and formulas are available to all users, although the algorithm details are sometimes kept secret. Some algorithms can be used with keys of various lengths. The greater the length of the key used to encrypt the data, the more difficult it is for an unauthorized person to use a trial-and-error approach to determine the key and successfully decrypt the data.

Cryptanalysis is the steps and operations performed in converting encrypted messages into plaintext without initial knowledge of the key employed in the encryption algorithm.

Encryption or cryptography is a method of converting information to an unintelligible code. The process can then be reversed, returning the information to an understandable form. The information is encrypted (encoded) and decrypted (decoded) by what are commonly referred to as cryptographic keys. These "keys" are actual values used by a mathematical algorithm to transform the data. The effectiveness of encryption technology is determined by the strength of the algorithm, the length of the key, and the appropriateness of the encryption system selected.

Because encryption renders information unreadable to any party without the ability to decrypt it, the information remains private and confidential, whether transmitted or stored on a computer system. Unauthorized parties will see nothing but an unorganized assembly of characters. Furthermore, encryption technology provides data integrity assurance as some algorithms offer protection against forgery and tampering. The ability of the technology to protect information requires that authorized parties properly manage the encryption and decryption keys.

(ii) Methods of Encryption

In general, the encryption mechanism effectively seals the information within an object inside an additional (logical) container. Used primarily to provide confidentiality, general encryption can be used to ensure the detection of integrity violations and to otherwise hinder integrity attacks. Encryption is not absolute protection, as the sealing process may be only as safe as the encryption key. Also, encryption of an object does not in and of itself prevent damage to its integrity. However, encryption does provide an additional level of protection that must be circumvented in order to violate protection policies or to succeed at making violations without detection. Distinct advantages of encryption are its flexibility of use, which includes its ability to be used either as blanket protection or "on demand," and its applicability to a wide array of object types. For example, digital signatures are intended to produce the same effect as a real signature, an unforgettable proof of authenticity.

The four major methods of encryption include one-time pads, substitution ciphers, transposition ciphers, and substitutions and permutations, described next.

1. **One-time pads.** A one-time pad is unbreakable, given infinite resources. It is a large nonrepeating set of truly random key letters. Each cipher key is used exactly once, for only one message. The sender encrypts the message and then destroys the pad's pages. The receiver does the same thing after decrypting the message. A requirement is that the key letters have to be generated randomly. Any attacks will target the method used to generate the key sequence. An advantage is that one-time pads are used in ultra-secure and low-bandwidth channels, hence they provide security over the transmitted key. A disadvantage is that they require an amount of key information equal to the size of the plaintext being enciphered.

2. **Substitution ciphers.** In a substitution cipher, each letter or group of letters is replaced by another letter or group of letters to disguise it. Probable words or phrases are guessed. Substitution ciphers preserve the order of the plaintext symbols but disguise them. Substitutions are performed by substitution boxes (S-boxes).

3. **Transposition ciphers.** In contrast to substitution ciphers, transposition ciphers reorder the letters but do not disguise them. The cipher is keyed by a word or phrase not containing any repeated letters. Permutation boxes (P-boxes) are used to effect a transposition.

4. **Substitutions and permutations.** An S-box is a nonlinear substitution table box used in several byte substitution transformations and in the key expansion routine to perform a one-for-one substitution of a byte value. S-boxes are used in the AES. Cipher keys are used in various permutations and combinations to keep the encryption scheme much stronger and highly secure. DES is not secure.

(iii) Types of Encryption
There are at least three types of encryption: stream ciphers, block ciphers, and product ciphers.

(A) Stream Ciphers
Stream ciphers are algorithms that convert plaintext to ciphertext one bit at a time. Their security depends entirely on the insides of the key-stream generator. Because it is necessary to change the key with each message, stream ciphers are not usually used to encrypt discrete messages. They are useful in encrypting nondiscrete messages, such as a T-1 link between two computers. In other words, they are good for continuous streams of communication traffic. The key-stream generator produces the same output on both the encryption and decryption ends.

There are three variants of stream ciphers: synchronous stream ciphers, self-synchronous stream ciphers, and using block ciphers as stream ciphers. In a synchronous stream cipher, the key-stream is generated independent of the message stream and is vulnerable to an insertion attack. A countermeasure is to not use the same key-stream to encrypt two different messages. In a self-synchronous stream cipher, each key-stream bit is a function of a fixed number of previous ciphertext bits. In the third variant, the block cipher algorithms are used as key-stream generators.

Protocols that use stream ciphers with no cryptographic checksums (e.g., Cyclical Redundancy Checks-32 [CRC-32]) are vulnerable to attacks.

The major characteristics of stream ciphers are listed next.

- They are not suitable for software implementation due to time-consuming manipulation of bits.
- They are easier to analyze mathematically than block ciphers.
- A single error can damage only a single bit of data.
- A good application is a T-1 link between two computers.
- A key-stream reuse attack is possible when the same key and initialization vector pair is used twice.

(B) Block Ciphers

A **block cipher** is a family of functions and their inverse functions that are parameterized by cryptographic keys. The functions map bit strings of a fixed length to bit strings of the same length. Several modes of operation are used with symmetric key block cipher algorithms.

Major characteristics of block ciphers are listed next.

- They are easy to implement in software due to less time consumption.
- They are more general in use.
- Algorithms are stronger.
- A single error can damage a block's worth of data.
- A good application is data on a computer.
- They take an n-bit block of plaintext as input and transform it using the key into an n-bit block of ciphertext.
- They are subject to cryptanalysis attacks, such as differential and simple power analysis and timing analysis.

(C) Product Ciphers

Product ciphers are a whole series of combinations of P-boxes and S-boxes cascaded. In each iteration, or round, first there is an S-box followed by a P-box. In addition, there is one P-box at the beginning and one P-box at the end of each round. Common product ciphers operate on k-bit inputs to product k-bit outputs. P-boxes and S-boxes can be implemented on hardware with electrical circuits.

(iv) Modes of Encryption

There are basically two modes of encryption in a network: link (online) encryption and end-to-end encryption. It is possible to combine both modes of encryption.

Link encryption encrypts all of the data along a communications path (e.g., a satellite link, telephone circuit, or T-1 line), including headers, addresses, and routing information. Since link encryption also encrypts routing data, communications nodes need to decrypt the data to continue routing.

WHO PERFORMS LINK ENCRYPTION AND END-TO-END ENCRYPTION?

- Data communications service providers generally perform link encryption.

- End user organizations generally perform end-to-end encryption.

- Link encryption occurs at the lower levels of the International Organization for Standardization/Open System Interconnection (ISO/OSI) model and encrypts both headers and trailers of the packet. This provides a strong security.

- End-to-end encryption occurs at the higher levels of the ISO/OSI model and does not encrypt headers and trailers. This does not provide a strong security.

Link encryption provides good protection against external threats, such as traffic analysis, because all data flowing on links can be encrypted, thus providing traffic-flow security. Entire packets are encrypted on exit from and decrypted on entry to a node. Link encryption also protects against packet sniffing and eavesdropping threats. Link encryption is easy to incorporate into network protocols.

However, link encryption has a major disadvantage: A message is encrypted and decrypted several times. If a node is compromised, all traffic flowing through that node is also compromised. A secondary disadvantage is that the individual user loses control over algorithms used. Another disadvantage is that key distribution and management is more complex.

In **end-to-end encryption**, a message is encrypted and decrypted only at endpoints, thereby largely circumventing problems that compromise intermediate nodes. However, some address information (data link headers and routing information) must be left unencrypted to allow nodes to route packets. Although data remains encrypted when being passed through a network, header and routing information remains visible. High-level network protocols must be augmented with a separate set of cryptographic protocols.

SUMMARY OF ENCRYPTION METHODS

- In link encryption, all data including addresses flowing on links can be encrypted.

- In end-to-end encryption, a message is encrypted and decrypted only at endpoints by hardware and software techniques.

- Bulk (trunk) encryption is simultaneous encryption of all channels of a multichannel telecommunications trunk. No bulk encryption is needed when a public key cryptographic is used to distribute keys since the keys are generally short.

- Session key encryption is used to encrypt data between applications and end users. It is effective in preventing an eavesdropping attack from remote access to firewalls. A secure server supports server authentication and session key encryption.

- Stream encryption encrypts and decrypts messages of arbitrary sizes.

- Line encryption protects data in transfer, which can be used to achieve confidentiality.

- File encryption protects data in storage. It is the process of encrypting individual files on a storage medium and permitting access to the encrypted data only after proper authentication is provided.

- Field-level encryption is stronger than file-, record-, and packet-level encryption.

- Folder encryption is the process of encrypting individual folders on a storage medium and permitting access to the encrypted files within the folders only after proper authentication is provided.

- Full (whole) disk encryption is the process of encrypting all the data on the hard drive used to boot a computer, including the computer's operating system, and permitting access to the data only after successful authentication with the full disk encryption product is made.

- Virtual disk encryption is the process of encrypting a container, which can hold many files and folders, and permitting access to the data within a container only after proper authentication is provided.

- Volume encryption is the process of encrypting an entire volume and permitting access to the data on the volume only after proper authentication is provided.

- Multiple (e.g., triple) encryption is stronger than single encryption but costs may increase and system performance may decrease.

- NULL encryption is used when integrity protection is required for an IPsec system, not for confidentiality.

- Superencryption is a process of encrypting information that is already encrypted. It occurs when a message, encrypted offline, is transmitted over a secured, online circuit or when information encrypted by the originator is multiplexed onto a communication trunk, with the information then bulk encrypted. In other words, superencryption is encryption plus encryption and from offline to online.

- Between authentication and encryption steps, encryption should be done first and authentication is done later (i.e., encrypt then authenticate), which provides the most secure approach.

- Encryption requires the use of either passwords or passphrases.

(v) Alternatives to Encryption

Full disk, virtual disk and volume, and file/folder encryption technologies are used for storage encryption on end user devices. Many other acceptable alternative methods to encryption are available to achieve the same objective. Alternatives are listed next.

- Backup utility programs to encrypt backups

- Compression utility programs to encrypt archives

- Cryptographic hashes of passwords instead of regular passwords

- Digital rights management (DRM) software to restrict access to files

- Virtual machines to access and store sensitive information

Sometimes the best way to address the problem of protecting sensitive information on end user devices is not to store the information on higher-risk devices (e.g., mobile devices or removable media) and to remove unneeded sensitive information from files or databases. If certain network traffic does not need to be encrypted or should not be encrypted, then other security controls, such as IDS sensors, can monitor the contents of traffic.

Other alternative approaches to encryption include:

- Using a thin client solution, such as terminal services, a thin Web-based application, or a portal to access the information and configuring the thin client solution to prohibit file transfers of the sensitive information to the end user device.

■ Configuring the organization's devices, including desktop computers, to prevent writing sensitive information to removable media (e.g., compact disks, flash drives, flash drives, thumb drives, or pen drives) unless the information is properly encrypted.

(vi) Basic Types of Cryptographic Key Systems

Cryptography relies on two basic components: an algorithm and a key. Algorithms are complex mathematical formulas, and keys are strings of bits. For two parties to communicate, they must use the same algorithm(s). In some cases, they must also use the same key. Most cryptographic keys must be kept secret; sometimes algorithms are also kept secret.

There are two basic types of cryptographic key systems: secret or private key systems (also called symmetric key systems) and public key systems (also called asymmetric key systems). Often the two are combined to form a hybrid system to exploit the strengths of each type. The type of key that is needed depends on security requirements and the operating environment of the organization. Exhibit 2.5 shows the basic types of cryptographic key systems.

EXHIBIT 2.5 Types of Cryptographic Key Systems

Secret (private) key system	Uses a single key, shared by parties; also called symmetric key system (e.g., DES, 3DES, and AES)
Public key system	Uses two keys, both private and public, not shared by parties; also called asymmetric key system (e.g., RSA, DSS, and DH)
Hybrid key system	Combines the best of secret and public key systems

(A) Secret Key System

In a secret (private) key system, two (or more) parties share the same key, and that key is used to encrypt and decrypt data. If the key is compromised, the security offered by cryptography is severely reduced or eliminated. Secret key cryptography assumes that the parties who share a key rely on each other not to disclose the key and to protect it against modification. Note that secret key systems are often used for bulk data encryption. The best-known secret key system is DES, which is used as the basis for encryption, integrity, access control, and key management standards.

The primary advantage of a secret key system is speed. Popular secret key encryption methods are significantly faster than any currently available public key encryption method. Alternatively, public key cryptography can be used with secret key cryptography to get the best of both worlds—the security advantages of public key systems and the speed advantages of secret key systems. The public key system can be used to encrypt a secret key used to encrypt the bulk of a file or message.

In some situations, a public key system is not necessary, and a secret key system alone is sufficient. This includes computing environments where (1) a secure secret key agreement can take place, (2) a single authority knows and manages all the keys, and (3) there is a single user. In general, the public key system is best suited for an open multiuser environment.

(B) Public Key System

Whereas a secret key system uses a single key shared by two (or more) parties, a public key system uses a pair of keys for each party. One of the keys of the pair is public and the other is private. The public key can be made known to other parties; the private key must be kept confidential and must be known only to its owner. Both keys, however, need to be protected against modification. Note that public key systems are used for automated key distribution.

The public key system is particularly useful when the parties wishing to communicate cannot rely on each other or do not share a common key. Examples of public key systems include RSA and the DSS. **Zero-knowledge proof** is used in the public key system.

The primary advantage of the public key system is increased security and convenience; private keys never need to be transmitted or revealed to anyone. In a private, secret key system, the secret keys must be transmitted, either manually or through a communication channel. There may be a chance that an unauthorized individual can access the secret keys during their transmission.

(C) Strengths and Weaknesses of Private Keys and Public Keys

A computer system can use both types of keys, private and public, in a complementary manner, with each performing different functions. Typically, the speed advantage of secret key (private key) cryptography means that it is used for encrypting bulk data.

Although public key cryptography does not require users to share a common key, secret key cryptography is much faster. Public key cryptography is used for applications that are less demanding to a computer system's resources, such as encrypting the keys used by secret key cryptography for distribution or to sign messages. Exhibit 2.6 compares the strengths and weaknesses of private keys with public keys.

Exhibit 2.6 presents the strengths and weaknesses of private and public keys.

EXHIBIT 2.6 Strengths and Weaknesses of Private and Public Keys

Distinctive Features	Private Keys	Public Keys
Number of keys	Single key shared by two or more parties	Pair of keys for each party
Types of keys	Key is secret	One key is private and one key is public
Protection of keys	Disclosure and modification	Disclosure and modification for private keys and modification for public keys
Relative speeds	Faster	Slower
Performance	Protocols are more efficient	Protocols are less efficient
Key length	Fixed key lengths	Variable key lengths
Application	Ideal for encrypting files and communication channels	Ideal for encrypting and distributing keys and for providing authentication

(vii) Basic Uses of Cryptography

Cryptography creates a high degree of trust in the electronic world. It is used to perform five basic security services: confidentiality, data integrity, authentication, authorization, and nonrepudiation.

(A) Confidentiality

Confidentiality is the property whereby information is not disclosed to unauthorized parties. The term "secrecy" is often used synonymously with confidentiality. Confidentiality is achieved using encryption to render the information unintelligible except by authorized entities. The information may become intelligible again by using decryption. In order for encryption to provide confidentiality, the cryptographic algorithm and mode of operation must be designed and implemented so that an unauthorized party cannot determine the secret or private keys associated with the encryption or be able to derive the plaintext directly without deriving any keys.

(B) Data Integrity

Data integrity is a property whereby data has not been altered in an unauthorized manner since it was created, transmitted, or stored. This includes the insertion, deletion, and substitution of data. Cryptographic mechanisms, such as message authentication codes or digital signatures, can be used to detect (with a high probability) both accidental modifications (e.g., modifications that sometimes occur during noisy transmissions or by hardware memory failures) and deliberate modifications (unauthorized alterations) by an adversary with a very high probability. Noncryptographic mechanisms are also often used to detect accidental modifications but cannot be relied on to detect deliberate modifications.

(C) Authentication

Authentication is a service that is used to establish the origin of information. That is, authentication services verify the identity of the user or system that created information (e.g., a transaction or message). This service supports the receiver in security-relevant decisions, such as Is the sender an authorized user of this system? or Is the sender permitted to read sensitive information? Several cryptographic mechanisms may be used to provide authentication services. Most commonly, authentication is provided by digital signatures or message authentication codes; some key agreement techniques also provide authentication. When multiple individuals are permitted to share the same authentication information (such as a password or cryptographic key), it is sometimes called role-based authentication.

WHAT ARE THE MAJOR USES AND TYPES OF CRYPTOGRAPHY?

Cryptography is used to provide confidentiality, data integrity, authentication, authorization, and nonrepudiation security services. Two basic types of cryptography exist: symmetric and asymmetric. Each has its own strengths and weaknesses. Most current cryptographic applications combine both symmetric and asymmetric cryptography (in what is called hybrid cryptography) to exploit the strengths of each type.

(D) Authorization

Authorization is concerned with providing an official sanction or permission to perform a security function or activity. Normally, authorization is granted following a process of authentication. A noncryptographic analog of the interaction between authentication and authorization is the examination of an individual's credentials to establish his or her identity (authentication); once the individual proves his or her identity, the person is then provided with the key or password that will allow access to some resource, such as a locked room (authorization). Authentication can be used to authorize a role rather than to identify an individual. Once an entity is authenticated to a role, that entity is authorized for all the privileges associated with the role.

(E) Nonrepudiation

Nonrepudiation is a service that is used to provide assurance of the integrity and origin of data in such a way that the integrity and origin can be verified by a third party. This service prevents an entity from successfully denying involvement in a previous action. Nonrepudiation is supported cryptographically by the use of a digital signature that is calculated by a private key known only by the entity that computes the digital signature.

(viii) Digital Signatures, Digitized Signatures, Electronic Signatures, and Digital Certificates

A **digital signature** is an electronic analog of a handwritten signature in that it can be used to prove to the recipient, or a third party, that the originator in fact signed the message. Digital signatures are also generated for stored data and programs to verify data and program integrity at any later time.

Digital signatures authenticate the integrity of the signed data and the identity of the signatory. They verify to a third party that data were actually signed by the generator of the signature. Digital signatures are used in email, electronic funds transfer, electronic data interchange, software distribution, data storage, and other applications requiring data integrity assurance and data origin authentication. Digital signatures can address potential threats, such as spoofing, masquerading, replay attacks, and password compromise. They cannot address DoS attacks.

The security of a digital signature system is dependent on maintaining the secrecy of users' private keys. Users must, therefore, guard against the unauthorized acquisition of their private keys. A digital signature can also be used to verify that information has not been altered after it was signed; this provides message integrity. A simpler alternative to a digital signature is a hash function.

Digital signatures offer protection not available by alternative signature techniques, such as a digitized signature. Converting a visual form of a handwritten signature to an electronic image generates a **digitized signature**. Although a digitized signature resembles its handwritten counterpart, it does not provide the same protection as a digital signature. Digitized signatures can be forged as well as duplicated and appended to other electronic data. Digitized signatures cannot be used to determine whether information has been altered after it is signed.

An **electronic signature** is a cryptographic mechanism that performs a function similar to a handwritten signature. It is used to verify the origin and contents of a message.

ELECTRONIC SIGNATURES VERSUS HANDWRITTEN SIGNATURES

Electronic signatures are very difficult to forge, although handwritten signatures are easily forged. In general, electronic signatures have the same legal status as written signatures. Cryptography can provide a means of linking a document with a particular person, as is done with a written signature. If a cryptographic key is compromised due to a social engineering attack, then the electronic originator of a message may not be the same as the owner of the key. Trickery and coercion are problems for both electronic and handwritten signatures (i.e., social engineering attacks).

Digital certificates are basically containers for public keys and act as a means of electronic identification. The certificate and public keys are public documents that, in principle, anyone can possess. An associated private key, possessed only by the entity to which the certificate was issued, is used as a means of binding the certificate to that entity. Users not possessing this private key cannot use the certificate as a means of authentication. Entities can prove their possession of the private key by digitally signing known data or by demonstrating knowledge of a secret key exchanged using public key cryptographic methods. A digital certificate is a password-protected and encrypted file. It should not contain any owner-related information that changes frequently. In practice, anyone can generate public–private key pairs and digital certificates; consequently, it is necessary to determine whether the certificate holder is trustworthy.

(ix) Cryptographic Mechanisms to Protect Data at Rest

The scope of data at rest, data in storage, or data on a hard drive includes protecting the confidentiality, integrity, and availability of data residing on servers, workstations, computers, storage/disk arrays (e.g., RAID), network-attached storage appliances, disk drives, tape drives, and removable media such as flash drives, thumb drives, and pen drives.

The need for encrypting the storage media is increasing, and selecting an encryption algorithm with the right strength is important to protect the media from internal and external attacks. Use of encryption algorithms (e.g., DES and 3DES) and hashing algorithms (e.g., MD5 and SHA-1) are considered to be no longer secure. Encrypting the storage media with AES-256 and providing end-to-end security is advised due to its strong and secure algorithm. When using AES-256, do not store the encryption keys in cleartext or leave them in an open operating system because the keys can be compromised.

Cryptographic mechanisms to protect data at rest include storage encryption technologies, such as full (whole) disk, virtual disk, volume, file, and/or folder encryption. Information stored on end user devices can be encrypted in many ways. For example, an application that accesses sensitive information could be responsible for encrypting that information. Applications such as backup programs might also offer encryption options. Another method for protecting files is DRM software.

Technologies such as firewalls, intrusion prevention systems, and VPNs seek to secure data by protecting the perimeter of the network. Unfortunately, these technologies do not adequately secure data in storage, as data is still stored in cleartext and thus is open to a wide range of internal and external attacks. Encrypting data at rest on tape and disk will mitigate such attacks and secure data while maintaining the current service levels.

Adding encryption to data at rest poses some challenges, such as changing the application code, data compression problems, slow response time, user unfriendliness, complexity, and additional cost to storage systems. The other challenge includes the impact of encryption on cryptographic key management. For example, keys:

- Can be lost, resulting in loss of data.
- Need to be kept secure but should be available.
- Have to be retained until the data is retained.
- Need to be created, changed, or destroyed.
- Need to be managed without excessive operational and administrative complexity.

Storage encryption can be applied as a part of a data-at-rest solution in several places. For example, encryption can be used:

- In the application.
- In the file system or operating system.

- In the device driver or network interface.

- On the network.

- In the storage controller.

- In the storage device using single-factor authentication (e.g., password, user ID, or, hardware token) and multiple-factor authentication (e.g., password, user ID, smart card, or cryptographic token).

(x) Cryptographic Mechanisms to Protect Data in Transit

The scope of data in transit or in flight or on the wire includes protecting the confidentiality, integrity, and availability of data as it is transferred across the storage network, LAN, and WAN.

Cryptographic mechanisms in controlling data in transit through remote access to an information system are listed next.

- Use encryption with a strong key in relation to the security categorization of the information.

- Restrict execution of privileged commands.

- Use standard bulk or session layer encryption, such as SSH and VPNs with blocking mode enabled.

- Route all remote accesses through a limited number of managed access control points.

- Do not use Bluetooth or peer-to-peer networking protocols because they are less secure than other protocols.

(xi) Alternatives to Cryptography

There are at least three alternatives methods to cryptography in order to hide information: steganography, digital watermarking, and reversible data hiding.

Steganography (concealed writing) deals with hiding messages and obscuring who is sending or receiving them. It is the art and science of writing hidden messages in such a way that no one, apart from the sender and intended recipient, suspects the existence of the message, which provides a form of security through obscurity.

Steganography includes the concealment of information within computer files. In digital steganography, electronic communications may include steganographic coding inside of a transport layer, such as a document file, image file, program, or protocol.

The advantage of steganography over cryptography alone is that messages do not attract attention to themselves. Plainly visible encrypted messages—no matter how unbreakable—will arouse suspicion and may be incriminating in countries where encryption is illegal. Therefore, whereas cryptography protects the contents of a message, steganography can be said to protect both messages and communicating parties. Media files are ideal for steganographic transmission because of their large sizes and the fact that changes are so subtle that someone not specifically looking for them is unlikely to notice them.

Digital watermarking is a type of marking that embeds copyright information about the copyright owner. Digital watermarking is the process of irreversibly embedding information into a digital signal.

Steganography is sometimes applied in digital watermarking, where two parties communicate a secret message embedded in the digital signal. Annotation of digital photographs with descriptive information is another application of invisible watermarking. While some file formats for digital media can contain additional information called metadata, digital watermarking is distinct in that the data is carried in the signal itself.

A digital watermark is called robust with respect to transformations if the embedded information can be reliably detected from the marked signal even if degraded by any number of transformations. Typical image degradations are compression, rotation, cropping, additive noise, and quantization.

A digital watermark is called imperceptible if the cover signal and marked signal are indistinguishable with respect to an appropriate perceptual metric. In general, it is easy to create either robust or imperceptible watermarks, but the creation of robust *and* imperceptible watermarks has proven to be quite challenging. Robust and imperceptible watermarks have been proposed as tools for the protection of digital content—for example, as an embedded no-copy-allowed flag in professional video content.

Reversible data hiding is a technique that enables images to be authenticated and then restored to their original form by removing the watermark and replacing the image data that had been overwritten. This method would make the images acceptable for legal purposes.

(x) A Summary of Cryptographic Algorithms and Key Lengths

The following is a summary of various cryptographic algorithms and key lengths used in various processes.

- Symmetric (secret and private) key cryptography includes Data Encryption Standard (DES), International Data Encryption Algorithm (IDEA), Tripe DES (3DES), Message Digest (MD), SKIPJACK, Kerberos, Rivest Cipher (RC) series, and message authentication code.

- Asymmetric (public) key cryptography includes Rivest Shamir-Adelman (RSA) algorithm, Diffie-Hellman (DH) Algorithm, digital signatures, Digital Signature Standard (DSS), Digital Signature Algorithm (DSA), and Key Exchange Algorithm (KEA).

- Hash functions include Secure Hash Algorithm (SHA), SHA-1, Message Digest 4 (MD4), and MD5.

- Both SHA and MD5 are the two principal algorithms used in cryptographic applications for compressing data.

- DES is a block cipher and an example of a symmetric-key encryption algorithm.

- Triple DES (3DES), a variant of DES, operates on a block of data three times either with two keys or three keys. The sequence of operations with two keys is as follows: first with one key, then with the second key, and finally with the first key again.

  □ The sequence of operations with two keys includes encrypt-decrypt-encrypt.

  □ The sequence of operations with three keys includes encrypt-encrypt-encrypt.

- International Data Encryption Algorithm (IDEA) is a replacement for DES. It resists most attacks due to its long key.

- One-time pad encryption algorithm is absolutely unbreakable.

- SKIPJACK is a symmetric-key encryption algorithm used to encrypt sensitive but unclassified data telecommunications.

- RSA is an asymmetric-key algorithm that can be used to provide both a digital signature and encryption service. The normal key length can range from 512 to 1,024 bits; the latter has become the standard practice. It has the potential to go even higher, say to 2,048 bits depending on the specific need.

- The Diffie-Hellman (DH) Algorithm is an example of asymmetric-key algorithm and is used to perform encryption service and key exchange. Its key length is 192 bits.

- The Digital Signature Algorithm (DSA) provides only a digital signature service, not an encryption service.

- Pretty Good Privacy (PGP) uses IDEA with 128-bit key to encrypt files or messages.

2.4 Data Privacy Management

This section defines privacy, explains privacy concerns, shows privacy risks, defines privacy impact assessments, focuses on compliance with privacy laws, and explains the nature of global privacy concerns. It establishes a privacy risk model and compares privacy with security.

(a) Privacy Defined

Privacy deals with balancing individual rights in a society. Two definitions exist: (1) the individual right to determine the degree to which one is willing to share information about oneself that may be compromised by unauthorized exchange of such information among other individuals or organizations, and (2) individual and organizational rights to control the collection, storage, and dissemination of information.

Privacy is the right of an individual to limit access to information regarding that individual. Privacy refers to the social balance between an individual's right to keep information confidential and the societal benefit derived from sharing information, and how this balance is codified to give individuals the means to control personal information. **Confidentiality** refers to disclosure of information only to authorized individuals and entities.

Privacy means that the rights of the accused (suspect) cannot be violated during an investigation. The accused can use protective orders if his or her privacy rights are ignored or handled improperly. If accused persons can prove that evidence brought against them would do more harm to them than good, the courts will favor the accused in suppressing such evidence from being presented.

(b) Privacy Concerns

With respect to information systems, privacy deals with the collection and use or misuse of personal data. The issue of privacy deals with the right to be left alone or to be withdrawn from public view. Privacy at work creates conflict between employers wanting to monitor employees' work activities and employees who resent such monitoring. For example, computer workstation software can track employee keystrokes made at keyboards. Another privacy issue is email at work. Courts have ruled that a privileged communication does not lose its privileged character if it is communicated or transmitted electronically. Email is a controversial topic; many state and federal laws have been passed in this area.

A BASIC PRIVACY RULE

A basic privacy policy or rule to protect an individual's privacy right is to provide a simple opt-in and opt-out choice for online services, such as web service providers and social media platform providers.

Another area of privacy concern is the Internet, where a website collects personal information (e.g., cookies) when potential or actual customers are buying or selling goods or services or simply inquiring. Individuals should protect their personal information by finding out what data is stored and how it is used, by not using a work email system to send personal emails, and by not sharing personal information without written consent.

One-half of online households reported that privacy or security concerns have stopped them from conducting financial transactions online, buying goods or services online, posting on social media networks, or expressing opinions on controversial or political issues via the Internet.

(c) Privacy Risks

Privacy risk originates from divulging or releasing personal financial information, personal medical information, trade secret formulas, and other sensitive information (e.g., salaries) about an individual to unauthorized parties.

Best practices to reduce privacy risks are listed next.

- Install a privacy officer or its equivalent.
- Develop and communicate privacy policies that contain consequences for not complying with them.
- Understand privacy laws and regulations.
- Implement policies and procedures for controlling and releasing personal information to third parties.
- Provide employee orientation classes by the human resources department at the time of hiring.
- Conduct privacy audits, special management reviews, and privacy self-assessment reviews periodically and proactively to reduce privacy risks.

(d) Privacy Impact Assessments

Organizations should conduct privacy impact assessments, which are processes for examining the risks and ramifications of collecting, maintaining, and disseminating information in identifiable form in an electronic information system. The assessments also include the means for identifying and evaluating protections and alternative processes to mitigate the impact to privacy of collecting information in identifiable form.

Privacy impact assessments should be performed and updated when a system change creates new privacy risks. Examples of system changes are listed next.

- When converting paper-based records into electronic-based records
- When anonymous information changes to non-anonymous state (i.e., information from nonidentifiable form to an identifiable form)

- When significant system changes occur in technology and databases
- When user-authenticating mechanisms (e.g., passwords, digital certificates, and biometrics) are new to an automated system

Privacy impact assessments must address the next issues.

- What information is to be collected (e.g., to determine eligibility)
- Why the information is being collected (e.g., nature and source)
- The intended use of the information (e.g., to verify data)
- With whom the information will be shared (e.g., internal and external)
- What notice or opportunities for consent would be provided to individuals regarding what information is collected and how that information is shared (e.g., choice of declining voluntary information or consenting to particular use of that information)
- How the information will be secured (e.g., administrative and technical controls)
- Whether a system of records is being created (e.g., audit trails)

(e) Compliance with Privacy Laws and Information Protection Laws and Regulations

Many laws and regulations apply to privacy of information and information protection both inside and outside the United States. For example:

- The U.S. Privacy Act of 1988 requires protection of information related to individuals maintained in the U.S. federal information systems and grants individuals access to the information concerning them. This act is applicable to both public sector and private sector organizations. This act defines 11 privacy principles, as follows:

  1. Manner and purpose of collection of personal information
  2. Solicitation of personal information from individual concerned
  3. Solicitation of personal information generally
  4. Storage and security of personal information
  5. Information relating to records kept by the record keeper
  6. Access to records containing personal information
  7. Alteration of records containing personal information
  8. Record keeper to check accuracy and completeness of personal information before use
  9. Personal information to be used only for relevant purposes
  10. Limits on use of personal information
  11. Limits on disclosure of personal information

- The U.S. Computer Security Act of 1987 requires U.S. federal government agencies to identify sensitive systems, conduct computer security training, develop computer security plans, and protect computer-related assets.

- The U.S. Computer Fraud and Abuse Act, as amended in 1996, deals with computers used in interstate commerce and makes it a crime and fraud to alter, damage, or destroy information, steal passwords, or introduce viruses or worms. The act covers classified defense and foreign relations information, records of financial institutions and credit-reporting agencies, and government computers. Unauthorized access and access in excess of authorization became felonies for incidents involving classified information and misdemeanors for incidents involving financial information. The act provides for limited imprisonment for the unintentional damage to one year and civil penalties in terms of compensatory damages.

- The U.S. Fair Credit Reporting Act protects consumer report information.

- The U.S. Gramm-Leach-Bliley Financial Modernization Act of 1999 protects nonpublic personal information collected and used by financial institutions.

- The U.S. Health Insurance Portability and Accountability Act (HIPAA) of 1996 protects health information collected by health plans, healthcare clearinghouses, and healthcare providers.

- The U.S. Federal Trade Commission is responsible for ensuring consumer protection and market competition.

- The European Union's (EU's) new directive General Data Protection Regulation (GDPR) is effective from May 2018 and replaces the Data Protection Directive. The scope of GDPR applies to all EU companies and all international companies operating in or doing business with individuals in EU member nations. Organizations dealing with personal data (e.g., medical, financial, or other sensitive data) whether it is for customers, employees, or third parties (e.g., suppliers, vendors, contractors, outsourced firms), must be protected at all times with security safeguards to prevent data breaches and unauthorized disclosure.

The GDPR requires that personal data and information is protected regardless of where the data is sent, processed, or stored that could negatively impact a company's financial condition and business operations, including IT operations. The GDPR requires that appropriate security and privacy controls must be in place during the six stages of data life cycle: data collection, data processing, data access, data storage, data usage, and data disposition, as shown next.

Collection → Processing → Access → Storage → Usage → Disposition

The GDPR requires the installation of a Data Protection Officer who has the expert knowledge of data protection laws and regulations and the best control practices. It also requires companies to notify or report a data breach incident to supervisory authorities or law enforcement agencies within 72 hours of the incident discovery (i.e., after becoming aware of the incident). Noncompliance to the GDPR imposes administrative fines based on the worldwide annual sales volume and revenue for the preceding financial year. A **data breach** is defined as unauthorized loss of data (e.g., data stealing and sharing), destruction of data, disclosure of data, modification of data, and access to data.

We suggest that companies develop and monitor the following metrics for data breaches so they can address and manage them:

☐ The mean time to identify, detect, or discover a data breach in days

☐ The mean time to contain a data breach in days

☐ The mean time to recover from a data breach in days

☐ The mean time to operate or normalize operations from a data breach in days

☐ The mean time to notify or report a data breach in hours

- The Organisation for Economic Co-operation and Development (OECD; www.oecd. org) issued guidelines to protect privacy and personal data and on obviating unnecessary restrictions to transborder data flows, both online and offline. It also issued guidelines to control:

  □ Spam attacks

  □ Cross-border cooperation in protecting privacy

  □ Cryptography

  □ Electronic authentication

  □ Identity management

  □ Protecting consumers from fraudulent and deceptive practices across borders

  □ Security of information systems and networks

(f) Global Privacy Concerns

Countries treat privacy matters differently based on their cultures, treaties, and practices. Globalization of business due to the Internet has meant many new laws and regulations to address concerns over specific rights to control personal information. Privacy provisions range from confidentiality of communications to specific access rights. The global privacy landscape involves legislative, regulatory, and cultural considerations of overlapping or conflicting requirements that range from generally acceptable use to more restriction in certain countries.

(g) Privacy Risk Model

Risk models define the risk factors to be assessed and the relationships among those factors where risk factors are inputs to determining levels of risk. Three privacy risk factors include likelihood, data action (information action), and impact. Likelihood is a contextual analysis that a data action is likely to create a problem for an individual or a group of individuals. Impact is an analysis of the costs should the problem occur and is represented as (1) big impact or small impact, (2) major impact or minor impact, or (3) significant impact or insignificant impact.

Exhibit 2.7 links the three privacy objectives of predictability, manageability, and disassociability with their corresponding system capabilities supporting both a privacy policy and a control mapping (i.e., tracing controls back to requirements).

EXHIBIT 2.7 Linking Privacy Objectives with System Capabilities

Privacy Objectives	System Capabilities
Predictability	Enabling reliable assumptions by individual, owners, and operators about personal information and its processing by an information system
Manageability	Providing the capability for granular administration of personal information including alteration, deletion, and selective disclosure
Disassociability	Enabling the processing of personal information or events without association to individuals or devices beyond the operational requirements of the system

(h) Privacy versus Security

Privacy and security are not the same, but they do overlap. Privacy concerns arise from by-products of authorized processing of personal information; security concerns arise from unauthorized system behavior dealing with bypassing security controls and sabotaging application systems or user behavior dealing with using weak passwords, stealing data, and sabotaging data files. The overlap is personal information, where the personal information can create problems for individuals and organizations such as loss of trust, discrimination (e.g., stigmatization, exclusion/inclusion, and power imbalance), economic loss (e.g., revenue and profits), loss of self-determination (e.g., loss of autonomy, loss of liberty, and physical harm), and loss of competitive advantage (not protecting privacy-preserving functions, as in the case of selling customer's email addresses and divulging sensitive personal information such as medical records). Another overlap is shown below between risk models:

Privacy risk model	Deals with privacy risk factors such as likelihood, data action, and impact
Security risk model	Deals with security risk factors such as likelihood, vulnerability, threat, and impact
Common risk factors	Deal with likelihood (probability) and impact (consequences)

2.5 Emerging Technology Practices

The overall goals of discussing emerging technology practices are to determine whether an organization's board members and senior management develop strategies, provide funding, and pay attention to the technology in the same way as they do with the products and services; and use technology as a strategic opportunity to increase sales, revenues, profits, stock price, and market share and to reduce costs. Regarding technology, organizations can take on one of these dichotomous variables:

- Encourage innovation or discourage innovation
- Enable technology or inhibit technology
- Technology leader or technology follower
- Competitive advantage or competitive disadvantage

(a) Uses of Technology

Technology can be put to good use to achieve several major benefits to any industry. For example, technology squarely fits with retail businesses because retailers generate vast amounts of data (big data) collected from, say, hundreds of retail stores, millions of customers, thousands of stock keeping units (SKUs of merchandise), thousands of employees, and hundreds of manufacturers and suppliers. Technology can process and summarize this big data faster and better than humans. Basically, uses of technology in retail can be discussed from two major perspectives: strategic uses and operational uses.

Strategic Uses	Senior management can measure and monitor store-related performance data through metrics and dashboards. Examples of metrics include year-over-year sales, comparable store sales per year, sales by region and quarter, net margins, and net income.

	Marketing management can use sales and customer data to open new stores, expand existing stores, close existing stores, and introduce new products into current markets or new markets. Advertising and promotional activities can be tailored based on the big data collected. For example, time to market a new product is a marketing metric.
Operational Uses	Operations management can use the store-related data, such as store traffic data, to tailor employee work schedules, sales data to increase or decrease in-store sales promotions and advertisements, and store traffic data to automate store operations. For example, time to hire new employees is a human resource metric; speed in processing and speed to deliver are operations metrics.

Example 1: In 2014, according to *Fast Company* magazine, Warby Parker, an e-commerce eyewear maker, Amazon, the Internet giant, and Walmart, the department store giant for mobile commerce, were named the world's most innovative retailers in technology.

Example 2: In 2016, Wayfair, a pure-play online furniture retailer, won the title of Internet retailer of the year.

Example 3: Amazon.com is an excellent example of an online and offline retailer that is fully capitalizing on existing technologies and creating new, unheard-of technologies. It is becoming a mega retailer and a model retailer for all other retailers to follow. It is entering into several areas of consumers' lives with innovative technologies (e.g., books, music, apparel, fashion, food service, fashion, and drones for fast delivery). It has created a simple, quick, and hassle-free shopping experience to customers with 1-click buy button strategy, variable pricing strategy, and faster delivery services, even on Sundays. Other retailers perceive Amazon as a real threat to their survival due to Amazon's great accomplishments. Amazon found the technology as the real solution to solve all the built-in problems that existed in retail for decades, from order to delivery.

Example 4: The customer retention rate for Amazon Prime members is a very high percentage, which is very impressive. Amazon achieves this rate in part by introducing products and services to Prime members, making them loyal customers, and in part due to its use of sophisticated technology.

Example 5: Google's 2-click instant buy app is a two-click mobile checkout process that eliminates the need for a customer to manually enter billing and shipping information. This is a result of efficiencies gained in technology.

(b) Specific Technologies

Sixteen specific technology areas are discussed; some are mature while others are new and emerging. These technology areas, which are not all-inclusive, are not listed in the order of their importance or use. For example, manufacturers can install and implement 3D and robotic technologies; retailers can install and implement retail technologies such as point-of-sale (POS) systems, radio frequency identification (RFID) systems; and both manufacturers and retailers can install and implement mobile, text messaging, website, and social media technologies.

Sixteen specific technology areas include:

1. Mobile technology
2. IoT technology

3. AI technologies

4. Augmented reality (AR) technology

5. Virtual reality (VR) technology

6. Robotic technology

7. Wearable technology

8. 3D technology

9. Bots and chatbots technology

10. Text messaging technology

11. Website technology

12. Search engine technology

13. Blockchain technology

14. Social media technology

15. Enterprise network technology

16. Retail technologies

(i) Mobile Technology

Mobile technology, pocket technology, or portable technology is exploding and is used in mobile commerce with mobile devices (e.g., smartphones and digital tablets) to place mobile orders, to make mobile checkouts, and to make mobile payments using mobile wallets. These are major functions of a retailer.

Mobile technology is also used in several supporting functions of a retailer with mobile apps; mobile marketing with SMS and multimedia message service (MMS); digital coupons, rebates, and gift cards; and wearable-device-based customer services. The goal of a retailer managing mobile technology is to increase the mobile conversion rates, turning each mobile shopper into a real customer of buying a product.

In the past, most customers browsed merchandise on mobile devices to compare prices and read reviews and then made purchases on the desktop/laptop computer. Today, most customers are browsing and buying using mobile devices, mainly due to convenience and heavy use of mobile apps. More than 50% of all digital purchases are purchased through mobile devices. It has been reported mobile apps are converting more shoppers into customers than desktop computers.

Past ⟶ Browsing on Mobile Devices and Buying on Desktop

Present ⟶ Browsing on Mobile Devices and Buying on Mobile Devices

A major concern with mobile technology is that most mobile shoppers abandon their shopping carts before completing a purchase, which decreases mobile conversion rates. Some reasons for mobile cart abandonment problems include screen freezes, slow performance in loading and displaying a page, blank screens, meaningless error messages, disruptive ads, and limited payment options. These problems can be fixed by redesigning and retesting mobile sites with better-quality features and functions.

(A) Mobile Device Use Policies

Management needs to create acceptable-use policies for all portable media devices and educate/train employees about those policies. Management needs to conduct cost-benefit analysis and perform risk-return analysis with either distributing locked-down, corporate-controlled devices or asking employees to bring or choose their own devices. An organization's mobile device use policy can have positive or negative consequences. For example, these choices can lead to risks such as data leakage, data loss, and data stealing. Consider banning from the workplace personal portable media devices that management cannot control and monitor.

1. **Bring your own device (BYOD)** is a policy that permits employees to bring personally owned devices to the workplace and use them to access restricted company's data, information, and applications. This policy is risky.

2. **Bring your own applications (BYOA)** is a policy similar to BYOD that involves employees using third-party applications in the workplace or on a work device. This policy is risky.

3. **Choose your own device (CYOD)** is a program that differs from BYOD by allowing end users to select from a predetermined and company-approved list of personal device types for work rather than any device. This policy is not risky.

4. **Wear your own device (WYOD)** is a program similar to BYOD that allows end users to use personal wearable devices (watches and VR goggles) to perform a company's tasks and functions. This policy is risky.

BYOD mobile devices that employees are allowed to bring to their workplace are called **rogue devices** due to the risk that they can pose to a company. These mobile devices become rogue devices when they are unofficially connected to unauthorized, unsecured, and controlled non-business external websites, such as social media, sports, gaming, and film networks. Hackers can insert rogue software (i.e., malware and bots) into these BYOD devices and can reach a company's official network to cause a data breach or other damage. This means that hackers use these mobile devices as an entry point to access a company's official network.

(B) Mobile Apps

Mobile apps are small-size computer programs that operate on mobile devices using the mobile operating system for users' convenience. These apps are primarily used on mobile devices, such as smartphones, digital tablets, and secondarily on personal, laptop, and notebook computers. Data loss, data theft, and security glitches are examples of potential risks in apps. Mobile apps are different from applets; applets are small computer applications written in various programming languages that are automatically downloaded and executed by applet-enabled Internet browsers. Examples include Active-X and Java applets, both of which have security concerns in that applets are much riskier than apps.

Design Features of Mobile Apps. Mobile apps are developed at a faster rate per day by all types of organizations to enable customers to do business with them, such as to place orders, pay, and track products and services; to receive marketing ads and promotional programs; to make appointments and schedules; and to download coupons and rewards.

Mobile apps are very popular and efficient tools for retail customers and retail store associates alike. Apps are convenient tools for customers to use during shopping, and they are productivity tools for retail store associates (retail employees) to assist customers. Regardless of the person, apps must be easy to use on a regular basis and must be designed keeping the context of their use in mind. Here, the **context** means that the app's format and function are carefully aligned to fully engage customers.

Specifically, **format** means layout, size, font, appearance, graphics resolution, readable and relevant information, display quality, appealing presentation, and form. Similarly, **function** means substance, features, usability, and applicability. Format and function are an example of the classic discussion of substance over form or form over substance.

One way to classify mobile apps is to divide them into basic apps and advanced apps. Going from a basic app to an advanced app requires a huge investment in development; the difference is the number and type of features and functions built into the app. Note that the features of advanced apps contain the features of basic apps and more.

- **Basic app features**—Accessing a retailer's coupons, rebates, price discounts, and special deals with sales promotions; browsing a retailer's inventory system to find a product; locating retail stores; and downloading a store's navigation map.

- **Advanced app features**—Scanning a product's bar code inside a store to show a product's price, description, availability, and customer reviews; searching for a product and finding matching products; connecting customer purchases to the loyalty program for rewards and points, which links customer engagement with customer retention; and mobile checkout to pay for purchases from anywhere in the store (i.e., tap-and-go).

Security Risks in Mobile Apps. Several security risks exist in mobile apps, including:

- Improper platform usage—Misuse of a platform's features or failure to use the platform's security controls

- Insecure data storage—Unintended data leakages and insecure authentication

- Insecure communication—Poor handshaking and weak negotiations between systems and devices and cleartext communication of sensitive information, such as passwords

- Insecure authentication—Failure to identify the user at all when that should be required and weaknesses in a computer session-management; it also means granting anonymous access to some system resources or services during the authentication process

- Insecure authorization due to incorrect authorization decisions

- Poor programming quality resulting in buffer overflow attacks

- Code tampering—Provides an attacker a direct method of subverting the intended use of the software for personal or financial gain

- Unauthorized functionality—Software developers insert a hidden backdoor, place a password as a comment in the programming code, and disable the 2FA mechanism during software testing

- Reverse engineering the final binary code to reveal its source code to understand the functions of back-end servers and to analyze the inner workings of intellectual property, such as trademarks and patents

Security Controls over Mobile Apps. In a rush to shorten the time-to-market metric, app software developers often focus on improving app functions and features and not so much on establishing security controls over apps. Apps can be classified as complex or simple; complex apps require maximum security controls, and simple apps require minimum security controls. In other words, apps require a customized security approach, not a one-size-fits-all approach. The absence of effective and strong security controls can lead to vulnerabilities, such as data breaches, data snoops, and identity theft attacks. Apps that are more complex may rely on remote servers for storing and manipulating users' data; app developers must be familiar with securing app software, securing transmission of data between two points, and securing servers.

A list of suggested security guidelines over apps is presented next.

- Take an inventory of the data you collect and retain. Doing this requires practicing the data minimization principle, meaning collecting all the relevant data needed and ignoring all the irrelevant data not needed.

- Understand the differences between mobile platforms. Each mobile operating system uses different application programming interfaces (APIs) and provides its own minimum security features, which may require add-on security features to make them security strong.

- Use the transit-encryption feature for storing and validating user credentials (e.g., usernames, passwords, passcodes, and API keys), and recognize that the apps will be used on unsecure Wi-Fi access points in public places, such as airports, coffee shops, restaurants, and retail stores. Hackers use these access points to conduct data snooping and data interception attacks. **Data snooping** is an attack where data is read off a network while in transit without modifying or destroying the data. **Data interception** can occur when an attacker is eavesdropping on communications originating from or being sent to a mobile device. Electronic eavesdropping is possible through various techniques, such as man-in-the-middle attacks, which occur when a mobile device connects to an unsecured Wi-Fi network and an attacker intercepts and alters the communication; and Wi-Fi sniffing, which occurs when data is sent to or from a mobile device over an unsecured network connection without encryption, thus allowing an eavesdropper to listen to and record information that is exchanged.

- Use due diligence reviews on programming libraries and software development kits that third-party providers use to make apps and to ensure that the apps are secure.

- If an app is communicating with a cloud provider's server, make sure that there is a division of responsibility between securing the app and updating the app (i.e., separation of duties) to make it conflict-free.

- Protect users' data stored on their mobile devices, including data stored on central or local servers, with encryption. Note that servers can be subjected to injection attacks, cross-site scripting, and other threats. **Injection attacks** occur when untrusted data is sent to a system interpreter as part of a command or query. An attacker's hostile data can trick the interpreter into executing unintended commands or accessing data without proper authorization. **Cross-site scripting** attacks occur whenever an application includes untrusted data in a new web page without proper validation. These attacks allow attackers to execute scripts in the victim's browser that can hijack user sessions, deface websites, or redirect the user to malicious websites.

- Do not store users' passwords in plaintext, and consider using an iterated cryptographic hash function to hash passwords and then verify against those hash values. That way, if your server suffers a data breach, passwords are not left totally exposed.

- Keep improving apps functions and features, including security controls, with frequent updates and patches. Solicit feedback from users on this matter.

■ Pay attention to laws and regulations dealing with financial data, health data, and children's data, as these laws are very strict, requiring full compliance. Protect users' privacy rights.

(ii) Internet-of-Things Technology

The IoT is a collection of several, diverse, and disparate technologies aimed at providing efficiency gains to a business and convenience and comfort to consumers' day-to-day life at home. Within a business environment, the IoT means connecting or networking several systems and devices and passing data between them to operate as a one seamless and cohesive system, providing insights and requiring decisions and actions, as shown next:

$$\text{Systems + Devices} \longrightarrow \text{Data} \longrightarrow \text{Insights}$$

$$\text{Insights} \longrightarrow \text{Decisions} \longrightarrow \text{Actions}$$

The growth of IoT devices is increasing at a faster rate than before. The connected IoT devices are as diverse as CCTV security cameras, digital video recorders, printers, scanners, wearable devices (e.g., watches, goggles, and headsets), Internet-connected home appliances, health monitoring system devices, and home security monitoring system devices—all have come to be collectively known as IoT devices. These IoT devices, which are a part of edge devices, are designed to collect, exchange, and process data over the Internet to provide users with convenient access to an array of services and information.

(A) Examples of IoT Applications

Some call the IoT technology breakthrough technology, smart technology, or even overhyped technology, enabling a programmatic commerce, meaning decision making is programmed and built-in. Features of the IoT technology are listed next.

■ It can connect a retail store's POS system, RFID system, mobile devices and apps, SMS text messaging, sensors, and cameras to alert a loss prevention staff member about a shoplifting incident soon to occur or that has just taken place.

■ It can measure peak times of store traffic.

■ It can monitor remote security alarms in a retail store, warehouse, distribution center, or fulfillment center.

■ It monitors temperatures in a grocery store's food freezers and sends alarms through mobile devices when the temperature is outside of a defined range.

■ It can help trace a product's recall from a manufacturer (producer) to a supplier to a retailer using the RFID tags attached to the product. These tags can help in tracking a shipment.

■ It can help a retailer know the exact amount of inventory and its shelf position in all online and offline locations using omnichannel access, which will ensure product availability and prevent out-of-stock situations.

■ It can help a manufacturer predict when and what equipment or machines require preventive maintenance or disposal

■ It can help a retailer up-sell or cross-sell in a store, to lower total cost of ownership, and to improve inventory turns or churns.

Here are some examples of use cases of the IoT technologies and the resulting data from ComQi (www.comqi.com).

Example 1: Walmart's data shows that sales for salad ingredients rise when the weather forecast suggests temperatures above 80 and light winds.

Example 2: Nordstrom tracks pins on Pinterest to see what products are trending and uses that on signs in-store to show shoppers what interests their peers.

Example 3: Disney has RFID-enabled wristbands that provide theme park access, entry access for guest hotel rooms, and cash- and card-free payment for food and merchandise. All that activity is also tracked data that helps build a better picture of how guests use Disney services.

Example 4: Amazon introduced a Dash Button, a Wi-Fi enabled device that is mapped to specific consumer packaged goods like laundry detergent at home. When the detergent is running low, the button generates an order transaction and delivers a fresh supply of detergent to a customer's home.

(B) Network of Things and Location of Things
Two topics related to the IoT are NoT and LoT technologies, which are discussed next.

Network-of-Things Technology. The relationship between IoT and NoT is subtle. In the NoT, "things" could be software, hardware, sensors, software and hardware, and people. A NoT may or may not employ "things" connected to the Internet. A typical example of NoT could be a LAN with none of its "things" connected to the Internet whereas the IoT is strongly anchored to the Internet. Social media networks (e.g., Facebook), sensor technology, and RFID tags are some variants of NoTs. For example, a sensor can transmit an RFID device's identification information to a nearby data collector (e.g., a POS system). IoT is one type of a NoT and a NoT is one type of a distributed system.

Sensors can provide surveillance features with cameras and microphones. However, sensors have security and reliability concerns such as data tampering, data stealing, data deleting, data dropping, and incorrect transmission of data. A sensor's data could be accessed by unauthorized parties. A **security control** is to install encryption methods in sensors.

Location-of-Things Technology. LoT technology provides IoT devices with sensing features that can communicate their geographic position (i.e., it knows where an IoT device is located). For example, retail stores, hospitals, and hotels can use Bluetooth Low Energy technology for indoor location services to track resources (e.g., people, furniture, people, and mobile devices, such as smartwatches, badges, or tags) to provide personalized experience to customers. The Bluetooth technology is an alternative to GPS technology since GPS cannot be used or reached in a specific indoor service facility.

Management can utilize LoT data to understand what is happening with the resources in a service facility, where it is happening, and what is expected to happen in a specific location.

(iii) Artificial Intelligence Technologies
The scope of artificial intelligence (AI) technologies consists of several topics, such as artificial intelligence, machine learning, neural networks, and expert systems. The AI is the umbrella type technology representing a group of several technologies.

Artificial intelligence (AI) is the simulation of human intelligence processing by machines and computer software. These processes contain learning rules, logical reasoning, and self-correction methods. For example, AI uses natural language processing technology, so it can process a retail shopper's questions and requests and provide answers. Other applications can be found in expert systems and speech recognition systems. AI can be thought of as an umbrella type of technology covering several topics.

Machine learning (ML) is a type of AI that provides computers with the ability to learn without being explicitly programmed. ML focuses on the development of computer programs that can change their behavior when exposed to new data. Computers can handle new situations through analysis, self-training, observation, and experience, all with minimal supervision and involvement by people. ML is a part of predictive analytics and is related to cognitive computing.

EXAMPLES

- Macy's is testing AI technology to improve sales. Customers can ask Macy's mobile tool designed with AI technology to receive answers related to the visited store, such as where a particular brand is located or what is in stock. Normally customers would ask a sales associate about these questions face to face.

- Retailers are using AI technology so customers can receive answers to their questions on the retailer's websites, not face to face.

- Transportation and package delivery companies can use AI-based chatbots so internal employees and external customers can track delivery of customer packages.

Neural networks (NNs) are a type of AI technologies built around concepts similar to the way the human brain's web of neural connections, known as synapses, is believed to work to identify patterns, learn, and reach conclusions. NNs have the ability to learn and to utilize accumulated experience to make decisions that rival those of human beings. NNs have nothing to do with telecommunications-related networks. NN systems are particularly apt for risk management and forecasting activities, in which the ability to identify intricate patterns is crucial to making predictions. In theory, an NN can be put to work in any application in which substantial amounts of data are used to predict an outcome.

NNs can be applied to:

- Trade securities and options
- Identify fraudulent use of credit cards
- Decide whether to approve a mortgage application

An NN develops the ability to decide and then learns to improve its performance through massive trial-and-error decision making. NNs are trained by being supplied with key data from a sample group of transactions. The NNs are able to use fuzzy or incomplete data successfully and to discover patterns in decision making that conventional rule-based systems would not pick up.

NNs can be used in reviewing credit card transactions to detect anomalies and fraudulent activities. Text-mining tools are used to scan unstructured documents, such as emails, web pages, and audio/video files, and to scan structured data found in databases or data warehouses.

Expert systems use AI programming languages to help human beings make better decisions. In the business world, managers at all levels make decisions based on incomplete data and ambiguous information and under uncertain conditions. Expert systems are built by a knowledge system builder, a knowledge engineer, a human expert in the subject matter based on rules of thumb, facts, and an expert's advice. Knowledge system builders are like programmers, and knowledge engineers are similar to systems analysts in a conventional systems development environment. Human experts are people knowledgeable in the subject matter located either inside the organization or outside. More than one expert can participate in an expert system project to develop the knowledge base.

DIFFERENCE BETWEEN CONVENTIONAL SYSTEMS AND EXPERT SYSTEMS

- Conventional systems are aimed at problems that can be solved using a purely algorithmic approach but can be solved using a system development life cycle methodology.

- Expert systems are aimed at problems that cannot be solved using a purely algorithmic approach but can be solved using a heuristic methodology.

Expert systems have an inference engine, which decides how to execute an application or how the rules are fired. The inference methods include forward and backward chaining (or reasoning). In forward chaining, data is subjected to rules to achieve system goals, whereas in backward chaining, the system starts with goals and works backward through the rules to determine what data is required. Facts (data) and rules are stored in the system's knowledge base and are used in the question-and-answer session with the end user. The system can be designed with a multiple-choice question format with a list of alternatives provided, and the end user chooses one. In a way, the expert system becomes a personal consultant or guide to the end user in solving problems.

SAFETY AND SECURITY RISKS IN EXPERT SYSTEMS

- If the rules in expert systems are not formulated properly and tested correctly, the outcomes could lead to loss of life or damage to property in medical and military systems.

- Use of too many rules in expert systems can complicate the programming work and access control decisions, thus compromising the system's security.

The operation of an expert system can be viewed in terms of the interaction of distinct components, such as the knowledge base, inference engine, and end user interface. The **knowledge base** stores knowledge about how to solve problems. A software module called the **inference engine** executes inference procedures. If the user of the expert system is a person, communications with the end user are handled via an **end user interface**.

(iv) Augmented Reality Technology

AR technology is an emerging technology applied to retail that uses cameras and images to provide seamless, positive, and meaningful interactions between customers (subjects) and products (objects) through smart mirrors. It creates 3D graphic models to interact with images. It improves how customers can view, see, and interact with a product using an AR app. The goal of retailers with AR technology is to turn viewers into buyers. AR technology is being used in several areas, such as playing video games, designing greeting cards, drawing visual art, showing beauty products, and designing an office or a store layout.

Similar to VR, AR is a prepurchase effort because it facilitates and influences a customer's decision to purchase. A major benefit of AR to retailers is that customer purchases increase and customer returns decrease because customers are trying out the products and they purchase those that fit or suit them, thus making them happy. This means that customers keep their purchases and do not return them. It says try it, like it, and keep it.

Fashion retailers are adding AR technology to visual search technology to create more compelling and immersive experiences in print media, such as catalogs and magazines.

> **Example 1:** Covergirl, a beauty retailer, has created an AR mobile app for use in mass merchandise stores and drugstores. This app scans a person's face using her mobile device's front-facing camera to identify skin tone, then shows different makeup looks. Customers can scan products to access additional information including costs and reviews.

> **Example 2:** Various retailers are launching AR apps to their catalog products in order to make them interactive so customers can zoom in and out, turn products 360 degrees, and play videos. Customers can purchase these products directly from the retailer's app.

> **Example 3:** Office Depot, an office supply retailer, is using AR technology to help with store design and layout planning in order to create shopping excitement in its physical stores.

> **Example 4:** Lacoste, a French tennis apparel retailer, is promoting its tennis brand shoes with AR collection with an interactive book that gives history of tennis, which is connected to a collection of short videos. The AR app gives a reading experience of the book's contents.

> **Example 5:** Wayfair, an online furniture retailer, is launching a new app for smartphones that uses AR technology to let shoppers visualize furniture and décor in their homes at full scale prior to making a purchase decision.

(v) Virtual Reality Technology

VR technology is a leading-edge technology applied to retail that replicates or simulates the real world through images and sounds that can be heard from speakers and headphones (headsets). It creates 3D graphic models to interact with images. A user of the VR equipment is immersed in an experience like real life while interacting with a computer-simulated environment. VR technology began started in video games, pilot training, and movie and motion pictures. VR technology has entered into medical training, military training, and other kinds of training. The goal of retailers with VR technology is to turn viewers into buyers.

Similar to AR, VR is a prepurchase effort because it facilitates and influences a customer's decision to purchase. A major benefit of VR to retailers is that customer purchases are increased and customer returns are decreased because customers try out the products and purchase those that fit or suit them, thus making them happy. This means that customers keep their purchases and do not return them. It is: try it, like it, keep it.

> **Example 1:** IKEA, global furniture chain retailer, is testing VR technology to see how a kitchen looks like after changing cabinet colors and how new furniture fits into an office without using a measuring tape.

> **Example 2:** eBay, an online resale retailer, opened its VR department store (not a physical store) where customers or shoppers can view and select products using VR viewers and cardboard headsets. Viewers can add products to a shopping cart by fixing their gaze on a specific product.

(vi) Robotic Technology

Proactive retailers are either operating or testing robots in their physical stores, fulfillment centers, distribution centers, and warehouses to automate routine and mechanical tasks faster and better than humans can do. Manufacturers are also using robots in their factories. Retailers are achieving multiple benefits from the use of robots, such as decreased costs, increased output from efficient production, increased accuracy, and faster movement of goods within a stockroom.

> **Example 1:** Hudson's Bay, a major retailer, is using robots in its fulfillment centers to reduce costs while improving output volume and accuracy for its e-commerce customers.

> **Example 2:** Amazon, the Internet giant retailer, is using robots in its fulfillment centers to help sort packages, move around the warehouses carrying inventory, reduce truck loading and unloading time, and reduce the overall order processing time.

> **Example 3:** Adidas, a shoe retailer, is planning to manufacture its shoes in a fully automated and robot-staffed factory in Atlanta.

> **Example 4:** Target, a major department store retailer, is testing robots to assist with inventory and supply-chain efforts inside a physical store, such as keeping track of inventory from shelves to carts, identifying misplaced or mispriced inventory, and recognizing low levels of inventory.

(vii) Wearable Technology

Wearable technology is an example of novel technology that is aimed to help both customers and retailers with smartwatches (Apple and Google watches), smart eyewear glasses (Google Glass), clothes, smart cameras (Google Helpouts), digital badges, and wristbands. Smartwatches are important to retailers to engage customers when they shop at a physical store. Retailers are hoping that customers who do not normally like shopping at a physical store may shop using wearable smartwatches due to convenience and comfort. After gaining popularity, wearable technology can become a new retail commerce channel. Apple and Google are the major players in the wearable technology market.

> **Example 1:** The Container Store, a household goods retailer, is known for giving wearable smartwatches to its employees to achieve several benefits in a physical store, such as improved communications, streamlined operations, improved customer service, and increased employee efficiency. For example, smartwatches: replaced old clunky walkie-talkies and overhead speakers previously used for in-store communications; allow employees to access product information from anywhere in the store, which improves customer service; and (3) track employees' day-to-day work activities and performance, which boosts their productivity and efficiency.

> **Example 2:** Early adopters of wearable technology stated that the technology helped them in their customer service function where service associates have real-time access to customers' previous purchase and return data when they are processing current returns. This access positively improved customers' experience.

(viii) 3D Technology

3D printing technology represents a paradigm shift from traditional production methods. It is a mature technology because it was born in 1980s and has been used as a rapid prototyping method in automotive, aerospace, consumer goods, and electronics industries.

However, the technology is new to the retail industry to create objects (goods) in glass, plastic, rubber, metal, and ceramic to make dresses and other goods. 3D models are used in AR and VR platforms. The demand for 3D printing is rising as customers want to make customized products for less money.

Two major concerns related to 3D printing are (1) intellectual property risks resulting from violation of trademark and copyright ownership and (2) recycling risk of unused raw materials. 3D printing is a great innovation for home-based makers in the maker movement.

> **Example 1:** Sephora, a beauty retailer, launched a 3D AR mirror that can simulate cosmetics on a customer's face in real time in 3D view and can get in-store makeovers.

> **Example 2:** Sportswear retailers such as Nike, Adidas, Reebok, DSW, and New Balance are either experimenting with or using the 3D printing technology to create football boots, running shoes, walking shoes, and sneakers.

> **Example 3:** Fashion retailers are using 3D technology to make garments, shoes, bags, belt buckles, jewelry, eyewear (e.g., Luxottica), and watches.

> **Example 4:** Wayfair, a pure-play online furniture retailer, has implemented the 3D technology on its website so customers can experiment with different textures and fabrics by viewing furniture in 360 degrees.

> **Example 5:** Target, a major department store retailer, launched 3D printing for holiday gifts, such as charms, rings, and holiday ornaments, that can be customized online and mailed to friends and family.

(ix) Bots and Chatbots Technology

Bots, pieces of software that mimic or impersonate a human being, are examples of emerging technologies. Bots can become human helpers in terms of personalization and customization that can be applied, say, to a customer service function. Chatbots are capable of providing organic (natural) conversations and communications to customers.

With respect to technology, a bot (robot) or zombie is a special class of malware, which is one of the largest malware problems. It is a mass hacking scheme infecting a network of computers with criminal malware. Bots are remote-control software agents installed on a user's computer system. They are often controlled remotely via Internet Relay Chat. Once a system is infected with a bot, it becomes part of a bot network (botnet [a robot network]) and is used in conjunction with other botnet members to carry out the wishes of the bot owner or bot herder. Bots can scan networks for vulnerabilities, install various distributed denial of service (DDoS) tools, capture network packets, or download and execute arbitrary dangerous programs. Often bots contain additional spyware and install it. Computers, networks, and computer systems infected with bots can be used to distribute spam software to make it harder to track and prosecute the spammers. Moreover, a botnet typically operates without obvious visible evidence and can remain operational and hidden for years.

Botnets are key cybersecurity threats with several negative purposes:

- They invade the privacy of the victim users by installing key logging software to steal sensitive information (e.g., personal, financial, and medical) online or by secretly activating computer cameras in victims' computers.

- They install ransomware software that holds a user's critical information hostage (data hijacking) by encrypting it unless the user agrees to pay a ransom amount.

- They use a victim's computer to attack other victims' computers, thus committing DDoS attacks.

- They deceive marketing advertisers to perpetrate click fraud to increase ad billing amounts (e.g., malvertising using adware).

In summary, major **risks** from bots include stealing sensitive information (i.e., data exfiltration), conducting ransomware attacks, introducing DDoS attacks, doing click-fraud activities, and involving in campaign propaganda on social media platforms

> **Example 1:** Bots combined with social media platforms can handle customer service issues better than phone calls or emails. This technology can reduce negative online posts and can avoid nasty tweet storms done by customers when they are upset with a retailer's specific brand and brand-related experiences.

> **Example 2:** Retail marketers at a travel company can use bots and chatbots installed on their websites to help customers in providing hotel options, comparing prices between hotels, and then booking the hotel that a customer liked the best. Bots can also locate a good pizza restaurant nearby.

(x) Text Messaging Technology

Retailers can deliver marketing messages to mobile customers using several communication channels, such as phone, email, social media, mobile apps, and text messages (i.e., SMS and MMS). Several studies have shown that only 30% of retailers are actually using SMS text messages; thus text messaging is an underused communication channel. Other companies actively using SMS technology include airlines, hotels, restaurants, doctor's offices, pharmacies, and hospitals. Note that there are alternative messaging services to SMS, including Facebook Messenger, Viber, and Whats App on smartphones.

According to a RetailNext survey (www.retailnext.com), 97% of text messages are opened as compared to just 20% of emails; 75% of customers would prefer to receive marketing offers via SMS text; and an average of 67 text messages are sent daily by each and every millennial. This survey strongly reminds the retailers that they should utilize SMS text messages as another revenue-generating opportunity. However, companies should not bombard and annoy customers with so many text messages that customers become insensitive to them.

In addition to or as an extension of SMS, MMS is available to retailers that use multimedia content to send messages over a cellular network. The content of MMS can include text messages greater than 160 characters in length, video, single or multiple images, and audio up to 40 seconds in length.

SMS versus MMS

- SMS sends content consisting of text-only messages.
- MMS sends content consisting of text, video, image, and audio.
- SMS can send a text message no longer than 160 characters.
- MMS can send a text message longer than 160 characters.
- MMS technology is an extension of SMS technology.
- Both SMS and MMS are customer-engagement channels.

- Group and bulk MMS, similar to group and bulk emails, are more effective than a single SMS because MMS can reach more customers at the same time and saves time and effort compared to sending single SMSs.

Several benefits can accrue to a retailer actively using text messaging technology, including:

- Efficiency (i.e., speed and savings in time)
- Reach (i.e., direct and immediate communication)
- Impact (i.e., increase in sales to a retailer and a value to a customer)
- Above all, a positive experience to customers who are actively engaged with mobile devices

Example 1: Some marketing-savvy retailers are using group or bulk MMS as a marketing tool to deliver scannable coupon codes, product images, video shows, and expert audio presentations.

Example 2: Customers with Kohl's department store cards receive several daily text messages and emails from Kohl's promoting sales events, special discounts, rebates, and coupons to a point that customers do not know what sales are good and for what length of time, thus causing confusion among customers. A downside to this unrelenting stream of communications is that customers do not buy anything at regular prices and simply wait for sales, which hurts a retailer's regular sales.

(xi) Website Technology

In this section, we discuss a retailer's technology in terms of its website, mobile site, and mobile apps. These sites and apps are the first touch points and digital storefronts to online stores. Because online sales are increasing through online stores and offline sales are decreasing through physical stores, it is important for retailers to pay more attention to and focus on how these sites and apps are designed and how they are inviting or disinviting customers to visit these sites and stores. The design of these sites and apps, which are the entry points to online business, is directly related to customer traffic to them. Simply stated, a retailer's sites and apps are revenue-generating opportunities and profit-making mechanisms.

Planning, designing, and developing a retailer's website and mobile site involve art, science, and creativity, resulting in inviting and inspiring work. In general, a site must be engaging through simple navigation tools and feature-rich designs for customers to want to purchase a product, which improves customer conversion rates. Website and mobile sites are online stores, not just symbols of cutting-edge technology; instead, they are a reflection of a retailer's business strategy because these sites can either bring sales or lose sales. Because of the importance of websites and mobile sites, their development should not be delegated to lower levels of technology and marketing staff; instead, senior management of both departments should take the lead to ensure their success.

Designing, developing, maintaining, and managing websites and mobile sites are part of a retailer's technology strategy. Websites operate on the Internet with mainframe computers and operating systems using desktop, laptop, and notebook computers (e.g., IBM's operating system for mainframe computers). Mobile sites operate on the mobile operating system (e.g., Apple's iOS and Google's Android) using mobile devices such as smartphones and digital tablets. Both websites and mobile sites are the heart of e-commerce and mobile commerce, respectively, for a retailer's online business.

Access possibilities to these sites include: customers accessing websites using desktop, laptop, or notebook computers; accessing retailer websites and accessing mobile sites using mobile devices, such as smartphones and tablets.

According to Supermarket News (www.supermarketnews.com), traditional retailers lack website functionality. Supermarket News suggests the following to add to a food retailer's website.

- Shopping list for customers
- Strong search and sort features for products of interest
- Strong product imagery through clear and readable graphics
- Clear and complete descriptions of products
- Reviews and recommendations posted from previous customer shoppers
- Technology integration between among (in-store), online, and mobile platforms

(A) Design of Websites and Mobile Sites

Today, retailer websites and mobile sites are growing in size and getting very complex because they display thousands of SKUs online. The greater the complexity, the harder it is to navigate the site. A good design should be simple after reducing the complexity factor. Websites and mobile sites must be designed in such a way that they are robust and responsive, and avoid site crashes.

Robust design means building with resilience principles combined with high-technical capacity in terms of larger-size bandwidth, large-size memory, and large-size data storage to handle heavy workloads, especially during holiday season; high-powered processing speeds in seconds, not in minutes; and the ability to withstand system errors and human errors.

Responsive means the ability to handle customers' heavy traffic demand for inquiries, searches, and processes in a timely manner either at a primary site (original site) or at a secondary site (backup site) to handle unforeseen contingencies. A key requirement for both the original site and the backup site is testing and retesting to ensure reliability and operational readiness.

(B) Original Site versus Backup Site

Both the original site and the backup site must have the same configuration in terms of using the same computer hardware and software in order to operate the same ways at all times. This means that when the original site is down or crashes due to a major or minor disaster, the backup site must kick in and be ready to take over (i.e., it must be disaster ready), as if nothing ever happened to the original site. The aim is that no one notices the difference between the original site and the backup site during their normal operation.

The backup site could be owned by the same retailer that operates the original site or it could be rented, leased, or hosted by commercial third parties. Additional problems can occur when the backup site is leased or hosted by the third parties, including how much testing was done to ensure preparedness and how quickly the site is disaster ready. Commercial banks, financial institutions, and airline companies have well-managed and well-tested backup sites due to the time sensitivity and customer-heavy nature of their businesses. Each minute a website is down is a loss of revenues and profits with associated reputation risk and customer defection.

(C) Good Design versus Bad Design

In reality, a retailer's website and mobile site are developed using either good design features or bad design features. Sites with good design features will be successful; those with bad design features will be unsuccessful. Metrics are the best way to measure whether a retailer's site design is successful or not because metrics are objective and quantify outcomes.

(D) Shopping Cart Abandonment

According to a RetailNext study (www.retailnext.net), the impact of online shopping cart abandonment accounts for a loss of $18 billion in sales each year for all retailers combined. The shopping cart is the final stage of a customer's shopping journey and decision-making process, whether to buy a product or not. It is a major decision with financial consequences to both customers and retailers alike. It is also the last touch point between an online retailer and an online customer.

Note that online shopping cart abandonment is similar to a physical store abandonment, where a customer visits a store and leaves without buying anything (i.e., browse and leave). Some reasons to abandon a physical store could be that: (1) customers did not like the look and feel of the store; (2) customers did not find what they were looking for; (3) store associates were not friendly or knowledgeable about products; (4) prices were too high; and (5) product quality appeared poor.

For retailers, the success of an online business greatly depends on how well the websites and mobile sites containing shopping carts are designed, developed, tested, operated, and managed. All these areas can affect retailers' sales, profits, and reputation, either positively or negatively. This means that a poorly designed website can lead to shopping cart abandonment and customer defection, reflecting in a loss of sales and profits to retailers. In contrast, a website with a good design can increase sales and profits for retailers. This is summarized next.

- Poorly designed websites can lead to online shopping cart abandonment, which is risky to e-commerce, resulting in lost sale and customer defection.
- Poorly designed mobile sites can lead to mobile shopping cart abandonment, which is risky to mobile commerce, resulting in lost sale and customer defection.

(E) Reasons for Shopping Cart Abandonment

According to a RetailNext study (www.retailnext.net), approximately 70% of e-commerce customers abandon their online shopping carts for these reasons:

- High prices
- High shipping costs
- Long delivery times
- Lack of delivery details
- Complicated checkout process
- Poor or lack of basic security and privacy features
- Poor layout of the website
- Distracting visual elements on screens and pages

- No option for a guest checkout
- Hidden fees

In addition to poor and uninviting design features and functions in websites and mobile sites, three major reasons for abandoning shopping carts are (1) high total cost of purchase, which includes final price, shipping costs, sales tax, and any other warranty/protection plan costs; (2) payment issues, such as not having enough money left on a charge card or not having more than one charge card; and (3) simply not being able to afford the item at this time.

(F) Recovery Methods for Shopping Cart Abandonment

Because retailers lose large amounts of sales and customers due to shopping cart abandonment, they need to develop effective and workable recovery methods to bring back lost customers and lost sales.

Current recovery methods for shopping cart abandonment include remarketing or retargeting those customers who abandoned their carts. This includes sending repeated, gentle reminder emails to customers as a follow-up, which may not work all the time. The first personalized and reminder email is sent to a lost customer within 24 hours without any financial remedy. Some kind of financial remedy is made either in the third or fourth email, which is too late to change the customer's mind to come back.

To recover from shopping cart abandonment, retailers should offer but do not offer any financial remedies before the customer finally leaves the website or during the first email, where the latter is practical than the former. This is a critical juncture because it is a financial-related decision for both retailers and customers alike. Moreover, a physical store's sales associates helping the customer are not empowered to offer any financial remedies, nor is the computer system programmed to do so, so the customer abandons and simply leaves the site.

Retailers can offer one or more of these financial remedies to an online customer before leaving their sites or during their first email to the customer after shopping cart abandonment so as to close the sale and to increase the conversion rate:

- Special price discounts, say 10% or 20% based on the customer's previous purchase history and whether the customer is a repeat, loyal, or first-time customer
- Free shipping for both inbound (returns) and outbound (deliveries)
- Waiver of 50% or 100% of sales tax, which is an out-of-pocket cost to retailers
- One-time discount, say 10% or 20%, on warranty/protection plan costs, which can be an out-of-pocket cost to retailers
- Special payment options, such as pay after delivery; delayed one-time and lump-sum payment; and installment payments of equal or unequal amounts; or a combination

    Example: Shoes.com ships shoes to its customers with a pay-after-delivery option, which is a revolutionary idea and a big departure from traditional retail business practice. Traditionally, customers pay first for a product and later receive the product from a retailer. With Shoes.com, customers receive a product first and pay for it after they try it on and see if they like it. Although it competes with Zappos.com and Shoebuy.com, Shoes.com has increased its sales due to payment convenience factor, which leads to repeat and happy customers. To identify and prevent fraud, Shoes.com uses the customer's IP address to determine if he or she is real or using a spoofed IP address.

(xii) Search Engine Technology

A major aspect of a digital marketing technology is the use of search engine optimization (SEO) techniques, which are based on the Internet marketing strategy. Basically, new and random visitors enter a keyword into search engines to access a retailer's website from anywhere in the world for browsing and buying products. In addition to using a keyword search, visitors can access a retailer's website through the use of image search, video search, news search, and other types of searches. A retailer's online business and a public search engine (e.g., Google) are related and connected to each other because they both deal with the same retailer's Internet-based website.

Popular and official search engine service providers include Google, Yahoo, and Bing, and they are free for visitors to access. Although not recognized as an official search engine service provider, Amazon.com has become a de facto search engine provider because Amazon is the Internet giant retailer and because Amazon sells almost anything and everything. This is why consumers and customers often go to Amazon first to find something.

A website that receives frequent searches with a large number of visitors gets a higher rank on the search results page, which advertising companies, such as retailers, prefer. A retailer's goal for SEO is to convert as many visitors as possible into customers and to convert these customers into buyers, as shown next.

Visitors $\longrightarrow$ Customers

Customers $\longrightarrow$ Buyers

Because the SEO is the first touch point between visitors and retailers and because the SEO is the first entry point into a retailer's website, it is very important for retail websites to be designed effectively with the right content to bring visitor traffic. A retailer's traffic analogy is shown below.

- Physical stores bring customer traffic through walk-ins.
- Online stores bring customer traffic through a retailer's website and mobile site.
- Search engines bring visitor traffic through the Internet-based website.

Regardless of the type of traffic, a retailer's goal is to convert the customers into buyers, that is, to increase conversion rates and consequently to increase in sales and profits. When the SEO approach proves ineffective for a retailer, an alternative method is to use paid advertising through a pay-per-click approach.

There is a direct relationship between search engines and a retailer's website design, as follows:

- An efficient search engine can amplify visitor traffic if the website is well designed.
- An efficient search engine can deamplify visitor traffic if the website is poorly designed.

    Example: According to Media Post's (www.mediapost.com) survey results, two-thirds of shoppers start searches for products and services directly on retailers' websites, such as Walmart, Target, and Best Buy. One-third of shoppers start searches on official search engines, such as Google, Yahoo, and Bing.

(xiii) Blockchain Technology

Blockchain or hash chain technology supports bitcoins where the disruptive technology facilitates transactions between mutually distrusting entities without the need for a trusted arbiter (i.e., no trusted middleperson, intermediary, or central bank). Blockchain is a fully distributed and decentralized ledger that is synchronized through consensus between entities or parties. It facilitates fully decentralized operations, processes peer-to-peer transactions, and is tamper evident and resistant.

Bitcoins, also called Litecoins and Peercoins, are technically called cryptocurrencies with cryptography as the supporting technology. They also are called virtual currency, digital currency, digital gold, or digital wallets. Bitcoins are called virtual currency because there is no real currency (real money or flat money, such as U.S. dollars) involved. Credit/debit cards or wire transfer funds from banks, cash, prepaid/money/cash cards can be used to buy the digital currency through standard bitcoin exchanges or smartphone apps, including major retail stores (e.g., Walmart and Amazon), local convenience stores, local currency exchanges, and local pharmacies. Bitcoins can also be used to purchase gift cards from retail stores. The key point is that a virtual currency is exchanged for flat currency, funds, or other forms of virtual currency, all for a fee.

Blockchain uses a cryptographic hash function (e.g., secure hash algorithm) and digital signature algorithm to create a continuous list of records (blocks) that are linked and secured. **Hash functions** are computational functions that take a variable-length data input and produce a fixed-length result (output) that can be used as evidence representing the original data. Therefore, if the hash of two messages is identical, it can be reasonably assumed that the messages are identical as well.

A hash function, which is a many-to-one function, compresses the bits of a message to a fixed-size hash value in a way that distributes the possible messages evenly among the possible hash values. A cryptographic hash function does this in a way that makes it extremely difficult to come up with a message that would hash to a previously computed hash value. For example, a password hashing is storing a hash of the password.

A **digital signature** is an electronic analog of a written signature in that it can be used to prove to the recipient, or a third party, that the originator in fact signed the message. Digital signatures are also generated for stored data and programs to verify data and program integrity at any later time.

The bitcoin technology platform contains two layers: the bottom layer is the blockchain protocol, which is not susceptible to hacking; the top layer is the bitcoin exchanges or websites, which are susceptible to hacking. Blockchains can be permissioned or permission-less with different characteristics and challenges.

Permissioned blockchains may lead to cost savings, workflow improvements, automation, and improved auditing with current business processes. Permissioned blockchains have these characteristics:

- Participation is private (closed) and/or controlled.
- The participants are trusted.
- They are more efficient than many public blockchains.
- They can support privacy and confidentiality requirements.

A major challenge is establishing a level of centralized trusting body through a governing authority and controlled mechanisms.

Permission-less blockchains are a symbol of utilizing disruptive technology that can dramatically change the way traditional business activities are conducted. Permission-less blockchains have these characteristics:

- Participation is open to the public at large and uncontrolled.
- They facilitate peer-to-peer transactions.
- They have fully decentralized operations.
- They handle irreversible transactions.

A major challenge is establishing operational security's best practices over network nodes and public blockchains.

In summary, bitcoin is a virtual currency and blockchain is a real technology, and they work together.

(A) Risks of Using Bitcoins

Bitcoins can be used legally for making and receiving business payments. They can also be used for illegal purposes, such as drug deals, money laundering, hacking, fraudulent activities, and other related crimes. For example, hackers often demand payment through bitcoins during ransomware attacks.

- Bitcoins and blockchains together deploy a disruptive technology that is not fully tested or proven, resulting in major risks to businesses and individuals.
- Public participation in bitcoin transactions is riskier than private participation.
- Privacy rights of participants can be violated due to lack of centralized record keeping for controlling and monitoring purposes.
- There is a lack of security best practices over digital wallets used for bitcoins.
- Lack of mitigating controls associated with the risk of irreversible transactions. This means that incorrect transactions cannot be corrected; once transactions are added to a blockchain, they cannot be changed. Buyers can get a refund for their purchases only if the seller is willing (i.e., voluntary or discretionary).
- Lack of effective identity and access management practices for validating users' electronic credentials.
- The bitcoin currency market is volatile due to its speculative nature (i.e., sudden high or low prices).
- There is a risk of data loss by potential hackers when they break into bitcoins distributed ledger.
- Bitcoin data cannot be changed when necessary because bitcoins were not designed to allow changes. Data source data immutability is not helpful when there are accusations of tampering after the fact.
- Fraudsters are ready to cheat innocent people with fake opportunities or deals using a variety of bitcoin scams, such as:
  - ☐ High investment returns guaranteed but never delivered
  - ☐ No net worth or no income requirements
  - ☐ Pressure to buy right now

- ☐ Unsolicited offers for selling and buying virtual currency
- ☐ Unlicensed individuals and unregistered firms offering and selling investments in bitcoins
- ☐ Above all, the entire deal sounds too good to be true (i.e., a high risk).
- ☐ Bitcoin has its own network called bitcoin network using a distributed ledger technology.

- ■ Bitcoins use open ledgers with distributed ledger technology, where membership is open to all participants. This means that open ledgers do not by default restrict participant membership as they are permission-less blockchains.

- ■ In contrast, closed ledgers are permissioned blockchains as they are entering a proof-of-concept phase application among financial institutions.

- ■ Bitcoins traded in the primary market must be registered under the U.S. federal securities laws to provide full protections for investors.

- ■ Bitcoins traded in the secondary market may not be registered under the U.S. federal securities, thus not providing the needed full protections for investors. Hence, investors are exposed to fraud risk or loss of money.

- ■ Bitcoins could offer penny stocks, meaning shares of a company with no assets, no products, and no staff, or shares in a pure Ponzi scheme.

- ■ Victims not receiving their cryptocurrency after they paid for it.

- ■ Attackers hack into victims' **virtual wallets** first, then blackmail the victims to get the attackers' ransom money back.

(B) Controls over Bitcoins

Victim organizations should implement Internet-safe computing practices and install antivirus and anti-malware software on computers. Software signatures should be current with updates.

(xiv) Social Media Technology

Social media platforms with extensive and sophisticated use of technologies include Facebook, Twitter, YouTube, Google+, Instagram, Pinterest, Snapchat, and several others. Social media can drive customer traffic into physical stores (offline stores) and nonphysical stores (online stores). Today's retailers are using YouTube, Google+, and Pinterest more than Facebook and Twitter. Members of the millennial generation (Generations Y and Z) use social media more than other generations. It is difficult for retailers to keep up with social media technology, as it changes constantly and continuously.

Today more and more customers are interacting and transacting with social media platforms (e.g., Facebook or Google) rather than directly with retailers. Retailers now have to have a greater presence on social media and offer personalized services. Customers ignore security and privacy concerns and are willing to share their information in exchange for more personalized services. Customers are using social channels to place and track their purchase orders with retailers. When most customers go to social media, retailers must follow.

Management must make sure that only authorized company employees can respond to comments posted by customers on social media platforms. Unauthorized employees responding to customer posts and comments can lead to an increase the company's negative reputation risk. The marketing staff, public relations office, or social media administrator should be given authority to respond to customer comments.

A retailer's marketing strategy today must use social channels to introduce new products, announce improvements made to existing products, and offer sales promotions. *Marketing management's goal is to turn social media into sales media.*

Because it is common for customers to post negative comments about a retailer's products on social media, retailers should publish "comment and post" policies describing what types of comments are allowed or acceptable for posting. Retailers should also provide a procedure to handle negative comments and posts to escalate and resolve problems and issues. Be aware that besides customers, disgruntled employees (former and current) can post negative comments.

Social channels should be viewed as a modern "suggestion box" system where employees and customers can suggest new products, improvements to existing products, and better ways of doing things, all online and instantly.

At least three fraudulent methods were identified in social media:

1. **Click-jacking** is concealing hyperlinks beneath legitimate clickable content that, when clicked, cause innocent users to unknowingly perform actions, such as download malware or send personal information to an unknown website. Fraudsters use "Like" and "Share" buttons to carry out these scams. A security control is to change browser options and settings to maximize security.

2. **Doxing** is publicly releasing a person's identifying information online without authorization. A security control is to exercise caution when sharing or posting personal information on social media, including that of friends and family.

3. **Pharming** is redirecting users from a legitimate website to an illegitimate (fake) website for the purpose of extracting confidential and sensitive data. A security control is to type in an official website's URL, instead of linking to it from an unsolicited and deceiving source. Never click the link.

   Example 1: Target, a major department store, has increased its budget on social media spending by 30%, reflecting its greater presence, priority, and strategic importance to social media.

   Example 2: Nordstrom, an upscale retailer, has increased its budget spending on mobile technology, social media technology, and multichannel growth strategies. Nordstrom claims that it has more followers on Pinterest than likes on Facebook. The keys to Nordstrom's success in social media are to bring rich content, showcasing fashion trends, and even using customer pins on trends to merchandise displays in stores. Nordstrom believes that social media is an important touch point to engage customers, build long-term relationships with customers, and turn regular customers into loyal customers. These efforts have increased Nordstrom's online sales.

   Example 3: Nordstrom is launching Like2Buy campaign to shop on Instagram where its e-commerce site is seamlessly connected to its Instagram page, thus allowing customers to purchase products they see posted (i.e., look and buy). Nordstrom also adding video screens in stores to showcase social shopping, especially by millennial customers.

   Example 4: Nordstrom is integrating social media technology with its physical stores. It encourages customers to pin their favorite Nordstrom products (e.g., shoes and handbags) on Pinterest and shows them an interactive display of those products within a store. Then a store's sales associates attach a Pinterest tag to those products and swap those pinned products based on other customers' demands.

Example 5: Publix Super Markets, a grocery store chain retailer, is big on social media to engage with its customers where they are and to extend in-store services to online customers. Publix is active on Facebook for posting comments and reviews, Twitter for promoting brands, Instagram for sharing photos and videos, and Pinterest for providing recipes and event planning ideas. Publix has benefited from social media through customer engagement, loyalty, and relationships, and eventual increase in sales.

Example 6: Williams-Sonoma, a general retailer, is using YouTube technology to show shoppable videos. Online customers can purchase everything they need from the videos with just a few clicks. The retailer has established a social media council as part of its social media strategy.

Example 7: Pottery Barn, a division of Williams-Sonoma, credits social media technology for its success. It works with Pinterest, an online pin board, which became a great source of referral traffic to its online business and helped its brand get market exposure.

Example 8: Target's website was crashed and went down for 20 minutes when the website could not keep up with the sales frenzy of a Lilly Pulitzer product, a designer limited edition collection. Later, social media members got frustrated with the out-of-stock condition and blasted Target to express their anger and disappointment. This shows the power of the social media on retailers and on society in general.

Example 9: According to the UPS Company's survey (www.solvers.ups.com), 43% of customers discover new products through social media.

Example 10: Amazon and eBay are the most active retailers on Twitter, a popular social media platform. Apparel retailers also use Twitter very heavily.

Example 11: Kohl's, a department store retailer, is ranked as number one in social media presence in terms of conversations and mentions. Kohl's is deploying omnichannel initiatives, including buy online and pick up in-store, and mobile features, such as the ability to pay with a mobile wallet.

(xv) Enterprise Network Technology

Enterprise networks are composed of locally connected devices (e.g., PCs, printers, scanners, routers, and modems) and locally connected sub-LANs using a private IP address space or alternative protocols (e.g., Bluetooth Low Energy). A robust infrastructure with a solid cybersecurity framework is needed that connects all disparate technical domains into a single domain-based integrated system. Enterprise networks are new visionary and integrated approaches connecting traditional networks and edge devices (e.g., PCs, mobile devices, and servers); traditional networks are disparately and loosely connected without integration and edge devices.

(A) Cybersecurity Framework

A foundational step toward the robust infrastructure would be increased enterprise application of the principles contained in the National Institute of Standards and Technology (NIST) Cybersecurity Framework (www.nist.gov) consisting of five concurrent and continuous functions of identify, protect, detect, respond, and recover:

1. **Identify.** Enterprises locate legacy devices (e.g., mainframe computer devices, such as workstations and servers, and PC devices, such as printers and scanners) and other devices that cannot be secured. Enterprises remove these high-risk devices from service wherever possible and replace them with devices that are inherently secure or can be secured.

2. **Protect.** The system architecture provides additional layers of protection to any remaining high-risk devices (e.g., access to legacy devices would be restricted by network architecture). Enterprises deploy or procure on-premise and off-premise DDoS mitigation services. Enterprises' network architectures limit exposure of devices to malicious actors and limit damage from compromised devices. Ingress and egress filtering are implemented to prevent network address spoofing, and attack amplifiers (e.g., open resolvers) are reconfigured. Efficient update processes minimize the window of vulnerability for all devices on the network. Multitenant infrastructures (i.e., multiple vendors and multiple subscribers) also enforce ingress and egress filtering to reduce the impact of cloud-based botnets.

3. **Detect.** A combination of Internet service provider-based (ISP-based) detection services and enterprise-operated network and service monitoring activities can detect outbound malicious traffic and inbound attacks and can identify compromised devices in near real time.

4. **Respond.** Enterprises have policies and procedures to address compromised devices (e.g., replace, mitigate, or patch a device participating in a botnet) when detected by the enterprise or ISP. Enterprises also have processes in place to contact their ISP(s) or other anti-DDoS service providers when attacks are detected locally. Key operational resources continue to operate with constrained resources.

5. **Recover.** Enterprises have the ability to reconstitute compromised systems (e.g., from backup) rather than make ransomware payments to resume operations.

(B) Edge Devices Technology

Edge devices include PCs, mobile devices, servers, IoT devices, NoT devices, LoT devices, and other connected devices, which are the heavy targets for hackers to attack and require the greatest protection. Broad advances in the edge device technical domain are both possible and essential to build a more resilient Internet and communications ecosystem. To be effective, these advances must be global, since the majority of Internet devices are located outside the United States. This global action will require globally accepted security standards and practices to be robust, widely understood, and applied ubiquitously. Those standards should be flexible, appropriately timed, open, voluntary, and industry-driven.

Devices must be able to resist attacks throughout their deployment life cycles—at the time of shipment, during use, and through to end of life. For this to occur, security must become a primary design requirement. Vendors must not ship devices with known serious security flaws, must include a secure update mechanism, and must follow best current practices (e.g., no hard-coded passwords, disabling software features that are not critical to operation) for system configuration and administration. Vendors should disclose the minimum duration of support to customers, and device manufacturers should maintain secure update services for the promised duration.

Hardware roots of trust and trusted execution technologies are now a component of many off-the-shelf computing platforms to provide trustworthiness to customers. Future products will need to leverage these technologies to demonstrate authenticity and integrity at initial deployment and throughout the period of use. Modern software and hardware development techniques rely on a combination of open-source and commercially available components. To meet future security demands, such components must be traceable through the supply chain and offer greater assurance of trust.

Such technological advances will require significant steps in awareness and education for product developers. All product developers must be equipped with the knowledge and skills required to apply the available tools for secure product development. The tool kits and components used by these vendors must reflect security concerns to achieve scale and keep pace with a changing developer workforce, and the partnerships and consortia driving standardized technology must empower developers to make and communicate security decisions. Meanwhile, operational-technology product developers must add basic security requirements to their product-specific knowledge and skills. At the same time, customers must be equipped with sufficient knowledge and information to select products designed to be secure in their environments, and they must be aware of the risks presented by all devices, including legacy devices.

Last, market incentives will need to align with these security advances, so that product developers who prioritize security and resilience equally with time to market and innovative functionality are rewarded. Clear signals regarding product security and resilience that are accessible to customers will help improve these incentives. However, the value proposition for better security will likely start in the enterprise environment due to its economies of scale; once there is a generally accepted security posture in a given product class, few manufacturers would be likely to ignore it.

(xvi) Retail Technologies

The retail industry as a whole is investing huge sums of money in emerging technologies to acquire new customers, to keep current customers, and to prevent customer defection as it deals with millions of customers. The scope of retail technologies can include POS, RFID, store (e.g., beacon technology), drone, interactive, visual search, kiosks and vending machines, loss prevention, and charge card technology.

(A) Point-of-Sale Technology

Today's POS technology is electronic and sophisticated compared to old, mechanical, and unsophisticated cash registers. The POS system is a mature technology and is the heart of a retail store. Simply presented, POS systems collect customer purchases by SKU, match the SKU with the pricing system to charge the right price, process customer payments, and produce a purchase receipt for customers. Behind the scenes, the POS system subtracts the SKUs sold from the SKUs on hand, resulting in the end balance of SKUs.

The POS system is electronically connected to several systems, such as an RFID system to pick up the SKU number from a product's label, the pricing system to pull a product's price, the inventory system to subtract the sold product, and the merchandising system to place a new order for the product sold.

Several variations of POS systems exist, including: (1) mainframe POS, where a physical store's cashier at the checkout station works with the POS system residing on a retailer's mainframe computers; (2) mobile POS, where customers with mobile devices can place a product order from anywhere and at any time; and (3) wearable POS, where a customer with a wearable device (watch-like device) can place a product order. The real challenge for a retailer is to coordinate and integrate all these variations of POS systems using technology to provide a comprehensive view of all customer orders with a unified POS system. In other words, the unified POS system provides a flexible connectivity solution between the various types of POSs that it integrates, the business application systems it uses, and the types of hardware devices it operates, such as terminals, scanners, and scales.

(B) Radio Frequency Identification Technology

The scope of RFID technology includes chips, sensors, and tags. RFID technology is a mature technology going through constant changes and improvements. The POS technology is electronically and directly connected and integrated with the RFID technology.

The RFID chip is a paper tag attached to products, such as clothes, shoes, bags, cans, bottles, packages, and boxes, sold in a store. These RFID chips do not use batteries or electricity to operate; instead, they use sensors with light beams. These chips contain information about a product, say, a shoe's size, color, price, materials, weight, and maker.

An RFID reader reads the SKU number in the Universal Product Code (UPC) on the RFID tag and displays product-related information. The UPC contains more information than traditional bar code.

RFID Tag $\longrightarrow$ RFID Reader $\longrightarrow$ Product-Related Information
(e.g., size, color, price, and weight)

All products in a store are tagged at the source by a manufacturer, wholesaler, supplier, distributor, vendor, or assembler, called source tagging. The tags are not made in a retailer's store, warehouse, or distribution center. The tag stays with a product or an item and travels from its origination point to its destination point (i.e., origin to destination). The tags should be designed around low-level, item-based, and SKU-based criteria because the tags provide needed, detailed, and useful information, and RFID is better than other high-level criteria, such as brand level, category level, or subcategory level.

Problems before RFID. There were several problems in physical stores prior to the implementation of the RFID technology, as follows.

- Inventory shortages occurred frequently due to improper and incorrect tracking of merchandise movement in and out of a store; clerical and procedural errors (human errors); and incorrect and untimely updates to computer-based inventory system (system errors).

- Accuracy of inventory was questionable due to counting it at a high level and category level.

- Inventory visibility and inventory availability could not be guaranteed due to lack of integration of inventory at a physical store, online store, warehouse, or distribution centers. This means that an omnichannel access strategy was not in place. Invisible inventory is unsellable inventory, resulting in lost sales revenues, margins, and profits.

- Customers did not have a seamless, stress-free, and hassle-free shopping experience because an omnichannel strategy was not implemented, thus making customers unhappy and dissatisfied.

- Use of the traditional bar code system, which increases store employees' time and labor costs, slowed down inventory counts in stores.

Solutions after RFID. The RFID technology provides several solutions and benefits to retailers. Some solutions and benefits follow.

- It is an inventory management tool in terms of locating out-of-place merchandise and replenishing out-of-stock merchandise in a store. It reduces human and system errors in managing the inventory.

- It improves customers' shopping experience by providing valuable information about a product (e.g., size, color, and cost) and product availability.

- The omnichannel strategy provides a seamless, stress-free, and hassle-free shopping experience to a store's customers, making them happy and satisfied.

- It is very useful in tracing and investigating a product's recall from source to store; watching for a product's expiration dates; and monitoring the performance of a supplier in the supply chain. This is possible due to item level–based source tagging.

- It tracks product returns by manufacturer, store, brand, supplier, and customer.

- It speeds up cycle counting of inventory in a store, thus saving store employees' time and costs.

- In the aggregate, it increases sales revenues, margins, and profits of a physical store.

   Example 1: Target, a major retailer, is working with its key vendors to insert "smart labels" on the RFID price tags that help the company to enhance the accuracy of inventory and to ensure product availability.

   Example 2: Zara, a fashion clothing retailer, is gaining greater insight into its store's inventory status through RFID technology. It knows exactly where each garment is located in a store, which increases inventory accuracy and sales. Consequently, store employees' manual efforts and costs in handling inventory-related problems and issues were reduced.

   Example 3: Macy's is leveraging the RFID technology with the idea of picking to the last unit as a part of its omnichannel fulfillment strategy. This idea yielded several benefits to Macy's, including increased accuracy of inventory, increased order fill rates, reduced need for frequent markdowns, and above all increased sales. Macy's is achieving its goal of "buy anywhere, fulfill anywhere" model, which is a game-changer strategy for the retailer.

RFID Risks. For RFID implementations to be successful, organizations should effectively manage four types of risks:

1. **Business process risk** includes:
   a. Failure of part or all of the RFID system leading to loss of critical business or operational records
   b. Human actions (e.g., either benign or malicious)
   c. Location of RFID technology
   d. Lack of robustness of business continuity planning
   e. Cloning of tags and attacks on enterprise subsystem networks

2. **Business intelligence risk** involves threats and vulnerabilities that could permit unauthorized parties to gain access to sensitive or proprietary information. A competitor or adversary can gain information from the RFID system in a number of ways, including eavesdropping on RFID transactions, reading tags, and gaining access to RFID-related databases. The risk of unauthorized access is realized when the entity engaging in the unauthorized behavior does something harmful with that information. In some cases, the information may trigger an immediate response, such as breaking into a container holding valuable goods. In other cases, data may also be aggregated over time to provide intelligence related to an organization's customers, operations, business strategy, or proprietary methods.

3. **Privacy risk** results from a compromised RFID system when the system uses a personal information for a purpose other than originally intended or if a third party uses the presence of tagged items to profile individuals. In the latter case, the primary privacy

risk is likely borne by the consumer, not the organization that implemented the RFID system. Nevertheless, the RFID-implementing organization still has privacy-related risks, including penalties from noncompliance with existing privacy regulations, legal liability, and the reaction of consumers, employees, public interest groups, and other stakeholders.

4. **External risk** for an enterprise subsystem includes successful attacks on networked hosts and critical applications. Computer network attacks can involve malware or attack tools that exploit software vulnerabilities and configuration weaknesses to gain access to systems, perform a DoS, or cause other damages. The impact of computer network attacks can range from performance degradation to complete compromise of a mission-critical application.

Because external risk by definition involves risks outside of the RFID system, it is distinct from both business process and business intelligence risks; external risks can be realized without having any effect on RFID-supported business processes or without revealing any information to adversaries. Two examples of external risks include hazards of electromagnetic radiation and computer network attacks.

RFID Attacks and Security Controls. Exhibit 2.8 presents several attacks or threats on RFID systems and associated security controls to mitigate such attacks or threats.

EXHIBIT 2.8 Attacks or Threats on RFID Systems and Associated Security Controls to Mitigate Them

Attacks or Threats	Security Controls
Rogue scanning of and eavesdropping on tags	Implement mandatory cover-coding technique to obscure certain transmissions from readers to tags. Encrypt the data-in-transit over-the-air. Install electromagnetic shielding material to limit rogue scanning of and eavesdropping on tags.
Spoofing, jamming, and skimming of readers	Install antispoofing countermeasures, such as digital signatures, to prevent the unauthorized use of legitimate authenticated data. Install antijamming countermeasures to ensure that transmitted information can be received despite deliberate jamming attempts. Install antiskimming material using electromagnetic shields.
Dictionary attacks on readers	Install strong, unique administrative passwords to perform reader authentication.
Improper authentication of tags	Use digital signatures to provide evidence of the authenticity of a tag and chain of custody events. Install strong, unique passwords to access tags.
Propagation of radio-frequency signals through radio interferences and radiation emissions	Use mandatory cover-coding techniques to obscure the content of messages from readers to tags. Encrypt data prior to its transmission, data in transit, and data at rest. Install electromagnetic shielding material to limit rogue scanning of and eavesdropping on tags. Keep readers and tags away from other radios.

Attacks or Threats	Security Controls
Traffic analysis	Implement traffic-flow protection methods by encrypting source and destination addresses with link encryption.
Modifying, damaging, and stealing of RFID system components	Install physical access controls, such as a panel or walls of grounded wire fences between radio-frequency sources or partitioned stalls to prevent unauthorized radio communications, interferences, and commands.

(C) Beacon Technology

Beacons are electronic sensors equipped with Bluetooth signals and are installed in a retailer's physical stores at the entrance doors. Sensors are small plastic transmitters that are mounted on store walls near the entrance. Beacons know who is walking into the store based on their smartphone number because they connect customers' names to their phone numbers.

Beacons send push alerts and notifications to customers' mobile devices about upcoming sales, promotions, price discount, coupons, rebates, and rewards, and special deals to make a purchase at future date or immediate use. Beacons also deliver recipes for customers who choose to opt in to the program.

Personalized marketing is possible with beacon technology using a Wi-Fi connection combined with location-based (proximity-based) marketing; it is also called targeted marketing. Beacon technology is most applicable to a consumer-packaged goods retailer selling goods such as wine and spirits, dry or frozen food, snacks, soft drinks, condiments, soups, soaps, shampoos, over-the-counter medications, and deli food items.

Example 1: Walgreens, a pharmacy retailer, has launched beacon technology to track shoppers inside stores and send digital incentives (coupons and rewards) to their smartphones. This is an example of personalized marketing.

Example 2: Barneys New York, a fashion retailer, is introducing a new personalization platform to offer shoppers a unique in-store digital experience. This includes using beacon technology and a cloud personalization platform, all to connect online and offline purchase preferences and to help sales associates better service clients using a mobile app. This is an example of personalized marketing.

Example 3: Apple, Inc., has launched beacon technology in all of its stores to provide personalized services to its customers.

Example 4: Kenneth Cole, a clothing retailer, and Oscar Mayer, a producer of packaged lunch meats sold in grocery stores, are reported to be successfully using the personalized marketing approach with beacon technology.

(D) Drone Technology

Drone technology is an example of an emerging technology. As a part of improving customer service and satisfaction, all retailers face a major challenge of delivering product orders to customers in a timely manner because there is a physical distance between customers and retailers. Proactive retailers then turned to flying drone technology, a form of mini aircrafts, for faster delivery services.

Example 1: Amazon is testing drones for delivering packages to customers' homes.

Example 2: Walmart is testing drones for delivering to customers' homes in small residential neighborhoods; grocery pickup services for customer orders; stock deliveries between Walmart stores, distribution centers, and fulfillment centers; and security protection over warehouses and stores from theft, robbery, and vandalism.

Example 3: Retailers such as Domino's pizza and Flower Delivery Express are testing drones for a faster delivery of orders to their customers.

(E) Interactive Technology
Progressive retailers are implementing interactive technologies in several ways to provide in-store shopping experiences.

- Some retailers have designed interactive tables with large touchscreens that allow customers to browse and locate inventory, whether it is located inside a store or outside the store.
- Some retailers have implemented interactive fitting rooms with mirrors to provide an immersive shopping experience so customers can try out the products of their choice.
- Some retailers launched interactive digital displays to give product information when a customer approaches a product or before picking up a product.

Example 1: Neiman Marcus, a high-end retailer, launched interactive tables for customers to add a product to a wish list after browsing, which is then emailed for later purchase.

Example 2: Ralph Lauren, a clothing retailer, added interactive fitting rooms with mirrors that are embedded with RFID chips. The mirror shows the selected products, displays additional colors and sizes, and makes recommendations. Customers can check out the products via mobile devices directly from the fitting room.

(F) Visual Search Technology
Visual search technology is an emerging technology that allows customers to use their smartphones to take a picture of a store's product, then search and find the same product or a similar one in a retailer's entire merchandise stock regardless of its location, whether offline or online. A retailer needs to implement an omnichannel access strategy to locate the merchandise stock. The technology behind the visual search is image recognition technology. The goal of retailers that use visual search technology is to turn browsers into buyers.

Example 1: Amazon is adding the visual search technology into its mobile app with scan-to-buy feature so customers with Apple phones can scan the UPC on a product's label, which is then added to their shopping cart for later purchase from Amazon. Google's app has the same kind of feature as Amazon's app.

Example 2: Target and Wayfair are using the visual search technology to convert pages of a catalog or magazine into shoppable content.

Example 3: Macy's is using the visual search technology to link printed content or online content to a customer's smartphone.

Example 4: Retailers such as Neiman Marcus and JC Penney are implementing visual search technology.

(G) Kiosks and Vending Machines Technology
A **kiosk** is a small or large box with a free-standing physical structure installed in a retailer's store, shopping malls, airports, or other public places to sell merchandise directly to customers. Kiosks are self-service equipment. A **vending machine** is self-service equipment, similar to

a kiosk, filled with soft drinks, snacks, gift cards, beauty supplies, or branded products for a quick purchase.

Example 1: Celiairis, a shopping mall kiosk company, is very successful in selling accessories such as chargers, batteries, and decorative cases for wireless devices in shopping malls.

Example 2: Samsung is partnering with Best Buy to open store-in-store boutique kiosks with their own payment and checkout systems. Similarly, Samsung is opening kiosks for its smartphones. These partnerships are called experience shops.

Example 3: Rite Aid, a drugstore chain retailer, is installing glasses-free 3D videos in the chain's new loyalty program kiosks. The kiosks, which project holographic 3D images in front of the kiosk touchscreens, provide wellness information, promotions, rewards, coupons, and product samples to customers.

Example 4: Eddie Bauer, an outdoor retailer, is opening pop-up stores with smart vending machines. These smart machines will dispense the brand's products, gift cards, and discount promotions to customers.

(H) Loss Prevention Technology

A major purpose of a retail store's loss prevention function is to protect assets (i.e., physical buildings, merchandise, equipment, and cash) and to keep people (i.e., employees, customers, and others) safe and secure at all times. For this to happen, a loss prevention function in a store must be a core function, not simply a support function, to highlight its significance to overall store operations. The loss prevention function, once considered a low-tech operation where security staff members walk around the store and watch over cameras all day long, is now a high-tech operation with many store technologies integrated and connected together to provide a real-time picture of store events taking place.

Today's loss prevention technology integrates video technology with store technology. This store technology, in turn, consists of several diverse technologies, such as traffic counting system, POS system, RFID system, and beacon system.

- The video technology can show the number of post-voids, no-sales transactions and cash given to customers for product returns in the physical absence of customers.

- The store traffic counting system consists of traffic sensors providing customers' foot traffic into and out of a store.

- The POS system shows all sales transaction, voided transactions, and overrides at the cash register with time and day.

- With its readers and tags, the RFID system presents product movement from store shelves to cash registers.

- The beacon system (also called a proximity-based or location-sensing system) sends push alerts and notifications of sale events and coupons to mobile customers based on their specific location in a store. For example, it shows lunch meat coupons when a customer is looking at or around a lunch meat section. In summary, loss prevention technology helps loss prevention staff members to watch customer foot traffic, to trace fraudulent activities by employees and customers during suspected fraud transactions, and to prevent shoplifting, all to protect a retailer's physical, financial, and human assets from loss, damage, or harm.

Example: A retail store's RFID reader showed a price of $100 for a jacket scanned from its tag at a cashier's check-out station. However, the POS transaction log showed the same jacket was sold as a T-shirt at a price of $10. This implies a fraudulent attempt on a cashier's part to do favors to family or friends or simply human error. A system override or intervention must have taken place for this to occur, requiring a loss prevention staff member's investigation.

(I) Charge Card Technology

American consumers and retailers have long used charge cards (credit cards and debit cards) that are designed with magnetic stripe technology, which is subject to data breaches by hackers and fraud by phony customers and employees. Currently debit cards require a PIN and a signature during payments to a retailer. Unfortunately, the signatures are not secure and are subject to hacking; the PIN is secure and not subject to hacking.

After a series of data breaches, retailers started to implement a new technology, such as the Europay MasterCard Visa (EMV) chip cards (smart cards), to prevent data breaches. Banks required all retailers to switch from using the magnetic-stripe cards to EMV cards for improved security for both credit cards and debit cards. EMV cards are of two types: chip and PIN and chip and signature.

Chip-and-PIN EMV cards that require a PIN to submit because the PIN is encrypted and is difficult for hackers to break into. These cards have a built-in and superior security defenses against fraud and data breaches. The old magnetic-stripe cards did not have such built-in security features due to lack of a chip. Retailers complained that EMV cards with the chip and signature is not as secure as the EMV card with a chip and PIN because signatures can be forged. Retailers want all the EMV cards to contain chip and PIN only. The required switch is shown next.

Magnetic-Stripe Cards ⟶ EMV Chip Cards

Chip-and-Signature Cards ⟶ Less Secure

Chip-and-PIN Cards ⟶ More Secure

Example 1: Prior to implementation of the EMV chip cards, major retailers were hacked due to poor security controls. (e.g., a major data breach at Target Corporation).

Example 2: After several hacking incidents, large-size retailers have switched to implement the EMV chip cards for a better security protection for their customers.

Example 3: Small-size retailers have objected to switching to EMV chip card due to the cost required to replace the magnetic-stripe terminals with EMV terminals. Costs include hardware and software, installation, employee training, customer-notification, and disruption costs (lost sales) due to installation time. If the terminals are not switched, costs related to fraud and data breaches can increase.

2.6 Cybersecurity Risks, Controls, and Policies

This section first presents a cybersecurity framework and a cyberattack life cycle model, including strategies of attackers and defenders. Next, it discusses cybersecurity risks in terms of threats, exploits, vulnerabilities, and attacks primarily against organizations in cyberspace (i.e., the Internet, wired and wireless networks, connected devices, cloud systems, and business computer systems). Topics such as cyber-resiliency techniques and digital forensics are highlighted, including cyber defenses. This section then presents cybersecurity and information systems policies required to mitigate cyber risks. The need for risk management concepts applied to cybersecurity is explored, including cybersecurity metrics and audits. Best practices in cybersecurity controls and mitigations are presented.

(a) Cybersecurity Framework

NIST developed a cybersecurity framework that is critical for industries vital to national and economic security in that the framework should be used as a first line of defense by every organization to manage and control its cyber risks.[4]

The framework defines two major items: five core functions (identify, protect, detect, respond, and recover) that should be performed concurrently and continuously to form an operational culture that addresses the dynamic nature of cybersecurity risks; (2) four implementation tiers (partial, risk informed, repeatable, and adaptive), which provide the context on how an organization views cybersecurity risk and the processes in place to manage that risk. In addition, the cybersecurity framework serves as the first line of defense against potential threats, vulnerabilities, and attacks facing an organization. The five core functions are shown next.

$$\text{Identify} \longrightarrow \text{Protect} \longrightarrow \text{Detect} \longrightarrow \text{Respond} \longrightarrow \text{Recover}$$

(i) Framework Core Functions
The five core functions are not intended to form a serial path or lead to a static desired end state but rather to a dynamic desired end state.

> **Core Function 1—Identify.** Identify requires developing an organizational understanding to manage cybersecurity risk to systems, people, assets, data, and capabilities. The activities in this function are foundational for effective use of the framework. Outcomes include asset management, business environment, governance, risk assessment, and risk management strategy.

> **Core Function 2—Protect.** Protect requires developing and implementing appropriate safeguards to ensure delivery of critical services. This function supports the ability to limit or contain the impact of a potential cybersecurity event. Outcomes include identity management and access control, awareness and training, data security, information protection processes and procedures, maintenance, and protective technology.

> **Core Function 3—Detect.** Detect requires developing and implementing appropriate activities to identify the occurrence of a cybersecurity event. This function enables timely discovery of cybersecurity events. Outcomes include anomalies and events, security continuous monitoring, and detection processes.

> **Core Function 4—Respond.** Respond requires developing and implementing appropriate activities to take action regarding a detected cybersecurity incident. This function supports the ability to contain the impact of a potential cybersecurity incident. Outcomes include response planning, communications, analysis, mitigation, and improvements.

---

[4] National Institute of Standards and Technology, *Framework for Improving Critical Infrastructure Cybersecurity*, Version 1.1, 2018, www.nist.gov.

Core Function 5—Recover. Recover requires developing and implementing appropriate activities to maintain plans for resilience and to restore any capabilities or services that were impaired due to a cybersecurity incident. The recovery function supports timely recovery to normal operations to reduce the impact from a cybersecurity incident. Outcomes include recovery planning, recovery improvements, and recovery communications.

(ii) Framework Implementation Tiers

The framework implementation tiers provide context on how an organization views cybersecurity risk and the processes in place to manage that risk. Ranging from partial (Tier 1) to adaptive (Tier 4), tiers describe an increasing degree of rigor and sophistication in cybersecurity risk management practices. They help determine the extent to which cybersecurity risk management is informed by business needs and is integrated into an organization's overall risk management practices. Risk management considerations include many aspects of cybersecurity, including the degree to which privacy and civil liberties considerations are integrated into an organization's management of cybersecurity risk and potential risk responses.

The tier selection process considers an organization's current risk management practices, threat environment, legal and regulatory requirements, information sharing practices, business/mission objectives, supply-chain cybersecurity requirements, and organizational constraints. Organizations should determine the desired tier, ensuring that the selected level meets the organizational goals, is feasible to implement, and reduces cybersecurity risk to critical assets and resources to levels acceptable to the organization.

While organizations identified as Tier 1 (partial) are encouraged to consider moving toward Tier 2 or greater, tiers do not represent maturity levels. Tiers are meant to support organizational decision making about how to manage cybersecurity risk as well as which dimensions of the organization are higher priority and could receive additional resources. Progression to higher tiers is encouraged when a cost-benefit analysis indicates a feasible and cost-effective reduction of cybersecurity risk. The four implementation tiers are shown next.

Partial → Risk Informed → Repeatable → Adaptive

For each tier, three elements—risk management process, integrated risk management program, and external participation—are presented. The four tier definitions are as follows.

Tier 1: Partial

Risk Management Process: Organizational cybersecurity risk management practices are not formalized, and risk is managed in an ad hoc and sometimes reactive manner. Prioritization of cybersecurity activities may not be directly informed by organizational risk objectives, the threat environment, or business/mission requirements.

Integrated Risk Management Program: There is limited awareness of cybersecurity risk at the organizational level. The organization implements cybersecurity risk management on an irregular, case-by-case basis due to varied experience or information gained from outside sources. The organization may not have processes that enable cybersecurity information to be shared within the organization.

External Participation: The organization does not understand its role in the larger ecosystem with respect to either its dependencies or its dependents. The organization does not collaborate with or receive information (e.g., threat intelligence, best practices, technologies) from other entities (e.g., buyers, suppliers, dependencies, dependents, information security officers, researchers, governments), nor does it share information. The organization is generally unaware of cyber supply chain risks of the products and services that it provides and uses.

Tier 2: Risk Informed

Risk Management Process: Risk management practices are approved by management but may not be established as organization-wide policy. Prioritization of cybersecurity activities and protection needs is directly informed by organizational risk objectives, the threat environment, or business/mission requirements.

Integrated Risk Management Program: There is an awareness of cybersecurity risk at the organizational level, but an organization-wide approach to managing cybersecurity risk has not been established. Cybersecurity information is shared within the organization on an informal basis. Consideration of cybersecurity in organizational objectives and programs may occur at some but not all levels of the organization. Cyber risk assessment of organizational and external assets occurs but is not typically repeatable or recurring.

External Participation: Generally, the organization understands its role in the larger ecosystem with respect to its own dependencies or those of its dependents, but not both. The organization collaborates with and receives some information from other entities and generates some of its own information but may not share information with others. Additionally, the organization is aware of the cyber supply chain risks associated with the products and services it provides and uses but does not act consistently or formally on those risks.

Tier 3: Repeatable

Risk Management Process: The organization's risk management practices are formally approved and expressed as policy. Organizational cybersecurity practices are regularly updated based on the application of risk management processes to changes in business/ mission requirements and a changing threat and technology landscape.

Integrated Risk Management Program: There is an organization-wide approach to managing cybersecurity risk. Risk-informed policies, processes, and procedures are defined, implemented as intended, and reviewed. Consistent methods are in place to respond effectively to changes in risk. Personnel possess the knowledge and skills to perform their appointed roles and responsibilities. The organization consistently and accurately monitors cybersecurity risk of organizational assets. Senior cybersecurity and non-cybersecurity executives communicate regularly regarding cybersecurity risk. Senior executives ensure consideration of cybersecurity through all lines of operation in the organization.

External Participation: The organization understands its role, dependencies, and dependents in the larger ecosystem and may contribute to the community's broader understanding of risks. It collaborates with and receives information from other entities regularly that complements internally generated information, and shares information with other entities. The organization is aware of the cyber supply chain risks associated with the products and services it provides and uses. Additionally, it usually acts formally on those risks, including mechanisms such as written agreements to communicate baseline requirements, governance structures (e.g., risk councils), and policy implementation and monitoring.

Tier 4: Adaptive

Risk Management Process: The organization adapts its cybersecurity practices based on previous and current cybersecurity activities, including lessons learned and predictive indicators. Through a process of continuous improvement incorporating advanced cybersecurity technologies and practices, the organization actively adapts to a changing threat and technology landscape and responds in a timely and effective manner to evolving, sophisticated threats.

Integrated Risk Management Program: There is an organization-wide approach to managing cybersecurity risk that uses risk-informed policies, processes, and procedures to address potential cybersecurity events. The relationship between cybersecurity risk and organizational objectives is clearly understood and considered when making decisions. Senior executives monitor cybersecurity risk in the same way as financial risk and other organizational risks. The organizational budget is based on an understanding of the current and predicted risk environment and risk tolerance. Business units implement executive vision and analyze system-level risks in the context of the organizational risk tolerances. Cybersecurity risk management is part of the organizational culture and evolves from an awareness of previous activities and continuous awareness of activities on their systems and networks. The organization can quickly and efficiently account for changes to business/mission objectives in how risk is approached and communicated.

External Participation: The organization understands its role, dependencies, and dependents in the larger ecosystem and contributes to the community's broader understanding of risks. It receives, generates, and reviews prioritized information that informs continuous analysis of its risks as threat and technology landscapes evolve. The organization shares that information internally and externally with other collaborators. The organization uses real-time or near-real-time information to understand and consistently act on cyber supply chain risks associated with the products and services it provides and uses. Additionally, it communicates proactively, using formal (e.g., agreements) and informal mechanisms to develop and maintain strong supply chain relationships.

(b) Cyberattack Life Cycle Model

There are at least two major parties involved in cyberspace and cybercrime: offenders (hackers and attackers) and defenders (attack-victim user organizations). Offenders target defenders to exploit or take advantage of a security weakness for personal and financial gain. Attackers are known as adversaries, hackers, and intruders; defenders are potential victim individuals, organizations, corporations, or institutions in the public or the private sector. A third-party such as law enforcement authorities (i.e., incident analysts, digital forensic specialists, and recovery analysts) can be involved when their help is requested to participate in an after-the-fact analysis. Although it is not feasible to fully predict an attacker's behavior, a cyberattack life cycle model can provide a simple and useful basis for analyzing potential threats.

The interaction between offenders and defenders is shown next.

- Offenders are hackers and attackers who are aggressors.
- Defenders are attack-victim individuals or organizations who are reactors.

- Offenders exploit defenders.
- Defenders protect from offenders.

(i) Attackers' Life Cycle Phases

According to the Lockheed Martin Corporation's Cyber Kill Chain Framework, there are seven phases in the attack life cycle: reconnaissance, weaponize, deliver, exploit, install, command and control, and act on objectives.[5] The first three phases—reconnaissance, weaponize, and deliver—are proactive so that protective and detective measures (e.g., honeypots and decoys) can be taken. The install, command and control, and act on objectives phases are reactive so that response and recovery measures (e.g., intrusion detection software, firewalls, and antivirus software) can be taken. The exploit phase between proactive and reactive measures separates these from the proactive and reactive phases.

Each phase in this life cycle is an opportunity for a defender to take actions against an attacker. By using this life cycle, in concert with both internal and external threat intelligence, defenders can craft proactive incident response strategies that focus on disrupting an attacker earlier in the life cycle, even before an exploit has occurred. These seven phases can enhance visibility into an attack and enrich a defender's understanding of an attacker's tools, techniques, tactics, and procedures (i.e., an attacker's tool kit).

Phase 1—Reconnaissance means an attacker identifies and selects a target organization (victim) to attack based on research, visiting websites, harvesting email addresses, attending conferences, and social relationships. *Countermeasures* for defenders in this phase include web analytics to detect and firewall-based ACLs (firewall ACLs) to deny.

Phase 2—Weaponize means an attacker packages an exploit into a payload designed to execute on the targeted computer network. It also means coupling exploit with a backdoor into a deliverable payload. *Countermeasures* for defenders in this phase include network-based intrusion detection systems (NIDS) to detect and network-based intrusion prevention system (NIPS) to deny.

Phase 3—Deliver means an attacker delivers the payload to the target system(s). It also means delivering a weaponized bundle to the victim via email, web, and USB. *Countermeasures* for defenders in this phase include vigilant users, proxy filters, in-line antivirus software, and email queuing.

Phase 4—Exploit means an attacker's code is executed on the target system(s). It also means exploiting a vulnerability to execute code on the victim's system. Defenders should develop proactive incident response strategies that focus on disrupting an attacker earlier in the life cycle, that is, before an exploit has occurred. *Countermeasures* for defenders in this phase include host intrusion detection system (HIDS), vendor patches, and data execution prevention (DEP). HIDS can passively detect exploits, patching can deny exploitation, and DEP can disrupt the exploit once it initiates.

Phase 5—Install means an attacker installs remote access software that provides a persistent presence within the targeted environment or system. It also means installing malware on the asset. *Countermeasures* for defenders in this phase include HIDS, "chroot" directory jail, and antivirus software.

---

[5] Adapted from Lockheed Martin Corporation's Cyber Kill Chain Framework, www.lockheedmartin.com.

Phase 6—Command and control means an attacker employs remote access mechanisms to establish a command and control channel with the compromised device. It also means the command channel is used for remote manipulation of the victim. *Countermeasures* for defenders in this phase include NIDS, firewall ACL, NIPS, URL redirect, and DNS redirect.

Phase 7—Act on objectives means an attacker pursues intended objectives, such as data exfiltration, lateral movement to other targets, or advanced (escalated) movement on the same target. It also means attackers accomplish their original goals using hands-on keyboard access. *Countermeasures* for defenders in this phase include audit logs, quality of service (QoS) throttles, honeypots, and hack-back on the attacker.

(ii) Attackers' Strategies

Attackers' strategies are part of their game plan; attackers have strategies in attacking victim organizations for personal reasons or financial gains. At a minimum, four specific strategies can be identified: attack-in-depth strategy, zero-day attacks, expansion of attack surfaces, and detection evasion tactics.

1. **Attack-in-depth strategy.** Malicious code attackers use this strategy to carry out their goals. Single-point solutions will not stop all of their attacks because a single countermeasure cannot be depended on to mitigate all security issues. In addition, a single-point solution can become a single point of failure (or compromise) that can provide extended access due to preexisting trust established among interconnected resources.

   The attack-in-depth strategy can create advanced persistent threats (APTs) where an adversary that possesses sophisticated levels of technical expertise and significant resources (i.e., money and time) which allow the adversary to create opportunities to achieve its objectives by using multiple attack vectors such as cyber, physical, logical, and social deceptive schemes (e.g., URL obfuscation, DNS and URL redirects, URL shortening, spear phishing (whaling), and killing the features of antivirus software). APTs can be mitigated with agile defenses combined with boundary protection controls. Agile defense employs the concept of information system resilience. Endpoint security controls can also help in protecting from APTs.

   Multiple countermeasures against attack-in-depth strategy include agile defenses, boundary protection controls (e.g., firewalls, routers, and software/hardware guards), defense-in-depth strategy, and defense-in-breadth strategy because they can disseminate risks over an aggregate of security mitigation techniques.

2. **Zero-day attacks.** Be aware of zero-day exploits and zero-day incidents (attacks). Attackers use or share security vulnerabilities to carry out attacks before software vendors fix those vulnerabilities. The term "zero-day exploit" refers to the actual code attackers use. A "zero-day attack (or threat)" is a computer threat that tries to exploit computer application vulnerabilities that are unknown to others, undisclosed to software vendors, or for which no security fix is available. Sophisticated attackers play this timing game on user organizations. Most organizations are helpless against zero-day attacks.

3. **Expansion of attack surfaces.** An **attack surface** is an accessible area where weaknesses or deficiencies in systems (e.g., hardware, software, and firmware components) provide opportunities for attackers to exploit vulnerabilities. As attackers fail in their current attack plans, they do not sit idle; rather, they expand the attack surface by pursuing several actions, such as:

□ Data exfiltration (data stealing and hiding) in the current targeted victim;

□ Advanced or escalated movement on the same targeted victim;

□ Lateral movement to other targeted victims; and

□ Writing new programming code to launch new, strong, and severe attacks.

All these actions can be labeled APTs.

4. **Detection evasion tactics.** Be aware of detection evasion tactics practiced by hackers and attackers where a detection mechanism does not work as intended. This means, hackers try to evade their detection by user organizations. Antivirus software, IDSs, and intrusion prevention systems (IPSs) generally perform detection work by looking for specific patterns in content. If a "known bad" pattern is detected, then the appropriate detective actions can take place to protect the user. Because of the dynamic nature of programming languages, bad actors can use scripting tools, such as JavaScript, VBScript, Cross-Site Scripting, and Cross-Zone Scripting, to evade such prevention and detection mechanisms. This means that hackers can make an organization's prevention and detection mechanisms ineffective by deactivating (killing) them. File-less attacks using macros, scripts, and exploits are examples of evasion detection tactics.

(iii) Defenders' Strategies

Defenders, or attack-victim user organizations, can take several courses actions to defend against attackers' exploits and attacks. Broad actions include:

- **Detect.** Specific actions here include web analytics, NIDS, HIDS, vigilant users, and audit logs.

- **Deny.** Specific actions here include firewall ACL, NIPS, proxy filters, vendor patches, and "chroot jail"

- **Disrupt.** Specific actions here include in-line antivirus software, data execution prevention, anti-spam software, anti-spyware tools, and NIPS.

- **Degrade.** Specific actions here include email queuing and QoS throttles.

- **Deceive.** Specific actions here include honeypots and DNS redirects.

- **Destroy.** Specific actions here include hacking back on the attacker.

The overall goals of a defender are to reduce a hacker's attack surface and to increase an attacker's work factor and to establish a digital defense team to develop digital strategies. Defenders should be aware that some advertised anti-spyware tools can be false, meaning that they themselves introduce spyware instead of detecting or removing it. Also, hackers can deactivate (kill) some or all of the features of anti-malware software to make it useless, which could create a false sense of security for user organizations.

(iv) Defenders' Defensive and Offensive Strategies

Both offenders and defenders can establish their own defensive and offensive strategies to achieve their own goals and objectives. Here, the real question is who should use what strategies—that is, defensive or offensive—and whether the strategy should be a proactive or reactive one. Exhibit 2.9 presents a combination of these strategies from the defenders' viewpoint.

EXHIBIT 2.9 Defenders' Courses of Actions

Actions	Description
Proactive and defensive actions	Deploy protective and detective measures.
	Implement best practices in security controls.
	Deploy defense-in-depth, defense-in-breadth, defense-in-time, defense-in-technology, defense-in-density, and defense-in-intensity strategies.
	Practice silent security mechanisms.
	Employ threat models and collect threat intelligence.
	Develop a cyberattack life cycle model (e.g., Lockheed Martin's Cyber Kill Chain Framework).
	Implement cyber-resiliency techniques.
	Understand hackers' detection evasion tactics.
	Understand hackers' attack-in-depth strategies and their behaviors.
	Reduce hackers' attack surface and increase their work factor.
	Acquire tool kits that attackers use.
	Install honeypot, honeynet, and decoy systems to trap, catch, and fool attackers.
	Install trusted antivirus and anti-spyware tools with updated signatures.
	Develop a strong computer forensic capability with digital forensics.
	Conduct penetration and continuous testing to make computer systems and networks cyber-ready and robust.
	Use web bugs, web beacons, and hop points to trace and find a company's stolen data by attackers (i.e., data exfiltration).
	Use sinkhole routers, servers, and DNSs to help in digital forensic identification by cyber researchers.
	Monitor web analytics and mobile analytics to improve performance.
	Do self-hacking, not hacking back.
	Purchase a cyber insurance policy to cover threats and attacks.
Reactive and defensive actions	Deploy response and recovery measures.
	Install IDS signatures.
	Install file integrity checking software.
	Install rootkit detection.
	Install configuration change monitoring software.
	Perform advanced threat protection acts and conduct threat analysis on demand.
	Train employees to think and act like hackers.
Proactive and offensive actions	Detect anomalies in inbound and outbound network traffic.
	Monitor against a baseline of security actions.
Reactive and offensive actions	Hacking back attackers could be illegal and/or unethical and could result in unintended, negative, and damaging consequences. Hacking back is not advised.

(v) Defenders' Defensive Actions Explained

Defensive cyber actions are security control activities to protect an organization's "crown jewels"—critical assets, such as data, technology, and human assets. Defenders' automated prevention mechanisms must be faster and harder than offenders' automated attack mechanisms. Proactive prevention is the best defense there is. Examples of these defensive actions include:

■ Gather cyber threat intelligence data through lawful monitoring of the infrastructure commonly used by intruders, hackers, and attackers (e.g., hop points) to store exfiltrated data (i.e., stolen data). The scope of intelligence covers intruders' targets, tools, tactics, and procedures.

■ An organization's legal counsel could be placing roadblocks regarding electronic surveillance due to legal uncertainty such as monitoring employees BYOD devices connected to company networks and employees participating in discussions in hacker chatrooms on the dark web. Here, legal counsel could be worried about public perception of a company rather than purely legal concerns.

■ Purchase a cyber insurance policy to protect from cyber threats and attacks such as data breaches, identity theft, Internet fraud, data integrity attacks, bitcoin fraud, and ransomware attacks.

■ Proactively hire an experienced and honest hacker from outside to launch self-attacks on an organization's computer systems and networks (i.e., a form of self-testing and self-hacking). Security weaknesses can be found based on the attack results. Here, the goal is to pick the hacker's brain and see how a hacker thinks and acts. Hackers' perspectives can offer great lessons. An alternative to a hacker is to hire a cybersecurity researcher to do self-testing and self-hacking. Attack-victim organizations is should do a self-hack on their own computer systems and network for self-testing purposes and then fight back or push back at hackers. However, attack-victim organizations should not hack back at attackers; that could lead to unexpected and legal consequences.

■ Train IT and non-IT employees to think and act like hackers, similar to internal auditors who think and act like fraudsters during fraud audits, which is like putting oneself in others' shoes. Conduct training classes to:

  □ Teach how hackers deploy attack-in-depth strategies;

  □ Establish the scope and size of attack surface;

  □ Exhibit the nature and extent of attacker behaviors and motivations;

  □ Practice detection evasion tactics; and

  □ Formulate overall offensive and defensive strategies.

■ Implement silent security mechanisms. Silent security works in the background or behind the scenes to provide seamless and borderless access protection to computer systems, devices, and networks at all times. These mechanisms intervene when something is going wrong or already went wrong from a security standpoint and provide the needed security protection. The term "silent security" does not mean weak security. In fact, it means strong and powerful security controls without much noise, secrecy, and publicity.

■ Practice sinkholing a DNS, which is re-registering domain names used for malware command and control servers, which is common and effective. Also, practice sinkholing a router as a part of forensic identification, which mitigates extraneous and dangerous network traffic. For example, law enforcement officers can take down an infected server from further damage by hackers and put it in a shadow and safe place, called sinkholing. These sinkholed servers are called shadow servers for law enforcement officers and cybersecurity research purposes.

Infected Server $\longrightarrow$ Sinkholed $\longrightarrow$ Shadow Server

- Use web bugs or web beacons and get assistance from ISPs to find data stolen from the organization by intruders.

- Although some organizations want to hack back against attackers, legal counsel may advise them not to do so due to unintended consequences of hack-back actions. Penetration testing is better and safer because it involves self-hacking into an organization's own computer networks and systems to find out strengths and weaknesses of security controls that can defend against attacks. Later, weaknesses can be fixed to become strengths.

- Establish a computer forensic capability with a digital forensic methodology to provide digital evidence to handle cybercrime legal cases. Be aware of antiforensic capabilities where some people (e.g., police or lawyers) try to suppress digital forensic evidence in order to protect themselves and their clients.

- Deploy countermeasures to crush attackers' attack-in-depth strategies or zero-day attacks against organizations. The attack-in-depth strategy can create APTs, where adversaries with expertise and resources create opportunities by using multiple attack vectors, such as cyber, physical, logical, and social deceptive schemes. For example, attackers can use URL obfuscation (i.e., hyperlink trick) as a part of their attack-in-depth strategy.

- Mitigate APTs with agile defenses combined with boundary protection controls. Agile defense employs the concept of information system resilience. Multiple countermeasures against attack-in-depth strategies include endpoint security controls, agile defenses, boundary protection controls (e.g., firewalls, routers, and software/hardware guards), defense-in-depth strategy, and defense-in-breadth strategy because they can disseminate risks over an aggregate of security mitigation techniques.

- Reduce hackers' attack surface, which is the total amount of free cyberspace attackers occupy when conducting attacks. The attack surface is an attacker's landscape and workspace to launch attacks. Hackers must have drawn a blueprint of the total attack surface divided into geographic areas (e.g., local, regional, domestic, or global), industries (e.g., public sector, private sector, healthcare, entertainment, energy, and military), countries (e.g., North America, South America, etc.), and technology platforms (e.g., social media, cloud services, mobile devices, servers, host computers, networks, and websites). This well-defined attack surface provides a greater number of permutations and combinations of attack lists from which to launch attacks. Practices such as network segmentation, hardening tools, hardware segmentation, application system portioning, and managing access to privileged accounts can reduce the attack surface.

- Understand attackers' destructive behavior and motivation. Management of an organization that has suffered a cyberattack must understand a great deal about the attackers, including whether they are insiders (e.g., employees and contractors) or outsiders (e.g., hackers and intruders). Management needs to understand the attackers' ambition, disruptive behavior, opportunities, and resources. In other words, organizations need to ask what critical assets attackers want that they have and how they can protect those assets from attacks.

- Increase hackers' work factor. The amount of work, cost, and effort necessary for hackers to break into computer systems and networks should exceed the value and the benefits that hackers would gain or receive from successful attacks. Defenders' primary goal is to make offenders fail in all of their efforts and actions. Defenders' specific actions to increase hackers' work factor include:

☐ Degrading or disrupting hackers' ability to exfiltrate sensitive information.

☐ Increasing the overall costs to attack, operate, and sponsor attacks. For example, data breach costs to hackers should exceed the benefits to hackers from such data breach.

☐ Sending hackers back to the drawing board to write new programming code for a new attack because the current code did not work. Writing new code takes time.

☐ Seeding uncertainty and a fear in the minds of hackers that law enforcement authorities are watching their attack movements.

☐ Deploying multifactor authentication factors to identify and authenticate system users and end users when they are trying to access a computer system, network, or mobile device, whether locally or remotely. MFA greatly increases hackers' work factor over 1FA.

■ The defensive actions may defeat or scare novice-threat actors but may not defeat or scare advanced-threat actors due to their increased technological sophistication, knowledge, and skill levels.

(c) Cyber Threats, Attacks, Risks, and Controls

This section discusses several types of cyber threat sources and cyber-based attacks (exploits and vulnerabilities), all of which create major cyber risks that require mitigating controls. Specific and broad types of cyber threats, attacks, risks, and controls are presented.

(i) Cyber Threat Sources

Cyber-based threat sources can be unintentional and intentional. Unintentional threats can be caused by software upgrades or defective equipment that inadvertently disrupts computer systems and networks. Intentional threats include both targeted and untargeted attacks from a variety of sources, such as business competitors (domestic and foreign), dishonest or disgruntled employees (insiders), criminal groups, hackers, bot network operators, phishers, spammers, spyware writers, malware writers, and foreign nations engaged in espionage and information warfare activities. These sources of cybersecurity threats make use of various techniques to compromise information or adversely affect computers, software, networks, an organization's operations, an industry, or the Internet itself.

Hacking is done by hackers who are mostly bad actors because they do bad things (i.e., illegal and unethical things) to individuals and organizations. Hackers break into networks for the thrill of the challenge, bragging rights in the hacker community, revenge, stalking, monetary gain, and political activism, among other reasons. While gaining unauthorized access once required a fair amount of skill and computer knowledge, hackers can now download attack scripts and protocols from the Internet and launch them against victim websites. Thus, while attack tools have become more sophisticated and innovative, they have also become easier to use and pose a big challenge to IT security staff who try to catch up with hackers. In a way, hackers are outthinking or outsmarting the IT security staff. Attackers, intruders, adversaries, scammers, crackers, cyber criminals, spammers, spoofers, data hijackers, threat actors, bad actors, and malicious actors are other names given to hackers.

The hacker literature defines three types of hackers:

1. **Black-hat hackers** break into computer systems and networks illegally and cause harm and damage by stealing or destroying data.

2. **White-hat hackers** (ethical hackers) use their technical skills to help organizations develop robust computer systems and networks after demonstrating strengths and exposing weaknesses in security.

3. **Gray-hat hackers** perform illegal hacking activities to show off their skills rather than to achieve personal or financial gain.

A fourth type of hackers is Red-hat hackers coined by the IBM Corporation with a theme of "hack anything to secure everything." These hackers will test the Internet of Things (IoT) technologies, automotive equipment, automated teller machines (ATMs), hardware/software devices, and other computer systems and technologies. Their goal is to find security vulnerabilities in computer systems and devices before and after they are deployed to customers. To this end, they are penetration testers who can break security (hacking) and fix security (remediation).

(ii) Specific Cyber Threats, Attacks, Risks, and Controls

The unique nature of cyber-based attacks can vastly enhance their reach and impact, resulting in the loss of sensitive data (e.g., personal, medical, financial, and customer), the loss of privacy (i.e., unauthorized information disclosure), identity theft (i.e., stealing of sensitive data), ransomware attacks (i.e., hijacking of sensitive data), the compromise of proprietary information (trade secrets), and the violation of intellectual property asset rights, such as copyrights.

Some specific cyber-based attacks and controls are listed next.

- **Tampering attack. Tampering** is modifying data, software, firmware, or hardware without authorization. It includes modifying data in transit, inserting tampered hardware or software into a supply chain, repackaging legitimate apps with malware, and modifying network or device configurations (e.g., jailbreaking or rooting a phone). A *security control* is to use an anti-tampering tool to make the data, software, firmware, or hardware tamper-proof.

- **Jamming attack. Jamming** is an attack in which a mobile device is used to emit electromagnetic energy on a wireless network's frequency to make the network unusable. Jamming is used in DoS attacks. A *security control* is to use anti-jamming and anti-skimming tools.

- **Spoofing attack. Spoofing** is impersonating something or someone, such as emails or SMS messages pretending to be from a boss or colleague (social engineering) or establishing fraudulent Wi-Fi access points or a cellular base station mimicking a legitimate one. A *security control* is to use anti-spoofing software, such as digital signatures.

- **Malware attacks. Malware attacks** are the most destructive and disruptive attacks. There are many forms and sizes of these attacks. Malware is often disguised as a game, patch, utility software, or other useful third-party software app. It includes adware, spyware, Trojan horses, keystroke logging, unauthorized location tracking, logic bombs, worms, and viruses. It is self-spreading and repackaging. A *security control* is to use antivirus, anti-spyware, and anti-malware software and make sure to keep their signatures current. Some Internet sites sell false anti-spyware tools that actually introduce spyware.

- **Adware attack. Adware** is a form of spyware program intended for marketing purposes, such as to deliver and display advertising banners or pop-ups to users' computer screens or to track users' online usage or purchasing activity. Adware tracks user activity and passes it to third parties without user knowledge or consent. Click fraud is possible with adware because it involves deceptions and scams that inflate advertising bills with improper usage and charges per click in online web advertisements. A *security control* is to use anti-spyware software.

- **Spyware attack. Spyware** is adware intended to violate users' privacy. It is placed on a computer to secretly gather and report information about users. Types of spyware include web bugs (tiny graphics on a website that are referenced within the hypertext markup language (HTML) content of a web page or email to collect information about users) and tracking cookies, described earlier. A *security control* is to use anti-spyware software, which specializes in detecting both malware and non-malware forms of spyware.

- **Autonomous spyware attack.** As a class, **autonomous spyware** operates as a separate process or injects itself into other processes running on users' computer systems. This type of spyware often starts up when users log onto their computers. Frequently it can access anything on user systems. Because autonomous spyware is simply a malicious application, it can be designed to perform almost any type of spying function. Spyware in this class often includes keyloggers, bots, email and web monitoring tools, packet sniffers, and mechanisms that permit intruders to remotely access and control an infected system. A *security control* is to use anti-spyware software.

- **Spamming attack. Spamming** is the abuse of an email system in the form of sending unsolicited bulk and junk emails. Recipients who click links in spam messages can inadvertently download spyware, viruses, and other malware. Spam can appear in text messages and email and can be used for phishing attempts and as a delivery mechanism for malware. A *security control* is to use anti-spamming software or spam filtering software, which analyzes email to look for characteristics of spam and places messages that appear to be spam in a separate email folder.

- **Social engineering attacks. Social engineering** attacks occur in many ways when malware is combined with socially deceptive techniques to accomplish complex attacks on unsuspecting users. In some cases, deception is used to trick users into downloading and executing malicious code. Phishing is also a deception technique, although it does not require malicious code. In other cases, malware is used to enable a deception, as in pharming. Both phishing and pharming are different and digital forms of social engineering. A nondigital (manual) and nontechnical version of social engineering is also available to deceive people through a phone or in person. A *security control* is for all employees to be vigilant and use common sense.

- **Phishing attack. Phishing** is the fraudulent practice of sending mass emails or pop-up messages to innocent people (untargeted victims) claiming to be from legitimate sources, such as companies and individuals, to induce victims to reveal sensitive, personal, and financial information, such as passwords and credit/debit card details, online. Phishing is a criminal act using a digital social engineering approach of masquerading as a trustworthy individual or entity. Internet scammers use email bait to "phish" for passwords and financial information from mobile and Internet users.

  Phishing is the creation and use of fraudulent but legitimate-looking emails and websites to obtain Internet users' identity, authentication, or financial information or to trick users into doing something they would not do. In many cases, perpetrators embed the URLs of illegitimate websites in spam, in hoping that recipients will click on those links and trigger the download of the malware or initiate the phishing attack.

  Specifically, phishing uses authentic-looking but fake emails to request sensitive information from users or direct them to fake websites that request such information. A *security control* is to use anti-phishing software. Vishing and smishing, described later, are variants of phishing and of social engineering approaches.

- **Spear phishing (or whaling) attack. Spear phishing** is a targeted form of email deception through social engineering, resulting in exploitation or compromise of an individual's mobile device and a company's networks. This deception is an entry point into the target's networks and computer systems. Attackers glean personal information about an individual, which allows them to masquerade as a trusted source in an electronic communication. This may lead the individual to click on links, accept software updates, or open attachments via email, social media messages, or electronic pop-up messages. *Security controls* include installing anti-phishing software, user education and training to become phishing aware, users acting as the second line of defense, and users becoming more vigilant at work.

- **Vishing attack. Vishing** is the act of using the telephone voice calls (cell/mobile, landline, or interactive voice recording system) in an attempt to scam users into surrendering private information that will be used for identity theft (e.g., credit/debit card activation, income tax refund, rewards redemption, winning a lottery, receiving a job promotion, and free vacation, travel, and gifts). Advanced vishing attacks can take place by exploiting voice over Internet protocol (VoIP) solutions and broadcasting services. VoIP easily allows caller ID to be spoofed. *Security controls* can include using anti-spoofing and anti-phishing software and installing voice encryption.

- **Smishing attack. Smishing** is a type of phishing attack where cell/mobile phone users receive text and multimedia messages containing website hyperlinks that, if clicked, would download a Trojan horse to the cell/mobile phone to spread viruses. Smishing exploits SMS and MMS messages. A *security control* is to use anti-phishing software.

- **Pharming attack. Pharming** is the redirection of legitimate web traffic (e.g., browser requests) to an illegitimate website for the purpose of obtaining private information. Pharming often uses Trojan horses, worms, or virus technologies to attack the Internet browser's address bar so that the valid URL typed by the user is modified to that of the illegitimate website. Pharming may also exploit the DNS server by causing it to transform the legitimate host name into the invalid website's IP address; this form of pharming is also known as DNS cache poisoning. A *security control* is to use anti-pharming software.

- **Supply-chain attacks.** A **supply-chain** threat can come from a failure or disruption in the production of a critical product or reliance on a malicious or unqualified service provider for the performance of technical services. Other exploits or threats can include insertion of malicious code, such as a logic bomb, Trojan horse, or virus; unintentional vulnerability, such as a program coding error or defective product; and implanting counterfeit parts into a final product that lead to product failures. A *security control* is to implement a defense-in-breadth strategy.

- **Click fraud attack. Click fraud** involves deceptions and scams that inflate online ad bills with improper, inaccurate, and illegal numbers of clicks made on the web. Either software bots are deployed or imposter users are hired by ad firms to keep clicking on ads to increase the number of users seeing the ad. Later, the advertising firm bills its client for the number of clicks made because the billing rate is based on cost per click. A *security control* against click fraud is to use heat maps that track website visitors' click behavior and browsing habits. Heat maps help web administrators visualize how web visitors are interacting with websites.

- **Network exploits attacks. Network exploits** take advantage of software flaws in a system that operates on local Bluetooth, Wi-Fi, or cellular networks. These exploits can propagate malware and hijack user credentials to impersonate users online. A bluesnarfing attack enables attackers to gain access to contact data by exploiting a software flaw in a Bluetooth-enabled device. A *security control* is to turn off the Bluetooth and Wi-Fi services when they are not needed.

- **Information disclosure attack. Information disclosure** is unauthorized access to information or service. It includes interception of data in transit; leakage or exfiltration of user, app, or enterprise data; tracking of user physical location (geolocation); eavesdropping on voice or data communications; and surreptitiously activating the phone's microphone or camera to spy on the user. A *security control* is to use encryption with passwords and passphrases.

- **Insider attacks.** Full-time employees, part-time employees, and independent contractors are known as **insiders** of an organization. Due to their IT skills, they can create insider attacks on computer assets and resources. Insiders pose a major threat to computer assets and information security due to their job duties; they work closely with other employees, know the ins and outs (strengths and weaknesses) of computer systems (i.e., know what works and what does not work), and can hide fraudulent activities on computer systems (i.e., covering their tracks). Insiders are trusted more than outsiders, and insiders can abuse or misuse that trust.

  The scope of insider attacks includes stealing financial assets (e.g., money from cash payments or from cash receipts, wire transfer fraud, and stealing blank checks and blank stock certificates), information assets (e.g., stealing customer, personal, and intellectual property assets data), and physical assets (e.g., stealing finished goods inventory, parts, components, and supplies). These insiders can steal, share, disclose, and sell sensitive and confidential data that could destroy brand image and create a bad reputation for the company.

Insiders can cause these additional risks:

- ☐ Employees can bring their own devices to the workplace to copy and steal company data.

- ☐ Lack of security controls over connected devices (e.g., mobile, legacy, edge, and endpoint devices) makes it easier for employees to accomplish insider attacks.

- ☐ Employees can use other employees' access credentials (e.g., user IDs and passwords) to gain access to higher levels of access to privileged accounts and to bypass separation-of-duties controls.

Security controls to prevent and/or detect insider attacks include:

- ☐ Conducting background checks at the time of employment focusing on honesty and integrity

- ☐ Submitting signed statements of conflicts of interest and confidentiality agreements by an employee to an employer

- ☐ Acknowledging the receipt of security policies, procedures, and practices documents from an employer that explain consequences for unethical and illegal behavior by an employee on the job

- ☐ Receiving rules of behavior and rules of engagement guidelines

- ☐ Implementing rule-based and role-based access controls

- ☐ Developing ACLs linking subjects to objects

- ☐ Implementing electronic separation-of-duties controls

- ☐ Implementing the principles of least privilege, and need to know, and need to access

- ☐ Providing user education, awareness, training, and retraining programs to all end users

(iii) Attacks on Privileged Access Accounts

Whether they work in a business function (e.g., operations, marketing, and finance) or an IT function (e.g., system development, computer operations, and network operations), end users are normal employees with regular access rights to computer systems and special employees with privileged access rights to computer systems. Normal employees (nonprivileged users) are given lower levels of access rights to sensitive and confidential data. Special employees (privileged users), such as team leaders, supervisors, managers, and executives, are given access rights to the privileged accounts. that normal employees do not get. These special employees are trusted employees with higher levels of access rights to sensitive and confidential data, such pay scales, job grades, and salary amounts. For example, a privileged user can alter or bypass application system controls to access and change sensitive data silently and then reset the controls back to the normal level. Therefore, privileged users pose greater risks to the company and highly attractive and opportunity for attackers to hack.

Normal Employees = Regular Access = Lower Levels of Access Rights = Low Attraction to Hackers

Special Employees = Privileged Access = Higher Levels of Access Rights = High Attraction to Hackers

These privileged users can abuse and misuse their trusted access rights to sensitive data to favor some employees over others and to perpetrate fraudulent acts for their own benefit. Hackers target these privileged access accounts because they can gain so much more from those accounts compared to normal employee accounts. Therefore, effectively managing access rights to privileged accounts can reduce hackers' attack surfaces because the reduced workspace affords hackers fewer incentives to launch their attacks.

Security controls to prevent and detect attacks on privileged access accounts include:

- Conducting background checks at the time of employment focusing on honesty and integrity
- Submitting signed statements of conflict-of-interest and confidentiality agreements
- Acknowledging receipt of security policies, procedures, and practices documents that explain consequences for unethical and illegal behavior on the job
- Implementing risk-based access rules
- Enforcing SSO mechanisms
- Implementing multifactor authentication controls
- Deciding what application systems to run on what servers and mobile devices to separate applications and servers from each other
- Implementing the principles of least privilege, need to know, and need to access
- Conducting periodic audits of privileged access accounts to detect anomalies

(iv) Denial-of-Service Attacks

DoS attacks deny or degrade service to users, jam wireless communications, overload networks with bogus traffic, help ransomware attacks, and facilitate theft of mobile devices or mobile services. DoS attacks prevent or impair authorized access to and use of networks, operating systems, or application systems by exhausting computing resources. These attacks also delay time-critical operations, where the time delay can be milliseconds or hours, depending on the service provided. DoS is synonymous with interdiction.

DoS attacks are types of computer attacks that deny service to users by either clogging the system with irrelevant messages or sending disruptive commands to the system. They are direct attacks on the system availability feature. They also can prevent a financial system service provider from receiving or responding to messages from a requester (customer). Such attacks on the financial system service provider would not be detected by a firewall or an IDS because these countermeasures are based on either entry-point or per-host computer specific but not on a per-transaction or per-operation basis. *Security controls* include implementing QoS and quality of protection (QoP) techniques. Note that DoS is related to QoS, QoP and a denial of quality. Also, install system availability standards and use anti-jamming tools.

Distributed Denial-of-Service Attacks. A **DDoS** attack is a variant of the DoS attack that uses numerous host computers to perform the attack. Heavy use of botnets has increased the number of DDoS attacks. *Security controls* include implementing QoS and QoP techniques, increasing the size and shape of network capacity, and installing ingress filtering and egress filtering methods to filter incoming and outgoing network traffic.

Email Configuration Attacks. Email users can configure email programs to send and display email content using plaintext instead of HTML. This can eliminate most of the risks from embedded scripts, web bugs, and other HTML-enabled threat techniques used by attackers. But just as disabling active content in web browsers reduces the functionality of some features, using plaintext can reduce the usability of some features. Also, many email developers are now offering the ability to disable scripting and block images until a user takes some action to display them. Some Internet-based frauds conducted using email configuration settings are identity, payment, and funds transfer fraud.

Zero-Day Attacks. A **zero-day attack** takes advantage of a security vulnerability before an update for the vulnerability is available. By writing an exploit for an unknown vulnerability, attackers create a potential threat because mobile devices generally will not have software patches to prevent the exploit from succeeding. A *security control* is to install all software patches and updates without fail.

Cross-Site Scripting Attack. Cross-site scripting (XSS) is an attack that uses third-party web resources to run a script within the victim's web browser or scriptable application. This attack occurs when a browser visits a malicious website or a browser clicks a malicious link. The most dangerous consequences occur when this method is used to exploit additional vulnerabilities that may permit attackers to steal cookies (i.e., data exchanged between a web server and a browser), log key strokes, capture screen shots, discover and collect network information, and remotely access and control the victim's computer.

Attackers may use XML injection attacks to perform the equivalent of a XSS, in which requesters of a valid web service have their requests rerouted to an attacker-controlled web service that performs malicious operations. Security controls over XSS attacks and XML injection attacks include installing web server-based controls and web browser-based controls.

Passive Wiretapping Attack. Passive wiretapping is the monitoring or recording of data, such as passwords transmitted in cleartext, while they are being transmitted over a telecommunications link. This tapping is done without altering or affecting the data. A *security control* is encrypting the passwords.

Structured Query Language Injection Attack. An **SQL injection** is an attack that involves the alteration of a database search in a web-based application. This alteration can be used to obtain unauthorized access to sensitive information in a database.

War Driving Attack. War driving is the method of driving through cities and neighborhoods with a wireless-equipped computer and antenna searching for unsecured wireless networks.

Theft or Loss of Mobile Devices. Because of their small size and use outside the office, mobile devices can be easier to misplace or steal than laptop or notebook computers. If mobile devices are lost, it may be relatively easy to gain access to the information they store. *Security controls* are to exercise the kill option on the device, use a remote data-wiping tool, and turn on the device's GPS.

(v) Data Integrity Attacks

Data integrity is the heart of any computer system. Here, data integrity refers to five control attributes: completeness, accuracy, authorization, consistency, and timeliness. If anyone of these attributes is missing, then the data is not reliable. Management makes decisions based on data mainly from computer systems. If a computer system's data is not reliable, then management's decisions will not be accurate.

Data integrity attacks are the most pressing cybersecurity challenges facing management due to their serious and dangerous results and negative outcomes.

General attacks on data that can compromise data integrity include data stealing, data sharing, data leaking, data modification, and data manipulation by insiders (employees) and data stealing, data destruction, data hijacking, and data corruption by outsiders (hackers).

Specific attacks that can target data at different stages of data life cycle include

- Data at entry (i.e., data entry from local devices, computers, and terminals; data entry from suppliers' and business partners' computers; and data entry from remote devices, computers, and terminals). These devices can be mobile, edge, legacy, and endpoint devices, collectively known as connected devices.

- Data in processing (i.e., manual, computer, or a combination).

- Data in transit (i.e., data in motion, data in flight, and data on the wire). For example, attacks on data in transit over a communication channel are eavesdropping, sniffing, session hijacking, and man-in-the-middle attacks.

- Data in transfer (i.e., data in exchange, say, between cloud services and mobile devices).

- Data at rest (i.e., data in internal storage or external storage (cloud); data on hard drives, on disks, in backups, and on USB drives).

- Data in use (i.e., data on hard drives or in cloud storage devices; data on disks, in backup files, and on USB drives).

Security controls to prevent data integrity attacks include:

- Establishing security policies.

- Enforcing security restrictions on who can enter, modify, view, or copy data; limiting access rights and privileges.

- Installing ACLs defining who can access what and do what.

■ Installing various encryption methods (e.g., end to end, session, link, bulk, stream, line, file, folder, full disk, volume, field level, and super-encryption). Exhibit 2.10 presents specific attacks on data and specific security controls that can mitigate such attacks.

EXHIBIT 2.10 Specific Attacks on Data and Specific Security Controls

Specific attack	Attack Description	Security Controls
Data at entry	Data stealing, sharing, leaking, modification, and manipulation	ACLs, user IDs, robust passwords, PINs, and pass codes Security restrictions on who can enter, modify, view, or copy data Access rights and privileges
Data in processing	Data modification, manipulation, and diddling	Data editing and validation controls Data integrity controls
Data in transit	Eavesdropping, sniffing, session hijacking, and man-in-the-middle attacks	Security filters; super-encryption; session key, link, and bulk encryption; passwords or passphrases
Data in transfer	Masquerading attacks Also known as impersonating, spoofing, mimicking attacks, and meet-in-the-middle attacks	Security filters: line, end-to-end, and bulk encryption; digital signatures, passwords, or passphrases
Data-at-rest	Data stealing, data destruction, data hijacking, data corruption, and data diddling.	Encryption: file-, folder-, or field-level; full-disk; virtual disk; and volume. Full, incremental, differential, and hybrid backups. Data sanitization methods Passwords or passphrases
Data in use	Data stealing, sharing, leaking, modification, and manipulation.	ACLs, user IDs, robust passwords, PINs, and pass codes Security restrictions on who can enter, modify, view, or copy data Access rights and privileges.

(vi) Internet-Based Fraudulent Attacks

Internet fraud is the use of Internet services or software with Internet access to defraud victims or to otherwise take advantage of them. A number of high-profile methods are discussed next.

Funds transfer fraud is a sophisticated scam targeting businesses working with foreign suppliers and companies that regularly perform wire transfer payments. The scam is carried out by compromising legitimate business email accounts through social engineering or computer intrusion techniques to conduct unauthorized transfers of funds.

Data breaches are leaks or spills of data that is released from a secure location to an untrusted environment. Data breaches can occur at personal and corporate levels and involve sensitive, protected, or confidential information that is copied, transmitted, viewed, stolen, or used by an individual unauthorized to do so.

Denial of service attacks are interruptions of an authorized user's access to any system or network, typically caused with malicious intent.

Payments fraud, similar to funds transfer fraud, targets the general public and professionals associated with, but not limited to, financial and lending institutions, real estate companies, and law firms. Perpetrators of payment fraud use compromised emails to request payments to fraudulent locations.

Malware/scareware attacks involve malicious software that is intended to damage or disable computers and computer systems. Sometimes perpetrators use scare tactics to solicit funds from victims.

Phishing/spoofing attacks deal with forged or faked electronic documents. **Spoofing** generally refers to the dissemination of email that is forged to appear as if it were sent by someone other than the actual source. **Phishing**, also referred to as vishing, smishing, or pharming, is often used in conjunction with a spoofed email. It is the act of sending an email falsely claiming to be from an established legitimate business in an attempt to deceive unsuspecting recipients into divulging personal, sensitive information, such as passwords, credit card numbers, and bank account information, after directing users to visit a specified website. The website, however, is not genuine and was set up only to steal users' information.

Ransomware attacks are forms of malware targeting both human and technical weaknesses in organizations and individual networks in an effort to deny the availability of critical data and/or systems. Ransomware is frequently delivered through spear phishing emails to end users, resulting in the rapid encryption of sensitive files on a corporate network. The cyber perpetrator demands the payment of a ransom, typically in virtual currency such as bitcoin, when members of the victim organization determine they are no longer able to access their data. After payment, the cyber perpetrator supposedly will purportedly provide an avenue to the organization to regain access to its data.

Technical support scams involve perpetrators claiming to be employees (or affiliates) of a major computer software or security company and offering technical support to victims. Some perpetrators claim to be support for cable and Internet companies and offer technical assistance with digital cable boxes and connections, modems, and routers. They claim the company has received notifications of errors, viruses, or security issues from the victim's Internet connection. Perpetrators also claim to work on behalf of government agencies to resolve computer viruses and threats from possible foreign countries or terrorist organizations.

In this scam, initial contact with the victims occurs by different methods, including telephone, pop-up message, and locked screen on a device. Any electronic device with Internet capabilities can be affected.

> **Telephone** is the traditional contact method. Victims receive a "cold" call from someone who claims the victim's computer is sending error messages and that numerous viruses were detected.

> **Pop-up messages** appear on victims' screens that claim viruses are attacking the device. Messages include a phone number to call to receive assistance.

> **Locked device screens** (blue screen of death) often display a phone number and instructions to contact a (phony) tech support company. Some victims report being redirected to alternate websites before the blue screen of death appears. This often occurs when victims are accessing social media and financial websites.

Pop-up messages and locked screens are sometimes accompanied by a recorded verbal message to contact a phone number for assistance.

Once phony tech support representatives (perpetrators) make verbal contact with the victim, they try to convince the victim to provide remote access to the device. If the device is mobile (e.g., digital tablet and smartphone), perpetrators often instruct the victim to connect it to a computer. After gaining remote access, perpetrators claim to have found multiple viruses, malware, and/or scareware, which can be removed for a fee. They usually collect fees via a personal debit or credit card, electronic check, wire transfer, or prepaid card.

(A) Software Piracy Risks

Software piracy risks for user organizations include legal risks (i.e., lawsuits and negative reputation) and financial liabilities (i.e., fines and penalties) with software vendors who are the owners of the software. Ineffective and inefficient management of software license issues can lead to software piracy risks. Here, the major issue facing user organizations is violation of the U.S. Copyright Act, because software is copyrighted by its owner. Developing and monitoring a software inventory management system is an effective control to detect illegal use of copyrighted software. Illegal copying of licensed software for personal use is called softlifting. Other acts of piracy include stealing movies, games, music, books, and sports. *Security controls* to minimize software piracy risks are to conduct periodic audits of software licenses and end user education and training.

Risks resulting from the use of illegal software are several and include:

- Telecommuting employees may install illegal software on their home computers, which they also use for business purposes, and that software is not authorized by their employers.

- Regular employees may bring software from home to work that is not authorized by their employers.

- Disgruntled employees may report illegal copying and using of vendor-developed software to government officers, internal company's hotline reporting, software vendor representatives, software vendor alliances, or external watchdog groups.

Software monitoring can be performed to determine illegal acquisition and unauthorized use of software. For example, vendor-provided audit software running on a user computer can detect illegal acquisition, which is using unofficially acquired software. This audit can be performed either manually or with automated tools. For example, an organization may audit systems for illegal copies of copyrighted software. This problem is primarily associated with PCs and LANs but can apply to any type of computer system or mobile devices. Another audit requirement is retention of business records to comply with legal, tax, audit, and regulatory authorities.

User organizations can use a **software metering program** to ensure that software is properly licensed, as required by the licensing agreement. System users are defined to the software metering product, and the product controls and monitors who is using the system and determines whether the user is authorized to use it. Unauthorized users will be denied access to the system.

(vii) File-Based Attacks and File-Less Attacks

Hackers deploy two types of attacks related to files: file-based and file-less attacks. **File-based attacks** are old practices that hackers deploy to defeat security controls. They use files containing extensions such as .exe, .doc, .pdf, or .bat with downloading malicious executable files. Traditional anti-malware (antivirus) software can protect these attacks with scan and block features. However, a protection gap exists with these attacks due to the large number of false positives and security alerts which are not detectable until it is too late. Moreover, file-based attacks require an extensive amount of security monitoring using significant staff and time resources. Unfortunately, hackers have been successful in deactivating (killing) the functions and features of anti-malware to make it useless. A *security control* to prevent file-based attacks is to install file encryption, full-disk encryption, and end-to-end encryption and to use VPN connections.

File-less attacks are new practices that hackers deploy to evade detection. A file-less attack, by definition does not use files; it is an attack that avoids downloading malicious executable files. Instead, hackers use macros, scripts, and exploits executing directly from computer memory (in-memory attacks) without being detected.

A **macro** is a compressed programming code with a certain sequence of commands that is repeated more than once. A macro can replace a repetitive series of keyboard strokes and mouse actions. A *hotkey* is assigned to the macro for even faster access. Although macros are used for good purposes (i.e., for efficiency reasons), hackers can turn them into malicious macros (bad macros, such as macro viruses) to introduce malicious software.

A **script** is a list of commands executed by computer programs or scripting languages. Scripts are used to customize and automate repeated tasks and to control overall computer functions. Scripts include autoexec.bat, Visual Basic Script, and JavaScript. Scripts are stored on servers or written to web pages and are used to install new software on computers. In addition, scripts are used to create dynamic web pages using JavaScript in conjunction with HTML programming language. Hackers can change the official scripts to insert malicious scripts.

An **exploit** takes advantage of a vulnerability, which is a security weakness in a computer system. For example, a vulnerability in an operating system can arise from unpatched and unsecured servers. Exploits are easy attack paths for hackers.

Once computers have been compromised, these attacks can nullify system administration tools, elevate access privileges, and spread laterally across the network. Anti-malware software cannot scan and block file-less attacks. A security control to prevent file-less attacks is to install AI tools and ML systems.

(viii) Device-Based Attacks and Controls

Organizations use several types of connected devices in their daily computing work. Although these devices are taken for granted for their simplicity and ease of use, they pose significant risks if not controlled properly and timely because they are the entry points to an organization's website, computing systems, and networks. If these devices are not secured, the organization's website, computing systems, and networks are not secured. A centralized inventory control system is needed to keep track of these devices for security and monitoring purposes. These connected devices are the major targets for attackers and present major challenges to user organizations in terms of preventing, detecting, blocking, and responding to attacks. Management's primary goal is to detect and stop these attacks right at their initiation; sometimes the attacks cannot be prevented due to their silent and deceptive acts. The major reason for security vulnerabilities in all these connected devices is because basic security features, protections, and controls were not built in. Developers paid more attention to device functions than to device controls.

Four types of connected devices are discussed next: mobile, legacy, edge, and endpoint devices.

Mobile devices are smartphones, digital tablets, electronic readers, USB flash drives, memory sticks, and digital cards. Mobile devices are called rogue devices because they are more vulnerable to risk than legacy devices because employees often are allowed to bring in their own devices.

Legacy devices are infrastructure devices consisting of traditional equipment related to mainframe computers and devices such as workstations, terminals, computer operator consoles, PCs (e.g., desktop, laptop, and notebook), scanners, printers, servers, routers, switches, firewalls, storage devices (e.g., RAID and network access storage devices), and hardware controllers.

Edge devices are devices used in the IoT, NoT, LoT technologies, and more. Examples include several gadgets and tools, such as edge servers, sensors, wearable devices (watches, goggles, and headsets), Internet-connected home appliances, printers, closed circuit television (CCTV) security cameras, digital video recorders, health monitoring devices, and home security monitoring systems, personal computers, and mobile devices.

Endpoint devices are connected to a network on both sides of the network: One point is at the Internet side, and the other point is at the personal computer side. Examples include servers, routers, firewalls, modems, sockets, ports, network nodes, port protection devices, hubs, gateways, backbone networks, portals, bridges, and switches.

Next, we discuss risks and controls of mobile devices, edge devices, and endpoint devices.

(A) Mobile Device Risks and Controls

Attacks against mobile devices generally occur through four different channels of activities: software downloads, visiting a malicious website, direct attack through the communication network, and physical attacks. These risks are described next.

1. **Software downloads.** Malicious applications may be disguised as games, device patches, or utility programs that are available for download by unsuspecting users. These applications provide the means for unauthorized users to gain unauthorized use of mobile devices and to access to private information or system resources on the devices.

2. **Visiting a malicious website.** Malicious websites may automatically download malware to mobile devices when users visit those sites. In some cases, users must take an action (such as clicking on a hyperlink) to download the application; in other cases the application may download automatically.

3. **Direct attack through the communication network.** Rather than targeting mobile devices themselves, some attacks try to intercept communications to and from devices in order to gain unauthorized use of the devices and access to sensitive information.

4. **Physical attacks.** Unauthorized individuals may gain possession of lost or stolen devices and use them to access sensitive information stored on them.

Security Controls over Mobile Devices and Their Associated Attacks

- Be suspicious of unsolicited phone calls, visits, email messages, or text messages from individuals asking about employees or other internal information. If an unknown individual claims to be from a legitimate organization, try to verify his or her identity directly with the organization.

- Do not provide personal information, customer information, or information about your organization, including its organizational structure, computer networks, or data centers, unless you are certain of a person's identity and authority to request this information.

- Do not reveal personal or financial information in email, and do not respond to email solicitations for this information. Do not follow the links sent in email.

- Do not send sensitive information over the Internet before checking a website's security.

- Pay attention to the URL of a website you receive by watching the domain extension names. Malicious websites may look identical to legitimate websites, but the URL may use a variation in spelling or a different domain (e.g., .com versus .net). If you are unsure of about the URL, contact the original company directly. Information about known phishing attacks is available online from groups such as the Anti-Phishing Working Group.

- Install and maintain antivirus software, firewalls, and email filters to reduce some of this unwanted network traffic. Also, take advantage of anti-phishing features offered by email servicers and web browser providers.

- Do not jailbreak or root mobile devices. **Jailbreaking** or **rooting** is removing the limitations imposed on a device by the manufacturer, often through the installation of custom operating system components or other third-party software. Jailbreaking makes a device more vulnerable to attacks because it removes important safeguards against malware attacks. Some users prefer to bypass the operating system's lockout features in order to install apps that could be malicious in nature. Doing jailbreaking and rooting is risky.

- Secure all sensitive data stored on USB drives (e.g., jump drives, flash drives, and thumb drives), CDs, and DVDs using strong encryption. Consider using jump drives with onboard antivirus capability to perform automatic virus scans. Also, use anti-malware software on mobile devices.

- Set up a local firewall on the device to filter inbound and outbound traffic and to block malicious software.

- If a device is lost, stolen, or misplaced, activate GPS to track its location and enable a remote-wiping feature to erase all data on the device.

- Disable Bluetooth and Wi-Fi services when not using them. When using Wi-Fi, encrypt the network or use a VPN connection. When using the Bluetooth, set it to "nondiscoverable" mode to make the device invisible to unauthenticated devices.

- Create acceptable-use policies for all portable media devices, and educate/train users about those policies.

- Develop an inventory of mobile devices that carry sensitive company information, and audit the inventory on a regular basis.

- Configure Secure Socket Layer (SSL) security features on organizational web servers to encrypt data being transmitted.

(B) Edge Device Risks and Controls

Edge devices have become increasingly attractive targets for criminal hackers, raising new risks. To attack edge devices, hackers often probe devices for security vulnerabilities and then install malware to surreptitiously control or damage the device, gain unauthorized access to the data on the device, and/or otherwise affect the device's operation without permission. In addition to manipulating edge devices, hackers can penetrate into other devices on the same network. Unless appropriate security controls are installed, malware can quickly spread across networks of IoT devices without users opening a file, clicking on a link, or doing anything other than turning on an Internet-controlled device. A common attack using edge devices infected with malware is a DDoS attack.

Security Controls over Edge Devices and Their Associated Attacks

- Secure edge devices immediately after purchase by resetting any default passwords with secure passwords.

- Adopt secure password practices with robust passwords.

- Continue to update firmware and software with patches.

- Consider disconnecting insecure edge devices.

- Turn off edge devices when not in use or periodically if otherwise always on.

- Protect routers and Wi-Fi networks with security controls, such as firewalls.

- Consider using antivirus and IDS products that protect edge devices.

- Avoid a single point of failure by segmenting networks.

- Disable universal plug-and-play feature on routers to increase network security.

- Disable all device terminal and management ports that are not explicitly required or actively being used for device management access.

- Enforce idle timeouts and keepalives (i.e., the time for a session to stay active) to detect and close inactive or hung sessions.

- Enforce an active session timeout to restrict the maximum duration of a session prior to re-authentication.

- Enforce a lockout period upon multiple authentication failure attempts.

- Limit the rate of login attempts (e.g., three times).

- Deny outgoing access unless explicitly required.

- Log all successful and failed access attempts for tracing and tracking purposes.

- Enforce strong encryption methods for locally stored information (e.g., computer hard drives and USB drives).

(C) Endpoint Device Risks and Controls

A variety of endpoint device risks exist, including man-in-the-middle attacks, meet-in-the-middle attacks, breaking into password files or encryption keys, launching DDoS attacks using bots, nullifying firewall protections, deactivating (killing) antivirus and anti-malware software features and functions, and implanting hacker-made dangerous malware into an organization's computers and networks.

Security Controls over Endpoint Devices

- Use anti-malware software. Anti-malware applications should be part of the standard secure configuration settings for system components. Anti-malware software (antivirus software) employs a wide range of signatures and detection schemes, automatically updates signatures, disallows modification by users, runs scans on a frequently scheduled basis, has an auto-protect feature set to scan automatically when a user action is performed (e.g., opening or copying a file), and may provide protection from zero-day attacks. For platforms for which anti-malware software is not available, other forms of anti-malware, such as rootkit detectors, may be employed. Similarly, anti-spyware and anti-phishing software tools can be used.

- Use personal firewalls. Personal firewalls provide a wide range of protection for host machines, including restriction on ports and services, control against malicious programs executing on the host, control of removable devices (e.g., USB flash drives, digital cards, and memory sticks), and auditing and logging capability.

- Use host-based intrusion detection and prevention system. Host-based intrusion detection and prevention system is an application that monitors the characteristics of a single host and the events occurring within that host to identify and stop suspicious activity. This is distinguished from network-based intrusion detection and prevention system that monitors network traffic for particular network segments or devices and analyzes the network and application protocol activity to identify and stop suspicious activity.

- Control the use of mobile code. Organizations should restrict the use of mobile code, such as ActiveX, Java, and JavaScript. An attacker can easily attach a script to a URL in a web page or email that, when clicked, will execute malicious code within the computer's browser.

- Use cryptography. In many systems, especially those processing, storing, or transmitting information that is moderate impact or higher for confidentiality, cryptography should be considered as a part of an information system's secure configuration. There are a variety of places to implement cryptography to protect data, including individual file encryption, full-disk encryption, and VPN connections.

- Implement end-to-end security. Transport layer security mechanisms (e.g., SSL/TLS) provide security of messages only during transmission, not at the intermediary level. Also, an intrusion prevention system becomes ineffective as the SSL-VPN can be controlled at the two endpoints (i.e., one point at the desktop and the other point at the Internet). Message layer security mechanisms (e.g., XML gateways or firewalls) provide security for messages that are stored and then forwarded. It is important to deal with security concerns at the transport layer independently of the message layer. In addition, end-to-end QoS and QoP should be guaranteed.

- Control the remote access servers. Endpoint remote access servers should be placed in the organization's DMZs to allow a perimeter firewalls to limit access to the servers from both internal and external hosts and to avoid the security concerns of external traffic entering into the internal network.

- Use thin nodes and clients. The deployment of information system components with minimal functionality (e.g., diskless nodes and thin client technologies) reduces the need to secure every user endpoint and may reduce the exposure of information, information systems, and services to a successful attack.

Identity Theft Attacks. Identity theft or fraud happens when someone steals personal information and uses it without the owner's permission. It is a serious crime that can wreak havoc with people's finances, credit history, and reputation—and can take time, money, and patience to resolve. There are three specific types of identity theft: tax-related identity theft using someone's Social Security number, child identity theft using a child's personal information, and medical identity theft using someone's personal information to get medical care or services.

COMMON IDENTITY THEFT SCHEMES

- Sending suspicious email and/or phishing attempts to trick victims into revealing personally identifiable information, such as bank account numbers, passwords, and credit card numbers.

- Involving smash-and-grab burglaries to steal hardcopy drivers' licenses, credit cards, and checkbooks and performing computer and network intrusion schemes that could result in the loss of personally identifiable information.

Identity theft can occur in several ways:

- Data breaches by hackers in a retail environment where hackers steal customers' personal and financial information.

- Data leakages by company insiders, such as employees and contractors.

- **Pretext calling** by a fraudster in a banking environment. Pretext callers use pieces of a customer's personal information to impersonate an account holder to gain access to that individual's account information. Armed with personal information, such as an individual's name, address, and Social Security number, a pretext caller may try to convince a bank employee to provide confidential account information. While pretext calling may be difficult to spot, banks can take measures to reduce the incidence of pretext calling, such as limiting the circumstances under which customer information may be disclosed over the telephone. A bank's policy could be that customer information is disclosed only through email, text message, a letter, or in-person meeting.

Specific Control Actions to Prevent Identity Theft

- Place both extended fraud alerts and credit freezes on credit reports to make it more difficult for an identity thief to open new accounts in your name.

- Repair credit after identity theft by disputing fraudulent charges and accounts related to identity theft.

- Reissuing lost or stolen credit/debit/automated teller machine cards to victim customers because federal law limits liability, but that liability may depend on how quickly the loss or theft is reported.

If identity thieves have your personal information, they can drain your bank accounts, run up charges on your credit cards, open new utility accounts, or get medical treatment on your health insurance. It is important to safeguard your personal information, whether it is on paper, online, or on computers and mobile devices.

The U.S. **Red Flags Rule** was issued in 2007 under the Fair and Accurate Credit Transactions Act, clarified with the issuance of the Red Flag Program Clarification Act of 2010. This rule, which amended the Fair Credit Reporting Act, requires many businesses and organizations to implement a written identity theft prevention program designed to detect the red flags of identity theft in their day-to-day operations, take steps to prevent the crime, and mitigate its damage. The bottom line is that a program can help businesses spot suspicious patterns and prevent the costly consequences of identity theft.

(D) Ransomware Attacks

Ransomware is malicious software (malware) that denies access to computer files until the victim pays a ransom. Ransomware is a type of cyberattack that prevents a user from using a computer until the user pays a certain amount of digital money (e.g., bitcoins or Green Dot cards). It is essentially extortion with all the data on the victim's computer at risk unless the victim pays.[6]

How Does Ransomware Work? Scammers, data-nappers, or computer kidnappers send emails that look like courtesy messages from legitimate companies—especially shipping companies —to spread ransomware called CryptoLocker botnet. Other names for this type of malware include WannaCry, WannaCrypt, CryptoWall, or Cryptomining. CryptoLocker works by encrypting all the files (e.g., photos, documents, and tax refunds) that victims have saved to the hard drive or to any shared folders. Once the files are encrypted, victims will not be able to open the files without the decryption key, which they can get only from the criminals behind CryptoLocker. Hackers or criminals hold user files hostage, often encrypting them and demanding payment, typically in virtual currency such as bitcoin, for victims to get the files back.

After CryptoLocker has encrypted the files, it displays a message like this: "Your personal files are encrypted." The criminals demand payment through an anonymous payment type, such as bitcoin or Green Dot cards, and promise to supply the decryption key if the victim pays the ransom amount in time (e.g., $300 to be paid within 72 hours). Unfortunately, once CryptoLocker has encrypted the files, there is no way to recover them. Paying the ransom is no guarantee that the decryption key to open the files will be supplied.

Common Ransomware Attacks. Ransomware attacks can occur on any organization's computer systems and networks and on any individual's PCs (i.e., Windows and other platforms). At least four common attack methods exist in ransomware: exploit kits, malicious email attachments, malicious email links, and multiple attack vectors.

Exploit kits are sophisticated tool kits that exploit vulnerabilities. Most often these kits are executed when a user (victim) visits a compromised website. Malicious code hidden on the site, often in an advertisement (adware), redirects the user to the exploit kit landing page without his or her knowledge. If websites are vulnerable to attacks, a drive by download of a malicious payload will be executed, the system will become infected, and the files will be held for ransom.

---

[6] U.S. Federal Trade Commission, *Ransomware* (Washington, DC: 2017), www.ftc.gov.

SOURCES OF RANSOMWARE ATTACKS

Sources of ransomware attacks include portable executable files, Word documents, JS files, compressed file attachments, zip file attachments, and double extension files, such as a .pdf.exe. Specifically, sources include:

- Clicking on email links

- Downloading attachments and apps

- Spear phishing emails (most common)

- Visiting a compromised website

- Opening malicious online advertisements (spam emails)

- Using outdated and unpatched software (e.g., applications software, operating system software, and antivirus software)

Malicious email attachments are crafted emails likely from a believable internal source (e.g., a human resource or an IT department) with a malicious file attached (e.g., a portable executable file, Word document, or .JS file). Recipients open the attachment, thinking the email came from a trusted source. Once the file is opened, the ransomware payload is downloaded, the system is infected, and the files are held for ransom.

Malicious email links are URLs in the body of an email. Likewise, these emails are sent from someone or some organization that a recipient believes to be a trusted source. When clicked, these URLs download malicious files over the web. The system is then infected, and the files are held for ransom.

Multiple attack vectors include regular networks, cloud-based networks, and network endpoints.

Security Measures over Ransomware Attacks. As they can against other computer attacks, organizations can develop security measures over ransomware attacks, including prevention, detection, and response (recovery) measures. It has been said that recovery costs from ransomware attacks will be much higher than the ransom money paid to hackers due to damage-control costs and loss of revenue, employee productivity, employee morale, and company reputation (i.e., increase in reputation costs).

Specific Preventive Measures over Ransomware

- Do not click on links in an email unless you know who sent it and what it is. Instead, type the URL.

- Minimize drive-by downloads. CryptoWall ransomware is spread primarily via spam email and infects victims through drive-by downloads and malvertising (i.e., advertising with malware attached).

- Do not open double extension files, such as .pdf.exe.

- Use a cloud-based backup method with add-on system that is secure, scalable, and effective that can move large amounts of data from the data center, thus avoiding network bottle-necks. A cloud backup is like an insurance policy.

- Make sure that all applications, operating system, antivirus, and mobile device software have been patched with the latest updates.

- Set up your operating system, web browser, and security software to update automatically.

- Use an external hard drive to back up all PC files every day. However, disconnect the backup device from the computer when it is not actively baking up the files. In other words, never use the automatic option for backing up files when you are using the computer for work. If the CryptoLocker program strikes while your backup device is connected to your computer, the program will try to encrypt both internal and external hard drive files. Consequently, the damage is multiplied.

- Use the application whitelisting feature, where only known computer programs can execute, based on security policy permissions.

- Separate networks and data categories by implementing physical security and logical security controls for different organizational units.

- Configure access controls on data files, data directories, and network share permissions with least privilege in mind. If a user needs only read-access to specific files, the user should not have write-access to those files, directories, or shares.

- Execute operating system software or specific application programs in a virtualized environment.

- Manage the use of privileged accounts based on the principle of least privilege. This means that no users should be assigned administrative access unless it is absolutely needed, and those with a need for administrator accounts should use them only when necessary.

Other Preventive Measures over Ransomware

- Conduct user awareness and training programs.

- Use spam filters to prevent phishing emails.

- Authenticate inbound emails to prevent email spoofing attacks.

- Scan all incoming and outgoing emails to detect threats and to filter executable files from reaching end users.

- Configure firewalls to block access to known malicious IP addresses.

- Patch operating system software and firmware on devices using a centralized patch management system.

- Install antivirus and anti-malware programs to conduct regular file scans automatically.

Specific Recovery Measures over Ransomware. All organizations and all individuals using computer systems and networks should develop a recovery plan with the details about the backup source methods, backup storage policy, backup schedules, backup duration, and rotation and retention of backup files. Verify the integrity of the backup files and programs and test the restoration process to ensure it is working.

- Contain the attack, meaning disconnect the infected devices from the network to keep ransomware from spreading.

- Isolate or power-off affected devices that have not yet been completely corrupted.

- Immediately secure backup data or systems by taking them offline and by ensuring that those backups are free of malware.

- Restore the computer only after all files have been backed up and any malware has been removed. Then reboot the computer.

■ Change all online account passwords and network passwords after the system is removed from the network. Furthermore, change all system passwords once malware is removed from the system.

■ Contact law enforcement authorities immediately with information such as criminals' email addresses or bitcoin wallet numbers.

■ Implement security incident responses and business continuity plans. Having a data backup can eliminate the need to pay a ransom to recover data. Conduct an annual penetration test and vulnerability assessment. Store backups in the cloud or physically offline. Backups are critical in ransomware recovery and response. If computer files are infected, a backup may be the best way to recover critical data.

Best Practices to Protect from Ransomware Attacks. Best practices are critical in protecting a company's computer system and networks from ransomware attacks. The following questions need to be answered:

Backups: Do we back up all critical information? Are the backups stored offline? Have we tested our ability to revert to backups during an incident?

Risk analysis: Have we conducted a cybersecurity risk analysis of the organization?

Staff training: Have we trained staff on cybersecurity best practices?

Vulnerability patching: Have we implemented appropriate patching of known system vulnerabilities?

Application whitelisting: Do we allow only approved programs to run on our networks?

Incident response: Do we have an incident response plan and have we exercised it?

Business continuity: Are we able to sustain business operations without access to certain systems? For how long? Have we tested this?

Penetration testing: Have we attempted to hack into our own systems to test the security of our systems and our ability to defend against attacks?

Risk Factors for Ransomware Victims. The cryptocurrency bitcoin is a payment mechanism that is increasing the success rate of ransomware attacks because bitcoin has no central authority. For that reason, law enforcement authorities cannot take any action against the attackers. Other payment mechanisms include Green Dot cards. Law enforcement authorities do not recommend paying ransom to criminals because doing so could send a signal to the criminals that the user files are not backed up and protected, which could increase the ransom price and increase the criminals' bargaining power.

Ransomware victims may wish to consider the next risk factors either before or after paying the ransom amount. Law enforcement authorities do not encourage or recommend that victims pay ransom to criminal actors. Victims will want to evaluate the technical feasibility, timeliness, and cost of restarting systems from backup. Ransomware victims may also wish to consider these factors:

■ Paying a ransom does not guarantee that an organization will regain access to their data; some individuals or organizations were never provided with decryption keys even though they paid a ransom.

■ Some victims who paid the ransom were targeted again by cyber actors (bad actors).

- After paying the original ransom amount, some victims were asked to pay more to get the promised decryption key.

- Paying the ransom amount could inadvertently encourage this criminal business model.

Data Breaches and Leak Attacks.   Data breaches are cybersecurity incidents that have occurred at several public sector organizations (e.g., the U.S. Office of Personnel Management (OPM), governmental agencies, and cities) and private-sector organizations (e.g., Target, Marriott, Yahoo, Sony, and Equifax) with severe financial losses and poor public relations with a high reputation risk. Hackers stole information affecting millions of customers, including financial and personal data, and sold that data to others, causing more identity fraud.

WHAT CUSTOMER INFORMATION IS STOLEN IN DATA BREACHES?

Hackers are interested in stealing this type of customer information: online login data, debit/credit card number, bank account information, Social Security number, date of birth, driver's license number, financial data, personal data, medical data, tax data, phone numbers, name and address, and biometric data. They use this information to re-create charge cards and perform other fraudulent activities.

Major reasons for data breaches are poor authentication, authorization, and identity controls combined with weak session management procedures placed at the front door to security. For example, sometimes retail customers use plain credit and debit cards without using a combination of smart chip and a PIN at retailers' POS registers. In the past, most retailers used weak and unsecure methods that combined (1) card and no signature, (2) card and signature, (3) card and PIN, (4) card and no PIN, and (5) card chip and no PIN. The best security control at the retail POS register is a combination of card chip and PIN, which can protect every customer, every retailer, and every card-issuing company. For online shopping, the best security control is username, password, passcode, charge card number, and personal security questions where customers provide answers to such questions. This type of authentication is referred to as multifactor authentication.

Organizations can protect customer data with basic user identification and authentication (e.g., username, passwords, passcodes, and personal security questions); strong encryption for data in storage, data in process, and data in transit; cloud storage; multilevel firewalls; and multifactor authentication mechanisms. Of course, user education and training always help in avoiding phishing and spamming emails, answering pretexting phone calls and robotic phone calls, and analyzing system logs. In summary, organizations need to invest resources to prevent data breaches with timely prevention, detection, and response capabilities.

Whereas data breaches are primarily conducted by outsiders (hackers), data leaks are primarily performed by insiders (employees and contractors). It has been reported that more than one-third of cybercrime incidents were caused by inside knowledge workers (employees) of a company due to their familiarity and access to internal computer systems. Of these one-third insiders, two-thirds were found to be negligent employees and one-third were found to be malicious employees. These inside threat sources include disgruntled employees and contractors, either actively employed or departing employees who are stealing sensitive company information (e.g., customer data, email lists, strategic plans, and research and development materials) and proprietary information (e.g., intellectual property data, such as software code, trademarks, and patents). These insiders are abusing their positions of trust.

This type of data leakage includes data loss, data stealing, and data destruction acts, which are possible when employees are given permission to bring their own devices and due to the availability of online file-sharing apps. Insiders think that it is acceptable to transfer work documents that they have created to their PCs, removable storage media, cloud-based data storage services, digital tablets, and smartphones. Some disgruntled employees and contractors even destroy company data by deleting or erasing it. These insiders are ignoring or violating confidentiality agreements, conflict-of-interest statements, code of conduct rules, code of ethics documents, noncompete agreements, and intellectual property agreements that they have signed, thus showing their lack of respect for laws.

Recommended Security Controls Against Insider Incidents

- Automatic daily data file backup systems.

- Endpoint backup systems that enable restoration to the last known good state of data files, thus providing visibility into when and how data was deleted.

- Filing lawsuits against inside cyber criminals.

- Restricting access to file-sharing services and cloud-based data storage services.

- Developing acceptable-use policies for mobile devices.

- Establishing a legal hold policy where courts require companies to document their security controls and the steps taken to prevent negligent or intentional destruction of data when the company brings lawsuits against inside cyber criminals. The security controls that are in place to prevent data leakage, data loss, and data stealing must be presented to the courts. This shows that the company has taken due care to protect data.

A PRIMER ON DATA BREACH COSTS, REASONS, AND REMEDIES

Organizations that are victims of data breach attacks must calculate the total costs of such attacks. Victim organizations will quickly find out that the actual costs are much higher than the expected costs. These total costs can be classified into four ways: direct, indirect, opportunity, and one-time costs.

Direct costs include external digital forensic costs; costs incurred to increase an attacker's work factor by delaying, nullifying, or deactivating the attacker's efforts; costs incurred to quickly identify, delay, and stop an attacker's detection evasion techniques; internal hotline support costs; external technical consulting costs and external legal consulting costs. Costs incurred for postbreach remedies include discounts given to the affected customers toward future purchase of products and services; credit monitoring services for affected customers; and reestablishing accounts for old customers and opening accounts for new customers.

Indirect costs include internal investigation costs, internal communication costs, lost sales, lost profits, and lost goodwill and reputation.

Opportunity costs include increased customer defection rates and costs resulting from increased turnover of current customers and increased customer acquisition rates and costs resulting from searching for new customers.

One-time costs include legal costs resulting from customer lawsuits; court fines and penalties; and related court filing fees and handling costs.

Reasons for Data Breaches

Management often is surprised and disappointed to learn the reasons for data breaches. The major reason is the lack of proactive security measures. Specific reasons include:

(Continued)

A PRIMER ON DATA BREACH COSTS, REASONS, AND REMEDIES (*Continued*)

- Poor security controls

- Failure to comply with security policies and procedures

- Lack of security metrics

- Extensive use of a variety of mobile platforms with poor security features

- Lack of an in-house incident response team

- Increased mean time to contain the data breach, which increases the recovery time and costs (The longer the mean time to contain, the higher the recovery cost and total cost.)

Remedies for Data Breaches

Management needs to take proactive, remedial security measures to reduce total costs of data breaches. Specific examples include:

- Installing an in-house incident response team with 24/7 support

- Making extensive use of encryption to reduce damages and total costs

- Utilizing modern tools and techniques by the incident response team

- Continuously monitoring computer systems and networks for red flags and incident clues and alerts

Automated and Distributed Attacks. The goal of attack-victim organizations is to dramatically reduce threats perpetrated by automated and distributed (A&D) attacks (e.g., botnets), as these attacks are growing at a faster rate than the other types of attacks. A&D attacks form a threat that reaches beyond any single company or industry. These threats are used for a variety of malicious activities, including DDoS attacks that overwhelm networked resources, sending massive quantities of spam; disseminating keylogger software and other malware; and ransomware attacks distributed by botnets that hold systems and data hostage. Traditional DDoS mitigation techniques, such as network providers building in excess capacity to absorb the effects of botnets, are designed to protect against botnets of an anticipated size. With new botnets that capitalize on the sheer number of IoT devices, DDoS attacks have grown in size and speed, far outstripping expected size and excess capacity. As a result, recovery time from these types of attacks may be too slow, particularly when mission-critical services are involved. Further, mitigation techniques were not designed to remedy other classes of malicious activities facilitated by botnets, such as ransomware.

Multiple types of **security controls** need to be installed to handle A&D attacks. Such controls include implementing ingress filtering and egress filtering to filter incoming and outgoing network traffic, increasing the size of network capacity, and hiring commercial anti-DDoS service providers.

Web Browser Attacks. Web browsers installed on PCs are entry points to websites, computer systems, and networks of any person or organization. Web browsers (e.g., Microsoft Edge, Google Chrome, Mozilla Firefox, and Apple Safari) are installed on almost all computers. Because web browsers are used so frequently, it is vital to configure and protect them securely. Often the web browser that comes with an operating system is not set up in a secure default configuration. Not securing a web browser can lead quickly to a variety of computer problems caused by anything from spyware being installed without your knowledge to intruders taking control of your computer.[7] It is

---

[7] Will Dormann and Jason Rafail, "Securing Your Web Browser," www.us-cert.gov/publications/securing-your-web-browser.

important to understand the functionality and features of the web browser you use. Enabling some web browser features may lower security. Often, vendors will enable features by default to improve the computing experience, but these features may end up increasing the risk to the computer.

BROWSER ATTACKS

Browser attacks (exploits) are designed to take advantage of vulnerabilities in software used to access websites. Visiting certain web pages and/or clicking on certain hyperlinks can trigger browser exploits that install malware or perform other adverse actions on a mobile device. A security control is to avoid clicking on unknown hyperlinks.

Attackers focus on exploiting client-side systems (your computer) through various vulnerabilities. They use these vulnerabilities to take control of your computer, steal your information, destroy your files, and use your computer to attack other computers. A low-cost method used to do this type of attack is by exploiting vulnerabilities in web browsers. Attackers can create a malicious web page that will install Trojan software or spyware that will steal your information. Rather than actively targeting and attacking vulnerable systems, a malicious website can passively compromise systems as the site is visited. A malicious HTML document can also be emailed to victims. In these cases, the act of opening the email or attachment can compromise the system.

Some specific web browser features and associated risks are briefly described next. Understanding what different features do will help you understand how they affect your web browser's functionality and the security of your computer.

ActiveX is a technology used by Microsoft Internet Explorer on Microsoft Windows systems. ActiveX allows applications or parts of applications to be utilized by the web browser. A web page can use ActiveX components that may already reside on a Windows system, or a site may provide the component as a downloadable object. This gives extra functionality to traditional web browsing but may also introduce more severe vulnerabilities if not properly implemented.

ActiveX has been plagued with various vulnerabilities and implementation issues. One problem with using ActiveX in a web browser is that it greatly increases the attack surface of a system. Installing any Windows application introduces the possibility of new ActiveX controls being installed. Vulnerabilities in ActiveX objects may be exploited via Internet Explorer, even if the object was never designed to be used in a web browser. Many ActiveX vulnerabilities lead to severe impacts. Often attackers can take control of the computer.

Java is an object-oriented programming language that can be used to develop active content for websites. A Java Virtual Machine (JVM) is used to execute the Java code or applet provided by the website. Some operating systems come with a JVM while others require the installation of a JVM before Java can be used. Java applets are operating system independent. Java applets usually execute within a sandbox where the interaction with the rest of the system is limited. However, various implementations of a JVM contain vulnerabilities that allow an applet to bypass these restrictions. Signed Java applets can also bypass sandbox restrictions, but they generally prompt the user before they can execute.

Plug-ins are applications intended for use in the web browser. Netscape has developed the standard for developing plug-ins, but this standard is used by multiple web browsers, including Mozilla Firefox and Safari. Plug-ins are similar to ActiveX controls but cannot be executed outside of a web browser. Adobe

Flash is an example of an application that is available as a plug-in. Plug-ins can contain programming flaws, such as buffer overflows, or they may contain design flaws, such as cross-domain violations.

Cookies are files placed on your system to store data for specific websites. A cookie can contain any information that a website is designed to store in it. Cookies may contain information about the sites you visited or may even contain credentials for accessing the sites. Cookies are designed to be readable only by the website that created them. Session cookies are cleared when the browser is closed; persistent cookies remain on the computer until the specified expiration date is reached. Cookies can be used to uniquely identify visitors of a website, which some people consider a violation of privacy. If a website uses cookies for authentication, then an attacker may be able to acquire unauthorized access to that site by obtaining the cookie. Persistent cookies pose a higher risk than session cookies because they remain on the computer longer.

JavaScript, also known as ECMAScript, is a scripting language that is used to make websites more interactive. Specifications in the JavaScript standard restrict certain features, such as accessing local files.

VBScript is another scripting language that is unique to Microsoft Windows Internet Explorer. VBScript is similar to JavaScript, but it is not as widely used because of its limited compatibility with other browsers. The ability to run a scripting language such as JavaScript or VBScript allows web page authors to add a significant number of features and interactivity to a web page. However, attackers can abuse this same capability. The default configuration for most web browsers enables scripting support, which can introduce multiple vulnerabilities, such as these:

- **Cross-site scripting vulnerability** (XSS), permits an attacker to leverage the trust relationship a user has with a website. XSS is not usually caused by a failure in the web browser.

- **Cross-zone and cross-domain vulnerabilities** occur when attackers can cross into the local machine zone or other protected areas and execute arbitrary commands on the vulnerable system. Most web browsers employ security models to prevent script in a website from accessing data in a different domain. Vulnerabilities that violate these security models can be used to perform actions that a site could not normally perform. The impact can be similar to an XSS vulnerability.

- **Detection evasion.** Antivirus, IDSs, and IPSs generally work by looking for specific patterns in content. If a known bad pattern is detected, then the appropriate actions can take place to protect the user. But because of the dynamic nature of programming languages, scripting in web pages can be used to evade such protective systems.

Recommended Security Practices over Web Browsers

Some software features that provide functionality to a web browser, such as ActiveX, Java, and scripting languages may also introduce vulnerabilities to computer systems. These may stem from poor implementation, poor design, or insecure configurations. For these reasons, you should understand which browsers support which features and the risks they could introduce. Some web browsers permit you to fully disable the use of these technologies, while others may permit you to enable features on a per-site basis.

Multiple web browsers may be installed on your computer. Other computer software applications, such as email clients or document viewers, may use a different browser from the one you normally use to access the web. Also, certain file types may be configured to open with a different web browser. Using one web browser to manually interact with websites does not mean other applications will automatically use the same browser. For this reason, it is important to securely configure each web browser that may be installed on your computer. One advantage to having multiple web browsers is that one browser can be used for only sensitive activities, such as online banking, and the other can be used for general-purpose web browsing. This can minimize the chances that a vulnerability in a web browser, website, or related software can be used to compromise sensitive information. Suggested controls are listed next.

1. **Keep the computer secure.** Enable automatic software updates if available. Some applications will automatically check for available updates, and many vendors offer automatic notification of updates via a mailing list. Look on your vendor's website for information about automatic notification. If no mailing list or other automated notification mechanism is offered, you may need to check the vendor's website periodically for updates.

2. **Install and use antivirus software.** Although an up-to-date antivirus software package cannot protect against all malicious code, for most users it remains the best first line of defense against malicious code attacks. Many antivirus packages support automatic updates of virus definitions. We recommend using these automatic updates when available.

3. **Avoid unsafe behavior.** For example:

   □ Use caution when opening email attachments or when using peer-to-peer file sharing, instant messaging, or chat rooms.

   □ Don't enable file sharing on network interfaces exposed directly to the internet.

4. **Follow the principle of least privilege—don't enable it if you don't need it.** Consider creating and using an account with limited privileges instead of an administrator- or root-level account for everyday tasks. Depending on the operating system, you only need to use administrator-level access when installing new software, changing system configurations, and the like. Many vulnerability exploits (e.g., viruses and Trojan horses) are executed with the privileges of the user that runs them, which makes it riskier to be logged in as an administrator all the time.

5. **Install browser settings properly and timely.** Proper and timely configuration settings of the browser can block (disable) active content (i.e., risky harmful content) like ActiveX, Java, scripting, pop-ups, images, and other potentially harmful content. These settings, in turn, can increase online security but decrease website functionality, resulting in a trade-off situation. One way to manage security is to utilize the "security zones" feature offered by some browsers (i.e., Microsoft Edge) to choose preset levels of security.

(d) Broad Cyber Defenses

This section presents broad topics: defense strategies, cyber-resiliency techniques, digital forensics, and web and mobile analytics.

(i) Defense Strategies

Deploy six defense strategies—defense in depth, defense in breadth, defense in time, defense in technology, defense in density, and defense in intensity. Together, these strategies provide a strong and robust cyber defense mechanism.

(ii) Cyber-Resiliency Techniques

A general definition of resilience as it relates to a computer system is its ability to continue to function correctly despite the existence of a fault or faults in one or more of its component parts. Cyber-resiliency techniques are a set or class of technologies and processes intended to achieve one or more objectives by providing capabilities to anticipate, withstand, recover from, and adapt to adverse conditions, stresses, attacks, or compromises on systems that include cyber resources. The cyber-resiliency techniques must be incorporated into a system development life cycle when developing a new system or maintaining an existing system. Exhibit 2.11 presents five strategic design principles linked to risk management strategies.

EXHIBIT 2.11 Linking of Strategic Design Principles with Risk Management Strategies

Strategic Design Principles	Analytical Practices	Risk Management Strategies
Focus on common critical assets	Criticality analysis, business impact analysis, mission impact analysis, and mission thread analysis	Engineering design: Physical redundancy, layered defense, and loose coupling Survivability design: Failure mode reduction, fail-safe, and evolution Constraints: Limited knowledge-based resources Priorities: Anticipate, withstand, and recover
Support agility and adaptability	Standards conformance analysis, interoperability analysis, and reusability analysis	Engineering design: Reorganization, human backup, inter-node interaction Survivability design: Mobility and evolution Constraints: Missions to be supported and mission needs can change rapidly Priorities: Recover and adapt
Reduce attack surfaces	Supply-chain risk management analysis, vulnerability and exposure analysis, operations security analysis, and cyber-attack modeling and simulation	Engineering design: Complexity avoidance and drift correction Survivability design: Prevention and failure-mode reduction Constraints: Limited operational resources to monitor and actively defend systems Priorities: Anticipate
Assume compromised resources	Cascading failure analysis, insider threat analysis, and cyber-attack modeling and simulation	Engineering design: Human backup, localized capacity, and loose coupling Survivability design: None Constraints: Ability to assure trustworthiness of system elements is limited Priorities: Anticipate and withstand
Expect adversaries to adapt and evolve	Adversary-driven cyber-resiliency analysis and red team tests	Engineering design: Reorganization and drift correction Survivability design: Evolution Assumptions: Adversaries can change their goals unpredictably Priorities: Anticipate and adapt

The following is a list of expanded definition of terms used in engineering design and survivability design in the exhibit.

Cyber-Resilience Engineering Design Principles

- **Absorption**—Allow the system to withstand threats to a specified level

- **Human-in-the-loop**—Allow the system to employ human elements when there is a need for human cognition

- **Internode interaction**—Allow the nodes of the system to communicate, cooperate, and collaborate with other nodes when this interaction is essential

- **Modularity**—Construct the system of relatively independent but interlocking components or system elements; also called localized capacity

- **Neutral state**—Allow the system to incorporate time delays that will allow human operators to consider actions to prevent further damage

- **Complexity avoidance**—Incorporate features that enable the system to limit its own complexity to a level not more than necessary

- **Hidden interactions avoidance**—Incorporate features that assure that potentially harmful interactions between nodes are avoided

- **Functional redundancy**—Employ an architecture with two or more independent and identical branches

- **Physical redundancy**—Employ an architecture with two or more different branches; also called diversity

- **Loose coupling**—Construct the system of elements that depend on each other to the least extent practicable

- **Defense-in-depth**—Provide multiple means to avoid failure; also called Layered Defense

- **Restructuring**—Incorporate features that allow the system to restructure itself; also known as reorganization

- **Reparability**—Incorporate features that allow the system to be brought up to partial or full functionality over a specified period of time and in a specified environment

Survivability Design Principles

- **Prevention** —Suppress a future or potential future disturbance

- **Mobility**—Relocate to avoid detection by an external change agent

- **Concealment**—Reduce the visibility of a system from an external change agent

- **Deterrence**—Dissuade a rational external agent from committing a disturbance

- **Preemption**—Suppress an imminent disturbance

- **Avoidance**—Maneuver away from an ongoing disturbance

- **Hardness**—Resist deformation

- **Redundancy**—Duplicate critical system functions to increase reliability

- **Margin**—Allow extra capability to maintain value delivery despite losses

- **Heterogeneity**—Vary system elements to mitigate homogeneous disturbances

- **Distribution**—Separate critical system elements to mitigate local disturbances

- **Failure mode reduction**—Eliminate system hazards through intrinsic design: substitute, simplify, decouple, and reduce hazardous materials

- **Fail-Safe**—Prevent or delay degradation via physics of incipient failure

- **Evolution**—Alter system elements to reduce disturbance effectiveness

- **Containment**—Isolate or minimize the propagation of failure

- **Replacement**—Substitute system elements to improve value delivery

- **Repair**—Restore the system to improve value delivery

(iii) Digital Forensics

Forensics is the process of using scientific knowledge for collecting, analyzing, and presenting evidence to the courts. Forensics deals primarily with the recovery and analysis of latent (hidden) evidence. Computer forensics is defined as the discipline that combines elements of law and computer science to collect and analyze data from computer systems, wired networks, wireless communications, mobile devices, and storage devices in a way that is admissible as evidence in a court of law. The admissibility of evidence is one of the requirements of the U.S. Federal Rules of Evidence. Different types of evidence include relevant evidence, authenticating or identifying evidence, and hearsay evidence.

An organization is said to possess a solid computer forensic capability when it:

- Develops a robust cyber-incident response plan; uses security monitoring tools

- Conducts vulnerability assessment exercises periodically

- Deploys IPSs

- Deploys IDSs

- Uses web application proxies

- Places firewalls at multiple levels for a stronger protection

- Uses web content filtering software to block unwanted website traffic

- Rotates regular data backup files between onsite and offsite

- Hires competent staff

All these combined capabilities are aimed at reporting on the security status of an organization's computer systems and networks with a defense-in-depth protection strategy.

Having a computer forensics capability offers an organization several benefits:

- It provides a defense-in-depth approach to network and computer security in that it provides multiple layers of different types of protection from different computer vendors, thus giving a substantially better protection than a single layer of protection.

- Should a computer intrusion or security incident lead to a court case, the organization with computer forensics capability will be at a distinct advantage because it followed the "due care" legal principle and safeguarded the security and privacy of the company's data.

- It is proof that the organization complies with computer security best practices and sound security policies.

- It can potentially avoid lawsuits by customers and employees or regulatory audits by government agencies, resulting from negligence.

- It shows the organization is complying with laws that hold businesses liable for breaches in the security or integrity of computer systems and networks, resulting in data theft, data loss, and data destruction. These federal laws include SOX, HIPAA, GLB, and the Privacy Act.

Simply stated, the court system prefers to see that organizations are proactive in establishing and monitoring strong security control mechanisms to handle computer incidents.

Two basic types of data are collected in computer forensics: persistent data and volatile data. **Persistent data** is the data that is stored on a local hard drive or cloud storage and is preserved when the computer is tuned off. **Volatile data** is any data that is stored in computer memory, or exists in transit, that is lost when the computer loses power or is turned off. Volatile data resides in computer registers, caches, and random access memory. Since volatile data is temporary, investigators must know reliable ways to capture it for evidence before it disappears. In addition, system administrators, security analysts, and network administrators must understand the computer forensic process and methods to recover data from backup files, computer hard drives, and mobile devices so they can help identify and analyze a security incident.

In a computer crime—for that matter, in any crime—successful prosecution depends heavily on presenting good evidence to the court. Computer forensics is used to provide that good evidence. It is the art of retrieving computer data in such a way that will make it admissible in court. It can be used to convict a computer criminal.

SAFEGUARDS TO PROTECT EVIDENCE

- Regular backups
- Off-site storage of backups
- Transaction logs
- Data storage on disks
- Chain-of-custody rules

The attack-victim organization should be able to know who used a computer system and why, trace the criminal's activity through transaction logs, and protect the evidence. From a court's viewpoint, the evidence needs to be understandable to a judge and jury, credible, and defensible. This requires forensic auditors to think like lawyers, investigators, and criminals.

Guidelines to Successful Computer Forensics

- If you suspect that a computer system has been used in a crime, cut off its links to the network immediately.

- Do not touch evidence that you find. Doing this requires freezing or taking a snapshot of the computer records and data.

- Do not present a "reasonable doubt" situation to a judge or jury.

- Prove when each transaction has occurred with a time and date stamp.

- Protect the evidential matter (e.g., programs, data, and hardware) in such a way that it will not be modified, tainted, or fabricated. This is very important to the court.

- Store that evidential matter in an immutable form (e.g., disks) so that it is inexpensive; defensible in a court; and easy to handle, present, and protect.

(A) Digital Forensics Analysis Methodology

A systematic and structured methodology is required to collect, extract, and analyze forensically needed data so that a forensic report can be issued to interested parties. Whether the data resides on computers (e.g., files on a hard drive of desktop, laptop, or notebook computers) or on mobile devices (e.g., smartphones, digital tablets, and flash drives), it must be secured. This systematic methodology should occur in these five steps:

1. Collect imaging forensic data.

2. Extract the required data.

3. Identify relevant data.

4. Analyze the relevant data.

5. Issue a forensic report.

Each step is explained next.

1. **Collecting imaging forensic data** means receiving an exact, sector-by-sector copy of a hard disk. Software capable of creating such copies of hard drives preserves deleted files, slack space, system files, and executable files (program files), which can be critical for later analysis of a security incident.

2. **Extracting the required data** means verifying the integrity of forensic data, selecting forensic tools, and extracting the requested data.

Forensic Tools

☐ Virus and spyware detection software

☐ Login scripts

☐ Sinkhole routers

☐ IPS and IDS software

☐ Packet sniffers

☐ Host and file scans

☐ File sharing tools

☐ Antivirus and anti-spyware software

☐ Network device logs

☐ Protocol analyzers

☐ Audit software

□ Password cracking programs

□ Disk imaging software

□ Auditing tools

□ Operating system file utility programs

□ File zip and unzip utility programs

□ Cable testers

□ Network line monitors

These and other tools can help investigators identify deleted, files, files, or encrypted files, where the latter can represent ransomware attacks.

3. **Identifying relevant data** requires deciding whether the data is relevant to the forensic request and making a relevant data list with all the associated metadata elements with data attributes.

4. **Analyzing the relevant data** asks a basic question: Is the collected data enough to proceed further or is more data? If more data is needed, relevant questions include "what," "where," "when," "who," and "how" to get the more data. At this time, the data is analyzed and the findings are documented.

5. **Issue a forensic report** to all the interested parties based on the findings noted.

Relatively speaking, extracting data from computers can be easier than extracting data from mobile devices for several reasons: There are so many small, novelty data devices on the market; it is difficult to know where the data is located (i.e., local on the device or remote on the cloud); and it is difficult to differentiate between employee-owned mobile devices and company-owned mobile devices. In order to inventory all the data needed in order to preserve and perform data extraction and recovery efforts, investigators need to determine the number of web-based email accounts, text messages, social media accounts, apps, and file storage locations.

Investigators can collect the following data from mobile devices:

■ Stand-alone data files, such as audio, graphic, and video files

■ Phone call logs showing incoming, outgoing, and missed calls

■ Text messages, such as SMS and enhanced message service (EMS) messages

■ MMS messages showing audio, graphic, and video files without a text message

■ Browser and email data

■ Social media data containing user profiles with or without pictures, video, or audio files

■ Data on subscriber identity module (SIM) cards on smartphones

■ Other data of interest, including equipment and subscriber data, digital wallet data, and data in personal notes and calendars.

Note that some people, such as law enforcement authorities, attorneys, and family and friends of criminals, can look for anti-forensic techniques to stop or discount the forensic work because they do not trust the results (outcomes) of digital forensic work. These techniques are methods to prevent or act against the application of science to those criminal and civil laws that are enforced by police agencies in a criminal justice system.

(iv) Web and Mobile Analytics

This section starts with five web generations so readers can understand the evolution of the World Wide Web (the Internet).

In addition, this section presents two types of analytics: web analytics based on websites and the Internet, and mobile analytics based on mobile operating systems and devices. Both types present metrics that should be measured and monitored to improve the performance of web and mobile platforms.

(A) Web Generations

The World Wide Web (www), the Internet, has been evolving at a rapid pace moving from web 0.0 to web 5.0 generations.

- **Web 0.0**—The birth of the Internet and its development. In a way, web 0.0 was in the concept stage of innovation with a proof of concept.

- **Web 1.0**—Basic web features, such as browsing, static web format, mostly read-only, owner-published content. Used portals and directories, banner advertising, directories, home pages, page views, web forms, online shopping carts, and minimal interactive publishing. Technologies and programming languages used include HTTP, TCP/IP, HTML, XML, and XHTML. Threats include viruses, worms, phishing, and social engineering approaches.

- **Web 2.0**—Read-write (writing and participating web), social media platforms, cloud computing networks, blogs, wikis, tweets, audio/video images, tweets, tagging, podcasts, collaboration, sharing content, connected devices, web applications (apps), mashups, search engines, mobile computing, and interactive advertising. All these features increased attacks on networks, computers, and devices with malware, spyware, adware, capturing user keystrokes, XSS, and phishing attacks. Web 2.0 provided an expanded bandwidth and greater computing power.

- **Web 3.0**—Personal and portable; executing web; content consolidation; represents smart applications such as artificial intelligence, robots, augmented/VR, and the IoT. Focuses on user behavior and engagement; promotes behavioral advertising and outsourced emails.

- **Web 4.0**—Mobile web connecting all devices in the real world and virtual world in real time.

- **Web 5.0**—Open connection, linked and intelligent web, and emotional web.

(B) Web Analytics

Similar to business, data, and audit analytics, web analytics are quantitative measurements of a company's website performance, functioning of online computer systems and networks, and overall Internet performance. These web analytics, which can be called web metrics and web key performance indicators (web-KPIs), must be tracked and improved similar to any other business-related KPIs. As e-commerce is increasing at a fast rate, it is important to pay special attention to web analytics. As with any other KPIs, web-KPIs should be a few in number, significant in size, and big in impact to be of any value.

Web Analytics

- Number of online shopping cart abandonments per day, week, month, quarter, and year. Shopping cart abandonments are a reflection of a poorly designed company website for customer orders with limited features and functions, followed by difficult flow of web screens with poor descriptions of a product's features. Overall, the online order system is unattractive and uninviting to customers, resulting in loss of sales orders and lost profits.

- Number of website crashes or shutdowns per day, week, month, quarter, and year. Crashes reflect poor system design, development, and testing of software followed by lack of preventive and regular maintenance. They result in loss of sales revenues, bad reputation, and loss of customer goodwill. The computer systems could be a legacy system that needs redesign or replacement.

- Number of online software glitches per day, week, month, quarter, and year. Software glitches are reflections of untested software containing processing flaws and file updating errors, requiring software patches and fixes.

- Number of data breaches from external hackers or internal employees per day, week, month, quarter, and year. Data breaches are reflections of lack of adequate security controls due to antiquated security design principles and practices. They are proof that hackers know more about system security weaknesses than the internal IT security staff.

- Number of marketing emails opened or not opened by targeted customers for advertising and promotional programs. This metric can reflect an aggressive marketing email campaign coming from the same company repeatedly, that turn their customers off. Customers may be bombarded or overwhelmed by frequent and unnecessary mass emails.

- Number of marketing emails responded to or not responded to by targeted customers for advertising and promotional programs. This metric reflects that customers are not interested in purchasing the company's products and services. Busy customers will not waste their time responding, and silence is their answer.

- Number of marketing text messages replied to or not replied to by targeted customers for advertising and promotional programs. The text messages could be annoying and irrelevant to customers, and can turn them off.

- Number of browser clicks made on a marketing ad campaign. An abnormal number of clicks could be a sign of **click fraud** and web fraud perpetrated by a hired advertising company. The hired company is cheating its customers by using employees or software bots to do fraud-clicking. A control is to replace the hired advertising company and focus on the reputation of a company before hiring.

- Percentage of system uptime (e.g., 90%) and system downtime (e.g., 10%) per day, week, month, quarter, and year. System uptime represents robust and resilient computer systems and networks; system downtime represents the opposite. Frequent system downtimes and crashes could lead to lost sales and customers switching to competitors due to frustration. Backup computer systems and alternative computer processing sites may be required to keep customers with the company.

- Number of times system maintenance (whether preventive or scheduled) work is done in a time period. Infrequent system maintenance work could lead to a higher percentage of system downtime.

- Social media metrics, such as revenue per pin (Pinterest), average time to respond on Twitter's customer feedback, percentage of Twitter customers' comments replied or ignored, and percentage of Facebook customers' comments answered or ignored.

- Using email as a sales channel, email metrics relevant to email campaigns are click-through rates, email open rates, and revenue per email.

- The click-through rate is the number of times a website user clicks on a web page ad compared to the total number of users viewing the same ad. The higher the **click-through rate**, the greater the interest in an ad and the higher the possibility of larger dollar amounts converted to online sales revenue (i.e., click-through conversion amount). As the click fraud rate increases, the click-through rate increases, showing a direct relationship. However, having a greater number of click-through rates may or may not increase online sales revenue, because the conversion depends on whether the clicks have actually turned into sales orders.

    Click-through rate = (Number of visitors clicked) / (Total number of visitors) × 100

- **Click to conversion time** for a product or service is the elapsed time between the number of browser clicks made, number of website navigation paths taken, and number of online ads read before a purchase decision was made. Comparisons can be made between different products and at different times to shorten the click-to-conversion time. The shorter the conversion time, the faster the sales revenue, and vice versa. Customer data is classified, stored, and analyzed to study purchasing trends and patterns. As the click fraud rate increases, the click-to-conversion time and the click-through-conversion amount decreases, showing an inverse relationship.

(C) Mobile Analytics

- Number of customer visits (traffic count) to a retailer's website classified as new customers or repeat customers. This website traffic is similar to foot traffic into physical stores. The simpler the design of the website, the better attraction it is to the site and vice versa.

- Number of customers who purchased a product using a smartphone after visiting a site and after going to a physical store. This metric is a measure of the online customer conversion rate because the customer purchased a product after visiting a site.

- Number of customers who abandoned a shopping cart, expressed as a percentage of total customers who ordered online. The higher the abandoned rate, the more poorly designed the site is.

- Number of page views on a retailer's site, expressed as above average, average, or below average. This metric represents the proper use of relevant search terms in product listings, which can enhance or diminish the visibility of page views to customers. Using pictures, photos, and other graphics in product listings can draw customer attention better than an average page view full of text.

- Number of bounced emails, classified as hard bounces and soft bounces. Hard bounces are messages that are permanently rejected due to an invalid email address or a blocked server. Soft bounces are messages that are temporarily rejected because a recipient's inbox is full or a server is down.

- System response time to reach a site's homepage and the size of the homepage. Average response time for the homepage should be three seconds or less, and average size of the homepage should be two pages or less.

- Volume of mobile device user traffic not going through a company's trusted Internet connection, the official communication channel.

(e) Cybersecurity and Information Security Policies

This section presents several policies that organizations should develop and enforce against cyber threats, exploits, and attacks, such as ransomware attacks as well as developing and enforcing general information security and network security policies. These policies can prevent and detect security incidents such as data breaches, malware infections, and insider threats (i.e., employee and contractor threats).

Overall benefits of such policies are to control or change the behavior of system users (employees and contractors) with rules of behavior and rules of engagement principles so that system users do not harm a company's data, technology, and human assets or so that system users do not help or support others to do such harm (i.e., loss of data, stealing of data, damaging [deleting] data, modifying data, sharing data, and selling data). Here, security controls are embedded or built into the security policies through manual procedure and/or automated procedures. Six security policies are listed next.

1. Establish basic security policies

2. Establish cybersecurity policies against ransomware and other malware attacks

3. Issue rules of behavior and rules of engagement documents

4. Establish access control policies

5. Establish telework, remote access, and mobile device policies

6. Establish information security and network security policies

(i) Establish Basic Security Policies

Effective security policies and procedures are the first step or the first line-of-defenses to ensure secure systems and networks. To make the security policy effective, it must be practical and enforceable, and it must be possible to comply with the policy. The policy must not significantly impact productivity, be cost prohibitive, or lack support. This delicate balance is best accomplished by including both functional management and information security management in the policy development process.

Four basic types of security policies exist: program policies, issue-specific policies, system-specific policies, and context-based policies. The context-based policies are further divided into several targeted contexts such as acceptable use policies, business-only Internet use policies, software restriction policies, mobile device use policies, social media use policies, telework and remote server access policies, and cloud service use policies. Each type of policy is discussed next.

1. **Program policies** are used to create an organization's information security program. Contents of program policy include purpose, scope, responsibilities, and compliance (i.e., penalties and disciplinary actions). It contains scope, responsibilities, strategic direction, and resources.

2. **Issue-specific policies** address specific issues of concern to the organization. Examples of specific issues include: Internet access; email privacy; approach to risk management and contingency planning; protection of confidential and proprietary information; use of unauthorized software; acquisition of software; doing computer work at home; bringing in disks from outside the workplace; access to other employees' files; encryption of files and email; rights of privacy; responsibilities for correctness of data; suspected malicious

code; and physical emergencies such as fire and flood. It contains contingency planning, risk management, and implementation of new regulations or laws.

3. **System-specific policies** focus on decisions taken by management to protect particular system, such as an application system or network system (i.e., management controls). Components of system-specific policies include security objectives and operational security rules. System-specific policies are often implemented through the use of logical access controls. They contain ACLs for a specific system, training users, and email/fax security policy. Some system-specific policies, where both functional management and information security management work together to develop, include: (1) creating a gold disk in configuration management; (2) modem usage policy; and (3) wireless security policy for planning, deploying, and configuring wireless access points to prevent war-driving attacks.

4. **Context-based policies** focus on several topics such as:

   (a) Acceptable use policies which require that a system user, an end-user, or an administrator (e.g., system, security, and network administrator) agrees to comply with such policies prior to accessing computer systems, internal networks, and external networks (the Internet). These policies also discuss how guest accounts, temporary accounts, terminated accounts, and privileged accounts are treated and maintained. Acceptable use is based on authorized access.

   (b) Business-only Internet use policies which deal with whether employees can access outside, nonbusiness websites during their work hours. This type of access includes employees checking baseball scores at lunchtime, accessing dating websites, placing online gambling bets, playing online games, and checking stock market prices.

   (c) Software restriction policies which should state what type of employees are allowed to bring their own software from home for use at work and under what circumstances. The types of restricted software can include game, entertainment (movies), sports, investment, open-source, and other non-business-related software. Software policies should also state which of the company's official computer programs can be run from temporary folders supporting popular Internet browsers, compression and decompression programs, or app folders. Running computer programs from the temporary folders is very risky due to their poor code quality and possibility of malware.

   (d) Mobile device use policies that require turning off Bluetooth and Wi-Fi connections when not used. This action, in turn, reduces the threat surface to which a mobile device is exposed. These policies should also state that important functions are deactivated to reduce the security exposure until requested by users.

   (e) Social media use policies should state what type of employees are allowed to access the organization's approved social media networks and under what circumstances. They should also spell out whether unauthorized employees can post their own comments in response to a customer's negative postings and whether employees can post personal opinions on political, economic, and social events occurring either domestically or internationally.

   (f) Telework and remote server access policies should state what type of employees are allowed to do telework and remote access and under what circumstances. They should also spell out what type of employees can bring their own devices and whether those devices can be used within an organization, for telework, or by remote access.

   (g) Cloud service use policies should state what type of employees can use the organization's approved cloud services and for what purposes. They should also spell out whether employees can use the company's cloud storage for personal and family use.

For example, in a cloud computing environment, subscribers ensure that all subscriber personnel read and understand the provider's acceptable use policy and negotiate an agreement for resolution of agreed-on policy violations in advance with the provider. The agreement also includes resolving disputes over possible policy violations.

(ii) Establish Cybersecurity Policies Against Ransomware and Other Malware Attacks

Proactive preventive mechanisms are the best defenses available. Specific preventive measures and policies to protect computer systems and networks from falling victims to a ransomware infections and attacks can include these:

- Train and remind employees to never click unsolicited links or open unsolicited attachments in emails. Attackers often enter organizations by tricking users into disclosing a password or clicking on a virus-laden email attachment.

- Enable strong spam filters to prevent phishing emails from reaching end users, and authenticate inbound email to prevent email spoofing.

- Scan all incoming and outgoing email to detect threats and filter executable files from reaching end users.

- Configure firewalls to block access to known malicious IP addresses.

- Patch operating systems, applications software, and firmware on mobile devices. Consider using a centralized patch management system.

- Set antivirus and anti-malware programs to conduct regular scans automatically.

- Manage the use of privileged accounts based on the principle of least privilege. This means that no users should be assigned administrative access unless they absolutely need it; those who need administrator accounts should use them only when necessary.

- Configure access controls, including file, directory, and network share permissions, with least privilege in mind. If a user only needs to read specific files, the user should not have write access to those files, directories, or network shares.

- Disable macro scripts from office files transmitted via email.

- Implement software restriction policies or other controls to prevent programs from executing from common ransomware locations, such as temporary folders supporting popular Internet browsers or compression or decompression programs.

- Consider disabling remote desktop protocol if it is not being used.

- Use application whitelisting, which only allows systems to execute programs known and permitted by security policy.

- Execute operating system environments or specific programs in a virtualized environment.

- Categorize data assets based on organizational value, and implement physical and logical separation of networks and data assets for different organizational units.

- Back up data regularly. Verify the integrity of those backups and test the restoration process to ensure it is working.

- Conduct an annual penetration test and vulnerability assessment exercise.

- Ensure backups are not connected permanently to the computers and networks they are backing up. Acceptable procedures include securing backups in the cloud or physically storing backups offline. Some attackers can lock cloud-based backups when systems continuously back up in real time (known as persistent synchronization). Backups are critical in ransomware recovery and response. *Note that a backup may be the best way to recover from infected data.*

(iii) Issue Rules of Behavior and Rules of Engagement Documents

Rules of behavior and rules of engagement must be considered to exact proper behavior from employees, outside contractors, and vendors with regard to computer systems and their security and use.

A **rules of behavior document** describes the rules established and implemented concerning use of, security in, and acceptable level of risk of the system. Rules clearly delineate responsibilities and expected behavior of all individuals with access to the system. The organization establishes and makes readily available to all information system users a set of rules that describes their responsibilities and expected behavior with regard to information system usage.

A rules of behavior document:

- Defines scope of coverage, including work at home; dial-in access; connection to the Internet; use of copyrighted work; unofficial use of organization equipment; assignment and limitations of system privileges and individual accountability in using passwords; searching databases; and divulging sensitive information.

- Delineates responsibilities, expected use of system, and behavior of all users.

- Describes appropriate limits on interconnections of systems.

- Defines service provisions and restoration priorities.

- Clarifies consequences of behavior not consistent with rules of behavior.

A **rules of engagement document** provides detailed guidelines and constraints regarding the execution of information security testing. The rules of engagement are established before the start of a security test. The rules give the test team authority to conduct the defined activities without the need for additional permissions. Rules of engagement are aimed at outside contractors and vendors before they perform work for an organization.

(iv) Establish Access Control Policies

- Define the access control policies to enforce the principles of least privilege and separation of duties.

- Develop an attack model to help determine the type of security incidents that should generate alerts.

- Grant only a very few users (e.g., human resource administrators) the authority to modify (i.e., initiate, change, or delete) employee access information. Require the approval of more than one individual (dual-person control) to update employee access information. Log all employee access information modifications. Define workflows to enforce these requirements.

- Grant only a very few users (e.g., access rules administrators) the authority to modify (i.e., initiate, change, or delete) access rules. Require the approval of more than one individual (dual-person control) to update access rules. Log all access rule modifications. Define workflows to enforce these requirements.

- Grant only a very few users (e.g., security analysts) the authority to modify (i.e., initiate, change, or delete) the access analytics that are applied to access log information by the monitoring capability to determine what constitute an anomaly and generates an alert. Any changes made to the access analytics should, by policy, require the approval of more than one individual, and these changes should themselves be logged, with the logs sent to a monitor-of-monitors system other than the monitoring system and to all security analysts and affected system users. Define workflows to enforce these requirements. In addition, the monitoring system should have the ability to notify individuals when it goes offline or stops functioning and should generate alerts in these cases.

- Equip the access control monitoring system with a complete set of access rules to take full advantage of the ability to identify anomalous situations that can signal a cyber incident. Define organization-wide workflows that include business rules and security rules to determine each user's access control authorizations and ensure that the organization-wide access control policy is enforced as completely and accurately as possible.

- Deploy a system that audits and analyzes access directory content to create a description of who has access to what resources. Validate that these access permissions correctly implement the organization's intended business processes and access control policies.

(v) Establish Telework, Remote Access, and Mobile Device Policies

Numerous organizations permit the use of devices that are outside organizational control. In addition, organizations allow devices controlled by contractors, business partners, and vendors, referred to as third-party-controlled technologies. Even though the organization may have written agreements or contracts with employees and third parties that require client devices to be properly secured, those agreements generally cannot be enforced automatically. Unsecured, malware-infected, and/or otherwise compromised devices may end up connected to sensitive organizational resources, such as computer systems and networks. The next policies are required to correct these security-related problems:

- Plan telework-related security policies and controls based on the assumption that external computing environments contain hostile threats with little or no trust.

- Develop a telework security policy that defines network, remote access, and BYOD requirements.

- Ensure that remote access servers are secured effectively and are configured to enforce telework security policies.

- Secure organization-controlled telework client devices against common threats, and regularly maintain their security controls.

- If external device use (e.g., BYOD and third-party-controlled devices) is permitted within the organization's facilities and systems, strongly consider establishing a separate, external, dedicated network for this use.

(vi) Establish Information Security and Network Security Policies

- Build cybersecurity controls into application system development methodology to produce robust and resilient systems. This practice is based on prevention more than on detection and correction.

- Isolate certain capabilities on separate subnetworks protected by firewalls, intrusion detection devices, VPNs, or port-based authentication mechanisms.

- Implement a management network to isolate log and management traffic from the production networks that are operational networks.

- Secure critical user access information and logs to protect them from unauthorized insertion, modification, or deletion.

- Log all privileged user access activities.

- Use encryption and integrity-checking mechanisms to protect user access information and associated logs while this information is in transit (i.e., data in transit) between endpoints.

- Keep operating system software up to date by patching, version control, and monitoring indicators of compromise. Perform virus and malware detection, and keep antivirus signatures up to date.

- Harden all system capabilities by deploying them on securely configured operating systems that use long and complex passwords and are configured per best practices.

- Scan operating system software for vulnerabilities.

- Change default passwords when installing software.

- Identify and understand which predefined administrative accounts and guest accounts come with default options. Remove these default options to eliminate any inadvertent backdoors into these accounts. Disable all unnecessary predefined accounts. Even though the accounts are disabled, change the default passwords in case a future patch enables them.

- Restrict all permitted communication to specific protocols, IP addresses, and port communications.

- Monitor firewall configurations to ensure that they perform network traffic filtering and blocking activities.

- Apply encryption and integrity-checking mechanisms to networks, user access, and log information so that tampering activities can be detected.

- Establish a gold disk policy—baseline configuration management of an operating system that contains only the essential ports, services, login credentials, and software needed to effectively run the system environment in a safe and efficient manner. This approach greatly increases an organization's security posture and lowers the attack surface that attackers can exploit by.

- In addition, a gold disk (master disk) can take advantage of removing all guest and unnecessary user accounts on a system and enforcing that the system be run with individual user IDs that have the least amount of privileges that are needed in order to properly operate the system. In doing so, the system can be modified or changed only if an account with the appropriate escalated privileges has been entered. This can significantly reduce the amount of improper use on a system and can make it much more difficult to install unwanted malicious code on a system.

- Install counter-action software tools on computers and mobile devices to prevent and detect malware and other destructive software implanted by hackers to kill the anti-tools. Examples of these tools include antivirus, anti-spyware, anti-skimming, anti-debugging software, anti-jittering, anti-phishing, anti-spoofing, anti-jamming, anti-tampering, and anti-spamming software. Be aware that hackers can nullify (kill) these anti-tools to carry out their malicious work. A hacker's goal is to make these user anti-tools ineffective and substitute their infected anti-tools. Some Internet sites sell false anti-spyware tools that actually introduce spyware.

(f) Cybersecurity Risk Management

Cybersecurity breaches are a major concern at all levels of management due to their frequent occurrence in all industries and the severe damages that they can cause. The best way to address security breaches is to have a clear understanding of the risks an organization faces and to develop strong mitigating options and remedial choices to control or reduce such risks.

Hackers are constantly developing and introducing sophisticated new threats and attacks on organizations of all sizes. Cyberspace is expanding rapidly, getting busier, and drawing a significant amount of hacker attention due to many new activities taking place in cyberspace. Examples of these new activities include heavy interaction between cloud computing, social media networks, connected devices (e.g., mobile devices, legacy devices, edge devices, and endpoint devices), and enterprise networks. New threats are emerging, including identity theft, Internet fraud, data breaches, data integrity attacks, and ransomware attacks. The expanded cyberspace is a gold mine into which hackers launch attacks.

(i) Cybersecurity Risk Management Concepts

Cyber threats and attacks create new and major cyber risks that were not observed or heard before because hackers are becoming more creative and innovative in coming up with new and destructive and disruptive attacks. Cyber risks are significant in size and impact, and the corresponding cyber controls are weak, inadequate, incomplete, ineffective, and inefficient. A gap exists between strong cyber risks and weak cyber controls; stronger cyber controls are needed. Strengthening security controls requires time, cost, and effort for an organization's IT security staff. They must write a new and customized computer security program, purchase new security hardware devices, or acquire off-the-shelf commercially available security software products. For this reason, management must be strongly committed to support, strategy, and funding of the IT department. Even with sufficient funding, there is always a lingering doubt whether an organization's IT staff possesses the right kind of knowledge, skills, and abilities (KSAs) to outthink, outgrow, and outsmart hackers' KSAs. This disparity in KSAs is seen when hackers launch advanced attacks against an organization; the hackers are ahead of the learning curve in this and similar situations.

A risk management program can assist in handling and addressing such risks. Mitigation options and remediation choices are needed to manage cyber risks. This section presents major risk management concepts as they relate to information systems and IT environment.

(A) Risk Management

Risk management is the total process of identifying, assessing, controlling, and mitigating risks (uncertainty). Risk management includes: risk assessment (risk analysis); cost-benefit analysis; the selection, implementation, test, and evaluation of safeguards (risk mitigation); risk financing (risk funding); and risk monitoring (reporting, feedback, and evaluation). It is expressed as:

Risk Management = Risk Assessment + Risk Mitigation + Risk Financing + Risk Monitoring

The ultimate goal of risk management is to minimize the adverse effects of losses and uncertainty connected with pure risks. Risk management is also defined as consisting of risk control and risk financing or categories. Note that risk assessment, risk mitigation, and risk monitoring are part of risk control.

(B) Risk Assessment

Risk assessment (risk analysis) includes identification, analysis, measurement, and prioritization of risks. It is the process of identifying the risks and determining the probability of occurrence, the resulting impact, and additional safeguards that would mitigate this impact. It includes risk measurement and prioritization.

(C) Risk Mitigation

Risk mitigation involves implementation of preventive, detective, and corrective controls along with management, operational, and technical controls to reduce the effects of risks. Risk mitigation includes designing and implementing controls and control-related procedures to minimize risks.

Risk mitigation is a systematic methodology used by senior management to reduce organization risks. Risk mitigation can be achieved through any one or combination of the next risk mitigation options or remediation choices.

Risk Mitigation Options or Remediation Choices

- **Risk rejection** or risk ignorance is not a wise choice, as all major risks must be managed.

- **Risk Assumption (acceptance)** is recognizing a risk and its potential consequences and accepting that risk. This usually occurs when no alternate risk mitigation strategy is more cost effective or feasible. Risk acceptance is associated with risk tolerance and risk appetite.

  Risk assumption involves accepting the potential risks and continuing to operate the system or process. At some point, management needs to decide if the operation, function, or system is acceptable, given the kind and severity of remaining risks. Risk acceptance is linked to the selection of safeguards since, in some cases, risk may have to be accepted because safeguards (countermeasures) are too expensive (in either monetary or nonmonetary factors).

  Merely selecting safeguards does not reduce risk; those safeguards need to be implemented effectively. Moreover, to continue to be effective, risk management needs to be an ongoing process. This requires a periodic assessment and improvement of safeguards and reanalysis of risks.

- **Risk avoidance** involves avoiding risk by eliminating the cause and/or consequence of the risk by, for example, adding controls that prevent the risk from occurring, removing certain functions from the system, or shutting down the system when risks are identified. Risk avoidance is appropriate when it is possible to reduce either the severity or the frequency of a risk.

- **Risk reduction (limitation)** limiting the risk by implementing controls (supporting, preventive, and detective controls) that minimize the adverse impact of a threat or vulnerability.

- **Risk transfer** means transferring the risk by using other options to compensate for the loss, such as purchasing insurance, coinsurance, or outsourcing. It involves finding another person or organization that can manage project risk(s) better. Risk transfer is appropriate for a risk with a low expected frequency and a high potential severity.

- **Risk protection** can be thought of as insurance against certain events. It involves doing something to allow the project to fall back on additional or alternate resources should the scheduled resource(s) fail.

- **Risk contingency** involves proper planning to define the necessary backup or alternative steps needed if an identified risk event should occur.

- **Risk compliance** means complying with all applicable laws and regulations in a timely and proper manner in order to reduce compliance risk.

- **Residual risk** refers to the risk remaining after the implementation of new or enhanced controls. Organizations can analyze the extent of the risk reduction generated by the new or enhanced controls in terms of reduced threat likelihood or impact. Practically no system or process is risk free, and not all implemented controls can eliminate the risks they are intended to address or reduce the risk level to zero. More is said later in this section about residual risk.

Implementation of new or enhanced controls can mitigate risks by:

- Eliminating some of the system's vulnerabilities (flaws and weaknesses), thereby reducing the number of possible threat source/vulnerability pairs.

- Adding a targeted control to reduce the capacity and motivation of a threat source (e.g., if technical controls are expensive, then consider administrative and physical controls).

- Reducing the magnitude of the adverse impact (e.g., limiting the extent of a vulnerability or modifying the nature of the relationship between the IT system and the organization's mission).

If the residual risk has not been reduced to an acceptable level, the risk management cycle must be repeated to identify a way of lowering the residual risk to an acceptable level.

(D) Risk Financing

Risk financing concentrates on arranging the availability of internal funds to meet financial losses that occur. It also involves the external transfer of risk. Risk financing includes risk retention and risk transfer, a tool used by captive insurers. Risk retention applies to risks that have a low expected frequency and a low potential severity. Risk transfer applies to risks that have a low expected frequency and a high potential severity. Insurance should be purchased for losses in excess of a firm's risk retention level.

When losses have both high expected frequency and high potential severity, it is likely that risk retention, risk transfer, and loss control all will need to be used in varying degrees. Common methods of loss control include reducing the probability of losses (i.e., frequency and severity reduction) and decreasing the cost of losses that do occur (i.e., cost reduction). Note that "high" and "low" loss frequency and severity rates are defined differently for different firms.

Risk financing includes internal funding for risks (self-insurance and residual risk) and external transfer of risks, such as insurance and hedging. It can be unfunded or funded retention. The unfunded retention is treated as part of the overall cost of doing business. A firm may decide to practice funded retention by making various preloss arrangements to ensure that money is readily available to pay for losses that occur. Examples of funded retention include use of credit, reserve funds, self-insurance, and captive insurers.

(E) Risk Monitoring

Risk monitoring (or risk evaluation) addresses internal and external reporting and provides feedback into the risk assessment process, continuing the loop. The third and final process of risk management, risk monitoring is a continual evaluation process since change is constant in most organizations. Eight changes are possible:

1. New businesses are acquired.

2. New products are introduced.

3. New services are provided.

4. Networks are updated and expanded.

5. Network components are added or removed.

6. Application software is replaced or updated with newer versions.

7. Personnel changes are made.

8. Security policies are updated.

These changes mean that new risks will surface and risks previously mitigated may again become a concern. Thus, the risk monitoring process is ongoing and evolving.

(F) Risk Pursuance

Risk pursuance means acknowledging increased risks and analyzing or exploring different approaches and methods to fully understand the size, scope, and severity of those risks for increased performance. The organization adopts aggressive growth strategies, such as introducing new and emerging technologies and associated hardware devices and software products (e.g., AI, 3D printing, robotics, VR, AR, and beacon technology). It sends a positive signal to further study and exploit risks that can result in either risk acceptance or risk rejection, not to exceed the target residual risk. This increased performance can result from greater changes in organizational strategies, policies, procedures, practices, and programs. However, if implementation of these new technologies is not successful, then total risks and residual risks will increase.

(G) Risk Appetite

Risk appetite is the level of risk that an organization is willing to accept. It documents the overall principles that an organization follows with respect to risk taking, given its business strategy, financial objectives, and capital resources. Often stated in qualitative terms, a risk appetite defines how an organization weighs strategic decisions and communicates its risk-taking strategy to key stakeholders. It is designed to enhance management's ability to make informed and effective business decisions while keeping risk exposures within acceptable boundaries.

An organization's risk appetite statement must be matched with its risk policy; otherwise, a risk policy gap can exist. A **risk policy gap** is the difference between the risk policy and risk appetite. Note that risk policy is derived from risk strategy.

Specific points regarding risk appetite are listed next.

- Risk appetite must balance risk-based decisions and risk-based rewards or returns.
- Risk appetite changes with changes in a nation's economy, business conditions, and competitive forces.

■ Risk appetite should be developed and implemented based on the organization's risk capacity (i.e., the maximum amount of risk to handle) and risk maturity (i.e., mature versus immature), meaning that mature organizations have already utilized all of their risk capacity or the risk-handling capabilities at their disposal with their resources.

■ Risk appetite is directly related to value at risk, meaning that the higher the risk appetite, the larger the amount of value at risk. The implication is that more value is at risk the higher the risk appetite is.

■ Risk appetite is closely linked with risk tolerance in terms of an organization's performance levels.

■ Risk appetite must remain within the outer boundaries and inner boundaries of risk tolerance

   Risk tolerance has a range of minimum and maximum amounts and levels of risk, and risk appetite falls within this defined range. An example of risk tolerance is when a retailer states that customer merchandise returns should fall between 1% and 2% of gross merchandise sales revenue.

The relationship between risk appetite, risk tolerance, and risk universe is shown next:

$$\text{Risk Appetite} < \text{Risk Tolerance} < \text{Risk Universe}$$

(H) Inherent Risk

Inherent risk is increased when an organization deploys a new technology because, by definition, risks are inherent in a new technology where outcomes from such technology are unexpected. For example, technical risks (i.e., whether technology works or not) and implementation risks (whether implementation efforts are successful or not) can be higher with new technologies. In a way, inherent risks are built-in risks in the absence of any action management might take to alter or reduce the risk's likelihood or impact.

(I) Residual Risk

Residual risk is the risk remaining after management takes necessary action to reduce the impact and likelihood of an adverse event, including control activities in responding to a risk. Residual risk is current risk; it is also called unmanaged risk, leftover risk, or net risk after existing controls are applied.

Several equations express the difficult concept of residual risks:

$$\text{Residual Risks} = \text{Total Risks} - \text{Mitigated Risks} = \text{Unmitigated Risks}$$
$$\text{Residual Risks} = \text{Unmitigated Risks} = \text{Unmanaged Risks}$$
$$\text{Residual Risks} = \text{Accepted Risks} = \text{Retained Risks}$$
$$\text{Residual Risks} = \text{Potential Risks} - \text{Covered Risks} = \text{Uncovered Risks}$$
$$\text{Residual Risks} = \text{Total Risks} - \text{Control Measures (Controls) Applied}$$
$$\text{Residual Risks} = \text{Total Risks} - \text{Transferred Risks or Shared Risks}$$
$$\text{Residual Risks} = \text{Potential Risks} - \text{Countermeasures (Controls) Applied}$$
$$\text{Residual Risks} = \text{Uncovered Risks} = \text{Unaddressed Risks} = \text{Unresolved Risks}$$
$$\text{Residual Risks} = \text{Uncommitted Risks} = \text{Untreated Risks}$$

With respect to IS and IT environment, the goal is to decrease the amount of residual risk as much as possible. The next list presents whether that goal can be achieved.

- Legacy technologies increase residual risk because (1) these technologies are old and inflexible with little or no interaction with other technologies and computer systems; (2) they have few or no built-in controls; and (3) they use old and obsolete programming languages to write computer programs that are difficult to maintain and patch today, and the required programmers are not available in the workforce due to their nonmarketable skills. Consequently, many risks are built-in and unaddressed.

- Poorly designed and implemented business application systems increase residual risk because controls were not built into such systems. Designing system functions was the priority, not security controls. Many risks are unaddressed or uncovered.

- Use of connected devices (mobile, legacy, edge, and endpoint devices) increases residual risk because they open up many new attack doors for hackers. Many new risks are introduced at a faster rate than they can be mitigated.

- Residual data—the data left over after data is sanitized, cleansed, or disposed of—can increase the residual risk. Hackers can dig into the residual data and can launch attacks. The larger the residual data is, the larger the residual risks will be.

- Limited resources in the IT function (budget and staff) can increase residual risks because the IT staff is not able to defend against hacker attacks.

- Limited expertise (i.e., limited KSAs) in IT staff can increase residual risks because hackers can outthink and outsmart the staff.

- As a hacker's attack surface increases, the residual risk increases, as there will be more risks to handle or mitigate.

- As a hacker's detection evasion strategies are successful, residual risks will increase because they are not stopped or controlled.

- Noncompliance with technology-related laws, rules, or regulations can increase residual risks.

- Improperly introducing new technologies into user organizations can increase residual risks when these technologies are not controlled fully or are implemented poorly.

- As the cost of a data breach to a hacker is much less than the benefits to a hacker, this situation increase the residual risk due to more attacks that can be launched. Here, residual risks are increased due to increased attacks that are cheaper than its benefits.

- Use of a combination of user ID and password, which represents 1FA, increases total residual risks. 1FA cannot fight against attacks when hackers break into 1FA. The total risks and residual risks will decrease when the number of authentication factors are increased (i.e., moving from 1FA to 2FA to 3FA to 4FA), showing an inverse (reverse) relationship between authentication factors and total risks and residual risks. The rationale is that as the number of authentication factors increases, it is more difficult for hackers to break in.

- Hiring an experienced and honest hacker to do self-hacking on the organization's computer systems and networks for a fee can decrease the total amount of residual risk.

Derisking. If risking means risk taking, **derisking** means risk lessening, risk downsizing, risk modifying, or risk reducing. With respect to IS and IT environment, the goal is to increase the derisking effort as much as possible. The next list describes whether that goal can be achieved.

- Derisking can be achieved when an offender's (hacker's) attack surface is decreased through proactive measures by a defender's (victim's) organization.

- Derisking can be achieved when a hacker's detection evasion strategies are deactivated (killed or nullified) by a defender's proactive measures.

- Derisking can be achieved when a victim organization complies with technology-related laws, rules, and regulations.

- Derisking can be achieved when a victim organization's IT staff outthink and outsmart a hacker's aggressive attack strategies.

- Derisking can be achieved when an organization hires an experienced and honest hacker to do self-hacking on the organization's computer systems and networks for a fee.

- Derisking can be achieved when an organization manages its privileged access accounts in an effective manner because this will, in turn, decreases a hacker's attack surface.

Information Value at Risk. Information value at risk (IVaR) is the maximum amount of loss that can occur in a given time period (e.g., one year) and at a given confidence level (e.g., 95%). The IVaR needs to be established for each critical asset (each crown jewel) that is documented in risk descriptions and risk discussions. The best way to quantify the IVaR is to compute the cost of not protecting the valuable information, including consequences from hacking, stealing, modifying, damaging, destroying, sharing, selling, and disclosing data and information and defaming organizations and individuals.

Risk Appetite versus Residual Risk. There is an inverse or indirect relationship between risk appetite and residual risk. Risk appetite is defined as the amount of risk that an organization is willing to *accept*. Residual risk is defined as the amount of risk that an organization is willing to *reject*. Hence, a reverse relationship exists; that is, risk appetite is high when the residual risk is low and vice versa.

$$\text{Residual Risk} = (1 - \text{Risk Appetite})$$

Derisking versus Residual Risk. Derisking has an inverse (indirect and opposite) relationship with residual risk in that while derisking efforts reduce overall risk, residual risk decisions result in adding risk to the overall risk.

(ii) Cybersecurity Risk Management Tools

Risk management tools to conduct cybersecurity analysis are risk maps, risk registers, risk heat maps, risk and control matrix.

Risk Maps

A **risk map** ties risk events to their sources (i.e., threats and vulnerabilities), determining their impact levels (i.e., low, medium, or high), and evaluates the presence of or lack of effective controls to mitigate risks. Risks are associated with a business area that will be affected. A risk map describes the primary control procedures in place and indicates the areas that need control-related investment. Risk maps are a part of developing risk profiles and risk appetite.

Risk Registers

A **risk register** (risk log) documents accepted risks below the strategic level (i.e., operational level and functional level) and includes inherent risks (high or higher), unchanged residual risks (net risks), ineffective key internal controls, and lack of mitigating factors (e.g., contingency plans and monitoring activities). Risk registers provide direct links among risk categories, risk aspects, risk descriptions, risk discussions, audit universe, and internal controls. Risk registers maintain centralized records of information about current and identified risks. Current risks include accepted risks and risks to be mitigated.

Risk Heat Maps

A **heat map** is a visual map highlighting a major activity of interest, using a data visualization technology. A risk heat map can show the impact (consequences) and probability (likelihoods) on a matrix. The impact can be labeled as very low, low, medium, high, and very high impact on a scale of 1 to 5. Similarly, the likelihood (riskiness) can be labeled as very low, low, medium, high, and very high probability between 0% and 100%. Color-coded heat maps highlight a major risk element of concern or a data outlier to draw attention.

Risk-and-Control Matrix

A **risk-and-control matrix** documents the links among risks, controls, testing approaches, summaries of interviews, internal auditor or security analyst observations, audit test results, audit evidence, and auditor/analyst conclusions that can be documented in audit workpapers. This matrix identifies the risks that may impact an auditable area's objectives, resources, systems, processes, and operations. Moreover, this matrix provides important feedback on the key risks that were identified, including mitigating controls.

(g) Cybersecurity Metrics

The best way to assess an organization's efforts in addressing cyberattacks it has experienced is to objectively and quantitatively measure those efforts through metrics. The organization's management can compile data related to attacks and develop metrics for each major attack to reveal strengths and weaknesses in its efforts in dealing with such attacks. A lessons learned report from these metrics can be used to improve future efforts. Exhibit 2.12 presents metric types, a defender's (attack victim) goals, and a defender's actions.

EXHIBIT 2.12   Metric Types, a Defender's Goals, and a Defender's Actions

Metric Types	Defender Goals	Defender Actions
Time to prevent	Shorter time	Install preventive mechanisms and controls.
Time to detect	Shorter time	Install detective mechanisms and controls.

Metric Types	Defender Goals	Defender Actions
Time to defend	Shorter time	Deploy several defensive mechanisms (e.g., defense in depth).
Time to exploit	Longer time for a defender but a shorter time for a hacker	Install decoy mechanisms. Increase attackers' work factor.
Time to hack	Zero time for a defender but a longer time for a hacker	Deploy several defensive mechanisms (e.g., defense in depth).
Time to evade	Longer time for a defender but a shorter time for a hacker	Install counter-evasion tactics. Increase attackers' work factor.
Time to pay	Longer time for a defender but a shorter time for a hacker	Install delayed payment strategies.
Time to contain	Shorter time	Install containment strategies.
Time to recover	Shorter time	Implement recovery mechanisms and controls.
Time to operate	Shorter time	Implement operational strategies.
Elapsed time between detection and recovery	Partial measure: shorter time	Lessons learned report.
Elapsed time between prevention or detection and operation	Overall measure: shorter time	Lessons learned report.
Elapsed time between a hack and a rehack	Infinite time for a defender but a shorter time for a hacker	If hackers come back to hack again quickly, they found a gold mine to attack and many security weaknesses in the victim's organization.

(h) Cybersecurity Audit

In this section, we first look at the three layers of cyber defense model followed by an audit program to conduct cyber audits.

(i) Three Layers of Cyber Defense

DoubleCheck Software Company recommends a three-layer cyber defense model to manage cyber-based risks.[8] The first layer deals with governance and oversight functions by executive management. The second layer focuses on five specific actions: identify, protect, detect, respond, and recover by the risk management department. These five specific actions are the same as the five core functions in the cybersecurity framework. The third layer emphasizes actions such as investigate, evaluate, validate, and document by audit management. These three layers together must be strong and robust in protecting against cyber threats and attacks.

---

[8] Simon Goldstein, "Audit Processes Add Value and Objectivity to Cyber Risk and Security Programming—Part 1," blog, October 2018, DoubleCheck Software Company, www.doublechecksoftware.com/audit-processes-add-value-and-objectivity-to-cyber-risk-and-security-programming/.

As part of the responsibility of audit management, auditors need to focus on four specific areas:

1. Internal controls testing (i.e., determining whether IT management: identifies critical assets to protect; performs periodic vulnerability scanning exercises; deploys intrusion prevention and detection systems; maintains incident or event logging records; and undertakes system hardening, network segmentation, domain separation, resource isolation, hardware segmentation, and application system partitioning practices to protect against cyberattacks).

2. Cybersecurity compliance reviews (i.e., determining whether a company's cybersecurity policies, procedures, practices, and controls are adhered to and that applicable cyber laws are followed).

3. Validating risk assessment results (i.e., determining whether assumptions and constraints used in the risk assessment exercises are valid and appropriate and that the results are useful).

4. Evaluating cyber incident investigations (i.e., determining how a company's IT management works with law enforcement authorities and digital forensic specialists in addressing and recovering from cyber incidents and attacks).

(ii) Audit Program

In light of frequent and severe attacks against organizations in cyberspace, internal auditors can conduct an audit of the cybersecurity framework, risks, controls, and metrics to determine whether the organization is cyber-ready. The next audit program is suggested.

- Study the cybersecurity framework and determine if it is still current, relevant, and effective.

- Select the most recent attacks on the organization and determine whether they were minor or major. Collect the necessary background information on these attacks from IT, operational, and senior management and from law enforcement authorities to ascertain what happened and how it happened.

- Analyze the root causes for these attacks, and trace them to published cybersecurity policies, procedures, practices, and controls.

- Take an inventory of what went wrong and determine if any gaps in policies, procedures, and practices contributed to ineffectiveness and inefficiency.

- Determine if there are any control gaps in terms of design, development, and implementation (i.e., fit-gap analysis). Assess whether controls have addressed the attacks or protected from the attacks.

- Issue an audit report discussing the findings and lessons learned and presenting recommendations to management for improvement.

(iii) Best Practices in Cybersecurity Controls and Mitigations

The following is a summary list of best practices in cybersecurity controls and mitigations that can help organizations to become cyber ready.

- Do not hack-back the attacker or hide-back, but do fight back. Practice threat-hunting and threat-defending tasks. Hack-back and hide-back are reactive tasks whereas threat-hunting and threat-defending are proactive tasks. Threat-hunting is a careful exercise in searching for unusual and unknown domain name system (DNS) requests and in learning about the number of queries an endpoint device receives and sends out to the requesters. Examples of endpoint devices include servers, routers, firewalls, modems, sockets, ports, network nodes, port protection devices, hubs, gateways, backbone networks, portals, bridges, and switches. Proactive and defensive actions are better than reactive and offensive actions.

- The ultimate goal of threat-hunting is to uncover hidden threats and vulnerabilities as much as possible in a much shorter timeframe. Threat-defending means deploying all available multiple defenses to become cyber ready.

- Restrict the policy of employees bring your own device (BYOD) to the workplace for a limited group of employees for inventorying, tracking, and monitoring the device uses and misuses and to prevent unwanted risks resulting from data breaches and computer viruses with the use of such devices.

- Implement a strong password policy and multifactor authentication (also known as two-factor authentication or two-step authentication) to reduce the impact of password compromises such as password reuse. Passwords should be difficult to guess and use long and strong passphrases or passwords consisting of between 8 and 16 characters with a combination of letters, numbers, and special characters. Use different passwords for different systems and devices.

- Change default usernames and passwords because they are readily available to hackers. Change them as soon as possible to a sufficiently strong and unique passwords, similar to other systems and devices.

- Protect connected devices (e.g., mobile, legacy, edge, and endpoint) and networks by keeping them up to date. Use the latest supported versions, apply security patches promptly, and use antivirus software and scan regularly to guard against known malware threats. Network administrators should monitor both normal and abnormal CPU activity on computer workstations, mobile devices, and network servers for processing degradation.

- Keep systems software and operating systems current with updates, patches, and fixes. Hackers cannot take advantage of known problems or vulnerabilities.

- Implement controls to achieve network segregation or segmentation. Analyze network intrusions regularly.

- Use modern systems and software products because they have better security features built into them. If not, update them.

- Control privileged accounts with access to vital IT assets. Review user accounts and verify that users with administrative access rights have a need for those privileges. Restrict general user accounts from performing administrative functions.

- Control entry points into computer systems and networks from connected devices and websites, especially from third-party systems with onward access to a company's core networks.

- Consider whitelisting of permitted application systems to prevent malicious application systems from running or to prevent unknown executable programs from launching attacks automatically.

- Monitor blacklists of websites that are hosting and distributing malware. Block the Internet Protocol (IP) addresses of known malicious websites to prevent connected devices from being able to access them.

- Manage macros carefully, disable them when not needed, and ensure antivirus programs scan macros.

- Use anti-virus programs, keep them up to date, and consider using a cloud-backed version of antivirus products. Be aware that hackers can deactivate or kill the features and functions of antivirus program making it useless. They can even install their own infected anti-virus program to launch attacks.

- Establish a layered defense strategy to handle phishing attacks and malware attacks. Use multiple layers of defenses such as defense-in-depth, defense-in-breadth, defense-in-time, and defense-in-technology strategies.

- Treat employees and security guards as the first line of defense (LOD) and the last LOD. As the first LOD, employees should report all phishing emails to management. If the first LOD does not work, then the last LOD should work.

- Deploy a host-based intrusion detection system. Build an incident response team internally to address cyber threats and attacks. Review and refresh the incident management processes.

- Defend computer systems and networks against denial-of-service (DoS), distributed DoS, and ransomware attacks. Keep safe copies of backup files, protect them from malware, and do not pay the ransom to hackers because it may not get the data back.

- Secure customer data and employee data carefully at all times to protect their privacy. Secure business data too (e.g., intellectual property assets and financial assets) to protect business advantage and to retain competitive advantage.

- Avoid downloading files from untrusted websites. Look for an authentic website certificate when downloading files from a secure site. Do not click on URLs directly; instead copy and paste them on the browser line.

- Disable unnecessary services, uninstall unused software to prevent hackers from exploiting them, validate input into web applications to mitigate injection attacks, and install a firewall to control inbound and outbound traffic. Disabling or blocking some unnecessary services may create problems in other places by obstructing access to files, data, or devices.

- Audit the use of scripts in web pages and inspect logs to identify anomalies. Scripts (e.g., JavaScript) can be used to evade system protection and detection offered by antivirus software, intrusion detection systems, and intrusion prevention systems. Scripts help in detection evasion efforts for hackers.

- Audit the third-parties for services rendered and programming code received. Acquiring services (e.g., marketing advertisements and data analytics) from third-parties and receiving programming code from third-parties can be risky. The programming code must be validated to ensure that no unexpected code or dangerous code is delivered to the end user. The types of validations can be vetting before loading into the website, vetting before hosting on the web server, vetting before paying the bill, and vetting before signing the contract with a due diligence review. Here, no validation means loading the programming code directly from the third party without any vetting process.

2.7 Sample Practice Questions

In the actual CIA Exam for Part 3, 100 multiple-choice (M/C) test questions appear. This book contains 100 M/C sample practice questions divided into syllabus-based domains using the approximate domain weight given in the exam. These questions are added at the end of each applicable domain of this book with the sole purpose of showing the flavor and structure of the exam questions and of creating a self-quiz experience. The answers and explanations for these questions are shown in a separate section at the end of this book just before the Glossary section. This separate section is titled "Sample Practice Questions, Answers, and Explanations." If CIA Exam candidates need to practice more sample questions to obtain a higher level of confidence, Wiley offers a separate online test bank software product with hundreds of similar, sample practice questions.

1. Between authentication and encryption activities, which one of the following items is **more** secure than the other three items?
   a. Authenticate and encrypt
   b. Authenticate then encrypt
   c. Encrypt and authenticate
   d. Encrypt then authenticate

2. Which of the following can help recover from ransomware attacks?
   a. Encryption key
   b. File and system backups
   c. Decryption key
   d. Patched and updated software

3. Social media platforms or networks were born during which of the following web generations?
   a. Web 1.0
   b. Web 2.0
   c. Web 3.0
   d. Web 4.0

4. Regarding mobile devices, the features of which one of the following items is different from the features of the other three items?
   a. Jailbreaking
   b. Tampering
   c. Jamming
   d. Rooting

5. Which of the following can help hackers in detection evasion situations?
   a. Scripting tools
   b. Antivirus software
   c. Intrusion detection system
   d. Intrusion prevention system

6. Regarding cybersecurity, defenders are the victim organizations and hackers are attacking individuals and organizations. Which of the following strategic aspect takes a completely opposite viewpoint between defenders and hackers?
   a. Expertise
   b. Resources
   c. Attack surface
   d. Tool kits

7. Which of the following is **not** a variant of phishing attacks?
   a. Spear phishing
   b. Vishing
   c. Smishing
   d. SIM card swapping

8. Bitcoins deploy which of the following technologies?
   I. Investment chain
   II. Blockchain
   III. Incident chain
   IV. Hash chain
   a. I and II
   b. II only
   c. II and IV
   d. I and III

9. The cybersecurity framework should act as a:
   a. First line of defense.
   b. Second line of defense.
   c. Third line of defense.
   d. Last line of defense.

10. In which of the following cybersecurity functions are system resilience plans developed and implemented?
   a. Protect
   b. Detect
   c. Recover
   d. Respond

11. Regarding mobile security, encryption can be used to protect which of the following with efforts to prevent data loss?
   I.   Data at rest
   II. Data in motion
   III. Data in processing
   IV. Data in use

   a. I and II
   b. II and III
   c. I and IV
   d. III and IV

12. Which of the following statement is **not** true about bitcoins?
   a. Bitcoins use a distributed ledger.
   b. Bitcoins use a centralized ledger.
   c. Bitcoins use a decentralized ledger.
   d. Bitcoins use a community ledger.

13. Which of the following are the common variants of ransomware attacks?
   I.   Bots and botnets
   II. Spam emails
   III. Drive-by downloads
   IV. Malvertising

   a. I only
   b. I and II
   c. I, II, and IV
   d. I, II, III, and IV

14. During an audit, an internal auditor observed that an employee at the audit-client department is watching online sports on his desktop computer during working hours. Which of the following policies should the auditor refer to determine whether the employee's actions are acceptable?
   a. Acceptable use policies
   b. Business-only Internet use policies
   c. Software restriction policies
   d. Mobile device use policies

15. Which of the following **cannot** reduce the total costs of data breaches?
   a. Security metrics
   b. Incident response team
   c. Encryption
   d. Mobile platforms

16. Authorization controls are a part of which of the following?
   a. Directive controls
   b. Preventive controls
   c. Detective controls
   d. Corrective controls

17. Which of the following is **not** an example of nondiscretionary access control?
   a. Identity-based access control
   b. Mandatory access control
   c. Role-based access control
   d. Temporal constraints

18. Which of the following statements are true about access controls, safety, trust, and separation of duty?
   I.   No leakage of access permissions is allowed to an unauthorized principal.
   II. No access privileges can be escalated to an unauthorized principal.
   III. No principals' trust means no safety.
   IV. No separation of duty means no safety.

   a. I only
   b. II only
   c. I, II, and III
   d. I, II, III, and IV

19. For privilege management, which of the following is the correct order?

a. Access Control $\longrightarrow$ Access Management $\longrightarrow$ Authentication Management $\longrightarrow$ Privilege Management

b. Access Management $\longrightarrow$ Access Control $\longrightarrow$ Privilege Management $\longrightarrow$ Authentication Management

c. Authentication Management $\longrightarrow$ Privilege Management $\longrightarrow$ Access Control $\longrightarrow$ Access Management

d. Privilege Management $\longrightarrow$ Access Management $\longrightarrow$ Access Control $\longrightarrow$ Authentication Management

20. The encryption technique that requires two keys, a public key that is available to anyone for encrypting messages and a private key that is known only to the recipient for decrypting messages, is

a. Rivest, Shamir, and Adelman (RSA).

b. Data encryption standard (DES).

c. Modulator-demodulator.

d. A cipher lock.

21. The use of message encryption software:

a. Guarantees the secrecy of data.

b. Requires manual distribution of keys.

c. Increases system overhead.

d. Reduces the need for periodic password changes.

22. The information systems and audit directors agreed on the need to maintain security and integrity of transmissions and the data they represent. The best means of ensuring the confidentiality of satellite transmissions would be:

a. Encryption.

b. Access control.

c. Monitoring software.

d. Cyclic redundancy checks.

23. For application user authenticator management purposes, use of which of the following is risky and leads to stronger alternatives?

a. A single sign-on mechanism

b. Same user identifier and different user authenticators on all systems

c. Same user identifier and same user authenticator on all systems

d. Different user identifiers and different user authenticators on each system

24. Which of the following statements is true about an intrusion detection system (IDS) and firewalls?

a. Firewalls are a substitute for an IDS.

b. Firewalls are an alternative to an IDS.

c. Firewalls are a complement to an IDS.

d. Firewalls are a replacement for an IDS.

25. Which one of the following is **not** an authentication mechanism?

a. What the user knows

b. What the user has

c. What the user can do

d. What the user is

Information Technology (20%)

This domain focuses on key theoretical topics. It discusses how application and system software is built with a system development life cycle methodology. This domain explains the basic database terms and the Internet terms. It identifies the key characteristics of business software systems such as the governance, risk, and compliance (GRC) system, enterprise resource planning (ERP) system, customer relationship management (CRM) system, and electronic data systems. It explains the basic information technology (IT) infrastructure and network concepts, including the roles of IT staff with separation of duties. It recognizes the purpose of and applications of IT control frameworks and basic IT controls. It explains disaster recovery site planning concepts, data recovery procedures, and data backup methods. All these topics are tested at the basic cognitive levels in Part 3 of the CIA Exam with a 20% weight given.

With respect to the CIA Exam, cognitive levels are labeled as proficient level and basic level. These cognitive levels suggest that more time and effort should be spent in studying and mastering the subject-matter covered in the topics labeled as the proficient level. Comparatively, less time and effort should be spent on the topics labeled as the basic level.

3.1 System Development Life Cycle

In this section, several topics are discussed, including system development methodology using a system development life cycle (SDLC) approach, information systems development, application development, change management and control, and end user computing.

(a) Systems Development Methodology

In this section, approaches to develop or acquire information systems or application systems are presented. In addition, models deployed in and tools to be applied in software development are discussed. The need for conducting due care and due diligence reviews during system development or acquisition is highlighted.

(i) Traditional Approaches to Develop Systems internally

Two approaches or methodologies exist to develop or to acquire information systems or application systems: traditional approaches and alternative approaches. The traditional approach requires systematic and disciplined work internally using a system SDLC methodology with phases to ensure consistency and quality of work. Five phases of SDLC include:

1. Planning/initiation
2. Development/acquisition
3. Implementation/assessment
4. Operation/maintenance
5. Disposal/decommissioning

Usually, the traditional approach combined with the SDLC methodology is used in developing custom software.

System-related activities and security-related activities are presented next for each phase of the SDLC.

(A) Phase 1: Planning/Initiation

System-related activities are listed next.

- Understanding a functional user's request for a new system
- Conducting a feasibility study (i.e., costs and benefits)
- Performing high-level needs assessment
- Doing a preliminary risk assessment
- Using decision tables, flowcharts, data-flow diagrams, and finite-state-machine models to express user needs and system requirements

Security-related activities include developing the security planning document, conducting a sensitivity assessment, and security assurance (cost driver). The security planning document contains several elements, such as those listed next.

- Security awareness and training plans
- Rules of behavior
- Risk assessment
- Configuration management (CM) plan
- Contingency plan
- Incident response plan
- System interconnection agreements

- Security tests and evaluation results
- Plan of actions and milestones

However, the security planning document does not contain a request for proposal, vendor contract plans, or a statement of work, as they are related to project management, not to security management.

(B) Phase 2: Development/Acquisition
System-related activities are listed next.

- Performing an in-depth analysis of user needs
- Performing general and detailed system design work
- Developing computer programs
- Conducting unit and system testing
- Planning desk reviews, mutation analysis, sensitivity analysis for analyzing changes, boundary-value analysis, and error seeding methods during testing
- Performing quality assurance (QA) and quality control (QC) reviews
- Doing a detailed risk assessment

During this phase, the system is designed, purchased, programmed, developed, or otherwise constructed.

Security-related activities are listed next.

- Determining security features, controls, assurances, and operational practices
- Incorporating these security requirements into security design specifications
- Actually building or buying these security requirements into the system
- Conducting design reviews through walkthroughs
- Preparing test documents with test cases and test procedures with formal specific programming languages
- Conducting certification and accreditation activities

Possible security threats or vulnerabilities that should be considered during this phase include Trojan horses, incorrect/incomplete program code, poorly functioning software development tools, manipulation of program code, and malicious insiders.

(C) Phase 3: Implementation/Assessment
System-related activities are listed next.

- Providing training to end users and system users
- Conducting acceptance testing for end users
- Converting the old system into the new system

- Developing instruction manuals for system use
- Performing QA and QC reviews

After acceptance testing and conversion, the system is installed or fielded with a formal authorization from management to put into production status.

Security-related activities include installing or turning on security controls, performing security tests (e.g., functional tests, penetration tests), and security evaluation report and accreditation statement.

(D) Phase 4: Operation/Maintenance
System-related activities are listed next.

- Doing production operations and support work
- Performing a postimplementation review
- Undertaking system maintenance and modification work
- Monitoring the system's performance

During this phase, the system is fully operational and doing its work as intended and planned. The system is frequently modified by the addition of new hardware and software and by new functional requirements. The CM process is implemented with baselines and change controls.

Security-related activities are listed next.

- Security operations and administration (e.g., performing backups, managing cryptographic keys, setting user access accounts, and updating security software)
- Operational assurance (e.g., conducting system audits and continuous monitoring)
- Periodic reaccreditation when security is insufficient and when the changes made are significant

---

WHAT IS THE FOCUS OF SYSTEM REQUIREMENTS, DESIGN, AND IMPLEMENTATION IN SYSTEM DEVELOPMENT?

System requirements describe external behavior of a computer system. They focus on what the software is to accomplish. Requirements present unmet user needs and unsolved business problems.

System design describes the internal behavior of a computer system. It focuses on how to develop solutions to unmet user needs and business problems. Design satisfies user needs and solves business problems.

System implementation focuses on how to use and operate the software.

(E) Phase 5: Disposal/Decommissioning
System-related activities include system retirement or replacement plans and media sanitization procedures. The computer system is disposed of (terminated) once the transition to a new computer system is completed.

Security-related activities are listed next.

- Disposition of information (i.e., data sanitization), hardware, and software

- Moving information to archives after considering legal and audit requirements for records retention and the method of retrieving the information in the future

- Disposition of software after considering licensing terms and agreements (site specific) with the developer, if the agreement prevents the software from being transferred

- Taking appropriate steps to ensure secure long-term storage of cryptographic keys and for the future use of data if the data have been encrypted

Some organizations may not have software disposal or decommissioning policies and procedures; in other organizations, such procedures might have been overlooked. Software acquirers should ensure that such policies and procedures are developed and followed to ensure the safe and secure disposal or decommissioning of software and to ensure that data are destroyed or migrated safely and securely. When a software-intensive system is retired or replaced, the data must be migrated by validated means to the new software-intensive system or must be made unreadable before disposal. Note that encrypted data may not be adequately protected if they are weakly encrypted. *Simply stated, residual data equals residual risk.*

Another consideration in this phase concerns storage devices used in virtualization process. Before a device using a virtualization process permanently leaves an organization (such as when a leased server's lease expires or when an obsolete personal computer [PC] is being recycled), the organization should remove any sensitive data from the host. Data may also need to be wiped if an organization provides loaner devices to teleworkers, particularly for travel. Note that sensitive data may be found nearly anywhere on a device because of the nature of virtualization. For this reason, an organization should strongly consider erasing all storage devices completely.

Another related concern in this phase is removing or destroying any sensitive data from the basic input/output system (BIOS) to reduce the chances of accidental data leakage. The configuration baseline should be reset to the manufacturer's default profile; in particular, sensitive settings, such as passwords, should be deleted from the system, and cryptographic keys should be removed from the key store.

(ii) Models in System Development

Several models exist to either develop or acquire information systems, and each model may be suitable to a particular environment. In practice, a combination of these models may be deployed after considering the time, cost, and skills constraints and trade-offs.

- The **waterfall model** takes a linear, sequential view of the software engineering process, similar to an SDLC model.

- The **rapid application development model** is quite opposite to the waterfall model. That is, it is good when requirements are not fully understood by both parties. It uses computer-aided software engineering (CASE) tools, fourth-generation programming languages (4GLs), and software reuse modules to quickly prototype an information system.

- Although the **incremental development model** and the evolutionary development models are better than the waterfall model, they are not as good as rapid prototyping in terms of bringing the operational viewpoint to the requirements specification. Successive versions of the system are developed reflecting constrained technology or resources.

- The **spiral model** is another type of evolutionary model. It was developed to provide the best feature of both the classic life cycle approach and prototyping.

- The **rapid prototyping model** is a process that enables the developer to create a model of the software built in an evolutionary manner. Rapid prototyping uses special software and a special output device to create a prototype to design and test a system in three dimensions.

- The **object-oriented development model** is applied once the design model has been created. The software developer browses a library or repository that contains existing program components to determine if any of the components can be used in the design at hand. If reusable components are found, they are used as building blocks to construct a prototype of the software.

(iii) Tools in Systems Development

At least three tools exist to development systems quickly and completely: prototyping, cleanroom software engineering, and computer-aided software engineering.

(A) Prototyping

Defining software requirements is the biggest and most troublesome area to handle and control for functional users, IT staff, and auditors. Yet it is the foundation upon which the entire applications software system is built. It is a very simple concept to grasp. If software requirements are incompletely defined and documented, the final product will be incomplete.

A major problem with software requirements is that the software development staff is working against a moving target. This occurs because software requirements are constantly changing due to functional users' inability to define their requirements clearly and completely, communication problems between functional users and IT staff, and natural changes in business functional requirements from internal and external sources over the time frame of the software development project.

Defining software requirements is often taken very lightly; most of the time, the step is skipped or skimped on. Consequently, excessive software maintenance is needed after the system becomes operational to meet the missing requirements, which should have been addressed earlier.

PROTOTYPING VERSUS COMMUNICATION

Prototyping increases communication between people, which solves one of the major problems in the traditional definition and documentation of software requirements.

An approach that rapidly brings a working version of the system into the hands of users seems to be a better strategy. This is because users sometimes cannot actually define system requirements correctly the first time until they have used some or all parts of the system. Prototyping is one way of dealing with the uncertainty, impreciseness, inconsistency, difficulty, and ambiguity involved in defining software requirements and design work. User requirements are not frozen; in fact, changing of users' minds is encouraged. Prototyping assures that system requirements are adequately defined and correct through actual user experience in using the model. Prototyping also addresses the question of timely delivery of completed systems. It is especially useful in the development of unstructured application systems.

In practice, software prototyping is done in many ways. For example, a prototyped system may be:

- Developed for a single user or multiple users.

- Programmed in one language for model development and later programmed in or combined with other language(s) to suit the operational (production) environment.

- Developed for both accounting/financial and nonfinancial systems.

- Developed to address partial or full system functions.

- Developed to build the final (real) system to operate in a production environment.

Different approaches are used to achieve the prototype variations mentioned, which is accomplished either by shortening or replacing the traditional SDLC phases. Prototyping can be viewed as the development of a **working model** with test or real (preferred) data using an iterative approach supported by user and developer interaction. Here the user is a functional user, and the developer is a data processing staff member (a programmer or systems analyst). Prototyping is done with the use of a **workbench or workstation concept** where functional user(s) and systems analyst(s) interact with the prototyping software in developing a working model. In some organizations, the information center staff assists functional users in developing prototyping models. Prototyping is meant to be a learning process in developing usable systems.

Functional users working with the system analyst or programmer/analyst use the model to experiment and understand the system/business requirements. With this approach, system fallacies can be eliminated or minimized quickly before they can get bigger. Usually models include online terminal screens with editing functions for data input and output, flow logic between screens, error handling rules, and batch reports. System users can define system input, process, and output functions; indicate the sequence of screens and functions; and specify data editing and validation rules to the system analyst. This method leads to accurate data collection and processing, which improves the reliability and integrity of the system.

The system model with its inputs, processes, and outputs can be mocked up either on paper or on computer (preferred) with real data. The model is tested, changed, and retested until users are satisfied with it. With this approach, end users will get a sense of the look and feel of a proposed system. All changes are handled during successive iterations of the model. Later these prototyped models are either expanded in the same programming language or rewritten in another programming language to include all functions and features that are expected in a final system.

Typically, the final system may use multiple programming languages. Data flow diagrams and a data dictionary (DD) are some of the important tools used to document the prototype features and functions.

Often a major question is whether prototyped systems can be directly moved into production operations. The answer depends on the size, type, and nature of the system (i.e., whether it is a heavy-duty, large and complex, and transaction-based business application system; a decision support system; a small system; a onetime system; or an ad hoc inquiry system).

Generally, heavy-duty, large and complex, and transaction-based prototyped systems should not be moved as is (directly) into production operations until full-scale design, programming, and testing activities are completed. However, for small and simple systems, onetime systems, decision support systems, and ad hoc systems, the prototyped system and the production system could be the same.

An organization has at least three choices after a prototype is completed: (1) discard the prototype (i.e., throwaway prototype), (2) move the prototype into production operations as is, or (3) use the prototype as a starting point for the full-scale design work.

1. **Throwaway prototype.** The prototype could be discarded because it is not serving the system objectives or may be addressing wrong problems. In some cases, the model is thrown away because system performance is so bad that it cannot be improved or the system cannot be used in multiuser environment.

2. **Use as is.** The prototype could become the actual system that can be operated in a production environment. Usually this choice is good for application systems with low-volume transactions, operated on a regular or an irregular basis. Examples are decision support systems, ad hoc inquiry systems, onetime systems, small and simple systems, and single-user systems.

3. **Input to full-scale design.** The prototype could become the basis for a full-scale system design, programming, and testing work using the SDLC approach. Usually this choice is good for application systems with large-volume transactions, with a need for quick response time and to operate on a scheduled basis. In this case, a programming language other than the one used in developing the prototyping model may be implemented for the production environment. Under these conditions, the original prototype model could be thrown away. Examples are heavy-duty, large and complex, and transaction-based business application systems, whether accounting/financial systems or not.

(B) Cleanroom Software Engineering

The primary goal of software quality assurance (SQA) is to enhance the quality of software. Cleanroom process or cleanroom software engineering is deployed to ensure software quality. With cleanroom processes, programmers do not compile their code. Instead, they spend more time on design, using a box structure method and analyzing their own work. When programmers are confident of their work, it is submitted to another group, whose members then compile and test the code. Cleanroom experiments have shown that a lower error rate in the finished software product and an increase in productivity across a system's life cycle are possible.

Cleanroom software engineering, which is a concept borrowed from cleanroom hardware engineering, is the result of the combined effect of statistical QC and proof-of-correctness principles. The first priority of the cleanroom process is defect prevention, not defect removal. It is understood that any defects not prevented should be removed. This priority is achieved through human verification procedures to ensure proof of correctness instead of program debugging to prepare the software for system test. The next priority is to provide QA, which is measured in terms of mean time to failure (MTTF). Both of these priorities eventually reflect in lowering the number of defects per 1,000 lines of code before the first executable tests are conducted.

(C) Computer-Aided Software Engineering

Computer-aided software engineering (CASE) tools, compilers, and assemblers are used to expedite and improve the productivity of software developers' work. CASE tools provide a 4GL or application generator for fast code writing, flowcharting, data flow diagramming, DD facility, and word processing in order to develop and document the new software. The CASE tools are used in prototyping the system by developing online screens and reports for the end user to view and change, as needed. Modern CASE tools are often called i-CASE tools due to their integration of several tools.

(iv) Alternative Approaches to Acquire Software Externally

Several alternative approaches or sources are available to user organizations from outside or commercial software vendors when planning to acquire software externally. Unavailability of source code from a commercial software vendor is a major risk in terms of not accessing and maintaining the source code to operate computer systems. Examples are listed next.

- Commercial off-the-shelf software
- Custom software
- Modifiable off-the-shelf software
- Government off-the-shelf software
- Mobile code software
- Freeware
- Shareware
- Open source software
- Embedded software
- Integrated software
- Software service from an application service provider (ASP)

Each approach is described in the paragraphs that follow.

Commercial-off-the-shelf (COTS) is a term for proprietary software products (including software appliances) that are ready-made and available for sale to customers.

Custom software is developed for either a specific organization or a function that differs from other already available software, such as COTS. It generally is not targeted to the mass market but usually is created for interested organizations.

Modifiable off-the-shelf (MOTS) software is typically a COTS product whose source code can be modified. The product may be customized by the purchaser, the vendor, or another party to meet customer requirements.

Government off-the shelf (GOTS) software products typically are developed by the internal IT staff of a specific government agency and can be used by other agencies. GOTS sometimes are developed by an external contractor, but with funding and product specification from the agency.

Mobile code software modules are obtained from remote systems, transferred across a network, and then downloaded and executed on local systems without explicit installation or execution by the recipient. Mobile code is risky because it is passed from one system to another and is used to describe applets within web browsers.

Freeware is copyrighted software that is available for use free of charge for an unlimited time.

Shareware is a marketing method for commercial software, whereby a trial version is distributed in advance and without payment, as is common for proprietary software. Shareware software typically is obtained free of charge; it is also known as try before you buy, demo-ware, and trial-ware.

Although it is typically obtained free of charge, payment is often required once a set period of time has elapsed after installation.

Open source software is computer software whose source code is available under a copyright license that permits users to study, change, and improve the software as well as to redistribute it in modified or unmodified form. Usually it is not obtained by a contract, but a fee may be charged for use.

There are eight possible risks from the use of open source software. These include not knowing whether:

1. The software is original source or a modified version (modified software can introduce malicious code or other vulnerabilities)
2. The software infringes on any copyright or patent
3. The software validates (e.g., filter with whitelisting) inputs from untrusted sources before being used
4. The software is designed to execute within a constrained execution environment (e.g., virtual machine, sandbox, chroot jail, single-purpose pseudo-user, and system isolation)
5. The software was measured or assessed for its resistance to identified relevant attack patterns
6. The software was subjected to thorough security testing with results posted
7. Patches are distributed or whether patches can be uninstalled
8. The vendor practices version management

Embedded software is part of a larger physical system and performs some of the requirements of that system (e.g., software used in an automobile or rapid transit, traffic control, or aircraft system) and may or may not provide an interface with the user. Embedded software is internally built within the physical system.

Integrated software results from when there is a prime contractor with multiple subcontractors, as in a supply chain environment. Each subcontractor provides a specific piece of software product and/or service for the software-intensive system. The prime contractor is responsible for integrating all the pieces into a whole software-intensive system, or that contractor may hire a separate contractor to integrate it. Because multiple contractors and subcontractors are involved in supply chain environments, security risks to user organizations can increase.

If a supplier is acting as an **application service provider (ASP)** and offering to provide software as a service, instead of a stand-alone software package product, software acquirers should consider the governance of these services. Here "governance" refers to the computer programs, processes, and procedures that the ASP organization puts in place to ensure that things are done right in accordance with best practices and principles. The ASP should provide appropriate access controls, audit, monitoring, and alerting activities. Note that with the ASP, a user organization is acquiring services, not products.

When considering these alternative approaches to software, application owners and acquirers should seek to reduce or manage the risks because each alternative can introduce its own, new risks. It is highly recommended that due care principles be applied and due diligence reviews be performed to reduce such risks.

Specifically, application owners and acquirers should perform these analyses to reduce risks:

- Evaluate alternatives for treatment of risks (i.e., accept, mitigate, avoid, transfer, or share with a third-party supplier).

- Identify protection strategies (i.e., security objectives and security controls) that reduce risks to levels within acceptable tolerance.

- Identify potential trade-offs among decreased risks, increased costs, and decreased operational effectiveness and efficiency.

- Identify approaches for managing residual risks that remain after protection strategies are adopted.

(v) Due Care and Due Diligence Reviews in Software Development and Acquisition

Regardless of the software alternative selected, due care and due diligence reviews are required because each software source code can introduce its own risks. This is because there are many third parties involved (e.g., integrators, suppliers, prime contractors, and subcontractors) in the development, maintenance, and distribution of software chain, which is a risky to manage. It is a good business practice to vet a third-parry source code before signing a contract, before loading the code, before hosting the software, and before paying any bills to the third-party.

Due care means reasonable care that promotes the common good. It is maintaining minimal and customary practices and/or following the best practices. Due care is the responsibility that managers and their organizations have a duty to provide for information security to ensure that the type, cost, and deployment of control are appropriate for the system being managed. Another related concept of due care is good faith, which means showing both honesty in fact and honesty in intent. Both due care and due diligence are similar to the prudent man concept.

Due diligence requires organizations to develop and implement an effective system of controls, policies, and procedures to prevent and detect violation of policies and laws. It requires that the organization has taken minimum and necessary steps in its power and authority to prevent and detect violation of policies and laws. In other words, due diligence is the care that a reasonable person exercises under the circumstances to avoid harm to other persons or to their property. Due diligence is another way of saying due care. Both due care and due diligence are similar to the prudent man concept. Note that a due diligence defense is available to a defendant in a legal case in that the defendant is not liable when he or she follows all the prescribed legal procedures.

Some examples of applications of due diligence reviews are listed next.

- An information security team reviews policies, procedures, and controls during acquisition and divestiture of security-related products and services, including initial screening of vendors and suppliers, performing make-or-buy or lease-or-purchase analysis, understanding contracts, and negotiating with suppliers and contractors.

- A software acquirer requires potential software suppliers to be evaluated qualitatively and quantitatively to ensure software quality prior to contract negotiations in order to make a go/no-go decision in selecting suppliers.

- Suppliers that provide computer products and services for regulated pharmaceutical operations are audited.

- Software suppliers that claim mature process capabilities prove their software assurance practices.

- The appropriate set of security controls to adequately mitigate risk and to protect the confidentiality, integrity, and availability of data/information and information systems is selected.

- A user organization outsources media sanitization work with a contractual agreement.

- Encryption mechanisms are used for web sessions whenever a rented application requires the confidentiality of application interfaces with other applications, data transfers, and data storage.

(b) Information Systems Development

This section covers applying security engineering principles; practicing defensive programming techniques; using system design principles; and implementing software assurance, safety, security, and quality techniques. These principles and techniques should be considered during information systems development to lay a strong foundation for information systems.

(i) Security Engineering Principles
(A) Purpose

A **principle** is a rule or standard for good cause or behavior. Principles will provide a baseline for achieving security. IT security is a critical element in the system life cycle. The purpose of the engineering principles for IT security is to present a list of system-level security principles to be considered in the design, development, and operation of an information system. Ideally, the principles would be used from the onset of a program—at the beginning of or during the initiation phase—and then would be employed throughout the system's life cycle. However, these principles are also helpful in affirming and confirming the security posture of already deployed information systems. The principles are short and concise and can be used by organizations to develop their system life cycle policies.[1]

Effective information assurance rests on five system security concepts:

1. Managing, not preventing, risk

2. Acknowledging that security is a system-level attribute

3. Recognizing that changing mission or business processes results in the increased need for technical protection methods

4. Recognizing that the enterprise is made up of interrelated security domains

5. Providing security mechanisms and services to support security implementation, both domain-specific and interdomain implementation

(B) Principle

The 33 IT engineering security principles are grouped into six categories:

1. Security foundation

2. Risk based

3. Ease of use

---

[1] Security Engineering Principles (NIST SP-800-27), U.S. Department of Commerce, National Institute of Standards and Technology (NIST), Gaithersburg, Maryland, March 2006.

4. Greater resilience

5. Reduce vulnerabilities

6. Use network-minded design

Category 1: Security Foundation

- Principle 1. Establish a sound security policy as the foundation for design.

- Principle 2. Treat security as an integral part of the overall system design.

- Principle 3. Clearly delineate the physical and logical security boundaries governed by associated security policies.

- Principle 4. Ensure that developers are trained in how to develop secure software.

Category 2: Risk Based

- Principle 5. Reduce risk to an acceptable level.

- Principle 6. Assume that external systems are insecure.

- Principle 7. Identify potential trade-offs between reducing risk and increased costs and decrease in other aspects of operational effectiveness.

- Principle 8. Implement tailored system security measures to meet organizational security goals.

- Principle 9. Protect information while it is being processed, in transit, and in storage.

- Principle 10. Consider custom-developed products to achieve adequate security. Here, "adequate security" is defined as security commensurate with risk, including the magnitude of harm resulting from the unauthorized access, use, disclosure, disruption, modification, or destruction of information.

- Principle 11. Protect against all likely classes of attacks.

Category 3: Ease of Use

- Principle 12. Where possible, base security on open standards for portability and interoperability.

- Principle 13. Use a common computer language in developing security requirements.

- Principle 14. Design security to allow for regular adoption of new technology, including a secure and logical technology upgrade process.

- Principle 15. Strive for operational ease of use.

Category 4: Greater Resilience

- Principle 16. Implement layered security to ensure no single point of vulnerability exists.

- Principle 17. Design and operate an IT system to limit damage and to be resilient in response.

- Principle 18. Provide assurance that the system is, and continues to be, resilient in the face of expected threats.

- Principle 19. Limit or contain vulnerabilities.

- Principle 20. Isolate public access systems from mission-critical resources (e.g., data and processes).

- Principle 21. Use boundary mechanisms to separate computing systems and network infrastructures.

- Principle 22. Design and implement audit mechanisms to detect unauthorized use and to support incident investigations.

- Principle 23. Develop and exercise contingency or disaster recovery procedures to ensure appropriate availability.

Category 5: Reduce Vulnerabilities

- Principle 24. Strive for simplicity.

- Principle 25. Minimize the system elements to be trusted.

- Principle 26. Implement the least-privilege access principle.

- Principle 27. Do not implement unnecessary security mechanisms.

- Principle 28. Ensure proper security in the shutdown or disposal of a system.

- Principle 29. Identify and prevent common errors and vulnerabilities.

Category 6: Use Network-Minded Design

- Principle 30. Implement security through a combination of measures distributed physically and logically.

- Principle 31. Formulate security measures to address multiple overlapping information domains.

- Principle 32. Authenticate users and processes to ensure appropriate access control decisions both within and across domains.

- Principle 33. Use unique identities to ensure individual accountability.

(ii) Defensive Programming Techniques

Defensive programming techniques include robust programming, N-version programming, fault-tolerant programming, secure coding practices, and parsing.

Robust programming makes a computer system more reliable with various programming techniques. It has five attributes:

1. It addresses interface faults during program routine invocations.

2. It practices the use of GOTO-less programming commands to minimize program complexity and errors.

3. It performs type-checking to detect human typing errors occurring during program coding.

4. It properly handles standard domains for correct inputs and exception domains for incorrect inputs.

5. It keeps the domain of unexpected exceptions, which are not caught, as small as possible because this category makes the system unreliable. The category of expected exception domain, which is caught, makes the system reliable.

N-version programming is based on design or version diversity. Different versions of the software are developed independently. It is hoped that these versions are independent in their failure behavior. The different versions are executed in parallel, and the results are voted on.

Fault-tolerant programming is robust programming plus redundancy features and is somewhat similar to N-version programming. In summary, in fault-tolerant programming,

1. The programming language is studied to identify error-prone program constructs and to ensure that only safe program constructs are used.

2. Program components are tested for faulty inputs.

3. Redundancy features are added to repair inadvertent events later.

Secure coding practices include good programming techniques with security-relevant functions. Some examples are listed next.

- Using the principles of data abstraction
- Using key attributes, such as low coupling and high cohesion, to bind modules together
- Using regression testing to verify compliance of library functions
- Using short functions and single-purpose functions
- Using single entry and single exit points in subsystems
- Minimizing interface ambiguities
- Checking for error conditions
- Encrypting important code
- Controlling the application program interfaces (APIs)
- Separating test libraries from production libraries so that the latter ones are not corrupted
- Validating inputs
- Using tools, such as static code and runtime code checkers and profiling, penetration testing, and application scanning tools
- Sanitizing data sent to other systems

Parsing is the procedure of breaking the program code, comments, or sentences into logical parts and then explaining the form, function, and interaction of these parts. Parsers (either self-generated or user-loaded) recognize syntactic and semantic constructs in the source code and load them as object-oriented representations into a repository.

(iii) System Design and Coding Principles

Both application systems and information systems should be designed and developed based on proven principles so systems are operated in a controlled environment. Some examples of system design principles are listed next.

The **principle of separation of privileges** asserts that protection mechanisms where two cryptographic keys or dual controls by different parties are required for access are stronger mechanisms than those requiring only one key. This principle is often implemented with access rules.

The **principle of least privilege** specifies that every program and user of the system should operate using the least set of privileges necessary to complete the job. One effect of this principle is that the potential for damage caused by an accident or an error is limited. This principle addresses the need for minimal interactions between privileged programs and the need to prevent improper uses of privilege.

The **principle of least functionality** (or minimal functionality) states that an information system's security functions should configure the system to provide only essential capabilities and specifically prohibits or restricts the use of risky (by default) and unnecessary functions, ports, protocols, and/or services. Note that the principle of least functionality facilitates the implementation of the principle of separation of privileges and the principle of least privileges.

The **principle of security by obscurity** (Kerckhoff's principle) does not work in practice because attackers can compromise the security system at any time. This principle means that trying to keep something secret when it is not does more harm than good.

The **principle of data hiding** is tied closely to modularity and abstraction and subsequently to maintainability. "Data hiding" means data and procedures in a module are hidden from other parts of the software. Errors contained in one module are restricted to that module only, not passed to other modules. Data hiding prevents components' actions from interfering with other components and advocates developing independent modules that communicate with one another only that information necessary to achieve software function. Abstraction helps to define the procedures, while data hiding defines access restrictions to procedures and local data structures. The concept of data hiding is useful during program testing and software maintenance. Note that layering, abstraction, and data hiding are protection mechanisms in security design architecture.

The **principle of process isolation, system isolation, and component isolation** is employed to preserve the object's wholeness and the subject's adherence to a code of behavior. It is necessary to prevent objects from colliding or interfering with one another and to prevent actions of active agents (subjects) from interfering or colluding with one another. Further, it is necessary to ensure that objects and active agents maintain a correspondence to one another so that (1) the actions of one agent cannot affect the states of objects to which that agent should not have correspondence and (2) the states of objects cannot affect the actions of agents to which they should not have correspondence. Isolation can exist at process, system, or component level.

Process isolation prevents data leakages and data modification problems. Techniques such as encapsulation, time multiplexing of shared resources, naming distinctions, and virtual mapping are used to employ the process isolation or separation concept. These separation concepts are supported by incorporating the principle of least privilege.

System isolation can be achieved in four ways:

1. Physical/logical isolation at the system level
2. Virtualization using virtual machines
3. Isolating tightly bounded and proprietary program components
4. Implementing standard interfaces and protocols rather than proprietary interfaces and protocols

Another related concept is component isolation, where components critical to system safety, security, and integrity are isolated from other parts of the system. Safety functions should be kept separate from one another. "Security isolation" means the information system isolates security functions from nonsecurity functions implemented via partitions and domains that control access to and protect the integrity of the hardware, software, and firmware that perform those security functions.

The **principle of fail-safe defaults** asserts that access decisions should be based on permission rather than exclusion. This equates to the condition in which lack of access is the default, and the protection scheme recognizes permissible actions rather than prohibited actions. Also, failures due to flaws in exclusion-based systems tend to grant (unauthorized) permission, whereas permission-based systems tend to fail-safe with permission denied.

The **principle of application system portioning** states that the information system should separate user functionality, including user interface services, from information system management functionality, including databases, network components, workstations, or servers. This separation is achieved through physical or logical methods using different computers, different central processing units (CPUs), different instances of the operating system (OS), different network addresses, or a combination of these methods. Similarly, security functions should be separated from nonsecurity functions. One way to prevent access to information system management functions is to use a gray-out option for nonprivileged users, separating them from privileged users with administrator privileges.

The **principle of silent security** states that security must be strong and should work in the background or behind the scenes to provide a seamless and borderless access and to intervene only when something is going wrong or went wrong with timely notifications and alerts.

The **principles of secure coding** include those listed next.

- Minimize the attack surface area.

- Establish secure defaults.

- Follow the principle of least privilege.

- Implement the strategy of defense in depth and defense in breadth.

- Fail securely in a known state.

- Do not trust servers and do verify.

- Implement separation of duties by separating job functions between designers and programmers, between programmers and testers, and between production staff and nonproduction staff.

- Avoid security by obscurity, security by default, or security by choice.

- Keep security simple, silent, and strong.

- Fix security problems and patches correctly.

(iv) Software Assurance, Safety, Security, and Quality

Critical software is software the failure of which could have an impact on security, safety, or privacy or could cause large financial, property, human, or social loss. It is also referred to as high-consequence software and software-intensive system. A software-intensive system is a system in which the majority of components are implemented in or by software and the functional objectives are achieved through software components.

Security controls over the critical software are listed next.

- Defensive design and programming techniques
- Robust identity and authentication methods
- Resilient/robust/trustworthy software
- Agile defenses to protect supply chain software and against advanced persistent threats using boundary protection mechanisms and information system resilience concepts
- Built-in software defenses
- Defense-in-depth strategies
- Defense-in-breadth strategies
- Defense-in-technology strategies
- Defense-in-time strategies
- Defense-in-density strategies
- Defense-in-intensity strategies

The scope of a secure software environment consists of software safety and software quality because security of an information system depends on both safety and quality elements of the system. An information system should have the right amounts of security controls, software safety functions, and software quality features.

(A) Software Assurance
Software assurance is related to reducing the level of uncertainty in software in terms of estimation, prediction, information, inference, or achievement of a specific goal. Such a reduction can provide an improved basis for justified confidence in software.

Contrast software assurance to information assurance, where the latter is related to measures that protect and defend information and information systems by ensuring their availability, integrity, authentication, confidentiality, and nonrepudiation. These measures include providing for restoration of information systems by incorporating protection, detection, and reaction capabilities.

(B) Software Safety
Software safety is important, since lack of safety considerations in a computer-based application system can cause danger or injury to people and/or damage to equipment and property. It could also create financial or other loss to people using or affected by the system. For example, an incorrectly programmed and incompletely tested medical diagnostic and treatment prescription system could kill a patient or injure people receiving the treatment. Another example is a process control system in a pharmaceutical company; drugs that are incorrectly formulated by a computer system could kill or injure patients due to errors in software. Similarly, incorrect and obsolete documentation, especially after a program change was made, could lead to improperly functioning software, loss of life, failed missions, and lost time.

Software needs to be developed using specific software development and software assurance processes to protect against or mitigate software failure. A complete software safety standard references other standards that address these processes and includes a software safety policy usually identifying required functionality to protect against or mitigate failure.

WHAT ARE THE MAJOR ATTRIBUTES OF SOFTWARE?

Polls and surveys have revealed that the top two most important attributes of software are (1) reliable software that functions as promised and (2) software free from security vulnerabilities and malicious code.

As software is included in more and more critical systems (e.g., medical devices, nuclear power plants, and transportation systems), the need for software safety programs becomes crucial. These software safety programs should consist not only of software safety analyses but of methodologies that assist in the assurance of developing quality software.

Software safety should not be confused with software reliability. "Reliability" is the ability of a system to perform its required functions under stated conditions for a specified period of time. "Safety" is the probability that conditions (hazards) that can lead to a mishap do not occur, whether the intended function is performed or not. Reliability concerns all possible software errors, while safety is concerned only with those errors that cause actual system hazards. Software safety and software reliability are part of software quality. "Quality" is the degree to which a system meets specified requirements and customer or user needs or expectations.

The overall purpose of the software safety evaluation review is to assess how well the product meets its software quality objectives. Quality objectives include reliability, safety, functionality, maintainability, and reviewability. To perform this evaluation, reviewers need sufficient information about the product requirements, product development guidelines, and product overall quality.

The next general types of questions can guide the reviewer regarding the product evaluation.

- How thoroughly has the developer or vendor analyzed the safety of critical functions of the software?

- How well has the developer or vendor established the appropriateness of the functions, algorithms, and knowledge on which the software is based?

- How carefully has the developer or vendor implemented the safety and performance requirements of the software?

Specific Safety Questions for the Requirements and Design Phases

1. Are the safety requirements consistent with the hazard analysis?
2. How was failure analysis of the software conducted?

3. Are there requirements for self-supervision of the software?

4. Is there modularity in the design?

5. Have critical components been isolated?

6. Were design reviews performed and documented?

Specific Safety Questions for the Implementation Phase

1. Do the test cases produce results identical with the expected output?

2. Does the operations procedure manual adequately describe diagnostic procedures and tools?

3. Does the operations procedure manual adequately describe emergency procedures and fault recovery procedures?

Specific Safety Questions for the Maintenance Phase

1. Is there a formal procedure to start maintenance when problems are found?

2. Is there a formal change control procedure?

(C) Software Quality Assurance

SQA is a planned systematic pattern for all actions necessary to provide adequate confidence that the product, or process by which the product is developed, conforms to established requirements.

The primary goal of SQA is to enhance the quality of software. Its thrust is product or service assurance. Quality of process is related to the quality of product. New SQA focuses on evaluating the processes by which products are developed or manufactured.

The major objectives of the SQA process are to ensure that the software development and software assurance processes comply with software assurance plans and standards and to recommend process improvements. The process uses the system requirements and information about the purpose and criticality of the software to evaluate the outputs of the software development and software assurance processes. It begins before the software requirements process and ends when its objectives have been met. An SQA plan and review/audit reports are produced during the SQA process.

(c) Application Development

This section covers scope of application systems; responsibilities of information systems management; software testing objectives, approaches, methods, and controls; software reviews, inspections, traceability analysis, and walkthroughs; risks and threats in systems development and in systems operation; and sample audit findings in application development.

(i) Scope of Application Systems

Application-oriented information systems encompass all areas of business functions, such as manufacturing and service (operations), marketing and sales, human resources (HR), quality, accounting, finance, logistics, IT, and customer service. These application systems represent mission-critical systems with a strategic focus, and they are used by internal managers and executives to make decisions and by employees at all levels to perform their job duties.

EXAMPLES OF APPLICATION SYSTEMS

- General ledger
- Insurance claims processing
- Accounts payable
- Demand deposits
- Payroll
- Welfare payments
- Order entry
- Tax administration
- Sales forecasting
- License administration
- Manufacturing scheduling
- Accounts receivable

Each application system is designed to perform specific functions, similar to a manual system, with clearly defined input, processing, and output activities and boundaries. Each application system under design and development should incorporate an appropriate type and amount of application controls and security controls. Application controls are primarily concerned with data being originated, prepared, entered, processed, stored, accessed, transmitted, secured, controlled, and used. Security controls are primarily concerned with access controls, identification and authentication controls for users and applications, encryption, and password management.

(A) Data Origination, Preparation, and Input

Several approaches exist to prepare and enter data into the application system. In some cases, data are captured on a paper (source) document, such as a sales order or purchase order. The source documents are batched into small groups and entered into the system either by functional users or central data entry operators through the use of terminals. In other cases, there is no externally generated source document; instead, the customer calls in and places an order with the organization.

Regardless of the method used to capture the data, the entered data are edited and validated to prevent or detect errors and omissions. Therefore, access controls and data editing and validation controls are important to ensure that quality data are entering into the application system.

Program-based controls are embedded in online data entry programs in the form of data editing and validation routines. These routines will ensure data integrity. The sequence of events followed by the computer center in a typical batch data entry and batch updating or online data entry and batch updating environment includes:

- Batching records of transactions or source documents.
- Converting (keying) transactions or documents to machine-readable form.
- Validating input transactions.
- Updating the master file with new transactions.
- Generating hard-copy reports.

(B) Data Processing

Processing controls should satisfy these objectives:

- All transactions are authorized prior to processing.
- All approved transactions are entered quickly in their entirety and accepted by the system.
- All transactions are accurately and quickly processed.

Understanding the nature of computer processing is critical. Although there are some common controls, controls will be different between batch and online processing. Similar to data input, data editing and validation controls are important during computer processing. Therefore, more program-based processing controls should be used to ensure data integrity and security.

DATA PROCESSING RULES

If an error occurs when processing a transaction, processing should be continued with that transaction. All errors and rejected transactions should be listed in a report or displayed on a computer terminal.

When updating a batched file, and if end-of-file condition is reached on the master file before end of file is reached on the transaction file, the application program should post the remaining transactions to the master file.

The process of carrying forward control totals from one run to another is known as **run-to-run balancing**. Run-to-run control totals are program processing-based controls. Examples could be the number of records in a file and amount totals for certain data fields. The objective is to maintain the accuracy and completeness of data as they pass through computer programs and processing operations (i.e., processing control). It is good to automate the batch report balancing and reconciliation procedures and return this function to functional user departments. Functional user control of report balancing activity increases the chances of correcting the source of out-of-balance conditions. This is because functional users have intimate knowledge about the nature of transactions and their interrelationships. Computer operators should not perform run-to-run balancing procedures.

(C) Data Output

There are many output devices in use. Some examples are terminals, printers, plotters, microfilm, microfiche, and voice response units. System output documents are photographed onto a roll of film and stored on microfilm, microfiche, and optical disk. Audio response systems will help people to inquire about a customer's bank balance, get the time and temperature readings, and obtain a telephone number from a directory. Usually system outputs are in the form of hard-copy reports. Balancing, distribution, and retention of system outputs are major concerns to management and auditors alike since they affect the quality and timeliness of data and usefulness of the system.

(D) Documentation

System documentation is a key element of system operations. Without correct and complete documentation, new users cannot be trained properly, programmers cannot maintain the system correctly, system users cannot make any meaningful references to the system functions and features, management or anyone else cannot understand the system functions and features, and system reviewers (e.g., auditors) cannot make objective evaluation of the system functions and controls. Application system documentation is classified into six categories:

1. System
2. Program
3. Computer operations
4. Help desk
5. Network control
6. User

This classification is based on the major user of the documentation. For example, help desk documentation is used by help desk staff.

(E) Data Integrity

Integrity is binary in nature: It exists or it does not. Likewise, information quality is binary: It meets system user requirements or it does not. Quality is a matter of characteristics.

The perception of quality depends on the purpose for which information is to be used. For information to be useful, it should be available where, when, and in the form it is required with costs equal to or less than benefits to be derived from it.

The data have a certain degree of quality, and the user has some expectations of quality. If the data quality equals or exceeds the expectations of quality, the data have integrity; otherwise, they do not. Other factors of data quality, in addition to completeness, accuracy, and timeliness, are relevance and validity. **Relevance** is a measure of the appropriateness of the data item in relation to the user's problem or need. **Validity** is a notion of external reference or correspondence. Data may be valid but not relevant or may have low validity but still be relevant.

Data integrity is the heart of any application system. Data integrity controls ensure the reliability and usability of data and information in making management decisions. The higher the integrity of controls, the greater the credibility and reliability of application systems. Here, "data integrity" refers to five control attributes: completeness, accuracy, authorization, consistency, and timeliness.

DATA INTEGRITY RULES AND CONTROLS

- A directive control will ensure that people follow data integrity rules consistently.
- A preventive control will stop a data integrity violation from happening.
- A detective control will recognize a data integrity violation.
- A corrective control will fix or repair the damage done by a data integrity violation.
- A recovery control will help in recovering or restoring from a disaster caused by a data integrity violation.

(ii) Responsibilities of Information Systems Management

A brief list of responsibilities of information systems management in developing or acquiring systems follows. Information systems management:

- Develops, disseminates, and reviews/updates at defined frequency:
  - A formal, documented system and services acquisition policy that includes information security considerations and that addresses purpose, scope, roles, responsibilities, management commitment, coordination among organizational entities, and compliance.
  - Formal, documented procedures to facilitate the implementation of the system and services acquisition policy and associated system and services acquisition controls.
- Determines, documents, and allocates the resources required to protect the information system as part of its capital planning and investment control process.
- Manages the information system using an SDLC methodology that includes information security considerations.
- Defines and documents information system security roles and responsibilities throughout the SDLC.
- Identifies individuals having information system security roles and responsibilities.
- Includes security functional requirements and specifications.
- Includes security-related documentation requirements.
- Includes developmental and evaluation-related assurance requirements.
- Obtains, protects as required, and makes available to authorized personnel administrator documentation for the information system that:
  - Implements secure configuration, installation, and operation of the information system.
  - Ensures effective use and maintenance of security features or functions.
  - Understands known vulnerabilities regarding configuration and use of administrative (i.e., privileged) functions.
- Obtains, protects as required, and makes available to authorized personnel user documentation for the information system that:
  - Develops user-accessible security features and functions and explains how to use those security features or functions effectively.
  - Implements methods for user interaction with the information system, which enables individuals to use the system in a more secure manner.
  - Defines user responsibilities in maintaining the security of the information and information system.
- Documents attempts to obtain information system documentation when such documentation is either unavailable or nonexistent.
- Uses software and associated documentation in accordance with contract agreements and copyright law.
- Employs tracking systems for software and associated documentation protected by quantity licenses to control copying and distribution.

- Controls and documents the use of peer-to-peer (P2P) file-sharing technology to ensure that this capability is not used for the unauthorized distribution, display, performance, or reproduction of copyrighted work.

- Prohibits the use of binary or machine-executable code from sources with limited or no warranty without accompanying source code.

- Enforces explicit rules governing the installation of software by users. If provided the necessary privileges, users have the ability to install software. The organization identifies what types of software installations are permitted (e.g., updates and security patches to existing software) and what types of installations are prohibited (e.g., software whose pedigree with regard to being potentially malicious is unknown or suspect).

- Conducts due care and due diligence reviews during software development and acquisition processes.

(iii) Software Testing Objectives, Approaches, Methods, and Controls

Several testing objectives exist to test either developed or acquired information systems, and each objective may be suitable to a specific program, module, subsystem, or the entire system. In practice, compatible test objectives should be combined after considering the time, cost, and skills constraints (e.g., recovery, security, and configuration tests). Testing is important to ensure that security-related functions and business-related functions work correctly whether the system is developed internally for internal use or developed commercially for external customers.

Testing approaches include the big-bang, top-down, bottom-up, and sandwich approach. The big-bang testing approach puts all the units or modules together at once, with no stubs (throwaway code that takes the place of the actual code) or drivers. In it, all the program units are compiled and tested at once. The top-down testing approach uses stubs. The actual code for lower-level units is replaced by a stub. The bottom-up testing approach uses drivers (a form of throwaway code). Units at higher levels are replaced by drivers that emulate the procedure calls. Sandwich testing approach uses a combination of top-down (stubs) and bottom-up (drivers) approaches.

Several testing methods are available to test computer programs at a detailed level, each with a different focus. Specific and detailed application software testing methods with their objectives are listed next.

- **Resiliency test.** Measures durability of a system in withstanding system failures.

- **Conformance test.** Determines if a product satisfies the criteria specified in standard documents.

- **Conversion test.** Determines whether old data files and record balances are carried forward accurately, completely, and properly to the new system.

- **Interface test.** Demonstrates that all systems work in concert. (Input/output description errors are detected in the interface testing phase.)

- **Recovery test.** Determines whether the system can function normally after a system failure, error, or other malfunction and determines the ability to operate within the fallback and recovery structure.

- **Security test.** Determines whether unauthorized people can use computer resources using red team and blue team testing approaches.

- **Configuration test.** Verifies that the product can be installed and operated in different hardware and software environments without using vendor default settings.

- **Integration test.** Tests a group of programs to see that a transaction or data passes between programs. It is least understood by software developers and end users due to lack of specification documents and the variety of testing methods used. A formal change control mechanism should start after completion of an integration test.

- **Regression test.** Verifies that changes do not introduce new errors. A significant amount of testing repetition occurs by design.

- **Stress test.** Verifies boundary conditions of a program.

- **Parallel test.** Verifies test results by comparing two systems with each other.

- **Performance test.** Measures resources required (e.g., memory and disk) and to determine online system response time and batch job throughput.

- **Interoperability test.** Ensures that two or more communications products (e.g., hosts or routers) can interwork and exchange data.

- **Network security test.** Ensures that network protection devices (e.g., firewalls and intrusion detection systems [IDSs]) selectively block packet traffic based on application system configurations.

- **Production acceptance test.** Tests operational preparedness of a new system prior to moving from the testing to the production environment. This performed by IT production staff.

- **Pilot test.** Tests a new system in one department or division at a time until enough experience is gained prior to launching an all-out implementation throughout the organization.

- **Program unit/module test.** Tests individual programs, modules, subroutines, or subprograms to verify their functionality.

- **Systems test.** Tests the entire system to prove the validity of the software requirements definition and design specifications including its interfaces. It should include a representative sample of data for both valid and invalid conditions using test data or copies of live data, not real live data.

- **User acceptance test.** Tests software functions and features to determine if the system meets business needs and user needs and to see if the system was developed according to end user requirements. The end user must accept the system before moving it into the production environment. The user acceptance test is performed functional user staff.

- **Load/volume test.** Tests whether simultaneous users can overload the system.

- **Concurrency test.** Tests whether multiple users can create system deadlocks or damage each other's work.

- **Quality assurance test.** Makes sure the software product fails only after meeting quality standards and specifications. It also tests the quality of service (QoS) features such as network bandwidth, traffic, collision, congestion, and performance levels; and jitters and latency factors,

- **Function test.** Verifies that each required capability and system operation is implemented correctly.

- **End-to-end test.** Verifies that a defined set of interrelated systems, which collectively support an organizational core business area or function, interoperate as intended in an operational environment (either actual or simulated). This test is conducted extensively when an internal system exchanges data with an external system.

- **Fault injection test.** Unfiltered and invalid data are injected as input into an application program to detect faults in resource operations and execution functions.

- **Fuzz test.** Similar to fault injection test in that invalid data is input into the application via the environment or input by one process into another process. Fuzz testing is implemented by tools called fuzzers, which are programs or scripts that submit some combination of inputs to the test target to reveal how it responds.

- **Alpha test.** End users who are independent of end users who participated in a new system development project conduct a field-based alpha test on a new system to ensure that its functions and features work as designed and to discover bugs and errors. Based on the outcome of the alpha test phase, the system is adjusted and refined and later moved to beta test phase. Mainly applies to commercially developed software, not to internally developed software.

  Alpha System $\longrightarrow$ Beta System

- **Beta test.** A group of volunteered people outside of a company (i.e., customers or others) conduct a beta test of the system, after it is alpha tested fully, to make sure it works and to discover any last-minute problems before it is released for commercialization (i.e., ready to market). A beta test is a prerelease test. Note that both the alpha test and the beta test apply to commercially developed software for sale to customers and not to internally developed software for internal use of a company.

  Alpha System $\longrightarrow$ Beta System $\longrightarrow$ Final System

In addition, four broad testing methods are used:

1. Black box testing
2. Gray box testing
3. White box testing
4. Independent testing

Black box testing is a basic test methodology that assumes no knowledge of the internal structure and implementation detail of the assessment object. It examines the software from the user's viewpoint and determines if the data are processed according to the specifications. It does not consider implementation details. It verifies that software functions are performed correctly and that advertised security mechanisms are tested under operational conditions. This testing focuses on the external behavior of a system and uses the system's functional specifications to generate test cases. It ensures that the system does what it is supposed to do and does not do what it is not supposed to do. Black box testing is also known as generalized testing or functional testing. Black box testing should be combined with white box testing for maximum benefit because neither type of testing by itself does a thorough testing job. Black box testing is functional analysis of a system.

Gray box testing is a test methodology that assumes some knowledge of the internal structure and implementation detail of the assessment object. It is also known as focused testing.

White box testing is a comprehensive test methodology that assumes explicit and substantial knowledge of the internal structure and implementation detail of the assessment object. It focuses on the internal behavior of a system (program structure and logic) and uses the code itself to generate test cases. The degree of coverage is used as a measure of the completeness of the test cases and test effort. White box testing is performed at the individual component level, such as program or module, not at the entire system level. It is also known as detailed testing or logic testing. White box testing should be combined with black box testing for maximum benefit because neither type of testing by itself does a thorough testing job. White box testing is structured testing since it focuses on the structural analysis of a system. It is also called glass box testing because testers can see the inside of a system as through a glass.

Independent testing is conducted by an independent accredited software testing organization as per the International organization for standardization (ISO) 17025 standard to verify that it meets both functional requirements and SQA requirements. The testing organization can use either a white box or black box scenario, depending on the need.

Testing controls bring disciple and structure to the testing process. Examples of controls to be exercised during application software testing are listed next.

- Activity logs, incident reports, and software versioning are the controls used during testing.
- There is a tendency to compress system initiation, requirements definition, design, programming, and training activities. However, for QA and security reasons, the testing activities should not be compressed.
- The correct sequence of tests is:

    Unit Test $\longrightarrow$ Integration Test $\longrightarrow$ System Test $\longrightarrow$ Acceptance Test
- The correct sequence of test tasks is:

    Prepare $\longrightarrow$ Execute $\longrightarrow$ Delete

(iv) Software Reviews, Inspections, Traceability Analysis, and Walkthroughs

Reviews, inspections, traceability analysis, and walkthroughs are examples of QA and QC tools used during the SDLC to ensure a safe, secure, and quality product.

Reviews are conducted in meetings at which the requirements, design, code, or other products of software development project are presented to the user, sponsor, or other interested parties for comment and approval, often as a prerequisite for concluding a given phase of the software development process. Reviews are more formal than walkthroughs.

Inspections are evaluation techniques in which software requirements, design, code, or other products are examined by a person or group other than the author to detect faults, violations of development standards, and other problems. The type of errors detected in inspections includes incomplete requirements errors, infeasible requirements errors, and conflicting requirements errors. Inspections are more formal than walkthroughs.

> ### DYNAMIC ANALYSIS VERSUS STATIC ANALYSIS
>
> An application system's functions and features can be analyzed in two ways: dynamic and static.
>
> The most common **dynamic analysis** technique is testing, which involves the execution of a software product and analysis of its response to sets of input data to determine its validity and to detect errors. The behavioral properties of the program are also observed. Software testing is usually conducted on individual components (e.g., subroutines and modules) as they are developed, on software subsystems when they are integrated with one another or with other system components, and on the complete system.
>
> Inspections, code reading, and tracing are examples of **static analysis**, which is the analysis of requirements, design, code, or other items, either manually or automatically, without executing the software product itself to determine its lexical and syntactic properties as opposed to its behavioral properties.

Traceability analysis is the process of verifying that each specified requirement has been implemented in the design or code, that all aspects of the design or code have their basis in the specified requirements, and that testing produces results that are compatible with the specified requirements. Traceability analysis is more formal than walkthroughs.

A **walkthrough** is an evaluation technique in which a designer or programmer leads one or more other members of the development team through a segment of design or code while the other members ask questions and make comments about technique and style and identify possible errors, violations of development standards, and other problems. Walkthroughs are similar to reviews but are less formal.

(v) Risks and Threats in Systems Development and in Systems Operation

When a computer system is being developed or operated, it is subject to several risks and threats from insiders (i.e., current and previous employees) and outsiders (i.e., hackers, adversaries, contractors, suppliers, and vendors) with different threat sources and threat objectives. These risks and threats are divided into three categories, as described next.

(A) Categories of Malware Inserted during Software Development and Maintenance Work

Malware refers to malicious software or malicious code that is designed to deny, destroy, modify, or impede the software's logic, configuration settings, data, or program library routines. Malware can be inserted during software development, preparation for distribution, deployment, installation, and/or update. It can be planted manually or through automated means. It can also be inserted during a system's operation. Regardless of when the malware is embedded during the software life cycle, it effectively becomes part of the software and can present substantial dangers and risks. Malware has become the most significant external threat to most systems, causing widespread damage and disruption and necessitating extensive recovery efforts within user organizations.

Malware is likely to be inserted in several ways during software development or maintenance: through back doors or trapdoors, time bombs, logic bombs, and software holes. This malware is introduced into a system due to unnoticed, forgotten, or neglected functions or when unnecessary functions are disregarded. It can be discovered through tabletop reviews, periodic assessments, and war-dialing, war-driving, wireless scanning, and penetration testing. Not having a source code escrow is a risk in itself.

Back doors are hidden software mechanisms used to circumvent the system's perimeter defenses and security controls, often to enable an attacker to gain unauthorized remote access to the system. A **trapdoor** is a hidden software or hardware mechanism that can be triggered to permit circumvention of system protection mechanisms. It is activated in some innocent-appearing manner (e.g., a special random key sequence at a terminal). Software developers often introduce trapdoors in their code to enable them to reenter the system and perform certain functions. Note that both back doors and trapdoors are undocumented ways of gaining access to a computer system. Both are potential security risks to user organizations as they completely circumvent perimeter defenses. The terms "back door" and "trapdoor" are used synonymously.

One frequently used back door method is inserting a malicious program that listens for system commands on a particular Transmission Control Protocol (TCP) or User Datagram Protocol (UDP) port. Usually, both back doors and trapdoors are introduced through software maintenance hooks (i.e., entry points into a program) because they are special instructions in software that allow easy maintenance and additional feature development. They are not clearly defined during system access or design specification and are not documented. Maintenance hooks frequently allow entry into the code at unusual points or without the usual checks, so they are serious security risks if they are not removed prior to live implementation.

A **time bomb** is a resident computer program that triggers an unauthorized or damaging action at a predefined time.

A **logic bomb** is a resident computer program that triggers an unauthorized or damaging action when a particular event or state in the system's operation is realized—for example, when a particular packet is received.

Software holes penetrate through lack of perimeter defenses, which is risky. A software hole can reside any of the three layers (i.e., networking, OS, or application). Software vendors or developers should provide security mechanisms to mitigate the risks. Defending the perimeter requires installing appropriate security controls at all entry points into the network, including the Internet connection. Testing the perimeter to identify back doors and software holes requires tabletop reviews, periodic assessments, and war-dialing, war-driving, wireless-scanning, and penetration testing.

Source code escrow can be risky as it is an arrangement with a third party (e.g., a bank) to hold the software under its custody and make it available to user organizations under unusual business circumstances. This arrangement is applicable to vendor-developed applications software packages either purchased or leased by user organizations. Usually vendors do not give the source code to user organizations for proprietary reasons; only the object is provided with the package. The vendor has the obligation to ensure that the escrowed source code is an exact copy of the production source code. The concept is similar to cryptographic key escrow.

The purpose of software escrow is to provide user organizations the ability to access the source code under unusual business circumstances, such as when the vendor is going out of business or merging with or being acquired by another organization. In the absence of an escrow arrangement, two risks are possible: User organizations cannot access the source code when needed, and applications software ceases to perform its functions or the application system cannot be recovered from a disaster. There should be a written contract for the escrow arrangement signed by the vendor and reviewed by an attorney specializing in such contracts.

(B) Categories of Malware Planted on Operational Systems

Malware is likely to be planted on operational systems in a number of ways, including those listed next.

- Viruses
- Worms
- Easter eggs (viruses)
- Trojan horses
- Zombies
- Cross-site scripting (XSS)
- Robots (botnets)
- Rootkits
- Cookies
- Adware
- Spyware
- Active content
- Applets
- Electronic dumpster diving
- API issues
- Buffer overflow

A **virus** is a self-replicating computer program (i.e., it makes copies of itself) that runs and spreads by modifying other programs or files and distributes the copies to other files, programs, or computers. It is a malware program and may attach itself to and become part of another executable program—for example, to become a delivery mechanism for malicious code or for a denial of service (DoS) attack. A virus can replicate by attaching a copy of itself to other programs or files and can trigger an additional payload when specific conditions are met.

A number of different types of viruses, which are listed next, exist.

- Boot sector viruses infect the master boot record of a hard drive or removable disk media (e.g., thumb drives and flash drives).
- File infector viruses attach themselves to executable programs, such as word processing, spreadsheet applications, and computer games.
- Macro viruses attach themselves to application documents, such as word processing files and spreadsheets, then use the application's macro programming language to execute and propagate.
- Compiled viruses have their source code converted by a compiler program into a format that can be directly executed by the OS.
- Interpreted viruses are composed of source code that can be executed only by a particular application or service.

- Multipartite viruses use multiple infection methods, typically to infect both files and boot sectors.

- Morphing viruses change as they propagate, thus making them extremely difficult to eradicate using conventional antivirus software tools because the virus signature is constantly changing.

Some examples of virus behaviors are listed next.

- Increase in file size

- Change in update timestamp

- Sudden increase in free space

- Numerous unexpected disk accesses

- Gradual loss of available storage space

- Unusual screen activity

To protect against viruses, install antivirus software, which is a program that monitors a computer or network to identify all major types of malware and prevent or contain malware incidents. This software detects malicious code, prevents system infection, and removes malicious code that has infected the system. There are two drawbacks associated with antivirus software tools: Virus-specific software may fail to detect viruses more recent than the software, and detection software may fail to detect some viruses that are already resident in memory when the software is loaded.

A **worm** is a computer program that copies itself (i.e., self-replicating) from system to system via a network and is self-contained and self-propagating. It exploits weaknesses in the OS or inadequate system management. Releasing a worm usually results in brief but spectacular outbreaks, shutting down entire networks. Most worms infect computers as a result of a user directly executing the worm (i.e., by clicking on it). It is unrealistic to assume that users will become cautious about executing unknown files. Countermeasures against worms include:

- Identification and authentication controls.

- Configuration review tools.

- Checksum-based change detection tools.

- Intrusion detection tools.

- Wrapper programs to filter network connections.

- Stackguarding technology to control worms.

- Firewalls to protect an organization's network from other networks.

Easter eggs are viruses, and they trigger when a program code is placed in software for the amusement of its developer or users. They are nuisances to users.

A **Trojan** or **Trojan horse** is a nonreplicating program that appears to be benign (i.e., looks innocent) but actually has a hidden malicious purpose. When the program is invoked, so is the undesired function whose effects may not be immediately obvious.

A **zombie** is a program that is installed on one computer system with the intent of causing it to attack other computer systems in a chainlike manner.

Cross-site scripting (XSS) is an attack technique in which an attacker subverts a valid website, forcing it to send malicious scripting to an unsuspecting user's browser. XSS is a delivery technique for malicious code.

A **robot (bot)** is an automated software program that executes certain commands when it receives a specific input. Bots are often the technology used to implement Trojan horses, logic bombs, back doors, and spyware.

Botnet is a term for a collection of software robots (bots) that run autonomously. A bot's originator can control the group remotely, usually through a means such as Internet Relay Chat (IRC) and usually for nefarious purposes. A botnet can comprise a collection of cracked computers running programs (usually referred to as worms, Trojan horses, or backdoors) under a common command-and-control infrastructure. Botnets are often used to send spam emails and to launch DoS phishing and virus attacks.

A **rootkit** is a collection of files that is installed on a system to alter its standard functionality in a malicious and stealthy way. It is a set of tools used by an attacker after gaining root-level access to a host computer. The rootkit conceals an attacker's activities on the host and permits the attacker to maintain root-level access to the host through covert means. Here are some examples of protection methods against botnets and rootkits:

- Use and maintain antivirus software.
- Install a firewall.
- Use strong passwords.
- Update software with patches.
- Take precautions when using email and web browsers to not trigger an infection.

Cookies are small computer files that store information for a website on a user's computer. This information is supplied by a web server to a browser, in a response for a requested resource, for the browser to store temporarily and return to the server on any subsequent visits or request. Cookies have two mandatory parameters: name and value. They have four optional parameters: expiration date, path, domain, and secure. Four types of cookies exist: persistent, session, tracking, and encrypted cookies.

Adware is any software program intended for marketing purposes, such as to deliver and display advertising banners or pop-ups to the user's computer screen or to track the user's online usage or purchasing activity. Adware tracks a user's activity and passes it to third parties without the user's knowledge or consent.

Click fraud is possible with adware because it involves deceptions and scams that inflate advertising bills with improper charges per click in an online advertisement on the Web.

Spyware is adware intended to violate a user's privacy. Spyware is placed on a computer to secretly gather information about the user and report it. The various types of spyware include web bugs, which are tiny graphics on a website that are referenced within the Hypertext Markup Language (HTML) content of a web page or email to collect information about the user viewing the HTML content, and tracking cookies, which are placed on the user's computer to track activity on different websites and create a detailed profile of the user's behavior. To protect against spyware, install antispyware software, which is a program that specializes in detecting both malware and nonmalware forms of spyware.

Active content technologies allow code, often in the form of a script, macro, or other mobile code representation, to execute when the document is rendered. HTML and other related markup-language documents, whether delivered via HTTP or another means, provide rich mechanisms for conveying executable content. Examples of active content include Postscript and portable document format (PDF) documents, web pages containing Java applets and JavaScript instructions, and word processor files containing macros, spreadsheet formulas, and other interpretable content. Active content may also be distributed embedded in email or as executable mail attachments. Countermeasures against active content documents include security policy, application settings, automated filters, software version control, software readers, and system isolation.

Applets are small computer applications written in various programming languages that are automatically downloaded and executed by applet-enabled Internet browsers. Examples include Active-X and Java applets, both of which have security concerns.

Electronic dumpster diving involves scanning and enumerating systems and ports to discover passwords and to investigate open source intelligence using domain name system (DNS) lookups and web searches to discover the characteristics of the system being attacked and particularly to pinpoint any potentially exploitable vulnerabilities.

API issues include calls, subroutines, or software interrupts that comprise a documented interface so that a higher-level program, such as an application program, can make use of the lower-level services and functions of another application, OS, network OS, or a driver. APIs can be used to write a file in an application program's proprietary format, communicate over a transmission control protocol/Internet protocol (TCP/IP) network, access a structured query language (SQL) database, or surf the Internet, which can be risky because APIs can cause buffer overflow exploits, which, in turn, lead to worm attacks.

Buffer overflow is a condition likely to occur in APIs in which more input is placed into a buffer or data-holding area than the capacity allocated, thus causing the information in the area to be overwritten. Attackers and adversaries can exploit such a condition to crash a system or to insert specially crafted code that allows them to gain control of the system. Some countermeasures are listed next.

- Use appropriate security controls across operational, network, and host layers, combined with applying updated antivirus software and patches.
- Install firewalls.
- Practice secure programming techniques.
- Install IDS software.
- Use APIs with stackguarding technology.
- Monitor with security event management tools.

(C) Categories of Nonmalware Deployed on Operational Systems

Sometimes malware is combined with nonmalware deceptive practices, such as social engineering techniques, to accomplish complex attacks on unsuspecting users. Three major categories of social engineering attacks include spamming, phishing, and pharming.

In some cases, deception is used to trick the user into downloading and executing malicious code (e.g., spamming attack). Phishing attack is also a deception technique, although it does not require malicious code. In other cases, malware is used to enable a deception, as in a pharming attack. Both phishing and pharming attacks are different forms of social engineering.

Spamming is the abuse of an email system in the form of sending unsolicited bulk and junk emails. Recipients who click links in spam messages can inadvertently download spyware, viruses, and other malware. To protect against spamming, install a spam filtering software (a computer program that analyzes email to look for characteristics of a spam and typically places the messages that appear to be spam in a separate email folder).

Phishing is the creation and use of fraudulent but legitimate looking emails and websites to obtain Internet users' identity, authentication, or financial information or to trick users into doing something they would not do. In many cases, the perpetrators embed the illegitimate website's universal resource locators (URLs) in spam, in hoping that a curious recipient will click on those links and trigger the malware download or initiate the phishing attack.

Pharming is the redirection of legitimate web traffic (e.g., browser requests) to an illegitimate website for the purpose of obtaining private information. Pharming often uses Trojan horses, worms, or virus technologies to attack the Internet browser's address bar so that the valid URL typed by the user is modified to that of the illegitimate website. Pharming may also exploit the DNS server by causing it to transform the legitimate host name into the invalid website's Internet Protocol (IP) address; this form of pharming is also known as DNS cache poisoning.

(vi) Security Risks in Web Applications

Several security risks exist in web applications that should be considered and mitigated with security controls during an SDLC.[2] **Injection flaws** (e.g., SQL and OS) can occur when untrusted data is sent to a system's interpreter as part of a command or query. An attacker's hostile data can trick the system's interpreter into executing unintended commands or accessing data without proper authorization. *Security controls* include implementing database access controls.

Broken authentication flaws can occur in application functions when authentication and session management are implemented incorrectly. This broken situation allows attackers to compromise passwords, steal encryption keys and session tokens, or exploit other implementation flaws to assume the other individuals' identities and credentials either temporarily or permanently. *Security controls* such as multifactor authentication techniques can prevent broken authentication flaws.

Sensitive data exposure situations can occur when web applications and APIs do not properly protect sensitive data, such as financial, medical, and personal information. Attackers may steal or modify the poorly protected data to conduct credit card fraud, identity theft, or other crimes. An API is an interface between an application system and OS component or other software service module. An API is a subroutine library. *Security controls* such as encryption is needed to protect data at rest, data in transit, and data in exchange with web browsers.

XML external entity attacks can occur when older XML processors are poorly configured. External entities can be used to disclose internal files using the file URL handler, internal file shares, internal port scanning, and remote and code execution and to launch DoS attacks. *Security controls* include installing QoS methods to prevent DoS attacks.

Broken access control flaws can occur when authentication restrictions are not properly enforced. Attackers can exploit these flaws to access unauthorized functions and data, such as access other users' accounts, to view sensitive data files, to modify other users' data, and to change access rights and privileges for some users. *Strong access controls* can prevent broken access control flaws.

---

[2] OWASP Web Applications Security Risks, 2017, www.owasp.org.

Security misconfiguration flaws can occur from insecure default configurations, incomplete or ad hoc configurations, open cloud storage, misconfigured HTTP headers, and error messages containing sensitive information. *Security controls* include configuring OSs, libraries, and applications and keeping them up-to-date with patches and upgrades.

Cross-site scripting (XSS) flaws can occur whenever an application includes untrusted data in a new web page without proper validation. This flaw allows an attacker to execute scripts in the victim's browser that can hijack user sessions, deface websites, or redirect the user to malicious websites. A user's web browser's API, HTML, and JavaScript are involved in XSS flaws. Fileless attacks can be performed with XSS. *Security controls* include the application of artificial intelligence systems and machine learning software.

Insecure deserialization flaw can lead to remote code execution. In addition, it can be used to perform replay attacks, injection attacks, and privilege escalation attacks. *Strong access controls* can prevent insecure deserialization flaws.

Using components with known vulnerabilities, such as libraries and software modules, create risks when those components are allowed to run with applications with privileges and without vulnerabilities. If a vulnerable component is exploited, such an attack can facilitate serious data loss or server takeover and can undermine an application's defensive actions. *Security controls* include strong access controls over software libraries and programming modules.

Insufficient logging and monitoring activities, when combined with missing or ineffective integration with incident response program, allow hackers to further attack systems; maintain persistent threats; pivot to more systems; and tamper, extract, or destroy data. *Security controls* include installing system logging facilities and monitoring software.

(vii) SDLC and Cyber Resiliency

The SDLC phases and processes and the cyber resiliency techniques and constructs can be used together for developing new systems, system upgrades, or repurposed systems. They can be utilized at any phase of the SDLC and can take advantage of any system development methodology, such as waterfall, spiral, or agile methods.

The processes and associated cyber resiliency techniques can also be applied recursively, iteratively, concurrently, sequentially, or in parallel and to any system regardless of its size, complexity, purpose, scope, environment of operation, or special nature.

In addition, these processes and techniques can ensure that the systems resulting from the application of the security and cyber resiliency design principles have the level of trustworthiness deemed sufficient to protect stakeholders from suffering unacceptable losses of their assets and associated consequences from a hacker's attacks. Trustworthiness is made possible in part by the rigorous application of security and cyber resiliency design principles, constructs, and concepts within a structured set of SDLC processes that provides the necessary traceability of requirements, transparency, and evidence to support risk-based and informed decision-making objectives.

(d) Change Management and Control

Change management (CM) configuration control, access controls over changes, check-in and check-out procedures, system stages, and application software maintenance controls are presented in this section.

(i) Change Management

A formal CM program should be established, and procedures should be used to ensure that all modifications to a computer system or network meet the same security requirements as the original components identified in the asset evaluation and the associated risk assessment and mitigation plan. The change control procedures for a software-intensive system should ensure that software assurance requirements are not compromised when changes are requested. Each change control request should include a specific section that addresses the impact of the requested change on software assurance requirements.

Risk assessment should be performed on all changes to the system or network that could affect security, including configuration changes, the addition of network components, and installation of software. Changes to policies and procedures may also be required. The current network configuration must always be known and documented.

For example, in object-oriented database management system model, version management is a method for tracking and recording changes made to data over time through the history of design changes. The version management system tracks version successors and predecessors. When objects constituting a portion of the design are retrieved, the system must ensure that versions of these objects are consistent and compatible.

WHAT IS THE DIFFERENCE BETWEEN VERSION CONTROL AND VERSION MANAGEMENT?

- **Version control** involves controlling the different versions of software, uniquely identifying versions and configurations, and providing version change history to ensure stability, traceability, and repeatability.
- A **version management system** tracks version successors and predecessors.
- Both version control and version management ensure that all versions are consistent and compatible with each other.

(ii) Configuration Management

The three essential features of CM include stability, traceability, and repeatability.

- **Stability** means that an information system will not crash, shut down, or fail. Even if it fails, it fails in a known secure state.

- **Traceability** means that the change activities can be followed from origin to destination and in between.

- **Repeatability** is the ability to reproduce any version of the software at any given time.

    The correct sequence of CM activities:

    Item Identification $\longrightarrow$ Change Control $\longrightarrow$ Item Status Accounting $\longrightarrow$ Audit

- **Configuration item (CI) identification.** A methodology for selection and naming of CIs that need to be placed under CM.

- **Configuration change control.** A process for managing updates to the baselines for the CIs.

- **CI status accounting.** Consists of recording and reporting of information needed to manage a configuration effectively.

- **Configuration audit.** Consists of periodically performing a review to ensure that the CM practices and procedures are rigorously followed. CM answers two questions:

    1. What constitutes a software product at any point in time?

    2. What changes have been made to the software product?

(iii) Configuration Control

Configuration control is the process of controlling modifications to hardware, firmware, software, and documentation to protect the information system against improper modification prior to, during, and after system implementation. Change control is related to configuration control.

The information security management:

- Determines the types of changes to the information system that are configuration controlled.

- Approves configuration-controlled changes to the system with explicit consideration of security impact analyses.

- Documents approved configuration-controlled changes to the system.

- Retains and reviews records of configuration-controlled changes to the system.

- Audits activities associated with configuration-controlled changes to the system.

- Coordinates and provides oversight for configuration change control activities through a committee or board.

Information security management and functional management determine the types of changes to the information system that are configuration controlled. Configuration change control for the information system involves the systematic proposal, justification, implementation, test/evaluation, review, and disposition of changes to the system, including upgrades and modifications. Configuration change control includes changes to information system components, changes to the configuration settings for IT products (e.g., OSs, applications, firewalls, and routers), emergency changes, and changes to remediate flaws.

A typical process for managing configuration changes to the information system includes, for example, a chartered configuration control board that approves proposed changes to the system. The board is made up of a group of qualified individuals with responsibility for regulating and approving changes to hardware, firmware, software, and documentation throughout the development and operation life cycle phases of an information system. The term "auditing of changes" refers to changes in activity before and after a change is made to the system and the auditing activities required to implement the change. It is important for an information security representative to be a member of the board.

Information security management employs automated mechanisms to:

- Document proposed changes to the information system.

- Notify designated approval authorities.

- Highlight approvals that have not been received by a certain date.

- Inhibit change until designated approvals are received.

- Document completed changes to the information system.

Functional management conducts tests and validates and documents changes to the information system before implementing the changes on the operational system. Functional management ensures that testing does not interfere with information system operations. The individual/ group conducting the tests understands the organization's: information security policies and procedures; information system security policies and procedures; and specific health, safety, and environmental risks associated with a particular facility and/or process. An operational system may need to be taken offline or replicated to the extent feasible before testing can be conducted. If an information system must be taken offline for testing, the tests are scheduled to occur during planned system outages whenever possible. In situations where the organization cannot conduct testing of an operational system, the organization employs compensating controls (e.g., providing a replicated system to conduct testing).

The IT software development management and the information security management employ automated mechanisms to implement changes to the current information system baseline and deploy the updated baseline across the installed base.

(iv) Access Controls over Program Changes

The information security management defines, documents, approves, and enforces physical and logical access restrictions associated with changes to the information system.

Any changes to information system hardware, software, and/or firmware components can potentially have significant effects on the overall security of the system. Accordingly, only qualified and authorized individuals are allowed to obtain access to information system components for purposes of initiating changes, including upgrades and modifications. Additionally, maintaining records of access is essential for ensuring that configuration change control is being implemented as intended and for supporting after-the-fact actions should the organization become aware of an unauthorized change to the information system. Access restrictions for change also include software libraries.

The next list presents examples of access restrictions.

- Physical and logical access controls
- Workflow automation
- Media libraries
- Abstract layers (e.g., changes are implemented into a third-party interface rather than directly into the information system component)
- Change windows (e.g., changes occur only during specified times and making unauthorized changes outside the time limits can lead to quick and early discovery of changes.)
- Authorizations to make changes to the information system
- Auditing changes
- Retaining and review records of changes

Specific access controls over changes include those listed next.

- Employ automated mechanisms to enforce access restrictions and support auditing of the enforcement actions.
- Conduct audits of information system changes at defined frequencies and when indications warrant, whether unauthorized changes have occurred or not.

- Prevent the installation of critical software programs and/or modules (e.g., patches, service packs, and device drivers) that are not signed with a certificate that is recognized and approved by the organization.

- Limit information system developer/integrator privileges to change hardware, software, and firmware components and system information directly within a production environment.

- Review and reevaluate information system developer/integrator privileges at defined frequencies.

- Limit privileges to change software resident within software libraries, including privileged programs.

- Implement automated safeguards if security functions or mechanisms are changed inappropriately.

The information system reacts automatically when inappropriate and/or unauthorized modifications occur to security functions or mechanisms. Automatic implementation of safeguards and countermeasures includes, for example, reversing the change, halting the information system, or triggering an audit alert when an unauthorized modification to a critical security file occurs.

(v) Check-in and Check-out Procedures

Check-in and check-out procedures, as they relate to a CI, are expressed in terms of a state-transition diagram that deals with events, transitions, and actions. System requirements and analysis are the major emphases in processing a request for change. These events and actions (i.e., initial, check-out, modify, and check-in) take place when the CIs are checked in and out:

- **Initial.** The initial state assumes that the CI is checked into the CM workspace and locked without a flag.

- **Check-out.** The action here is to copy the CI to the software developer's workspace in the unlocked state. The CI is flagged as out and locked.

- **Modify.** The action is to modify the contents of the developer's workspace.

- **Check-in.** The action is to copy the modified CI to the CM workspace, remove the flag in the CM workspace, and delete the CI from the developer's workspace.

(vi) System Stages

Whether a system is database or nondatabase, a new system should go through four stages during its development: development, testing, staging (QA), and production libraries. Although all these stages require the same type of security controls, the staging library requires additional controls, because that library often is copied into production library. Nonproduction environments pose a security risk due to the use of production data without proper controls. Therefore, nonproduction environments should be treated with the same care as the production environment. The sequence of stages is:

Development ⟶ Testing ⟶ Staging ⟶ Production

(vii) Application Software Maintenance Controls

The scope of application software maintenance controls includes controls used to monitor the installation of and updates to application software to ensure that the software functions as expected and that a historical record is maintained of system changes. Such controls also help to ensure that only authorized software is allowed on the system. These controls may include a software configuration policy that grants managerial approval to modification and then documents the changes. They may also include some products used for virus protection.

(e) End User Computing

This section discusses end user computing (EUC) scope, audit challenges, audit and control risks, and suggested controls.

(i) Scope

The scope of EUC can be limited or extended; "limited" means that end user systems are developed to automate an individual's day-to-day work functions using small computer programs or spreadsheet applications, which is a low risk. But the risk is high with extended systems when these end user systems are uploading or downloading end user data files back and forth to local area network (LAN) or mainframe computer systems in order to exchange and share data between these systems.

This is because end user systems, by definition, often have inadequate and incomplete application-based controls and lack effective security controls, thus compromising data integrity in all connected systems. Usually end users utilize PCs and/or desktop computers to facilitate their work and seek help through help desk staff and IT technical support staff.

The ideal EUC system is a system that is well confined to its scope and contained within its boundary. When this is not possible, end users should obtain design and development assistance either from internal IT staff or external contractors.

(ii) Audit Challenges

According to the Institute of Internal Auditors' study results, there are seven audit challenges in EUC. Organizations and auditors must:

1. Understand the current use or impact of EUC.
2. Need to link EUC activities with business objectives.
3. Coordinate potentially synergistic EUC activities.
4. Ensure connectivity and interoperability.
5. Assist end user department managers and staff to identify business risks, control points, and benefits for adopting application-based controls and security controls.
6. Implement the application selection and development methodologies.
7. Expand audit programs to include EUC when significant financial or operational issues exist.[3]

(iii) Audit and Control Risks

A list of audit and control risks in end user-developed systems is presented next.

- Information (audit) trails, controls, and security features may not be available in the end user-developed application systems.

---

[3] Rittenberg, Senn, and Martin Bariff, *Audit and Control of End User Computing* (Altamonte Springs, FL: Institute of Internal Auditors Research Foundation, 1990).

- Data storage and file retention, backup, purging, archiving, and rotating procedures may not be available or adequate.

- Documentation may not be available, or it is inadequate or incorrect.

- Backup and recovery procedures may not be available or effective in the application systems developed by end users.

- Program change controls may not be available or effective.

(iv) Suggested Controls

Lack of adequate separation of duties is a potential control weakness in end user systems. Direct supervision, training, and frequent work reviews should be conducted to balance the control weaknesses.

When uploading data from a PC to a host computer, the data conversion programs residing on the host computer should reject inaccurate or incomplete data before updating any host-resident data files. Control totals should be developed between the PC and the host computer and reconciled automatically by the program. Uploading files is one source of computer viruses, and its effects on other programs and data files are unknown.

Exhibit 3.1 presents a summary of preventive, detective, and recovery controls as they relate to PCs and EUC. Implementation of these controls would help IT management and end user management in strengthening overall controls.

EXHIBIT 3.1 Preventive, Detective, and Corrective Controls for PCs and End User computing

Preventive Controls	Detective Controls	Corrective Controls
Establish a PC support function. Issue policies, procedures, and standards. Establish controls in application programs used for mini- and midrange computers (e.g., label checking, recovery procedures, batch and file balancing, audit trails). Require a user ID and a password prior to accessing the PC system. Initiate a preventive maintenance program for PCs. Install program change controls for end user–developed systems. Require documentation for end user–developed and maintained systems.	Install physical security devices. Implement logical security mechanisms. Test end user-developed software.	Develop control reports. Develop audit trail reports. Develop exception reports. Develop error reports. Develop activity aging reports.

3.2 Database Terms and Internet Terms

In this section, two major topics are discussed: basic database terms (e.g., data, database, record, object, field, and schema) and Internet terms (e.g., HTML, HTTP, URL, USB, domain name, browser, click-through, and cookies).

(a) Database Terms

Database terms presented here include data, record, file, directory, dataset, database, database system, DD, schema, subschema, subject, object, access, checkpoint, deadlock, tuple, rollback, rollforward, and recovery.

Data: The smallest unit of information, such as an employee's hourly wage rate (e.g., $15 per hour). Data resides in a data field. In computers, data is processed and stored as bits and bytes. Data is raw numbers (e.g., hours worked and hourly wage rate), and information is processed data (e.g., a paycheck).

Record: A log of an employee's hourly wage rate, hours worked in a week, employee ID number, and payroll workweek.

File: A collection of related records. An example is a payroll file containing payroll records.

Directory: The list of files stored on a disk (e.g., payroll directory).

Dataset: A collection of related bytes, or characters, of secondary storage. For example, a dataset may be a file of payroll records or a library of payroll programs.

Database: A collection of interrelated data stored together, using a common and controlled approach (e.g., payroll).

Database system: In a database system, data are maintained independently of the application programs. Data can be shared by many programs and users. Database management system (DBMS) software manages and controls the data and the database software.

Data dictionary: Contains attributes and characteristics of each data element or field in a computer record. It also includes file organization and structure and edit and validation rules.

Schema: A set of specifications that defines a database. Specifically, it includes entity names, sets, groups, data items, areas, sort sequences, access keys, and security locks.

Subschema: A subset of a schema. It represents a portion of a database as it appears to a user or application program.

Subject: A person who is using a computer system (e.g., employee, contractor, and consultant).

Object: A passive entity that contains or receives information. Examples of objects are data, records, blocks, files, and programs.

Access: A specific type of interaction between a subject (e.g., user) and an object (e.g., data) that results in the flow of information from one to the other.

Check-point: A point, generally taken at regular intervals, at which a program's intermediate results are dumped to a secondary storage (e.g., disk) to minimize the risk of work loss. Databases operate on checkpoints.

Deadlock: A consequence of poor resource management that occurs when two programs each control a resource (e.g., printer, data file, database, and record) needed by the other and neither is willing to give in its resource. Databases can run into deadlocks.

Tuple: A row of a relational table in a relational database.

Rollback: Restores the database from one point in time to an earlier point.

Rollforward: Restores the database from a point in time when it is known to be correct to a later time.

Recovery: The process of reconstituting a database to its correct and current state following a partial or complete hardware, software, network, operational, or processing error or failure.

(b) Database Management System

Topics discussed include DBMS software, including its advantages and disadvantages; database design approaches; database checkpoints; database compression techniques; database reorganization; database restructuring; database performance monitoring; database utility programs; and DD systems software.

(i) Database Management Systems Software

A database contains facts and figures on various types of information, such as sales, costs, and personnel. These files are collectively called the firm's database, which is used and shared by several employees inside a company. The DBMS is comprised of software, hardware, and procedures. It acts as a software controller enabling different application systems to access large numbers of distinct data records stored on direct access storage devices (e.g., disk).

The DBMS should be compatible with the OS environment as it handles complex data structures. Unauthorized access to data elements is a major concern in a database system due to concentration of data. The DBMS helps in providing users an interface with the application system through increased accessibility and flexibility by means of data views.

Advantages (objectives) of a DBMS are listed next. A DBMS provides:

- Minimum data redundancy resulting in data consistency.
- Data independence from application programs except during computer processing.
- Consistent and quality information for decision-making purposes.
- Adequate security and integrity controls.
- Shared access to data.
- A single storage location for each data item.
- Built-in backup and recovery procedures.

In addition, a DBMS:

- Facilitates uniform development and maintenance of application systems.
- Ensures that all applicable standards (e.g., documentation, data naming, data formats) are observed in the representation of the data.
- Improves program maintenance due to separation of data from programs.
- Separates file management tasks from application programs.
- Programs access data according to predefined subschema.

Disadvantages of a DBMS are that it:

- Can be expensive to acquire, operate, and maintain.
- Requires additional main memory.
- Requires additional disk storage.
- Requires knowledgeable and technically skilled staff (e.g., database administrator [DBA] and data administrator).
- Results in additional system overhead, thereby slowing down the system response time.
- Needs additional CPU processing time.
- Requires sophisticated and efficient security mechanisms.
- Is difficult to enforce security protection policies.

Redundancy of data is sometimes necessary when high system performance and high data availability are required. The trade-off here is the cost of collecting and maintaining the redundant data and the system overhead it requires to process the data. Another concern is synchronization of data updates in terms of timing and sequence. Ideally, the synchronization should be done at the system level rather than the application level.

A DBMS understands the structure of the data and provides a language for defining and manipulating stored data. The primary functions of the DBMS are to store data and to provide operations on the database. The operations usually include create, delete, update, and search of data. Most DBMS products require extensive file backup and recovery procedures and require more processing time.

Some essential features supported by most DBMSs are listed next.

- **Persistence** is the property wherein the state of the database survives the execution of a process in order to be reused later in another process.
- **Data sharing** is the property that permits simultaneous use of the database by multiple users. A DBMS that permits sharing must provide some **concurrency control** (locking) mechanism that prevents users from executing inconsistent actions on the database.
- **Recovery** refers to the capability of the DBMS to return its data to a consistent and coherent state after a hardware or software failure.
- **Database language** permits external access to the DBMS. The language may be the Data Definition Language (DDL), the Data Manipulation Language (DML), the Data Control Language (DCL), or an ad hoc query language. The DDL is used to define the database schema and subschema. The DML is used to examine and manipulate contents of the database. The DCL is used to specify parameters needed to define the internal organization of the database, such as indexes and buffer size. Ad hoc query language is provided for interactive specification of queries.
- **Security and integrity.** Security and authorization control, integrity checking, utility programs, backup/archiving, versioning, and view definition are other features of most DBMS. Integrity checking involves two types: semantic and referential.

Semantic integrity refers to the declaration of semantic and structural integrity rules (e.g., typing constraints, values of domain constraints, and uniqueness constraints) and the enforcement of these rules. Semantic integrity rules may be automatically enforced at program run time or at compile time or may be performed only when a message is sent. **Referential integrity** means that no record may contain a reference to the primary key of a nonexistent record. Cascading of deletes, one of the features of referential integrity checking, occurs when a record is deleted and all other referenced records are automatically deleted.

(ii) Database Design Approaches

User requirements are specified to the conceptual model first, which represents "user views" of the database. When the conceptual model is presented to the DBMS, it becomes a logical model, external model, or schema/subschema. The type of DBMS is not a factor in designing a conceptual model, but the design of a logical model is dependent on the type of DBMS to be used. This means that the conceptual model is, or should be, independent of a DBMS.

Next, the logical model is converted to a physical model in terms of physical storage media, such as magnetic disks, tapes, and disk arrays. The physical model, which is also called an internal model, considers the type of access methods needed, the type of indexing techniques required, and the data distribution methods available.

SCHEMAS/SUBSCHEMAS

- A logical view of an entire database is called a schema. Schemas may be external, conceptual, or internal. A synonym for the word "schema" is "view."

- A subschema is a part of schema. In other words, a schema is made up of one or more subschemas.

- A logical data model presents a view of data.

Logical database design is the process of determining an information system structure that is independent of software or hardware considerations. It produces logical data structures consisting of a number of entities connected by one-to-one or one-to-many relationships, subject to appropriate integrity checking. The objective is to improve the effectiveness of an information system by maximizing the accuracy, consistency, integrity, security, and completeness of the database.

Physical database design is the implementation of a logical design in a particular computer system environment. It deals with retrieval and update workloads for the system and the parameters required (i.e., average time required for random/sequential access to a track, length of a track, and disk cylinder sizes) for the hardware environment. The objective is to improve information system performance by minimizing the data entry time, data retrieval time, data update time, data query time, and storage space and costs.

For large, logically complex databases, physical design is an extremely difficult task. Typically, an enormous number of alternatives must be explored in searching for a good physical design. Often optimal or near-optimal designs cannot be discovered, resulting in the creation of inefficient and costly databases. Suggested action steps required in a physical database design are listed next.

- Analyze workload complexity and characteristics.

- Translate the relationships specified in the logical data structures into physical records and hardware devices, and determine their relationships. This includes consideration of symbolic and direct pointers. **Symbolic pointers** contain the other's logical identifier. **Direct pointers** contain the other's physical address. Both pointers can coexist.

- Fine-tune the design by determining the initial record loading factors, record segmentations, record and file indexes, primary and secondary access methods, file block sizes, and secondary memory management for overflow handling.

Exhibit 3.2 depicts the relationships among conceptual, logical, and physical database models.

EXHIBIT 3.2 Relationships among Database Models

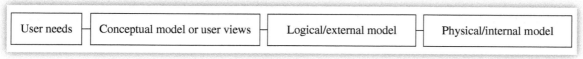

Prior to developing a full-scale database, a prototype may be undertaken to finalize user/technical requirements of the application system. Later, the prototype can be merged into normal system design phase for security, controls, recovery, and performance considerations.

Another way of looking at the database models is from the design focus and features of the database itself. Exhibit 3.3 lists features of a physical data model and a logical data model.

EXHIBIT 3.3 Features of Physical and Logical Data Models

Physical Data Model	Logical Data Model
Concerned with physical storage of data (internal schema)	Concerned with user-oriented data views (external schema)
Concerned with entities for which data are collected	Concerned with entities for which data are collected
Describes how data are arranged in the defined storage media (e.g., disk) from program and programmer viewpoints	Describes how data can be viewed by the designated end user
Physical in nature in the sense that it describes the way data are physically located in the database	Conceptual in nature (conceptual schema) in the sense that it describes the overall logical view of the database

A **data model** describes relationships between the data elements and is used as a tool to represent the conceptual organization of data. A relationship within a data model can be one to one (e.g., between patient and bed in a hospital environment; at any given time, one bed is assigned to one patient), one to many (e.g., between hospital room and patients; one hospital room accommodates more than one patient), and many to many (e.g., between patient and surgeon; one surgeon may attend to many patients, and a patient may be attended by more than one surgeon). A data model can be considered as consisting of three components.

1. **Data structure**—The basic building blocks describing the way data are organized
2. **Operators**—The set of functions that can be used to act on the data structures
3. **Integrity rules**—The valid states in which the data stored in the database may exist

The primary purpose of any data model is to provide a formal means of representing information and a formal means of manipulating the representation. A good data model can help describe and model the application effectively. A DBMS uses one or more data models, as described.

DATA MODEL TYPES

Relational

Hierarchical

Network

Inverted file

Object

Distributed

(A) Relational Data Model

The relational data model (e.g., DB2) consists of **columns**, equal to data fields in a conventional file, and **rows**, equal to data records in a conventional file, represented in a **table**. Data is stored in tables with keys or indexes outside the program. For example, in a hospital environment, a patient table may consist of columns (patient number, name, and address); the values in the columns (patient number, 1234; patient name, John Jones; patient address, 100 Main Street, Any Town, U.S.A.) are represented in rows.

The columns of the table are called *attributes* while the rows are called *tuples*. A set of actual values an attribute may take are drawn from a domain. The primary key to the patient table is patient number. The properties of a relational data model are described next.

- All "key" values are defined.
- Duplicate rows do not exist.
- Column order is not significant.
- Row order is not significant.

Major *advantages* of a relational model are its simplicity in use and true data independence from data storage structures and access methods. Some major *disadvantages* are low system performance and operational efficiency compared to other data models.

(B) Hierarchical Data Model

From a comparison point of view, the hierarchical data model (e.g., IP Multimedia Subsystem) can be related to a family **tree concept**, where the parents can have no children, one child, or more than one child. Similarly, a tree is composed of a number of branches or nodes. A number of trees, or data records, form a database. Every branch has a number of leaves, or data fields. Hence, a hierarchical tree structure consists of nodes and branches. The highest node is called a "root" (parent—level 1), and its every occurrence begins a logical database record. The dependent nodes are at the lower levels (children—level 2, 3, …).

The properties of a hierarchical data model are described next.

- A model always starts with a root node.

- A parent node must have at least one dependent node.

- Every node except the root must be accessed through its parent node.

- Except at level 1, the root node, the dependent node can be added horizontally as well as vertically with no limitations.

- There can be a number of occurrences of each node at each level.

- Every node occurring at level 2 must be connected with one and only one node occurring at level 1, and is repeated down.

Some major advantages of a hierarchical data model are its proven performance, simplicity, ease of use, and reduction of data dependency. Some major disadvantages are that addition and deletion of parent/children nodes can become complex, and deletion of the parent results in the deletion of the children.

(C) Network Data Model

The network data model (e.g., IDMS/R) is depicted using blocks and arrows. A block represents a record type or an entity. Each record type, in turn, is composed of zero, one, or more data elements/fields or attributes. An arrow linking two blocks shows the relationship between two record types. A network database consists of a number of areas. An area contains records, which in turn contain data elements or fields. A set, which is a grouping of records, may reside in an area or span a number of areas. Each area can have its own unique physical attributes. Areas can be operated independently of, or in conjunction with, other areas.

Exhibit 3.4 depicts the network data model, where a patient is described as an owner record type and surgery is denoted as member record type in the set type patient-has-surgery.

EXHIBIT 3.4 Network Model

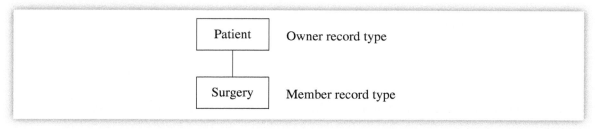

(D) Inverted File Data Model

In the inverted file data model (e.g., Adaptable Data Base System [ADABAS]), each entity is represented by a file. Each record in the file represents an occurrence of the entity. Each attribute becomes a data field or element in the inverted file.

The properties of a network data model are described next.

- A set is composed of related records.
- There is only a single "owner" in a set.
- There may be zero, one, or many members in a set.

Some major advantages of a network data model are its proven performance and the accommodation of many-to-many relationships that occur quite frequently in real life. Some major disadvantages are its complexity in programming and loss of data independence during database reorganization and when sets are removed.

In the inverted file data model (e.g., ADABAS), each entity is represented by a file. Each record in the file represents an occurrence of the entity. Each attribute becomes data field or element in the file. Data fields are inverted to allow efficient access to individual files. To accomplish this, an index file is created containing all the values taken by the inverted field and pointers to all records in the file.

Some major advantages of the inverted file data model are its simplicity, data independence, and ease of adding new files and fields. Some major disadvantages are difficulty in synchronizing changes between database records/fields and index file.

(E) Object Data Model

The object data model is developed by combining the special nature of object-oriented programming languages (e.g., Lisp, C++) with DBMS. Objects, classes, and inheritance form the basis for the structural aspects of the object data model. Objects are basic entities that have data structures and operations. Every object has an object ID that is a unique, system-provided identifier. Classes describe generic object types. All objects are members of a class. Classes are related through inheritance. Classes can be related to each other by superclass or subclass relationships, similar to entity-relationship-attribute model, to form class hierarchies. Class definitions are the mechanism for specifying the database schema for an application. For example, the class PERSON has an attribute SPOUSE whose data type is also PERSON.

Object DBMS also supports data sharing, provides concurrency controls and system recovery, and handles cooperative transaction processing and data versioning. Engineering applications such as computer-aided design systems, office information systems, and artificial intelligence (knowledge-based) systems require the use of cooperative transaction processing and data versioning techniques.

Version management is a facility for tracking and recording changes made to data over time through the history of design changes. The version management system tracks version successors and predecessors. When objects constituting a portion of the design are retrieved, the system must ensure that versions of these objects are consistent and compatible. Some advantages of the object data model are system development efficiency and handling of complex data structures. Some disadvantages include new technology and new risks, which requires training and learning curves.

(F) Distributed Data Model

The distributed database model can be thought of as having many network nodes and access paths between the central and local computers and within the local computer sites. Database security becomes a major issue in a truly distributed environment, where the actual data are distributed and there are many access paths to the data from far-flung locations.

Data in a distributed database reside in more than one physical database in the network. **Location transparency**, in which the user does not need to know where data are stored, is one of the major goals of a distributed database data model. Similarly, programmers do not have to rewrite applications and can move data from one location to another, depending on need.

(iii) Database Checkpoints

A technique used to start at certain points in the execution of a program after the system fails or detects an error is called **checkpoints**. In the case of a backout of programs, it is possible to go back to the last checkpoint instead of starting at the beginning of a program. Checkpoints are relatively easy to implement in batch programs and cumbersome for online programs due to concurrent processing.

A drawback of checkpoints is that they degrade system performance. The database designer needs to balance the number of checkpoints and the time interval between two checkpoints. Usually the higher the number of checkpoints, the greater the degradation of performance, even though the recovery process is easier. If the time interval between two checkpoints is long, however, performance degradation is reduced but recovery is more difficult. A tradeoff exists between the number of checkpoints and the time interval between two checkpoints.

Some criteria for designing and implementing checkpoints are listed next.

- Time interval
- Operator action
- Number of changes to the database
- Number of records written to the log tape
- Number of transactions processed

(iv) Database Compression Techniques

In some DBMSs, it is common to find unused space in the database due to the deletion of many records. This unused space widens the distance between the active database records, resulting in longer time for data retrieval. Compression or compaction techniques can be used to reduce the amount of storage space required for a given collection of data records. In addition to saving storage space, compression saves disk input/output operations. However, CPU activity will increase to decompress the data after it has been retrieved. A trade-off exists between the input/output savings and additional CPU activity. Indexes always gain from the use of a compression technique. Both pointers and data values can be compressed too.

(v) Database Reorganization

A deletion of some records in the database results in a fragmentation of space or unused space. This could happen during initial loading or after the reloading of the database. A normal practice is to reorganize the database by:

- Copying the old database onto another device, such as disk or tape (where tape can act as a backup copy of the database).
- Reblocking the valid records.

- Reloading the valid records.

- Excluding the records marked "deleted" during this process.

Besides reclaiming unused space, reorganization can arrange the records in such a way that their physical sequence is the same or nearly the same as their logical sequence. It is also possible to arrange the records so that the more frequently accessed ones are stored on a disk, whereas the rarely accessed or less frequently accessed records are stored on tape. Other reorganization efforts could result from changing block sizes, buffer pool sizes, prime areas, and overflow areas.

(vi) Database Restructuring

Databases go through changes after their creation, usually because of usage patterns, application systems priorities, or performance requirements. New record types and new data elements may be added to the database. Access controls and database procedures may need to be changed. Implementing all of these changes is called **restructuring the database** at the logical and physical level.

Relatively speaking, database reorganization is a minor activity, and restructuring is a major activity. Usually reorganization does not affect the existing application systems and procedures, whereas restructuring does affect them. Normally, there are three types of changes in restructuring.

1. **Logical changes** in terms of adding or deleting data elements, combining a number of records, changing the relationship between records

2. **Physical changes** in terms of channels and disk configuration to minimize contention (delays) by adding or removing some pointers

3. **Procedural changes** in terms of backup and recovery procedures and access control security rules

(vii) Database Performance Monitoring

An important responsibility of a DBA is to monitor the performance of the database. The DBMS can consume large amounts of computer resources (i.e., memory, disk space) and can take long processing times due to design complexity. Often a performance-monitoring tool and/or utility programs are utilized to take internal readings of the database and its components. The objective is to identify performance-related problems and take corrective action as quickly as possible.

(viii) Database Utility Programs

The DBA needs uses these utility programs to make his or her work more effective and efficient:

- Load and restore routines can be used to create the initial version of the database.

- Dump and reload routines can be used to dump (unload) the database to backup storage for recovery purposes and to reload the database from such a backup copy.

- Statistical routines can be used to compute and analyze various performance statistics, such as file sizes and database values.

- Reorganization routines can be used to rearrange the data in the database to improve performance.

- Programs can be used to analyze database pointers and broken chains.

- Reconfiguring routines can be used to reconfigure the pointers in the database.

- Programs can be used to archive journal files.

- Programs can be used to initialize database files.

- Routines can be used to fix journal problems.

- Programs can be used to rollback or rollforward database updates.

- Routines can be used to expand database page size.

- Programs can be used to restructure database contents.

- Routines can be used to print and clear the log area of the DD.

(ix) Data Dictionary Systems Software

A **data dictionary or directory** is an alphabetical listing that describes all the data elements (fields) in an application system and tells how and where they are used. It defines each data element's characteristics, properties, and processes, including the size of the data field and record, the volume of records, the data field editing and validation rules with maximum and minimum values, the security levels or ratings, and the frequency of use and of changes of data elements.

Used properly, a DD presents a top-down structure or definition of a complex data element. The data editing and validation rules available in the DD can be used to prevent the entry of inaccurate data into the system. The DD can be used as a corrective control because of its "where-used" information, which can be used to trace data backward and forward through the transaction as an audit trail.

The DD is a central repository of an organization's data elements and their relationships. The DD stores critical information, such as data sources, formats, usages, and relationships. In this regard, a DD can be a database itself—storing data about data. A DD provides cross-references between groups of data elements and databases and indicates which computer programs use which databases. A DD is a tool to develop and maintain database as well as nondatabase application systems. Usually automated software is used to manage and control the DD. A manual DD can become inconsistent with what is actually in the system in a very short time. An automated DD supports the objectives of minimum data redundancy, maximum data consistency, and adequate data integrity and security.

The DD can be dependent on a DBMS, or it can be stand-alone. A dependent DD uses the underlying DBMS to manage and control its data, and it is a part of the DBMS. A stand-alone DD is a separate package from the DBMS package. *A DD may be active or passive with the DBMS software.* An active DD requires all data descriptions for a database defined or available at one time. A passive DD may or may not require a check for currency of data descriptions before a program is executed. Some major advantages of each approach are described next.

Advantages of an Active DD System

- Provides quick access to the data in the database

- Tracks database accesses and actions

- Provides valuable statistics for improving system performance

- Minimizes redundancy in storage of data descriptions

- Facilitates system documentation

- Improves data editing and validation controls
- Works well with database files

Advantages of a Passive DD System

- Less risk of commitment to a DBMS
- Easier to implementation
- Can describe data descriptions on a piecemeal basis
- Works well with conventional data files
- Serves as a documentation and communication tool

The major reports that can be obtained from a DD and its interface systems include these:

- Access control reports
- Audit trail reports
- Cross-reference reports
- Data elements and their relationships with their usage frequencies
- Summary, change, error, and ad hoc reports

In summary, a DD provides these benefits:

- It provides a consistent description of data as well as consistent data names for programming and data retrieval. This in turn provides consistent descriptive names and meanings.
- It shows where-used information, such as what programs used the data items, which files contain the data items, and which printed reports display the data items.
- It provides data integrity through data editing and validation routines.
- It supports elimination of data redundancy.
- It supports tracing of data item's path through several application programs.
- It describes the relationships among the entities.

(c) Internet Terms

This section defines several technical terms related to the Internet. Basic familiarity with these terms can help internal auditors to communicate clearly and concisely during their IT audit projects and when working with the IT staff.

Transmission control protocol/Internet protocol contains two protocols, TCP and IP, and is the protocol suite used by the Internet. A protocol suite is the set of message types, their formats, and the rules that control how messages are processed by computers on the network. The TCP is a reliable connection and byte-oriented transport layer protocol within the TCP/IP suite. The IP is the network-layer protocol in the TCP/IP stack used in the Internet. The IP is a connectionless protocol that fits well with the connectionless Ethernet protocol. However, the IP does not fit well with the connection-oriented asynchronous transfer mode (ATM) network.

An **internet protocol (IP) address** is a unique number for a computer that is used to determine where messages transmitted on the Internet should be delivered. The IP address is analogous to a house number for ordinary postal mail. Some websites can identify a user's location from the IP address associated with that user's PCs.

Internet protocol (IP) spoofing refers to sending a network packet that appears to come from a source other than its actual source.

Internet protocol security (IPsec) provides security capabilities at the IP layer of communications. IPsec's key management protocol is used to negotiate the secret keys that protect virtual private network (VPN) communications and the level and type of security protections that will characterize the VPN. The most widely used key management protocol is the Internet key exchange protocol. IPsec features provide confidentiality, data integrity, and nonrepudiation services.

Hypertext markup language (HTML) is a markup language that is a subset of standard generalized markup language (SGML) and is used to create hypertext and hypermedia documents on the web incorporating text, graphics, sound, video, and hyperlinks. SGML is used to define the structure and to manage documents in electronic form. HTML is a mechanism used to create web pages on the Internet. A malicious HTML document can be emailed to system user victims where the act of opening the email or attachment can compromise the system.

(i) Digital Certificates

Trusted certificate authorities (CAs), which are third-party companies and who are trusted by browser software and operating systems are authorized to issue original digital certificates on behalf of domain users.

Websites use these digital certificates to create hypertext transfer protocol secure (HTTPS) connection, which gives confidence to browsers that they are visiting a "real" website and that it is valid, safe, and secure to visit. The certificate is a computer file containing the domain name, a digital signature, an expiration date, and a cryptographic public key.

When a website presents a certificate to a browser during an HTTPS connection, the browser uses the information and the signature in the certificate to confirm that a CA it trusts has decided to trust the information in the certificate. However, be aware of "rogue" certificates obtained by manipulating and compromising a certificate authority.

(ii) Domain Name System

A major purpose of the domain name system (DNS) protocol on the Internet is to translate domain names into domain numbers (i.e., Internet Protocol (IP) address). Bad actors on the Internet can manipulate the DNS to conduct distributed denial-of-service (DDoS) attacks, DNS exfiltration, DNS spoofing, electronic dumpster diving, and DNS cache poisoning attacks.

Each entity in a network, such as a computer, requires a uniquely identifiable network address for proper delivery of message information. DNS is a protocol used to manage name lookups for converting between decimal and domain name versions of an address. It uses a name server (DNS server), which contains a universe of names called name space. Each name server is identified by one or more IP addresses. Hackers can intercept and forge traffic for arbitrary name nodes, thus impersonating IP addresses. Secure DNS can be accomplished with cryptographic protocols for message exchanges between name servers. DNS transactions include DNS query/response, zone transfers, dynamic updates, DNS lookups, and DNS NOTIFY.

Electronic dumpster diving involves scanning and enumeration of systems and ports to discover passwords and to investigate open source intelligence using DNS lookups and web searches to discover the characteristics of the system being attacked and particularly to pinpoint any potentially exploitable vulnerabilities.

DNS collects passive network data that can provide new insights into suspicious network connections. This passive data when combined with data from firewalls and intrusion detection systems can (1) reveal hackers attack tactics that can be used to block malicious domains attacking an organization and (2) perform threat-hunting exercises. Threat-hunting is a careful exercise in searching for unusual and unknown DNS requests and in learning about the number of queries an endpoint device receives and sends out to the requesters. Examples of endpoint devices are servers, routers, firewalls, modems, sockets, ports, network nodes, port protection devices, hubs, gateways, backbone networks, portals, bridges, and switches. The overall goal of the threat-hunting exercise is to uncover hidden cyber threats and vulnerabilities as much as possible in much a shorter timeframe.

(iii) Hypertext Transfer Protocol

Hypertext transfer protocol (HTTP) is not secure because it uses an unencrypted protocol and does not protect data from interception or alteration, which can subject users to eavesdropping, impersonation, tracking, and the modification of received data.

Because the HTTP uses an unencrypted connection, it creates a privacy vulnerability and exposes potentially sensitive information about website users and visitors to public. In addition, HTTP does not achieve the objectives of confidentiality, authenticity, and integrity while hypertext transfer protocol secure (HTTPS) does. Hence, HTTP is subject to several attacks such as data tampering, impersonation, obfuscated universal resource locators (URLs), or "man-in-the-middle" scenario.

HTTP is the plain and native protocol of the Web, used to transfer hypertext documents on the Internet. It is a standard method for communication between clients and Web servers. A plain HTTP connection can be easily monitored, modified, and impersonated and can even be attacked by a novice hacker at large scale and at low cost.

(iv) Hypertext Transfer Protocol Secure

Hypertext transfer protocol secure (HTTPS) is a variation of HTTP that provides encryption and transmission through a secure port. HTTPS allows HTTP to run over transport layer security (TLS). TLS is a network protocol that establishes an encrypted connection to an authenticated peer over an untrusted network.

$$HTTPS = HTTP + TLS$$

HTTPS verifies the identity of a website or web service for a connecting client, and encrypts nearly all information sent between the website and the client-user. Protected information includes web cookies, user-agent details, universal resource locator (URL) paths, web form submissions, and query string parameters. HTTPS is designed to prevent this information from being read or changed while in transit.

HTTP and HTTPS contain a mixed content. This mixing happens when a secure HTTPS website references its resources to an unsecure HTTP website resource. Moving an existing website from HTTP to HTTPS means identifying and fixing or replacing the mixed content. External resources such as images, scripts, frames, and fonts, which are part of mixed content could be unsecure.

When properly configured, HTTPS connection guarantees the website visitor about three things:

1. **Confidentiality.** The visitor's connection is encrypted, obscuring URLs, web cookies, and other sensitive metadata.

2. **Authenticity.** The visitor is talking to the "real" website, and not to an impersonator or through a "man-in-the-middle" scenario.

3. **Integrity.** The data sent between the visitor and the website has not been tampered with or modified.

However, HTTPS can be attacked by a sophisticated and advanced hacker through performing cryptanalysis, exploiting other protocol weaknesses, installing a malicious root certificate into a browser, or obtaining a "rogue" certificate.

However, HTTPS has several important limitations. IP addresses and destination domain names are not encrypted during communication. Even encrypted traffic can reveal some information indirectly, such as time spent on a website, the size of requested resources, or the size of submitted information.

HTTPS only guarantees the integrity of the connection between two systems, not the systems themselves. It is not designed to protect a web server from being hacked or compromised or to prevent the web service from exposing user information during its normal operation. Similarly, if a user's system is compromised by an attacker, that system can be altered so that its future HTTPS connections are under the attacker's control. The guarantees of HTTPS may also be weakened or eliminated by compromised or malicious certificate authorities issuing "rogue" certificates.

(v) HTTPS and HSTS

Hypertext transfer protocol secure (HTTPS) and HTTP strict transport security (HSTS) together can provide encrypted communications between the website and visitors/system users to ensure their privacy rights are protected. A strong protection is facilitated solely through the use of encrypted communications.

$$HSTS = HTTP + TLS$$

To ensure that a hacker cannot use a DNS spoofing attack to direct the user to a plain HTTP connection where traffic can be intercepted, websites can use HSTS to instruct browsers to require an HTTPS connection for their domain at all times. This means that an attacker that successfully spoofs DNS resolution must also create a valid HTTPS connection. This makes DNS spoofing as challenging and expensive as attacking HTTPS generally.

If the attacker spoofs DNS but does not compromise HTTPS, users will receive warning messages from their browser that will prevent them from visiting the possibly malicious website. If the site uses HSTS, there will be no option for the visitor to disregard and click through the warning. Thus, HTTPS and HSTS work together to protect a domain against DNS spoofing attack.

(vi) Secure Hypertext Transfer Protocol

Secure hypertext transfer protocol (SHTTP) is used to support encryption and decryption of specific Web-based documents sent over the Internet. It is a message-oriented communication protocol that extends the HTTP protocol. It coexists with HTTP's messaging model and can be easily integrated with HTTP applications.

SHTTP employs Rivest Shamir Adelman (RSA) public-key encryption technology. Its major purpose is to provide end-to-end confidentiality, integrity, non-repudiation, and authentication of electronic payments made through the Internet. SHTTP contains HTTP and secure sockets layer (SSL). The combination of hypertext transfer protocol secure (HTTPS) and HTTP strict transport security (HSTS) is much stronger and highly secure than the secure hypertext transfer protocol (SHTTP) because the HTTPS and HSTS contains transport layer security (TLS). In other words, the transport layer security (TLS) is much stronger than the secure sockets layer (SSL).

$$SHTTP = HTTP + SSL$$

The **Secure Shell (SSH)** protocol uses a hybrid cryptosystem similar to secure sockets layer (SSL). A shared secret is exchanged using public key cryptography, and then data is encrypted using a symmetric cipher based on the shared secret. Server authentication is performed using public key cryptographic methods, whereas several possibilities are provided for client authentication without needing password exchanges.

PROTOCOLS AND ENCRYPTION

Use secure protocols that can provide encryption of both passwords and data (e.g., SSH and HTTPS); do not use less secure protocols (e.g., TELNET, trivial FTP, NFS, and HTTP) unless absolutely required and tunneled over an encrypted protocol, such as SSH, SSL, transport layer security (TLS), or IPsec.

SSH has grown in popularity since its introduction and is considered an Internet standard. The software has been ported to a wide variety of UNIX platforms; both commercial and noncommercial versions are available. SSH offers these features: (1) it prevents identity spoofing and Trojan horse viruses due to strong authentication, (2) it provides data encryption and compression and (3) it provides a secure means for file transfer. SSH protects UNIX remote shell commands against the possibility of unauthorized clients masquerading as the server host.

The **SSH-2** protocol authenticates the client to the server by establishing an encrypted tunnel between the SSH client and the SSH server. SSH-2 meets the confidentiality and integrity goals. It is used for remote access and includes a transport layer protocol, a user authentication protocol, and a connection protocol.

The **Secure Electronic Transaction (SET)** protocol supports secure transactions over the Internet. It is based on RSA's encryption technology and data encryption standard (DES). It is backed by major credit card processing companies, such as MasterCard and Visa and technology companies, such as IBM, and Microsoft. This protocol is used for buying goods and services by paying with charge cards. SET uses the SSL, secure HTTP, or both in online transactions. SET is based on public key encryption and authentication technology and involves three-way transactions among the buyer, the seller, and a financial institution (a bank).

The **secure sockets layer (SSL)** is a protocol that provides end-to-end encryption of application layer network traffic. It provides privacy and reliability between two communicating applications. It is designed to encapsulate other protocols, such as HTTP. SSL is an authentication and security protocol widely implemented in browsers and web servers for protecting private information during transmission via the Internet.

SSL is a protocol developed for transmitting private documents via the Internet. SSL is based on public key cryptography, used to generate a cryptographic session that is private to a Web server and a client browser. SSL works by using a public key to encrypt data that is transferred over the SSL connection. Most web browsers support SSL, and many websites use the protocol to obtain confidential user information, such as credit card numbers. By convention, URLs that require an SSL connection start with "https" instead of "http." SSL has been superseded by the newer transport layer security protocol.

Transport layer security (TLS) is an authentication and security protocol widely implemented in web browsers and web servers. It provides security at the layer responsible for end-to-end communications. TLS provides privacy and data integrity between two communicating applications. It is designed to encapsulate other protocols, such as HTTP. TLS is new and SSL is old.

Sockets (SOCKS) protocol is an Internet protocol to allow client applications to form a circuit-level gateway to a network firewall via a proxy service. This protocol supports application-layer firewall traversal. The SOCKS protocol supports both reliable TCP and UDP transport services by creating a shim layer between the application and the transport layers. The SOCKS protocol includes a negotiation step whereby the server can dictate which authentication mechanism it supports.

As a server, SOCKS is a networking-proxy protocol that enables full access across the SOCKS server from one host to another without requiring direct IP reachability. The SOCKS server authenticates and authorizes the requests, establishes a proxy connection, and transmits the data. SOCKS is commonly used as a network firewall that enables hosts behind a SOCKS server to gain full access to the Internet while preventing unauthorized access from the Internet to the internal hosts.

Session initiation protocol (SIP) is a text-based protocol, like simple mail transfer protocol (SMTP) and hypertext transfer protocol (HTTP), for initiating interactive communication sessions between users. Such sessions include voice, video, data, instant messaging, chat, interactive games, and virtual reality. SIP is the protocol used to set up conferencing, telephony, multimedia, and other types of communication sessions on the Internet. SIP operates over Transmission Control Protocol (TCP) or User Datagram Protocol (UDP).

SIP is described as a control protocol for creating, modifying, and terminating sessions with one or more participants in an IP-based network. These sessions include Internet multimedia conferences, Internet telephone calls, and multimedia distribution. Session members can communicate via multicast, through a mesh of unicast relations, or by a combination of these. SIP supports session descriptions that allow participants to agree on a set of compatible media types. It also supports user mobility by proxying and redirecting requests to the user's current location. SIP is not tied to any particular conference related control protocol.

SIP authentication is between a user agent client and a user agent server (i.e., two-party sessions). Although one application may act as both client and server, the authentication is usually not end to end (i.e., user to user). Instead, authentication is usually between a user and a server or between two servers. For conference calls, all participants in the conference must authenticate a conference control application (i.e., multiparty sessions).

HOW MANY SESSIONS ARE THERE IN A SIP?

- Two-party sessions between a caller and a receiver in an ordinary telephone call

- Multiparty sessions between several individuals in a telephone conference call where everyone can hear and speak

- Multicast sessions between one sender and many receivers (like broadcasting to several individuals simultaneously)

SIP just handles setup, management, and termination of sessions. Other protocols, such as Real-Time Transport Protocol (RTP) and Real-Time Transport Control Protocol (RTCP) are used for data transport. Telephone numbers in SIP are represented as uniform resource locator (URL) and domain name system (DNS) in that the SIP URL may contain IPv4 and IPv6 addresses. SIP is one of the leading signaling protocols for voice over IP (VoIP), along with H.225gatekeeper, H.245 telephony protocol, and H.323 gateway protocol.

The **H.323 gateway protocol** is a cornerstone technology for the transmission of real-time audio, video, and data communications over packet-based networks. It is an umbrella standard that specifies the components, protocols, and procedures that provide multimedia communication over packet-based networks that do not provide a guaranteed QoS. H.323 protocol can be applied in a variety of mechanisms: audio only (IP telephony); audio and video (video telephony); audio and data; audio, video, and data; and multipoint multimedia communications. The official title of H.323 is "visual telephone systems and equipment for local-area networks (LANs) which provide a non-guaranteed quality of service."

A **peer-to-peer (P2P) file sharing program** is free and easily accessible software that poses risks to individuals and organizations. The P2P program unknowingly enables users to copy private files, download material that is protected by the copyright laws, download a virus, or facilitate a security breach.

A **universal resource locator (URL)** or uniform resource locator (URL) provides a web address for an organization's website. This means that an URL is an entry point (i.e., a key to a door) to an organization's website, computers, networks, and devices, which can be risky. The most commonly used protocols with a URL are HTTP and HTTPS. Some URLs pose a risk to organizations because hackers can manipulate them to conduct their own illegal and unethical actions. The best advice is to pay attention to the URL of a received website. Malicious websites may look identical to legitimate websites, but the URL may use a variation in spelling or a different domain (e.g., .com versus .net). Users who are unsure about the authenticity of a URL should contact the original company directly for validation.

At least two types of URLs exist: static and dynamic. The content on the web page of a **static URL** does not change unless a web programmer changes the page's HTML code (e.g., www.gao.gov). Search engines (e.g., Google) often prioritize static URLs over dynamic URLs. A web administrator can do URL rewriting to make dynamic URLs more attractive.

The content of a web page with a **dynamic URL** changes because the page is generated from automated queries to the website's database (e.g., a dynamic URL contains special characters, such as & $ + = ?). A dynamic URL is convenient for a web programmer to change a website's appearance because the change is an automated process without changing the web page's HTML code. Instead, the change is made in the website's associated database.

Examples of URLs that can be used for good and bad purposes include redirected URLs, obfuscated URLs, and shortened URLs.

In an openly **redirected URL**, a user victim is tricked into selecting a URL that has been modified to direct him or her to an external and malicious website, which may contain malware (phishing attack) that can compromise the victim's computers. Here, the redirected URL is an exploit. Sometimes a redirected URL is done for a good reason when a company's business name and its URL is changed (i.e., URL forwarding or domain forwarding). In other words, a redirected URL is used for good and bad purposes.

An **obfuscated URL** is a situation where a fraud (fake) URL imitates the original (real) URL to deceive innocent users to divulge login data and release financial and personal information to attackers. A domain or URL name is misspelled to trick users into visiting a hacker's website; this is called a hyperlink trick. An obfuscated URL is a concealed URL used to: (1) launch spamming, phishing, and XSS attacks by hackers; (2) hide the true URL of certain web pages for legitimate reasons and control purposes; (3) act as an anti-hacking procedure for organizations; and (4) act as an attack-in-depth strategy for hackers. In other words, an obfuscated URL is used for good and bad purposes.

A **shortened URL** is a shorter URL or IP address that is used to direct to the same web page as the longer web address. Using an HTTP redirect feature, multiple URLs can be used to reach a specific web page (e.g., special and loyal customers may be given unique URLs to buy products and services). Organizations should develop their own shorter URLs with appropriate security and logging controls in place. Short URLs are used to accommodate character limitations on a social media platforms (Twitter) and text messages (short message service, or SMS) and to address privacy concerns. Unfortunately, short URLs are also used to introduce spyware (malware) or launch a phishing attack. Attackers can use shortened URLs to obscure the actual website name. URL shortening is also known as URL redirecting. In other words, a shortened URL is used for good and bad purposes.

Universal serial bus (USB) is a hardware device and a common interface mechanism that enables communication between devices and a PC. The USB port connects several devices, such as mice, keyboard, printers, scanners, cameras, external hard drives, flash drives, and electrical power outlets. Compared to optical disk drives, USB flash drives can store large volumes of data with faster data transfer rates.

Similar to a web browser software and a URL address, the USB port is an entry point (i.e., a key to a door) to an organization's website, computers, networks, and devices, which can be risky. For example, employees who are permitted to bring their own devices to the workplace can bring in an infected flash drive and infect the company's computer systems and networks, which is risky.

USB drives such as flash drives are perfect for data backup purposes as they are small, durable, reliable, handy, and easy to backup data, although they can easily be lost or stolen. It is good to secure all sensitive data stored on USB drives (e.g., jump, flash, pen, smart, and thumb drives), CDs, and DVDs using strong encryption. Consider using jump drives with onboard antivirus capability to perform automatic virus scans. Also use anti-malware software on mobile devices. Note that hackers can install their own malware on USB devices and can kill the anti-malware software already on these devices using scripting programming languages as part of their detection evasion strategy.

Network address translation (NAT) is a routing technology used by many firewalls to hide internal system addresses from an external network through use of an addressing schema. It is a mechanism for mapping addresses on one network to addresses on another network, typically private addresses to public addresses. **Port address translation (PAT)** does the same thing with the ports.

Both NAT and PAT are used to hide internal system addresses from an external network by (1) mapping internal addresses to external addresses, (2) mapping internal addresses to a single external address, or (3) using port numbers to link external system addresses with internal systems.

The Internet's interactive **file transfer protocol (FTP)** is a part of the application layer protocols of the TCP/IP that requires users to log in to the remote computer to download files placed on the FTP server. From this viewpoint, FTP is better than HTTP because FTP allows a user on a computer A to transfer a file from computer B to a computer C.

Local files can be accessed using the file protocol without requiring a FTP server. However, FTP requires a FTP server for remote files. FTP cannot work on local files, only on remote files.

FTP also cannot work with the network address translation (NAT) because both FTP and NAT do not know the IP addresses they are handling. Anonymous FTP (trivial FTP; TFTP) allows users to log in using the username "anonymous" and using email address as the password. TFTP is not secure; secure FTP (SFTP) is more secure.

Use an SFTP or secure copy protocol (SCP) instead of FTP or TFTP, as shown:

$$\text{FTP/TFTP} \longrightarrow \text{SFTP/SCP}$$

Web browser software is a client program (i.e., a computer user program) designed to interact on the web and to view web content through a graphical user interface (GUI) and other helper applications in order to make it easy for computer users to do their work (e.g., Microsoft Edge and Google Chrome).

Browser software is an entry point (i.e., a key to a door) for computer users to access an organization's website, computers, networks, and devices. At the same time, browser software provides a risky entry door to hackers, attackers, and bad actors to initiate their illegal and unethical.

The enable and disable features should be of concern to computer users. Enabling some web browser features may lower security and vice versa. Often vendors enable features by default to improve the computing experience, but these features may end up increasing computer user risk.

Attackers actively focus on exploiting client-side systems (user computers) through various vulnerabilities that are part of a browser's design. They use these vulnerabilities to take control of users' computers, steal valuable user information, destroy user data files, and use one computer to attack other computers.

An attacker can create a malicious web page that will install Trojan virus software or spyware that will steal user information. Rather than actively targeting and attacking vulnerable systems, a malicious website can passively compromise systems as the site is visited. A malicious HTML document can also be emailed to user victims. In these cases, the act of opening the email or attachment can compromise the system.

Some specific web browser risks include vulnerabilities in Active X technologies, Java programming languages, plug-in applications, website cookies, and scripting languages (e.g., JavaScript, VBScript, and XSS).

Website cookies are small computer files that store information for a website on a user's computer. This information is supplied by a web server to a browser, in a response for a requested resource, for the browser to store temporarily and return to the server on any subsequent visits or requests. Cookies may contain information about the websites a user visited or even credentials for accessing the website. Cookies are designed to be readable only by the websites that created them, meaning cookies are unique to each website. Cookies can be used to uniquely identify all visitors of a website, which some people consider a violation of privacy. If a website uses cookies for authentication, then an attacker may be able to acquire unauthorized access to that site by obtaining the cookie.

Cookies have two mandatory parameters—name and value—and four optional parameters: expiration date, path, domain, and secure parameters. Four types of cookies exist: encrypted, persistent, session, and tracking cookies. Some websites create **encrypted cookies** to protect the data from unauthorized access. **Persistent cookies** are stored on a computer's hard drive indefinitely so that a website can identify the user during subsequent visits. These cookies are set with expiration dates and are valid until the user deletes them. Hence, persistent cookies pose a higher risk than session cookies because they remain on the computer longer. **Session cookies** are temporary cookies that are valid only for a single website session; they are cleared or erased when the browser is closed, and they are stored in a temporary memory. **Tracking cookies** are cookies placed on a user's computer to track the user's activity on different websites, creating a detailed profile of user behavior.

Click-through rate is the number of times a website user clicks on a web page advertisement compared to the total number of users viewing the same advertisement. The higher the click-through rate, the greater the interest in an advertisement, and the larger the dollar amounts converted to online sales revenue (i.e., click-through conversion amount). As the click-fraud rate increases, the click-through rate increases, showing a direct relationship. Higher click-through rates may or may not increase online sales revenue; it depends on whether the number of clicks have actually turned into sales orders.

Click-through rate = (Number of visitors clicked) / (Total number of visitors) × 100

Click to conversion time for a product or service is the elapsed time between a number of browser clicks made, the number of website navigation paths taken, and the number of online ads read before a purchase decision is made. Comparisons can be made between different products and at different times to shorten the click to conversion time. The shorter the conversion time, the faster the sales revenue, and vice versa. Customer data is classified, stored, and analyzed to study purchasing trends and patterns. As the click fraud rate increases, the click to conversion time and the click-through conversion amount decreases, showing an inverse relationship.

Click fraud involves deceptions and scams that inflate online advertising bills with improper, inaccurate, and illegal number of clicks made on the web. Either software bots are deployed or imposter users are hired by advertising firms to keep clicking on the ad either continuously or periodically to indicate that actual users are reading the ad. Later, the advertising firm bills clients for the number of clicks made. (The billing rate is based on cost per click.) Click fraud is possible with adware software because it involves deceptions and scam that inflate advertising bills with improper usage and charges per click in online web advertisements. A security control against click fraud is to use heat maps that track website visitors' click behavior and browsing habits. Heat maps help web administrators visualize how web visitors are interacting with website.

A **web bug** or **web beacon** is a tiny image, invisible to a user, placed on web pages in such a way to enable third parties to track use of Web servers and collect information about the user, including

IP address, host name, browser type and version, OS name and version, and web browser cookies. It is a tiny graphic on a website that is referenced within the HTML content of a Web page or email to collect information about the user viewing the HTML content.

Demilitarized zone: A demilitarized zone (DMZ) is an interface on a routing firewall that is similar to the interfaces found on the firewall's protected side. Traffic moving between the DMZ and other interfaces on the protected side of the firewall still goes through the firewall and can have firewall protection policies applied. It is a host or network segment inserted as a "neutral zone" between an organization's private network and the Internet. A DMZ is a network created by connecting to firewalls. Systems that are externally accessible but need some protections are usually located on DMZ networks.

Web-based threats: Web-based threats include security assertions markup language (SAML) threats and extensible markup language (XML) threats. Examples of SAML threats include assertion manufacture, modification, disclosure, repudiation, redirect, reuse, and substitution. Examples of XML threats include dictionary attacks, DoS attacks, SQL command injection attacks, confidentiality and integrity attacks, and XML injection attacks.

SAML is an XML-based security specification for exchanging authentication and authorization information between trusted entities over the Internet. Security typically involves checking the credentials presented by a party for authentication and authorization. SAML standardizes the representation of these credentials in an XML format called "assertions," enhancing the interoperability between disparate applications. SAML is a specification for encoding security assertions in the XML. SAML is a protocol consisting of XML-based request and response message formats for exchanging security information, expressed in the form of assertions about subjects and between online business partners. XML is a metalanguage that is in a flexible text format designed to describe data for electronic publishing. The web browser interprets the XML, and the XML takes over the HTML for creating dynamic web documents.

Variations of XML include XHTML, XML encryption, XML gateways, XML schema, and XML signature. **Extended hypertext markup language (XHTML)** is a unifying standard that brings the benefits of XML to those of HTML. XHTML is the new web standard and should be used for all new web pages to achieve maximum portability across platforms and browsers. **XML encryption** is a process or mechanism for encrypting and decrypting XML documents or parts of documents.

XML gateways provide sophisticated authentication and authorization services, potentially improving the security of the web service by having all simple object access protocol (SOAP) messages pass through a hardened gateway before reaching any of the custom-developed code. XML gateways can restrict access based on source, destination, or WS-Security authentication tokens.

XML schema is a language for describing and defining the structure, content, and semantics of XML documents.

XML signature is a mechanism for ensuring the origin and integrity of XML documents. XML signatures provide integrity, message authentication, or signer authentication services for data of any type, whether located within the XML that includes the signature or elsewhere.

A **script** is a sequence of instructions, ranging from a simple list of OS commands to full-blown programming language statements, which can be executed automatically by an interpreter.

Script commands reside in text files. Unlike compiled programs, which execute directly on a computer processor, a script must be processed by another program that carries out the indicated actions.

Scripting language is a definition of the syntax and semantics for writing and interpreting scripts. Typically, scripting languages follow the conventions of a simple programming language, but they can also take on a more basic form, such as a macro or a batch file. JavaScript, VBScript, Tcl (Tool Command Language), PHP (Personal Home Page), and Perl are examples of scripting languages.

Client-side scripts, which include JavaScript, Java applets, and Active-X controls, are used to generate dynamic web pages. Server-side scripts include CGI, ASP, JSP, PHP, and Perl are used to generate dynamic web pages.

Multipurpose Internet Mail Extension (MIME) is a standard method for sending and receiving attachments to Internet email messages. MIME works across different computing platforms. All email messages have message headers that identify the sender, destination, subject, and other information needed to transfer the message. MIME can be used to support security features like digital signatures and encrypted messages. It also facilitates mailing virus-infected executables and malign active content.

S/MIME (secure MIME) is an extension of MIME, which uses encryption to protect against unintended recipients reading, changing, or forging email messages. This Internet email security-oriented protocol adds public key encryption and digital signatures support to the MIME email protocol.

S/MIME is CPU intensive as it uses a combination of public and private key encryption, hash codes, and digital certificates. A major part of S/MIME is the consideration of the encryption algorithm and key length, as a wide variety of these are used. S/MIME is implemented with X.509 V3 protocol.

There are two S/MIME message types: signed messages, and signed and enveloped messages. Signed messages provide integrity and sender authentication, while the signed and enveloped messages provide integrity, sender authentication, and confidentiality.

Privacy Enhanced Mail (PEM) is an Internet standard for email systems using encryption techniques to ensure message privacy and security by providing encryption, authentication, message integrity, and key management.

PEM is an application-layer security protocol to add confidentiality and authentication services to electronic messages. Its major features include sender and forwarder authentication, end-to-end confidentiality, algorithm independence, and originator non-repudiation. PEM supports DES for data encryption, DES and RSA for key management, and RSA for digital signatures and message integrity. PEM works with both secret key and public key approaches for encryption of data encrypting keys. It can be implemented selectively, by site or by user, and without impacting the rest of the network. PEM is a superset of X.509 protocols.

Pretty Good Privacy (PGP) is used to encrypt files or messages. It is implemented exclusively in software and available in source code. It is the encryption mechanism to facilitate confidential communication (email) among individuals over the Internet. It uses the IDEA algorithm to encrypt files or messages and an asymmetric key algorithm for key exchange.

PGP is a product, not a standard. It does not interoperate with any other security product, either PEM or non-PEM. PGP is portable to a wide variety of hardware platforms. It encrypts and signs messages. The owner of the private key needs to remember an arbitrarily long pass-phrase for the private key, which is a difficult thing to do. PGP stores keys in files called key-rings. A key fingerprint is used to verify the identity of a key. A limitation of PGP is that someone can be duped into using the wrong key.

PEM VERSUS PGP

- PEM and PGP have different philosophies.
- PEM is based on the concept of a hierarchical organization.
- PGP is based on the concept of distributed network of individuals.
- PEM is suited for application systems in all organizations.
- PGP is suited for communicating among individuals on the Internet.
- Both PEM and PGP can encrypt and sign messages.
- Both PEM and PGP are based on public key cryptography

OpenPGP is a nonproprietary protocol for encrypting email using public key cryptography. The most widely used email encryption standard in the world, it is based on PGP, and its protocol defines standard formats for encrypted messages, signatures, and certificates for exchanging public keys.

3.3 Business Software Systems

The section covers several topics in business software systems such as GRC systems, ERP systems, CRM systems, and electronic data systems (EDS). Specifically, this section discusses the strategic issues facing the GRC system, advantages and disadvantages of the ERP system, benefits from the CRM system, and operational issues in the EDS systems.

(a) Governance, Risk, and Compliance System

(i) Overview

Today, a GRC system is an automated and integrated reporting system describing how an organization is meeting its reporting requirements on GRC matters. In the past, GRC systems were manual and/or spreadsheet systems systems with data inputs from siloed departments. The reporting structure was not timely and was decentralized, with individual business functions collecting data and developing reports, independent of each function. These manual reports were fraught with problems, such as time delays, inaccuracies, and inconsistencies in data collection and data coding efforts. Moreover, the aggregated results in these reports were often difficult to interpret and failed to provide a comprehensive picture on the GRC matters. Decision making was difficult with manual reports due to lack of reporting accuracy with low confidence such reports provided. Moreover, management was unable to take timely corrective actions for noncompliance with laws and regulations. Consequently, organizations were fined for missed, delayed, and inaccurate reporting and noncompliance with laws and regulations. The automated GRC system eliminates most of these problems due to its consistency in data collection, data coding, and data aggregation and timely centralized reporting structure. GRC reporting is a part of and an extension of the Sarbanes-Oxley Act of 2002 reporting requirements. Exhibit 3.5 shows how a corporation's GRC reporting system has evolved from yesterday's inadequate system to today's adequate system.

EXHIBIT 3.5 Evolution of a GRC Reporting System

GRC Yesterday	Manual reporting system; reports were prepared in siloed departments with decentralized reporting structures; reports were delayed, inaccurate, and inconsistent; data collection, coding, and reporting efforts were disorganized; decision making was difficult with the aggregated data that could not provide meaningful insights; management was unable to make timely decisions to correct noncompliance problems; and workflows were rigid and static with multiple sources of data input. Spreadsheet systems were used to do the GRC work, but they did not provide accurate, timely, and consistent results and reports.
GRC Today	Automated reporting system; reports are prepared in cross-departments, cross-functions, and cross-divisions with centralized reporting structures; reports are timely, accurate, and consistent; data collection, coding, and reporting efforts are systematic; decision making is relatively easier with the aggregated data that provides meaningful insights; management is able to make timely decisions to correct noncompliance problems; and workflows are flexible and dynamic with a single source of data input.

Internal recipients of the GRC reports are board members, the chief executive officer (CEO), chief governance officer, chief risk officer, chief compliance officer, other executives, senior managers, and internal audit management. External recipients are shareholders, regulators, and other stakeholders (e.g., corporate activists and watchdog groups). Internal risk owners or process owners who are functional managers and department managers collect data and prepare the GRC reports. Management of any organization prefer the GRC reporting system to be credible, useful, and timely to facilitate well-informed decisions. Here, management is seeking a clear answer to the question: Are we fully meeting the GRC reporting requirements?

(ii) GRC's Core Functions

A GRC system should have these five core functions to support its full capabilities in standardized and centralized data management and reporting structure:

1. Centralized data management

2. Process and incident management

3. Workflow management

4. Automated monitoring and alerting

5. Automated reporting

Exhibit 3.6 lists benefits from these core functions in terms of productivity gains, visibility and clarity, and risk mitigation.

EXHIBIT 3.6 Benefits of Core GRC Functionality

Benefit Item	Benefit Description	Source of Benefits
Productivity gains	Reduction in time spent updating data	Uniform and controlled system of record
	Reduction in time spent distributing data	Automation of processes, alerts, and reporting
	Reduction in time spent compiling data	Centralized access to compliance and risk information
	Reduction in time spent responding to department, regulatory, and auditor requests	Ability to customize delivery of compliance and risk data to business context
	Reduction in business process delays	
Visibility and clarity	Reduction in errors and inaccurate data	Uniform and controlled system of record
	Improved understanding of requirements	Automation of processes alerts, and reporting
	Improved insight into changing performance and exposure	Centralized access to compliance and risk information
	Improved insight into consequences of decisions	Retention of information and performance data
Risk mitigation	Reduction in exposure to penalties or liability	Improved understanding of requirements
	Reduction in exposure to poor business outcomes and financial harm	Improved insight into changing performance and exposures
	Increased trust and "benefit of the doubt" of regulators	Improved ability to demonstrate compliance and efforts made
		Increase in risk and compliance projects undertaken

Source: Adapted from Blue Hill Research, *Analyst Insight, Four Components of an Enterprise Risk Reporting and Management Platform*, 2017. www.rims.org/RiskKnowledge/RISKKnowledgeDocs/DoubleCheck_FourComponents_WhitePaper_10182017_143847.pdf

(iii) Four Components of a GRC Reporting System

Further research on the five core GRC functions has explored the need for four major areas of differentiation, described next: (1) use-case sensitive work environments, (2) incorporation of business intelligence analytics, (3) data visualization capabilities, and (4) configurable workflows.

(A) Use-Case Sensitive Work Environments

Risk management and compliance management collect big data with multiple overlapping information types, sources, and applications. The complexity of the information itself combined with the number of stakeholders inside and outside of an organization gives process owners a major challenge in collecting and reporting this information.

Use-case work environments need a "single source of truth" to help an organization obtain consistent and meaningful insight into its GRC performance across the organization. This single source provides a consistent and meaningful data management and centralized reporting process. This means that the new reporting system provides only one view of data, not multiple views of data.

Exhibit 3.7 summarizes the potential benefits that the adaption of data management to specific use cases and stakeholder contexts over a data-centric view and the factors to consider as organizations evaluate how GRC solutions provide for this need.

EXHIBIT 3.7 Use-Case Sensitive Work Environments

Advantages	Improved operational performance by risk and process owners
	Faster identification of relevant data and potential impacts
	Faster application of relevant data with operational functions of data users
	Improved understanding of risks and broader risk implications
Factors to consider	Number of workflow and use-case contexts that the solution supports
	Adaptability of solution workflow and interface to individual needs
	Future workflow and use-case contexts that might be needed
	Amount of customization required to support users
	Ability to drill down or roll up from personal use-case views to enterprise data views

(B) Incorporation of Business Intelligence Analytics

Although the automated GRC reporting system, which is better than a manual reporting system, provides a system of records to track and maintain historical data and relationships between data elements, the automated reports represent static snapshots of information that cannot be interacted or lack intelligence to assist in interpretation or the identification of trends.

Business intelligence (BI) analytics tools embedded within the GRC platform provide the ability to recognize these relationships and to identify trends and insights in a way that is not provided by basic static reports. Core aspects of BI solutions, such as the ability to draw connections across data, roll up conclusions, or drill down into underlying factors, have tremendous impact in helping organizations manage the various constraints, risk tolerances, key risk indicators, and key performance indicators at the heart of compliance and risk operations. A further advantage lies in the combination of real-time intelligence capabilities that allow the organization to automate oversight and the generation of meaningful reports and alerts as circumstances change, requiring new action or changes in strategy.

This ability to derive connections between data to drive new insights is the core difference between the BI analytics and simple (basic) reporting capabilities. For example, where an automated report might be used to report the number of open risk projects within an organization and the percentage at a given stage of remediation, a BI solution can permit the organization to rank and prioritize incidents based on potential exposure, consequences to business operations, and other factors set by the organization. See Exhibit 3.8.

EXHIBIT 3.8 Business Intelligence Analytics

Advantages	Earlier identification of risks and incidents
	Understanding of relationships between risk factors and performance
	Superior insight into risks, potential impact, and consequences
Factors to consider	Fit of embedded algorithms to organization needs
	Range of unstructured and structured data included
	Ability to support causal analysis by line of business users
	Time required to set up and complete analyses

(C) Data Visualization Capabilities

Both risk and compliance management can involve large amounts of numerical or unstructured text data. Understanding the scope of change or making comparisons between numerical data often is difficult for human reviewers. Even for the most numerically savvy, a quick review of simple data outputs often requires a great deal of "cognition" and calculation to make sense of the results. All of this slows the process of reviewing data and works to erode its value to users. This is particularly true for stakeholders who are not familiar with risk management. While many risk managers may be comfortable with risk scoring methods, Monte Carlo simulations, and other quantitative risk measures, the nuances can be lost on non-risk managers.

Data visualization technology is a response to these challenges, offering visual representations of data to speed interpretation and context insight to assist human review. Visualization tools run the gamut: heat maps, pie charts, bar charts, simple line graphs, progress indicators, star charts, scorecards, and dashboards. For example, heat maps are color-coded and graphics-based matrixes that can be used to analyze risks facing an organization. Heat maps can show data outliers for further analysis. While the particular modes and presentations of a visualization tool may differ, the underlying purpose is the same: to allow for quick comprehension of data. As such, these tools contribute benefits in the efficiency and effectiveness of risk and compliance staff. See Exhibit 3.9.

EXHIBIT 3.9 Visualization Capabilities

Advantages	Faster human review of data
	Easier identification of outliers, anomalies, and exposures
	Improved data use and speed of insight
Factors to consider	Variety of visualization formats offered
	Ability to tailor data visualization to reporting needs
	Automation of data incorporation and display
	Ability to filter and drill down data as needed

(D) Configurable Workflows

GRC tools often employ automated workflow rules and alerts that can improve tasks and projects that can benefit stakeholders and process owners.

In the past, most workflows were rigid, static (i.e., nonconfigurable), and could not change or adapt to new work environments. Overly rigid workflows can create impediments to the value of a GRC solution by requiring either that: (1) internal processes be adapted to a universal or generic process of the solution, or (2) the software environment itself be customized to fit internal processes and use cases. The former impediment erodes the value of the solution in much the same way as generic data management does; the latter introduces new costs and delays into solution implementation as well as subsequent upgrades and expansions.

By contrast, today's GRC solutions with "configurable" workflows are flexible, dynamic, and predesigned to be adaptable to particular use cases without customization. While not necessarily offering the level of tailoring available through customization, a configurable solution offers a closer fit to the organization's processes without incurring the additional costs and delays of customizing the solution. In this way, configurable solutions help to control the implementation costs of the investment. Ultimately, this helps to speed time to value of the investment and increase the return on investment. It also helps to enhance the total impact of the solution by helping to match the solution's workflow capabilities to the organization's needs. See Exhibit 3.10.

EXHIBIT 3.10 Configurable Workflows

Advantages	Reduction in time to value on the GRC investment
	Reduction in the implementation cost of the solution
	Reduction in the total cost of ownership of the solution
	Improved operational performance in managed processes
	Avoidance of constraints placed on processes by limitations of the tool
Factors to consider	Degree of definition and particular requirements in organization's processes
	Number of varying processes and workflows across stakeholders
	Amount of customization required to fit solution to needs

(iv) Conclusions

The increased complexity and stakes of risk and compliance functions have resulted in strengthened demand for an understanding of the risks that face an organization. While this raises the profile of compliance and risk management with corporate leadership, it also presents new challenges. Few directors or senior executives outside of risk and compliance management have in-depth exposure to the methods and measurements used by practitioners. As a result, they are often unable to engage in detailed discussion of risk data. Combined with lingering perceptions regarding the lack of active business contribution by risk and compliance management, this creates obstacles to meaningful discussion of risk that highlights the business consequences without providing excessive detail. To this end, research interviews identified three crucial aspects of the board of directors' engagement with organizational risk and compliance activities:

- Set risk appetite or tolerance

- Risk prioritization

- High-level management of risk and compliance management operations

Attention to these activities encouraged the research participants to focus on limiting the kind of information they provide to directors. The top concerns cited include:

- Identification of current exposure

- Performance tracking of risk appetite or tolerance

- Top risks facing the organization with the highest value at risk

- Identification of emergent risks

- Demonstration of remediation action or organizational preparedness

- The cost of operations to the organization

- Impact on business operations

In all of these areas, participants highlighted the need to avoid providing overly detailed or drill-down data. Rather, organizations emphasized a focus on overall trends and "peaks and valleys" changes in their portfolios that required action or attention.

The GRC system can assist organizations in presenting risk and compliance management performance in a meaningful context for compliance and risk management purposes. In particular, the core capabilities of GRC offer:

- Aggregation of how risks and activities impact the organization's risk profile
- Cross-divisional and cross-functional view of risk and compliance
- Insight into risk interdependencies
- Insight into relationships between key risk indicators and key performance indicators
- High-level progression of activities and performance of risk and compliance tasks

(b) Enterprise Resource Planning System

(i) Overview of ERP System

An ERP system is software that can help organizations to optimize their value chain, which requires integrating business processes across organizational boundaries through IT.

$$\text{Value Chain} = \text{Business Process Reengineering} + \text{CM} + \text{ERP}$$

ERP systems allow employees to access a full database of information that will allow them to complete their tasks. The information can also be shared with customers and suppliers as needed. The ERP system can track business transactions from their origin (at the customer) to order entry through operations and accounting until the transaction is completed. The objective of ERP systems is to integrate all functions within an organization and to become customer-oriented (customer-centric). Companies are using ERP systems for increased business competitiveness.

The SAP R3 system is an example of ERP. Its objective is to standardize business processes across business units, functional departments, and product lines. R3 is the broadest and most feature-rich ERP system. SAP provides collaborative ebusiness solutions between companies and their customers and suppliers. More specifically, SAP integrates front-office and back-office systems, internal and external systems, and unstructured and structured information. The IT department will play a major role in implementing ERP systems.

SAP and other vendors use push technology to deliver critical software or information over the Internet to their customers. **Push technology** is an automatic transmission of information over the Internet rather than making users search for it with their browsers. Advantages of push technology are speed and convenience; disadvantages include information overload and clogging up the Internet communications links with data traffic.

(ii) Advantages and Disadvantages of ERP Systems

Advantages of ERP systems include: elimination of costly, inflexible legacy systems; improvement of work processes; increase in access to data for operational decision making; and standardization of IT infrastructure (hardware, software, OSs, and databases). *Disadvantages* of ERP systems include: expense and time in implementation, difficulty in implementing change in the organization, risks in using a single vendor, and difficulty in integrating with other computer systems.

(c) Customer Relationship Management System

Marketing departments are acquiring or developing CRM systems to survive in the customer-centric environment and to establish a one-to-one business relationship with customers.

Some define CRM as a call center solution. Some view it as sales force automation; to others, it is direct mail, marketing automation, or simply a web page. Many companies see it as a front-end application only, interacting at the point of contact, point of purchase, or customer support. Others believe the secret to CRM success is in the back-end activities, such as data mining, data warehousing, data distribution, and data sharing. A properly designed and implemented CRM system encompasses all of these and much more. It is better to view the CRM system as a bridge system, not as a front-end system or back-end system.

To derive benefits from a CRM system, organizations *must*:

- Understand that customers come first, products and services come next.
- Understand the customer cycle as "get, keep, grow" or "acquire, support, retain."
- Understand that customers "pull" the company's products or services of their choice.
- Understand that marketers "push" company's products or services on to customers.
- Understand that pull and push concepts must be linked together to create interactive, learning relationships between the company and its customers. This linkage, in turn, results in increasing customer satisfaction and loyalty, share of customer, return on sales, and return on investment.
- Establish a strong linkage between the CRM system and financial performance, such as return on sales and return on investment.

(d) Electronic Data Systems

The scope of electronic data systems includes a discussion of electronic funds transfer, electronic commerce, mobile commerce, electronic auctions, and electronic data interchange.

(i) Electronic Funds Transfer

Basically, an electronic funds transfer (EFT) system transfers money and other information electronically from one institution to another. A by-product of this service is the reduction of mountains of paper and time delays, thereby gaining cost efficiencies. For example, banks can transfer money from an account in one bank to another account in another bank, and the federal government can deposit benefits directly into recipients' bank accounts.

A trend in EFT systems is the transmittal of tax information electronically to tax authorities at a central processor. Information such as the amount, tax due, and employer identification number are provided to the central processor. Some advantages of this approach include fewer errors, lower costs, more timely deposits, and increased elimination of float associated with delays in moving funds.

Some state governments distribute public aid benefits electronically. Benefit recipients who use this system are given magnetic cards with their photographs, which they insert into special electronic devices at the participating check-cashing centers or banks. The cards access computer records to tell the agents the amounts of benefits due.

Other applications include payment of unemployment insurance benefits. Claimants can call the government agency and enter their Social Security number and personal identification number (PIN). After successfully answering certification questions, claimants are informed that they are to receive their benefits. Participants then gain access to their weekly payments with a plastic card and a PIN through automated teller machines (ATMs) or point-of-sale (POS) terminals.

Those who already have a bank account are given the option to directly deposit their benefits, and those who prefer to receive state-issued checks may continue to do so. This is a clear example of integration of such diverse technologies such as POS, EFT, and ATMs.

(ii) Electronic Commerce
(A) Overview

Electronic commerce (e-commerce) is defined as a place where buyers and sellers are connected using computers and networks (the Internet) to buy and sell goods and services. The term "electronic business" (e-business) is much broader than e-commerce because the former includes distribution of information and customer support, which are lacking in the latter. In other words, e-commerce is a subset of e-business.

E-COMMERCE AND VALUE CHAIN

E-commerce is a web-enabled value chain since the Internet is the enabling technology. Business applications are located on web servers for wide access to employees and selective access to customers and suppliers.

A value chain is created in e-commerce among demand planning, supply planning, and demand fulfillment. **Demand planning** consists of analyzing buying patterns and developing customer demand forecasts. **Supply planning** consists of supply allocation, inventory planning, distribution planning, procurement planning, and transportation planning. **Demand fulfillment** consists of order capturing, customer verification, order promising, backlog management, and order fulfillment.

(B) Electronic Commerce Models

E-commerce is the process of buying, selling, or exchanging products, services, or information via computer networks. At least ten e-commerce models exist between four parties such as businesses, retailers, consumers, and governments where these parties are constantly interacting with each other.

These ten e-commerce models are: retailer-to-retailer (R2R), direct-to-consumer (D2C), maker-to-buyer (M2B), business-to-consumer (B2C), business-to-business (B2B), consumer-to-consumer (C2C), government-to-citizen (G2C), government-to-business (G2B), consumer-to-business (C2B), and exchange-to-exchange (E2E).

In the R2R model, a retailer establishes an informal business partnership arrangement with non-competing retailers so they co-exist in customers' minds in terms of cross-selling of complementary and supplementary products. This is a win-win situation for both retail partners.

Example 1: Birchbox, a beauty retailer, is a digital subscription service provider for its members. When a new customer signs up at Birchbox, these customers can buy beauty products from other beauty retailers such as Sephora and Ulta. Birchbox uses the R2R model.

In the D2C model, retailers sell their goods directly to consumers without any middleman such as suppliers or distributors.

Example 2: Fashion show retailers such as Ralph Lauren and Burberry are selling the fashion clothes worn by models in the show directly to the show audience without any middlemen.

This new marketing them is called "see now, buy now." These fashion show retailers are using the D2C model.

Example 3: Everlane Company, an online fashion retailer, sells goods directly to consumers at a lower price because it eliminated the cost of all the middlemen such as wholesalers, distributors, suppliers, and vendors. Everlane uses the D2C model.

In the M2B model, ordinary consumers make their own products at their home (makers) and sell them to other ordinary consumers (buyers). They use e-commerce websites such as Etsy.com and Amazon.com to sell their products.

Example 4: The maker movement products that are self-made and self-sold include clothes, food, beer, home decorating items, crochet, craft work, jewelry, canning of fruits and vegetables, making of pickles with vegetables, making of jams and jellies with fruits, and growing of fruits and vegetables in the backyard of homes.

In the B2C model, online retail stores sell goods directly to consumers through their websites. Both electronic data interchange (EDI) and electronic funds transfer (EFT) systems are critical components of the sales process for many online retailers.

Example 5: Retailers such as Walmart, Amazon, Target, Macy's, Best Buy, and eBay operate using the B2C model.

In the B2B model, the Internet enables existing relationships between two or more companies in exchanging and procuring goods and services. Both EDI and EFT systems are the underlying technologies in both B2C and B2B enabling online buyers and sellers through a supply chain.

Example 6: Walmart and other major retailers procure merchandise from their manufacturers, wholesalers, suppliers, distributors, and vendors using the B2B model. Procurement managers at retail companies can also use the B2B model to buy goods through electronic auctioning sites.

In the C2C model, consumers buy and sell goods (used or unused) with other consumers through online ordering, bidding, and auction sites.

Example 7: Two popular applications of the C2C model are classified advertisements and auctions. Regular customers buy and sell goods (used or unused) to other regular customers through websites such as eBay, PayPal, Amazon, Craigslist, and Zaplye. The website for Zaplye deals with pre-owned luxury goods market.

In the G2C model, the federal government, for example, uses the Internet to reach its citizens and consumers for a variety of information-dissemination purposes and financial transactions

Example 8: The U.S. Office of Personnel Management (OPM) uses the Internet to announce job openings in the federal government to the U.S. citizens though a program called USAJOBS.

In the G2B model, all levels of government deals with business entities, vendors, contractors, and suppliers to procure goods and services.

Example 9: Various governmental agencies at federal, state, and local levels use the G2B model for electronic procurement purposes with request for information (RFI) and request for proposal (RFP) documents.

In the C2B model, mostly individual consumers and some business customers request lower prices from selling companies, and these companies, in turn, come back with the lowest price. These requests include prices for airline tickets; hotels; car rentals; vacations; cruises; resorts; and insurance policies for life, health, auto, and home coverage.

Example 10: John, a consumer, buys vacation tickets from discounted airline companies using the C2B model.

In the E2E model, the electronic exchanges formally connect to one another for the purpose of exchanging information.

Example 11: Electronic exchanges of buying and selling stocks and bonds occur between stock brokers/dealers and stock market exchanges using the E2E model. The New York Stock Exchange and the London Stock Exchange are examples of E2E model and auction model.

(C) E-Commerce Security Risks and Controls

E-commerce security risks arising from technical threats include DoSs, zombies, phishing, web server and web page hijacking, botnets, and malicious code (e.g., viruses, worms, and Trojan horses). Risks arising from nontechnical threats include pretexting (impersonating) and social engineering.

E-commerce requires robust authentication due to potential risks, such as cyberattacks and intrusions. The next security controls help to prevent and detect such attacks and intrusions:

- Multifactor authentication methods
- One-time passwords
- Continuous authentication with digital signatures and digital certificates
- Defense-in-depth strategies
- Need-to-know and least-privilege access privileges
- Role-based access controls
- Logging and monitoring practices
- Software patch management program
- Security incident response handling capabilities

(D) E-Commerce Security Classes

For the purposes of exploring the relevant security issues, e-commerce can be divided into four basic classes: (1) electronic mail (email), (2) EDI, (3) information transactions, and (4) financial transactions.

E-mail Security Issues. The use of Internet email to carry business-critical communications is growing exponentially. While email provides a low-cost means of communication with customers, suppliers, and partners, a number of security issues are related to the use of email. The security issues include: Internet email addresses are easily spoofed.

- It is nearly impossible to be certain who created and sent an email message based on the address alone.
- Internet email messages can be easily modified.

- SMTP mail provides no integrity checking.

- The contents of an email message can be read by unintended recipients at a number of points.

- There is usually no guarantee of delivery with Internet email. Although some mail systems support return receipts, when such receipts work at all, they often signify only that the user's server (not necessarily the user) has received the message.

These weaknesses make it important for organizations to issue policies defining acceptable use of email for business purposes.

Electronic Data Interchange Security Issues. Traditional EDI systems allow preestablished trading partners to electronically exchange business data through value-added networks (VANs). The Internet can provide the connectivity needed to support EDI at a substantial cost savings over VANs. However, the Internet does not provide the security services (integrity, confidentiality, and nonrepudiation) required for business EDI. Similar to email over the Internet, EDI transactions are vulnerable to modification, disclosure, or interruption when sent over the Internet. The use of cryptography to provide the required security services has changed this; consequently, many companies and government agencies are moving to Internet-based EDI.

SCOPE OF E-COMMERCE

E-commerce encompasses a broader commerce environment than EDI. Because of this, EDI is a subset of e-commerce. Similarly, e-commerce is a subset of e-business.

Information Transactions Security Issues. Providing information (e.g., stock quotes, news) is a major and costly element of commerce. Using the Internet to provide these services is substantially less expensive than fax, telephone, or postal mail services. Integrity and availability of the information provided are key security concerns that require security controls and policy.

Financial Transactions Security Issues. Computer networks are used to process financial transactions, such as checks, debit cards, credit cards, and EFT. Similar to EDI over VANs, the connectivity options have been limited, and leased lines are expensive. The Internet provides an opportunity for cost savings in electronic financial transactions. The use of the Internet to carry these types of transactions replaces the physical presentation or exchange of cash, checks, or debit/credit cards with the electronic equivalent. Each of these forms of transactions involves the use of cryptography to provide for integrity, confidentiality, authentication, and nonrepudiation. For example, a standard known as Secure Electronic Transactions SET is used for processing credit card transactions over public networks. Use of SET involves three-way transactions among buyer, seller, and a financial institution (a bank).

(E) E-Commerce Software

E-commerce software should support these tasks:

- **Catalog management.** Catalog management software combines different product data formats into a standard format for uniform viewing, aggregating, and integrating catalog data into a central repository for easy access, retrieval, and updating of pricing and availability changes.

- **Product configuration.** Customers need help when an item they are purchasing has many components and options. Buyers use web-based product configuration software to build the product they need online with little or no help from salespeople.

- **Shopping cart facilities.** Today many e-commerce sites use an electronic shopping cart to track the items selected for purchase, allowing shoppers to view what is in their cart and add new items to it or remove items from it.

- **E-commerce transaction processing.** E-commerce transaction processing software takes data from the shopping cart and calculates volume discounts, sales tax, and shipping costs to arrive at the total cost.

- **Website traffic data analysis software** captures visitor information, including who is visiting the website, what search engine and keywords they used to find the site, how long their web browser viewed the site, the date and time of each visit, and which pages were displayed. These data are placed into a web log file for future analysis to improve the website's performance.

(F) E-Commerce Infrastructure

Key technology infrastructure for e-commerce applications include web server hardware, server OS, server software, e-commerce software, VPN, value-added network (VAN), and the Internet, intranet, or extranet. Four strategies for successful e-commerce are listed next.

1. Develop an effective website that creates an attractive presence and that meets the needs of its visitors (customers).

2. Contract out with website hosting service providers or storefront brokers.

3. Build traffic into the website through a metatag, which is a special HTML tag that contains keywords about the website.

4. Analyze website traffic to identify which search engines are effective for the business.

EXAMPLES OF BEST PRACTICES IN E-COMMERCE

- There should be a set of security mechanisms and procedures that, taken together, constitute a security architecture for e-commerce (deals with architecture).

- There should be measures in place to ensure the choice of the correct protocols for the application and the environment as well as the proper use and exploitation of their features and compensation for their limitations (deals with infrastructure/protocol).

- There should be a mechanism in place to mediate between the public network (the Internet) and an organization's private network (deals with infrastructure or firewall).

- There should be a means to communicate across the Internet in a secure manner (deals with infrastructure/virtual private network).

- There should be a process whereby participants in an e-commerce transaction can be uniquely and positively identified (deals with authentication/digital certificates).

- There should be a mechanism by which the initiator of an e-commerce transaction can be uniquely associated with it (deals with authentication/digital signatures).

- There should be an infrastructure to manage and control public key pairs and their corresponding certificates (deals with authentication/PKI).

- There should be procedures in place to control changes to an e-commerce presence (deals with applications/change control).

- E-commerce applications should maintain logs of their use, which should be monitored by responsible personnel (deals with applications/logs and monitoring).

- There should be methods and procedures to recognize security breaches when they occur (deals with applications/intrusion detection).

- There should be features in e-commerce applications to reconstruct the activity performed by the applications (deals with applications/auditability).

- There should be a means to maintain a provable association between an e-commerce transaction and the person who entered it (deals with applications or nonrepudiation).

- There should be protections in place to ensure that data collected about individuals is not disclosed without their consent or used for purposes other than that for which it was collected (deals with applications/privacy).

- There should be a means to ensure the confidentiality of data communicated between customers and vendors (deals with data protection/encryption).

- There should be mechanisms to protect e-commerce presences and their supporting private networks from computer viruses and to prevent them from propagating viruses to customers and vendors (deals with data protection/virus scanning).

- There should be protection over the devices used to access the Internet (deals with availability/protecting the user environment).

- There should be features within e-commerce architecture to keep all components from failing and for components to repair themselves if they should fail (deals with availability/fault tolerance).

- There should be a plan and procedures to continue e-commerce activities in the event of an extended outage of required resources for normal processing (deals with availability/business continuity planning).

- There should be a commonly understood set of practices and procedures to define management's intentions for the security of e-commerce (deals with policy and governance/policy).

- There should be measures in place to prevent information about customers from being disclosed and not used for purposes other than that for which it was obtained, without the customer's permission (deals with policy and governance or privacy).

- There should be shared responsibility within an organization for e-commerce security (deals with policy and governance/oversight).

- There should be communication from vendors to customers about the level of security in an e-commerce presence (deals with policy and governance or notification).

- There should be a regular program of audit and assessment of the security of e-commerce environments and applications to provide assurance that controls are present and effective (deals with policy and governance/auditing and assurance).

Source: E-Commerce Security, Enterprise Best Practices, Information Systems Audit and Control Research Foundation (ISACRF), now known as the IT Governance Institute, Rolling Meadows, IL, 2000.

(iii) Mobile Commerce

Mobile commerce (m-commerce) is conducted using mobile devices, such as smartphones, digital tablets, digital phones, and mobile computers, requiring a connection to the Internet. Consumers use these devices from any location to research product information, compare prices, make purchases, and communicate with customer support. Retailers can use these devices for tasks such as price checks, inventory inquiries, and payment processing. M-commerce uses the wireless application protocol. M-commerce is any business activity conducted over a wireless telecommunications network. Both B2B and B2C e-commerce transactions can use m-commerce technology. Security risks for m-commerce are more severe than those of e-commerce due to heavily and extensively connected mobile devices.

(A) Cyber Threats to Mobile Devices Used in M-Commerce

A multitude of threats exist for mobile devices, such as application of social engineering methods (i.e., using deceptive marketing practices on system users by creating illegal and unethical websites, emails, text messages, faxes, and voice mails); exploitation of social networking media due to blind sharing of information from unauthenticated users; use of mobile botnets controlling computers remotely; spreading of mobile malware, such as viruses and worms; exploitation of mobile applications (e.g., creating fraudulent banking apps for checking balances, paying bills, transferring funds, or locating nearby automated teller machines and banking centers); and exploitation of day-to-day m-commerce work using illegal mobile devices and apps.

(B) Risks to M-Commerce

Several risks exist in m-commerce, similar to e-commerce. For example, the credit card reader functionality of smartphones has the potential risk to enable criminal activity, such as skimming and carding. **Skimming** is the theft of credit card information using card readers, or skimmers, to record and store victim's data, which is accomplished with legitimate transactions. **Carding** is the process of testing the validity of stolen credit card numbers, which can be done on websites that support real-time transaction processing, to determine if the credit card information can be successfully processed.

(iv) Electronic Auctions

Another extension of e-commerce is electronic auctions (e-auctions), which are conducted online through the Internet. Near-perfect market information is available about prices, products, current supply, and current demand, which benefits all parties. Several variations of e-auctions exist:

- A seller invites consecutive bids from multiple buyers, and the bidding price either increases or decreases sequentially (forward auction). This is a model of one seller and many buyers. The forward auction is practiced mostly with the C2C e-commerce model.

- A buyer invites bids, and multiple sellers respond with the price reduced sequentially, and the lowest bid wins (backward or reverse auction). This is a model of one buyer and multiple sellers. The reverse auction is practiced with B2B, G2B, and C2B e-commerce models.

- Multiple buyers propose bidding prices, and multiple sellers respond with asking prices simultaneously. Both prices are matched based on the quantities of items available on both sides (double auction). This is a model of many buyers and many sellers.

- Negotiations and bargaining power can take place between one buyer and one seller due to supply and demand. This is a model of one buyer and one seller.

- Sellers and buyers interact in one industry or for one commodity (vertical auction). Prices are determined dynamically through the bidding process.

Limitations of e-auctions include minimal security for C2C auctions (i.e., no encryption), possibility of fraud (i.e., shipping defective products), and limited buyer participation because the e-auctions may be invitation only or open to dealers only. B2B, G2B, and C2B auctions are secure due to use of private, leased lines.

(v) Electronic Data Interchange

EDI systems provide computer-to-computer communication. These systems are becoming a normal way of exchanging or transmitting documents, transactions, records, quantitative and financial information, and computer-related messages from one computer to another. Some examples of transactions and documents involved include purchase orders, invoices, shipping notices, receiving advice, acknowledgments, and payments. When payment is involved, the EDI system can be referred to as an EFT system.

(A) EDI System

Essentially, the EDI system works in this way:

- The buyer identifies the item to be purchased. Data is entered into the purchasing application system. Translation software creates an EDI purchase order, which is sent electronically to the supplier. The same order is sent to the buyer's accounts payable and goods receiving system.

- A functional acknowledgment, indicating receipt of the order, is automatically generated and electronically transmitted to the buyer.

- The supplier's computer sends the order information to the supplier's shipping and invoicing systems.

- When the buyer receives the ship notice, the data is electronically entered into the receiving system file.

- The receipt notice is electronically transmitted to the accounts payable application system.

- The ship notice is electronically transmitted to the invoicing application system.

- An invoice is electronically generated by the supplier and transmitted to the buyer. The same information is sent to the supplier's accounts receivable system.

- The invoice is received by the buyer's computer and is translated into the buyer's format. The invoice, receiving notice, and purchase order are electronically matched and reconciled.

- The buyer electronically transmits payment to the supplier's bank through their bank. An electronic remittance advice is transmitted to the supplier.

- Upon receipt of the remittance and notice of payment, the data is transmitted into the accounts receivable system, and the buyer account is updated. The buyer is given credit for payment.

(B) Components of an EDI System

The components of an EDI system are standards, software, and networks. EDI standards consist of formatting standards and communication standards. **Formatting standards** deal with the type, sequence, and content of an electronic document. **Communication standards** cover baud rate, protocols, electronic envelopes, and message transmission times. Standards provide a set of common rules, in terms of syntax and formatting, for the development of electronic communications.

In terms of software, a translation program is needed to translate company-specific data to EDI standard format for transmission. A reverse translation is performed when data arrive at the organization from external sources.

In terms of networks, there are two approaches in common use. In a direct network, the computers of the trading partners are linked directly, usually through dial-up modems. A direct network is effective for a limited number of trading partners. As the number of trading partners increases, it is difficult to maintain open lines for all trading partners. The second choice is to use a third-party network (VAN) that acts as an intermediary between trading partners. A VAN maintains a mailbox for both the sender and the receiver.

The VAN receives purchase orders from the sender (buyer), sorts them by seller, and places each seller's purchase orders in his mailbox. At a later time, the seller can dial in to the VAN and retrieve its mail in the form of electronic purchase orders. This approach allows each trading partner to create only one electronic transmission to the VAN rather than each trading partner having to create a separate electronic transmission.

(C) Benefits of EDI

A major benefit of EDI is the ability to load data, without rekeying, from various formats and place it where it is needed in a different format for further processing. Besides savings due to reductions in document mailing and processing costs, decreases in data entry personnel costs, and reductions in inventory stock levels, organizations are realizing other significant benefits, including:

- Improved operational efficiency in warehousing, shipping, purchasing, and receiving areas
- Increased sales
- Increased customer responsiveness
- Increased ability to compete
- Quick access to better information in a timely manner

The users of EDI include organizations in the trucking, retail, shipping, grocery, health care, pharmaceutical, and automotive industries; government; and others.

3.4 IT Infrastructure and Networks

Three major topics are presented in this section: (1) OSs, mainframe computers, terminals, work-stations, and servers; (2) network communications, such as LAN, wide area network (WAN), and VPN; and (3) network connections, such as routers, switches, bridges, and gateways. In addition, the operational roles and responsibilities of IT staff are defined with required separation of duties among them, including service-level agreements with the user community.

(a) Operating Systems, Mainframe Computers, Terminals, Workstations, and Servers

This section discusses highly interrelated and integrated topics—OSs, mainframe computers, terminals, workstations, and servers—because they all work together with their vast amount of computing power to process users' data In addition, security over web servers is highlighted in terms of their security levels and security controls.

(i) Operating Systems

An OS is an integrated collection of software routines that service the sequencing and processing of computer programs by a computer; it is often called systems software. Many control operations are concentrated in systems software, which is defined as a collection of programs or systems that help interconnect and/or control the elements of input devices, computer processing operations, output devices, data files, application programs, and hardware. Typically, systems software is provided by outside vendors.

The OS may provide many services, such as computer resource allocation, computer job scheduling, input/output (I/O) control, and data management. The OS software controls the allocation and usage of hardware resources, such as memory, CPU time, disk space, and peripheral devices. The OS is often called the brain of a computer, whether it is a mainframe computer, PC, desktop computer, palm computer, laptop computer, tablet computer, or mobile devices (e.g., smartphones, digital pads and tablets). The OS is the foundation software on which applications' software depends. Popular OSs for workstations include Windows, Mac OS, Linux, and UNIX. Network connectivity devices, such as routers, have proprietary OSs; and many embedded systems, such as cell phones, digital cameras, and audio players, also use OSs. Although OSs are predominantly software based, partial or full implementations can be made in hardware in the form of firmware.

An OS is a program that runs on a computer and provides a software platform on which other programs can run. In addition, an OS is responsible for processing user input commands, sending output to a display, interacting with storage devices to store and retrieve data, and controlling peripheral devices, such as printers and modems.

OS data exist in both nonvolatile and volatile states. **Nonvolatile data** is data that persists even after a computer is powered down, such as a file system stored on a hard drive. **Volatile data** is data on a live system that is lost after a computer is powered down, such as the current network connections to and from the system. *Both types of data are useful to internal auditors when they perform IT system audits.*

(A) Nonvolatile Data

The primary source of nonvolatile data within an OS is the file system. The file system is also usually the largest and richest source of data within the OS, containing most of the information recovered during a typical forensic event. The file system provides storage for the OS on one or more media. It typically contains many types of files, each of which may be of value to analysts in different situations. In addition, important residual data can be recovered from unused file system space. Several types of nonvolatile data commonly found within OS file systems are discussed next.

- **Configuration files.** The OS may use configuration files to store OS and application settings. For example, configuration files could list the services to be started automatically after system boot and specify the location of log files and temporary files. Users might also have individual OS and application configuration files that contain user-specific information and preferences, such as hardware-related settings (e.g., screen resolution and printer settings) and file associations. Configuration files can contain users and groups, password files, and scheduled jobs.

- **Users and groups.** The OS keeps a record of its user accounts and groups. Account information may this information:

  - Group membership

  - Account name and description

  - Account permissions

  - Account status (e.g., active, disabled)

  - Path to the account's home directory

- **Password files.** The OS may store password hashes in data files. Various password-cracking utilities may be used to convert a password hash to its cleartext equivalent for certain OSs.

- **Scheduled jobs.** The OS maintains a list of scheduled tasks that are to be performed automatically at certain times (e.g., perform a virus scan every week). Information that can be gleaned from this list includes the task name, the program used to perform the task, command line switches and arguments, and the days and times when the task is to be performed.

- **Logs.** OS log files contain information about various OS events and may also hold application-specific event information. Depending on the OS, logs may be stored in text files, proprietary-format binary files, or databases. Some OSs write log entries to two or more separate files. The OS logs can contain this information:

  □ Systems events

  □ Audit records

  □ Application events

  □ Command history

  □ Recently accessed files

  □ Application files

  □ Data files

  □ Swap files

  □ Dump files

  □ Hibernation files

  □ Temporary files

- **System events.** System events are operational actions performed by OS components, such as shutting down the system or starting a service. Typically, failed events and the most significant successful events are logged, but many OSs permit system administrators to specify which types of events will be logged. The details logged for each event also vary widely. Each event is usually time-stamped; other supporting information could include event codes, status codes, and usernames.

- **Audit records.** Audit records contain security event information, such as successful and failed authentication attempts and security policy changes. OSs typically permit system administrators to specify which types of events should be audited. Administrators also can configure some OSs to log successful, failed, or all attempts to perform certain actions.

- **Application events.** Application events are significant operational actions performed by applications, such as application startup and shutdown, application failures, and major application configuration changes.

- **Command history.** Some OSs have separate log files (typically for each user) that contain a history of the OS commands performed by each user.

- **Recently accessed files.** An OS might log the most recent file accesses or other usage, creating a list of the most recently accessed files.

- **Application files.** Applications can be composed of many types of files, including these:

  □ Executables

  □ Scripts

- ☐ Documentation
- ☐ Configuration files
- ☐ Log files
- ☐ History files
- ☐ Graphics
- ☐ Sounds
- ☐ Icons

- **Data files.** Data files store information for applications. Examples of common data files are listed next.

  - ☐ Text files
  - ☐ Word processing documents
  - ☐ Spreadsheets
  - ☐ Databases
  - ☐ Audio files
  - ☐ Graphics files

  In addition, when data are printed, most OSs create one or more temporary print files that contain the print-ready version of the data.

- **Swap files.** Most OSs use swap files in conjunction with random access memory (RAM) to provide temporary storage for data often used by applications. Swap files essentially extend the amount of memory available to a program by allowing pages (or segments) of data to be swapped in and out of RAM. Swap files may contain a broad range of OS and application information, such as usernames, password hashes, and contact information.

- **Dump files.** Some OSs have the ability to store the contents of memory automatically during an error condition to assist in subsequent troubleshooting. The file that holds the stored memory contents is known as a dump file.

- **Hibernation file.** A hibernation file is created to preserve the current state of a system (typically a laptop) by recording memory and open files before shutting off the system. When the system is next turned on, the state of the system is restored.

- **Temporary files.** During the installation of an OS, application, or OS or application updates and upgrades, temporary files are often created. Although such files typically are deleted at the end of the installation process, this does not always occur. In addition, temporary files are created when many applications are run; again, such files are usually deleted when the application is terminated, but this does not always happen. Temporary files could contain copies of other files on the system, application data, or other information.

- **BIOS.** Although file systems are the primary source of nonvolatile data, another source of interest is the BIOS. The BIOS contains many types of hardware-related information, such as the attached devices (e.g., CD-ROM drives and hard drives), the types of connections and interrupt request line assignments (e.g., serial, USB, and network card), motherboard components (e.g., processor type and speed, cache size, and memory information), system security settings, and hot keys. The BIOS also communicates with redundant array of independent disk (RAID) drivers and displays the information provided by the drivers. For example, the BIOS views a hardware RAID as a single drive and a software RAID as multiple drives. The BIOS typically permits the user to set passwords, which restrict access to the BIOS settings and may prevent the system from booting if the password is not supplied. The BIOS also holds the system date and time.

(B) Volatile Data

OSs execute within system RAM. While the OS is functioning, the contents of RAM are constantly changing. At any given time, RAM might contain many types of data and information that could be of interest. For example, RAM often contains frequently and recently accessed data, such as data files, password hashes, and recent commands. In addition, like file systems, RAM can contain residual data in slack and free space. Other significant types of volatile data that might exist within an OS include network configuration, network connections, running processes, open files, login sessions, and OS time.

Slack Space. Memory slack space is much less deterministic than file slack space. For example, an OS generally manages memory in units known as pages or blocks and allocates them to requesting applications. Sometimes, although an application might not request an entire unit, it is given one anyway. Residual data could therefore reside in the unit of memory allocated to an application, although it might not be addressable by the application. For performance and efficiency, some OSs vary the size of the units they allocate, which tends to result in smaller memory slack spaces.

Free Space. Memory pages are allocated and deallocated much like file clusters. When they are not allocated, memory pages are often collected into a common pool of available pages, a process often referred to as garbage collection. It is not uncommon for residual data to reside in these reusable memory pages, which are analogous to unallocated file clusters.

Network Configuration. Although many elements of networking, such as network interface card (NIC) drivers and configuration settings, are typically stored in the file system, networking is dynamic in nature. For example, many hosts are assigned IP addresses dynamically by another host, meaning that their IP addresses are not part of the stored configuration. Many hosts also have multiple network interfaces defined, such as wired, wireless, VPN, and modem; the current network configuration indicates which interfaces are currently in use. Users also may be able to alter network interface configurations from the defaults, such as manually changing IP addresses. Accordingly, analysts should use the current network configuration, not the stored configuration, whenever possible.

Network Connections. The OS facilitates connections between the system and other systems. Most OSs can provide a list of current incoming and outgoing network connections, and some OSs can list recent connections as well. For incoming connections, the OS typically indicates which resources are being used, such as file shares and printers. Most OSs can also provide a list of the ports and IP addresses at which the system is listening for connections.

Running Processes. Processes are the programs that are currently executing on a computer. They include services offered by the OS and applications run by administrators and users. Most OSs offer ways to view a list of the currently running processes. This list can be studied to determine the services that are active on the system, such as a Web server, and the programs that individual users are running (e.g., encryption utility, word processor, and email client). Process lists may also indicate which command options were used. Identifying the running processes is also helpful to identify programs that should be running but have been disabled or removed, such as antivirus software and firewalls.

Open Files. OSs may maintain a list of open files, which typically include the user or process that opened each file.

Login Sessions. OSs typically maintain information about currently logged in users (and the start time and duration of each session), previous successful and failed logons, privileged usage, and impersonation. However, login session information might be available only if the computer has been configured to audit logon attempts. Logon records can help to determine a user's computer usage habits and confirm whether a user account was active when a given event occurred.

Operating System Time. The OS maintains the current time and stores daylight savings time and time zone information. This information can be useful when building a timeline of events or correlating events among different systems. Analysts should be aware that the time presented by the OS might differ from that presented by the BIOS because of OS-specific settings, such as time zone.

(C) OS Response to Failures

OS response to failures can be classified into three general categories: system reboot, emergency system restart, and system cold start.

System reboot is performed after shutting down the system in a controlled manner in response to a trusted computing base (TCB) failure. For example, when the TCB detects that space in some of its critical tables is exhausted or finds inconsistent object data structures, it closes all objects, aborts all active user processes, and restarts with no user process in execution. Before restart, however, the recovery mechanisms make a best effort to correct the source of inconsistency. Occasionally the mere termination of all processes frees up some important resources, allowing restart with enough resources available. Note that system rebooting is useful when the recovery mechanisms can determine that TCB and user data structures affecting system security and integrity are, in fact, in a consistent and synchronized state.

Emergency system restart is done after a system fails in an uncontrolled manner in response to a TCB or media failure. In such cases, TCB and user objects on nonvolatile storage belonging to processes active at the time of TCB or media failure may be left in an inconsistent state. The system enters maintenance mode, recovery is performed automatically, and the system restarts with no user processes in progress after bringing up the system in a consistent state.

System cold start takes place when unexpected TCB or media failure takes place and the recovery procedures cannot bring the system to a consistent state. TCB and user objects may remain in an inconsistent state following attempts to recover automatically. Intervention of administrative personnel is required to bring the system to a consistent state from maintenance mode.

(ii) Mainframe Computers, Terminals, and Workstations

OS software, mainframe computers, PCs, terminals, workstations, and servers are tightly connected in a network, and they work in harmonious ways in handling computing jobs and services.

- **Mainframe computers** are big computers in terms of their memory, size, speed, and processing power. They are suitable to handling heavy-duty computing tasks required in databases and complex networks. They have the ability to support many users connected to the computer by terminals. Other computers, such as PCs and terminals, are connected to mainframes to share resources and computing power.

- A **terminal** is a networking device consisting of a video adapter, a monitor, and a keyboard. It is capable of sending and/or receiving information over a communications channel. A terminal does little no or no computer processing on its own; instead, it is connected to a computer with a communications link over a cable.

- A **workstation** is a hardware device that can be defined in several ways, depending on its configuration. A workstation can be:

  □ A combination of input, output, and computing hardware that an individual can use for work.

  □ A powerful stand-alone computer used in computer-aided design work requiring heavy-duty calculations and graphics.

  □ A PC or terminal connected to a network.

  □ Workstations also can provide an operator–system interface, and they may not require external access.

(iii) Servers

A **server** is a host computer that provides one or more services for other hosts over a network as a primary function. A server is deployed in several ways, as discussed next. A server can be:

- A computer or device on a network that manages network resources such as files, programs, and data.

- A computer program that provides services to other computer programs in the same or another computer.

- A computer program running a server program and is based on client/server architecture, where the server software receives requests from the client, processes the requests, and returns data to the client.

- A computer running administrative software that controls access to the network and its resources, such as printers and disk drives, and provides resources to computers functioning as workstations on the network.

One of the most common motivations for using a server is resource sharing. The goal is to provide transparent access to organization-wide data distributed across PCs and mainframe computers while protecting the security and integrity of that data.

The database management system (DBMS) handles the logical organization of the data and communicates with the server OS to access the data storage devices. A server can be either a LAN database server or a host database accessed via a gateway. The network OS provides software connectivity between the server database management systems software and the LAN.

There are many types of servers, and each server has its own specific purpose. Servers pose specific risks due to the concentration of data in one place. For example, a file server is a computer and storage device for storing files; a web server, for access to web content; a DNS server, for domain name services; a database server, for access to relational tables; and an email server, for access to email services.

Today's servers are very powerful and fast and perform diverse functions, such as transferring files, storing data, communicating outside the network, and processing databases. Because a LAN server is charged with moving large quantities of data from disk and memory onto the network, it is by nature I/O bound rather than computer bound, resulting in degraded performance. One way to curb memory operations is with caching, a performance-enhancing technique that establishes a small, very-high-speed static RAM cache (or buffer) between main memory and the processor. This approach frees the LAN server from repeated calls to memory. The next time the processor goes looking for data, it first tries to retrieve it from cache memory.

Basically, there are two types of servers: dedicated and nondedicated. Which one is chosen depends on the significance and risk level of the work done on the network.

In a **dedicated server**, the computer running the server software cannot be used as a workstation, hence the name "dedicated." *Advantages* of dedicated servers include the fact that they are easier to manage because all data are in one place, and they are faster to run because servers do not have a local user to serve. *Disadvantages* of dedicated servers are: it is harder to make resources available on an ad hoc basis because setting up a server is difficult and time consuming; and if the server fails, all users are forced to discontinue their work because all resources are centralized (i.e., all users either work or do not work).

A **nondedicated server** can work as both a computer and a workstation. *Advantages* of nondedicated servers include that: They allow flexibility to users because users can make resources available on their computers as necessary; and they make users LAN-literate, requiring them to take some administrative responsibilities for system backup and security. The second item can be viewed as either an advantage or a disadvantage, because with LAN literacy, users can now be network administrators. Convenience is the advantage, and unlimited access to system resources is the disadvantage of being a network administrator. *Disadvantages* of nondedicated servers include that: servers can suffer some performance degradation when being used simultaneously as workstations and computers; and users must be LAN-literate, requiring them to back up the shared data, set up security, and establish access rights to the system.

HOW TO DECIDE BETWEEN A DEDICATED SERVER AND A NONDEDICATED SERVER

- Multitasking OSs require a dedicated file server.
- Single-task OSs require a nondedicated file server.

A number of specific servers are described next.

File servers send and receive data between a workstation and the server. A file server is the heart of a LAN. Its primary purpose is to make files, printers, and plotters available to users. The file server has to transfer the entire file across the network in order to process it. In a file server approach, each workstation has to provide the services of both a front end and a back end. The bandwidth is limited too. For these reasons, database servers are better. A file server cannot be a diskless workstation. An FTP server is an example of a file server. In mobile devices, the FTP server could result in arbitrary code execution, which is a risky situation. Possible mitigations include installing patches and software updates.

Database servers (e.g., SQL) can access data from mainframes, minicomputers, and other servers, providing a critical link in distributed database systems. They employ client/server architecture for application systems in a distributed computing environment. Distributed computing enables a standard set of resources and services (i.e., directories, files, print queues, named pipes, communications queues, data, and programs) residing on different machines in different locations to be available to any workstation connected to the network. Simply stated, the client part of the client/server issues a request to the server, and the server part processes the request and returns the requested information to the client.

Client/server architecture makes it possible for a wide range of front-end client applications, such as databases, spreadsheets, and word processors, to share the same data simultaneously. A database server supports a high-performance, multi-user, relational database management system. Client/server architecture provides a high level of data integrity, concurrency control, and improved performance.

The database server's distributed update capability allows databases on multiple database servers located in different places to be updated by a single transaction. This ability to scale a system in response to database server requirements provides greater flexibility in accessing geographically dispersed data. Some database servers provide transaction buffering, automatic disk repair, and a real-time tape backup option to guard against hardware problems.

Print servers allow multiple users and multiple PCs to share an expensive printer, such as a high-speed and high-quality laser printer, and a plotter. Spooling software may come with the printer software to queue jobs ready to be printed.

Communication servers (terminal servers) allow LANs to be connected to WANs and enable a stand-alone PC to connect directly to a WAN. Communications servers share LAN user files and password files. The terminal server is a dedicated computer with an asynchronous communications controller and a network interface. Its job is to take keystrokes entered by a user and deliver them to one or more host computers on a network. Terminal servers tie together character-based terminals, printers, and their host computers. An example is a terminal server giving each teleworker access to a separate standardized virtual desktop. The terminal server simulates the look and feel of a desktop OS and provides access to applications.

A communications server can be used to provide interconnectivity between all managed network elements and the out-of-band management gateway router for administrative access to the device's console port. In the event the out-of-band management network is not able to provide connectivity due to an outage, the communications server can provide a dial-up, point-to-point protocol connection to access a network element. The auxiliary port, console port, and low-speed asynchronous serial port with an analog modem connected to the managed device also provide the capability for direct dial-up administrative access for infrastructures that do not have a communications server for management access.

Facsimile (fax) servers allow a single user or many users to transmit high-quality and high-volume documents straight from the PC or workstation disk without passing the document through the scanner of a stand-alone fax machine. Documents can be sent to and received from any fax machine. With fax modules integrated into the system, both background (fax application) and foreground (other application) processing can take place simultaneously, which increases productivity.

Image servers store and process documents, such as loan, credit, and employment applications; invoices; and purchase orders. Stored documents can be retrieved later, further transmitted to the host computer, or downloaded to a PC.

Network servers (super servers) connect LAN users to host (e.g., mainframe) computer sessions and public data networks. These interconnections become fully transparent to users. Super servers are hardware based, unlike others that are software based (e.g., disk mirroring). Fault tolerance is a major feature of these servers, using techniques such as disk duplexing. Network servers can handle heavy traffic generated by hundreds or thousands of users with faster I/O rates, and they usually come with more disk space.

Mail servers are a part of a network, acting as the central email drop for a set of users (i.e., an electronic post office). All email messages are routed to this server, which delivers them to the addressees. The recipients run their email program to read the messages. Email servers can store and forward messages across all computing resources of an organization. Email servers and clients can be configured to block specific email attachments with certain file extensions. This can help to reduce the likelihood of computer infections.

An **application server** is a computer responsible for hosting applications to user workstations. Application servers include directory services providing organization-wide distributed directories and document management services implementing a lending library concept that lets users "check out" documents for review and revision. Most server-level applications have extensive auditing capabilities, which can be of value in tracking down suspected or actual intrusions.

Redundant servers record data on two servers simultaneously. When the primary server fails for any reason, the backup server takes over.

X Window servers create and manipulate windows in response to requests from clients and send events to notify clients of user input or changes in a window's state. The server provides a portable layer between all applications and the display hardware. The X Window server typically runs on a workstation or PC with a graphics display, although some vendors offer dedicated X terminals that implement all or part of the X Window server in hardware or firmware.

Video servers are specialized versions of network servers. They store digitized video images (movies) that require far greater storage and network capacity than text files, and they distribute those images across LANs/WANs to desktop PCs. Video servers require higher levels of bandwidth to carry the data loads that video imposes. Zipf's law can be helpful in estimating the storage capacity of a video server for a movie distributor in storing movies. The law states that the most popular movie is seven times as popular as the seventh most popular movie. It is assumed that most customers will order the most popular movie more often.

Web servers on the Internet provide knowledge bases in various organizations. These servers, connected through hyperlinks, provide a global interconnected document of knowledge bases, permitting corporations, individuals, universities, and research centers all over the world to share and use common information. In other words, they make information more accessible and products more user friendly and easier to configure remotely. However, they may also add cyber risks and create new security vulnerabilities that need to be addressed. For example, software components, such as ActiveX controls or Java applets, must be installed or downloaded onto each client machine accessing the web server. In addition, FTP and email servers are used to configure remotely and to generate email notifications when certain adverse conditions occur. From a strong security viewpoint, HTTPS should be used instead of HTTP; SFTP or SCP should be used instead of FTP or TFTP; and inbound FTP and email traffic should be blocked.

HTTP server is server software that uses HTTP to serve up HTML documents and any associated files and scripts when requested by a client, such as a web browser. The connection between client and server is usually broken after the requested document or file has been served. HTTP servers are used on web and intranet sites. HTTP servers are also called web servers.

WHAT ARE SERVER-BASED THREATS?

Server-based threats occur due to poorly implemented session tracking, which may provide an avenue of attack. Similarly, user-provided input might eventually be passed to an application interface that interprets the input as part of a command, such as a SQL command. Attackers may also inject custom code into the website for subsequent browsers to process via XSS. Subtle changes introduced into the web server can radically change its behavior (e.g., turning a trusted entity into malicious one), the accuracy of the computation (e.g., changing computational algorithms to yield incorrect results), or the confidentiality of the information (e.g., disclosing collected information).

Authentication servers can be used to solve identification and authentication problems in distributed systems. Third-party authentication based on Kerberos and X.509 certificates is widely used to communicate between previously unknown entities and across heterogeneous OSs. An authentication server is used to distribute shared session keys to parties, and its responsibility is to authenticate the identity of entities in the network. Both Kerberos and X.509 certificates rely on reusable passwords, which have been subject to offline password cracking attacks. Other examples of authentication servers include RADIUS, TACACS, and DIAMETER, which are often called authentication, authorization, and accounting servers. Regardless of the type of authentication server used, an organization must install an IDS to monitor the system for password cracking attacks.

Using standardized authentication servers, such as RADIUS, TACACS+, and Kerberos, an authentication server provides centralized and robust authentication services for the management of network components. An authentication server is very scalable as it supports many user accounts and authentication sessions with the network components. It allows for the construction of template profiles or groups that are given authorization for specific tasks and access to specific resources. Users are then given an account that has been configured in the authentication server and has been assigned to a group.

Remote access servers/network access servers (RASs/NASs) are devices that provide for the initial entry point into a network. The NAS provides all the services that are normally available to a locally connected user (e.g., file and printer sharing and database and Web server access). Permission to dial into the local network is controlled by the NAS and can be granted to single users, groups, or all users. The RAS allows access to a network via a dial-up phone connection.

RAS and NAS devices can interface with authentication servers, such as RADIUS and TACACS. Regarding configuration of RAS or NAS, it is a sound approach to place dial-in users under the same access policy as those connecting via a VPN. This can be accomplished by placing the RAS either in the DMZ or within a screened subnet where the VPN gateway resides. The screened subnet architecture provides a layered defense. It ensures that only authorized users are permitted access to the internal network while still providing protection for the RAS. Only services that are needed should be allowed through the firewall from the RAS. The network administrator will ensure that logs provide a call audit trail, and, if callback procedures are used, upon establishment of the callback connection, the communications device requires the user to authenticate to the system.

RASs are devices such as VPN gateways and modem servers that facilitate connections between networks. This connection often involves systems connecting to internal systems through the RAS but can also include internal systems connecting to external or internal systems. RASs typically record the origin of each connection and might also indicate which user account was authenticated for each session. If the RAS assigns an IP address to the remote user, this is also likely to be logged. Some RASs also provide packet filtering functions, which typically perform logging similar to that provided by firewalls and routers. RASs typically work at a network level, supporting the use of many different applications. Because the servers have no understanding of the applications' functions, they usually do not record any application-specific data.

In addition to RASs, organizations typically use multiple applications that are specifically designed to provide remote access to a particular host's OSs. Examples include Secure Shell (SSH), TELNET, terminal servers, and remote control software. Such applications typically can be configured to log basic information for each connection, including source IP address and user account. Organizations also typically use many applications that are accessed remotely, such as client/server applications. Some of these applications also log basic information for connections. Although most remote access–related logging occurs on the RAS or the application server, in some cases the client also logs information related to the connection.

A **quarantine server** is used for protection at the network gateway from malicious code attacks. A common technique used in protecting networks is to use a firewall. In this technique, if a user attempts to retrieve an infected program via FTP, HTTP, or SMTP, the program is stopped at the quarantine server before it reaches the individual workstations. The firewall will direct suspicious traffic to the antivirus scanner on the quarantine server. This technique scales well since LAN administrators can add multiple firewalls or gateway scanners to manage network traffic for improved performance. In addition, users cannot bypass this architecture, and LAN administrators do not need to configure clients at user workstations. Other useful scanning techniques for a network include continuous, automated malicious code scanning using numerous scripts. Simple commands can be executed, and numerous computers in a network can be scanned for possible infections. Other scripts can be used to search for possible security holes through which future malicious code could attack the network. Only after fixing these security holes can a network withstand many attacks from malicious code.

WHAT IS A SERVER FARM AND HOW IS IT CONTROLLED?

A **server farm** is a physical security control that uses a network configuration mechanism to monitor and minimize theft of or damage to servers because all servers are kept in a single, secure physical location with a key and lock. If not controlled well, server farms can become a single point of failure and can be a target of internally originated attacks. Only those individuals (e.g., server administrators) who require physical access to the server farm should be given a key to open and close the doors. Two-person control is better.

Examples of logical security controls over a server farm include host- and network-based IDSs, private virtual LANs (VLANs), access controls with strong passwords, and good system administration practices (e.g., keeping systems up to date with the latest patches).

A **virtual server** is built on top of off-the-shelf servers for designing certification authority services. The virtual server can become very robust evidence of attacks on or errors made by other servers. Virtual servers are much easier to migrate between physical hosts in an infrastructure, and this movement may have unintended security consequences. For example, moving a virtual server from a lower-risk (more trusted) to a higher-risk (less trusted) domain may expose the sensitive information the server contains or is allowed to process unless its configuration is hardened appropriately. Conversely, when a virtual server is moved from a higher-risk (less trusted) domain to a lower-risk (more trusted) domain, its hardening configuration may interfere with normal operations unless it is matched to that appropriate for the lower-risk domain.

A domain name system (**DNS**) **server** is an example of an information system that provides name/address resolution service. To eliminate single points of failure and to enhance redundancy, there are typically at least two authoritative DNS servers, one configured as primary and the other as secondary. Additionally, the two servers are commonly located in two different network subnets and are geographically separated (i.e., not located in the same physical facility).

Transport-layer security (TLS) proxy servers provide network, transport, or application-layer VPNs (depending on the configuration). Typically, remote users connect to the proxy server using TLS-protected HTTP and authenticate themselves; users can then access designated applications indirectly through the proxy server, which establishes its own separate connections with the application servers. Non-web-based applications can be accessed by deploying special programs to clients and then tunneling the application data over HTTPS or another protocol; another method is to use a terminal server and to give users a web-based terminal server client. Unlike IPsec, TLS proxy servers cannot protect IP header characteristics, such as IP addresses. The TLS/SSL proxy server provides a more robust VPN solution for remote users than other means.

HOW TO MAINTAIN SERVER INTEGRITY

To ensure and maintain the integrity of the network servers, it is important to constantly monitor them for signs of malicious activity and other vulnerabilities. Integrity controls include a server farm, a secure DMZ, a secure server network with firewalls, or using routers behind the firewall.

A **network time protocol (NTP) server** is maintained to synchronize clocks and logs in different time zones throughout the world. NTP helps organizations with systems in multiple time zones to convert all logged times to a single time zone. NTP provides an efficient and scalable method for network elements to synchronize to an accurate time source referred to as the reference clock or stratum-0 server. The reference clock synchronizes to the Coordinated Universal Time derived from a set of atomic clocks using Global Positioning System (GPS), code division multiple access (CDMA), or other time signals.

A **system log server** (syslog server) provides the network administrator the ability to configure all of the communication devices on a network to send log messages to a centralized host for review, correlation, reporting, and storage. This implementation provides for easier management of network events and is an effective way to monitor and automatically generate alert notifications. The repository of messages facilitates troubleshooting when problems are encountered and can assist analysts in performing root cause analysis. Syslog files can also be parsed in real time to identify suspicious behavior or can be archived for review at a later time for research and analysis. Syslog is a protocol that specifies a general log entry format and a log entry transport mechanism.

A **management server** is a centralized device that receives information from the sensors or agents and manages them. The management server performs correlation analysis, such as finding events triggered by the same IP address, and identifies events that the individual sensors or agents cannot. Some small intrusion detection and prevention system (IDPS) deployments do not use management servers, but most large IDPS deployments do. In large IDPS deployments, there are often multiple management servers; in some cases, there are two tiers of management servers.

A **Dynamic Host Configuration Protocol (DHCP) server** can be configured to log each IP address assignment and the associated media access control (MAC) address, along with a time-stamp. This information can be helpful to security analysts in identifying which host performed an activity using a particular IP address. However, analysts should be mindful of the possibility that attackers on an organization's internal networks falsified MAC or IP addresses, a practice known as spoofing.

DHCP is a set of rules used by communications devices, such as computers, routers, or network adapters, to allow the device to request and obtain an IP address from a server that has a list of addresses available for assignment. The DHCP service assigns IP addresses to hosts on a network as needed. Some hosts might have static IP addresses, meaning that they always receive the same IP address assignment; however, typically most hosts receive dynamic assignments. This means that the hosts are required to renew their IP address assignments regularly and that there is no guarantee that they will be assigned the same addresses. DHCP servers may contain assignment logs that include the MAC address, the IP address assigned to that MAC address, and the time the assignment occurred.

The MAC address, also known as the hardware address or Ethernet address, is a unique identifier specific to the network card inside a computer. MAC allows the DHCP server to confirm that the computer is allowed to access the network.

An **anonymizer server** is an intermediate server that performs activity on a user's behalf to preserve the user's privacy. Because IP addresses are often assigned dynamically, the system currently at a particular IP address might not be the same system that was there when the attack occurred. In addition, many IP addresses do not belong to end user systems but instead to network infrastructure components that substitute their IP address for the actual source address, such as a firewall performing network address translation. Some attackers use anonymizer servers.

A **warez server** is a file server that is used to distribute illegal content, such as copies of copy-righted songs and movies as well as pirated software. "Warez" is a term widely used by hackers to denote illegally copied and distributed commercial software from which all copy protection has been removed. Warez often contain viruses, Trojan horses, and other malicious code and thus are very risky to download and use (legal issues notwithstanding).

A **Kerberos security server** provides a means by which constituents of the network (principals) can trust each other. These principals may be any hardware or software that communicates across the network. Kerberos protocol is used for local logins, remote authentication, and client/server requests. It uses a symmetric-key cryptography and a trusted third party. The principals involved in the Kerberos model are the user, the client, the key distribution center, the ticket-granting service, and the server providing the requested service.

A **SOCKS server** (socket server) is a networking-proxy protocol that enables full access across the SOCKS server from one host to another without requiring direct IP reachability.

Load-balancing servers distribute HTTP requests over multiple Web servers, allowing organizations to increase the capacity of their website by transparently adding additional servers. Load balancers act as virtual servers, receiving all HTTP requests to the website. These requests are forwarded, based on the load balancer's policy, to one of the servers that hosts the website. The load balancer's policy attempts to ensure that each server receives a similar number of requests. Many load balancers are capable of monitoring the servers and compensating if one server becomes unavailable.

WHAT IS SERVER LOAD BALANCING AND HOW IS IT RELATED TO SERVER CLUSTERING?

Server load balancing refers to fine-tuning a computer system, network, or disk subsystem in order to more evenly distribute the data and/or processing across available resources. The load balancing occurs when network traffic is distributed dynamically across groups of servers running a common application so that no one server is overwhelmed. It increases server availability and application system availability and could be a viable contingency measure when it is implemented among different websites. In this regard, the application system continues to operate as long as one or more websites remain operational.

Server clustering means multiple servers providing the same service. It implies resilience to failure and/ or some kind of load balancing between the servers. For example, in clustering, load balancing might distribute the incoming transactions evenly to all servers, or it might redirect them to the next available server. The stronger the server clustering, the smoother is load balancing among servers.

Load balancers are often augmented by caching mechanisms. Many of the HTTP requests an organization's Web server receives are identical and return identical HTTP responses. However, when dynamic content generation is in use, these identical responses need to be regenerated each time the request is made. To alleviate this requirement and further reduce the load on individual web servers, organizations can deploy caching servers.

Like network switches, load balancers are not specifically security appliances, but they are essential tools for maintaining the availability of a website. By ensuring that several individual web servers are sharing the load, rather than placing the load on a single web server, the organization is better able to withstand the high volume of requests used in many DoS attacks. Firewalls, switches, and routers should also be configured (when possible) to limit the amount of traffic that is passed to the web servers, which further reduces the risk of successful DoS attacks.

(iv) Security over Web Servers
(A) Security Levels
Recent attacks on websites have shown that computers supporting websites are vulnerable to attacks ranging from minor nuisances to significant service interruptions. Each organization has to decide its sensitivity to risk and how open it wants to be to the external world. When resources are limited, the cost of security incidents should be considered, and the investment in protective measures should be concentrated in areas of highest sensitivity.

Three levels of web security techniques can be applied to web servers. They operate in a cumulative manner, meaning that techniques in level 3 are stronger than those in level 1.

Level 1 Minimum Security

1. Upgrade software/install patches.

2. Use single-purpose servers.

3. Remove unnecessary applications.

Level 2 Penetration Resistance

1. Install external firewalls.

2. Administer remote security.

3. Restrict server scripts.

4. Shield the web server with packet filtering.

5. Educate and allocate resources.

6. Plus techniques listed in level 1.

Level 3 Attack Detection and Mitigation

1. Apply separation of privileges principles.

2. Install hardware-based solutions.

3. Install internal firewalls.

4. Installing network-based IDSs.

5. Installing host-based IDSs.

6. Plus techniques listed in levels 1 and 2.

Security controls over Web servers are discussed next.

Upgrade Software/Install Patches. One of the simplest and yet most effective techniques for reducing risk is the installation of the latest software upgrades and patches. Web servers should be examined frequently to determine what software needs to be updated or patched.

Use Single-Purpose Servers. Organizations should run Web servers on computers dedicated exclusively to that task. A common mistake is to save money by running multiple servers on the same host. For example, it is common to run an email server, web server, and database server on the same computer. However, each server running on a host provides an attacker with avenues for attack. Each newly installed server increases the organization's reliance on that host while simultaneously decreasing the host's security. Given the decreasing cost of hardware and the increasing importance of having fast web servers, it generally is effective to buy a dedicated host for each web server. Also, in situations where a web server constantly interacts with a database, it is best to use two separate hosts.

Remove Unnecessary Applications. Privileged software is defined as software that runs with administrator privileges or that receives packets from the network. All privileged software not specifically required by the web server should be removed.

OSs often run a variety of privilege programs by default. System administrators may not even be aware that these programs exist. Each privileged program provides another avenue by which an attacker can compromise a web server. It is therefore crucial that web servers are purged of unnecessary programs. For greater security and because it is often difficult to identify what software is privileged, many system administrators remove all software not needed by a web server.

Install External Firewalls. Install public web servers outside of an organization's firewall. In this configuration, the firewall prevents the web server from sending packets into an organization's network. If attackers on the Internet penetrate the external web server, they have no more access to the organization's internal network than they had before. If a web server is inside the organization's firewall and is penetrated by attackers on the Internet, the attackers can use the web server as a launching point for attacks on internal systems. Thus, these attacks completely bypass the security provided by the firewall.

Administer Remote Security. Since it is often inconvenient to administer a host from the physical console, system administrators often install software on web servers to allow remote administration. From a security perspective, this practice is dangerous and should be minimized or eliminated. In order to increase security where this practice is necessary:

- Encrypt remote administration traffic such that attackers monitoring network traffic cannot obtain passwords or inject malicious commands into conversations.
- Use packet filtering to allow remote administration only from a designated set of hosts.
- Maintain this designated set of hosts at a higher degree of security than normal hosts.
- Do not use packet filtering as a replacement for encryption because attackers can spoof IP addresses. With IP spoofing, attackers lie about their location by sending messages from an IP address other than their own.

Restrict Server Scripts. Most websites contain scripts (small programs) created locally by website developers. A web server runs these scripts when a user requests a particular page. Attackers can use these scripts to penetrate websites by finding and exercising flaws in the code. Scripts must be carefully written with security in mind, and system administrators should inspect them before placing them on a website. Do not allow scripts to run arbitrary commands on a system or to launch insecure or nonpatched programs. Scripts should restrict users to doing a small set of well-defined tasks. They should carefully restrict the size of input parameters so that an attacker cannot give a script more data than it expects. If an attacker is allowed to add more data, often a system can be penetrated using a buffer overflow technique. With this type of attack, an attacker convinces a web server to run arbitrary code by giving it more information than it expected to receive. Run scripts with nonadministrator privileges to prevent an attacker from compromising the entire web server in the event that a script contains flaws.

Shield the Web Server with Packet Filtering. A router set up to separate a web server from the rest of the network can shield a web server from many attacks. It can thwart attacks before they reach the web server by dropping all packets that do not access valid web server services. Typically, the router should drop all network packets that do not go either to the web server or to the remote administration server. For additional security, only allow a preapproved list of hosts to send traffic to a web server's remote administration server. This way, an attacker can compromise a web server only by using the remote administration server via a restricted set of network paths. The filtering router shield offers protection similar to that of removing all unneeded software from a host because it prevents an attacker from requesting certain vulnerable services. Be aware that setting up a router with many filtering rules may noticeably slow its ability to forward packets.

Educate and Allocate Resources. Attackers are able to penetrate most web servers because system administrators are either not knowledgeable about web server security or do not take the time to properly secure the system. Website administrators must be trained about web server security techniques and rewarded for spending time securing the sites.

Apply Separation of Privileges Principles. Regardless of the security measures established for a Web server, penetration may still occur. If this happens, it is important to limit the attacker's actions on the penetrated host. Separation of privileges is a key concept for restricting actions once a part of the host is penetrated. To establish such control, partition the various host resources among a set of user accounts. An attacker who penetrates some software will then be limited to acting within that single user account instead of having control over the entire system. For example, a web server can run as one user, but another user can own the web pages, with the web server given read-only access. Then, if attackers penetrate the web server, they cannot change the web pages owned by other users. Likewise, IDS can run as another user to protect it from being modified by an attacker penetrating the web server user. For the best security, run the web server process as a user who has write privilege only in a few privately owned temporary directories. This requires storing the web server software as read-only under one user but running it as a different user.

Install Hardware-Based Solutions. Hardware can implement separation of privilege concepts with a greater degree of security than software because hardware is not as easily modified as software. With software implementation, if the underlying OS is penetrated, the attacker has complete control of all files on a web server. Using read-only external hard disk or CD-ROMs, web pages and even critical software can be stored in a way that an attacker cannot modify the files. The usual configuration is for web servers to have a read-write port so that the web pages can be updated. Note that an attacker who penetrates a protected web server can still copy data, change the copied data, and serve up the changed pages.

Install Internal Firewalls. Modern web servers often serve as front ends to complex and possibly distributed applications. In this situation, a web server often communicates with several other hosts, each of which contains particular data or performs particular computations. It is tempting to locate these computers inside an organization's firewall for ease of maintenance and to protect these important computers. However, if an attacker can compromise a web server, these back-end systems may be penetrated using the web server as a launching point. Instead, it is a good idea to separate web server back-end systems from the rest of the organization's networks using an internal firewall. Then penetration of the web server and subsequently the web server's back-end systems does not provide access to the rest of the organization's networks.

Install Network-Based Intrusion Detection Systems. Despite all attempts to patch a web server and to configure it securely, vulnerability may still exist. Also, the web server may be perfectly secure, but an attacker may cleverly overwhelm the host's services such that it ceases to operate. In this kind of environment, it is important to know when your web server has been compromised or shut down so that service can be quickly restored. Network-based IDSs monitor network traffic to determine whether a web server is under attack or has been compromised or disabled. Modern IDSs have the ability to launch a limited response to attacks or notify system administrators via email, pagers, or messages on a security console. Typical automated responses include killing network connections and blocking IP addresses.

Install Host-Based Intrusion Detection Systems. Host-based IDSs reside on a web server. Thus, they are better positioned to determine the state of the web server than a network-based IDS. They provide the same benefits as network-based IDSs and in some circumstances can better detect attacks since they have finer-grained access to the web server's state. However, some drawbacks exist. An attacker penetrating a web server can disable a host-based IDS, thereby preventing it from issuing a warning. In addition, remote DoS attacks often disable host-based IDSs while disabling the web server. Remote DoS attacks enable an attacker to remotely shut down a web server without actually penetrating it. Thus, host-based IDSs are useful, but they should be used in conjunction with the typically more secure network-based IDSs.

(B) Limitations of Techniques to Secure Web Servers

Today's software is not 100% secure, and applications of standard web security techniques cannot guarantee that a web server will be impenetrable. A web server should use its stated web server security techniques in addition to using trustworthy software. "Trustworthy" means software that can be assessed by studying past vulnerabilities, using software specifically created with security as the principal goal, and using software evaluated by trusted third parties.

Three issues can be raised here with web servers:

1. Some level of assurance in software can be gained by looking at past vulnerabilities discovered in different web server software. The number of past vulnerabilities is an indicator of future vulnerabilities and also reflects how well the software was crafted. Trustworthiness is directly related to the quality of the software product. A poorly crafted product built explicitly to meet security needs remains a poorly crafted product and therefore is not trustworthy.

2. Some companies specialize in creating very secure web server software, and some boast that no vulnerabilities have ever been discovered. Users have to balance a vendor's security claims against any security-performance trade-offs that have been made.

3. A way to gain a level of assurance in software is to use evaluated and validated software. Many private sector organizations perform third-party evaluations of commercial products in order to verify a particular level of security.

(C) Security Testing Web Servers

Periodic security testing of public web servers is critical. Without periodic testing, there is no assurance that current protective measures are working or that the security patch applied by the web server administrator is functioning as advertised. Although a variety of security testing techniques exist, vulnerability scanning is the most common. Vulnerability scanning assists a web server administrator in identifying vulnerabilities and verifying whether the existing security measures are effective. Penetration testing is also used, but it is used less frequently and usually only as part of an overall penetration test of the organization's network.

(D) Remotely Administering a Web Server

It is strongly recommended that remote administration and remote updating of content for a web server be allowed only after careful consideration of the risks. The most secure configuration is to disallow any remote administration or content updates. However, that might not be viable for all organizations. The risk of enabling remote administration or content updates varies considerably depending on the location of the web server on the network. For a web server that is located behind a firewall, remote administration or content updating can be implemented relatively securely from the internal network but not without added risk. Remote administration or content updating generally should not be allowed from a host located outside the organization's network unless it is performed from an organization-controlled computer through the organization's remote access solution, such as a VPN.

If an organization determines that it is necessary to remotely administer or update content on a web server, the next steps should ensure that content is implemented in as secure a manner as possible:

- Use a strong authentication mechanism (e.g., public/private key pair and two-factor authentication).

- Restrict which hosts can be used to remotely administer or update content on the Web server.

  □ Restrict by authorized users.

  □ Restrict by IP address (not host name).

  □ Restrict to hosts on the internal network or those using the organization's enterprise remote access solution.

- Use secure protocols that can provide encryption of both passwords and data (e.g., SSH, HSTS, and HTTPS); do not use less secure protocols (e.g., TELNET, trivial FTP, NFS, and HTTP) unless absolutely required and tunneled over an encrypted protocol, such as SSH, SSL, or IPsec.

- Enforce the concept of least privilege on remote administration and content updating (e.g., attempt to minimize the access rights for the remote administration/update accounts).

- Do not allow remote administration from the Internet through the firewall unless accomplished via strong mechanisms, such as VPNs.

- Change any default accounts or passwords for the remote administration utility or application.

- Do not mount any file shares on the internal network from the web server or vice versa.

(b) Network Communications

Computer data and communications networks can be classified according to their scale and location similar to classifying multiple processors based on their physical size. Wired networks include personal area networks (PANs), LANs, metropolitan area networks (MANs), WANs, and the Internet. Wireless networks include wireless PANs (WPANs), wireless LANs (WLANs), wireless MANs (WMANs), wireless WANs (WWANs), and wireless cellular networks. In addition, client/server architecture, campus area networks, broadband networks, VoIP, voice mail network systems, cloud networks, social media networks, VPNs, multimedia collaborative computing systems, ad hoc networks, content delivery networks (CDNs), VANs, wireless sensor networks, digital cellular networks, P2P networks, converged networks, optical networks, body area networks, and radio frequency identification (RFID) networks are presented.

MAJOR RISKS IN NETWORKS

- **Jamming** is an attack in which a mobile device is used to emit electromagnetic energy on a wireless network's frequency to make the network unusable.

- Loss of data packets in a network (called black holes) can occur when network traffic is sent to a router where it drops some or all of the packets. Sometimes incoming data packets can be destroyed, displaced, or discarded without informing the sender or recipient of their failed delivery status.

(Continued)

> ### MAJOR RISKS IN NETWORKS (*Continued*)
>
> - **Jitters** are nonuniform delays that can cause network packets to arrive and be processed in an out-of-sequence fashion.
>
> - **Network congestion** is an undesirable overload condition caused by network traffic in excess of its capacity to handle, resulting in a degradation of network performance. Inadequate and insufficient bandwidth can also cause congestion.
>
> - **Message collision** is a condition in which two data packets are transmitted over a network medium at the same time from two or more stations. When a collision is detected, both messages should be retransmitted after a random interval.
>
> - **Network latency** is the total time or delay when a network component is waiting for another component to complete the latter component's task. Several delays can occur: transmission delay from fiber optics to coaxial cable, travel delay from one node to the next node, processing delay by a router, and storage delay in disk drives.

(A) Wired Networks

The lowest scale of wired network is a **PAN,** or home network, in a room for an individual's use or to conduct home-based business. For example, a wireless network connecting a computer (e.g., desktop PC, laptop PC, notebook PC, and tablet PC) with its mouse, keyboard, and printer is a PAN.

The next highest scale of wired network is a **LAN** for use in a single building or campus of buildings connected by PCs and workstations to share peripheral resources (e.g., printers and scanners) and to exchange information. Several topologies are possible for broadcast LANs, such as bus, star, tree, ring, and mesh. The combination of a cable and host forms a LAN, and there is no subnet for LANs.

The next highest scale of wired network is a **MAN** for use in a city for a cable television network. MANs are also called wireless local loops. It interfaces to the network layer and uses packet protocols (e.g., IP, point-to-point protocol, and Ethernet), which are connectionless, and ATM, which is connection oriented. It requires mapping the ATM connection to the other connections.

The next highest scale of wired network is **WAN** for use in a country or continent to run user application systems. A WAN consists of hosts (PCs) that are connected by a communication subnet. The subnet consists of transmission lines and switching elements (routers). Transmission lines move bits between computers using copper wire, optical fiber, or radio links. Routers connect three or more transmission lines. Customers own the hosts whereas telephone companies or Internet service providers (ISPs) own and operate the communication subnet. The combination of a subnet and its hosts forms a WAN.

The highest scale of wired network is the Internet for use on all continents (i.e., the entire planet). An internetwork (Internet) is established when distinct networks are interconnected (e.g., connecting a LAN and a WAN or connecting two LANs).

(B) Wireless Networks

WPANs are short-range wireless networks (e.g., Bluetooth), using the IEEE 802.15 standard. They connect computer components without wires and using short-range radio and use open standards for short-range communications.

WLANs, using the IEEE 802.11 standard (Wi-Fi), communicate with other systems through a radio modem and antenna. They are used when it is not feasible to install Ethernet, as in office buildings, airports, hotels, restaurants, and campuses. WLANs serve as an extension to existing wired LANs.

The IEEE 802.11 standard defines how to design interoperable WLAN equipment that provides a variety of capabilities, including a wide range of data rates, QoS, reliability, range optimization, device link options, network management, and security.

WLANs provide five distribution services (association, disassociation, reassociation, distribution, and integration) and four station services (authentication, de-authentication, privacy, and data delivery). Distribution services relate to managing cell activities and interacting with stations outside the cell. Station services relate to activity within a single cell (intracell) and occur only after the distribution services have taken place.

WMANs, which are fixed broadband networks, are used for high-speed wireless Internet access jobs in a city using the IEEE802.16 standard known as Worldwide Interoperability for Microwave Access (WiMAX). It is intended for wireless MAN and provides seamless mobile access in much the same as wide area cellular networks with higher transmission speeds. Security advantages of WiMAX include mutual device/user authentication, improved traffic encryption, and options for securing data within the core network.

WWANs, using the IEEE 802.11 standard, are installed for cellular telephone systems using the radio network. A WLAN bridge can connect multiple LANS to form a WAN. Wireless supports varying distances with a direct line of sight. WWANs are similar to WLANs except that the distances involved are much greater and the bit rates are much slower. WWANs use low bandwidth.

Wireless cellular networks are managed by service providers that provide coverage based on dividing a large geographical service area into smaller areas of coverage called cells. As a mobile phone moves from one cell to another, a cellular arrangement requires active connections to be monitored and effectively passed along between cells to maintain the connection.

Cellular networks support cellular phones, smartphones, and cellular data cards. Smartphones offer more functionality than basic cellular phones, including email and wireless Web browsing (e.g., Bluetooth and Wi-Fi). Cellular data cards allow laptop users to connect to the Internet anywhere cellular service is available. However, cellular data cards can access the Internet only if the user is within the service provider's network coverage area.

WHAT ARE WIRELESS TECHNOLOGIES?

Wireless technologies include:

- Bluetooth technology is used in laptop computers and other mobile devices.
- Wireless closed circuit television technology is used in surveillance and monitoring.
- RFID technology is used in identification and tracking of items.
- 802.11 technology is used in WLANs.
- Mobile radio technology is used in radio transmissions.

(Continued)

- Wireless mesh network technology is used in transporting data.

- Cellular technology is used in cellular modems, routers, and bridges for high-speed wireless data.

- WiMAX technology used in WMANs.

- Microwave and satellite technology is used in cell phones, radio, cable, infrared, and air lasers.

(C) Wired Local Area Networks

A wired LAN is a network that interconnects systems located in a small geographic area, such as an office, all the computers in one building, or all the computers in several buildings in close proximity (i.e., in a campus). LANs can be classified in a number of different ways. Four commonly used classifications include topology, transmission controls, transmission medium, and architectural design.

LAN Architecture. Choosing a LAN software or hardware configuration that will support the desired functional and security features requires an understanding of LAN architectures. Two popular logical architectures that are supported on PC-LANs today include client/server architecture and P2P architecture.

LAN Concepts. Various concepts in wired LANs are listed next.

- LAN basic topologies include star, bus, ring, tree, and mesh.

- LAN media access control methods include Ethernet (IEEE 802.3), token bus (IEEE 802.4), IBM token ring (IEEE 802.5), and Fiber Distributed Data Interface (FDDI).

- IP, which is a packet protocol, is a connectionless protocol so it fits well with the connectionless Ethernet protocol.

- The LAN transmission media include twisted-pair wire, coaxial cable, and fiber optic cable.

- LAN transmission methods include unicast, broadcast, and multicast.

- LAN internetworking devices include routers, bridges, brouters, repeaters, switches, hubs, and gateways.

- FDDI and fiber channel are two ring-based optical LANs, used as backbone networks. They are not successful for desktop-level use.

- FDDI offers an optional bypass switch at each node for addressing failures.

- LANs can link to WANs and other networks using the Internet.

- LANs may use client/server or P2P architecture.

- Transmission media can be guided or unguided. Examples of guided transmission media include twisted-pair wire, coaxial cable, and fiber optic cable.

- Examples of unguided transmission media include radio, microwave, infrared, and air lasers.

LAN Security Goals and Features. There are four LAN security goals.

1. Maintain the confidentiality of data as it is stored, processed, or transmitted on a LAN.

2. Maintain the integrity of data as it is stored, processed, or transmitted on a LAN.

3. Maintain the availability of data stored on a LAN and the ability to process and transmit the data in a timely manner.

4. Ensure the identity of the sender and receiver of a message.

LAN Security Concerns and Risks. Major security concerns and risks of LANs are listed next.

- Distributed file storing (file servers controlling user access to files)
- Remote computing (servers authenticating remote users, system components and applications)
- Topologies and protocols (messages reaching the desired destination)
- Messaging services (protecting email during transit and in storage)

Other security concerns and risks are listed next.

- Possible inherent threats in LANs include both active and passive wiretapping.
- Passive wiretapping includes not only information release but also traffic analysis (using addresses, other header data, message length, and message frequency).
- Active wiretapping includes message stream modifications, including delay, duplication, modification, deletion, or counterfeiting.
- A single-link failure, a repeater failure, or a break in the cable could disable a large part or the entire network.
- When two or more stations transmit at the same time, data frames will collide, leading to unpredictable results and garbled transmission. Neither one gets through. "Who goes next?" is the problem to be resolved. The number of **collisions** will increase as the channel's load increases. When two frames collide, the medium remains unusable for the duration of transmission of both damaged frames. Collision detectors are needed to resolve collision.
- There may not be a backup person for the LAN administrator.
- The backup person, even though designated, may not have been trained adequately to take over the LAN administrator's job duties when needed.
- Changes made to the LAN network may not be transparent to end users.
- LANs can become single points of failure due to vulnerable cables and connectivity hardware.
- Inadequate LAN management and security policies.
- Lack of training of employees for proper LAN usage and security.
- Inadequate protection mechanisms in the workstation environment.
- Inadequate protection during transmission.

LAN High-Security and Low-Security Features. A **high-security LAN** might include these features:

- Dedicated file server using client/server architecture
- Diskless PCs or workstations remotely booted

- Logical access security control down to the lowest level possible (i.e., byte level)
- Encryption of passwords
- Password format control
- Security monitoring, accounting, and reporting
- Network encryption devices
- No disk format command
- Image backup utility programs
- Fault-tolerance design with the use of disk-mirroring, disk-duplicating, or server-mirroring methods
- Reduced system privileges to directories, files, or records
- No remote log-in feature
- Automatic log-out feature after some dormant period
- Printers attached to secured file server

A **low-security LAN** might include these features:

- P2P architecture
- Allows disk format command
- Shareable printers across the network
- Bootable workstations with local storage facilities
- No directory-, file-, record-, byte-level access controls
- Basic, simple password protection

(D) Client/Server Architecture

Many definitions exist for client/server systems. One broad definition is the coordination of data as application systems are distributed. The application system's processing is divided into two parts: (1) client, where users request data services, and (2) server, which furnishes the requested data to the user client. In other words, web pages, documents, and files (e.g., data, video, and audio) are transferred from the server to the client.

Client/server architecture or configuration is similar to cooperative processing, which enables the application system to be divided across multiple, different hardware platforms. In other words, the computing process is distributed across multiple, different hardware platforms. This contrasts with distributed processing in that the entire computing process is distributed among several similar platforms. In cooperative processing, a single computing process uses several different connected platforms. With distributed processing, a single computing process runs independently on multiple, similar platforms.

Typical hardware components required in a client/server environment include a PC or workstation capable of storing data, a terminal emulation device, and a physical connection to the host computer system. Servers are powerful computers providing the client computers with a variety of data services. The client and the server are linked via a LAN or other data communications system. The flow of data is mostly one way (i.e., from the server to the client).

There are six basic elements of the client/server computing process:

1. Data storage
2. Database management system
3. Application system
4. Operating system
5. Display device
6. User interface

Elements 1 and 2 are located on the server or host platform, and elements 3 through 6 are located on the client platform.

The normal client/server implementation is a two-tiered architecture for simple networks (i.e., one client and one server). Multitiered (*n*-tier) architecture is possible for complex networks. In *n*-tier architecture, there is one client and several servers (e.g., web server, application server, database server, etc.) where client requests are handled by different levels of servers.

Most client/server systems are designed for PCs and LAN-based OSs. The processing of an application is split between a front-end portion executing on a PC or workstation (client) and a back-end portion running on a server. Exhibit 3.11 provides an overview of the client/server functions.

EXHIBIT 3.11 Overview of Client/Server Functions

Client Functions	Server Functions
Contains front-end programs	Contains back-end programs
Provides data entry and data manipulation	Facilitates access to the data
Handles ad hoc queries	Accepts and process the data
Invoked by a user	Invoked by a client
Provides management reporting	Provides locking and logging mechanisms
Runs batch jobs	Places data in the database
Users cannot access the data in the server directly	Returns the data and status codes to the client on request
Needs heavy user interface	Needs no user interface
Provides user-friendly interaction	Provides system backups, database synchronization, and database protection
Uses diskless PCs or workstations for better security	Uses strong security controls to protect servers (e.g., SSL/TLS for authentication and encryption; mirrored or shadowed disks; shared buffering; fault tolerance mechanisms, such as automatic fail-over)

Four client/server implementation approaches are listed next.

1. Simple file transfer
2. API
3. GUI-based OS
4. P2P communications

The **simple file transfer approach** involves the transfer of data from a host server to a client workstation, PC, or LAN. The client application then accesses and processes the data. In addition to the physical connection, the workstation requires emulation software to allow it to function as a host terminal. This approach is least costly and least complex to implement, costs little to integrate data, and is good for situations where access to real-time data is not required. With this approach, information associated with each physical database access must flow across the network. This approach assumes that the database resides on one processor and that the application program that accesses the database resides on some other processor.

The **API approach** links the client application with existing host applications. It requires no modifications to existing applications and requires no specialized programming skills. This approach is a first step in implementing more client/server strategies. The API provides a GUI with an existing character-based mainframe application system.

The **GUI-based OS approach** conforms to the true client/server model and is used in combination with an SQL database. Development costs may be high if there is a lack of in-house IT expertise and retraining is required. This approach is suited for situations where there is a need for access to updated information and multiple client applications access the database. With this approach, only the initial query and the final result need to flow across the network. This approach assumes that the database resides on one processor and that the application program that accesses the database resides on some other processor. A GUI-based application and user-centered applications would reduce the amount of end user training required on applications software.

The **P2P communications approach** does not use a hierarchical configuration, unlike the other three approaches. It allows applications to interact with each other on an equal basis. Any platform may act as a client, a server, or both. This approach is expensive, uses more system resources, requires greater programming skills, and is highly complex. Extensive rewrites of existing software are needed. This approach is well suited for situations where there is an availability of host data and there is a need to access or integrate data on multiple platforms and for a common interface.

P2P architecture requires no dedicated file server because any node on the network may selectively share its local hard disk with other nodes on the network. Other peripherals, such as printers, may also be shared across the LAN. This is a good choice for smaller LAN installations as it has a lower cost per node rate. However, significant security problems exist because of the lack of centralized data storage across the network. Typically, the architecture also has lower performance and requires greater administrative effort to configure and maintain security definition.

(E) Virtual Local Area Networks

VLAN technology is an efficient way of grouping users into workgroups to share the same network address space regardless of their physical location on the network. VLAN separates the logical topology of the LANs from their physical topology and employs the IEEE 802.1Q standard. Users can be organized into separate VLANs according to their department, location, function, application, physical address, logical address, or protocol. Regardless of the organization method used, the goal with any VLAN is to group users into separate communities that share the same resource, thereby enabling the majority of their traffic to stay within the boundaries of the VLAN.

The logical separation of users and traffic results in better performance management (i.e., broadcast and bandwidth utilization control). It also facilitates a reduction in CM overhead, enabling networks to scale at ease. By default, all ports are configured to be members of VLAN1, which is all untagged traffic. As a consequence, VLAN1 may span the entire network if not appropriately controlled. The risk is even greater if VLAN1 is also used for user VLANs or the management of VLAN. In addition, it is unwise to mix management traffic with user traffic, which makes the VLAN an easier target for exploitation.

Trunk links can carry the traffic of multiple VLANs simultaneously. Therein lies a potential security exposure. Trunk links have a native or default VLAN that is used to negotiate trunk status and exchange VLAN configuration information. Trunking also enables a single port to become part of multiple VLANs—another potential security exposure.

The system administrator for VLAN will ensure that:

- VLAN1 is not used for in-band management traffic. It is good to use a dedicated management VLAN to keep management traffic separate from user data and control plane traffic.
- Management of a VLAN is not configured on any trunk or access port that does not require it.
- VLAN1 is not used for user VLANs.
- VLAN1 is pruned from all trunk and access ports that do not require it.
- Trunking is disabled on all access ports.
- When trunking is necessary, a dedicated VLAN is configured for all trunk ports.
- Access ports are not assigned to the dedicated trunk VLAN.

Eliminating unauthorized access to the network from inside the enclave is vital to keeping a network secure. Unauthorized internal access leads to the possibility of hackers or disgruntled employees gaining control of network resources, eavesdropping, or causing DoS on the network. Simply connecting a workstation or laptop to a wall plate or access point located in the work area enables internal access to the private network.

The port security feature provided by most switch vendors can be used to block input to the access port when the MAC address of the station attempting to access the port does not match any of the MAC addresses specified for that port (i.e., those addresses statically configured or autoconfigured [i.e., learned]). The maximum number of MAC addresses that can be configured or learned (or combination of both) is also configurable.

The system administrator for VLAN will ensure that:

- Disabled ports are placed in an unused VLAN.
- Port security or port authentication is used on all access ports.
- Port security has been implemented; the MAC addresses are statically configured on all access ports.
- If port authentication is implemented, reauthentication occurs every 60 minutes.
- If port authentication is implemented, all access ports must start in the unauthorized state.

(F) Wireless Local Area Networks

The most widely implemented legacy WLAN technologies are based on the IEEE 802.11 standard and its amendments, which are not capable of using the new IEEE 802.11i standard that is used in robust security networks (RSNs). WLAN transmission protocols include Carrier Sense

Multiple Access (CSMA), with Collision Avoidance (CSMA/CA) and with Collision Detection (CSMA/CD).

Legacy WLANs. WLANs are groups of wireless networking nodes within a limited geographic area (e.g., an office building or building campus) that are capable of radio communication. WLANs are usually implemented as extensions to existing wired LANs to provide enhanced user mobility and network access. Legacy WLANs have limited and weak security controls and are particularly susceptible to loss of confidentiality, integrity, and availability. Unauthorized users have access to well-documented security flaws and exploits that can easily compromise an organization's systems and information, corrupt its data, consume network bandwidth, degrade network performance, launch attacks that prevent authorized users from accessing the network, or use organizational resources to launch attacks on other networks.

WHAT ARE THE POTENTIAL RISKS IN WLAN TECHNOLOGY?

Despite the availability of strong encryption for user communication, the management frames of IEEE 802.11 messages are not encrypted, leaving the door open for DoS attacks. Several tools (e.g., Wi-Fi jammers and rogue access points) are available that can cause users to drop off the network or send messages to hamper the functionality of wireless endpoints. Wi-Fi jammers are designed to block IEEE 802.11 transmissions. Rogue access points are set up in the hope of attracting connections, then stealing sensitive information or altering communications.

Note that Wi-Fi access points are often set up quickly and without security foresight. This results in the use of weak or no encryption, allowing attackers to impersonate wireless endpoints in the hope of providing false data. It also may result in users not changing default passwords for device management, allowing attackers to gain full control of the access point. There is also a possibility of worms and other malicious code propagating on the local network.

Robust Security Networks for WLANs. Based on the IEEE 802.11i standard, RSNs were found to remedy the security problems of wired equivalent piracy as RSNs provide moderate to high levels of assurance against WLAN security threats through use of a variety of cryptographic techniques. The three types of RSN components are stations, access points, and authentication servers.

(G) Campus Area Networks

A campus area network consists of LANs interconnected within multiple buildings or a small geographic area (e.g., a school campus, office towers, or military base). It can be safely assumed that all the threats, vulnerabilities, and risks applicable to LANs are equally applicable to campus area networks due to a common architecture.

(H) Wired Metropolitan Area Networks

A wired MAN is configured for a larger geographical area than a LAN, ranging from several blocks of buildings to an entire city, for cable television networks. MANs can be owned and operated either as public utilities or as individual organizations. MANs interconnect two or more LANs. Although MANs depend on moderate to high data rates as required for LANs, the error rates and delays would be higher than might be obtained on a LAN. MAN is based on the IEEE 802.6 standard—distributed-queue dual-bus standard. Physically, a MAN consists of a transmission medium and nodes that provide user access to the medium. The distributed-queue dual-bus standard is divided into three layers: upper, middle, and lower.

(I) Wireless Metropolitan Area Network

A WMAN employs the WiMAX communication technology using the IEEE 802.16 standard. WiMAX network threats focus on compromising the radio links between WiMAX nodes. These radio links support both line-of-sight (LOS) and non-line-of-sight (NLOS) signal propagation. Links from LOS WiMAX systems are generally harder to attack than those from NLOS systems because an adversary (attacker) would have to physically locate equipment between the transmitting nodes to compromise the confidentiality or integrity of the wireless link. WiMAX NLOS systems provide wireless coverage over large geographic regions (e.g., the size of a city), which expands the potential staging area for both clients and adversaries. Like other wireless networking technologies, all WiMAX systems are susceptible to DoS attacks, eavesdropping, man-in-the-middle (MitM) attacks, message modification, and resource misappropriations.

(J) Wired Wide Area Networks

A wired WAN is a network that interconnects systems located in a large geographic area, such as a city, a continent, or several continents. A complex network can consist of WANs that span continents or geographic regions within continents and connect smaller, more localized LANs.

WANs connect intelligent terminals, workstations, PCs, minicomputers, and LANs together. They use public as well as private telecommunication facilities to accomplish this connection. For example, a WAN data link interconnection can be used to connect two or more physical LANs in different geographical locations. Some popular WAN protocols include Synchronous Data Link Control (SDLC), High-Level Data Link Control (HDLC), Link Access Procedure, Balanced (LAPB), and High-Speed Serial Interface (HSSI). The sequence of SDLC evolution is as follows:

$$SDLC \longrightarrow HDLC \longrightarrow LAPB$$

Switching networks are a type of WAN network. Switching is used to share communication channels between many users and can take place in the telephone exchange office, where the user dials into it using a telephone. The exchange can even take place on the user's premises, which enables many users to share a small number of access lines.

The four popular types of switching are message switching, circuit switching, packet switching and hybrid switching. With **message switching,** users can be interconnected on demand without using circuit switches. Messages are forwarded to a final destination (e.g., email systems). In **circuit switching**, all the lines are connected to telephone exchange or switching offices. Individual users can lease telephone channels and install their own switches. **Packet switching** is another form of message switching used to interconnect all types of users on a general-purpose public data network. In this type, messages are broken up into smaller packets, which are routed independently through the network. The X.25 protocol standard is used in a packet switching network. **Hybrid switching** combines circuit switching and packet switching. Computer networks are usually packet switched, occasionally circuit switched, but seldom message switched due to transmission delays and throughput problems.

Fast packet networks, using fiber optic transmission, provide the necessary processing power to keep up with increases in link bandwidth and the necessary flexibility to support different kinds of services and a range of bandwidth requirements. Fast packet networks overcome the main weakness of traditional packet networks by using special control mechanisms to provide the consistent network performance required for video and other real-time services. In traditional packet networks, such as the current Internet, the network may become heavily loaded in a way that degrades these services.

WHAT ARE THE MAJOR CONCEPTS IN A WIRED WIDE AREA NETWORK?

Some examples of major concepts in a wired WAN are listed next.

- WANs are packet-switched networks, meaning they use routers.

- WAN interconnection devices include bridges, repeaters, routers, switches, multiplexers, modems, and protocol converters.

- WAN networks include: private circuit networks (e.g., Integrated Services Digital Network [ISDN], Digital Subscriber Line (XDSL), and public and leased lines), circuit-switched networks used in telephone company networks, and packet-switched networks (e.g., X.25, Frame Relay, link access procedure B [LAPB], Switched Multimegabit Data Services [SMDS], asynchronous transfer mode (ATM), packet transfer mode (PTM), and Voice over Internet Protocol (VoIP)).

- WANs can become a single point of failure due to connecting several Internet Service Providers (ISPs), networks, protocols, and communication lines and because of problems with their incompatibility and vulnerability.

The differences between a private (leased) line and a public line are listed next.

- A private line provides voice and data transmission services without public exchange.
- A public line provides voice and data transmission services with public exchange.
- If a private line fails, its users are cut off from the connection.
- If a public line fails, its users are provided with fallback procedures to recover from a disaster or malfunction.

The **X.25 standard** is an international standard that defines the interface between a computing device and a packet-switched data network WAN. X.25 implements point-to-point (PTP) connections between two or more user computers. It is a single point of connection for one user computer and a logical PTP connection for a number of user computers. This is accomplished through a concept called virtual circuits operating in either a permanent or a switched mode. The virtual circuits function in the network layer of the ISO/OSI Reference Model. By using X.25, one pays only for the bits sent, unlike circuit-switched or leased lines, where one pays for the time regardless of how much was sent. X.25 uses a high-speed shared connection, which is a predecessor to Frame Relay. Charging is typically by the packet, segment, or character and requires a connection before exchanging data, similar to a telephone call.

Advantages of X.25 virtual circuits include flexibility in providing a range of functions for implementing multiple-protocol enterprise internetworks when compared with the conventional telecommunication data links. *Disadvantages* of X.25 include additional overhead due to handling of multiple protocols and lower throughput due to complex routing decisions.

(K) Broadband Networks

The capacity of a network, measured as the number of bits it can transmit every second, is called **bandwidth**. Broadband networks are high-bandwidth networks due in part to the use of optical fiber and high-speed switches. They carry video, sound, data, and image services. Broadband networks also allow a closer coupling of the computers on a network. Today, any kind of network transmitting at more than 100 million bits per second is considered a broadband network.

WHAT IS THE DIFFERENCE BETWEEN NARROWBAND NETWORKS AND BROADBAND NETWORKS?

- Narrowband network services include switching networks (WANs) and X.25 standard.

- Broadband networks include Frame Relay, Switched Multimegabit Data Services SMDS, ATM, PTM, ISDN, Digital Subscriber Line (DSL/ADSL), T lines and carriers, and cable Internet connections.

- Narrowband networks are low-bandwidth networks.

- Broadband networks are high-bandwidth networks.

- The dividing line between the two networks is not always clear and changes as technology evolves.

(L) Voice over Internet Protocol

VoIP Risks and Opportunities.   VoIP is the transmission of voice over packet-switched IP networks. VoIP systems take a wide variety of forms, including traditional telephone handsets, conferencing units, and mobile units. In addition to end user equipment, VoIP systems include a variety of other components, including call processors/call managers, gateways, routers, firewalls, and protocols. Because VoIP adds a number of complications to existing network technology, problems are magnified by security considerations.

Current VoIP systems use either a proprietary protocol or one of two standards: the H.323 gateway standard and the Session Initiation Protocol (SIP). An extension of SIP, the SIP Instant Messaging and Presence Leverage Extensions (SIMPLE) standard, is being incorporated into products that support IM. In addition to H.323 and SIP, there are two other standards, Media Gateway Control Protocol (MGCP) and Megaco/H.248, which may be used in large deployments for gateway decomposition. Until a truly dominant standard emerges, organizations moving to VoIP should consider gateways and other network elements that support both H.323 and SIP.

The IPsec protocol was designed to provide interoperable, cryptographically based security for IPv4 and IPv6. The set of security services includes access control, connectionless integrity, data origin authentication, protection against replays, confidentiality, and limited traffic flow confidentiality. These services are provided at the IP layer, offering protection for IP and/or upper layer protocols. Thus, IPsec can be used to protect both VoIP signaling (i.e., SIP and H.323) and VoIP user traffic (i.e., Real-Time Transport Protocol (RTP).

VoIP Control Guidelines.   VoIP can provide more flexible service at lower cost, but there are significant trade-offs that must be considered. VoIP systems can be expected to be more vulnerable than conventional telephone systems, in part because they are tied into the data network, resulting in additional security weaknesses and avenues of attack.

Confidentiality and privacy may be at greater risk in VoIP systems unless strong controls are implemented and maintained. An additional concern is the relative instability of VoIP compared with established telephony systems.

VoIP systems are unstable due to their reliance on packet networks as a transport medium. The public switched telephone network (PSTN) is ultra-reliable. Internet service is generally much less reliable, and VoIP cannot function without Internet connections. Essential telephone services, unless carefully planned, deployed, and maintained, will be at greater risk if based on VoIP.

VoIP General Controls. An overview of general controls over VoIP is presented next.

■ Separate voice and data on logically different networks. Different subnets with separate address blocks should be used for voice and data traffic, with separate DHCP servers for each.

■ At the voice gateway, which interfaces with the PSTN, disallow H.323, SIP, MGCP, or Megaco/H.248 connections from the data network. Use strong authentication and access control on the voice gateway system, as with any other critical network management components. Strong authentication of clients toward a gateway is often very difficult. Here access control mechanisms and policy enforcement may help.

■ Use firewalls designed for VoIP traffic, through either application-level gateways or firewall control proxies. Stateful packet filters can track the state of connections, denying packets that are not part of a properly originated call.

■ Use IPsec or SSH protocol for all remote management and auditing access. If practical, avoid using remote management at all and do IP-based Private Branch Exchange (PBX) access from a physically secure system.

■ If performance is a problem, use encryption at the router or other gateway, not at the individual endpoints, to provide for IPsec tunneling. Since some VoIP endpoints are not computationally powerful enough to perform encryption, placing this burden at a central point ensures that all VoIP traffic emanating from the enterprise network has been encrypted.

VoIP Physical Controls. Unless the VoIP network is encrypted, anyone with physical access to the office LAN could potentially connect network-monitoring tools and tap into telephone conversations. Even if encryption is used, physical access to VoIP servers and gateways may allow an attacker to monitor network traffic. Organizations therefore should ensure that adequate physical security is in place to restrict access to VoIP network components. Physical security measures, such as barriers, locks, access control systems, and security guards, are the first line of defense. Organizations must make sure that the proper physical countermeasures are in place to mitigate some of the biggest risks, such as insertion of sniffers or other network-monitoring devices. For example, installation of a sniffer could result in the interception of not just data but all voice communications.

(M) Voicemail Systems

Voicemail or voice messaging systems are computer-based systems with their own input, editing, storage, retrieval, and transmission of information in the form of natural (human) or synthetic speech. Voicemail systems can be PC based or PBX based. Each user is given a voice mailbox for his or her own use. Outgoing and incoming messages can be of any length, or they can be fixed. All messages are date- and time-stamped.

Voicemail systems interface with PBX systems, voice-response systems to place purchase orders or inquire status of an account balance in a financial/retail institution, and email systems to remind that a voicemail message is waiting while the user is on the email session. See Exhibit 3.12 for risks and suggested controls for voicemail systems.

There are two **advantages** for attackers to attack the phone system. The first advantage is that phone system attacks are hard to trace. It is possible to make connections through multiple switching units or to use unlisted or unused phone numbers to confound a tracing effort. Also, by being in the phone system, it is sometimes possible to monitor the phone company to see if a trace is initiated.

EXHIBIT 3.12 Risks and Controls for Voice-Mail Systems

Potential or Actual Risks and Exposures	Suggested Controls
Various scams (social engineering schemes and toll fraud through voicemail	Ensure that PINs are truly random; periodically change all PINs; use a lockout feature on failed attempts; remove all unassigned or unused mailboxes; unpublish the remote access number; block access to long-distance trunks and local lines; deactivate any mailboxes used by intruders; use voice encryption; restrict collect calls; and review telephone bills.

There are two advantages for attackers to attack the phone system. The first advantage is that phone system attacks are hard to trace. It is possible to make connections through multiple switching units or to use unlisted or unused phone numbers to confound a tracing effort. Also, by being in the phone system, it is sometimes possible to monitor the phone company to see if a trace is initiated.

The second advantage is that a sophisticated host machine is not needed to originate an attack. Also, there is no need to have a direct access to the network to which the target system is attached. A simple unintelligent terminal connected to a modem can be used to initiate an attack. Often an attack consists of several hops, a procedure whereby one system is broken into and from that system another system is broken into, and so on. This again makes tracing more difficult.

(N) Cloud Networks
Cloud computing is a model for enabling ubiquitous, convenient, on-demand network access to a shared pool of configurable computing resources (e.g., networks, servers, storage, applications, and services) that can be rapidly provisioned and released with minimal management effort or service provider interaction. This cloud model promotes availability and is composed of five essential characteristics—on-demand self-service, broad network access, resource pooling, rapid elasticity, and measured service—three service models—cloud software as a service, cloud platform as a service, and cloud infrastructure as a service—and four deployment models—private cloud, community cloud, public cloud, and hybrid cloud. Cloud technology provides three major services: computing, storage, and networking. The major issues in cloud computing include security and privacy of data.

The emergence of cloud computing promises to have far-reaching effects on the systems and networks of many organizations. Many of the features that make cloud computing attractive, however, can also be at odds with traditional security models and controls. The major issues include security and privacy of data. Next, we discuss the security downside (bad news) and the security upside (good news) of cloud computing environment.

Security Downside. Some of the more fundamental concerns in cloud computing are listed next.

- System complexity
- Shared multitenant environment
- Internet-facing service
- Loss of control

As with any technology, cloud computing services can be turned toward improper or illicit activities, such as botnets and cracking mechanisms, such as a Wi-Fi Protected Access cracker.

Solutions to the Security Downside.   The next security controls can mitigate the security downside of a cloud computing environment.

- Deploy access control and intrusion detection technologies at the cloud provider, and conduct an independent assessment to verify that they are in place. Doing this includes traditional perimeter security measures in combination with the domain security controls. Traditional perimeter security includes:
    - Restricting physical access to network and devices.
    - Protecting individual components from exploitation through security patch deployment.
    - Setting as default the most secure configurations.
    - Disabling all unused ports and services.
    - Using role-based access control.
    - Monitoring audit trails.
    - Minimizing the use of privileges.
    - Using antivirus software.
    - Encrypting communications.
- Define trust boundaries between service providers and consumers to ensure that the responsibility for providing security is clear.
- Support application and data portability such that the customer can take action to change cloud service providers when needed to satisfy availability, confidentiality, and integrity requirements. Doing this includes the ability to close an account on a particular date and time and to copy data from one service provider to another.

Security Upside.   The cloud computing paradigm provides opportunities for innovation in provisioning security service that holds the prospect of improving the overall security of some organizations. The biggest beneficiaries are likely to be smaller organizations that have limited numbers of IT administrators and security personnel and lack the economies of scale available for larger organizations with sizable data centers. Potential areas of improvement where organizations may derive security benefits from transitioning to a public cloud computing environment are listed next.

- Staff specialization
- Platform strength
- Resource availability
- Backup and recovery
- Mobile endpoints
- Data concentration
- Data center oriented (e.g., redirecting email records to a cloud provide via mail exchange records to discover widespread spam, phishing, and malware campaigns and to carry out remedial actions, such as quarantining suspect messages and content)
- Cloud oriented (e.g., reverse proxy products are available that enable unfettered access to a cloud environment yet maintain the data stored in that environment in encrypted form)

Key Security Considerations. Major security considerations in cloud computing include the need to:

- Carefully define security and privacy requirements during the initial planning stage at the start of the SDLC.

- Determine the extent to which negotiated service agreements are required to satisfy security requirements and the alternatives of using negotiated service agreements or cloud computing deployment models, which offer greater oversight and control over security and privacy.

- Assess the extent to which the server and client-side computing environments meet the organizational security and privacy requirements.

- Continue to maintain security management practices, controls, and accountability over the privacy and security of data and applications.

Potential Vulnerabilities. Potential vulnerabilities associated with various cloud computing service and deployment models are listed next.

- The inherent system complexity of a cloud computing environment and the dependency on the correctness of these components and the interactions among them

- The dependency on the service provider to maintain logical separation in a multitenant environment, which is not unique to the cloud computing model

- The need to ensure that the organization retains an appropriate level of controls to obtain situational awareness, weigh alternatives, set priorities, and effect changes in security and privacy that are in the best interests of an organization

Security Requirements. The goal is to ensure that a safe and secure cloud solution is available to provide a prospective IT service. The following security needs must be considered:

- Statutory compliance to laws, regulations, and organization requirements

- Data characteristics to assess which fundamental protections an application's data set requires

- Privacy and confidentiality to protect against accidental and nefarious access to information

- Integrity to ensure data are authorized, complete, and accurate

- Data controls and access policies to determine where data can be stored and who can access physical locations

- Governance to ensure that cloud computing service providers are sufficiently transparent, have adequate security and management controls, and provide the information necessary for the organization to appropriately and independently assess and monitor the efficacy of those controls

Potential Security Benefits. Potential security benefits of using cloud computing services are listed next.

- The ability to focus resources on areas of high concern as more general security services are assumed by the cloud provider

- Potential platform strength resulting from greater uniformity and homogeneity and the resulting improved information assurance, security response, system management, reliability, and maintainability

- Improved resource availability through scalability, redundancy, and disaster recovery capabilities; improved resilience to unanticipated service demands

- Improved backup and recovery capabilities, policies, procedures, and consistency

- Ability to leverage alternate cloud services to improve the overall security posture, including that of traditional data centers

- Reduced time-to-market metric regarding access provisioning of new applicants

General and Specific Security and Privacy Issues. Data processed in a public cloud computing environment and applications running in a public cloud facility can experience different security and privacy exposures than would be the case in an onsite hosted environment. For example, cloud subscribers, who are ultimately responsible for their data processed on providers' systems, must require assurances from providers that they are in compliance with the appropriate regulations.

Examples of **general security and privacy issues** in a public cloud environment include *not*:

- Meeting the subscriber's data protection requirements.

- Providing encryption of data at rest in storage.

- Knowing the strengths of the encryption algorithm.

- Knowing the attack surface of a cloud and the likely pool of attackers.

- Knowing the expertise level of cloud administrators.

Examples of **specific security and privacy issues** in public cloud computing environment include:

- Storing sensitive data without adequate protection due to risk of unintended data disclosure.

- Lack of subscriber awareness over where data are stored and who has or can have access, leading to privacy concerns due to the distributed nature of clouds.

- Inability to partition access rights among subscribers, providers, and administrators, thus compromising system integrity.

- Not having both logical and physical separation of systems required to protect a subscriber's resources due to multitenancy.

- Using a subscriber's browser as a graphical interface, an account setup, and resource access administration, all leading to security flaws.

- Lack of proper protection of a subscriber's cryptographic keys to ensure a safe use of cryptography from inside a cloud.

(O) Social Media Networks

Social media platforms with extensive use of technologies include Facebook, Twitter, YouTube, Google+, Instagram, Pinterest, Snapchat, and several others. Social media can drive customer traffic into both physical stores (offline stores) and nonphysical stores (online stores). Retailers are using YouTube, Google+, and Pinterest more than the Facebook and Twitter.

The millennial generation (Generations Y and Z) uses the social media more than the other generations. A retailer trying to understand and keep up with the social media technology is finding it very difficult to do as it is changing constantly and continuously.

Today, more and more customers are interacting and transacting with social media platforms (e.g., Facebook or Google) than with retailers directly. This new direction requires retailers to establish and maintain a greater presence in social media with their products and brands combined with personalized services to loyal customers. These customers, in turn, are willing to give up their security and privacy concerns and are willing to share their information in exchange for more personalized services. It is a marketing reality that retailers must go where customers go, even if that means to social media. The goal of marketing management is to turn social media into sales media due to massive numbers of potential customers present in social media.

A survey of women shoppers by Influence Central (www.influence-central.com) shows that:

- 86% buy a brand for the first time when they begin interacting with that brand on social media.

- 87% of them are more likely to buy a brand more regularly if it engages with them on social media platforms, which can make them more loyal.

- 82% said that insights and recommendations received through social media channels have changed how they gather information.

- 81% are influenced by product reviews.

- 72% said the ability to check social media recommendations takes the guesswork out of buying a new product.

- More than 50% said that recipes, images with photos and videos, testimonials, and comments received through social media had value to them.

- Generation Z, teenagers, take inspiration and product recommendations from Pinterest, Instagram, and Snapchat.

- Generation Z customers are more frugal and value-oriented than Generation Y customers.

- Generation Z customers like to buy their clothes from retailers such as H&M, Forever 21, and Zara.

- Generation Z customers want everything quickly and do not care about buying popular brand names and logos; instead, they prefer buying unbranded products.

- More than 60% of customers said they would not interact with a retailer's social media site while shopping at the store; instead they would love to use the general or public social media platforms, such as Facebook.

- 98% of millennials said they do not want to be texted or called by retailers about sales promotions; instead they prefer sales promotions sent by email.

- Millennial customers want retailers to engage them only on social media, not to sell their products to them.

   Example 1: Target Corporation, a major retailer has increased its budget on social media spending by 30%, reflecting its greater presence, priority, and strategic importance to social media.

Example 2: Nordstrom has increased its budget spending on mobile technology, social media technology, and multichannel growth strategies. Nordstrom claims that it has more followers on Pinterest than likes on Facebook. The keys to Nordstrom's success in social media are to bring rich content, showcase fashion trends, and even use customer pins on trends to merchandise displays in stores. Nordstrom believes that social media is an important touch point to engage customers, build long-term relationships with customers, and turn regular customers into loyal customers, more than with traditional product advertising and quick sales. These efforts have increased the Nordstrom's online sales.

Example 3: Nordstrom is launching its Like2Buy campaign to shop on Instagram where its e-commerce site is seamlessly connected to its Instagram page, thus allowing customers to purchase products they see posted (i.e., look and buy). Nordstrom also adding video screens in stores to showcase social shopping, especially by millennial customers.

Example 4: Nordstrom is integrating social media technology with its physical stores. It encourages customers to pin their favorite Nordstrom products (e.g., shoes and handbags) on Pinterest and shows them interactive display of those products within a store. Then a store's sales associates attach a Pinterest tag to those products and swap those pinned products based on other customer's' demands.

Example 5: Publix Super Markets, a grocery store chain retailer, is big on social media to engage with its customers where they are and to extend in-store services to online customers. Publix is active on Facebook for posting comments and reviews, Twitter for promoting brands, Instagram for sharing photos and videos, and Pinterest for providing recipes and event-planning ideas. Publix has benefited from social media through customer engagement, loyalty, and relationships, and eventual increase in sales.

Example 6: Williams-Sonoma, a general retailer, is using YouTube technology to show shoppable videos. Online customers can purchase everything they need from the videos with just a few clicks. The retailer has established a social media council as part of its social media strategy.

Example 7: Pottery Barn, a division of Williams-Sonoma, credits social media technology for its success. It works with Pinterest, an online pin board, which has become a great source of referral traffic to its online business and helped its brand get market exposure.

Example 8: Target's website crashed and went down for 20 minutes when the website could not keep up with the sales frenzy of a Lilly Pulitzer product, a designer limited edition collection. Later, social media members got frustrated with the out-of-stock condition and blasted Target to express their anger and disappointment. This shows the power of social media on retailers and on society in general.

(P) Virtual Private Networks

A VPN is a virtual network, built on top of existing physical networks, that provides a secure communications tunnel for data/information transmitted between networks. A VPN is a protected information system link utilizing tunneling, security controls, and endpoint address translation giving the impression of a dedicated (leased) line. Because a VPN can be used over existing networks, such as the Internet, it can facilitate the secure transfer of sensitive data across public networks. VPNs are usually established and managed by VPN gateway devices owned and managed by the organization being protected. Although VPNs can be implemented on top of ATM or Frame Relay, or over WAN connections, an increasingly popular approach is to build VPNs directly over the Internet. The leased lines (e.g., T-1 and T-3) are secure but expensive, and the Internet is less expensive.

The main components that make VPN secure are encrypted traffic and a protected authentication mechanism. The authentication method used can be a security token, known key, securely distributed certificate, password, or a combination of any of these methods. Once the authentication is complete, the VPN should encrypt all traffic between endpoints to ensure that no data is leaked and to prevent MitM attacks. Multifactor identification and authentication is strongly advised to neutralize the effectiveness of brute-force attacks. A common multifactor identification is a combination of a security token, known key, certificate, password, PIN, or biometrics.

A VPN can allow employees to connect to the intranet securely, so there are no fears of sensitive information leaving the network unprotected. The Internet alone cannot remove this fear.

A VPN is a private network composed of computers owned by a single organization that share information with each other in that organization (e.g., LAN or WAN). A public network is a large collection of organizations or computers that exchange information with each other (e.g., a public telephone system and the Internet).

A VPN blurs the line between a private network and a public one. With a VPN, a secure, private network can be created over a public network, such as the Internet. A VPN can be created using software, hardware, or a combination of the two that provides a secure link between peers over a public network. Control techniques, such as encryption, packet tunneling, and firewalls, are used in a VPN. Tunneling encapsulates a packet within a packet to accommodate incompatible protocols. The packet within the packet could be of the same protocol or of a completely different one.

The private network is called "virtual" because it uses temporary connections that have no real physical presence but consist of packets routed over various computers on the Internet on an ad hoc basis. Secure virtual connections are created between two computers, a computer and a network, or two networks. A VPN does not exist physically.

A VPN is a distributed collection of networks or systems that are interconnected via a public and/or private network but that protects their communications using encryption. In effect, a VPN is a private secure distributed network that is transported or tunneled across a public and/or private network. Typically, VPN encryption is implemented at the local network entry points (i.e., the firewall or premise router), thereby freeing the end systems from having to provide the necessary encryption or communication security functions.

The VPN is configured to maintain the security of the enclave and the requirement that all traffic must pass through the enclave security architecture. This is not to say that encrypted data (e.g., SSL, SSH, and TLS) that entered the VPN tunnel must also be unencrypted prior to leaving the tunnel. However, the data would still have to pass through the respective application proxy. If host-to-host VPN is required, it will be established between trusted known hosts.

A VPN solution can be cheaper than conventional networks that run over WAN connections. VPN devices and software provide not only encryption functions but also network access control to secure Internet tunnels between remote sites. A VPN must provide privacy and integrity of data as it traverses the public network. At a minimum, it should provide user authentication, address management, and data encryption security services.

Four types of VPNs exist: SSL VPNs, IPsec VPNs, Encapsulating Security Payload (ESP) in tunnel mode, and firewall-based VPNs. Three primary models for IPsec VPN architectures include gateway to gateway, host to gateway, and host to host. Alternatives to IPsec VPNs include the ESP tunnel mode and firewall-based VPNs.

(Q) Multimedia Collaborative Computing Networks

Multimedia collaborative computing networks include Instant Messaging (IM) architecture, IRC architecture, remote (virtual) meeting technology, networked whiteboards, cameras, and microphones. Explicit indication of use includes signals to users when collaborative computing devices are activated.

The IM architectures vary in design depending on the services being provided to end users. There are four possible architectural designs for IM systems:

1. Private hosting (i.e., client to server)

2. Public hosting

3. Client to client

4. Public switched network

The four architectures differ in the location of the session data.

The IRC architecture consists of servers and clients. Servers form the backbone of the network, linking components together and using routing capabilities to relay messages to their destinations. All packets are relayed through the server, hence the name of the protocol. Clients reside on the machines of users who are chatting on the network. Currently, the IRC is mainly designed for group (many-to-many) communication in discussion forums called channels, but it also allows one-to-one communications via private message. IRC networks that are in operation need to migrate to newer IM technologies due to the inherent security vulnerabilities with IRC.

(R) Ad Hoc Networks

Networks of nodes that are near each other are called ad hoc networks, where both the routers and the hosts are mobile and running on the same computer (i.e., Nodes = Routers + Hosts). In traditional wired networks, the routers are fixed and the hosts are mobile. In ad hoc networks, topologies are changing all the time without warning. An ad hoc network is used when a group of users with notebook computers are gathered in an area where the IEEE 802.11 standard is not available. A common routing algorithm used in ad hoc networks is ad-hoc on-demand distance vector, where it determines a route to some destination only when someone wants to send a packet to that destination (i.e., as needed, meaning ad hoc). A local Wi-Fi or Bluetooth are very popular ad hoc network standards.

(S) Content Delivery Networks

CDNs are used to deliver the contents of music, movie, sports, or news from content owners' websites to end users quickly with the use of tools and techniques such as client caching, server replication, client's request redirection, and a proxy content server to enhance Web performance in terms of optimizing the disk size and preload time.

Three parties exist in the CDN process to deliver content to end users: the CDN provider (contractor), the ISP, and the content owner (music or news provider). The CDN contractor delivers the content owner's material to end users via the ISP for a fee. Server replication is called server mirroring, where the content is replicated at multiple, dispersed locations for end users' easy and quick access, especially during a disaster. The content is redirected without changing the DNS. Similar to caching, which improves the client's performance, mirroring improves a server's performance.

(T) Value-Added Networks

Value-added carriers lease channels from other common carriers and then provide additional services to customers using these leased channels. They operate a public data network, where the equipment breaks up the user's data into packets, routes the packets over its network between one location and another, and reassembles them into their original form on the other end. VANs take advantage of economies of scale. Usually they share a wider bandwidth, which gives a faster response time. Some examples of services provided by VANs include bulletin board services, Internet, EDI, and dial-in services. The last two topics are covered next.

Electronic Data Interchange. EDI uses proprietary communication structures and provides the exchange of routine business transactions in a computer-processable format, covering such traditional applications as inquiries, planning, purchasing, acknowledgments, pricing, order status, scheduling, shipping and receiving, invoices, and payments. New ways of implementing EDI include the use of standardized communication structures such as eXtensible Markup Language (XML), Simple Object Access Protocol (SOAP), and web services; and moving away from using proprietary communication structures (e.g., VANs) to allow more interoperability and to facilitate better maintenance work.

Dial-in Services. Many external, commercial electronic databases and online systems exist to satisfy the needs of specific customers. Some systems provide general services, such as email, real-time conferences, file transfer, game playing, and online news. Online search systems contain indexes from major magazines and other periodicals on all topics.

(U) Wireless Sensor Networks

Wireless sensor networks are networks of interconnected wireless devices that are embedded in the physical environment to provide measurements of, for example, building security. These devices have built-in processing, storage, and radio frequency (RF) sensors and antennas. These sensors start with a low-level sensors and progress toward nodes for high-level data aggregation, analysis, and storage, where data is routed over a network to an automated computer facility. Typical applications of wireless sensor networks are listed next.

- Monitoring traffic or military activity

- Protecting physical property

- Monitoring environmental changes in a building (e.g., humidity, voltage, and temperature)

- Managing machinery and vehicle operation

- Establishing physical security perimeters for building and facilities

- Monitoring supply-chain management activities

- Detecting the presence of chemical, biological, or radiological substances

(V) Digital Cellular Networks

Today, separate networks are used for voice traffic (telephone traffic), computer communications (data networks such as the Internet), and video (broadcast or cable television or other specialized networks). These separate networks are expensive, time consuming, and complicated. A single digital network is needed that can potentially be used to transmit all types of data and information (i.e., voice, data, video, and images).

Digital cellular network standards in the world are varied and incompatible with each other. For example, the United States uses a Code Division Multiple Access (CDMA) standard whereas the rest of the world uses a Global System for Mobile Communications standard. Today's cellular network systems are used to transmit both voice and data (e.g., SMS to send and receive text messages).

(W) Peer-to-Peer Networks

Broadly defined, a P2P network is a distributed computing software architecture that enables individual computers to connect to and communicate directly with other computers. Through this connection, computer users (known as peers) can share communications, processing power, and data files. With respect to file sharing specifically, P2P technology allows decentralized sharing. That is, rather than storing files in a central location to which individual computers must connect to retrieve the files, P2P technology enables individual computers to share directly among themselves files stored on the individual computers. P2P file-sharing programs themselves do not perform the sharing or copying of files; rather, they employ a protocol that facilitates communication between the two peers who wish to share or copy a particular file. Peers can share myriad types of files, including audio, video, software, word processing, and photographs.

By eliminating the need for a central storage point for files, P2P file-sharing technology allows for faster file transfers and conservation of bandwidth (i.e., the capacity to transmit information to and from a computer). In addition, because P2P technology decreases the need for businesses and consumers to store files on their hard drives, it can lower costs by conserving on storage requirements and saving on maintenance and energy costs related to data retrieval, sharing, and processing.

Uses of and risks from P2P technology include the following:

- P2P technology enables users to share communications, processing power, and data files with other users. Use of P2P technology can enhance efficiency by allowing faster file transfers, conserving bandwidth, and reducing or eliminating the need for central storage of files.

- P2P technology has a variety of applications, but the most common application by far is commercial file-sharing software programs used by consumers to exchange files, such as music, movies, television programs, video games, software, and pornography.

- P2P technology continues to evolve in response to market and legal forces. It appears likely that the uses of P2P technology will expand in the future.

- Consumers face risks when using commercial P2P file-sharing software programs, including risks related to data security, spyware and adware, viruses, copyright infringement, and unwanted pornography.

(X) Converged Network

A **converged network** occurs when two different networks are combined, as in the case of data and voice networks. A converged network is subject to vulnerabilities and threats. For example, the same openings that allow voice traffic to pass unimpeded may also either create high-bandwidth covert channels for data infiltration or exfiltration or provide a point of entry for other probes and attacks. Although it may be impossible to examine voice traffic in real time without incurring unacceptable delay, it may be possible to isolate the voice traffic in some way from the rest of the network to minimize the vulnerabilities introduced by opening these entry points.

Although firewalls, hardware and software guards, and software downgraders (i.e., lowers a network grade) serve to separate an enclave from the outside world or the rest of the network, they may not limit latency, jitter, and delay problems in the context of the converged network.

A converged network is a single point of failure in a way that totally separate data and voice infrastructures were not because the converged network may not have uninterruptible power supply (UPS) and fault tolerance mechanisms to facilitate graceful degradation.

Until the technology improves, it might be preferable to isolate the packet-switched digital voice on a separate network from the data network. This isolation is a better approach rather than an ad hoc box-based mix-and-match solution focused on individual functions.

(Y) Optical Networks

Optical networks use fiber optic cables, which are strands of clear glass fiber. These cables are faster and lighter than non-optical networks. They are, secure, durable, expensive, and difficult to install. An optical network can transmit voice, data, and video with greater bandwidth. Existing optical networks can increase their capacity with dense wavelength division multiplexing (DWDM), which enables a single communications channel to carry simultaneous data transmissions from multiple sources without any extra cable. DWDM uses different wavelengths to carry separate streams of data over the same cable at the same time. Prior to DWDM, optical networks could use only a single wavelength per strand.

Synchronous Optical Network (SONET) is popular in transmitting voice, data, and video over optical networks. Most of the world's long-distance telephone systems use SONET to standardize and connect multiple and different long-distance carriers. The goals of SONET are to: (1) interwork the multiple carriers with a common signaling standard regarding wavelength, timing, and framing structures; (2) unify the pulse code modulation channels, which are incompatible with each other; (3) multiplex different digital channels with different speed in terms of data rates; and (4) provide support for operations, administration, and maintenance systems. SONET is a synchronous system, meaning that the sender and receiver are tied to a common clock, whereas ATM system is not tied to a common clock because it permits irregular cell arrivals. SONET operates at the physical layer of the ISO/OSI model and supports gigabit transmission rates. SONET has a fault tolerance mechanism (i.e., redundancy) in that it has a backup ring to ensure continued transmission if the primary ring fails.

(Z) Body Area Networks

A body area network is a technology that allows communication between ultra-small and ultra-low-power intelligent sensors/devices that are located on the body surface or implanted inside the body. In addition, the wearable/implantable nodes can also communicate to a controller device that is located in the vicinity of the body. These radio-enabled sensors can be used to continuously gather a variety of important health and/or physiological data (i.e., information critical to providing health care) wirelessly.

Radio-enabled implantable medical devices offer a revolutionary set of possible applications, including smart pills for precision drug delivery, intelligent endoscope capsules, glucose monitors, and eye pressure sensing systems. Similarly, wearable sensors allow for various medical and physiological monitoring (e.g., electrocardiogram, temperature, respiration, heart rate, and blood pressure) and disability assistance.

(AA) Radio Frequency Identification Networks

RFID network systems share information across organizational boundaries, such as supply chain applications. RFID systems provide a method for tracking the movement of goods throughout the supply chain. These systems use small tags with embedded microchips containing data about an item and its location to transmit radio signals over a short distance to special RFID readers. These readers then pass the data over a network to a computer for processing the tag data. These tags, unlike bar codes, do not need LOS contact to be read. RFID systems can be very complex, and implementations vary greatly across industries and organizations.

An RFID system is composed of three components: an RF subsystem, an enterprise subsystem, and an inter-enterprise subsystem. The four major categories of RFID risk are: (1) business process risk (loss of critical and operational records and cloning of tags); (2) BI risk (access to sensitive or proprietary information); (3) privacy risk (profiling individuals using the tagged items); and (4) externality risk (health hazards from electromagnetic radiation).

(c) Network Connections

Network connections consist of connectivity hardware devices and software to share resources and information among the networks. This connection would enable a network user to establish a communication link with a user from another network, and vice versa. The hardware devices and software move data frames and packets from one cable segment to another. They may use a piggybacking technique of temporarily delaying outgoing acknowledgments of data frames so that they can be attached to the next outgoing data frames.

In this section, we discuss these types of network connectivity hardware devices and software: routers; sensors; hardware and software guards; network switches; bridges; brouters; repeaters; gateways; proxies and reverse proxies; modems; port protection devices; multiplexers; hardware controllers; protocol converters; protocol analyzers; backbone networks; concentrators; hubs; connectors; NICs; front-end processors; network nodes; sockets; ports; subnets; portals; wireless devices such as smartphones, and Bluetooth; wireless access points; domain controller; programmable logic controllers; and network access storage devices. In addition, measurement metrics, such as quality of service and quality of protection, are addressed to reduce network congestion and to improve network performance.

(i) Routers

A **router** is a network connectivity device that establishes a path through one or more computer networks. Routers offer a complex form of interconnectivity. They keep a record of node addresses and current network status. Routers are known to the end-stations, as they are device dependent. LANs connect PCs, terminals, printers, and plotters within a limited geographical area. An extended LAN is achieved through the use of bridges and routers. In other words, the capabilities of a single LAN are extended by connecting LANs at distant locations. A router operates in the network layer of the Open System Interconnection (OSI) Reference Model.

Routers convert between different data link protocols and re-segment transport-level protocol data units as necessary to accomplish this. These protocol data units are reassembled by the destination endpoint transport protocol entity. Several routing protocols are in common use. Routers must have more detailed knowledge than bridges about the protocols used to carry messages through the internetwork. When routers are used to connect FDDI to other networks, it is important to ensure that the routers support the needed network-level protocols.

WHAT IS AN INFORMATION TECHNOLOGY PERIMETER SECURITY DEFENSE?

An IT perimeter security defense is a method that integrates security of all layers of the architecture, including router, switch, network, OS, file system, database, and applications layers.

Router Accounts and Passwords. Restricting access to all routers is critical in safeguarding the network. In order to control and authorize access, an authentication server that provides extended user authentication and authority levels should be implemented.

For router accounts and passwords, the router administrator will ensure:

- An authentication server is used to gain administrative access to all routers.
- When an authentication server is used for administrative access to the router, only one account is defined locally on the router for use in an emergency (i.e., authentication server or connection to the server is down).
- Each user has his or her own account to access the router with username and password.
- All user accounts are assigned the lowest privilege level that allows them to perform their duties.
- Accounts that are no longer required should be removed immediately from the authentication server or router.
- A password is required to gain access to the router's diagnostic port (management port used for troubleshooting).
- The enable secret password must not match any other username and passwords, enable password, or other enable secret password.
- Passwords are not viewable when displaying the router configuration.

Routing Table Integrity. A rogue router could send a fictitious routing table to convince a site's premise router to send traffic to an incorrect or even a rogue destination. This diverted traffic could be analyzed to learn confidential information from the site's network or to disrupt the network's ability to communicate effectively with other networks.

Router Packet Filtering and Logging. Access control lists (ACLs) are used to separate data traffic into that which it will route (permitted packets) and that which it will not route (denied packets). Secure configuration of routers makes use of ACLs for restricting access to services on the router itself as well as for filtering passing through the router.

Router Configuration Management. CM activities can be extended to routers using rule sets, similar to firewalls. The rule set can be a file that the router examines from top to bottom when making routing decisions, using routing tables.

(ii) Sensors

Sensors are IDSs and are composed of monitors and scanners, and they fill the gap left by firewalls. Monitors are of two types: network and host. Both types of monitors perform intrusion detection and malicious code detection. Scanners also are of two types: network and host. Network scanners provide vulnerability scanning and war dialing. Host scanners provide vulnerability scanning and file integrity checking. Both monitors and sensors must have detect and respond capabilities.

IDSs are hardware and software products that gather and analyze information from various areas within a computer or network to identify possible security breaches. These breaches include intrusions from outside the organization and misuse from within. An IDS is a system to detect, report, and provide limited response to an activity that may be harmful to an information system. Some IDSs can even prevent the intrusion activities. Tools to complement IDSs include antimalware products (i.e., antivirus and antispyware software), firewalls, routers, honeypots, honeynets, padded cell systems, and canaries.

(iii) Hardware and Software Guards

Hardware and/or software guards enable users to exchange data between private and public networks, which is normally prohibited because of information confidentiality. A combination of hardware and/or software guards is used to allow secure LAN connectivity between enclave boundaries operating at different security classification levels (i.e., one private and the other public).

A guard is a device used to defend the network boundary by employing these functions and properties:

- Guards typically are subjected to a high degree of assurance during development.
- They support limited services.
- Services are at the application level only.
- Guards may support application data filtering reviews.
- Guards may support sanitization of data.
- Typically, they are used to connect networks with differing levels of trust (i.e., provide regrading of data).

Guard technology can bridge across security boundaries by providing some of the interconnectivity required between systems operating at different security levels. Several types of guards exist. These protection approaches employ various processing, filtering and data-blocking techniques in an attempt to provide data sanitization (e.g., downgrade) or separation between networks. Some approaches involve human review of the data flow and support data flow in one or both directions. Information flowing from public to private networks is considered an upgrade. This type of transfer may not require a review cycle but should always require a verification of the integrity of the information originating from the public source system and network. Guards can be used to counteract attacks made on the enclave.

A guard is designed to provide a secure information path for sharing data between multiple system networks operating at different security levels. The guard system is composed of a server, workstations, malicious code detection, a firewall and/or filtering routers, all configured to allow transfer of information among communities of users operating at different security levels.

Most guard implementations use a dual network approach, which physically separates private and public sides from each other. Guards are application specific; therefore, all information will enter and exit by first passing through the Application Layer, Layer 7 of the Open System Interconnection (OSI) model. In addition, most guard processes are high-assurance platforms that host some form of trusted OS and trusted networking software.

Enclave boundaries need protection from the establishment of unauthorized network connections. The focus is on attacks into an enclave by malicious email transfer, file transfer, or message transfer. Guards can be implemented to provide a high level of assurance for networks by preventing certain types of malicious messages from entering the enclave.

(iv) Network Switches

A computer network has three main components: computers, links, and **switches**. The web of links and switches carry data between the computers. Links are made of copper (either twisted pair or coaxial cable) or fiber optics. Transmission equipment at each end of the fiber or copper generates the electrical or optical signals. There are also satellite and microwave links that send radio waves through the air. Fiber optics has several advantages over other types of links—most notably its very high bandwidth.

As the information travels through the network, the switches decide which link it will have to traverse next in order to reach its destination. The rules by which the switches and the users' computers coordinate the transmission of information through the network are called protocols.

Bridges and repeaters share the same physical transmission medium to interconnect or extend a LAN. Switches and hardware devices are designed for the opposite purpose of bridges and repeaters. Switches, in the form of routers, interconnect when the systems forming one workgroup are physically separated from the systems forming other workgroups. Switches do not extend LANs as bridges and repeaters do. Switches are used primarily to implement multiple, parallel transmission medium segments to which different groups of workstations can be connected and to provide full network bandwidth to multiple groups of systems.

Network switches are devices that provide connectivity between two or more hosts located on the same network segment. They are similar to hubs in that they allow communications between hosts; but, unlike hubs, the switches have more intelligence and send communications to only those hosts to which the communications are addressed. The benefit of switches from a security standpoint is that when they are employed on a network, it is much more difficult to eavesdrop on communications between other hosts on the network segment. This is extremely important when a web server is on a network segment that is used by other hosts. For example, if a hub is used and a host on the DMZ is compromised, an attacker may be able to eavesdrop on the communications of other hosts on the DMZ, possibly leading to the compromise of those hosts or the information they communicate across the network. For example, email servers in their default configurations receive unencrypted passwords; a compromise of the web server would lead to the exposure of email passwords by sniffing them from the compromised web server.

Switches can have a negative impact on network-based IDPSs. Most network switches allow network administrators to configure a specific port on the switch, known as a span port, so that it replicates the entire switch's traffic to the port used by the IDPS. This allows a network-based IDPS to see all traffic on a particular network segment. However, under high loads, the switch might have to stop sending traffic to the span port, causing the IDPS to be unable to monitor network activity. Also, other devices use span ports, and there are typically very few span ports on a switch; therefore, it might not be possible to connect an IDPS to a particular switch because its span ports are all in use.

WHAT ARE THE FUNCTIONS OF ROUTERS, SENSORS, HARDWARE AND/OR SOFTWARE GUARDS, SWITCHES, BRIDGES, REPEATERS, AND GATEWAYS?

- Routers are limited to particular routing protocols, while bridges may be transparent to most routing protocols.
- Sensors are intrusion detection systems and are composed of monitors and scanners. They fill the gap left by firewalls.
- Hardware and/or software guards enable users to exchange data between private and public networks, which is normally prohibited because of information confidentiality.
- Switches decide which link it will have to traverse next in order to reach its destination. Unlike bridges and repeaters, switches do not extend LANs.
- Bridges are generally considered to be faster than routers since the processing they perform is simpler.
- Bridging protocols are semiautomatic. Routers are automatic and depend on routing tables, which typically must be maintained.
- Bridge protocols limit the size of any extended LAN network while routers do not. Routers are used to connect LANs, WANs, and WANs.
- Repeaters are the simplest form of interconnectivity hardware devices.
- A gateway is an interface providing compatibility between networks by converting transmission speeds, protocols, codes, or security measures.
- Routers do not propagate network broadcasts. Bridges do.
- Bridges and repeaters share the same physical transmission medium to interconnect or extend a LAN.
- Routers and switches provide the simplest method of local authentication for network infrastructure devices.
- Repeaters and hubs are similar in function.
- Bridges and switches are similar in function.

(v) Bridges

A **bridge** is a device that connects together two or more LANs that are similar or dissimilar to form an extended LAN. Bridges are protocol-independent devices and are designed to store and then forward frames destined for another LAN. Bridges are transparent to the end stations connecting through the bridge. Bridges can reduce total traffic on the extended LAN by filtering unnecessary traffic from the overall network. A bridge functions in a MAC/Data Link layer of the ISO/OSI Reference Model. Bridges are similar to switches.

Various types of bridges are discussed briefly next.

Local bridges connect to LANs together directly at one bridge. Remote bridges connect two distant LANs through a long-distance circuit, which is invisible to the stations on the LANs.

Learning bridges learn whether they must forward packets by observing the source addresses of packets on the networks to which they are connected. The bridge maintains a table of source addresses for each subnetwork. Learning bridges generally participate in a spanning tree algorithm, in which the bridges communicate with each other to establish a tree through the extended LAN so that there is one and only one path between any two stations, preventing endlessly circulating packets. The spanning tree algorithm is used to build plug-and-play bridges.

With source routing bridges, the source and destination stations explicitly participate in the routing through the bridges. The source station inserts the route through the bridges to the information field of the packet. The bridge, in turn, just uses the routing information supplied by the source station to route packets.

Bridges and routers are lower-level network interconnection devices. Typically network interconnection strategies involve some combination of bridges and routers. The decision regarding when to use a bridge and when to use a router is a difficult one. Enterprises may use bridging to connect LANs between different buildings on corporate or university campuses. Bridging access point (AP) devices are typically placed on top of buildings to achieve greater antenna reception.

(vi) Brouters

Brouters are routers that can also bridge; they route one or more protocols and bridge all other network traffic. Routing bridges are capable of maintaining the protocol transparency of a standard bridge while also making intelligent path selections, just like routers. Brouters merge the capabilities of bridges and routers into a single, multifunctional device.

(vii) Repeaters

Repeaters offer the simplest form of interconnectivity hardware devices. Multiple cables can be connected by repeaters to make larger networks. Repeaters merely generate or repeat data packets or electrical signals between cable segments. They also perform data insertion and reception functions. They receive a message, amplify it, and then retransmit it, regenerating the signal at its original strength in both directions. In their purest form, repeaters physically extend a network. They also provide a level of fault tolerance by isolating networks electrically, so problems on one cable segment do not affect other segments. However, repeaters exert stress on a network's bandwidth due to difficulty in isolating network traffic. Repeaters are independent of protocols and media. A repeater operates in a Physical Layer of the ISO/OSI Reference Model and performs no Data Link Level functions. Repeaters are similar to hubs.

(viii) Gateways

A **gateway** is an interface providing compatibility between networks by converting transmission speeds, protocols, codes, or security measures. In general, a gateway is a device that connects incompatible networks using different communications protocols so that information can be passed from one to the other (i.e., two connection-oriented protocols, such as TCP/IP and ATM transport protocol). A gateway transfers information and converts it to a form compatible with the receiving network's protocols (e.g., an email gateway could translate the Internet messages into SMS messages for mobile phones). Several types of gateway exist, including data, email, application, secure, XML, and VPN gateways.

WHICH CONNECTIVITY DEVICE OPERATES WHERE IN THE OPEN SYSTEM INTERCONNECTION LAYER?

- A gateway operates in the application layer and transport layer.
- A router operates in the network layer.
- A bridge and switch operate in the data-link layer.

(Continued)

> ### WHICH CONNECTIVITY DEVICE OPERATES WHERE IN THE OPEN SYSTEM INTERCONNECTION LAYER? (*Continued*)
>
> - A repeater and hub operate in the physical layer.
>
> - A NIC operates at the data-link layer.
>
> - Firewalls operate at lower layers and higher layers of the ISO/OSI model. Basic firewalls operate on one or a few lower layers while more advanced firewalls examine all of the layers. Firewalls that examine more layers can perform more granular and thorough examinations. A firewall that handles lower layers only (e.g., data-link layer) cannot usually identify specific users.

(ix) Proxies and Reverse Proxies

A **proxy** is a computer with software acting as a barrier between a private network and the Internet by presenting only a single network address to external sites. By acting as a go-between representing all internal computers, the web proxy protects network identities while still providing access to the Internet. Proxy servers forward application traffic through a firewall. Proxies tend to be specific to the protocol they are designed to forward and may provide increased access control or audit. A proxy server is a firewall component that manages Internet traffic to and from a LAN. The proxy server also provides document caching and access control. A proxy server can improve performance by supplying frequently requested data (e.g., a popular web page) and can filter and discard requests that the owner does not consider appropriate (e.g., unauthorized access requests).

Reverse proxies are devices that sit between a web server and the server's clients. The term "reverse proxy" is used because the data flow is the reverse of a traditional (forward) proxy. Reverse proxies can serve as a valuable addition to the security of a web server. The term is used rather loosely in the industry and can include some or all of these functionalities:

- Encryption accelerators, which offload the computationally expensive processing required for initiating SSL/TLS connections

- Security gateways, which monitor HTTP traffic to and from the web server for potential attacks and take action as necessary, acting in essence as application-level firewalls

- Content filters, which can monitor traffic to and from the web server for potentially sensitive or inappropriate data and take action as necessary

- Authentication gateways, which authenticate users via a variety of authentication mechanisms and control access to URLs hosted on the web server itself

Reverse proxies should be considered for any high-risk web server deployment. While they do add risk by requiring the deployment of additional hardware and software, the risk is generally outweighed by the benefits. In addition to the functionality just listed, web proxies are valuable because they add an additional layer between a web server and its less trusted users. Due to their highly specialized nature, proxies are easier to secure than web servers. Proxies also further obfuscate a web server's configuration, type, location, and other details that are pertinent to attackers. For example, web servers have banners that frequently reveal the web server type and version, and these banners sometimes cannot be changed. With a reverse proxy, this is not an issue because the proxy can rewrite the banner before it is sent to users.

(x) Modems

If computers are connected over long distances, modems are needed. The term "modem" is an acronym for *mo*dulator and *dem*odulator. A **modem** is a device that modulates and demodulates signals. Modems are used primarily for converting digital signals into quasi-analog signals for transmission over analog communication channels and for reconverting the quasi-analog signals into digital signals. Many additional functions may be added to a modem to provide customer service and control features. Modems can be installed either internally or externally to a computer.

The range of options available on modems is quite large. Simple units do little more than perform the digital-to-analog signal conversion, but more intelligent units can automatically dial phone numbers, store messages for delayed transmission, and perform a number of other functions.

These factors should be considered in modem selection:

- The requirements of the communications software and target computer
- Speed (measured in baud)
- Physical connection (RS-232 or V.35)
- Duplex (full or half)
- Synchronization scheme (asynchronous or synchronous)
- Dialing (manual or automated)

Basic modems have two major uses: They are attached to a stand-alone PC, either internally or externally, and they are attached to network-based PCs. Other modems include cable and digital modems.

A **cable modem** provides high-speed access to the Internet. Its drawbacks include inadequate security due to shared media, such as coaxial trunks, and lower throughput due to several users using the service at the same time. Some cable data providers offer limited firewall protection and packet filtering services, where the latter is meant to protect against broadcasts.

A **digital modem** provides high-speed access to the Internet with Digital Subscriber Line (XDSL) constantly connected with the fixed IP address, which is less vulnerable to attacks than dial-up lines.

(xi) Port Protection Devices

A **port protection device (PPD)** is fitted to a communications port of a host computer and authorizes access to the port itself, prior to and independent of the computer's own access control functions. A PPD can be a separate device in the communications stream (typically PPDs are found only in serial communications streams), or it may be incorporated into a communications device (e.g., a modem). PPDs typically require a separate authenticator, such as a password, in order to access the communications port.

One of the most common PPDs is the dial-back modem. In a typical dial-back modem sequence, a user calls the dial-back modem and enters a password. The modem hangs up on the user and performs a table lookup for the password provided. If the password is found, the modem places a return call to the user (at a previously specified number) to initiate the session. The return call itself also helps to protect against the use of lost or compromised accounts. This is, however, not always the case. Malicious hackers can use the call forwarding feature to reroute calls. A terminal server can act as a PPD for remote maintenance connections, such as router maintenance ports.

(xii) Multiplexers

A **multiplexer** is a device for combining two or more channels. A **channel** is a single path provided from a transmission medium, either by physical separation (e.g., cable) or by electrical separation (e.g., frequency- or time-division multiplexing). In optical communications, wavelength-division multiplexing involves the use of several distinct optical sources (e.g., lasers) with each having a distinct center frequency. In general, multiplexing is the combining of two or more information channels onto a common transmission medium.

(xiii) Hardware Controllers

A **controller** is a hardware device that coordinates and manages the operation of one or more I/O devices, such as computer terminals, workstations, disks, and printers. It synchronizes the operations of these devices with the operation of the computer system as a whole. A controller organizes a series of actions from requests received from computer terminals, other controllers, or host computer systems. Many varieties of controllers exist, including communication, store, cluster, and terminal controllers.

A **communication controller** manages the details of communication line control and the routing of data and messages through a network in which a series of computer programs are stored and executed. A **store controller** is a programmable unit in a network used to collect data, direct inquiries, and control communication within a computer system. It stores information such as tables, lists, and control blocks used by the host processor to work with the store controller. A **cluster controller** is a device that controls the I/O operations of more than one device connected to it through a series of computer programs stored and executed in the unit. A **terminal controller** is used in WANs in accessing mainframe computers.

(xiv) Protocol Converters

Protocol converters are devices that change one type of coded data to another type of coded data for computer processing. Conversion facilities allow an application system conforming to one network architecture to communicate with an application system conforming to some other network architecture.

(xv) Protocol Analyzers

Protocol analyzers are software tools that vary widely in functions and user friendliness. Examples of their functions include password sniffing and packet sniffing performed by sniffers. Protocol analyzers perform password sniffing to capture passwords for unauthorized reuse.

Sniffers are LAN protocol analyzers that capture packets and analyze them for certain attributes. They capture illegally short or long frames typically discarded by standard LAN adapters. Sniffers are programs to capture, interpret, and store packets traversing a network used for later analysis and debugging network problems. Sensitive data, such as a username (user ID) and password combination, confidential email messages, and file transfers of proprietary data can be sniffed.

The protocol analyzer allows the LAN administrator to see what is happening on the LAN in real time and observe problems as they occur. It is a valuable tool for online testing of service degradation.

(xvi) Backbone Network

A **backbone network** is a central network to which other networks connect. Users are not attached directly to a backbone network; they are connected to the access networks, which in turn connect to the backbone. A backbone network provides connection between LANs and

WANs. Dumb terminals can be attached directly to the backbone through terminal servers. The backbone network is a high-speed connection within a network that connects shorter, usually slower circuits.

HOW DO NETWORKS GET CONNECTED?

- Front-end networks connect workstations and servers for file sharing and application processing.
- Back-end networks connect peripherals, such as disk drives and high-speed printers.
- A backbone network is a central network to which other networks connect.

(xvii) Concentrators

The major function of **concentrators** is to gather together several lines in one central location. Concentrators are the foundation of an FDDI network and are attached directly to the FDDI dual ring. Concentrators provide highly fault-tolerant connections to the FDDI rings.

Concentrators allow stations to be inserted and removed with minimal effect on the operation of the ring. One function of the concentrator is to ensure ports (stations) are automatically bypassed in response to a detected fault connection, a high error rate, or when a user powers down the station. This bypass function of the concentrator enhances the reliability of the FDDI ring.

(xviii) Hubs

A **hub** can be thought of a central place from which all connecting lines are made. All the lines coming into a hub must operate at the same speed. Unlike repeaters, hubs do not amplify the incoming signals. Like repeaters, hubs do not examine IEEE 802 addresses. If two frames arrive at the same time, they will collide, as with a coaxial cable. Hubs are similar to repeaters.

There are a number of definitions of the term "hub," including:

- The link from remote end users to the central satellite and back to the central satellite dish
- The link from Ethernet LANs to host computers
- Another name for the Ethernet concentrator

Although hubs are cheaper than switches, they are becoming obsolete due to falling switch prices and better performance of switches. However, legacy hubs still exist. The backbone network was also used as a hub, but that is not common now.

(xix) Connectors

A **connector** is an electro-mechanical device on the ends of cables that permit them to be connected with and disconnected from other cables. For example, connectors join controllers to peripherals (e.g., printers and hard disk drive) and computers. The type of cable used determines the type of connector needed (e.g., a thicknet coaxial cable needs Type N connector).

(xx) Network Interface Cards

NICs are circuit boards used to transmit and receive commands and messages between a PC and a LAN. They are expansion cards, and they mediate between the computer and the physical media (e.g., cable) over which transmissions take place. When the NIC fails, workstations and file servers also fail. Network adapters, which function like NICs, establish a connection to other computers or peripherals, such as a printer in the network. NICs operate at the data-link layer.

To establish connections to the wireless LAN, mobile wireless stations need an add-on card called a wireless NIC with a built-in radio and antenna signals. In a wireless LAN, a station or client can be a laptop/notebook/desktop computer or device with a wireless NIC. Usually the wireless NIC is inserted in the client's PC card slot or USB port.

(xxi) Front-End Processors

A **front-end processor (FEP)** is a programmed logic or stored program device that interfaces data communication equipment with an I/O bus or the memory of a data processing computer. It reduces the workload of a host computer by performing certain tasks that the host computer would otherwise do. A programmable FEP (PFEP) puts less demand on the host computer by sharing some tasks with the host. The PFEP performs polling, code conversion, and data formatting functions.

(xxii) Network Nodes

The term **network node** has multiple definitions:

- A physical connection (junction) point where communication lines come to and leave from
- The point at an end of a branch
- The representation of a state or event in terms of a point on a diagram
- In network topology, it is a terminal of any branch of a network or an interconnection common to two or more branches of a network
- In a tree structure, it is a point at which subordinate items of data originate.
- In a switched network, it is one of the switches forming the network backbone

Nodes can be distributed to host processors, communication controllers, or terminals. Nodes are labeled as major, minor, endpoint, host, master, intermediate, or terminal.

WHICH NETWORK USES WHAT TOPOLOGY?

Topology affects security, so proper selection and functioning of topology is important to ensure proper security. Several types of topologies exist.

Star topology—All nodes are connected to a single central hub. Traffic is in both directions.

Bus topology—All nodes are connected to a central cable, called the bus or backbone. Traffic is in both directions.

Ring topology—All nodes are connected to one another in the shape of a closed loop, so that each node is connected directly to two other nodes, one on either side of it. Traffic is in one direction.

Mesh topology—Networked components are connected with many redundant interconnections between network nodes. In a true mesh topology, every node has a connection to every other node in the network.

Hybrid topology—A linear bus backbone connects with the star-configured network. Dial-up telephone services and PBX systems use the star topology. Ethernet mostly uses the bus topology. FDDI uses the ring topology. The Internet uses the mesh topology.

(xxiii) Sockets

Sockets are end points created in a TCP service by both the sender and the receiver. Each socket has a socket number consisting of the IP address of the host and a port number. For a TCP service to be obtained, a connection must be made between a socket on the sending computer and a socket on the receiving computer. Two or more connections can terminate at the same socket. Connections are identified by the socket number at both ends, and no virtual circuit numbers are used. In TCP/IP, the socket number is the concatenation of the sender's or receiver's IP address and the port number for the service being used. The pair of these sender's and receiver's socket numbers uniquely specifies the connection to the Internet.

(xxiv) Ports

The term "port" has multiple definitions.

- An access point for data entry or exit

- A connector on a device to which cables for other devices such as terminals and printers are attached

- In a communication network, a point at which signals can enter or leave the network en route to or from another network

- A port is identified by a port number assigned either ephemerally or permanently to enable IP packets to be sent to do a particular task on a computer connected to the Internet. Ephemeral port numbers go out of use when the session ends. All ports should be closed when they are not in use because open and unused ports invite attackers.

Some protocols, such as FTP and SMTP use the same permanent port number in all TCP/IP implementations. Note that some connections use TCP protocol for FTP, SMTP, and TELNET services; some use UDP protocol for DNS service; and while others use either TCP or UDP for Packet Internet groper (PING) echo service.

Telnet is the TCP/IP standard network virtual terminal protocol that is used for remote terminal connection service. It allows a user terminal at one site to interact with systems at other sites as if that user terminal were directly connected to computers at those sites.

PING is a TCP/IP diagnostic program that sends one or a series of Internet Control Message Protocol echo packets to a user-specified IP address. The echo packet requests that the receiver reply with an echo reply packet. The PING program measures and displays the round-trip time for replies to return, the number of hosts that are operational, the number of IP addresses that are valid, and the percentage of returned or lost packets. The PING protocol tests the ability of a computer to communicate with a remote computer by sending a query and receiving a confirmation response.

There are a number of ports, including serial, parallel, terminal, I/O, protocol, disabled, and communication ports. Ports should be closed when not in use because open ports invite attackers.

(xxv) Subnets

There are a number of definitions for the term "subnet" (also called subnetwork):

- A network that forms part of a larger network

- A group of nodes with the same network ID

- The Ethernet part of a main network

- In TCP/IP, a part of a network that is identified by a portion of the Internet address

In terms of the ISO/OSI Reference Model, the subnet comprises the layers below the transport layer (i.e., the network, data-link, and physical layers). The network layer operates ATM networks, ad hoc networks, P2P networks, and WANs. The medium access control sublayer of the data-link layer operates wired LANs and MANs, wireless LANs and MANs, and virtual LANs. The physical layer operates ISDN, PSTN, and SONET.

The application layer operates the Internet (wired web and wireless web), client/server network, CDN, and VoIP network. There are no networks operating either at the transport layer or at the session layer because the transport layer provides an understanding of layered protocols and end-to-end connection-oriented services, and the session layer provides services such as dialog control and token management.

WAN machines are called host computers, which are connected by a communications subnet. Individual customers own the host (personal) computers whereas the telephone company or the ISPs own and operate subnets. In most WAN networks, the subnet consists of two distinct components: transmission lines to move bits between machines and switching elements, which are special computers (routers) that connect three or more transmission lines.

All host computers in a main network must have the same network number to the outside world. Since IP addresses are limited in supply, the subnets are created by splitting the main network into several parts for internal use with different IP addresses, but they still act like a single network to the outside world. Hence, subnets are not visible to the outside the world.

In an IP address, a subnet address is an extension that allows users in a network to use a single IP network address for multiple physical subnetworks. To implement subnetworking, the main router needs a subnet mask that indicates the split among network, subnet, and host. To accomplish this, routing tables need to be changed to add new entries of subnets.

Subnets face traffic congestion problems for packets (e.g., increased delay and decreased throughput) and QoS issues. Some solutions to handle the congestion problems include:

- Increasing the resources.
- Decreasing the load.
- Designing open-loop and closed-loop controls.
- Establishing caching, retransmission, and flow control policies, where discarded or choked packets are retransmitted or sent back or the load can be reduced.

Some methods to improve QoS include:

- Buffering at the client side.
- Increasing the router capacity.
- Traffic shaping.
- Resource reservation.
- Packet scheduling.

(xxvi) Portals

A **portal** is a website that acts as a gateway to the Internet. It is a collection of links, content, and services designed to guide end users to search for information on the Internet (e.g., Yahoo,

Google, and Bing). A portal is a server that offers access to one or more applications through a single centralized interface. Most portals are web based—for them, the portal client is a regular web browser. The application client software is installed on the portal server, and it communicates with application server software on servers within the organization. The portal server communicates securely with the portal client as needed; the exact nature of this communication depends on the type of portal solution in use.

Examples of portals include:

- Application portals, such as a secure socket layer (SSL) portal
- VPN, which is a web-based portal providing a user with access to multiple Web-based applications from a single portal website
- An Ethernet portal connected to the Internet
- Mobile (wireless) portals that provide content and services on users' mobile devices

(xxvii) Wireless Devices

The most frequently used handheld wireless devices include **smartphones** and digital tablets using text-messaging technology (e.g., short message service-SMS and multimedia messaging service-MMS) and Bluetooth technology. Mobile (cell) phones with information-processing and data-networking capabilities are called smartphones. Digital tablets are very popular in use and they look like notebook computers with no data input from outside.

Text-messaging technology is designed to monitor a user's inbox for new email and relay the email to the user's wireless handheld device via the Internet and wireless network.

Bluetooth is a popular ad hoc network standard, which describes how mobile phones, computers, and PDAs should interconnect with each other, with home/business phones, and with computers using short-range wireless connections. Bluetooth network applications include wireless synchronization; email, Internet, and intranet access using local PC connections; hidden computing through automated applications and networking; and applications that can be used for hands-free devices.

(xxviii) Wireless Access Points

Wireless APs are devices that act as conduits to connect wireless communication devices together to allow them to communicate and create a wireless network. For example, employees traveling on business work with wireless-enabled devices can connect to an organization's network via any of the many public Internet access points or public hot spots.

The two fundamental types of WLAN components are client devices (e.g., computers, PDAs, and smartphones) and access points, where the latter logically connect client devices with a distribution system, which is typically an organization's wired network infrastructure. The distribution system is the means by which client devices can communicate with the organization's wired LANs and external networks, such as the Internet. Some WLANs also use wireless switches, which act as intermediaries between APs and the distribution system. The purpose of the wireless switch is to assist network administrators in managing the WLAN infrastructure. The security of each of the WLAN components, including client devices, APs, and wireless switches, is heavily dependent on its WLAN security configuration.

The AP, which acts a bridge between the wireless and wired networks, typically comprises a radio, a wired network interface (e.g., IEEE 802.3), and bridging software. The AP functions as a base station for the wireless network, aggregating multiple wireless stations onto the wired network.

APs generally have only three encryption settings available: none, 40-bit shared key, and 104-bit setting. The setting of "none" represents the most serious risk since unencrypted data traversing the network can easily be intercepted, read, and altered. A 40-bit shared key will encrypt the network communications data, but there is still a risk of compromise (broken by brute-force attack using a high-end graphics computer or even a low-end computer). In general, 104-bit encryption is more secure than 40-bit encryption because of the significant difference in the size of the cryptographic keyspace.

Attackers can introduce rogue devices and create rogue APs to conduct their attacks. A **rogue device** is an unauthorized node on a network; a **rogue AP** is an unauthorized entry point.

Some examples of attacks using wireless vulnerabilities are listed next.

- Passive attacks include eavesdropping and traffic analysis
- Active attacks include masquerading, replay, message modification, DoS, and misappropriation of assets

The deployment of rogue WLAN devices is a form of active attack. For example, an attacker deploys an AP that has been configured to appear as part of an organization's WLAN infrastructure. This can provide a backdoor into the wired network, bypassing perimeter security mechanisms, such as firewalls. In addition, if client devices inadvertently connect to the rogue AP, the attacker can view and manipulate communications on the client devices (i.e., conducting a MitM attack) and potentially gain access to the client devices themselves.

- In a dual-connect scenario when a wireless network is connected to the wired network, an attacker exploits insecure laptop configurations to gain unauthorized access to an organization's core network.
- Wireless MitM attacks use an insecure laptop configuration to intercept or alter information transmitted wirelessly between the target laptop and a wireless access point.
- Attacks on smartphones can involve stealing data or injecting malicious code using phone memory cards.

Some examples of security controls to mitigate wireless vulnerabilities are listed next.

- Use a personal firewall when accessing public wireless networks in airports and conference centers.
- Obtain vendor upgrades to software and firmware.
- Install a VPN to stop leakage of data through hot spots because a VPN can encrypt the data transmitted in public places.
- Install personal firewalls in public places, where possible.
- Establish proper configuration settings.
- Incorporate wireless and mobile device security component topics in training.
- Implement handheld scanner or network authentication mechanisms to detect rogue wireless client devices.

- Install a wireless intrusion detection system (WIDS) to continuously monitor, detect, and respond to malicious activities before they inflict damage. Use of WIDS is better than using handheld scanners or network authentication mechanisms to find rogue APs.

WLAN monitoring tools can detect these devices and intrusion attempts:

- Unauthorized WLAN devices (rogue devices), including rogue APs and unauthorized client devices

- WLAN devices that are misconfigured or using weak WLAN protocols and protocol implementations

- Unusual WLAN usage patterns (e.g., extremely high number of client devices using a particular AP, abnormally high volumes of WLAN traffic involving a particular client device, or many failed attempts to join the WLANs in a short period of time)

- DoS attacks and conditions (e.g., network interference; a large number of events involving the termination of WLAN services can indicate a DoS attack)

- Impersonation and MitM attacks (e.g., some WIDS sensors can detect when a device is attempting to spoof the identity of another device)

Organizations should be able to identify the physical location of a detected WLAN threat by using triangulation, which involves estimating the threat's approximate distance from multiple sensors by the strength of the threat's signal received by each sensor, then calculating the physical location at which the threat would be the estimated distance from each sensor. This method allows an organization to send physical security staff to the location to handle the threat.

(xxix) Domain Controller

A **domain controller** is a server responsible for managing domain information, such as login identification and passwords.

(xxx) Programmable Logic Controller

A **programmable logic controller (PLC),** used in industrial control systems, is a programmable microprocessor-based device designed to control and monitor various inputs and outputs used to automate industrial processes. Since a PLC is a first-level decision-making device controlling safety interlocks, it can become a single point of failure.

(xxxi) Network Access Storage

An **NAS device** is a dedicated hardware device made up of several hard drives used to store data in a single location. This device offers an easy way for multiple users to access the same data, which is important in situations where users are collaborating on projects.

(xxxii) Quality of Service and Quality of Protection

Network congestion occurs when too many network packets are present in the subnet (i.e., too much traffic), thus degrading network performance in terms of some lost packets or all packets undelivered. The presence of congestion means that the load is temporarily greater than the system resources can handle. Two solutions are available to the congestion problem: Either increase the resources or decrease the load.

A critical requirement of networks is the delivery of messages in a timely and predictable manner, and it is addressed with adequate network bandwidth and reliability. Bandwidth resources can be managed with QoS management where resources are allocated and conflicts are resolved using established security policies.

Quality of service (QoS) is a network performance property that specifies a guaranteed throughput level for end-to-end services, which is critical for most composite web services in delivering enterprise-wide service-oriented distributed systems. Examples of network performance properties include throughput (bandwidth), transit delay (latency), error rates, priority, security, packet loss, and packet jitter.

Quality of protection (QoP) requires that overall performance of a system should be improved by prioritizing traffic and considering rate of failure or average latency at the lower layer protocols.

Denial of quality (DoQ) results from lack of QA methods and QC techniques used in delivering messages, packets, and services. QA is the planned systematic activities necessary to ensure that a component, module, or system conforms to established technical requirements. QC is the prevention of defective components, modules, and systems. Proper implementation of QA methods and QC techniques can prevent DoQ and DoS and support QoS and QoP.

Denial of service (DoS) is the prevention of authorized access to resources or the delaying of time-critical operations.

Ways to improve QoS and QoP are listed next.

- Implement service-to-service authentication services as a part of authentication, authorization, and accountability concepts.

- Implement traffic prioritization rules to improve overall performance of the system.

- Implement Web Service Reliability (WS-Reliability) and WS-Reliable Messaging standards for guaranteed message delivery and message ordering. These standards also address rate of failure or average latency at the lower layer protocols. Through WS-Reliable Messaging, web services can ensure that messages are not lost even if the network is saturated.

- Use queuing networks and simulation techniques for both single service and composite services to ensure quality and availability of web services. For example, enterprise systems with several business partners must complete business processes in a timely manner to meet real-time market conditions. The dynamic and compositional nature of web services makes end-to-end QoS and QoP management a major challenge for service-oriented distributed systems.

- Ensure that packets corresponding to individual web service messages are routed accordingly.

- Practice defensive programming techniques and information hiding to make web service software more robust.

- Implement service-level agreements (SLAs) between an end user organization and a service provider to satisfy specific end user (customer) application system requirements.

(d) Operational Roles of IT Staff

The operational roles and responsibilities of IT staff are defined with required separation of duties among them. Examples of IT staff job titles include network administrator, DBA, data administrator, help-desk staff, security administrator, web master, web server administrator, system administrator, web programmer, web administrator, systems analyst, applications programmer, systems programmer, computer operator, SQA analyst, web designer, and web developer. These IT staff members are deeply committed to service-level management practices with the ultimate goal of providing excellent service to end users. Understanding the IT staff roles and responsibilities can help internal auditors during IT audits so auditors can approach the right IT staff to work with.

(i) Roles and Responsibilities

Network administrator is a person responsible for the overall design, implementation, and maintenance of a network. The scope of responsibilities includes overseeing network security, installing new applications, distributing software upgrades, monitoring the daily network activity, enforcing software licensing agreements, developing a storage management program, and providing for routine backups.

Database administrator is a person responsible for the day-to-day control and monitoring of databases, including data warehouse and data mining activities. The DBA deals with the physical design of the database while the data administrator (DA) deals with the logical design.

Data administrator is responsible for the planning, acquisition, and maintenance of database management software, including the design, validation, and security of database files. The DA is fully responsible for the data model and the DD software. The DA focuses on data architecture and big data. **Data architecture** deals with data compilation, including who creates and uses the data and how. It presents a stable basis for the processes and information used by the organization to accomplish its mission.

Help desk staff make up the end user support function in many computer centers. This function includes an information center, help desk, 24-hour hotline services, call center agents for helping customers, technical support analysts, telephone voice response system, and automated problem and CM systems.

A help desk function can implement telephone hotline services so that end users can call in and ask questions. These questions could be related to problems as diverse as printer/terminal operations, OS malfunctions, troubleshooting of problems, downloading on-demand software, and fixing telecommunications software incompatibilities, or applications software glitches and bugs. The help desk person will try to solve a problem; if he or she cannot, the person will route the problem to the right person, it is hoped. Problem logging, routing, and escalation procedures are needed to resolve problems in a timely and proper manner.

Voice response systems could supplement the help desk function in terms of directing end users to the appropriate person. Other developments include the implementation of Artificial Intelligence (AI) technology and Expert Systems that aid help desk staff to diagnose and resolve problems.

Security administrator is a person dedicated to performing information security functions for servers and other hosts as well as networks.

Web master is a person responsible for the maintenance of a website, including adding new content, organizing and reorganizing the content, removing older and incorrect content, and monitoring website traffic. Web masters must be proficient in HTML and one or more scripting and interface languages, such as JavaScript and Perl. They collect and compile web-related performance data to develop web analytics (e.g., click-through rates). They could be web developers in building a website. They may or may not be responsible for the underlying server, which is traditionally the responsibility of the web server administrator.

Web server administrator is a system architect responsible for the overall design, implementation, and maintenance of a web server. Web server administrators may or may not be responsible for web content, which is traditionally the responsibility of the web master.

System administrator is a person who manages a multiuser computer system, including its OS and applications, and whose responsibilities are similar to that of a network administrator. A system administrator performs systems programmer activities with regard to the OS and network control programs.

Web programmer develops programs for web pages using the HTML and XML code. Web programmers work with static URLs and dynamic URLs; improve user experience on the client side; and improve data retrieval, security, and performance features on the server side.

Web administrator is responsible for supporting web servers, websites, and web applications, including troubleshooting. Web administrators work with search engines (e.g., Google), which automatically prioritizes static URLs over dynamic URLs. The reprioritization of URLs is called rewriting the URL with the goal of making dynamic URLs more interactive and attractive in display.

Systems analyst breaks down a large problem into several smaller problems to make system analysis, system requirements, and system design work much simpler and easier. The output of a systems analyst's work becomes an input to an application programmer's work so the latter can develop computer programs.

Application programmer writes or develops computer programs using the system analysis work results from a system analyst. An application program or system is intended to serve a business or nonbusiness function and has a specific input, processing, and output activities (e.g., accounts receivable and general ledger system or a general support system). Applications software comprises the functions of data entry, update, query, and report programs that process an organization's business data.

Systems programmer works on system software, which is a major category of programs used to control the computer and process other programs, such as OSs, communications control programs, security software, and database managers. The OS and accompanying utility programs enable a computer user to control, configure, and maintain the computer system, software, and data.

Systems programmers also work on system partitioning tasks, where system user functionality and user interface services are separated from information system management functionality, including databases, network components, workstations, and servers. This separation is achieved through physical or logical methods using different computers, different CPUs, different instances of the OS, different network addresses, or combination of these methods.

Computer operator is a person whose activities include console operations, system commands and parameters, system backups and backup alternatives, data file backup methods, and hardware preventive maintenance work. Other activities include reviewing and monitoring system logs and coordinating with the help desk function.

Software quality assurance analyst ensures that all SQA requirements are met using peer reviews where two or more programmers review and critique each other's work for accuracy and consistency with other parts of the system and detect program errors. This analyst participates in a new system development work, ongoing system maintenance work, and routine system operations work.

SQA is a planned and systematic method of all actions necessary to provide adequate confidence that a developed software product conforms to established SQA requirements.

Web designer prepares content for a website in terms of styling and layout of web pages with content, including text and images. Web designers use HTML technologies and tools and focus on website aesthetics (e.g., style and color schemes).

Web developer writes application programs for the Internet or distributed networks to run the HTTP protocols. Web developers use HTML programming languages connected with the back-end programs of the Internet or web applications.

(ii) Separation of Duties

The objective of separation of duties is to ensure that no one person has complete control over a transaction or an activity throughout its initiation, authorization, recording, processing, and reporting. This means that an employee cannot approve his or her own travel expense report; a supervisor must approve. A similar concept applies equally to any operation performed by IT or user department employees. The rationale is to minimize incompatible functions, which are not conducive to good internal control structure. Incompatible functions can create conflict-of-interest and uncontrolled situations whereas compatible functions can promote conflict-free and controlled situations. The separation of duties provides checks and balances between employees performing different job duties so no errors, fraud, collusion, abuse, misuse, and other irregularities can occur.

The degree of separation of duties depends on the job level. More separation of duties is practiced at the lower levels of the organization than at higher levels. The rationale is that someone at higher levels needs to be in charge of many functions, activities, and operations to facilitate integration and coordination. At a minimum, the listed functions in the IT department should be separated from each other at lower levels.

Incompatible IT Functions

- Web administrator and web server administrator
- Web designer and web developer
- Web programmer and web master
- Computer operations and applications programming
- Computer operations and systems programming
- Application programming and systems programming
- Systems programming and data security administration
- Data security administration and data administration
- Data security administration and database administration
- Data security administration and system administration
- Data administration and QA
- Database administration and applications programming
- Telecommunication network and computer operations

- QA and applications development/maintenance
- QA and systems programming

Compatible IT Functions

- QA and data security administration
- Call center agent and network administrator
- Web master and web server administrator
- Help desk and computer operations
- Systems analysis and application programming
- Web developer and web programmer
- Web master and web developer
- Call center agent and technical support analyst

(iii) Service-Level Management

Service-level management is an effective way for computer center management to improve the quality of computing services for system users. Computer center management must define a set of user service levels or service objectives that describe application systems, volume of transactions, processing windows, online system response times, and batch job turnaround times. Without defined service levels to monitor against actual performance determined in the resource utilization function, the capacity limit of a computer system is difficult to identify. Without managed service levels, computer center management will consider that computer capacity is near its limits only when users begin to complain about computer performance.

By monitoring performance against service levels, computer center management can identify approaching problems in meeting service objectives. In order to achieve these goals, computer center management needs to develop service-level objectives for internal use. Some examples of areas requiring service-level objectives are listed next.

- System capacity during peak hours in terms of average CPU busy, average demand paging rate, and maximum channel busy
- Number of: online users, online transactions per minute, and batch jobs per hour
- Online system average response time in seconds by application
- Percentage of time the online system is available
- Turnaround time for test and production batch jobs processed under each job class by application
- Number of job reruns and time lost due to job reruns
- Number of abnormal terminations by application program per operating shift

Where applicable, maximum and minimum numbers (range) should be identified for each of these objectives. The rationale behind developing service-level objectives internally first is that they provide a basis for negotiating SLAs with the user community.

After developing service-level objectives internally, computer center management is ready to negotiate with each business user to develop formal SLAs. Some examples of SLAs are listed next.

- Average response times for each online application system

- Turnaround times for each batch job by application system

- System availability time (system up-time) by each application system

- Accuracy limits in terms of number of errors by cause for each application system

- Number of job reruns by each application system

- Number of transactions to be processed during peak hours in each application system

- Number of production problems by application system per week

- Computer report delivery times by application system

- Plan for reporting service-level problems

- Action priorities if services cannot be delivered

- Scheduled meetings to discuss service levels between end users and computer center management

It is important to remember that these SLAs are not static. They require periodic adjustments and refinements, such as at least once a year or preferably at the time of renegotiation of the agreement with customers (users).

3.5 IT Control Frameworks and Basic Controls

IT control frameworks and basic IT controls are presented in this section.

(a) Information Technology Control Frameworks

IT control frameworks provide overall guidance to user organizations as a frame of reference for security, governance, and implementation of security-related controls. Several organizations within and outside the United States provide such guidance.

Eleven major types of IT control frameworks are discussed in this section:

1. The Institute of Internal Auditors' Electronic Systems Assurance and Control

2. The IT Governance Institute's Control Objectives for Information and Related Technology

3. The Information Systems Audit and Control Foundation's Control Objectives for Net Centric Technology

4. The SysTrust Principles and Criteria for Systems Reliability from the American Institute of Certified Public Accountants/Canadian Institute of Certified Accountants

5. The International Federation of Accountants' Managing Security of Information

6. The Information Security Forum's standard

7. U.S. Department of Homeland Security

8. The European Union's security directives

9. The Organisation for Economic Co-operation and Development's Guidelines for the Security of Information Systems

10. International Common Criteria

11. The International Organization for Standardization standards

In addition, guidelines for implementing minimum security requirements, regardless of the type of IT control framework adopted, are presented.

(i) The Institute of Internal Auditors' Electronic Systems Assurance and Control

The Institute of Internal Auditors' Electronic Systems Assurance and Control (eSAC) sets the stage for effective technology and risk management by providing a framework for evaluating the e-business control environment. Within the context of an organization's mission, values, objectives, and strategies, the different eSAC modules will assist in gaining an objective perspective on the organization's IT culture. This knowledge will then aid in providing assurance to customers, regulators, management, and boards that IT risks are understood and managed.

eSAC brings executive management, corporate governance entities, and auditors new information to understand, monitor, assess, and mitigate IT risks. It examines and assesses risks that accompany each organizational component, including customers, competitors, regulators, the community at large, and owners and investors. The eSAC title is enhanced by changing "Auditability" to "Assurance" to recognize the important perspectives of governance and the alliances—both within an organization and between business partners—needed to ensure effective security, auditability, and control of information.

(A) Technology Challenge of Components

The technology challenge of components include open systems, technology complexity, information security, privacy concerns, and development and distribution processes.

Open Systems. Internet-based distributed systems have very different characteristics from internally focused, closed private computer information systems. Open systems that use the Internet are the first truly pubic systems and as such are exposed to more and different risks. Never before have organizations been so accessible to so many. The Internet is a global client/server environment that evolved due to low-cost powerful computers with large storage capacity, mass communications, and user-friendly software.

Technology Complexity. Dispersion of technology into every department, division, or business unit provides new challenges to control and assurance. Over both proprietary and Internet connections, organizational system boundaries will blur into those of allies, partners, suppliers, and end users. Such widespread distribution will challenge already inadequate abilities to provide security, control, and privacy.

Control migration from application code to the environment is a growing trend. Traditional applications—accounting, purchasing, scheduling, manufacturing, inventory, sales, delivery, and collection—are often integrated into ERP systems. Data reside in one central database, with more responsibility for control. The HR system and its database may support all employee-related activities, such as payroll, evaluations, training and skills, benefits, and retirement benefits. ERP systems integrate traditional applications, databases, and HR systems.

The proliferation of computers and the Internet has brought technology services into even the smallest of businesses and organizations. Common applications offer enormous economies of scale, and even niche applications can thrive. Software size and complexity has consumed new capability faster than computer chips can make it available. As more people acquire computers and access spreads to more countries, the current Web will expand to even more products, services, and languages, challenging controls over users' interaction while providing the information and services they seek.

Information Security. Effective security is not only a technology problem; it is a business issue. It must address people's awareness and actions, training, and especially the corporate culture, influenced by management's security consciousness and the tone at the top.

Access to a computer system is not an issue; rather the issue is how much access is enough. When access exists, there is the potential for inappropriate access, introduction of errors, possible disclosure, corruption, and destruction of information. Since security is a moving target, there must be a continual risk assessment and management process to examine changing vulnerabilities and consequences and to prioritize risks and probabilities. This focuses security resources on things that must be protected and threats that can be mitigated at appropriate cost based on a cost/benefit analysis.

Privacy Concerns. Countries treat privacy matters differently based on their cultures, treaties, and practices. Globalization of business due to the Internet has meant many new laws and regulations to address concerns over specific rights to control personal information. Privacy provisions range from confidentiality of communications to specific access rights. The global privacy landscape involves legislative, regulatory, and cultural considerations of overlapping or conflicting requirements that range from generally acceptable use to more restrictions in certain countries. A new regulation is European Union's General Data Protection Regulation (GDPR) effective in 2018, which addresses privacy concerns, risks, and controls.

Development and Distribution of Processes. The design and development process for systems has changed. Formerly, systems were developed to facilitate existing business operations, but today they are frequently seen as a new line of business. E-business and the need to get to market faster often mean expansion of the IT infrastructure outside the organization. Hardware and software, telecommunications, and web hosting are often outsourced to ISPs. The provision of controls, and assurance that controls are deserving of reliance placed on them, grows exponentially more complex as the number of parties and layers grows.

Responses to the Technology Challenge. Risk assessment, internal control, and e-assurance are suggested as responses to the technology challenge.

Risk Assessment. Functional and technology managers must reject the silo attitude or inept behavior toward risks. An organization may do its strategic planning too quickly or not at all; it may not align strategy and enterprise design with market requirements; managers may not look beyond strict areas of their authority; compensating controls may not be designed to mitigate local risks; or teamwork among cross functions may not exist to communicate the nature and severity of risks to senior management.

There is no standard way to measure risks and associated losses since e-commerce risks affect businesses differently. Therefore, each business unit should conduct its own risk assessment, addressing such questions as:

- What are the risks?
- How large is the adverse effect of an exposure?
- Are preventive, detective, and corrective controls in place, and are they effective?

- How much security protection against risks is justified?
- Which risks threaten survivability of the business?
- Which risks can be mitigated at relatively low cost?

Internal Control. Internal control comprises the activities an organization uses to reduce risks that can affect its mission. The tone at the top (senior management) determines the focus for the entire organization, including the system of internal control. Management has direct responsibility for control and must coordinate efforts to achieve objectives. Although changes in technology present new risks and require different control techniques, basic control objectives remain essentially unchanged.

While definitions of internal control vary, they address the same objectives. The system of internal control is processes and procedures to provide reasonable assurance that goals and objectives are achieved and to ensure that risk is reduced to an acceptable level.

A cost/benefit analysis should decide which controls—internal or external—mitigate the risks most effectively. To devise an IT risk strategy, management must decide which risks are serious, which can be insured, which controls can be relied on, and which risks require compensating controls. Monitoring for compliance and constant update are essential.

E-assurance. Systems are imperfect, things go wrong, and people seek assurance that prudent controls minimize risk. Assurance services check the degree to which a system deviates from industry standards or management requirements for reliability. Whenever one party makes an assertion that requires review before others can rely on it, there must be an agreed-on set of criteria against which to measure it and a process to collect such evidence. When there are few agreed-on standards, attaining such a goal becomes difficult at best.

Traditional assurance services are being revamped to meet the new challenges. The problem is the ever-shifting nature of risks and controls. As a body of data is developed, these services, along with improvements in firewalls and intelligence being built into routers, third-party certifications, trusted certificate authorities, digital signatures, and encryption using PKI and the like will combine to improve controls over e-business.

An issue exists as to whether the marketplace—internal or external—will accept that internally provided assurance by internal auditors is effective in enhancing trust. The trust marks and website seals that external assurance service providers can provide are increasingly seen as viable methods to reassure users of e-business services. For most organizations, an appropriate balance between using internal and external assurance is the best path.

(B) eSAC Model

The eSAC model's assurance objectives or control attributes, such as availability, capability, functionality, protectability, and accountability, are integrated with the objectives of the Committee of Sponsoring Organizations (COSO), such as effectiveness and efficiency of operations, financial and other management reporting, compliance with laws and regulations, and safeguarding of assets. Privacy concerns are discussed under protectability and accountability. Next, we discuss the five assurance objectives of the eSAC model:

1. Availability
2. Capability

3. Functionality

4. Protectability

5. Accountability

Availability. Information, processes, and services must be available when needed. Specifically, the organization must be able to receive, accept, process, and support transactions in a manner acceptable to its customers. Access via the Internet can mean 24/7/365 availability. To ensure availability, the auditor evaluates controls that deal with potential causes of business interruption. These might include:

- Physical and logical security of system resources.
- Mechanical failure of computer file storage devices.
- Malfunction of software or unexpected incompatibilities.
- Inadequate computer capacity planning.

In the event of a problem, controls must provide for swift recovery to the normal position.

Capability. **Capability** means end-to-end reliable and timely completion and fulfillment of all transactions. This means that the system has adequate capacity, communications, and other aspects to consistently meet needs even at peak demand. For systems to provide such services, important controls are monitoring of usage, SLAs with ISPs, ASPs, and others. It is critical that system and process bottlenecks be identified and eliminated or carefully managed—the goal is to achieve and maintain an efficient and effective balance across the organization.

Efficiency of systems is an aspect of capability that leads to effective use of resources. A key is controlling system development and acquisition methodologies to prevent cost overruns and systems that do not perform as required. To help ensure efficiency of IT, the auditor evaluates controls that deal with causes and risks of excessive costs, characterized as waste and inefficiency. Some of the problems might include weaknesses in controls that result in excessive correction of errors; prevention is usually more efficient; and controls that consume more resources than the benefits they deliver. Systems that are inefficient may lead users to create shadow systems that work around the official system. Such duplicate costs are clearly inefficient. The unreliable system must be fixed before the shadow system is halted. The objectives of system development controls are to avoid such issues. Methodologies should result in efficient and appropriate design and development of an application and ensure that controls, auditability, and security are built into the system.

An information system that is not maintained effectively becomes unreliable. Controls over system maintenance, often called change controls, provide continuity while hardware or software changes are made and ensure that all changes are documented, approved, and confirmed. System maintenance controls include:

- Adequate user involvement in requesting, testing, and approving program changes.
- Creating appropriate audit trails, including program change history logs.
- IT and user personnel approval.
- Sufficient documentation of program changes.

Once these controls are complete, controlled production transfer procedures reduce the risk of programmers having the ability to introduce unapproved test versions of programs into production environment.

Functionality. **Functionality** means the system provides the facilities, responsiveness, and ease of use to meet user needs. Good functionality goes well beyond minimum transaction processing. It should also provide for recording control information and other issues of concern to management. Preventing problems in functionality includes considering the perspective of untrained, possibly unknown online users. Users can become impatient and may quit without completing a transaction or may resubmit input, causing duplicates. To help ensure functionality, the auditor evaluates controls that monitor and provide feedback. Some of these might include:

- The display of progress indicators following input.
- Positive confirmation of transactions.
- Monitoring user abandonment of transactions.
- Monitoring system hang-ups.

Effective information is information that is relevant to the business process, delivered by a functional system. Relevance of information is based on system design, which requires user and management participation to reach functionality. Problems often stem from inadequate specifications due to lack of user involvement in system development, which usually means the resulting application will be ineffective.

To help ensure effectiveness, the auditor evaluates controls over timely, correct, consistent, and usable information. The system should permit flexible displays and reports that can be tailored to different audiences. The format in which information is delivered can have a substantial impact on how effective the communication is.

Protectability. **Protectability** includes protection of hardware, software, and data from unauthorized access, use, or harm. Robust security is difficult to maintain due to the vast access possible via the Internet, the structure of which has inherent weaknesses. Controls are needed to safeguard IT assets against loss and to identify when such loss has occurred. Many current controls focus on reducing risks of catastrophic damage, internal fraud, or embezzlement. To ensure protectability, the auditor evaluates general controls over IT that are often grouped as shown next.

- **Data security and confidentiality.** Access to data, an important asset, should be limited to those authorized to process or maintain specific data or records. Protecting organizational data is the key responsibility of the information security function and its administrators. The security functions may include restricting access to data through various logical access paths, based on user requirements; restricting access to program libraries and data files on a need-to-know basis; and providing the ability to hold users accountable for activities performed.

- **Program security.** Access to program files and libraries should be restricted to authorized personnel through the use of access control and other security software. Program updates should be monitored and controlled using library management software. Appropriate segregation of duties should ensure that the programming function does not have unrestricted access to production programs.

- **Physical security.** Access to computer processors and storage devices should be limited to those (e.g., data center management and computer operations staff) requiring access to perform job functions. Access to the host server computer room should be monitored and controlled (e.g., card access control systems). Physical control over reports containing confidential data should be implemented (e.g., report distribution procedures). Physical safeguards include fire prevention, preventive maintenance, backup of data files, and property insurance.

Many protectability objectives are designed to ensure that data retains its integrity—in other words, that data is complete, accurate, and up to date and cannot be changed on an unauthorized basis. To help ensure integrity, the auditor evaluates controls over causes of erroneous data, which often are known as application controls, plus by general controls over access to computer resources. More detailed integrity control objectives are listed next.

- Authorized transactions are initially and completely recorded.

- All transactions are completely and accurately entered into the system for processing.

- Approved transactions entered are accepted by the system and processed to completion.

- All transactions are processed only once; no duplicate transactions are processed.

- All transactions are processed accurately, updating the correct files and records.

Procedures should minimize the opportunity for application programmers and users to make unauthorized changes to production programs. Access to system software should be controlled to avoid direct compromise of the integrity of program code, data on file, or results of processing.

Confidentiality and privacy are issues of accountability in compliance and protectability of information. There is no privacy without security. Confidentiality refers to intellectual property, trade secrets, and strategic plans. Privacy is usually viewed in the context of personal information, including customers, employees, and stockholders, but not corporate entities.

Accountability. Accountability identifies individual roles, actions, and responsibilities. It includes the concepts of data ownership, identification, and authentication, all fundamental to being able to identify who or what caused a transaction. The audit or transaction trail should have enough information—and be retained long enough—for transactions to be confirmed, if necessary.

Accountability also includes the concept of nonrepudiation. This means that once authenticated, a user cannot disclaim a transaction, as might happen when an online brokerage user seeks to break a trade that turned out to be a bad idea that he or she nonetheless actually caused.

Accountability also includes issues in granting traceable access to restricted information and software functions. This is a particular problem in IT, where systems analysts, programmers, system administrators, and the like resist controls over their own activities. In some cases, monitoring of such use, while seemingly appropriate, can be turned off by the very system administrator it is designed to watch.

Organizations need to authenticate the identity of people entrusted with authority to change data files or software. Similarly, an organization holding private information has an obligation to authenticate the identity of people making inquiries before disclosing such information. In such cases, accountability and privacy may appear to be in conflict. Accountability means identifying the source of a transaction, while privacy might deny meaningful identification. These objectives can be reconciled with care. Accountability protects everyone—for example, where a seller has a legitimate need to authenticate the identity of a buyer for credit purposes, while the holder of the credit card has a legitimate need to authenticate the seller to prevent fraudulent misrepresentation.

To support accountability, information must be sufficient, accurate, timely, and available to management to meet its responsibilities. To help ensure reliability of information, the auditor evaluates controls over unacceptable processing and reporting. Some of these controls are listed next.

- Information can be supported irrefutably. Controls that provide support are variously known as transaction trails or audit trails.

- Information should be timely. It must be available when decisions are made. This is a common criticism of financial statements issued months after the events.

- Information must be consistent, in accordance with applicable policies. Errors of inappropriate processing, whether programmed or not, are common causes of this effect. Management override can be another.

(ii) IT Governance Institute's Control Objectives for Information and Related Technology

The control objectives make a clear and distinct link to business objectives in order to support significant use outside the audit community. Control objectives are defined in a process-oriented manner following the principle of business reengineering.

An internal control system or framework must be in place to support business processes, and it must be clear how each individual control activity satisfies the information requirements and impacts the resources. Impact on IT resources is highlighted in the Control Objectives for Information and Related Technology (COBIT) framework together with the business requirements for effectiveness, efficiency, confidentiality, integrity, availability, compliance, and reliability of information that need to be satisfied. Control, which includes policies, organizational structures, practices, and procedures, is management's responsibility. Management, through its corporate governance, must ensure that due diligence is exercised by all individuals involved in the management, use, design, development, maintenance, or operation of information systems.

Business orientation is the main theme of COBIT. It is designed not only to be employed by users and auditors but also—and more important—as a comprehensive checklist for business process owners. Increasingly, business practice involves the full empowerment of business process owners as they have total responsibility for all aspects of the business process. In particular, this includes providing adequate controls. The COBIT framework provides a tool for the business process owner that facilitates the discharge of this responsibility.

The COBIT framework starts from a simple and pragmatic premise: In order to provide the information that the organization needs to achieve its objectives, IT resources need to be managed by a set of naturally grouped processes.

The COBIT framework includes (1) the classification of domains where high-level control objectives apply (domains and processes), (2) an indication of the business requirements for information in that domain, and (3) the IT resources primarily impacted by the control objectives.

COBIT continues with a set of high-level control objectives, one for each of the IT processes, grouped into four domains:

1. Planning and organization

2. Acquisition and implementation

3. Delivery and support

4. Monitoring

In establishing the list of business requirements, COBIT combines the principles embedded in existing and known reference models.

- Quality requirements cover quality, cost, and delivery.

- Fiduciary requirements (COSO report) cover effectiveness and efficiency of operations, reliability of information, and compliance with laws and regulations.

- Security requirements cover confidentiality, integrity, and availability.

The COBIT framework consists of high-level control objectives and an overall structure for their classification. The underlying theory behind the classification is three levels of IT efforts when considering the management of IT resources (see Exhibit 3.13). Starting at the bottom, there are activities and tasks needed to achieve a measurable result. Activities have a life cycle concept with a clear start and end dates and goals, while tasks are more discrete in nature. The life cycle concept has typical control requirements that are different from discrete activities. Processes are then defined one layer up as a series of joined activities or tasks with natural (control) breaks. At the highest level, processes are naturally grouped together into domains.

EXHIBIT 3.13 COBIT Classification System

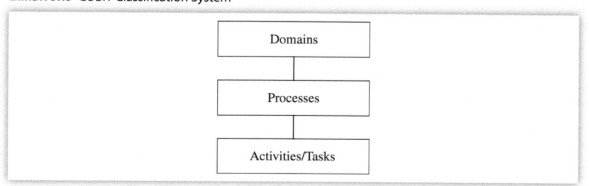

Domain 1: Planning and organization. This domain covers strategy and tactics and concerns the identification of the ways IT can best contribute to the achievement of business objectives. Furthermore, the realization of the strategic vision needs to be planned, communicated, and managed for different perspectives. Finally, a proper organization as well as a technological infrastructure must be put in place.

Domain 2: Acquisition and implementation. To realize the IT strategy, IT solutions need to be identified, developed, or acquired as well as implemented and integrated into the business process. In addition, changes in and maintenance of existing systems are covered by this domain to make sure that the life cycle is continued for these systems.

Domain 3: Delivery and support. This domain is concerned with the actual delivery of required services, which range from traditional operations of security to the continuity of training. In order to deliver services, the necessary support processes must be set up. This domain includes the actual processing of data by application systems, often classified under application controls.

Domain 4: Monitoring. All IT processes need to be regularly assessed over time for their quality and compliance with control requirements. This domain thus addresses management's oversight of the organization's control process and independent assurance provided by internal and external audit or obtained from alternative sources.

In summary, in order to provide the information that the organization needs to achieve its objectives, the organization must exercise IT governance to ensure that IT resources are managed by a set of naturally grouped IT processes.

(iii) The Information Systems Audit and Control Foundation's Control Objectives for Net Centric Technology

Control Objectives for Net Centric Technology (CONCT), issued by the Information Systems Audit and Control Foundation, focuses on these activities: intranet, extranet, Internet; data warehouses; and online transaction processing systems. CONCT provides well-structured ways of understanding and assessing the very complex centric technology environment that exists.

The IT governance model for centric technology has three dimensions: IT control objectives for information services, IT activities, and the IT resources required for the accomplishment of these activities.

(iv) American Institute of Certified Public Accountants/Canadian Institute of Certified Accountants' SysTrust Principles and Criteria for Systems Reliability

Several organizations, such as American Institute of Certified Public Accountants/Canadian Institute of Certified Accountants, provide guidance on information security in terms of principles, standards, management, assurance, and measurement.

SysTrust is an assurance service designed to increase the comfort of management, customers, and business partners with the systems that support a business or a particular activity. The SysTrust service entails a public accountant providing an assurance service in which he or she evaluates and tests whether a system is reliable when measured against four essential principles: availability, security, integrity, and maintainability. For each of the four principles, 58 reliability criteria have been established against which a system can be evaluated.

Potential users of this service are shareholders, creditors, bankers, business partners, third-party users who outsource functions to other entities, stakeholders, and anyone who in some way relies on the continued availability, integrity, security, and maintainability of a system. The SysTrust service will help differentiate entities from their competitors because entities that undergo the rigors of a SysTrust engagement will presumably be better service providers—attuned to the risks posed by their environment and equipped with the controls that address those risks.

(v) The International Federation of Accountants' Managing Security of Information

International Information Technology Guidelines are issued by the Information Technology Committee of the International Federation of Accountants.

Threats to information systems may arise from intentional or unintentional acts and may come from internal or external sources. Threats may emanate from, among others, technical conditions (e.g., program bugs and disk crashes), natural disasters (e.g., fires and floods), environmental conditions (e.g., electrical surges), human factors (e.g., lack of training, errors, and omissions), unauthorized access (e.g., hacking), or viruses. In addition to these, other threats, such as business dependencies (reliance on third-party communications carriers, outsourced operations) that can potentially result in a loss of management control and oversight are increasing in significance.

The objective of information security is the protection of the interests of those relying on information, and the information systems and communications that deliver the information, from harm resulting from failures of availability, confidentiality, and integrity. For any organization, the security objective is met when:

- Information systems are available and usable when required (availability objective).

- Data and information are disclosed only to those who have a right to know it (confidentiality objective).

- Data and information are protected against unauthorized modification (integrity objective).

The relative priority and significance of availability, confidentiality, and integrity vary according to the data within the information systems and the business context in which it is used. Core information security principles presented by the IFAC are derived from the Guidelines published by the Organisation for Economic Co-operation and Development.

(vi) The Information Security Forum's Standard

The standard of good practices for information security of the Information Security Forum is based on research and the practical experience for forum members. The standard divides security into five component areas:

1. Security management

2. Critical business applications

3. Computer installations

4. Networks

5. System development

(vii) U.S. Department of Homeland Security

The U.S. Department of Homeland Security cohosted a National Cyber Security Summit in 2003 and formed five task forces, including the Corporate Governance Task Force. In its report, the task force called on all organizations to make information security governance a corporate board-level priority. The report requires COSO of the Treadway Commission to revise its document entitled "Internal Controls—An Integrated Framework" so it explicitly addresses information security governance.

(viii) European Union Security Directives

The European Union has issued several directives covering:

- Information security

- Attacks against information systems

- Legal aspects of electronic commerce
- Access to electronic communications networks
- Protection of personal data
- Safer Internet Plus Programme (i.e., no illegal or harmful content)
- Unfair commercial practices
- Copyrights in the information society
- International safe harbor privacy principles

(ix) Guidelines for the Security of Information Systems of the Organisation for Economic Co-operation and Development

The Organisation for Economic Co-operation and Development has developed a critical information infrastructure framework and has issued several guidelines as they relate to IT and information security. These guidelines cover data collection limitations, quality of data, limitations on data use, IT security safeguards, accountability of the data controller, trans-border data flow laws dealing with personal data, cross-border threats, privacy laws, cryptography guidelines, anti-spam regulations, electronic authentication guidelines and cross-border cooperation in the enforcement of laws protecting privacy.

(x) International Common Criteria

The International Common Criteria (CC) is a product evaluation model that represents the outcome of efforts to develop criteria for evaluation of IT security. These criteria will be used throughout the international community. The CC defines a set of IT requirements of known validity used in establishing security requirements for prospective products and systems. The CC also defines the "protection profile" construct that allows prospective consumers or developers to create standardized sets of security requirements that will meet their needs. The CC presents requirements for the IT security of a product under the distinct categories of functional requirements and assurance requirements (www.commoncriteriaportal.org).

Examples of functional requirements include requirements for identification and authentication and security classes of products and systems. In essence, the CC is a standard security specification "language." Products whose security properties have been specified using the CC may then be validated (tested) for conformance to their CC specifications. Such a validation, when performed by an accredited testing laboratory, confirms that the product meets its security specification(s). Note that ISO/IEC standard 15408 addresses the CC in the form of evaluation criteria for IT security.

The CC is a repeatable methodology for documenting IT security requirements, documenting and validating product security capabilities, and promoting international cooperation in the IT security area. It supports security in depth and security layering concepts.

Using CC protection profiles and security targets greatly aids the development of products or systems that have IT security functions. The rigor and repeatability of the CC methodology provides thorough definition of user security needs. Validated security targets provide system integrators with key information needed to procure security components and implement secure IT functions and features.

The protection profile contains a set of security requirements either from the CC or stated explicitly, which should include evaluation assurance levels. The security target contains a set of security requirements that may be made by reference to a protection profile, directly by reference to CC functional or assurance components, or stated explicitly.

The CC permits comparability between the results of independent security evaluations. It does so by providing a common set of requirements for the security functionality of IT products and for assurance measures applied to these IT products during a security evaluation. The evaluation results may help consumers to determine whether these IT products fulfill their security needs. The CC is useful as a guide for the development, evaluation, and/or procurement of products with IT security functionality.

The CC uses the term "product" to refer to an IT product, a part of an IT product, and a set of IT products. Examples of IT products are listed next.

- A software application
- An OS
- A software application in combination with an OS
- A software application in combination with an OS and a workstation
- An OS in combination with a workstation
- A smart card integrated circuit
- The cryptographic coprocessor of a smart card integrated circuit
- A LAN including all terminals, servers, network equipment, and software
- A database application excluding the remote client software normally associated with that database application

The CC addresses protection of information from unauthorized disclosure (confidentiality), modification (integrity), or loss of use (availability). The CC is also applicable to risks arising from human activities (malicious or otherwise) and to risks arising from nonhuman activities. The CC is applicable to IT security functionality implemented in hardware, firmware, or software.

Because the next topics involve specialized techniques or because they are somewhat peripheral to IT security, they are considered to be outside the scope of the CC:

- The CC does not contain security evaluation criteria pertaining to administrative security measures not related directly to the IT security functionality. Administrative security controls, such as organizational, personnel, physical, and procedural controls, are important in other areas.
- The evaluation of technical physical aspects of IT security, such as electromagnetic emanation control, is not specifically covered. The CC does address some aspects of physical protection.
- The CC addresses neither the evaluation methodology nor the administrative and legal framework under which the criteria may be applied by evaluation authorities.

- The procedures for use of evaluation in accreditation are outside the scope of the CC. The results of the evaluation process are an input to the accreditation process.

- The CC does not cover the subject of criteria for the assessment of the inherent qualities of cryptographic algorithms.

- The CC does not state requirements for the regulatory framework.

By establishing a CC base, the results of an IT security evaluation will be meaningful to a wider audience. There are three groups with a general interest in evaluation of the security properties of target of evaluations (TOEs): consumers, developers, and evaluators. The CC gives consumers, especially in consumer groups and communities of interest, an implementation-independent structure termed the "protection profile" in which to express their special security requirements. The CC is intended to support developers in preparing for and assisting in the evaluation of their TOEs and in identifying security requirements to be satisfied by those TOEs. These requirements are contained in an implementation-dependent construct termed the security target. This security target may be based on one or more protection profiles. The CC contains criteria to be used by evaluators when forming judgments about the conformance of TOEs to their security requirements. The CC describes the set of general actions the evaluator is to carry out but does not specify procedures to be followed in carrying out those actions.

Some of the additional interest groups that can benefit from information contained in the CC are listed next.

- System custodians and system security officers responsible for determining and meeting organizational IT security policies and requirements

- Auditors, both internal and external, responsible for assessing the adequacy of the security of an IT solution

- Security architects and designers responsible for the specification of security properties of IT products

- Accreditors responsible for accepting an IT solution for use within a particular environment

- Sponsors of evaluation responsible for requesting and supporting an evaluation

- Evaluation authorities responsible for the management and oversight of IT security evaluation programs

In order to achieve greater comparability between evaluation results, evaluations should be performed within the framework of an authoritative evaluation scheme that sets the standards, monitors the quality of the evaluations, and administers the regulations to which the evaluation facilities and evaluators must conform.

Use of a common evaluation methodology contributes to the repeatability and objectivity of the results but is not by itself sufficient. Many of the evaluation criteria require the application of expert judgment and background knowledge for which consistency is more difficult to achieve. As the application of criteria contains objective and subjective elements, precise and universal ratings for IT security are infeasible.

The certification process is the independent inspection of the results of the evaluation leading to the production of the final certificate or approval. It is noted that the certification process is a means of gaining greater consistency in the application of IT security criteria.

The evaluation scheme, methodology, and certification process are the responsibility of the evaluation authorities who run evaluation schemes and are outside the scope of the CC. However, the evaluation base is part of the CC.

The outcome of an evaluation is a statement about the extent to which assurance is gained that the TOE can be trusted to reduce the risks to the protected assets and does not itself possess exploitable vulnerabilities. The statement assigns an assurance rating to the TOE, assurance being that property of a TOE that gives grounds for confidence in its proper operation. This statement can be used by the asset owner in deciding whether to accept the risk of exposing the assets to the threats. This mandates that evaluation leads to objective and repeatable results that are defensible and can be cited as evidence.

(xi) International Organization for Standardization Standards

The International Organization for Standardization (ISO) in collaboration with the International Electro-Technical Commission (IEC) issues several standards to business, government, and society for economic, environmental, and social development. It develops standards for which there is a clear market requirement, as these standards provide specific solutions to achieve specific benefits. The ISO issued several standards relating to information technology and information security.

ISO 27001:2005—INFORMATION TECHNOLOGY SECURITY TECHNIQUES—REQUIREMENTS OF INFORMATION SECURITY MANAGEMENT SYSTEMS

The ISO/IEC 27001:2005 standard covers all types of organizations (e.g., commercial enterprises, government agencies, and not-for-profit organizations). It specifies the requirements for establishing, implementing, operating, monitoring, reviewing, maintaining, and improving a documented information security management system within the context of the organization's overall business risks. It specifies requirements for the implementation of security controls customized to the needs of individual organizations or parts thereof. This standard is designed to ensure the selection of adequate and proportionate security controls that protect information assets and give confidence to interested parties. This standard uses the Plan-Do-Check-Act (PDCA) cycle framework.

The ISO/IEC 27001:2005 standard is intended to be suitable for several different types of use, including:

- Within organizations to formulate security requirements and objectives.

- Within organizations as a way to ensure that security risks are cost-effectively managed.

- Within organizations to ensure compliance with laws and regulations.

- Within organizations as a process framework for the implementation and management of controls to ensure that the specific security objectives of an organization are met.

- In the definition of new information security management processes.

- In the identification and clarification of existing information security management processes.

- By the management of organizations to determine the status of information security management activities.

- By internal and external auditors of organizations to determine the degree of compliance with the policies, directives, and standards adopted by an organization.

- By organizations to provide relevant information about information security policies, directives, standards, and procedures to trading partners and other organizations with which they interact for operational or commercial reasons.

- In implementation of business-enabling information security.

- By organizations to provide relevant information about information security to customers.

ISO 27002:2005—INFORMATION TECHNOLOGY SECURITY TECHNIQUES—CODE OF PRACTICE FOR INFORMATION SECURITY MANAGEMENT

The ISO/IEC 27002:2005 standard (formerly known as ISO/IEC 17799 standard and the British Standard Institute's BS 7799 standard) establishes guidelines and general principles for initiating, implementing, maintaining, and improving information security management in an organization. This standard provides a comprehensive set of controls addressing information security, including security governance. It is intended to serve as a single reference point for identifying controls needed for most situations where information systems are used in industry and commerce for large, medium, and small organizations. The standard has three major components: confidentiality, integrity, and availability. The control objectives provide general guidance on the commonly accepted goals of information security management.

This standard contains best practices of control objectives and controls in the next areas of information security management:

- Security policy deals with management direction, including risk assessment.

- Organization of information security deals with governance of information security.

- Asset management deals with inventory and classification of information assets.

- HR security deals with security aspects for employees joining, in moving within, and leaving an organization.

- Physical and environmental security deals with protection of the computer facilities.

- Communications and operations management deals with management of technical security controls in systems and networks.

- Access control deals with restriction of access rights to networks, systems, applications, functions, and data.

- Information systems acquisition, development, and maintenance deals with building security into applications.

- Information security incident management deals with anticipating and responding appropriately to information security breaches.

- Business continuity management deals with protecting, maintaining, and recovering business-critical processes and systems.

- Compliance deals with ensuring conformance with information security policies, standards, laws, and regulations.

The control objectives and controls just listed are intended to be implemented to meet the requirements identified by a risk assessment. They are intended as a common basis and practical guidelines for developing organizational security standards and effective security management practices and to help build confidence in interorganizational activities.

ISO 28000—SECURITY MANAGEMENT SYSTEMS FOR THE SUPPLY CHAIN

The ISO 28000:2007 standard specifies the requirements for a security management system, including those aspects critical to security assurance of the supply chain. Managers responsible for selecting suppliers for purchasing decisions can refer to ISO 9001 for the supply chain. Security management is linked to many other aspects of business management. Aspects include all activities controlled or influenced by organizations that impact on supply chain security. These other aspects should be considered directly, where and when they have an impact on security management, including transporting these goods along the supply chain. Some examples of risks in the supply chain include piracy, fraud, and terrorism.

The ISO 28000:2007 standard is applicable to all sizes of organizations, from small to multinational, in manufacturing (including software and hardware), service, storage, or transportation at any stage of the production or supply chain that wishes to:

- Establish, implement, maintain, and improve a security management system.

- Assure conformance with stated security management policy.

- Demonstrate such conformance to others.

- Seek certification/registration of its security management system by an accredited third-party certification body.

- Alternately, make a self-determination and self-declaration of conformance with ISO 28000:2007. It is not the intention of ISO 28000:2007 to require duplicative demonstration of conformance. Organizations that choose third-party certification can further demonstrate that they are contributing significantly to supply chain security.

OTHER ISO STANDARDS

- The ISO/IEC 15026 standard addresses software assurance in terms of managing risks and assuring safety, security, and dependability in the context of system and software life cycles.

- The ISO/IEC 15026-3:2011 standard addresses software assurance in terms of managing risks and assuring safety, security, and dependability in the context of system and software life cycles. This standard is intended for use by:

  - Definers of integrity levels, such as industry and professional organizations, standards organizations, and government agencies.

  - Users of integrity levels, such as developers and maintainers, suppliers and acquirers, users, assessors of systems or software, and for the administrative and technical support of systems and/or software products.

- The ISO/IEC 17025 standard addresses independent testing of software using either the white box or the black box testing method.

- The ISO/IES 22301 standard provides guidance on business continuity management, including IT contingency planning.

- The ISO/IEC 15048 standard addresses evaluation criteria for IT security (i.e., CC).

- The ISO/IEC 27003:2010 standard deals with IT security techniques regarding system implementation guidance in accordance with the ISO/IEC 27001:2005 standard.

- The ISO/IEC 27004:2009 standard deals with IT security techniques regarding measurement of controls in accordance with the ISO/IEC 27001:2005 standard.

- The ISO/IEC 27005:2011standard deals with IT security techniques regarding risk management in accordance with the ISO/IEC 27001:2005 standard.

- The ISO/IEC 27006 standard provides requirements for bodies providing audit and certification of information security management systems.

(Continued)

OTHER ISO STANDARDS (*Continued*)

- The ISO/IEC 27007:2011 standard deals with IT security techniques regarding management systems auditing in accordance with the ISO 19011 standard and the ISO 19001 standard dealing with auditing management systems.

- The ISO/IEC 90003:2004 standard deals with software engineering guidelines for the application of ISO 9001:2000 to computer software. This standard provides guidance for organizations in the application of ISO 9001:2000 to the acquisition, supply, development, operation, and maintenance of computer software and related support services. This standard does not add to or otherwise change the requirements of ISO 9001:2000. The 90003:2004 guidelines are not intended to be used as assessment criteria in quality management system registration or certification. The application of ISO/IEC 90003:2004 is appropriate to software that is:

  - ☐ Part of a commercial contract with another organization.

  - ☐ A product available for a specific market sector.

  - ☐ Used to support the processes of an organization.

  - ☐ Embedded in a hardware product.

  - ☐ Related to software services.

- The ISO/IEC 18033 standard deals with encryption algorithms.

- The ISO/IEC 10116 standard deals with security techniques for modes of operation for an *n*-bit block cipher.

- The ISO/IEC 11770 standard deals with security techniques for cryptographic key management framework and mechanisms for using symmetric key techniques.

SUMMARY OF INFORMATION TECHNOLOGY CONTROL FRAMEWORKS

A summary of IT control frameworks presented in this section and more follows.

- **The Institute of Internal Auditors' eSAC** sets the stage for effective technology and risk management by providing a framework for evaluating the e-business control environment.

- **The IT Governance Institute's COBIT** states that control objectives make a clear and distinct link to business objectives in order to support significant use outside the audit community. Control objectives are defined in a process-oriented manner following the principle of business reengineering. COBIT focuses on processes and process ownership; looks at fiduciary, quality, and security needs of enterprises; and provides seven information criteria in terms of what a business requires from IT: effectiveness, efficiency, availability, integrity, confidentiality, reliability, and compliance.

- **The Information Systems Audit and Control Foundation's CONCT** focuses on intranet, extranet, and Internet; data warehouses; and online TPSs.

- **The American Institute of Certified Public Accountants/Canadian Institute of Certified Accountants' SysTrust Principles and Criteria for Systems Reliability** provide guidance on information security in terms of principles, standards, management, assurance, and measurement.

- **The International Federation of Accountants' Managing Security of Information** states that the objective of information security is to protect the interests of those relying on information, and the information systems and communications that deliver the information, from harm resulting from failures of availability, confidentiality, and integrity.

■ **The Information Security Forum's standard** divides security into five component areas:

1. Security management

2. Critical business applications

3. Computer installations

4. Networks

5. System development

■ **The U.S. Department of Homeland Security's** task force on corporate governance calls on all organizations to make information security governance a corporate board-level priority.

■ **The European Union's Security Directives** cover these areas:

☐ Information security

☐ Attacks against information systems

☐ Legal aspects of electronic commerce

☐ Access to electronic communications networks

☐ Protection of personal data

☐ Safer Internet Plus Programme (i.e., no illegal or harmful content)

☐ Unfair commercial practices

☐ Copyrights in the information society

☐ International safe harbor privacy principles

■ **The Organisation for Economic Co-operation and Development's Guidelines for the Security of Information Systems** cover these areas:

☐ Data collection limitations

☐ Quality of data

☐ Limitations on data use

☐ IT security safeguards

☐ Accountability of the data controller

☐ Transborder data flow laws dealing with personal data

☐ Cross-border threats

☐ Privacy laws

☐ Cryptography guidelines

☐ Antispam regulations

☐ Electronic authentication guidelines

☐ Cross-border cooperation in the enforcement of laws protecting privacy

(Continued)

(b) Basic IT Controls

Basic IT controls are further divided into three types: controls based on action, controls based on objects and subjects, and controls based on requirements.

(i) Controls Based on Action

One way of presenting the security controls is to classify them from a technical viewpoint and according to their action, such as preventive, detective, and recovery controls. These controls are described next.

(A) Preventive Controls

Preventive controls focus on inhibiting or stopping security breaches from occurring in the first place. They include identification, authentication, authorization, access control enforcement, cryptographic key management, nonrepudiation, system protections, transaction privacy, protected communications, and security administration.

> The **identification** control provides the ability to uniquely identify users, processes, and information resources. To implement other security controls (e.g., discretionary access control, mandatory access control, and accountability), it is essential that both subjects and objects be identifiable. Identification control recognizes an entity (e.g., user, program, device, or process) prior to access.

> The **authentication** control provides the means of verifying the identity of a subject to ensure that a claimed identity is valid. Weak authentication mechanisms include passwords and personal identification numbers (PINs). Strong authentication mechanisms include token, smart card, digital certificate, and Kerberos. Authentication often acts as a prerequisite to allowing access to resources in a computer system.

> The **authorization** control enables specification and subsequent management of the allowed actions for a given system (e.g., the information owner or the DBA determines who can update a shared file accessed by a group of online users).

> **Access control enforcement** relates to data integrity and confidentiality. When the subject requesting access has been authorized and validated to access particular computer processes, it is necessary to enforce the defined security policy (i.e., discretionary or mandatory access control). These policy-based access controls are enforced via access control mechanisms distributed throughout the system (e.g., mandatory access

control–based sensitivity labels; discretionary access–based control file permission sets, access control lists, roles, file encryption, and user profiles). The effectiveness and the strength of access control depend on the correctness of the access control decisions (e.g., how the security rules are configured) and the strength of access control enforcement (e.g., the design of software or hardware security). Examples of access control enforcement mechanisms are checking identity and requested access against ACLs and using file encryption methods.

The correct sequence of access to a computer or information resource is shown next.

Identification ⟶ Authentication ⟶ Authorization ⟶ Access Control Enforcement

Cryptographic key management is important when cryptographic functions are implemented in other controls. The scope of key management includes key generation, distribution, storage, and maintenance.

The **nonrepudiation** control provides an unforgeable proof of sending and/or receiving data, and its scope spans prevention and detection categories. System accountability depends on the ability to ensure that senders cannot deny sending data and that receivers cannot deny receiving it. This control has been placed in the prevention category because the mechanism implemented prevents the successful repudiation of an action (e.g., the digital certificate that contains the owner's private key is known only to the owner). Consequently, this control typically is applied at the point of transmission or reception.

System protections ensure confidence in the system's technical implementation. This protection represents the quality of the implementation from the perspective of both the design processes used and the manner in which the implementation was accomplished. Some examples of system protections are residual information protection (also known as object reuse), least privilege (need to know), process separation, modularity, layering, abstraction, encryption, data hiding, and minimization of what needs to be trusted.

Transaction privacy controls are important to both government and private-sector systems, which are increasingly required to maintain the privacy of individuals using the systems. Transaction privacy controls (e.g., SSL and secure shell) protect against loss of privacy with respect to transactions performed by an individual.

Protected communications controls ensure trustworthy communications in distributed systems. Protected communications controls ensure the integrity, availability, and confidentiality of sensitive and critical information while it is in transit. Protected communications use data encryption methods (e.g., VPN and IPsec protocol), and deployment of cryptographic technologies (e.g., Data DES, Triple DES, RSA, Message Digest 4 (MD4), MD5, and secure hash standard), and escrowed encryption algorithms (e.g., Clipper) to minimize such network threats as replay, interception, packet sniffing, wiretapping, and eavesdropping. Protected communications must be safe from disclosure, substitution, modification, and replay attacks.

Security administration controls ensure that the security features of an IT system are configured (e.g., enabled or disabled) to meet the needs of a specific installation and to account for changes in the operational environment. System security can be built into OS security or the application system. Commercial off-the-shelf add-on security products are available.

(B) Detective Controls

Detective controls focus on identifying and discovering security breaches. Specifically, detective controls warn of violations or attempted violations of security policies and procedures. They are needed to complement or supplement the preventive controls, which are not perfect. Detective controls include audits, audit trails, checksums, intrusion detection and containment, proof of wholeness, and virus detection and eradication.

Audits of security-relevant events and the monitoring and tracking of system abnormalities are key elements in the after-the-fact detection of and recovery from security breaches. After-the-fact events include audits, investigations, and court evidence.

Audit trails show a chronological record of system activities that is sufficient to enable the reconstruction and examination of the sequence of events surrounding or leading to an operation, procedure, or event, from beginning to the end. They show who has accessed a system and what operations are carried out in aiding tracing system activities.

Checksums show a value automatically computed on data to detect errors or manipulations during transmission and to ensure the accuracy of data transmission. The number of bits in a data unit is summed and transmitted along with the data. The receiving computer then checks the sum and compares, and any changes are noticed.

Intrusion detection and containment is essential to detect security breaches (e.g., network break-ins and suspicious activities) so that a response can occur in a timely manner.

Proof-of-wholeness control (e.g., a system integrity tool) analyzes system integrity and irregularities and identifies exposures and potential threats. It determines whether integrity has been compromised and whether the information state or system state has been corrupted. However, this control does not prevent violations of security policy; it detects violations and helps determine the types of corrective action needed.

Virus detection and eradication software installed on servers and user workstations detects, identifies, and removes software viruses to ensure system and data integrity.

(C) Recovery Controls

Recovery controls focus on normalizing operations from security breaches as they restore lost computing resources. Recovery controls are needed as a complement or supplement to preventive controls and detective controls, both of which are not perfect. Recovery controls include backups, checkpoints, contingency plans, and controls to restore a system to its secure state.

Backup methods copy files and programs to facilitate recovery in a timely manner.

Checkpoints provide restore procedures before, during, or after completion of certain transactions or events to ensure acceptable level of fault recovery.

Contingency plans provide policies and procedures designed to maintain or restore business operations and computer operations, at the primary processing center and/or at an alternate processing site.

Restore to a secure state control enables a system to return, after a security breach occurs, to a state known to be secure.

(ii) Controls Based on Objects and Subjects

Preventive, detective, corrective, and recovery controls are needed to control unauthorized or illegal access to objects (e.g., computer programs, data files, and devices) by subjects (e.g., employees and contractors).

Examples of Preventive Controls

- Access control and accountability policies and procedures
- Access rules
- Account management
- Identification and authentication techniques for internal users, external users, cryptographic modules, and mobile and nonmobile devices
- Identifier management
- Authenticator management
- Session lock
- Access control enforcement by checking identity and requested access against ACLs and file encryption
- Information flow enforcement
- Separation of duties principle
- Least privilege principle
- Permitted actions without identification or authentication for emergencies and accessing public websites
- Security labels, attributes, tags, and markings
- Trust relationships in using external information systems
- Allowed and disallowed access to remote networks
- Usage restrictions for wireless access
- Restrictions in sharing information with business partners
- Separating public information from nonpublic information (e.g., personnel privacy and vendor proprietary data)
- Information system monitoring for information disclosure
- Timestamps
- Protection of audit-related information
- Audit record retention and storage capacity
- Security advisories and directives
- Information input restrictions
- Predictable failure prevention
- Security functionality verification
- Malicious code protection, including spam
- Trustworthy communications in distributed systems
- Intrusion prevention system
- Single sign-on, reduced sign-on, and single logout
- Web content filtering software

- Application content filters
- Security policy filters
- Blacklisting of user IDs and IP addresses
- Security banners on computer screens

Examples of Detective Controls

- Unsuccessful login attempts
- System use notification
- Previous access logon notification to detect false logons
- Concurrent session control
- System logs
- Session audit
- Audit review, analysis, and reporting
- Security alerts
- Error handling
- Proof of wholeness
- Intrusion detection system

Examples of Corrective Controls

- Authenticator feedback
- Response to audit-related data processing failures
- Audit reports
- Error correction

Examples of Recovery Controls

- Fail in a known secure state
- Recover/restore to a known secure state
- Flaw remediation
- Information output handling and retention
- Audit recovery from security breaches

(iii) Controls Based on Requirements

Regardless of the control framework used, there are 17 minimum security requirements that all IT departments should adhere to. These security requirements are expressed in terms of security safeguards or controls. Security controls are the management, operational, and technical safeguards and countermeasures that are needed to protect the confidentiality, integrity, and availability of a computer system and its information. These security controls constitute the minimum security requirements for information systems and the information processed, stored, and transmitted by those systems.

(A) Management Controls

Management safeguards or controls range from risk assessments to security planning.

1. **Risk assessment.** Organizations must periodically assess the risk to organizational operations (including mission, function, image, or reputation), organizational assets, and individuals resulting from the operation of organizational information systems and the associated processing, storage, or transmission of organizational information.

2. **Planning.** Organizations must develop, document, periodically update, and implement security plans for organizational information systems that describe the security controls in place or planned for the information systems and rules of behavior for individuals accessing the information systems.

3. **Systems and services acquisition.** Organizations must:

   a. Allocate sufficient resources to adequately protect organizational information systems.

   b. Employ SDLC processes that incorporate information security considerations.

   c. Employ software usage and installation restrictions.

   d. Ensure that third-party providers employ adequate security measures to protect information, applications, and/or services outsourced from the organization.

4. **Certification, accreditation, and security assessments.** Organizations must:

   a. Periodically assess the security controls in organizational information systems to determine if the controls are effective in their application.

   b. Develop and implement plans of action designed to correct deficiencies and reduce or eliminate vulnerabilities in organizational information systems.

   c. Authorize the operation of organizational information systems and any associated information system connections.

   d. Monitor information system security controls on an ongoing basis to ensure the continued effectiveness of the controls.

(B) Operational Controls

Operational safeguards or controls include factors such as personnel security and basic hardware/software maintenance.

5. **Personnel security.** Organizations must:

   a. Ensure that individuals occupying positions of responsibility within organizations (including third-party service providers) are trustworthy and meet established security criteria for those positions.

   b. Ensure that organizational information and information systems are protected during and after personnel actions, such as terminations and transfers.

   c. Employ formal sanctions for personnel failing to comply with organizational security policies and procedures.

6. **Physical and environmental protection.** Organizations must:

   a. Limit physical access to information systems, equipment, and the respective operating environments to authorized individuals.

   b. Protect the physical plant and support infrastructure for information systems.

   c. Provide supporting utilities (e.g., heating, air conditioning, and humidity levels) for information systems.

   d. Protect information systems against environmental hazards.

   e. Provide appropriate environmental controls in facilities containing information systems.

7. **Contingency planning.** Organizations must establish, maintain, and effectively implement plans for emergency response, backup operations, and post disaster recovery for organizational information systems to ensure the availability of critical information resources and continuity of operations in emergency situations.

8. **Configuration management.** Organizations must:

   a. Establish and maintain baseline configurations and inventories of organizational information systems (including hardware, software, firmware, and documentation) throughout the respective SDLCs.

   b. Establish and enforce security configuration settings for IT products employed in organizational information systems.

9. **Maintenance.** Organizations must:

   a. Perform periodic and timely maintenance on organizational information systems.

   b. Provide effective controls on the tools, techniques, mechanisms, and personnel used to conduct information system maintenance.

10. **System and information integrity.** Organizations must:

    a. Identify, report, and correct information and information system flaws in a timely manner.

    b. Provide protection from malicious code at appropriate locations within organizational information systems.

    c. Monitor information system security alerts and advisories and take appropriate actions in response.

11. **Media protection.** Organizations must:

    a. Protect information system media, both paper and digital.

    b. Limit access to information on information system media to authorized users.

    c. Sanitize or destroy information system media before disposal or release for reuse.

12. **Incident response.** Organizations must:

    a. Establish an operational incident handling capability for organizational information systems that include adequate preparation, detection, analysis, containment, recovery, and user response activities.

    b. Track, document, and report incidents to appropriate organizational officials and/or authorities.

13. **Awareness and training.** Organizations must:

   a. Ensure that managers and users of organizational information systems are made aware of the security risks associated with their activities and of the applicable laws, executive orders, directives, policies, standards, instructions, regulations, or procedures related to security of organizational information systems.

   b. Ensure that organizational personnel are adequately trained to carry out their assigned information security-related duties and responsibilities.

(C) Technical Controls

Technical safeguards or controls include items such as audit trails and communications protection.

14. **Identification and authentication.** Organizations must identify information system users, processes, acting on behalf of users, or devices and authenticate (or verify) the identities of those users, processes, or devices as a prerequisite to allowing access to organizational information systems.

15. **Access control.** Organizations must limit information system access to authorized users, processes acting on behalf of authorized users, or devices (including other information systems) and to the types of transactions and functions that authorized users are permitted to exercise.

16. **Audit and accountability.** Organizations must:

   a. Create, protect, and retain information system audit records to the extent needed to enable the monitoring, analysis, investigation, and reporting of unlawful, unauthorized or inappropriate information system activity.

   b. Ensure that the actions of individual information system users can be uniquely traced to those users so they can be held accountable for their actions.

17. **System and communications protection.** Organizations must:

   a. Monitor, control, and protect organizational communications (i.e., information transmitted or received by organizational information systems) at the external boundaries and key internal boundaries of the information systems.

   b. Employ architectural designs, software development techniques, and systems engineering principles that promote effective information security within organizational information systems.

SUMMARY OF MANAGEMENT, OPERATIONAL, AND TECHNICAL CONTROLS DEFINED AS MINIMUM SECURITY REQUIREMENTS

Management controls include risk assessment; planning; systems and services acquisition; and certification, accreditation, and security assessments.

Operational controls include personnel security; physical and environmental protection; contingency planning; configuration management; maintenance; system and information integrity; media protection; incident response; and awareness and training.

Technical controls include identification and authentication; access control; audit and accountability; and system and communications protection.

3.6 Disaster Recovery and Backup Methods

This section focuses on the need for business continuity management and IT continuity management. It defines the roles and responsibilities of business continuity manager or executive. This section establishes the relationship between business continuity management and ISO standards. It looks at the systems and data backup methods.

(a) Business-Focused Continuity Management

The entire scope of business continuity management (BCM) should be broader and more comprehensive than before. Its scope should be elevated to the enterprise level, similar to enterprise risk management, enterprise-wide resource planning software, enterprise CRM systems, enterprise-wide internal control systems, and enterprise-wide total quality management programs. The reason for elevating BCM to the enterprise level is to integrate all the relevant elements to determine the magnitude of disasters and incidents occurring in the entire enterprise in a timely manner for better and more complete action. The new BCM function should become a business-led initiative, not an IT-led initiative.

In the past, the BCM activities were focused more on the IT function and less on business functions (e.g., operations, marketing, accounting, HR, and finance), leaving huge gaps and unmitigated risks to the overall enterprise.

The business-led processes should focus on these topics, for example:

- Addressing all business functions, including the IT function
- Handling IT continuity plans and disaster recovery plans (DRPs)
- Handling nature-made, man-made, and technology-used disasters
- Handling kidnapping of key executives and officers
- Understanding the applicable legal and regulatory requirements
- Ensuring that suppliers/vendors and business partners would continue to provide key raw materials, products, and services, even during disasters or incidents
- Handling cyber-based and terrorism-based attacks targeted at companies by hacking their computer systems and networks and stealing intellectual property information
- Implementing a vital records retention program
- Obtaining adequate insurance coverage for assets to recover losses

Implementing a vital records retention program and obtaining adequate insurance coverage is essential to ensuring BCM in order to protect assets from accidents, errors, disruptions, attacks, losses, damages, and disasters.

(i) Vital Record Retention Program

Vital records, whether maintained on paper or computer, should be retained according to internal requirements (e.g., management's policies and procedures on record keeping, record retention, storage, and disposal; and internal legal and audit requirements) and external requirements (e.g., legal, audit, regulatory, and tax guidelines). With respect to computer operations, record retention deals with retaining computer records, software, data files, directories, and libraries.

Regarding electronic records, user organizations must ensure that the original software version that was used to create these records is still available and operable to retrieve the needed records. This requires policies and procedures to archive and test the original software and data quality.

(A) Retention of Email Messages

Email messages should be treated the same way as paper documents that do the same things. Email is no more and no less important than other information used to transact business. All employees must apply the same decision-making process to email that they apply to other documentary materials regardless of the media used to create them.

Records may not be retained in an email directory. Any paper document can become an electronic record if issued via email. Normally, only the originator copy is the record copy. Record documents may be retained in word processing directories or in hard-copy files, as long as they can be maintained in accordance with approved record schedules. Nonrecord material (e.g., transitory documents, copies, and drafts) may be retained in an email directory for short periods. Delete all such material as soon as it has served its purpose.

Email directories should be purged routinely of material that is more than a certain period (e.g., 90 days) old. System administrators should accomplish this deletion after notice to system users that record material must be transferred from email to appropriate scheduled files or directories.

(B) Retention of Tapes

Tape management systems, which are used for data backup, have a vault management system that controls the movement of tape volumes from one storage location to another. Typically, critical tape volumes are cycled out of the central tape library to progressively more secure and less accessible storage areas, such as vaults, and then are finally transferred back to the central library. The retention of a vault tape can be based on one or more criteria, such as number of days elapsed since placed in the vault, number of days since the tape was created, a specific hold time, or several others. Alternatively, an electronic vault can be used.

(C) Location of Electronic Records

Because electronic records provide electronic evidence to a court of law as well as for fraud/crime investigators and law enforcement authorities, key challenges include whether these records will be available when needed or requested and how long they are available. Usually the data custodian of an organization decides how long to maintain them. ISPs retain records for a limited period, depending on what records are involved. For example, text messages may be retained for only a short time (e.g., two days). Another challenge is that electronic or paper records may often be stored in more than one place. Regarding email messages, there could be multiple co-conspirators and multiple computers involved in a legal case, thus complicating the case analysis. Investigators need to search multiple locations to piece the key events together in order to issue simultaneous search warrants. It is even more challenging to deal with electronic records stored outside the country that were involved in trade secret and economic espionage cases. Efforts to obtain this electronic evidence from abroad can cause legal complications and delays.

(ii) Insurance Coverage

Implementing an effective insurance recovery program can complement the DRP. Insurance is a recovery control. Some organizations are self-insured and assume all risks while others take insurance coverage from insurance companies. Obtaining insurance coverage for computer-related property or equipment is no different from obtaining insurance for other types of property (e.g., building, machinery, and personal property). The insurance coverage should include software, hardware, and data. A complete property inventory is important not only for insurance purposes but also for disaster recovery planning. Four steps are involved in this process:

1. Determine the cost to replace each inventoried item.
2. Inquire where the item can be replaced.
3. Know the items that are irreplaceable.
4. Determine consequences if the items are lost.

There are at least three methods of property valuation: actual cash value, replacement value, and functional replacement value. Each is discussed next.

1. **Actual cash value** accounts for the replacement value of an item minus the actual depreciation and obsolescence that have lessened its value. The amount likely will not be enough to adequately replace what was lost.
2. **Replacement value** is the amount it costs to buy the exact piece of property, new, without deducting for depreciation. This is the most commonly used method of all.
3. **Functional replacement value** is the amount paid to replace obsolete machinery with up-to-date models. In rare cases, this cost actually may be less than the original value of the item being replaced.

(A) Coinsurance Requirements

Once accurate values have been determined for all property items, the decision is the amount of insurance to carry. Usually, 80% coinsurance (insurance to value) is the standard, and it represents the percentage of recovery entitled in the event of a total loss. If less than 80% coinsurance is purchased, the cost of any loss sustained will be shared with the insurance company according to the percentage of coverage purchased.

(b) IT-Focused Continuity Management

This section covers the scope of contingency planning and of incident management; contingency planning strategies; scope of disaster recovery planning; developing recovery site strategies and alternate recovery site strategies; implementation, documentation, training, and testing; contingency plan maintenance; and fault-tolerance mechanisms.

(i) Scope of Contingency Planning

Computer-based application systems and business-related information systems must be available at all times to continue normal business operations and to handle and recover from disasters.

A **computer security contingency** is an event, incident, or disaster with the potential to disrupt computer operations, thereby disrupting critical mission and business functions. Such an event could be a power outage, hardware failure, software malfunction, fire, or storm. Disruptive events are of three types: man made, nature made, or technology used. Examples of man-made disruptions include vandalism, terrorism, economic espionage, sabotage, malicious mischief, arson, strikes, riots, and collisions from vehicles, trains, boats, and aircraft. Examples of nature-made disruptions include wind, rain, snow, sleet, lightning, flooding, tidal waves, moving ice, fire, earthquakes, and slides. Technology-used disruptions include cyberattacks and other attacks. To avert potential contingencies and disasters or to minimize the damage they cause, organizations can take steps early to control these events.

Generally called contingency planning, this activity is closely related to incident handling, which primarily addresses malicious technical threats, such as hackers and viruses. Other names given to contingency planning include disaster recovery, business continuity, continuity of operations, or business resumption planning. The contingency planning document and procedures must be useful in time of emergency. Computer hardware or software must have built-in fail-soft controls to provide continuity of operations.

Contingency planning involves more than planning for a move offsite after a disaster destroys a data center. It also addresses how to keep an organization's critical functions operating in the event of disruptions, both large and small. This broader perspective on contingency planning is based on the distribution of computer support throughout an organization. Physical disaster prevention and preparedness begins when a data center site is first constructed. For example, the best location for a data center in a multistory building is any floor other than the first floor, basement level, or top floor.

Disasters can happen without warning. The great losses that accrue as a result of a disaster are directly related to the side effects of the disaster, not the disaster itself. Management cannot prevent disasters; it can only detect, correct, or recover from them. DRPs and security policies are separate but complementary. The public relations department of an organization should act immediately after a disaster has occurred to notify the press and the public.

(A) Contingency Plan

Undesirable events occur regardless of a security program's effectiveness. Contingency planning provides a controlled response that minimizes damage and restores operations as quickly as possible. A **contingency plan** is a document or set of documents that provides a course of action to be followed before, during, and after an undesirable event that disrupts or interrupts IT operations. The document should include procedures for data recovery, hardware recovery, and updating the contingency plan. The planning process should focus on providing a minimum acceptable level of outputs and services, using a combination of top-down and bottom-up approaches. It should also focus on a vital records program considering legal, tax, audit, regulatory, and business requirements.

A contingency plan should detail:

- Individual roles and responsibilities.
- Actions to be taken before an undesirable event occurs.
- Actions to be taken at the onset of an undesirable event to limit the level of damage, loss, or compromise of assets.
- Actions to be taken to restore critical IT functions.
- Actions to be taken to reestablish normal IT operations.

Contingency plans address both catastrophic events that cause major destruction to IT assets and less-than-catastrophic events that interrupt IT operations but do not cause major destruction. Contingency plans do not concentrate on disaster recovery planning to the detriment of planning for less-than-catastrophic occurrences. As a general rule, the greater the adverse impact of an undesirable event, the lower its probability of occurring. Contingency plans are stored onsite for use in less-than-catastrophic occurrences and offsite so that they will be available when needed.

To handle these undesirable events, organizations should do the following:

- Develop risk profiles.
- Establish security priorities.
- Identify critical applications.

(B) Business Impact Analysis

The business impact analysis (BIA) is a critical step in implementing the contingency plan controls and in the contingency planning process overall. The BIA enables management to characterize the system components, supported business functions, and their interdependencies. The results of the BIA characterize the consequences of a disruption and are used to determine contingency planning requirements and priorities.

The BIA should critically:

1. Examine the business processes and their dependencies.
2. Assess costs and benefits.
3. Locate single points of failure.
4. Identify risks and threats (both physical and environmental).

For example, a single point of failure occurs when there is no redundancy in data, equipment, facilities, systems, and programs. Risks in the use of cellular radio and telephone networks during a disaster include security systems and switching offices.

The BIA should be performed during the initiation phase of the SDLC using both quantitative and qualitative tools. Three steps typically are involved in accomplishing the BIA:

1. **Determine mission or business functions and recovery criticality.** Business functions supported by the system are identified and the impact of a system disruption to those functions is determined along with outage impacts and estimated downtime. The downtime should reflect the maximum time that an organization can tolerate while still maintaining the business functions.

2. **Identify resource requirements.** Realistic recovery efforts require a thorough evaluation of the resources needed to resume business functions and related interdependencies as quickly as possible. Examples of resources that should be identified include facilities, personnel, equipment, software, data files, system components, supplies, and vital records.

3. **Identify recovery priorities for system resources.** Based on the results from the previous activities, system resources can be linked more clearly to critical business processes and functions. Priority levels can be established for sequencing recovery activities and resources.

(C) Identify and Prioritize Critical Business Functions

When developing an IT contingency plan, the first step is to establish a contingency planning policy within the organization. This policy may exist at the department, division, and/or program level of the organization. The statement should do three things:

1. Define the organization's overall contingency objectives.

2. Identify leadership roles and responsibilities; resource requirements; and test, training, and exercise schedules.

3. Develop maintenance schedules and determine the minimum required backup frequency.

Protecting the continuity of an organization's mission or business is very difficult if it is not clearly identified. Managers need to understand the organization from a point of view that usually extends beyond the area they control. The definition of an organization's critical mission or business function is often called a business plan.

Since the business plan will be used to support contingency planning, it is necessary not only to identify critical missions and businesses but also to set priorities for them. A fully redundant capability for each function is prohibitively expensive for most organizations. In the event of a disaster, certain functions will not be performed based on careful decisions. The setting and approval of appropriate priorities by senior management could mean the difference in the organization's ability to survive a disaster.

After identifying critical missions and business functions, it is necessary to identify the supporting resources, the time frames in which each resource is used (e.g., is the resource needed constantly or only at the end of the month?), and the effect on the mission or business of the unavailability of the resource. In identifying resources, a traditional problem has been that different managers oversee different resources. They may not realize how resources interact to support the organization's mission or business. Many of these resources are not computer resources. Contingency planning should address all the resources needed to perform a function, regardless of whether they directly relate to a computer.

The analysis of needed resources should be controlled by those who understand how the function is performed and the dependencies of various resources on other resources and other critical relationships. This will allow an organization to assign priorities to resources since not all elements of all resources are crucial to the critical functions. *In many cases, the longer an organization is without a resource, the more critical the situation becomes.*

(D) Maximum Tolerable Downtime

Maximum tolerable downtime (MTD) represents the total amount of time the system owner is willing to accept for a business process outage or disruption and includes all impact considerations. Determining MTD is important because it could leave continuity planners with imprecise direction on (1) selection of an appropriate recovery method and (2) the depth of detail required when developing recovery procedures, including their scope and content. MTD is also known as maximum allowable outage (MAO), which describes the downtime threshold.

Additional processing time (APT) is required when a system outage may prevent a particular process from being completed. Because it takes time to reprocess the data, that APT must be added to the RTO to stay within the time limit established by the MTD.

(E) Assess Exposure to Outages (Local, Regional, National, or Global)

Although it is impossible to think of all the things that can go wrong (i.e., outages), the next step is to identify a likely range of problems. The development of *scenarios* will help an organization develop a plan to address the wide range of things that can go wrong. Scenarios should include small and large contingencies and best, worst, and most likely cases. Creating them requires imagination and creativity.

(F) Recovery Objectives

Two types of recovery objectives exist: RTO and recovery point objective (RPO).

RTO defines the maximum amount of time that a system resource can remain unavailable before there is an unacceptable impact on other system resources, supported business functions, and the MTD. Determining the information system resource RTO is important for selecting appropriate technologies that are best suited for meeting the MTD. When it is not feasible to immediately meet the RTO and when the MTD is inflexible, a plan of action and milestone should be initiated to document the situation and plan for its mitigation.

RTOs for essential business functions must be sustained within 12 hours and for up to 30 days from an alternate site, what are determined by the system-based BIA. Nonessential business functions do not require an alternate site as part of the recovery strategy but may require security controls similar to an alternate site.

The contingency plan coordinator, working with management, should determine the optimum point to recover the information system by addressing the factors mentioned earlier while balancing the cost of system inoperability against the cost of resources required for restoring the system and its overall support for critical business functions.

The longer a disruption is allowed to continue, the more costly it can become to the organization and its operations. Conversely, the shorter the RTO, the more expensive the recovery solutions cost to implement. For example, if the system must be recovered immediately for a high-impact system, zero-downtime solutions and alternate processing site costs will be much higher. A low-impact system with a longer RTO would be able to implement a less costly simple tape backup system. Plotting a graph between the cost and the length of disruption time will show an optimal point called the cost balance point, where the cost to recover line intersects with the cost of disruption line (business downtime). The cost balance point will be different for every organization and system based on financial constraints and operating requirements. Note that the cost to recover a mirrored system is high and the cost to recover a tape backup system is low.

WHAT IS RECOVERY POINT OBJECTIVE, RECOVERY TIME OBJECTIVE, AND MAXIMUM TOLERABLE DOWNTIME, AND HOW ARE THEY RELATED TO BUSINESS IMPACT ANALYSIS?

- An RPO is the point in time in which data must be restored in order to resume computer processing.

- An RTO is the maximum acceptable length of time that elapses before the unavailability of the system severely affects the organization.

- An MTD is the total amount of time the system owner is willing to accept for a business process outage or disruption and includes all impact considerations.

- Note that the BIA must consider the RPO, RTO, and MTD since they are related to and affect each other.

- Note that RPO and RTO are a part of disaster recovery controls and procedures.

The RPO represents the point in time, prior to a disruption or system outage, to which business process data can be recovered (given the most recent backup copy of the data) after an outage.

Because the RTO must ensure that the MTD is not exceeded, the RTO normally must be shorter than the MTD. For example, a system outage may prevent a particular process from being completed, and because it takes time to reprocess the data, that APT must be added to the RTO to stay within the time limit established by the MTD. These relationships are shown next.

$$BIA \longrightarrow MTD, RTO, \text{ and } RPO$$

$$RTO < MTD$$

$$RTO + APT < MTD$$

(ii) Scope of Incident Management
(A) Security Incident Triad

The security incident triad includes three elements: detect, respond, and recover. An organization should have the ability to detect an attack, respond to an attack, and recover from an attack by limiting consequences of or impacts from an attack.

The security incident triad is the emergency response capability for various technical threats, such as hackers and viruses. Incident handling can also help an organization prevent future incidents. These questions should be raised:

- Are there procedures for reporting incidents handled either by system personnel or externally?

- Are there procedures for recognizing and handling incidents (i.e., what files and logs should be kept, whom to contact, and when)?

- Who receives and responds to alerts or advisories (e.g., vendor patches or exploited vulnerabilities)?

- What preventive measures are in place (i.e., intrusion detection tools, automated audit logs, or penetration testing)?

Root cause analysis can be used in the remediation step of the incident response. **Root cause analysis** is a problem-solving tool, using a cause-and-effect diagram. This diagram is used for analyzing when a series of events or steps in a process creates a problem and it is not clear which event or step is the major cause of the problem. After examination, significant root causes of the problem are discovered, verified, and corrected. The cause-and-effect diagram is also called a fishbone or Ishikawa diagram and is a good application in managing a computer security incident response as a remediation step.

(B) Symptoms of an Incident

It is always possible that a computer system or network is compromised by an intentional or unintentional incident. When several symptoms start to appear, a pattern may indicate that a system is under attack, and the situation may be worth investigating further. If the adversary is skilled, it may not be very obvious that an attack is under way. The symptoms of an incident could include any of the following:

- Unusually heavy network traffic

- Out-of-disk space alert or significantly reduced free disk space

- Unusually high CPU usage

- Creation of new user accounts and accounts in use when the user is not at work

- Attempted or actual use of administrator-level accounts and locked-out accounts
- Cleared log files and full log files with unusually large numbers of events
- Antivirus alerts or alerts from the intrusion detection system and disabled antivirus software
- Unexpected patch changes and unexpected changes in configuration settings
- Computers and communication devices connecting to outside IP addresses
- Requests for information about a system-related data such as user IDs and passwords (i.e., social engineering attempts)
- Unexpected system shutdown or slowdown

INCIDENT HANDLING VERSUS CONTINGENCY PLANNING

An incident-handling capability may be viewed as a component of contingency planning because it provides the ability to react quickly and efficiently to disruptions in normal processing. Broadly speaking, contingency planning addresses events with the potential to interrupt system operations. Incident handling can be considered that portion of contingency planning that responds to malicious technical threats.

(C) Benefits

Two types of benefits are accrued from incident management: primary and secondary (side benefits). The primary benefits are containing and repairing damage from incidents and preventing future damage. The side benefits include use of threat and vulnerability of data, enhancing internal communications and organization preparedness, and enhancing the training and awareness program.

(D) Help Desk

The help desk function should be closely linked to an organization's incident response handling capability because in many cases the same staff members perform these two functions.

(iii) Contingency Planning Strategies

Procedures for executing the recovery strategy should be outlined in the contingency plan. The plan must be written in a format that will provide the users (recovery team leadership and members) the context in which the plan is to be implemented and the direct procedures, based on role, to execute. The plan includes notification and activation procedures, damage assessment, sequence of recovery activities, restore original site, testing systems, and terminating operations.

The next thing is to plan how to recover needed resources. It is a fact that there is no recovery without a backup. In evaluating alternatives, it is necessary to consider what controls are in place to prevent and minimize contingencies. Since no set of controls can cost-effectively prevent all contingencies, it is necessary to coordinate prevention and recovery efforts.

A contingency planning strategy normally consists of three parts: emergency response, recovery, and resumption (restoration). **Emergency response** encompasses the initial actions taken to protect lives, limit property damage, and minimize the impact of the emergency. Contingency planning for LANs should consider security incident response, backup operations, and recovery plans. **Recovery** refers to the steps taken to continue support for critical functions. A proactive

DRP includes a UPS, an emergency procedure, and a fire extinguisher. **Resumption** is the return to normal operations. The relationship between recovery and resumption is important. The longer it takes to resume normal operations, the longer the organization will have to operate in the recovery mode.

The selection of a strategy needs to be based on practical considerations, including feasibility and cost. The different categories of resources should be considered separately. Risk assessment can be used to help estimate the cost of options to decide on an optimal strategy. For example, is it more expensive to purchase and maintain a power generator or to move computer processing to an alternate site, considering the likelihood of losing electrical power for various lengths of time? Are the consequences of a loss of computer-related resources sufficiently high to warrant the cost of various recovery strategies? The risk assessment should focus on areas where it is unclear which strategy is best.

An incident-handling capability plan might call for at least one manager and one or more technical staff members to accomplish program objectives. Depending on the scope of the effort, however, full-time staff members may not be required. In some situations, some staff may be needed part time or on an on-call basis. Personnel may be performing incident-handling duties as an adjunct responsibility to their normal assignments.

A training and awareness program can benefit from lessons learned during incident handling. Incident-handling staff will be able to help assess the level of user awareness about current threats and vulnerabilities. Staff members may be able to help train system administrators, system operators, and other users and systems personnel. Knowledge of security precautions (resulting from such training) helps reduce future incidents. It is also important that users are trained what to report and how to report it.

Incident-handling staff will need to keep current with computer system and security developments. Budget allowances need to be made, therefore, for attending conferences, security seminars, and other continuing education events. If an organization is located in more than one geographic area, funds probably will be needed for travel to other sites for handling incidents.

(iv) Scope of Disaster Recovery Planning

A DRP is essential to continued availability of computer systems. The DRP should include the following items:

- Required response to events or conditions of varying duration and severity that would activate the recovery plan

- Procedures for operating the computer system in manual mode without external electronic connections

- Roles and responsibilities of responders (first and second responders)

- Processes and procedures for the backup and secure storage of information

- Complete and up-to-date logical network diagrams

- Personnel list for authorized physical and cyber-access to computer systems

- Communication procedures and list of personnel to contact in the case of an emergency including vendors, network administrators, and support staff (call tree list)

- Current configuration information for all components of systems
- Replacement for hard-to-obtain critical components kept in inventory

The DRP plan should define a comprehensive backup and restore policy. In formulating this policy, these issues should be considered:

- The speed at which data or the system must be restored. This requirement may justify the need for a redundant system, spare offline computer, or valid file-level system backups.
- The frequency at which critical data and configurations are changing. This will dictate the frequency and completeness of backups.
- The safe onsite and offsite storage of full and incremental backups.
- The safe storage of installation media, license keys, and configuration information.
- Identification of individuals responsible for performing, testing, storing, and restoring backups.

(v) Develop Recovery Site Strategies

Recovery strategies provide a means to restore IT operations quickly and effectively following a service disruption. The strategies should address disruption impacts and MAO times identified in the BIA. Several alternatives should be considered when developing the strategy, including cost, allowable outage time, security, and integration with larger, organization-level contingency plans.

The selected recovery strategy should address the potential impacts identified in the BIA and should be integrated into the system architecture during the design and implementation phases of the system life cycle. The strategy should include a combination of methods that complement one another to provide recovery capability over the full spectrum of incidents. A wide variety of recovery approaches may be considered; the appropriate choice depends on the incident, type of system, and its operational requirements. Specific recovery methods should be considered and may include these types:

- Commercial contracts with cold, warm, or hot site vendors
- Mobile sites
- Mirrored sites
- Reciprocal agreements with internal or external organizations
- SLAs with equipment vendors

In addition, technologies such as RAID, automatic fail-over, UPS, and mirrored systems should be considered when developing a system recovery strategy.

When a disruption occurs despite the preventive measures implemented, a recovery strategy must be in place to recover and restore data and system operations within the RTO period. The recovery strategy is designed from a combination of methods that together address the full spectrum of information system risks. Several options may be evaluated during the development phase; the most cost-effective option, based on potential impact, should be selected and integrated into the information system architecture and operating procedures.

The contingency planning coordinator should determine the optimum point to recover the IT system by balancing the cost of system inoperability against the cost of resources required for restoring the system. This is called *recovery cost balancing.* Where the cost-of-disruption line and the cost-to-recover line (on a cost versus time graph) meet defines how long the organization can afford to allow the system to be disrupted or unavailable.

Systems and data must be backed up regularly; therefore, all IT contingency plans should include a method and frequency for conducting data backups. The frequency of backup methods—daily or weekly, incremental, differential, or full—should be selected based on system criticality when new information is introduced. The backup method selected should be based on system and data availability and integrity requirements (as defined in the BIA). Data that is backed up may need to be stored offsite and rotated frequently, depending on the criticality of the system. A backup-in-depth strategy is better than a single-level backup strategy.

Major disruptions to system operations may require restoration activities to be implemented at an alternate site. The type of alternate site selected must be based on RTO requirements and budget limitations. Equipment for recovering and/or replacing the information system must be provided as part of the recovery strategy. Cost, delivery time, and compatibility factors must also be considered when determining how to provide the necessary equipment. Organizations must also plan for an alternate site that, at a minimum, provides workspace for all contingency plan personnel, equipment, and the appropriate IT infrastructure necessary to execute IT contingency plan and system recovery activities. The level of operational readiness of the alternate site is an important characteristic to determine when developing the recovery strategy.

(A) Offsite Storage

Offsite storage locations should be identified to store magnetic media, paper documentation, and forms needed to run the backup computer in the event of a disaster. Care should be taken to select an offsite storage location, whether it is a part of the organization or an outside commercial storage center situated locally or remotely to the primary computer center. Regardless of the choice, the offsite storage location should be well controlled in terms of record keeping of movement of media and documentation between onsite and offsite, adequate physical security over the facilities, and environmental controls within the facility.

It is good business practice to store backed-up data offsite. Commercial data storage facilities are specially designed to archive media and protect data from threatening elements. If using offsite storage, data are backed up at the organization's facility and then labeled, packed, and transported to the storage facility. If the data is required for recovery or testing purposes, the organization contacts the storage facility requesting transport of specific data to the organization or to an alternate facility. Backup tapes should be tested regularly to ensure that data is being stored correctly and that the files may be retrieved without errors or lost data. Also, the contingency planning coordinator should test the backup tapes at the alternate site, if applicable, to ensure that the site supports the same backup configuration that the organization has implemented. Commercial storage facilities often offer media transportation and response and recovery services.

Full-volume backups and incremental backups are two common methods used to back up system/file contents. In full-volume backups, the entire disk volume is backed up regardless of the changes made to individual files in a volume. In incremental backups, only changes since the last backup are backed up, which saves time. Storing backup files and documentation offsite is the best corrective control.

The backup files should include current and critical master files, transaction files, OS application source programs, and compiled object programs. Other documentation should include system-related documentation, the phone contact list, and a supply of special forms.

The type of data to be stored offsite depends on legal, business, and regulatory requirements. The frequency of backup depends on whether it is an online or a database system. For example, online systems require a periodic dump of transaction logs, and the database is backed up hourly. To restore a file, the previous day's backup file and the current transaction file are needed. Inadequate documentation, lack of audit trails, inability to resolve system deadlocks, or lack of passwords could delay system recovery at an offsite backup facility.

When selecting an offsite storage facility and vendor, these criteria should be considered:

- **Geographic area.** Distance from the organization and the probability of the storage site being affected by the same disaster as the organization
- **Accessibility.** Length of time necessary to retrieve the data from storage and the storage facility's operating hours
- **Security.** Security capabilities of the storage facility and employee confidentiality, which must meet the data's sensitivity and security requirements
- **Environment.** Structural and environmental conditions of the storage facility (i.e., temperature, humidity, fire prevention, and power management controls)
- **Cost.** Cost of shipping, operational fees, and disaster response/recovery services

(B) Tape Rotation
Usually tape files are backed up using a three-generation (son, father, and grandfather) concept, where each generation represents a time period (e.g., seven or five operating days). Disk files are saved for five or seven generations. Each generation can have multiple copies and be rotated between onsite and offsite. Tape files are a major obstacle to unattended computer center operation due to their labor-intensive nature.

(C) Electronic Vaulting
The manual mode of performing system backups is time consuming, labor intensive, and costly because physical tape vaulting and tape rotation are required. **Electronic vaulting** is the ability to store and retrieve backups electronically, in a site remote from the primary computer center. The backup information can be transmitted to offsite from onsite and vice versa. Optical disks, magnetic disks, mass storage devices, and an automated tape library are some examples of storage media devices used on the receiving end of an electronic vault. Electronic vaulting exploits the significant cost/performance improvements made in telecommunications technologies. The higher bandwidth and lower costs associated with fiber optics and satellite links have made it possible to send complete backup image copies electronically. It is also possible to vault current transaction recovery information (log or journal data) to the remote site in a timely manner.

The *benefits* of electronic vaulting are: improved system availability, system performance, and system reliability; quality of the backup and recovery processes; and increased customer (user) service and satisfaction. Electronic vaulting makes backup information more accessible by reducing retrieval time from hours or days to minutes during an interruption or a disaster when time is most valuable. Depending on the application, less information can be maintained online in the computer center, which in turn reduces the amount of onsite backup storage needed.

This method supports automated or unattended computer center operations because minimal or no human intervention is required.

An electronic vault can be located in these areas:

- At a primary recovery site
- At an alternate recovery site
- At a reciprocal site (i.e., recovery at the development site and production on the other site)
- In a third-party location close to the primary recovery site
- At a commercial hot/cold site facility

(vi) Develop Alternate Recovery Site Strategies

Although major disruptions with long-term effects may be rare, they should be accounted for in the contingency plan. Thus, for all high-impact and moderate-impact systems, the plan should include a strategy to recover and perform system operations at an alternate site/facility for an extended period. Organizations may consider low-impact systems for alternate site processing, but such a site is not required due to their low risk and is dependent on management's decision.

- High-impact systems require mirrored systems with disk replication; high-availability systems; and a hot site, mobile site, or mirrored site, or a combination of these sites.
- Medium-impact systems require a warm site.
- Low-impact systems require a cold site or a reciprocal agreement.

In general, three types of alternate sites are available:

1. Dedicated site owned or operated by the organization (i.e., company owned or operated, which is very expensive).
2. Reciprocal agreement requiring a memorandum of agreement (MOA) or a memorandum of understanding (MOU) with an internal or external entity. Internal entities may require an MOU while external entities may require an MOA.
3. Commercially leased facility (e.g., cold site, warm site, or hot site).

Regardless of the type of alternate site chosen, the facility must be able to support system operations as defined in the contingency plan. The three alternate site types commonly categorized in terms of their operational readiness are cold sites, warm sites, and hot sites, progressing from basic to advanced, as follows:

Cold Site $\longrightarrow$ Warm Site $\longrightarrow$ Hot Site

Other variations of the three common sites include mobile sites and mirrored sites with similar core features. A brief discussion of cold sites, warm sites, hot sites, mobile sites, mirrored sites, reciprocal agreements, SLAs, and hybrid approaches follows.

(A) Cold Sites

Cold sites are locations that have the basic infrastructure and environmental controls available (e.g., electrical, heating, and air conditioning), but no equipment or telecommunications established or in place. There is sufficient room to house needed equipment to sustain a system's critical functions. Examples of cold sites include unused areas of a data center and unused office space (if specialized data center environments are not required). Cold sites are normally the least expensive alternate processing site solution, as the primary costs are only the lease or maintenance of the required square footage for recovery purposes. However, the recovery time is the longest, as all system equipment (including telecommunications) will need to be acquired or purchased, installed, tested, and have backup software and data loaded and tested before the system can be operational. Depending on the size and complexity of a system, recovery could take several days to weeks to complete. The cold site method is most difficult and expensive to test compared to the hot or warm site method.

(B) Warm Sites

Warm sites are locations that have the basic infrastructure of cold sites but also have sufficient computer and telecommunications equipment installed and available to operate the system at the site. However, the equipment is not loaded with the software or data required to operate the system. Warm sites should have backup media readers that are compatible with the system's backup strategy. Warm sites may not have equipment to run all systems or all components of a system, just enough to operate critical mission/business functions. An example of a warm site is a test or development site that is geographically separate from the production system. Equipment may be in place to operate the system but would require reverting to the current production level of the software, loading the data from backup media, and establishing communications to users. Another example is available equipment at an alternate facility that is running noncritical systems and that could be transitioned to run a critical system during a contingency event. A warm site is more expensive than a cold site, as equipment is purchased and maintained at the site, with telecommunications in place. Some costs may be offset by using equipment for noncritical functions or for testing. Recovery to a warm site can take several hours to several days, depending on system complexity and the amount of data to be restored.

(C) Hot Sites

Hot sites are locations with fully operational equipment and capacity to quickly take over system operations after loss of the primary system facility. A hot site has sufficient equipment and the most current version of production software installed and adequate storage for the production system data. Hot sites should have the most recent version of backed-up data loaded, requiring only updating with data since the last backup. In many cases, hot site data and databases are updated concurrently with or soon after the primary data and databases are updated. Hot sites also need a way to quickly move system users' connectivity from the primary site. One example of a hot site is two identical systems at alternate locations that are in production, serving different geographical locations or load-balancing production workloads. Each location is built to handle the full workload, and data are continuously synchronized between the systems. This is the most expensive option, requiring full operation of a system at an alternate location and all telecommunications capacity, with the ability to maintain or quickly update the operational data and databases. Hot sites also require having operational support nearly equal to the production location. Recovery to a hot site can take minutes to hours, depending on the time needed to move user connectivity to the new location and make data current at the hot site location. A hot site is used for short-term needs while a cold site is used for long-term needs.

(D) Mobile Sites

Mobile sites are self-contained, transportable shells custom-fitted with specific telecommunications and system equipment necessary to meet system requirements.

(E) Mirrored Sites

Mirrored sites are fully redundant facilities with automated real-time information mirroring. A mirrored site (redundant site) is equipped and configured exactly like the primary site in all technical respects. Some organizations plan on having partial redundancy for disaster recovery purposes and partial processing for normal operations. The stocking of spare PCs and their parts or LAN servers also provide some redundancy. Exhibit 3.14 summarizes the five alternate sites.

EXHIBIT 3.14 Five Alternate Sites

Alternate Site	Cost	Hardware/ Equipment	Tele- communications	Setup Time	Location
Cold site	Low	None	None	Long	Fixed
Warm site	Medium	Partial	Partial/full	Medium	Fixed
Hot site	Medium/high	Full	Full	Short	Fixed
Mobile site	High	Dependent	Dependent	Dependent	Not fixed
Mirrored site	High	Full	Full	None	Fixed

(F) Reciprocal Agreements

Reciprocal agreements occur when two or more organizations with similar or identical system configurations and backup technologies enter into a formal agreement to serve as alternate sites for each other or enter into a joint contract for an alternate site. This type of site is set up via a reciprocal agreement with an MOA or MOU. A reciprocal agreement should be entered into carefully because each site must be able to support the other, in addition to its own workload, in the event of a disaster. This type of agreement requires the recovery sequence for the applications from both organizations to be prioritized from a joint perspective, favorable to both parties. Testing should be conducted at the partnering sites to evaluate the extra processing thresholds, compatible system and backup configurations, sufficient telecommunications connections, compatible security measures, and the sensitivity of data that might be accessible by other privileged users, in addition to functionality of the recovery strategy. Consideration should also be given to system interconnections and possible interconnection security agreements.

(G) Service-Level Agreements for Alternate Recovery Sites

An MOA/MOU or an SLA for an alternate site should be developed specific to the organization's needs and the partner organization's capabilities. The legal department and audit department of each party must review and approve the agreement. In general, the SLA should address at a minimum, each of these elements:

- Contract/agreement duration
- Cost/fee structure for disaster declaration and occupancy (daily usage), administration, maintenance, testing, annual cost/fee increases, transportation support cost (receipt and return of offsite data/supplies, as applicable), cost/expense allocation (as applicable), and billing and payment schedules
- Disaster declaration (i.e., circumstances constituting a disaster, notification procedures)
- Site/facility priority access and/or use

- Site availability

- Site guarantee

- Other clients subscribing to same resources and site, and the total number of site sub-scribers, as applicable

- Contract/agreement change or modification process

- Contract/agreement termination conditions

- Process to negotiate extension of service

- Guarantee of compatibility

- Information system requirements (including data and telecommunication requirements) for hardware, software, and any special system needs (hardware and software)

- CM and notification requirements, including hardware, software, and infrastructure

- Security requirements, including special security needs

- Staff support provided/not provided

- Facility services provided/not provided (e.g., use of onsite office equipment and cafeteria)

- Testing, including scheduling, availability, test time duration, and additional testing, if required

- Records management (onsite and offsite), including electronic media and hard copy

- Service-level management (performance measures and management of quality of information system services provided)

- Workspace requirements (e.g., chairs, desks, telephones, and PCs)

- Supplies provided/not provided (e.g., office supplies)

- Additional costs not covered elsewhere

- Other contractual issues, as applicable

- Other technical requirements, as applicable

(H) Hybrid Approaches to Alternate Sites
Some organizations use any combination of the preceding approaches in what is called a hybrid approach. It includes having a hot site as a backup in case a redundant or reciprocal agreement site is damaged by a separate contingency.

(vii) Implementation, Documentation, Training, and Testing
Once the contingency planning strategies have been selected, it is necessary to make appropriate preparations for implementation and to document the strategies, train employees, and test. Many of these tasks are ongoing.

(A) Implementation
Much preparation is needed to implement the strategies for protecting critical functions and their supporting resources. For example, one common preparation is to establish procedures for backing up files and applications. Another is to establish contracts and agreements, if the contingency strategy calls for them. Existing service contracts may need to be renegotiated to add contingency services. Another preparation may be to purchase equipment, especially to support a redundant capability.

It is important to keep preparations, including documentation, up to date. Computer systems change rapidly, and so should backup services and redundant equipment. Contracts and agreements also may need to reflect the changes. If additional equipment is needed, it must be maintained and periodically replaced when it is no longer dependable or no longer fits the organization's architecture.

Preparation should also include formally designating people who are responsible for various tasks in the event of a contingency. These people often are referred to as the contingency response team. This team often is composed of people who were a part of the contingency planning team.

There are many important implementation issues for an organization. Two of the most important are: How many plans should be developed? and Who prepares each plan? Both of these questions revolve around the organization's overall strategy for contingency planning. The answers should be documented in an organization's policy and procedures manual.

(B) Documentation

The contingency plan needs to be written, kept up to date as the system and other factors change, and stored in a safe place. A written plan is critical during a contingency, especially if the person who developed the plan is unavailable. The plan should clearly state in simple language the sequence of tasks to be performed in the event of a contingency so that someone with minimal knowledge can immediately begin to execute it. It is generally helpful to store up-to-date copies of the contingency plan in several locations, including any offsite locations, such as alternate processing sites or backup data storage facilities.

(C) Training

All personnel should be trained in their contingency-related duties. New personnel should be trained as they join the organization, refresher training may be needed, and personnel will need to practice their skills.

Training is particularly important for effective employee response during emergencies. If there is a fire, there is no time to check a manual to determine correct procedures. Depending on the nature of the emergency, there may or may not be time to protect equipment and other assets. Practice is necessary in order to react correctly, especially when human safety is involved.

(D) Testing

A contingency plan should be tested periodically because there will undoubtedly be flaws in the plan and in its implementation. The plan will become dated as time passes and as the resources used to support critical functions change. Responsibility for keeping the contingency plan current should be specially assigned. The extent and frequency of testing will vary between organizations and among systems. Regardless, recovery strategy should be revised based on the test results and lessons learned. There are several types of testing, including reviews, analyses, disaster simulations, end-to-end testing, and full-scale testing, as discussed later in this chapter.

Reviews.   A **review** can be a simple test to check the accuracy of contingency plan documentation. For instance, a reviewer could check if individuals listed are still in the organization and still have the responsibilities that caused them to be included in the plan. This test can check home, cell/mobile, and work telephone numbers, organizational codes, and building and room numbers. The review can determine if files can be restored from backup tapes or if employees know emergency procedures. A checklist is used during reviews to ensure that all items are addressed.

Analyses.   An analysis, or desk checking, may be performed on the entire plan or portions of it, such as emergency response procedures. It is beneficial if the analysis is performed by someone who did not help develop the contingency plan but has a good working knowledge of the critical function and supporting resources. The analyst(s) may mentally follow the strategies in the contingency plan, looking for flaws in the logic or processes used by the plan's developers. The analyst also may interview functional managers, resource managers, and their staff to uncover missing or unworkable pieces of the plan.

Disaster Simulations.   Organizations may also arrange disaster simulations, which provide valuable information about flaws in the contingency plan and provide practice for a real emergency. While they can be expensive, disaster simulations can provide critical information that can be used to ensure the continuity of important functions. In general, the more critical the functions and the resources addressed in the contingency plan, the more cost beneficial it is to perform a disaster simulation.

End-to-End Testing.   The purpose of end-to-end testing is to verify that a defined set of interrelated systems, which collectively support an organizational core business area or function, interoperate as intended in an operational environment (either actual or simulated). These interrelated systems include not only those owned and managed by the organization but also the external systems with which they interface.

Generally, end-to-end testing is conducted when one major system in the end-to-end chain is modified or replaced, and attention is rightfully focused on the changed or new system. The boundaries on end-to-end tests are not fixed or predetermined but vary depending on a given business area's system dependencies (internal and external) and criticality to the mission of the organization. Therefore, in planning end-to-end tests, it is critical to analyze the organization's core business functions, the interrelationships among systems supporting these functions, and potential risk exposure due to system failures in the chain of support. It is also important to work early and continuously with the organization's data exchange partners so that end-to-end tests can be effectively planned and executed.

Full-Scale Testing.   Full-scale (full-interruption) testing is costly and disruptive while end-to-end testing is least costly and less disruptive. Management of a firm will not allow normal production operations to be stopped for the sake of full-interruption testing. Some businesses operate on a 24/7 schedule, and losing several hours or days of production time is equal to another disaster, financial or otherwise. Hence, full-scale testing is not advised unless overruled by management.

(E) A Summary of Training, Testing, and Exercise Documents

A *personnel training program* document should include these items:

- Purpose of the plan
- Cross-team coordination and communication
- Reporting procedures
- Security requirements
- Team-specific processes (i.e., activation/notification, recovery, and reconstitution phases)
- Individual responsibilities (i.e., activation/notification, recovery, and reconstitution phases)

A *testing program* document should include these items:

- System recovery on an alternate site from backup media
- System performance using alternate equipment

- Coordination among recovery teams (e.g., business continuity planners)
- Restoration of normal operations
- Internal and external connectivity
- Notification procedures

An *exercise program* document should include these items:

- Tabletop exercises (Discussion-based only, without deployment of equipment, is useful for low-impact systems.)
- Functional exercises (Validation of operational readiness for emergencies is useful for moderate-impact systems with system recovery from backup media.)
- Full-scale functional exercises (A system failover to the alternate site, recovery of a server or database from backup media, and processing from a server at an alternate site are useful for high-impact systems with full system recovery and reconstitution to a known state.)
- Personnel exercises (i.e., execution of staff roles and responsibilities)
- Scenario-driven exercises (i.e., simulation of operational emergency environment, such as a power failure or a fire in a data center) functional, full-scale functional, and personnel exercises are examples of scenario-driven exercises.

(viii) Contingency Plan Maintenance

The IT contingency plan must always be maintained in a ready state for use immediately upon notification. Periodic reviews of the plan must be conducted for currency of key personnel and vendor information, system components and dependencies, the recovery strategy, vital records, and operational requirements. While some changes may be obvious (e.g., personnel turnover or vendor changes), others will require analysis. The BIA should be reviewed periodically and updated with new information to identify new contingency requirements and priorities. Changes made to the plan are noted in a record of changes, dated, and signed or initialed by the person making the change. The revised plan (or plan sections) is circulated to those with plan responsibilities. Because of the impact that plan changes may have on interdependent business processes or information systems, the changes must be clearly communicated and properly annotated in the beginning of the document.

Modern fault-tolerance mechanisms can play an important role in maintaining data and system integrity as they increase system resilience. **Resilience** is the ability of a computer system to continue to perform its tasks after the occurrence of faults and to operate correctly even though one or more of its component parts are malfunctioning. Traditional system fault-tolerance mechanisms, such as logs and locks, cannot handle serious malicious code attacks or cyberattacks. The ultimate goal is to ensure that computer systems are reliable and available for system users.

Some examples of fault-tolerance mechanisms are listed next.

- Develop error detection, error correction, and redundant processing policies and procedures to maintain integrity of data and systems.
- Install mechanisms such as fail-stop processors and redundancy mechanisms with built-in fault detection, error recovery, and failure recovery abilities combined with system reliability

measurement metrics (e.g., MTTF, mean time to repair [MTTR], and mean time between failures [MTBF]).

■ Install fault-tolerant hardware methods, as they increase system resilience.

■ Install a robust OS so it can handle unexpected system failures.

System Redundancy Mechanisms. Some concepts regarding system redundancy mechanisms are listed next.

■ Increasing system redundancy will increase system reliability, availability, and serviceability.

■ The need for redundant electrical power is often overlooked during contingency plan development.

■ Network availability is increased with redundancy in electrical power.

■ Meshed network topology provides a high degree of fault tolerance when compared to star, bus, and ring topologies.

■ Network reliability is increased with alternate telecommunications carriers.

■ Normal Ethernet does not have built-in redundancy. Fast Ethernet, FDDI, and SONET have built-in redundancy or have options for it.

■ Implement disk mirroring, disk shadowing, server mirroring, disk duplexing, block mirroring, check-pointing, disk farming, and disk arrays concepts to reduce or eliminate downtime from disk failure or loss of data.

System Reliability Measurement Metrics. Some examples of system reliability measurement metrics are listed next.

■ MTTF is the average time to the next failure. It is the time taken for a part or system to fail for the first time. MTTF assumes that the failed system is not repaired. A high MTTF means high system reliability.

■ MTTR is the amount of time it takes to resume normal operation. It is the total corrective maintenance time divided by the total number of corrective maintenance actions during a given period of time. A low MTTR means high system reliability.

■ MTBF is the average length of time a system is functional or the average time interval between failures. It is the total functioning life of an item divided by the total number of failures during the measurement interval of minutes, hours, and days. It is the average length of time a system or a component works without fault between consecutive failures. MTBF assumes that the failed system is immediately repaired, as in MTTR (repair). A high MTBF means high system reliability.

$$MTBF = MTTF + MTTR \text{ (repair)}$$

SYSTEM RELIABILITY VERSUS SYSTEM AVAILABILITY

■ The reliability of a computer system is defined as the probability that the system will be able to process work correctly and completely without its being terminated or corrupted.

■ The availability of a computer system is a measure of the amount of time that the system is actually capable of accepting and performing a user's work.

- System reliability can be thought of as the quality of service. System availability can be thought of as the quantity of service. In other words, availability can be considered a component of reliability.

- A system that fails frequently but is restarted quickly has high availability even though its reliability is low.

- System reliability is related to system safety and quality, not system availability.

- Note that the terms "reliability" and "availability" are closely related but are often incorrectly used as synonyms.

- MTTR is the time following a failure to restore a RAID disk array to its normal failure-tolerant mode of operation. This time includes replacement of the failed disk and the time to rebuild the disk array. A low MTTR means high system availability.

- Mean time between outages (MTBO) is the mean time between equipment failures that result in a loss of system continuity or unacceptable degradation, as expressed by:

$$MTBO = MTBF / (1-FFAS)$$

where

MTBF = nonredundant mean time between failures

FFAS = fraction of failures for which the failed hardware or software is bypassed automatically

A low MTBO means high system availability.

- MTTR is the average time to restore service following system failures that result in service outages. The time to restore includes all time from the occurrence of the failure until the restoral of service. A low MTTR means high system availability.

- Mean time to data loss (MTTDL) is the average time before a loss of data occurs in a given disk array and is applicable to RAID technology. A low MTTDL means high data reliability.

- Time to recover (TTR) is the time required for any computer resources to be recovered from disruptive events. It is the time required to reestablish an activity from an emergency or degraded mode to a normal mode. Note that TTR is also defined as emergency response time (EMRT).

Fault-Tolerance Hardware Methods. These next fault-tolerant hardware methods should be implemented in combination to improve the performance of data storage media regardless of the type of computer used:

- Disk arrays

- Disk striping

- Disk mirroring

- Server mirroring

- Disk duplexing

- Block mirroring

- Disk replication

- Disk imaging
- Disk farming
- Check-pointing

A gap between CPU and data storage subsystem performance causes imbalance in performance, which in turn degrades online system response time and batch job turnaround time.

Disk arrays use a parity disk scheme to keep track of data stored in a domain of the storage subsystem and to regenerate it in case of hardware/software failure. A disk array unit contains many ready-to-use and standby disks. When one disk in the array fails, a spare disk automatically fills in and operates. Data is rebuilt from the parity disk. Disk arrays consume less overhead than disk mirroring and hence can be thought of as an alternative to disk mirroring. Disk arrays can be used to improve data transmission rates by improving input and output rates. They can fill the performance gap between the CPU and the storage subsystem. RAID has seven categories from 0 through 6; RAID-0 provides lower performance; and RAID-6 provides higher performance characteristics when used with larger number of physical disks (i.e., 10 to 20). RAID technology increases fault tolerance of hardware and uses several disks in a single logical subsystem. The main purpose of RAID is to provide backup so if one disk fails, all of the data are immediately available from the other disks. RAID storage units offer fault-tolerant hardware. The purpose of disk arrays is same as the disk striping, disk mirroring, and server mirroring.

Disk striping uses more than one disk and more than one partition, and is the same as disk arrays. An advantage of disk arrays include running multiple drives in parallel, and a disadvantage includes the fact that its organization is more complicated than disk farming and highly sensitive to multiple failures.

Disk mirroring means that the file server contains duplicate disks, and all information is written to both disks simultaneously. It is same as disk shadowing.

Server mirroring means that the server is duplicated instead of the disk, which is expensive. All information is written to both servers simultaneously. Server mirroring serves the same purpose as disk arrays do.

Disk duplexing means that the disk controller is duplicated. When one disk controller fails, the other one is ready to operate.

Block mirroring is a method to provide backup, redundancy, and failover processes to ensure high availability of systems. Block mirroring is performed on an alternate site, preferably separate from the primary site. Whenever a data write is made to a block on a primary storage device at the primary site, the same write is made to an alternate storage device at the alternate site, either within the same storage system or between separate storage systems, at different locations.

In **disk replication**, data are written to two different disks to ensure that two valid copies of the data are always available. Disk replication minimizes the time windows for recovery.

Disk imaging is generating a bit-for-bit copy of the original media, including free space and slack space. Disk imaging is used in forensics evidence.

In **disk farming**, data are stored on multiple disks for reliability and performance reasons.

Check-pointing is a fault-recovery and restore procedure that is needed before, during, or after completion of certain transactions or events to ensure acceptable fault recovery.

(B) Robust Operating Systems

An OS must be robust enough to withstand system failures. The OS response to failures can be classified into three general categories: system reboot, emergency system restart, and system cold start.

A *system reboot* is performed after shutting down the system in a controlled manner in response to a TCB failure. For example, when the TCB detects the exhaustion of space in some of its critical tables or finds inconsistent object data structures, it closes all objects, aborts all active user processes, and restarts with no user process in execution. Before restart, however, the recovery mechanisms make a best effort to correct the source of inconsistency. Occasionally the mere termination of all processes frees up some important resources, allowing restart with enough resources available. Note that system rebooting is useful when the recovery mechanisms can determine that TCB and user data structures affecting system security and integrity are, in fact, in a consistent state.

An *emergency system restart* is done after a system fails in an uncontrolled manner in response to a TCB or media failure. In such cases, TCB and user objects on nonvolatile storage belonging to processes active at the time of TCB or media failure may be left in an inconsistent state. The system enters maintenance mode, recovery is performed automatically, and the system restarts with no user processes in progress after bringing up the system in a consistent state.

A *system cold start* takes place when unexpected TCB or media failure takes place and the recovery procedures cannot bring the system to a consistent state. TCB and user objects may remain in an inconsistent state following attempts to recover automatically. Administrative personnel intervention is required to bring the system to a consistent state from maintenance mode.

(c) Roles and Responsibilities of Business Continuity Manager or Executive

Because the size and scope of each organization are different, the roles and responsibilities of a business continuity manager or executive are different too. This position is diversified and unique, and it should serve in more of a liaison role with coordination and cooperation from several functions within the organization. Regarding reporting relationships, the business continuity manager or executive should functionally report to the chief executive officer (CEO) and administratively report to the chief information officer (CIO) for independence and objectivity reasons. This reporting relationship is similar to cases when CIO reports to the chief financial officer (CFO) instead of the CEO and when the chief audit executive reports to the CFO instead of functionally reporting to the board of directors and administratively to the CEO.

Specific roles and responsibilities of a business continuity manager or executive are listed next.

- Develop policies and procedures in handling normal (regular) and emergency disasters and incidents.
- Coordinate with business functional managers (e.g., accounting, finance, operations, and marketing), insurance manager, physical security officer, information security manager, and risk manager.

- Work with the insurance department to understand various insurance policy types, coverage, and limits, for equipment, buildings, and machinery. Also, understand the reinsurance provisions and limits.

- Work with the record-keeping department to ensure that both manual records and electronic records are properly retained, labeled, preserved, and stored in a safe and secure place. Ensure that the electronic records can be retrieved at a later date, so the corresponding software must be retained. Be familiar with the ISO standard issued on record keeping (ISO 15489).

- Regularly meet with various stakeholders (offsite organizations, vendors, suppliers, regulatory authorities, and insurance companies) to understand their issues and concerns.

- Work with U.S. federal or state emergency management administrators or authorities to obtain the needed help and assistance during a disaster or incident in a timely manner.

- Familiarize yourself with management of alternate recovery sites (e.g., hot, cold, or warm sites) to understand their operations, policies, and procedures.

(d) Relationship between Business Continuity Management and ISO Standards

International Organization for Standardization (ISO) standard 22301 focuses on BCM systems and requirements in order to prepare for, to protect against, and to reduce the likelihood of occurrence of disasters or disruptive incidents (i.e., man made, nature made, or technology used). The goal is to respond to and recover from disasters and incidents and to improve business continuity capabilities. Organizations are able to obtain certification to ISO 22301 similar to other certifiable standards, such as ISO 9000, ISO 14000, ISO 27001, and ISO 28000. Note that the standard previously known as British Institute's BS25999 standard has been transitioned to the ISO 22301 standard.

Other ISO standards related to BCM include ISO 15489, which provides general guidance regarding records management, and ISO 13606, which provides guidance regarding electronic health record communications.

(e) Backup Methods

This section defines system backups and presents system backups based on frequency and on storage media, and data file rotation methods.

(i) System Backups Defined

Hardware failures, disk crashes, power outages, software failures, and other disruptions are normal in computer center operation. Periodic **system backups** provide the ability to recover and restart from a failure or disaster and prevent the destruction of information. System backups include backing up operational application programs, data files, databases, systems software products, configuration files, system development programs, utility programs, and others.

Timely system backups help in reconstructing any damaged files (recovery) and resuming computer program execution (restart). For example, online and real-time systems and database systems require duplicate backup arrangements and extensive backup and recovery and restart procedures.

For online systems, restart procedures identify transactions that were lost when the online process failed. Another related backup mechanism is *checkpoints* that allow program restarts.

Checkpoints are most effective for batch (sequential processing), online data entry, and batch update processing and multiprogramming and are least effective for online real-time systems due to their instant access and updates. Checkpoints are needed to recover from hardware failures and are usually applicable to sequential files, direct (random) access files, and tape or disk files. Exhibit 3.15 compares the backup requirements between online and batch systems.

EXHIBIT 3.15 Backup Requirements for Online and Batch Systems

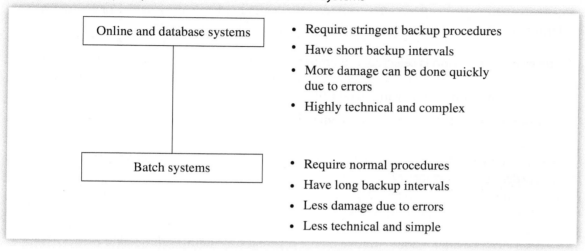

A prerequisite to the performance of timely system backups is the availability of accurate and up-to-date operations documentation (run books), which includes run-time instructions, backup schedules, and recovery/restart procedures for each application system in the production environment. The decision on how often to back up a file is dependent on cost of backup versus expected cost of failure, ability to re-create the file without a backup, and time needed to create a copy.

(ii) System Backups Based on Frequency

System/data backups are maintained through a combination of full-volume backups and incremental backups.

Full-volume backups, which are common, involve compressing the image copy of an entire magnetic disk volume to a tape. This is also known as the brute-force approach since it takes copies of all files regardless of the need or regardless file changes. Full-volume backups take less time to perform and are less error-prone than the incremental backups, but require more storage media to store and more manual intervention.

This method is most applicable to database programs and data files due to the logical relationships between data. System recovery is achieved by restoring the database and reapplying transactions from the journal or log. Journals and logs are records of all the transactions that have been processed against a database. Logs contain before-and-after images of transactions for all changes. In the event of a failure, the database is restored, and all the changes that have occurred up to the point of failure are reapplied to the database. Some databases are so large that record-level backup is performed whenever a change to the logical database record occurs.

Incremental backups, a different approach, focus only on backing up data sets that have changed since the last full backup. The need for continuous, uninterrupted online system availability leaves a reduced time window for full backups, which, in turn, justifies the use of incremental backups.

(iii) System Backups Based on Storage Media

Another way of looking at the backup methods is to determine where the data is to be stored. Three possible options exist: (1) remote backup in cloud storage, (2) internal hard disk drives, and (3) removable storage media, consisting of external hard disk drive, solid-state storage, optical storage, and digital tape system.[4]

Large businesses or organizations should consider keeping one backup copy onsite and another offsite either through a separate data service (such as a cloud service provider or remote server backup) or on the organization's own offsite servers or digital tape system.

Whatever backup option is selected, remember to follow the 3-2-1 rule of backups:

3 — Keep 3 copies of any important file: 1 primary and 2 backups.

2 — Keep the files on 2 different media types to protect against different types of hazards.

1 — Store 1 copy offsite (e.g., outside of a business facility).

(A) Remote Backup—Cloud Storage

Recent expansions of broadband Internet service have made cloud storage available to a wide range of computer users. Cloud service customers use the Internet to access a shared pool of computing resources (e.g., networks, servers, storage, applications, and services) owned by a cloud service provider. Cloud storage is a secure backup method to quickly recover from a ransomware attack.

Pros. Remote backup services can help protect data against some worst-case scenarios, such as natural disasters or critical failures of local devices due to malware. Additionally, cloud services provide anytime access to data and applications anywhere there is an Internet connection, with no need for the user to invest in networks, servers, and other hardware. More or less cloud service can be purchased as needed, and the service provider transparently manages resource usage as it grows or shrinks. Some providers can also ensure regulatory compliance in the handling of sensitive data, which may benefit small businesses.

Cons. The cloud's dependence on the Internet can delay communications between users and the cloud. In addition, there are no universal standards, platforms, or languages for cloud computing, so users may become locked into one provider. The physical distribution of cloud data over many geographically dispersed servers may cause some organizations, especially ones handling sensitive data, problems with jurisdiction and fair information practices. Cloud customers have little or no knowledge of their service provider's cloud infrastructure or its reliability, and users surrender most of their control over their own data.

Security. Cloud service providers can often encrypt user data, making it harder for attackers to access critical information. However, cloud users have little or no direct control over their data or knowledge of their cloud service provider's security practices. Shared clouds store one user's data along with data from many other users in the same cloud infrastructure, posing a security risk.

Before entrusting critical data to a cloud service provider, carefully check the service agreement for security practices. To increase the security of data in the cloud, look for a cloud service provider that will:

---

[4] *Data Backup Options*, produced for US-CERT, a government organization, by Carnegie Mellon University, 2012, www.us-cert.gov.

- Encrypt data with established encryption algorithms, such as Advanced Encryption Standard or Blowfish.

- Transfer the data via a SSL connection.

- Follow established network security recommended practices, such as the use of firewalls.

- Physically protect the hardware that stores, processes, and transmits data.

- Prevent one customer's data from leaking to other customers on its cloud.

(B) Internal Hard Disk Drives

Hard disk drives store data on a spinning magnetic platter read by a moving read/write head. Nearly all desktop and laptop computers use their internal hard drive to store most of the information they need in order to run as well as the user's working, primary files. Secondary systems and backup servers also store data on internal hard drives. Because hard drives are rewritable, they can be used to perform rolling backups, a method that automatically and periodically updates the backup files with the most recent versions of the primary files.

Pros. Keeping primary file copies and backup copies on the same internal hard drive allows users to quickly update backup files and maintain a simple file structure, all without purchasing any other storage device.

Cons. Rolling backups can silently propagate any corruption or malware in the primary files to the backup files. Worse, if the internal hard drive is damaged, stolen, or corrupted, users could lose both primary and backup files. In addition, the computer constantly uses the internal hard drive, so the more backup files stored there, the less space the computer has to operate. Last, the working life span of hard drives varies, and installing new internal hard drives requires some technical expertise.

Security. Backup files stored on the internal hard drive are just as vulnerable to damage and corruption as primary files. Additionally, internal hard drives are only as physically secure as the computers that house them. Hard drives can be encrypted to prevent unauthorized access to stored data, but data can be erased—and the hard drive rendered unusable—via magnetic degaussing without accessing the drive electronically. To increase the security of an internal hard drive, encrypt the drive's contents, physically secure the computer, and follow network security recommended practices, such as the use of firewalls and antivirus.

(C) Removable Storage Media

Storage media that can be connected to and disconnected from a computer are a more versatile backup option than a computer's internal hard drive. Physically separating backups from the computer helps keep data safe, from both online attackers (e.g., ransomware attacks) and power surges.

Pros. Removable media are a flexible data storage alternative because most are portable and work on most computers. They are also available in a wide variety of storage capacities and prices, so users can find a device that fits their needs and budget. Most removable media are also reusable.

Cons. Portability makes removable storage devices convenient but also makes them prone to loss or theft. Rolling backups may spread corruption and malware from the primary files to the backups.

Security. Unlike remote storage, removable storage media give users direct control over their data. However, that means users are responsible for protecting that data, especially when traveling with it. To increase the security of removable media devices:

- Password-protect them.
- Encrypt their data when possible.
- Connect them only to systems that follow network security recommended practices, such as the use of firewalls and antivirus.
- Remove them from the computer when the backup is completed.
- Secure them physically.

(D) Types of Removable Storage Media

Four types of removable storage media include external hard disk drives, solid-state storage, optical storage, and digital tape systems. A gold disk or master disk is an example of removable storage media where the final version of mainframe computer configuration files is permanently stored, saved, archived, and secured as a master copy for backup, recovery, and update purposes. The gold disk serves as an insurance policy.

External Hard Disk Drives. External hard drives are the same as internal hard drives, but they are portable and easy to install. They are still prone to physical damage and degaussing, and they are bulkier than solid-state storage of similar capacity.

Solid-State Storage. Solid-state storage—also known as flash drives, USB flash drives, thumb drives (pen drives), SD and micro-SD cards, memory sticks, and solid-state drives (SSDs)—is at the heart of many portable storage media, including most digital music players and smartphones. Unlike hard drives, solid-state devices contain no moving parts, which allows them to be small, resist shock, and access data quickly. Use plug-and-play USB drives and cards primarily for data storage; use more complex SSDs, which can be internal or external, for data storage and processing.

USB drives are small enough to slip into a pocket and are plug-and-play compatible with most computers. Solid-state media are rewritable, though they do not store data magnetically and so are not in danger of degaussing. Some USB drives can store hundreds of gigabytes of data, and SSDs can store even more. However, solid-state media still do not offer as much storage capacity as hard disk drives or digital tapes. Additionally, solid-state media are more expensive per gigabyte than hard drives, although the price gap has been steadily narrowing. Writing data to a solid-state device will eventually wear it out, though modern device controllers extend media life spans. Many SSDs and even USB drives now come with built-in password protection and data encryption.

Optical Storage. Optical storage media (e.g., CDs, DVDs, and Blu-ray discs) store data on reflective discs read by a moving laser head that can also write data onto rewritable discs with varying storage capacities.

Many computers come with some kind of internal optical disc drive, and external drives can be bought. Although the kinds of discs may change, newer optical disc drives usually read older discs, making optical storage a forward-compatible backup option good for disaster recovery. Nonrewritable discs do not allow for rolling backups, so they might not contain the most recent version of primary files. However, data on nonrewritable discs cannot be accidentally erased or inherit corruptions or malware from later versions of primary files. Optical discs are also relatively inexpensive, although they do not come with built-in data encryption, so a third-party solution would be required. Optical discs, especially CDs and rewritable discs, do not last forever. Handling can shorten their life spans and, short of multidisc hardware, optical discs must be individually handled.

Digital Tape Systems. A digital tape system comprises a tape deck, individual tapes, and, optionally, a tape auto-loader. Individual digital tapes can provide capacities of more than a terabyte, or roughly 1,000 gigabytes, and are fairly cheap. Once installed, digital tape systems require little user interaction and access data very quickly. The reusable tapes enable rolling backups but are less vulnerable to viruses than hard disks, if older versions of files are adequately archived. Although digital tapes are one of the least expensive storage media per gigabyte, digital tape systems are expensive and may require additional costs to install.

(iv) Data File Rotation Methods

Usually tape data files are backed up and rotated between onsite storage and offsite storage using a three-generation concept (i.e., son, father, and grandfather), where each generation represents a time period. Disk data files are saved for five or seven generations. Each generation can have multiple copies and be rotated between onsite and offsite. Tape files are a major obstacle to unattended computer center operation due to their labor-intensive nature and are mainly used as a transportation mechanism to third-party service providers.

3.7 Sample Practice Questions

In the actual CIA Exam for Part 3, 100 multiple-choice (M/C) test questions appear. This book contains 100 M/C sample practice questions divided into syllabus-based domains using the approximate domain weight given in the exam. These questions are added at the end of each applicable domain of this book with the sole purpose of showing the flavor and structure of the exam questions and of creating a self-quiz experience. The answers and explanations for these questions are shown in a separate section at the end of this book just before the Glossary section. This separate section is titled "Sample Practice Questions, Answers, and Explanations." If CIA Exam candidates need to practice more sample questions to obtain a higher level of confidence, Wiley offers a separate online test bank software product with hundreds of similar, sample practice questions.

1. In the preliminary risk assessment task of the system development life cycle initiation phase, integrity needs from a user's or owner's perspective are defined in terms of which of the following?
   a. Place of data
   b. Timeliness of data
   c. Form of data
   d. Quality of data

2. Which of the following is required when an organization uncovers deficiencies in the security controls deployed to protect an information system?
   a. Develop preventive security controls.
   b. Develop plan of action and milestones.
   c. Develop detective security controls.
   d. Modify ineffective security controls.

3. Which of the following occurs after delivery and installation of a new information system under acquisition?
   a. Unit testing
   b. Subsystem testing
   c. Full system testing
   d. Integration and acceptance testing

4. Effective control is achieved when configuration management control is established prior to the start of which of the following?
   a. Requirements analysis
   b. Design
   c. Coding
   d. Testing

5. Media sanitization activity is usually **most** intense during which of the following phases of the system development life cycle?
   a. Development/acquisition
   b. Implementation
   c. Operation/maintenance
   d. Disposal

6. Which of the following is the correct sequence of steps to be followed in an application software change control process?
   I.   Test the changes.
   II. Plan for changes.
   III. Initiate change request.
   IV. Release software changes.

   a. I, II, III, and IV
   b. II, I, III, and IV
   c. III, II, I, and IV
   d. IV, III, I, and II

7. Software configuration management (SCM) should primarily address which of the following questions?
   a. How does software evolve during system development?
   b. How does software evolve during system maintenance?
   c. What constitutes a software product at any point in time?
   d. How is a software product planned?

8. Security controls are designed and implemented in which of the following system development life cycle phases?
   a. Planning/initiation
   b. Development/acquisition
   c. Implementation/assessment
   d. Disposal/decommissioning

9. Which of the following tests is driven by system requirements?
   a. Black box testing
   b. White box testing
   c. Gray box testing
   d. Glass box testing

10. Which of the following volatile data generated by operating system software installed on workstations and servers should be collected first prior to conducting computer forensic auditing work?
   I. Network connections
   II. Login sessions
   III. Network configuration
   IV. Operating system time

   a. I and II
   b. I and III
   c. II and III
   d. III and IV

11. Which of the following are the potential advantages of using cloud computing technology to user organizations?
   I. They can access data and documents from anywhere and at any time.
   II. They can reduce the cost of purchasing additional hardware and software.
   III. They can reduce the cost of purchasing additional storage memory devices.
   IV. They can implement pay-as-you-go method.

   a. I and II
   b. I and IV
   c. I and III
   d. I, II, III, and IV

12. Which of the following statements is **not** true? A data warehouse is:
   a. Distributed.
   b. Subject oriented.
   c. Time variant.
   d. Static in nature.

13. Which of the following provides an effective security control over the Internet access points or hot spots during remote access and telework?
   a. Virtual private network
   b. Wireless personal area network
   c. Wireless local area network
   d. Virtual local area network

14. What does an effective backup method for handling large volumes of data in a local area network (LAN) environment include?
   a. Backing up at the workstation.
   b. Backing up at the file server.
   c. Using a faster network connection.
   d. Using redundant array of independent disks technology.

15. All of the following are examples of security risks over servers **except**:
   a. Client/server architecture.
   b. Data concentration.
   c. Attack targets.
   d. A single point of failure.

16. Which of the following server types is used for protection from malicious code attacks at the network gateway?
   a. A web server
   b. An image server
   c. A mail server
   d. A quarantine server

17. Which of the following information technology contingency solutions for servers minimizes the recovery time window?

   a. Electronic vaulting
   b. Remote journaling
   c. Load balancing
   d. Disk replication

18. Contingency plans for information technology operations should include appropriate backup agreements. Which of the following arrangements would be considered too vendor dependent when vital operations require almost immediate availability of computer resources?

   a. A hot site arrangement
   b. A cold site arrangement
   c. A cold site and hot site combination arrangement.
   d. Using excess capacity at another data center within the organization

19. From an operations viewpoint, the first step in contingency planning is to perform a(n):

   a. Operating system software backup.
   b. Applications software backup.
   c. Documentation backup.
   d. Hardware backup.

20. The primary contingency strategy for application systems and data is regular backup and secure offsite storage. From an operations viewpoint, which of the following decisions is least important to address?

   a. How often the backup is performed
   b. How often the backup is stored offsite
   c. How often the backup is used
   d. How often the backup is transported

Financial Management (20%)

This domain focuses on key theoretical topics. It presents basic, intermediate, and advanced financial accounting concepts at a basic level. This domain helps to interpret the outcomes of financial statement analysis at a proficient level. It describes asset and liability management, financial instruments, and valuation models at a basic level. It describes capital budgeting; capital structure; taxation schemes; and mergers, acquisitions, and divestitures at a basic level. This domain explains the general concepts of managerial accounting, costing systems, cost concepts, transfer pricing, responsibility accounting, and operating budgets at a basic level. All these topics are tested at the basic and proficient cognitive levels in Part 3 of the CIA Exam with a 20% weight given.

With respect to the CIA Exam, cognitive levels are labeled as proficient level and basic level. These cognitive levels suggest that more time and effort should be spent in studying and mastering the subject matter covered in the topics labeled as the proficient level. Comparatively less time and effort should be spent on the topics labeled as the basic level.

4.1 Financial Accounting and Finance

Various topics are included in this section, including those listed next.

- Basic concepts
- Intermediate concepts
- Advanced concepts
- Financial statement analysis
- Types of debt and equity
- Financial instruments
- Cash management
- Valuation models

- Capital budgeting methods and decisions
- Cost of capital evaluations
- Taxation schemes
- Mergers, acquisitions, and divestitures

(a) Basic Concepts and Underlying Principles of Financial Accounting

Financial accounting (FA) is the language of business. All business transactions eventually end up in financial statements. Accounting principles are used to classify, record, post, summarize, and report the business transactions among various parties involved. Accountants apply their professional standards to analyze business transactions, prepare estimations, and report business events. The business transactions data accumulated in the chart of accounts are used to prepare the financial statements of an organization. Accounting principles and qualities of accounting information, the accounting cycle, different formats of financial statements, and account analysis are discussed in this section.

(i) Accounting Principles and Qualities of Accounting Information
(A) Accounting Principles

If company management could record and report financial data as it saw fit, comparisons among companies would be difficult, if not impossible. Thus, financial accountants follow generally accepted accounting principles (GAAP) in preparing reports. These reports allow investors and other stakeholders to compare one company to another.

Accounting principles and concepts are developed from research, accepted accounting practices, and pronouncements of authoritative bodies. Currently, the Financial Accounting Standards Board (FASB) is the authoritative body having the primary responsibility for developing accounting principles. The FASB publishes *Statements of Financial Accounting Standards* and *Interpretations* to those *Standards*.

Next, we emphasize accounting principles and concepts. It is through this emphasis on the "why" of accounting as well as the "how" that you will gain an understanding of the full significance of accounting. In the following paragraphs, we discuss the business entity concept, the cost concept, the matching concept, and other accounting concepts.

Business Entity Concept. The individual business unit is the business entity for which economic data are needed. This entity could be an automobile dealer, a department store, or a grocery store. The business entity must be identified so that the accountant can determine which economic data should be analyzed, recorded, and summarized in reports.

The business entity concept is important because it limits the economic data in the accounting system to data related directly to the activities of the business. In other words, the business is viewed as an entity separate from its owners, creditors, or other stakeholders. For example, the accountant for a business with one owner (a proprietorship) would record the activities of the business only, not the personal activities, property, or debts of the owner. The business entity concept can be related to the economic entity assumption, which states that economic activity can be identified with a particular unit of accountability; the going-concern assumption, where the accountant assumes that, unless there is evidence to the contrary, the reporting entity will have a life long enough to fulfill its objectives and commitments; and the monetary unit assumption, where it provides that all transactions and events can be measured in terms of a common denominator—the dollar.

Cost Concept. The historical cost concept is the basis for entering the exchange price or cost of an asset into the accounting records. Using the cost concept involves two other important accounting concepts: objectivity and the unit of measure. The objectivity concept requires that the accounting records and reports be based on objective evidence. In exchanges between a buyer and a seller, both try to get the best price. Only the final agreed-on amount is objective enough for accounting purposes. If the amounts at which properties were recorded were constantly being revised upward and downward based on offers, appraisals, and opinions, accounting reports would soon become unstable and unreliable. The unit of measure concept requires that economic data be recorded in dollars. Money is a common unit of measurement for reporting uniform financial data and reports.

Matching Concept. The matching concept, which is based on accrual accounting, refers to the matching of expenses and revenues (hence net income) for an accounting period. Under the accrual basis, revenues are reported in the income statement in which they are earned. Similarly, expenses are reported in the same period as the revenues to which they relate. Under the cash basis of accounting, revenues and expenses are reported in the income statement in the period in which cash is received or paid.

Other Accounting Concepts. The materiality concept implies that errors, which could occur during journalizing and posting transactions, should be significant enough to affect the decision-making process. All material errors should be discovered and corrected. The accounting period concept breaks the economic life of a business into time periods and requires that accounting reports be prepared at periodic intervals. The revenue recognition concept, which is based on accrual accounting, refers to the recognition of revenues in the period in which they are earned.

(B) Qualities of Accounting Information

The accounting function collects the raw data from business transactions and converts it into information useful to the decision maker. In this regard, the accounting information should contain two qualitative characteristics: primary and secondary qualities.

Primary Qualities. The two primary qualities that distinguish useful accounting information are relevance and reliability. If either of these qualities is missing, accounting information will not be useful. **Relevance** means the information must have a bearing on a particular decision situation. Relevant accounting information possesses at least two characteristics: timeliness and predictive value or feedback value. **Timeliness** means accounting information must be provided in time to influence a particular decision. **Predictive value** means accounting information can be used to predict the future and timing of cash flows. **Feedback value** means the accounting function must provide decision makers with information that allows them to assess the progress or economic worth of an investment.

To be considered reliable, accounting information must possess three qualities: verifiability, representational faithfulness, and neutrality. Information is considered verifiable if several individuals, working independently, would arrive at similar conclusions using the same data. **Representational faithfulness** means accounting information must report what actually happened. **Neutrality** means accounting information must be free of bias or distortion.

Secondary Qualities. The term "secondary qualities" does not mean that these characteristics are of lesser importance than the primary qualities. If a secondary characteristic is missing, the accounting information is not necessarily useless. The secondary qualities of useful information are comparability and consistency. **Comparability** means accounting reports generated for one firm may be easily and usefully compared with the accounting reports generated for other firms. If the two firms use totally different accounting methods, it would be very difficult to make a useful comparison of their data and information. **Consistency** means that a firm systematically uses the same accounting methods and procedures from one accounting period to the next accounting period.

In addition to the primary and secondary qualities, the accounting information must be understandable to economic decision makers. The earnings management strategy can destroy the primary and secondary qualities of accounting information.

(ii) Accounting Cycle

FA provides accounting information for use by those outside and inside the organization. This information is used by current and potential investors to determine the future benefits they will receive if they hold or acquire ownership in a business. Creditors and lenders use this information to assess the creditworthiness of an organization. Other users of this information include employees, unions, customers, the general public, and governmental units.

Transactions, in accounting, are the result of the exchange of goods and/or services. Two factors allow the recording of a transaction: evidence and measurement. An exchange is an observable event and, therefore, provides evidence of business activity. This exchange takes place at a set price and thus provides an objective measure of the economic activity. The accounting cycle is one of four business cycles; the other three are sales, finance, and production.

With the traditional accounting model, a double-entry system of record keeping is used. The fundamental equation used with this system is

$$\text{Assets} = \text{Liabilities} + \text{Owners' equity}$$

All transactions are analyzed and then recorded based on their effect on assets, liabilities, and owners' equity. The increases and decreases in these accounts are recorded as debits or credits. In recording these transactions, the total amount of debits must equal the total amount of credits. The requirement that debits and credits must be equal gives rise to the double-entry method of record keeping. The rules of debits and credits are listed next.

Debits	**Credits**
Increase assets	Decrease assets
Decrease liabilities	Increase liabilities
Decrease owners' equity	Increase owners' equity
Increase owners' drawing	Decrease owners' drawing
Decrease revenues	Increase revenues
Increase expenses	Decrease expenses

(A) Cash-Basis versus Accrual-Basis Accounting

The two approaches of accounting are cash-basis accounting and accrual-basis accounting. With **cash-basis accounting**, revenues are recognized when cash is received, and expenses are recognized when cash is paid out. The primary advantages of cash-basis accounting are increased reliability due to the fact that transactions are not recorded until complete and simplicity due to the fact that fewer estimates and judgments are required.

For most businesses, cash-basis accounting for a period requires recognition and measurement of noncash resources and obligations. Cash-basis accounting is not in accordance with GAAP.

With **accrual-basis accounting**, revenues are recognized when sales are made or services are performed, and expenses are recognized as incurred. Revenues and expenses are recognized in the period in which they occur rather than when cash is received or paid out.

In accrual accounting, the financial effect of transactions that have cash consequences are recorded in the periods in which those transactions occur rather than in the periods in which cash is received or paid.

(B) Steps in the Accounting Cycle

The accounting cycle records the effect of economic transactions on the assets, liabilities, and owners' equity of an organization. The accounting cycle involves the eight steps shown in Exhibit 4.1.

EXHIBIT 4.1 Eight Steps in the Accounting Cycle

1. Analysis of transactions
2. Journalizing of transactions
3. Posting to ledger
4. Trial balance and working papers
5. Adjusting journal entries
6. Closing journal entries
7. Preparing financial statements
8. Reversing journal entries

Analysis of Transactions. Each transaction must be analyzed before being recorded to determine the effect on assets, liabilities, and owners' equity accounts. Asset, liability, and equity accounts are known as real accounts because they are not closed at the end of an accounting period. Revenue and expense accounts, however, are referred to as nominal accounts because they are closed at the end of an accounting period (usually a year), and their balances are reduced to zero. Therefore, real accounts represent the financial position of an organization at any point in time. Nominal accounts represent the results of operations over a given period of time.

Journalizing of Transactions. After analysis to determine the affected accounts, transactions are recorded in the accounting journal, or journalized. Each account affected, the amount of the changes, and the direction of the changes (increases or decreases) are recorded. These transactions are recorded in the general journal or special journals, which serve as a chronological record of all the economic transactions of an organization. Special journals group similar types of transactions to provide more efficient processing of data. These journals systematize the original recording of major recurring types of transactions, such as cash receipts, cash disbursements, purchases, and sales.

The general journal is used to make entries that do not fit in the special journals, to make adjusting entries at the end of the accounting period, and to make closing entries at the end of the accounting period.

Posting to the Ledger. The **ledger** is the complete collection of all the accounts of an organization. Transactions are posted to individual ledger accounts after being journalized. The ledger maintains the current balance of all the accounts.

Most organizations maintain subsidiary ledgers for accounts receivable (A/R) and accounts payable (A/P), because it is difficult to determine amounts due from specific customers and amounts due to specific suppliers using the master A/R account in the ledger. When using subsidiary ledgers, entries to the general ledger are totals for a specific period of time—for example, weekly totals—from the special journals. The sums of all subsidiary ledgers should be equal to the master account in the general ledger.

Trial Balance and Working Papers. The first step in the preparation of working papers is the preparation of a trial balance. The **trial balance** lists all accounts with balances as of the end of the accounting period. Account balances are entered in the columns and totaled. If postings for the period are arithmetically correct, then debits will equal credits. The trial balance does not provide a means of determining whether transactions have been posted to the correct accounts or journalized and/or posted to the general journal.

Working papers are large columnar sheets of paper for entering and summarizing the information necessary for making adjusting and closing entries and preparing financial statements. Working papers are prepared at the end of an accounting period and are for internal use only.

Adjusting Journal Entries. With the accrual system of accounting, certain adjustments must be made at the end of each accounting period. These adjusting entries convert the amounts actually in the accounts to the amounts that should be in the accounts for proper financial reporting. These adjusting entries allocate the cost of assets used in several accounting periods and revenues earned in several accounting periods, accrue revenues and expenses attributable to the current period that have not been recorded, and make appropriate end-of-period adjustments in the carrying value of certain assets (i.e., marketable securities and inventories).

With accrual accounting, the cost of long-term assets must be apportioned to the periods that benefit from their use. The three types of long-term assets are productive assets, such as buildings and machinery, wasting assets, such as minerals, and intangible assets, such as patents and copyrights. These assets are apportioned to periods through depreciation, depletion, and amortization.

Another type of revenue and expense apportionment is to record the portion of unearned revenues earned during the year and the portion of a prepaid expense that expired during the year. Three steps are necessary to make adjusting entries:

1. Determine the current balance in an account.

2. Determine the appropriate balance for the account.

3. Make the appropriate entry or entries to achieve the desired ending balances.

An adjusting entry may be necessary to reduce an asset to its market value. Some common adjustments are A/R, inventories, and marketable securities. These accounts are adjusted by debiting an expense or loss account and crediting a contra asset account.

Closing Journal Entries. After posting adjusting entries, all nominal accounts with existing balances are closed to real accounts. These closing entries reduce the nominal account balances to zero to show the effect of these accounts on owners' equity and so that information for the next accounting period may be accumulated. Three steps are required:

1. Close all revenue, gain, expense, and loss accounts to the expense and revenue summary account. This account is used only at the end of an accounting period to summarize revenues and expenses for the period.

2. Close the expense and revenue summary account to retained earnings.

3. Close the dividend account to retained earnings.

A postclosing trial balance is prepared after making all necessary closing entries. This provides a check against partial posting of closing entries. The postclosing trial balance reflects the balances to be included in the balance sheet at the end of the period.

Preparing Financial Statements. After preparing the adjusting entries and posting them to the working papers, an income statement can be prepared using the income statement numbers from the working papers.

After preparing the closing entries and posting them to the working papers, the only accounts with balances should be the asset, liability, and owners' equity accounts. At this time, a statement of stockholders' equity or statement of retained earnings should be prepared. This statement summarizes the transactions affecting the owners' capital account balance or retained earnings. Such a statement shows the beginning capital account, plus net income or less net loss, less owners' withdrawals or dividends. The ending capital account is then carried forward to the balance sheet, which helps to relate income statement information to balance sheet information.

Now it is time to prepare the balance sheet. The balance sheet is divided into assets, liabilities, and owners' equity and reflects the balances in these accounts at the end of the year.

Reversing Journal Entries. Reversing entries, the final step in the accounting cycle, are recorded on the first day of the next accounting period. Reversing entries are prepared to reverse the effects of certain adjusting entries to which they relate. These entries reduce the possibility of including a revenue or expense at the time of the adjusting entry and including it again when the economic transaction occurs. The general rule on reversing entries is that all adjusting entries that increase assets or liabilities may be reversed. Therefore, the only adjusting entries that should be reversed are those that accrue revenues or expenses. Reversing entries are optional and are dependent on an organization's bookkeeping system.

JOURNAL ENTRIES

Next we present varied examples of journal entries for better understanding of recording of business transactions with accounting implications.

Example 1

Debiting the prepaid insurance account and crediting the A/P account would correctly record the purchase of a liability insurance policy on account.

(Continued)

JOURNAL ENTRIES (*Continued*)

Example 2

Debiting the interest expense account and crediting the interest payable account would correctly record the accrued expense transaction.

Example 3

A company has been sued for $100 million for producing and selling an unsafe product. Attorneys for the company cannot predict the outcome of the litigation. In its financial statements, the company should disclose the existence of the lawsuits in a footnote without making a journal entry. The situation did not meet the criteria for setting up as a contingent liability. Only disclosure is required when a loss contingency is possible. No accrual is required because the loss could not be reasonably estimated.

Example 4

In the December 31, 2018, balance sheet, ending inventory was valued at $140,000. An investigation revealed the true balance should have been $150,000. In the December 31, 2019, balance sheet, ending inventory was shown at $200,000. The correct balance should have been $180,000. All errors were discovered during an investigation in 2020 before the books were closed. Ignoring tax effects, the appropriate journal entry that should be made in 2020 to correct the errors would be debiting the retained earnings for $20,000 to correct the decreased income and crediting the inventory for $20,000 to correct the decreased inventory.

This is an example of counterbalancing error affecting both the balance sheet and the income statement. An entry to adjust the beginning balance of the retained earnings is necessary as it takes two years for the error to be counterbalanced naturally. Note that the books were not closed for 2020.

Example 5

A retail shoe store purchases a copy machine for its office. The copier is priced at $5,000. The store gives cash of $2,000 and a 10% one-year promissory note in exchange for the copier. The acquisition of the copy machine could be recorded by debiting the office equipment account, crediting the cash account for $2,000, and crediting the note payable account for $3,000.

The 10% interest rate seems reasonable and the note can be recorded at its face value since it is only for one year. Otherwise, present value (PV) should be used to record the note.

Example 6

A retail company purchases advertising services on account. The appropriate journal entry to record the purchase would be debiting the advertising expense account and crediting the A/P account.

Example 7

A company allows customers to redeem 20 coupons for a toy (cost $3.00). Estimates are that 40% of coupons distributed will result in redemption. Since beginning the promotion this year, 4 million coupons were distributed and 1 million were redeemed. The adjusting journal entry to accrue for unredeemed coupons at year-end is debiting premium expense account for $90,000 and crediting estimated liability for premiums account for $90,000.

All expenses must be accrued at the end of accounting (fiscal) year. In this case, all unredeemed coupons that are still outstanding at year-end must be accrued. The liability of $90,000 is calculated as follows:

Unredeemed coupons: 4,000,000 × 0.40 − 1,000,000 = 600,000

Equivalent toys: 600,000 / 20 = 30,000 toys

Liability: 30,000 toys × $3.00 cost per toy = $90,000

Example 8

The debit to supplies and credit to supplies expense is indication of an end-of-period adjusting journal entry. These adjustments may include inventory adjustments.

Example 9

When a perpetual inventory system is used and a difference exists between the perpetual inventory amount balance and the physical inventory count, the following journal entry is needed to adjust the perpetual inventory amount: a debit to inventory "over and short" account and a credit to inventory. A write-down of inventory has occurred, which is reported as an adjustment of cost of goods sold (COGS) or as another expense on the income statement.

(iii) Different Formats of Financial Statements

A full set of four financial statements discussed in this section is based on the concept of financial capital maintenance. For a period, the full set should show these items:

1. Financial position at the end of the period

2. Earnings and comprehensive income for the period

3. Cash flows during the period

4. Investments by and distributions to owners during the period

A statement of financial position provides information about an entity's assets, liabilities, and equity and their relationships to each other at a moment in time. The statement delineates the entity's resources structure—major classes and amounts of assets—and its financial structure—major classes and amounts of liabilities and equity.

A statement of financial position does not purport to show the value of a business enterprise but, together with other financial statements and other information, should provide information that is useful to those who desire to make their own estimates of the enterprise's value. Those estimates are part of financial analysis, not of financial reporting, but FA aids financial analysis.

Statements of earnings and of comprehensive income together reflect the extent to which and the ways in which the equity of an entity increased or decreased from all sources other than transactions with owners during a period.

The concept of earnings in these statements is similar to net income for a period in current practice; however, it excludes certain accounting adjustments of earlier periods that are recognized in the current period—cumulative effects of a change in accounting principle is the principal example from current practice. Other names given to earnings are net income, profit, or net loss.

The next list presents different meanings of the term "earnings."

- **Earnings** are a measure of entity performance during a period. They measure the extent to which assets inflows (revenues and gains) associated with cash-to-cash cycles substantially completed during the period exceed asset outflows (expenses and losses) associated, directly or indirectly, with the same cycle.

- **Comprehensive income** is a broad measure of the effects of transactions and other events on an entity. It comprises all recognized changes in equity (net assets) of the entity during a period from transactions and other events and circumstances except those resulting from investments by owners and distributions to owners. Other names given to comprehensive income include total nonowner changes in equity or comprehensive loss.

- Earnings and comprehensive income are not the same. Certain gains and losses are included in comprehensive income but are excluded from earnings. Those items fall into two classes that are illustrated by certain current practices: (1) effects of certain accounting adjustments of earlier periods that are recognized in the current period; and (2) certain other changes in entity assets (principally certain holding gains and losses) that are recognized in the period but are excluded from earnings, such as some changes in market values of investments in marketable equity securities classified as noncurrent assets, some changes in market values of investments in industries having specialized accounting practices for marketable securities, and foreign currency translation adjustments.

A statement of cash flows (SCF) directly or indirectly reflects an entity's cash receipts classified by major sources and its cash payments classified by major uses during a period, including cash flow information about its operating, financing, and investing activities.

A statement of investments by and distributions to owners reflects an entity's capital transactions during a period—the extent to which and in what ways the equity of the entity increased or decreased from transactions with investors as owners. Exhibits 4.2 through 4.5 present each of these four statements with explanations.

EXHIBIT 4.2 Statement of Financial Position

The statement of financial position (balance sheet) presents assets, liabilities, and shareholders' equity. The balance sheet provides a basis for assessing the liquidity and financial flexibility of an entity, computing rates of return on investments (ROIs), and evaluating the capital structure of an entity. It reflects the financial status (health) of an enterprise in conformity with GAAP. The balance sheet reports the aggregate (and cumulative) effect of transactions at a point in time, whereas the statement of income, statement of retained earnings, and statement of cash flows report the effect of transactions over a period of time. The balance sheet is based on historical cost, the exchange price principle, or at the acquisition price.

Assets are classified as current if they are reasonably expected to be converted into cash, sold, or consumed either in one year or in the operating cycle, whichever is longer.

Liabilities are classified as current if they are expected to be liquidated through the use of current assets or the creation of other current liabilities.

Shareholders' equity arises from the ownership relation and is the source of enterprise distribution to the owners. Equity is increased by owners' investments and comprehensive income and is reduced by distributions to the owners.

Limitations of the balance sheet are listed next.

- The balance sheet does not reflect current values. Items are recorded at a mixture of historical cost and current values. Historical cost used to record assets and liabilities does not always reflect current value. Monetary assets, such as cash, short-term investments, and receivables, closely approximate current values. Similarly, current liabilities closely approximate current value and should be shown on the balance sheet at face value.

- Fixed assets are reported at cost less depreciation, depletion, or amortization. Inventories and marketable equity securities are exceptions to historical cost, where they are allowed to be reported at lower of cost or market. Similarly, certain long-term investments, which are another exception, are reported under the equity method. Long-term liabilities are recorded at the discounted value of future payments.

- Judgments and estimates are used to determine the carrying value or book value of many assets. Examples include determining the collectibility of receivables, salability of inventory, and useful life of fixed (long-term) assets. Estimations are not necessarily bad; however, there is no accounting guidance available.

- Appreciation of assets is not recorded except when realized through an arm's-length transaction.

- Internally generated goodwill, customer base, managerial skills and talent, reputation, technical innovation, human resources, and secret processes and formulas are not recorded in the balance sheet. Only assets obtained in a market transaction are recorded.

- The balance sheet ignores the time value of its elements. Most items are stated at face value regardless of the timing of the cash flows that they will generate. Exceptions are certain long-term receivables and payables, which are discounted.

- The balance sheet omits off–balance sheet items (mostly liabilities), such as sales of receivables with recourse, leases, throughput arrangements, and take-or-pay contracts.

- **Classification of assets.** In order to properly value an asset on the balance sheet, any related valuation allowance account should be reported contra to the particular asset account. Assets include current assets, noncurrent assets, and other assets.

- **Current assets** include cash, short-term investments, receivables, inventories, and prepaid expenses. The key criterion as to whether something should be included in current assets is the length of the operating cycle. When the cycle is less than one year, the one-year concept is used. When the cycle is very long, the usefulness of the concept of current assets diminishes. Specific components of current assets are listed next.

- **Cash and cash equivalents** include cash on hand consisting of coins, currency, undeposited checks, money orders and drafts, and deposits in banks. Certificates of deposit (CDs) are not considered cash because of the time restrictions on withdrawal. Cash that is restricted in use or cash restricted for a noncurrent use would not be included in current assets. Cash equivalents include: short-term, highly liquid investments that are readily convertible to known amounts of cash and are near their maturity period; Treasury bills; commercial paper; and money market funds.

- **Short-term investments** are readily marketable securities acquired through the use of temporarily idle cash.

- **Receivables** include A/R and notes receivable, receivables from affiliates, and receivables from officers and employees. Allowances due to uncollectibility and any amounts discounted or pledged should be clearly stated.

- **Inventories** are goods on hand and available for sale. The basis of valuation and the methods of pricing should be disclosed.

- **Prepaid expenses** are assets created by the prepayment of cash or incurrence of a liability. They expire and become expenses with the passage of time, usage, or events. Examples include prepaid rent, insurance, and deferred taxes.

- **Noncurrent assets** include long-term investments; property, plant, and equipment; and intangible assets. Specific components are listed next.

- **Long-term investments** include investments that are intended to be held for longer than one operating cycle. Examples are debt and equity securities, tangible assets, investments held in sinking funds, pension funds, amounts held for plant expansion, and cash-surrender values of life insurance policies.

- **Property, plant, and equipment** includes machinery and equipment, buildings, furniture and fixtures, natural resources, and land. These assets are of a durable nature that are to be used in the production or sale of goods, sale of other assets, or rendering of services.

- **Intangible assets** include goodwill, trademarks, patents, copyrights, and organizational costs. Generally, the amortization of an intangible asset is credited directly to the asset account, although it is acceptable to use an accumulated amortization account.

- **Other assets** include accounts that do not fit in the preceding asset categories. Examples include long-term prepaid expenses, deferred taxes, bond issue costs, noncurrent receivables, and restricted cash.

- **Classification of liabilities.** The liabilities are presented in the balance sheet in the order of payment. They are grouped into three categories: current, noncurrent, and other.

- **Current liabilities** include obligations arising from the acquisition of goods and services entering the operating cycle, collections of money in advance for the future delivery of goods or performance of services, and other obligations maturing within the current operating cycle to be met through the use of current assets. **Exceptions** that are treated as noncurrent liabilities are debt expected to be refinanced through another long-term issue after the balance sheet date but prior to the issuance of the balance sheet and debt that will be retired through the use of noncurrent assets (bond sinking fund). The reason is that liquidation does not require the use of current assets or the creation of other current liabilities. The excess of total current assets over the current liabilities is called working capital. Working capital provides a margin of safety or liquid buffer available to meet the financial demands of the operating cycle.

- **Noncurrent liabilities** include obligations arising through the acquisition of assets, obligations arising out of the normal course of operations, and contingent liabilities involving uncertainty as to possible losses.

- **Other liabilities** include deferred charges, noncurrent receivables, intangible assets, deferred income taxes, and deferred investment tax credits.

- **Classification of shareholders' equity. Shareholders' equity** is the interest of the stockholders in the assets of an enterprise. It shows the cumulative net results of past transactions. Specific components are listed next.

- **Capital stock** consists of par/stated value of common and preferred stock.

- **Additional paid-in capital** includes: paid-in capital in excess of par/stated value, which is the difference between the actual issue price and par/stated value; paid-in-capital stock from other transactions, which includes treasury stock, retirements of stock, stock dividends recorded at market, lapse of stock purchase warrants, and conversion of convertible bonds in excess of the par value of the stock.

- **Donated capital** includes donations of noncash property such as land, securities, buildings, and equipment by either stockholders or outside parties.

- **Retained earnings** are accumulated earnings not distributed to the shareholders. They are divided into appropriated (certain amount is not available for dividends) and unappropriated (available for dividends).

- **Treasury stock** represents issued shares reacquired by the issuer. Treasury stock is stated at its cost of acquisition and as a reduction of shareholders' equity.

- **Adjustments of equity** include net unrealized losses on noncurrent portfolios of marketable equity securities, the excess of minimum pension liability over unrecognized prior service cost, and unrealized gains or losses on foreign currency transactions.

EXHIBIT 4.3 Statement of Income

The statement of income, also known as the income statement, statement of earnings, or statement of operations, summarizes the results of an entity's economic activities or performance for a period of time (i.e., an accounting period). It also measures a firm's profitability over a specific period. Enterprise managements refer to the income statement to determine how efficiently or effectively resources are used and how investors and creditors view the income statement.

Forms of Income Statement

- Single step

- Multiple step

- Condensed

Many accountants prefer the single-step form of income statement with two groups: revenues and expenses. The **single-step income statement** is simple to present, and all items within expenses and revenues are treated similarly in terms of priorities. Expenses are deducted from revenues to arrive at net income or loss, hence the name "single step." One exception is income taxes, which are reported separately as the last item.

However, some accountants prefer a **multiple-step income statement** to present more information and to show better relationships with many classifications. The multiple-step statement separates operating transactions from nonoperating transactions and matches costs and expenses with related revenues. For example, the multiple-step income statement further classifies the item "administrative expenses" from the single-step income statement into office salaries, officers' salaries, utilities expenses, depreciation of buildings, and so on. Similarly, it breaks down the item "interest expenses" into interest on bonds, interest on notes, and so forth. Income taxes can be broken into current and deferred.

(Continued)

EXHIBIT 4.3 Statement of Income (*Continued*)

An unrealized loss resulting from a temporary decline in the market value of short-term investments in marketable equity securities should be reported as another expense or loss item on the multiple-step income statement. The short-term investments in marketable equity securities are carried at the lower of aggregate cost or market. The excess of aggregate cost over market is credited to a valuation account. Any increase in the valuation allowance is reported as a charge to income. These unrealized losses do not meet the criteria for classification as extraordinary and are not to be handled as prior-period adjustments. Unrealized losses on noncurrent marketable equity securities are to be classified as contra stockholders' equity.

The major distinction between the multiple-step and single-step income statement formats is the separation of operating and nonoperating data.

A condensed income statement presents, in addition to revenue, only the totals of expense groups, which it supports with supplementary schedules. These schedules can be found in the notes to the income statement.

An example of income statement sections in the order of presentation follows.

Income Statement Sections

1. Operating section
2. Nonoperating section
3. Income from continuing operations before income taxes
4. Income taxes
5. Income from continuing operations
6. Results from discontinued operations (gain/loss)
7. Extraordinary items (gain or loss)
8. Cumulative effect of a change in accounting principle
9. Net income
10. Earnings per share

Single-step income statements report irregular transactions, such as items 6 through 8, separately following income from continuing operations.

Limitations of income statements are presented next.

- Items that cannot be quantified with any degree of reliability are not included in determining income (i.e., economic income versus accounting income).
- Income numbers are often affected by the accounting methods employed (e.g., depreciation).
- Increases in income may result from a nonoperating or nonrecurring event that is not sustainable over a period of time (e.g., onetime tax forgiveness, exchange of preferred stock).

Limitations of accrual-based accounting for earnings are listed next.

- Information about the liquidity and potential cash flows of an organization is absent.
- The income statement does not reflect earnings in current dollars.
- Estimates and judgments must be used in preparing the income statement.

Major Components of the Income Statement

The major components and items that must be presented in the income statement include income from continuing operations, results from discontinued operations, extraordinary items, accounting changes, net income, and earnings per share.

Income from Continuing Operations

- **Sales or revenues** are charges to customers for the goods and/or services provided during the period. Both gross and net sales/revenues should be presented by showing discounts, allowances, and returns.

- **Cost of goods sold** is the cost of the inventory items sold during the period for a manufacturing or retail company.

- **Operating expenses** are primary recurring costs associated with business operations to generate sales or revenues. It does not include COGS, but includes selling expenses (e.g., salesperson salaries, commissions, advertising) and general and administrative expenses (e.g., salaries, office supplies, telephone, postage, utilities, accounting and legal services). An expense is to be recognized whenever economic benefits have been consumed.

- **Gains and losses** stem from the peripheral transactions of the enterprise. Examples are write-downs of inventories and receivables, effects of a strike, and foreign currency exchange gains and losses.

- **Expenses versus losses**. Losses result from peripheral or incidental transactions whereas expenses result from ongoing major or central operations of the entity. Expense accounts are costs related to revenue whereas loss accounts are not related to revenue.

- **Other revenues and expenses** are revenues and expenses not related to the operations of the enterprise. Examples include gains and losses on the disposal of equipment, interest revenues and expenses, and dividend revenues. A material gain on the sale of a fully depreciated asset should be classified on the income statement as part of other revenues and gains. Since the sale of an asset is not an operating item, it should be classified as other revenues and gains.

- **Income tax expense** related to continuing operations.

Results from Discontinued Operations

It contains two components.

- The first component, income (loss) from operations, is disclosed for the current year only if the decision to discontinue operations is made after the beginning of the fiscal year for which the financial statements are being prepared.

- The second component, gain (loss) on the disposal, contains income (loss) from operations during the phase-out period and gain (loss) from disposal of segment assets. Discontinued operations are presented after income from continuing operations and before extraordinary income on the income statement. The disposal of a line of business is normal, and any loss should be treated as an ordinary loss.

Extraordinary Items

Per Accounting Principles Board (APB) Opinion 30, two criteria must be met to classify an event or transaction as an extraordinary item: unusual nature (high degree of abnormality, clearly unrelated to, or only incidentally related to) and infrequency of occurrence (not reasonably be expected to recur in the foreseeable future). Various Statements of Financial Accounting Standards (SFAS) required

(Continued)

EXHIBIT 4.3 Statement of Income (*Continued*)

these exceptional items to be presented as extraordinary even though they do not meet the criteria stated above. (Remember that SFAS override the APB Opinions.)

- Material gains and losses from the extinguishment of debt except for sinking-fund requirements
- Profit or loss resulting from the disposal of a significant part of the assets or a separable segment of previously separate companies, provided the profit or loss is material and the disposal is within two years after a pooling of interest
- Write-off of operating rights of motor carriers
- The investor's share of an investee's extraordinary item when the investor uses the equity method of accounting for the investee
- Gains of a debtor related to a troubled debt restructuring

Extraordinary items should be segregated from the results of ordinary operations and be shown net of taxes in a separate section of the income statement, following discontinued operations and preceding cumulative effect of a change in accounting principle. Extraordinary losses must be both unusual and nonrecurring. Sales price minus net book value is gain or loss. A loss because of an expropriation of assets by a foreign government is classified as an extraordinary item in the income statement.

APB 28 requires that extraordinary items be disclosed separately and included in the determination of net income for the interim period in which they occur. Extraordinary gain should not be prorated or loss should not be deferred.

Accounting Changes

A change in accounting principles (including methods of applying them) results from adoption of a GAAP different from the one previously used for reporting purposes. The effect on net income of adopting the new accounting principle should be disclosed as a separate item following extraordinary items in the income statement. Changes in accounting estimates (lives of fixed assets, adjustments of the costs) are not considered errors or extraordinary items; instead, they are considered prior-period adjustments.

Net Income

Obviously, net income is a derived item by subtracting results from discontinued operations, extraordinary items, and cumulative effect of changes in accounting principles from income from continuing operations.

Earnings per share

Earnings per share (EPS) is a compact indicator of a company's financial performance. It is used to evaluate a firm's stock price, assess the firm's future earnings potential, and determine the firm's ability to pay dividends. EPS is calculated as net income minus preferred dividends divided by the weighted average of common shares outstanding. EPS must be disclosed on the face of the income statement. EPS may be disclosed parenthetically when only a one per-share amount is involved.

EPS must be reported for the following items:

- Income from continuing operations

- Income before extraordinary items and cumulative effect of changes in accounting principles

- Cumulative effect of changes in accounting principles

- Net income

- Results from (gain/loss on) discontinued operations (optional)

- Gain or loss on extraordinary items (optional)

EXHIBIT 4.4 Statement of Retained Earnings

The statement of retained earnings is a reconciliation of the balance of the retained earnings account from the beginning to the end of the year. This statement tells the reader how much money management is plowing back into the business. Prior-period adjustments, including correction of errors (net of taxes), are charged or credited to the opening balance of retained earnings.

Net income is added and dividends declared are subtracted to arrive at the ending balance of retained earnings. This statement may report two separate amounts: retained earnings free (unrestricted) and retained earnings appropriated (restricted). Statement of Financial Accounting Standards (SFAS) 16, *Prior Period Adjustments*, provides additional guidelines.

The statement of income and the statement of retained earnings can be shown separately. It is an acceptable practice to combine them into a single statement called the statement of income and retained earnings for convenience. Net income is computed in the same manner as in a multiple- or single-step income statement. The beginning balance in retained earnings is added to the net income (loss) figure. Any prior-period adjustments are included in the retained earnings to obtain adjusted retained earnings. Declared dividends (for both preferred stock and common stock) are deducted to obtain the retained earnings ending balance.

EXHIBIT 4.5 Statement of Cash Flows

The SCF replaces the previous statement of changes in financial position. The primary purpose of the SCF is to provide relevant information about the cash receipts and cash payments of an enterprise during a period. A secondary purpose is to provide information about the investing and financing activities of the enterprise during the same period. The emphasis in the SCF is on gross cash receipts and cash payments. For example, the SCF is the most useful financial statement for a banker to evaluate the ability of a commercial loan customer to meet current obligations. Cash flow per share should not be reported in the financial statements. Foreign currency exchange rate effects should be used in the preparation of the consolidated SCF.

Noncash exchange gains and losses recognized on the income statement should be reported as a separate item when reconciling net income and operating activities. The SCF includes net income, depreciation, investing activities, financing activities, and operating activities.

Specifically, the SCF should help investors and creditors assess:

- Ability to generate future positive cash flows.
- Ability to meet obligations and pay dividends.
- Reasons for differences between income and cash receipts and cash payments.
- Both cash and noncash aspects of an entity's investing and financing transactions.

(A) Classification

The SCF requires three classifications: investing activities, financing activities, and operating activities.

Investing activities show the acquisition and disposition of long-term productive assets or securities that are not considered cash equivalents. This category also includes the lending of money and collection of loans.

Financing activities include obtaining resources from and returning resources to the owners. This category also includes resources obtained from creditors and repaying the amount borrowed.

Operating activities include all transactions that are not investing and financing activities. This category includes delivering or producing goods for sale and providing services to customers. It involves cash effects of transactions that enter into the determination of net income for the period.

Although the FASB has expressed a preference for the direct method of presenting net cash from operating activities, the indirect method can also be used. The **direct method** shows the items that affected cash flow. This method allows the user to clarify the relationship between the company's net income and its cash flows. It reports only the items that affect cash flow (e.g., real cash inflows and real cash outflows) and ignores items that do not affect cash flow (e.g., depreciation and gains).

Entities using the direct method are required to report the following classes of operating cash receipts and payments:

- Cash collected from customers
- Interest and dividend received
- Cash paid to employees and other suppliers
- Interest and income taxes paid
- Other operating cash receipts and payments

The **indirect method** of presenting net cash from operating activities is most widely used and easy to prepare. It focuses on the difference between net income and cash flows. It emphasizes changes in the components of most current asset and current liability accounts. The amount of interest and income tax paid should be included in the related disclosures. Depreciation expense should be presented as an addition to net income in converting net income to net cash flows from operating activities.

The next tables present examples of the SCF classifications in terms of cash inflows and cash outflows.

CASH INFLOWS

Operating	Investing	Financing
Cash receipts exceed cash expenditures	Principal collections from loans	Proceeds from issuing equity securities
Receipts from sale of goods or services	Sale of long-term debt or equity securities	Proceeds from issuing short-term or long-term debt (e.g., bonds, notes)
Returns on loans (interest)	Sale of property, plant, and equipment	
Returns on equity securities (dividends)		

CASH OUTFLOWS

Operating	Investing	Financing
Cash expenditures exceed cash receipts	Loans made to others	Payment of dividends
Payments for inventory	Purchase of long-term debt or equity securities	Repurchase of entity's capital stock (e.g., treasury stock)
Payments to employees	Purchase of property, plant, and equipment	Repayment of debt principal
Payments of taxes		
Payments of interest		
Payments to suppliers		

EXAMPLE OF SINGLE-STEP INCOME STATEMENTS

Revenues

Net sales

Dividend revenue

Rental revenue

Total revenues

Expenses

COGS

Selling expenses

Administrative expenses

Interest expense

Income tax expense

Total expenses

Net income

Earnings per common share

EXAMPLE CALCULATION OF PURCHASING POWER GAIN OR LOSS ON NET MONETARY ITEMS

A corporation has gathered the following data in order to compute the purchasing power gain or loss to be included in its supplementary information for the year ended December 31, 20X1:

	Amount in nominal dollars	
	December 31, 20X0	**December 31, 20X1**
Net monetary assets	$800,000	$943,000

	Amount in nominal dollars
	Index number
Consumer price index at December 31, 20X0	200
Consumer price index at December 31, 20X1	230
Average consumer price index for 20X1	220

Question: What is the purchasing power gain or loss on net monetary items (expressed in average-for-the-year dollars for 20X1) reported at what amount for the year ended December 31, 20X1?

Answer: $121,000 purchasing power loss, as shown below.

The net monetary asset position at the beginning of the period ($800,000) is restated to $880,000 average constant dollars ($800,000 × 220/200 = $880,000). The actual increase in net monetary assets ($943,000 − $800,000 = $143,000) is assumed to have occurred evenly throughout the year so it is already stated in terms of average-for-the-year dollars. The restated beginning balance ($880,000) plus the increase ($143,000) yields a subtotal of $1,023,000. This subtotal is compared with the ending balance restated to an average basis ($943,000 × 220/230 = $902,000) to yield a purchasing power loss of $121,000.

EXAMPLE OF RETAINED EARNINGS STATEMENTS

Retained earnings balance at the beginning of the period

Prior period adjustments, net of taxes (+/−)

Correction of an error, net of taxes (+/−)

Net income (+)

Dividends declared (−)

Retained earnings balance at the end of the period

(iv) Account Analysis

Account analysis helps the internal auditor reconstruct balance sheet accounts from account balances and journal entries and understand the account classifications and posting error correction process through journal entries.

The composition of accounts with their balances and the nature of business transactions and their effect on account balances can be analyzed using two approaches: worksheet (columnar) approach and T-account approach. (See Exhibit 4.6.)

EXHIBIT 4.6 Techniques to Analyze Accounts

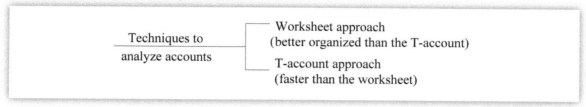

(A) Techniques to Analyze Accounts

The **worksheet approach** analyzes the changes that occurred in the balance sheet accounts by considering the income statement items. This approach is better organized than the T-account approach.

The **T-account approach** analyzes the changes in the noncash accounts and provides details on the cash flows during the period. This approach is faster than the worksheet approach.

It should be noted that there will always be a cause-and-effect relationship between and among accounts due to interlinking of those accounts. Consideration should be given to the characteristics of accounts, such as the number of accounts affected, the time frame involved, and the nature of the effect.

At least two accounts will be related to each other, and usually more. For example, an income statement classification error has no effect on the balance sheet and no effect on net income.

The time horizons for these causes and effects to materialize would be the past, present, and future accounting periods, due to lagging and leading effects of accounts. For example, it takes two accounting periods to correct a counterbalancing error itself while it takes more than two periods to correct a noncounterbalancing error itself.

Two types of effects can be seen: direct and indirect. An example of direct effect is overstatement of net income when wage expense is understated. An example of an indirect effect is liability being understated when wage expense is understated.

The internal auditor needs to understand account relationships when conducting audits, whether financial or operational. This understanding helps the auditor know what to look for during the account examination and verification process and how to conduct tracing and vouching work. This, in turn, will ensure that all related accounts and their effects are reviewed. Such account analysis will most likely help the auditor in reviewing the completeness, accuracy, and appropriateness of accounting journal entries and not so much who made the entries.

A partial, independent list of accounts with established interrelationships is presented next.

- The balance in inventory accounts will increase prior to sales while the balance in customer receivable accounts will increase after the sales. The reason is that adequate inventories must be available in advance for sales to take place. Here sales, inventories, and receivable accounts are being affected.

- The effects of misstating unearned interest as revenue would overstate revenue and receivables for this period and understate revenue for later periods. Examples of accounts that would be affected include interest, receivables, and income.

- When receivables are collected, the balance in cash accounts rises and the balance in receivable accounts falls. Working capital, which is current assets minus current liabilities, stays the same. Here the working capital composition has just been rearranged. These transactions have an inverse effect on each other since only asset accounts with opposite change are involved.

- During recession, receivables will likely increase as customers attempt to squeeze their trade credit limits to the maximum. This, in turn, increases funds tied up in working capital. Such an increase in working capital would reduce available cash and increase the need for financing. Cash, receivables, and liabilities accounts are affected here.

- Equal changes in A/R and A/P would alter the balance of cash but have no affect on working capital. Here the change has an offsetting effect since receivables and payables move in the opposite direction of the balance sheet.

- Issuance of common stock will increase cash, thereby increasing working capital. Cash accounts, stock accounts, and liability accounts are involved here.

- The longer the sales cycle is, the more working capital required. This is an example of the effect on interrelationships among accounting cycles and accounts within a cycle. Here both sales cycle and finance cycle are affected.

- An increase in the average length of time to collect receivables from customers would increase bad debts for the same type of customers.

- If credit-granting policies become too strict, the company will lose customers. If inventory balances are reduced too much, stock-out costs will be increased. Both situations will result in lower profits to the company.

- The just-in-time (JIT) inventory concept minimizes working capital investment because the firm maintains only a minimum amount of inventory. This is a result of vendors continuously making small deliveries of raw materials and parts that are immediately used on the factory floor.

- Payment of the current portion of the mortgage payable would not affect the net working capital situation.

(b) Intermediate Concepts of Financial Accounting

(i) Bonds

(A) Overview

Bonds result from a single agreement. However, a bond is intended to be broken up into various subunits. Notes and bonds have similar characteristics, including a written agreement stating the amount of the principal to be paid, the interest rate, when the interest and principal are to be paid, and the restrictive covenants.

The stated interest rate on a note or bond often differs from the market interest rate at the time of issuance. When this occurs, the PV of the interest and principal payments will differ from the maturity, or face value. Possible scenarios include:

- When the market rate exceeds the stated rate, the instrument is sold at a discount, meaning that the cash proceeds are less than the face value.

- When the stated rate exceeds the market rate, the instrument is sold at a premium, meaning that the cash proceeds are more than the face value.

- When the market and stated rates are the same at the time of issuance, no discount or premium exists, and the instrument will be sold at its face value.

The proper valuation is the PV of the future payments using the market rate of interest, either stated or implied in the transaction, at the date the debt was incurred.

EXCEPTIONS TO PRESENT VALUE OR MARKET INTEREST RATES

- Deferred income tax debits should not be discounted.

- Deferred income tax credits should not be discounted.

- Long-term notes should be valued using an imputed interest rate with no stated interest rate.

Nominal rate, stated rate, or coupon rate are all names for the interest rate stated on a bond. The periodic interest payments on a bond are determined by this rate. However, the price at which the bonds are sold determines the actual interest expense incurred on the bond issue. The actual rate of interest incurred is called the effective rate, yield rate, or market rate and is determined by the investment market.

When a bond sells at par value or face amount, the effective interest rate and the stated rate are equal. When a bond sells at a discount (below par), the effective rate is greater than the stated rate. When a bond sells at a premium (above par), the stated rate is greater than the effective rate of the bond; then the bond will sell at a discount. If the prevailing market rate of interest is less than the stated rate, then the bond will sell at a premium.

When a bond sells at a discount, a contra liability account, discount on bonds payable, is debited for the amount of the discount (excess of face value over cash proceeds). This contra liability account is shown as a deduction from bonds payable on the balance sheet. This discount is then amortized over the life of the bonds by one of two methods.

1. **Straight-line method.** Under this method, the amount to be amortized each period is determined by dividing the discount by the number of periods in the life of the bonds. Therefore, an equal amount of discount is charged to expense each period.

2. **Effective interest method.** This method computes bond interest expense for the period by multiplying the effective interest rate (at the bond issue date) by the bond's carrying value at the beginning of the period.

The difference between interest expense for the period and interest payable for the period is the discount amortized for the period.

The carrying value of the bonds issued at a discount increases as they mature. Therefore, the effective interest expense increases as the bonds mature, since it is based on the carrying value of the bonds.

When a bond sells at a premium, a valuation account, premium on bonds payable, is credited for the amount of the premium (excess of cash proceeds over face amount). This valuation account is shown as an addition to bonds payable on the balance sheet. One of two methods can be used to amortize the premium over the life of the bonds.

1. **Straight-line method.** This method is calculated the same as it is for a discount. Premium amortization reduces interest expense for the period. The carrying value of the bonds decreases each period by the amount of bond premium amortization.

2. **Effective interest method.** The periodic bond interest expense for this method is computed in the same manner as for a bond discount. The difference between bond interest payable in cash (stated interest rate times face amount of bonds) and effective bond interest expense (effective interest rate times carrying value of bonds) is the bond premium amortization for the period.

DEFINITIONS OF KEY TERMS: LONG-TERM DEBT

Bond—A debt instrument that contains a promise to pay a specified principal amount at a determinable future date together with interest at specified times. Bonds are a good financing arrangement when relatively large sums of money are required for long periods.

Bond indenture—A contract between the corporation issuing the bonds and the bondholders. It includes items such as the amount of bonds authorized, due date, interest rate, any dividend or other restrictions, and any property pledged as security.

Callable bonds—Can be purchased from the bondholder by the issuing corporation at the issuer's option prior to maturity. If interest rates fall or an organization wishes to reduce its outstanding debt, then it may call a bond issue.

Convertible bonds—Allow the bondholder the option to convert the bonds into a specified number of shares of common stock.

Income bonds—Unsecured debt where interest is paid only to the extent of an organization's current earnings. If interest is not paid due to a lack of earnings, bondholders have no claim against future earnings for the interest not paid in the current period.

Registered bonds and coupon bonds—With **registered bonds**, interest is paid to the registered owner. With **coupon bonds**, interest is paid to the individual presenting the periodic interest coupons.

Revenue bonds—Generally are issued by local governmental units, and interest and principal can be paid only from specific revenue sources.

Secured debt and unsecured debt—**Secured debt** has legal agreements that provide the creditor with liens on certain specified property. These liens allow creditors to sell the property pledged as security on the loan to obtain money to satisfy any unpaid balance of interest and principal. Unsecured debt has no liens.

Term bonds and serial bonds—**Term bonds** occur when an entire bond issue matures on a single fixed maturity date. **Serial bonds** are issues that mature in installments over a period of time.

Trustee—Typically, the entity holding the bond indenture and acting as an independent third party to protect the interests of the bond issuer and the bondholder.

The carrying value of bonds issued at a premium decreases as they mature. Therefore, the effective interest expense decreases as the bonds mature.

Any costs incurred related to the issuance of bonds, such as advertising costs, printing costs, and fees paid to underwriters, accountants, and attorneys, should be charged to a prepaid expense account. These costs should then be amortized over the life of the bond issue, because revenue results from the use of the proceeds over this period.

The reacquisition of a debt security or instrument before its scheduled maturity (except through conversion by the holder) is early extinguishment of debt. Upon early extinguishment, the bond can be formally retired or held as a treasury bond.

The net carrying amount of debt is the amount payable at maturity, adjusted for any unamortized discount, premium, or debt issue costs. The amount paid on early extinguishment, including the call premium and other reacquisition costs, is the reacquisition price of debt. A gain on early extinguishment occurs when the net carrying amount exceeds the reacquisition price. A loss occurs when the reacquisition price exceeds the net carrying amount. A gain or loss on early extinguishment should be recognized in the period in which extinguishment occurred and reflected as a separate line item on the income statement.

When serial bonds are sold and each maturity sells at a different yield rate, each maturity should be treated as a separate bond issue. The entire bond issue's discount or premium should be debited or credited to a single account. The amount of discount or premium amortization for each period is determined by performing a separate computation for each maturity. Either amortization method, straight-line or effective interest, may be applied to the discount or premium for each maturity. The amortization amounts for all maturities are then summarized and totaled to determine the periodic amortization.

When a note is issued solely for cash, the PV of the note is the cash proceeds. The PV of the note minus its face amount is the amount of the discount or premium. The interest expense on such a note is the stated or coupon interest plus or minus the amortization of any discount or premium.

When a note is issued in a noncash transaction and no interest rate is stated, the stated interest rate is unreasonable, or the stated face amount of the note is materially different from the current cash sales price for similar items or from the market value of the note at the date of the transaction, then the note issued and the property, goods, or services received should be recorded at the fair value of the property, goods, or services. If the fair value of the noncash item cannot be determined, then the market value of the note should be used.

A discount or premium is recognized when there is a difference between the face amount of the note and its fair value.

INTEREST RATES ON NOTES AND BONDS

The interest rate is affected by many factors, including:

- Cost of money
- Business risk factors
- Inflationary expectations associated with the business

This discount or premium should be amortized over the life of the note. If neither the fair value of the noncash item nor the market value of the note is determinable, then the PV of the note should be determined by discounting all future payments on the note using an imputed interest rate.

Short-term obligations that are expected to be refinanced on a long-term basis may be classified as long-term liabilities on the balance sheet. The requirements for classification as long-term are that management intends to refinance the obligations on a long-term basis and demonstrates the ability to obtain the refinancing.

According to APB Opinion 21, *Interest on Receivables and Payables*, *all* contractual rights to receive money or contractual obligations to pay money on fixed or determinable dates are subject to PV techniques including interest imputation.

SUGGESTED DISCLOSURES—NOTES AND BONDS

- The aggregate amount of debt net of the current portion due within one year (i.e., a short-term debt) and any discount or premium must be disclosed.

- The current portion of the long-term debt is shown as a current liability unless something other than current assets will be used to satisfy the obligation.

- Details of each debt, including nature of the liability, maturity dates, interest rates, call provisions, conversion privileges, restrictive covenants, and assets pledged as collateral must be disclosed.

Examples of APB Opinion 21 include secured and unsecured notes, debentures, bonds, mortgage notes, equipment obligations, and some A/R and A/P. However, the following items are **exceptions**:

- Receivable and payables arising from transactions with customers or suppliers in the normal course of business that are due in customary terms not exceeding approximately one year

- Amounts that do not require repayment in the future but rather will be applied to the purchase price of the property, goods, or service involved (e.g., deposits or progress payments on construction contracts, advance payments for acquisition of resources and raw materials, advances to encourage exploration in the extractive industries)

- Amounts intended to provide security for one party to an agreement (security deposits, retainages on contracts)

- The customary cash lending activities and demand or savings deposit activities of financial institutions whose primary business is lending money

- Transactions where interest rates are affected by the tax attributes or legal restrictions prescribed by a governmental agency (e.g., industrial revenue bonds, tax-exempt obligations, government-guaranteed obligations, and income tax settlements)

- Transactions between parent and subsidiary companies and between subsidiaries of a common parent

- Warranty for product performance

- Convertible debt securities

APB Opinion 21 requires the amortization of a bond discount or premium using the effective interest rate method. Under this method, the total interest expense is the carrying value (book value) of the bonds at the start of the period multiplied by the effective interest rate. The objective of this method is to arrive at a periodic interest cost that will result in a constant effective rate on the carrying value of the bond at the beginning of each period. By the time the bond matures, the carrying value of the bond will be equal to the face value.

Other methods, such as the straight-line method, can be used if the results are not materially different. Under this method, interest expense is equal to the cash interest paid plus the amortized portion of the discount or minus the amortized portion of the premium. The amortized portion is equal to the total amount of the discount or premium divided by the life of the debt from issuance in months multiplied by the number of months the debt has been outstanding that year.

Bondholders have a prior claim to the earnings and assets of the issuing organization. They rank ahead of preferred and common stockholders. Interest must be paid to bondholders before dividends can be distributed to stockholders. Bondholders have a prior claim on assets in the case of dissolution or bankruptcy.

The next list shows the hierarchy of stakeholders.

High priority	Bondholders	<ul><li>Prior claim on assets in case of dissolution or bankruptcy.</li><li>Interest must be paid first, before dividends are paid to stockholders.</li></ul>
	Preferred Stockholders	<ul><li>Prior claim on assets and dividends are paid during liquidation.</li><li>Dividends in arrears are paid.</li></ul>
Low priority	Common stockholders	<ul><li>Low priority in case of dissolution or bankruptcy.</li><li>Receive highest benefit if the organization is successful.</li></ul>

(B) Extinguishment of Debt

Outstanding debt may be reacquired or retired before its scheduled maturity. Usually this is caused by changes in interest rates or in cash flows. SFAS 76, *Extinguishment of Debt*, presents accounting treatment for *early* extinguishment of debt. SFAS 76 is applicable to all debt extinguishment other than debt conversions and troubled debt restructuring. (The latter is addressed by SFAS 15). Debt is now considered extinguished for financial reporting purposes in these circumstances:

- The debtor pays the creditor and is relieved of all of its obligations, regardless of whether the securities are canceled or held as so-called treasury bonds.

- The debtor is legally released from being the primary obligor, either judicially or by the creditor, and it is probable that the debtor will not be required to make future payments.

- The debtor irrevocably places cash or other assets in a trust to be used solely for satisfying scheduled payments of both interest and principal of a specific obligation, and the possibility that the debtor will be required to make future payments with respect to that debt is remote. In this circumstance, debt is extinguished even though the debtor is not legally released from being the primary obligor under the debt obligation.

  The trust shall be restricted to owing only monetary assets that are essentially risk free as to the amount, timing, and collection of interest and principal. A monetary asset is money or a claim to receive a sum of money that is fixed or determinable without reference to future prices of specific goods or services.

SUGGESTED DISCLOSURES—EXTINGUISHMENT OF DEBT

- Aggregated gains or losses and unconditionally classified as extraordinary items
- Description of the transaction and sources of the funds used
- Income tax effect of the transaction
- Per-share amount of the aggregate gain or loss, net of tax

The monetary assets shall be denominated in the currency in which the debt is payable. For debt denominated in U.S. dollars, essentially risk-free monetary assets shall be limited to:

☐ Direct obligations of the U.S. government.

☐ Obligations guaranteed by the U.S. government.

☐ Securities that are backed by U.S. government obligations as collateral under an arrangement by which the interest and principal payments on the collateral generally flow immediately through to the holder of the security.

According to APB Opinion 26, *Early Extinguishment of Debt*, the difference between the net carrying value and the acquisition price is to be recorded as a gain or loss.

KEY CONCEPTS TO REMEMBER: Rules for Gains and Losses

- If the acquisition price is greater than the carrying value, a loss exists.

- If the acquisition price is less than the carrying value, a gain is generated.

- These gains or losses are to be recognized in the period in which the retirement took place.

- All gains and losses, if material in amount, should be treated as extraordinary items.

- Any gains or losses resulting from satisfying sinking fund requirements within one year are exempted from extraordinary item treatment.

(ii) Leases

A lease agreement involves at least two parties (lessor, lessee) and an asset. The lessor, who owns the asset, agrees to allow the lessee to use it for a specified period of time for rent payments. The key point in leases is the transfer of risk of ownership. If the transaction effectively transfers ownership to the lessee, then it should be treated as a sale even though the transaction takes the form of a lease. Here the substance, not the form, dictates the accounting treatment. Two types of leases exist: capital and operating leases.

(A) Accounting by Lessees

SFAS 13, *Accounting for Leases*, requires lessees to classify every lease as either an operating lease or a capital lease. A capital lease, not an operating lease, is an installment purchase of the property.

The lessee records a capital lease as an asset and an obligation at an amount equal to the PV at the beginning of the lease term of minimum lease payments during the lease term, excluding that portion of the payments representing executory costs, such as insurance, maintenance, and taxes to be paid by the lessor, together with any profit thereon.

However, if the amount so determined exceeds the fair value of the leased property at the inception of the lease, the amount recorded as the asset and obligation shall be the fair value. If the portion of the minimum lease payments representing executory costs, including profit thereon, is not determinable from the provisions of the lease, an estimate of the amount shall be made. At the inception of a capital lease, the guaranteed residual value should be included as part of minimum lease payments at PV.

SUGGESTED DISCLOSURES: LESSEE

For capital leases:

- Gross amount of assets recorded
- Future minimum lease payments in the aggregate
- Total of minimum sublease rentals to be received
- Total contingent rentals actually incurred for each period
- Depreciation

For operating leases:

- Future minimum lease payments in the aggregate
- Total of minimum rentals that will be received under noncancelable subleases
- Rental expenses separated into minimum rentals, contingent rentals, and sublease rentals

A lease meeting any one of the four criteria listed under Criterion 1 should be accounted for as a capital lease by the lessee:

Criterion 1

1. The lease transfers ownership of the property to the lessee by the end of the lease term. If the title is transferred, the lease is assumed to be a purchase and the assets should be capitalized.

2. The lease contains a bargain purchase option.

3. The lease term is equal to 75% or more of the estimated economic life of the leased property. However, if the beginning of the lease term falls within the last 25% of the total estimated economic life of the leased property, including earlier years of use, this criterion shall not be used for purposes of classifying the lease.

4. The PV at the beginning of the lease term of the minimum lease payments, excluding that portion of the payments representing executory costs such as insurance, maintenance, and taxes to be paid by the lessor, including any profit thereon, equals or exceeds 90% of the excess of the fair value of the leased property.

Normally, rental on an operating lease shall be charged to expense over the lease term as it becomes payable. If rental payments are not made on a straight-line basis, rental expense nevertheless shall be recognized on a straight-line basis unless another systematic and rational basis is more representative of the time pattern in which use benefit is derived from the leased property, in which case that basis shall be used. The most significant reason for choosing an operating lease over a capital lease would be to avoid an increase in the debt to equity ratio.

(B) Accounting by Lessor

From the standpoint of the lessor, if at inception a lease meets any one of the four criteria listed under Criterion 1 and in addition meets *both* of the criteria listed under Criterion 2, it shall be classified as a sales-type lease or a direct financing lease. Otherwise, it shall be classified as an operating lease.

Criterion 2

1. Collectibility of the minimum lease payments is reasonably predictable. Estimation of uncollectibility based on experience with groups of similar receivables is not a reason for applying this criterion.

2. No important uncertainties surround the amount of unreimbursable costs yet to be incurred by the lessor under the lease. The necessity of estimating executory costs, such as insurance, maintenance, and taxes to be paid by the lessor, shall not by itself constitute an important uncertainty.

SUGGESTED DISCLOSURES: LESSOR

For sales-type and direct financing leases:

- Components of the net investment in leases including future minimum lease payments, unguaranteed residual values, initial direct costs for direct financing leases, and unearned interest revenue

- Future minimum lease payments

- Total contingent rentals included in income

For operating leases:

- The cost and carrying amount of property leased

- Minimum rentals on noncancelable leases in the aggregate

- Total contingent rentals included in income

A lessor can classify a lease in four ways:

1. Sales-type leases
2. Direct financing leases
3. Operating leases
4. Participation by third parties

Sales-Type Leases. The lessor should account for sales-type leases as follows:

- The minimum lease payments (net of amounts, if any, included therein with respect to executory costs such as maintenance, taxes, and insurance to be paid by the lessor, together with any profit thereon) plus the unguaranteed residual value accruing to the benefit of the lessor shall be recorded as the gross investment in the lease.

- The difference between the gross investment in the lease and the sum of the PVs of the two components of the gross investment shall be recorded as unearned income. The interest rate to be used in determining the PVs shall be the interest rate implicit in the lease. *The net investment in the lease consists of the gross investment less the unearned income.* The unearned income shall be amortized to income over the lease term so as to produce a constant periodic rate of return on the net investment in the lease. Contingent rentals, including rentals based on variables such as the prime interest rate, shall be credited to income when they become receivable.

- The PV of the minimum lease payments (net of executory costs, including any profit thereon), computed at the interest rate implicit in the lease, shall be recorded as the sales price. The cost or carrying amount, if different, of the leased property plus any initial direct costs, less the PV of the unguaranteed residual value accruing to the benefit of the lessor, computed at the interest rate implicit in the lease, shall be charged against income in the same period.

- The estimated residual value shall be reviewed at least annually. An upward adjustment of the estimated residual value should not be made while permanent reduction in the net investment should be recognized as a loss in the period in which the estimate is changed.

Direct Financing Leases. The lessor should account for direct financing leases as follows:

- The minimum lease payments (as defined earlier) plus the unguaranteed residual value accruing to the benefit of the lessor should be recorded as the gross investment in the lease.

INITIAL DIRECT COST DEFINITION

Those incremental direct costs incurred by the lessor in negotiating and consummating leasing transaction including commissions and legal fees.

- The difference between the gross investment in the lease and the cost or carrying amount, if different, of the leased property shall be recorded as unearned income. The net investment in the lease should consist of the gross investment less the unearned income.

Initial direct cost shall be charged against income as incurred, and a portion of the unearned income equal to the initial direct costs shall be recognized as income in the same period. The remaining unearned income shall be amortized to income over the lease term so as to produce a constant periodic rate of return on the net investment in the lease. Contingent rentals, including rentals based on variables such as the prime interest rate, shall be credited to income when they become receivable.

- The estimated residual value shall be reviewed at least annually and, if necessary, adjusted in the manner prescribed in sales-type leases.

Operating Leases. The lessor should account for operating leases as follows:

- The leased property shall be included with or near property, plant, and equipment in the balance sheet. The property shall be depreciated following the lessor's normal depreciation policy, and in the balance sheet the accumulated depreciation shall be deducted from the investment in the leased property.

- Rent shall be reported as income over the lease term as it becomes receivable according to the provisions of the lease. However, if the rentals vary from a straight-line basis, the income shall be recognized on a straight-line basis unless another systematic and rational basis is more representative of the time pattern in which use benefit from the leased property is diminished, in which case the straight-line basis shall be used.

- Initial direct costs shall be deferred and allocated over the lease term in proportion to the recognition of rental income. However, initial direct costs may be charged to expense as incurred if the effect is not materially different from that which would have resulted from the use of the method prescribed in the preceding sentence.

Participation by Third Parties. The lessor should account for participation-by-third-parties leases as follows:

- The sale or assignment of the lease or of property subject to a lease that was accounted for as a sales-type lease or direct financing lease shall not negate the original accounting treatment accorded the lease. Any profit or loss on the sale or assignment shall be recognized at the time of the transaction except that (1) when the sale or assignment is between related parties or (2) when the sale or assignment is with recourse, the profit or loss shall be deferred and recognized over the lease term in a systematic manner (e.g., in proportion to the minimum lease payments).

- The sale of property subject to an operating lease, or of property that is leased by or intended to be leased by the third-party purchaser to another party, shall not be treated as a sale if the seller or any party related to the seller retains substantial risks of ownership in the leased property.

  A seller may be by various arrangements assured recovery of the investment by the third-party purchaser in some operating lease transactions and thus retain substantial risks in connection with the property. For example, in the case of default by the lessee or termination of the lease, the arrangements may involve a formal or informal commitment by the seller to acquire the lease or the property, substitute an existing lease, or secure a replacement lessee or a buyer for the property under a remarketing agreement.

- If a sale to a third party of property subject to an operating lease or of property that is leased by or intended to be leased by the third-party purchaser to another party is not to be recorded as a sale. Instead, the transaction should be accounted for as a borrowing.

(C) Lease Involving Real Estate

Lease involving real estate can be divided into four categories:

1. Leases involving land only
2. Leases involving land and buildings
3. Leases involving equipment as well as real estate
4. Leases involving only part of a building

(D) Sale-Leaseback Transaction

Sale-leaseback transactions involve the sale of property by the owner and a lease of the property back to the seller. If the lease meets one of the criteria (Criterion 1) for treatment as a capital lease, the seller-lessee shall account for the lease as a capital lease; otherwise, as an operating lease.

Except as noted below, any profit or loss on the sale shall be deferred and amortized in proportion to the amortization of the leased asset, if a capital lease, or in proportion to rental payments over the period of time the asset is expected to be used, if an operating lease. However, when the fair value of the property at the time of the transaction is less than its undepreciated cost, a loss shall be recognized immediately up to the amount of the difference between undepreciated cost and fair value.

If the lease meets Criteria 1 and 2, the purchaser-lessor shall record the transaction as a purchase and a direct financing lease; otherwise, he or she shall record the transaction as a purchase and an operating lease.

(E) Accounting and Reporting for Leveraged Leases

From the standpoint of the lessee, leveraged leases shall be classified and accounted for in the same manner as nonleveraged leases. The balance of this section deals with leveraged leases from the standpoint of the lessor.

A leveraged lease is defined as one having all of the following characteristics:

- It involves at least three parties: a lessee, a long-term creditor, and a lessor (commonly called the equity participant).
- Direct financing and sales-type leases are not included.

BALANCE SHEET PRESENTATION

The accounts of subsidiaries (regardless of when organized or acquired) whose principal business activity is leasing property or facilities to the parent or other affiliated companies shall be consolidated. The equity method is not adequate for fair presentation of the subsidiaries because their assets and liabilities are significant to the consolidated financial position of the enterprise.

- The financing provided by the long-term creditor is nonrecourse as to the general credit of the lessor. The amount of the financing is sufficient to provide the lessor with substantial leverage in the transaction.

- The lessor's net investment declines during the early years once the investment has been completed and rises during the later years of the lease before its final elimination. Such decrease and increase in the net investment balance may occur more than once.

The lessor shall record this investment in a leveraged lease net of the nonrecourse debt. The net of the balances of the following accounts shall represent the initial and continuing investment in leveraged leases:

- Rentals receivables, net of that portion of the rental applicable to principal and interest on the nonrecourse debt

- A receivable for the amount of investment tax credit to be realized on the transaction

- The estimated residual value of the leased asset

- Unearned and deferred income consisting of (1) the estimated pretax lease income (or loss), after deducting initial direct costs, remaining to be allocated to income over the lease term and (2) the investment tax credit remaining to be allocated to income over the lease term

The investment in leveraged leases less deferred taxes arising from difference between pretax accounting income and taxable income shall represent the lessor's net investment in leveraged leases for purposes of computing periodic net income from the lease.

For purposes of presenting the investment in a leveraged lease in the lessor's *balance sheet*, the amount of related deferred taxes shall be presented separately from the remainder of the net investment. In the *income statement* or the notes thereto, separate presentation shall be made of pretax income from the leveraged lease, the tax effect of pretax income, and the amount of investment tax credit recognized as income during the period.

KEY CONCEPTS TO REMEMBER: Leases

- A major difference between operating and financial leases is that operating leases frequently contain a cancellation clause, while financial leases are not cancelable.

- Lessee corporation has leased manufacturing equipment from lessor corporation in a transaction that is to be accounted for as a capital lease. Lessee has guaranteed lessor a residual value for the equipment. The PV of the residual guarantee should be capitalized as part of the cost of the equipment and be reflected in the financial statements of lessee.

- In accounting for a 20-year operating lease of machinery, lease expense and cash outflow would both be the same in total for the 20-year term of the lease as if the lease were capitalized.

- Rent expense is recognized for operating leases only.

(Continued)

> **KEY CONCEPTS TO REMEMBER: Leases (*Continued*)**
>
> ■ Prepaid rent is not reported for a capital lease by lessee.
>
> ■ Depreciation expense is a part of items reported by a lessee for a capital lease.
>
> ■ Interest expense is a part of items reported by a lessee for a capital lease.

(iii) Pensions

SFAS 87, *Employers' Accounting for Pensions*, and SFAS 88, *Employers' Accounting for Settlements and Curtailments of Defined Benefit Pension Plans and for Termination Benefits*, are the sources of GAAP in the pension area. The principal focuses of SFAS 87 are the PV of the pension obligation, the fair value of plan assets, and the disclosure of the makeup of net pension costs and of the projected benefit obligation. The critical accounting issues are the amount to be expensed on the income statement and the amount to be accrued on the balance sheet.

> **APPLICATION OF SFAS 87 AND 88**
>
> The scope includes unfunded, insured, trust fund, defined contribution, defined benefit plans, and deferred compensation contracts.
>
> The scope does not include (1) independent deferred profit-sharing plans and pension payments to selected employees on a case-by-case basis; (2) plans providing only life or health insurance benefits or both; or (3) postemployment health care benefits, related assets, and obligations.

Employer commitment to employees takes the form of contributions to an independent trustee. The trustee then invests the contributions in various plan assets, such as Treasury bills and bonds, CDs, annuities, marketable securities, corporate bonds and stock. The plan assets generate interest and/or appreciate in asset value. The return on the plan assets provides the trustee the money to pay the benefits to which the employees are entitled. These benefits are defined by the terms of the pension plan using a plan's benefit formula. The formula is used to determine the pension cost for each year. The formula takes into account factors such as employee compensation, service length, age, and other factors to determine pension costs. (See Exhibit 4.7.)

EXHIBIT 4.7 Components of Pension Expense

Component	Effect
1. Service cost	Increases
2. Interest cost	Increases
3. Actual return on plan assets	Generally decreases
4. Prior service cost	Generally decreases
5. Net total of other components (gain or loss)	Increases or decreases
$\quad 5 = 1 + 2 + 3 + 4$	

■ Pension expense is determined by adding up five components that affect the pension expense amount, as shown in Exhibit 4.7. The service cost component is determined by the actuarial PV of benefits attributed by the pension benefit formula to employee service during that period.

■ Past service cost is the portion of pension plan expense that relates to years prior to inception of the pension plan.

- The interest cost component is the interest for the period on the projected benefit obligation outstanding during the period.

- The actual return on plan assets is determined based on the fair value of plan assets at the beginning and the end of the period, adjusted for contributions and benefit payments.

- The prior service cost component is the PV of future benefits payable as a result of work done before the start of or change in a pension plan. The cost is amortized over the average remaining service period of the employees expected to receive benefits.

- Gains and losses are changes in the amount of either the projected benefit obligation or plan assets resulting from experience different from that assumed and from changes in assumptions.

(iv) Intangible Assets

Typically intangibles lack physical existence and have a high degree of uncertainty regarding their future benefits. These assets have value because of the business advantages of exclusive rights and privileges they provide. The two sources of intangible assets are listed next.

1. Exclusive privileges granted by authority of the government or legal contract, which includes patents, copyrights, trademarks, franchises, and so forth

2. Superior entrepreneurial capacity or management know-how and customer loyalty that is goodwill

Intangible assets are initially recorded at cost. Therefore, the costs of intangible assets, except for goodwill, are relatively easy to determine. These assets must be amortized over their expected useful life but not to exceed 40 years. An organization must use straight-line amortization, unless it can prove that another method is more appropriate. The amortization of intangible assets over their useful lives is justified by the going-concern assumption.

(A) Copyrights, Trademarks, and Patents

Those intangibles that have a separate identity apart from the enterprise as a whole are identifiable as **intangible assets**. The most common types are listed next.

- **Copyrights** protect the owner from illegal reproductions of designs, writings, music, and literary productions. Purchased copyrights are recorded at cost. Research and development (R&D) costs incurred to produce a copyright internally must be expensed. The only costs that can be capitalized are the legal costs to obtain and defend the copyright. Generally, copyrights are amortized over a period of five years or less.

  A material amount of legal fees and other costs incurred by a holder of a copyright in successfully defending a copyright suit should be capitalized as part of the cost of the copyright and amortized over the remaining estimated useful life of the copyright, not to exceed 40 years. All costs should be charged to the copyright account.

SUMMARY OF AMORTIZATION PERIODS

- Copyrights not to exceed 40 years
- Trademarks not to exceed 40 years
- Patents not to exceed 17 years
- Organization costs not to exceed 40 years
- Goodwill not to exceed 40 years

- **Trademarks** are features such as designs, brand names, or symbols that allow easy recognition of a product. The costs to develop or acquire a trademark, except for R&D costs, are capitalized. Trademarks must be amortized over a period not to exceed 40 years.

- **Patents** are granted by the U.S. government and allow the owner exclusive benefits to a product or process over a 17-year period. Purchased patents are recorded at cost. An internally developed patent includes all costs except R&D. Legal fees incurred to successfully defend the patent should also be capitalized. A patent should be amortized over its useful life or 17 years, whichever is shorter.

TREATMENT OF R&D COSTS

R&D costs are normally expensed while organization costs, equipment costs, and goodwill costs are capitalized.

- **Organization costs** are incurred in the process of organizing a business. Legal fees, payments to officers for organization activities, and various state fees may be included in organization costs. A material amount of organization costs should be amortized over five years. The period of their useful life should not exceed 40 years.

- **Franchises** grant the right to provide a product or service or use a property. Franchise fees that are paid in advance should be capitalized and amortized over the useful life of the asset.

- **Leases** are contracts between the owner of property (lessor) and another party (lessee) that grant the right to use the property in exchange for payments. Any portion of the lease payments made in advance are capitalized in the leasehold account, an intangible asset account. Another intangible account, leasehold improvements, is established for any improvements to the leased property by the lessee. Leasehold improvements should be amortized over their useful life or the remaining life of the lease, whichever is shorter. The leasehold is amortized over the life of the lease.

(B) Goodwill

Some intangible assets, since they cannot be separated from the business as a whole, are not specifically identifiable. Goodwill is a prime example of this type of intangible.

Goodwill arises when an organization's value as a whole exceeds the fair market value of its net assets. This typically occurs when an organization generates more income than other organizations with the same assets and capital structure. Superior management, a superior reputation, and a valuable customer list are factors that may contribute to these excess earnings.

SUGGESTED DISCLOSURES FOR INTANGIBLE ASSETS

- Description of the nature of the assets
- Amount of amortization expense for the period and the method used
- Amortization period used
- Amount of accumulated amortization

Goodwill is something that develops over time through the generation of these excess earnings. However, since no objective measure of the total value of a business is available until it is sold, goodwill is not recorded unless a business is purchased.

To calculate goodwill, a portion of the total cost of the acquired organization should be allocated to the tangible and intangible assets based on their fair market values. Goodwill is the difference between the cost allocated to these assets and the total cost of the acquisition.

Negative goodwill is created when the fair market value of the acquired net assets exceeds the cost of the acquired company. This excess is allocated proportionately to reduce noncurrent assets except for long-term investments in marketable securities. If noncurrent assets are reduced to zero, then the excess should be recorded as a deferred credit and amortized over a period not to exceed 40 years.

Estimating the value of goodwill prior to the consummation of a purchase requires estimating future expected excess earnings and calculating their PV. The same result should be achieved by determining the PV of the total expected future earnings of the organization, which is the total value of the firm. The total value of the firm minus the value of the identifiable tangible and intangible net assets is estimated goodwill.

RULES FOR GOODWILL

- If goodwill is internally generated, expense it.
- If goodwill is purchased, capitalize it.

(v) Research and Development
(A) R&D Costs
SFAS 2, *Accounting for Research and Development (R&D) Costs*, requires R&D costs to be expensed as incurred except for intangible or fixed assets purchased from others having alternative future uses. Thus, the cost of patents and R&D equipment purchased from third parties may be deferred, capitalized, and amortized over the assets' useful life. However, internally developed R&D may not be deferred and therefore should be expensed. R&D done under contract for others is not required to be expensed per SFAS 2. The costs incurred would be matched with revenue using the completed-contract or percentage-of-completion method. The key accounting concept is expense R&D costs as incurred and disclose total R&D expenses per period on the face of income statement or notes.

Under R&D activities, SFAS 2 includes laboratory research to discover new knowledge, formulation, and design of product alternatives (e.g., testing and modifications); preproduction prototypes and models (e.g., tools, dies, and pilot plants); and engineering activity until product is ready for manufacture.

SFAS 2 excludes these nine R&D activities:

1. Engineering during an early phase of commercial production
2. Quality control for commercial production

3. Troubleshooting during commercial production breakdowns

4. Routine, ongoing efforts to improve products

5. Adaptation of existing capability for a specific customer

6. Seasonal design changes to products

7. Routine design of tools and dies

8. Design, construction, and start-up of equipment except that used solely for R&D

9. Legal work for patents or litigation

Item 9 is capitalized while all the other eight items are expensed.

Elements of R&D costs are listed next.

- Materials, equipment, and facilities

- Salaries, wages, and related costs

- Intangibles purchased from others are treated as materials

- R&D services performed by others

- Reasonable allocation of indirect costs, excluding general and administrative costs not clearly related to R&D

(B) Software Developed for Sale or Lease

The costs that are incurred internally to create software should be expensed as R&D costs until technological feasibility is established. Thereafter, all costs should be capitalized and reported at the lower of unamortized cost or net realizable value. Capitalization should cease when the software is available for general release to customers.

The annual amortization of capitalized computer software costs will be the greater of the ratio of current revenues to anticipated total revenues or the straight-line amortization that is based on the estimated economic life. Once the software is available for general release to customers, the inventory costs should include costs for duplicating software and for physically packaging the product. The cost of maintenance and customer support should be charged to expense in the period incurred.

(C) Software Developed for Internal Use

Software must meet two criteria to be accounted for as internally developed software:

1. The software's specifications must be designed or modified to meet the reporting entity's internal needs, including costs to customize purchased software.

2. During the period in which the software is being developed, there can be no plan or intent to market the software externally, although development of the software can be jointly funded by several entities that each plan to use the software internally.

In order to justify capitalization of related costs, it is necessary for management to conclude that it is probable that the project will be completed and that the software will be used as intended. Absent that level of expectation, costs must be expensed currently as R&D costs are required to be. Entities that historically were engaged in both R&D of software for internal use and for sale to others would have to carefully identify costs with one or the other activity, since the former would be subject to capitalization while the latter might be expensed as R&D costs until technological feasibility had been demonstrated.

Under terms of SFAS 2, cost capitalization commences when an entity has completed the conceptual formulation, design, and testing of possible project alternatives, including the process of vendor selection for purchased software, if any. These early-phase costs (i.e., preliminary project stage costs) are similar to R&D costs and must be expensed as incurred.

Costs incurred subsequent to the preliminary project stage, and that meet the criteria under GAAP as long-lived assets, can be capitalized and amortized over the asset's expected economic life. Capitalization of costs will begin when both of two conditions are met:

1. Management having the relevant authority approves and commits to funding the project and believes that it is probable that it will be completed and that the resulting software will be used as intended.

2. The conceptual formulation, design, and testing of possible software project alternatives (i.e., the preliminary project stage) have been completed.

(c) Advanced Concepts of Financial Accounting

This section discusses business combination, consolidation, partnerships, and foreign currency transactions.

(i) Business Combination
(A) Overview

According to FASB, a **business combination** occurs when an entity acquires net assets that constitute a business or acquires equity interests of one or more other entities and obtains control over that entity or entities. Business combinations may be friendly or hostile takeovers. Purchase accounting is the only acceptable accounting method for all business combinations; the pooling-of-interest method is not.

FASB Statement 141 identified these key components of the purchase method of accounting:

- **Initial recognition.** Assets are commonly acquired in exchange transactions that trigger the initial recognition of the assets acquired and any liabilities assumed.

- **Initial measurement.** Like other exchange transactions generally, acquisitions are measured on the basis of the fair values exchanged.

- **Allocating costs.** Acquiring assets in groups requires not only ascertaining the cost of the asset (or net asset) group but also allocating that cost to the individual assets (or individual assets and liabilities) that make up the group.

- **Accounting after acquisition.** The nature of an asset and not the manner of its acquisitions determines an acquiring entity's subsequent accounting for the asset.

According to the FASB, the **combinor** is a constituent company entering into a purchase-type business combination whose stockholders as a group retain or receive the largest portion of the voting rights and control over the combined enterprise and thereby can elect a majority of the governing board of directors or other group of the combined enterprise. The **combinee** is a constituent company other than the combinor involved in a business combination.

(B) Computation and Allocation of Cost of a Combinee

The cost of a combinee is the total of the amount of consideration paid by the combinor, the combinor's direct out-of-pocket costs of the combination, and any contingent consideration that is determinable on the date of the business combination.

The amount of consideration is the total amount of cash paid, the current fair value of other assets distributed, the PV of debt securities issued, and the current fair value (or market) value of equity securities issued by the combinor.

The direct out-of-pocket costs include some legal fees, some accounting fees, and finder's fees (paid to an investment banking firm). Costs of registering with the Securities and Exchange Commission (SEC) and issuing debt securities are not part of the direct cost of the combinee. Costs of registering with the SEC and issuing equity securities are not part of direct costs either but can be offset against the proceeds from the issuance of the equity securities.

Contingent consideration is additional cash, other assets, or securities that may be issuable in the future, contingent on future events, such as a specified level of earnings or a designated market price for a security that had been issued to complete the business combination. Contingent consideration can be determinable or not determinable for recording as part of the cost of the combination.

The FASB requires that the cost of a combinee must be allocated to assets (other than goodwill) acquired and liabilities assumed based on their estimated fair values on the date of the combination. Any excess of total costs over the amounts thus allocated is assigned to goodwill. Methods for determining fair values are listed next.

- PVs for receivables and most liabilities
- Net realizable value less a reasonable profit for work in process (WIP) and finished goods inventories
- Appraised values for land, natural resources, and nonmarketable securities
- Individual fair values for patents, copyrights, franchises, customer lists, and unpatented technology

(ii) Consolidation

The purpose of consolidated financial statements is to present for a single accounting entity the combined resources, obligations, and operating results of a group of related corporations, such as parent and subsidiaries. Only subsidiaries not actually controlled should be exempted from consolidation. A controlling interest is defined when an investor's direct or indirect ownership of more than 50% of an investee's outstanding common stock.

Actual control is more important than the controlling interest in situations such as liquidation or reorganization (bankruptcy) of a subsidiary or control of a foreign subsidiary by a foreign government. GAAP requires the use of the cost method of accounting for investments in unconsolidated subsidiaries because the subsidiaries generally are neither controlled nor significantly influenced by the parent company.

Assets, liabilities, revenues, and expenses of the parent company and its subsidiaries are totaled; intercompany transactions and balances are eliminated; and the final consolidated amounts are reported in the consolidated balance sheet, income statement, statement of stockholders' equity, statement of retained earnings, and SCFs.

(A) Consolidation of Wholly Owned Subsidiary Using Purchase Accounting Method (on Date of Purchase Combination)

The parent company's investment account and the subsidiary's stockholders' equity accounts do not appear in the consolidated balance sheet because they are intercompany (reciprocal) accounts. Under purchase accounting theory, the parent company assets and liabilities (except intercompany) are reflected at carrying amounts, and the subsidiary assets and liabilities (except intercompany) are reflected at current fair values, in the consolidated balance sheet. Goodwill is recognized to the extent the cost of the parent's investment in 100% (wholly owned) of the subsidiary's outstanding common stock exceeds the current fair value of the subsidiary's identifiable net assets.

(B) Consolidation of Partially Owned Subsidiary Using Purchase Accounting Method (on Date of Purchase Combination)

The recognition of minority interest is handled differently between the wholly owned subsidiary and the partially owned subsidiary. **Minority or noncontrolling interest** refers to the claims of stockholders other than the parent company to the net income or losses and net assets of the subsidiary. The minority interest in the subsidiary's net income or losses is displayed in the consolidated income statement, and the minority interest in the subsidiary's net assets is displayed in the consolidated balance sheet.

Minority interest is accounted for in two ways: the parent company concept, which emphasizes the interests of the parent's shareholders, and the economic unit concept, which emphasizes the legal aspect and the entity theory. The parent company concept treats the minority interest in net assets of a subsidiary as a liability. This liability is increased each accounting period subsequent to the date of a purchase-type business combination by an expense representing the minority's share of the subsidiary's net income or decreased by the minority's share of the subsidiary's net loss. Dividends declared by the subsidiary to minority stockholders decrease the liability to them. Consolidated net income is net of the minority's share of the subsidiary's net income. In the economic unit concept, the minority interest in the subsidiary's net assets is displayed in the stockholders' equity section of the consolidated balance sheet. The consolidated income statement displays the minority interest in the subsidiary's net income as a subdivision of total consolidated net income, similar to the distribution of net income of a partnership.

(C) Consolidation of Wholly Owned Subsidiary Using Purchase Accounting Method (Subsequent to Date of Purchase Combination)

Subsequent to the date of a business combination, the parent company must account for the operating results of the subsidiary: The net income or net loss and dividends declared are paid by the subsidiary. In addition, a number of intercompany transactions and events that occur in a parent–subsidiary relationship must be recorded.

In accounting for the operating results of consolidated purchased subsidiaries, a parent company may choose the equity method or the cost method of accounting. In the equity method, the parent company recognizes its share of the subsidiary's net income or net loss, adjusted for depreciation and amortization of differences between current fair values and carrying amounts of a purchased subsidiary's net assets on the date of the business combination, as well as its share of dividends declared by the subsidiary. In the cost method, the parent company accounts for the operations of a subsidiary only to the extent that dividends are declared by the subsidiary. Dividends declared by the subsidiary from net income subsequent to the business combination are recognized as revenue by the parent company; dividends declared by the subsidiary in excess of postcombination net income constitute a reduction of the carrying amount of the parent company's investment in the subsidiary. Net income or net loss of the subsidiary is not recognized by the parent company when using the cost method.

The equity method is consistent with the accrual basis of accounting and stresses the economic substance of the parent–subsidiary relationship due to the single economic entity concept. The equity method is appropriate for pooled subsidiaries as well as purchased subsidiaries. The cost method recognizes the legal form of the parent–subsidiary relationship. The cost method is compatible with purchase accounting only, and there is no cost to pooled subsidiary. Consolidated financial statement amounts are the same, regardless of whether a parent company uses the equity method or the cost method to account for a subsidiary's operations.

(D) Consolidation of Partially Owned Subsidiary Using Purchase Accounting Method (Subsequent to Date of Purchase Combination)

Accounting for the operating results of a partially owned subsidiary requires the computation of the minority interest in net income or net losses of the subsidiary. Thus, under the parent company concept of consolidated financial statements, the consolidated income statement of a parent company and its partially owned purchased subsidiary includes an expense—minority interest in net income (or loss) of subsidiary. The minority interest in net assets of the subsidiary is displayed among liabilities in the consolidated balance sheet.

(E) Accounting for Intercompany Transactions Not Involving Profit (Gain) or Loss

Subsequent to the date of a business combination, a parent company and its subsidiaries may enter into a number of transactions with each other. Both the parent and the subsidiary should account for these intercompany transactions in a manner that facilitates the consolidation process. Separate ledger accounts should be established for all intercompany assets, liabilities, revenues, and expenses. These separate accounts clearly identify the intercompany items that must be eliminated in the preparation of consolidated financial statements. After elimination, the consolidated financial statements include only those balances and transactions resulting from outside entities.

(F) Accounting for Intercompany Transactions Involving Profit (Gain) or Loss

Many business transactions between a parent company and its subsidiaries involve a profit (gain) or loss. Among these transactions are intercompany sales of merchandise, of plant assets, and of intangible assets and intercompany leases of property under capital lease or sales-type leases. Until intercompany profits or losses in such transactions are realized through the sales of the asset to an outsider or otherwise, the profits or losses must be eliminated in the preparation of consolidated financial statements.

In addition, a parent or subsidiary company's acquisition of its affiliate's bonds in the open market may result in a realized gain or loss to the consolidated entity. Such a realized gain or loss is not recognized in the separate income statement of either the parent company or the subsidiary, but it must be recognized in the consolidated income statement.

(iii) Partnerships

A **partnership** is an association of two or more people to carry on as co-owners of a business for profit. Competent parties agree to place their money, property, or labor in a business and to divide the profits and losses. Each person is personally liable for the debts of the partnership. Express partnership agreements may be oral or written.

Partnerships are not subject to the income tax. The partnership net profit or loss is allocated to each partner according to the partnership's profit-sharing agreement. Each partner reports these items on his or her own tax return. Several separately reported items (e.g., capital gains, charitable contributions) retain their character when passed through to the partners.

DEFINITIONS OF KEY TERMS: PARTNERSHIPS

Dormant partner—A partner who is both silent and secret

General partner—A partner who is liable for all partnership liabilities plus any unpaid contributions

Limited partner—A partner who is obligated to the partnership to make any contribution stated in the certificate, even if he or she is unable to perform because of death, disability, or any other reason

Secret partner—A partner who may advise management and participate in decisions, but his or her interest is not known to third parties

Silent partner—A partner who does not participate in management

---

(A) Duties, Rights, and Powers of Partners

The duties, rights, and powers of partners are both expressed (in the agreement) and implied (created by law). In most states, the statutory law is the Uniform Partnership Act.

All partners have equal rights in management and conduct of business, even if their capital contributions are not equal. The partners may agree to place management within the control of one or more partners.

Ordinary matters are decided by a majority of the partners. If the partnership consists of two persons who are unable to agree and the partnership agreement makes no provision for arbitration, then dissolution is the only remedy.

The next matters require the unanimous consent of the partners:

- Changing the essential nature of the business by altering the original agreement or reducing or increasing the partners' capital
- Embarking on a new business or admit new members
- Modifying a limited partnership agreement
- Assigning partnership property to a trustee for the benefit of creditors
- Confessing a judgment
- Disposing of the partnership's goodwill
- Submitting a partnership agreement to arbitration
- Performing an act that would make impossible the conduct of the partnership business

However, the process of "engaging a new client" does not require unanimous consent of the partners.

Partners are not entitled to payment for services rendered in conducting partnership business, but they may receive a salary. The payment of a salary to a partner requires either an express agreement stating such or may be implied from the partner's conduct.

Capital contributions are not entitled to draw interest; a partner's earnings on his or her capital investment are his or her share of the profits. Interest may be paid on advances to the partnership above the amount of original contributed capital. Profits that are not withdrawn but left in the partnership are not entitled to draw interest.

Each partner has the duty to give the person responsible for record keeping any information necessary to efficiently and effectively carry on business. Each partner has the right to inspect the records at any time, but no partner can remove the records from the agreed-on location without the other partners' consent. Copies of the records can be made.

Knowledge known to one partner and not revealed to the other partners is considered notice to the partnership. A partner should communicate known facts to the other partners and have them added to the partnership records. A partner who possesses knowledge and does not reveal it to the other partners has committed an act of fraud.

Every partner has an equal right to possess partnership property for partnership purposes. Possession of partnership property for other purposes requires the other partners' permission. A partner cannot transfer partnership property or use partnership property in satisfaction of personal debts.

In the case of a partner's death, his or her interest in specific partnership property passes to the surviving partners. The surviving partners wind up the affairs of the partnership in accordance with the partnership agreement and the applicable laws.

Partners owe each other the duty of undivided loyalty, since a partnership is a fiduciary relationship. Each partner must exercise good faith and consider the mutual welfare of all the partners in conducting business.

Partners have the following powers.

- **Power to contract.** The general laws of agency apply to partnerships, since a partner is considered an agent for the partnership business. A partner may bind the partnership with contractual liability whenever he or she is apparently carrying on the partnership business in the usual manner. Otherwise, a partner cannot bind the partnership without the authorization of the other partners.

- The **common implied powers** of a partner include the ability to
  - □ Compromise, adjust, and settle claims or debts owed by or to the partnership.
  - □ Sell goods in the regular course of business and make warranties.
  - □ Buy property within the scope of the business for cash or on credit.
  - □ Buy insurance.
  - □ Hire employees.
  - □ Make admissions against interest.
  - □ Enter into contracts within the scope of the firm.
  - □ Receive notices.

- **Power to impose tort liability.** The law imposes tort liability on a partnership for all wrongful acts or omissions of any partner acting in the ordinary course of the partnership and for its benefit. The partnership has the right of indemnity against the partner at fault.

- **Power over property.** Partners have implied authority to sell to good-faith purchasers personal property that is held for resale and to execute the necessary documents to transfer title. Selling the fixtures and equipment used in the business requires the other partners' authorization.

   The right to sell a business's real property is implied only if it is in the real estate business. Other transfers of real property require partnership authorization.

- **Financial transactions.** Partnerships are divided into general classes, trading and non-trading partnerships, to determine the limit of a partner's financial powers. A trading partnership engages in the business of buying and selling merchandise. Each partner has an implied power to borrow money and to extend the credit of the firm, in the usual course of business, by signing negotiable paper.

   A nontrading partnership engages in the production of merchandise or sells services. In these partnerships, a partner's powers are more limited. A partner does not have the implied power to borrow money.

(B) Liabilities and Authorities of a General Partner

General partners are liable for:

- Fraudulent acts of other partners.
- Debts attributable to limited partner notes to the partnership.
- Debts related to the purchase of real property without each partner's consent.

General partners have no authority to:

- Do any act in violation of the certificate.
- Do any act that would make it impossible to carry on the ordinary business of the partnership.
- Confess a judgment against the partnership.
- Possess or assign partnership property for other than partnership purposes.
- Admit a person as a general partner.
- Admit a person as a limited partner unless the right to do so is given in the certificate.
- Continue the business with partnership property on the death, retirement, or incapacity of a general partner unless the right to do so is given in the certificate.

(C) Partnership Accounting

A partner's share of the partnership assets or profits may be determined in a suit for an accounting. These suits are equitable in nature and must be filed in a court of equity. A partner is entitled to a formal accounting in these situations:

- The partnership has been dissolved.
- An agreement calls for an accounting at a definite date.
- A partner has withheld profits arising from secret transactions.
- An execution has been levied against the interest of one of the partners.

- One partner does not have access to the books.

- The partnership is approaching insolvency, and all parties are not available.

Partners may make a complete accounting and settle their claims without resort to a court of equity. An accounting is performed on the dissolution of a solvent partnership and winding up of its business. All firm creditors other than partners are entitled to be paid before the partners are entitled to participate in any of the assets.

The assets are distributed among the partners in these ways:

- Any partner who has made advances to the firm or has incurred liability for, or on behalf of, the firm is entitled to reimbursement.

- Each partner is entitled to return of his or her capital contributions.

- Any remaining balance is distributed as profits in accordance with the partnership agreement.

(D) Actions Against Other Partners
Typically a partner cannot maintain an action at law against the other partners, because the indebtedness among the partners is undetermined until there is an accounting and all partnership affairs are settled. The three exceptions to this rule are if

1. The partnership is formed to carry out a single venture or transaction;

2. The action involves a segregated or single unadjusted item or account; or

3. The action involves a personal covenant or transaction entirely independent of the partnership affairs.

(E) Admitting a New Partner
If a partnership admits a new partner, the new partner is liable to the extent of his or her capital contribution for all obligations incurred before his or her admission. The new partner is not personally liable for such obligations.

(F) Asset Distribution of Partnership
If a firm is insolvent and a court of equity is responsible for the distribution of the partnership assets, the assets are distributed in accordance with a rule known as marshalling of assets. The firm's creditors may seek payment out of the firm's assets and then the individual partner assets. The firm's creditors must exhaust the firm's assets before recourse to the partners' individual assets. The descending order of asset distribution of a limited partnership is listed next.

1. Secured creditors other than partners

2. Unsecured creditors other than partners

3. Limited partners in respect of their profits

4. Limited partners in respect of their capital contributions

5. General partners in respect of any loans to the partnership

6. General partners in respect of their profits

7. General partners in respect of their capital contributions

The asset distribution hierarchy of a limited partnership is shown in Exhibit 4.8.

EXHIBIT 4.8 Asset Distribution Hierarchy

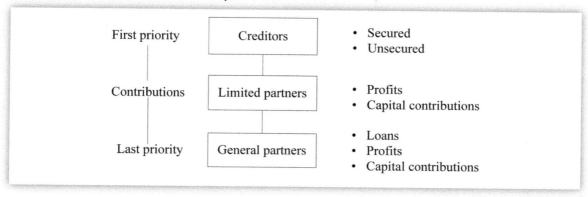

(iv) Foreign Currency Transactions

The buying and selling of foreign currencies result in variations in the exchange rate between the currencies of two countries. The bank's selling spot rate is what it charges for current sales of the foreign currency. The bank's buying spot rate for the currency is less than the selling spot rate; the spread between the selling and buying spot rates represents gross profit to a trader in foreign currency. Factors influencing fluctuations in exchange rates include: a nation's balance of payments surplus or deficit; differing global rates of inflation; and money market variations, such as interest rates, capital investment levels, and monetary policies and actions of central banks.

A multinational corporation (MNC) headquartered in the United States engages in sales, purchases, and loans with foreign companies as well as with its own branches, divisions, investees, and subsidiaries in other countries. If the transactions with foreign companies are denominated in terms of the U.S. dollar, no accounting problems arise for the U.S.-based MNC. If the transactions are negotiated and settled in terms of the foreign companies' local currency unit, then the U.S. company must account for the transaction denominated in foreign currency in terms of U.S. dollars. This foreign currency translation is accomplished by applying the appropriate exchange rate between the foreign currency and the U.S. dollar.

In addition to spot rates, forward rates apply to foreign currency transactions to be completed on a future date. Forward rates apply to forward exchange contracts, which are agreements to exchange currencies of different countries on a specified future date at the forward rate in effect when the contract was made. Forward rates may be larger or smaller than spot rates for a foreign currency, depending on the foreign currency dealer's expectations regarding fluctuations in exchange rates for the currency.

Increases in the selling spot rate for a foreign currency required by a U.S.-based MNC to settle a liability denominated in that currency generate transaction losses to the company because more dollars are required to obtain the foreign currency. Conversely, decreases in the selling spot rate produce transaction gains to the company because fewer U.S. dollars are required to obtain the foreign currency. In contrast, increases in the buying spot rate for a foreign currency to be received by a U.S.-based MNC in settlement of a receivable denominated in that currency generate transaction gains to the company; decreases in the buying spot rate produce transaction losses.

(A) Translation of Foreign Currency Financial Statements

When a U.S.-based MNC prepares consolidated or combined financial statements that include the operating results, financial position (balance sheet), and cash flows of foreign subsidiaries or branches, the U.S. company must translate the amounts in the final statements of the foreign entities from the entities' functional currency to U.S. dollar. Similar treatment must be given to investments in other foreign investees for which the U.S. company uses the equity method of accounting.

Three methods are available to translate foreign currency: current/noncurrent, monetary/nonmonetary (also known as temporal method), and current rate.

Current/Noncurrent Method. Current assets and current liabilities are translated at the exchange rate in effect on the balance sheet date of the foreign entity (i.e., the current rate). All other assets and liabilities, and the components of owners' equity, are translated at the historical rates in effect at the time the assets, liabilities, and equities first were recognized in the foreign entity's accounting records. In the income statement, depreciation expense and amortization expense are translated at historical rates applicable to the related assets, while all other revenue and expenses are translated at an average exchange rate for the accounting period.

This method reflects the liquidity aspects of the foreign entity's financial position by showing the current U.S. dollar equivalents of its working capital components. Inventories are translated at the current rate, which is a departure of the historical rate.

Monetary/Nonmonetary Method. Monetary assets and liabilities, which are expressed in a fixed amount, are translated at the current exchange rate. All other assets, liabilities, and owners' equity amounts are translated at appropriate historical rates. In the income statement, average exchange rates are applied to all revenue and expenses except depreciation expense, amortization expense, and cost of goods sold (COGS), which are translated at appropriate historical rates.

This method emphasizes the retention of the historical-cost principle in the foreign entity's financial statements and parent company aspects of a foreign entity's financial position and operating results. Due to use of the parent company's reporting currency, this method misstates the actual financial position and operating results of the foreign entity.

Current Rate Method. All balance sheet accounts other than owners' equity are translated at the current exchange rate. Owners' equity amounts are translated at historical rates. To emphasize the functional currency aspects of the foreign entity's operations, all revenue and expenses may be translated at the current rate on the respective transaction dates, if practical. Otherwise, an average exchange rate is used for all revenue and expenses.

(B) Transaction Gains and Losses Excluded from Net Income

Gains and losses from the next foreign currency transactions should be accounted for in the same manner as translation adjustments:

- Foreign currency transactions that are designated, and are effective, as economic hedges of a net investment in a foreign entity, commencing as of the designation date

■ Intercompany foreign currency transactions that are of a long-term investment nature, when the entities to the transaction are consolidated, combined, or accounted for by the equity method

(C) Functional Currency in Highly Inflationary Economies

The functional currency of a foreign entity in a highly inflationary economy can be identified as the reporting currency (e.g., the U.S. dollar for a U.S.-based MNC). A **highly inflationary economy** is defined as the one having cumulative inflation of 100% or more over a three-year period. The financial statements of a foreign entity in a country experiencing severe inflation are remeasured in U.S. dollars.

(D) Income Taxes Related to Foreign Currency Translation

The procedures for the interperiod and intraperiod tax allocation to determine the effects of foreign currency translation are listed next.

■ Interperiod tax allocation for temporary differences associated with transaction gains and losses are reported in different accounting periods for FA and income taxes.

■ Interperiod tax allocation for temporary differences associated with translation adjustments that do not meet the criteria for nonrecognition of deferred tax liabilities for undistributed earnings of foreign subsidiaries.

■ Intraperiod tax allocation for translation adjustments are included in the stockholders' equity section of the balance sheet.

(E) Disclosure of Foreign Currency Translation

Aggregate transaction gains or losses of an accounting period should be disclosed in the income statement or in a note to the financial statements. Changes in cumulative translation adjustments during an accounting period should be disclosed in a separate financial statement, in a note to financial statements, or in a statement of stockholders' equity.

The minimum required disclosures include:

■ Beginning and ending amounts of cumulative translation adjustments.

■ Aggregate adjustments during the accounting period for translation adjustments, hedges of net investments, and long-term intercompany transactions.

■ Income taxes allocated to translation adjustments during an accounting period.

■ Decreases resulting from sale or liquidation of an investment in a foreign entity.

(d) Financial Statement Analysis

(i) Overview

Financial statement analysis requires a comparison of the firm's performance with that of other firms in the same industry, with its own previous performance, and/or both. Three major parties who analyze financial statements from their own perspectives are managers of the firm to gauge performance; potential investors who want to invest in the firm by purchasing stocks and bonds; and creditors and lenders (e.g., bankers) who analyze data in financial statements to assess the financial strength of the firm and its ability to pay interest and principal for the money they lent to the firm. Investors use data in financial statements to form expectations about future earnings and dividends and to determine the riskiness of these expected values. The real value of financial statements is in their predictive power about the firm's future earnings potential and dividends payment strength.

WHO LOOKS FOR WHAT?

- Investors look for earnings and dividends, and this is reflected in security values. Therefore, cash flows are the major basis for security values.
- Creditors look for asset strength and the ability to pay off the debt.
- Financial statements report accounting profits.
- High accounting profits generally mean high cash flows and the ability to pay high dividends and debt payments.

A company's **annual report** presents four basic financial statements, including a statement of income (income statement), a statement of financial position (balance sheet), a statement of retained earnings, and an SCF. The income statement summarizes the firm's revenues and expenses over an accounting period.

An **income statement** presents the results of operations for a given time period. Net sales are shown at the top; then various costs, including income taxes, are subtracted to obtain the net income available to common stockholders. A report on earnings and dividends per share is given at the bottom of the statement.

A **balance sheet** is a statement of the firm's financial position at a specific point in time. The firm's assets are shown on the left-hand side of the balance sheet while liabilities and equity (the claims against these assets) are shown on the right-hand side. The assets are listed in the order of their liquidity or the length of time it takes to convert assets into cash. The liabilities are listed in the order in which they must be paid.

A **statement of retained earnings** shows how much of the firm's earnings were not paid out in dividends. Retained earnings represent a claim against assets, not assets per se. Retained earnings do not represent cash and are not "available" for the payment of dividends or anything else. A positive retained earnings means that the firm has earned an income, but its dividends have been less than its reported income. Due to differences between accrual and cash accounting practices, a firm may earn money, which shows an increase in the retained earnings, but still be short of cash.

A **statement of cash flows** (SCF) reports the impact of a firm's operating, investing, and financing activities on cash flows over an accounting period. This statement shows how the firm's operations have affected its cash flows and presents the relationships among cash flows from operating, investing, and financing activities of the firm.

(ii) Types of Financial Statement Analysis

Four types of measures that are used to analyze a company's financial statements and its financial position include common size analysis, trend analysis, comparative ratios, and single ratios. (See Exhibit 4.9.)

EXHIBIT 4.9 Types of Financial Statement Analysis

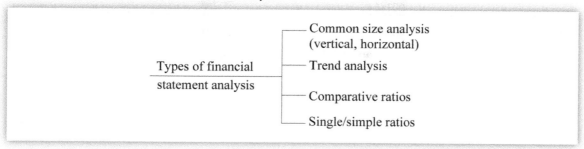

Common size analysis expresses items in percentages, which can be compared with similar items of other firms or with those of the same firm over time. For example, common size balance sheet line items (both assets and liabilities) are expressed as a percentage of total assets (e.g., receivables as X% of total assets). Similarly, common size income statement line items are expressed as a percentage of total sales (e.g., COGS as X% of total sales).

Variations of common size analysis include vertical analysis and horizontal analysis. **Vertical analysis** expresses all items on a financial statement as a percentage of some base figure, such as total assets or total sales. Comparing these relationships between competing organizations helps to isolate strengths and areas of concern.

In **horizontal analysis**, the financial statements for two years are shown together with additional columns showing dollar differences and percentage changes. Thus, the direction, absolute amount, and relative amount of change in account balances can be calculated. Trends that are difficult to isolate through examining the financial statements of individual years or comparing with competitors can be identified.

Trend analysis shows trends in ratios, which gives insight as to whether the financial situation of a firm is improving, declining, or stable. It shows a graph of ratios over time, which can be compared with a firm's own performance as well as that of its industry.

Comparative ratios show key financial ratios, such as current ratio and net sales to inventory, by industry, such as beverages and bakery products. These ratios represent average financial ratios for all firms within an industry category. Many organizations that supply ratio data exist; each designs ratios for its own purpose, such as small firms or large firms. Also, the focus of these ratios is different, such as creditors' viewpoint or investors' viewpoint. Another characteristic of organizations that supply ratio data is that each has its own definitions of the ratios and their components. Due to these differences, caution is required when interpreting these ratios.

Another type of comparative analysis is comparing the financial statements for the current year with those of the most recent year. By comparing summaries of financial statements for the last five to 10 years, an individual can identify trends in operations, capital structure, and the composition of assets. This comparative analysis provides insight into the normal or expected account balance or ratio, information about the direction of changes in ratios and account balances, and insight into the variability or fluctuation in an organization's assets or operations.

TREND ANALYSIS VERSUS COMPARATIVE RATIO ANALYSIS

- In trend analysis, trends are shown over time between the firm and its industry.

- In comparative ratio analysis, a single point (one-to-one) comparison is shown between the firm and its industry.

- In both analyses, the industry's ratio is an average ratio while the firm's ratio is not.

Next, our major focus shifts to single ratios or simple ratios. Certain accounts or items in an organization's financial statements have logical relationships with each other. If the dollar amounts of these related accounts or items are expressed in fraction form, they are called **ratios**. These ratios are grouped into five categories:

1. Liquidity ratios

2. Asset management ratios

3. Debt management ratios

4. Profitability ratios

5. Market value ratios

Exhibit 4.10 presents individual ratios for each ratio category.

EXHIBIT 4.10 Individual Financial Ratios

Ratio Category	Individual Ratios
Liquidity (1)	Current ratio, quick ratio, or acid-test ratio
Asset management (2)	Inventory turnover ratio, days sales outstanding ratio, fixed assets turnover ratio, total assets turnover ratio
Debt management (3)	Debt to total assets ratio, times-interest-earned ratio, fixed charge coverage ratio, cash flow coverage ratio
Profitability (4) = (1) + (2) + (3)	Profit margin on sales ratio, basic earning power ratio, return on total assets ratio, return on common equity ratio, earnings per share ratio, payout ratio
Market value (5) = (1) + (2) + (3) + (4)	Price/earnings ratio, book value per share ratio, market/book ratio

(iii) Single/Simple Ratios

Details on liquidity ratios, asset management ratios, debt management ratios, profitability ratios, and market value ratios are presented next.

(A) Liquidity Ratios

Liquidity ratios measure an organization's debt-paying ability, especially in the short term. Examples include current ratio, quick ratio, and free cash flows. These ratios indicate an organization's capacity to meet maturing current liabilities and its ability to generate cash to pay these liabilities.

Current Ratio (Working Capital Ratio)

Current assets / Current liabilities

Current ratios indicate an organization's ability to pay its current liabilities with its current assets and therefore show the strength of its working capital position. A high current ratio indicates a strong liquidity and vice versa. While a high current ratio is good, it could also mean excessive cash, which is not good.

Both short-term and long-term creditors are interested in the current ratio, because a firm unable to meet its short-term obligations may be forced into bankruptcy. Many bond indentures require the borrower to maintain at least a certain minimum current ratio.

Acid-Test Ratio (Quick Ratio)

$$\text{Quick assets / Current liabilities}$$

Quick assets are cash, marketable securities, and net receivables. This ratio is particularly important to short-term creditors since it relates cash and immediate cash inflows to immediate cash outflows. Purchases of inventory on account would make the quick ratio decrease since it does not include inventory. Current liabilities increase, not current assets. Quick assets are current assets minus inventory.

Free Cash Flows. **Free cash flows** are the amount of cash flows available to investors, creditors, and equity owners after the firm has met all operating needs and paid for investments in net fixed assets and net current assets. These cash flows are calculated as:

$$\text{After-tax operating cash flows} - \text{Net fixed asset investment} - \text{Net current asset investment}$$

Here the term "free cash flows" does not mean that the cash is "free"; it means that cash is available for other useful purposes.

(B) Asset Management Ratios

Asset management ratios or **activity ratios** measure the liquidity of certain assets and relate information on how efficiently assets are being utilized.

Inventory Turnover Ratio

$$\text{Sales / Average inventory or COGS / Average inventory}$$

Inventory turnover indicates how quickly inventory is sold. Typically, a high turnover indicates that an organization is performing well. This ratio can be used in determining whether there is obsolete inventory or if pricing problems exist. The use of different inventory valuation methods (last in, first out [LIFO], first in, first out [FIFO], etc.) can affect the turnover ratio. It is also called the inventory utilization ratio. As the obsolete inventory increases, the inventory turnover decreases.

Days Sales Outstanding Ratio

$$\text{Receivables / Average sales per day}$$

The **days sales outstanding (DSO)** ratio indicates the average length of time that a firm must wait to receive cash after making a sale. It measures the number of days sales are tied up in receivables. If the calculated ratio for a company is 45 days, its sales terms are 30 days, and the industry average ratio is 35 days, it indicates that customers, on average, are not paying their bills on time. In the absence of a change in the credit policy about sales terms, the higher the company's actual ratio, the greater its need to speed up collection efforts. A decrease in the DSO ratio is an indication of effective collection efforts.

Another related ratio is **A/R turnover ratio**, which is net credit sales divided by average net trade receivables outstanding. The A/R outstanding can be calculated by using the beginning and ending balance of the trade receivables. This ratio provides information on the quality of an organization's receivables and how successful it is in collecting outstanding receivables. A fast turnover lends credibility to the current ratio and acid-test ratio.

Fixed Asset Turnover Ratio

$$\text{Net sales} / \text{Net fixed assets}$$

The **fixed asset turnover ratio** shows how effectively the firm uses its fixed assets, such as plant, equipment, machinery, and buildings. Note: Inflation erodes the historical cost base of old assets, thus reporting a higher turnover. This inflation problem makes it hard to compare fixed asset turnover between old and new fixed assets. Assets reported on current value basis would eliminate the inflation problem. The fixed asset turnover ratio is also called fixed assets utilization ratio and is similar to the inventory utilization ratio. A high fixed asset turnover ratio may mean either that a firm was efficient in using its fixed assets or that the firm is undercapitalized and could not afford to buy enough fixed assets.

Total Assets Turnover Ratio

$$\text{Net sales} / \text{Average total assets}$$

The **total assets turnover** indicates how efficiently an organization utilizes its capital invested in assets. A high turnover ratio indicates that an organization is effectively using its assets to generate sales. This ratio relates the volume of a business (i.e., sales, revenue) to the size of its total asset investment. In order to improve this ratio, management needs to increase sales, dispose of some assets, or a combination of both.

(C) Debt Management Ratios

Debt management ratios or coverage ratios are used in predicting the long-run solvency of organizations. Bondholders are interested in these ratios because they provide some indication of the measure of protection available to bondholders. For those interested in investing in an organization's common stock, these ratios indicate some of the risk, since the addition of debt increases the uncertainty of the return on common stock.

Debt Ratio

$$\text{Total debt} / \text{Total assets}$$

The **debt ratio** impacts an organization's ability to obtain additional financing. It is important to creditors because it indicates an organization's ability to withstand losses without impairing the creditor's interest. A creditor prefers a low ratio since it means there is more cushion available to it if the organization becomes insolvent. However, owners prefer a high debt ratio to magnify earnings due to leverage or to minimize loss of control if new stock is issued instead of taking on more debt. Total debt includes both current liabilities and long-term debt.

The capitalization of a lease by a lessee will result in an increase in the debt-to-equity ratio. If a firm purchases a new machine by borrowing the required funds from a bank as a short-term loan, the direct impact of this transaction will be to decrease the current ratio and increase the debt ratio.

Times-Interest-Earned Ratio

$$\text{Earnings before interest and taxes} / \text{Interest charges}$$

The **times-interest-earned ratio** provides an indication of whether an organization can meet its required interest payments when they become due and not go bankrupt. This ratio also provides a rough measure of cash flow from operations and cash outflow as interest on debt. This information is important to creditors, since a low or negative ratio suggests that an organization could default on required interest payments. This ratio measures the extent to which operating income can decline before the firm is unable to meet its annual interest costs. The ability to pay current interest is not affected by taxes since the interest expense is tax deductible. In other words, the interest expense is paid out of income before taxes are calculated.

Fixed Charge Coverage Ratio

Earnings before interest and taxes + Lease payments / Interest charges + Lease payments

The **fixed charge coverage ratio** is similar to times-interest-earned ratio except that the former ratio includes long-term lease obligations. When a company's ratio is less than the industry average, the company may have difficulty in increasing its debt.

Cash Flow Coverage Ratio

Earnings before interest and taxes + Lease payments + Depreciation / Interest charges + Lease payments + Preferred stock dividends (before tax) + Debt repayment (before tax)

The **cash flow coverage** ratio shows the margin by which the firm's operating cash flows cover its financial obligations. This ratio considers principal repayment of debt, dividends on preferred stock, lease payments, and interest charges. The reason for putting the dividends on preferred stock and debt repayment amounts before the tax basis is due to the fact that they are not tax deductible, meaning that they are paid out of the income before taxes are paid.

(D) Profitability Ratios

Profitability ratios, the ultimate test of management's effectiveness, indicate how well an organization operated during a year. They are a culmination of many policies and decisions made by management during the current year as well as previous years. Typically these ratios are calculated using sales or total assets. Profitability ratios show the combined effect of liquidity, asset management, and debt management performance on operating results.

Profit Margin on the Sales Ratio

Net income available to common stockholders / Sales

The profit margin on the sales ratio indicates the proportion of the sales dollar that remains after deducting expenses. Here the net income after taxes is divided by sales to give the profit per dollar of sales.

Basic Earning Power Ratio

Earnings before interest and taxes / Total assets

The **basic earning power ratio** shows the raw earning power of the firm's assets, before the influence of taxes and impact of the financial leverage. It indicates the ability of the firm's assets to generate operating income. A low total asset turnover and low profit margin on sales gives a low basic earning power ratio. ROI may be calculated by multiplying total asset turnover by profit margin.

Return on Total Assets Ratio

Net income available to common stockholders / Total assets

The **return on total assets (ROA) ratio** measures the ROA after interest and taxes are paid. The net income used in the equation is net income after taxes. A low ratio indicates a low basic earning power ratio and a high use of debt.

Another way of looking at the ROA ratio is by breaking it down into subcomponents: net income divided by net sales (i.e., profit margin on sales) as one component and net sales divided by total average assets (i.e., total asset turnover) as another component. This breakdown helps in pinpointing problems and opportunities for improvement.

Return on Common Equity Ratio

$$\text{Net income available to common stockholders / Common equity}$$

The **return on common equity (ROE)** measures the rate of return on common stockholders' investments. The net income used in the equation is the net income after taxes, and common equity is the average stockholders' equity. A low ratio compared to the industry indicates high use of debt. This ratio reflects the return earned by an organization on each dollar of owners' equity invested.

Earnings per Share Ratio

$$\text{Net income} - \text{Current-year preferred dividends / Weighted-average number of shares outstanding}$$

The **earnings per share ratio** is probably the most widely used ratio for evaluating an organization's operating ability. The complexity of the calculation of EPS is determined by a corporation's capital structure.

An organization with no outstanding convertible securities, warrants, or options has a simple capital structure. An organization has a complex structure if it has such items outstanding. Investors should be careful not to concentrate on this number to the exclusion of the organization as a whole. One danger in concentrating on this number is that EPS can easily be increased by purchasing treasury stock that reduces the outstanding shares.

Payout Ratio

$$\text{Cash dividends / Net income or dividends per share / EPS}$$

The **payout ratio** indicates the ability to meet dividend obligations from net income earned. There is a relationship between the payout ratio and the need for obtaining external capital. The higher the payout ratio, the smaller the addition to retained earnings and, hence, the greater the requirements for external capital. This says that dividend policy affects external capital requirements. If d is the dividend payout ratio, $(1 - d)$ is called the earnings retention rate.

Depending on their tax status, certain investors are attracted to the stock of organizations that pay out a large percentage of their earnings. Others are attracted to organizations that retain and reinvest a large percentage of their earnings. Growth organizations typically reinvest a large percentage of their earnings; therefore, they have low payout ratios.

(E) Market Value Ratios

Market value ratios relate the firm's stock price to its earnings and book value per share. They show the combined effects of liquidity ratios, profitability ratios, asset management ratios, and debt management ratios. The viewpoint is from outside in (i.e., from an investors' view about the company's financial performance—past and future).

Price/Earnings Ratio

Price per share / EPS

The price/earnings (P/E) ratio shows how much investors are willing to pay per dollar of reported profits. Financial analysts, stock market analysts, and investors in general use this value to determine whether a stock is overpriced or underpriced. Different analysts have differing views as to the proper P/E ratio for a certain stock or the future earnings prospects of the firm. Several factors, such as relative risk, trends in earnings, stability of earnings, and the market's perception of the growth potential of the stock, affect the P/E ratio.

P/E RATIOS VERSUS GROWTH VERSUS RISK

- P/E ratios are higher for firms with high growth prospects and low risk.
- P/E ratios are lower for firms with low growth prospects and high risk.

Book Value per Share

Common equity / Shares outstanding

The **book value per share ratio** is used as an intermediate step in calculating the market/book ratio. The book value per share ratio is used in evaluating an organization's net worth and any changes in it from year to year. If an organization were liquidated based on the amounts reported on the balance sheet, the book value per share indicates the amount that each share of stock would receive. If the asset amounts on the balance sheet do not approximate fair market value, then the ratio loses much of its relevance.

Market/Book Ratio

Market price per share / Book value per share

The **market/book ratio** reveals how investors think about the company. This ratio is related to the ROE ratio in that a high ratio of ROE gives a high market/book ratio and vice versa. In other words, companies with higher ROEs sell their stock at higher multiples of book value. Similarly, companies with high rates of return on their assets can have market values in excess of their book values. A low rate of return on assets gives a low market/book value ratio.

EXAMPLES: CALCULATION OF FINANCIAL RATIOS

Examples 1 through 3 are based on the following selected data that pertain to a company at December 31, 20X1:

Quick Assets	$208,000
Acid-test ratio	2.6 to 1
Current ratio	3.5 to 1
Net sales for 20X4	$1,800,000
Cost of sales for 20X1	$990,000
Average total assets for 20x1	$1,200,000

(Continued)

EXAMPLES: CALCULATION OF FINANCIAL RATIOS (*Continued*)

Example 1

Based on the data, the company's current liabilities at December 31, 20X1, amount to:

a. $ 59,429

b. $ 80,000

c. $342,857

d. $187,200

Choice (b) is the correct answer. Computations follow.

$$\frac{\text{Quick assets}}{\text{Current liabilities}} = \text{Acid-test ratio}$$

$$\frac{\$208,000}{\text{Current liabilities}} = 2.6$$

$$\text{Current liabilities} = \frac{\$208,000}{2.6} = \underline{\$80,000}$$

Choice (a) is incorrect. This answer incorrectly reflects the computation quick assets ($208,000) divided by the current ratio (3.5). Choice (c) is incorrect. This answer reflects the incorrect computation of average total assets ($1,200,000) divided by the current ratio (3.5). Choice (d) is incorrect. This answer reflects the incorrect computation of quick assets ($208,000) multiplied by the excess of the current ratio (3.5) over the acid-test ratio (2.6).

Example 2

Based on the data listed, the company's inventory balance at December 31, 20X1, is:

a. $ 72,000

b. $187,200

c. $231,111

d. $282,857

Choice (a) is the correct answer. Computations follow.

$$\frac{\$208,000}{\text{Current liabilities}} = 2.6$$

$$\frac{\$208,000}{2.6} = \$80,000 = \text{Current liabilities}$$

$$\frac{\text{Current assets}}{\text{Current liabilities}} = \text{Current ratio}$$

$$\frac{\text{Current assets}}{\$80,000} = 3.5$$

Choice (b) is incorrect. This answer reflects the incorrect computation of the current ratio (3.5) minus the acid-test ratio (2.6) multiplied by quick assets ($208,000). Choice (c) is incorrect. This answer reflects the incorrect computation of quick assets ($208,000) divided by the excess of the current ratio (3.5) over the quick ratio (2.6). Choice (d) is incorrect. This answer reflects the incorrect computation of cost of sales ($990,000) divided by the current ratio (3.5).

Example 3

Based on the data listed, the company's asset turnover for 20X1 is:

a. 0.675

b. 0.825

c. 1.21

d. 1.50

Choice **(d)** is the correct answer. Computations follow.

$$\frac{\text{Net sales}}{\text{Average total assets}} = \frac{\$1,800,000}{\$1,200,000} = 1.5$$

Choice (a) is incorrect. This answer reflects the incorrect computation of gross profit ($1,800,000 – $990,000) divided by average total assets ($1,200,000). Choice (b) is incorrect. This answer reflects the incorrect computation of cost of sales ($990,000) divided by average total assets ($1,200,000). Choice (c) is incorrect. This answer reflects the incorrect computation of average total assets ($1,200,000) divided by cost of sales ($990,000).

(iv) Limitations of Financial Statement Ratios

Because ratios are simple to compute, convenient, and precise, they are attractive, and a high degree of importance is attached to them. Since these ratios are only as good as the data on which they are based, the next limitations exist:

- The use of ratio analysis could be limiting for large, multidivisional firms due to their size and complexity—two conditions that mask the results. However, they might be useful to small firms.

- Typically, financial statements are not adjusted for price-level changes. Inflation or deflation can have a large effect on the financial data.

- Since transactions are accounted for on a cost basis, unrealized gains and losses on different asset balances are not reflected in the financial statements.

- Income ratios tend to lose credibility in cases where a significant number of estimated items exist, such as amortization and depreciation.

- Seasonal factors affect and distort ratio analysis, which can be minimized by using average figures in calculations.

- Be aware of window-dressing and earnings management techniques used by firms to make them look financially better than they really are. Often management manipulates the financial statements to impress credit analysts and stock market investors (i.e., management fraud).

- Certain off–balance sheet items do not show up on the financial statements. For example, leased assets do not appear on the balance sheet, and the lease liability may not be shown as a debt. Therefore, leasing can improve both the asset turnover and the debt ratios.

- Attaining comparability among organizations in a given industry is an extremely difficult problem, since different organizations apply different accounting procedures. For this reason, auditors must identify the basic differences in accounting from organization to organization and adjust balances to achieve comparability.

- Auditors should not take ratios at their face value since a "good" ratio does not mean that the company is a strong one and a "bad" ratio does not mean that the company is a weak one. Ratios should be evaluated and interpreted with judgment and experience and considering the firm's characteristics and the industry's uniqueness.

(e) Types of Debt and Equity

(i) Types of Debt

Debt is of two types: short-term debt and long-term debt. Debt maturities affect both risk and expected returns. For example, short-term debt:

- Is riskier than long-term debt.

- Is less expensive than long-term debt.

- Can be obtained faster than long-term debt.

- Is more flexible than long-term debt.

(A) Sources of Short-Term Financing

By definition, **short-term debt (credit)** is any liability originally scheduled for payment within one year. The four major sources of short-term credit are: accruals, A/P, bank loans, and commercial paper. The order of short-term credit sources is shown next from both cost and importance viewpoints.

Order of Importance	Order of Cost
A. Trade credit (most important)	A. Trade credit (free, no interest paid)
B. Bank loans	B. Accruals
C. Commercial paper	C. Commercial paper
D. Accruals (least important)	D. Bank loans (not free, interest paid)

Trade Credit. Trade credit is granted by suppliers of goods as a sales promotion device. All firms, regardless of their size, depend on A/P or trade credit as a source of short-term financing. Small firms rely more heavily on trade credit than larger firms due to the former's inability to raise money from other sources. **Trade credit**, a major part of current liability, is an interfirm debt arising from credit sales and recorded as an A/R by the seller and as an A/P by the buyer. Trade credit is a spontaneous source of financing arising from normal course of business operations.

When payment terms are extended, the amount in A/P is expanded to provide an additional source of financing. Therefore, lengthening the credit period generates additional financing.

Payment terms vary and usually call for "net 30," meaning that a company must pay for goods 30 days after the invoice date. Other terms include "1/10, net 30," which means that a 1% discount is given if payment is made within 10 days of the invoice date, but the full invoice amount is due and payable within 30 days if the discount is not taken. The finance manager has a choice of taking or not taking the discount and needs to calculate the cost of not taking discounts on purchases. The equation is

$$\text{Percentage cost of not taking discount} = \frac{\text{Discount percent}}{100\% - \text{Discount \%}} \times \frac{360}{A - B}$$

where

A = days credit outstanding

B = discount period

EXAMPLE: COST OF NOT TAKING A DISCOUNT

The approximate cost of not taking a discount when the payment terms are 1/10, net 30, is calculated as follows:

$$\text{Percentage cost of not taking discount} = \frac{1}{100\% - 1\%} \times \frac{360}{30 - 10} = 0.18 = 18\%$$

By paying late (stretching A/P), the cost of trade credit is reduced. This is shown next. When a 30-day bill is paid in 60 days, the approximate cost drops from 18% to 7.2%. That, is 1/99 × 360 / (60 − 10) = 0.072 = 7.2%.

KEY CONCEPTS TO REMEMBER: Cost of Trade Discounts

- The cost of not taking trade discounts can be substantial.
- The cost can be doubled when payment (credit) terms are changed from 1/10, net 30 to 1/10, net 20.
- The cost can be doubled when payment (credit) terms are changed from 1/10, net 30 to 2/10, net 30.
- The cost can be quadrupled when payment (credit) terms are changed from 1/10, net 30 to 2/10, net 20.
- The cost can be reduced by paying late (i.e., from 2/10, net 30 to 2/10, net 60).

A firm's policy with regard to taking or not taking trade discounts can have a significant effect on its financial statements. A dichotomy exists here in terms of taking discounts or not taking discounts. Careful analysis needs to be performed showing relevant costs and their effects on net income.

Decision Conditions

1. If the company does not take discounts (i.e., uses maximum trade credit), its interest expense will be zero (i.e., no borrowing is necessary), but it will have an expense equivalent to lost discounts.

2. If the company does take discounts (i.e., borrows money from bank), it will incur interest expense on the loan, but it will avoid the cost of discounts lost. The company gives up some of the trade credit, and it has to raise money from other sources, such as bank credit, common stock, or long-term bonds.

Decision Rules

1. If the discount amount lost exceeds the interest expense, a take-discounts policy would result in a higher net income and eventually a higher stock price.

2. If the interest expense exceeds the discount amount lost, a does-not-take-discounts policy would result in a higher net income and eventually a higher stock price.

Bank Loans. Bank loans appear on firms' balance sheets under the notes payable account category. A promissory note is signed by the borrower (customer) specifying the amount borrowed, the percentage interest rate, the repayment schedule, any collateral, and any other terms and conditions. Banks require a compensating balance in the form of a minimum checking account balance equal to a specified percentage (i.e., 10%–20%) of the face amount of the loan. A compensating balance raises the effective interest rate on the loan.

EXAMPLES OF BANK LOAN FEATURES

- Promissory note
- Compensating balance
- Line of credit
- Revolving credit agreement

Banks also give a line of credit to a borrower, which works like a credit card limit. A line of credit can be based on either formal or informal understanding. It includes the maximum amount of credit the bank will extend to the borrower. A revolving credit agreement, which is similar to a line of credit, is a formal line of credit often used by large firms. The bank has a legal obligation to honor a revolving credit agreement; no legal obligation exists under the line of credit.

The cost of a bank loan (i.e., interest rate) varies depending on economic conditions and Federal Reserve (Fed) money supply policy. Generally, interest rates are higher for riskier borrowers and for smaller loans due to fixed costs of servicing the loan. If a firm is financially strong, it can borrow at the prime rate, which traditionally has been the lowest rates bank charge. If a firm is financially weak, the bank will charge higher than prime rate to compensate for the risk involved.

 KEY CONCEPTS TO REMEMBER: Loan Demand and Interest Rates

- When the economy is weak (i.e., loan demand is weak), the Fed increases the money supply. Consequently, the interest rates on all types of loans decline.
- When the economy is strong (i.e., loan demand is strong), the Fed decreases the money supply. Consequently, the interest rates on all types of loans increases.

Interest rates on bank loans are quoted in three ways: simple interest, discount interest, and add-on interest. Each method is discussed briefly.

In a **simple (regular) interest** loan, the borrower receives the face value of the loan and then repays the principal and interest at maturity.

$$\text{Effective rate} = \text{Interest} / \text{Amount received}$$

If a loan period is one year or more, the nominal (stated) rate equals the effective rate. If a loan period is less than one year, the effective rate is higher than the nominal (stated) rate.

In a **discount interest loan**, the borrower receives less than the face value of the loan since the bank deducts the interest in advance.

Because of discounting, the effective rate is always higher than a simple interest loan regardless of the loan period. However, the discount interest imposes less of a penalty on a shorter-term than on a longer-term loan because the interest is paid closer to the average date of use of the funds (half the life of the loan).

Small installment loans employ the **add-on interest** method. The interest is calculated based on the nominal rate and then added to the amount received to obtain the loan's face value.

$$\text{Effective rate} = \text{Interest} / 0.5 \text{ (Amount received)}$$

The effective rate can be almost double the stated rate since the average amount actually outstanding is less than the original amount of the loan.

The situation is different when compensating balances are introduced to the simple interest method and discount interest method. In general, compensating balances tend to raise the effective interest rate on a loan because some money is tied up in a checking account (i.e., cannot be used). There are two exceptions: (1) If the firm can use transaction balances as compensating balances, the effective interest rate will be less than otherwise; and (2) if the firm can earn interest on its bank deposits, including the compensating balance, the effective interest rate will be decreased.

Commercial Paper. **Commercial paper** represents short-term, unsecured promissory notes of large, strong firms and is highly liquid in nature. The interest rate charged on commercial paper is somewhat below the prime rate, and its maturity ranges from two to six months. Even though compensating balances are not required for commercial paper, its effective interest rate is higher due to the loan commitment fees involved.

Firms issuing commercial paper are required by commercial paper dealers to have unused revolving credit agreements to back up their outstanding commercial paper. A commitment fee is charged on the unused credit line.

Unlike bank loans, the commercial paper market is impersonal. However, it also is flexible and provides a wide range of credit sources generally available to financially strong firms with low credit risks.

Accruals. **Accruals** are short-term liabilities arising from wages owed to employees and taxes owed to government. These accruals increase automatically as a firm's operations expand; hence little control exists over their levels. No explicit interest is paid on funds raised through accruals.

(B) Use of Security in Short-Term Financing

The security agreement of the Uniform Commercial Code provides guidelines for establishing loan security. Secured loans are expensive due to record-keeping costs. Financially weak companies are required to put up some type of collateral to protect the lender, while financially strong companies generally are not so required, even though they are encouraged to do so. Most commonly used collateral for short-term credit is A/R and inventories, which are described in Exhibit 4.11.

EXHIBIT 4.11 Collateral for Short-Term and Long-Term Loans

Short-Term Loan Collateral	Long-Term Loan Collateral
Accounts receivable	Land
Inventories	Building
Stocks	Equipment
Bonds	Stocks
	Bonds

Accounts Receivable Financing. **A/R financing** involves either the pledging of receivables or the selling of receivables (i.e., factoring) to obtain a short-term loan. Usually either commercial banks or industrial finance companies are involved in pledging and factoring, and a legally binding agent is established between the borrower and the lender. (See Exhibit 4.12.)

EXHIBIT 4.12 Accounts Receivable Financing Methods

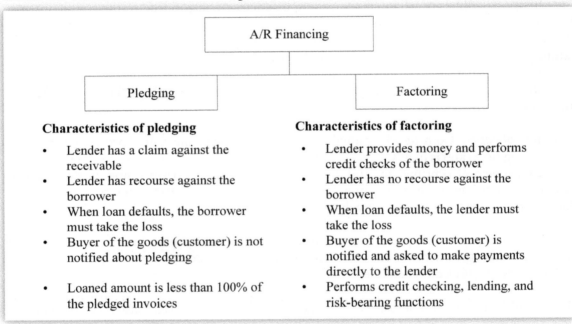

The expensive operation of pledging and factoring functions today will become less expensive tomorrow due to automation and use of debit cards and credit cards. This makes it affordable for small companies to finance their receivables. When a credit card is used to purchase an item, the seller is in effect factoring receivables.

Advantages and disadvantages of A/R financing are listed next.

Advantages

- Flexibility because the financing is tied to the growth of receivables. As sales increase, financing increases.

- Receivables are put to better use than would be the case otherwise.

- Benefit of an in-house credit department without having one.

Disadvantages

- Administrative costs could be higher to handle a large volume of invoices with small dollar amounts.

- Trade creditors may object to selling their goods on credit because receivables (noncash assets) are being pledged or factored. They may be uneasy about this type of financing arrangement.

Inventory Financing. **Inventory financing** involves the use of inventory as a security to obtain a short-term loan. Three methods exist: inventory blanket liens, trust receipts, and warehouse receipts. (See Exhibit 4.13.)

EXHIBIT 4.13 Inventory Financing Methods

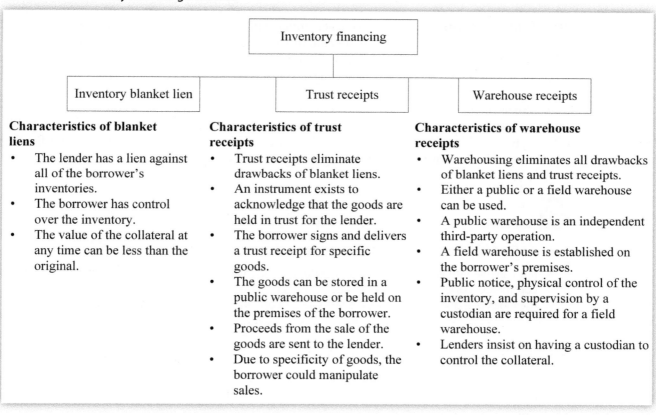

Advantages and Disadvantages of Field Warehouse Financing. Advantages and disadvantages of field warehouse financing are listed next.

Advantages

- Flexibility because the financing is tied to the growth of inventories.

- More sales means more inventory buildup is required and more financing is needed.

- A convenient method is loan collateral.

- Better inventory control and warehousing practices, which in turn save handling costs, insurance charges, and theft losses.

Disadvantages

- An extensive amount of paperwork is required.

- Goods are physically separated using fences and signs.

- The cost of supervision by a custodian of the field warehousing company is high, especially for small firms obtaining the loan.

(C) Long-Term Debt

Long-term debt is often called funded debt, a term used to define the replacement of short-term debt with securities of longer maturity (e.g., stocks, bonds). Many types of long-term debt instruments are available, including term loans, bonds, secured notes, unsecured notes, marketable debt, and nonmarketable debt. Term loans and bonds are discussed next.

Term Loans. A **term "loan"** is a contract under which a borrower agrees to make a series of payments (interest and principal) at specific times to the lender. Most term loans are amortized, which means they are paid off in equal installments over the life of the loan, ranging from three to 15 years. Amortization protects the lender against inadequate loan provisions made by the borrower.

Since the agreement is between the lender and the borrower, documentation requirements are lower, the speed and future flexibility are greater, and the cost is lower compared to a public offering involved in a stock or bond issue. The interest rate on a term loan can be either fixed or variable, and lenders are reluctant to make long-term, fixed rate loans.

KEY CONCEPTS TO REMEMBER: Term Loans

- If a fixed rate is used, it is set close to the rate on bonds of equivalent maturity and risk.

- If a variable rate is used, it is set at a certain number of percentage points over the prime rate, commercial paper rate, Treasury bill rate, Treasury bond rate, or London Interbank Offered Rate. When the index rate goes up or down, the rate charged on the outstanding balance will vary accordingly.

Bonds. A **bond** is a long-term contract (seven to 10 years or more) under which a borrower agrees to make payments (interest and principal) on specific dates to the holder of the bond. The interest rates paid on bonds can be fixed or variable (floating rate bonds); generally, they are fixed.

Some debts have specific contractual requirements to meet. The effective cost of the debt is high, and the debt contracts contain many restrictions, which limit a firm's future flexibility. In order to protect the rights of the bondholders and the issuing firm, a legal document called an indenture is created, which includes restrictive covenants. A trustee, usually a bank, is assigned to represent the bondholders. The role of the trustee is to enforce the terms of the indenture and to ensure compliance with restrictive covenants.

WHAT IS INCLUDED IN RESTRICTIVE COVENANTS?

- Conditions under which the issuer can pay off the bonds prior to maturity

- The level at which the issuer's times-interest-earned ratio must be maintained if the firm is to sell additional bonds

- Restrictions against the payment of dividends when earnings fall below a certain level

Most bonds contain a **call provision** that gives the issuing firm the right to call the bonds for redemption before maturity. The bondholder is paid an amount greater than par value (call premium) for the bond when it is called. The call premium is set equal to one year's interest if the bond is called during the first year, and the premium declines at a constant rate of I/N each year thereafter, where I equals annual interest and N equals original maturity in years.

TERM LOANS VERSUS BONDS

- Bonds and term loans are similar in that both require payments of interest and principal amounts on specific dates.

- Only one lender is involved in a term loan. Thousands of investors are involved in a bond issue.

- A bond issue is advertised and sold to many investors. A term loan is not advertised and only one borrower is involved.

- Syndicates of many financial institutions can grant very large term loans.

- A bond issue can be sold to one or a few lenders (privately placed) for speed, flexibility, and low issuance costs.

Another example of specific debt contract features is sinking fund requirements. A **sinking fund** is a provision that requires an annual payment designed to amortize a bond or preferred stock issue. It retires a portion of the bond issue each year. It can also be viewed as buying back a certain percentage of the issue each year. Annual payments are a cash drain on the firm, and nonpayment could cause default or force the company into bankruptcy. The firm may deposit money with a trustee who will retire the bonds when they mature.

KEY CONCEPTS TO REMEMBER: Call Provision and Sinking Fund

- A bond without a call provision will protect the bondholder. The investor is not subject to interest rate fluctuations.

- A bond with a sinking fund call provision will not protect the bondholder when interest rates fall. The investor loses money on interest.

- Bonds with a sinking fund provision are safer than bonds without such a provision. Sinking fund bonds results in lower coupon rates.

The sinking fund retirement is handled either by calling in for redemption (at par) a certain percentage of the bonds each year or by buying the required amount of bonds on the open market. A sinking fund call requires no call premium; a refunding operation does require such a premium. A sinking fund requires that a small percentage of the issue is callable in any one year.

The refunding operation works as follows: When a firm sold bonds or preferred stock at high interest rates, and if the issue is callable, the firm could sell a new issue at low interest rates. Then the firm could retire the expensive old issue. This refunding operation reduces interest costs and preferred dividend expenses.

> **INTEREST RATES VERSUS BOND PRICES**
>
> - There is an inverse relationship between bond prices and interest rates.
> - If interest rates are increased, the firm will buy bonds in the open market at a discount.
> - If interest rates are decreased, the firm will call the bonds.

Types of long-term bonds are discussed next.

Mortgage Bonds. Under a **mortgage bond**, the corporation pledges certain fixed assets as security for the bond. Mortgage bonds can be of two types: senior (first) mortgage bonds and junior (second) mortgage bonds. Second mortgage bondholders are paid only after the first mortgage bondholders have been paid off in full. All mortgage bonds are written subject to an indenture. Details regarding the nature of secured assets are contained in the mortgage instrument. From the viewpoint of the investor, mortgage bonds provide lower risk and junk bonds provide greater risk.

> **BOND RATING CRITERIA**
>
> - Debt ratio
> - Times-interest-earned ratio
> - Current ratio
> - Fixed charge coverage ratio
> - Mortgage or other provisions
> - Sinking fund requirements

Debentures. A **debenture** is an unsecured bond. Consequently, it provides no lien against specific property as security for the obligation. Debenture holders are general creditors. Financially strong companies do not need to put up property as security when they issue debentures. Debentures can be subordinate or not. In the event of liquidation, reorganization, or bankruptcy, subordinate debt has claims on assets only after senior debt has been paid off. Subordinate debentures may be subordinated either to designated notes payable or to all other debt.

Convertible Bonds. **Convertible bonds** are securities that are convertible into shares of common stock, at a fixed price, at the option of the bondholder. Convertible bonds have a lower coupon rate than nonconvertible debt and have a chance for capital gains.

Warrants. **Warrants** are options that permit the holder to buy stock for a stated price, thereby providing a capital gain if the price of the stock rises. Bonds that are issued with warrants, such as convertible bonds, carry lower coupon rates than straight bonds.

Income Bonds. As the name implies, **income bonds** pay interest only when the interest is earned. These bonds are safer to a company but riskier to an investor than "regular" bonds.

Putable Bonds. **Putable bonds** may be turned in and exchanged for cash at the holder's option. The put option can be exercised only if the issuer is being acquired or is increasing its outstanding debt or other specified action.

Treasury Bonds. A **treasury bond** will have the lowest risk and low opportunity for return to an investor. It has the highest interest rate risk at the date of issue to an issuer. (See Exhibit 4.14.)

EXHIBIT 4.14 Bonds and Risks

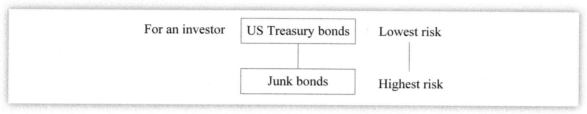

Indexed Bonds. Countries faced with high inflation rates issue **indexed bonds**, also known as purchasing power bonds. The interest paid is based on an inflation index (e.g., Consumer Price Index) so that the interest paid rises automatically when the inflation rate rises. This bond protects the bondholder against inflation.

Floating Rate Bonds. The interest rate on **floating rate bonds** fluctuates with shifts in the general level of interest rates. The interest rate on these bonds is adjusted periodically, and it benefits the investor and the lender. Corporations also benefit from not having to commit themselves to paying a high rate of interest for the entire life of the loan.

Zero-Coupon Bonds. The major attraction of zero-coupon bonds is capital appreciation rather than interest income. Therefore, **zero-coupon bonds** pay no interest and are offered at a discount below their par values. Both private and public organizations are offering zero-coupon bonds to raise money. Zero-coupon bonds are also called original issue discount bonds.

Junk Bonds. **Junk bonds** are high-risk, high-yield bonds issued to finance a leveraged buyout (LBO), a merger, or a troubled company. In junk bond deals, the debt ratio is high, so bondholders share as much risk as stockholders would. Since the interest expense on bonds is tax deductible, it increases after-tax cash flows of the bond issuer.

So many different types of long-term securities are available because different investors have different risk/return trade-off preferences. Different securities are issued to accommodate different tastes of investors and at different points in time. Short-term U.S. Treasury bills are risk-free and low-return securities (they act as a reference point); warrants are high-risk and high-return securities.

(D) Factors Influencing Long-Term Financing Decisions

Long-term financing decisions require a great deal of planning since a firm commits itself for many years to come. The long-term nature combined with uncertainty makes long-term financing risky, requiring careful consideration of all factors involved. Examples of important factors are listed next.

- **Target capital structure.** A firm should compare its actual capital structure to its target structure and keep them in balance over a longer period of time. Exact matching of capital structure is not economically feasible on a yearly financing basis due to increased flotation costs involved. It has been shown that small fluctuations about the optimal capital structure have little effect either on a firm's cost of debt and equity or on its overall cost of capital.

- **Maturity matching.** The maturity-matching concept proposes matching the maturity of the liabilities (debt) with the maturity of the assets being financed. This factor has a major influence on the type of debt securities used.

- **Interest rate levels.** Consideration of both absolute and relative interest rate levels is crucial in making long-term financing decisions. The issuance of a long-term debt with a call provision is one example where the interest rate fluctuates. The callability of a bond permits the firm to refund the issue, should interest rates drop. Companies base their financing decisions on expectations about future interest rates.

- **The firm's current and forecasted financial conditions.** The firm's financial condition, earnings forecasts, status of R&D programs, and introduction of new products all have a major influence on what type of long-term security is issued. For example, these decision rules apply:

  - If management forecasts higher earnings, the firm could use debt now rather than issuing common stock. After earnings have risen and pushed up the stock price, the firm should issue common stock to restore the capital structure to its target level.

  - If a firm is financially weak but forecasts better earnings, permanent financing should be delayed until conditions have improved.

  - If a firm is financially strong now but forecasts poor earnings, it should use long-term financing now rather than waiting.

- **Restrictions in existing debt contracts and availability of collateral.** Restrictions on the current ratio, debt ratio, times-interest-earned ratio, and fixed charge coverage ratio can also restrict a firm's ability to use different types of financing at a given time. Also, secured long-term debt will be less costly than unsecured debt. Firms with large amounts of fixed assets (with a ready resale value) are likely to use a relatively large amount of debt.

(ii) Types of Equity

When management decides to acquire new assets, it has the option of financing these assets with equity, debt, or a combination. A good financial management policy is to finance:

- Long-term assets with long-term capital.
- Short-term assets with short-term capital.

Common equity means the sum of the firm's common stock, additional paid-in capital, preferred stock, and retained earnings. Common equity is the common stockholders' total investment in the firm. The sources of long-term capital are shown in Exhibit 4.15.

EXHIBIT 4.15 Sources of Long-Term Capital

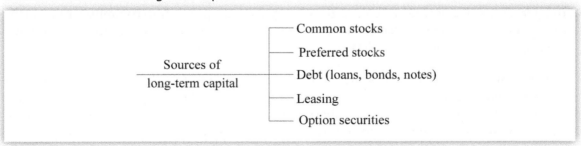

Common stocks and preferred stocks are discussed in this section. Debt was discussed in the previous section, and leasing was presented earlier in this chapter.

(A) Common Stocks

The common stockholders are the owners of a corporation. **Common stock** is the amount of stock management has actually issued (sold) at par value. **Par value** is the nominal or face value of a stock and is the minimum amount for which new shares can be issued. The component "additional paid-in capital" represents the difference between the stock's par value and what new stockholders paid when they bought newly issued shares. **Retained earnings** are the money that belongs to the stockholders and that they could have received in the form of dividends. Retained earnings are also the money that was plowed back into the firm for reinvestment.

Book value of firm = Common stock + Paid-in capital + Retained earnings = Common equity

Book value per share = Book value of firm / Common shares outstanding

It is interesting to note that par value, book value, and market value will never be equal due to conflicting relationships.

KEY CONCEPTS TO REMEMBER: Relationships among Book Value, Par Value, and Market Value

- If a company had lost money since its inception, it would have had negative retained earnings, the book value would have been below par value, and the market price could have been below the book value.

- When a stock is sold at a price above book value per share, the book value increases.

- When a stock is sold at a price below book value per share, the book value decreases.

Most firms have one type of common stock; other firms may have multiple types of stock called classified stock. Usually newer firms issue classified stock to raise funds from outside sources. For example, Class A stock may be sold to the public with a dividend payment but no voting rights. Class B stock may be kept by the founder of the firm to gain control with full voting rights. A restriction might be placed on Class B stock not to pay dividends until the firm reaches a predesignated retained earnings level.

Legal Rights of Common Stockholders. Since the common stockholders are the owners of a firm, they have these rights: the right to elect the firm's directors and the right to remove the management of the firm if they decide a management team is not effective. Stockholders can transfer their right to vote to a second party by means of an instrument known as a proxy. A **proxy fight** is a situation where outsiders plan to take control of the business by requesting that stockholders transfer their rights to outsiders in order to remove the current management and to bring in a new management team.

Common stock holders have preemptive rights to purchase any additional shares sold by the firm. Preemptive rights protect the power of control of current stockholders and protect stockholders against a dilution of stock value. Selling common stock at a price below the market value would dilute its price. This would transfer wealth from current stockholders to new stockholders. Preemptive rights prevent such transfer.

Put and Call Options. A **put option** is the right to sell stock at a given price within a certain period. A **call option** is the right to purchase stock at a given price within a certain period. Selling a put option could force the company to purchase additional stock if the option is exercised. The holder of a put option for a particular common stock would make a profit if the option is exercised during the option term after the stock price has declined below the put price. A warrant option gives the holder a right to purchase stock from the issuer at a given price.

Exhibit 4.16 presents the advantages and disadvantages associated with common stock financing.

EXHIBIT 4.16 Advantages and Disadvantages of Common Stock Financing

Advantages	Disadvantages
It gives the benefits of ownership and expected returns in terms of dividends and capital gains.	It gives voting rights and control to new stockholders when a stock is sold.
It does not obligate the firm to make dividend payments to stockholders; dividends are optional and dependent on earnings, investment plans, and management practices. This gives flexibility to management.	It gives new stockholders the right to share in the income of the firm.
It has no fixed maturity date.	It increases the cost of underwriting and distributing common stock. Flotation costs are higher than incurred for debt.
It provides a cushion against losses from the creditors' viewpoint since it increases a firm's creditworthiness. It lowers the firm's cost of debt due to a good bond rating.	Its average cost of capital will be higher when a firm has more equity than is called for in its optimal capital structure.
It provides investors with a better hedge against unanticipated inflation.	Its dividend payments are not tax deductible for corporations.
It provides financing flexibility in that it permits companies to finance with common stock during good times and to finance with debt during bad times. This practice is called "reserve borrowing capacity."	

(B) Preferred Stock

Preferred stock is issued to raise long-term capital for many reasons:

- When neither common stock nor long-term debt can be issued on reasonable terms.
- During adverse business conditions, a firm can issue preferred stock with warrants when the common stock is depressed in order to bolster the equity component of a firm's capital structure.
- A firm can issue convertible preferred stock in connection with mergers and acquisitions (M&A).
- A firm can issue a floating rate preferred stock to stabilize the market price.

Preferred stock is the stock whose dividend rate fluctuates with changes in the general level of interest rates. Thus, this stock is good for liquidity portfolios (e.g., marketable securities). Preferred stock is a clear way to obtain new capital at a low cost due to its floating dividend rates, stable market price, and tax exemption for dividends received.

Under U.S. tax laws, if preferred stock with conversion privilege is exchanged for the acquired company's common stock, this constitutes a tax-free exchange of securities (i.e., no gain or loss is recognized for tax purposes). Also, if the buyout was for cash, the acquired company's stockholders would have to pay capital gain taxes.

Preferred stock is a hybrid stock, meaning that it is similar to bonds in some respects and similar to common stock in others. Therefore, preferred stock can be classified as either bonds or common stock. (See Exhibit 4.17.)

EXHIBIT 4.17 Characteristics of Preferred Stock

Preferred Stocks as Bonds (Debt)	Preferred Stocks as Common Stocks (Equity)
Like bonds, preferred stock has a par value and a call provision.	Like most common stock, preferred stock has a par value.
Preferred dividends are fixed similar to interest payments on bonds and must be paid before common stock dividends can be paid.	Like common stock, preferred stocks have no maturity date and are not callable. Hence they are perpetuity stocks.
During financial difficulty, preferred dividends can be omitted without leading the firm to bankruptcy.	Unlike common stock, most preferred stock requires dividend payments. This reduces earnings available for common stock shareholders. Preferred stock dividends must be paid before common stock dividends can be paid.
Financial analysts sometimes treat preferred stock as debt.	
Like debt, preferred stocks have coverage requirements for the amount of preferred stock and the level of retained earnings.	Like common stock, preferred stock carries a voting right to vote for director.
Preferred stock may be redeemed at a given time, at the option of the holder, or at a time not controlled by the issuer—called transient preferreds.	Unlike common stock, there is no share in control of the firm.
	Like common stock dividends, preferred dividends can be omitted without bankrupting the firm.
	Financial analysts sometimes treat preferred stock as common stock.

Preferred stock is usually reported in the equity section of the balance sheet under "preferred stock" or "preferred equity." Accountants and financial analysts treat the preferred stock differently. Accountants treat preferred stock as equity, and financial analysts treat it as equity or debt, depending on who benefits from the analysis being made. Preferred stock has an advantage in that it has a higher priority claim than common stock. (See Exhibit 4.18.)

EXHIBIT 4.18 Features of Preferred Stock

Features of preferred stock
— Has priority over common stock in the assets and earnings
— Can be convertible into common stock
— May be participating
— Cumulative preferred dividends must be paid before common dividends are paid
— Can be treated as a debt due to redeemable feature
— Requires reporting to SEC about redeemable preferred and nonredeemable preferred

KEY CONCEPTS TO REMEMBER: Preferred Stock from Whose Viewpoint?

- From the point of view of common stockholders, preferred stock is similar to debt due to the fixed dividend payment and reduced earnings for common stock.

- From the point of view of debt holders, preferred stock is similar to common equity due to the high priority of the debt holder's claim on assets when the firm is liquidated.

- From the point of view of management, preferred stock is safer to use than debt since it will not force the company to bankruptcy for lack of dividend payment. Loan defaults would force the company to bankruptcy.

Exhibit 4.19 shows the relative priorities over assets when the firm is in the liquidation stage.

EXHIBIT 4.19 Relative Priorities over Assets

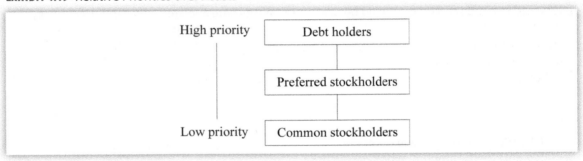

Major Provisions of Preferred Stocks. Major provisions of preferred stocks are listed next.

- Priority to assets and earnings
- Par value
- Cumulative dividends
- Convertibility into common stock
- Voting rights
- Participation in sharing the firm's earnings
- Sinking fund requirements
- Maturity date
- Call provisions

Some of these provisions are explained next.

- **Cumulative dividends.** All preferred dividends in arrears must be paid before common dividends can be paid. This is a protection feature for preferred stock to receive a preferred position and to avoid paying huge common stock dividends at the expense of paying stipulated annual dividend to the preferred stockholders.

- **Sinking fund requirements.** Most newly issued preferred stocks have sinking fund requirements that call for the purchase and retirement of a given percentage (e.g., 2–3%) of the preferred stock each year.

■ **Call provisions.** A call provision gives the issuing corporation the right to call in the preferred stock for redemption. A call premium may be attached where a company has to pay more than par value when it calls the preferred stock.

Pros and Cons of Preferred Stock from Issuer and Investor Viewpoints. From an issuer's viewpoint, the *advantages* of financing with preferred stock are: fixed financial cost, no danger of bankruptcy if earnings are too low to meet fixed charges, and avoidance of sharing control of the firm with new investors.

From an issuer's viewpoint, the *disadvantage* of financing with preferred stock is a higher after-tax cost of capital than debt due to nondeductibility of preferred dividends. The lower a company's tax bracket, the more likely it is to issue preferred stock.

From an investor's viewpoint, the *advantages* of financing with preferred stock are: steadier and more assured income than common stock, preference over common stock in the case of liquidation, and tax exemption for preferred dividends received.

From an investor's viewpoint, the *disadvantages* of financing with preferred stock are: no legally enforceable right to dividends, even if a company earns a profit; and for individual investors, after-tax bond yields could be higher than those on preferred stock, even though the preferred stock is riskier.

(f) Financial Instruments

Financial instruments (currency and credit derivatives) are used by large and small businesses in every industry to hedge against financial risk. One means to hedge currency exposure and risk is through the currency market, which includes forward contracts, futures contracts, currency options, currency swaps, and credit derivatives. This section also discusses hidden financial reporting risks and financial engineering topics.

(i) Forward Contracts

In the forward exchange market, one buys a forward contract for the exchange of one currency for another at a specific future date and at a specific exchange ratio. This differs from the spot market, where currencies are traded for immediate delivery. A **forward contract** provides assurance of being able to convert into a desired currency at a price set in advance. A foreign currency sells at a forward discount if its forward price is less than its spot price. If the forward price exceeds the spot price, it is said to sell at a forward premium. Forward contracts provide a two-sided hedge against currency movements. Forward contracts are settled only at expiration, and they can be issued at any size.

(ii) Futures Contracts

A **futures contract** is a standardized agreement that calls for delivery of a currency at some specified future date. These contracts are formed with a clearinghouse, not directly between the two parties. Futures contracts provide a two-sided hedge against currency movements.

Each day, the futures contract is marked to market, meaning it is valued at the closing price. Price movements affect buyers and sellers in opposite ways. Every day there is a winner and a loser, depending on the direction of price movement. Losers must come up with more margin (a small deposit), while winners can draw off excess margin. Future contracts come only in multiples of standard-size contracts.

(iii) Currency Options

An **option** is a contract that gives its holder the right to buy or sell an asset at some predetermined price within a specified period of time. Pure options (financial options) are created by outsiders (investment banking firms) rather than by a firm itself; they are bought and sold by investors or speculators. The leverage involved makes it possible for speculators to make more money with just a few dollars. Also, investors with sizable portfolios can sell options against their stocks and earn the value of the options (minus brokerage commissions) even if the stocks' prices remain constant. Option contracts enable the hedging of one-sided risk. Only adverse currency movements are hedged, either with a call option to buy the foreign currency or with a put option to sell it.

Both the value of the underlying stock and the striking price of the option are very important in determining whether an option is in the money or out of the money. If an option is out of the money on its expiration date, it is worthless. Therefore, the stock price and the striking price are important for determining the market value of an option. In fact, options are called derivative securities because their values are dependent on, or derived from, the value of the underlying asset and the striking price. In addition to the stock's market price and the striking price, the value of an option also depends on the option's time to maturity, the level of strike price, the risk-free rate, and the variability of the underlying stock's price. The higher the strike price, the lower the call option price. The higher the stock's market price in relation to the strike price, the higher will be the call option price. The longer the option period, the higher the option price and the larger its premium. The exercise value of an option is the maximum of the current price of the stock minus the strike price. The price of an option is the cost of stock minus the PV of portfolio. The Black-Scholes model is used to estimate the value of a call option.

Warrants are options issued by a company that give the holder the right to buy a stated number of shares of the company's stock at a specified price. Warrants are distributed along with debt, and they are used to induce investors to buy a firm's long-term debt at a lower interest rate than otherwise would be required.

Real options are used for investment in real assets. Their value is determined as follows:

$$\text{Project discounted cash flow value} = (\text{Cash flows}) / (1 + \text{Risk-free cash flow})$$

(iv) Currency Swaps

A **swap** exchanges a floating rate obligation for a fixed rate one, or vice versa. There are two types of swaps: currency and interest rate swaps. With the currency swaps, two parties exchange interest obligations on debt denominated in different currencies. At maturity, the principal amounts are exchanged, usually at a rate of exchange agreed on in advance. With an interest rate swap, interest-payment obligations are exchanged between two parties, but they are denominated in the same currency. There is not an actual exchange of principal. If one party defaults, there is no loss of principal per se. However, there is the opportunity cost associated with currency movements after the swap's initiation. These movements affect both interest and principal payments. In this respect, currency swaps are riskier than interest rate swaps, where the exposure is only to interest. Currency swaps are combined with interest rate swaps; there is an exchange of fixed rate for floating rate payments where the two payments are in different currencies. Financing hedges provide a means to hedge on a longer-term basis, as do currency swaps.

The swap can be longer term in nature (15 years or more) than either forward or futures contracts (five years). Swaps are like a series of forward contracts corresponding to the future settlement dates at which difference checks are paid. However, a comparable forward market does not exist, nor do lengthy futures or options contracts.

The most common swap is the floating/fixed rate exchange. The exchange itself is on a net settlement basis. That is, the party that owes more interest than it receives in the swap pays the difference. A basis swap is another popular swap where two floating rate obligations are exchanged.

Various options exist for swap transactions, which are known as swaptions. One is to enter a swap at a future date. The terms of the swap are set at the time of the option, and they give the holder the right, but not the obligation, to take a swap position.

(v) Credit Derivatives

The scope of credit derivatives includes total return swaps, credit swaps, and other credit derivatives.

(A) Total Return Swaps

Credit derivatives unbundle default risk from the other features of a loan. The original lender no longer needs to bear the risk; it can be transferred to others for a price. The party who wishes to transfer is known as the protection buyer. The protection seller assumes the credit risk and receives a premium for providing this insurance. The premium is based on the probability and likely severity of default.

The protection buyer is assumed to hold a risky debt instrument and agrees to pay out its total return to the protection seller. This return consists of the stream of interest payments together with the change in the instrument's market value. The protection seller agrees to pay some reference rate and perhaps a negative or positive spread from this rate.

(B) Credit Swaps

A credit swap, also known as a default swap, is similar in concept to the total return swap but different in the detail. The protection buyer pays a specific premium to the protection seller, insurance against a risky debt instrument deteriorating in quality. The annuity premium is paid each period until the earlier of the maturity of the credit swap agreement or a specific credit event occurring, usually default. If the credit event occurs, the protection seller pays the protection buyer a contingent amount. This often takes the form of physical settlement, where the protection buyer "puts" the defaulted obligation to the protection seller at its face value. The economic cash flow is the difference between the face value of the instrument and its market value. Thus, the protection buyer receives payment only when a specific credit event occurs; otherwise, the cash flow from the protection seller is zero. The periodic premium paid is called the credit swap spread. This cost of protection depends on the credit rating of the company, risk mitigation, and likely recovery should default occur.

(C) Other Credit Derivatives

Other credit derivatives include spread-adjusted notes, credit options, and credit-sensitive notes.

Spread-adjusted notes involve resets based on the spread of a particular grade of security over Treasury securities. An index is specified, and quarterly and semiannual resets occur, where one counterparty must pay the other depending on whether the quality yield spread widens or narrows. Usually the spread is collared with a floor and cap.

Credit options involve puts and calls based on a basket of corporate fixed income securities. The strike price often is a specified amount over Treasury securities.

With **credit-sensitive notes**, the coupon rate changes with the credit rating of the company involved. If the company is downgraded, the investor receives more interest income; if the company is upgraded, the investor receives less interest income.

DEFINITIONS OF KEY TERMS: CURRENCY AND CREDIT DERIVATIVES

Abandonment options—Options that can be structured so that they provide the option to reduce capacity or temporarily suspend operations.

Basis risk—The difference between two risks or prices.

Call option—An option to buy (call) a share of stock at a certain price within a specific period.

Call swaption—Involves paying floating rate and receiving fixed rate in the swap.

Cap—A put option on a fixed income security's value.

Collar— A combination of a cap and a floor, with variation only in the midrange.

Flexibility options—Permit the firm to alter operations depending on how conditions change during the life of the project.

Floor—A call option.

Growth option—Allows a company to increase its capacity if market conditions are better than expected. Variations of growth options include increasing capacity of an existing product line, expanding into new geographic markets, and adding new products.

Interest rate risk—The risk that interest rates will change in an unfavorable direction.

In-the-money option—Occurs when it is beneficial financially for the option holder to exercise the option. A gain will be realized if the option is exercised.

Liquidity risk—Refers to the ability to find a counterparty to enter or terminate a transaction.

Managerial (strategic) options—Give managers a chance to influence project outcomes. These options are used with large and strategic projects.

Market risk—The risk that the value of the agreement will change.

Out-of-the-money option—Occurs when it is not beneficial financially for the option holder to exercise the option. A loss would be incurred if the option is exercised.

Protection buyer—Pays the protection seller to assume the credit risk.

Put option—The option to sell a specified number of shares of stock at a prespecified price during a particular period.

Put swaption—Involves paying a fixed rate and receiving a floating rate in the swap.

Striking price or exercise price—The price that must be paid (buying or selling) for a share of common stock when an option is exercised.

(vi) Hidden Financial Reporting Risks

Off–balance sheet accounting practices include hiding debt with the equity method, with lease accounting, with pension accounting, and with special-purpose entities. In all these cases, debt is underreported, which creates a financial reporting risk. Investors and creditors charge a premium for the financial reporting risk. Consequently, the cost of capital goes up and stock prices and bond prices go down.

The equity method hides liabilities because it nets the assets and liabilities of the investee. Since assets are greater than liabilities, this net amount goes on the left-hand side of the balance sheet. This type of accounting practice hides all of the investee's debts.

Use of operating lease accounting "gains" managers an understatement of their firm's financial structure by 10 to 15 percentage points. Footnotes to financial statements can help investors, creditors, and analysts to unravel the truth.

Huge amounts of money are involved in pension accounting. Pension expenses include the service cost plus the interest on the projected benefit obligation minus the expected return on plan assets plus the amortization of various unrecognized items, such as the unrecognized prior service cost. The only item found on the balance sheet is the prepaid pension asset or the accrual pension cost, which in turn equals the pension assets minus the projected benefit obligation minus various unrecognized items. The netting of the projected benefit obligations and the pension assets is incorrect; consequently, investors, creditors, and analysts must "un-net" them to gain a better understanding of the truth. Another area of concern is the assumptions about interest rates and the need to assess their appropriateness.

Special-purpose entity debt includes securitizations and synthetic leases. Securitizations take a pool of homogeneous assets and turn them into securities. The idea is to borrow money from investors, who in turn are repaid by the cash generated by the asset pool. This process includes mortgages, credit card receivables, transportation equipment, energy contracts, water utilities, and trade A/R. Securitizations are big business and represent a financial risk since these amounts are not shown on the balance sheet. Synthetic leases constitute a technique by which firms can assert that they have capital leases for tax purposes but operating leases for financial reporting purposes. They form a way for companies to decrease income taxes without admitting any debt on their balance sheets.

(vii) Financial Engineering

The scope of financial engineering involves creating new financial instruments (derivative securities) or combining existing derivatives to accomplish specific hedging goals (e.g., reduce financial risk). A derivative security is a financial asset that represents a claim to another financial asset (e.g., a stock option that gives the owner the right to buy or sell stock). Financial risk may result from changes in domestic and international interest rates, foreign exchange rates, and commodity prices.

Tools for managing financial risk include hedging with forwards, futures, currency options, and currency swap contracts. These tools allow a firm to reduce or even eliminate its exposure to financial risks. Hedging avoids a firm's expensive and troublesome disruptions that result from short-run and temporary price fluctuations. It gives a firm the ability to react and adapt to changing financial market conditions.

Financial engineering can also be applied to insurance and reinsurance areas using captive insurance methods and alternate risk transfer methods as part of a company's risk management and risk mitigation strategy.

(g) Cash Management

(i) Cash Controls

The standard medium of exchange is cash, which provides the basis for measuring and accounting for all other items. To be presented as cash on the balance sheet, cash must be available to meet current obligations. Cash includes such items as coins, currency, checks, bank drafts, checks from customers, and money orders. Cash in savings accounts and cash in CDs maturing within one year can be included as current assets, preferably under the caption of short-term investments, but not as cash. Petty cash and other imprest cash accounts can be included in other cash accounts.

Current assets are those assets expected to be converted into cash, sold, or consumed within one year or within the operating cycle, whichever is longer. Current assets are properly presented in the balance sheet in the order of their liquidity. Some of the more common current assets are cash, marketable securities, A/R, inventories, and prepaid items.

(A) Cash Items Excluded

The portion of an entity's cash account that is a compensating balance must be segregated and shown as a noncurrent asset if the related borrowings are noncurrent liabilities. If the borrowings are current liabilities, it is acceptable to show the compensating balance as a separately captioned current asset.

RULES FOR COMPENSATED BALANCES

- If related borrowings are noncurrent liabilities, then show the compensated balance as a noncurrent asset.
- If related borrowings are current liabilities, then show the compensated balance as a current asset.

Certain cash items are not presented in the general cash section of the balance sheet. They include compensating balances, other restricted cash, and exclusions from cash.

Compensating Balances. The SEC defines compensating balances as "that portion of any demand deposit (or any time deposit or certificate of deposit) maintained by a corporation which constitutes support for existing borrowing arrangements of the corporation with a lending institution. Such arrangements would include both outstanding borrowing and the assurance of future credit availability."

The classification of compensating balances on the balance sheet depends on whether the compensation relates to short-term or long-term borrowing. If held for short-term borrowing, it should be presented separately in current assets. If held for long-term borrowing, it should be classified as a noncurrent asset under investments or other assets.

Where compensating balance arrangements exist but do not legally restrict the use of cash, the arrangements and amounts should be disclosed in the footnotes of the financial statements.

Other Restricted Cash. Cash balances can be restricted for special purposes, such as dividend payments, acquisition of fixed assets, retirement of debt, plant expansion, or deposits made in connection with contracts or bids. Since these cash balances are not immediately available for just any use, they should be presented separately in the balance sheet. Classification as current or noncurrent is dependent on the date of availability or disbursement.

Exclusions from Cash. Items that should not be presented as cash are postage stamps, postdated checks, travel advances, IOUs, securities, investments in federal funds, and checks deposited and returned because of insufficient funds. CDs should be reflected in the temporary investment account, since they are not available for use until the maturity date.

As mentioned earlier, cash includes coins and currency on hand and demand deposits available without restrictions. Cash in a demand deposit account that is being held for the retirement of long-term debts not maturing currently should not be included in the current assets. Instead, it should be shown as a noncurrent investment. The key criterion is management's intention that the cash be available for current purposes. Cash equivalents include other forms of near cash as well as demand deposits and liquid, short-term securities. The key point is that the cash equivalents must be available on demand similar to cash.

SUGGESTED DISCLOSURES FOR CASH

- Amount and nature of restricted cash
- Amount and nature of compensating balances
- Overdrafts presented as current liabilities

(B) Bank Reconciliation

Every organization should prepare a bank reconciliation schedule periodically (e.g., monthly) to reconcile the organization's cash record with the bank's record of the organization's cash. It is unusual for these two sets of records to be the same due to errors and timing differences, such as

- Bank or depositor (customer) errors
- Bank credits
- Bank charges
- Deposits in transit
- Outstanding checks

A widely used method reconciles both the bank balance and the book balance to a correct cash balance. This is shown in Exhibit 4.20.

EXHIBIT 4.20 Reconciliation of Bank Balance with Book Balance

Balance per bank statement	
Add:	Deposits in transit
	Undeposited cash receipts
	Bank errors (understating the bank balance)
Deduct:	Outstanding checks
	Bank errors (overstating the bank balance)
Correct cash balance (item 1)	
Balance per depositors' books	
Add:	Bank credits and collections not yet recorded in the books
	Book errors (understating the book balance)
Deduct:	Bank charges not yet recorded in the books
	Book errors (overstating the book balance)
Correct cash balance (item 2)	

The goal is to make item 1 and item 2 equal.

Cash requires a good system of internal control, since it is so liquid and easy to conceal and transport. Segregation of duties is an important part of the system of internal control for cash. No one person should both record a transaction and have custody of the asset. Without proper segregation, it is easier for an employee to engage in lapping. **Lapping** is a type of fraud in which an employee misappropriates receipts from customers and covers the shortages in these customers' accounts with receipts from subsequent customers. Therefore, the shortage is never eliminated but rather is transferred to other accounts. Lapping schemes do not require employees to divert funds for personal use. The funds can be diverted for other business expenses.

Kiting is a scheme in which a depositor with accounts in two or more banks takes advantage of the time required for checks to clear in order to obtain unauthorized credit. The scheme would not exist if depositors were not allowed to draw against uncollected funds. The use of uncollected funds does not always indicate a kite; such use can be authorized by an officer of the bank. Kiting schemes can be as simple as cashing checks a few days before payday, then depositing the funds to cover checks previously written. Or they can be as complex as a systematic buildup of uncollected deposits, pyramiding for the "big hit." Kiting can be eliminated or reduced through electronic funds transfer (EFT) systems. It can be detected when reviewing accounts to determine if a customer or employee is drawing a check against an account in which he or she has deposited another check that has not yet cleared.

Float is an amount of money represented by items (both check and noncheck) outstanding and in the process of collection. The amount of float incurred is determined by two factors: the dollar volume of checks cleared and the speed with which the checks are cleared. The relationship between float and these two factors can be expressed as

$$\text{Float} = \text{Dollar volume} \times \text{Collection speed}$$

The cost of float pertains to the potential for earning income from nonearning assets, as represented by items in the process of collection. This cost of float is an opportunity cost—the firm could have fully invested and earned income had the funds been available for investment and not incurred float.

In a financial futures **hedging** transaction, a firm takes a futures position that is opposite to its existing economic or, to use the more common name, "cash" position. By taking the opposite position in the financial futures market, the firm can protect itself against adverse interest rate fluctuations by locking in a given yield or interest rate.

(ii) Controls over Cash

Cash is a precious resource in any organization. Cash is required to pay employee wages and salaries, buy raw materials and parts to produce finished goods, pay off debt, and pay dividends, among other things. Cash is received from customers for the sale of goods and the rendering of services. Customer payments come into the organization in various forms, such as checks, bank drafts, wire transfers, money orders, charge cards, and lockbox systems. The cash manager's primary job is to ensure that all customer payments funnel into the company's checking accounts as fast as possible with greater accuracy. Payments received at lockboxes located at regional banks flow into cash concentration accounts, preferably on the same day of deposit.

The cash manager should focus on reducing the elapsed time from customer payment date to the day funds are available for use in the company's bank account. This elapsed time is called the float.

A major objective of the cash manager is to accelerate the cash inflow and slow the cash outflow without damaging the company's reputation in the industry. To do this, the cash manager needs to find ways to accelerate cash flows into the company, which, in turn, reduce investment in working capital. Similarly, the cash manager needs to find ways to slow the outflow of cash by increasing the time for payments to clear the bank. Another major objective is not to allow funds to sit idle without earning interest.

The cash manager needs to focus on seven major areas for effective cash management. (See Exhibit 4.21.)

EXHIBIT 4.21 Cash Control Items

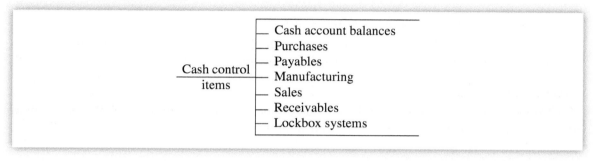

(A) Cash Account Balances

The following actions are advised to strengthen controls in cash accounts:

- Take an inventory of cash accounts open. Since each account maintains cash balances, the potential exists to improve control over cash.

- Perform account reconciliations periodically, and ensure that the person doing the reconciliations has no cash management duties.

- Review the account of compensating balances held at the banks. Focus on eliminating or reducing the amount of compensating balances.

- Review cash account balances to see if they are kept too high for fear of being overdrawn. Try to bring these balances down to the bare minimum without being overdrawn. Doing this will improve the idle cash situation.

- Review the fees charged by the bank for the number of accounts open, and understand the reasons for the service fees charged.

CASH CONTROLS

The more accounts there are, the fewer the controls are over cash balances. Consequently, the higher the likelihood that significant idle funds are sitting in those accounts.

(B) Purchases

The method of payment and the payment date can impact the firm's cash situation. An early payment date demanded by a vendor could add to the interest expense. Payment discounts should be taken by making payment within a specified time. The cash manager should review any purchase contracts containing clauses with unusual late fees and interest rates on unpaid balances.

(C) Payables

The following actions are advised to strengthen controls in payables:

- Establish policies concerning the average payment period. The payment period is calculated by dividing the A/P balance by the average daily credit purchases.

- Use remote disbursement banks, preferably with zero balance.

- Perform periodic aging of the A/P.

(D) Manufacturing

The following actions are advised to strengthen controls in manufacturing:

- Understand that labor union contract negotiations will affect cash balances.

- Understand that the sale of obsolete or overstocked inventory will suddenly increase the inflow of cash that must be put to work (i.e., invested).

(E) Sales

Credit policies should be balanced. Overly lenient credit policies will cause a rise in payment delinquencies and bad debt, which will create a funding gap in the cash position.

- If bad debts are increasing due to lenient credit policies, see if the sales force commission payment policy can be changed from a gross sales basis to a collected balances basis.

- If credit policies are overly stringent, the firm will lose its customers to competition.

(F) Receivables

The following actions are advised to strengthen controls in receivables:

- Review billing and collection policies and procedures.

- Minimize the elapsed time between sale and release of invoice to the customer.

- Reduce the long time between invoice preparation and entry of the invoice into the receivables system.

- Identify receivable backlogs, and determine their impact on cash position.

- Minimize the time required to record the payment and to remove it from the receivable subledger. If the time lag is too long, collection resources will be wasted pursuing accounts that have already paid.

- Perform aging of receivables.

- Establish procedures related to the types of collection efforts, including customer statements, dunning letters, phone calls by trained in-house staff, referral to a collection agency, and so forth.

- Establish policies toward selling the receivables or clarify the policies toward using the receivables as collateral for financing purposes.

(G) Lockbox Systems

Most banks offer both retail and wholesale lockbox services. Wholesale lockboxes collect payments from other companies; here the volume of transactions is small and the dollar amount of each transaction is large. Retail lockboxes receive payments from individual customers; here the volume of transactions is large and the dollar amount of each transaction is small.

SELECTION CRITERIA FOR LOCKBOX BANKS

If the company has customers scattered around the country and payments are all sent to a single centralized location, use of a lockbox is advisable. Banks servicing the lockboxes are chosen for their proximity to the lockbox, their processing capability, their ability to transfer funds quickly to the cash concentration system, and geographic concentration of customers.

With lockbox systems, most of the float has been squeezed from the cash management systems of both vendor and customer. These cash acceleration techniques have been referred to as a zero-sum game with no advantage for either side of the transaction (i.e., vendor and customer). Lockbox systems help sellers stay even with their customers in the race to accelerate cash inflow and delay its outflow. Elimination of float accelerates cash inflow.

Two types of lockbox systems are in use: manual and electronic. The **manual lockbox** system collects and processes the checks and deposits them into the customer's account. Then the bank sends the money to the cash concentration account and sends the payment information to the customer via a magnetic tape or telecommunication transmission for entry into the A/R system. The funds are transferred from the lockbox account to the cash concentration account through the use of depository transfer checks, wire transfers, or ETFs through an automated clearinghouse (ACH).

Electronic lockboxes eliminate checks and automate the transfer payment data from company to company as a wholesale transaction. When a customer receives a vendor's invoice, the customer calls the third-party computer to make payment. The third party can be a bank or a service bureau, which acts as a payment collector. After the daily cutoff, the payment collector transmits the daily payment receipts file to the vendor's computer for automatic processing by the vendor's A/R system.

Some *advantages* of an electronic lockbox system are listed next.

- Cash inflow accelerates because there is no float.
- Misapplied and partial payments do not exist since the payment collector does not accept partial payment, and the customer account is verified prior to payment entry applied properly.
- Information about nonsufficient funds comes back faster than for returned checks.
- Credit controls can be tightened for high-risk or slow-paying customers.
- The days of sales outstanding ratio, which measures the velocity of collections, is reduced.

Disadvantages of an electronic lockbox system are the high initial system design cost and cost per transaction and service fees by the third-party payment collector.

(iii) Electronic Techniques to Control Cash

In addition to the electronic lockboxes just discussed, two other electronic techniques to control cash need to be mentioned. These include EFT and electronic data interchange (EDI) systems.

(A) Electronic Funds Transfer

EFT systems allow organizations to pay their bills without actually writing checks. EFT eliminates bank float as "good" funds move quickly from customer accounts to vendor accounts at their respective banks. EFT accelerates cash inflow for the company receiving payment.

The EFT system removes several days from the entire payment cycle of cutting a paper check, mailing it, depositing it, clearing it through the bank, recording its payment in the customer's A/P system, and recording the cash receipts in the vendor's A/R system. The only cycle time is the time for physically receiving the goods or services through truck, car, by rail, or other.

The ACH clears debits and credits created by ETFs. The ACH clears all transactions each day by properly debiting and crediting them to the correct accounts. The ACH then routes these cleared transactions to the proper member banks.

(B) Electronic Data Interchange

The EDI system is another major step toward a payment acceleration scheme. EDI is used not only to place purchase orders with vendors for raw materials and finished goods but also to send invoices and receive payments. The EDI system automatically creates the invoice and sends it to the customer. After receiving the goods, the customer authorizes an electronic payment with virtually no float. EDI involves a third party as a middleman to transmit and receive electronic messages between vendors and customers.

The data transferred between vendor and customer contain this information:

- Dollar amount
- Invoice number
- Purchase order number
- Customer number
- Discounts taken
- Shipping instructions
- Product delivery dates
- Payment due dates

Electronic payments are posted automatically to the vendor's A/R system. A major advantage of EDI is that the posting is fast, not subject to human errors, and cash inflows are accelerated. A major drawback of the EDI system is the need to have a standardized format of data transmitted between vendors and customers. This could limit the flexibility of doing business with many parties.

(iv) Management of Current Assets

Effective cash management requires a working capital policy, which refers to the firm's policies regarding the desired level for each category of current assets and how current assets will be financed. The components of current assets in order of liquidity are shown in Exhibit 4.22.

EXHIBIT 4.22 Components of Current Assets

Cash (most liquid)
Marketable securities
Accounts receivable
Prepaid expenses
Inventories (least liquid)

Current assets fluctuate with sales and represent a large portion (usually greater than 40%) of total assets. Working capital management is important for large and small firms alike.

DEFINITIONS OF KEY TERMS: WORKING CAPITAL

Net working capital—Current assets minus current liabilities

Working capital or **gross working capital**—Current assets

Working capital management—Involves the administration of current assets and current liabilities

For financing current assets, most small firms rely on trade credit and short-term bank loans, both of which affect working capital by increasing current liabilities. A/P represents "free" trade credit when discounts are taken. This is similar to an interest-free loan. However, current liabilities are used to finance current assets and in part represent current maturities of long-term debt. Large firms usually rely on long-term capital markets, such as stocks. The components of current liabilities are shown in Exhibit 4.23 with their associated costs.

EXHIBIT 4.23 Components of Current Liabilities

Accounts payable (free trade credit)
Accrued wages
Accrued taxes
Notes payable (not free)
Current maturities of long-term debt

The relationship between sales and the need to invest in current assets is direct. As sales increase, A/R increases, inventory will increase, and cash needs increase. Any increase in an account on the left-hand side of the balance sheet must be matched by an increase on the right-hand side. It involves matching maturities of assets and liabilities. That is, current assets are financed with current liabilities, and fixed assets are financed with long-term debt or stock. This is done to reduce interest rate risk.

EXAMPLE COMPUTATION OF CHANGES IN CASH AND NET WORKING CAPITAL

Example 1

Partial balance sheet information for a company for the years ending December 31, 20X1 and 20X2 is shown next.

(Continued)

EXAMPLE COMPUTATION OF CHANGES IN CASH AND NET WORKING CAPITAL (*Continued*)

	December 31	
	20X1	**20X2**
Current assets (except for cash):		
Accounts receivable	$20,000	$ 5,000
Inventories	50,000	14,000
Prepaid expenses	3,000	6,000
Current liabilities:		
Accounts payable	32,000	16,000
Property tax payable	4,000	3,000

Working capital (WC) is assumed to increase in 20X2 by $12,000.

Question: What is the change in cash in 20X2?

Answer: The change is −$19,000, as shown next, where CA refers to capital assets, CL refers to capital liabilities and ▲ refers to change

$$\text{▲Cash} = \text{▲WC} - \text{▲Noncash CA} + \text{▲CL}$$

$$= 12,000 - (15,000 + 36,000 - 3,000)$$

$$+ (16,000 + 1,000)$$

$$= -19,000$$

Example 2

The next amounts pertain to the ABC Corporation at December 31, 20X2.

Total current assets	$ 300,000
Total fixed assets	2,200,000
Total assets	2,500,000
Total current liabilities	120,000
Total liabilities	1,600,000
Total paid-in capital	400,000
Total stockholders' equity	900,000

Question: What is the ABC's net working capital at December 31, 20X2?

Answer: It is $180,000. Net working capital is computed by subtracting total current liabilities ($120,000) from total current assets ($300,000), which in this case yields an answer of $180,000.

(A) Cash Conversion Cycle Model

The cash conversion model defines the length of time from the payment for the purchase of raw materials to the collection of A/R generated by the sale of the final product. It is an important model since it focuses on the conversion of materials and labor to cash. The model is represented in Exhibit 4.24.

EXHIBIT 4.24 Cash Conversion Model

| Cash conversion cycle | = | Inventory conversion period | + | Receivables conversion period | − | Payables deferral period |

Where:

Inventory conversion period = Length of time required to convert raw materials into finished goods and then to sell these goods

Receivables conversion period = Length of time required to convert the firm's receivables into cash

Payables deferral period = Average length of time between the purchase of raw material and labor and the payment of cash for them

The cash conversion cycle begins the day a bill for labor and/or supplies is paid and runs to the day receivables are collected. The cycle measures the length of time the firm has funds tied up in working capital. The shorter the cash conversion cycle, the smaller the need for external financing and thus the lower the cost of such financing. This would result in increase in profits.

EXAMPLE CALCULATION OF CASH CONVERSION CYCLE

It takes a firm 70 days from the purchase of raw materials to the sale of finished goods, 50 days after a sale to convert a receivable into cash, and 30 days to pay for labor and materials. The firm's cash conversion cycle is 90 days, as shown next.

70 days + 50 days − 30 days = 90 days or

(Delay in receipt of cash) − (Payment delay) = Net delay

The firm needs to finance the costs of processing for a 90-day period. Its goals should be to shorten its cash conversion cycle without jeopardizing business operations (i.e., without increasing costs or decreasing sales).

(B) Approaches to Shorten the Cash Conversion Cycle
The next list presents ways to shorten the cash conversion cycle.

- Reduce the inventory conversion period by processing and selling goods more quickly.
- Reduce the receivables conversion period or days sales outstanding by speeding up collections.
- Lengthen the payables deferral period by slowing down payments.

(C) Working Capital Asset Investment Policies
Appropriate working capital policies are needed to support various levels of sales. Three such policies include relaxed, moderate, and restricted. (See Exhibit 4.25.)

EXHIBIT 4.25 Working Capital Asset Policies

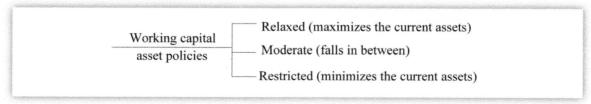

Working capital asset policies
- Relaxed (maximizes the current assets)
- Moderate (falls in between)
- Restricted (minimizes the current assets)

- **Relaxed (liberal) working capital policy.** Sales are stimulated by the use of a credit policy that provides liberal financing to customers, which results in a high level of A/R. This policy maximizes current assets. A/R will increase as credit sales increase for a relaxed policy; the opposite is true for the restricted policy.

- **Moderate working capital policy.** This policy falls between the liberal and tight working capital policies.

- **Restricted (tight) working capital policy.** This policy minimizes current assets. A tight policy lowers the receivables for any given level of sales or even the risk of a decline in sales. This policy provides the highest expected ROI and entails the greatest risk. The firm would hold minimal levels of safety stocks for cash and inventories.

CERTAINTY VERSUS UNCERTAINTY OF BUSINESS CONDITIONS

- Under conditions of **certainty**, the firm knows the sales, costs, order lead times, and collection periods. All firms would hold the same level of current assets. Any larger amounts would increase the need for external funding without a corresponding increase in profits. Any decrease in amounts would involve late payments to suppliers, lost sales, and production inefficiencies because of inventory shortages.

- Under conditions of **uncertainty**, the firm does not know the sales, costs, order lead times, and collection periods. The firm requires some minimum amount of cash and inventories based on expected payments, sales, safety stocks, and order lead times. Safety stocks help deal with deviations of sales from expected values.

(D) Working Capital Financing Policies

A good working capital financing policy is needed to handle seasonal or cyclical business fluctuations and a strong or weak economy. When the economy is strong, working capital is built up and inventories and receivables go up. When the economy is weak, working capital goes down along with inventories and receivables. Current assets are divided into permanent and temporary, and the manner in which these assets are financed constitutes the firm's working capital financing policy.

A firm's working capital asset policy, including its cash conversion cycle, is always established in conjunction with the firm's working capital financing policy. Three financing policies are available to manage working capital: maturity matching, an aggressive approach, and a conservative approach.

EXAMPLE CALCULATION OF TOTAL ASSETS

	January 1 (million)	June 30 (million)
Cash and marketable securities	4	4
Accounts receivable	6	8
Inventories	15	20
Current assets	25 (1)	32 (2)
Fixed assets	40	40
Total assets	65	72

1. Permanent current assets that are still on hand at the trough of a firm's cycles

2. Temporary assets that fluctuate with seasonal or cyclical sales variation that fluctuates from zero to a maximum of $7 million (i.e., $32 - 25 = 7$)

The maturity matching, or self-liquidating, approach requires that asset maturities are matched with liability maturities. This means permanent assets are financed with long-term capital to reduce risk. Each loan would be paid off with cash flows generated by assets financed by the loan, so loans would be self-liquidating. Uncertainty about the lives of assets prevents exact matching in an *ex post* sense.

MATURITY MATCHING—ASSETS VERSUS DEBT

- If long-term assets are financed with short-term debt, there might be a problem in making the required loan payments if cash inflows are not sufficient. The loan may not be renewed.

- If long-term assets are financed with long-term debt, the required loan payments would have been matched with cash flows from profits and depreciation. No question of loan renewals will come up.

Two approaches are used in maturity matching: the aggressive (nonconservative) approach and the conservative approach. Exhibit 4.26 presents characteristics of these two approaches.

EXHIBIT 4.26 Characteristics of Aggressive and Conservative Approaches to Maturity Matching

Aggressive Approach	Conservative Approach
Financing of part of permanent current assets is accomplished with short-term credit.	Financing of all permanent assets is accomplished with long-term capital.
Financing of all current assets and part of fixed assets is accomplished with short-term credit.	The firm uses a small amount of short-term credit to meet its peak requirements.
There is a trade-off between safety and profits since short-term debt is cheaper than long-term debt.	
The length of the cash conversion cycle is shorter since the firm holds a minimal level of cash, securities, inventories, and receivables. Inventories and receivables conversion periods would be shorter.	The length of the cash conversion cycle is longer because higher levels of inventories and receivables lengthen the inventory and receivables conversion periods.

(E) Advantages and Disadvantages of Short-Term Credit

Short-term credit is generally riskier and cheaper than using long-term credit. There is a trade-off between risk and profits in using short-term credit. Although short-term credit has some disadvantages, it also has some advantages such as easy and quick to finance.

The three financing policies discussed earlier differ in the relative amount of short-term debt financing each uses, as shown in Exhibit 4.27.

EXHIBIT 4.27 Debt Financing with Short-Term Credit

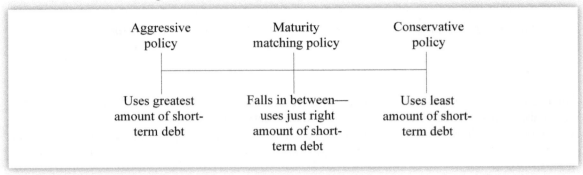

(F) Management of Cash

On one hand, adequate cash serves as protection against a weak economy and can be used to pay off debts and to acquire companies. On the other hand, too much cash makes a firm vulnerable to corporate raiding or takeovers.

$$\text{Cash} = \text{Currency} + \text{Bank demand deposits} + \text{Near-cash marketable securities}$$

$$\text{Near-cash marketable securities} = \text{U.S. Treasury bills} + \text{Bank CDs}$$

Effective cash management is important to all organizations, whether profit oriented or not. The scope of cash management encompasses cash gathering (collection) and disbursement techniques and investment of cash. Since cash is a "nonearning" asset until it is put to use, the goal of cash management is to reduce cash holdings to the minimum necessary to conduct normal business. See Exhibit 4.28 for advantages and disadvantages of short-term and long-term credit.

EXHIBIT 4.28 Advantages and Disadvantages of Short-Term and Long-Term Credit

Short-Term Credit	Long-Term Credit
Advantages	**Advantages**
A short-term loan can be obtained much more quickly than a long-term loan.	Interest costs are fixed and stable over time.
A short-term loan can accommodate seasonal or cyclical needs for funds.	Long-term debt is subject to less risk than short-term debt.
Short-term credit provides flexible repayment schedules.	Temporary changes in either the general level of interest rates or the firm's own financial position do not adversely affect long-term debt.
Short-term credit has less restrictive provisions.	Long-run performance can overcome short-run recession.
Interest rates are generally lower than on long-term debt due to upward sloping of the yield curve.	Lenders require thorough financial examination before granting a long-term loan, which takes time for approval.
Financing is less expensive than long-term debt.	

Short-Term Credit	Long-Term Credit
Disadvantages	**Disadvantages**
Net income and the rate of return on equity will be higher than on long-term debt due to lower interest rates for short-term debt.	Long-term loans require a detailed loan agreement.
	Flotation costs are higher.
Short-term debt is subject to more risk (interest-rate risk) than long-term debt due to fluctuating interest expense and the possibility of bankruptcy.	Prepayment penalties can be expensive.
	Long-term loans can contain provisions or covenants that may constrain the firm's future actions.
It runs the risk of having to refinance the short-term debt at a higher interest rate, which would lower the rate of return on equity.	Interest rates are higher than on short-term debt due to downward sloping of the yield curve.
There is the possibility of being unable to renew the debt when its loans mature, thus of facing maturity risk. Also, tight money supply, labor problems, extreme competition, low demand for products, and higher interest rates will make creditors raise interest rates.	

There are four reasons for holding cash by organizations, as shown in Exhibit 4.29.

EXHIBIT 4.29 Reasons for Holding Cash

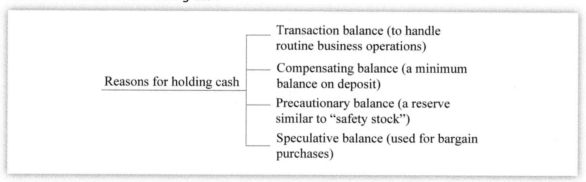

1. **Transaction balance.** Payments and collections are handled through the cash account. These routine transactions are necessary in business operations.

2. **Compensating balance.** A bank requires the customer to leave a minimum balance on deposit to help offset the costs of providing the banking services. The balance is compensation paid to banks for providing loans and services. Some loan agreements also require compensating balances.

3. **Precautionary balance.** Firms hold some cash in reserve to accommodate for random, unforeseen fluctuations in cash inflows and outflows. These are similar to the safety stocks used in inventories.

4. **Speculative balance.** Cash may be held to enable the firm to take advantage of any bargain purchases that might arise. Similar to precautionary balances, firms could rely on reserve borrowing capacity and on marketable securities rather than on cash for speculative purposes.

KEY CONCEPTS TO REMEMBER: Management of Cash

- The less predictable the firm's cash flows, the longer the need for a precautionary balance, and vice versa. The easier the access to borrowed funds on short notice, the lower the need to hold cash for precautionary purposes, and vice versa.

- Marketable securities can be an attractive alternative to holding cash for precautionary purposes since they can provide greater interest income than cash.

A total desired cash balance for a firm is not simply the sum of cash in transaction, compensating, precautionary, and speculative balances. This is because the same money often serves more than one purpose. For example, precautionary and speculative balances can also be used to satisfy compensating balance requirements. A firm needs to consider these four factors when establishing its target cash position.

(G) Advantages of Holding Adequate Cash and Near-Cash Assets

In addition to the motives for transaction, compensating, precautionary, and speculative balances, there exist other reasons for firms to hold adequate cash and near-cash assets. These *advantages* are listed next.

- Taking trade discounts. Suppliers offer customers trade discounts—discounts for prompt payment of bills. Cash is needed to take advantage of trade discounts. The cost of not taking trade discounts could be high.

- Keeping current ratios and acid-test ratios in line with those of other firms in the industry requires adequate holdings of cash. Higher ratios give a strong credit rating. A strong credit rating enables the firm to purchase goods and services from suppliers and provide favorable terms and to maintain an ample line of credit with the bank. A weak credit rating does the opposite.

- Holding an ample supply of cash could help a firm to acquire another firm, to handle contingencies such as labor strikes, to attack competitors' marketing campaigns, and to take advantage of special offers by suppliers.

(H) Cash Management Efficiency Techniques

A cash budget, showing cash inflows and outflows and cash status, is the starting point in the cash management system. The techniques used to increase the efficiency of management are listed next.

- Cash flow synchronization

- Use of float

- Speeding collections

- Slowing disbursements

- Transfer mechanisms

These techniques are shown in Exhibit 4.30.

EXHIBIT 4.30 Cash Management Efficiency Techniques

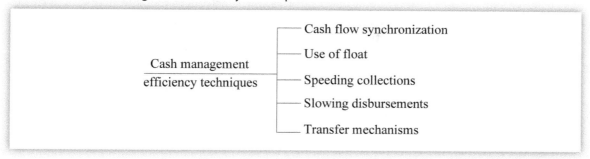

Cash Flow Synchronization. When cash inflows coincide with cash outflows, the need for transaction balances will be low. The benefits would be to reduce cash balances, decrease bank loan needs, reduce interest expenses, and increase profits.

Use of Float. Two kinds of float exist: disbursement float and collection float. The difference is net float. Disbursement float arises when one makes a payment by a check. It is defined as the amount of checks that one has written but are still being processed and thus have not yet been deducted from the checking account balances by the bank. Collection float arises when one receives a check for payment. It is defined as the amount of checks that have been received but that are in the collection process. It takes time to deposit the check, for the bank to process it, and to credit an account for the amount collected.

Net float = Disbursement float − Collection float

Net float = One's checkbook balance − Bank's book balance

A positive net float is better than a negative net float because the positive net float collects checks written to a firm faster than clearing checks written to others. Net float is a function of the ability to speed up collections on checks received and to slow down collections on checks written. The key is to put the funds received to work faster and to stretch payments longer.

Speeding Collections. Funds are available to the receiving firm only after the check-clearing process has been completed satisfactorily. There is a time delay between a firm processing its incoming checks and in making use of them. Three parties are involved in the check-clearing process: the payer, payee, and the Federal Reserve System (requires a maximum of two days to clear a check). Traditionally, the length of time required for checks to clear is a function of the distance between the payer's and the payee's banks. This has improved significantly due to information technology (IT). The greater the distance, the longer the delay due to regular mail, especially for remote locations. If the payer's and the payee's bank are the same, there is less delay than if they are different.

KEY CONCEPTS TO REMEMBER: Techniques to Speed Up Collections

- Lockboxes are used to reduce mail delays and check-clearing delays. Both mail and check collection times are reduced using lockboxes. Lockboxes are mailboxes at the post office.

- Preauthorized debt (checkless transactions) allows funds to be automatically transferred from a customer's account to the firm's account on specified dates. Both mail and check-clearing times are eliminated. Examples include payroll checks, mortgage payments, tax bills, utility bills.

Slowing Disbursements.   Three techniques are available to slow down disbursements: delaying payments, writing checks on banks in different locations, and using drafts. Delaying payments has negative consequences, such as a bad credit rating. Customers can sue firms for writing checks on banks in distant locations—playing West Coast banks against East Coast banks in the United States. Speeding the collection process and slowing down disbursements have the same objectives. Both keep cash on hand for longer periods.

Use of drafts seems normal. A check is payable on demand while a draft is not. A draft must be transmitted to the issuer, who approves it and then deposits funds to cover it, after which it can be collected.

Transfer Mechanisms.   A transfer mechanism is a system for moving funds among accounts at different banks. Three types of transfer mechanisms are depository transfer checks, wire transfers, and electronic depository transfer checks. Each is described next.

- **Depository transfer check (DTC).** Such a check is restricted for deposit into a particular account at a particular bank. A DTC is payable only to the bank of deposit for credit to the firm's specific account. DTCs provide a means of moving money from local depository banks to regional concentration banks and to the firm's primary bank, as shown in Exhibit 4.31.

- **Wire transfer.** A wire transfer is the electronic transfer of funds via a telecommunications network that makes funds collected at one bank immediately available from another bank. The wire transfer eliminates transit float and reduces the required level of transaction and precautionary cash balances.

- **Electronic depository transfer check (EDTC).** EDTC is a combination of a wire transfer and a DTC. It provides one-day availability in check clearing time because it avoids the use of the mail. EDTC is a paperless transaction. EDTC is also called ACH, which is a telecommunication network that provides an electronic means of sending data from one financial institution to another. Magnetic tape files are processed by the ACH, and direct computer-to-computer links are also available.

EXHIBIT 4.31 Movement of Depository Transfer Checks

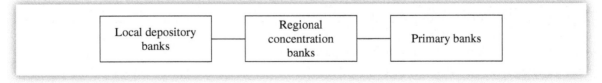

(v) Management of Marketable Securities

Two basic reasons for holding marketable securities (e.g., U.S. Treasury bills, commercial paper, and CDs) are that they are used as a temporary investment and they serve as a substitute for cash balances. Temporary investment occurs when the firm must:

- Finance seasonal or cyclical operations;
- Meet some known financial requirements, such as new plant construction program, a bond about to mature, or quarterly tax payments; and
- Uses proceeds from stocks and bonds to pay for operating assets.

Actually, the choice is between taking out short-term loans or holding marketable securities. There is a trade-off between risks and return. Similar to cash management policy, a firm's marketable security policy should be an integral part of its overall working capital policy. The working capital financing policy may be conservative, aggressive, or moderate. (See Exhibit 4.32.)

EXHIBIT 4.32 Types of Marketable Securities Policies

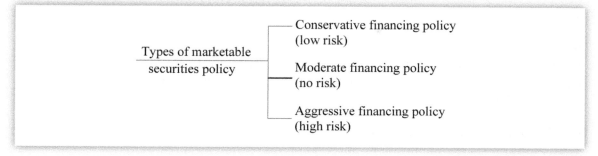

- If the firm has a conservative working capital financing policy, its long-term capital will exceed its permanent assets, and it will hold marketable securities when inventories and receivables are low. This policy is less risky than the others. There is no liquidity problem since the firm has no short-term debt. However, the firm incurs higher interest rates when borrowing than the return it receives from marketable securities. It is evident that a less risky strategy costs more.

- If the firm has a moderate working capital financing policy, the firm will match permanent assets with long-term financing and meet most seasonal increases in inventories and receivables with short-term loans. The firm also carries marketable securities at certain times. With this policy, asset maturities are matched with those of liabilities. No risk exists, at least theoretically.

- If the firm has an aggressive working capital financing policy, it will never carry any securities and will borrow heavily to meet peak needs. This is the riskiest method, and the firm will face difficulties in borrowing new funds or repaying the loan, due to its low current ratio. The expected rate of return on both total assets and equity will be higher.

(A) Criteria for Selecting Marketable Securities

The selection criteria for a marketable security portfolio include default risk, taxability, and relative yields. The financial manager has several choices available in selecting a marketable securities portfolio, and they all differ in risk and return. Most financial managers are averse to risk and unwilling to sacrifice safety for higher rates of return. The higher a security's risk, the higher its expected and required return, and vice versa. A trade-off exists between risk and return.

Exhibit 4.33 presents the types of marketable securities that are available to financial managers for investment of surplus cash.

EXHIBIT 4.33 Marketable Securities Available for Investment of Surplus Cash

Securities Suitable to Hold as Near-Cash Reserve	Securities Not Suitable to Hold as Near-Cash Reserve
Treasury bills	U.S. Treasury notes and bonds
Commercial paper	Corporate bonds
Negotiable CDs	Common stock and preferred stock
Money market mutual funds	State and local government bonds
Eurodollar time deposits	All of the above with more than one year maturity
All of the above with less than one year maturity	

Large corporations tend to make direct purchases of U.S. Treasury bills, commercial paper, CDs, and Eurodollar time deposits. Small corporations are more likely to use money market mutual funds as near-cash reserves (because they can be quickly and easily converted to cash). Interest rates on money market mutual funds are lower and net returns are higher than on Treasury bills.

(B) Risks in Marketable Securities

Here we review the different types of risk—default, interest rate, purchasing power, and liquidity risk—facing financial managers in managing the portfolio of marketable securities. (See Exhibit 4.34.)

EXHIBIT 4.34 Risks in Marketable Securities

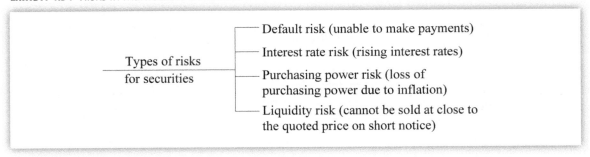

Default Risk. **Default risk** is the risk that a borrower will be unable to make interest payments or to repay the principal amount upon maturity. For example, the default risk for securities issued by the U.S. Treasury is negligible while securities issued by a corporation and others have some degree of default risk. The higher the earning power of a firm, the lower its default risk, and vice versa.

Interest Rate Risk. **Interest rate risk** is the risk to which investors are exposed due to rising interest rates. Interest rate fluctuations are what cause interest rate risk. Even U.S. Treasury bonds are subject to interest rate risk.

Bond prices vary with changes in interest rates. Long-term bonds have more interest rate risk. Short-term bonds have less interest rate risk.

Purchasing Power Risk. **Purchasing power risk** is the risk that inflation will reduce the purchasing power of a given sum of money. Purchasing power risk is lower on assets whose returns tend to rise during inflation. It is higher on assets whose returns are fixed during inflation. The variability of returns during inflation determines the purchasing power risk.

Real estate, short-term debt, and common stocks are better hedges against inflation than cash or certificate of deposits. Bonds and other long-term fixed income securities are not better hedges against inflation because they lose value over time with inflation.

Liquidity (Marketability) Risk. **Liquidity risk** is the risk that securities cannot be sold at close to the quoted market price on short notice. For example, securities issued by the U.S. Treasury and larger corporations have little liquidity risk while securities issued by small and unknown companies are subject to liquidity risk. Illiquidity of a firm is the situation where the firm's maturing obligations are greater than the cash immediately available to pay.

An asset that can be sold quickly for close to its quoted price is highly liquid. An asset that cannot be sold quickly and is sold at a reduced price is not highly liquid.

(C) Inventory Management

Inventories are the least liquid of all tangible assets because they take a long time to convert into cash. They can be damaged, outdated, spoiled, or stolen.

(h) Valuation Models

Three type of valuation models are discussed in this section: inventory valuation (e.g., cost flow methods, valuation methods, and estimation methods), financial asset valuation (e.g., stocks and bonds), and business valuation (e.g., book value model, liquidation value model, and price replacement cost model).

(i) Inventory Valuation

Accounting Research Bulletin 43, *Restatement and Revision of Accounting Research Bulletins*, defines **inventory** as "the sum of those items of tangible personal property which are held for sale in the ordinary course of business, in process of production for sale, or to be currently consumed in the production of goods for sale." The three types of manufacturing inventory are raw materials, WIP, and finished goods, which represent the largest current asset. A committee of the American Institute of Certified Public Accountants said: "A major objective of accounting for inventories is the proper determination of income through the process of matching appropriate costs against revenues."

(A) Inventory Cost Flow Methods

Five inventory costing methods are used based on differing inventory flow assumptions.

1. **Specific identification method**, where the cost of the specific items sold are included in the COGS, while the costs of the specific items on hand are included in the inventory. This method is used for valuing jewelry, fur coats, automobiles, and high-priced furniture.

   Advantages are accuracy; if done properly, cost flow matches the physical flow of the goods. *Disadvantages* are that the method requires detailed record keeping and elaborate manual and/or computer systems.

2. **Average cost method**, where the items in inventory are priced on the basis of the average cost of all similar goods available during the period. The weighted-average method or moving-average technique is used for calculating the ending inventory and the COGS.

   The *advantage* of the average cost method is that it is simple to apply, and it is objective. The *disadvantage* is that the inventory is priced on the basis of average prices paid, which is not realistic.

3. **FIFO method**, where goods are used in the order in which they are purchased; the first goods purchased are the first used. The inventory remaining must represent the most recent purchase. Cost flow matches the physical flow of the goods, similar to the specific identification method.

   An *advantage* of the FIFO method is that the ending inventory is close to current cost and provides a reasonable approximation of replacement cost on the balance sheet when price changes have not occurred since the most recent purchases.

   A *disadvantage* of FIFO is that current costs are not matched against current revenues on the income statement. The oldest costs are charged against the more current revenue, which can lead to distortions in gross profit and net income. This creates transitory or inventory profits (paper profits).

4. **LIFO method**, where the cost of the last goods purchased is matched against revenue. The ending inventory would be priced at the oldest unit cost. LIFO is the most commonly used method.

   The LIFO method matches the cost of the last goods purchased against revenue, and the ending inventory is costed at the oldest units remaining in the inventory. In other words, in LIFO, the inventory with current costs becomes part of the COGS for the current period, and this COGS is matched against revenues and sales for that current period. Ending inventory contains the oldest inventory with the oldest costs.

   LIFO *advantages* are listed next.

   □ During periods of inflation, current costs are matched against current revenues, and inventory profits are thereby reduced. Inventory profits occur when the inventory costs matched against sales are less than the inventory replacement cost. The COGS is understated, and profit is considered overstated.

   □ Lower tax payments. The tax law requires that if a firm uses LIFO for tax purposes, it must also use LIFO for FA and reporting purposes.

   □ Improved cash flow due to lower tax payments, which could be invested for a return unavailable to those using FIFO.

   LIFO *disadvantages* are listed next.

   □ Lower profits reported under inflationary times. The company's stock could fall.

   □ Inventory is understated on the balance sheet because the oldest costs remain in ending inventory. This understatement of inventory makes the firm's working capital position appear worse than it really is.

   □ LIFO does not approximate the physical flow of the items.

   □ LIFO falls short of measuring current cost (replacement cost) income, though not as far as FIFO.

   □ Manipulation of income at the end of the year could occur by simply altering a firm's pattern of purchases.

5. **Next-in, first-out (NIFO) method**, which is not currently acceptable for purposes of inventory valuation. NIFO uses replacement cost. When measuring current cost income, the COGS should consist not of the most recently incurred costs but rather of the cost that will be incurred to replace the goods that have been sold.

KEY CONCEPTS TO REMEMBER: Inflation, LIFO, FIFO, and Taxes

■ During general and prolonged inflation, income tends to be overstated because of holding gains.

■ The LIFO method results in a significantly understated value of inventory when prices move up steadily. LIFO helps to exclude inventory profits from the determination of net income, resulting in lower income.

■ During a period of rising prices, taxable income and income taxes are reduced through the use of LIFO.

■ Under LIFO, the most recent costs of goods acquired are assigned to COGS, thus resulting in a more realistic matching of costs and revenues.

- Under the FIFO method, the inventory is valued at the most recently incurred costs; thus, the cost assigned to inventory tends to be relatively close to the current replacement cost. Earliest costs are assigned to the COGS, thus resulting in the reporting of holding gains in net income.

- During a period of rising prices, taxable income and income taxes are increased through the use of FIFO.

- The FIFO method results in a significantly overstated value of inventory when prices move up steadily.

- During inflationary periods, LIFO is usually considered preferable to FIFO. However, with LIFO, a major problem exists in evaluating inventory on the balance sheet when reviewing a company's financial statements.

(B) Inventory Valuation Method

Generally, historical cost is used to value inventories and COGS. In certain circumstances, though, departure from cost is justified. Some other methods of costing inventory are listed next.

- **Net realizable value.** Damaged, obsolete, or shopworn goods should never be carried at an amount greater than net realizable value. Net realizable value is equal to the estimated selling price of an item minus all costs to complete and dispose of the item.

- **Lower of cost or market.** If the value of inventory declines below its historical cost, then the inventory should be written down to reflect this loss. A departure from the historical cost principle is required when the future utility of the item is not as great as its original cost. When the purchase price of an item falls, it is assumed that its selling price has fallen or will fall. The loss of the future utility of the item should be charged against the revenues of the period in which it occurred. Market in this context generally means the replacement cost of the item.

  However, market cost is limited by a floor and ceiling cost. Market cannot exceed net realizable value, which is the estimated selling price minus the cost of completion and disposal (ceiling). Market cannot be less than net realizable value minus a normal profit margin (floor). Lower of cost or market can be applied to each inventory item, each inventory class, or total inventory.

EFFECTS OF INVENTORY ERRORS

- If ending inventory is overstated, assets, gross margin, net income, and owners' equity will be overstated, and COGS will be understated.

- If ending inventory is understated, assets, gross margin, net income, and owners' equity will be understated, and COGS will be overstated.

(C) Inventory Estimation Methods

An organization may estimate its inventory to compare with physical inventories to determine whether shortages exist, to determine the amount of inventory destroyed in a fire or stolen, or to obtain an inventory cost figure to use in monthly or quarterly (interim) financial statements. Two methods of estimating the cost of ending inventory are the gross margin (GM) method and the retail inventory method. (See Exhibit 4.35.)

EXHIBIT 4.35 Inventory Estimation Methods

- Gross margin method (establishes a relationship between GM and sales; prior-period GM rates are used to estimate the current inventory cost)
- Retail inventory method (establishes a relationship between prices and costs; cost/price ratio is used to estimate the current inventory cost)

The **gross margin method** is based on the assumption that the relationship between GM and sales has been fairly stable. GM rates from prior periods are used to calculate estimated gross margin. The estimated GM is deducted from sales to determine estimated COGS. The estimated COGS is then deducted from cost of goods available for sale to determine estimated inventory cost.

The **retail inventory method** is used by organizations that mark their inventory with selling prices. These prices are converted to cost using a cost/price (cost-to-retail) ratio. The cost/price ratio is simply what proportion cost is to each sales dollar. This cost/price ratio is applied to ending inventory stated at retail prices to estimate the cost of ending inventory.

The proper treatment of net additional markups and markdowns in the cost-to-retail ratio calculation is to include the net additional markups in the ratio and to exclude net markdowns. This approach approximates the lower-of-average-cost-or-market valuation.

EXAMPLE CALCULATION OF INVENTORY LOST DUE TO FIRE

A division of a company experienced a fire in 20X2, which destroyed all but $6,000 of inventory (at cost). Data available is listed next.

	20X1	20X2 (to date of fire)
Sales	$100,000	$40,000
Purchases	70,000	35,000
Cost of goods sold		60,000
Ending inventory		10,000

Question: What is the approximate inventory lost (destroyed) to the fire in 20X2?

Answer: Inventory lost to the fire in 20X2 is $15,000, as shown next.

20X2 sales	$40,000
20X2 COGS using 20X1 ratio ($60,000 / $100,000) × $40,000 =	$24,000 COGS in 20X2
	$10,000 Beginning inventory 20X2
	$35,000 Purchases in 20X2
	$45,000 Goods available for sale in 20X2
	$24,000 COGS in 20X2
	$21,000 Ending inventory in 20X2
	$6,000 Undestroyed inventory in 20X2
	$15,000 Destroyed inventory in 20X2

(ii) Financial Asset Valuation

Policy decisions that are most likely to affect the value of the firm include: investment in a project with large net present value (NPV), sale of a risky operating division that will now increase the credit rating of the entire company, and use of more highly leveraged capital structure that results in a lower cost of capital.

Establishing or predicting the value of a firm is an important task of the financial manager since maximizing the value of the firm is a major goal. Here the focus is on maximizing shareholders' wealth. Similar to capital budgeting decisions, the financial manager can use discounted cash flow (DCF) techniques to establish the worth of any assets (e.g., stocks, bonds, real estate, equipment) whose value is derived from future cash flows. *The* key concept of DCF is that it takes time value of money into account. The value of a firm is a combination of bond valuation, common stock valuation, and preferred stock valuation. (See Exhibit 4.36.)

EXHIBIT 4.36 Valuation of a Firm

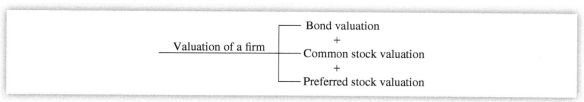

(A) Bond Valuation

A **bond valuation model** shows the mathematical relationships between a bond's market price and the set of variables that determine the price. For example, bond prices and interest rates are inversely related. Corporate bonds are traded in the over-the-counter market.

DEFINITIONS OF KEY TERMS: BONDS

Call provision—A provision that allows the issuer to pay off (redeem) the bond prior to its maturity date. This provision enables issuers to substitute low-interest-rate bonds for high-interest-rate bonds. When interest rates decline, issuers can sell a new issue of low-interest-rate bonds and use the proceeds to retire the old high-interest-rate bond.

Coupon interest payment—The specified number of dollars of interest paid each period on a bond.

Coupon interest rate—The coupon interest payment divided by the par value. It is the stated amount rate of interest on a bond and remains fixed.

Maturity date—A specified date on which the par value of the bond must be repaid.

Par value—The stated face value of the bond. The par value represents the amount of money the firm borrows and promises to repay at some future date (i.e., maturity date)

Reinvestment rate risk—A bond with a shorter (e.g., one year) maturity exposes the buyer to more such risk than a bond with a longer maturity (e.g., 10 years). Reinvestment rate risk is the risk that income will decline when the funds received from maturing short-term bonds are reinvested.

Yield to call—The rate of return earned on a bond if it is called before the maturity date.

Yield to maturity—The rate of return earned on a bond if it is held to maturity.

Treasuries raise money by issuing bonds and offering common equity. A bond that has just been issued is known as a new issue. Newly issued bonds are sold close to par value. A bond that has been on the market for a while is called a seasoned issue and is classified as an outstanding bond. The prices of outstanding bonds vary from par value. A bond's market price is determined primarily by its coupon interest payments. The coupon interest payment is set at a level that will cause the market price of the bond to equal its par value.

KEY CONCEPTS TO REMEMBER: Bond Valuation

- The higher the coupon interest payment, the higher the market price of the bond.
- The lower the coupon interest payment, the lower the market price of the bond.
- At constant coupon interest payment and changing economic conditions, the market price of the bond is more or less equal to its par value.
- A bond's interest rate depends on its riskiness, liquidity, yield to maturity, and supply and demand conditions of money in the capital markets.

A bond represents an annuity (i.e., interest payments) plus a lump sum (i.e., repayment of the par value), and its value is found as the PV of this payment stream. The equation to find a bond's value is

Value of bond = I (Present value of annuity) + M (Present value of lump sum)

where

I = Dollars of interest paid each year (i.e., Coupon interest rate × Par value = Coupon interest payment)

M = Par (maturity) value

Both the PV of the annuity and the lump-sum amount are discounted at an appropriate rate of interest (Kd) on the bond for a number of years (n) until the bond matures. The value of n declines each year after the bond is issued.

PREMIUM VERSUS DISCOUNT OF A BOND

- When interest rates fall after bonds are issued, the value of the firm's bonds would increase, and the bonds would sell at a premium, or above its par value.
- Bond premium = Bond price + Par value
- When interest rates rise after bonds are issued, the value of the firm's bonds would decline, and the bonds would sell at a discount, or below their par value.

Bond discount = Bond price − Par value

The discount or premium on a bond may be calculated as follows:

Discount or premium = (Interest payment on old bond − Interest payment on new bond) × PV of annuity

The PV is calculated for n years to maturity on the old bond and at current rate of interest (Kd) on a new bond. Total rate of return or yield on a bond is equal to Interest (Current yield) + Current gains yield.

A graph can be drawn to show the values of a bond in relation to interest rate changes. Note that regardless of what the future interest rates are, the bond's market value will always approach its par value as it nears the maturity date, except in bankruptcy. If the firm went bankrupt, the value of the bond might drop to zero.

KEY CONCEPTS TO REMEMBER: Interrelationships among the Coupon Interest Rate, Par Value, and Going Rate of Interest

- Whenever the going rate of interest is equal to the coupon interest rate, a bond will sell at its par value.

- Whenever the going rate of interest is greater than the coupon rate, a bond will sell below its par value. This bond is called a discount bond.

- Whenever the going rate of interest is less than the coupon rate, a bond will sell above its par value. This bond is called a premium bond.

- The longer the maturity of the bond, the greater its price changes in response to a given change in interest rates.

- An increase in interest rates will cause the price of an outstanding bond to fall.

- A decrease in interest rates will cause the price of an outstanding bond to rise.

- Those who invest in bonds are exposed to interest rate risk (i.e., a risk due to changing interest rates).

- The bond with a longer maturity is exposed to more risk than a shorter maturity bond from a rise in interest rates.

(B) Common Stock Valuation

Investors buy common stock for two main reasons: to receive dividends and to enjoy capital gain. Dividends are paid to stockholders at management's discretion since there is no legal obligation to pay dividends. Usually stockholders expect to receive dividends, even though, in reality, they may not. If the stock is sold at a price above its purchase price, the investor will receive a capital gain. Similarly, if the stock is sold at a price below its purchase price, the investor will suffer capital losses.

The value of a common stock is calculated at the PV of the expected future cash flow stream (i.e., expected dividends, original investment, and capital gain or loss). Different aspects of these cash flow streams involve the determination of the amount of cash flow and the riskiness of the amounts, and knowing what alternative actions affect stock prices.

Next, the stock values are determined using four different scenarios.

Scenario 1: Expected dividends as the basis for stock values

$$\text{value of stock } (Po) = \sum \frac{Dt}{(1+Ks)^t}$$

where

Po = Actual market price of the stock today

Dt = Dividend the stockholder expects to receive at the end of year t (can vary from one year to infinity)

Ks = Minimum acceptable or required rate of return on the stock

Scenario 2: Stock values with zero growth

A stock reaches a zero-growth stage (i.e., $g = 0$) when future dividends are not expected to grow at all (i.e., $D1 = D2 = D3 \ldots Dn$). Dividends will be constant over time. The value of a zero-growth stock is defined as $Po = D/Ks$. Zero-growth stock is a perpetuity since it is expected to pay a constant amount of dividend each year.

Scenario 3: Stock values with normal growth

Most firms experience an increase in earnings and dividends, but some firms may not. Dividends growth rate is expected to be equal to nominal gross national product (i.e., real GNP + Inflation). The value of a stock with normal (constant) growth is defined by Myron Gordon as $Po = D1 / (Ks - g)$, which is called the Gordon model. When using the Gordon model, the investor's required rate of return on the firm's stock is used in determining the value of a stock. This value, in turn, is used to calculate the cost of equity.

KEY CONCEPTS TO REMEMBER: Common Stock Valuation

- A company's stock price decreases as a result of the increase in nominal interest rates.
- Growth in dividends occurs as a result of growth in EPS.
- Earnings growth, in turn, results from these factors:
  - Inflation. If output is stable and if both sales prices and input costs rise at the inflation rate, EPS will grow at the inflation rate.
  - The amount of earnings the firm reinvests. EPS will grow as a result of retained earnings.
  - The rate of return the firm earns on its equity.

Scenario 4: Stock values with supernormal growth

Some companies experience supernormal (nonconstant) growth, where their growth rate is much faster than that of the economy as a whole. The growth rate depends on what stage a company is in its business cycle (i.e., introduction, mature).

STOCK PRICES VERSUS GROWTH RATES

- The stock price of a zero-growth firm is expected to be constant.
- The stock price of a declining firm is expected to be falling.
- The stock price of a constant-growth firm is expected to grow at a constant rate.
- The stock price of a supernormal-growth firm is expected to be higher in the beginning and then to decline as the growth period ends.

(C) Preferred Stock Valuation

As mentioned earlier, preferred stock is a hybrid stock—it has elements of both bonds and common stock. Most preferred stocks entitle their owners to regular fixed dividend payments. The value of the preferred stock can be found as follows:

$$Vps = \frac{Dps}{Kps}$$

where

Vps = Value of the preferred stock

Dps = Preferred dividend

Kps = Required rate of return on preferred stock

(iii) Business Valuation

Business valuation means valuing the worth of a business entity, whether in whole or in part. The value of a business is derived from its ability to generate cash flows consistently period after period over the long term. Business valuation can be performed at various milestones, such as these:

- New product introduction
- Mergers, acquisitions, divestitures, recapitalization, and stock repurchases
- Capital expenditures and improvements
- Joint venture agreements
- Ongoing review of performance of business unit operations

There are 12 models to help management make sound decisions during valuation of a business opportunity. These models, in the order of importance and usefulness, are listed next.

1. Book value model
2. Accounting profit model
3. Liquidation value model
4. Replacement cost model
5. Discounted abnormal earnings model
6. Price multiples model
7. Financial analysis model
8. Economic-value-added model
9. Market-value-added model
10. Economic profit model
11. NPV model
12. DCF model

Each model is briefly discussed.

(A) Book Value Model

The **book value** (net worth, net assets, or stockholders' equity) of a company's stock represents the total assets of the company less its liabilities. The book value per share has no relation to market value per share, as book values are based on historical cost of assets, not at the current value at which they could be sold. Book values are not meaningful because they are distorted by inflation factors and different accounting assumptions used in valuing assets. These net assets are undervalued when the inflation rate increases. One use of book value is to provide a floor value, with the true value of the company being some amount higher. Sales prices of companies are usually expressed as multiples of book values within each industry.

(B) Accounting Profit Model

Accounting profit is total revenue minus total accounting cost, which is used in the calculation of the EPS ratio. The **total accounting cost** is the explicit costs of production or service inputs, where these costs represent the actual monies paid to acquire inputs. The price of a product or service is often determined with accounting costs, not economic costs. The resources (e.g., labor, money, materials, energy, and machinery) used to produce goods and services are known as factors of production or simply production inputs. Accounting profits and costs are objectively determined based on the application of GAAP. The accounting profit model is mainly based on the book value model. The relationship is as follows:

$$\text{Accounting profit} = \text{Total revenues} - \text{Total explicit costs}$$

(C) Liquidation Value Model

The **liquidation value** of a firm is total assets minus all liabilities and preferred stock minus all liquidation costs incurred. Liquidation value may be a more realistic measure of a firm than book value in that a liquidation price reflects the current market value of the assets and liabilities if the firm is in a growing, profitable industry. Depending on the power of negotiations, the liquidation prices may be set at fire-sale prices. There is no terminal value here.

(D) Replacement Cost Model

The replacement cost model is based on the estimated cost to replace a company's assets, which include both tangible (e.g., plant, and equipment) and intangible assets (e.g., patents and copyrights). Only tangible assets are replaceable; intangible ones are not. Because of this fact, the replacement cost is lower than the market value of the company; sometimes it could be higher than the market value.

(E) Discounted Abnormal Earnings Model

If a firm can earn only a normal rate of return on its book value, then investors will pay no more than the book value. Abnormal earnings are equal to total earnings minus normal earnings. The estimated value of a firm's equity is the sum of the current book values plus the discounted future abnormal earnings.

(F) Price Multiples Model

The value of a firm is based on price multiples of comparable firms in the industry. This model requires calculating the desired price multiples and then applying the multiple to the firm being valued—that is,

$$\text{Price multiple} = \text{EPS} \times \text{P/E}$$

where

EPS = Earnings per share

P/E = Price earnings

Examples of price multiples include the price/earnings (P/E) ratio, price-to-book ratio, price-to-sales ratio, price-to-cash-flow ratio, and market-to-book ratio.

(G) Financial Analysis Model

Financial analysis includes ratio analysis and cash flow analysis. In ratio analysis, the analyst can compare ratios for a firm over several years, compare ratios for the firm and other firms in the industry, and compare ratios to some benchmark data. While ratio analysis focuses on analyzing a firm's income statement or its balance sheet, cash flow analysis focuses on operating, investing, and financing policies of a firm by reviewing its SOF. Cash flow analysis also provides an indication of the quality of the information in the firm's income statement and balance sheet.

(H) Economic-Value-Added Model

Economic value added (EVA) is operating profit minus a charge for the opportunity cost of capital. An *advantage* of the EVA method is its integration of revenues and costs of short-term decisions into the long-term capital budgeting process. *Disadvantages* of EVA are that it focuses only on a single period and does not consider risk. The EVA model can be combined with market-value-added (MVA) model to address this disadvantage. The formula for calculating the EVA is:

Operating profit – (Weighted-average cost of capital [WACC] × Capital invested.

(I) Market-Value-Added Model

The **MVA model** is the difference between the market value of a company's debt and equity and the amount of capital invested since its origin. The MVA measures the amount by which stock market capitalization increases in a period. Market capitalization is simply the number of shares outstanding multiplied by share price. MVA is calculated as:

PV of debt + Market value of equity – Capital invested

(J) Economic Profit Model

According to the economic profit model, the value of a company equals the amount of capital invested plus a premium equal to the PV of the cash flows created each year. Economic profit measures the value created in a company in a single period, and it is calculated as:

Invested capital × (return on invested capital – WACC)

Economic profit is total revenue minus total economic cost, where (1) total revenue is the total money received from selling goods or rendering services and (2) economic cost is the total cost of inputs used in the production of goods and services; it is equal to explicit costs (product/service costs) plus implicit costs (opportunity costs). Economic costs are greater than accounting costs and economic profits are less than accounting profits because accounting costs do not include opportunity (implicit) costs. Note that the traditional corporate accounting system does not record economic profits and costs because they are subjectively determined and are not derived from GAAP.

Economic profit = Total revenues – Total explicit costs – Total implicit costs

Opportunity cost is the cost of a forgone choice when selecting some other choice (i.e., it is the amount of sacrifice to get something). It is a trade-off between two choices and is an example of implicit cost that does not require money payments to acquire inputs. Opportunity costs should be considered in decision making and capital investments. However, opportunity costs are considered in economic costs but not in accounting costs because opportunity costs are not recorded by the formal accounting system. Examples of implicit costs include opportunity cost, cost of capital (interest costs), and cost of management talent.

Opportunity costs = Total implicit costs

(K) Net Present Value Model

Basically, the NPV model compares the benefits of a proposed project or firm with the costs, including financing costs, and approves those projects or firms whose benefits exceed costs. The NPV model incorporates the time value of money and the riskiness of the cash flows, which are the vital elements of a valuation model. The approach is to calculate the NPV of each alternative and then select the alternative with the highest NPV. NPV is calculated as:

$$PV \text{ of all cash inflows} - PV \text{ of all cash outflows}$$

(L) Discounted Cash Flow Model

The total value of a firm is value of its debt plus value of its equity. The DCF model goes beyond the NPV model and uses free cash flows. The DCF model focuses on discounting cash flows from operations after investment in working capital, less capital expenditures. The model does not consider interest expenses and cash dividends.

The calculation involves the generation of detailed, multiple-year forecasts of cash flows available to all providers of capital (debt and equity). The forecasts are then discounted at the WACC to arrive at an estimated PV of the firm. The value of debt is subtracted from the total value of the firm to arrive at the value of equity. Note that the DCF model considers the time value of money but does not consider the riskiness and uncertainty of specific cash flows (both inflows and outflows) in terms of their amounts.

(i) Capital Budgeting Methods and Decisions

Capital budgeting decisions deal with long-term future of a firm's course of action. **Capital budgeting** is the process of analyzing investment projects and deciding whether they should be included in the capital budget, which, in turn, outlines the planned expenditures on fixed assets, such as buildings, plant, machinery, equipment, warehouses, computer hardware and software, and offices.

CURRENT ASSETS VERSUS FIXED ASSETS

- Working capital decisions focus on increasing current assets.
- Investment decisions focus on increasing fixed assets.

A firm needs to develop capital budget plans several years in advance to synchronize the timing of funds availability with the timing of fixed asset acquisitions. Capital budgeting projects are initiated and selected by the company's management to be in line with the strategic business plan (e.g., M&A, introduction of new products). Generally, the larger the required investment, the more detailed the analysis and the higher the level of management approval required to authorize the expenditure.

SIMULATION AND CAPITAL BUDGETING

A firm is evaluating a large project; it wants to develop not only the best guess of the outcome of the project but also a list of outcomes that might occur. The firm would best achieve its objective by using simulation as applied to capital budgeting.

The process of capital budgeting is similar to securities valuation (i.e., stocks and bonds) in that the value of the firm increases when the asset's PV exceeds its cost. A link between capital budgeting and stock values exists in that the more effective the firm's capital budgeting procedures, the higher the price of its stock. From an economics point of view, an optimal capital budget is determined by the point where the marginal cost of capital is equal to the marginal rate of ROI.

(i) Methods to Rank Investment Projects

Four methods used to rank investment projects and to decide whether they should be accepted for inclusion in the capital budget are payback method (regular and discounted), NPV method, regular internal rate of return (IRR), and modified internal rate of return (MIRR). (See Exhibit 4.37.) Each is discussed next.

EXHIBIT 4.37 Methods to Rank Investment Projects

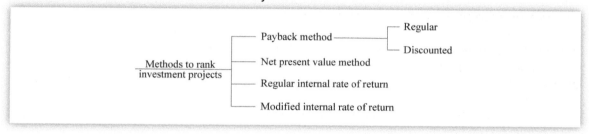

(A) Payback Method

The **payback period** is investment divided by after-tax cash flows. It is the expected number of years required to recover the original investment in a capital budgeting project. The procedure calls for accumulating the project's net cash flows until the cumulative total becomes positive. The shorter the payback period, the greater the acceptance of the project and the greater the project's liquidity. Risk can be minimized by selecting the investment alternative with the shortest payback period. Initial investment money can be recouped quickly.

A variation of the regular payback method is the discounted payback period, where the expected cash flows are discounted by the project's cost of capital or the required rate of return for the project. The next list compares regular payback and discounted payback.

- A **regular payback period** is the number of years required to recover the investment from the project's net cash flows. It does not take into account the cost of capital. The cost of debt and equity used to finance the project is not reflected in the cash flows.

- A **discounted payback period** is the number of years required to recover the investment from DCFs. It does take into account the cost of capital. It shows the breakeven years after covering debt and equity costs.

- Both methods are deficient in that they do not consider the time value of money.

- Both methods ignore cash flows after the payback period.

It is possible for the regular payback and the discounted payback methods to produce conflicting ranking of projects. The payback method is often used as a rough measure of both the liquidity and the riskiness of a project since longer-term cash flows are riskier than near-term cash flows. This method is used as a screening device to weed out projects with high and marginal payback periods. A low-payback period is preferred. The payback method can be used to reduce the uncertainty surrounding a capital budgeting decision and is often used in conjunction with NPV and IRR methods.

(B) Net Present Value Method

A simple way to accommodate the uncertainty inherent in estimating future cash flows is to adjust the minimum desired rate of return. DCF techniques, which consider the time value of money, were developed to compensate for the weakness of the payback method. Two examples of DCF techniques are the NPV method and the IRR method.

NPV is equal to the PV of future net cash flows, discounted at the marginal cost of capital. The approach calls for finding the PV of cash inflows and cash outflows, discounted at the project's cost of capital, and adding these DCFs to give the project's NPV. The rationale for the NPV method is that the value of a firm is the sum of the values of its parts.

$$\text{NPV} = (\text{After-tax cash flows}) \times (\text{Present value of annuity}) - (\text{Initial investment})$$

The **NPV index** or profitability index is the PV of after-tax cash flows divided by initial investment. Accounting rate of return is annual after-tax net income divided by initial or average investment. When the profitability index or cost/benefit ratio is 1, the NPV is zero.

Decision Rules

- If the NPV is positive, the project should be accepted since the wealth of the current stockholders would be increased.

PRESENT VALUES AND FUTURE VALUES

The relationship between the PV of a future sum and the future value of a present sum can be expressed in terms of their respective interest rate factors. The interest factor for the future value of a present sum is equal to the reciprocal of the interest factor for the PV of a future sum.

- If the NPV is negative, the project should be rejected since the wealth of the current stockholders would be reduced.

- If the NPV is zero, the project should be accepted even though the wealth of the current stockholders is unchanged. (The firm's investment base increases but the value of its stock remains constant.)

- If two projects are mutually exclusive, the one with the higher positive NPV should be chosen.

- If two projects are independent, there is no conflict in selection. Capital rationing is the only limiting factor.

- If money is available, invest in all projects in which the NPV is greater than zero.

- If a project's return exceeds the company's cost of capital, select the combination of projects that will fully utilize the budget and maximize the sum of the NPVs.

(C) Regular Internal Rate of Return

In the regular IRR method, the discount rate that equates the PV of future cash inflows to the investment's cost is found. In other words, the **IRR method** is the discount rate at which a project's NPV equals zero. Similarities and differences between the NPV and IRR methods are listed next.

Similarities

- Both NPV and IRR methods consider the time value of money.

- Both methods use the same basic mathematical equation for solving the project's problems.

Differences

- In the NPV method, the discount rate is specified, and the NPV is found.

- In the IRR method, the NPV is specified to equal zero, and the value of IRR that forces this equality is determined.

- The NPV method assumes reinvestment of project cash flows at the cost of capital.

- The IRR method assumes reinvestment of project cash flows at the IRR.

When a project's IRR is greater than its marginal cost of capital, the value of the firm's stock increases since a surplus remains after paying for the capital. Similarly, when a project's IRR is less than its marginal cost of capital, the value of the firm's stock decreases since the project reduces the profits of the existing stockholders.

EVALUATING CAPITAL PROJECTS

The payback method, NPV method, and IRR method all show an investment "breakeven" point for the project in an accounting sense, which would be useful in evaluating capital projects. The IRR method, NPV method, and NPV index consider risk only indirectly through the selection of a discount rate used in the PV computations.

Two kinds of projects exist: normal and nonnormal. A normal project is one that has one or more cash outflows followed by a series of cash inflows. When evaluated by the IRR method, the project does not present any difficulties. However, when a nonnormal project (i.e., a project that calls for a large cash outflow either sometime during or at the end of its life) is evaluated by the IRR method, unique difficulties can arise.

Which Method Is Best: Payback, NPV, or IRR. Any capital budgeting method should meet three criteria in order to produce consistent and correct investment decisions:

1. **The method must consider all cash flows throughout the entire life of a project**. The payback method does not meet this property. The NPV and IRR methods do.

2. **The method must consider the time value of money**. A dollar received today is more valuable than a dollar received tomorrow. The payback method does not meet this property. The IRR and NPV methods do.

3. **The method must choose the project that maximizes the firm's stock price among a set of mutually exclusive projects**. The payback method and the IRR methods do not meet this property. The NPV method meet this property all the time.

The NPV method is better for evaluating mutually exclusive projects. However, when two projects are independent, both the NPV and the IRR criteria always lead to the same accept or reject decision.

The critical issue in resolving NPV/IRR conflicts between mutually exclusive projects is the different reinvestment rate assumptions made. The reinvestment rate is the opportunity cost rate at which a firm can invest differential early year's cash flows generated from NPV or IRR methods.

The next list presents assumptions in NPV and IRR methods.

NPV assumptions: The cash flows generated by a project can be reinvested at the cost of capital. The NPV method discounts cash flows at the cost of capital.

IRR assumptions: The cash flows generated by a project can be reinvested at the IRR. The IRR method discounts cash flows at the project's IRR.

It has been demonstrated that the best assumption is that cash flows of projects are reinvested at the cost of capital. Therefore, the NPV method is better.

(D) Modified Internal Rate of Return

Academics prefer the NPV method while business executives favor the IRR method. The reason business executives prefer the IRR method is that they find IRR "more natural" to analyze investments in terms of percentage rates of return rather than dollars of NPV.

The regular IRR method can be modified to make it a better indicator of relative profitability and hence better for use in capital budgeting. The new measure is called the modified IRR, and it is the discount rate at which the PV of a project's cost is equal to the PV of its terminal value. The **terminal value** is the sum of the future values of the cash inflows, compounded at the firm's cost of capital. In other words, the MIRR is the discount rate that forces the PV of the costs to equal the PV of the terminal value.

The MIRR method is better than the regular IRR method because MIRR assumes that cash flows from all projects are reinvested at the firm's cost of capital, whereas the regular IRR method assumes that the cash flows from each project are reinvested at the project's own IRR. Therefore, the MIRR method is better indicator of a project's true profitability.

MODIFIED INTERNAL RATE OF RETURN VERSUS NET PRESENT VALUE

- If two projects are of equal size, NPV and MIRR will always lead to the same project selection decision. No conflict is present.

- If the projects differ in size, conflicts can occur similar to NPV and regular IRR. NPV is better because it provides a better indicator of how much each project will cause the value of the firm to increase.

- The MIRR method is superior to the regular IRR method as an indicator of a project's "true" rate of return.

(ii) Postaudit of Capital Projects

A **postaudit** is a comparison of the actual and expected results (both costs and savings) for a given capital project and explanation of variances, if any. A postaudit is a good learning exercise and is practiced by most successful organizations. The lessons learned from the postaudit can be used to fine-tune forecasts of costs and benefits and to improve business operations.

The postaudit is a complicated process to review since factors occur that are beyond the control of most managers in the firm, such as demand uncertainty and unexpected deviations from plans. Actual savings may not materialize as expected due to unexpected costs. Despite these problems, conducting a postaudit of capital projects is a good approach, as long as the blame is on the process, not on the people involved.

(iii) Project Cash Flows and Risk Assessment
(A) Project Cash Flows

It is important to note that capital budgeting decisions must be based on annual cash flows, not accounting income, and that only incremental cash flows are relevant to the accept or reject decision. Cash flows and accounting income can be different due to depreciation expense, which is a noncash expense. Net cash flows are obtained by adding depreciation expense to the net income after taxes.

Incremental cash flows represent the changes in the firm's total cash flows that occur as a direct result of accepting or rejecting the project. They are the net cash flow that can be traceable to an investment project. A project's terminal cash flows should be considered here.

Four special problems occur in determining incremental cash flows: sunk costs, opportunity costs, externalities, and shipping and installation costs. (See Exhibit 4.38.)

EXHIBIT 4.38 Problems in Determining Incremental Cash Flows

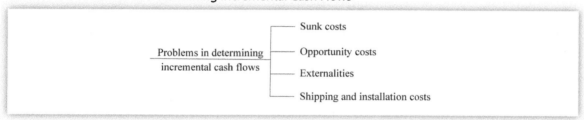

Sunk costs are not incremental costs, and they should not be included in the project analysis. A sunk cost is an outlay that has already been committed or has already occurred. Hence it is not affected by the "accept" or "reject" decision under consideration. Only incremental cash flows should be compared with the incremental investment.

Opportunity costs are the cash flows that can be generated from assets the firm already owns, provided they are not used for the project in question. These costs are the return on the best alternative use of an asset that is forgone due to funds invested in a particular project. Opportunity costs are not incremental costs.

Externalities are the indirect effects of a project on cash flows in other parts of the firm. Revenues produced from the effects of externalities should not be treated as incremental income.

Shipping and installation costs incurred on a new fixed asset (e.g., equipment) should be added to the invoice price of the fixed asset. The depreciation base for calculating the depreciation expense is the total invoice price including shipping and installation costs. Therefore, shipping and installation costs should not be treated as incremental cash flows; if they were, they would be double-counted.

(B) Project Risk Assessment

Risk analysis is important to capital budgeting decisions. Three separate and distinct types of project risk are the project's own stand-alone risk, corporate (within-firm) risk, and market risk (beta risk). (See Exhibit 4.39.)

EXHIBIT 4.39 Capital Project Risk Categories

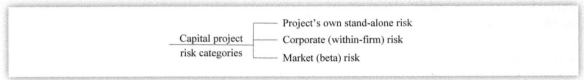

A project's own **stand-alone risk** is measured by the variability of the project's expected returns. A project's **corporate risk** is measured by the project's impact on the firm's earnings variability. Corporate risk does not consider the effects of stockholders' diversification. Corporate risk measures risk within a firm.

A project's **market (beta) risk** is measured by the project's effect on the firm's beta coefficient. Market risk cannot be eliminated by diversification. If the project has highly uncertain returns, and if those returns are highly correlated with those of the firm's other assets and with most other assets in the economy, the project will have a high degree of all types of risk. A company whose beta value has decreased due to a change in its marketing strategy would apply a lower discount rate to expected cash flows of potential projects.

Market risk is important because of its direct effect on a firm's stock prices. Both market risk and capital risk affect stock prices. Corporate risk for weak firms increases significantly compared to strong firms. This is because weak firms would have difficulty in borrowing money at reasonable interest rates, which, in turn, would decrease profits. The decrease in profits would be reflected in the price of the stock.

KEY CONCEPTS TO REMEMBER: Capital Project Risks

- It is much easier to estimate a project's stand-alone risk than its corporate risk.
- It is far easier to measure stand-alone risk than market risk.
- Stand-alone risk, corporate risk, and market risk are highly correlated.

    Economy ⟶ Firm ⟶ Project

If the economy is good, both the firm and the projects are good, and vice versa.

- Stand-alone risk is a good proxy for hard-to-measure market risk.

Risk to a company is affected by both project variability and how project returns correlate with those of the company's prevailing business. Overall company risk will be lowest when a project's returns exhibit low variability and negative correlation.

(C) Techniques for Measuring Stand-Alone Risk

Here we are interested in determining the uncertainty inherent in the project's cash flows. Three techniques are available for assessing a project's stand-alone risk: sensitivity analysis, scenario analysis, and Monte Carlo simulation. (See Exhibit 4.40.)

EXHIBIT 4.40 Techniques for Measuring Stand-Alone Risk

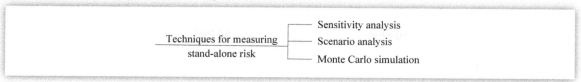

Sensitivity analysis (what-if analysis) can provide useful insights into the riskiness of a project. It is a technique that indicates exactly how much the NPV will change in response to a given change in an input variable, other things held constant. For example, if each input variable can be changed by several percentage points above and below the expected value, then a new NPV can be calculated for each of those values. Finally, the set of NPVs can be plotted against the variable that was changed. The slope of the lines in the graphs show how sensitive NPV is to changes in each of the inputs; the steeper the slope, the more sensitive the NPV is to a change in the variable.

Scenario analysis is a risk analysis technique that considers both the sensitivity of NPV to changes in key variables and the range of likely variable values. NPV is calculated under bad conditions (i.e., low sales, high variable cost per unit) and good conditions (i.e., high sales and low variable cost per unit) and compared to the expected (i.e., base case) NPV. Highlights of these relationships are shown next.

Bad condition ⟶ Worst-case scenario ⟶ (All input variables are set at their worst forecasted values)

Good condition ⟶ Best-case scenario ⟶ (All input variables are set at their best forecasted values)

Base case condition ⟶ Most likely scenario ⟶ (All input variables are set at their most likely values)

The results of the scenario analysis are used to determine the expected NPV, the standard deviation of NPV, and the coefficient of variation. Even though scenario analysis provides useful information about a project's stand-alone risk, it is limited in that it only considers a few discrete NPV outcomes for a project. In reality, there are an infinite number of outcomes.

Monte Carlo simulation ties together sensitivities and input variable probability distributions. Probability distributions of each uncertain cash flow variable are specified. The computer chooses at random a value for each uncertain variable based on the variable's specified probability distributions. The model then determines the net cash flows for each year, which, in turn, are used to determine the project's NPV in the first run. Since this is a simulation technique, this model is repeated many times to yield a probability distribution.

The primary advantage of simulation is that it shows a range of possible outcomes along with their attached probabilities. Scenario analysis shows only a few point estimates of the NPV. Both the standard deviation of the NPV and the coefficient of variation are calculated in Monte Carlo simulations, providing additional information in assessing the riskiness of a project.

It is difficult to obtain valid estimates of probability distributions and correlations among variables. No clear-cut decision rule emerges from both scenario analysis and simulation analysis. Both techniques ignore the effects of the project as well as investor diversification—which is the major drawback.

(iv) Market or Beta Risk

As mentioned earlier, **beta risk** is that part of a project's risk that cannot be eliminated by diversification. It is measured by the project's beta coefficient. Two methods are available to estimate the betas of individual projects: the pure-play method and the accounting beta method.

In the **pure-play method,** the company tries to find several single-product firms in the same line of business as the project being evaluated, and it then applies these betas to determine the cost of capital for its own project. A major drawback of the pure-play method is that the approach can be applied only for major assets, such as whole divisions, not individual projects. Therefore, it is difficult to find comparable business firms of the size in question.

> **CAPITAL ASSET PRICING MODEL TO MEASURE RISK**
>
> The capital asset pricing model (CAPM) can be used to measure market (beta) risk. A major drawback of CAPM is that it ignores bankruptcy costs. The probability of bankruptcy depends on a firm's corporate risk, not on its market risk. Therefore, management should give careful consideration to corporate risk instead of concentrating entirely on market risk.

The **accounting beta method** fills the gap of the pure-play method in finding single-product, publicly traded firms by applying against a large sample of firms. The project's beta is determined by regressing the returns of a particular company's stock against returns on a stock market index. Betas determined by using accounting data rather than stock market data are called accounting betas. In practice, accounting betas are normally calculated for divisions or other large units, not for single assets, and divisional betas are then imputed to the asset.

(v) Project Risks and Capital Budgeting

Capital budgeting can affect a firm's market risk, its corporate risk, or both. It is difficult to develop a good measure of project risk due to difficulty in quantifying either risk.

Two methods for incorporating project risk into the capital budgeting decision process include the certainty equivalent approach and the risk-adjusted discount rate approach.

Under the **certainty equivalent approach**, the expected cash flows are adjusted to reflect project risk. All unknown cash flows will have low certainty equivalent values. This approach is difficult to implement in practice despite its theoretical appeal.

Under the **risk-adjusted discount rate approach**, differential project risk is dealt with by changing the discount rate. Risk adjustments are subjective and take these decision paths:

- Average-risk projects are discounted at the firm's average cost of capital.
- Above-average-risk projects are discounted at a higher cost of capital.
- Below-average-risk projects are discounted at a rate below the firm's average.

(vi) Capital Rationing

Although there are many acceptable capital budget projects, the amount of funds available to a firm is limited. A firm will approve an independent project if its NPV is positive. When faced with mutually exclusive projects, a firm selects the project with the highest NPV. Management cannot or would not want to raise whatever funds are required to finance all of the acceptable projects. When capital budget must be limited, this situation is called capital rationing.

Capital rationing is a constraint placed on the total size of the firm's capital investment. A drawback of capital rationing is that it is not maximizing a firm's stock value since it deliberately forgoes profitable projects. Because of this negative effect, only a few firms ration their capital.

(vii) Key Principles and Practices in Capital Budgeting

Five key principles and practices to be employed during capital budgeting decision-making process are listed next.

Principle 1. Integrate organizational goals into the capital decision-making process.

Practice 1a. Conduct comprehensive assessment of needs to meet results-oriented goals and objectives.

Practice 1b. Identify current capabilities including the use of an inventory of assets and their condition, and determine if there is a gap between current and needed capabilities.

Practice 1c. Decide how best to meet the gap by identifying and evaluating alternative approaches.

Principle 2. Evaluate and select capital assets using an investment approach.

Practice 2a. Establish review and approval framework.

Practice 2b. Rank and select projects based on established criteria.

Practice 2c. Decide a long-term capital plan that defines capital asset decisions.

Principle 3. Balance budgetary control and managerial flexibility when funding capital projects.

Practice 3a. Budget for projects in useful segments.

Practice 3b. Consider innovative approaches to full up-front funding.

Principle 4. Use project management techniques to optimize project success.

Practice 4a. Monitor project performance and establish incentives for accountability.

Practice 4b. Use cross-functional teams to plan for and manage projects.

Principle 5. Evaluate results and incorporate lessons learned into the decision-making process.

Practice 5a. Evaluate results to determine if organization-wide goals have been met.

Practice 5b. Evaluate the decision-making process; reappraise and update to ensure those organization-wide goals are met.

(viii) International Capital Budgeting

The techniques presented in this section for domestic capital budgeting are equally applicable to the international capital budgeting process. However, three types of risks exist in the international area: cash flow risk (i.e., cash flow estimation is much more difficult); (2) exchange rate risk (i.e., exchange rate fluctuations add to the riskiness of the foreign investment); and sovereignty risk (i.e., the possibility of deliberate foreign government acts that reduce or eliminate cash flows).

In terms of cash flows, the relevant cash flows are the dollar cash flows that the subsidiary can turn over to the parent. Since the foreign currency cash flows turned over to the parent must be converted to U.S. dollar values by translating them at expected future exchange rates, an exchange rate premium should be added to the domestic cost of capital. This is done to reflect the exchange rate risk inherent in the investment. The exchange rate risk can be minimized by hedging, which adds to the cost of the project.

Sovereignty risk includes the possibility of expropriation or nationalization without adequate compensation and also the possibility of unanticipated restrictions of cash flows to the parent company, such as tighter controls on repatriation of dividends or higher taxes. Generally, sovereignty risk premiums are not added to the cost of capital to adjust for sovereignty risk. Companies can take three major steps to reduce the potential loss from expropriation: (1) finance the subsidiary with local sources of capital, (2) structure operations so that the subsidiary has value only as a part of the integrated corporate system, and (3) obtain insurance against economic losses from expropriations. When insurance is obtained, its cost should be added to the project's cost.

(j) Cost of Capital Evaluations

The rate of return on a security to an investor is the same as the cost of capital to a firm, which is a required return on its investments. Any increase in total assets of a firm's balance sheet must be financed by an increase in one or more of capital components (i.e., debt, preferred stock, retained earnings, common stock). Like any other resources, capital has a cost. The cost of capital must reflect the average cost of the various sources of long-term funds used (i.e., one or more of the capital components used. (See Exhibit 4.41.)

EXHIBIT 4.41 Components of Cost of Capital

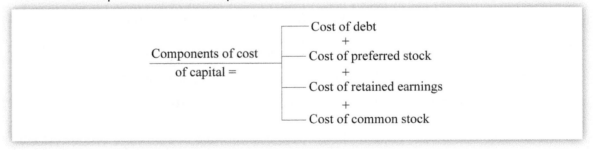

Next we briefly review each component of capital.

(i) Cost of Debt

The cost of debt is calculated as $Kd\ (1-T)$, where Kd is the interest rate on debt and T is the firm's marginal tax rate. The government pays part of the cost of debt (equal to tax rate) because interest is deductible for tax purposes. The value of the firm's stock depends on after-tax cash flows. Here we are interested in acquiring a new debt (marginal cost of debt) to finance a new asset, and past financing is a sunk cost and is irrelevant for cost of capital calculation purposes.

The key point is to compare the rate of return with after-tax flows. After-tax cost of debt is less than before-tax cost due to tax savings resulting from an interest expense deduction that reduces the net cost of debt.

(ii) Cost of Preferred Stock

The cost of preferred stock (Kp) is the preferred dividend (Dp) divided by the net issuing price (Pn) or the price the firm receives after deducting flotation costs. This is $Kp = Dp \,/\, Pn$. Since preferred dividends are not tax deductible, there are no tax savings, unlike interest expense on debt.

(iii) Cost of Retained Earnings

If management decides to retain earnings, an opportunity cost is involved (i.e., stockholders could have received the earnings as dividends and invested this money somewhere else). Because of this opportunity cost, the firm should earn on its retained earnings at least as much as the stockholders themselves could earn in alternative investments of comparable risk, such as the cost of common stock equity.

WHO REQUIRES WHAT?

- The costs of debt are based on the returns investors require on debt.

- The costs of preferred stock are based on the returns investors require on preferred stock.

- The costs of retained earnings are based on the returns stockholders require on equity capital (e.g., common stock).

(iv) Cost of Common Stock

The cost of common stock (Ke) is higher than the cost of retained earnings (ks) due to flotation costs involved in selling new common stock. The equation is

$$Ke = \frac{D1}{Po\,(1-F)} + g$$

where

$D1 =$ Dividends

$Po =$ Stock price

$F =$ Percentage flotation cost incurred in selling the new stock

$Po\,(1-F) =$ Net price per share received by the firm

$g =$ Stock's expected growth rate

When a stock is in equilibrium, its required rate of return (Ks) should be equal to its expected rate of return (Kes).

$$Ks = Krf = Rp \text{ or } Kes = (D1 \ / \ Po) + g$$

where

Krf = Risk-free rate

Rp = Risk premium

$D1 \ / \ Po$ = Stock's dividend yield

g = Stock's expected growth rate

Three methods are commonly used to calculate the cost of common stock: the CAPM approach, the bond-yield-plus-risk-premium approach, and the DCF approach. (See Exhibit 4.42.) The DCF approach does not consider risk explicitly; the other two approaches do consider risk explicitly.

EXHIBIT 4.42 Methods to Calculate the Cost of Common Stock

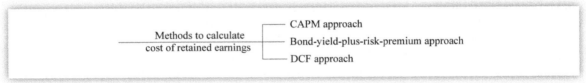

(A) Capital Asset Pricing Model Approach

The CAPM model is used to determine the required rate of return on an asset, which is based on the idea that any asset's return should be equal to the risk-free rate of return plus a risk premium rate that reflects the asset's non diversifiable risk. Note that the non-diversifiable risk cannot be eliminated through diversification because it is a part of systematic risk.

The CAPM model equation is:

$$Ks = Krf + (Km - Krf) \ bi$$

where

Krf = Risk-free rate (e.g., U.S. Treasury bond or bill rate)

$(Km - Krf)$ = Risk premium

Km = Expected rate of return on the market or on "average" stock

bi = Stock's beta coefficient (an index of the stock's risk)

Drawbacks of the CAPM approach include:

- A stockholder may be concerned with total risk rather than with market risk only.
- Beta coefficient may not measure the firm's true investment risk.
- This approach understates the correct value of the required rate of return on the stock, Ks.
- It is difficult to obtain correct estimates of the inputs to the model to make it operational.

Examples of the CAPM approach include deciding whether to use long-term or short-term Treasury bonds for the risk-free rate. Some problems when using the CAPM approach include (1) difficulty in estimating the beta coefficient that investors expect the firm to have in the future and (2) difficulty in estimating the market risk premium.

(B) Bond-Yield-Plus-Risk-Premium Approach

This method provides a ballpark estimate of the cost of equity, not a precise number, since it uses ad hoc, subjective, and judgmental estimates.

$$Ks = \text{Bond rate} + \text{Risk premium}$$

A firm's cost on common equity is found by adding a risk premium (say, 2%–4%) based on judgment to the interest rate on the firm's own long-term debt.

(C) Discounted Cash Flow Approach

The DCF approach is also called the dividend-yield-plus-growth rate approach. It is calculated as

$$Ks = Kes = D1 \,/\, Po + \text{Expected growth } (g)$$

Investors expected to receive a dividend yield $(D1/Po)$ plus a capital gain (g) for a total expected return of Kes. At equilibrium, this expected return would be equal to the required return (Ks).

$$Ks = Kes$$

EFFECTS OF COST OF COMMON STOCK

■ The firm must earn more than the cost of common stock (Ke) due to flotation cost.

■ When a firm earns more than Ke, the price of the stock will rise.

■ When a firm earns exactly Ke, EPS will not fall, expected dividend can be maintained, and consequently the price per share will not decline.

■ When a firm earns less than Ke, then earnings, dividends, and growth will fall below expectations, causing the price of the stock to decline.

(v) Weighted-Average and Marginal Cost of Capital Concepts

An optimal (target) capital structure is a mix of debt, preferred stock, and common stock that maximizes a firm's stock price. The goal of the finance manager should be then to raise new capital in a manner that will keep the actual capital structure on target over time. The firm's WACC is calculated based on the target proportions of capital and the cost of the capital components, all based on after-tax costs. The WACC could be used as a hurdle rate for capital investment projects and is computed as:

$$\text{WACC} = WdKd\,(1 - T) + WpKp + WsKs$$

where

Wd = Weight used for debt

Wp = Weight used for preferred stock

Ws = Weight used for common stock

Kd = Interest rate on the debt

Kp = Cost of preferred stock

Ks = Required rate of return on the stock

The weights could be based on either book values or market values. The latter is preferred over the former. If a firm's book value weights are close to its market value weight, book weights can be used.

As the firm tries to raise more money, the cost of each dollar will rise at some point. The marginal cost concept can be applied here: The marginal cost of any item is the cost of another unit of that item, whether the item is labor or production. The marginal cost of capital (MCC) is the cost of the last dollar of new capital that the firm raises, and the MCC rises as more and more capital is raised during a given period. The MCC schedule shows how the WACC changes as more and more new capital is raised during a given year.

KEY CONCEPTS TO REMEMBER: Break Point, Investment Opportunity Schedule, and Marginal Cost of Capital

- A break point will occur in the MCC schedule whenever the cost of one or more of the capital components rises. If there are n separate breaks, there will be $n + 1$ different weighted-average costs of capital.

- The investment opportunity schedule (IOS) curve is a graph of the firm's investment opportunities, with the projects having the highest return plotted first.

- The intersection of the MCC schedule and the IOS schedule is called the corporate cost of capital, which is used to evaluate average-risk capital budgeting projects.

The **break point** is the dollar value of new capital that can be raised before an increase in the firm's WACC occurs. It is the total amount of lower cost of capital of a given type divided by a fraction of this type of capital in the capital structure.

(vi) Issues in Cost of Capital

There are three major issues in cost of capital: depreciation-generated funds, privately owned and small business firms, and measurement problems.

1. **Depreciation-generated funds**. Depreciation is a source of capital, and its cash flows can be either reinvested or returned to investors. The cost of depreciation-generated funds is equal to the WACC in which capital comes from retained earnings and low-cost debt.

2. **Privately owned and small business firms**. The same principles of cost of capital estimation can be applied to both privately held and publicly owned firms. Input data are difficult to obtain for privately owned firms since their stock is not publicly traded.

3. **Measurement problems**. It is difficult to estimate the cost of equity, obtain input data for the CAPM approach, estimate stock growth rate, and assign different risk-adjusted discount rates to capital budgeting projects of differing degrees of riskiness.

Capital budgeting and cost of capital estimates deal with *ex ante* (estimated) data rather than *ex post* (historical) data. Because of this, we can be wrong about the location of the IOS schedule and the MCC schedule. Consequently, a project that looked good could turn out to be a bad one. Despite these issues, the cost of capital estimates used in this section are reasonably accurate. By solving these issues, refinements can be made.

(k) Taxation Schemes

Taxes are assessed for various purposes, such as to collect revenues, encourage or discourage different kinds of investments, or redistribute income among citizens. The different types of taxes differ in:

- Classes of taxable income.
- Which expenses are allowed for deduction from revenues and how they are to be calculated.
- What kind of taxes (e.g., direct or indirect) are to be collected.
- The extent to which companies report income honestly.

Exhibit 4.43 presents different types of taxes.

EXHIBIT 4.43 Different Types of Taxes

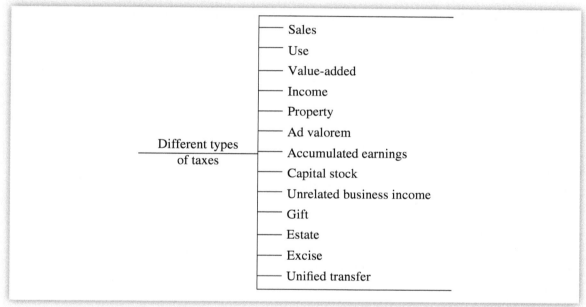

(i) Sales Tax

A **sales tax** is a state-level or local-level (e.g., county, city) tax on the retail sale of specified property. Generally, the purchaser pays the tax, but the seller collects it, as an agent for the government. Various taxing jurisdictions allow exemptions for purchases of specific items, including certain foods, services, and manufacturing equipment. If the purchaser and seller are in different states, a use tax usually applies.

THREE CONCEPTS OF AN INCOME TAX SYSTEM

A tax system should be equitable and nondistorting. Three different concepts of equity as it applies to the tax system include: the ability-to-pay principle, the benefit principle, and equal treatment of those equally situated.

(Continued)

THREE CONCEPTS OF AN INCOME TAX SYSTEM (*Continued*)

Ability-to-Pay Principle

Under this concept, people with higher incomes should pay more than those with lower incomes. It is based on the assumption that a more equal distribution of income would be more equitable. The real question is at what rate different incomes should be taxed. Some argue that the tax rate should be proportional—that is, the same percentage of each person's income.

Some argue that the tax rate should be progressive—that is, a higher-percentage tax on high incomes than on low incomes. All ability-to-pay advocates argue against regressive taxation, which takes a larger percentage of income from lower-income groups. Regressive taxes will not take a larger absolute amount of income as income rises. There is no objective way of deciding whether tax rates should be proportional or progressive or, if progressive, how steeply progressive.

Benefit Principle

This concept proposes that people should be taxed only to pay for the benefits they choose to buy from the government. This concept is more revolutionary in that each individual should have the income that he or she earns by helping to produce what consumers choose to buy. A direct sale of government services to the user would prevent redistribution of income.

Equal Treatment of Those Equally Situated

This concept states that persons equally situated should be taxed equally. The term "equally situated" is not clear and may have many meanings. Are two people with the same income always equally situated? What about the differences among disabled people, or retired persons and healthy young persons with the same income?

(ii) Use Tax

A **use tax** is a sales tax that is collectible by the seller when the purchaser is domiciled in a different state.

(iii) Value-Added Tax

A **value-added tax (VAT)** is a form of sales tax. Many European countries use VATs. The firm pays a percentage of tax based on the value that its production process adds to the final product. VAT is less complex and easier to calculate than an income tax and is easier to monitor. VAT encourages honesty whereas income tax does not.

(iv) Income Tax

Income tax is a tax imposed on income earned after deducting allowable expenses from all sources of revenues. Income tax rates vary depending on the amount of income earned. Corporations are subject to an alternative minimum tax, which has a more expansive tax base than does the regular tax. The corporation is required to apply a minimum tax rate to the expanded base and pay the difference between the tax liability for the alternative minimum tax and the regular tax.

(v) Property Tax

Property tax is an ad valorem tax, usually levied by a city or county government, on the value of real or personal property that the taxpayer owns on a specified date. Most states exclude intangible property and assets owned by exempt organizations from the tax base; some exclude inventory, pollution control, or manufacturing equipment and other items to provide relocation or retention incentives to the taxpayer.

(vi) Ad Valorem Tax

An **ad valorem tax** is a tax imposed on the value of property. The most common ad valorem tax is that imposed by states, counties, and cities on real estate. Ad valorem taxes can, however, be imposed on personal property as well.

(vii) Accumulated Earnings Tax

An **accumulated earnings tax** is a special tax imposed on corporations that accumulate (rather than distribute) their earnings beyond the reasonable needs of the business. This tax and related interest are imposed on accumulated taxable income in addition to the corporate income tax.

(viii) Capital Stock Tax

A **capital stock tax**, which is a state-level tax, is usually imposed on out-of-state corporations for the privilege of doing business in the state. The tax may be based on the entity's apportionable income or payroll or on its apportioned net worth as of a specified date.

(ix) Unrelated Business Income Tax

Unrelated business income tax is levied on the unrelated business taxable income of an exempt organization.

(x) Gift Tax

A **gift tax** is a tax imposed on the transfer of property by gift. Such tax is imposed on the donor of a gift and is based on the fair market value of the property on the date of the gift.

(xi) Estate Tax

An **estate tax** is a tax imposed on the right to transfer property by death. Thus, an estate tax is levied on the decedent's estate, not on the heir receiving the property.

(xii) Excise Tax

An **excise tax** is a tax on the manufacture, sale, or use of goods or on the carrying on of an occupation or activity, or a tax on the transfer of property. Thus, the federal estate and gift taxes are theoretically excise taxes.

(xiii) Unified Transfer Tax

Unified transfer tax is a set of tax rates applicable to transfers by gift and death made after 1976. It is a tax imposed on the transfer of property.

(l) Differences Between Tax Reporting and Financial Reporting

The net income computed for FA purposes will be different from taxable income reported on the corporation's income tax return. Therefore, reconciliation between these two types of income is essential to ensure accuracy. The starting point for the reconciliation is net income per books, which is the FA net income. Additions and subtractions are entered for items that affect net income per books and taxable income differently.[1]

$$\text{Net income per books} + \text{Additions} - \text{Subtractions} = \text{Taxable income}$$

---

[1] William H. Hoffman, William A. Raabe, James E. Smith, and David M. Maloney, *Corporations, Partnerships, Estates, and Trusts* (St.Paul, MN: West's Federal Taxation, West Publishing Company, 1993).

The following items are added to the net income per books:

- Federal income tax liability (deducted in computing net income per books but not deductible in computing taxable income)

- Excess of capital losses over capital gains (deducted for FA purposes but not deductible by corporations for income tax purposes)

- Income that is reported in the current year for tax purposes that is not reported in computing net income per books (e.g., prepaid income)

- Various expenses that are deducted in computing net income per books but not allowed in computing taxable income (e.g., charitable contributions in excess of the 10% ceiling applicable to corporations)

The following items are subtracted from the net income per books:

- Income reported for FA purposes but not included in taxable income (e.g., tax-exempt interest)

- Expenses deducted on the tax return but not deducted in computing net income per books (e.g., a charitable contributions carryover deducted in a prior year for FA purposes but deductible in the current year for tax purposes. The result is taxable income before net operating loss deduction and the dividends received deduction.)

(m) Mergers, Acquisitions, and Divestitures

This section discusses mergers and acquisitions as one topic due to their similarities; divestitures are presented as a separate topic due to their uniqueness from M&A; LBOs are discussed briefly; advantages and disadvantages of holding companies are highlighted briefly; the role of investment banker in mergers, acquisitions, and divestitures is discussed; and key terms, actions, and tactics used in M&A and divestitures are pointed out for a better understanding of the complex subject matter. Similarities and differences between acquisitions and divestitures are also presented.

(i) Mergers and Acquisitions

A **merger or acquisition** is defined as the combination of two or more firms to form a single large firm. An **acquiring company** is a firm in a merger transaction that is attempting to acquire or buy another firm. **A target company** is a firm in a merger transaction that the acquiring company is attempting to buy or combine. The preferred financial profile of a target company includes high-liquidity (high solvency), low-leverage (less debt), low P/E ratio, high EPS, and an upward trend in cash flows. In M&A, one firm is targeting to buy another firm either in part or whole with an offer to start the process.

A merger can be friendly or hostile, depending on some unknown situations that can occur (e.g., changes in management's attitudes and behaviors) that are beyond each party's control. In a friendly merger, the terms and conditions of a merger are approved by the management of both companies; in a hostile merger, the target firm's management resists acquisition, leading to use takeover defenses to fight the takeover. Of course, a friendly merger is better than a hostile one.

It has been pointed out that many mergers today are designed to benefit managers of the firm more than stockholders—who are really the owners of the firm. As shown in Exhibit 4.44, five motives have been given to account for the high levels of U.S. merger activity and for the huge amounts of money spent using cash, stock, or both:

1. Synergy

2. Tax considerations

3. Purchase of assets below their replacement cost

4. Diversification

5. Maintaining control

EXHIBIT 4.44 Motives for Mergers and Acquisitions

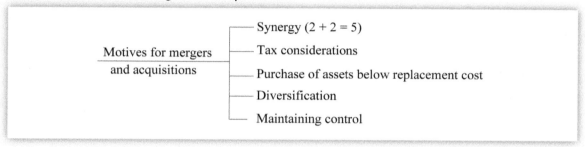

Synergy is defined as the whole is greater than the sum of the parts (i.e., 2 + 2 = 5). It means outputs are more than the sum of inputs. Synergy is the basic rationale for any operating merger. The word also refers to when a company's income and stock prices are higher than before, but only after it acquired another company. Synergistic effects can arise from four sources:

1. Operating economies of scale in production or distribution

2. Financial economies, which include a higher price/earnings ratio, a lower cost of debt, or a greater debt capacity

3. Differential management efficiency (one firm's management is seen as inefficient)

4. Increased market power resulting from reduced competition

Tax considerations include using tax status to the firm's advantage and using excess cash in mergers. Using excess cash to acquire another firm has no immediate tax consequences for either the acquiring firm or its stockholders.

TAXES AND ACQUISITIONS
_____

- A firm that is highly profitable and in the highest tax brackets could acquire a company with large accumulated tax losses, then use those losses to offset its own income. This method reduces the total tax bill and is one reason for making the acquisition.

- A firm with large losses could acquire a profitable firm and minimize the tax bill. Example: A young profitable company acquires an older company in a different industry that has experienced losses recently.

When the **replacement value of a firm's assets** is considerably higher than its market value, the firm becomes an acquisition candidate. The purchase price will be less than the replacement value of the assets.

Diversification was thought to be a stabilizing factor on a firm's earnings and thus reduce risk. There is a controversy about this practice. Stabilization of earnings is beneficial to a firm's employees, suppliers, and customers, but its value to stockholders and debt holders is not clear. This is because investors can diversify their risk on their own; a merger is not the answer.

Maintaining control is a major motivation and based on human psychology. Managers of acquired companies generally lose their jobs or their autonomy. Therefore, managers who own less than 51% of the stock in their firms look to mergers that will lessen the chances of their firm's being taken over. Defensive merger tactics are practiced by using much higher debt to acquire other firms so that the debt level will be hard for any potential acquirer to digest.

As shown in Exhibit 4.45, economists classify mergers into five groups:

1. Horizontal
2. Vertical
3. Congeneric
4. Conglomerate
5. Beachhead

EXHIBIT 4.45 Types of Mergers

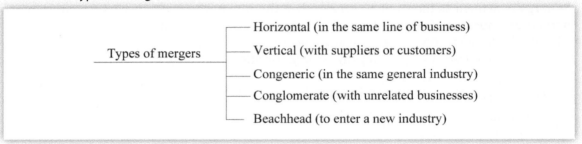

A **horizontal merger** occurs when one firm combines with another competing firm in its same line of business or market. Such a merger can occur between a producer and another producer in the same industry (e.g., an automobile manufacturing firm combines with another automobile manufacturing firm). This kind of merger provides the greatest synergistic operating benefits and could be subjected to investigations by the U.S. Department of Justice or SEC. It is most likely to be attacked as a restraint of trade because both companies are in the same line of business and in the same industry.

A **vertical merger** occurs between a firm and one of its suppliers or customers. The goal is to integrate operations from both sides. It can occur between a producer and its supplier (e.g., a steel manufacturing firm acquires one of its own suppliers or customers). The suppliers are the firm's own suppliers in the supply-chain line. Two types of vertical merger can occur: A forward vertical merger occurs when a supplier acquires a customer; a backward vertical merger occurs when a customer acquires a supplier.

A **congeneric merger** is a merger of firms in the same general industry but for which no customer or supplier relationship exists. Also, the lines of businesses are different. Here the word "congeneric" means allied in nature or action involving related businesses. It is neither a horizontal merger nor a vertical merger.

A **conglomerate merger** occurs when two or more unrelated enterprises combine. It is an acquisition by one company of another that is not a competitor, customer, or supplier. An example is when a retail firm acquires both a financial institution and a real estate firm.

A **beachhead merger** takes on a new risk and opportunity, entering a new industry to exploit perceived opportunities.

(A) Merger Analysis

Whatever type of merger is used, the underlying concept of merger analysis is capital budgeting techniques. The objective is to determine whether the PV of the cash flows expected to result from the merger exceeds the price that must be paid for the target company. The acquiring firm performs the capital budgeting analysis.

CAPITAL BUDGETING TECHNIQUES AND MERGERS

- If the NPV is positive, the acquiring firm acquires the target firm.
- If the NPV is negative, the acquiring firm does not acquire the target firm.

The merger analysis can focus on four areas: strategic mergers, operating mergers, financial mergers, or strategic alliance arrangements. In a **strategic merger**, the economies-of-scale concept is the focus, which means:

- Increasing market share for products and services.
- Eliminating duplicate functions, departments, divisions, manufacturing plants, warehouses, or offices.
- Reducing the raw material suppliers' source base.
- Decreasing the number of marketing distribution channels.
- Increasing the overall efficiency of the entire company.

Senior management expects that after a strategic merger, the performance of the postmerged firm is significantly better than that of the premerged firm. A strategic merger appears to be the best type of merger due to its long-term survivability or sustainability compared to other types of mergers.

An **operating merger** is a merger in which operations of the firms involved are integrated in the hope of achieving synergistic benefits. In most cases, an operating merger is similar to a strategic merger in terms of common goals and objectives to achieve.

ANALYTICAL TECHNIQUES USED IN MERGERS, ACQUISITIONS, AND DIVESTITURES

- Strengths, weaknesses, opportunities, and threats (SWOT) analysis
- Investment analysis (capital budgeting, NPV, and IRR)
- Sensitivity analysis (using what-if questions, finding out what it is, and knowing what it should be after changing the inputs to determine corresponding outputs)

(Continued)

ANALYTICAL TECHNIQUES USED IN MERGERS, ACQUISITIONS, AND DIVESTITURES (*Continued*)

- Scenario analysis (building scenarios such as A, B, C, or D with best-case, most likely, and worst-case outcomes with or without the help of simulations)

- Simulation analysis (using computers, models, and statistics to determine different outcomes with different assumptions)

- Normal due diligence reviews (initial screening, analysis, and negotiations) prior to closing the M&A (If such reviews are done properly, the defendant is not liable.)

- Reverse due diligence reviews (initial screening, analysis, and negotiations) prior to closing the divestitures (If such reviews are done properly, the defendant is not liable.)

- Fit-gap analysis (how much fit is there, how much gap is there, and where is the real value)

- Consequence-based analysis (understanding competitors' unexpected and aggressive moves; government's negative reactions by the SEC and Federal Trade Commission in the United States; current customers' acceptance and retention rates; changes in technology in both IT and non-IT areas; buyers becoming competitors in divestitures; positive or negative impact on sales, costs, profits, stock prices, and business growth levels; and employee morale issues)

A **financial merger** is one in which the merged companies will be operated independently and from which no significant operating economies of scale are expected. The postmerger cash flows are simply the sum of the expected cash flows of the two companies if they continued to operate independently. A financial merger also means restructuring the acquired company to improve the cash flows and unlock its hidden value.

A **strategic alliance arrangement**, although not a merger in its true meaning, occurs when a large and highly established company with proven products, markets, and distribution channels wishes to invest its money in a small and emerging company in the areas of new R&D activities that could help the large company in its growth.

After completing the merger analysis, a value of the target firm should be assessed in order to determine an educated price. Both cash flows and a discount rate are essential in valuing the target firm, although accurate estimates of future cash flows are difficult to obtain. Cash flows can be developed using a set of pro forma income statements and balance sheets for a number of years (say, five years). These net cash flows are discounted at the firm's overall cost of capital, if both debt and equity are used to finance the merger. If only equity is used, then the firm's cost of equity should be used. The price paid to acquire the target firm is a summation of the discounted net cash flows at the appropriate cost of capital.

EXAMPLE REASON FOR ACQUISITION

A company acquired an older and more established competitor in the same industry. The company being acquired had consistently earned lower (but positive) net income and has a low debt-to-equity ratio. The reason for the acquisition probably was to increase financing capacity.

(ii) Divestitures

While M&As focus on buying new businesses and new assets from outside sellers either as a whole or in parts, divestitures focus on selling a company's existing businesses or assets to outside buyers either as a whole or in parts. The reason divestitures are undertaken is that these businesses or assets have little or no value to the selling company due to their underperformance or money losses and the fact that they do not fit with the core business of the selling company.

Divestiture actions can be thought of as cleaning up or strengthening the balance sheet or cleaning the closet or garage. They also can be thought of as treating nonproducing assets the same as dead assets (assets that are not making the company money and at the same time are cluttering the balance sheet). These nonproducing assets should not be taken lightly; their hidden values could be valuable to some other companies.

At least three types of divestitures can exist: spin-offs, selloffs, and close-offs.

Spin-offs occur where a large company establishes a new corporation based on the assets from one of its operating divisions. The stock of the new corporation is titled to the stockholders of the parent firm. The operating division or business unit becomes an independent company through the issuance of shares in it, on a pro rata basis, to the parent company's shareholders. A spin-off also occurs when a company sells one of its operating divisions to its existing shareholders, and the shareholders receive new stock representing separate ownership rights in the division.

Sell-offs include selling the entire business unit or its assets, whether as a whole or in parts. The total value of a firm is greater than the sum of the values of its individual operating units if each unit were sold separately. This means some units are good with hidden value while other units are bad with little or no value.

Close-offs include discontinuing an unprofitable product line and closing a losing department, facility, business unit, or division.

(iii) Leveraged Buyouts

Often, an LBO method is an alternative to a merger. An **LBO** is a financial transaction in which a firm's publicly owned stock is bought up in a mostly debt-financed tender offer. The result is a privately owned and highly leveraged firm. There is a controversy as to whether LBOs are good or bad ideas for companies or the economy as a whole. Some argue that LBOs might destabilize the economy because of the disruptive forces involved in the deals. Others argue that LBOs can stimulate lethargic or complacent management.

The existence of potential bargains, situations in which companies were using insufficient leverage, and the development of the so-called junk bond market all facilitated the use of leverage in takeovers. LBOs can be initiated in one of two ways.

1. The firm's own managers can set up a new company whose equity comes from the managers themselves plus equity from outside sources. This new company then arranges to borrow a large amount of money by selling junk bonds through an investment banking firm.

2. A specialized LBO firm identifies a potential target company, goes to the management, and suggests that an LBO deal be done.

Whatever method is used in an LBO, the newly formed company will have a high debt ratio, ranging from 80% to 98%, hence the term "highly leveraged."

(iv) Holding Companies

A **holding company** is a company that owns stock in another company and exercises control. The holding company is called the parent company, and the controlled companies are called subsidiaries or operating companies. A holding company is taxed on profits, cannot issue tax-free bonds, and is subject to normal government regulations. Consolidation accounting-type transactions are needed between the parent company and its subsidiaries.

Although holding companies have advantages and disadvantages similar to those of large corporations, they differ in the following areas.

Advantages of a holding company include: (1) control with fractional ownership (anywhere between 5% and 100% of another company's stock; 10% to 25% of common stock ownership is considered to have a working control); (2) isolation of risk to a single unit; and (3) legal and accounting separation when regulations make such separation desirable.

Disadvantages of a holding company include: partial multiple taxation due to not requiring a consolidated tax return when the ownership is less than 80% of a subsidiary's voting stock and ease of enforced dissolution by the Justice Department if it finds the ownership of a holding company unacceptable. The parent company is required to pay tax on dividends from the subsidiary, thus leading to partial and multiple taxations.

(v) Role of Investment Bankers in Mergers, Acquisitions, and Divestitures

An investment banker and a lawyer are usually involved with a merger by helping to arrange mergers, advising target companies in developing and implementing defensive tactics, and helping to value target companies. An investment banker is also consulted for divestitures. For these services, a fee and commissions are paid to the investment banker.

(vi) Key Terms, Actions, and Tactics Used in Mergers, Acquisitions, and Divestitures

Business mergers can be friendly or hostile. Of particular importance is developing defensive tactics to block hostile mergers. Some commonly used tactics are listed next.

- Changing the bylaws to require a supermajority of directors instead of a simple majority to approve a merger
- Educating the target firm's stockholders that the price being offered is too low
- Raising antitrust issues in the hope that the Justice Department will intervene
- Persuading a white knight (i.e., last minute helping-hand) more acceptable to the target firm's management that it should compete with the potential acquirer
- Taking a "poison pill," which includes:
  - Management committing suicide to avoid a takeover
  - Borrowing on terms that require immediate repayment of all loans if the firm is acquired
  - Selling off the assets at bargain prices to make the firm less attractive to the potential acquirer
  - Granting lucrative golden parachutes to the firm's executives to drain off some cash
  - Taking on a huge debt
  - Leaving behind assets of questionable value

Corporate management often uses the following terms, actions, and tactics during the merger, acquisition, and divestiture processes either to delay the process or to deny the offer, especially if it is a hostile one. Specific examples of these terms, actions, and tactics follow.

- A **friendly merger** is a merger whose terms are amicable and approved by management of both the acquiring and the target firms. There is a higher chance of completing the friendly merger transaction and a small chance of its becoming a hostile merger.

- A **tender offer** occurs when one firm buys the stock of another firm by going directly to the stockholders, frequently over the opposition of the target firm's management. The intent is to bypass the target firm's management. This is an example of a defensive takeover attempt.

- A **golden parachute** is a legal employment contract in which a corporation agrees to make payment to key officers (e.g., directors, executives, and managers) if a hostile takeover or a major change in the control of the corporation takes place. This is an added financial incentive for key officers to aggressively focus on M&A of other companies and stop worrying about their fear of job loss and losses of: bonuses, stock options, profit sharing, job status and prestige, and perks. A major downside of the golden parachute is that key officers get paid huge amounts of money even though their company's financial and operational performance is bad or not as expected. This occurs because the golden parachute is based on a legal employment contract. Here the golden parachute is used in a hostile merger or as a bad merger tactic.

- A **hostile merger** is a merger transaction that the target firm's management does not support. The acquiring company is forced to try to gain control of the firm by buying shares in the marketplace. Varieties of defensive tactics are available to stop the hostile takeover attempts.

- A **Pac-Man defense** is a threat to undertake a hostile takeover of the prospective combinor.

- A **poison pill** is a takeover defense in which an acquiring firm issues new securities that give its current shareholders certain rights that become effective when a takeover is attempted; these rights make the target firm less desirable to a hostile acquirer. The poison pill action will seriously damage a target company if it is acquired by a hostile firm. It may involve an amendment of the articles of incorporation or bylaws to make it more difficult to obtain stockholders' approval for a hostile takeover. A poison pill is a shareholder rights plan aimed at discouraging or preventing hostile takeovers. Typically, the poison pill provides that when a hostile suitor acquires more than a certain percentage of a company's stock, other shareholders receive share purchase rights designed to dilute the suitor's holdings and make the acquisition prohibitively expensive. Here the poison pill is a bad merger tactic and a takeover defense.

- A **poison put** is a variation of the poison pill as it forces a firm to buy its securities (e.g., stocks) back at some set price. Here the poison put is a bad merger tactic.

- A **scorched earth strategy** is the disposal of assets either by sale or by spin-off to stockholders of one or more profitable business segments. Target firms often sell or threaten to sell their major assets (i.e., crown jewels) when faced with a hostile takeover threat. This tactic often involves a lockup (another name for a scorched earth strategy).

- A **lockup** is an option granted to a friendly suitor (e.g., a white knight) giving it the right to purchase stock or some of the major assets (e.g., crown jewels) of a larger firm at a fixed price in the event of an unfriendly takeover.

- A **shark repellent** is any tactic (e.g., poison pill) designed to discourage hostile or unwanted merger offers. It may involve acquisition of substantial amounts of outstanding common stock in exchange for treasury stock or for retirement of stock, or incurring of substantial long-term debt in exchange for the outstanding common stock.

- A **white knight** occurs when the target firm finds a friendly new acquiring firm that is more acceptable to its management than the initial hostile acquirer. Then the white knight and the target firm together can compete to take over the acquiring firm. The friendly firm is the white knight. This it is a good merger tactic.

- A **greenmail** occurs when a target firm repurchases, through private negotiations, a large block of stock at a premium price from one or more shareholders to end a hostile takeover attempt by those shareholders. The target companies pay the greenmail to end the threat of a takeover attempt. Here greenmail is a bad merger tactic.

- A **whitemail** occurs when white knights or others are granted exceptional merger terms or otherwise well compensated. Here the whitemail is a good merger tactic.

- A leveraged buyout (LBO) is a transaction in which a firm's publicly owned stock is bought up in a mostly debt-financed tender offer. The result is a privately owned and highly leveraged firm. It is an example of a financial merger.

- An initial public offering (IPO) or going public means that a privately owned firm is offering its shares to public ownership the first time. After an IPO, the public owns a part of the private firm for the first time.

- A holding company is a corporation that has voting control of one or more other corporations.

Key terms, actions, and tactics used in a *friendly merger* include: up front, honest, and amicable communication, and use of white knight and whitemail as needed and only after thorough research, keen observations, expert advice, and detailed analysis and evaluations are performed.

Key terms, actions, and tactics used in a *hostile merger* include: tender offer, poison pill, poison put, shark repellent, scorched earth, greenmail, Pac-Man defense, and golden parachute.

Key terms, actions, and tactics used in a *divestiture* include: scorched earth, selling crown jewels, lockup, spin-offs, and selling a profitable division and setting it up as a new company for existing stockholders.

(vii) Similarities and Differences Between Acquisitions and Divestitures

Most companies actively perform acquisition (includes both M&A) activities in buying new businesses or assets and passively perform selling some of their existing businesses and assets for glamour, recognition, and status, to name a few reasons. There is nothing wrong with selling underperforming and money-losing businesses or assets that do not fit well with a company's core business and that could prove more valuable to other firms. This is because both acquisitions and divestitures have the same goal of increasing returns to shareholders (e.g., wealth, profit, and stock price maximization, and all leading to the ultimate goal of maximizing shareholders' value).

- Acquisitions need a team approach to perform buy-side activities in a systematic, disciplined, and structured manner.

- Divestitures need a team approach to perform sell-side activities in a systematic, disciplined, and structured manner.

- Both require the same amount of planning, time, effort, and analysis from a strategic, operational, technical, and cultural viewpoint before making a final decision.

- Both should perform a fit-gap analysis to determine what new business or assets to be acquired and what existing businesses or assets should be disposed of, either in whole or in part. This fit-gap analysis should follow the core business objectives and goals.

- Both have the same problem of buying or selling assets at the wrong time, at the wrong price, to a wrong party, and in a wrong manner.

- Both operate on the assumption that there is always a buyer and a seller available to start and complete a business transaction.

- Acquisitions need an integration plan and approach to combine the new business with the current business.

- Divestitures need a deintegration plan and approach to separate the sold business from the current business.

- Both have a negative impact on current employees in terms of their job performance levels: job motivation levels, pay levels, job security needs; pension and retirement benefits; medical and health care benefits; severance pay amounts, outplacement services, and job seniority levels.

- In divestitures, each potential buyer can become a potential competitor later on.

- In acquisitions, a normal due diligence review should be conducted by a buyer through the seller' eyes to quantify risks, opportunities, costs, profits, and revenue synergies for potential sellers.

- In divestitures, a reverse due diligence review should be conducted by a seller through the buyer's eyes to quantify risks, opportunities, costs, profits, and revenue synergies for potential buyers.

- Both sides should bring a win-win attitude to the negotiating table during acquisition and divestiture discussions. However, the real outcome is not known until after the acquisition or divestiture is fully completed and has operated for some time.

4.2 Managerial Accounting

The scope of managerial accounting (MA) topics include a discussion of costing systems, cost concepts, relevant costs, cost-volume-profit (CVP) analysis, transfer pricing, responsibility accounting, and operating budgets. In addition, general concepts in MA are briefly presented and compared with FA where necessary.

(a) Managerial Accounting: General Concepts

The topics of MA and FA can be thought of as two sides of a coin. One side provides information to the other side, and each side shares some common information with each other. For example, internal managers and executives share and use some FA reports, such as balance sheets, income statements, statements of cash flows, and other customized financial reports. Some activities are similar between MA and FA (e.g., record keeping) while some activities (e.g., decision making) are different.

- The major focus of MA is satisfying the internal needs of an organization by helping the board of directors, executives, managers, and employees. The focus of FA is meeting the external needs of an organization by helping investors, owners, creditors, governmental agencies, suppliers and vendors, and labor unions through publishing financial statements and filing tax reports.

- Most MA decisions are future oriented (i.e., focusing on incremental revenues, costs, and profits) instead of past oriented (historical costs, revenues, and profits) as in FA.

- Inventory valuation methods are different between MA and FA, thus affecting the value of inventory assets, costs, and net incomes. FA uses GAAP; MA does not use GAAP. GAAP offers more flexibility to MA than to the FA because the focus of MA is internal to a company.

- MA looks at incremental and differential costs, revenues, and profits prior to making decisions.

- MA considers opportunity costs (implicit costs) in decision making; these costs are not recorded in FA transactions.

- MA separates relevant costs from irrelevant costs, handles transfer pricing issues between departments and divisions, and fosters responsibility accounting in making managers and executives more accountable to their actions or inactions.

- Both MA and FA have a similar policy in terms of financing long-term assets with long-term liabilities and financing short-term assets with short-term liabilities. It is called maturity matching. Any misuse of this matching policy can lead to financial volatility and to loss of profitability and solvency.

- MA helps managers and executives understand the basic cost concepts and their behaviors (e.g., period costs versus product costs; variable costs versus fixed/mixed costs; direct costs versus indirect costs; short-run costs versus long-run costs; avoidable costs versus unavoidable costs; controllable costs versus uncontrollable costs; discretionary costs versus nondiscretionary costs; and committed costs versus uncommitted costs) when establishing long-term prices for products and services and after considering changes in production, sales, and workforce volumes and their effects on profit and growth levels.

- MA experiments with or researches new costing systems for products and services, such as activity-based or target-based costing methods, to determine the true cost of a product and service and to see how such costs can be decreased and profits can be increased without decreasing quality.

- MA works with technologies and innovations, such as flexible manufacturing systems, computer-aided manufacturing, bar-coding systems, point-of-sale terminals, robotics, JIT philosophies, lean production methods, total quality management principles, Six Sigma tools, international organization for standardization (ISO) standards, and cellular manufacturing systems.

- MA's goal is to identify and remove non-value-adding activities and waste from value-adding activities in manufacturing and services to conserve resources, decrease costs, and increase profits.

- MA uses both capital budgeting and operating budgets as control devices in managing cash inflows and cash outflows and in estimating cash needs for both the short and the long term.

- MA deals with nonprogrammed and nonroutine decisions for managers and executives. These decisions include:

  - Building a new manufacturing plant, warehouse, or office

  - Handling mergers, acquisitions, and divestitures

  - Introducing new products and services

  - Divesting an existing product or service

  - Making lease-or-buy decisions

  - Analyzing make-or-buy decisions

  - Entering new markets with new or existing distribution channels or exiting from such markets and channels

  - Setting long-term pricing policies (i.e., price leader or follower)

  - Deciding between insourcing or outsourcing of products and services

  - Addressing workforce staffing, planning, and diversity management issues

  - Understanding the cost of compliance versus cost of noncompliance with laws and regulations

  - Abandoning a specific nonperforming product/product line or service or closing a money-losing department or division

  - Setting short-term prices for certain products or services based on a one-time big order from a major customer at least to recover variable costs, increase contribution margins (CMs), ignoring long-term fixed costs, all of which can increase short-term profits

In summary, MA concepts and decisions are nonsequential, unstructured, nonprogrammed, and nonroutine in nature and are handled mostly by high-level management. The reverse is not true with FA.

(b) Costing Systems

Product cost control systems can be viewed in terms of target, traditional, activity-based, JIT, and standard costing.

(i) Target Costing

Target costing is a better way of controlling a product's cost. A **target cost** is the allowable amount of cost that can be incurred on a given product and still earn the required profit margin. It is a market-driven cost in which cost targets are set by considering customer requirements and competitive environment. Cost targets are achieved by focusing and improving both process design and product design. Market research indicates the target price customers are willing to pay.

$$\text{Target cost} = \text{Target price} - \text{Profit margin}$$

$$\text{Target price} = \text{Target cost} + \text{Profit margin}$$

The need for target costing arises due to sophisticated customers demanding better-quality products with more features and functions at an affordable price. This is made real by aggressive competitors who are willing to take risks and provide a product at a target price with the hope of achieving efficiencies in cost management and production operations.

Target costing is not the same as design to cost or design for manufacturability, which are issues for engineering and manufacturing management, respectively. Target costing integrates strategic business planning with cost/profit planning. To achieve this integration, a target-costing system requires cross-functional teams to take ownership and responsibility for costs. These teams consist of representatives from finance/accounting, marketing, engineering, manufacturing, and other functions.

(ii) Traditional Costing

Traditional costing systems use a cost-plus approach, where production costs are first estimated, then a profit margin is added to it to obtain a product price that the market is going to pay. If the price is too high, cost reductions are initiated. Traditional costing systems are cost-driven approaches where customer requirements and competitive environment are not considered.

$$\text{Traditional cost} = \text{Traditional price} - \text{Profit margin}$$

$$\text{Traditional price} = \text{Traditional cost} + \text{Profit margin}$$

The cost to manufacture a product is necessary for external reporting (e.g., inventory valuation and COGS determination) and internal management decisions (e.g., price determination, product mix decisions, and sensitivity analysis). One of the goals of cost accounting is to provide information for management planning and control and determination of product or service costs. This is achieved through the accumulation of costs by department and/or by product. Although the terminology differs between manufacturing and service industries, the principles of cost accounting are the same.

Two methods exist to accumulate product costs: job order costing systems and process (operations) costing systems. Both methods help management in planning and control of business operations. A job order cost system provides a separate record for the cost of each quantity of product that passes through the factory. This system is best suited to industries that manufacture custom goods to fill special orders from customers or that produce a high variety of products for stock (job shops). Under a process cost system, costs are accumulated for each of the departments or processes within the factory. This system is best suited for manufacturers of units of products that are not distinguishable from each other during a continuous production process (e.g., oil refineries and food processing). See Exhibit 4.46.

TRADITIONAL COST SYSTEMS VERSUS TARGET COST SYSTEMS

- Traditional cost systems are closed systems where the focus is on internal measures of efficiency. Suppliers are involved after the product is designed. Cost reduction is initiated after the fact based on product standards or budgets with the aim of reducing or eliminating waste and inefficiency. Costs determine price.

■ Target cost systems are open systems where the focus is on external market demands. Suppliers are involved before the product is designed. Cost reduction is initiated before the fact based on continuous improvement opportunities with the aim of enhancing the product's design. Prices determine costs.

Exhibit 4.46 compares these two product cost systems.

EXHIBIT 4.46 Comparison of Product Costing Methods

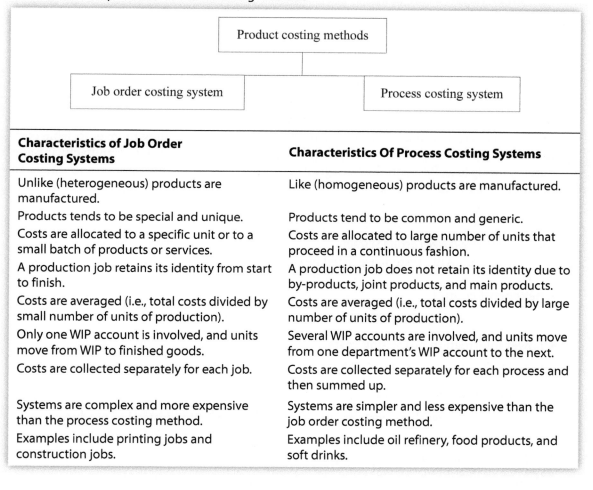

Characteristics of Job Order Costing Systems	Characteristics Of Process Costing Systems
Unlike (heterogeneous) products are manufactured.	Like (homogeneous) products are manufactured.
Products tends to be special and unique.	Products tend to be common and generic.
Costs are allocated to a specific unit or to a small batch of products or services.	Costs are allocated to large number of units that proceed in a continuous fashion.
A production job retains its identity from start to finish.	A production job does not retain its identity due to by-products, joint products, and main products.
Costs are averaged (i.e., total costs divided by small number of units of production).	Costs are averaged (i.e., total costs divided by large number of units of production).
Only one WIP account is involved, and units move from WIP to finished goods.	Several WIP accounts are involved, and units move from one department's WIP account to the next.
Costs are collected separately for each job.	Costs are collected separately for each process and then summed up.
Systems are complex and more expensive than the process costing method.	Systems are simpler and less expensive than the job order costing method.
Examples include printing jobs and construction jobs.	Examples include oil refinery, food products, and soft drinks.

(iii) Activity-Based Costing

Activity-based costing (ABC) is a management system that focuses on activities as the fundamental cost objects and uses the costs of these activities as building blocks for compiling the costs of other cost objects. ABC helps management in controlling costs through its focus on cost drivers. ABC can provide more accurate product cost data by using multiple cost drivers that more accurately reflect the causes of costs. Inaccurate product cost information can lead to cross-subsidization of products. This results in systematic under-costing of products due to lower overhead rate. These cost drivers can be both non-volume-based as well as volume-based drivers.

KEY CONCEPTS TO REMEMBER: Activity-Based Costing

- The key focus of ABC is on activities, not on products. This is in line with the philosophy of executives in managing costs. The scope of activities may range from start to finish for a product or service (i.e., from R&D to customer service).

- If the manufacturing process is described as machine-paced, then machine hours should be used as the cost driver.

- If the manufacturing process is described as labor-paced, then direct labor hours should be used as the cost driver.

- If direct labor is a small percentage (e.g., 5%) of total manufacturing costs, it should be regarded as a part of indirect costs, not direct costs.

- ABC can be a part of a job-costing or process-costing system.

ABC builds the cost of a product from the bottom up for all activities involved (A1 through An) in all departments (D1 through Dn) in a manufacturing function yielding to inventoriable cost. The full cost of a product is obtained similarly by adding costs for functions. Manufacturing and nonmanufacturing (e.g., R&D, product design, marketing, customer service) costs are accumulated for each activity as a separate cost object. The costs collected at each cost object can be variable costs of the activity or both variable and fixed costs of the activity.

(A) Benefits of Activity-Based Costing System

Major benefits of an ABC system are listed next.

- Better cost control

- Accurate product cost information

- Lower information processing costs

- Individual costs allocated to products via several cost drivers

- Better make-or-buy decisions

- Focus on activities where costs are incurred and accumulated instead of products

(B) When to Use an Activity-Based Costing System

An ABC system should be used in companies that have these characteristics:

- High overhead costs

- A widely diverse range of products and operating activities

- Wide variation in number of production runs and costly setups

- The accounting system lags behind the production system's advancements

(C) Comparison of a Traditional Accounting System with an Activity-Based Costing System

A better appreciation of an ABC system can be made when it is compared with the traditional, typical accounting system. (See Exhibit 4.47.)

EXHIBIT 4.47 Comparison of Traditional Accounting System with Activity-Based Costing System

Traditional Accounting System	Activity-Based Costing System
Functions are divided into departments.	Departments are divided into activities.
The system fails to highlight interrelationships among activities in different departments or functions.	The system highlights interrelationships among activities in different departments or functions.
Accountants need not possess interpersonal skills to interact with production staff.	Accountants need to possess interpersonal skills to interact with production staff.
Accountants need not become knowledgeable in production operations.	Accountants need to become knowledgeable in production operations.
One or a few indirect cost pools are used for each department or whole plant.	Many indirect cost pools are used because there are many activity areas.
Indirect cost application bases are often financial, such as direct labor costs or direct material costs.	Indirect cost application bases are often nonfinancial variables, such as number of parts in a product or hours of test time.
Indirect costs are allocated to products using a single overhead rate.	Indirect costs are allocated to products using multiple cost drivers, preferably the same as the indirect cost application bases.

(iv) Just-in-Time Costing

A JIT costing system starts with completed production units (outputs) and then assigns manufacturing costs to units sold (sales) and units not sold (inventories). This is called backflush costing because it works backward by recording the costs of production when outputs are completed. It does not cost products as they move from raw materials stage to work-in-process stage and then to finished goods stage. JIT costing contrasts with standard costing, where the latter builds the costs of products as they move from raw materials stage to work-in-process stage and then to finished goods stage. Backflush costing is also called delayed costing or postdeduct costing.

(v) Standard Costing

Standard costs are predetermined costs or estimated costs requiring a start-up investment to develop them. Ongoing costs for maintenance of standards can be lower than for an actual-cost system. Standard costs should be attainable and are expressed on a per-unit basis. Without standard costs, there is no flexible budgeting system since the latter is developed at different volumes of production using standard costs per unit.

Standard costs, flexible budgets, and standards are equally applicable to manufacturing and nonmanufacturing firms. Standard costs and flexible budgets are interrelated. A **flexible budget** is a budget that is adjusted for changes in the unit level of the cost driver or revenue driver. In a standard cost system, the concept of a flexible budget is key to the analysis of variances.

A powerful benefit of standard costing is its feedback mechanism, where actual costs are compared with standard costs resulting in variances. This feedback helps users to explore better ways of adhering to standards, modifying standards, and accomplishing production goals. Standard costs can be developed for material, labor, and overhead. One drawback of a standard cost system is that actual direct material costs and actual direct labor costs cannot be traced to individual products.

STANDARD COST VERSUS BUDGETED COST

- "Standard cost" refers to the cost of a single unit of output (e.g., $50 per unit).

- "Budgeted cost" refers to a total amount ($500,000 at 10,000 units).

- A standard amount and a budgeted amount are the same when standards are attainable.

Major purposes of standard costs are listed next, in decreasing order of importance.

- Cost management
- Price-making policy
- Budgetary planning and control
- Financial statement preparation
- Lower record-keeping costs

Line management is responsible for standard setting and the budget-development process. The accounting department, which is a staff function, is responsible for expressing the physical standard in monetary terms, for coordinating the budgeting process throughout the firm, and for reporting operating performance in comparison with standards and budgets.

Standards help in evaluating the performance of responsibility centers. Most recently established standards should be used in variance analysis. Variances—differences between standards and actuals—can be developed, reported, and tracked for control purposes in a number of ways, as shown in Exhibit 4.48.

EXHIBIT 4.48 Different Ways of Tracking and Measuring Variances

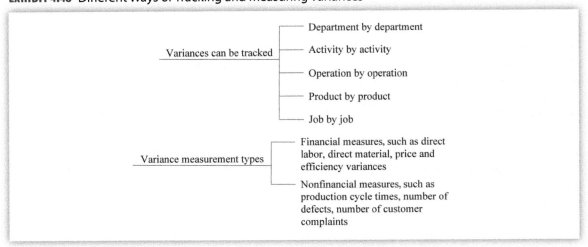

Organizations are moving away from financial measures to nonfinancial measures for better focus on the problem at hand because numbers cannot tell everything and to gain different perspectives. For example, one reason for moving away from direct labor as a measurement of variance is its minor role in total cost for firms with automated production operations.

(A) Types of Standards

Two concepts prevail in standards: perfection (ideal or theoretical) and currently attainable. Their features are shown in the Exhibit 4.49.

EXHIBIT 4.49 Characteristics of Standards

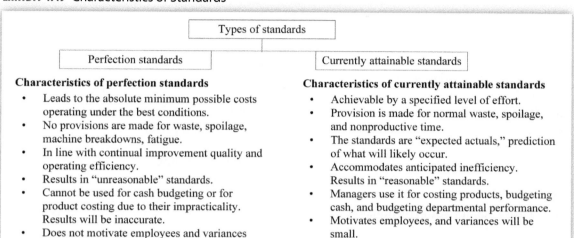

(B) Types of Variances

In general, **price variance** is the difference between actual unit prices and budgeted unit prices multiplied by the actual quantity of goods sold, used, or purchased.

$$\text{Price variance} = (\text{Actual unit price} - \text{Standard unit price}) \times \text{Actual inputs purchased}$$

Companies that use fewer suppliers and longer-term contracts are less likely to have significant material price variances. This is because contracts specify unchanging prices for fixed time spans and the buying firm has leverage against the selling firm.

Companies that use several suppliers and short-term contracts are more likely to have significant material price variances. This is because contracts are frequently changed or canceled and the buying firm has little or no leverage against the selling firm.

The purchasing manager is responsible for the material price variance and can help control it by:

- Getting many price quotations.
- Buying in economical lot sizes.
- Taking advantage of cash discounts.
- Selecting the most economical means of material delivery.

These variances could result in a favorable material price variance, depending on how material standards are set.

Due to labor union contracts, labor price variance is relatively insignificant since management knows the future labor rates, unlike material prices.

In general, efficiency variance is of two types: material efficiency and labor efficiency. Possible reasons for material efficiency variances are listed next.

- Quality of materials
- Workmanship
- Choice of materials
- Mix of materials
- Incorrect standards

Efficiency variance is the difference between the quantity of actual inputs used and the quantity of inputs that should have been used multiplied by the budgeted price.

$$\text{Efficiency variance} = (\text{Inputs actually used} - \text{Inputs that should have been used}) \times \text{Standard unit price of inputs}$$

The factory supervisor is responsible for the efficiency variance. Efficiency variance is quantity or usage variance with respect to direct materials.

Direct materials variance is of two types: price and quantity. The price variance is actual price paid per unit of input (AP) minus standard price established per unit of input (SP) multiplied by actual quantity of input used in production (AQ); in other words:

$$\text{Direct materials price variance} = (AP - SP) \times AQ$$

The materials price variance is unfavorable if AP is greater than SP and favorable if AP is less than SP.

The quantity variance is actual quantity of input used in production (AQ) minus standard quantity of input that should have been used in production (SQ) multiplied by standard price established per unit of input (SP), or:

$$\text{Direct materials quantity variance} = (AQ - SQ) \times SP$$

The materials quantity variance is unfavorable if AQ is greater than SQ and favorable if AQ is less than SQ.

Direct labor variance is of two types: rate and efficiency. The rate variance is actual price paid per unit of input (AP) minus standard price established per unit of input (SP) multiplied by actual quantity of input used in production (AQ), or:

$$\text{Direct labor rate variance} = (AP - SP) \times AQ$$

The labor rate variance is unfavorable if AP is greater than SP and favorable if AP is less than SP.

The efficiency variance is actual quantity of input used in production (AQ) minus standard quantity of input that should have been used in production (SQ) multiplied by standard price established per unit of input (SP), or:

$$\text{Direct labor efficiency variance} = (AQ - SQ) \times SP$$

The labor efficiency variance is unfavorable if AQ is greater than SQ and favorable if AQ is less than SQ.

Overhead variance is of four types: spending, efficiency, budget, and volume. Spending and efficiency variances are part of variable overhead variances; budget and volume variances are part of fixed overhead variances.

$$\text{Spending variance} = \text{Actual variable overhead} - (\text{Actual hours} \times \text{Budget rate})$$

$$\text{Efficiency variance} = \text{Budget rate} \times (\text{Actual hours} - \text{Standard hours})$$

The budget variance is sometimes called the fixed overhead spending variance. It is calculated as the difference between actual fixed costs and budget fixed costs.

The volume variance is sometimes called the idle capacity variance. This is computed as:

$$\text{Budget fixed cost} - (\text{Standard hours allowed for actual output at standard rate})$$

EXAMPLE CALCULATION OF VARIANCES

Example 1

A manager prepared the following table by which to analyze labor costs for the month:

Actual hours at actual rate	Actual hours at standard rate	Standard hours at standard rate
$10,000	$9,800	$8,820

What variance was $980? It is the labor efficiency variance, which is the difference between actual and standard hours multiplied by standard wages— that is, $9,800 – $8,820 = $980.

Example 2

A firm's budget showed planned sales of 20,000 units at a $20 CM each, or $400,000. Actual sales totaled 21,000 units. There were no variable cost variances. What was the sales volume variance for the period? It is $20,000, as shown below.

The sales volume variance is the difference between actual results (21,000 units) and planned results (20,000 units) at planned CM ($20), or $20,000.

Example 3

The next exhibit reflects a summary of performance for a single item of a retail store's inventory for the month ended April 30, 20X2.

	Actual Results	Flexible Budget Variances	Flexible Budget	Static (Master) Budget
Sales (units		11,000	11,000	12,000
Revenue (sales)	$208,000	$12,000 U	$220,000	$240,000
Variable costs	121,000	11,000 U	110,000	120,000

(Continued)

EXAMPLE CALCULATION OF VARIANCES (*Continued*)

	Actual Results	Flexible Budget Variances	Flexible Budget	Static (Master) Budget
Contribution margin	$121,000	$23,000 U	$110,000	$120,000
Fixed costs	72,000	72,000	72,000	
Operating income	49,000	$23,000 U	$38,000	$48,000

What is the sales volume variance? It is $10,000 U, where U means unfavorable. Sales volume variance is defined as the difference between the flexible budget amounts and the static (master) budget amounts: ($38,000 − $48,000 = $10,000 U).

KEY CONCEPTS TO REMEMBER: Price and Efficiency Variance

■ A manager has less control over price variance because of outside influences. Variance is the difference in price multiplied by actual inputs purchased.

■ A manager has better control over efficiency variance because the quantity of inputs used is affected by factors inside the firm. Efficiency variance is the difference in quantity multiplied by the standard unit price.

■ Price and efficiency variances are either written off immediately to COGS or prorated among the inventories and COGS.

A performance measurement and reward system for a firm should emphasize total organizational objectives, not individual departments' variances. The goal is to reduce the total costs of the company as a whole, not price variance or efficiency variance (i.e., single performance measure).

Although labor rates are known from union contracts, unfavorable labor price variance can occur due to:

■ The use of a single average standard labor rate for a given activity that requires different labor rates (the averaging effect).

■ The assignment of a high-skilled worker earning more money to an activity that should have been assigned to a less-skilled worker earning less money.

The control of direct labor is more important to firms with less automation and less important to firms with more automation. The source documents for variance reports are time tickets showing the actual time used. Codes are used to indicate the departmental responsibility and causes of the variance. Employee absenteeism can affect labor efficiency.

Variance analysis should be subjected to the same cost/benefit test as any other managerial decision. No fixed guidance can be given as to how much unfavorable or favorable variance ought to be analyzed. However, it is important to separate variances caused by random events (uncontrollable) from variances that are controllable. Random variances are attributable to chance rather than to management's implementation decisions. Note that (1) a credit balance in the cost variance account means that the actual costs are less than the standard costs, and (2) a debit balance in the cost variance account means that the actual costs are more than the standard costs.

KEY CONCEPTS TO REMEMBER: What Is a Standard?

- A standard is not a single acceptable measure.

- A standard is a range of possible acceptable outcomes.

- Variances are expected to fluctuate randomly within some normal limits. A random variance per se is within this range and requires no corrective action. Only nonrandom variance requires corrective action by management.

(C) Effects of Variance Prorations

GAAP and income tax laws require that financial statements show actual costs of inventories and COGS. Consequently, variance prorations are required if they result in a material change in inventories or operating income. **Variance** is the difference between actual costs and standard costs. A good benefit of proration is that it prevents managers from setting standards aimed at manipulating income. By setting loose standards, managers can bring the resulting favorable variance into current income. If managers do not have to prorate variances, how they set standards can more easily affect a year's operating income. The relevant questions are listed next.

- **How should variances occurring during the first stages of new operations be accounted for?** Standards might initially be set at a loose level to allow for start-up inefficiencies, and later they should be tightened. If the standards are currently attainable, variances should be carried forward as assets and written off in future periods.

- **How should variances be prorated?** First, a decision should be made whether proration should occur, and it usually depends on whether the variances are material in amount.

Decision Rules to Handle Variances

1. Immaterial variances should be written off immediately and adjusted to COGS.

2. Material variances should be prorated as follows: (a) to affect current incomes by posting to COGS and income accounts; (b) to affect inventories by apportioning among WIP, finished goods, and COGS.

Some contend that variances are measures of inefficiency and should be completely written off to the accounting period instead of being prorated among inventories and COGS. They argue that inventory costs will be more representative of desirable and attainable costs.

KEY CONCEPTS TO REMEMBER: Variances

- Variance proration tends to carry costs of inefficiency as assets.

- Variances need not be prorated to inventories as long as standards are currently attainable.

- If ideal or obsolete standards are used, variances should be split: (1) The portion of the variance that reflects departures from currently attainable standards should be written off as period costs, and (2) the portion that does not reflect departures from currently attainable standards should be prorated to inventories and COGS.

Adjustments to inventory accounts are made to satisfy external reporting requirements. The adjustments include:

- Converting a variable-costing inventory valuation to absorption-costing valuation.

- Prorating variances. The journal entry to accomplish this adjustment would be to debit the finished goods inventory adjustment account and to credit either the fixed factory overhead or cost variance accounts (e.g., direct material price variance).

(D) Reporting of Variances

Interim reporting of variance differs among companies. Some firms write off all variances monthly or quarterly to COGS while others prorate the variances among inventories and COGS. Most firms follow the same reporting practices for both interim and annual financial statements.

Interim overhead variances are often called "planned" variances and are deferred. These variances include direct material price variances and factory overhead production volume variances. The rationale is that these variances are expected to disappear by the end of the year through the use of averaging as costs are applied to the product. The "unplanned," unanticipated, underapplied, or overapplied overhead should be reported at the end of an interim period following the same procedures used at the end of a fiscal year (according to APB Opinion 28).

UNDERAPPLIED VERSUS OVERAPPLIED MANUFACTURING OVERHEAD

- If underapplied manufacturing overhead is carried forward during the year, it would appear on an interim balance sheet as a current asset, a prepaid expense.

- If overapplied manufacturing overhead is carried forward during the year, it would appear on an interim balance sheet as a current liability, a deferred credit.

WHO IS RESPONSIBLE FOR WHAT TYPE OF VARIANCES?

- The human resources department is responsible for direct labor price variance due to its ineffectiveness in negotiating favorable labor wage rates with unions.

- The production or manufacturing department is responsible for direct labor efficiency variance due to its ineffectiveness in utilizing labor hours favorably without abnormal delays and bottlenecks in the production flows.

- The purchasing or procurement department is responsible for direct material price variance due to its ineffectiveness in negotiating favorable material prices paid to suppliers and vendors.

- The production or manufacturing department is responsible for material efficiency variance due to its ineffectiveness in utilizing materials favorably without abnormal spillage, spoilage, loss, and waste in the production process.

- The marketing and sales department is responsible for unit sales volume variance due to its inability to sell the products at the budgeted units.

- The marketing or sales department is responsible for sales revenue variance due to its inability to sell the products at the budgeted prices.

- The production or manufacturing department is responsible for variable overhead variance, not fixed overhead variance, due to its ineffectiveness in controlling day-to-day spending and efficiency levels in the factory on items such as nonproduction supplies, repair costs, factory upkeep (maintenance) costs, energy costs, indirect labor time utilization, indirect materials utilization, and other expenses related to nonproduction variable overhead items.

- The plant manager is responsible for underapplied or overapplied manufacturing overhead variance due to differences between planned and actual production volumes.

(c) Cost Concepts

Various cost concepts are introduced in this section along with their specific meanings, application, behavior with changes in sales and production volumes, and estimation methods.

(i) Absorption and Variable Costing Methods

The COGS, which is larger than all of the other expenses combined in a product cost, can be determined under either the absorption costing or variable costing method.

Under **absorption costing**, all manufacturing costs are included in finished goods and remain there as an inventory asset until the goods are sold. Management could misinterpret increases or decreases in income from operations due to mere changes in inventory levels to be the result of business events, such as changes in sales volume, prices, or costs. Absorption costing is necessary in determining historical costs for financial reporting to external users and for tax reporting.

Variable costing may be more useful to management in making decisions. In **variable costing (direct costing)**, the cost of goods manufactured is composed only of variable manufacturing costs—costs that increase or decrease as the volume of production rises or falls. These costs are the direct materials, direct labor, and only those factory overhead costs that vary with the rate of production. The remaining factory overhead costs, which are fixed or nonvariable costs, are generally related to the productive capacity of the manufacturing plant and are not affected by changes in the quantity of product manufactured. Thus, the fixed factory overhead does not become a part of the cost of goods manufactured but is treated as an expense of the period (period cost) in which it is incurred.

The income from operations under variable costing can differ from the income from operations under absorption costing. This difference results from changes in the quantity of the finished goods inventory that are caused by differences in the levels of sales and production.

The following decision rules apply.

- If units sold are less than units produced, then variable costing income is less than absorption costing income.

- If units sold are greater than units produced, then variable costing income is greater than the absorption costing income.

Many accountants believe that the variable costing method should be used for evaluating operating performance because absorption costing encourages management to produce inventory. This is because producing inventory absorbs fixed costs and causes the income from operations to appear higher. In the long run, building inventory without the promise of future sales may lead to higher handling, storage, financing, and obsolescence costs.

(ii) Management's Use of Absorption and Variable Costing Methods

Management's use of absorption costing and variable costing includes controlling costs, pricing products, planning production, analyzing market segments (sales territory and product profitability analysis), and analyzing the CM. Preparing comparative reports under both concepts provides useful insights.

(A) Controlling Costs

All costs are controllable in the long run by someone within a business, but they are not all controllable at the same level of management. For example, plant supervisors, as members of operating management, are responsible for controlling the use of direct materials in their departments. They have no control, however, of insurance costs related to the buildings housing their departments. For a specific level of management, **controllable costs** are costs that can be influenced by management at that level, and **noncontrollable costs** are costs that another level of management controls. This distinction is useful in fixing the responsibility for incurring costs and for reporting costs to those responsible for their control.

Variable manufacturing costs are controlled at the operating level. If the product's cost includes only variable manufacturing costs, operating management can control these costs. The fixed factory overhead costs are normally the responsibility of a higher level of management. Fixed factory overhead costs that are reported as a separate item in the variable costing income statement are easier to identify and control than when they are spread among units of product, as they are under absorption costing.

As in the case with the fixed and variable manufacturing costs, the control of variable and fixed operating expenses is usually the responsibility of different levels of management. Under variable costing, the variable selling and administrative expenses are reported separately from the fixed selling and administrative expenses. Because they are reported in this manner, both types of operating expenses are easier to identify and control than is the case under absorption costing.

(B) Pricing Products

Many factors enter into determining the selling price of a product. The cost of making the product is clearly significant. Microeconomic theory states that income is maximized by expanding output to the volume where the revenue realized by the sale of an additional unit (marginal revenue) equals the cost of that unit (marginal cost). Although the degree of accuracy assumed in economic theory is rarely achieved, the concepts of marginal revenue and marginal cost are useful in setting selling prices.

In the short run, a business is committed to its existing manufacturing facilities. The pricing decision should be based on making the best use of such capacity. The fixed costs cannot be avoided, but the variable costs can be eliminated if the company does not manufacture the product. The selling price of a product, therefore, should at least be equal to the variable costs of making and selling it. Any price above this minimum selling price contributes an amount toward covering fixed costs and providing income. Variable costing procedures yield data that emphasize these relationships.

In the long run, plant capacity can be increased or decreased. If a business is to continue operating, the selling prices of its products must cover all costs and provide a reasonable income. Hence, in establishing pricing policies for the long run, information provided by absorption costing procedures is needed. The results of a research study indicated that the companies studied used absorption costing in making routine pricing decisions. However, these companies regularly used variable costing as a basis for setting prices in many short-run situations.

(C) Planning Production

Planning production also has both short-run and long-run implications. In the short run, production is limited to existing capacity. Operating decisions must be made quickly before opportunities are lost. For example, a company manufacturing products with a seasonal demand may have an opportunity to obtain an off-season order that will not interfere with its production schedule or reduce the sales of its other products. The relevant factors for such a short-run decision are the additional revenues and the additional variable costs associated with the off-season order. If the revenues from the special order will provide a CM, the order should be accepted because it will increase the company's income from operations. For long-run planning, management must also consider the fixed costs.

(D) Analyzing Market Segments

Market analysis is performed by the sales and marketing function in order to determine the profit contributed by market segments. A **market segment** is a portion of business that can be assigned to a manager for profit responsibility. Examples of market segments include sales territories, products, salespersons, and customer distribution channels. Variable costing can provide significant insight to decision making regarding such segments.

(E) Analyzing Contribution Margins

Another use of the CM concept to assist management in planning and controlling operations focuses on differences between planned and actual CMs. However, mere knowledge of the differences is insufficient. Management needs information about the causes of the differences. The systematic examination of the differences between planned and actual CMs is termed **contribution margin analysis.**

Since CM is the excess of sales over variable costs, a difference between the planned and actual CM can be caused by an increase or decrease in the amount of either sales or variable costs. An increase or decrease in either element may in turn be due to an increase or decrease in the (1) number of units sold (quantity factor) or (2) unit sales price or unit cost (unit price or unit cost factor). The effect of these two factors on either sales or variable costs may be stated as follows:

1. **Quantity factor.** It is the effect of a difference in the number of units sold, assuming no change in unit sales price or unit cost. The quantity factor is the difference between the actual quantity sold and the planned quantity sold, multiplied by the planned unit sales price or unit cost.

2. **Unit price factor or unit cost factor.** It is the effect of a difference in unit sales price or unit cost on the number of units sold. The unit price or unit cost factor is the difference between the actual unit price or unit cost and the planned unit price or unit cost, multiplied by the actual quantity sold.

(iii) Technical Aspects of Absorption and Variable Costing Methods

An understanding of the inventory costing method is important for several reasons, such as:

- Measuring product costs and inventories.
- Determining income.
- Deciding between making or buying a product.
- Setting prices.
- Planning product mix to produce or sell.

Two major methods of inventory costing are absorption costing and variable costing (see Exhibit 4.50), and they differ in whether fixed manufacturing overhead is an inventoriable cost (i.e., whether such overhead is included in the inventory or not). Other names used for fixed manufacturing overhead are fixed factory overhead and indirect manufacturing cost.

EXHIBIT 4.50 Two Major Methods of Inventory Costing

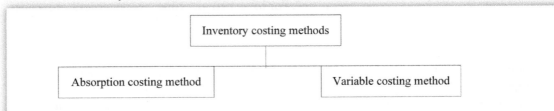

Characteristics of absorption costing method

- Also called full costing method.
- Includes all direct manufacturing costs and both variable and fixed indirect manufacturing costs as inventoriable costs.
- Production volume variance exists.
- All nonmanufacturing costs are expensed.
- Greater incentive to build inventory levels.
- Fixed manufacturing cost is held back in inventory.
- Income statement classifies cost by business function (i.e., marketing, manufacturing).
- Gross margin is different from contribution margin.
- Variable marketing and administrative costs are expensed (i.e., become period costs) in the period incurred along with fixed components, and deducted from gross margin to arrive at operating income.

Characteristics of variable costing method

- Also called direct or marginal costing method.
- Includes all direct manufacturing costs and variable indirect manufacturing costs only as inventoriable cost (fixed indirect manufacturing costs are excluded from the inventoriable costs).
- No production volume variance exists.
- All nonmanufacturing costs are expensed.
- No incentive to build up inventory levels.
- Fixed manufacturing cost is expensed in the period incurred.
- Income statement classifies cost by cost behavior (i.e., fixed, variable).
- Contribution is different from gross margin.
- Variable marketing and administrative costs are expensed (i.e., become period costs) in the period incurred. However, they are included to compute contribution margin.
- All fixed indirect costs including manufacturing, marketing, and administrative costs are deducted from the contribution margin to arrive at operating income.

Operating Income under the Absorption and Variable Costing Methods

Absorption costing method		Variable costing method	
Sales	$xxx	Sales	$xxx
Less variable manufacturing costs	xxx	Less variable manufacturing cost of goods sold	xxx
Less fixed manufacturing costs	xxx		
Deduct ending inventory	xxx		
Equals **gross margin**	xxx		
Deduct total marketing and administrative costs including variable costs	xxx		
		Less variable marketing costs	xxx
		Less variable administrative costs	xxx
		Total variable costs	xxx
		Contribution margin	xxx
		Deduct all fixed costs	xxx
Operating income	xxx	Operating income	xxx

The difference in operating income between these two methods arises from the difference in the amount of inventories. The CM and GM highlight the conflict of the underlying concepts of variable cost and absorption cost. Both methods can operate in conjunction with actual, normal, or standard costing systems.

The arguments for and against variable costing method are listed next. Fixed portion of factory overhead is relevant to overall plant capacity, not to the production of a specific product. Hence, the focus should be on all variable costs. Inventories should contain fixed costs in addition to variable costs since both are needed to produce goods. Hence, all costs should be inventoried.

KEY CONCEPTS TO REMEMBER: Relationships between Variable Costing and Absorption Costing Methods

- If inventories increase during a period, the variable costing method will generally report less operating income than will the absorption costing method.

- If inventories decrease, the variable costing method will report more operating income than the absorption costing method.

- The differences in operating income are due solely to moving fixed overhead in and out of inventories.

  Absorption costing operating income − Variable costing operating income = Fixed overhead in ending inventory in absorption cost − Fixed overhead in beginning inventory in absorption costing

- The difference between variable costing and absorption costing incomes is a matter of timing. Under the variable costing method, fixed overhead is expensed in the period incurred. Under the absorption costing method, fixed overhead is inventoried and expensed when the related units are sold.

(Continued)

KEY CONCEPTS TO REMEMBER: Relationships between Variable Costing and Absorption Costing Methods (*Continued*)

- Under the variable costing method, operating income is drawn by fluctuations in sales volume. Operating income should increase as sales increase and vice versa. Operating income rises at the rate of the CM per unit. This dovetails precisely with CVP analysis, and the breakeven point can be calculated easily. There are no temptations to manipulate income.

- Under the absorption costing method, both sales volume and production volume drive the operating income. Changes in inventory levels and choice of production schedule and volume can dramatically affect income. There are great temptations to manipulate income.

- Under the absorption costing method, it is possible to report a lower operating income even though sales volume increased due to the unusually large amounts of fixed overhead being charged to a single accounting period.

- If the number of units produced exceeds the number of units sold, ending inventory increases. Since absorption defers some fixed overhead in the increased ending inventory, absorption costing income is generally higher than variable costing income.

- A manager whose performance bonus is based on absorption costing income could increase production levels to obtain favorable production volume variance by hiding fixed overhead expenses as inventoriable costs in order to increase income. A manager can also choose to decrease absorption costing income by decreasing inventory if he or she has met this year's targeted income. Thus, managers are tempted to make short-run decisions at the expense of long-run objectives of the organization.

- To balance the negative effects of the absorption costing method (such as buildup of inventory), a manager's performance should be based on both financial and nonfinancial criteria. Examples of nonfinancial performance criteria include meeting inventory levels, meeting product delivery dates, adhering to plant maintenance schedules, and meeting or exceeding product quality and customer service levels.

- Variable cost is not acceptable for tax or external financial reporting purposes. Variable cost is heavily used for internal management reporting.

- GAAP requires that all manufacturing overhead is inventoried. Some firms may choose not to include depreciation on factory equipment as part of inventory cost.

- The U.S. Internal Revenue Code requires that all manufacturing and some marketing, distribution, and administrative costs are included in inventory.

APPLICATION OF ABSORPTION AND VARIABLE COSTING METHODS

During the first year of operations, a company produced 275,000 units and sold 250,000 units. The following costs were incurred during the year:

Variable costs per unit	
Direct material	$ 15.00
Direct labor	10.00
Manufacturing overhead	12.50
Selling and administrative	2.50
Total fixed costs	
Manufacturing overhead	$ 2,200,000
Selling and administrative	1,375,000

What would be the difference between operating income calculated on the absorption (full) costing basis and on the variable (direct) costing basis?

a. Absorption costing operating income would be greater than variable costing operating income by $200,000.

b. Absorption costing operating income would be greater than variable costing operating income by $220,000.

c. Absorption costing operating income would be greater than variable costing operating income by $325,000.

d. Variable costing operating income would be greater than absorption costing operating income by $62,500.

Choice (a) is the correct answer. Absorption costing operating income will exceed variable costing operating income because production exceeds sales, resulting in a deferral of fixed manufacturing overhead in the inventory under absorption. The amount of difference is the fixed manufacturing overhead per unit ($2,200,000 / 275,000 = $8.00) times the difference between production and sales (275,000 − 250,000 = 25,000 units; this could also be stated as the inventory change in units). That is, $8.00 × 25,000 units = $200,000.

Choice (b) is incorrect. The reasoning is the same as response choice (a) except fixed manufacturing overhead per unit is calculated by using unit sales rather than production units ($2,200,000/250,000 = $8.80; $8.80 × 25,000 = $220,000).

Choice (c) is incorrect. The reasoning is the same as response choice (a) except all fixed costs treated as being inventoriable under absorption costing and production units used as the base [($2,200,000 + 1,375,000)/275,000 = $13.00; $13.00 × 25,000 = $325,000)].

Choice (d) is incorrect. This response assumes that the difference between variable and absorption costing is that variable selling and administrative costs are inventoriable for variable costing and not inventoriable for absorption costing; thus, a portion of the variable selling and administrative expenses would be deferred in the inventory, meaning variable operating income would exceed absorption operating income ($2.50 × 25,000 = $62,500).

(iv) Other Cost Concepts

The next list provides a brief description of cost concepts other than absorption or variable costs.

Actual costs—The amounts determined on the basis of cost incurred for making a product or delivering a service to customers.

Average costs—The total cost divided by the activity (i.e., number of units).

Budgeted costs—Costs that were predetermined for managerial planning and controlling purposes.

Common costs—Costs of facilities and services shared by several functional departments. These are costs incurred for the benefit of more than one cost objective.

Conversion costs—A combination of direct labor costs, indirect material costs, and factory overhead. Assembly workers' wages in a factory are an example of conversion costs since their time is charged to direct labor.

Current costs—Costs that represent fair market value at current date.

Direct costs—Costs that can be directly identified with or traced to a specific product, service, or activity (e.g., direct labor and direct materials). In a manufacturing operation, direct material costs would include wood in a furniture factory since wood is a basic raw material of furniture. Direct labor costs are wages paid to workers.

Other examples of direct costs include insurance on the corporate headquarters building since it is not a cost of production, depreciation on salespersons' automobiles, salary of a sales manager, commissions paid to sales personnel, and advertising and rent expenses.

Expired costs—The portions of cost that are expensed. An expired cost is a period cost, and it is either an expense or a loss.

Fixed costs—Costs that remain constant in total but change per unit over a relevant range of production or sales volume (e.g., rent and depreciation). A fixed cost is a unit cost that decreases with an increase in activity. It is constant in total but varies per unit in direct proportion to changes in total activity or volume. It is a cost that remains unchanged in total for a given period despite fluctuations in volume or activity as long as the production is within the relevant range. A fixed cost may change in total between different periods or when production is outside the relevant range. Therefore, unit fixed cost decreases as output increases at a given relevant range.

Full costs—A combination of direct costs and a fair share of the indirect costs for a cost objective. "Full costs" refer to a unit of finished product. They consist of prime costs and overhead and are the entire sacrifice related to a cost objective.

Historical costs—Costs incurred at the time of occurrence of a business transaction. They represent what costs were.

Indirect costs—Costs that cannot be identified with or traced to a specific product, activity, or department (e.g., salaries, taxes, utilities, machine repairs). An example is a factory manager's salary. Another term for indirect costs is factory overhead. It consists of all costs other than direct labor and direct materials associated with the manufacturing process.

Joint costs—Costs of manufactured goods of relatively significant sales values that are simultaneously produced by a process.

Long-run costs—Costs that vary as plant capacity changes over a long period of time.

Marginal costs—Costs to make an additional unit or the last unit. They are the incremental or variable costs of producing an additional or extra unit.

Mixed costs—Costs that fluctuate with volume but not in direct proportion to production or sales. Mixed costs (semivariable or semifixed costs) have elements of both fixed and variable costs (e.g., supervision and inspection). A salesperson's compensation is an example of mixed costs since salary is fixed and commissions are variable.

Period costs—Costs that can be associated with the passage of time, not the production of goods. Period costs are always expensed to the same period in which they are incurred, not to a particular product. Period costs are not identifiable with a product and are not inventoried. Only product costs are included in manufacturing overhead. Period costs are those costs deducted as expenses during the current period without having been previously classified as costs of inventory.

Prime costs—A combination of direct labor and direct material costs. Overhead is not a part of prime costs. The term "prime costs" refers to a unit of finished product. The costs can be identified with and physically traceable to a cost objective.

Product costs—Costs that can be associated with production of certain goods or services. Product costs are those that are properly assigned to inventory when incurred. Inventoriable costs are those costs incurred to produce the inventory and that stay with the inventory as an asset until they are sold. Product costs are expensed (as COGS) in the period the product is sold.

Examples include property taxes on a factory in a manufacturing company, direct materials, direct labor, and factory overhead. Product costs include direct labor, direct material, and plant manufacturing overhead.

Short-run costs—Costs that vary as output varies for a short period or for a given production capacity.

Standard costs—Predetermined or engineered costs that should be attained under normal conditions of operations. They represent what costs should be.

Step costs—Costs that are constant over small ranges of volume (output) but increase in discrete steps as volume increases. A supervisor of the second shift is an example of step cost. If the step is narrow, it is equal to the variable cost and fixed cost of a wider step.

Sunk costs—Past cost outlays that have already been incurred (e.g., installed factory machinery and equipment cost that becomes a historical cost) or committed to be incurred. Sunk costs are not relevant to most future costs and current decisions since they cannot be changed by any decision made now or in the future. These costs are irreversible and cannot be affected by choices already made.

APPLICATION OF A SUNK COST CONCEPT

A company has an old machine with a book value of $75,000, with no salvage value, and an estimated remaining life of 12 years. A new machine is available at a cost of $190,000. It has the same estimated remaining life and the same capacity as the old machine, but it would reduce operating costs by $17,000 per year. Which of the following amounts is a sunk cost in the decision whether to replace the old machine?

a. $0

b. $17,000

c. $75,000

d. $190,000

Choice (c) is the correct answer. The old machine's book value of $75,000 is an outlay made in the past that cannot be changed. Choice (a) is incorrect. The salvage value does not dictate sunk costs. Choice (b) is incorrect. The $17,000 is a future cost that can be avoided. Choice (d) is incorrect. The $190,000 is a future cost that can be avoided.

Unexpired costs—Portions of cost that remain as assets and continue to generate future benefits.

Variable costs—Costs that fluctuate in total but remain constant per unit as the volume of production or sales changes. For example, a variable cost is constant per unit produced but varies in total in direct proportion to changes in production. The cost of fabricator wages should be considered variable because they change in total in direct proportion to the number of similar cables fabricated. General and administrative and other indirect costs can be either fixed or variable. In general, variable costs vary directly with volume or activity. For example, if indirect materials vary directly with volume, then indirect materials can be classified as variable costs.

Avoidable costs—Costs that will not be incurred or costs that may be saved if an ongoing activity is discontinued, changed, or deleted, as in a make-or-buy decision. These costs are relevant costs.

Unavoidable costs—The opposite of avoidable costs. These are costs that are irrelevant; they are sunk costs.

Controllable costs—Costs that can be definitely influenced by a given manager within a given time span. An example includes office supplies purchased by an office manager. In the long run, all costs are controllable. In the short run, costs also are controllable, but they are controlled at different management levels. The higher the management level, the greater the possibility of control.

Noncontrollable costs—The opposite of the controllable costs. These are costs that are unaffected by a manager's decision (e.g., plant rent expense by a plant foreman).

Out-of-pocket costs—Costs that require the consumption of current economic resources (e.g., taxes, insurance). They are the current or near-future expenditures that will require cash outlays to execute a decision.

Embodied costs—Measure sacrifices in terms of their origins, reflecting what was originally given up to acquire and convert the object being costed.

Displaced costs—Measure sacrifices in terms of their ultimate effects on the group making the sacrifice, reflecting the opportunity lost by, or the adverse consequences resulting from, the sacrifice in question. Displaced costs are also called opportunity costs.

Discretionary costs—Costs that arise from periodic budgeting decisions and that have no strong input/output relationship.

Opportunity costs—The maximum net benefit that is forgone by the choice of one course of action over another course of action. They are the economic sacrifice attributable to a given decision. They are the loss associated with choosing the alternative that does not maximize the benefit.

Incremental costs—The increase in total sacrifice identifiable with the specific object, or group of objects, being costed, recognizing that fixed and otherwise joint sacrifices may be increased little, if at all, because of what was done to or for the specific object being costed. Incremental costs also are called differential costs.

Differential costs—The difference in total costs between alternatives.

APPLICATION OF A DIFFERENTIAL COST CONCEPT

ABC Company receives a onetime special order for 5,000 units of Kleen. Variable costs per unit are as follows: direct materials $1.50, direct labor $2.50, variable overhead $0.80, and variable selling $2.00. Fixed costs per year include fixed overhead of $100,000 and fixed selling and administrative cost of $50,000. Acceptance of this special order will not affect the regular sales of 80,000 units. Variable selling costs for each of these 5,000 units will be $1.00.

Question: What is the differential cost to the company of accepting this special order?

Answer: The differential cost is $29,000, as shown below.

We need to consider all differential or incremental costs that would change as a result of the changes in production operations. It should include all variable manufacturing costs and variable selling costs. That is, $1.50 (materials) + $2.50 (direct labor) + $0.80 (variable overhead) + $1.00 (new variable selling cost for 5,000 units) = $5.80. This is multiplied by 5,000 units and gives $29,000. Here fixed costs and variable selling costs for sales of 80,000 units are not relevant.

Replacement costs—Costs that would have to be incurred to replace an asset.

Implicit costs—Imputed costs. They are used in the analysis of opportunity costs.

Imputed costs—Costs that can be associated with an economic event when no exchange transaction has occurred (e.g., the rent for a building when a company "rents to itself" a building).

Committed costs—Two types of committed costs exist: manageable and unmanageable. Manageable committed costs are sacrifices influenced to an important degree by managers' decisions and actions, but these influences have already had most of their effect, setting in motion the chain of events that largely determine the sacrifice in question. Most fixed costs are committed costs. Unmanageable committed costs are sacrifices largely influenced by factors or forces outside managers' control and already set in motion to such an extent that influences have had most of their effect.

Uncommitted costs—Two types of uncommitted costs exist: manageable and unmanageable. Manageable uncommitted costs are sacrifices influenced to an important degree by managers' decisions and actions with plenty of time for these influences to have their effect. Unmanageable uncommitted costs are sacrifices largely influenced by factors or forces outside managers' control with plenty of time for these influences to have their effect.

Rework costs—Costs incurred to turn an unacceptable product into an acceptable product and sell it as a normal finished good.

Engineered costs—Costs resulting from a measured relationship between inputs and outputs.

(v) Cost Behavior

Costs have a behavior pattern. For example, costs vary with volumes of production, sales, or service levels; with the application of the amount of resources; and with the time frame used. Knowing cost-behavior information helps in developing budgets, interpreting variances from standards, and making critical decisions. The manager who can predict costs and their behavior is a step ahead in planning, budgeting, controlling, product pricing, and nonroutine decisions (i.e., make or buy, keep or drop) and in separating cost into its components (i.e., fixed, variable, and mixed costs). In order to make more accurate cost predictions, managers must have superior cost estimates at their disposal.

COST ESTIMATION VERSUS COST PREDICTION

- In cost estimation, an equation is formulated to measure and describe past cost relationships.

- In cost prediction, future costs are forecasted using the cost estimation equation. Here the behavior of past costs will help in predicting future costs.

Two assumptions are made in the estimation of cost functions: (1) cost behavior is a linear function within the relevant range, and (2) variations in the total cost level can be explained by variations in a single cost driver. A **cost driver** is any factor whose change causes a change in the total cost of a related cost object. Machine hours and direct labor hours are examples of cost drivers in a manufacturing firm.

A cost function is an equation showing the cost-behavior pattern for all changes in the level of the cost driver. A linear cost function is described next.

$$y = a + bx$$

where

y = Estimated value

a = Constant or intercept (does not vary with changes in the level of the cost driver within a relevant range)

b = Slope coefficient (the amount of change in total cost [y] for each unit change in the cost driver [x] within the relevant range)

The intercept includes fixed costs that cannot be avoided even at shutdown of the operations. The relevant range is the range of the cost driver in which a valid relationship exists between total cost and the level of the cost driver.

Three types of linear cost functions exist:

1. **Variable cost function,** where its total cost changes in direct proportion to changes in x within the relevant range because the intercept, a, is zero.

2. **Fixed cost function,** where the total cost will be constant regardless of the changes in the level of the cost driver.

3. **Mixed cost function,** also known as **semivariable cost**, which has both fixed and variable elements. The total costs in the mixed cost function change as the number of units of the cost driver changes, not proportionately.

TECHNIQUES TO SEPARATE COSTS

- Statistics (regression analysis, scatter graphs, and least squares methods)
- High-low method
- Spreadsheet analysis
- Sensitivity analysis
- Managerial judgment

(A) Assumptions Underlying Cost Classifications

The classification of costs into their variable cost or fixed cost components is based on three assumptions.

1. The cost object must be specified since costs are variable or fixed with respect to a chosen cost object. Cost objects can be product based or activity based.

2. The time span must be specified. Costs are affected by the time span. The longer the time span, the higher the proportion of total costs that are variable and the lower the fixed costs. Costs that are fixed in the short run may be variable in the long run. There should be a cause-and-effect relationship between the cost driver and the resulting costs. A cost driver may be either an input (e.g., direct labor hour or machine hour) or an output (finished goods). For example, fixed manufacturing costs decline as a proportion of total manufacturing costs as the time span is lengthened from the short run to the medium run to the long run.

3. The relevant range for changes in the cost driver must be specified. Each of the cost-behavior patterns, such as variable cost, fixed cost, or mixed cost, has a relevant range within which the specified cost relationship will be valid. Constraints such as labor agreements and plant capacity levels set the relevant range. If volume exceeds the relevant range, total fixed costs would increase if a new plant is built, and unit variable costs would increase if overtime must be paid.

(B) Cost Estimation Approaches

There are four approaches to estimate costs:

1. Industrial engineering method

2. Conference method

3. Account analysis method

4. Quantitative analysis method of current or past cost relationships

(See Exhibit 4.51.) The first three approaches require less historical data than do most quantitative analyses. Therefore, cost estimations for a new product will begin with one or more of the first three methods. Quantitative analysis may be adopted later, after experience is gained. These cost estimation approaches, which are not mutually exclusive, differ in the cost of conducting the analysis, the assumptions they make, and the evidence they yield about the accuracy of the estimated cost function.

EXHIBIT 4.51 Four Approaches of Cost Estimation

1. Industrial engineering method (analyzes relationships between inputs and outputs in physical terms)

2. Conference method (incorporates analysis and opinions gathered from various departments of the firm)

3. Account analysis method (classifies cost accounts in the ledger as variable, fixed, or mixed costs)

4. Quantitative analysis methods (uses time-series data based on past cost relationships, regression analysis)

The **industrial engineering method** analyzes the relationship between inputs and outputs in physical terms. Using time and motion studies, physical measures are transformed into standard or budgeted costs. The drawbacks of this method are that it can be time consuming and costly. This method is most often used for significant costs, such as direct labor and direct material costs that are relatively easy to trace to the products. It is used less often or not used for indirect cost categories, such as manufacturing overhead, due to difficulty in specifying physical relationships between inputs and outputs.

The **conference method** develops cost estimates based on analysis and opinions gathered from various departments of an organization. Product costs are developed on consensus of the relevant departments. The advantages of this method include the speed at which cost estimates can be developed, the pooling of knowledge from experts in the functional area, and the resulting credibility of the cost estimates. The disadvantage of this method is that the accuracy of the cost estimates depends on the care taken and attention to detail by those people providing the inputs.

The **account analysis method**, which is widely used, classifies cost accounts in the ledger as variable, fixed, or mixed costs. The method can be thought of as a first step in cost classification and estimation. The conference method is used as a supplement to the account analysis method, which improves the credibility of the latter.

Quantitative analysis methods, such as time-series data or cross-sectional data based on past cost relationships, are often used to estimate cost functions. Time-series data pertain to the same entity over a sequence of past time periods while cross-sectional data pertain to different entities for the same time period.

STEPS IN ESTIMATING COST FUNCTION

The six steps in estimating the cost function based on an analysis of current or past cost relationships are listed next.

1. Choose the dependent variable (the variable to be predicted). The choice is guided by the purpose for estimating a cost function.

2. Choose the cost driver that is economically plausible (logical and common sense) and accurately measurable. There should be a cause-and-effect relationship between the cost driver and the resulting costs. For example, number of employees is a cost driver for measuring health benefit costs.

3. Collect data on the dependent variable and on the cost driver. The time period (e.g., daily, weekly) used to measure the dependent variable and the cost driver should be identical.

4. Plot the data. The general relationship between the dependent variable and the cost driver (i.e., correlation) can be observed in a plot of the data. A plot of data will reveal whether the cost relation is linear or whether there are outliers. Extreme observations, or outliers, can occur due to errors in recording the data or from an unusual event, such as a labor strike, fire, or flood.

5. Estimate the cost function by using either regression analysis or the high-low method.

6. Evaluate the estimated cost function. The relationship between the dependent variable and the cost driver should be economically plausible. The closer the actual cost observations are to the values predicted by a cost function, the better the goodness of fit of the cost function. In other words, the cost function should be economically plausible and fit the data.

Next we review quantitative methods, including regression analysis and high-low methods, used to estimate cost function.

(C) Regression Analysis

Regression analysis provides a model for estimating a cost function and probable error for cost estimates. It measures the average amount of change in the dependent variable, Y, that is associated with a unit change in the amount of one or more independent (or explanatory) variables, x. x is also called the cost driver.

$$Y' = a + bx$$

where

a = Constant or intercept

b = Slope coefficient

When only one independent variable (e.g., machine hours) is used, the analysis is called simple regression; when more than one independent variable is used (e.g., machine hours and direct labor hours), it is called multiple regression.

Regression analysis offers a structured approach, based on past data relationships, for identifying cost drivers. All independent variables in a regression model should satisfy these four selection criteria for qualifying as a cost driver:

1. **Economic plausibility.** The relationship between the dependent variable and the independent variable(s) should make economic sense and be intuitive.

2. **Goodness of fit.** The coefficient of determination, r^2, measures the extent to which the independent variable(s) accounts for the variability in the dependent variable. The range of r^2 is from zero to 1, where zero implies no explanatory ability and 1 implies perfect explanatory ability. The goal of maximizing r^2 is called data mining and should not be done at the expense of economic plausibility. A balance is required.

3. **Significance of independent variable(s).** The t-value is computed by dividing the slope coefficient by its standard error. The t-value of a slope coefficient (b) measures the significance of the relationship between changes in the dependent variable and changes in the independent variable. The coefficient of the chosen independent variable(s) should be significantly different from zero for that independent variable to be considered a possible cost driver.

4. **Specification analysis.** Cost function models make assumptions, such as linearity within the relevant range, constant variance of residuals, independence of residuals, and normality of residuals. When these assumptions are met, the sample values of a and b from a regression model are the best available linear, unbiased estimates of the population parameters alpha and beta. Testing the assumptions underlying regression analysis is termed specification analysis.

Multicollinearity can exist in a multiple regression when two or more independent variables are highly correlated with each other. This is indicated when a coefficient of correlation (r) is greater than 0.70. Multicollinearity has the effect of increasing the standard error of the coefficients of the individual independent variable(s), thus increasing their uncertainty.

Regression analysis and interviews with operating personnel are used to identify cost drivers. For example: The number of products is a cost driver in product design function, the number of suppliers can be a cost driver in a manufacturing operation, and the number of advertisements can be a cost driver in a marketing function.

(D) High-Low Method
The high-low method uses two extreme data points (i.e., highest, lowest) to calculate the formula for a line. These two data points could be outliers or may not be representative of all the observations. This method ignores information on all but two observations when estimating the cost function.

EXAMPLE APPLICATION OF HIGH-LOW METHOD

	Machine Hours	Indirect Manufacturing Costs
Highest observation of cost driver	5,000	$400,000
Lowest observation of cost driver	2,000	$190,000
Difference	3,000	$210,000

Slope coefficient (**b**) = $210,000 / 3,000 = $70 per machine hour

Constant (**a**) can be calculated using either highest or lowest observations.

Using the highest observation = $400,000 − $70 (5,000) = $50,000

The high-low estimate of the cost function is $Y' = a + bx$ = $50,000 + $70 (machine hours)

(E) Nonlinearity and Cost Functions

A **nonlinear cost function** is a cost function in which a single constant and a single slope coefficient do not describe in an additive manner the behavior of costs for all changes in the level of the cost driver. For example, even direct materials costs are not always linear variable costs due to quantity discounts. The cost per unit decreases with large orders, but the total costs increase slowly as the cost driver increases.

Step function cost is a situation where the cost of the input is constant over various small ranges of the cost driver but the cost increases by discrete amounts (in steps) as the cost driver moves from one relevant range to the next. This step-pattern behavior occurs when the input is acquired in discrete quantities but is used in fractional quantities (e.g., vehicle-leasing costs for a package-delivery company).

Batch costs are increased when products are made in batches and a changeover (setup) cost is needed to run a different type of batch. These batch costs are incurred regardless of the size of each batch and have no linear relationship with the number of items in a batch.

(F) Learning Curves and Cost Functions

A **learning curve** is a function that shows how labor hours per unit decline as units of output increase. The learning curve helps managers predict how labor hours or costs will change as more units are produced. The idea behind the learning curve is that workers handling repetitive tasks will become more efficient as they become more familiar with the operation.

Management must be cautious in using the learning curve to establish standards. A steady-state condition can be reached when the effect of the learning curve ceases, and the standard costs would be lower per unit. The corresponding standard cost for the learning curve phase will be higher per unit. If the steady-state standards are imposed during the learning-curve phase, an unfavorable efficiency variance between standards and actual performance may persist, and employees might reject the standards as unattainable. This situation will lead to low morale and low productivity.

The benefit of the learning curve can be clearly seen with new products, new workers, and new machines. Learning curves are applied more frequently to direct labor and overhead and less frequently to direct materials. In addition to volume as a driver of learning, product design and process configuration are being researched as possible drivers of learning.

EXAMPLE APPLICATION OF LEARNING CURVE PRINCIPLE

Sun Corporation has received an order to supply 240 units of a product. The average direct labor cost was estimated to be $40,000 per unit for the first lot of 30 units. The direct labor is subject to a 90% learning curve.

Question: What is the cumulative average unit cost of labor for production of 240 units?

Answer: The cumulative average unit cost of labor for production of 240 units is $29,160, as shown.

Cumulative lots	# Cumulative Units	#Cumulative average unit cost of labor
1	30	($40,000 × 1) = $40,000
2	60	($40,000 × .9) = 36,000
4	120	($36,000 × .9) = 32,400
8	240	($32,400 × .9) = 29,160

The term "experience curve" describes the broader application of the learning curve to include not only manufacturing cost but also marketing, distribution, and customer service areas. An **experience curve** is a function that shows how full costs per unit decline as units of output increase.

(G) Learning Curve Models
Two learning curve models exist: the cumulative average-time learning model and the incremental unit-time learning model.

In the cumulative average-time learning model, the cumulative average time per unit is reduced by a constant percentage each time the cumulative quantity of units produced is doubled. Learning occurs at a faster rate with this method as compared to the incremental unit-time model.

In the incremental unit-time learning model, the time needed to produce the last unit is reduced by a constant percentage each time the cumulative quantity of units produced is doubled. This method requires a higher cumulative total time to produce two or more units as compared with cumulative average-time model.

The deciding factor between the cumulative average-time and incremental unit-time learning model is the ability to approximate the behavior of labor-hour usage as output levels increase.

(d) Relevant Costs

(i) Differential Analysis
Managers must consider the effects of alternative decisions on their businesses. We discuss differential analysis, which reports the effects of alternative decisions on total revenues and costs. Planning for future operations involves decision making. For some decisions, revenue and cost data from the accounting records may be useful. However, often the revenue and cost data for

use in evaluating courses of future operations or choosing among competing alternatives are not available in the accounting records and must be estimated. These estimates include relevant revenues and costs. The relevant revenues and costs focus on the differences between each alternative. Costs that have been incurred in the past, called **sunk costs,** are not relevant to the decision.

FOCUS OF RELEVANT COSTS

Relevant revenues and costs focus on the difference between each alternative.

Differential revenue is the amount of increase or decrease in revenue expected from a course of action as compared with an alternative. To illustrate, assume that certain equipment is being used to manufacture calculators, which are expected to generate revenue of $150,000. If the equipment could be used to make digital clocks, which would generate revenue of $175,000, the differential revenue from making and selling digital clocks would be $25,000.

Differential cost is the amount of increase or decrease in cost that is expected from a course of action as compared with an alternative. For example, if an increase in advertising expenditures from $100,000 to $150,000 is being considered, the differential cost of the action is $50,000.

Differential income or loss is the difference between the differential revenue and the differential costs. Differential income indicates that a particular decision is expected to be profitable, while a differential loss indicates the opposite.

Differential analysis focuses on the effect of alternative courses of action on the relevant revenues and costs. For example, if a manager must decide between two alternatives, differential analysis would involve comparing the differential revenues of the two alternatives with the differential costs.

Differential analysis can be used in analyzing these alternatives:

- Leasing or selling equipment
- Discontinuing an unprofitable segment
- Manufacturing or purchasing a needed part (make-or-buy analysis)
- Replacing usable fixed assets
- Processing further or selling an intermediate product
- Accepting additional business at a special price

(ii) Application of Relevant Cost Concept

When deciding whether to accept a special order from a customer, the best thing to do is to compare the total revenue to be derived from this order with the total relevant costs incurred for this order. The key terms are incremental relevant costs and incremental relevant revenues. The relevant costs are those that vary with the decision.

Long-term fixed costs should be excluded from the analysis since they will be incurred regardless of whether the order is accepted. Direct labor, direct materials, variable manufacturing overhead, and variable selling and administrative costs are relevant because they will not be incurred if the special order is not accepted. Incremental fixed costs would be relevant in short-term decision making under certain situations.

(e) Cost-Volume-Profit Analysis

Cost-volume-profit (CVP) analysis helps managers who are making decisions about short-term duration and for specific cases where revenue and cost behaviors are linear and where volume is assumed to be the only cost and revenue driver. CVP is an approximation and low-cost tool.

KEY CONCEPTS TO REMEMBER: What Are Cost or Revenue Drivers?

- A cost driver is any factor whose change causes a change in the total cost of a related cost object.

- A revenue driver is any factor whose change causes a change in the total revenue of a related product or service.

- There are many cost drivers and revenue drivers besides volume of units produced or sold. Examples affecting total cost and revenue include changes in quantity of materials and changes in setting prices, respectively.

CVP analysis is a straightforward, simple-to-apply, widely used management tool. It answers questions such as: How will costs and revenues be affected if sales units are up or down by X%? If price is decreased or increased by X%? A decision model can be built using CVP relationships for choosing among courses of action. CVP analysis tells management what will happen to financial results if a specific level of production or sales volume fluctuates or if costs change.

An example of a decision model is the breakeven point (BEP), which shows the interrelationships of changes in costs, volume, and profits. It is the point of volume where total revenues and total costs are equal. No profit is gained or loss incurred at the BEP.

(i) Methods for Calculating Breakeven Point

Three methods available for calculating the BEP are shown in Exhibit 4.52.

EXHIBIT 4.52 Breakeven Point Methods

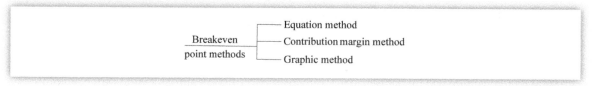

An increase in the BEP is a red flag for management to analyze all its CVP relationships more closely.

(A) Equation Method

The equation method is general and thus easier to apply with multiple products, multiple costs and revenue drivers, and changes in the cost structure. The BEP tells how many units of product must be sold to generate enough contribution margin (CM) to cover total fixed costs

At BEP, the operating income is zero.

Formula

(Unit sales price × Number of units) − (Unit variable cost × Number of units) − Fixed costs

= Operating income or Sales − Variable costs − Fixed costs = Operating income

Example

Price is $100, variable cost is $60, fixed costs are $2,000. What are the breakeven units?

$$100N - 60N - 2,000 = 0$$

$$40N = 2,000$$

$$N = 2,000 \ / \ 40 = 50 \text{ units}$$

(B) Contribution Margin Method

CM is equal to sales minus all variable costs. BEP is calculated as follows:

$$BEP = Fixed \ costs \ / \ Unit \ CM$$

Using the same example,

$$BEP = 2,000 \ / \ (100 - 60) = 2,000/40 = 50 \text{ units}$$

A desired target operating income can be added to the fixed costs to give a new BEP that tells how many units must be sold to generate enough CM to cover total fixed costs plus target operating income.

The CM method is valid only for a single product and a single cost driver. The method is a restatement of the equation method in a different form. Either method can be used to calculate the BEP.

(C) Graphic Method

A CVP chart results when units are plotted on the x-axis and dollars on the y-axis. The BEP is where the total sales line and total cost line intersect. The total sales line begins at the origin because if volume is zero, sales revenue will be zero too.

- As volume increases, total fixed costs remain the same over the entire volume range.
- As volume increases, both total variable costs and sales increase.

The total fixed cost line will be flat because fixed costs are constant across a wide range of volumes. Linear CVP analysis is approximate under perfect competition, thus showing the link between cost accounting and economics. In economics, the slope of the total revenue (TR) function equals marginal revenue (MR), which equals sales per unit. The slope of the total cost (TC) function is marginal cost (MC), which equals variable cost per unit. The sales price per unit and variable cost per unit are constant across a wide range of volumes only if there is perfect competition in input and output markets. However, this is not true for imperfect competition, where sales price must be reduced to increase volume.

EXAMPLES: Volume versus Costs versus Sales

Use the following CVP chart for Examples 1 and 2.

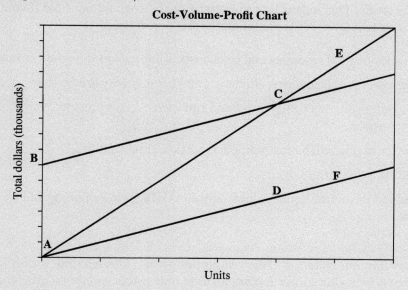

Example 1

Which of the following labeled points on this chart is the BEP?

a. Point A

b. Point B

c. Point C

d. Point D

Choice (c) is the correct answer. Point C is the intersection of the total cost line and the total revenue line, which is the BEP. Choice (a) is incorrect. Point A is the origin, where total revenues are zero and there is a loss equal to the amount of fixed costs. Choice (b) is incorrect. Point B is the total cost line at zero activity, which is the amount of total fixed costs. Choice (d) is incorrect. Point D is on the total variable cost curve and represents the total variable costs at the BEP.

Example 2

Which of the following items is graphically represented on the CVP chart as the difference between labeled points E and F?

a. Total profit

b. Total variable costs

c. Total fixed costs

d. Total CM

Choice (d) is the correct answer. The difference between labeled point E (which is on the total revenue line) and point F (which is on the total variable cost line) is total CM. Choice (a) is incorrect because it is on point C. Choice (b) is incorrect because it is on point D. Choice (c) is incorrect because it is on point B. Choices (a), (b), and (c) are not between points E and F.

(ii) CVP Assumptions and Their Limitations
(A) Assumptions

We already learned that the CVP relationships hold true for only a limited range of production or sales volume levels. This means that these relationships would not hold if volume fell below or rose above a certain level. A list of assumptions is presented next.

- The behavior of total revenues and total costs is linear over the relevant range of volume.
- Selling prices, total fixed costs, efficiency, and productivity are constant.
- All costs can be divided neatly into fixed and variable components. Variable cost per unit remains constant.
- A greater sales mix will be maintained as total volume changes.
- Volume is the only driver of costs.
- The production volume equals sales volume, or changes in beginning and ending inventory levels are zero.

(B) Limitations

There are many limitations to the CVP assumptions just made. Volume is only one of the factors affecting cost behavior. Other factors include unit prices of inputs, efficiency, changes in production technology, civil wars, employee strikes, laws, and regulations. Profits are affected by changes in factors besides volume. A CVP chart must be analyzed in total by considering all assumptions and their limitations.

(iii) Ways to Lower the Breakeven Point

The next strategies should help in lowering the BEP, which means fewer units need to be sold, which, in turn, contributes more to profits. (Note that the strategies are not order ranked).

- Reduce the overall fixed costs.
- Increase the CM per unit of product through an increase in sales prices.
- Increase the CM per unit of product through decreases in unit variable costs.
- Increase the CM per unit through both an increase in sales prices and a decrease in unit variable costs.
- Set a hiring freeze for new employees.
- Limit merit increases for senior executives.
- Cut the annual percentage salary rate increase for all salaried employees.
- Reduce overtime pay for all employees to reduce labor costs.
- Reduce the number of employees on the payroll.
- Improve employee productivity levels.
- Increase machine utilization rates.

(iv) Sensitivity Analysis in CVP

A CVP model developed in a dynamic environment determined that the estimated parameters used may vary between limits. Subsequent testing of the model with respect to all possible values of the estimated parameters is termed a sensitivity analysis.

Sensitivity analysis is a management tool that will answer questions such as: What will operating income be if volume changes from the original prediction? What will operating income be if variable costs per unit decrease or increase by X%? If sales drop, how far can they fall below budget before the BEP is reached? The last question can be answered by the margin of safety tool. The **margin of safety** is a tool of sensitivity analysis and is the excess of budgeted sales over the breakeven volume.

Sensitivity analysis is a what-if technique aimed at asking how a result will be changed if the original predicted data are not achieved or if an underlying assumption changes. It is a measure of changes in outputs resulting from changes in inputs. It reveals the impact of changes in one or more input variables on the output or results.

(v) Changes in Variable and Fixed Costs

Organizations often face a trade-off between fixed and variable costs. Fixed costs can be substituted for variable costs and vice versa. This is because variable costs and fixed costs are subject to various degrees of control at different volumes—boom or slack. For example, when a firm invests in automated machinery to offset increase in labor rates, its fixed costs increase, but unit variable costs decrease.

(vi) Contribution Margin and Gross Margin

CM is the excess of sales over all variable costs, including variable manufacturing, marketing, and administrative categories. GM, also called gross profit, is the excess of sales over the cost of the goods sold. CM and GM would be different for a manufacturing company. They are equal only when fixed manufacturing costs included in COGS are the same as the variable nonmanufacturing costs, which is a highly unlikely event.

- Variable manufacturing, marketing, and administrative costs are subtracted from sales to get CM but not GM.

- Fixed manufacturing overhead is subtracted from sales to get GM but not CM.

- Both CM and GM can be expressed as totals, as an amount per unit, or as percentages of sales in the form of ratios.

An example of GM and of CM is presented next.

Gross Margin		Contribution Margin	
Sales	$50,000	Sales	$50,000
Manufacturing		Variable manufacturing costs	$20,000
Cost of goods sold	$30,000	Variable nonmanufacturing costs	$ 5,000
Gross margin	$20,000	Total variable costs	$25,000
		Contribution margin	$25,000

EXAMPLE APPLICATION OF CONTRIBUTION MARGIN CONCEPT

A department store prepares segmented financial statements. During the past year, the income statement for the perfume department located near the front entrance was:

(Continued)

EXAMPLE APPLICATION OF CONTRIBUTION MARGIN CONCEPT (*Continued*)

Sales	$200,000
Cost of goods sold	120,000
Gross profit	80,000
Janitorial expense	5,000
Sales commissions	40,000
Heat and lighting	4,000
Depreciation	3,000
Income before taxes	$ 28,000

Janitorial expense, heat and lighting, and depreciation are allocated to the department based on square footage. Sales personnel work for only one department and are paid on commission. What is the perfume department's CM?

a. $28,000

b. $31,000

c. $37,000

d. $40,000

Choice (d) is the correct answer. CM is the gross profit of $80,000 minus the $40,000 of sales commissions, that is, $40,000. Choice (a) is incorrect. This is net income, as given. Choice (b) is incorrect. Janitorial and heat and light are fixed costs ($80,000 − $40,000 − $5,000 − $4,000). Choice (c) is incorrect. Depreciation is a fixed cost, hence not a part of CM ($80,000 − $40,000 − $3,000).

(vii) Profit-Volume Chart

The profit-volume chart is preferable to the cost-volume-profit chart because it is simpler to understand. The profit-volume chart shows a quick, condensed comparison of how alternatives on pricing, variable costs, or fixed costs affect operating income as volume changes. The y-axis shows the operating income, and the x-axis represents volume (units or dollars).

Due to operating leverage, profits increase during high volume because more of the costs are fixed and do not increase with volume. Profits decrease during low volume because fixed costs cannot be avoided despite the lower volume.

(viii) Effect of Sales Mix and Income Taxes

Sales mix is the relative combination of quantities of products that constitute total sales. A change in sales mix will cause actual profits to differ from budgeted profits. It is the combination of low-margin or high-margin products that causes the shift in profits, despite achievement of targeted sales volume.

There will be a different BEP for each different sales mix. A higher proportion of sales in high-CM products will reduce the BEP. A lower proportion of sales in small-CM products will increase the BEP. Shifting marketing efforts to high-CM products can increase the operating income and profits.

Management is interested in the effect of various production and sales strategies on the operating income, not so much on BEP. Both operating income and BEP are dependent on the assumptions made (i.e., if the assumptions change, operating income and BEP will also change).

The impact of income taxes is clear. The general equation method can be changed to allow for the impact of income taxes, as shown next.

$$\text{Target operating income} = (\text{Target net income}) / (1 - \text{Tax rate})$$

Each unit beyond the BEP adds to net income at the unit CM multiplied by $(1 - \text{Tax rate})$. However, the BEP itself is unchanged. This is because no income tax is paid at a level of zero income. In other words, an increase in income tax rates will not affect the BEP.

(f) Transfer Pricing

Transfer pricing involves inter- or intracompany transfers, whether domestic or international. A **transfer price** is the price one unit of a corporation charges for a product or service supplied to another unit of the same corporation. The units involved could be either domestic or international, and the products involved could be intermediate products or semifinished goods.

Reasons for establishing transfer pricing in either domestic or international operations are listed next.

- Performance evaluation of decentralized operations
- Overall minimization of taxes to a corporation
- Minimization of custom duties and tariffs
- Minimization of risks associated with movements in foreign currency exchange rates
- Circumventing restrictions on profit remittance to corporate headquarters
- Motivation of unit managers

KEY CONCEPTS TO REMEMBER: Supplying Unit and Receiving Unit

Supplying Unit (Seller)	Receiving Unit (Buyer)
Domestic	Domestic
Domestic	International
International	International
International	Domestic

- If the seller is a profit or investment center, transfer pricing is most likely to cause conflicts.
- If the seller is a cost center, it has less (no) incentive to maximize sales revenues. Hence, there is little or no conflict.

(i) Transfer Pricing Methods

Three methods are available for determining transfer prices: market based, cost based, and negotiated (see Exhibit 4.53).

EXHIBIT 4.53 Transfer Pricing Methods

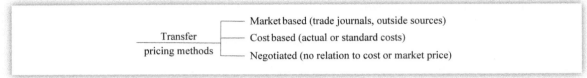

1. **Market-based transfer prices.** The price appearing in a trade journal or other independent (outside) sources establishes the transfer price of a product or service. Difficulty in obtaining market price forces corporations to resort to cost-based transfer prices. This method is in widespread use.

TRANSFER PRICES ALERT

There is no single best method to determine transfer prices. Ideally, the chosen method should help the unit manager to make optimal decisions for the organization as a whole.

---

2. **Cost-based transfer prices.** The costs used could be either actual costs or standard costs and include variable manufacturing costs or absorption (full) costs. Use of full cost-based prices leads to suboptimal decisions in the short run for the company as a whole. This method is also in widespread use. Standard costs are used more widely than actual costs to motivate the seller to produce efficiently. If transfer prices are based on actual costs, sellers can pass along costs of inefficiency to buyers.

3. **Negotiated transfer prices.** These are the negotiated prices between units of a corporation and may not have any relation to either cost or market-price data. Unit autonomy is preserved. Drawbacks include time-consuming and drawn-out negotiations, which may not lead to goal congruence. Weak bargaining units may lose out to strong ones.

The choice of a transfer pricing method affects the operating income of individual units. Next, we discuss how the criteria of goal congruence, managerial effort, and unit autonomy affect the choice of transfer pricing methods.

(ii) Transfer Pricing Management
Goal congruence exists when individual goals, group goals, and senior management goals coincide. Under these conditions, each unit manager acts in his or her own best interest, and the resulting decision is in the long-term best interest of the company as a whole. A transfer price method should lead to goal congruence.

A sustained high level of managerial effort can lead to achievement of goals. A transfer price method promotes management effort if sellers are motivated to hold down costs and buyers are motivated to use the purchased inputs efficiently.

Senior management should allow a high level of unit autonomy in decision making in a decentralized organization. This means that a transfer price method should preserve autonomy if unit managers are free to make their own decisions and are not forced to buy or sell products at a price that is unacceptable to them.

KEY CONCEPTS TO REMEMBER: Transfer Pricing

■ If no incremental fixed costs are incurred, variable costs are a floor transfer price since the seller will not sell for less than the incremental costs incurred to make the product.

■ Market price is a ceiling transfer price since the buyer will not pay more than market price.

■ Therefore, the final transfer price usually falls between variable cost and market price.

■ Corporations may use different transfer price methods for different items (i.e., market-based pricing for big-ticket items, variable cost-plus for low-value items, and negotiated prices for midrange items).

(iii) Dual Pricing

Dual pricing uses two separate transfer pricing methods to price each inter-unit transaction. It uses the two methods because a single transfer price seldom meets the criteria of goal congruence, managerial effort, and unit autonomy. An example of dual pricing is when the selling unit receives a full-cost plus markup-based price and the buying unit pays the market price for the internally transferred products.

The dual pricing method reduces the goal-congruence problems associated with a pure cost-plus-based transfer pricing method. Some of the drawbacks of dual pricing are listed next.

■ The manager of the supplying unit may not have sufficient incentives to control costs.

■ It does not provide clear signals to unit managers about the level of decentralization senior managers are seeking.

■ It tends to insulate managers from the frictions of the marketplace (i.e., knowledge of units' buying and selling market forces).

(iv) International Transfer Pricing

Because MNCs must deal with transfer pricing and international taxation, knowledge of international laws related to these areas is important. A transfer is a substitute for a market price and is recorded by the seller as revenue and by the buyer as COGS. The transfer pricing system should motivate unit managers not to make undesirable decisions at the expense of the corporation as a whole. The ideal manager would act in the best interests of the company as a whole, even at the expense of the reported profits of his or her own unit. For this to happen, managers must be rewarded when they choose companywide goal congruence over unit performance.

EXAMPLE APPLICATION OF TRANSFER PRICING METHOD

Example 1

Unit A sells 500 units of product X to Unit B for $5 per unit. The $5 selling price is the transfer price.

Example 2

Unit A sells 500 units of product X to Unit B for $6 per unit. The normal market price is $4 per unit. Unit A shows increased sales of $2 per unit and a higher profit. Unit B shows the COGS has increased by $2 per unit and therefore has a lower profit. This example clearly violates the goal-congruence principle since Unit A charges an inflated transfer price for products transferred to Unit B.

> **GOAL CONGRUENCE AND DECISION MAKING**
> ■ Desirable decisions enhance goal congruence.
> ■ Undesirable decisions stifle goal congruence.
> ■ Undesirable decisions can be minimized when the performance evaluation system is compatible with the transfer system.

According to Mueller and his coauthors,[2] the international transfer pricing system must also attempt to accomplish objectives that are irrelevant in a purely domestic operation. These objectives include:

■ Worldwide income tax minimization.

■ Minimization of worldwide import duties.

■ Avoidance of financial restrictions.

■ Managing currency fluctuations.

■ Winning host-country government approval.

Each objective is discussed briefly.

(A) Worldwide Income Tax Minimization

The transfer pricing system can be used to shift taxable profits from a country with a higher tax rate to a country with a lower tax rate; the result is that the MNC retains more profit after taxes. For example, the Cayman Islands have long been considered a tax haven for MNCs due to the zero corporate income tax rate. Pakistan has the highest corporate income tax rate: 50%.

(B) Minimization of Worldwide Import Duties

Transfer prices can reduce tariffs. Import duties are normally applied to intracompany transfers as well as sales to unaffiliated buyers. If the goods are transferred in at low prices, the resulting tariffs will be lower.

Tariffs interact with income taxes. Two associations exist: (1) low import duties and high income tax rates, and (2) high import duties and low income tax rates. There is a trade-off between income taxes and tariffs. The MNC has to evaluate the benefits of a lower (higher) income tax in the importing country against a higher (lower) import tariff as well as the potentially higher (lower) income tax paid by the MNC in the exporting country.

(C) Avoidance of Financial Restrictions

Foreign governments place certain types of economic restrictions on MNC operations with respect to the amount of cash transferred between the countries and the amount of a tax credit or subsidy allowed. A subsidy is a payment from the government to the subsidiary unit and the nondeductibility of certain expenses provided by the parent against taxable income. This includes R&D expenses, general and administrative expenses, and royalty fees.

Some ways to avoid these financial restrictions include setting a high transfer price on goods imported into the country, which would facilitate the desired movement of cash because the

---

[2] Gerard G. Mueller, Helen Gernon, and Gary Meek, *Accounting: An International Perspective* (Burr Ridge, Illinois: Irwin, 1994).

importing subsidiary must remit payment; charging a high transfer price on exported products, which will be followed by a larger tax credit or higher subsidy; or inflating the transfer price of imports to the subsidiary so that the nondeductibility of certain expenses can be recovered.

Two options are available to an MNC to avoid financial restrictions:

1. If the goal is to show lower profitability, high transfer prices on imports to subsidiaries can be used. This objective is appropriate to discourage potential competitors from entering the market or takeover by outsiders.

2. If the goal is to show higher profitability, lower transfer prices on imports to subsidiaries can be used. Higher profits may trigger the subsidiary's employees to demand higher wages or profit-sharing plans or takeover by outsiders. Lower transfer prices on imports could improve the subsidiary's financial position, which facilitates local financing and enjoys a competitive edge during its initial stages of growth.

(D) Managing Currency Fluctuations

A country suffering from balance-of-payments problems may decide to devalue its national currency. Losses from such devaluations may be avoided by using inflated transfer prices to transfer funds from the country to the parent country or to some other affiliate unit.

Balance-of-payments problems often result from an inflationary environment. Inflation erodes the purchasing power of an MNC's monetary assets. Using inflated transfer prices on goods imported to such an environment may offer a timely cash removal method.

(E) Winning Host-Country Government Approval

Maintaining positive relations with the host government is a good idea since the government is concerned about both intercorporate pricing and its effect on reported profits and continually changing and manipulating transfer prices. For example, using unfavorable transfer prices to a country's economic detriment could result in the loss of goodwill. It is a trade-off between sacrificing some profits and satisfying foreign government authorities. Factors such as tax rates, tariffs, inflation, foreign exchange controls, government price controls, and government stability need to be considered when analyzing the trade-offs.

(v) Transfer Pricing Choices

Basically, two choices exist in transfer pricing: market-based pricing and cost-based pricing. The *benefits* of using market-based pricing are listed next.

- Divisional profitability approaches the real economic contribution of the subsidiary to the total MNC.

- Such pricing creates a sense of competition among various subsidiaries.

- It facilitates better evaluation of a subsidiary's performance

- Market-based pricing incurs less scrutiny from foreign government tax authorities

Pitfalls of using market-based pricing are listed next.

- Subsidiaries need not be autonomous profit centers.

- Subsidiary managers may not have the authority to make autonomous decisions.

- There may not be an intermediate market in order to establish a free competitive market price.

- The MNC may not have much flexibility to manipulate profits and cash flows.

If market prices are either unavailable or cannot be reasonably estimated, then cost-based transfer prices are conveniently determined because the information on costs is available. Cost may be the full cost, a variable cost, or marginal cost with a markup added to allow the selling subsidiary some percentage of profit.

Disadvantages of cost-based transfer pricing are listed next.

- The selling party has no incentive to control costs or to operate efficiently.

- Since inefficiencies can be passed along to the purchasing subsidiary, undesirable behavior may result in the form of poor decision making.

KEY CONCEPTS TO REMEMBER: Transfer Pricing Choices

- A highly decentralized MNC would be expected to use market-based transfer prices. Smaller firms favor decentralized operations to achieve their objectives and to avoid foreign government scrutiny.

- A centralized MNC would control the setting of cost-based transfer prices. Large firms are generally more centralized due to worldwide optimization of objectives. Cost-based transfer pricing provides flexibility and control.

- The nationality of the parent company's management also affects whether the MNC uses market prices or costs in establishing a transfer price.

(vi) Taxes and Transfer Pricing

Intercompany transactions from an MNC point of view are subject to Section 482 of the Internal Revenue Code of the United States. Section 482 gives the Internal Revenue Service (IRS) the authority to reallocate income and deductions among subsidiaries if it determines that this is necessary to prevent tax evasion (the illegal reduction of taxes). The key test is whether intercompany sales of goods or services appear to be priced at arm's-length market values. Among items the IRS will scrutinize are trademarks, patents, R&D cost, and management services.

The IRS allows three pricing methods considered arm's length: (1) the comparable uncontrolled price method (i.e., market-based transfer pricing), (2) the resale price method (i.e., sales price less markup), and (3) the cost-plus method (i.e., cost-based transfer pricing).

TAX OBJECTIVES IN CONFLICT: IRS versus MNC

- The IRS's objective is to determine the MNC's tax liability.

- The MNC's objective is after-tax profit maximization.

- These two objectives conflict.

- It is possible that a U.S. MNC may use one transfer price for internal financial reporting and another for computing its U.S. tax liability.

(g) Responsibility Accounting

(i) Overview

Managers are responsible and accountable for their decisions and actions in planning and controlling the resources of the organization. Resources include physical, human, and financial ones. Resources are used to achieve the organization's goals and objectives. Budgets help to quantify the resources required to achieve goals.

The concept of responsibility accounting emerged because a few senior managers at the top cannot run all parts of a business effectively. To improve performance, the organization is divided into centers, product lines, divisions, and units so that a lower-level manager is responsible for a specific center, product line, division, or unit.

(ii) Definition of Responsibility Accounting

Each manager is in charge of a responsibility center and is accountable for a specified set of activities and operations within a segment of the organization. The degree of responsibility varies directly with the manager's level. **Responsibility accounting** is a system that measures the plans and actions of each responsibility center. Four types of responsibility centers are common, as shown in Exhibit 4.54.

EXHIBIT 4.54 Types of Responsibility Centers

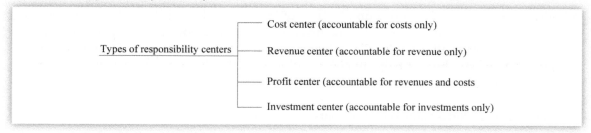

In a **cost center**, a manager is accountable for costs only (e.g., a manufacturing plant). In a **revenue center**, a manager is accountable for revenues only (e.g., a product manager or brand manager). In a **profit center**, a manager is accountable for revenues and costs (e.g., a division). In an **investment center**, a manager is accountable for investment (e.g., a division's revenues and costs).

A major advantage of the responsibility accounting approach is that costs can be traced to either the individual who has the best knowledge about the reasons for cost increase or the activity that caused the cost increase. A major disadvantage is the behavioral implications of the approach on managers whose performance is to be evaluated.

Managers should be held accountable for the costs that they have control over. **Controllability** is the degree of influence that a specific manager has over costs, revenues, and investment. A **controllable cost** is any cost that is subject to the influence of a given manager of a given responsibility center for a given time span. Controllable costs should be separated from uncontrollable costs in a manager's performance report.

KEY CONCEPTS TO REMEMBER: Responsibility Accounting

- Most managers have partial control over their costs; their rewards depend on factors they cannot control.

- Managers should be compensated according to risk taking regardless of who controls the costs. Otherwise, management turnover, frustration, and low motivation will set in.

- Managers should be able to influence activities even they he do not have full control over costs.

- Senior management can change a manager's behavior by switching costs from cost center to profit center if it helps the organization.

In responsibility accounting, feedback is crucial. When budgets are compared with actual results, variances occur. The key is to use variance information to raise questions and seek answers from the right party. Variance information should not be abused—in other words, it should not be used to lay blame on others. Variances invoke questions as to why and how, not who.

(h) Operating Budgets

A budgeting system includes both expected results and historical or actual results. Such a system builds on historical, or actual, results and expands to include consideration of future, or expected, results. A budgeting system guides managers into the future.

Budget system $\longrightarrow$ Forward looking

Historical cost system $\longrightarrow$ Backward looking

A budget is a quantitative expression of a plan of action. It aids in the coordination of various activities or functions throughout the organization. The **master budget** by definition summarizes the objectives of all subunits of an organization (i.e., both operating budgets and financial budgets). The master budget helps in coordinating activities, implementing plans, authorizing actions, and evaluating performance. (See Exhibit 4.55.)

EXHIBIT 4.55 Master Budget and Its Components

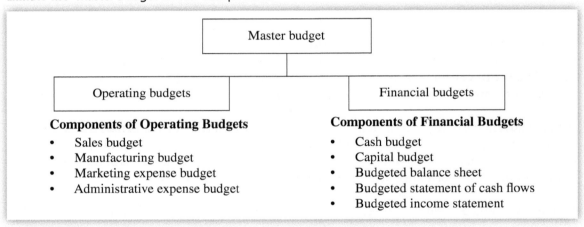

The master budget captures the financial impact of all the firm's other budgets and plans. Although the master budget itself is not a strategic plan, it helps managers to implement the strategic plans. The master budget focuses on both operating decisions and financing decisions. Operating decisions concentrate on the acquisition and use of scarce resources.

Financing decisions center on how to get the funds to acquire resources. It focuses on operating decisions and budgets.

(i) Benefits of Operating Budgets
Benefits to be derived from budgets are listed next.

- Budgets are planning tools. Budgets force managers to look into the future and make them prepare to meet uncertainties and changing business conditions.

- Budgets provide a starting point for discussing business strategies. In turn, these strategies direct long-term and short-term planning. Therefore, strategic plans and budgets are interrelated and affect one another.

- Budgeted performance is better than historical data for judging or evaluating employee performance. This is because employees know what is expected of their performance. A major drawback of using historical data is that inefficiencies and bad decisions may be buried in past actions.

- Budgets can be valuable vehicles for communication with interested parties. Budgets help coordinate activities of various functions within the organization to achieve overall goals and objectives.

- Budgets are control systems. They help to control waste of resources and search out weaknesses in the organizational structure.

- A budget should be implemented so as to gain acceptance by employees. This requires a buy-in by employees, senior management support, and lower-level management involvement.

- A budget should be set tight but attainable and flexible. A budget should be thought of as a means to an end, not the end in itself.

- A budget should not prevent managers from taking prudent action. Nonetheless, managers should not disregard the budget entirely.

(ii) Different Dimensions in Operating Budgets

The time period for budgets varies from one year to five or more years. The common budget period is one year, broken down by quarters and months. Four types of budgets emerge from the time coverage and update point of view: short-term, long-term, static, and continuous budgets.

1. Short-term budgets (operating budgets) have a time frame of one to two years.

2. Long-term budgets (strategic budgets) have a time frame of three to five or more years.

3. Static budgets are the original budgeted numbers, which are not changed. The time frame does not change.

4. Continuous budgets are also called rolling budgets. A 12-month forecast is always available by adding a month in the future as the month just ended is dropped. The time frame keeps changing in the continuous budgets.

Budgets should be viewed positively, not negatively. Although budget preparation is mechanical, its administration and interpretation require patience, education, and people skills. Budgets are a positive device designed to help managers choose and accomplish objectives. However, budgets are not a substitute for bad management or poor accounting system.

(iii) How Operating Budgets Are Prepared

The master budget (static budget) is developed after the goals, strategies, and long-range plans of the organization have been determined. It summarizes the goals of the subunits or segments of an organization. This master budget information summarizes, in a financial form, expectations regarding future income, cash flows, financial position, and supporting plans. Budget functions include planning, coordinating activities, communicating, evaluating performance, implementing plans, motivating, and authorizing actions. The master budget contains the operating budget.

A detailed budget is prepared for the coming fiscal year along with some less detailed amounts for the following years. Budgets may be developed from the top down or from bottom up. With the top-down approach, upper management determines what it expects from subordinate managers. Subordinate managers may then negotiate with upper management concerning the items they feel are unreasonable. With the bottom-up approach, lower-level managers propose what they expect to accomplish and the required resources. Upper management then makes suggestions and revisions. Budgets may be used for long-range planning, but the typical planning-and-control budget period is one year. This annual budget may be broken down into months or quarters and continuously updated.

HOW MANY BUDGETS ARE THERE?

Every company needs some combination of the following budgets every year. Manufacturing companies need labor budgets, production cost budgets, production budgets, and purchases budgets while service companies do not need them. However, all companies need finance-related budgets such as balance sheet, income, expense, and cash budgets.

- **Budgeted balance sheet.** This budget reflects the expected balance sheet at the end of the budget period. It is determined by combining the estimate of the balance sheet at the beginning of the budget period with the estimated results of operations for the period obtained from the budgeted income statements and estimating changes in assets and liabilities. These changes in assets and liabilities result from management's decisions regarding capital investment in long-term assets, investment in working capital, and financing decisions.

- **Budgeted income statement or operating budget.** This budget reflects the income expected for the budget period.

- **Budgets for other expenses.** These budgets may be broken down according to expense category, depending on the relative importance of the types of expenses (i.e., selling, administrative, R&D, etc.).

- **Cash budget.** This budget summarizes cash receipts and disbursements and indicates financing requirements. It is important in ensuring an organization's solvency, maximizing returns from cash balances, and determining whether the organization is generating enough cash for current and future operations.

- **Cash disbursements budget.** This budget is dependent on the pattern of payments for expenses. Cash disbursements typically do not match costs in a period, since expenses generally are paid later than they are incurred.

- **Cash receipts budget.** This budget estimates how much cash receipts can come from credit sales made to customers. The collection of sales depends on an organization's credit policies and its customer base. Most organizations must obtain cash to pay current bills while waiting for payment from customers. This cash represents an opportunity cost to the organization.

■ **Labor budget.** This budget may be broken down by type of worker required in hours or number of workers.

■ **Production cost budget.** This budget may be broken down by product or plant.

■ **Production budget.** This budget may be broken down by product or plant. Production must meet current sales demand and maintain sufficient inventory levels for expected activity levels during the budget period and on into the next period. This budget is reviewed with production managers to determine if it is realistic. If the budget is not attainable, management may revise the sales forecast or try to increase capacity. If production capacity will exceed requirements, other uses of the idle capacity may be considered.

■ **Purchases budget.** This budget typically is broken down by raw materials and parts. An organization's inventory policy determines its level of purchases.

■ **Sales budget.** This budget may be broken down by product, territory, plant, or other segment of interest.

■ **Service budget.** This budget may be broken down by the type of customer (commercial or residential), by territory (local, regional, and national), and by the type of skillsets needed (entry level or advanced).

(iv) Operating Budgeting Techniques

Budgets are a necessary component of financial decision making because they help provide an efficient allocation of resources. A budget is a profit-planning and a resource-controlling tool. It is a quantitative expression of management's intentions and plans for the coming year(s) to meet goals and objectives within the resource constraints. Budgets are prepared at the beginning of each year. Departmental or functional budgets are summarized and compared with revenue forecasts and revised as necessary.

As shown in Exhibit 4.56, five budgeting techniques are available.

EXHIBIT 4.56 Budgeting Techniques

1. Incremental budgeting (adds a percentage or fixed amount to the previous budget)
2. Flexible budgeting (reflects variation in activity levels)
3. Zero-based budgeting (uses decision packages to specify objectives and workloads)
4. Planning, programming, and budgeting systems (link performance levels with specific budget amounts)
5. Performance budgeting (focuses mainly on public sector)

A brief description of each budget is presented next.

Incremental budgeting is a traditional approach to budgeting focusing on incremental changes in detailed categories of revenues and expenses, called line items, to represent sales, salaries, travel, supplies, and so forth. The incremental approach to budgeting does not take into account variation in volume or change in activity levels. It operates on the principle of management by exception.

Flexible budgeting (variable or dynamic budgeting) adjusts the budget for changes in the unit level of the cost or revenue. It is also called a variable budget. The flexible budget is based on the knowledge of how revenues and costs should behave over a range of activity. Thus, it is appropriate for any relevant level of activity. The master budget is not adjusted after it is developed, regardless of changes in volume, cost, or other conditions during the budget period.

Zero-based budgeting, especially in the public sector, attempts to analyze the incremental change in a program's output at different levels of funding. For each program, a decision package specifies objectives and measures of efficiency, effectiveness, and workload for alternate levels of funding.

Planning, programming, and budgeting systems attempt to further advance budgeting techniques, especially in the public sector, by presenting budget choices more explicitly in terms of public objectives. With these budgets, the cost and effectiveness of programs are evaluated in a multiyear framework, and alternate approaches are considered.

Performance budgeting, which also focuses mainly on the public sector, links performance measures directly to agency missions and program objectives. Under the performance budgeting model, budgets are developed based on unit costs and service expectations followed by analysis of actual work performed compared with budget estimates.

BUDGET PURPOSES

The main purpose of a budget is to forecast and control the expenditures for a certain activity. A budget is an aid to planning and control. It helps managers to allocate resources efficiently and to achieve objectives effectively. A budget does not allow managers to estimate a firm's beta coefficient, which is a measure of stock market volatility.

(v) Advantages of Operating Budgets

Budgets are commonly used in both large and small organizations. No matter what the size of the organization, the benefits of budgeting typically exceed the costs. The *advantages* of budgets are listed next.

- Budgets compel planning. Management must have targets, and budgets reflect expected performance. Budgets affect strategies, which are the relatively general and permanent plans of an organization that change as conditions and/or objectives change. Budgets can give direction to operations, point out problems, and give meaning to results.

- Budgets provide performance criteria. Budgets allow employees to know what is expected of them. Comparing actual results to budgeted amounts provides more useful information than without comparing

- Budgets promote communication and coordination. Coordination deals with the interests of the organization as a whole, meshing and balancing the factors of production and other departments and functions so that objectives can be achieved. Budgets aid coordination because they require well-laid plans and isolate any problems.

(vi) Limitations of Operating Budgeting Techniques

Peculiarities and limitations of budgets are described next.

- Budgeted items are a mixture of fixed and variable cost components. Accordingly, mixed costs cannot be used for linear projections.

- Budgeted items include some direct costs and some allocated costs. Direct costs are more useful for decision making than allocated costs. Responsibility accounting favors direct and controllable costs, not allocated and uncontrollable costs.

- The nature of volume levels needs to be understood. Most budgets are based on a single level of volume (point estimates), but multiple volume levels (range estimates) would be better for decision making.

- The kinds of assumptions made during the budget development process need to be known. The budget preparer's state of mind must be understood: optimistic, most likely, or pessimistic outcomes. Each of these outcomes would bring a different type of realism to the budget numbers.

- The variances from budgets need to be analyzed very carefully. Performance reports show the variations between the actual and the budgets—an element of control. Corrective action requires determination of underlying causes of variation. Variation could be favorable or unfavorable.

4.3 Sample Practice Questions

In the actual CIA Exam for Part 3, 100 multiple-choice (M/C) test questions appear. This book contains 100 M/C sample practice questions divided into syllabus-based domains using the approximate domain weight given in the exam. These questions are added at the end of each applicable domain of this book with the sole purpose of showing the flavor and structure of the exam questions and of creating a self-quiz experience. The answers and explanations for these questions are shown in a separate section at the end of this book just before the Glossary section. This separate section is titled "Sample Practice Questions, Answers, and Explanations." If CIA Exam candidates need to practice more sample questions to obtain a higher level of confidence, Wiley offers a separate online test bank software product with hundreds of similar, sample practice questions.

1. The following information is available from the records of a manufacturing company that applies factory overhead based on direct labor hours:

Estimated overhead cost	$500,000
Estimated labor hours	200,000 hours
Actual overhead cost	$515,000
Actual labor hours	210,000 hours

Based on this information, overhead would be:

a. Underapplied by $9,524.

b. Overapplied by $10,000.

c. Overapplied by $15,000.

d. Overapplied by $40,750.

2. A company plans to implement a bonus plan based on segment performance. In addition, the company plans to convert to a responsibility accounting system for segment reporting. The following costs, which have been included in the segment performance reports that have been prepared under the current system, are being reviewed to determine if they should be included in the responsibility accounting segment reports.

I. Corporate administrative costs allocated on the basis of net segment sales

II. Personnel costs assigned on the basis of the number of employees in each segment

III. Fixed computer facility costs divided equally among each segment

IV. Variable computer operational costs charged to each segment based on actual hours used times a predetermined standard rate; any variable cost efficiency or inefficiency remains in the computer department

Of these four cost items, the only item that could logically be included in the segment performance reports prepared on a responsibility accounting basis would be the:

a. Corporate administrative costs.

b. Personnel costs.

c. Fixed computer facility costs.

d. Variable computer operational costs.

3. In a merger or acquisition transaction, usually two companies are involved such as an acquiring company and a target company (i.e., company to be acquired). All of the following are the preferred financial profile of a target company **except**:

a. High-liquidity

b. High price/earnings ratio

c. High earnings per share

d. Low leverage

4. What conclusion should a financial analyst draw if a company has a high fixed assets turnover ratio?

a. The company may be overcapitalized.

b. The company may have a problem with employees converting inventory to personal use.

c. The company may be undercapitalized.

d. The company has favorable profitability.

5. A company will finance next year's capital projects through debt rather than additional equity. The benchmark cost of capital for these projects should be:

a. The before-tax cost of new debt financing.

b. The after-tax cost of new debt financing.

c. The cost of equity financing.

d. The weighted-average cost of capital.

6. In the distribution of liquidation proceeds for a bankrupt firm, which of the following claimants has highest priority?

   a. Preferred stock

   b. Common stock

   c. Bonds payable

   d. Taxes payable

7. A company has a foreign-currency-denominated trade payable due in 60 days. In order to eliminate the foreign exchange risk associated with the payable, the company could:

   a. Sell foreign currency forward today.

   b. Wait 60 days and pay the invoice by purchasing foreign currency in the spot market at that time.

   c. Buy foreign currency forward today.

   d. Borrow foreign currency today, convert it to domestic currency on the spot market, and invest the funds in a domestic bank deposit until the invoice payment date.

8. A company has 7,000 obsolete toys, which are carried in inventory at a manufacturing cost of $6 per unit. If the toys are reworked for $2 per unit, they could be sold for $3 per unit. If the toys are scrapped, they could be sold for $1.85 per unit. Which alternative is more desirable (rework or scrap), and what is the total dollar amount of the advantage of that alternative?

   a. Scrap, $5,950

   b. Rework, $36,050

   c. Scrap, $47,950

   d. Rework, $8,050

9. Which of the following statements about activity-based costing (ABC) is **not** true?

   a. ABC is useful for allocating marketing and distribution costs.

   b. ABC is more likely to result in major differences from traditional costing systems if the firm manufactures only one product rather than multiple products.

   c. In ABC, cost drivers are what cause costs to be incurred.

   d. ABC differs from traditional costing systems in that products are not cross-subsidized.

10. The cost of materials has risen steadily over the year. The company uses its newest materials first when removing items from inventory. Which of the following methods of estimating the ending balance of the materials inventory account will result in the highest net income, all other variables held constant?

   a. Last in, first out (LIFO)

   b. First in, first out (FIFO)

   c. Weighted average

   d. Specific identification

11. In its first year of operations, a firm had $50,000 of fixed operating costs (F). It sold 10,000 units at a $10 unit price (P) and incurred variable costs (V) of $4 per unit. If all prices and costs will be the same in the second year and sales are projected to rise to 25,000 units (Q), what will the degree of operating leverage (DOL; the extent to which fixed costs are used in the firm's operations) be in the second year?

   a. 1.25

   b. 1.50

   c. 2.00

   d. 6.00

12. During the current accounting period, a manufacturing company purchased $70,000 of raw materials, of which $50,000 of direct materials and $5,000 of indirect materials was used in production. The company also incurred $45,000 of total labor costs and $20,000 of other factory overhead costs. An analysis of the work-in-process control account revealed $40,000 of direct labor costs. Based on the above information, what is the total amount accumulated in the factory overhead control account?

   a. $25,000

   b. $30,000

   c. $45,000

   d. $50,000

13. A company experienced a machinery breakdown on one of its production lines. As a consequence of the breakdown, manufacturing fell behind schedule, and a decision was made to schedule overtime in order to return manufacturing to schedule. Which one of the following methods is the proper way to account for the overtime paid to the direct laborers?

a. The overtime hours times the sum of the straight-time wages and overtime premium would be charged entirely to manufacturing overhead.

b. The overtime hours times the sum of the straight-time wages and overtime premium would be treated as direct labor.

c. The overtime hours times the overtime premium would be charged to repair and maintenance expense while the overtime hours times the straight-time wages would be treated as direct labor.

d. The overtime hours times the overtime premium would be charged to manufacturing overhead while the overtime hours times the straight-time wages would be treated as direct labor.

14. A company uses straight-line depreciation for financial reporting purposes, but uses accelerated depreciation for tax purposes. Which of the following account balances would be lower in the financial statements used for tax purposes than it would be in the general purpose financial statements?

a. Accumulated depreciation
b. Cash
c. Retained earnings
d. Gross fixed assets

15. An existing machine with estimated remaining life of five years that cost $100,000 can be sold for $20,000. The variable cost of output from this machine has been $1 per unit with 100,000 units per year produced. A new machine will cost $90,000 and is estimated to lower the variable cost to $.70 per unit over its five-year life. The **most** appropriate term for the decision process involved in this scenario is:

a. Capital budgeting.
b. Economic order quantity.
c. Flexible budgeting.
d. Sensitivity analysis.

16. Many service industries utilize a budgeting process to identify major programs and develop short-term operating budgets, such as expected revenues and expected direct expenses, for the identified programs. For example, a nursing home may develop one-year revenue and expense budgets for each of its different programs, such as day care for the elderly or Meals on Wheels. Which of the following is a **major** advantage of short-term program planning and budgeting?

a. It eliminates the need for periodic program evaluation.

b. It provides a rigid basis for periodic program evaluation.

c. It promotes communication and coordination within an organization.

d. It provides an important basis for strategic analysis of the goals of the organization.

17. Actual and projected sales of a company for September and October are:

	Cash Sales	Credit Sales
September (actual)	$20,000	$50,000
October (projected)	30,000	55,000

All credit sales are collected in the month following the month in which the sale is made. The September 30 cash balance is $23,000. Cash disbursements in October are projected to be $94,000. To maintain a minimum cash balance of $15,000 on October 31, the company will need to borrow:

a. $0.
b. $6,000.
c. $11,000.
d. $16,000.

18. Which of the following is **not** true about international transfer prices for a multinational firm?

a. They allow firms to attempt to minimize worldwide taxes.

b. They allow the firm to evaluate each division.

c. They provide each division with a profit-making orientation.

d. They allow firms to correctly price products in each country in which they operate.

19. One department of an organization, Final Assembly, is purchasing subcomponents from another department, Materials Fabrication. The price that Materials Fabrication will charge Final Assembly is to be determined. Outside market prices for the subcomponents are available. Which of the following is the **most** correct statement regarding a market-based transfer price?

a. Marginal production cost transfer prices provide incentives to use otherwise idle capacity.

b. Market transfer prices provide an incentive to use otherwise idle capacity.

c. Overall long-term competitiveness is enhanced with a market-based transfer price.

d. Corporate politics is more of a factor in a market-based transfer price than with other methods.

20. A company makes a product that sells for $30. During the coming year, fixed costs are expected to be $180,000, and variable costs are estimated at $26 per unit. How many units must the company sell in order to break even?

a. 6,000

b. 6,924

c. 45,000

d. 720,000

Sample Practice Questions, Answers, and Explanations

Domain 1: Business Acumen (35%)

1. Which of the following is very useful in developing succession plans for executives and senior management of a corporation?

   a. Depth charts

   Correct. Depth charts provide the board members a snapshot of the available, internal management staff and their readiness to take on increased leadership roles when the right time comes. So, depth charts are very useful in succession plans of key management positions.

   b. Organization charts

   Incorrect. Organization charts show who reports to whom in the management chain of command.

   c. Responsibility charts

   Incorrect. Responsibility charts can be considered part of organization charts.

   d. Accountability charts

   Incorrect. Accountability charts can be considered part of organization charts.

2. In addition to the four basic requirements of a contract, which of the following must also occur in order to have a valid contract?

   a. The agreement always must be in writing.

   Incorrect. See correct answer (c).

   b. There must be evidence of undue influence.

   Incorrect. See correct answer (c).

   c. There must be an absence of an invalidating contract.

   Correct. There must be an absence of an invalidating contract, such as duress, undue influence, misrepresentation, or mistake. That is, the purpose should be legal. The four basic requirements include mutual assent, consideration, legality of object, and capacity.

   d. A legal remedy need not be available for there to be a breach.

   Incorrect. See correct answer (c).

3. Some economic indicators lead the economy into a recovery or recession, and some lag it. An example of a lag variable would be:

   a. Chronic unemployment.

   Correct. Initial claims of unemployment is a lead indicator, but chronic unemployment is a lag variable.

   b. Orders for consumer and producer goods.

   Incorrect. Orders for consumer and producer goods lead the economy.

   c. Housing starts.

   Incorrect. Housing starts lead the economy.

   d. Consumer expectations.

   Incorrect. Consumer expectations lead the economy.

4. The relationship between organizational structure and technology suggests that in an organization using mass production technology (e.g., automobile manufacturing), the best structure would be:

a. Organic, emphasizing loose controls and flexibility.

Incorrect. Mass production technology should not be matched with an organic structure.

b. Matrix, in which individuals report to both product and functional area managers.

Incorrect. Matrix is not a type of structure but rather a type of departmentalization and should not be used with mass production.

c. **Mechanistic, that is, highly formalized, with tight controls.**

Correct. Mass production would be best matched with a mechanistic, highly formalized structure.

d. Integrated, emphasizing cooperation among departments.

Incorrect. There is no such thing as integrated structure, and integration is not conducive to mass production.

5. Routine tasks, which have few exceptions and problems that are easy to analyze, are conducive to:

a. **Formalized structure, where procedure manuals and job descriptions are common.**

Correct. Routine tasks are conducive to formalized structure.

b. Decentralized decision making, where decisions are pushed downward in the organization.

Incorrect. Routine tasks are conducive to centralization.

c. Organic structures that emphasize adaptability and flexibility to changing circumstances.

Incorrect. Routine tasks are conducive to mechanistic, not organic, structures.

d. High degrees of job satisfaction on the part of employees performing them.

Incorrect. Job satisfaction is often low in tasks that are routine and repetitive.

6. Which of the following theories predicts that employee behavior depends on the belief that good performance will be rewarded by continued employment?

a. Equity theory: Employees compare their job inputs and outcomes with those of others and then react to eliminate inequities.

Incorrect. In equity theory, employees compare their job inputs and outcomes with others and then respond to eliminate inequities.

b. **Expectation theory: The strength of a tendency to act in a certain way depends on the strength of an expectation that an act will be followed by a given outcome.**

Correct. The strength of a tendency to act in a certain way depends on the strength of an expectation that an act will be followed by a given outcome.

c. Goal-setting theory: Specific and difficult goals lead to higher performance.

Incorrect. Goal-setting theory postulates that specific and difficult goals lead to higher performance.

d. Reinforcement theory: Behavior is a function of its consequences.

Incorrect. Reinforcement theory states that behavior is a function of its consequences.

7. Which of the following has a flat organizational structure compared to others?

a. Organization A with 11 hierarchical levels

Incorrect. See correct answer (b).

b. **Organization B with three hierarchical levels**

Correct. A flat structure has a wide span, is horizontally dispersed, and has fewer hierarchical levels. Relative to a flat structure, a tall structure has a narrow span of management and more hierarchical levels.

c. Organization C with eight hierarchical levels

Incorrect. See correct answer (b).

d. Organization D with six hierarchical levels

Incorrect. See correct answer (b).

8. The **most** fundamental flaw of cost-plus pricing is that it:

a. Fails to account for competition.

Incorrect. See correct answer (b).

b. Ignores demand.

Correct. Price reflects some unit of value given up by one party in return for something gained from another party. The setting of price based on costs has become a common practice. Two approaches include standard markup pricing and target return pricing. The cost-plus pricing method ignores demand since costs are generated internally and since the demand is created externally to an organization.

c. Ignores industry-wide standard markup policies.

Incorrect. See correct answer (b).

d. Places too much emphasis on competition.

Incorrect. See correct answer (b).

9. "Selling price = Unit cost + Desired profit" represents which of the following pricing approaches?

a. Profit maximization

Incorrect. See correct answer (c).

b. Demand-based pricing

Incorrect. See correct answer (c).

c. Target return pricing

Correct. Two pricing approaches based on cost include standard markup pricing and target return pricing. Target return pricing adds both cost per unit and desired profit and is calculated as: Selling price per unit = Unit cost per unit + Desired profit per unit. A standard markup percentage based on management profit goal is added to the cost in the standard markup pricing approach.

d. Standard markup

Incorrect. See correct answer (c).

10. Choosing vendors based solely on which of the following factors is detrimental to the long-term success of a buying firm?

a. Quality

Incorrect. See correct answer (c).

b. Service

Incorrect. See correct answer (c).

c. Price

Correct. Suppliers should be viewed as outside partners who can contribute to the long-term success of a buying firm. If suppliers are selected on price only, they will be switched continuously, which will destabilize the purchasing process.

d. Delivery

Incorrect. See correct answer (c).

11. Supplier audits are an important first step in:

a. Supplier certification.

Correct. Supplier audits are an important first step in the supplier certification program.

b. Supplier relationships.

Incorrect. This choice occurs after supplier certification.

c. Supplier partnerships.

Incorrect. This choice occurs after supplier certification.

d. Strategic partnerships.

Incorrect. This choice occurs after supplier certification.

12. Customers in which of the following phases of the product life cycle are called laggards?

a. Introduction

Incorrect. See correct answer (d).

b. Growth

Incorrect. See correct answer (d).

c. Maturity

Incorrect. See correct answer (d).

d. Decline

Correct. Innovators and early adopters are those customers who are willing to take more risk and buy the product shortly after introduction. During the growth phase, product purchase begins to spread to the early majority of the mass market, with full penetration and adoption by the late majority occurring primarily in the maturity phase. Near the product's decline, only laggards are left purchasing the product.

13. Few competitors exist in which phase of the product life cycle?

    a. Introduction

    Correct. In the introduction phase of the product life cycle, few competitors exist. A growing number exists in the growth phase, many rivals exist in the maturity phase, and a declining number exists in the decline phase. Similarly, negative cash flows occur in the introduction phase, moderate cash flows occur in the growth phase, high cash flows occur in the maturity stage, and low cash flows occur in the decline phase.

    b. Growth

    Incorrect. See correct answer (a).

    c. Maturity

    Incorrect. See correct answer (a).

    d. Decline

    Incorrect. See correct answer (a).

14. Regarding the theory of constraints in operations, which of the following does **not** describe a bottleneck situation appropriately?

    a. A machine exists where jobs are processed at a slower rate than they are demanded.

    Incorrect. See correct answer (c).

    b. A work center exists where jobs are processed at a slower rate than they are demanded.

    Incorrect. See correct answer (c).

    c. An employee's skill levels are more than needed for a specific job but less than needed for any general job.

    Correct. A bottleneck is a constraint in a facility, function, department, or resource whose capacity is less than the demand placed on it. For example, a bottleneck machine or work center exists where (1) jobs are processed at a slower rate than they are demanded and (2) the demand for a company's product exceeds the ability to produce the product. Generally, bottlenecks deal with products, not people. That an employee's skill levels are more than needed for a specific job but less than needed for any general job is related to people.

    d. The demand for a company's product exceeds its ability to produce that product.

    Incorrect. See correct answer (c).

15. Regarding production process flows, which of the following is **not** a part of the levers for managing throughput of a process?

    a. Decrease resource idleness.

    Incorrect. This choice is an example of a lever in managing the throughput.

    b. Increase effective capacity.

    Incorrect. This choice is an example of a lever in managing the throughput.

    c. Reduce setup resources.

    Incorrect. This choice is an example of a lever in managing the throughput.

    d. Decrease theoretical capacity.

    Correct. Three operational process flow measures include flow time, inventory, and throughput. Theoretical capacity should not be decreased; instead, it should be increased by decreasing the unit load on the bottleneck resource pool.

16. Which of the following inventory items would be the **most** frequently reviewed in an ABC inventory control system?

    a. Expensive, frequently used, high stock-out cost items with short lead times

    Incorrect. Long, not short, lead times prompt more frequent reviews in the ABC inventory control system.

    b. Expensive, frequently used, low stock-out cost items with long lead times

    Incorrect. High, not low, stock-out costs prompt a more frequent review in an ABC inventory control system.

    c. Inexpensive, frequently used, high stock-out cost items with long lead times

    Incorrect. Expensive, not inexpensive, items prompt a more frequent review in an ABC inventory control system.

    d. Expensive, frequently used, high stock-out cost items with long lead times

    Correct. All of these items prompt a more frequent review in an ABC inventory control system.

17. What are the three factors a manager should consider in controlling stock-outs?

a. Holding costs, quality costs, and physical inventories

Incorrect. These are inventory-related terms, but none will controls stock-outs.

b. Economic order quantity, annual demand, and quality costs

Incorrect. The order quantity and annual demand are not factors in the stock-out problem.

c. **Time needed for delivery, rate of inventory usage, and safety stock**

Correct. Delivery time, usage rate, and level of safety stock are all considerations in controlling stock-outs.

d. Economic order quantity, production bottlenecks, and safety stock

Incorrect. Production bottlenecks are the results of a stock-out; they are not a method of control. Also, economic order quantity is irrelevant to stock-outs.

18. Reordering of specific items from vendors should be based on:

a. Computations on the basis of economic order quantities.

Incorrect. Computations on the basis of economic order quantities (EOQs) will minimize the EOQ objective, but EOQ assumes stationary demand, which is not the case here.

b. **Demand forecasting based on early orders for the items.**

Correct. A stated requirement is demand forecasting based on early orders for items, which means that company personnel have learned that the best predictor of subsequent sales of a specific item is sales in the first few days after it has been made available.

c. Market demographics.

Incorrect. This is not the critical ordering factor for a specific item.

d. Vendor quantity discounts and warehouse space.

Incorrect. Vendor quantity discounts and warehouse space are valid considerations only if the company would order the item in those quantities anyway.

19. A risk associated with just-in-time (JIT) production is the:

a. Increased potential for early obsolescence of inventories of finished goods.

Incorrect. To the contrary, finished goods inventories are virtually eliminated.

b. High cost of material handling equipment.

Incorrect. JIT does not necessarily require high-cost material handling equipment.

c. Potential for significant costs associated with reworking defective components.

Incorrect. If a defect is discovered, production is stopped.

d. **Critical dependency on a few vendors.**

Correct. Because materials are delivered as needed, it is imperative to establish and maintain good relations with those critical suppliers.

20. With regard to inventory management, an increase in the frequency of ordering will normally:

a. Reduce the total ordering costs.

Incorrect. Total ordering costs would increase.

b. Have no impact on total ordering costs.

Incorrect. Total ordering costs would increase.

c. **Reduce total carrying costs.**

Correct. As the frequency of ordering increases, total carrying costs are reduced by the average that inventory level is reduced.

d. Have no impact of total carrying costs.

Incorrect. Total carrying costs are reduced.

21. In which of the following phases of business development life cycle will both outputs and employment be declining?

a. Peak

Incorrect. See correct answer (b).

b. **Recession**

Correct. Economists suggest four phases of the business cycle: peak, recession, trough, and recovery. During the recession phase, both output and employment will decline, but prices tend to be relatively inflexible in a downward direction.

c. Trough

Incorrect. See correct answer (b).

d. Recovery

Incorrect. See correct answer (b).

22. Which of the following scope items for an outsourced vendor takes on a significant dimension in a supply chain environment?

a. **Liabilities and guarantees**

Correct. In a supply chain environment, there could be several suppliers and integrators in developing or delivering a specific product or service to a user customer or client. Liabilities and guarantees involve problems in performance levels where each party is accountable to its roles, responsibilities, and remedies to problems encountered. The other three choices are also important.

b. Well-defined service levels

Incorrect. See correct answer (a).

c. Licensing of services and products

Incorrect. See correct answer (a).

d. Changes to terms and conditions of services

Incorrect. See correct answer (a).

23. When managing a third-party organization such as an outsourcing vendor, which of the following is **not** applicable?

a. Due diligence review

Incorrect. This choice is applicable to outsourcing vendors.

b. Rules of engagement

Incorrect. This choice is applicable to outsourcing vendors.

c. **Rules of behavior**

Correct. The rules of behavior document is applicable to internal employees of an organization, not for external, third-party organizations.

d. Contractual agreement

Incorrect. This choice is applicable to outsourcing vendors.

24. Where does the information about opportunities and threats come from for a company?

a. An analysis of the organization's internal environment

Incorrect. See correct answer (c).

b. A department-by-department study of the organization

Incorrect. See correct answer (c).

c. **A scan of the external environments**

Correct. While information about strengths and weaknesses of an organization come from internal sources, information about opportunities and threats will come from external sources. The external sources can include competition, government, economy, and political, legal, demographic, and cultural changes.

d. An analysis of employee grievances

Incorrect. See correct answer (c).

25. The auditor has recognized that a problem exists because the organizational unit has been too narrow in its definition of goals. The goals of the unit focus on profits, but the overall organizational goals are much broader. The auditor also recognizes that the auditee will resist any recommendations about adopting broader goals. The **best** course of action would be to:

a. Avoid conflict and present only those goals that are consistent with the auditee's views since all others will be ignored.

Incorrect. Organizations cannot avoid conflict. It is now becoming accepted that some levels of conflict are necessary in order for organizations to grow and adapt to a changing environment.

b. **Identify the broader organizational goals and present a set of recommendations that attempts to meet both organizational and auditee goals.**

Correct. The auditor is responsible to the organization, not just the auditee, and should therefore report the problem to the auditee.

c. Subtly mix the suggested solution with the problem definition so that the auditee will identify the solution apparently independently of the auditor.

Incorrect. Mixing solutions with problem identification is a frequent problem cited in the managerial literature but is not an effective means of dealing with the problem identified.

d. Only report the conditions found and leave the rest of the analysis to the auditees.

Incorrect. This would be a violation of the Standards, which specify reporting criteria.

26. Which of the following problem-solving tools is an idea-generating and consensus-building technique?

a. Brainstorming

Incorrect. Brainstorming is a technique to generate a great number of ideas.

b. Synectics

Incorrect. Synectics involves the use of nontraditional activities, such as excursions, fantasies, and analogies.

c. Systems analysis

Incorrect. Systems analysis breaks down a large problem into many smaller problems.

d. Nominal group technique

Correct. The nominal group technique is an idea-generating and consensus-building problem-solving tool. This technique gives everyone an opportunity to express ideas without being interrupted by others in the group.

27. Job performance is **best** defined as follows:

a. Job performance = Motivation × Ability

Correct. Job performance is motivation multiplied by ability. The reason for the multiplication sign in the equation is because motivation cannot compensate for lack of ability. In addition to ability, skill, experience, and training are needed.

b. Job performance = Needs × Skills

Incorrect. See correct answer (a).

c. Job performance = Satisfaction × Job experience

Incorrect. See correct answer (a).

d. Job performance = Goals × Training

Incorrect. See correct answer (a).

28. Which of the following is a critical challenge in implementing the employee empowerment principle?

a. Pushing authority downward closer to front-line employees

Incorrect. This is not a critical challenge.

b. Expecting accountability from all employees

Incorrect. This is not a critical challenge.

c. Delegating employees with restrictive rules to achieve objectives

Correct. A critical challenge in implementing employee empowerment principle is to delegate only to the extent required to achieve objectives. This requires ensuring that risk acceptance is based on sound practices for identification and minimization of risk, including sizing risks and weighing potential losses against gains in arriving at good business decisions. This is a balancing act among risk, competence, and objectives.

The employee empowerment principle includes assignment of authority, responsibility for operating activities, and establishment of reporting relationships and authorization protocols. It involves the degree to which individuals and teams are encouraged to use initiative in addressing issues and solving problems as well as limits of their authority. It also deals with policies describing appropriate business practices, knowledge and experience of key personnel, and resources provided for carrying out duties. Specifically, employee empowerment also includes pushing authority downward closer to front-line employees (choice a), expecting accountability from all employees (choice b), and developing clear and complete job description for employees (choice d), but these are not critical challenges.

d. Developing clear and complete job descriptions for employees

Incorrect. This is not a critical challenge.

29. In light of rapidly changing technologies and increasing competition and to provide the ability to affect quality initiatives, which of the following human resources policies and practices is **not** enough?

a. Hiring competent employees

   Incorrect. See correct answer (b).

b. **Providing one-time training for employees**

   Correct. It is essential that employees be equipped for new challenges as issues that enterprises face change and become more complex, driven in part by rapidly changing technologies and increasing competition. Education and training, whether classroom instruction, self-study, or on-the-job training, must prepare an entity's people to keep pace and deal effectively with the evolving environment. They will also strengthen the entity's ability to affect quality initiatives. Hiring of competent people and one-time training are not enough. The education and training process must be ongoing and continuing.

c. Encouraging continuing education for employees

   Incorrect. See correct answer (b).

d. Conducting periodic performance evaluations for employees

   Incorrect. See correct answer (b).

30. From a human resources policies and practices viewpoint, which of the following sends a strong message to all interested parties?

a. Expected levels of integrity

   Incorrect. See correct answer (b).

b. **Expected levels of disciplinary actions**

   Correct. Human resources practices send messages to employees regarding expected levels of integrity, ethical behavior, and competence. Such practices relate to hiring, orientation, training, evaluating, counseling, promoting, compensating, and remedial actions. Out of all the practices, disciplinary actions send a strong message that violations of expected behavior will not be tolerated.

c. Expected levels of ethical behavior

   Incorrect. See correct answer (b).

d. Expected levels of competence and trust

   Incorrect. See correct answer (b).

31. Commitment falls under which of the following types of a leader's power?

a. Reward power

   Incorrect. Reward power is gaining compliance through rewards.

b. Coercive power

   Incorrect. Coercive power is gaining compliance through fear or threat of punishment.

c. Expert power

   Incorrect. Expert power is based on the ability to dispense valued information. An example of expert power is when a financial planner manages and advises an investment portfolio for a client.

d. **Referent power**

   Correct. Referent power comes from a leader's personality characteristics that command subordinates' identification, respect, admiration, and charisma. It is expressed through commitment.

32. Which of the following defines the process of evaluating an individual's contribution as a basis for making objective personnel decisions?

a. **Performance appraisal**

   Correct. Performance appraisal defines the process of evaluating an individual's contribution as a basis for making objective personnel decisions.

b. Environmental factors

   Incorrect. Environmental factors include intrinsic and extrinsic rewards.

c. Facilitation skills

   Incorrect. Facilitation skills include diplomacy, negotiating, and communicating skills.

d. Training and development

   Incorrect. Training and development are part of enabling an employee to learn new skills for career advancement.

33. Negotiation, manipulation, coercion, employee education, and increased communication are all ways in which managers can:

a. Improve employee morale.

   Incorrect. All five items listed may either increase or decrease morale.

b. **Overcome resistance to change.**

   Correct. The five items listed are generally recommended as means of overcoming resistance to change. Each technique is recommended in different situations and is likely to address specific resistance to change factors.

c. Maintain control of information.

   Incorrect. All five items listed may either increase or decrease a manager's control over information or the organization.

d. Demonstrate their power to both their supervisors and subordinates.

   Incorrect. Although use of manipulation and coercion may help a manager demonstrate power, education, communication, and negotiation would not.

34. The adoption of a new idea or behavior by an organization is known as organizational

a. Development.

   Incorrect. Organizational development is planned change programs intended to help people and organization function more effectively.

b. **Change.**

   Correct. Organizational change is defined as the adoption of a new idea or behavior by an organization.

c. Structure.

   Incorrect. Organizational structure refers to who reports to whom in the company.

d. Intervention.

   Incorrect. Organizational intervention refers to management's degree of involvement in the day-to-day operation.

35. In project management, which of the following outcomes of the schedule performance index (SPI) analysis should be worked on first?

a. A negative SPI of 1.0.

   Incorrect. See correct answer (c).

b. A positive SPI of 1.0.

   Incorrect. See correct answer (c).

c. **A negative SPI of 2.0.**

   Correct. A negative SPI means that the time a work is performed is not in keeping with the actual schedule. It also means that there is a gap between the earned value of the work performed and the planned value.

   An SPI of less than 1.0 means that for every planned hour actually expended, less than one hour of earned value was received. When the SPI goes below 1.0 or gradually gets smaller, corrective action should be taken. Here, the largest negative value of 2.0 should be given top priority to work on it first.

   In terms of negative values, the same logic equally applies to both SPI and the cost performance index (CPI). A negative cost variance means that the work performed is not in keeping with the actual cost. It also means that there is a gap between the value of the work performed and the actual costs incurred. A CPI of less than 1.0 means that for every dollar actually expended, less than one dollar of earned value was received. When the CPI goes below 1.0 or gradually gets smaller, corrective action should be taken.

d. A positive SPI of 2.0.

   Incorrect. See correct answer (c).

Domain 2: Information Security (25%)

1. Between authentication and encryption activities, which one of the following items is **more** secure than the other three items?

    a. Authenticate and encrypt

        Incorrect. Authentication and encryption at the same time is out of sequence and not secure. Encryption should be done first. There should be a time gap between encryption and authentication to be secure.

    b. Authenticate then encrypt

        Incorrect. Authentication first and encryption next is out of sequence and not secure. Encryption should be done first. There should be a time gap between encryption and authentication to be secure.

    c. Encrypt and authenticate

        Incorrect. Encryption and authentication should not be done at the same time as it is not secure. There should be a time gap between encryption and authentication to be secure.

    d. Encrypt then authenticate

        Correct. Which should be done first and which should be done next between authentication and encryption is the important issue here. Encrypting a plaintext should be done first. Later, authentication is done with a time gap. This is very secure.

2. Which of the following can help recover from ransomware attacks?

    a. Encryption key

        Incorrect. Hackers encrypt victims' files with an encryption key so that victims cannot use the files until they pay a ransom amount. An encryption key does not help recover from ransomware attacks.

    b. File and system backups

        Correct. File and system backups, especially maintained in a cloud storage system, are like insurance policies. When computer files are infected with ransomware, a backup version of the files is the best way to recover the critical data.

    c. Decryption key

        Incorrect. Hackers decrypt victims' encrypted files with a decryption key after victims pay a ransom amount. A decryption key does not help recover from ransomware attacks.

    d. Patched and updated software

        Incorrect. Using patched and updated software is a good practice, but it alone cannot help recover from ransomware attacks.

3. Social media platforms or networks were born during which of the following web generations?

    a. Web 1.0

        Incorrect. Web 1.0 provides the basic features, such as browsing, static web format, and mostly read-only features.

    b. Web 2.0

        Correct. Web 2.0 is the source for social media platforms or networks, providing expanded bandwidth and greater computing power.

    c. Web 3.0

        Incorrect. Web 3.0 is the personal, portable, and executable web.

    d. Web 4.0

        Incorrect. Web 4.0 focuses on mobile web connections.

4. Regarding mobile devices, the features of which one of the following items is different from the features of the other three items?

a. Jailbreaking

Incorrect. Jailbreaking is removing the limitations imposed on a device by the manufacturer, often through the installation of custom operating system components or other third-party software. Jailbreaking makes a device more vulnerable to attacks because it removes important safeguards against malware attacks. Some users prefer to bypass the operating system's lockout features in order to install apps that could be malicious in nature. Doing jailbreaking is risky.

b. Tampering

Incorrect. Tampering is modifying data, software, firmware, or hardware without authorization. It includes modifying data in transit, inserting tampered hardware or software into a supply chain, repackaging legitimate apps with malware, and modifying network or device configurations (e.g., jailbreaking or rooting a phone). Doing tampering is risky.

c. Jamming

Correct. Jamming is an attack in which a mobile device is used to emit electromagnetic energy on a wireless network's frequency to make the network unusable. Jamming is used in denial-of-service attacks. Jamming attacks occur based on how a mobile device was designed and developed; jailbreaking, tampering, and rooting attacks are based on what users are doing to their mobile devices.

d. Rooting

Incorrect. Rooting is removing the limitations imposed on a device by the manufacturer, often through the installation of custom operating system components or other third-party software. Rooting makes a device more vulnerable to attacks because it removes important safeguards against malware attacks. Some users prefer to bypass the operating system's lockout features in order to install apps that could be malicious in nature. Doing rooting is risky.

5. Which of the following can help hackers in detection evasion situations?

a. Scripting tools

Correct. Scripting tools are tools of the trade for bad actors, hackers, attackers, or intruders in cyberspace to conduct malicious acts. Scripting tools (e.g., JavaScript, VBscript, cross-site scripting, and cross-zone scripting) can help bad actors to evade detection.

b. Antivirus software

Incorrect. Antivirus software can help to detect bad actions and protect the user.

c. Intrusion detection system

Incorrect. An intrusion detection system can help to detect bad incidents and protect the user.

d. Intrusion prevention system

Incorrect. An intrusion prevention system can help to prevent bad incidents and protect the user.

6. Regarding cybersecurity, defenders are the victim organizations and hackers are attacking individuals and organizations. Which of the following strategic aspect takes a completely opposite viewpoint between defenders and hackers?

a. Expertise

Incorrect. Expertise (i.e., technical knowledge and skills) is different in terms of one party having more expertise than the other party.

b. Resources

Incorrect. Resources (i.e., money and staff) are different in terms of one party having more resources than the other party.

c. Attack surface

Correct. An attack surface is the total amount of cyberspace available for an attacker to exploit or target individuals or organizations, which is a strategic importance for attackers. Defenders' objectives are to reduce the attack surface to as small as possible; attackers' objectives are to expand the attack surface as large as possible. So, these two objectives reflect diverse or opposite viewpoints.

d. Tool kits

Incorrect. Tool kits (i.e., hardware and software) are different in terms of one party having more sophisticated tools than the other party.

7. Which of the following is **not** a variant of phishing attacks?

   a. Spear phishing

   Incorrect. Spear phishing or whaling is a variant of phishing attacks. It is a very serious and targeted attack.

   b. Vishing

   Incorrect. Vishing is a variant of phishing attacks. It uses voicemail to attack.

   c. Smishing

   Incorrect. Smishing is a variant of phishing attacks. It uses text messages to attack.

   d. SIM card swapping

   Correct. Subscriber identity module (SIM) card swapping involves an identity thief approaching a wireless carrier with a victim's fake proof of identity and obtaining a duplicate SIM card for a mobile/cell phone to perpetrate fraud. The wireless carrier deactivates the original SIM card and issues a replacement SIM card. Then the fraudster uses the new SIM card and carries out unauthorized and illegal account transactions without the victim's knowledge.

8. Bitcoins deploy which of the following technologies?

   I. Investment chain

   II. Blockchain

   III. Incident chain

   IV. Hash chain

   a. I and II

   Incorrect. This is partially true about the blockchain technology behind the bitcoin currency. The investment chain is not relevant.

   b. II only

   Incorrect. This is partially true about the blockchain technology behind the bitcoin currency.

   c. II and IV

   Correct. Both blockchain and hash chain are the technologies behind the bitcoin currency.

   d. I and III

   Incorrect. Both the investment chain and incident chain are unrelated to the blockchain technology behind the bitcoin currency.

9. The cybersecurity framework should act as a:

   a. First line of defense.

   Correct. The cybersecurity framework should act as the first line of defense for all organizations, whether in the public sector or the private sector, to protect against cyber threats and cyberattacks.

   b. Second line of defense.

   Incorrect. It is too late to act as the second line of defense.

   c. Third line of defense.

   Incorrect. It is too late to act as the third line of defense.

   d. Last line of defense.

   Incorrect. It is too late to act as the last line of defense.

10. In which of the following cybersecurity functions are system resilience plans developed and implemented?

    a. Protect

    Incorrect. Protect means developing and implementing the appropriate safeguards (controls) to ensure delivery of critical infrastructure services.

    b. Detect

    Incorrect. Detect means developing and implementing the appropriate activities to identify the occurrence of a cybersecurity event.

    c. Recover

    Correct. During the recover function, system resilience plans are developed and implemented, and any capabilities or services that were impaired due to a cybersecurity event are restored.

    d. Respond

    Incorrect. Respond means developing and implementing the appropriate activities to take action regarding a detected cybersecurity event.

11. Regarding mobile security, encryption can be used to protect which of the following with efforts to prevent data loss?

I. Data at rest

II. Data in motion

III. Data in processing

IV. Data in use

a. I and II

Correct. Encryption provides confidentiality for and integrity of sensitive information and can be used to protect data at rest and in motion (i.e., data in transit). Data at rest means data are temporarily or permanently stored on internal storage devices and external storage devices (e.g., cloud storage) and/or volatile or nonvolatile memory.

b. II and III

Incorrect. Encryption can be applied to data in motion, not to data in processing. Data in processing means that data are being acted on by an automated process, such as a program or command.

c. I and IV

Incorrect. Encryption can be applied to data at rest, not to data in use. Data in use means data are actively being updated, modified, or used by end users.

d. III and IV

Incorrect. Encryption cannot be applied to data in processing or data in use. Data in processing means that data are being acted on by an automated process such as a program or command. Data in use means data are actively being updated, modified, or used by end users.

12. Which of the following statement is **not** true about bitcoins?

a. Bitcoins use a distributed ledger.

Incorrect. It is true that bitcoins use a distributed ledger.

b. Bitcoins use a centralized ledger.

Correct. A ledger is a chronological listing of all business transactions in one place to provide a clear and complete picture of all transactions. Bitcoins do not use a centralized ledger.

c. Bitcoins use a decentralized ledger.

Incorrect. It is true that bitcoins use a decentralized ledger.

d. Bitcoins use a community ledger.

Incorrect. It is true that bitcoins use a community ledger.

13. Which of the following are the common variants of ransomware attacks?

I. Bots and botnets

II. Spam emails

III. Drive-by downloads

IV. Malvertizing

a. I only

Incorrect. Bots and botnets are a variation of ransomware attacks because they can spread through computer networks at a faster rate.

b. I and II

Incorrect. Bots, botnets, and spam emails are a common variation of ransomware attacks. Bots and botnets can spread through computer networks at a faster rate than the other types of malware (e.g., viruses and worms). Ransomware attacks can infect computers when a user clicks a spam email.

c. I, II, and IV

Incorrect. Bots, botnets, spam emails, and malvertizing are common variations of ransomware attacks. Bots and botnets can spread through computer networks at a faster rate than the other types of malware (e.g., viruses and worms). Ransomware attacks can infect computers when a user clicks a spam email. Malvertizing is the use of malicious advertisements (ads) on legitimate websites without any action from the user.

d. I, II, III, and IV

Correct. Bots, botnets, spam emails, drive-by downloads, and malvertizing are the common variants of ransomware attacks. Bots and botnets can spread through computer networks at a faster rate than the other types of malware (e.g., viruses and worms). Ransomware attacks can infect computers when a user clicks a spam email. Drive-by downloads is the transfer of malicious software to a victim's computer without any action by the victim. Malvertizing is the use of malicious advertisements (ads) on legitimate websites without any action from the user.

14. During an audit, an internal auditor observed that an employee at the audit-client department is watching online sports on his desktop computer during working hours. Which of the following policies should the auditor refer to determine whether the employee's actions are acceptable?

a. Acceptable use policies

Incorrect. Acceptable use policies require that a system user, an end user, or an administrator (e.g., system, security, and network administrator) agrees to comply with such policies prior to accessing computer systems, internal networks, and external networks (the Internet). These policies also discuss how guest, temporary, terminated, and privileged accounts are treated and maintained. Acceptable use is based on authorized access.

b. Business-only Internet use policies

Correct. Business-only Internet use policies deal with whether employees can access outside, nonbusiness websites during their work hours. Examples of this type of access include checking baseball scores at lunchtime, accessing a dating website, conducting online gambling, playing online games, and checking stock market prices. Here, the employee is accessing the Internet to watch online sports using his desktop computer.

c. Software restriction policies

Incorrect. Software restriction policies should state what types of employees are allowed to bring their own software from home for use at work and under what circumstances. The types of restricted software can include games, entertainment (movies), sports, investment, open-source, and other non-business-related software. Software policies should also state what the company's official computer programs can be run from temporary folders supporting popular Internet browsers, compression and decompression programs, or app folders. Running computer programs from the temporary folders is very risky due to their poor code-quality or corrupted code and possibility of malware.

d. Mobile device use policies

Incorrect. Mobile device use policies include turning off Bluetooth and Wi-Fi connections in order to reduce   the threat surface to which a mobile device is exposed. These policies should also state that important functions are deactivated to reduce the security exposure until requested by users. Here, the employee is using his desktop computer, not a mobile device.

15. Which of the following **cannot** reduce the total costs of data breaches?

a. Security metrics

Incorrect. Security metrics can reduce the total costs of data breaches due to the insights they provide regarding threats, attacks, and hackers. It is a proactive security measure.

b. Incident response team

Incorrect. The existence of an incident response team can reduce the total costs of data breaches due to the team's expertise and readiness to prevent, detect, and recover from threats and attacks. It is a proactive security measure.

c. Encryption

Incorrect. Use of encryption in computer programs and data files can reduce the total costs of data breaches because encryption protects against a hacker's attacks. It is a proactive security measure.

d. Mobile platforms

Correct. Extensive use of mobile platforms (e.g., operating systems and devices) can increase risks and costs due to their unchecked usage and uncontrolled growth, resulting in increased data breaches and their associated costs.

16. Authorization controls are a part of which of the following?

a. Directive controls

Incorrect. Directive controls are broad-based controls to handle security incidents, and they include management's policies, procedures, and directives.

b. Preventive controls

Correct. Authorization controls, such as access control matrices and capability tests, are a part of preventive controls because they block unauthorized access. Preventive controls deter security incidents from happening in the first place.

c. Detective controls

Incorrect. Detective controls enhance security by monitoring the effectiveness of preventive controls and by detecting security incidents where preventive controls were circumvented.

d. Corrective controls

Incorrect. Corrective controls are procedures to react to security incidents and to take remedial actions on a timely basis. Corrective controls require proper planning and preparation as they rely more on human judgment.

17. Which of the following is **not** an example of nondiscretionary access control?

a. Identity-based access control

Correct. Nondiscretionary access control policies have rules that are not established at the discretion of the user. These controls can be changed only through administrative action, not by users. An identity-based access control decision grants or denies a request based on the presence of an entity on an access control list. Identity-based access control and discretionary access control are considered equivalent and are not examples of nondiscretionary access controls.

b. Mandatory access control

Incorrect. This is an example of a nondiscretionary access control. Mandatory access control deals with rules.

c. Role-based access control

Incorrect. This is an example of a nondiscretionary access control. Role-based access control deals with job titles and functions.

d. Temporal constraints

Incorrect. This is an example of nondiscretionary access controls. Temporal constraints deal with time-based restrictions and control time-sensitive activities.

18. Which of the following statements are true about access controls, safety, trust, and separation of duty?

I. No leakage of access permissions is allowed to an unauthorized principal.

II. No access privileges can be escalated to an unauthorized principal.

III. No principals' trust means no safety.

IV. No separation of duty means no safety.

a. I only

Incorrect. See correct answer (d).

b. II only

Incorrect. See correct answer (d).

c. I, II, and III

Incorrect. See correct answer (d).

d. I, II, III, and IV

Correct. If complete trust by a principal is not practical, there is a possibility of a safety violation. The separation of duty concept is used to enforce safety and security in some access control models. In the event that there are many users (subjects), objects, and relations between subjects and objects, safety needs to be carefully considered.

19. For privilege management, which of the following is the correct order?

a. Access Control ⟶ Access Management ⟶ Authentication Management ⟶ Privilege Management

Incorrect. See correct answer (c).

b. Access Management ⟶ Access Control ⟶ Privilege Management ⟶ Authentication Management

Incorrect. See correct answer (c).

c. Authentication Management ⟶ Privilege Management ⟶ Access Control ⟶ Access Management

Correct. Privilege management is defined as a process that creates, manages, and stores the attributes and policies needed to establish criteria that can be used to decide whether an authenticated entity's request for access to some resource should be granted. Authentication management deals with identities, credentials, and any other authentication data needed to establish an identity. Access management, which includes privilege management and access control, encompasses the science and technology of creating, assigning, storing, and accessing attributes and policies. These attributes and policies are used to decide whether an entity's request for access should be allowed or denied. In other words, a typical access decision starts with authentication management and ends with access management. Privilege management falls in between.

d. Privilege Management ⟶ Access Management ⟶ Access Control ⟶ Authentication Management

Incorrect. See correct answer (c).

20. The encryption technique that requires two keys, a public key that is available to anyone for encrypting messages and a private key that is known only to the recipient for decrypting messages, is

    a. Rivest, Shamir, and Adelman (RSA).

    Correct. Rivest, Shamir, and Adelman (RSA) requires two keys: The public key for encrypting messages is widely known, but the private key for decrypting messages is kept secret by the recipient.

    b. Data encryption standard (DES).

    Incorrect. Data encryption standard (DES) requires only a single key for each pair of communicants that want to send each other encrypted messages.

    c. Modulator-demodulator.

    Incorrect. A modulator-demodulator (modem) is used for telecommunications.

    d. A cipher lock. It uses a series of transformations that converts plaintext to ciphertext using a cipher key.

21. The use of message encryption software:

    a. Guarantees the secrecy of data.

    Incorrect. No encryption approach absolutely guarantees the secrecy of data in transmission, although encryption approaches are considered to be less amenable to being broken than other approaches.

    b. Requires manual distribution of keys.

    Incorrect. Keys may be distributed manually, but they may also be distributed electronically via secure key transporters.

    c. Increases system overhead.

    Correct. The machine instructions necessary to encrypt and decrypt data constitute system overhead, which means that processing may be slowed down.

    d. Reduces the need for periodic password changes.

    Incorrect. Using encryption software does not reduce the need for periodic password changes because passwords are the typical means of validating users' access to unencrypted data.

22. The information systems and audit directors agreed on the need to maintain security and integrity of transmissions and the data they represent. The best means of ensuring the confidentiality of satellite transmissions would be:

    a. Encryption.

    Correct. Encryption is the best means of ensuring the confidentiality of satellite transmissions because even if an unauthorized individual recorded the transmissions, they would not be intelligible.

    b. Access control.

    Incorrect. Access control applies to gaining entrance to the application systems, not to the format of transmissions.

    c. Monitoring software.

    Incorrect. Monitoring software is designed to monitor performance (human or machine) for specified functions, such as the number of tasks performed or capacity utilized.

    d. Cyclic redundancy checks.

    Incorrect. Cyclic redundancy checks are complex computations performed with the data bits and the check bits in data transmissions to ensure the integrity, but not the confidentiality, of the data.

23. For application user authenticator management purposes, use of which of the following is risky and leads to stronger alternatives?

a. A single sign-on mechanism

Incorrect. See correct answer (c).

b. Same user identifier and different user authenticators on all systems

Incorrect. See correct answer (c).

c. Same user identifier and same user authenticator on all systems

Correct. Examples of user identifiers include internal users, contractors, external users, guests, passwords, tokens, and biometrics. Examples of application user authenticators include passwords, PINs, tokens, biometrics, digital certificates based on public key infrastructure, and key cards. When an individual has accounts on multiple information systems, there is the risk that if one account is compromised and the individual uses the same user identifier and authenticator, other accounts will be compromised as well. Possible alternatives include (1) having the same user identifier but different authenticators on all systems, (2) having different user identifiers and different user authenticators on each system, (3) employing a single sign-on mechanism, or (4) having one-time passwords on all systems.

d. Different user identifiers and different user authenticators on each system

Incorrect. See correct answer (c).

24. Which of the following statements is true about an intrusion detection system (IDS) and firewalls?

a. Firewalls are a substitute for an IDS.

Incorrect. See correct answer (c).

b. Firewalls are an alternative to an IDS.

Incorrect. See correct answer (c).

c. Firewalls are a complement to an IDS.

Correct. An IDS should be used as a complement to a firewall, not as a substitute for it. Together, they provide a synergistic effect.

d. Firewalls are a replacement for an IDS.

Incorrect. See correct answer (c).

25. Which one of the following is **not** an authentication mechanism?

a. What the user knows

Incorrect. This choice is part of an authentication process.

b. What the user has

Incorrect. This choice is part of an authentication process.

c. What the user can do

Correct. "What the user can do" is defined in access rules or user profiles, which come after a successful authentication. The other three choices are part of an authentication process. The authenticator factor "knows" means a password or PIN, "has" means key or card, and "is" means a biometric identity.

d. What the user is

Incorrect. This choice is part of an authentication process.

Domain 3: Information Technology (20%)

1. In the preliminary risk assessment task of the system development life cycle initiation phase, integrity needs from a user's or owner's perspective are defined in terms of which of the following?

   a. Place of data

   Incorrect. Place of data is not an attribute of integrity.

   b. Timeliness of data

   Incorrect. Timeliness of data is not an attribute of integrity.

   c. Form of data

   Incorrect. Form of data is not an attribute of integrity.

   d. Quality of data

   Correct. Integrity can be examined from several perspectives. From a user's or application owner's perspective, integrity is the quality of data that is based on attributes such as accuracy and completeness.

2. Which of the following is required when an organization uncovers deficiencies in the security controls deployed to protect an information system?

   a. Develop preventive security controls.

   Incorrect. Preventive security controls should have been established prior to uncovering deficiencies.

   b. Develop plan of action and milestones.

   Correct. Detailed plans of action and milestones schedules are required to document the corrective measures needed to increase the effectiveness of the security controls and to provide the requisite security for the information system prior to security authorization.

   c. Develop detective security controls.

   Incorrect. Detective security controls should have been established prior to uncovering deficiencies.

   d. Modify ineffective security controls.

   Incorrect. This choice is vague without a specific plan of action schedule.

3. Which of the following occurs after delivery and installation of a new information system under acquisition?

   a. Unit testing

   Incorrect. Unit testing is not conducted for an acquired system but is conducted for an in-house-developed system.

   b. Subsystem testing

   Incorrect. Subsystem testing is not conducted for an acquired system but is conducted for an in-house-developed system.

   c. Full system testing

   Incorrect. Full system testing is not conducted for an acquired system but is conducted for an in-house-developed system.

   d. Integration and acceptance testing

   Correct. Integration and acceptance testing occur after delivery and installation of the new information system. Both of these tests are conducted for an acquired system.

4. Effective control is achieved when configuration management control is established prior to the start of which of the following?

   a. Requirements analysis

   Incorrect. Requirements analysis focuses on gathering needs of system users to understand the nature of the programs to be built. It is too early to talk about the configuration management.

   b. Design

   Correct. The design phase translates requirements into a representation of the software. The design is placed under configuration management control before coding begins. It is the right time to talk about the configuration management.

   c. Coding

   Incorrect. The design must be translated into a programming code-readable form. The coding step performs this task. Code is verified, for example, through the inspection process and put under configuration management control prior to the start of formal testing. It is too late to talk about the configuration management.

   d. Testing

   Incorrect. Once code is generated, program testing begins. The testing focuses on the logical internals of the software, ensuring that all statements have been tested, and on the functional externals; that is, conducting tests to uncover errors to ensure that the defined input will produce actual results that agree with required results. It is too late to talk about the configuration management.

5. Media sanitization activity is usually **most** intense during which of the following phases of the system development life cycle?

a. Development/acquisition

Incorrect. It is too early to talk about the media sanitization.

b. Implementation

Incorrect. It is too early to talk about the media sanitization.

c. Operation/maintenance

Incorrect. It is too early to talk about the media sanitization.

d. Disposal

Correct. Media sanitization and information disposition activity is usually most intense during the disposal phase of the system life cycle, which is the last phase. This media sanitization activity (i.e., wiping the data clean and removing it from the storage devices) is also done for several maintenance reasons, such as operating system upgrades, application system upgrades, or during a configuration update.

6. Which of the following is the correct sequence of steps to be followed in an application software change control process?

I. Test the changes.

II. Plan for changes.

III. Initiate change request.

IV. Release software changes.

a. I, II, III, and IV

Incorrect. See correct answer (c).

b. II, I, III, and IV

Incorrect. See correct answer (c).

c. III, II, I, and IV

Correct. Any application software change must start with a change request from a functional user. An information technology person can plan, test, and release the change after approved by the functional user.

d. IV, III, I, and II

Incorrect. See correct answer (c).

7. Software configuration management (SCM) should primarily address which of the following questions?

a. How does software evolve during system development?

Incorrect. See correct answer (c).

b. How does software evolve during system maintenance?

Incorrect. See correct answer (c).

c. What constitutes a software product at any point in time?

Correct. SCM is a discipline for managing the evolution of computer products, during the initial stages of development and through to maintenance and final product termination. Visibility into the status of the evolving software product is provided through the adoption of SCM on a software project. Software developers, testers, project managers, QA staff, and the customer benefit from SCM information. SCM answers questions such as (1) What constitutes the software product at any point in time? and (2) What changes have been made to the software product? How a software product is planned, developed, or maintained does not matter; these issues refer to the history of a software product's evolution, as described in the other choices.

d. How is a software product planned?

Incorrect. See correct answer (c).

8. Security controls are designed and implemented in which of the following system development life cycle phases?

   a. Planning/initiation

   Incorrect. See correct answer (b).

   b. Development/acquisition

   Correct. Security controls are developed, designed, and implemented in the development/acquisition phase. Additional controls may be developed to support the controls already in place or planned. Security controls are not designed and implemented in the other three choices because they are either too early or too late in the life cycle.

   c. Implementation/assessment

   Incorrect. See correct answer (b).

   d. Disposal/decommissioning

   Incorrect. See correct answer (b).

9. Which of the following tests is driven by system requirements?

   a. Black box testing

   Correct. Black box testing, also known as functional testing, executes part or all the system to validate that the user requirement is satisfied.

   b. White box testing

   Incorrect. White box testing, also known as structural testing or glass box testing, examines the logic of the units and may be used to support software requirements for test coverage (i.e., how much of the program has been executed).

   c. Gray box testing

   Incorrect. Gray box testing can be looked at as anything that is not tested in white box or black box.

   d. Glass box testing

   Incorrect. Glass box testing is another name for white box testing.

10. Which of the following volatile data generated by operating system software installed on workstations and servers should be collected first prior to conducting computer forensic auditing work?

    I. Network connections

    II. Login sessions

    III. Network configuration

    IV. Operating system time

    a. I and II

    Correct. Operating system data exists in both nonvolatile and volatile data. "Nonvolatile data" refers to data that persists even after a PC is powered down, such as a file system stored on a hard drive or a flash drive. "Volatile data" refers to data on a live system that is lost after a PC is powered down, usually stored on a system's random access memory.

    Because volatile data has a propensity to change over time, the order and timeliness with which volatile data is collected is important. In most cases, system auditors and security analysts should first collect information on network connections and login sessions, because network connections may time out or be disconnected, and the list of users connected to a system at any single time may vary. Volatile data that is less likely to change, such as network configuration and operating system time (choice d), should be collected later, if needed.

    b. I and III

    Incorrect. See correct answer (a).

    c. II and III

    Incorrect. See correct answer (a).

    d. III and IV

    Incorrect. See correct answer (a).

11. Which of the following are the potential advantages of using cloud computing technology to user organizations?

I. They can access data and documents from anywhere and at any time.

II. They can reduce the cost of purchasing additional hardware and software.

III. They can reduce the cost of purchasing additional storage memory devices.

IV. They can implement pay-as-you-go method.

a. I and II

Incorrect. See correct answer (d).

b. I and IV

Incorrect. See correct answer (d).

c. I and III

Incorrect. See correct answer (d).

d. I, II, III, and IV

Correct. Cloud computing technology makes it possible to access a user's information stored by a cloud vendor from anywhere at any time. Now even small organizations can store their information in the cloud, obviating the need to purchase additional hardware and software and additional storage memory devices. User organizations need to buy only the amount of storage space that will be really needed and used, which is referred to as the pay-as-you-go method. The best feature of this method is that it allows user organizations to scale their needs either up or down based on the storage space required, and they pay a cloud vendor accordingly.

12. Which of the following statements is **not** true? A data warehouse is:

a. Distributed.

Correct. Databases can be distributed, but data warehouse cannot be. A distributed data warehouse would have all the security problems a distributed database faces. From a security viewpoint, data warehousing provides the ability to centrally manage access to an organization's data regardless of a specific location. A data warehouse is subject oriented, time variant, and static in nature.

b. Subject oriented.

Incorrect. See correct answer (a).

c. Time variant.

Incorrect. See correct answer (a).

d. Static in nature.

Incorrect. See correct answer (a).

13. Which of the following provides an effective security control over the Internet access points or hot spots during remote access and telework?

a. Virtual private network

Correct. A virtual private network (VPN) should be used to encrypt data for hot spot users. A VPN is a private network that is maintained across a shared or public network, such as the Internet, by means of specialized security procedures. VPNs are intended to provide secure connections between remote clients, such as branch offices or traveling employees and a central office. The networks listed in the other three choices do not have the same security features as VPNs and do not have the same geographic reach as VPNs. The other three networks have limitations in terms of access reach.

b. Wireless personal area network

Incorrect. A wireless personal area network is used to establish small-scale wireless networks, such as those using Bluetooth, which is an open standard for short-range communication.

c. Wireless local area network

Incorrect. A wireless local area network is a group of wireless networking nodes within a limited geographic area that serves as an extension to existing wired local area network.

d. Virtual local area network

Incorrect. A virtual local area network (VLAN) is a network configuration in which frames are broadcast within the VLAN and routed between VLANs. VLANs separate the logical topology of the LANs from their physical topology.

14. What does an effective backup method for handling large volumes of data in a local area network (LAN) environment include?

a. Backing up at the workstation.

Incorrect. A workstation lacks storage capacity to back up large volumes of data.

b. **Backing up at the file server.**

Correct. Backing up at the file server is effective for a LAN due to the file server's greater storage capacity.

c. Using a faster network connection.

Incorrect. Using a faster network connection increases the speed but does not perform backup.

d. Using redundant array of independent disks technology.

Incorrect. Redundant array of independent disks (RAID) technology is mostly used for mainframe computers.

15. All of the following are examples of security risks over servers **except**:

a. **Client/server architecture.**

Correct. Client/server architecture makes it possible for a wide range of front-end client applications, such as databases, spreadsheets, and word processors, to simultaneously share the same data. A database server supports a high-performance, multi-user, relational database management system. Client/server architecture provides a high level of data integrity, concurrency control, and improved performance.

b. Data concentration.

Incorrect. This is an example of security risks over servers.

c. Attack targets.

Incorrect. This is an example of security risks over servers.

d. A single point of failure.

Incorrect. This is an example of security risks over servers.

16. Which of the following server types is used for protection from malicious code attacks at the network gateway?

a. A web server

Incorrect. See correct answer (d).

b. An image server

Incorrect. See correct answer (d).

c. A mail server

Incorrect. See correct answer (d).

d. **A quarantine server**

Correct. A quarantine server is used for protection from malicious code attacks at the network gateway. A common technique applied in protecting networks is to use a firewall. In this technique, if a user attempts to retrieve an infected program via File Transfer Protocol, Hypertext Transfer Protocol, or Simple Mail Transfer Protocol, it is stopped at the quarantine server before it reaches individual workstations.

17. Which of the following information technology contingency solutions for servers minimizes the recovery time window?

a. Electronic vaulting

Incorrect. Electronic vaulting provides additional data backup capabilities, with backups made to remote tape or disk drives over communication links.

b. Remote journaling

Incorrect. Remote journaling provides additional data backup capabilities, with backups made to remote tape or disk drives over communication links.

c. Load balancing

Incorrect. Load balancing increases server and application system availability.

d. **Disk replication**

Correct. With disk replication, recovery windows are minimized because data is written to two different disks to ensure that two valid copies of the data are always available. The two disks are called the protected server (the main server) and the replicating server (the backup server). Electronic vaulting and remote journaling are similar technologies that provide additional data backup capabilities, with backups made to remote tape or disk drives over communication links.

18. Contingency plans for information technology operations should include appropriate backup agreements. Which of the following arrangements would be considered too vendor dependent when vital operations require almost immediate availability of computer resources?

a. A hot site arrangement

Incorrect. A hot site has all needed assets in place and is not vendor dependent.

b. A cold site arrangement

Correct. A cold site has all necessary assets in place except the needed computer equipment and is vendor dependent for timely delivery of equipment.

c. A cold site and hot site combination arrangement.

Incorrect. The combination of cold site and hot site allows the hot site to be used until the cold site is prepared and is thus not too vendor dependent.

d. Using excess capacity at another data center within the organization

Incorrect. Excess capacity would ensure that needed assets are available and would not be vendor dependent.

19. From an operations viewpoint, the first step in contingency planning is to perform a(n):

a. Operating system software backup.

Incorrect. See correct answer (d).

b. Applications software backup.

Incorrect. See correct answer (d).

c. Documentation backup.

Incorrect. See correct answer (d).

d. Hardware backup.

Correct. Hardware backup is the first step in contingency planning. All computer installations must include formal arrangements for alternative processing capability in the event their data center or any portion of the work environment becomes disabled. These plans can take several forms and involve the use of another data center. Hardware manufacturers and software vendors can be helpful in locating an alternative processing site and in some cases provide backup equipment under emergency conditions. The more common plans are service bureaus, reciprocal arrangements, and hot sites. After hardware is backed up, operating system software is backed up next, followed by applications software backup and documentation.

20. The primary contingency strategy for application systems and data is regular backup and secure offsite storage. From an operations viewpoint, which of the following decisions is least important to address?

a. How often the backup is performed

Incorrect. See correct answer (c).

b. How often the backup is stored offsite

Incorrect. See correct answer (c).

c. How often the backup is used

Correct. Normally, the primary contingency strategy for applications and data is regular backup and secure offsite storage. Important decisions to be addressed include how often the backup is performed, how often it is stored offsite, and how it is transported to storage, to an alternative processing site, or to support the resumption of normal operations. How often the backup is used is not relevant because it is hoped that it may never have to be used

d. How often the backup is transported

Incorrect. See correct answer (c).

Domain 4: Financial Management (20%)

1. The following information is available from the records of a manufacturing company that applies factory overhead based on direct labor hours:

Estimated overhead cost	$500,000
Estimated labor hours	200,000 hours
Actual overhead cost	$515,000
Actual labor hours	210,000 hours

Based on this information, overhead would be:

a. Underapplied by $9,524.

Incorrect. Factory overhead reflects overhead application based on the estimated volume times an application rate based on the actual overhead over the actual volume. The application rate would be $24,5238, and the applied overhead would be $490,476, which results in underapplied overhead by $9,524 (i.e., $500,000 − $490,476).

b. **Overapplied by $10,000.**

Correct. Overhead would be overapplied by $10,000 and is computed as:

Applied overhead = Actual labor hours × Estimated application rate ($2.50 per direct labor hour), or $525,000. This amount is $10,000 higher than the actual overhead cost incurred of $515,000 (i.e., $525,000 − $515,000).

c. Overapplied by $15,000.

Incorrect. This is simply the actual overhead cost less the estimated overhead cost and does not reflect any application, whether over or under (i.e., $515,000 − $500,000).

d. Overapplied by $40,750.

Incorrect. This reflects overhead application based on the actual volume times an application rate based on the actual overhead over the estimated volume. The application rate would be $2.575 per hour, and the applied overhead would be $540,750, resulting in overapplied overhead by $40,750 (i.e., $540,750 − $500,000).

2. A company plans to implement a bonus plan based on segment performance. In addition, the company plans to convert to a responsibility accounting system for segment reporting. The following costs, which have been included in the segment performance reports that have been prepared under the current system, are being reviewed to determine if they should be included in the responsibility accounting segment reports.

I. Corporate administrative costs allocated on the basis of net segment sales

II. Personnel costs assigned on the basis of the number of employees in each segment

III. Fixed computer facility costs divided equally among each segment

IV. Variable computer operational costs charged to each segment based on actual hours used times a predetermined standard rate; any variable cost efficiency or inefficiency remains in the computer department

Of these four cost items, the only item that could logically be included in the segment performance reports prepared on a responsibility accounting basis would be the:

a. Corporate administrative costs.

Incorrect. This item should be excluded from the performance report because the segments have no control over the cost incurrence or the allocation basis (i.e., the allocation depends on the segment sales [controllable] as well as the sales of other segments [uncontrollable]).

b. Personnel costs.

Incorrect. This item should be excluded from the performance report because the segments have no control over the cost incurrence or the method of assignment (i.e., the assignment depends on the number of employees in the segment [controllable] in proportion to the total number of employees in all segments [not controllable]).

c. Fixed computer facility costs.

Incorrect. This item should be excluded from the performance report because the segments have no control over the cost, and the equal assignment is arbitrary, bearing no relation to usage.

d. **Variable computer operational costs.**

Correct. This is the only cost item that can be included in the segment performance report. First, the segments are being charged for actual usage, which is under each segment's control. The predetermined standard rate is set at the beginning of the year, which is known by the segment managers, and the efficiencies and inefficiencies of the computer department are not being passed on to the segments; both of these procedural methods promote a degree of control by the segments.

3. In a merger or acquisition transaction, usually two companies are involved such as an acquiring company and a target company (i.e., company to be acquired). All of the following are the preferred financial profile of a target company **except**:

   a. High-liquidity

   Incorrect. High-liquidity means high-solvency, which is preferred.

   b. High price/earnings ratio

   Correct. Low price/earnings ratio is preferred. The lower the price/earnings ratio, the higher is the earnings per share (EPS) and vice versa. High EPS is referred.

   c. High earnings per share

   Incorrect. High earnings per share is preferred.

   d. Low leverage

   Incorrect. Low leverage means less debt, which is preferred.

4. What conclusion should a financial analyst draw if a company has a high fixed assets turnover ratio?

   a. The company may be overcapitalized.

   Incorrect. The ratio may indicate just the opposite.

   b. The company may have a problem with employees converting inventory to personal use.

   Incorrect. The fixed assets turnover ratio is sales divided by net fixed assets; fluctuations in inventory do not affect the ratio.

   c. The company may be undercapitalized.

   Correct. This high ratio could be an indicator that the company cannot afford to buy enough assets.

   d. The company has favorable profitability.

   Incorrect. The fixed assets turnover ratio is not a profitability indicator. It is sales divided by net fixed assets.

5. A company will finance next year's capital projects through debt rather than additional equity. The benchmark cost of capital for these projects should be:

   a. The before-tax cost of new debt financing.

   Incorrect. The cost of capital is a composite, or weighted average, of all financing sources in their usual proportions. The cost of capital should also be calculated on an after-tax basis.

   b. The after-tax cost of new debt financing.

   Incorrect. The cost of capital is a composite, or weighted average, of all financing sources in their usual proportions. It includes both the after-tax cost of debt and the cost of equity financing.

   c. The cost of equity financing.

   Incorrect. The cost of capital is a composite, or weighted average, of all financing sources in their usual proportions. It includes both the after-tax cost of debt and the cost of equity financing.

   d. The weighted-average cost of capital.

   Correct. A weighted average of the costs of all financing sources should be used, with the weights determined by the usual financing proportions. The terms of any financing raised at the time of initiating a particular project do not represent the cost of capital for the firm.

6. In the distribution of liquidation proceeds for a bankrupt firm, which of the following claimants has highest priority?

   a. Preferred stock

   Incorrect. Preferred shareholders are not among the high-priority claimants of a bankrupt firm, ranking ahead of only the common shareholders.

   b. Common stock

   Incorrect. Common shareholders are the residual claimants of a bankrupt firm. They receive a portion of the liquidation proceeds only after all other claims have been satisfied in full.

   c. Bonds payable

   Incorrect. Bonds payable are general, unsecured claims. They share in liquidation proceeds only after all priority claimants are satisfied.

   d. Taxes payable

   Correct. Taxes payable is a priority claim. Priority claims are paid in full before any liquidation proceeds are distributed to general claimants or shareholders.

7. A company has a foreign-currency-denominated trade payable due in 60 days. In order to eliminate the foreign exchange risk associated with the payable, the company could:

a. Sell foreign currency forward today.

Incorrect. The company needs to arrange to buy the foreign currency in order to make payment to the supplier. This cannot be accomplished by a forward market sale of foreign currency.

b. Wait 60 days and pay the invoice by purchasing foreign currency in the spot market at that time.

Incorrect. Waiting to convert the currency in 60 days' time does not eliminate the risk of exchange rate movements.

c. **Buy foreign currency forward today.**

Correct. The company can arrange today for the exchange rate at which it will purchase the foreign currency in 60 days' time by buying the currency in the forward market. This will eliminate the exchange risk associated with the trade payable.

d. Borrow foreign currency today, convert it to domestic currency on the spot market, and invest the funds in a domestic bank deposit until the invoice payment date.

Incorrect. This strategy would be comparable to a future sale of the foreign currency at a rate known today, which would not provide the currency needed to pay the invoice. The opposite strategy would be an effective money market hedge, however. If the company converted domestic currency to foreign currency in the spot market today and invested in a foreign bank deposit or Treasury bill, it could use the proceeds from the foreign investment to pay the invoice in 60 days' time.

8. A company has 7,000 obsolete toys, which are carried in inventory at a manufacturing cost of $6 per unit. If the toys are reworked for $2 per unit, they could be sold for $3 per unit. If the toys are scrapped, they could be sold for $1.85 per unit. Which alternative is more desirable (rework or scrap), and what is the total dollar amount of the advantage of that alternative?

a. **Scrap, $5,950**

Correct. The total dollar amount of the advantage of that alternative is scrap, $5,950, and is computed as:

(3 – 2) (7,000) = $7,000 for rework

(1.85) (7,000) = $12,950 for scrap

Advantage of scrap by $5,950. That is, $12,950 – $7,000 = $5,950.

b. Rework, $36,050

Incorrect. (6 + 3 – 2) (7,000) – (1.85) (7,000) = $36,050 (rework).

c. Scrap, $47,950

Incorrect. (1.85 + 6) (7,000) – (3 – 2) (7,000) = $47,950 (scrap).

d. Rework, $8,050

Incorrect. (3) (7,000) – (1.85) (7,000) = $8,050 (rework).

9. Which of the following statements about activity-based costing (ABC) is **not** true?

a. ABC is useful for allocating marketing and distribution costs.

Incorrect. This is a true statement.

b. **ABC is more likely to result in major differences from traditional costing systems if the firm manufactures only one product rather than multiple products.**

Correct. When there is only one product, the allocation of costs to the product is trivial. All of the cost is assigned to the one product; the particular method used to allocate the costs does not matter.

c. In ABC, cost drivers are what cause costs to be incurred.

Incorrect. This is a true statement.

d. ABC differs from traditional costing systems in that products are not cross-subsidized.

Incorrect. This is a true statement.

10. The cost of materials has risen steadily over the year. The company uses its newest materials first when removing items from inventory. Which of the following methods of estimating the ending balance of the materials inventory account will result in the highest net income, all other variables held constant?

a. Last in, first out (LIFO)

Incorrect. The LIFO method assumes that the most recent and hence costliest units have been removed from inventory. This method will result in the lowest inventory balance if costs rise steadily during the accounting period, the highest cost of goods sold, and the lowest net income.

b. First in, first out (FIFO)

Correct. The FIFO method assumes that the oldest and hence least costly units have been removed from inventory. This method will result in the highest inventory balance if costs rise steadily during the accounting period. This then results in the lowest cost of goods sold and therefore the highest net income.

c. Weighted average

Incorrect. The weighted-average cost method will average the cost of all inventory items and will result in a lower inventory balance and net income than does the FIFO method.

d. Specific identification

Incorrect. Specific identification charges the actual cost of each unit to cost of goods sold each period, leaving as inventory the actual cost of all items still in inventory. Since the question states that the newest and most costly items are removed from inventory first, the inventory balance and net income will be lower than that obtained using FIFO estimation.

11. In its first year of operations, a firm had $50,000 of fixed operating costs (F). It sold 10,000 units at a $10 unit price (P) and incurred variable costs (V) of $4 per unit. If all prices and costs will be the same in the second year and sales are projected to rise to 25,000 units (Q), what will the degree of operating leverage (DOL; the extent to which fixed costs are used in the firm's operations) be in the second year?

a. 1.25

Incorrect. This solution incorrectly uses total revenue rather than contribution to fixed costs in the DOL formula as:

$$DOL = Q(P) / [Q(P) - F]$$
$$= 25{,}000(\$10) / [25{,}000(\$10) - \$50{,}000]$$
$$= 250{,}000 / 200{,}000 = 1.25$$

b. 1.50

Correct. The projected DOL is 1.50 and is calculated as:

$$DOL = Q(P - V) / [Q(P - V) - F]$$
$$= 25{,}000(\$10 - \$4) / [25{,}000(\$10 - \$4) - \$50{,}000]$$
$$= 150{,}000 / 100{,}000 = 1.50$$

c. 2.00

Incorrect. This solution uses the year 1 sales level of 10,000 units and also uses total revenue rather than the contribution to fixed costs in calculating the DOL as:

$$DOL = Q(P) / [Q(P) - F]$$
$$= 10{,}000(\$10) / [10{,}000(\$10) - \$50{,}000]$$
$$= 100{,}000 / 50{,}000 = 2.00$$

d. 6.00

Incorrect. This solution incorrectly uses the year 1 sales level of 10,000 units in calculating the DOL as:

$$DOL = Q(P - V) / [Q(P - V) - F]$$
$$= 10{,}000(\$10 - \$4) / [10{,}000(\$10 - \$4) - \$50{,}000]$$
$$= 60{,}000/10{,}000 = 6.00$$

12. During the current accounting period, a manufacturing company purchased $70,000 of raw materials, of which $50,000 of direct materials and $5,000 of indirect materials was used in production. The company also incurred $45,000 of total labor costs and $20,000 of other factory overhead costs. An analysis of the work-in-process control account revealed $40,000 of direct labor costs. Based on the above information, what is the total amount accumulated in the factory overhead control account?

a. $25,000

Incorrect. The $25,000 amount includes only two of the three factory overhead costs.

b. **$30,000**

Correct. The total amount accumulated in the factory overhead control account is $30,000 and is computed as shown.

Indirect materials	**$5,000**
Indirect labor ($45,000 − $40,000)	**5,000**
Other factory overhead	**20,000**
Total overhead	**$30,000**

c. $45,000

Incorrect. The $45,000 amount includes additional costs, which are not classified as factory overhead costs.

d. $50,000

Incorrect. The $50,000 amount also includes additional costs, which are not classified as factory overhead costs.

13. A company experienced a machinery breakdown on one of its production lines. As a consequence of the breakdown, manufacturing fell behind schedule, and a decision was made to schedule overtime in order to return manufacturing to schedule. Which one of the following methods is the proper way to account for the overtime paid to the direct laborers?

a. The overtime hours times the sum of the straight-time wages and overtime premium would be charged entirely to manufacturing overhead.

Incorrect. This treatment is inappropriate; only the overtime premium times the overtime hours is charged to overhead. The straight-time wages times the overtime hours should still be treated as direct labor.

b. The overtime hours times the sum of the straight-time wages and overtime premium would be treated as direct labor.

Incorrect. This treatment is inappropriate; only the straight-time wages times the overtime hours should still be treated as direct labor. The overtime premium times the overtime hours is charged to overhead.

c. The overtime hours times the overtime premium would be charged to repair and maintenance expense while the overtime hours times the straight-time wages would be treated as direct labor.

Incorrect. While the second part of this response is correct, the first part is inappropriate. There is no way that the overtime hours times the premium can be charged to repair and maintenance expense because this cost is not related to any repairs. This work is production work, not repairs.

d. **The overtime hours times the overtime premium would be charged to manufacturing overhead while the overtime hours times the straight-time wages would be treated as direct labor.**

Correct. This treatment is appropriate because the overtime premium cost is a cost that should be borne by all production.

14. A company uses straight-line depreciation for financial reporting purposes, but uses accelerated depreciation for tax purposes. Which of the following account balances would be lower in the financial statements used for tax purposes than it would be in the general purpose financial statements?

    a. Accumulated depreciation

    Incorrect. The balance of accumulated depreciation would be higher in the financial statements for tax purposes, since higher depreciation expense would be reported under accelerated depreciation than under straight-line depreciation.

    b. Cash

    Incorrect. Depreciation expense is a noncash charge. The cash balance is unaffected by the depreciation method used.

    c. Retained earnings

    Correct. Under accelerated depreciation, depreciation expense is higher and net income is lower. Retained earnings would therefore be lower for tax-reporting purposes than for general-purpose financial reporting based on straight-line depreciation.

    d. Gross fixed assets

    Incorrect. The historic cost of fixed assets is recorded in the gross fixed assets account. The historic cost of the assets is unaffected by the depreciation method used.

15. An existing machine with estimated remaining life of five years that cost $100,000 can be sold for $20,000. The variable cost of output from this machine has been $1 per unit with 100,000 units per year produced. A new machine will cost $90,000 and is estimated to lower the variable cost to $.70 per unit over its five-year life. The **most** appropriate term for the decision process involved in this scenario is:

    a. Capital budgeting.

    Correct. Capital budgeting is the term for deciding on long-term investments such as the one described.

    b. Economic order quantity.

    Incorrect. Economic order quantity deals with the quantity of goods to order at a time, which will minimize the total of order and storage costs during the period.

    c. Flexible budgeting.

    Incorrect. Flexible budgeting deals with short-term adjustments of a budget to conform to actual production or sales.

    d. Sensitivity analysis.

    Incorrect. Sensitivity analysis deals with any instance in which a range of outcome is possible and is not restricted to long-term investment decisions.

16. Many service industries utilize a budgeting process to identify major programs and develop short-term operating budgets, such as expected revenues and expected direct expenses, for the identified programs. For example, a nursing home may develop one-year revenue and expense budgets for each of its different programs, such as day care for the elderly or Meals on Wheels. Which of the following is a **major** advantage of short-term program planning and budgeting?

a. It eliminates the need for periodic program evaluation.

Incorrect. Short-term program planning and budgeting provides the basis for periodic program evaluation.

b. It provides a rigid basis for periodic program evaluation.

Incorrect. The administration of budgets should never be rigid, as changed conditions call for changes in the budget.

c. It promotes communication and coordination within an organization.

Correct. Promotion of communication and coordination is a major advantage of short-term program planning and budgeting.

d. It provides an important basis for strategic analysis of the goals of the organization.

Incorrect. Strategic analysis is long-term rather than short-term in nature and usually precedes the development of short-term budgets.

17. Actual and projected sales of a company for September and October are:

	Cash Sales	Credit Sales
September (actual)	$20,000	$50,000
October (projected)	30,000	55,000

All credit sales are collected in the month following the month in which the sale is made. The September 30 cash balance is $23,000. Cash disbursements in October are projected to be $94,000. To maintain a minimum cash balance of $15,000 on October 31, the company will need to borrow:

a. $0.

Incorrect. See correct answer (b).

b. $ 6,000.

Correct. The company will need to borrow $6,000, computed as:

Ending cash balance

= Beginning cash balance + Cash collections

− Cash disbursements

= $23,000 + (50,000 + 30,000) − 94,000 = $ 9,000

Borrowing = $15,000 − 9,000 = $6,000

Therefore, the other choices are incorrect.

c. $11,000.

Incorrect. See correct answer (b).

d. $16,000.

Incorrect. See correct answer (b).

18. Which of the following is **not** true about international transfer prices for a multinational firm?

a. They allow firms to attempt to minimize worldwide taxes.

Incorrect. Properly chosen transfer prices allow firms to attempt to minimize worldwide taxes by producing various parts of the products in different countries and strategically transferring the parts at various systematically calculated prices.

b. They allow the firm to evaluate each division.

Incorrect. Properly chosen transfer prices allocate revenues and expenses to divisions in various countries. These numbers are used as part of the input for the performance evaluation of each division.

c. They provide each division with a profit-making orientation.

Incorrect. Transfer prices motivate division managers to buy parts and products (from either internal or external suppliers) at the lowest possible prices and to sell their products (to either internal or external customers) at the highest possible prices. This provides each division with a profit-making orientation.

d. **They allow firms to correctly price products in each country in which they operate.**

Correct. The calculation of transfer prices in the international arena must be systematic. A scheme for calculating transfer prices for a firm may correctly price the firm's product in Country A but not in Country B. The product may be overpriced in Country B, and sales will be lower than anticipated. Alternatively, the product may be underpriced in Country B, and authorities there may allege that the firm is dumping its product in Country B.

19. One department of an organization, Final Assembly, is purchasing subcomponents from another department, Materials Fabrication. The price that Materials Fabrication will charge Final Assembly is to be determined. Outside market prices for the subcomponents are available. Which of the following is the **most** correct statement regarding a market-based transfer price?

a. Marginal production cost transfer prices provide incentives to use otherwise idle capacity.

Incorrect. Marginal production cost does not relate to market-based transfer prices.

b. Market transfer prices provide an incentive to use otherwise idle capacity.

Incorrect. Transfer prices based on marginal cost provide more of an incentive to the purchasing division to buy internally and thus use idle facilities of the selling division than the usually higher market-based transfer price.

c. **Overall long-term competitiveness is enhanced with a market-based transfer price.**

Correct. Market-based transfer prices provide market discipline. Inefficient internal suppliers will tend to wither while efficient ones prosper, enhancing the overall long-term competitiveness of the firm.

d. Corporate politics is more of a factor in a market-based transfer price than with other methods.

Incorrect. Corporate politics is less of a factor in market-based prices than in other methods, such as a negotiated transfer price, because market-based prices are objective.

20. A company makes a product that sells for $30. During the coming year, fixed costs are expected to be $180,000, and variable costs are estimated at $26 per unit. How many units must the company sell in order to break even?

a. 6,000

Incorrect. This answer ignores variable costs. Total unit sales needed to cover fixed costs only are $180,000 / $30.

b. 6,924

Incorrect. This is total fixed costs divided by variable costs per unit.

c. 45,000

Correct. The company must sell 45,000 units to break even. This is computed as: The contribution to overhead for each unit is $4.00. Fixed costs of $180,000 divided by the contribution of $4.00 produces the answer of $45,000.

d. 720,000

Incorrect. This is total fixed costs multiplied by the contribution to overhead of $4.00 per unit instead of divided by it.

Business Glossary

This business glossary contains key terms useful to the CIA Exam candidates and students. Reading the glossary terms prior to studying the theoretical subject matter covered in Part 3 of the review book or the study guide and prior to answering the practice questions in Wiley's online test bank can help the candidate understand the domain content better. In addition, this glossary is a good review source for answering multiple-choice questions on the actual CIA Exam. This topical glossary provides a focused reading and study on a single topic for a better retention of key terms as opposed to multiple topics (i.e., business, financial, and technology glossary) put together. We strongly suggest that students read this glossary prior to studying the subject matter covered in the theoretical domains of this book.

30-day rule
30-day rule applies to U.S. online merchants and marketers where online orders must be shipped to customers within 30 days from the date of ordering.

40/30/30 rule
40/30/30 rule identifies the sources of scrap, rework, and waste in manufacturing operations which are approximated to 40% product design, 30% manufacturing processing, and 30% from suppliers.

80/20 rule
See Pareto's law.

ABC analysis
ABC analysis is an application of Pareto's law, or the 80/20 rule, to inventory or purchasing. It is a determination of the relative ratios between the number of items and the dollar value of the items purchased repetitively for stock.

Activity analysis
Activity analysis is a decision-making tool. All current activities can be labeled as either value-added or non-value-added using a T-account diagram. The goal is to eliminate or reduce non-value-added activities since they are adding little or no value to the process at hand. Decisions affecting costs incurred for non-value-added activities can then be challenged or revisited by performing a detailed analysis of all tasks and activities with the purpose of eliminating or reducing them. A T-column can be used with the headings "Value-added activities" and "Non-value-added activities" to facilitate the activity analysis.

Administered price
An administered price is a price determined by the policy of a seller rather than by the marketplace.

Alliances

Firms with unique strengths join alliances to be more effective and efficient than their competitors. *See* Partnership/alliance.

Anticipation inventory

An anticipation inventory is an inventory accumulated for a well-defined future need.

Authoritative decision making

The term "authoritative decision making" refers to a style of decision making in which the leader makes a decision and instructs followers what to do without consulting or involving them in the decision-making process.

Authority

Authority is the formal and legitimate right of a manager to make decisions, issue orders, and allocate resources to achieve organizationally desired outcomes.

Authorization

Authorization implies that the authorizing authority has verified and validated that the activity or transaction conforms to established policies and procedures. It is a process of verifying that approvals and procedures for recording and processing transactions have been obtained in accordance with management's general policies, standards, procedures, and specific instructions.

Autocratic leader

An autocratic leader is one who tends to centralize authority and rely on legitimate, reward, and coercive power to manage subordinates.

Autocratic management

In autocratic management, managers are focused on developing an efficient workplace and have little concern for people. They typically make decisions without input from subordinates, relying on their positional power. Autocratic management is conducted by a few key people who do not accept advice or participation from other employees.

Backflush

The term "backflush" means the deduction from inventory records of the component parts used in an assembly by exploding the bill of materials by the production count of assemblies produced.

Bar chart

The bar chart, or Gantt chart, is essentially a column chart on its side (set horizontally) and is used for the same purpose as a column chart. It is a tool that allows a manager to evaluate whether existing resources can handle work demand or whether activities should be postponed. The Gantt chart is used for milestone scheduling, where each milestone has both start and completion dates. A milestone represents a major activity or task to be accomplished (e.g., design phase in a computer system development project) on the Gantt chart.

Barrier elements

Barrier elements inhibit the implementation and maintenance of various business programs and strategies.

Barriers to entrants

Barriers to entrants are any and all of the measures that a business can take to prevent potential competitors from entering the market.

BCG matrix

The BCG matrix was developed by the Boston Consulting Group (BCG) and evaluates strategic business units with respect to the dimensions of the business growth rate and market share.

Behaviorally anchored rating scale

A behaviorally anchored rating scale (BARS) is a rating technique that relates an employee's performance to specific job-related incidents.

Benchmark

A benchmark is the measurement of performance against a uniform set of standards or environments.

Benchmark job

A benchmark job is a job found in many organizations and performed by several individuals who have similar duties that are relatively stable and require similar knowledge, skills, and abilities (KSAs).

Benchmarking

(1) Benchmarking is an improvement process in which a company measures its performance against that of best-in-class companies (or others that are good performers), determines how those companies achieved their performance levels, and uses the information to improve its own performance. The areas that can be benchmarked include strategies, operations, processes, and procedures. (2) "Benchmarking" means comparing specific measures of performance against data on those measures in other "best practice" organizations. (3) Benchmarking is the measurement of time intervals and other important characteristics of hardware and software, usually when testing them before a decision to purchase or reject. (4) Benchmarking is an ongoing, systematic approach by which a public affairs unit measures and compares itself with higher-performing and world-class units in order to generate knowledge and action about public affairs roles, practices, processes, products, services, and strategic issues that will lead to improvement in performance. Originated in the total quality management (TQM) movement.

In summary, benchmarking is the continuous process of measuring a company's products, services, costs, and practices against those of competitors or firms that display best-in-class achievements.

Benford's Law of First-Digit Test

As part of fraud investigations, internal auditors can apply Benford's law or the first-digit test to detect unusual data patterns arising from human errors, data manipulations, or fraudulent transactions. If the first digit is 1 in a financial account number or business transaction number, chances are good that it is a naturally occurring number (i.e., fraud-free). If the first digit is 9, chances are good that it might be a purposefully assigned number (i.e., fraudulent) to perpetrate fraud. The test looks at the first digit of the account or transaction number to see if it is 1 or 9 because the digit 1 occurs in that location 30% of the time while the digit 9 occurs in that location only 5% of the time. On a scale of 1 to 9, in general, lower numbers (1–5) are known to be fraud-free while the higher numbers (6–9), are known to be fraudulent. The following conditions apply:

The number is fraud-free if digits 1, 2, 3, 4, and 5 appear. They can occur in combination 78% of the time.

The number is fraudulent if digits 6, 7, 8, and 9 appear. They can occur in combination 22% of the time.

If first-digit analysis indicates that digits 6 through 9 are occurring more often than their expected frequency, it is an indication of fraud or other irregularities, and further investigation is required.

Best practices

Best practices are the processes, practices, and systems identified in public and private organizations that performed exceptionally well and are widely recognized as improving an organization's performance and efficiency in specific areas. Successfully identifying and applying best practices can reduce business expenses and improve organizational efficiency.

Bid-rigging

Bid-rigging is a fraud scheme which involves bidding. It is an agreement among competitors as to who will be the winning bidder (seller). Bid rigging occurs when a purchaser (buyer) solicits bids to purchase goods or services. The bidders agree in advance who will submit the winning bid. The purchaser, which depends on competition between the bidders to generate the lowest competitive price, receives instead a "lowest bid" that is higher than the competitive market would bear.

Bid rotation

Bid rotation is a form of bid-rigging scheme, where all co-conspirators submit bids, but by agreement, take turns being the low bidder on a series of contracts.

Bid suppression

Bid suppression is a form of bid-rigging scheme, where one or more competitors agree not to bid, or withdraw a previously submitted bid, so that a designated bidder will win. In return, the non-bidder may receive a subcontract or payoff.

Big data

As the name says, big data is vast amounts of data collected from a variety of sources, both internal and external to an organization. The data is big in terms of many data volumes, several datasets, and many data types. The purpose of big data is to analyze (data analytics) the data to develop insights, which, in turn, are turned into decisions that will produce the right results.

Big Five personality factors

The Big Five personality factors are dimensions that describe an individual's extroversion, agreeableness, conscientiousness, emotional stability, and openness to experience.

Big Q, little q

Big Q, little q is a quality-contrasting term where big Q focuses on all business products and processes in the entire company and little q focuses on all or parts of products and processes in one factory or plant. An example of Big Q is when an automobile company focuses on its three car brands 1, 2, and 3. An example of little q is when an automobile company focuses on its one car brand 1.

Bill of lading

A bill of lading is a carrier's contract and receipt for goods it agrees to transport from one place to another and to deliver to a designated location or person. There are many types of bills of lading.

Bill of materials

A bill of materials is a list containing the quantity and description of all materials required to manufacture a single unit of a component or product. There are many types of bills of material.

Bill of sale

A bill of sale is a written document formally transferring ownership of property specified in the document from the supplier to the purchaser.

Blanket order

A blanket order is a commitment to a supplier for certain goods over a predetermined period (one year) at predetermined prices or at prices to be determined.

Blasting, creating, and refining

Blasting, creating, and refining are used when a completely new way of thinking or speculation is required or when answering a question, such as "What else will do the job?" Blasting is good when group members are free to speculate and come up with totally new ideas that were never heard of or thought about before. Creativity comes into full play. It is a problem-solving tool.

Bottleneck

A bottleneck is a facility, function, department, or resource whose capacity is less than the demand placed on it.

Bottom-up approach

A bottom-up approach starts with the lowest-level software components of a hierarchy and proceeds through progressively higher levels to the top-level component.

Brainstorming

Brainstorming is a technique to generate a great number of ideas. The key is to let group members feel free to express whatever ideas come to mind without fear of judgment or criticism. It is a problem-solving tool.

Budgeted capacity

Budgeted capacity is the volume/mix of throughput on which financial budgets were set and overhead absorption rates were established.

Bullet chart

A bullet chart is good to compare two variables, such as sales dollars and salesperson. Actual sales data and target (quota) sales data can be compared for each salesperson to visualize which person meets assigned target sales quotas (i.e., above or below the quota). In bullet charts, two charts are combined with a bar chart showing actual sales dollars on the horizontal x-axis and a vertical reference line (quota line) on the vertical y-axis.

Bullwhip effect

The bullwhip effect, also known as the Forrester Effect, refers to a rippling and magnifying effect on inventory levels due to changes in product demand levels between producers and suppliers. This means a small change in demand at the first downstream supplier (DS-1) creates a big change in the demand at the first upstream supplier 1 (US-1) and generates a huge demand at the producer, as shown below.

$$US\text{-}1 \longrightarrow US\text{-}N \longrightarrow Producer \longleftarrow DS\text{-}N \longleftarrow DS\text{-}1$$

The same bullwhip effect can be seen in the supply-chain levels due to rippling and magnifying effect from the changes in product supply levels between producers and suppliers.

Bureaucratic control

The term "bureaucratic control" refers to the use of rules, policies, hierarchy of authority, reward systems, and other formal devices to influence employee behavior and assess performance.

Bureaucratic organization

A bureaucratic organization is a subfield of the classical management perspective that emphasizes management on an impersonal, rational basis through such elements as clearly defined authority and responsibility, formal record keeping, and separation of management and ownership.

Business acumen

Business acumen is a collective term representing the knowledge of business mission and vision; business strategies, goals, objectives, and plans; developing grand strategy; formulating strategic plans; executing (implementing) strategic plans; exercising strategic controls; complying with regulatory and legal requirements; developing an organization's management reporting structures and systems; creating and growing human talent; and understanding competitors' strategies and plans. This knowledge can help management and auditors to evaluate the effectiveness and efficiency of governance, risk management, and control processes in an organization.

Business ethics

Business ethics are concerned with good and bad or right and wrong behavior and practices that take place within a business context.

Business ethics gap

Compared with other capitalistic societies, the approach to ethics is more individualistic, legalistic, and universalistic in the United States.

Business ethics visibility gap

The people of the United States read and hear far more about business misconduct than people in other countries. Thus, there is a business ethics visibility gap in other countries.

Business-level strategy

Business-level strategy is the level of strategy concerned with the question "How do we compete?" It pertains to each business unit or product line within the organization.

Business market

The business market is comprised of all organizations that buy goods and services for use in the production of other goods and services or for resale.

Business model

A business model is the manner in which businesses generate income.

Business necessity

A business necessity is a practice necessary for safe and efficient organizational operations.

Business partnering

Business partnering involves the creation of cooperative business alliances between constituencies within an organization or between an organization and its customers or suppliers. Partnering occurs through a pooling of resources in a trusting atmosphere focused on continuous, mutual improvement.

Business plan

A business plan is a document specifying the business details prepared by an entrepreneur in preparation for opening a new business.

Business planning

Business planning is the general idea or explicit statement of where an organization wishes to be at some time in the future.

Business process reengineering

Business process reengineering is a systematic, disciplined improvement approach that critically examines, rethinks, and redesigns mission-delivery processes in order to achieve dramatic improvements in performance in areas important to customers and stakeholders.

Business processes

Business processes are processes that focus on what the organization does as a business and how it goes about doing it. A business has functional processes (generating output within a single department) and cross-functional processes (generating output across several functions or departments).

Business report

A business report is a report that covers many of the matters typically found in the management discussion and analysis part of company annual reports in North America.

Business risk

Business risk is the possibility that a company will not be able to meet ongoing operating expenditures. It is the risk associated with projections of a firm's future returns on assets or returns on equity if the firm uses no debt.

Business stakeholder

A business stakeholder is a person or entity that has an interest in the economic performance of the business.

Business transaction

A business transaction occurrence is an economic event or a condition that must be recorded in the accounting records.

Buying (sourcing) team

A buying (sourcing) team is composed of individuals from several functional departments of a company who pool their expertise to jointly make sourcing decisions.

C&E diagram

See Cause-and-effect diagram.

Capacity

Capacity refers to the capability of a worker, machine, work center, plant, or organization to produce output per time period. Also, it is the capability of a system to perform its expected functions. Capacity can be classified in several ways, such as budgeted, dedicated, demonstrated, productive, protective, excess, idle, rated, safety, and theoretical capacity.

Capacity strategy

Capacity strategy is part of a manufacturing (plant) strategy with three commonly recognized capacity strategies: lead, lag, and tracking. A lead strategy adds capacity in anticipation of increasing demand. A lag strategy does not add capacity until the firm is operating at or beyond full capacity. Both lead and lag capacity strategies are similar to the leading and lagging economic indicators.

A tracking strategy adds capacity in small amounts or takes capacity away in small amounts to attempt to respond to changing demand in the marketplace. The tracking strategy is also called a level production strategy, where production is leveled with the demand.

Lead capacity strategy + Lag capacity strategy = Chase capacity strategy

Tracking capacity strategy = Level production strategy

All plant capacity strategies are related to demand in the marketplace.

Cause-and-effect diagram (C&E diagram)

A C&E diagram (also called an Ishikawa, or fishbone, diagram), can be used to identify possible causes for a problem. The problem solver looks for the root causes by asking "why" five or six times to move from broad (possible) causes to specific (root) causes. The idea is that by repeating the same question, the true source of a problem will be discovered. This process helps identify the real problem. Then users choose the most likely cause for further review. Brainstorming can be used in developing the C&E diagrams.

Certification

Certification is a procedure by which a third party gives written assurance that a product, process, or service conforms to specified requirements. It is used in supplier certification and in issuing digital certificates.

Change management

Change management pertains to activities involved in (1) defining and instilling new values, attitudes, norms, and behaviors within an organization that support new ways of doing work and overcome resistance to change; (2) building consensus among customers and stakeholders on specific changes designed to better meet their needs; and (3) planning, testing, and implementing all aspects of the transition from one organizational structure or business process to another.

Charismatic leader

A charismatic leader is one who has the ability to motivate subordinates to transcend their expected performance.

Chart and graph

The basic purpose of a chart or graph is to give a visual comparison between two or more things. For example, changes in budget from one year to the next may be represented on a graph. One significant reason for visualizing a comparison is to reinforce its comprehension. Charts and graphs are used to dramatize a statement, fact, point of view, or idea. They are data presentation tools and visual aids assisting in the quick comprehension of simple and complex data, statistics, or problems. A chart should explain itself in silence; it should be completely understood without the assistance of a caption. The caption must act only as reinforcement to its comprehension.

Various charts include tabular, column, bar, pie, line, layer, and radar charts, as follows:

The **tabular chart** is used to represent items of interest. It requires a fair amount of study in order to grasp the full meaning of the figures. This is because it takes longer to digest the meaning of an itemization of compiled figures than if the same figures are presented graphically.

The **column chart** is most commonly used for demonstrating a comparison between two or more things. The column chart is vertical.

The **bar chart** or **Gantt chart** is essentially a column chart on its side, and is used for the same purpose. The bar chart is horizontal. It is a tool that allows a manager to evaluate whether existing resources can handle work demand or whether activities should be postponed. The Gantt chart is used for milestone scheduling where each milestone has start and completion dates. A milestone represents a major activity or task to be accomplished (e.g., design phase in a computer system development project). A **Gantt chart** is a graphical illustration of a scheduling technique. The structure of the chart shows output plotted against units of time. It does not include cost information. It highlights activities over the life of a project and contrasts actual times with projected times using a horizontal (bar) chart. It gives a quick picture of a project's progress in terms of actual time lines and projected time lines.

The **pie chart** is used to represent a 100% total of two or more items.

The **line chart** is very impressive when comparing several things but could present a visual problem if the comparisons are too many or too close in relation to one another. Advantages are that it is simple to draw. Disadvantages are that if the lines are close to each other, it is difficult to distinguish some of the plotted points.

The **layer chart** is linear in appearance but has a different representation. It depicts the accumulation of individual facts stacked one over the other to create the overall total. This chart is more complex than the others, since it illustrates much more. In addition to showing the comparison of layers that add up to the total, a layer chart also shows how each group of layers relates to subsequent groups. The layer chart requires more work to prepare than the other charts. There is more arithmetic involved, and it requires a good deal of concentration to draw the chart.

The **radar chart** is a visual method to show in graphic form the size of gaps in a number of areas, such as current performance versus ideal (expected) performance and current budget versus previous budget. Computer programs can be used to display radar charts.

Checklist

A checklist focuses one's attention on a logical list of diverse categories to which the problem could conceivably relate. It is a problem-solving tool.

Chief knowledge officer

The chief knowledge officer (CKO) is a relatively new position in some large organizations. The CKO is responsible for garnering knowledge and making it available for future operations in which employees can learn from previous experience. The CKO works closely with the chief information officer, who is in charge of the technical means for garnering the necessary information. In some firms, the position is called chief learning officer (CLO).

Chief learning officer

The chief learning officer (CLO) is responsible for developing on a worldwide scale the organization's human talent and for using the human knowledge present in the organization. *See* Chief knowledge officer.

Classical model

The classical model is a decision-making model based on the assumption that managers should make logical decisions that will be in the organization's best economic interests.

Closure

Closure is a perceptual process that allows a person to solve a complex problem with incomplete information. It is a problem-solving tool.

Coaching

Coaching is a continuous improvement technique by which people receive one-to-one learning through demonstration and practice. It is characterized by immediate feedback and correction.

Coercive power

Coercive power is power that stems from the authority to punish or recommend punishment.

Cognitive analytics

Cognitive analytics use artificial intelligence (AI) technology as it applies to cybersecurity, healthcare, transportation, and finance areas. The AI group of technologies such as machine learning and natural language processors can provide clear insights into problems with greater confidence, speed, and accuracy. For example, the AI technology can be used in cybersecurity in performing threat hunting and defending exercises; in healthcare, it can be used in diagnosing a patient's health risks; in transportation, in predicting airline delays; and in finance, in estimating the reasons for late bill payments from customers and business partners and how to improve accounts receivable collection frequency.

Cognitive biases and traps

Cognitive biases and traps are rooted in an individual's own personality zone (area). Examples include projection, analogy, and stereotyping traps.

Collective

In a social interaction paradigm, leaders look for opportunities that benefit the group as a whole.

Collectivism

The term "collectivism" refers to: (1) a preference for a tightly knit social framework in which individuals look after one another and organizations protect their members' interests; or (2) the belief that interests of the organization should have top priority.

Column chart

The column chart is most commonly used for demonstrating a comparison between two or more things. The column chart is vertical.

Commercial/industrial market

The term "commercial/industrial market" refers to business market customers who are described by variables such as location, Standard Industrial Classification (SIC) code, buyer industry, technological sophistication, purchasing process, size, ownership, and financial strength.

Common cause

A common cause is a source of variation inherent in a process over time. It can affect every outcome of the process and everyone in the process.

Compensating control

The compensating control concept states that the total environment should be considered when determining whether a specific policy, procedure, or control has been violated or a specific risk is present. If controls in one area are weak, they should be compensated for or mitigated in another area. Some examples of compensating controls are: strict personnel hiring procedures, bonding employees, information system risk insurance, increased supervision, rotation of duties, review of computer logs, user sign-off procedures, mandatory vacations, batch controls, user review of input and output, system activity reconciliations, and system access security controls.

Competence

Competence refers to a person's ability to learn and perform a particular activity. It generally consists of skill, knowledge, experience, and attitude components.

Competencies

Competencies are basic characteristics that can be linked to enhanced performance by individuals or teams.

Competitive advantage

Competitive advantage is defined as: (1) a position in which one dominates a market; also called strategic advantage; or (2) the ability to produce a good or service more cheaply than other countries due to favorable factor and demand conditions; strong related and supporting industries; and favorable firm strategy, structure, and rivalry conditions.

Competitive analysis

Competitive analysis involves the gathering of intelligence relative to competitors in order to identify opportunities or potential threats to current and future strategy.

Competitive assessment

Competitive assessment is a research process that consists of matching markets to corporate strengths and providing an analysis of the best potential for specific offerings.

Competitive disadvantage

The Trade-Related Investment Measures (TRIMs) agreement contains a provision concerning "competitive disadvantage." This provision would allow countries to apply existing TRIMs to new investing firms for the duration of the transition period when (1) the products of such investment were similar to the products of the established enterprises and (2) it was necessary to avoid distorting the conditions of competition between the new investment and the established enterprises.

Competitive environment

A competitive environment is affected by bribery and the existence of cartels.

Competitively advantaged product

A competitively advantaged product is a product that solves a set of customer problems better than any competitor's product. This product is made possible due to a firm's unique technical, manufacturing, managerial, or marketing capabilities, which are not easily copied by others.

Complementary bidding

Complementary bidding is a form of bid-rigging scheme, where co-conspirators submit token bids which are intentionally high or which intentionally fail to meet all of the bid requirements in order to lose a contract. It is also called courtesy bidding and it is the most commonly and frequently used form of bid-rigging.

Compliance

The term "compliance" refers to verifying that both manual and computer processing of transactions or events are in accordance with the organization's policies and procedures, generally accepted accounting principles, government laws, and regulatory agency rules and requirements.

Compliance testing

Compliance testing is the process of verifying compliance with the organization's internal controls, operations, policies, plans, procedures, guidelines, practices, and standards to evaluate efficiency and effectiveness. The process is called compliance auditing, and the tests performed are called compliance tests.

Concentration strategy

Concentration strategy is a market development strategy that involves focusing on a smaller number of markets.

Concurrent engineering

Concurrent engineering is defined as a systematic approach to the integrated and overlapping design of products and their related processes including design, manufacturing, and support. It requires that, from the beginning, all elements of a product's life cycle be evaluated across all design factors to include user requirements, quality, cost, and schedule.

Consideration

Consideration is a type of leadership behavior that describes the extent to which a leader is sensitive to subordinates, respects their ideas and feelings, and establishes mutual trust.

Consignment buying

Consignment buying is a method of procurement in which a supplier maintains inventory on the purchaser's premises. The purchaser's obligation to pay for the goods begins when goods are drawn from the stock for use.

Contingency table

A contingency table is a type of table presented in a matrix format displaying frequency distribution, showing their probabilities. Contingency tables (cross-tabulations) are used in business intelligence, market research, and customer surveys where interrelations and interactions between two or more variables can be studied to obtain greater insights of data. Due to their statistical focus, contingency tables show a measure of association between variables. For example, a table can be put together showing how male and female customers prefer to purchase product A and product B from a retailer.

Continuous improvement

Continuous improvement is an ongoing activity where problems are diagnosed, root causes are identified, solutions are developed, and controls are established to improve the overall performance of activities.

Continuous process improvement

Continuous process improvement is an ongoing effort to incrementally improve how products and services are provided and internal operations are conducted.

Control

A control is any protective action, device, procedure, technique, or other measure that reduces exposure. Controls can prevent, detect, or correct errors and can reduce loss or harm.

Control functions

Control functions (e.g., internal audit, accounting, finance, loss prevention, and risk management) in an organization have a responsibility to provide independent and objective assessment, reporting, and assurance to management and others. These functions perform internal audit, risk, and compliance reviews.

Cooperative purchasing

Cooperative purchasing is a volume-buying approach in which several organizations form or utilize a centralized buying service that purchases specified types of items for all members of the group.

Coordinated decentralization

Coordinated decentralization involves headquarters providing the overall corporate strategy while granting subsidiaries the freedom to implement it within established ranges.

Copyright

A copyright is a property right in an original work of authorship that arises automatically upon creation of such a work and belongs, in the first instance, to the author.

Core competence

Core competence is: (1) a business activity that an organization does particularly well in comparison to competitors; (2) a unique capability that creates high value and that differentiates the organization from its competition.

Core processes

Core processes have a major impact on the strategic goals of an organization.

Corporate culture

The term "corporate culture" refers to: (1) the collective beliefs, values, attitudes, manners, customs, behaviors, and artifacts unique to an organization; (2) an organization's practice, such as its symbols, heroes, and rituals; and its values, such as its employees' perception of good/ evil, beautiful/ugly, normal/abnormal, and rational/ irrational. The practice aspects differ from corporation to corporation within a national culture, and the value aspects vary from country to country.

Corporate-level strategy

The corporate-level strategy is the strategy concerned with the question "What business are we in?" It pertains to the organization as a whole and the combination of business units and product lines that make it up.

Cost of production

Cost of production refers to the sum of the cost of materials, fabrication, and/or other processing employed in producing the merchandise sold in a home market or to a third country, together with appropriate allocations of general administrative and selling expenses. The cost of production is based on the producer's actual experience and does not include any mandatory minimum general expenses or profit, as in "constructed value."

Cost/benefit analysis

Cost/benefit analysis is a decision-making tool in which the expected costs and benefits of alternative actions are compared. The action for which the expected value of the benefits minus the expected value of the costs is greatest is chosen. The expected value is the desirability of the alternative multiplied by the probability of success. The likelihood of an occurrence that is derived mathematically from reliable historical data is called objective probabilities. However, subjective probabilities do not have mathematical reliability since they are derived from the decision maker's intuition and gut feel.

Cost leadership

Cost leadership is a: (1) pricing tactic where a company offers an identical product or service at a lower cost than the competition; (2) type of competitive strategy with which the organization aggressively seeks efficient facilities, cuts costs, and employs tight cost controls to be more efficient than competitors.

Critical-to-quality

Critical-to-quality (CTQ) is a quality measurement technique that dictates a product's output specifications in terms of a customer's needs, wants, and expectations, whether the customer is internal or external to an organization. CTQ focuses on customer requirements, design and test parameters, mistake-proofing, quality robustness, and control charts.

Cultural environment

To develop an effective international business strategy, the critical aspects of culture must be identified.

Cultural leader

A cultural leader is an employee who uses signals and symbols to influence corporate culture.

Customer or market allocation

Customer or market allocation is a form of bid-rigging scheme, where co-conspirators agree to divide up customers or geographic areas. The result is that the coconspirators will not bid or will submit only complementary bids when a solicitation for bids is made by a customer or in an area not assigned to them. This scheme is most commonly found in the service sector and may involve quoted prices for services as opposed to bids.

Cycle count

A cycle count is a physical stock-checking system in which the inventory is divided into groups, one of which is physically counted each week.

Dashboard

A dashboard is a collection of performance indicators showing their status and quality levels in colors. A dashboard provides a concise and visual summary of overall performance. An example is showing an automobile's performance in terms of speed, revolutions per minute, oil pressure, and temperature.

Dashboards in general, and specifically business data dashboards, are a collection of performance indicators showing an object's or a device's status and quality levels in colors. They are used to present vital data in order to develop a strategy or plan. The dashboard provides a concise and visual summary of overall performance. Data dashboards are presented in several forms, including numerical, graphical, and interactive formats (exhibits, slides, audios, and videos). They use drill-down and drag-and-drop features. An example is showing an automobile's performance in terms of its speed, revolutions per minute, oil pressure, and temperature.

Dashboards are of two types: static and interactive (basic and advanced). Static dashboards show traditional reports that are mainly focused on financial information (e.g., sales, revenues, costs, and profits). Basic interactive dashboards show information about customers' buying habits and cross-sales to them. Advanced interactive dashboards can have built-in simulation models to do what-if type of analyses (i.e., sensitivity analysis).

Today, most organizations present only structured data on dashboards. Better insights and rewards can be achieved if they show structured, unstructured, and semi-structured data on their dashboards, because doing so provides a big-picture perspective of their business.

Data analytics
"Data analytics" means applying sophisticated analytical methods to data, whether it is big data or not. Data is subjected to various types of analysis to yield new insights, results, and decisions, as follows.

$$\text{Data} \longrightarrow \text{Analytics} \longrightarrow \text{Insights} \longrightarrow \text{Results} \longrightarrow \text{Decisions}$$

Sophisticated analytical methods include prescriptive, predictive, and descriptive analytics.

$$\text{Data Analytics} = \text{Prescriptive Analytics} + \text{Predictive Analytics} + \text{Descriptive Analytics}$$

Data filters
Data filters can be built into dashboards so data can be sliced from different perspectives or drilled down to a more detailed level using parameters such as: (1) transaction date, month, quarter, or year; (2) cost data by contract; (3) revenue or profit data by a retail store; (4) sales data by a market region; or (5) quarterly performance by a business segment. Data filters provide the ability to explore data at multiple levels and to customize user-driven data analysis. Data filters show only the requested data and ignore the rest of the data not requested.

Data mining
Data mining is the application of database technologies and advanced data-analytics programs to uncover hidden patterns, trends, correlations, outliers, anomalies, and subtle relationships in data and to infer rules that allow for the prediction of future results and outcomes. Data mining analyzes data for relationships that have not previously been discovered and other insights not suggested by a priori hypotheses or explicit assumptions. Big data is often used as input into data mining applications due to its vast amounts of data, meaning the more data available, the more it can be applied to. Data mining is mostly used in the marketing and advertising of products and services and gathering of business intelligence.

Data visualization tools
Data visualization tools are data presentation methods and include various reporting and information dissemination methods to report data results to management for their actions and decisions. These methods include charts and graphs (e.g., tabular, column, bar, pie, line, layer, Pareto, and radar charts) as well as dashboards, histograms, and scatter diagrams.

Decision table
A decision table is a decision-making tool that documents rules used to select one or more actions based on one or more conditions. These conditions and their corresponding actions can be presented either in a matrix or tabular form.

Decision tree
A decision tree is a graphical representation of possible decisions, events, or states of nature resulting from each decision with its associated probabilities, and the outcomes of the events or states of nature. The decision problem displays the sequential nature of the decision-making situation. The decision tree has nodes, branches, and circles to represent junction boxes, connectors between the nodes, and state-of-nature nodes, respectively. It is a decision-making tool.

Dedicated capacity
Dedicated capacity is designated to produce a single item or a limited number of similar items.

De facto and de jure factors

De facto factors are real and factual things, which are based on practices whereas de jure factors are official and right things, which are based on laws.

Delphi technique

The Delphi technique is a method used to avoid groupthink in which group members do not meet face to face to make decisions. Rather, each group member independently and anonymously writes down suggestions and submits comments, which are then centrally compiled. The compiled results are then distributed to the group members who, independently and anonymously, write additional comments. These comments are again centrally compiled, and the process is repeated until consensus is obtained. The Delphi technique is a problem-solving tool and a group decision-making method.

Demand-pull system

A demand-pull system is a material movement technique where a downstream work center pulls materials from the upstream work center when they are needed, not when on a schedule.

Demonstrated capacity

Demonstrated capacity is a proven capacity calculated from actual performance data. It is expressed as the average number of items produced multiplied by the standard hours per item.

Dependent demand

Dependent demand refers to the demand for an item that is derived from the demand for another component or a finished product.

Depth charts

Depth charts, coined by the U.S. Office of Personnel Management (OPM), provide the board of directors a snapshot of the available internal management staff and their readiness to take on new and increased leadership roles. As such, depth charts are very useful in developing succession plans for key management positions with several levels. Management succession plans are management backup plans that can be used in the case of (1) emergency situations such as crisis, death, and sudden departures of key management personnel; (2) position transitions during job demotions, promotions, and transfers; and (3) job rotations for career development. Management backup plans indicate who can step in when and where as needed. The board chairperson develops the level 1 charts for the board members, the board members together develop the level 2 charts for the CEO and president, the CEO develops the level 3 charts for key senior management such as executives and officers (C-level suite), and senior management develops the level 4 charts for key functional managers or operational managers.

Descriptive analytics

Descriptive analytics describes what already happened.

Design of experiments

Design of experiments (DOE) deals with planning, conducting, analyzing, and interpreting controlled tests to evaluate the factors that control the value of a parameter (e.g., design specification tolerance).

Devil's advocate technique

In the devil's advocate technique, the decision maker is focusing on failures and identifies ways an action or an alternative can be less than successful. It is a decision-making tool.

Differential analysis

Differential analysis is a technique to compare differences in revenues or costs of two or more alternatives. It is a decision-making tool.

Discriminant analysis

Discriminant analysis is a qualitative, subjective decision-making tool to differentiate between effective and ineffective procedures or actions.

Division

A division is a decentralized organizational unit that is structured around a common function, product, customer, or geographical territory. Divisions can be cost, profit, or investment centers.

Divisional structure

Divisional structure is an organizational structure in which departments are grouped based on similar organizational outputs.

Drip pricing

Drip pricing means back-end prices are different from front-end prices and vice versa, and it is illegal. In drip pricing, additional charges are added to a customer's final prices without disclosing them to the customer at the beginning. Drip pricing can be found in the hospitality industry, such as hotel reservations and vacation resorts, and in consumer financing, such as home mortgage loans and short-term loans. Legal liabilities exist with deceptive and discriminatory price practices in violation of the FTC's Robinson-Patman Act.

Drivers of quality

Drivers of quality include customers; suppliers; vendors; employees; products; services; organizational culture and ethics; organizational policies, procedures, and standards; and total organizational focus and commitment. Note that these drivers of quality can either increase or decrease quality based on how these drives move up and down.

Dual control

Dual control is the process of using two or more separate entities or individuals operating in concert to protect sensitive functions or information. The idea is that no single entity should be able to generate, access, or use keys to open sensitive containers or rooms. This is similar to dual control in physical access, such as opening a safe deposit vault in the presence of two individuals. All entities are equally responsible for all actions or inactions.

Dual-hat leadership

Dual-hat leadership, commonly practiced in the military sector, applies to situations where an incoming executive or officer has been given two job responsibilities in two different organizations, functions, or departments simultaneously. This military practice can be applied to nonmilitary sectors during a transition period where one executive leaves the organization and another executive assumes responsibilities for two functions simultaneously until a new executive is hired to replace the executive who left. Advantages of this leadership approach include (1) more in-depth coordination and collaboration, (2) faster decision making, and (3) more efficient use of resources. Disadvantages of this leadership approach include (1) concerns about unfair prioritization of requests for support services between the two functions at the same time; (2) broader span of control (i.e., increased breadth, depth, and magnitude of issues to deal with); (3) increased tension between the two functions for routine resource prioritization, allocation, and sharing; and (4) conflict-of-interest situations where the leader favors one function over others.

Econometrics

The application of statistical methods to economic data is called econometrics. It analyzes the relationships between two or more economic variables and uses multiple regression analysis.

Economics

Economics deals with the allocation and utilization of scarce resources (e.g., men, money, materials, and machinery; 4Ms) to produce goods and provide services. The 4Es (i.e., effectiveness, efficiency, economy, and economics) and 4Ms are connected with the common term "resources."

Economy or economical

Economy or economical means whether an organization is acquiring the appropriate type, quality, and amount of resources at an appropriate cost. It focuses on cost-benefit analysis.

Edisonian

Edisonian is a type of trial-and-error experimentation named after Thomas Edison. This method requires a tedious and persistent search for the solution. It is a problem-solving tool.

Effectiveness

Effectiveness is the degree to which an organization achieves a stated goal or objective. It is the measure of how well a job or task is performed.

Efficiency

Efficiency is the use of minimal resources—materials, money, machinery, and people—to provide a desired volume of output. It is a measurement (usually expressed as a percentage) of the actual output to the standard output expected. Efficiency measures how well a task or activity is performed relative to existing standards; in contrast, productivity measures output relative to a specific input, for example, tons per labor hour. Efficiency is the ratio of (1) actual units produced to the standard rate of production expected in a time period or (2) standard hours produced to actual hours worked (taking longer means less efficiency) or (3) actual dollar volume of output to a standard dollar volume in a time period. Illustrations of these calculations follow.

There is a standard of 100 pieces per hour and 780 units are produced in one eight-hour shift; the efficiency is 780/800 converted to a percentage, or 97.5%.

The work is measured in hours and took 8.21 hours to produce eight standard hours; the efficiency is 8/8.21 converted to a percentage, or 97.5%.

The work is measured in dollars and produces $780 with a standard of $800; the efficiency is $780/$800 converted to a percentage of 97.5%.

Enterprise-level strategy

An enterprise-level strategy is the overarching strategy level that poses these basic questions: "What is the role of the organization in society?" and "What do we stand for?"

Environmental quality engineering

Environmental quality engineering means designing products and their processes that are environmentally friendly using green manufacturing techniques, such as design for reuse (recycling), design for disassembly (repair), design for rework, and design for remanufacturing (restoration).

Design for recycling is an investment recovery and environmental improvement effort to recover revenues and reduce costs associated with scrap, surplus, obsolete, and waste materials. In design for repair, a nonconforming product is fixed so that it will fulfill the intended use requirements, although it may not conform to the originally specified requirements. A repaired product retains its original identity and only those parts that have failed or badly worn out are replaced or serviced. In design for rework, a nonconforming product is taken back to the production line to fix it in order to meet the originally specified requirements. In design for remanufacturing, worn-out products are restored to like-new condition.

Green manufacturing uses a life cycle design-approach that focuses on incoming materials, manufacturing processes, customer use of the product, and product disposal.

Complying with environmental quality standards such as ISO 14000 and 14001 is a part of the environmental quality engineering scope. The goal is to reduce the potential legal liabilities and respond to regulatory requirements (e.g., EPA in the United States) addressing human safety and health issues.

Ethical dilemma

An ethical dilemma is a situation that arises when all alternative choices or behaviors have been deemed undesirable because of potentially negative ethical consequence, making it difficult to distinguish right from wrong.

Ethical impact statement

An ethical impact statement is an attempt to assess the underlying moral justifications for corporate actions and the consequent results of those actions.

Ethical relativism

Ethical relativism refers to picking and choosing which source of norms to use based on what will justify current actions or maximize freedom.

Ethical responsibilities

Ethical responsibilities are those activities and practices that are expected or prohibited by societal members even though they are not codified into law.

Ethical values

Ethical values are moral values that enable a decision maker to determine an appropriate course of behavior; these values should be based on what is right, which may go beyond what is legal.

Ethical vigilance

Ethical vigilance involves paying constant attention to whether one's actions are right or wrong and, if ethically wrong, asking why one is behaving in that manner.

Ethics

Ethics is a: (1) code of conduct that is based on moral principles and tries to balance what is fair for individuals with what is right for society; (2) code of moral principles and values that govern the behaviors of a person or group with respect to what is right or wrong; and (3) discipline that deals with what is good and bad and with moral duty and obligation.

Excess capacity

Excess capacity is where the output capabilities at a non-constraint resource exceed the amount of productive or protective capacity required to achieve a given level of throughput at the constraint.

Execution time

See Cycle time.

Expectancy theory

Expectancy theory is a process theory that proposes that motivation depends on individuals' expectations about their ability to perform tasks and receive desired rewards.

Expert power

Expert power is power that stems from special knowledge of or skill in the tasks performed by subordinates.

Extrinsic reward

An extrinsic reward is a reward given by another person.

Fishbone diagram

A fishbone diagram is a graphic technique for identifying cause-and-effect relationships among factors in a given situation or problem. It is also called Ishikawa diagramming.

Fit-gap analysis

Fit-gap analysis, or gap-fit analysis, is a simple and powerful analytical exercise used by management that compares a company's current state to its desired state as indicated in its plans and budgets and compares a company's current state to its major competitors' state in order to determine what things fit and what things do not fit, thus leaving a gap in a given situation. The goal is to identify what needs to be done to eliminate or minimize the gap. Fit-gap analysis supports the strengths, weaknesses, opportunities, and threats (SWOT) analysis. Examples include (1) a gap between service providers' and service receivers' expectations, (2) a gap between supplier/vendor's goals and customer's goals, (3) a gap between business strategies and business processes, and (4) a gap between a computer's CPU performance and data storage subsystem performance.

Fit-gap analysis deals with how two or more things match or align with each other (what fits) or do not match or align (what does not fit, or gaps). This analysis reveals deeper insights into how things are working or not working. It is also defined as an exercise of comparing an actual outcome to a standard (expected) outcome, resulting in deficiencies and excesses.

Fixed-order quantity system

A fixed-order quantity system is one in which the order quantity is fixed and the time between orders varies.

Flowchart

A flowchart helps a decision maker in analyzing a large, complex problem. Flowcharts and decision trees both show flow or sequencing. Unlike the flowchart, a decision tree shows outcome probabilities. It is a problem-solving and decision-making tool.

Force-field analysis

Force-field analysis involves the identification of a problem, the factors or forces contributing to making it a problem, and steps for generating solutions. Two main sets of forces are identified: (1) inhibiting forces—those that resist the resolution of the problem; and (2) facilitating forces—those that push the problem toward resolution. It is a problem-solving tool.

Forward buying

Forward buying means buying in excess of current requirements as part of a strategy or because of anticipated shortages, strikes, or price increases.

Forward logistics versus reverse logistics

In forward logistics, raw materials and finished products are moved from upstream suppliers to downstream customers. In reverse logistics, already sold finished products are moved from downstream customers to upstream suppliers and eventually to manufacturers for returns and repairs.

Free alongside vessel

In a free alongside (FAS) vessel, the supplier agrees to deliver the goods in proper condition alongside the vessel. The buyer assumes all subsequent risks and expenses after delivery to the port or pier.

Free on board

Free on board (FOB) is a contractual arrangement in which title is transferred between supplier and purchaser at the FOB point. There are many variations of FOB.

Functional-level strategy

A functional-level strategy addresses the questions: How should a firm integrate its various subfunctional activities, and how should these activities be related to changes taking place in the various functional areas? The strategy pertains to all of the organization's major departments.

Functional organization

A functional organization is structured by discrete functions (e.g., marketing/sales, engineering, production, finance, human resources).

Functional organization structure

Functional organization structure is an organizational structure in which groups are made up of individuals who perform the same function, such as engineering or manufacturing, or have the same expertise or skills, such as electronics engineering or testing.

Functional structure

Functional structure is an organization structure in which positions are grouped into departments based on similar skills, expertise, and resource use.

Futures contract

A futures contract is used for the purchase or sale and delivery of commodities at a future date. It is primarily used as a hedging device against market price fluctuations or unforeseen supply shortages.

Gainsharing

Gainsharing is a type of program that rewards individuals financially on the basis of organizational performance.

Gantt chart

A Gantt chart is a project management technique to pictorially represent the tasks to be performed and the interrelationships among tasks in a project. It is also called a bar chart. It shows the time frame (e.g., hours, days) for each task.

A Gantt chart is a graphical illustration of a scheduling technique. The structure of the chart shows output plotted against units of time. It does not include cost information. It highlights activities over the life of a project and contrasts actual times with projected times using a horizontal (bar) chart. It gives a quick picture of a project's progress in terms of actual timelines and projected timelines.

Gap-fit analysis

Gap-fit analysis is a technique that compares a company's existing state to its desired state (as expressed by its long-term plans) to determine what fits and what does not fit (gap) and what needs to be done to remove or minimize the gap. Examples include (1) a gap between service providers' and service receivers' expectations, (2) a gap between supplier/vendor's goals and customer's goals, (3) a gap between business strategies and business processes, and (4) a gap between a computer's CPU performance and data storage subsystem performance.

General semantics

General semantics includes approaches that help individuals to discover multiple meanings or relationships in words and expressions. It is a problem-solving tool.

Geographic organization

A geographic organization is one structured by geography, territory, region, and the like.

Goal

A goal is a desired future state that the organization attempts to realize; a statement of general intent, aim, or desire; it is the point toward which management directs its efforts and resources. Goals are often nonquantitative.

Goal conflict

Goal conflict occurs when an employee's self-interest differs from business objectives.

Grand strategy

A grand strategy is the general plan of major action by which an organization intends to achieve its long-term goals.

Grapevine

The grapevine consists of informal communication channels over which information flows within an organization, usually without a known origin of the information and without any confirmation of its accuracy or completeness (sometimes referred to as the rumor mill).

Graphic rating scale

A graphic rating scale is a scale that allows the rater to mark an employee's performance on a continuum.

Gray market

A gray market is a market entered in a way not intended by the manufacturer of the goods.

Gray marketing

Gray marketing is the marketing of authentic, legally trademarked goods through unauthorized channels.

Gresham's law of planning

Gresham's law of planning states that managers pay more attention and put more time and effort into planning programmed activities (i.e., routine and simple tasks) than planning for non-programmed activities (i.e., rare and complex tasks). This means that programmed activities overshadow nonprogrammed activities.

Halo effect

The halo effect is an overall impression of a person or situation based on one characteristic, either favorable or unfavorable. It is a type of rating error that occurs when an employee receives the same rating on all dimensions regardless of his or her performance on individual ones.

Hard controls

Controls can be classified into two categories: hard controls and soft controls. Hard controls are formal, tangible, objective, and much easier to measure and evaluate than the soft controls. Examples of hard controls include budgets, dual controls, written approvals, reconciliations, authorization levels, verifications, and segregation of duties. Tools to evaluate hard controls include flowcharts, system narratives, testing, and counting. Higher-level managers and executives need more depth in soft skills and soft controls and less depth in hard skills and hard controls. Lower-level managers and executives need more depth in hard skills and hard controls and less depth in soft skills and soft controls.

Hard skills

An individual's skills can be divided into two types: hard skills and soft skills. Hard skills are mostly quantitative in nature and include analytical, technical, and functional skills; problem identification and solving skills; and decision-making, managing, application, and integration skills. Higher-level managers and executives need more depth in soft skills and soft controls and less depth in hard skills and hard controls. Lower-level managers and executives need more depth in hard skills and hard controls and less depth in soft skills and soft controls.

Histogram

A histogram is a graphic summary of variations in a dataset. It shows data patterns that are difficult to notice in a simple table of numbers. A histogram is a vertical bar chart providing a frequency distribution of measured data.

Horizontal analysis

Horizontal analysis is financial analysis that compares an item in a current statement with the same item in prior statements.

Horizontal communication

Horizontal communication is the lateral or diagonal exchange of messages among peers or coworkers.

Horizontal dependency

Horizontal dependency is the relationship between the components at the same level in the bill of material, in which all must be available at the same time and in sufficient quantity to manufacture the parent assembly.

Horizontal information interchange

Horizontal information interchange means sharing information by organizations in a horizontal market.

Horizontal market

A horizontal market is a market in which all players buy or sell the same type of product, making them competitors.

Horizontal price fixing

Horizontal price fixing occurs between two or more competing retailers because they are in the same hierarchical level in the marketplace. It is illegal.

Horizontal promotion

In a horizontal promotion, instead of slowly climbing the organizational ladder, a worker or manager makes lateral movements, acquiring expertise in different functions, such as marketing or manufacturing.

Horizontal structure

A horizontal structure is an organization that is organized along a process or value-added chain, eliminating hierarchy and functional boundaries (also referred to as a systems structure).

Horizontal team

A horizontal team is a formal team composed of employees from about the same hierarchical level but from different areas of expertise.

Hoshin planning

Hoshin planning is a type of Japanese strategic planning process in which an organization develops up to four vision statements that indicate where the organization should be in the next five years. Company goals and work plans are developed based on the vision statements. Periodic audits are then conducted to monitor progress. It is a breakthrough planning process.

Hostile environment

A hostile environment involves harassment, where an individual's work performance or psychological well-being is unreasonably affected by intimidating or offensive working conditions.

House of quality

The house of quality (HOQ) is a diagram that clarifies the relationship between customer needs and product features. It helps correlate market or customer requirements and analysis of competitive products with higher-level technical and product characteristics. The diagram, which makes it possible to bring several factors into a single figure, is named for its house-shaped appearance; however, sometimes it is referred to as quality function deployment (QFD), a sign of the connection between the three approaches of voice of the customer (VOC), QFD, and HOQ.

Humor

In addition to being a powerful tool to relieve tension and hostility, humor is a problem-solving tool. When correctly executed, it opens the mind to seeking creative solutions to a problem. Humor can be in the form of detached jokes, quips, games, puns, and anecdotes. Humor gives perspective and solves problems. Stepping back and viewing a problem with a certain level of detachment restores perspective. A sense of humor sends messages of self-confidence, security, and control of the situation. However, humor should not be sarcastic or scornful.

Hygiene factors

Hygiene factors are factors that involve the presence or absence of job dissatisfiers, including working conditions, pay, company policies, and interpersonal relationships. "Hygiene factor" is a term used by Frederick Herzberg to label "dissatisfiers."

Idle capacity

Idle capacity is the capacity not used in a system of linked resources. It consists of protective capacity and excess capacity.

Imagineering

Imagineering is a problem-solving tool that involves the visualization of a complex process, procedure, or operation with all waste eliminated. The imagineer assumes the role of dreamer, realist, and critic. The steps in imagineering consist of taking an action, comparing the results with the person's imagined perfect situation, and making a mental correction for the next time. This approach eventually improves the situation and brings it to the desired level. Imagineering is similar to value analysis.

Implemented practices

Implemented practices can consist of a combination of legacy, promising, leading, and best practices. Implemented practices reflect the current business situation.

Industrial engineering

Industrial engineering, also known as management engineering, ensures the economical, efficient, and effective use of an organization's resources in manufacturing and service industries.

Industrial engineers (management engineers) are known as efficiency experts in manufacturing or service firms as they deal with the five Ms of a company's resources: men, machines, materials, methods, and measurements. Specifically, industrial engineers participate in the design of jobs, products, and processes; schedule machines for greater utilization; schedule operators for maximum productivity; measure material-usage efficiency; measure labor productivity through motion and time studies; measure energy-usage efficiency; participate in layout design for equipment and facilities; analyze materials handling and warehousing operations for efficiency; analyze work steps to identify value-added and non-value-added activities; review product specifications for accuracy and improvement; and enhance production systems, methods, and procedures to eliminate waste and duplication. They approach production or service activities with an eye toward continual improvement using integrated systems, methods, and procedures.

Informal communication

Informal communication is unofficial communication that takes place in an organization as people talk freely and easily; examples include impromptu meetings and personal conversations (verbal or email).

Informal communication channel

An informal communication channel is a communication channel that exists outside formally authorized channels without regard for the organization's hierarchy of authority.

Interactive leadership

Interactive leadership is a leadership style characterized by values such as inclusion, collaboration, relationship building, and caring.

Internal economies of scale

Internal economies of scale are lower production costs resulting from greater production for an enlarged market.

Interval data

Interval data arises when the data have ordinal properties, such as measuring the distance between the two data items.

Interval variable

The interval variable is a quantitative variable the attributes of which are ordered and for which the numerical differences between adjacent attributes are interpreted as equal.

Intuitive approach

The intuitive approach is a problem-solving tool based on hunches. It does not use a scientific approach and uses subjective estimates or probabilities, which are difficult to replicate.

Investigative questions

Six investigative questions are used to understand the root causes of issues and problems better: who, what, when, where, why, and how. The questions are a problem-solving tool.

ISO 9000 standards

The International Organization for Standardization (ISO) 9000 standards address quality system processes but not product performance specifications. In other words, ISO 9000 covers how products are made but not necessarily how they work. ISO 9000 focuses on processes, not on products or people. It is based on the concept that one will fix the product by fixing the process. ISO 9000 is a standard by which to judge the quality of suppliers. It assumes that suppliers have a sound quality system in place and are following it. ISO 9000 can be used as a baseline quality system to achieve quality objectives.

Two kinds of ISO 9000 standards exist: product standards dealing with technical specifications and quality standards dealing with management systems. Four quality measures for ISO 9000 are: (1) leadership, (2) human resource development and management, (3) management of process quality, and (4) customer focus and satisfaction.

ISO 14000 environmental standards

The ISO 14000 environmental standards are divided into two broad categories: (1) environmental management systems consisting of environmental performance evaluation and environmental auditing and (2) life cycle assessment consisting of environmental labeling and environmental aspects in product standards.

ISO 14001 environmental standard

The ISO 14001 environmental standard is a framework for planning, developing, and implementing environmental strategies in an organization. The framework includes a policy, a planning process, organizational structure, specific objectives and targets, specific implementation programs, communications and training programs, management review, monitoring, and corrective action in terms of environmental audit.

Jidoka

Jidoka (a Japanese word) means stopping a production line or a process step when a defect or problem is discovered so that it will not cause additional or new problems further down the production line. Jidoka requires employee training and empowerment to stop the running production line. A production worker and/or a programmed machine can accomplish the jidoka goals.

Job analysis

Job analysis is a systematic way to gather and analyze information about the content, context, and human requirements of jobs.

Job characteristics model

The job characteristics model is a model of job design that comprises core job dimensions, critical psychological states, and employee growth-need strength.

Job criteria

Job criteria are important elements in a given job.

Job description

A job description is a narrative explanation of the work, responsibilities, and basic requirements of a job.

Job design

Job design is the application of motivational theories to the structure of work for improving productivity and satisfaction. It involves organizing tasks, duties, and responsibilities into a productive unit of work.

Job enlargement

Job enlargement is a job design that combines a series of tasks into one new, broader job to give employees variety and challenge.

Job enrichment

Job enrichment is a job design that incorporates achievement, recognition, and other high-level motivators into the work. It is the process of increasing the depth of a job by adding the responsibility for planning, organizing, controlling, and evaluating the job.

Job evaluation

Job evaluation is the process of determining the value of jobs within an organization through an examination of job content.

Job rotation

Job rotation is a job design that systematically moves employees from one job to another to provide them with variety and stimulation.

Job satisfaction

Job satisfaction is a positive emotional state resulting from evaluating one's job experience.

Job simplification

Job simplification is a job design whose purpose is to improve task efficiency by reducing the number of tasks a single person must do.

Job specifications

Job specifications are the knowledge, skills, and abilities (KSAs) an individual needs to perform a job satisfactorily.

Job statement
A job statement is a statement used to separate and identify jobs.

Joint venture
A joint venture is the product of two or more firms that have banded together to establish operations in foreign markets in order to capitalize on each other's resources and reduce risk. They share profits, liabilities, and duties. A joint venture results from the participation of two or more companies in an enterprise in which each party contributes assets, owns the new entity to some degree, and shares risk.

Just-in-time
Just-in-time (JIT) philosophy reduces the cost of quality (COQ) and improves quality. It is related to continuous improvement.

Kaizen
Kaizen (a Japanese word) is an ongoing process of unending improvement, that is, establishing and achieving higher goals of improvement all the time. PDCA, JIT, and kaizen are related to quality or continuous improvement. In manufacturing, it relates to finding and eliminating waste in machinery, labor, or production methods. Journalist tools such as Five Ws and One H can be used to understand a process deeply and to improve a process continuously. These tools include Who, What, Where, When, Why, and How. Answers to these six questions help guide the problem solving and quality improvement process.

Kanban
"Kanban" is a Japanese term used to describe a method of just-in-time production that uses standard containers or lot sizes with a single card attached to each.

Kano principles
Kano principles focus on customer survey, which can be applied to customers knowing about their purchases and experiences with a specific product or service. The principles ask the customers questions such as whether they are delighted, satisfied, neutral, or dissatisfied with a product or service. The same principles can be applied to stakeholders' opinions of an internal audit's performance. An effective audit function can obtain 360-degree feedback from audit clients or stakeholders, such as internal customers (e.g., audit committee members, senior managers, and functional managers), and external customers (e.g., external and regulatory auditors). Kano principles can be applied to this feedback process using three rating scales, such as satisfied, neutral, and dissatisfied, for measuring the effectiveness of an internal audit. Each rating must give reasons and explanations. In a way, the Kano principles can validate what audit stakeholders value the most.

Key value drivers
Key value drivers are core elements that can make an organization either a value creator or a value destroyer. These core elements together form a solid value chain. Six core elements include (1) mission and vision; (2) strategies and goals; (3) culture and ethics; (4) people (e.g., employees, managers, executives, officers, and directors); (5) products, services, and technologies; and (6) stakeholders, especially customers, suppliers, and vendors. All six elements must work together in harmony to create a real value to the organization. If any one of these core elements is broken, the entire value chain is broken.

Kiertsu
"Kiertsu" is a Japanese term used to describe a situation where both supplier and customer organizations have a financial interest in each other; often represented as members of the board of directors in both organizations.

Layer chart

The layer chart is linear in appearance but depicts the accumulation of individual facts stacked one over the other to create the overall total. This chart is more complex than the others since it illustrates much more. Besides showing the comparison of layers that add up to the total, the layer chart also shows how each group of layers relates to subsequent groups. The layer chart requires more work to prepare than the other charts. There is more arithmetic involved, and drawing the chart requires a good deal of concentration.

Leader

A leader is an individual recognized by others as the person to lead an effort. One cannot be a leader without one or more followers. The term is often used interchangeably with manager. A leader may or may not hold an officially designated management-type position.

Leadership in quality management

Leadership is an essential part of a quality improvement effort. Organization leaders must establish a vision; communicate that vision to those in the organization; and provide the tools, knowledge, and motivation necessary to accomplish the vision.

Leadership grid

A leadership grid is a two-dimensional leadership theory that measures a leader's concern for people and for production.

Leading

Leading is a management function that involves the use of influence to motivate employees to achieve the organization's goals. Leading is a strategy used by a firm to accelerate payments, normally in response to exchange rate expectations; it is the practice of accelerating collections or payments.

Leading practices

Leading practices are successful strategies, actions, and polices that were true, tried, tested, and proven over a time period that resulted in an increase in revenues and profits, reduced costs, and gained a competitive advantage in the marketplace. Leading practices can become best practices when more and more organizations implement and benefit from them.

Leapfrogging

Leapfrogging is taking a big step forward in thinking up idealistic solutions to a problem. For example, leapfrogging can be applied to value-analyzing comparable products to identify their best features and design. These ideas are then combined into a hybrid product that, in turn, can bring new superior products to enter a new market. It is a problem-solving tool.

Learning organization

A learning organization is an organization in which everyone is engaged in identifying and solving problems, which enables the organization to continuously experiment, improve, and increase its capability. It is an organization that has a policy to continue to learn and improve its products, services, processes and outcomes; an organization that is continually expanding its capacity to create its future. The term also refers to an organization that accumulates knowledge through the experiences of its employees. Information systems facilitate learning by organizations.

Legacy practices

Legacy practices are old, inefficient, and ineffective practices found in many departments or functions of an organization due to their age. Legacy practices should be documented in a report to communicate and share their mission failures and lessons learned with other departments and functions so the corporation can possibly avoid repetitions of the same problems and progress to promising, leading, or even best practices.

Legal concepts

Several legal concepts exist as they apply to managers, executives, officers, and boards of directors in any organization. For example, officers and directors need to follow duty of due care, duty of loyalty, and duty of obedience, not duty of absolute care or duty of utmost care. Only reasonable and ordinary care is expected of the officers and the boards of directors because no one can anticipate all problems or protect from all disasters or losses. Officers and boards of directors especially are expected to follow the highest levels of legal concepts due to their fiduciary and governance responsibilities (i.e., duty of loyalty and duty of obedience). Examples of legal concepts follow:

"Due process" means following rules and principles so that an individual is treated fairly and uniformly at all times with basic rights protected. It also means fair and equitable treatment to all concerned parties so that no person is deprived of life, liberty, or property without due process of the law, which is the right to notice and a hearing. Due process means each person is given an equal and fair chance of being represented or heard and that everybody goes through the same process for consideration and approval. It means all people are equal in the eyes of the law. Due law covers due process and due care. Due process requires due care and due diligence.

Two types of due process exist: procedural due process and substantive due process. Procedural due process ensures that a formal proceeding is carried out regularly and in accordance with the established rules and principles. Substantive due process deals with a judicial requirement that enacted laws may not contain provisions that result in the unfair, arbitrary, or unreasonable treatment of an individual. It protects personal property from government interference or possession.

"Due care" means reasonable care in promoting the common good, maintaining the minimal and customary practices, and following the best practices. Due law covers due process and due care. For example, it is the responsibility that managers and their organizations have a duty to provide for information security to ensure that the type of control, the cost of control, and the deployment of control are appropriate for the system being managed. Another related concept of due care is good faith, which means showing "honesty in fact" and "honesty in intent." Both due care and due diligence are similar to the "prudent man" or "reasonable person" concept.

"Due diligence" reviews involve pre-assessment, examination, analysis, and reporting on major activities with due care before they are finalized or approved by management. Its purpose is to minimize potential risks from undertaking new businesses and ventures and analyzing all mergers, acquisitions, and divestitures. Due diligence requires organizations to develop and implement an effective system of controls, policies, and procedures to prevent and detect violation of policies and laws. It requires that the organization has taken minimum and necessary steps in its power and authority to prevent and detect violation of policies and laws. In other words, due diligence is the care that a reasonable person exercises under the circumstances to avoid harm to other persons or to their property. Due diligence is another way of saying due care. Both due care and due diligence are similar to the "prudent man" or "reasonable person" concept. A due diligence defense is available to a defendant in that it makes the defendant not liable if the defendant's actions are reasonable and they are proven.

"Due professional care" calls for the application of the care and skill expected of a reasonably prudent and competent person in the same or similar circumstances. For example, due professional care is exercised when internal audits are performed in accordance with the IIA Standards. The exercise of due professional care requires that: (1) internal auditors be independent of the activities they audit; (2) internal audits be performed by those persons who collectively possess the necessary knowledge, skills, and disciplines to conduct the audit properly; (3) audit work be planned and supervised; (4) audit reports be objective, clear, concise, constructive, and timely; and (5) internal auditors follow up on reported audit findings to ascertain that appropriate action was taken.

"Duty of loyalty" is applicable to the officers and the directors of a corporation not to act adversely to the interests of the corporation and not to subordinate their personal interests to those of the corporation and its shareholders.

"Duty of care" is the legal obligation that each person has to others not to cause any unreasonable harm or risk of harm resulting from careless acts. A breach of the duty of care is negligence. An example is that corporate directors and officers must use due care and due diligence when acting on behalf of a corporation. Duty of reasonable care is the same as the duty of care.

"Duty of obedience" is expected of officers and directors of a corporation to act within the authority conferred upon them by the state corporation statute, the articles of incorporation, the corporate bylaws, and the resolutions adopted by the board of directors.

Legal environment
The legal environment includes rules of competition, packaging laws, patents, trademarks, copyright laws and practices, labor laws, and contract enforcement.

Legitimate power
Legitimate power is power that stems from a formal management position in an organization and the authority granted to it.

Line chart
A line chart is exceptionally impressive when comparing several things but could present a visual problem if the comparisons are too many or too close in relation to one another. Advantages are that line charts are simple to draw. Disadvantages are that if the lines are close to each other, it is difficult to distinguish some of the plotted points.

Locus of control
A locus of control in a person is the tendency to place the primary responsibility for one's success or failure either within oneself (internally) or on outside forces (externally).

Loss leader pricing
Loss leader pricing is legal as it is a retail pricing practice where a primary product is priced at near or below cost to bring more customers into retail stores, whether they are physical or online stores. Retailers hope that when customers come to their stores to buy the primary product, they will also purchase secondary products, such as accessories, derivative products, or complementary products related to the primary product, thus bringing additional sales revenues. Here, primary products are sold at lower prices and secondary products are sold at higher prices because they are connected to make them complete and wholesome. Selling eggs at low prices on or before the Easter Day holiday and selling Turkey birds at low prices on or before the Thanksgiving Day holiday are examples of loss-leader pricing.

Lot size
A lot size is the quantity of goods purchased or produced in anticipation of demand.

Machiavellianism
Machiavellianism is the tendency to direct much of one's behavior toward the acquisition of power and the manipulation of others for personal gain.

Machine productivity

Machine productivity is a partial productivity measure. It is the rate of output of a machine per unit of time compared with an established standard or rate of output. Machine productivity can be expressed as output per unit of time or output per machine-hour.

Machine utilization

Machine utilization is a measure of how intensively a machine is being used. It compares the actual machine time (setup and run time) to available time.

Magnuson Moss Warranty Act

The Magnuson Moss Warranty Act directs the FTC to establish disclosure and designation standards for written warranties, specific standards for full warranties, and establishes consumer remedies for breach of warranty or service contract obligations.

Management science

Management science or operations research provides management an approach that focuses on decision making and reliance on formal mathematical models. It is a decision-making tool.

Manager

A manager is an individual who manages and is responsible for resources (people, material, money, and time); a person officially designated with a management-type position title. A manager is granted authority from above, whereas a leader derives his or her role by virtue of having followers. However, the terms "manager" and "leader" are often used interchangeably.

Managerial grid

A managerial grid is part of a management theory developed by Robert Blake and Jane Mouton that maintains that a manager's management style is based on his or her mindset toward people; it focuses on attitudes rather than behavior. The grid is used to measure concern with production and people.

Manifest

A manifest is an itemization of the items shipped; a copy of the freight bill.

Market entry strategy

A market entry strategy is an organizational strategy for entering a foreign market.

Market grade

If a product is market grade, it is of fair, average quality. The grade is used in applying the implied warranty of merchantability.

Maslow's Hierarchy of Needs

Maslow's Hierarchy of Needs is a classification scheme of needs satisfaction where higher-level needs are dormant until lower-level needs are satisfied.

Matrix approach

The matrix approach is an organization structure that uses functional and divisional chains of command simultaneously in the same part of the organization.

Matrix organization

A matrix organization is an organization in which managers report to both a divisional executive and a functional executive. For instance, the marketing manager of the manufacturing division reports both to the division's president and to the corporate vice president of marketing.

Matrix organization structure

The matrix organization structure is a hybrid of the functional and project organizational structures, in which resources from appropriate functional components of a company are temporarily assigned to particular projects.

Matrix structure

The term "matrix structure" describes an organization that is organized into a combination of functional and product departments. It brings together teams of people to work on projects and is driven by product scope. Matrix structure refers to an organizational structure that uses functional and divisional structures simultaneously. This structure is strongly decentralized: It allows local subsidiaries to develop products that fit into local markets. Yet, at its core, it is very centralized: It allows companies to coordinate activities across the globe and capitalize on synergies and economies of scale.

Metrics

Metrics are measurements that provide a basis for comparison. They provide an accurate baseline against which an individual department's progress can be assessed. Metrics may or may not have warning mechanisms, signals, and alerts. Some companies could combine the metrics with key performance indicators (KPIs) due to their similarity in function and focus.

Miller-Tydings Resale Price Maintenance Act

The Miller-Tydings Resale Price Maintenance Act of 1937 exempts the interstate fair trade contracts from compliance with antitrust requirements.

Morphological analysis

Morphological analysis is a system involving the methodical interrelating of all elements of a problem in order to discover new approaches to a solution. It is a problem-solving tool.

Natural team

A natural team is a work group having responsibility for a particular process.

Needs

The term "needs" refers to unsatisfactory conditions of the consumer that prompt him or her to an action that will make the condition better.

Negotiation

Negotiation is a process of formal communication, either face to face or electronic, where two or more people come together to seek mutual agreement about an issue or issues.

Nominal data

Nominal data arises when numbers or other symbols are used to describe an item, category, or attribute.

Nominal group technique

The nominal group technique is an idea-generating, consensus-building tool for problem solving. No real group exists; it is a group in name only. A strength of this technique is that it permits a problem to become focused in a short period of time.

Nominal variable

A nominal variable is a quantitative variable the attributes of which have no inherent order.

Norming

Norming is the stage of team development in which conflicts developed during the storming stage are resolved and team harmony and unity emerge.

Norms

Norms are behavioral expectations, mutually agreed-on rules of conduct, protocols to be followed, and social practice.

An open-end order is an order specifying all terms except quantity; it is similar to a blanket order.

Operational goals
Operational goals are specific, measurable results expected from departments, work groups, and individuals within the organization.

Operational managers
Operational managers are individuals who are in charge of small groups of workers.

Operational plans
Operational plans are plans developed at the organization's lower levels that specify action steps toward achieving operational goals and that support tactical planning activities.

Operational risk
Operational risk is a risk related to the organization's internal systems, products, services, processes, technology, and people.

Operations
Operations is the collection of people, technology, and systems within a company that has primary responsibility for providing the organization's products or services. Operations used with "objectives" or "controls," has to do with the effectiveness and efficiency of an entity's operations, including performance and profitability goals and safeguarding resources.

Operations research
Operations research is a management science discipline attempting to find optimal solutions to business problems using mathematical techniques, such as simulation, linear programming, statistics, and computers. It is a problem-solving tool.

Operations strategy
Operations strategy is the recognition of the importance of operations to the firm's success and the involvement of operations managers in the organization's strategic planning.

Ordinal data
Ordinal data consists of data elements that can be rank-ordered on the basis of some relationship between them, such as strength.

Ordinal variable
An ordinal variable is a quantitative variable the attributes of which are ordered but for which the numerical difference between adjacent attributes is not necessarily interpreted as equal.

Organic organization
An organic organization allows employees considerable discretion in defining their roles and the organization's objectives. Historically, small organizations have tended to adopt the organic form.

Organization
An organization is a social entity that is goal directed and deliberately structured.

Organizational behavior
Organizational behavior is an interdisciplinary field dedicated to the study of how individuals and groups tend to act in organizations.

Organizational change
Organizational change refers to the adoption of a new idea or behavior by an organization.

Organizational control
Organizational control is the systematic process through which managers regulate organizational activities to make them consistent with expectations established in plans, targets, and standards of performance.

Organizational culture

Organizational culture is the pattern of basic assumptions that a given group has invented, discovered, or developed in learning to cope with its problems of external adaptation and internal integration; having worked well enough to be considered valid, the pattern may be taught to new members as the correct way to perceive, think, and feel in relation to those problems. "Organizational culture" is an umbrella term referring to the general tone of a corporate environment.

Organizational development

Organizational development is the application of behavioral science techniques to improve an organization's health and effectiveness through its ability to cope with environmental changes, improve internal relationships, and increase problem-solving capabilities. It is an organization-wide (usually) planned effort, managed from the top, to increase organization effectiveness and health through interventions in the organization's processes, using behavioral science knowledge.

Organization structure

Organization structure is the framework in which the organization defines how tasks are divided, resources are deployed, and departments are coordinated.

Outlier

An outlier is an extremely large or small observation; it applies to ordinal, interval, and ratio variables.

P > O expectancy

P > O expectancy is the expectancy that successful performance (P) of a task will lead to the desired outcome (O).

Panel consensus technique

The panel consensus technique is a way to process a large number of ideas, circumventing organizational restraints to idea creation, using extensive participation and emphasizing methods for selecting good ideas. It is a problem-solving tool.

Parent company

A parent company is the company owning a majority of the voting stock of another corporation.

Parent/subsidiary relationship

A parent/subsidiary relationship is a combination of companies where control of other companies, known as subsidiaries, is achieved by a company, known as the parent, through acquisition of voting stock.

Pareto chart

A Pareto chart can be drawn to separate the "vital few" from the "trivial many." It is based on the 80/20 rule: 20% of items contribute to 80% of problems. It is a problem-solving tool.

Pareto's law

Pareto's law, or the 80/20 rule, applies to many things in business and life, such as:

- 80% of problems in a factory, retail store, or office operation come from 20% of activities, tasks, areas, things, people, machines, or items. In other words, 80% of effects come from 20% of causes.

- 80% of an organization's problems are caused by management and 20% of problems are caused by employees.

- 80% of sales or profits for a company come from 20% of its customers.

- 80% of retail sales comes from 20 % of merchandise items.

- 80% of merchandise value and use comes from 20% of merchandise A items, and 80% of merchandise B and C items account for 20% of merchandise value and use.

- 80% of a manufacturer's or retailer's production materials come from 20% of suppliers.

- 80% of a new retail store's potential customers are located in the primary trading geographic area and 20% of its customers are located in the secondary trading geographic area.

- 80% of retail sales worldwide come from national (manufacturer) brands and 20% of retail sales worldwide come from private (store) brands.

- 80% of nonsignificant items and 20% of significant items exist in anything (known as the vital few and trivial many theory).

- 80% of the world's wealth is owned by 20% of the people.

Note that Pareto's law is also known as Pareto's principle, Pareto's chart, 80/20 rule, or 20/80 rule.

Participative management
Participative management is a management style that expects everyone in the organization to take ownership and responsibility for their conduct and duties; this allows input into decisions.

Partnership/alliance
A partnership/alliance is a strategy leading to a relationship with suppliers or customers aimed at reducing costs of ownership, maintenance of minimum stocks, just-in-time deliveries, joint participation in design, exchange of information on materials and technologies, new production methods, quality improvement strategies, and the exploitation of market synergy.

Passive investment strategy
A passive investment strategy involves a minimal amount of oversight and very few transactions once the portfolio has been selected.

Patent
A patent protects an invention by giving the inventor the right to exclude others from making, using, or selling a new, useful, nonobvious invention during a specific patent term.

Path-goal theory
Path-goal theory is a contingency approach to leadership specifying that the leader's responsibility is to increase subordinates' motivation by clarifying the behaviors necessary for task accomplishment and rewards.

Pay compression
Pay compression is a situation in which pay differences among individuals with different levels of experience and performance in the organization becomes small.

Pay equity
Pay equity is the similarity in pay for all jobs requiring comparable levels of knowledge, skill, and ability, even if actual duties and market rates differ significantly.

Pay for performance
Pay for performance refers to incentive pay that ties at least part of compensation to employee effort and performance.

Payoff table
A payoff table is a tabular representation of the payoffs for a decision problem. It shows losses and gains for each outcome of the decision alternatives. It is a decision-making tool.

Performance

Performance is the organization's ability to attain its goals by using resources in an efficient and effective manner. Performance is what an employee does or does not do in his or her job.

Performance appraisal

A performance appraisal is the process of evaluating how well employees perform their jobs when compared to a set of standards and then communicating that information to employees.

Performance-based pay

Performance-based pay is pay related to and directly derived from performance.

Performance consulting

Performance consulting is a process in which a trainer and the organizational client work together to boost workplace performance in support of business goals.

Performance gap

A performance gap is a disparity between existing and desired performance levels.

Performance management system

A performance management system is a system that supports and contributes to the creation of high-performance work and work systems by translating behavioral principles into procedures. It is a system where processes are used to identify, encourage, measure, evaluate, improve, and reward employee performance.

Performance measurement

Performance measurement is the process of developing measurable indicators that can be systematically tracked to assess progress made in achieving predetermined goals and using such indicators to assess progress in achieving these goals.

Performance plan

A performance plan is a performance management tool that describes desired performance and provides a way to assess the performance objectively.

Performance report

A performance report is a routine report that compares actual performance against budgetary goals.

Performance shares

Performance shares are used in incentive plans in which managers are awarded shares of stock on the basis of the firm's performance with respect to earnings per share or other measures.

Performance standards

Performance standards are expected levels of performance.

Performance test

A performance test is an assessment device that requires candidates to complete an actual work task in a controlled situation.

Performing

Performing is the stage of team development in which members focus on problem solving and accomplishing the team's assigned task.

Periodic review system

A periodic review system is a fixed-order interval inventory control system in which an item's inventory position is reviewed on a scheduled periodic basis.

Perpetual inventory system

A perpetual inventory system maintains information about both receipts and withdrawals for each item in the inventory. The system shows the current balance on hand, which can be reconciled to the actual physical inventory on the floor.

Pie chart

A pie chart is used to represent a 100% total of two or more items.

Pivot table

A pivot table is a second, revised table in rows and columns containing reformatted data using the raw data from the first, original table in rows and columns. A pivot table is also called a pivot chart.

> First Table ⟶ Original Table
>
> Second Table ⟶ Pivot Table

The basic data values are the same between the original table and the pivot table. However, the pivot table contains sorted, rearranged, and summarized data, providing better insights.

For example, a retail marketing manager can create a pivot table showing which salesperson has the highest sales dollars in a given month or quarter from original sales data tables.

Plan-Do-Check-Adjust cycle

The Plan-Do-Check-Adjust (PDCA) cycle is related to continuous improvement, where an improvement plan is developed (Plan), implemented (Do), monitored and evaluated (Check), and modified or refined (Adjust). Deming's PDCA cycle is a core management tool for problem solving and quality improvement, which can be used for planning and implementing quality improvements.

PM theory of leadership

The PM theory of leadership is a Japanese theory; the "P" stands for showing a concern for subordinates and leadership that is oriented toward forming and reaching group goals; the "M" stands for leadership that is oriented toward preserving group stability.

Poka-yoke

Poka-yoke is an approach for mistake-proofing a production or service process using automatic devices (failsafe methods) to avoid simple human or machine errors in order to improve quality. It is based on two aspects: prediction and detection of a defect or error. It is a simple, creative, and inexpensive method to implement and in part achieves zero defects, as suggested by Crosby.

Portfolio strategy

Portfolio strategy is a type of corporate-level strategy that pertains to the organization's mix of strategic business units and product lines that fit together in such a way as to provide the corporation with synergy and competitive advantage.

Power

Power refers to the potential ability to influence others' behavior.

Predatory pricing

Predatory pricing is a controversial and confusing topic in pricing where retailers charge lower prices to customers to drive competitors out of the marketplace. The U.S. Supreme Court has been skeptical about claims by the Federal Trade Commission (FTC) of predatory pricing practices, stating that they are illegal and unsustainable and that they destroy healthy competition. However, the Supreme Court did not agree with the FTC, stating that these pricing practices are temporary and unsustainable, and hence legal. Reduced prices for items in a clearance sale are legal and are not a predatory pricing practice.

Predictive analytics

Predictive analytics describes what could happen.

Prescriptive analytics

Prescriptive analytics helps decide what should happen.

Price discounts

Price discounts are heavily and frequently used to attract customers and to turn them into buyers. Price discounts are legal only when they are properly designed, represented, and advertised. Otherwise, they can be illegal.

Price discrimination

Price discrimination can be legal or illegal based on business circumstances. Price discrimination can occur when a seller (retailer) charges customers (buyers) different prices for the same commodity or product. This discrimination also applies to advertising and promotional allowances. Generally, price discriminations are legal, particularly if the price differences reflect the different costs of dealing with different buyers or are the result of a seller's attempts to meet a competitor's offering. If the price discriminations do not reflect these issues, they are illegal. Here, the price differences are justified by different costs incurred to manufacture, sell, or deliver, or the price concessions were given in good faith to meet a competitor's price (i.e., price matching). In the United States, the Robinson-Patman Act handles the price discrimination claims and lawsuits.

Price fixing

Price fixing is illegal in the United States because it restricts competition and the result is often higher prices. Price fixing occurs when competitors agree to raise prices, lower prices, stabilize prices, or change other competitive terms, such as shipping fees. Customers expect that retail prices are established based on supply and demand factors and that retailers set their own prices independently, not based on collusive agreements. The agreement can be written, verbal, or inferred from conduct (i.e., practice or intent). Price fixing relates not only to prices of products but also to other related items that affect the final cost to customers, such as shipping fees, warranties, discount programs, and financing rates. Price fixing is a common and major legal risk in marketing functions.

Prisoner's dilemma

The prisoner's dilemma is a type of business game situation where one firm is concerned about the actions of its rivals. It is a decision-making tool.

Process mapping

Process mapping is flowcharting of a work process in detail, showing key work steps and key measurements.

Process maps

A process map is a visual diagram showing inputs, transformation (conversion), and outputs of a task, activity, or function. It can show delays, duplicates, conflicts, and constraints that waste resources and increase inefficiencies. It can be used to determine whether quality and value are either created or destroyed in a process. Tools such as questionnaires, interviews, focus groups, and flowcharts can be used to understand and improve a process. The goal of any business process is to improve its effectiveness, increase its efficiency, and reduce its resource consumption.

Process owner

A process owner is an individual held accountable and responsible for the workings and improvement of one of the organization's defined processes and its related subprocesses.

Process theories

Process theories explain how employees select behaviors with which to meet their needs and determine whether their choices were successful.

Processed material

A processed material is a tangible product generated by transforming raw material into a desired state. This state can be liquid, gas, particulate, material, ingot, filament, or sheet.

Product

A product is the result of activities or processes.

Product cycle theory

Product cycle theory suggests that a firm initially establish itself locally and expanded into foreign markets in response to foreign demand for its product; over time, the multinational corporation will grow in foreign markets; after some point, its foreign business may decline unless it can differentiate its product from competitors. This theory views products as passing through four stages: introduction, growth, maturity, and decline. During these stages, the location of production moves from industrialized to lower-cost developing nations.

Product differentiation

Product differentiation is the effort to build unique differences or improvements into products.

Product division structure

Each of the enterprise's product divisions is responsible for the sale and profits of its product.

Productive capacity

Productive capacity is the maximum of the output capabilities of a resource or the market demand for that output for a given time period.

Productivity

Productivity is the organization's output of goods and services divided by its inputs. This means productivity can be improved by either increasing the amount of output using the same level of inputs or reducing the number of inputs required to produce the output. Number of dollars spent does not measure productivity, but number of goods produced per hour does.

Product life cycle

A product life cycle is a cycle of stages that a product goes through from birth to death: introduction, growth, maturity, and decline.

Product organization

In a product organization, each department focuses on a specific product type or family.

Product/service strategy

Managers are typically concerned with what the product or service should look like and what it should be able to do. In foreign markets, they must determine whether their product or service can be sold in standard form or be customized to fit differing foreign market needs.

Promising practices

When properly managed, promising practices can turn into either best practices or leading practices because they have been proven to be successful and effective. In order to achieve that goal, promising practices must be defined in terms of the context that led to their success; the challenges faced must be explained; problems and solutions applied must be indicated; and the results obtained must be documented.

Prospective pricing

Prospective pricing is a pricing decision made in advance of performance, based on an analysis of comparative prices, cost estimates, past costs, or combinations of such considerations.

Protective capacity

Protective capacity is the amount of extra capacity at non-constraints above the system constraint's capacity, used to protect against statistical fluctuations (e.g., equipment breakdowns, quality problems, late deliveries).

Psychodramatic approach

The psychodramatic approach is a problem-solving tool that involves role-playing and role-reversal behavior. In psychodrama, the attempt is made to bring into focus all elements of an individual's problem; here, as in sociodrama, the emphasis is on shared problems of group members.

Quality assurance

Quality assurance focuses on the inputs to a process or product, rather than the traditional controlling mode of inspecting and checking products at the end of operations, *after* errors have been made (i.e., quality control).

Quality audit

A quality audit is a systematic, independent examination and review to determine whether quality activities and related results comply with planned arrangements and whether these arrangements are implemented effectively and are suitable to achieve the objectives. Quality planning, quality assurance, and quality engineering focus on the front-end of a process, whereas quality control and quality audit focus on the back-end of a process.

Quality circles

Quality circles refer to a team of employees (6 to 12) voluntarily getting together periodically to discuss quality-related problems and issues and to devise strategies and plans to take corrective actions. Quality circles should be introduced in an evolutionary manner, so employees feel that they can tap their creative potential. Quality circles are a part of employee empowerment. Ishikawa is known as the "Father of Quality Circles."

Quality control

Quality control is an evaluation to indicate needed corrective action, the act of guiding, or the state of a process in which the variability is attributable to a constant system of chance causes. It compares and acts on the difference between actual performance and target performance (goal). Quality control includes the operational techniques and activities used to fulfill requirements for quality. Often, quality assurance and quality control are used interchangeably, referring to the actions performed to ensure the quality of a product, service, or process, but they are different in meaning in terms of timing.

Quality council

Quality council is a prerequisite of implementing a total quality management (TQM) program in an organization. The quality council is similar to an executive steering committee.

Quality engineering

Quality engineering focuses on combining product design engineering methods and statistical concepts to reduce costs and improve quality by optimizing product design and manufacturing processes. For example, Taguchi's quality loss function (QLF) is connected with quality engineering.

Quality function deployment

Quality function deployment (QFD) is a structured method in which customer requirements are translated into appropriate technical requirements for each stage of product development and manufacturing. Input for the QFD process comes from listening to the voice of the customer (VOC).

Quality improvement

Quality improvement is an ongoing activity where problems are diagnosed, root causes are identified, solutions are developed, and controls are established to improve quality.

Quality planning

Quality planning focuses on developing products, services, systems, processes, policies, and procedures needed to meet or exceed customer expectations. Quality planning is a part of the Japanese Hoshin planning method where it involves consensus at all levels as plans are cascaded throughout the organization, resulting in actionable plans and continual monitoring and measurement.

Radar chart

The radar chart is a visual method to show in graphic form the size of gaps in a number of areas, such as current performance versus ideal (expected) performance and current budget versus previous budget.

Rated capacity

Rated capacity is the expected output capability of a resource or system. It is equal to hours available times efficiency times utilization. It is synonymous with calculated capacity, standing capacity, and nominal capacity. In the theory of constraints, rated capacity is hours available times efficiency times activation, where activation is a function of scheduled production and availability is a function of uptime.

Ratio data

Ratio data are the highest level of data measurements and the strongest data measurement technique.

Ratio variable

A ratio variable is a quantitative variable the attributes of which are ordered, spaced equally, and have a true zero point.

Reality check

The reality check decision is tested in pseudo-real-world conditions. A T-column is used with headings "Our expectations" and "Our concerns" to facilitate the analysis. It is a decision-making tool.

Reasoning skills

Reasoning skills are based on logical thinking or logical reasoning. They are comprised of deductive, inductive, and abductive (inference) reasoning.

Recidivism

Recidivism is a tendency to relapse into a previous condition or repeat a mode of behavior.

Referent power

Referent power is power that results from characteristics that command subordinates' identification with, respect and admiration for, and desire to emulate the leader.

Refreezing

Refreezing is the reinforcement stage of organizational development in which individuals acquire a desired new skill or attitude and are rewarded for it by the organization.

Reorder point

A reorder point is a predetermined inventory level that triggers an order. This level provides inventory to meet anticipated demand during the time it takes to receive the order.

Reorder point system

A reorder point system is a continuous-review inventory control system in which an order is placed whenever a withdrawal brings the inventory position to a predetermined reorder point level.

Responsibility assignment matrix

A responsibility assignment matrix, or RACI diagram, deals with four items: responsible (R), accountable (A), consulted (C), and informed (I). Typically, a task is associated with one or more roles using the RACI diagram. Simply stated, the RACI diagram connects people to their assigned jobs, duties, tasks, activities, or projects so they can complete them.

This diagram describes and clarifies participation by several individuals assuming various roles in completing the assigned tasks or deliverables required in a project, process, or facility. It can be applied either in one business function or department or across several functions or departments.

Retroactive pricing

Retroactive pricing is a pricing decision made after some or all of the work specified under contract has been completed, based on a review of performance and recorded cost data.

Reverse marketing or reverse purchasing

In reverse marketing or reverse purchasing, a buyer takes the initiative in making the sourcing proposal to several suppliers in order to find a new supplier. It is a reversal of the traditional buyer/supplier marketing practice where a buyer goes to an existing supplier.

Reward power

Reward power is power that results from the authority to bestow rewards on others.

Robinson-Patman Act

The Robinson-Patman Act of 1936 further addresses the issue of price discrimination established in the Clayton Act. It prohibits sellers from offering a discriminatory price where the effect of discrimination may limit competition or create a monopoly. There is also a provision that prohibits purchasers from inducing a discriminatory price. While a seller may legally lower price as a concession during negotiations, the purchaser should not mislead or trick the seller, thus resulting in a price that is discriminatory to other buyers in the market.

Root cause

A root cause is a fundamental deficiency that results in a nonconformance, which must be corrected to prevent recurrence.

Root cause analysis

Root cause analysis is a technique used to identify the conditions that initiate the occurrence of an undesired activity or state.

Safety capacity

Safety capacity is the planned amount by which the available capacity exceeds current productive capacity. This capacity provides protection from planned activities, such as resource contention, preventive maintenance, and rework.

Safety capacity + Excess capacity = 100% of capacity

Scatter diagram

A scatter diagram is used to determine whether a relationship exists between the dependent variable (vertical, y-axis) and an independent variable (horizontal, x-axis) shown in a graph.

Scenario analysis

Scenario analysis is a risk analysis technique in which "bad" and "good" sets of financial circumstances are compared with a most likely, or base case, situation.

Scenario building

Scenario building involves the identification of crucial variables and determining their effects on different cases or approaches.

Scenario planning

Scenario planning is a strategic planning process that generates multiple stories about possible future conditions, allowing an organization to look at the potential impact on them and different ways the company could respond.

Scenario writing

Scenario writing is a qualitative forecasting method that consists of developing a conceptual scenario of the future based on a well-defined set of assumptions.

Self-managed team

A self-managed team is a team that requires little supervision and manages itself and the day-to-day work it does; such teams are responsible for whole work processes with each individual performing multiple tasks.

Sensitivity analysis

Sensitivity analysis refers to the study of how changes in the probability assessments for the states of nature and/or changes in the payoffs affect the recommended decision alternative. It involves using a model to determine the extent to which a change in a factor affects an outcome (what-if analysis). The analysis is done by repeating if-then calculations. Sensitivity analysis is a means of incorporating risk in financial outcomes that involves varying key inputs, one at a time, and observing the effect on the decision variable(s). For example, the analyst might vary the sales level and observe the effect on the company's cash forecast.

Sequential engineering

Sequential engineering (traditional engineering or over-the-wall engineering) is an approach to the product development process, where each stage is carried out separately and where the next stage cannot start until the previous stage is completed. The entire process takes time and costs money because the communication and coordination flows are only in one direction and all changes and corrections are relayed back to the beginning of the process or previous stages. The time-to-market for a new product is long, expensive, and inefficient with sequential engineering. The concurrent engineering approach is an improvement over the sequential engineering approach, as the former approach improves timing, communication, and coordination problems often encountered in the latter approach.

Servant leader

A servant leader is a leader who works to fulfill subordinates' needs and goals as well as to achieve the organization's larger mission.

Service

Service is a result generated by activities and the interface between the supplier and the customer and by supplier internal activities to meet customer needs. An organization can have both internal and external suppliers and customers.

Service-level agreements

Service-level agreements (SLAs) between service providers and receivers should, as a minimum, specify these points:

- Explicit definitions of both the user organization's roles and responsibilities and the service provider's roles and responsibilities.

- Period of performance and/or deliverables due dates.

- Defined service levels and their costs.

- Defined processes regarding how the managers will assess the service provider's compliance with the service level and due date targets, rules, laws, regulations, and performance levels.

- Specific remedies (e.g., financial, technical, and legal) for noncompliance or harm caused by the service provider.

- Explicit rules and processes for handling sensitive data to ensure privacy.

Services

Services, as defined in the Trade and Tariff Act of 1984, consist of economic activities whose outputs are other than tangible goods, including businesses such as accounting, advertising, banking, engineering, insurance, management consulting, retail, tourism, transportation, and wholesale trade.

Situation analysis

Situation analysis is an analysis of the strengths, weaknesses, opportunities, and threats (SWOT) that affect organizational performance.

Situational ethics

Situational ethics is a societal condition where "right" and "wrong" are determined by the specific situation rather than by universal moral principles.

Situational leadership

Situational leadership is a leadership theory that maintains that the leadership style should change based on the person and the situation, with the leader displaying varying degrees of directive and supportive behavior.

Situational theory

Situational theory is a contingency approach to leadership that links the leader's behavioral style with the task readiness of subordinates.

Soft controls

Controls can be classified into two categories: hard controls and soft controls. Soft controls are informal, intangible, subjective, and much harder to measure and evaluate than hard controls. Examples of soft controls include an organization's ethical climate, integrity, values, culture, vision, people's behaviors and attitudes, commitment to competence, tone at the top, management philosophy, management's operating style, level of understanding and commitment, and communication. Tools to evaluate soft controls include self-assessments, questionnaires, interviews, workshops, and role playing. Higher-level managers and executives need more depth in soft skills and soft controls and less depth in hard skills and hard controls. Lower-level managers and executives need more depth in hard skills and hard controls and less depth in soft skills and soft controls.

Soft skills

An individual's skills can be divided into two types: hard skills and soft skills. Soft skills are mostly qualitative in nature and include people (interpersonal); motivational; leadership; communications; presentation; coordination; project management; implementation; time management; creative; and critical thinking skills. Higher-level managers and executives need more depth in soft skills and soft controls and less depth in hard skills and hard controls. Lower-level managers and executives need more depth in hard skills and hard controls and less depth in soft skills and soft controls.

Spaghetti plot
A spaghetti plot (chart, diagram, or map) is a workflow system to visualize data flows through a system where flows appear as noodles. This plot is used to (1) track product routing and material movement through a factory; (2) reduce inefficiencies in an office, factory, or warehouse workflow system; and (3) show the effects of medical drugs on test patients during a new drug trial; among others. The results of a spaghetti plot can be useful in streamlining or simplifying workflow to save resources, such as time, money, materials, and energy.

Special-purpose team
A special-purpose team is an organizational team formed to address specific problems, improve work processes, and enhance product and service quality.

Specification
A specification is a requirement with which a product or service must conform.

Speculative buying
The term "speculative buying" refers to purchasing material in excess of current and future known requirements, with the intention of profiting on price movement.

Spend analysis
Spend analysis is a strategic approach to analyzing spending amounts and profiles in both private and public sector organizations. It is a process of analyzing an organization's spending levels (purchasing level) to develop a better picture of what and how much it is spending to make and sell goods or services. Spend analysis is a very useful technique during procurement of materials and services for the organization because huge amounts of money are spent acquiring materials and labor to make goods and provide services to customers.

Stages of team growth
The term "stages of team growth" refers to four development stages through which groups typically progress: forming, storming, norming, and performing. Knowledge of the stages helps team members accept the normal problems that occur on the path from forming a group to becoming a team.

Stakeholder audit
A stakeholder audit is a systematic attempt to identify and measure issues of an organization's stakeholders and measure and evaluate their opinions with respect to their effective resolution.

Stakeholder empowerment
Stakeholder empowerment means involving employees in every step of a production or service process to solicit their input. It is based on the idea that employees who are close to the action would better know the shortcomings of a system, machine, or process than those who are not. Quality circles are part of employee empowerment. Similarly, inviting suppliers and customers to participate in a product or service design to improve quality and features is also a part of stakeholder empowerment.

Stakeholder environment
A stakeholder environment is composed of trends, events, issues, expectations, and forecasts that may have a bearing on the strategic management process and the development of corporate public policy.

Stakeholders
Stakeholders are individuals or entities that have an interest in the well-being of a firm—stockholders, creditors, employees, customers, suppliers, and so forth.

Static gains

Static gains stem from the increased efficiency of resource allocation and improved consumption possibilities. Additional gains from trade may result from increasing returns to scale and from increased product and input variety for consumers and producers. Static gains imply a change in the amount of aggregate output but not its growth rate. In empirical studies of trade liberalization, static gains from trade are relatively small as a percentage of gross domestic product.

Stevens' power law

Stevens' power law states that four types of scales can be used to define how things or data can be measured, arranged, or counted: nominal, ordinal, interval, and ratio scales. These scales are used in big data analytics, as data counting methods.

Stockholders

Stockholders and shareholders are owners of a corporation.

Stockless purchasing

Stockless purchasing is an arrangement where a supplier holds inventory until the buyer places orders for specific items. Examples include blanket orders, open-end orders, and system contracts.

Storming

Storming is the stage of team development in which individual personalities and roles, and resulting conflicts, emerge.

Storyboard

A storyboard is a group problem-solving technique to create a picture of relevant information. A storyboard can be created for each group that is making decisions.

Storyboarding

Storyboarding is a technique that visually displays thoughts and ideas and groups them into categories, making all aspects of a process visible at once. Often it is used to communicate to others the activities performed by a team as they improve a process. A positive outcome of storyboarding is that it takes less time than interviewing, and many employees can get involved in problem solving, not just managers.

Strategic activities

Strategic activities are those activities that support the long-term objectives of an organization. Examples include strategic planning and strategic sourcing.

Strategic advantage

Strategic advantage is a position in which one dominates a market; also called competitive advantage.

Strategic alliance

A strategic alliance is a firm's collaboration with companies in other countries to share rights and responsibilities as well as revenues and expenses as defined in a written agreement. Some common types of strategic alliances are research collaboration, licensing programs, and copromotion deals. A strategic alliance is formed when two or more companies band together to attain efficiency. *See* Joint venture.

Strategic business unit

A strategic business unit (SBU) is a division of the organization that has a unique business mission, product line, competitors, and markets relative to other SBUs in the same corporation.

Strategic fit review
A strategic fit review is a process by which senior managers assess the future of each project of an organization in terms of its ability to advance the mission and goals of that organization.

Strategic goals
Strategic goals are broad statements of where the organization wants to be in the future; they pertain to the organization as a whole rather than to specific divisions or departments.

Strategic human resource management
Strategic human resource management is the organizational use of employees to gain or keep a competitive advantage against competitors.

Strategic information system
A strategic information system is any information system that gives its owner a competitive advantage.

Strategic leader
A strategic leader is a highly competent firm located in a strategically critical market.

Strategic management
Strategic management is the set of decisions and actions used to formulate and implement strategies that will provide a competitively superior fit between the organization and its environment so as to achieve organizational goals.

Strategic manager
A strategic manager is a person who makes decisions that affect an entire organization, or large parts of it, and leaves an impact in the long run.

Strategic marketing concept
A strategic marketing concept states the company's mission to identify, generate, and sustain competitive advantage through superior positioning and vision.

Strategic objectives
Guided by the enterprise's mission or purpose, strategic objectives associate the enterprise with its external environment and provide management with a basis for comparing performance with that of its competitors, in relation to environmental demands.

Strategic plan
A strategic plan is a plan that integrates an organization's major goals, policies, and action sequences into a cohesive whole. It is the action steps by which an organization intends to attain its strategic goals.

Strategic planning
Strategic planning is a process to set an organization's long-range goals and identify the actions needed to reach the goals.

Strategic risk
Strategic risk is a high-level and corporate-wide risk, which includes strategy, political, economic, regulatory, reputation, global, leadership, customer, and market brand management risk. It is also related to failure of strategy and changing customer needs and business conditions.

Strategy
A strategy is the plan of action that prescribes resource allocation and other activities for dealing with the environment and helping the organization attain its goals.

Strategy formulation

Strategy formulation is the stage of strategic management that involves the planning and decision making that lead to the establishment of the organization's goals and of a specific strategic plan.

Strategy implementation

Strategy implementation is the stage of strategic management that involves the use of managerial and organizational tools to direct resources toward achieving strategic outcomes.

Strategy map

A strategy map is a visual diagram showing an organization's grand strategy divided into strengths, weaknesses, threats, and opportunities (SWOT). It shows how strategic goals are derived from the grand strategy and how to define performance management outcomes from the established goals. Strategy maps are used in designing a company's balanced scorecard system in order to develop and communicate a company's strategy to insiders and outsiders.

Stretch goal

A stretch goal is one that requires a significant change in the performance (quality, quantity, time, cost) of a process. It forces an organization to think in a radically different way for major and incremental improvements.

Subcontracting arrangements

Subcontracting arrangements are often a part of a bid-rigging scheme where competitors who agree not to bid or to submit a losing bid frequently receive subcontracts or supply contracts in exchange from the successful low bidder. In some schemes, a low bidder will agree to withdraw its bid in favor of the next low bidder, in exchange for a lucrative sub-contract that divides the illegally obtained higher profits between them.

Success-failure analysis

Success-failure analysis is a qualitative approach to brainstorming conditions for both success and failure. A T-column can be used with headings "What will guarantee success" and "What will guarantee failure." It is a decision-making tool.

Supplier partnership

A supplier partnership is a business relationship between a supplying firm and a buying firm for mutual benefit of both parties. It requires a commitment, trust, and a common direction for the future. It is not a legal partnership but a strategic alliance.

Supply chain

A supply chain is a series of firms providing value-added activities from raw materials to finished goods purchased by a final customer. From an information technology viewpoint, it is a system of organizations, people, activities, information, and resources involved in moving a product or service from supplier/producer to consumer/customer. It involves several layers of suppliers. The scope can be domestic or international in nature, and it uses a defense-in-breadth strategy. It can be risky because several suppliers are involved.

Sustainable competitive advantage

A sustainable competitive advantage is a competitive edge that cannot be easily or quickly copied by competitors in the short run.

Sustainable growth

Sustainable growth is the rate of sales growth that is compatible with a firm's established financial policies including asset turnover, net profit margin, dividend payout, and debt to equity ratio. It assumes that new equity is derived only through retained earnings, not new common stock.

SWOT analysis

SWOT analysis is a self-assessment of a company's core capabilities and key strengths, weaknesses, opportunities, and threats (SWOT). It considers factors such as the organization's industry, the competitive position, functional areas, and management talent. SWOT analysis is useful in developing an organization's strategy and is the same as situation analysis or situation audit. The goal is to turn weaknesses into strengths, turn threats into opportunities, and turn opportunities into strengths through strategic planning and implementation processes, and game-changing plans. The company should conduct the same SWOT analysis on its major competitors to capitalize on the competitors' gaps found in unaddressed weaknesses, opportunities, threats, issues, and areas. Fit-gap analysis helps in a better understanding of the SWOT analysis.

Turn Weaknesses $\longrightarrow$ Strengths

Turn Threats $\longrightarrow$ Opportunities

Turn Opportunities $\longrightarrow$ Strengths

Synectics

Synectics is a technique for creating an environment that encourages creative approaches to problem solving. It is a problem-solving tool.

System of internal controls

A system of internal controls consists of both internal controls and information systems. Internal control is the systems, policies, procedures, and processes, effected by the board of directors and senior management, designed to safeguard assets, limit/control risks, and achieve goals and objectives. These objectives address effectiveness and efficiency of operations, reliability of financial reporting, and compliance with applicable laws and regulations. The system of internal controls varies with the size, scope, nature, and complexity of organizations, meaning small organizations may have an informal (loose) system of internal controls whereas large organizations may have a formal (tight) system of internal controls.

Systems analysis

Systems analysis breaks down a large problem into many smaller problems. It is an excellent technique if the desired outcome of the problem-solving session is a detailed understanding of a problem. It is a problem-solving tool.

Systems contract

A systems contract is a contract generated by the purchasing department that authorizes designated employees of the buying firm to place orders directly with the supplier. A release system is developed for specific materials during a given contract period.

Tabular chart

The tabular chart is used to represent items of interest. It requires a fair amount of study in order to grasp the full meaning of the figures. This is because it takes longer to digest the meaning of an itemization of compiled figures than if the same figures are presented graphically.

Tactical goals

Tactical goals are goals that define the outcomes that major divisions and departments must achieve in order for the organization to reach its overall goals.

Tactical managers

Tactical managers are individuals who receive general directions and goals from their superiors and, within those guidelines, make decisions for their subordinates; also called middle managers.

Tactical objectives

Tactical objectives are objectives that, guided by the enterprise's strategic objectives, identify the key result areas in which specific performance is essential for the success of the enterprise and aim to attain internal efficiency.

Tactical plans

Tactical plans are short-term plans, usually of one- to two-year duration, that describe actions the organization will take to meet its strategic business plan.

Tactics

Tactics are strategies and processes that help an organization meet its objectives.

Tall structure

A tall structure is a management structure characterized by an overall narrow span of management and a relatively large number of hierarchical levels.

T-analysis

T-analysis is a tabular presentation of strengths on one side and weaknesses on the other side of the letter "T." The goal is to address the weaknesses (problems). It is a problem-solving tool.

Target marketing

Target marketing involves promoting products and services to the people who are most likely to purchase them.

Target markets

Target markets are market segments whose needs and demands a company seeks to serve and satisfy.

Target pricing

In target pricing, a buying organization estimates the highest price it could pay to a supplier and still sell its product competitively in the marketplace. Further negotiations between the two parties can bring down costs and prices.

Task force

A task force is a temporary team or committee formed to solve a specific short-term problem involving several departments.

Task identity

Task identity is the extent to which the job includes a "whole" identifiable unit of work that is carried out from start to finish and that results in a visible outcome.

Task significance

Task significance is the impact the job has on other people.

Task specialist role

A task specialist role is a role in which an individual devotes personal time and energy to helping the team accomplish its task.

Team

A team is a set of two or more people who are equally accountable for the accomplishment of a purpose and specific performance goals; it is also defined as a small number of people with complementary skills who are committed to a common purpose. Many organizations manage themselves through empowered self-managed teams.

Team-based structure

A team-based structure is: (1) an organizational structure in which team members are organized around performing a specific function of the business, such as handling customer complaints or assembling an engine; (2) a structure in which the entire organization is made up of teams that coordinate their work and work directly with customers to accomplish the organization's goals.

Team building

Team building is a process that enhances the cohesiveness of a department or group by helping members learn how to organize their work and assume responsibility for it. Team building is a type of organizational development intervention that enhances the cohesiveness of departments by helping members learn to function as a team.

Team building/development

Team building/development is a process of transforming a group of people into a team and developing the team to achieve its purpose.

Team cohesiveness

Team cohesiveness is the extent to which team members are attracted to the team and motivated to remain in it.

Team dynamics

The term "team dynamics" refers to the interactions that occur among team members under different conditions.

Team facilitation

Team facilitation deals with both the role of the facilitator on the team and the techniques and tools for facilitating the team.

Team interview

A team interview is an interview in which the team members with whom they will work interview applicants.

Team performance evaluation, rewards, and recognition

Special metrics are needed to evaluate the work of a team (to avoid focus on any individual on the team) and as a basis for rewards and recognition for team achievements.

Theoretical capacity

Theoretical capacity is the maximum output capability, allowing no adjustments for preventive maintenance, machine downtime, and plant shutdown.

Theory of constraints

The theory of constraints is a management philosophy applied to manufacturing operations that can be viewed as three separate but interrelated areas: logistics, performance measurement, and logical thinking. Logistics include drum-buffer-rope schedule, buffer management, and logical product structure. Performance measurement includes throughput, inventory, and operating expenses. Logical thinking tools are important in identifying the root problem (current reality tree), identifying and expanding win-win solutions, and developing implementation plans.

Throughput

Throughput can be defined in a number of ways: (1) Machine throughput is the central processing unit run time divided by elapsed time. (2) Job throughput is the actual number of jobs processed during a specific period by the elapsed time. (3) Throughput is the total volume of production through a facility (machine, work center, department, plant, or network of plants). (4) In the theory of constraints, it is the rate at which the system (firm) generates money through sales. Throughput is a separate concept from output.

Throughput time

Throughput time is the total time required in processing a queue from concept to launch, from order received to delivery, or from raw materials received to delivery to customer.

Time-based competition

Time-based competition is a competitive strategy based on the ability to deliver products and services faster than competitors.

Top-down approach

A top-down approach is an approach that starts with the highest-level component of a hierarchy and proceeds through progressively lower levels.

Total factor productivity

The total factor productivity is a measure of the productivity of a department, plant, strategic business unit, or firm that combines the individual productivities of all its resources including labor, capital, energy, material, and equipment. For example, if material accounts for 50% of the cost of sales, labor 15% of the cost of sales, equipment 20% of the cost of sales, capital 10% of the cost of sales, and energy 5% of the cost of sales:

Total factor productivity = 0.50 (Material productivity) + 0.15 (Labor productivity) + 0.20 (Equipment productivity) + 0.10 (Capital productivity) + 0.05 (Energy productivity)

Total quality management

Total quality management (TQM) is an umbrella term and concept that focuses on doing things right in the first place, whether in producing goods or providing services. TQM encompasses the entire organization both internally from higher-level employees to lower-level employees and externally from suppliers to customers. A TQM strategy or program includes several elements such as quality concepts and tools, continuous improvement (kaizen), PDCA, JIT, stakeholder empowerment, benchmarking, ISO, Six Sigma, statistical process control (SPC), and Taguchi's quality loss function. Contrary to the popular belief, quality decreases costs and increases profits.

Transaction

A transaction is a logical unit of work for an end user. Also, the term is used to define a program or a dialog in a computer system.

Transactional leader

A transactional leader is a leader who clarifies subordinates' role and task requirements, initiates structure, provides rewards, and displays consideration for subordinates.

Transactional leadership

Transactional leadership is a style of leading whereby the leader sees the work as being done through clear definitions of tasks and responsibilities and the provision of resources as needed.

Transformational leader

A transformational leader is a leader distinguished by a special ability to bring about innovation and change.

Transformational leadership

Transformational leadership is a style of leading whereby the leader articulates the vision and values necessary for the organization to succeed.

TRIZ

TRIZ is a theory of solving inventive problems, and it is a Russian acronym. It supports the idea that unsolved problems are the result of contradicting goals (constraints) and nonproductive thinking. It suggests breaking out of the nonproductive thinking mold by reframing the contradicting and competing goals in such a way that the contradictions disappear. It is a problem-solving tool.

Turnaround time

Turnaround time is the time between job submission and job completion.

Two-bin system

A two-bin system is a simple, manual inventory system in which an item's inventory is stored in two different locations, with the first bin being the place where inventory is first withdrawn. When the first bin becomes empty, the second bin provides backup to cover the demand until a replenishment order arrives.

Two-tiered pricing

Two-tiered pricing occurs when a government charges a higher price for export than for domestic sales of a scarce natural resource input, thereby providing a competitive advantage to a domestic industry using this input.

Uncertainty

Managers know what goal they wish to achieve, but information about alternatives and future events is incomplete.

Uncertainty acceptance

Uncertainty acceptance is the extent to which uncertainty is considered a normal part of life; feeling comfortable with ambiguity and unfamiliar risks.

Uncertainty avoidance

Uncertainty avoidance is: (1) a value characterized by people's intolerance for uncertainty and ambiguity and their resulting support for beliefs that promise certainty and conformity; (2) a dimension of culture that refers to the preference of people in a country for structured rather than unstructured situations.

Unfreezing

Unfreezing is a stage of organizational development in which participants are made aware of problems in order to increase their willingness to change their behavior.

Upstream and downstream suppliers

Upstream and downstream suppliers are partnering firms in a supply-chain operation consisting of many suppliers (S-1 to S-N), whether local or global forming a chain presented as follows:

Upstream Suppliers 1, 2, and 3 ⟶ Manufacturer ⟶ Downstream Suppliers 4, 5, and 6 ⟶ Retailers ⟶ Customers

Here, suppliers 1, 2, and 3 are called upstream suppliers because they transport and deliver raw materials, ingredients, parts, and components to a manufacturer to make a full or partial product. Suppliers 4, 5, and 6 are called downstream suppliers because they transport and deliver a fully completed product from a manufacturer to a retailer and eventually to customers. Note that there could be only one manufacturer or multiple manufacturers in the supply chain.

Utilitarian approach

The utilitarian approach is an ethical concept that moral behaviors produce the greatest good for the greatest number.

Valuation

Valuation is a process of verifying that a recorded financial amount fairly represents an item's (e.g., equipment, inventory, furniture) real worth considering the market, cost, and economic and political conditions.

Value added

Value added in business processes are those activities or steps that add to or change a product or service as it goes through a process; these are the activities or steps that customers view as important and necessary.

Value analysis

Value analysis is a systematic study of a business process or product with a view to improving the process or product and reducing cost. Creative skills are required while doing value analysis. Its goal is to ensure that right activities are performed in the right way the first time. Industrial engineering techniques, such as work measurement and simplification methods, can be used to achieve the goals. It is a group approach that encourages free discussion and exchange of ideas is required to conduct value analysis in order to determine how the functions of particular parts, materials, or services can be performed as well or better at a lower cost. Techniques such as brainstorming, hitchhiking, and leapfrogging are used during value analysis. It is a problem-solving tool.

Value chain

Activities in an organization are related to what is sometimes referred to as the value chain: inbound (receiving), operations (production or service), outbound (shipping), marketing, sales, and service. Value chain is related to supply chain.

Value stream

A value stream consists of the processes of creating, producing, and delivering a good or service to the market. For a good, the value stream encompasses the raw material supplier, the manufacture and assembly of the good, and the distribution network. For a service, the value stream consists of suppliers, support personnel and technology, the service "producer," and the distribution channel. The value stream may be controlled by a single business or a network of several businesses.

Value stream mapping

Value stream mapping is a technique of mapping the value stream for products and services and for vendors and suppliers.

Verification

Verification is the act of reviewing, inspecting, testing, checking, auditing, or otherwise establishing and documenting whether activities, processes, services, or documents conform to specified requirements.

Vertical analysis

Vertical analysis is an analysis that compares each item in a current statement with a total amount within the same statement. It is a tool that converts financial statement numbers to percentages so that they are easy to understand and analyze.

Vertical market

A vertical market is a market in which the goods of one business are used as raw materials or components in the production or sale process of another business.

Vertical price fixing

Vertical price fixing occurs between a retailer and a manufacturer and between a wholesaler and a retailer because they are in the different hierarchical position in the marketplace and that they agreed together to maintain the same prices or increase prices. It is called price maintenance and is illegal.

Vertical team

A vertical team is a formal team composed of a manager and his or her subordinates in the organization's formal chain of command.

Vertically integrate

To vertically integrate is to bring together more of the steps involved in producing a product in order to form a continuous chain owned by the same firm; it typically involves taking on activities that were previously in the external portion of the supply chain.

Vintage analysis

Vintage analysis refers to comparing the performance of newer transactions, events, or things with older transactions, events, or things at comparable points in time. The idea is that this type of analysis provides early warning signs of potential performance problems in the newer transactions, events, or things so that the required corrective actions can be taken. One disadvantage is that vintage analysis assumes that the present repeats the past, which may not be true. However, such analysis is an advantage if the present does repeat the past.

Virtual organization

A virtual organization is an organization that has few full-time employees and temporarily hires outside specialists who form teams to work on specific opportunities, then disband when objectives are met. A virtual organization requires very little office space. Its employees telecommute, and services to customers are provided through telecommunications lines.

Virtual team

A virtual team is a team that uses advanced information and telecommunications technologies so that geographically distant members can collaborate on projects and reach common goals.

Vision

A vision is an attractive, ideal future that is credible yet not readily attainable. It is a statement that explains what the company wants to become and what it hopes to achieve.

Vroom-Jago model

The Vroom-Jago model is a model designed to help managers gauge the amount of subordinate participation in decision making.

Vulnerability

A vulnerability is a weakness or flaw that might be exploited to cause loss or harm.

Web mining

Web mining is a data mining technique for discovering and extracting information from web documents. Web mining explores both web content and web use.

What-if analysis

What-if analysis is a trial-and-error approach to learning about the range of possible outputs for a model. Trial values are chosen for the model inputs (these are the what-ifs) and the value of the output(s) is computed. It is an analysis that is conducted to test the degree to which one variable affects another. It is called sensitivity analysis.

Whistleblowing

Whistleblowing is the disclosure by an employee of illegal, immoral, or illegitimate practices by the organization.

The board and senior management of an organization should ensure that there is a process for employees to report legitimate concerns about suspected illegal, unethical, or questionable practices taking place within the organization with protection from reprisal. This process includes the ability to escalate operational problems, inappropriate conduct, policy violations, or other risks to the organization for investigation. The suspected individuals can be internal to the organizations (e.g., employees, supervisors, managers, executives, and the board members) and external to the organization (e.g., customers, contractors, consultants, suppliers, and vendors).

Work measurement

Work measurement is an industrial engineering program that applies some of the general principles of creative problem solving to the simplification of operations or procedures. It is a problem-solving tool.

Workflow

Workflow is a graphic representation of the flow of work in a process and its related subprocesses, including specific activities, information dependencies, and the sequence of decisions and activities.

World-class (leading) organizations

World-class (leading) organizations are organizations that are recognized as the best for at least one critical business process and are held as models for other organizations.

Worst-case scenario

A worst-case scenario is an analysis in which all of the input variables are set at their worst reasonably forecasted values.

Zen principles of leadership

Basically, the Zen principles of leadership tap into the creative and innovative side of a leader. The seven Zen principles are: (1) communicating in a plain, simple, clear, concise, and natural manner; (2) staying positive and achieving a balance in solving problems, despite differences, ambiguities, imperfections, and irregularities; (3) spending more time in guiding, mentoring, coaching, and delegating and less time in telling, micromanaging, and directing; (4) being more trusting and less doubting and behaving honestly and openly; (5) managing change very carefully while respecting the organizational culture; (6) striving for innovation by breaking away from tradition to achieve a competitive edge; and (7) motivating more and asserting less authority. The last principle includes creating harmony in the workplace, listening with an open mind, and establishing stretch goals.

- *Sources*: U.S. GAO's Financial Audit Manual Glossary. www.gao.gov.
- The Institute of Internal Auditors (IIA) Glossary. www.theiia.org.

Technology Glossary

This technology glossary contains key terms useful to CIA Exam candidates and students. Reading the glossary terms prior to studying the theoretical subject matter covered in Part 3 of the review book or the study guide and prior to answering the practice questions in Wiley's online test bank can help the candidate understand the domain content better. In addition, this glossary is a good review source for answering multiple-choice questions on the actual CIA Exam. This topical glossary provides a focused reading and study on a single topic for a better retention of key terms as opposed to multiple topics (i.e., business, financial, and technology glossary) put together. We strongly suggest that students read this glossary prior to studying the subject matter covered in the theoretical domains of this book.

Acceptance testing
Acceptance testing is one of the phases in the system development life cycle methodology where users and/or independent testers are involved in testing and accepting the system based on the test plan and results. It enables system users to determine whether to accept the system.

Access
Access is a specific type of interaction between a subject (e.g., user) and an object (e.g., data) that results in the flow of information from one to the other.

Access control list
The access control list (ACL) specifies who or what is allowed to access the object and what operations (e.g., modify or delete) are allowed to be performed on the object. It deals with relationships between subjects (e.g., individual users, group of users, processes, and devices) and objects (e.g., programs, files, databases, directories, and devices).

Access time
Access time is defined in several ways. For computer processing, it is the time it takes for the control section of the central processing unit (CPU) to locate program instructions and data for processing. For hard disks, it is the time that elapses between when the operating system issues an order for data retrieval and the time the data are ready for transfer from the disk. The access time of a PC disk drive is determined by: seek time (the time the disk heads take to move to the correct track), settle time (the time the heads take to settle down after reaching the correct track), and latency time (the time required for the correct sector to swing around under the head).

Active content technologies
Active content technologies allow code, often in the form of a script, macro, or other mobile code representation, to execute when the document is rendered. Hypertext Markup Language

(HTML) and other related markup language documents, whether delivered via Hypertext Transfer Protocol (HTTP) or another means, provide rich mechanisms for conveying executable content. Examples of active content include Postscript and PDF documents; web pages containing Java applets and JavaScript instructions; and word processor files containing macros, spreadsheet formulas, and other interpretable content. Active content may also be distributed embedded in email or as executable mail attachments. Countermeasures against active content documents include security policy, application settings, automated filters, software version control, software readers, and system isolation.

Active testing
Active testing is a hands-on security test of systems and networks to identity security vulnerabilities.

Adaptive maintenance
Adaptive maintenance is any effort initiated as a result of changes in the environment in which a software must operate.

Administrative security
Administrative security is the management constraints, operational procedures, accountability procedures, and supplemental controls established to provide an acceptable level of protection for sensitive data, programs, equipment, and physical facilities.

Advanced encryption standard
The advanced encryption standard (AES) specifies a cryptographic algorithm that can be used to protect electronic data that is sensitive but unclassified material. The AES algorithm is a symmetric block cipher that can encrypt (encipher) and decrypt (decipher) information.

Advanced persistent threats
A hacker's attack-in-depth strategy can create advanced persistent threats (APTs) where an adversary (a hacker) that possesses sophisticated levels of technical expertise and significant resources (money and time) can launch attacks. These resources allow a hacker to create opportunities to achieve her objectives by using multiple attack vectors such as cyber, physical, logical, and social deceptive schemes (e.g., URL obfuscation, DNS and URL redirects, URL shortening, spear phishing, and killing the features of antivirus software). APTs can be mitigated with agile defenses combined with boundary protection controls. Agile defense employs the concept of information system resilience. Endpoint security controls are also needed to protect from APTs.

Adware
Adware is a software program intended for marketing purposes, such as to deliver and display advertising banners or pop-ups to users' computer screen or track users' online use or purchasing activity. Adware tracks users' activity and passes it to third parties without the users' knowledge or consent. Click fraud is possible with adware because it involves deceptions and scams that inflate advertising bills with improper charges per click in an online advertisement on the web. This software application displays advertising in pop-up windows or a bar in the frame of the application window when the program is running. Adware can conduct malvertizing attacks.

Afterimage
An afterimage is the image of a database record after it has been updated by an application program.

Applets
Applets are small applications written in various programming languages that are automatically downloaded and executed by applet-enabled World Wide Web browsers. Examples include Active X and Java applets, both of which have security concerns.

Application program/system

An application program or system is intended to serve a business or nonbusiness function and has a specific input, processing, and output activities (e.g., accounts receivable and general ledger system).

Application program interfaces

Application program interfaces (APIs) include calls, subroutines, or software interrupts that comprise a documented interface so that a higher-level program, such as an application program, can make use of the lower-level services and functions of another application, operating system, network operating system, or a driver. APIs can be used to write a file in an application program's proprietary format, communicate over a TCP/IP network, access an SQL database, or surf the Internet, which can be risky because APIs can cause buffer overflow exploits that, in turn, lead to worm attacks.

Application system partitioning

The information system should separate user functionality, including user interface services, from information system management functionality, including databases, network components, workstations, or servers. This separation is achieved through physical or logical methods using different computers, different CPUs, different instances of the operating system, different network addresses, or a combination of these methods. Other separation approaches include sandboxing program modules and isolating application programs from their associated data files (i.e., separating code from data). Application system partitioning is a security control.

Archiving

Archiving is the practice of moving seldom-used data or programs from the active database to secondary storage media, such as magnetic tape or cartridge.

Asynchronous communication

Asynchronous communication is a method of data communication in which the transmission of bits of data is not synchronized by a clock signal but is accomplished by sending the bits one after another, with a start bit and a stop bit to mark the beginning and end of the data unit. The two communicating devices must be set to the same speed (the baud rate). Parity also may be used to check each byte transferred for accuracy. Asynchronous communication is popular among personal computers. Because of the lower communication speeds, normal telephone lines can be used for asynchronous communication.

Attacker's work factor

An attacker's work factor (i.e., time, cost, and effort) is the total amount of work necessary for an attacker to break a computer system or network. It should exceed the value and benefit that the attacker would gain from a successful compromise. One way to impose costs on an attacker is to make botnet takedown actions and malware eradication activities much faster so their negative effects are limited.

Auditability

The term "auditability" refers to features and characteristics that allow verification of the adequacy of procedures and controls and of the accuracy of processing transactions and results in either a manual or an automated system.

Authenticate

To authenticate is to establish the validity of a claimed identity.

Authentication

Authentication is the act of identifying or verifying the eligibility of a station, originator, or individual to access specific categories of information.

Authorization

Authorization implies that the authorizing authority has verified and validated that the activity or transaction conforms to established policies and procedures. It is a process of verifying that approvals and procedures for recording and processing transactions have been obtained in accordance with management's general policies, standards, procedures, and specific instructions.

Availability

Availability is the state that exists when required automated services or system data can be obtained within an acceptable period at a level and in the form the system user wants.

Backbone

A backbone is a central network to which other networks connect.

Back door or trapdoor

A back door or trapdoor is a means of access to a computer program that bypasses security mechanisms.

Backup

A backup is a duplicate of a hardware system, software, data, or documents intended as a replacement in the event of a malfunction or disaster.

Backup computer facility

A backup computer facility is a computer (data) center having hardware and software compatible with the primary computer facility. The backup computer is used only in the case of a major interruption or disaster at the primary computer facility. It provides the ability for continued computer operations, when needed, and should be established by a formal agreement.

Bandwidth

Bandwidth is the range of frequencies available to transmit signals. Hertz (cycles per second) is used to express the difference between the highest and lowest frequencies.

Baseband

Baseband is a transmission technique in which devices can share a single communication channel. It is used in twisted-pair and coaxial cable media.

Baseline

A baseline is a set of critical observations or data used for a comparison or a control. It indicates a cutoff point in the design and development of a configuration item beyond which configuration does not evolve without undergoing strict configuration control policies and procedures.

Black box testing

Black box testing is a basic test methodology that assumes no knowledge of the internal structure and implementation detail of the assessment object. It examines the software from the user's viewpoint and determines if the data are processed according to the specifications; it does not consider implementation details. It verifies that software functions are performed correctly. It focuses on the external behavior of a system and uses the system's functional specifications to generate test cases. It ensures that the system does what it is supposed to do and does not do what it is not supposed to do. It is also known as generalized testing or functional testing, and should be combined with white box testing for maximum benefit because neither one by itself does a thorough testing job. Black box testing is a functional analysis of a system.

Blackholing

Blackholing occurs when traffic is sent to routers that drop some or all of the packets. It is synonymous with blackhole.

Blacklisting

Blacklisting is the process of the system invalidating a user ID based on the user's inappropriate actions. A blacklisted user ID cannot be used to log on to the system, even with the correct authenticator. Blacklisting also applies to (1) blocks placed against IP addresses to prevent inappropriate or unauthorized use of Internet resources, (2) blocks placed on domain names known to attempt brute force attacks, (3) a list of email senders who have previously sent spam to a user, and (4) a list of discrete entities, such as hosts or applications, that have been previously determined to be associated with malicious activity. Placing blacklisting and lifting blacklisting are both security-relevant events. Web content filtering software uses blacklisting to prevent access to undesirable websites. Blacklisting is a security control.

Blue team

A blue team is a group of people conducting penetration tests. This team is responsible for defending an enterprise's use of information systems by maintaining its security posture against a group of mock attackers (i.e., red team). The blue team must defend against real or simulated attacks (1) over a significant period of time, (2) in a representative operational context, and (3) according to rules established and monitored with the help of a neutral group (i.e., white team) refereeing the simulation or exercise.

Boot-sector virus

A boot-sector virus works during computer booting, where the master boot sector and boot sector code is read and executed. Such viruses place either their starting code or a jump to their code in the boot sector of floppies. They can also place the code either at the boot sector or at the master boot sector of a hard disk. Most boot viruses infect by moving the original code of the master boot sector or boot sector to another location, such as slack space, and then placing their own code in the master boot sector or boot sector. Boot viruses also infect the boot sector of floppy disks; some of them, such as Form, also infect the boot sector of hard disks. Other boot viruses infect the master boot sector of hard disks.

Botnet

A botnet is a network of computers that cybercriminals or hackers have infected with malware that gives a hacker access to each computer and allows a hacker to control each computer remotely. Botnets are very damaging attacks.

"Botnet" is a term for a collection of software robots (bots) that run autonomously. A bot's originator can control the group remotely, usually through Internet relay chat, and usually for nefarious purposes. A botnet can comprise a collection of cracked computers running programs (usually referred to as worms, Trojan horses, or back doors) under a common command-and-control infrastructure. Botnets are often used to send spam emails and to launch denial-of-service (DoS) attacks, phishing attacks, and virus attacks.

Bridge

A bridge is a device used to link two or more homogeneous local area networks. A bridge does not change the contents of the frame that is being transmitted but acts as a relay.

Broadband

Broadband is a transmission technique in which devices can communicate with each other on dedicated frequencies.

Browser

A browser is a client program used to interact on the World Wide Web.

Browser-based attacks

Attacks can be launched against web browser components and technologies by a web server. The mobile code paradigm requires a browser to accept and execute code developed elsewhere. Incoming code has two main methods of attack. The first action is to gain unauthorized access to computational resources residing at the browser (e.g., security options) or its underlying platform (e.g., system registry). The second action is to use its authorized access based on the user's identity in an unexpected and disruptive fashion (e.g., invade privacy or deny service). Because browsers can support multiple associations with different web servers as separate windowed contexts, the mobile code of one context can also target another context. Unauthorized access may occur simply through a lack of adequate access control mechanisms or weak identification and authentication controls, which allow untrusted code to act or masquerade as a trusted component. Attackers may take advantage of browser vulnerabilities in mobile code execution environments. Once access is gained, information residing at the platform can be disclosed or altered. Attackers may install spyware, connect the platform to a botnet, or modify the platform's configuration. Depending on the level of access, complete control of the platform may be taken over by the mobile code. Even without gaining unauthorized access to resources, malicious code can deny platform services to other processes by exhausting computational resources, if resource constraints are not established or not set tightly.

Brute-force password attack

A brute-force password attack is a method of accessing an obstructed device by attempting multiple combinations of numeric and/or alphanumeric passwords, as found in simple passwords.

Buffer

A buffer is an area of random access memory or the central processing unit that is used to temporarily store data from a disk, communication port, program, or peripheral device.

Buffer overflow

Buffer overflow is a condition likely to occur in a programming interface under which more input is placed into a buffer or data-holding area than the capacity allocated, thus overwriting the information. Attackers and adversaries can exploit such a condition to crash a system or to insert specially crafted code that allows them to gain control of the system. As a countermeasure, appropriate security controls should be used across operational, network, and host layers, combined with updated antivirus software and patches, firewalls, secure programming techniques, intrusion detection system software, and monitoring with security event management (SEM) tools. In addition, secure File Transfer Protocol (SFTP) or Secure Copy Protocol (SCP) should be used instead of regular File Transfer Protocol (FTP) or Trivial File Transfer Protocol (TFTP).

Bug

A bug is an error or mistake in a computer program or data file.

Bus

A bus is a topology in which stations are attached to a shared transmission medium.

Byte

A byte is usually a group of eight bits. Bytes are the most convenient units for storing letters or characters, computer instructions, and system status indications.

Call-back

A call-back is a procedure established for positively identifying a terminal dialing into a computer system by disconnecting the calling terminal and reestablishing the connection by the computer system's dialing the telephone number of the calling terminal.

Canaries

Whereas honeypots analyze unauthorized connections, canaries flag that a connection attempt has taken place. Canaries provide passive network monitoring and work with network intrusion detection systems. Canaries can be standalone computers or unused network interface cards in existing hardware. Canaries complement intrusion detection systems.

Catalog

A catalog is a systematic method of keeping track of stored data and programs in system libraries.

Channel

A channel is a path for electrical transmission between two or more connecting points. It is also called path, link, line, or circuit.

Check digit

A check digit calculation helps ensure that the primary key or data are entered correctly.

Checkpoint

A checkpoint is a point, generally taken at regular intervals, at which a program's intermediate results are dumped to a secondary storage (e.g., disk) to minimize the risk of work loss.

Checksum

A checksum is an error-checking technique to ensure the accuracy of data transmission. The number of bits in a unit of data is summed and transmitted along with the data. The receiving computer then checks the sum and compares.

CIA triad

The CIA triad includes confidentiality, integrity, and availability, which are the primary objectives in information security.

Clearing

Clearing is the removal of sensitive data from storage media at the end of a period of processing, including from peripheral devices with storage capacity, in such a way that there is assurance, proportional to the sensitivity of the data, that the data may not be reconstructed using normal system capabilities (i.e., through the keyboard). Clearing may include use of advanced diagnostic utility programs. The storage media need not be disconnected from any external network before a clear. A potential risk is reconstruction of data if the clearing operation is not performed properly.

Click fraud

Click fraud involves deceptions and scams that inflate advertising bills with improper charges per click in an online advertisement on the Web. Advertisement firms hire several individuals to do repeat clicks in order to increase phony bills to their customers.

Client/server architecture

Client/server architecture is an architecture consisting of server programs that await and fulfill requests from client programs on the same or another computer.

Client/server authentication

Client/server authentication uses Secure Sockets Layer (SSL) and Transport Layer Security (TLS) to provide client and server authentication and encryption of Web communications.

Cloud computing

Cloud computing is a model for enabling ubiquitous, convenient, on-demand network access to a shared pool of configurable computing resources (e.g., networks, servers, storage, applications, and services) that can be rapidly provisioned and released with minimal management effort or service provider interaction. The cloud model promotes availability and is composed of five essential characteristics (i.e., on-demand self-service, broad network access, resource pooling, rapid elasticity, and measured service), three service models (i.e., cloud software as a service, cloud platform as a service, and cloud infrastructure as a service), and four deployment models (i.e., private, community, public, and hybrid cloud).

Coaxial cable

Coaxial cable is an electromagnetic transmission medium consisting of a center conductor and an outer, concentric conductor.

Cohesion

Cohesion is the degree to which the functions or processing elements within a module are related or bound together.

Cold site

A cold site is a backup, alternate computer processing location that has the basic infrastructure and environmental controls available (e.g., electrical, heating, and air conditioning) but no equipment or telecommunications established or in place. The cold site method is most difficult and expensive to test compared to the hot or warm site method. Cold sites are a part of information technology continuity planning.

Collision

A collision is a condition in which two data packets are being transmitted over a medium at the same time from two or more stations.

Collision detection

When a collision is detected, in data transmission, the message is retransmitted after a random interval.

Communications software

Communications software is a program that moves electronic messages from computer to terminals and vice versa.

Companion virus

A companion virus is a program that attaches to the operating system rather than files or sectors. In a disk operating system, when a user runs a file named "ABC," the rule is that ABC.COM would execute before ABC.EXE. A companion virus places its code in a .COM file whose first name matches the name of an existing .EXE. When a user runs the ABC file, the actual sequence of run is ABC.COM and ABC.EXE. In other words, a companion virus hides and spreads as a COM variant of a standard EXE file (e.g., clone war virus).

Compensating control

The compensating control concept states that the total environment should be considered when determining whether a specific policy, procedure, or control is violated, or a specific risk is present. If controls in one area are weak, they should be compensated for or mitigated in another area. Some examples of compensating controls are: strict personnel hiring procedures, bonding employees, information system risk insurance, increased supervision, rotation of duties, review of computer logs, user sign-off procedures, mandatory vacations, batch controls, user review of input and output, system activity reconciliations, and system access security controls.

Compiler

A compiler is a program that translates a source code module (statements written in a human readable programming language) to computer-readable machine language. It produces an object code module.

Compliance

The term "compliance" refers to verifying that both manual and computer processing of transactions or events are in accordance with the organization's policies and procedures, generally accepted accounting principles, government laws, and regulatory agency rules and requirements.

Compliance testing

Compliance testing is the process of verifying compliance with the organization's internal controls, operations, policies, plans, procedures, guidelines, practices, and standards to evaluate efficiency and effectiveness. The process is called compliance auditing, and the tests performed are called compliance tests.

Configuration accounting

The recording and reporting of configuration item descriptions and all departures from the baseline during design and production.

Configuration auditing

Configuration auditing is an independent review of computer software for the purpose of assessing compliance with established requirements, standards, and baseline controls.

Configuration control

Configuration control is the process of controlling modifications to the system's design, hardware, firmware, software, and documentation, thus providing sufficient assurance that the system is protected against the introduction of improper modification prior to, during, and after system implementation.

Configuration identification

Configuration identification is the identifying of the system configuration throughout the design, development, test, and production tasks.

Configuration item

A configuration item is the smallest component of hardware, software, firmware, documentation, or any of its discrete portions, that is tracked by the configuration management system.

Configuration management

Configuration management is management of security features and assurances through control of changes made to hardware, software, firmware, documentation, and actual test with test data and results throughout the life cycle of an information system.

Contention

Contention it is a state of busy condition between a terminal and a channel. If the channel in question is free, transmission is done. Otherwise, the terminal waits. Also, it is the condition when two or more stations attempt to use the same channel at the same time.

Contingency plan

A contingency plan is a plan that includes procedures for storing hardware, software, supplies, and personnel to operate the backup computer facilities in the case of a major interruption or disaster at the primary computer facility. It is also called disaster recovery plan, business resumption plan, or business continuity plan.

Control unit

A control unit is an electrical device that connects an input/output (I/O) device to a channel. I/O devices are connected to the central processing unit through channels and control units.

Cookies

Cookies are small text files on a computer that store information about what websites a user accessed while browsing the Internet. They are used to track a user across multiple websites in order to provide the best possible user experience to website visitors. Cookies are used for storing user authentication data. Cookies combined with web bugs are used to build user profiles. Often information collected with cookies is sold to third parties. A cookie consent form is needed so visitors can tell what cookies can and cannot be used on their computing devices (i.e., mobile or non-mobile). Four types of cookies exist: persistent, session, tracking, and encrypted, as follows:

A **persistent cookie** is stored on a computer's hard drive indefinitely so that a website can identify the user during subsequent visits. These cookies are set with expiration dates and are valid until the user deletes them.

A **session cookie** is a temporary cookie that is valid only for a single website session. It is stored in temporary memory and is erased when the user closes the web browser.

A **tracking cookie** is placed on a user's computer to track the user's activity on different websites, creating a detailed profile of the user's behavior.

Encrypted cookies are created by websites to protect the data from unauthorized access.

Coupling

The term "coupling" refers to the degree to which modules in a computer program depend on each other.

Cracking attack

Cracking is breaking and bypassing software controls in an electronic authentication system in order to obtain passwords, such as user registration.

Cryptocurrency

Cryptocurrency is a digital currency used as a medium of exchange, similar to other currencies such as a dollar. However, unlike other currencies, cryptocurrency operates independently of a central bank and uses encryption techniques and blockchain technologies to secure and verify crypto transactions. Examples of cryptocurrencies are bitcoin and litecoin.

Cryptography

Cryptography is the only known current practical means of securing data and information that are transmitted over communications lines such as cable, microwave, fiber optics, or satellite.

Cryptojacking

Cryptojacking is a security risk that occurs when malicious cyber actors exploit vulnerabilities in web pages, applications software, and operating systems to illicitly install cryptomining software on victims' mobile devices and computer systems. After installation, cyber actors hijack the processing power of the victims' devices and systems and further infect websites with cryptomining JavaScript code. The resulting consequences are:

- Degraded system and network performance because bandwidth and central processing unit (CPU) resources are monopolized by cryptomining activity.

- Increased electric power consumption, system crashes, and physical damage from equipment component failure due to the extreme temperatures caused by cryptomining.

- Disruption of regular IT operations.

- Financial loss due to system downtime caused by component failure and the cost of restoring systems and files to full operation, including the cost of the increased power consumption.

Cryptojacking involves maliciously installed programs that are persistent or non-persistent. Non-persistent cryptojacking occurs only while a user is visiting a particular web page or has an Internet browser open. Persistent cryptojacking continues to occur even after a user has stopped visiting the source that originally caused the system to perform mining activity.

Malicious actors distribute cryptojacking malware through weaponizing mobile applications (apps), Wi-Fi botnets, and social media platforms by exploiting flaws in applications and servers and by hijacking Wi-Fi hotspots.

In summary, computer systems and networks; mobile devices; and Internet of Things (IoT) devices such as printers, video cameras, and smart TVs, are at risk for cryptojacking malware attacks.

Cryptomining

Cryptocurrency mining, or cryptomining, is the way in which cryptocurrency such as bitcoin or litecoin is earned. Individuals mine cryptocurrency by using cryptomining software to solve complex mathematical problems involved in validating transactions. Each solved equation verifies a transaction and earns a reward paid out in the cryptocurrency. Solving cryptographic calculations to mine cryptocurrency requires a massive amount of computer processing (CPU) power.

Cycle checker

In a database system or program, a cycle checker detects and resolves deadlocks.

Cycle time

Cycle time represents the time interval between initiating a transfer of data to or from storage and the instant when this transfer is completed. Cycle time is the same as execution time.

Cyclic redundancy check

In a cyclic redundancy check (CRC), an algorithm is used to generate error detection bits in a data link protocol. The receiving station performs the same calculation as done by the transmitting station. If the results differ, then one or more bits are in error.

Dark web

The dark web is a private web unlike the Internet, which is a public web. The dark web uses a script-based language such as JavaScript for content whereas the Internet uses a HTML-based content. Most dark websites are not directly accessible by most people; they cannot be reached through a search engine service. The Internet Protocol (IP) addresses for dark websites are hidden but are popular in the black market, selling illegal drugs and guns and doing other illegal activities. Hackers and scammers have their own dark websites.

Darknet

The darknet is a collection of networks consisting of dark websites. "Deepweb" or "deepnet" includes websites and web pages that are invisible and known only to limited people in their community. These websites are not indexed by search engine services such as Google.

Data dictionary

A data dictionary contains attributes and characteristics of each data element or field in a computer record. It also includes file organization and structure and edit and validation rules.

Data encryption standard

Data encryption standard (DES) is an encryption standard established by the National Bureau of Standards. The use of DES or some other encryption algorithm is essential for securing telecommunications.

Data exfiltration

Data exfiltration is data theft where cyber criminals do unauthorized copying, transferring, and retrieving of data from a victim organization's computers and servers into their own storage space. Data exfiltration can occur when the victim organizations are using default or easy passwords. Intruders use hop points to store the stolen or exfiltrated data.

Data immutability

Data immutability means data cannot be changed or modified. It also means data can only be written as it applies to bitcoins and blockchain technology.

Data-in-transit attack

Data that is in transit between a source point and a destination point over a communication channel is vulnerable to attacks, such as eavesdropping, sniffing, session hijacking, and man-in-the-middle (MitM) attacks. Security controls include installing security filters and encryption methods.

Data remanence

Data remanence is residual data remaining on storage media after clearing. It is a residual risk.

Data sequencing

Data sequencing is an automated software tool that allows large volumes of data to conduct threat intelligence analysis. This software puts threat data in chronological order as it occurred in a fast, effective, and accurate manner.

Database

A database is a collection of interrelated data stored together, using a common and controlled approach.

Database system

In a database system, data are maintained independently of the application programs. Data can be shared by many programs and users. Database management system (DBMS) software manages and controls the data and the database software.

Dataset

A dataset is a collection of related bytes, or characters, of secondary storage. For example, a dataset may be a file of payroll records or a library of payroll programs.

Deadlock

A deadlock is a consequence of poor resource management that occurs when two programs each control a resource (e.g., printer, data file, and record) needed by the other and neither is willing to give in its resource.

Debugging

Debugging is the process of correcting mistakes or errors in a computer program.

Decipher

The term "decipher" means to convert, by use of the appropriate key, enciphered text into its equivalent plain text, respectively. It is a decision-making tool.

Decrypt

To decrypt is to convert, by use of the appropriate key, encrypted (encoded or enciphered) text into its equivalent plaintext.

Defense in breadth

Defense in breadth is a planned, systematic set of multidisciplinary activities that seek to identify, manage, and reduce risk of exploitable vulnerabilities at every stage of the system, network, or subcomponent life cycle (system, network, or product design and development; manufacturing; packaging; assembly; system integration; distribution; operations; maintenance; and retirement). It is a strategy dealing with scope of information protection coverage of a system.

Also called supply chain protection control, it supports an agile defense strategy. Defense in breadth is a security control.

Defense-in-density

Defense-in-density is a strategy requiring stronger security controls for high-risk and very complex systems. Defense-in-density is a security control.

Defense in depth

Defense in depth is an information security strategy integrating people, technology, and operations capabilities to establish variable barriers across multiple layers and dimensions of information systems. It is an approach for establishing an adequate information assurance (IA) posture whereby (1) IA solutions integrate people, technology, and operations; (2) IA solutions are layered within and among IT assets; and (3) IA solutions are selected based on their relative level of robustness. Implementation of this approach recognizes that the highly interactive nature of information systems and enclaves creates a shared risk environment; therefore, the adequate assurance of any single asset is dependent on the adequate assurance of all interconnecting assets. It is an information protection strategy dealing with controls placed at multiple levels and at multiple places in a given system. It supports agile defense strategy and is the same as security in depth. Defense in depth is a security control.

Defense-in-intensity

Defense-in-intensity is a strategy dealing with a range of controls and protection mechanisms designed into high-visibility and high-impact systems. Defense-in-intensity is a security control.

Defense-in-technology

Defense-in-technology is a strategy dealing with diversity of information technologies used in the implementation of a system. Complex technologies create complex security problems. Defense-in-technology is a security control.

Defense-in-time

Defense-in-time is a strategy of applying controls at the right time and at the right geographic location. It considers global systems operating at different time zones. Defense-in-time is a security control.

Degaussing

Degaussing, also called demagnetizing, is a procedure that reduces the magnetic flux to virtual zero by applying a reverse magnetizing field to magnetic media.

Deleted file

A deleted file has been logically, but not physically, erased from the operating system, perhaps to eliminate potentially incriminating evidence. Deleting files does not always necessarily eliminate the possibility of recovering all or part of the original data, which is an easy target for an electronic scavenging attack.

Demilitarized zone

A demilitarized zone (DMZ) is an interface on a routing firewall that is similar to the interfaces found on the firewall's protected side. Traffic moving between the DMZ and other interfaces on the protected side of the firewall still goes through the firewall and can have firewall protection policies applied. DMZ is a host or network segment inserted as a neutral zone between an organization's private network and the Internet. It is a network created by connecting to firewalls. Systems that are externally accessible but need some protections are usually located on DMZ networks.

Detailed design

Detailed design is a process where technical specifications are translated into more detailed programming specifications, from which computer programs are developed.

Digital certificate

A digital certificate is a password-protected and encrypted file that contains identification information about its holder. It includes a public key and a unique private key.

Digital signature

Digital signature is electronic information stored or transferred in digital form. It is a nonforgeable transformation of data that allows the proof of the source (with nonrepudiation) and the verification of the integrity of that data. Digital signatures provide authentication and integrity protection.

Digital watermarking

Digital watermarking is the process of irreversibly embedding information into a digital signal to hide sensitive data.

Direct access storage device

Direct access storage device (DASD) is a migration device (disk) that transfers files to tape or cartridge in order to efficiently use file space.

Directory

A directory is a list of files stored on a disk.

Discretionary access control policy

The basis for a discretionary access control (DAC) policy is that an individual user or program operating on the user's behalf is allowed to specify explicitly the types of access other users or programs executing on their behalf may have to the information under the user's control. A DAC is called a surrogate access control. *Compare* with mandatory access control policy.

Disk array

Disk array is a recovery control technique used to improve the performance of data storage media regardless of the type of computer used. Disk arrays use parity disk schema to keep track of data stored in a domain of the storage subsystem and to regenerate it in case of a hardware/software failure. Disk arrays use multiple disks. If one disk drive fails, the other one becomes available. They also have six levels from level zero through five (i.e., Redundant Array of Independent Disks [RAIDs]). They use several disks in a single logical subsystem. Disk arrays are also called disk striping.

Disk duplexing

The purpose of disk duplexing is the same as with disk arrays. The disk controller is duplicated. When one disk controller fails, the other one is ready to operate.

Disk farm

A disk farm is data that are stored on multiple disks for reliability and performance reasons.

Disk mirroring

The purpose of disk mirroring is the same as with disk arrays. A file server contains two physical disks and one channel, and all information is written to both disks simultaneously (disk-to-disk copy). If one disk fails, all of the data are immediately available from the other disk. Disk mirroring uses a copy/image technique to make an identical copy of the hard drive. It incurs some performance overhead during write operations and increases the cost of the disk subsystem since two disks are required. Disk mirroring should be used for critical applications that can accept little or no data loss. This is a technical and recovery control and ensures the availability goal. It is synonymous with disk shadowing.

Disk replication

Disk replication is data that are written to two different disks to ensure that two valid copies of the data are always available. It minimizes the time for recovery.

Disk striping

Disk striping contains more than one disk and more than one partition, and is the same as a disk array. An advantage of disk striping is running multiple drives in parallel. A disadvantage is that its organization is more complicated than disk farm and is highly sensitive to multiple failures.

Domain name sinkhole

A domain name sinkhole means re-registering a current domain name used for malware command-and-control servers. A potential problem is that the new owner of the domain name can receive data from computers in other victim networks, including those of business competitors.

Domain name system spoofing attack

A domain name system (DNS) spoofing attack occurs when hackers redirect an innocent website user to a plain and insecure HTTP connection where traffic can be intercepted. It will be safe if websites can use HTTP strictly transport security (HSTS) protocol to instruct browsers to require a secure HTTPS connection for their domain at all times. This means that an attacker that successfully spoofs DNS resolution must also create a valid HTTPS connection. This makes DNS spoofing attack much more challenging and expensive than attacking a plain HTTP generally.

Domain separation

Domain separation relates to the mechanisms that protect objects in the system. The term "domain" refers to the set of objects (e.g., data files, program files, libraries, directories, and databases) that a subject (e.g., end user and system user) is able to access.

Probably the most straightforward approach for implementing domain separation is to design a trusted computing base (TCB) that takes advantage of multistate hardware (i.e., a CPU that provides two or more hardware states such as rings, modes, and domains). For most hardware platforms, the domain separation requirement will mean that at least two hardware states are provided, where one state permits access of privileged instructions necessary to manipulate memory-mapping registers. Memory mapping alone is not sufficient to meet this requirement but may be used to enhance hardware isolation. However, the multistate mechanism need not be totally implemented in hardware. Software, including compilers, can be used.

Drive-by-download

Drive-by-download is a type of ransomware attack where it will transfer malicious software (malware) to a victim's computer without the knowledge of or any action required by the victim.

Driver

A driver is program code that sets up an environment and calls a module for testing.

Dual cable

In dual cable systems, two separate cables are used: one for transmission and one for reception.

Dual control

Dual control in information technology is the process of using two or more separate entities or two individuals operating in concert to protect sensitive functions or information. No single entity is able to generate, access, or use cryptographic keys. This is similar to dual control in physical access, such as opening a safe vault in the presence of two individuals. All entities are equally responsible. This approach generally involves the split knowledge of the physical or logical protection of security parameters.

Dump

A dump is a process of copying or printing the contents of computer program, central processing unit memory, or data file to find errors and to conduct analysis.

Easter egg

An Easter egg is a form of computer virus that triggers when a program code is placed in software for the amusement of its developer or users. It is a nuisance to users.

Eavesdropping attack

Several definitions of eavesdropping attack exist: (1) It is passively monitoring network communications for data and authentication credentials. (2) It is the unauthorized interception of information-bearing emanations through the use of methods other than wiretapping. (3) It is a passive attack in which an attacker listens to a private communication, and (4) it is also known as packet snarfing. The best way to thwart this attack is by making it very difficult for the attacker to make any sense of the communication by encrypting all messages (i.e., a security control).

Egress filtering

Egress filtering is the filtering of outgoing network traffic. It blocks outgoing packets that should not exit a network—those that use obviously false Internet Protocol (IP) addresses, such as source addresses—from internal networks.

Emanations attacks

Computer equipment and facilities routinely radiate electromagnetic energy that can be detected with special-purpose radio receivers. Successful interception depends on the signal strength at the receiver's location; the greater the separation between the system and the receiver, the lower the success rate. Tempest shielding, of either equipment or rooms, can be used to minimize the spread of electromagnetic signals. The signal-to-noise ratio at the receiver, determined in part by the number of competing emitters, will also affect the success rate. The more workstations of the same type in the same location performing random activity, the more difficult it is to intercept a given workstation's radiation. On the other hand, the trend toward wireless local area network (WLAN) connections may increase the likelihood of successful interception.

Countermeasures (controls) against emanations attacks include control zones and white noise. Control zones need to be addressed in two places or at two times. The first place, which is ideally preferred, is during the construction of the data center so that materials used in building walls will block the electrical signals generating from computer hardware, which will stop emitting the signals to outside intruders. The second place, which is practically preferred, is to segment the data center facilities and business offices into control zones (e.g., parking lot, front lobby, executive offices, research and development area, IT offices, and networks (e.g., local area and wide area). Then, access controls and firewalls should be designed to suit each of these control zones depending on the sensitivity levels of data they process and the nature and criticality of hardware devices used. Another control is white noise, which is a distribution of uniform spectrum of random electrical signals so that an intruder is unable to decipher real data from random (noise) data due to the use of constant bandwidth.

Emulate

To emulate is to use firmware to allow original code to run on target hardware, with no functional change.

Encipher

To encipher is to convert plaintext into unintelligible form by means of a code system.

Encrypt

To encrypt is to convert plaintext into unintelligible form by means of a cryptographic system.

Encrypted virus

An encrypted virus has two parts: a small decryptor and the encrypted virus body. When the virus is executed, the decryptor executes first and decrypts the virus body. Then the virus body executes by replicating or becoming resident. The virus body includes an encryptor to apply during replication. A variably encrypted virus uses different encryption keys or encryption algorithms. Encrypted viruses are more difficult to disassemble and study since the researcher must decrypt the code. The variably encrypted virus code begins with a decryption algorithm and continues with the scrambled or encrypted code of the remainder of the virus. When several identical files are infected with the same virus, they share a brief identical decryption algorithm but, beyond that, each copy may appear different. A scan string can be used to search for the decryption algorithm.

Enterprise resource planning system

Enterprise resource planning (ERP) is a system that integrates enterprise-wide information, including human resources, finance, manufacturing, and distribution, and connects the organization to its customers and suppliers.

Enterprise risk management program

Traditionally, corporate risk management focused on partial portfolio of risks (silo approach), specifically on financial and hazard risks. This narrow scope ignored all the other risks impacting the organization. It did not exploit the natural hedges and portfolio effects in the collective and tended to treat risk as downside phenomenon.

An enterprise risk management (ERM) program focuses on total portfolio risks, including financial, hazard, strategic, and operational risks. The scope of ERM is much broader than the traditional view with the objective of creating, protecting, and enhancing shareholder value. ERM treats risk as both upside and downside phenomenon since it integrates all risks. Scorecards, action plans, and monitoring are part of the ERM approach.

Execution time

See Cycle time.

Extensible Markup Language

Extensible Markup Language (XML) is a cross-platform, extensible, and text-based standard markup language for representing structured data. It provides a cross-platform, software- and hardware-independent tool for transmitting information. XML is a meta-language, a coding language for describing programming languages used on the web. XML uses standard generalized markup language (SGML) on the web, and it is like Hypertext Markup Language (HTML). The web browser interprets the XML tags for the right meaning of information in web documents and pages. It is a flexible text format designed to describe data for electronic publishing.

Extranet

An extranet is the Internet technology used to connect the intranet of an organization with the intranet from other organizations, such as suppliers and customers.

Failover

Failover is: (1) the capability to switch over automatically without human intervention or warning to a redundant or standby information system upon the failure or abnormal termination of the previously active system. (2) It is a backup concept in that when the primary system fails, the backup system is automatically activated. It is related to information technology.

Failsafe

A failsafe is an automatic protection of programs and/or processing systems when hardware or software failure is detected in a computer system. It is a condition to avoid compromise in the event of a failure or have no chance of failure. It is related to information technology.

Failsafe default

A failsafe default asserts that access decisions should be based on permission rather than exclusion. This equates to the condition in which lack of access is the default, and the protection scheme recognizes permissible actions rather than prohibited actions. Also, failures due to flaws in exclusion-based systems tend to grant (unauthorized) permissions, whereas permission-based systems tend to failsafe with permission denied. It is related to information technology.

Failsecure

In a failsecure system, the system preserves a secure condition during and after an identified failure. It is related to information technology.

Failsoft

A failsoft is a selective termination of affected nonessential processing when hardware or software failure is determined to be imminent in a computer system. The computer system continues to function because of its resilience. Failsoft methods are found in distributed data processing systems. They are related to information technology.

Failstop processor

A failstop processor is one that can constrain the failure rate and protects the integrity of data. However, it is likely to be more vulnerable to denial-of-service attacks. It is related to information technology.

Failure

Failure is a discrepancy between external results of a program's operation and software product requirements. A software failure is evidence of software faults. It is related to information technology.

Failure access

Failure access is a type of incident in which unauthorized access to data results from hardware or software failure. It is related to information technology.

Failure control

Failure control is a methodology used to detect imminent hardware or software failure and provide failsafe or failsoft recovery in a computer system. It is related to information technology.

Failure rate

The failure rate is the number of times the hardware ceases to function in a given time period. It is related to information technology.

Fair and Accurate Credit Transactions Act

The Fair and Accurate Credit Transactions Act in 2003, which amended the Fair Credit Reporting Act, adds provisions designed to improve the accuracy of consumers' credit-related records. It gives consumers the right to one free credit report a year from the credit reporting agencies, and consumers may also purchase for a reasonable fee a credit score along with information about how the credit score is calculated. The Act also adds provisions designed to prevent and mitigate identity theft, including a section that enables consumers to place fraud alerts in their credit files. Further, the Act grants consumers additional rights with respect to how their information is used.

The **Red Flags Rule** was issued in 2007 under this Act, clarified with the issuance of the Red Flag Program Clarification Act of 2010, and amended the Fair Credit Reporting Act, requires many businesses and organizations to implement a written identity theft prevention program designed to detect the "red flags" of identity theft in their day-to-day operations, take steps to prevent the crime, and mitigate its damage. The bottom line is that a program can help businesses spot suspicious patterns and prevent the costly consequences of identity theft.

Fallback procedure

A fallback procedure refers to the ability to: (1) fall back to the original or alternate method for continuation of processing in the event of a failure of transactions or the system; and (2) fall back to the original or alternate method for continuation of computer processing. It is related to information technology.

False negative

A false negative is an instance of incorrectly classifying malicious activity or content as benign. It is an instance in which a security tool intended to detect a particular threat fails to do so. A false negative also occurs when a tool does not report a security weakness where one is present.

False non-match rate

False non-match rate is an alternative to the false rejection rate. Used to avoid confusion in applications that reject the claimant if the biometric data matches with that of an applicant.

False positive

A false positive is an instance in which a security tool incorrectly classifies benign activity or content as malicious. It is an instance when a tool reports a security weakness where no weakness is present. A false positive is an alert that incorrectly indicates that malicious activity is occurring.

False positive rate

False positive rate is the number of false positives divided by the sum of the number of false positives and the number of true positives.

False rejection

False rejection occurs when a biometric system fails to identify an applicant or fails to verify the legitimate claimed identity of an applicant.

False rejection rate

False rejection rate (FRR) is the probability that a biometric system will fail to identify an applicant, or verify the legitimate claimed identity of an applicant. The FRR is stated as the ratio of the number of false rejections divided by the number of identification attempts.

Fault injection test

In a fault injection test, unfiltered and invalid data are injected as input into an application program to detect faults in resource operations and execution functions.

An alpha test is a field-based test of a new system by outside end users to ensure that its functions and features work as designed and to discover bugs and errors. Alpha test and Beta test are not a part of fault injection test. Put them in their right places separately and alphabetically. Based on the outcome of the alpha test phase, the system is adjusted and refined and later moved to the beta test phase. Note that both alpha and beta tests apply to commercially developed software for external customers and not for internally developed software for internal use of a company.

Alpha system ──→ Beta system

A beta test is when a group of volunteered people outside of a company (i.e., customers or others) test a new system, after it has been alpha tested, to make sure it works as intended and to discover any last-minute errors before it is released for commercialization (i.e., ready to market). It is a pre-release test. Note that both alpha and beta tests apply to commercially developed software for external customers and not for internally developed software for internal use of a company.

Alpha system ──→ Beta system ──→ Final system

Fault-tolerance mechanisms

Fault-tolerance mechanisms have the built-in capability to provide continued, correct execution of their assigned functions in the presence of hardware and/or software faults. Examples of such mechanisms include disk mirroring, server mirroring, disk duplexing, block mirroring, and checkpointing. Checkpointing is needed before, during, or after completion of critical transactions or events to ensure acceptable fault recovery.

Feasibility study

A feasibility study determines whether the needs of system users can be satisfied by a system's solution, considering the cost, capabilities, and benefits in developing, acquiring, operating, and maintaining a computer system.

File

A file is a collection of related records.

File allocation table

A file allocation is a table, stored on a disk, that contains an entry for each cluster on the disk.

File infector virus

A file infector virus attaches itself to (or replaces) .COM and .EXE files, although in some cases it can infect files with extension .SYS, .DRV, .BIN, .OVL, .OVR, and others. The most common file infector viruses are resident viruses, going into memory at the time the first copy runs and taking clandestine control of the computer. Such viruses commonly infect additional programs as they are run. Nonresident viruses simply infect one or more files whenever an infected file is run.

File organization

The term "file organization" refers to the manner in which records in a computer data file appear and are accessed for data entry, update, processing, retrieval, and query purposes (i.e., sequential, direct access).

File server

A file server sends and receives data between a workstation and the server.

File transfer protocol

File transfer protocol (FTP) is an Internet standard for transferring files over the Internet. It is a means to exchange files across a network. FTP programs and utility programs are used to upload and download web pages, graphics, and other files between local media and a remote server that allows FTP access. For example, in smartphones, the FTP server could result in arbitrary code execution, which is risky. Use of FTP is risky since it uses a weak security protocol.

Firewall

A firewall is a method of protecting a network against security threats from other systems and networks by centralizing and controlling access to the network using a combination of hardware and software controls. Several definitions exist for a firewall: (1) It is a process integrated with a computer operating system that detects and prevents undesirable applications and remote users from accessing or performing operations on a secure computer; security domains are established that require authorization to enter. (2) It is a product that acts as a barrier to prevent unauthorized or unwanted communications between sections of a computer network. (3) A firewall is a device or program that controls the flow of network traffic between networks or hosts that employ differing security postures. (4) It is a gateway that limits access between networks in accordance with local security policy. (5) It is a system designed to prevent unauthorized accesses to or from a private network. Firewalls often are used to prevent Internet users from accessing private networks connected to the Internet.

Firmware

The term "firmware" refers to computer programs and data loaded in a class of memory that cannot be easily modified by the user during processing.

Fragmentation

Fragmentation refers to chunks of unused space throughout primary memory or on a secondary storage device.

Frame

A frame is a group of bits that include data plus one or more addresses. It is the unit of data that is handled by the data link level layer (layer 2) of software in a data communication system.

Functional design

Functional design is a process in which the user's needs are translated into a system's technical specifications.

Fuzz testing

Fuzz testing is similar to fault injection testing in that invalid data is input into the application via the environment, or input by one process into another process. Fuzz testing is implemented by tools called fuzzers, which are programs or script that submit some combination of inputs to the test target to reveal how it responds.

Gateway

A gateway is a device to connect two different networks.

Gramm-Leach-Bliley Act

The Gramm-Leach-Bliley Act (GLBA) in 1999 also known as the Financial Services Modernization Act of 1999 requires financial institutions to protect their customers' information against security threats and maintain privacy. Three key rules under the Act dealing with privacy include the following:

(1) The financial privacy rule which governs the collection and disclosure of customers' personal financial information by financial institutions. It also applies to nonfinancial companies who receive and maintain such information. It requires financial institutions to provide a privacy notice to consumers that they have the right to opt out of the information being shared with unaffiliated parties pursuant to the provisions of the Federal Trade Commission's (FTC's) Fair Credit Reporting Act.

(2) The safeguards rule requires all financial institutions to design, implement, and maintain safeguards to protect customer information. It applies to financial institutions, credit reporting bureaus, property appraisers, and mortgage brokers who receive customer information either directly or indirectly.

(3) The pretexting protection deals with social engineering methods that occur when an unauthorized party tries to gain access to personal nonpublic information through impersonating the account holder by phone, by regular mail, by email, by texting, or by phishing (i.e., using a phony website or email to collect personal data).

Other provisions of the Act deal with designing, implementing, and monitoring computer logs that can be helpful in identifying possible privacy violations, security breaches, and resolving them effectively in a timely manner.

Gray box testing

Gray box testing is a software test methodology that assumes some knowledge of the internal structure and implementation detail of the assessment object. It is also known as focused testing.

Hacking back

A hacking back is a tempting reaction by an attack-victim organization to "hack back" the initial hacker who intruded the organization in the first place. It is not advised to hack back the hacker because it could be unethical and/or illegal, expensive, and time-consuming with unintended consequences. In a way, hacking back is fighting back.

Half-duplex

A half-duplex data communication line can transmit in both directions, but only in one direction at a time.

Hardware and software monitors

Hardware monitors work by attaching probes to processor circuits and detecting and recording events at those probes. Software monitors are programs that execute in a computer system to observe and report on the behavior of the system. Hardware and software monitors are security controls.

Hardware segmentation

The principle of hardware segmentation provides hardware transparency when hardware is designed in a modular fashion and when it is interconnected with other hardware modules. A failure in one module should not affect the operation of other modules. Similarly, a module attacked by an intruder should not compromise the entire system. System architecture should be arranged so that vulnerable networks or network segments can be quickly isolated or taken offline in the event of an attack. Examples of hardware that need to be segmented include network switches, physical circuits, and power supply equipment. Hardware segmentation is a security control.

Heat maps

A heat map is a visual map highlighting a major activity of interest, using a data visualization technology. It can be applied to several situations, such as a risk heat map; an attacker's heat map; a website's heat map; and an organization's governance, risk, and compliance (GRC) heat map showing data outliers and problem areas.

A **risk heat map** can show the impact (consequences) and probability (likelihoods) on a matrix. The impact can be labeled as very low, low, medium, high, and very high impact on a scale of 1 to 5. Similarly, the likelihood (riskiness) can be labeled as very less, less, medium, high, and very high probability between 0% and 100%. Color-coded heat maps highlight a major risk element of importance and data outliers.

An **attacker's heat map** shows an attacker's activity as an output from threat intelligence efforts. This map can help victim organizations build a profile of past and current attackers' activity, helping the organizations to better understand when, where, and how they will be attacked again in the future.

A **website's heat map** tracks website visitors' click behavior and browsing habits. These maps help a web administrator visualize how visitors are interacting with the website.

An **organization's GRC heat map** can show a quick comprehension of data when its reports are blended into its dashboards. These maps improve the efficiency and effectiveness of risk and compliance staff because they can highlight outliers or other problem areas quickly for their attention.

Hijacking attack

Hijacking is an attack that occurs during an authenticated session with a database system or non-database system. Hijacking can be data hijacking, as in a ransomware attack, or session hijacking, as in a data-in-transit attack.

Honeynet

Honeynet is a network of honeypot systems designed to attract hackers so that their intrusions can be detected and analyzed, and to study a hacker's behavior. Organizations should consult with their legal department before deploying a honeypot or honeynet for any legal ramifications of monitoring an attacker's activity. Honeypots and honeynets complement intrusion detection systems. A honeynet is a security control.

Honeypot systems

A honeypot system is a fake production system designed with firewalls, routers, web services, and database servers that look like a real production system, but acts as a decoy and is studied to see how attackers do their work. A honeypot could be a web server, a file on a server, or a host computer that is designed to be attractive to potential hackers in order to collect and study data on suspicious activity. Honeypots have no authorized users other than security administrators and attackers.

Honeypot systems are decoy systems that attempt to lure an attacker away from critical systems. These fake production systems are filled with information that is seemingly valuable but that has actually been fabricated and would not be accessed by an honest user. Thus, when access to the honeypot is detected, there is a high likelihood that it is an attacker. The purpose of the honeypot is to divert an attacker from accessing critical systems, collecting information about the attacker's activity, and encouraging the attacker to stay on the system long enough for a security administrator to respond. Organizations should consult their legal counsel before deploying a honeypot strategy for any legal ramifications of monitoring an attacker's activity. Honeypot systems are security controls.

Hop points

Hop points are remote servers where an attacker can hide stolen data from a victim's organization. Victims can trace and access these hop points for damage assessment, which is a difficult task to do. An alternate (and better) approach is to request the cooperation of an Internet service provider's (ISP's) technical help to locate and access these hop points so the stolen data can be retrieved and recovered.

Hot site

A hot site is a backup, alternate computer processing location with fully operational equipment and capacity to quickly take over system operations after loss of the primary system facility. A hot site has sufficient equipment and the most current version of production software installed, and adequate storage for the production system data. A hot site is used for short-term needs while a cold site is used for long-term needs. Hot sites are part of information technology continuity planning.

Hot spots

Hot spots consist of one or more Wi-Fi access points positioned on a ceiling or wall in a public place to provide maximum wireless coverage for a wireless LAN (WLAN). Hot spots have a security risk of eavesdropping and sniffing attacks.

Hypertext markup language

Hypertext markup language (HTML) is a mechanism used to create web pages on the Internet.

Hypertext transfer protocol

Hypertext transfer protocol (HTTP) is the native protocol of the web, used to transfer hypertext documents on the Internet.

Identity-based access control policy

Identity-based access control (IBAC) policy is an access control mechanism based only on the identity of the subject and object. An IBAC decision grants or denies a request based on the presence of an entity on an access control list. Identity-based access controls and discretionary access controls are considered equivalent.

Identity Theft Assumption and Deterrence Act

The Identity Theft Assumption and Deterrence Act of 1998 assigned the Federal Trade Commission (FTC) as a central clearinghouse for identity theft complaints. The ACT requires the FTC to log and acknowledge such complaints, provide victims with relevant information, and refer their complaints to appropriate law enforcement agencies and national consumer reporting agencies.

Independent testing of software

Independent testing of software is conducted by an independent accredited software testing organization as per the ISO/IEC 17025 standard to verify that it meets both functional requirements and software quality assurance requirements. The testing organization can use either a white or black box scenario, depending on the need.

Index

An index is a secondary path to data. Indexes are normally used to enhance the speed of data retrieval at the expense of update speed.

Information engineering

Information engineering (IE) is an approach to planning, analyzing, designing, and developing an information system with an enterprise-wide perspective and an emphasis on data and architectures.

Information security governance

Information security governance can be defined as the process of establishing and maintaining a framework and supporting management structure and processes to provide assurance that information security strategies are aligned with and support business objectives, are consistent with applicable laws and regulations through adherence to policies and internal controls, and provide assignment of responsibility, all in an effort to manage risk. Two organizational structures are recommended, including centralized and decentralized.

Information system

An information system (IS) is the organized collection, processing, transmission, and dissemination of information in accordance with defined procedures, whether automated or manual. Information systems include financial, nonfinancial, and mixed systems.

Information technology

Information technology (IT) is the hardware and software operated by an organization to accomplish a function, regardless of the technology involved (e.g., computers, telecommunications, etc.).

Information technology architecture

Information technology (IT) architecture is an integrated framework for evolving or maintaining existing IT and acquiring new IT to achieve the organization's strategic goals. A complete IT architecture should consist of both logical and technical components. The logical architecture provides the high-level description of the organization's mission, functional requirements, information requirements, system components, and information flows among the components. The technical architecture defines the specific IT standards and rules that will be used to implement the logical architecture.

Ingress filtering

Ingress filtering is the filtering of incoming network traffic. It blocks incoming packets that should not enter a network—those that use obviously false IP addresses, such as reserved source addresses.

Internet

The Internet is the worldwide network of networks that use the Transmission Control Protocol/ Internet Protocol (TCP/IP) protocol suite for communications.

Internet Protocol address

An Internet Protocol (IP) address is a globally unique number for a computer or other device that is used to determine where messages transmitted on the Internet should be delivered. The IP address routes Internet communications to and from the computer or device. The IP address is analogous to a house number for delivering postal mail.

Internet service provider

An Internet Service Provider (ISP) is an entity providing a network connection to the global Internet. The ISP can provide technical assistance to its customers during attacks on smart-phones, digital tablets, computers, and networks.

Internetworking

Internetworking is communication among devices across multiple networks.

Interpreter

An interpreter is the same as a compiler, in computer software, but an interpreter translates a single source statement and executes those machine-level instructions and then moves on to the next source statement.

Intranet

The Internet technology is used to develop a network within an organization for communicating among and between employees.

Intrusion detection system

An intrusion detection system (IDS) is a computer security system to detect, report, and provide a limited response to a security incident that may be harmful to an information system.

Intrusion prevention system

An intrusion prevention system (IPS) provides security policies and rules for network traffic along with an intrusion detection system for alerting system or network administrators to suspicious traffic, but allows the administrator to provide preventive action upon being alerted. IPS and IDS should be combined with a firewall for a stronger protection.

Jailbreaking

Jailbreaking is removing the limitations imposed on a device by the manufacturer, often through the installation of custom operating system components or other third-party software. Jail-breaking makes a device more vulnerable to attacks because it removes important safeguards against malware attacks. Some users prefer to bypass the operating system's lockout features in order to install apps that could be malicious in nature. Jailbreaking is risky.

Jamming attack

Jamming is an attack in which a mobile device is used to emit electromagnetic energy on a wireless network's frequency to make the network unusable. Jamming is used in denial-of-service attacks. Jamming attacks can take place based on how a mobile device was designed and developed; jailbreaking, tampering, and rooting attacks can take place based on what users are doing on their mobile devices.

Java

Java is a programming language invented by Sun Microsystems. It can be used as a general-purpose application programming language with built-in networking libraries. It can also be used to write small applications called applets. The execution environment for Java applets is intended to be safe (i.e., executing an applet should not modify anything outside the World Wide Web browser).

Kerberos

Kerberos is an authentication tool used in local logins, remote authentication, and client/server requests. It is a means of verifying the identities of principals on an open network. Kerberos accomplishes this without relying on the authentication, trustworthiness, or physical security of hosts while assuming all packets can be read, modified, and inserted at will. Kerberos uses a trust broker model and symmetric cryptography to provide authentication and authorization of users and systems on the network.

Kernel virus

A kernel is the base of an operating system of a computer system. A kernel virus loads into memory ahead of the operating system and avoids many traditional forms of virus detection. The virus operates at one level above the boot sector but within the heart of the operating system. The virus achieves "stealth" qualities such as hiding its code, making it difficult to trace.

Key

In cryptography, a key is a sequence of symbols that controls the operations of encryption and decryption.

Key logger

A key logger is a computer program designed to record which keys are pressed on a computer keyboard. It is used to obtain passwords or encryption leys and thus bypass other security measures.

Killer packet

A killer packet is a method of disabling a computer system by sending Ethernet or Internet Protocol (IP) packets that exploit bugs in the networking code to crash the system. A similar action is done by synchronized (SYN) floods, which is a method of disabling a computer system by sending more SYN packets than its networking code can handle.

Least privilege

The least privilege principle requires that each subject in a system be granted the most restrictive set of privileges (or lowest clearance) needed for the performance of authorized tasks. Application of this principle limits the damage that can result from accident, error, or unauthorized use.

Link virus

A link virus manipulates the directory structure of the media on which it is stored, pointing the operating system to virus code instead of legitimate code.

Local area network

A local area network (LAN) is a data communication network operating over a limited geographical area, typically within a building or group of buildings.

Logic bomb

A logic bomb is a resident computer program that triggers an unauthorized or damaging action when a particular event or state in the system's operation is realized (e.g., when a particular packet is received).

Macro virus

A specific type of computer virus that is encoded as a macro embedded in some document and activated when the document is handled. It is a virus that attaches itself to application documents, such as word processing files and spreadsheets, and uses that application's macro-programming language to execute and propagate.

Mailbombing

Mailbombing means flooding a site with enough mail to overwhelm its email system. It is used to hide or prevent receipt of email during an attack or as a retaliation against a site.

Main memory

Main memory is memory that can be directly accessed by the processor.

Maintenance hooks

Maintenance hooks are special instructions in software that allow easy maintenance and additional feature development. These are not clearly defined during access or design specification. Hooks frequently allow entry into the code at unusual points or without the usual checks, so they are a serious security risk if they are not removed prior to live implementation.

Maintenance hooks are special types of trapdoors. A trapdoor is a hidden software or hardware mechanism that can be triggered to permit system protection mechanisms to be circumvented. It is activated in some innocent-appearing manner, e.g., a special random key sequence at a terminal. Software developers often introduce trapdoors in their code to enable them to reenter the system and perform certain functions. Trapdoor is synonymous with back door.

Malvertizing attack

Malvertizing is the use of malicious advertisements (ads) on legitimate websites. These ads contain a programming code that will infect a user's computer without any action required from the user (i.e., the user does not have to click on the ad to become infected). Adware, which is a form of malware, can conduct malvertizing attacks.

Malware

Malware is malicious software, usually loaded onto a computer or device without the knowledge of the computer's owner or user. For example, computer viruses are malware. This malicious code contains computer instructions intended for abnormal program behavior. Contrast this behavior to unexpected program behavior due to errors or bugs introduced accidentally. Malware is designed to deny, destroy, modify, or impede the software's logic, configuration settings, data, or program library routines. It can be inserted during software development, preparation for distribution, deployment, installation, and/or update. It can be planted manually or through automated means, and it can also be inserted during a system's operation. Regardless of when in the software development life cycle the malware is embedded, it effectively becomes part of the software and can present substantial dangers and risks.

There are several ways in which malware is likely to be inserted during software development or maintenance through a back door or trapdoor, time bomb, logic bomb, and software holes. Malware is introduced into a system due to unnoticed, forgotten, or neglected functions or when unnecessary functions are disregarded. It can be discovered through table-top reviews, periodic assessments, war dialing, war driving, wireless scanning, and penetration testing. Examples of malware planted on operational systems include viruses, worms, Easter eggs, Trojan horses, zombies, cross-site scripts, botnets, rootkits, cookies, adware, spyware, vandalware, active content (Active X), applets, application program interface (API), electronic dumpster diving, and buffer overflow. A security control is to install anti-malware software and keep its attack signatures current, knowing that hackers can deactivate or kill the features and functions of anti-malware software to make it useless.

Malware router

A malware router (bad router) contains the capabilities of a normal router in the form of an Internet Protocol (IP) address and a domain name. The malware router conducts brute force attacks, exploits, or misconfigurations; steals data and program files; deletes files; escalates access privileges; and captures and logs keystrokes made on the keyboard.

Mandatory access control policy

Mandatory access control (MAC) policy is driven by the results of a comparison between the user's trust level/clearance and the sensitivity designation of the information. MAC is a means of restricting access to objects (system resources) based on the sensitivity (as represented by a label) of the information contained in the objects and the formal authorization (i.e., clearance) of subjects (users) to access information of such sensitivity. *Compare* with discretionary access control (DAC) policy.

Man-in-the-middle attack

A man-in-the-middle (MitM) attack results from using Wi-Fi wireless network communication technology. This is an attack on the authentication protocol run in which the attacker positions him- or herself between the claimant and verifier to intercept and alter data traveling between them.

MitM attacks occur in several forms.

- Using Wi-Fi wireless network communication technology.

- Taking advantage of the store-and-forward mechanism used by insecure networks such as the Internet (also called bucket brigade attack).

- Impersonating multiple legitimate parties, such as appearing as a client to an access point and appearing as an access point to a client. This allows an attacker to intercept communications between an access point and a client, thereby obtaining authentication credentials and data.

- Attacking on the authentication protocol run in which the attacker positions himself in between the claimant and verifier so that he or she can intercept and alter data traveling between them.

- Attacking public key algorithms, where an attacker substitutes his or her public key for the requested public key.

Security controls against MitM attacks include network segmentation tools, network hardening tools, system hardening tools, hardware segmentation practices, and software guards.

Masquerading

Several definitions exist for masquerading: (1) impersonating an authorized user and gaining unauthorized privileges; (2) an unauthorized agent claiming the identity of another agent; (3) an attempt to gain access to a computer system by posing as an authorized user; and (4) the pretense by which an entity pretends to be a different entity. It is synonymous with impersonating, mimicking, and spoofing. A security control is to install anti-spoofing countermeasures such as digital signatures to prevent the unauthorized use of legitimate authenticated data.

Mean time between failures

Mean time between failures (MTBF) is the average length of time a system is functional or the average time interval between failures. It is total functioning life of an item divided by the total number of failures during the measurement interval of minutes, hours, and days. It is the average length of time a system or a component works without fault between consecutive failures. MTBF assumes that the failed system is immediately repaired as in MTTR. A high MTBF means high system reliability. MTBF = MTTF + MTTR.

Mean time between outages

Mean time between outages (MTBO) is the mean time between equipment failures that result in a loss of system continuity or unacceptable degradation, as expressed by MTBO = MTBF/ (1 − FFAS), where MTBF is the non-redundant mean time between failures and FFAS is the fraction of failures for which the failed hardware or software is bypassed automatically. A low MTBO means high system availability.

Mean time to data loss

Mean time to data loss (MTTDL) is the average time before a loss of data occurs in a given disk array and is applicable to the redundant array of independent disk (RAID) technology. A low MTTDL means high data reliability.

Mean time to failure

Mean time to failure (MTTF) is the average time to the next failure. It is the time taken for a part of or an entire system to fail for the first time. MTTF assumes that the failed system is not repaired. A high MTTF means high system reliability.

Mean time to repair

Mean time to repair (MTTR) is the amount of time it takes to resume normal operation. It is the total corrective maintenance time divided by the total number of corrective maintenance actions during a given period of time. A low MTTR means high system reliability.

Meet-in-the-middle attack

Meet-in-the-middle attack (MiM) occurs when one end is encrypted and the other end is decrypted and the results are matched in the middle. MiM attacks are made on block ciphers. A block cipher is a sequence of binary bits that comprise the input and output data and encryption keys. A security control is to install robust encryption algorithms that cannot be easily broken.

Memory card

A memory card is a removable data storage device used for personal authentication, access authorization, card integrity, and application systems. A memory card is made up of nonvolatile flash memory chips.

Metropolitan area network

A metropolitan area network (MAN) is a network concept aimed at consolidating business operations and computers spread out in a town or city.

Migration

"Migration" is a term generally used to refer to the moving of data from an online storage device to an offline or low-priority storage device, as determined by the system or as requested by the system user.

Mirrored sites

Mirrored sites are fully redundant facilities with automated real-time information mirroring. A mirrored site (redundant site) is equipped and configured exactly like the primary site in all technical respects. Some organizations plan on having partial redundancy for disaster recovery purposes and partial processing for normal operations. The stocking of spare personal computers and their parts or local area network servers also provide some redundancy. Mirrored sites are a part of information technology continuity planning.

Mobile sites

Mobile sites are self-contained, transportable shells custom-fitted with specific telecommunications and system equipment necessary to meet system requirements. Mobile sites are a part of information technology continuity planning.

Modem

The term "modem" is an acronym for modulation/demodulation. During data transmission, the modem converts the computer representation of data into an audio signal for transmission on telephone, teletype, or intercom lines. When receiving data, the modem converts the audio signal to the computer data representation.

Modular design

Modular design is information system project design that breaks the development of a project into various pieces (modules) that each solve a specific part of the overall problem. These modules should be as narrow in scope and brief in duration as practicable. Such design minimizes the risk to an organization by delivering a net benefit that is separate from the development of other pieces.

Multipartite virus

A multipartite virus is a combination of both boot sector and file infector viruses, which can be spread by both methods.

Network

A network consists of two or more computers linked by communication lines.

Network-based attacks

Attacks can be launched against the network infrastructure used to communicate between the browser and server. An attacker can gain information by masquerading as a web server using a man-in-the-middle attack, whereby requests and responses are conveyed via the imposter as a watchful intermediary. Such a web spoofing attack allows the impostor to shadow not only a single targeted server, but also every subsequent server accessed. Other attack methods lie outside the browser-server framework and involve targeting the communications or the supporting platforms. For example, at a level of protocol below HTTP, an entity may eavesdrop on messages in transit between a browser and server to glean information. Many diagnostic tools, such as packet sniffers, can reconstruct HTTP traffic from captured IP packets. An attacking entity may also intercept messages in transit and modify their contents, substitute other contents, or simply replay the transmission dialogue later in an attempt to disrupt the synchronization or integrity of the information. For example, an attacker may modify the DNS mechanisms used by a computer to direct it to a false website. These techniques are often used to perform pharming attacks, where users may divulge sensitive information. Denial-of-service attacks through available network interfaces are another possibility, as well as exploits involving any existing platform vulnerability.

Network segmentation

Network segmentation requires isolating management networks and ports from the rest of the network components. Network segmentation is done to reduce a hacker's attack surface in that the greater the segmentation efforts, the smaller would be the attack surface's size. Network segmentation is a security control. Other segmentation efforts include:

- Isolating host computers, subscribers, and services to contain and protect them from one another

- Isolating computer operations consoles, access control lists (ACLs), and protocols such as hypertext transfer protocol (HTTP), HTTP security (HTTPS), secure shell (SSH), and Telnet.

Network sniffing

Network sniffing is software that monitors network communications, decodes protocols, and examines headers and payloads for information of interest. It is both a passive review technique and an attack-target identification and analysis technique. On a TCP/IP network protocol, network sniffers audit information packets. It is a network-monitoring tool, usually running on a personal computer. Network sniffing precedes either a spoofing attack or a hijacking attack.

Node

A node is a communication point at which subordinate items of data originate. Examples include cluster controllers, terminals, computers, networks.

Object

An object is a passive entity that contains or receives information. Examples of objects are records, blocks, files, and programs.

Object-based virus

Major office application programs are written in objects, so they can be reused. These objects are loaded into random access memory and linked together only when they are needed. An object-based virus infects the object and avoids normal methods of detection. Most antivirus software packages protect and monitor executable files, not objects.

Object code/module

An object code/module is source code compiled to convert to object code, a machine-level language or computer software.

Offline storage

Offline storage refers to the storage of data on media that are physically removed from the computer system and stored elsewhere (e.g., disks and flash drives).

Offsite storage

In offsite storage, backup programs, data files, forms, and documentation, including a contingency plan, are stored in a location remote from the primary computer facility. These are used at backup computer facilities during a disaster or major interruption at the primary computer facility.

Operating system

An operating system (OS) is an integrated collection of computer programs, service routines, and supervising procedures to operate a computer (i.e., scheduling of jobs, loading of programs, allocation of memory, file management, controlling of input/output operations).

Operating system (console) log

An operating system (console) log provides information on who used computer resources, for how long, and for what purpose. Unauthorized actions can be detected by analyzing the OS log.

Optical fiber

Optical fiber is a thin filament of glass or other transparent material through which a signal-encoded light beam may be transmitted by means of total internal reflection.

Overlay

Overlay refers to storing a program module in the main memory space previously allocated to another, no-longer-needed module of the same program.

Overwriting virus

An overwriting virus destroys code or data in the host program by replacing it with the virus code. Most viruses attempt to retain the original host program's code and functionality after infection because the virus is more likely to be detected and deleted if the program ceases to work. A non-overwriting virus is designed to append the virus code to the physical end of the program or to move the original code to another location.

Packet sniffer

A packet sniffer is software that observes and records network traffic. It is a passive review technique with little or no harm.

Padded cell systems

Padded cell systems take a different approach from honeypots and honeynets. Instead of trying to attract attackers with tempting data, a padded cell waits for traditional intrusion detection and prevention systems to detect an attacker. The attacker is then seamlessly transferred to a special padded cell host. The attacker may not realize anything has happened but is now in a simulated environment where it can not cause any harm. Like the honeypot, this simulated environment can be filled with interesting data to convince an attacker that the attack is going according to plan. Padded cells offer unique opportunities to monitor the actions of an attacker. Padded cell systems complement intrusion detection systems.

Parasitic virus

Parasitic viruses are more numerous but less prevalent than boot sector viruses. They are considered file infectors because they infect executable files.

Parity bit

A parity bit is a bit indicating whether the sum of a previous series of bits is even or odd.

Parity checking

Parity checking is a hardware control in computers that detects data errors during transmission. It compares the sum of a previous set of bits with the parity bit to determine if an error in the transmission or receiving of the message has occurred.

Passive testing

Passive testing is a non-intrusive security test, primarily involving reviews of documents such as policies, procedures, security requirements, software code, system configurations, and system logs.

Passphrase

A passphrase is a unique password, not like a simple password, and is both strong and easy to remember. It follows several safeguard guidelines: It is longer than a simple, or normal password, it is not a common phrase, and it includes numbers, both lowercase and uppercase letters, and special characters (e.g., dollar sign, pound sign, or punctuation).

Patch management

Patch management is the process of acquiring, testing, and distributing patches, fixes, and service packs to the appropriate system administrators and users throughout organizations.

Peer-to-peer network

A peer-to-peer (P2P) network refers to a means of networking computers such that they communicate directly with each other, rather than through a centralized management point. P2P is an Internet network in which a group of computer users, each equipped with the same networking program, can connect to each other and directly access files from one another's computers. Use of P2P can be risky due to data sharing and malware spreading.

Penetration testing

Penetration testing is a type of laboratory-based testing. It consists of: (1) pretest analysis based on full knowledge of the target system, (2) pretest identification of potential vulnerabilities based on pretest analysis, and (3) current testing designed to determine exploitability of identified vulnerabilities. Detailed rules of engagement are agreed on by all parties before the commencement of any penetration testing scenario.

Penetration testing is a test methodology in which test assessors, using all available documentation (e.g., system design, source code, and manuals) and working under specific constraints, attempt to circumvent or defeat the security features of an information system. It is a security testing method in which evaluators mimic real-world attacks in an attempt to identify ways to circumvent the security features of an application system, operating system, or network.

Penetration testing often involves issuing real attacks on real systems and data, using the common tools and techniques used by actual attackers. Most penetration tests involve looking for combinations of vulnerabilities on a single system or multiple systems that can be used to gain more access than could be achieved through a single vulnerability. It is good to consider penetration testing as a form of self-hacking into a company's own systems to test the security of them and the ability to defend against attacks. It is also a type of self-analysis of identifying strengths and weaknesses of a company's own computer systems and networks.

Another technique in penetration testing is network weaving in which different communication networks are linked to access an information system to avoid detection and trace-back.

A one-time penetration testing is not useful when attacks occur frequently. Hence, a continuous testing of security should be undertaken across all phases of a new system development and maintenance work. Costs for initial testing, retesting, retrofitting, and redeploying the system must be considered for each application and operating system.

Perfective maintenance

The term "perfective maintenance" refers to all changes, insertions, deletions, modifications, extensions, and enhancements made to a system to meet the user's evolving or expanding needs.

Pharming attack

Pharming is misdirecting users to fraudulent websites or proxy servers, typically through domain name system hijacking or poisoning. A pharming attack is a computer attack in which an attacker corrupts an infrastructure service, such as the domain name system (DNS), causing the subscriber to be misdirected to a forged verifier/relying party and to reveal sensitive information, download harmful software, or contribute to a fraudulent act. It uses DNS server software to redirect users into accessing a fake website masquerading as a legitimate one and divulging personal information. It is a digital form of social engineering technique.

Phishing attack

Phishing is tricking individuals into disclosing sensitive personal information through deceptive computer-based means. Phishing attacks use social engineering and technical subterfuge to steal consumers' personal identity data and financial account credentials. It involves Internet fraudsters who send spam or pop-up messages to obtain personal information (e.g., credit card numbers, bank account information, Social Security numbers, passwords, or other sensitive information) from unsuspecting victims.

A phishing attack is a computer attack in which the subscriber is lured (usually through an email) to interact with a counterfeit verifier and tricked into revealing information that can be used to masquerade as that subscriber to the real verifier. It is a digital form of social engineering technique that uses authentic-looking but phony (bogus) emails to request personal information from users or direct them to a fake website that requests such information. It tricks or deceives individuals into disclosing sensitive personal information through deceptive computer-based means.

Piggyback entry

A piggyback entry is one where unauthorized access to a system or information system facility is gained via another user's legitimate connection.

Ping-of-death attack

A ping-of-death attack sends a series of oversized packets via the Ping command. The ping server reassembles the packets at the host machine. The result is that the attack could hang, crash, or reboot the system. This is an example of a buffer overflow attack.

Platform

A platform is the foundation technology (bottommost layer) of a computer system. The term also refers to the type of computer (hardware) or operating system (software) being used.

Plug-ins

Plug-ins are computer applications intended for use in a web browser (e.g., Adobe Flash). Plug-ins are similar to Microsoft's Active X controls but cannot be executed outside of a web browser. Plug-ins can be risky because they can contain programming flaws, such as buffer overflows, or they may contain design flaws, such as cross-domain violations.

Polymorphic virus

During replication, a polymorphic virus creates instructions that are functionally equivalent but have distinctly different byte streams. To achieve this, the virus may randomly insert superfluous instructions, change the order of independent instructions, or choose from a number of different encryption schemes. This variable quality makes the virus difficult to locate, identify, or remove. A polymorphic virus produces varied copies of itself, in the hope that virus scanners will not be able to detect all instances of the virus. These copies are operational in nature. A simple boot sector or file virus is transformed into a polymorphic virus using a mutation engine, which further proliferates. Polymorphic viruses are difficult to detect due to their proliferation.

Pretty good privacy

Pretty good privacy (PGP) is a computer program used to encrypt and decrypt data, primarily email, over the Internet.

Privileged access accounts

Privileged access accounts are assigned to individuals who have access to a set of "access rights" on a given computer system. These are sometimes referred to as system or network administrative accounts, which are assigned to privileged users.

Privileged programs

Privileged programs are those programs that if unchecked could cause damage to computer files. For example, IBM's SUPERZAP is a powerful utility program that can destroy files if controls are circumvented.

Privileged user

A privileged user is an individual who has access to system control, monitoring, or administration functions (e.g., system administrator, information system security officer, system maintainer, and system programmer). Privileged users are trusted users.

Program race conditions

Race conditions can occur when a program or process has entered into a privileged mode but before the program or process has given up its privileged mode. A user can time an attack to take advantage of this program or process while it is still in the privileged mode. If an attacker successfully manages to compromise the program or process during its privileged state, then the attacker has won the "race." Common race conditions occur in signal handling and core-file manipulation, time-of-check to time-of-use (TOC–TOU) attacks, symbolic links, and object-oriented programming errors.

Protocol

A protocol is a set of rules that govern the way in which computers or other functional units transfer data.

Prototyping

Prototyping is a hardware and software development technique in which a preliminary version of part or all of the hardware or software is developed to permit user feedback, determine feasibility, or investigate timing or other issues in support of the development process.

Purging

Purging is the removal of sensitive data from storage media at the end of a period of processing, including from peripheral devices with storage capacity, in such a way that there is assurance, proportional to the sensitivity of the data, that the data may not be reconstructed through open-ended laboratory techniques (i.e., information scavenging through laboratory equipment). The storage media must be disconnected from any external network before a purge. A potential risk is reconstruction of data if the purging operation is not performed properly.

Rainbow attacks

Rainbow attacks occur in two ways: using rainbow tables, which are used in password cracking, and using pre-shared keys (PSKs) in a wireless local area network (WLAN) configuration. Password cracking threats include discovering a character string that produces the same encrypted hash as the target password. In PSK environments, a secret passphrase is shared between base stations and access points, and the keys are derived from a passphrase that is shorter than 20 characters, which are less secure and subject to dictionary and rainbow attacks. Rainbow tables are lookup tables that contain precomputed password hashes, often used during password cracking. These tables allow an attacker to crack a password with minimal time and effort.

Rapid prototyping

Rapid prototyping is a type of prototyping in which emphasis is placed on developing prototypes early in the development process to permit early feedback and analysis in support of the development process.

Recovery

Recovery is the process of reconstituting a database to its correct and current state following a partial or complete hardware, software, network, operational, or processing error or failure.

Recovery controls

Recovery controls are actions necessary to restore a system's computational and processing capability and data files after a system failure or penetration. Recovery controls for information technology continuity planning are related to recovery point objective and recovery time objective.

Recovery point objective

The recovery point objective (RPO) is a point in time in which data must be recovered after an outage in order to resume computer processing. RPO is a part of information technology continuity planning.

Recovery time objective

Recovery time objective (RTO) is the overall length of time an information system's components can be in the recovery phase before the organization's mission or business functions are negatively impacted. It is the maximum acceptable length of time that elapses before the unavailability of the system severely affects the organization. RTO is a part of information technology continuity planning.

Red team

A red team is a group of people authorized and organized to emulate a potential adversary's attack or exploitation capabilities against an enterprise's security posture by conducting penetration testing. The red team's objective is to improve enterprise information assurance by demonstrating the impacts of successful attacks and what works for the defenders (i.e., the blue team) in an operational environment. The red team is a test team that performs penetration security testing using covert methods and without the knowledge and consent of the organization's IT staff but with full knowledge and permission of upper management.

The red team's exercises reflect real-world conditions; the team's attacks are conducted as a simulated adversarial attempt to compromise organizational missions and/or business processes to provide a comprehensive assessment of the security capability of the information system and the organization itself

Redundant Array of Independent Disks

A Redundant array of independent disks (RAID) is a cluster of disks used to back up data onto multiple disk drives at the same time, providing increased data reliability and increased input/output performance. Seven classifications for RAID are numbered as RAID-0 through RAID-6. RAID storage units offer fault-tolerant hardware with varying degrees. Nested or hybrid RAID levels occur with two-deep levels. For example, a simple RAID configuration with six disks includes four data disks, one parity disk, and one hot spare disk.

Problems with RAID include correlated failures due to drive mechanical issues, atomic write semantics (meaning that the write of the data either occurred in its entirety or did not occur at all), write cache reliability due to a power outage, hardware incompatibility with software, data recovery in the event of a failed array, untimely drive errors recovery algorithm, increasing recovery times due to increased drive capacity, operator skills in terms of correct replacement and rebuild of failed disks, and exposure to computer viruses. RAID is a part of information technology continuity planning.

Regression testing

Regression testing means rerunning test cases that a program has previously executed correctly in order to detect errors created during software correction or modification activities.

Reliability

Reliability is the extent to which a computer system, hardware, or program can be expected to perform its intended function with required precision.

Remediation of threats

Remediation is the act of correcting a vulnerability or eliminating a threat. Three possible types of remediation are installing patches, adjusting configuration settings, and uninstalling a software application.

Research virus

A research virus is a virus that has been written but has never been unleashed on the public. These viruses include samples that have been sent to researchers by virus writers.

Resident virus

A resident virus installs itself as part of the operating system upon execution of an infected host program. The virus will remain resident until the system is shut down. Once installed in memory, a resident virus is available to infect all suitable hosts that are accessed. A resident virus loads into memory, hooks one or more interrupts, and remains inactive in memory until some trigger event. When the trigger event occurs, the virus becomes active, either infecting something or causing some other consequence (such as displaying something on the screen). All boot viruses are resident viruses, as are the most common file viruses. Macro viruses are nonresident viruses.

Resource isolation

Resource isolation is the containment of subjects and objects in a system in such a way that they are separated from one another, as well as from the protection controls of the operating system. The architecture should ensure that the trusted computing base (TCB) imposes its discretionary access controls and auditing on all of the subjects and objects under its control.

Response time

Response time is the time elapsed between entering a transaction or query and seeing the first character of the system's response appear on a computer or terminal screen.

Restore

A restore is the process of retrieving a dataset that has been migrated to offline storage and restoring it to online storage.

Retention program (documents)

A retention program is a management program to save documents, forms, history logs, master and transaction data files, computer programs (both source and object level), and other documents on the system until no longer needed. Retention periods should satisfy organization and legal requirements.

Rivest-Shamir-Adelman algorithm

The Rivest-Shamir-Adelman (RSA) algorithm is a public key algorithm used for key establishment and for generation and verification of digital signatures, encrypt messages, and provides key management for the data encryption standard (DES) and other secret key algorithms.

Role-based access control policy

Several definitions exist for role-based access control (RBAC) policy. It is: (1) access control based on user roles (e.g., a collection of access authorizations a user receives based on an explicit or implicit assumption of a given role). Role permissions may be inherited through a role hierarchy and typically reflect the permissions needed to perform defined functions within an organization. A given role may apply to a single individual or to several individuals. (2) It is a model for controlling access to resources where permitted actions on resources are identified with roles rather than with individual subject identities. RBAC is an access control based on specific job titles, functions, roles, and responsibilities.

Roll back

A roll back restores the database from one point in time to an earlier point.

Roll forward

A roll forward restores the database from a point in time when it is known to be correct to a later time.

Rooting

Rooting, similar to jailbreaking, is removing the limitations imposed on a device by the manufacturer, often through the installation of custom operating system components or other third-party software. Rooting makes a device more vulnerable to attacks because it removes important safeguards against malware attacks. Some users prefer to bypass the operating system's lockout features in order to install apps that could be malicious in nature. Rooting is risky.

Rootkit

A rootkit is a collection of computer files that is installed on a computer system to alter the standard functionality of the system in a malicious and stealthy way. It is a set of tools used by an attacker after gaining root-level access to a host computer to conceal an attacker's activities on the host and permit the attacker to maintain root-level access to the host through covert means. Some examples of protection methods against botnets and rootkits include using and maintaining antivirus software, installing a firewall, using strong passwords, updating software with patches, and taking precautions when using emails and web browsers not to trigger an infection.

Router

A router is a physical or logical entity that receives and transmits data packets or establishes logical connections among a diverse set of communicating entities (usually supports both hardwired and wireless communication devices simultaneously).

Rule-based access control policy

A rule-based access control (RuBAC) policy is based on specific rules relating to the nature of the subject and object, beyond its identity, such as a security label. A RuBAC decision requires authorization information and restriction information to compare before any access is granted. RuBAC and mandatory access control policy are considered equivalent.

Rules of behavior

Rules of behavior are rules that are established and implemented concerning use of, security in, and acceptable level of risk in a computer system. They clearly delineate responsibilities and expected behavior of all individuals with access to the system. The organization establishes and makes readily available to all information systems these rules, which describe their responsibilities and expected behavior with regard to information system use. Rules of behavior are established to control the business behavior of employees' on computer systems.

Rules of engagement

Rules of engagement are detailed guidelines and constraints regarding the execution of information security testing. These rules are established before the start of a security test. They give the test team authority to conduct the defined activities without the need for additional permissions. Rules of engagement are established to control the behavior of contractors, vendors, and suppliers during their work for an organization.

Rule set

A rule set is a table of instructions used by a controlled (managed) interface to determine what data are allowable and how the data are handled between interconnected computer systems. Rule sets govern access control functionality of a firewall or a router. The firewall uses these rule sets to determine how packets should be routed between its interfaces. A rule set is a collection of rules or signatures that network traffic or system activity is compared against to determine an action to take, such as forwarding or rejecting a packet, creating an alert, or allowing a system event.

Sandboxing

Sandboxing has several definitions:

(1) It is a method of isolating application modules into distinct fault domains enforced by software. The technique allows untrusted programs written in an unsafe language, such as C, to be executed safely within the single virtual address space of an application. Untrusted machine interpretable code modules are transformed so that all memory accesses are confined to code and data segments within their fault domain. Access to system resources can also be controlled through a unique identifier associated with each domain.

(2) New malicious code protection products introduce a "sandbox" technology allowing users the option to run programs such as Java and Active-X in quarantined subdirectories of systems. If malicious code is detected in a quarantined program, the system removes the associated files, protecting the rest of the system.

(3) It is a method of isolating each guest operating system from the others and restricting what resources they can access and what privileges they can have (i.e., restrictions and privileges).

Scamming attack

Scamming is impersonating a legitimate business using the Internet. Buyers should verify sellers before buying goods or services. Sellers should give out a physical address with a working telephone number.

Scanning attack

A scanning attack is sending network packets or requests to another system to gain information to be used in a subsequent attack.

Scanning check

Scanning checks are performed on computer files for evidence of unauthorized or malicious code. Two types of scanning exist: online scanning and offline scanning. Online scanning checks files as they are created, opened, closed, or executed. Online scanning is performed by memory-resident antivirus software. Other names for online scanning include automatic, background, resident, and active scanning. On the other hand, offline scanning is performed on-demand by a user or process. Other names for offline scanning include manual, foreground, nonresident, and inactive scanning. A scanning check is a security control.

Scavenging of data

Data scavenging is searching through the residual data on storage media for the purpose of unauthorized data acquisition.

Schema

A schema is a set of specifications that defines a database. Specifically, it includes entity names, sets, groups, data items, areas, sort sequences, access keys, and security locks.

Secondary storage

Secondary storage consists of nonvolatile, auxiliary memory such as disk or tape/cartridge used for the long-term storage of programs and data.

Secure Sockets Layer

Secure Sockets Layer (SSL) is a method for securing information exchange on the Internet. SSL uses data encryption and digital certificate authentication to secure the information exchange.

Security by obscurity

Security by obscurity is a countermeasure principle that does not work in practice because attackers can compromise the security of any system at any time. The meaning of this principle is that trying to keep something secret when it is not does more harm than good.

Security filters

A security filter is a secure subsystem of an information system that enforces security policy on the data passing through it.

Security functions

Security functions are the hardware, software, and/or firmware of the information system responsible for enforcing the system security policy and supporting the isolation of code and data on which the protection is based.

Self-recognition virus

A self-recognition virus is a virus that determines whether an executable is already infected. The procedure usually involves searching for a particular value at a known position in the executable. Self-recognition is required if the virus is to avoid multiple infections of a single executable. Multiple infections cause excessive growth in size of infected executables and corresponding excessive storage space, contributing to virus detection.

Sensitive data

Sensitive data are those that require a degree of protection due to the risk and magnitude of loss or harm that could result from inadvertent or deliberate disclosure, alteration, or destruction of the data (e.g., personal data, proprietary data).

Sensitive system

A sensitive system is a computer system that requires a degree of protection because it processes sensitive data or because of the risk and magnitude of loss or harm that could result from improper operation or deliberate manipulation of the application system.

Server-based attacks

Attacks can be launched against web server components and technologies by the browser. A browser can easily isolate and capture a response from a server, and may launch an attack by manipulating information and feeding back unexpected input to the server in a subsequent request. The idea is to induce the server to perform unauthorized commands provided by the browser, which in turn gains access to sensitive information or control of the server. For example, because HTTP is stateless, having no integrated mechanisms for maintaining persistent information between transactions, web-based applications often use tricks, such as session identifiers, to provide continuity between transactions. Poorly implemented session-tracking may provide an avenue of attack. Similarly, user-provided input might eventually be passed to an application interface that interprets the input as part of a command, such as a Structured Query Language (SQL) command. Attackers may also inject custom code into the website for subsequent browsers to process via cross-site scripting (XSS). Subtle changes introduced into the web server can radically change the server's behavior (e.g., turning a trusted entity into a malicious one), the accuracy of the computation (e.g., changing computational algorithms to yield incorrect results), or the confidentiality of the information (e.g., disclosing collected information).

Server mirroring

The purpose of server mirroring is the same as disk arrays, but a file server is duplicated instead of a disk. All information is written to both servers simultaneously to back up data.

Service

Service is a result generated by activities and the interface between suppliers and customers and by suppliers' internal activities to meet customers' needs. An organization can have both internal and external suppliers and customers.

Service-level agreements

Service-level agreements (SLAs) between service providers and receivers should, as a minimum, specify these points:

- Explicit definitions of the roles and responsibilities of both the user organization and the service provider.

- Period of performance and/or deliverables due dates.

- Defined service levels and their costs.

- Defined processes regarding how managers will assess the service provider's compliance with the service level and due date targets, rules, laws, regulations, and performance levels.

- Specific remedies (e.g., financial, technical, and legal) for noncompliance or harm caused by the service provider.

- Explicit rules and processes for handling sensitive data to ensure privacy.

Session hijack attack

Session hijacking is an attack in which the attacker can insert him- or herself between a claimant and a verifier subsequent to a successful authentication exchange between the latter two parties. The attacker can pose as a subscriber to the verifier or vice versa to control session data exchange. This attack results from using Bluetooth wireless technology due to its vulnerability in facilitating a key negotiation hijack attack during session initialization.

Shareware
Shareware is software that is distributed free of charge, often through electronic bulletin boards; it may be freely copied. Often, a nominal fee is requested if the program is found useful.

Shoulder surfing attack
Shoulder surfing attack is stealing passwords or personal identification numbers by looking over someone's shoulder. It is also called a keyboard logging attack because a keyboard is used to enter passwords and identification numbers. Shoulder surfing attacks can also be done at a distance using binoculars or other vision-enhancing devices, and these attacks are common when using automated teller machines and point-of-sale terminals. A simple and effective **security control** to avoid this type of attack is to shield the keypad while entering the required data.

Side-channel attacks
Side-channel attacks result from the physical implementation of a cryptosystem. Examples of these attacks include timing, power monitoring, TEMPEST, and thermal imaging attacks. Improper error handling in cryptographic operation can also allow side-channel attacks. In all these attacks, side-channel leakage of information occurs during the physical operation of a cryptosystem through monitoring of sound from computations, observing from a distance, and introducing faults into computations, thus revealing secrets such as the cryptographic key, system-state information, initialization vectors, and plaintext. Side-channel attacks are possible even when transmissions between a web browser and server are encrypted. Note that side-channel attacks are different from social engineering attacks, where the latter involves deceiving or coercing people who have the legitimate access to a cryptosystem. In other words, the focus of side-channel attacks are on data and information, not on people. Countermeasures against the side-channel attacks include implementing physical security over hardware, jamming the emitted channel with noise (white noise), designing isochronous software so it runs in a constant amount of time independent of secret values, designing software so that it is PC-secure, building secure CPUs (asynchronous CPUs) so they have no global timing reference, and retransmitting the failed (error prone) transmission with a predetermined number of times.

Sign-off
Functional users are requested and required to approve in writing their acceptance of the system at various stages or phases of the system development life cycle.

Signal injection attack
A signal injection attack can result from using a credit card or debit card during the card's transmission of signals using signal analyzers.

Signal interception attack
A signal interception attack can result from using a credit card or debit card during the card's transmission of signals using signal analyzers.

Simplicity in security
Security mechanisms and information systems in general should be as simple as possible. Here, simplicity refers to simplicity in design, operation, and use. Complexity is at the root of many security vulnerabilities and breaches.

Single-hop problem
A single-hop problem is a security risk resulting from a mobile software agent moving from its home platform to another platform.

Single point-of-failure

A single point-of-failure is a security risk due to concentration of risk in one place, system, process, or with one person. Examples include placement of web servers and DNS servers, primary telecommunication services, centralized identity management, central certification authority, password synchronization, single sign-on systems, firewalls, Kerberos, converged networks with voice and data, cloud storage services, and system administrators.

Single sign-on

A single sign-on (SSO) represents a technology that allows a user to authenticate once and then access all the resources the user is authorized to use.

Sinkhole

A sinkhole is the redirection of network traffic, which is typically malicious in nature, from its original destination to a new destination where its malicious function will instead have a harmless or limited effect. This technique is most commonly used by cybersecurity researchers to redirect a victim's infected computers in a botnet attack to specified research computers to capture data about the hackers. This technique is also occasionally used in conjunction with law enforcement operations to take control of infected attack-victim computers in a botnet attack away from hackers. Law enforcement staff call the infected computers as shadow computers, infected servers as shadow servers, and infected routers as shadow routers.

$$\text{Infected servers} \longrightarrow \text{Sinkholed} \longrightarrow \text{Shadow servers}$$

Sinkhole router

A sinkhole router is a part of computer forensic identification which mitigates extraneous and malicious traffic coming from an ongoing traffic. Sources of active identification include login scripts; customized network-based intrusion prevention system (IPS) or intrusion detection system (IDS) signatures; packet sniffers, vulnerability assessment software; host computer scans; and file scans. Routers and servers can be sinkholed.

Skimming attack

A skimming attack is the unauthorized use of a reader to read tags without the authorization or knowledge of the tag's owner or the individual in possession of the tag. An example of a skimming attack is on radio frequency identification (RFID) tags. A security control is to install anti-skimming material using electromagnetic shields.

Smart card

A smart card is a credit card–size card with embedded integrated circuits that can store, process, and communicate information. It has a built-in microprocessor and memory that is used for identification of individuals or financial transactions. When inserted into a reader, the card transfers data to and from a central computer. A smart card is more secure than a magnetic stripe card and can be programmed to self-destruct if the wrong password is entered too many times.

Smurf attack

A smurf attack occurs when a hacker sends a request for information to the special broadcast address of a network attached to the Internet. The request sparks a flood of responses from all the nodes on this first network. The answers are then sent to a second network that becomes a victim. If the first network has a larger capacity for sending out responses than the second network is capable of receiving, the second network experiences a DoS problem as its resources become saturated or strained.

Sniffer attack

A sniffer attack is performed by software that observes and records network traffic. On a TCP/IP network, a sniffer audits information packets. It is a network-monitoring tool, usually running on a PC.

Snooping attack

Snooping, scanning, and sniffing are all actions that search for sensitive and valuable information. They involve looking around for vulnerabilities (security weaknesses) while planning to attack. These are preparatory actions prior to launching serious penetration attacks.

Social engineering

Social engineering attacks are of two types: technical (digital) social engineering and non-technical social engineering. Examples of digital social engineering attacks include pretexting, phishing, and pharming activities. Some spyware software can trick users to run or install malware. Nontechnical social engineering attacks rely heavily on human interaction and often involve tricking other people into breaking normal security procedures. The best security control is to exercise caution when downloading anything from public websites, newsgroups, instant messaging sessions, or when opening email attachments from unknown persons.

Software escrow arrangement

A software escrow arrangement represents something (e.g., a document, software source code, or an encryption key) that is delivered to a third person to be given to the grantee only upon the fulfillment of a condition or a contract.

Software guard

A software guard is a security mechanism limiting the exchange of information between information systems or subsystems. It operates as a gatekeeper in the form of an application layer guard to implement firewall mechanisms, such as performing identification and authentication functions and enforcing security policies. Guard functionality includes such features as cryptographic invocation checks on information that is allowed outside the protected enclave and data content filtering to support sensitivity regrade decisions. The guard functionality, although effective for non-real-time applications (e.g., email on networks with low sensitivity), has been difficult to scale to highly classified networks and real-time applications. Software guards provide security controls.

Software holes

Software holes (software weaknesses) penetrate through lack of perimeter defenses, which is risky due to potential entry points into a computer system or network. Software holes can reside on any of the three layers (i.e., networking, operating system, or application), and software vendors or developers should provide security mechanisms to mitigate the risks. Defending the perimeter requires installing appropriate security controls at all entry points into the network, including the Internet connection. Testing the perimeter to identify back doors and software holes requires tabletop reviews, periodic risk assessments, war-dialing, war-driving, wireless scanning, and penetration testing.

Source code/module

Source code/module is the form of software used by programmers to create and modify software.

Source code escrow

Source code escrow is an arrangement with a third party (e.g., a bank) to hold the software under its custody and make it available to user organizations under unusual business circumstances. This arrangement is applicable to vendor-developed applications software packages either purchased or leased by user organizations. Because it is risky, vendors usually do not give the source code to users.

Source code virus

Visual Basic programming language is a good target for a source code virus where it looks for file extensions such as .C and .BAS.

Spamming

Spamming refers to posing identical messages to multiple unrelated newsgroups on the Internet (e.g., USENET). It is often used as cheap advertising, to promote pyramid schemes, or simply to annoy other people.

Split knowledge

Split knowledge is a process by which a cryptographic key is split into multiple key components, individually sharing no knowledge of the original key, which can be subsequently input into, or output from, a cryptographic module by separate entities and combined to re-create the original cryptographic key. It is the separation of data into two or more parts, with each part constantly kept under control of separate authorized individuals or teams so that no one individual will be knowledgeable of the total data involved. It is similar to using a dual control mechanism.

Split tunneling

Split tunneling has multiple definitions: (1) A virtual private network (VPN) client feature that tunnels all communications involving an organization's internal resources through the VPN, thus protecting them, and excludes all other communications from going through the tunnel. (2) A method that routes organization-specific traffic through the SSL-VPN tunnel, but other traffic uses the remote user's default gateway.

Spoofing

Spoofing is the deliberate inducement of a user or a resource to take an incorrect action. Many spoofing attacks exist. An example is the Internet Protocol spoofing attack, in which a network packet is sent that appears to come from a source other than its actual source. Spoofing involves the ability to receive a message by masquerading as the legitimate receiving destination or masquerading as the sending machine and sending a message to a destination.

Spoofing attack

Many spoofing attacks exist. An example is the Internet protocol (IP) spoofing attack, which refers to sending a network packet that appears to come from a source other than its actual source. It involves (1) the ability to receive a message by masquerading as the legitimate receiving destination or (2) masquerading as the sending machine and sending a message to a destination. A security control is to install anti-spoofing countermeasures such as digital signatures to prevent the unauthorized use of legitimate authenticated data.

Spoofing, in part, is using various techniques to subvert Internet Protocol (IP)–based access control by masquerading as another system by using its IP address. Spoofing is an attempt to gain access to a system by posing as an authorized user. Other examples of spoofing include spoofing packets to hide the origin of attack in a denial of service (DoS) situation, spoofing email headers to hide spam, and spoofing phone numbers to fool caller-ID. Spoofing involves the ability to receive a message by masquerading as the legitimate receiving destination or masquerading as the sending machine and sending a message to a destination.

Spoofing is synonymous with impersonating, masquerading, or mimicking and is not synonymous with sniffing.

Spyware

Spyware is adware that tracks user activity and passes it to third parties without the user's knowledge or consent. Its intent is to violate a user's privacy. Types of spyware include web bugs, which are tiny graphics on a website that are referenced within the Hypertext Markup Language (HTML) content of a web page or email to collect information about the user viewing the HTML content. Tracking cookies are another example where cookies are placed on the user's computer to track activity on different websites and create a detailed profile of the user's behavior. To combat spyware, install an antispyware software, which is a program that specializes in detecting both malware and non-malware forms of spyware.

Stackguarding technology

Stackguarding technology uses a layered defense approach, which makes it extremely difficult for attackers to exploit computer buffer overflows, the most common type of vulnerability discovered in network code. Stackguarding can also prevent worms from gaining increased privileges on that system. Worms that gain control of a low-privilege account may attempt to elevate their privilege. Hence, stackguarding can defend against buffer overflow and worm attacks.

State attacks

Asynchronous attacks deal with timing differences. An example of this type of attack is time-of-check/time-of-use (TOC-TOU) where one print job under one user's name is exchanged with the print job for another user. It is achieved through bypassing security controls by attacking information after the controls were exercised (i.e., when the print job is queued) but before the information is used (i.e., prior to printing the job). The best way to prevent these types of attacks is to apply task-sequencing rules combined with encryption.

Stealth virus

A stealth virus is a resident virus that attempts to evade detection by concealing its presence in infected files. To achieve this, the virus intercepts system calls that examine the contents or attributes of infected files. The results of these calls must be altered to correspond to the file's original state. For example, a stealth virus might remove the virus code from an executable when it is read (rather than executed) so that an antivirus software package examines the original, uninfected host program. A stealth virus uses any of a variety of techniques to make itself more difficult to detect. For example, a stealth boot virus typically intercepts attempts to view the sector in which it resides and instead shows the viewing program a copy of the sector as it looked prior to infection. An active stealth file virus typically does not reveal any size increase in infected files when a user issues the DIR command. Stealth viruses must be active, or running, in order to exhibit their stealth qualities.

Steering committee

A steering committee is a group of management representatives from each user area of information systems services that establishes plans and priorities and reviews a project's progress and problems for the purpose of making management decisions.

Stress testing of application programs

Computer application programs are tested with test data chosen for maximum, minimum, and trivial values, or parameters.

Strong authentication

Strong authentication requires the use of multiple factors for authentication using an advanced technology (i.e., dynamic passwords or digital certificates) to verify an entity's identity.

Structured techniques

Structured techniques are an orderly and systematic process that shows interrelationships of activities among all functions of a system and among programs, input data, and output reports. The techniques begin system analysis by specifying user system (output) needs first and then working backward to input data. Structured techniques can be applied to system requirements, design, programming, and testing activities. They can produce small, quality program modules that are easy to maintain.

Subschema

A subschema is a subset of a schema. It represents a portion of a database as it appears to a user or application program.

Synchronization flood attack

Synchronization (SYN) flood attacks can occur in several ways. (1) It can be a stealth attack because the attacker spoofs the source address of the SYN packet, thus making it difficult to identify the perpetrator. (2) It can be used as a method of overwhelming a host computer on the Internet by sending the host a high volume of SYN packets requesting a connection but never responding to the acknowledgment packets returned by the host. In some cases, the damage can be very serious. (3) A synchronization flood attack is a method of disabling a system by sending more SYN packets than its networking code can handle.

Synchronous communication

Synchronous communication is the transmission of data at very high speeds using circuits in which the transfer of data is synchronized by electronic clock signals. Synchronous communication is used within the computer and in high-speed mainframe computer networks.

System development life cycle

System development life cycle (SDLC) is a systematic process for planning, analyzing, designing, developing, implementing, operating, and maintaining a computer-based application system.

System hardening tools

The major purpose of system hardening is to eliminate as many security risks as possible in order to make the system secure and strong. System hardening is achieved by removing all nonessential software and dangerous utility programs from the computer. While some utility programs may offer useful features to users, if they provide back door access to the system, they must be removed during the system hardening process.

Hardening (strengthening) tools help configure a host's computer operating system and application systems to reduce the host's security weaknesses. Several tools and approaches include:

- Strengthen network infrastructure elements such as routers, servers, and switches.
- Remove default accounts and passwords.
- Log configuration change notifications and alerts.
- Strengthen transport, services, and application infrastructure elements.
- Enforce security policies.
- Harden protocols such as hypertext transfer protocol (HTTP), HTTP security (HTTPS), secure shell (SSH), Telnet, and simple network management protocol (SNMP).
- Place software objects in a secure state.
- Implement the failover feature in hardware elements.
- Partition application systems from each other and between data files.
- Install software guards, firewalls, and encryption methods.

Deploy defensive mechanisms with layered security controls.

System integrity

System integrity is the condition that exists when there is complete assurance that any program not authorized by a mechanism under the installation's control cannot (1) circumvent or disable store or fetch protection, (2) access a protected resource, and (3) obtain control in an authorized (supervisor) state. Also, it is the state that exists when there is complete assurance that under all conditions a computer system is based on (1) the logical correctness and reliability of the operating system, (2) the logical completeness of the hardware and software that implement the protection mechanisms, and (3) data integrity.

System integrity exposure

System integrity exposure is a condition that exists when there is a potential of one or more programs that can bypass the installation's control and (1) circumvent or disable store or fetch protection, (2) access a protected resource, and (3) obtain control in an authorized (supervisor) state. This condition can lead to compromise of systems protection mechanisms and data integrity.

System software

System software is the operating system and accompanying utility programs that enable a user to control, configure, and maintain the computer system, software, and data.

Systems analysis

Systems analysis breaks down a large problem into many smaller problems. It is an excellent technique if the desired outcome of the problem-solving session is a detailed understanding of a problem. It is a problem-solving tool.

Tampering attack

Tampering is modifying data, software, firmware, or hardware without authorization. Modifying data in transit, inserting tampered hardware or software into a supply chain, repackaging a legitimate app with malware, modifying network or device configuration (e.g., jailbreaking or rooting a phone) are examples of tampering. Tampering is risky.

Teardrop attack

A teardrop attack can freeze vulnerable hosts by exploiting a bug in the fragmented packet reassembly routines. A countermeasure is to install software patches and upgrades.

TEMPEST

TEMPEST is a short name that refers to the investigation, study, and control of compromising emanations from telecommunications and automated information systems equipment (i.e., spurious electronic signals emitted by electrical equipment). A low signal-to-ratio is preferred to control the TEMPEST-shielded equipment.

TEMPEST attack

A TEMPEST attack is based on leaked electromagnetic radiation, which can directly provide plaintext and other information that an attacker needs to attack. It is a general class of side channel attack.

Text message spam

Text message spam is to a person's cellphone what email spam is to a person's personal computer. Both acts may try to get a person to reveal personal information (e.g., bank account number and Social Security number) for the promise of free gifts or discounted product offers. Clicking on a link in the message can install malware that collects information from a person's phone. Once the spammer gets the needed information, it is sold to marketers or identity thieves. In addition to revealing personal information, the spam can lead to unwanted charges on a user's cellphone bill and it can even slow down the cellphone's performance (i.e., a triple threat). Note that it is illegal to send unsolicited commercial email messages to wireless devices, including cellphones and pagers, unless the sender gets permission first. It's also illegal to send unsolicited text messages from an auto-dialer—telephone equipment that stores and dials phone numbers using a random or sequential number generator. Exceptions to the law include (1) transactional or relationship types of messages. If a company has a prior relationship with an individual, it can send discounted product offers and or warranty information and (2) noncommercial messages such as political surveys or fundraising messages. Security controls include not to reply, not to click on the links provided in the text message, delete the text message, and report the spam to wireless carriers.

Threat

A threat is a potential violation of system security. It is any circumstance with the potential to cause loss or harm. Threats arise from internal failures, human errors, attacks, and natural catastrophes.

Tiger team

A tiger team conducts penetration testing to attempt a system break-in to discover system weaknesses and to recommend security controls. A tiger team is an old name for the new "red team" in IT testing, but some organizations still use it for a different purpose, as follows: In a product development strategy, the tiger team must:

- Understand business use cases and abstract models of a product.

- Develop functional requirements based on the business use cases and abstract models.

- Translate functional requirements into technical standards.

Time bomb

A time bomb is a resident computer program that triggers an unauthorized or damaging action at a predefined time.

Time to recover

Time to recover (TTR) is the time required for any computer resources to be recovered from disruptive events. It is the time required to reestablish an activity from an emergency or degraded mode to a normal mode. It is also defined as emergency response time (EMRT).

Timing attack

Timing attack is a side-channel attack in which the attacker attempts to compromise a cryptosystem by analyzing the time taken to execute cryptographic algorithms. Every logical operation in a computer takes time to execute, and the time can differ based on the input; with precise measurements of the time for each operation, an attacker can work backward to the input. Information can leak from a system through measurement of the time it takes to respond to certain queries. Timing attacks result from poor system/program design and implementation methods. Timing attacks and side-channel attacks are useful in identifying or reverse-engineering a cryptographic algorithm used by some device. Other examples of timing attacks include (1) a clock drift attack, where it can be used to build random number generators; (2) clock skew exploitation based on CPU heating; and (3) attackers who may find fixed Diffie-Hellman exponents and RSA keys to break cryptosystems.

TOC–TOU attack

TOC–TOU stands for time-of-check to time-of-use. An example of a TOC–TOU attack is when one print job under one user's name is exchanged with the print job for another user. It is achieved through bypassing security controls by attacking information after the controls were exercised (that is, when the print job is queued) but before the information is used (that is, prior to printing the job). This attack is based on timing differences and changing states.

Traffic analysis attack

Traffic analysis attacks come in several forms: (1) The act of passively monitoring transmissions to identify communication patterns and participants. (2) A form of passive attack in which an intruder observes information about calls (although not necessarily the contents of the messages) and makes inferences from the source and destination numbers or frequency and length of the messages. The goal is to gain intelligence about a system or its users. It may not require the examination of the content of the communications, which may or may not be decipherable. (3) A traffic flow signal from a reader could be used to detect a particular activity occurring in the communications path. (4) An inference attack occurs when a user or intruder is able to deduce information to which he has no privilege from information to which he has privilege. Traffic-flow security protection can be used to counter traffic analysis attacks.

Transborder data flow

Transborder data flow deals with the movement and storage of data by automatic means across national or federal boundaries. It may require data encryption when data are flowing over some borders or countries.

Tripwire

Tripwire is a network security tool used to monitor the permissions and checksums of important system files to detect if they have been replaced or corrupted. Tripwire can be configured to send an alert to the administrator should any file's recomputed checksum fail to match its baseline, indicating that the file has been altered.

Trojan horse

A Trojan horse is a computer program in which malicious or harmful programming code is packaged inside apparently harmless software or data.

True negative

A true negative occurs when a tool reports a weakness when it is not present.

True positive

A true positive occurs when a tool reports a weakness when it is present.

Tuple

A tuple is a row of a relational table.

Turnaround time

Turnaround time is the time between job submission and job completion.

User-based attacks

Increasingly, attackers use social engineering combined with other techniques to target web users. Often, these attacks occur in the form of phishing attacks, where attackers try to trick users into accessing a fake website and divulging personal information. In some phishing attacks, users receive a legitimate-looking email asking them to update their information on the company's website. Instead of legitimate links, however, the universal resource locators (URLs) in the email actually point to a rogue website. Other phishing attacks are more advanced and take advantage of vulnerabilities in the legitimate website's application. For example, a security flaw in the PayPal website was exploited to steal credit card numbers and other personal information belonging to its users. Visiting users were presented with a message that had been injected into the site that said, "Your account is currently disabled because we think it has been accessed by a third party. You will now be redirected to the Resolution Center." Rather than the Resolution Center, the user was redirected to the attacker's website.

Value-added network

A value-added network (VAN) is a network of computers owned or controlled by a single entity that can be used by subscribers for data transmission, email, information retrieval, and other functions.

Variant virus

A variant virus is a virus generated by modifying a known virus. Examples are modifications that add functionality or evade detection. The term "variant" is usually applied only when the modifications are minor in nature. An example would be changing the trigger date from Friday the 13th to Thursday the 12th.

Version configuration

A version configuration refers to a change to a baseline configuration item that modifies its functional capabilities. As functional capabilities are added to, modified within, or deleted from a baseline configuration item, its version identifier changes.

Virtual private network

A virtual private network (VPN) is a virtual network, built on top of existing physical networks, providing a secure communications tunnel for data and other information transmitted between networks. It uses a split tunneling method to route an organization's specific network traffic through the SSL-VPN tunnel, but other traffic uses the remote user's default gateway (gateway is a network interconnection).

Virtual reality

Virtual reality is a set of hardware and software that creates images, sounds, and possibly the sensation of touch that give the user the feeling of a real environment and experience. In advanced virtual reality systems, the user wears special goggles and gloves.

Virus

A virus is a self-replicating code segment attached to a host executable. (An executable is an abstraction for programs, command files, and other objects on a computer system that can be executed.) There are many types of viruses, including macro, worms, Trojan horse, resident, stealth, and polymorphic.

Vulnerability

A vulnerability is a weakness or flaw that might be exploited to cause loss or harm.

Walkthrough

A walkthrough is a project management technique or procedure where the programmer, project team leader, functional users, system analysts, or managers review system requirements, design, and programming and test plans; design specifications and program code to (1) prevent errors in logic and misinterpretation of user requirements, design, and program specifications, and (2) prevent omissions. It is a detective control.

In a system walkthrough, for example, functional users and information systems staff together review the design or program specifications, program code, test plans, and test cases to detect omissions or errors and to eliminate misinterpretation of system or user requirements. System walkthroughs can also occur within and among colleagues in the information systems and system user departments. It costs less to correct omissions and errors in the early stages of system development than it does later. This technique can be applied to both system development and system maintenance.

Warm site

A warm site is a backup, alternate computer processing location that has the basic infrastructure of a cold site but also has sufficient computer and telecommunications equipment installed and available to operate the system at the site. However, the equipment is not loaded with the software or data required to operate the system. Warm sites are a part of information technology continuity planning.

Watering hole attack

A watering hole attack is a malware attack in which a hacker watches an individual user or a group of users visiting a next (targeted) company's website using browser cookies. Later, the hacker analyzes the security vulnerabilities of the targeted company's website and implants it with malware. Any innocent new user visiting the targeted company's website is redirected to the hacker's malicious website where dangerous code and malvertisements or malvertizing (false advertisements with adware) are present. Later, any innocent new user's computer connected to the hacker's website is infected with the implanted malware. In a way, watering hole attack is a chain-of-attacks on a series of websites.

Watering hole attack = Original company's website 1 ———▶ Targeted company's website 2 ———▶ Hacker's malicious website 3

Security controls to fight against the watering hole attack are to (1) install web content filtering software to control web bugs, (2) educate users about the dangers of this type of attack, and (3) perform web scans to look for abnormal activities on the website.

Web bug

A web bug is a Hypertext Markup Language (HTML) element, often in the form of image tags, that retrieves information from a remote website. While the image may not be visible to the user, the act of making the request can provide information about the user. Web bugs are often embedded in web pages and HTML-enabled email messages.

White box testing

White box testing is a comprehensive software test methodology that assumes explicit and substantial knowledge of the internal structure and implementation detail of the assessment object. It focuses on the internal behavior of a system (program structure and logic) and uses the code itself to generate test cases. The degree of coverage is used as a measure of the completeness of the test cases and test effort. White box testing is performed at the individual components level, such as program or module, but not at the entire system level. It is also known as detailed testing or logic testing and should be combined with black box testing for maximum benefit because neither one by itself does a thorough testing job. White box testing is structured testing, since it focuses on structural analysis of a system. As such, it is also called glass box testing, because the tester can see the inside of a system through a glass using test cases, test data, and program code.

White team

A white team is a neutral team of employees acting as referees and judges between a red team of mock attackers (offenders) and a blue team of actual defenders of their enterprise's use of information systems. The white team establishes rules of engagement and performance metrics for security tests. The white team acts as observers during the red team activity, because it has prior knowledge of unannounced red team activities and ensures that the scope of testing does not exceed a predefined threshold. Occasionally, the white team also performs incident response activities and addresses bot attacks on an emergency basis.

Whitelisting

Several definitions exist for whitelisting: (1) It is a method for controlling the installation of software by ensuring that all software is checked against a list approved by the organization. (2) Whitelisting technology only allows known good applications and does not allow any new or unknown exploits to access a system. (3) It is a list of discrete entities, such as hosts or applications that are known to be benign. (4) It is a list of email senders known to be benign, such as a user's coworkers, friends, and family. Synonymous with whitelists. Whitelisting is a security control.

Wide area network

A wide area network (WAN) is a network concept to link business operations and computers used across geographical locations.

Worm

A worm is a self-replicating, self-propagating, self-contained computer program that uses networking mechanisms to spread itself.

Zap

Zap is a powerful computer utility program that can alter data file and program contents, directly bypassing integrity and security controls (e.g., IBM's Superzap).

Zombie

A zombie is a compromised web server on which an attacker has placed programming code that, when triggered, will launch with other zombies, leading to a denial-of-service attack. It is a program that is installed on one computer system with the intent of causing it to attack other computer systems in a chainlike manner.

- *Sources*: National Institute of Science and Technology (NIST) Glossary (NISTIR 7298), www.nist.gov.

- The Institute of Internal Auditors (IIA) Glossary. www.theiia.org.

Financial Glossary

This financial glossary contains key terms useful to the CIA Exam candidates and students. Reading the glossary terms prior to studying the theoretical subject matter covered in Part 3 of the review book or the study guide and prior to answering the practice questions in Wiley's online test bank can help the candidate understand the domain content better. In addition, this glossary is a good review source for answering multiple-choice questions on the actual CIA Exam. This topical glossary provides a focused reading and study on a single topic for a better retention of key terms as opposed to multiple topics (i.e., business, financial, and technology glossary) put together. We strongly suggest that students read this glossary prior to studying the subject matter covered in the theoretical domains of this book.

Antitrust laws
Antitrust laws are laws that prohibit monopolies, restraint of trade practices, and conspiracies to inhibit competition. They apply to unfair methods of competition that have a direct, substantial, and reasonably foreseeable effect on the domestic, import, or export commerce of the United States.

Arbitrage
Arbitrage is an equalization of foreign exchange rates involving more than two countries.

Business risk
Business risk is the possibility that a company will not be able to meet ongoing operating expenditures. It is the risk associated with projections of a firm's future returns on assets or returns on equity if the firm uses no debt.

Call option
A call option is an option to buy a currency. A call option gives an investor the right, but not the obligation, to buy stock. Therefore, a call option generally will increase in value as the price of the underlying stock increases. Unlike stock, which retains some value even if the price falls, a call option loses all value once it expires. A call option with a strike price that is greater than the stock's market price is referred to as being "out-of-the-money" because there is little to no value in the right to buy a stock at a price greater than its current market price.

Celler-Kefauver Antimerger Act
The Celler-Kefauver Antimerger Act of 1950 amended the Clayton Act to include major asset purchases that decrease competition in an industry.

Clayton Antitrust Act
The Clayton Antitrust Act of 1914 makes price discrimination illegal and prohibits sellers from exclusive arrangements with purchasers and/or product distributors. The Clayton Act

strengthens the Sherman Act by restricting such practices as price discrimination, exclusive dealing, tying contracts, and interlocking boards of directors where the effect may be to substantially lessen competition or tend to create a monopoly.

Credit memo
A credit memo is a document used to correct an overcharge, pay a rebate, or credit the value of goods returned.

Currency swap
A currency swap is an agreement to trade currencies at one date and reverse the trade at a later date. It is a financial market.

Cut-off
A cut-off is a process of verifying that all transactions are recorded in the proper accounting period to protect and provide consistency of input data and output results (based on specific beginning and ending dates).

Derivatives
Derivatives are financial securities where their prices are derived from the value of other financial instruments such as interest rates, foreign exchange rates, commodity prices, stock market prices, gold/silver prices, and gas/oil prices. Examples of derivatives that increase financial risk are future contracts, forward contracts, financial options, and security swaps.

Discount rate
A discount rate is the interest rate at which member banks can borrow from the Federal Reserve banks. It is a cost of borrowing to member banks.

Embargo
An embargo is the most restrictive barrier to exporting to a country, often resulting from political actions.

Federal Trade Commission Act
The Federal Trade Commission Act of 1914 authorizes the Federal Trade Commission (FTC) to interpret trade legislation, including the provisions of the Sherman Antitrust Act that deal with restraint of trade. The act also addresses unfair competition and unfair or deceptive trade practices.

Financial engineering
The goal of financial engineering is to reduce financial risks. Its goals are achieved through financial instruments, such as derivative securities (e.g., hedging with forward contracts). Financial engineering can also be applied to insurance and reinsurance areas using alternate risk transfer methods (e.g., captive insurance) as part of a company's risk mitigation strategy. In a way, financial engineering is related to risk engineering in terms of sharing common goals, such as risks, hedging, insurance, and captive insurance.

Financial risk
A financial risk is a risk arising from volatility in foreign currencies, interest rates, and commodities. It includes credit risk, liquidity risk (bankruptcy risk), interest rate risk, and market risk.

Foreign Corrupt Practices Act (FCPA)
FCPA is an established U.S. code of conduct in 1977 making it illegal for U.S. businesses to bribe foreign government officials, political parties, and political candidates to obtain business or license in foreign countries, even if it is an acceptable practice in the foreign country. It also requires appropriate accounting controls for full disclosure of firms' foreign transactions.

Foreign exchange balancing

Foreign exchange balancing restricts a company's imports by limiting the company's access to foreign exchange to pay for goods to some proportion of the amount of foreign exchange earned by the company.

Forward buying

Forward buying means buying in excess of current requirements as part of strategy or because of anticipated shortages, strikes, or price increases.

Forward market

A forward market is a financial market that buys and sells currencies to be delivered at a future date.

Futures contract

A futures contract is used for the purchase or sale and delivery of commodities at a future date. It is primarily used as a hedging device against market price fluctuations or unforeseen supply shortages.

Grease payments

Grease payments are minor, facilitating payments to officials for the primary purpose of getting them to do whatever they are supposed to do anyway.

Greenfield venture

A greenfield venture is a very risky type of direct investment, whereby a company builds a subsidiary from scratch in a foreign country.

Greenmail

The term "greenmail" refers to a situation in which a firm, trying to avoid a takeover, buys back stock at a price above the existing market price from the person(s) trying to gain control of the firm.

Hart-Scott-Rodino Antitrust Improvements Act

The Hart-Scott-Rodino Antitrust Improvements Act of 1976 amended the Clayton Act by requiring companies to file premerger notifications with the Federal Trade Commission (FTC) and the Antitrust Division of the Justice Department. The Act establishes waiting periods that must elapse before certain acquisitions or tender offers may be consummated and authorizes the enforcement agencies to stay those periods until the companies provide certain additional information about the proposed transaction.

Hedging operation

A hedging operation is done through matching the liability created by borrowing foreign currencies with the asset created by lending domestic currency, both to be repaid at the known future exchange rate.

Horizontal analysis

Horizontal analysis is financial analysis that compares an item in a current statement with the same item in prior statements.

Horizontal market

A horizontal market is a market in which all players buy or sell the same type of product, making them competitors.

Horizontal merger

A horizontal merger is a combination of two firms that produce the same type of good or service.

Hostile takeover
A hostile takeover is the acquisition of a company over the opposition of its management.

Kiting
Kiting is a scheme in which a depositor with accounts in two or more banks takes advantage of the time required for checks to clear in order to obtain unauthorized credit.

Lapping
Lapping is a type of fraud in which an employee misappropriates receipts from customers and covers the shortages in these customers' accounts with receipts from subsequent customers.

Miller-Tydings Resale Price Maintenance Act
The Miller-Tydings Resale Price Maintenance Act of 1937 exempts the interstate fair trade contracts from compliance with antitrust requirements.

Objective risk
Objective risk differs from subjective risk primarily in the sense that it is more precisely observable and therefore measurable. In general, objective risk is the probable variation of actual from expected experience.

Off-balance sheet accounting
Off-balance sheet accounting involves hiding debt or underreporting of liabilities on the balance sheet, thus increasing financial risk of a company and thereby deceiving investors and creditors.

Option contract
An option is a contract that provides the right to buy or sell a given amount of currency at a fixed exchange rate on or before the maturity date. An option contract gives the purchaser the right to buy or sell a given number of shares of the underlying stock before a specified deadline, known as the expiration date, for a predetermined price per share, known as the strike price. It is a financial market risk.

Parent company
A parent company is the company owning a majority of the voting stock of another corporation.

Parent/subsidiary relationship
A parent/subsidiary relationship is a combination of companies where control of other companies, known as subsidiaries, is achieved by a company, known as the parent, through acquisition of voting stock.

Partnership/alliance
A partnership/alliance is a strategy leading to a relationship with suppliers or customers aimed at reducing costs of ownership, maintenance of minimum stocks, just-in-time deliveries, joint participation in design, exchange of information on materials and technologies, new production methods, quality improvement strategies, and the exploitation of market synergy.

Passive investment strategy
A passive investment strategy involves a minimal amount of oversight and very few transactions once the portfolio has been selected.

Portfolio approach
The portfolio approach is a method used to manage economic exposure of a company by offsetting negative exposure in one country with positive exposure in another.

Portfolio risk
Portfolio risk considers risk and return of a firm when it is investing in acquisition or expansion projects. Management needs to find the relationship between the net present values (NPVs)

for new projects and the NPVs for existing projects. In a portfolio framework, the tradeoff between risk and expected NPV for different combinations of investments can be analyzed.

Portfolio strategy

Portfolio strategy is a type of corporate-level strategy that pertains to the organization's mix of strategic business units and product lines that fit together in such a way as to provide the corporation with synergy and competitive advantage.

Pure risk

Risk is a possibility of loss. Many types of risk exist, including pure, speculative, static, dynamic, subjective, and objective risk. Pure risk is a condition in which there is the possibility of loss or no loss (e.g., default of a debtor or disability). Pure risks are of several types, including personal, property, liability, and performance risks. Risk management is a scientific approach to the problem of dealing with the pure risks facing an individual or an organization. Insurance is viewed as simply one of several approaches for dealing with such risks. The techniques of insurance and self-insurance are commonly limited to the treatment of pure risks, such as fire, product liability, and worker's compensation. Traditionally, risk management tools—avoidance, loss control, and transfer—have been applied primarily to the pure or hazard risks facing a firm.

Put option

A put option is an option to sell a currency. It is a financial market risk.

Risk

Risk has several definitions. The term "risk" means the possibility of an event occurring that will have an impact on the achievement of objectives. Risk is measured in terms of impact and likelihood. It is the probability that an event or action may adversely affect the organization or activity under audit. Risk is uncertainty about loss. Risks should be avoided where possible; if not, they should be well managed. There are at least six specific types of risks, including pure, strategic, operational, financial, hazard, and speculative. Risks can be classified or categorized into three basic categories: static versus dynamic, subjective versus objective, and pure versus speculative.

Risk/exposure

A risk is the probability that an undesirable event will occur, resulting in financial or other loss, or otherwise creating a problem. Exposures are caused by the undesirable events. An example of exposure is the damage (loss of time and integrity of data) that errors (both data and processing) may cause. In other words, the causes must exist before exposures result. In this example, errors must exist before the damages occur.

Risk acceptance

The term "risk acceptance" means accepting a potential risk and continuing with operating a process or system. It is like accepting risks as part of doing business (a kind of self-insurance). Risk acceptance is also called risk tolerance and risk appetite in order to achieve a desired result.

Risk analysis

Risk analysis is: (1) an assessment of the vulnerability of a specific facility or organization to various types of occurrences (e.g., flood, power interruption) that affect their information systems operations; (2) the analysis of possible risks to be encountered and the means to handle them that can be performed. A T-column can be used with headings "Anticipated risks" and "Actions to overcome risks." It is a decision-making tool.

Risk appetite

The risk appetite of an organization is the level of risk that it is willing to accept.

Risk assessment

Risk assessment (or risk analysis) includes identification, analysis, measurement, and prioritization of risks. It is the process of identifying the risks and determining the probability of occurrence, the resulting impacts, and additional safeguards that would mitigate these impacts. Risk assessment is a systematic process for assessing and integrating professional judgments about probable adverse conditions and/or events. The risk assessment process should provide a means of organizing and integrating professional judgments for development of the audit work schedule.

Risk assignment

Risk assignment consists of transferring or assigning risk to a third party by using other options to compensate for the loss, such as an insurance company or outsourcing firm.

Risk avoidance

Risk avoidance eliminates the risk causes and/or consequences (e.g., add controls that prevent the risk from occurring, remove certain functions of the system, or shut down the system when risks are identified). It is like reducing, avoiding, or eliminating risks by implementing cost-effective safeguards and controls. Risk situations that have high severity and high frequency of loss should be either avoided or reduced. Risk reduction is appropriate when it is possible to reduce either risk severity or frequency. Otherwise, the risk should be avoided or transferred. Examples of risk avoidance controls include (1) separating threats from assets or assets from threats to minimize risks, and (2) separating resource allocation from resource use to prevent resource misuse.

Risk control

Risk control identifies the presence of or lack of effective controls to prevent, detect, or correct risks. Risk control focuses on minimizing the risk of loss to which an organization is exposed. The situation of high frequency and low severity should be managed with additional controls (loss control). Risk control includes risk avoidance and risk reduction.

Risk engineering

The goal of risk engineering is to reduce risks in traditional and nontraditional insurance activities, which is achieved, in part, through risk financing to fund financial losses. Risk financing includes internal funds for risks (e.g., self-insurance and residual risk) and external transfer of risks (e.g., insurance, hedging, and captive insurance). In a way, risk engineering is related to financial engineering in terms of sharing common goals, such as risks, hedging, insurance, and captive insurance.

Risk financing

Risk financing concentrates on arranging the availability of internal funds to meet occurring financial losses. It also involves external transfer of risk. Risk financing includes risk retention and risk transfer, which is a tool used by captive insurers. Risk retention applies to risks that have a low expected frequency and a low potential severity. Risk transfer applies to risks that have a low expected frequency and a high potential severity (e.g., buying insurance). Insurance should be purchased for losses in excess of a firm's risk retention level.

When losses have both high expected frequency and high potential severity, it is likely that risk retention, risk transfer, and loss control all will need to be used in varying degrees. Common methods of loss control include reducing the probability of losses (i.e., frequency and severity reduction) and decreasing the cost of losses that do occur (i.e., cost reduction). Note that "high" and "low" loss frequency and severity rates are defined differently for different firms.

Risk financing includes internal funding for risks (self-insurance and residual risk) and external transfer of risks, such as insurance and hedging. It can be unfunded or funded retention of risks. The unfunded retention is treated as part of the overall cost of doing business. A firm may decide to practice funded retention by making various pre-loss arrangements to ensure that money is readily available to pay for losses that occur. Examples of funded retention include use of credit, reserve funds, self-insurance, and captive insurers.

Risk limitation

The term "risk limitation" means limiting or containing risks by implementing controls that minimize the adverse impact of a threat's exercising a vulnerability (e.g., use of supporting, preventive, and detective controls) or by authorizing operation for a limited time during which additional risk mitigation efforts by other means is installed.

Risk management

Risk management is the total process of identifying, assessing, controlling, and mitigating risks as it deals with uncertainty. It includes risk assessment (risk analysis); cost/benefit analysis; the selection, implementation, testing, and evaluation of safeguards (risk mitigation); risk financing (risk funding); and risk monitoring (reporting, feedback, and evaluation). It is expressed as:

$$\text{Risk Management} = \text{Risk Assessment} + \text{Risk Mitigation} + \text{Risk Financing} + \underline{\text{Risk Monitoring}}$$

The ultimate goal of risk management is to minimize the adverse effects of losses and uncertainty connected with pure risks. Risk management is broken down into two major categories: risk control and risk financing.

Risk mapping

Risk mapping involves profiling risk events to their sources (i.e., threats and vulnerabilities), determining their impact levels (i.e., low, medium, or high), and evaluating the presence of or lack of effective controls to mitigate risks.

Risk mitigation

Risk mitigation involves implementation of preventive, detective, and corrective controls along with management, operational, and technical controls to reduce the effects of risks. It includes designing and implementing controls and control-related procedures to minimize risks.

Risk monitoring

Risk monitoring addresses internal and external reporting and provides feedback into the risk assessment process, continuing the loop.

Risk registers

Risk registers document the risks below the strategic level and include inherent risks (high or higher) and unchanged residual risks, lack of or ineffectiveness of key internal controls, and lack of mitigating factors (e.g., contingency plans and monitoring activities). Risk registers provide direct links among risk categories, risk aspects, audit universe, and internal controls.

Risk retention

Risk retention is retention of risks and is most appropriate for situations in which there is a low probability of occurrence (frequency) with a low potential severity for an event. These are situations that seldom occur, and, when they do happen, the financial impact is small or negligible. Severity dictates whether a risk should be retained. If the potential severity is more than the organization can afford, retention is not recommended. Frequency determines whether the risk is economically insurable. The higher the probabilities of loss, the higher the expected value of loss and the higher the cost of transfer.

Risk spreading or sharing

Risk spreading or sharing involves spreading or sharing risks with other divisions or business units of the same organization. It is viewed as a special case of risk transfer, in which the risk is transferred from an individual to a group, from one division to another, or from one business unit to another. It is a form of risk retention, depending on the success of the risk-sharing arrangement.

Risk transfer
Risk transfer involves payment by one party (the transferor) to another party (the transferee, or risk bearer). The five forms of risk transfer are: hold-harmless agreements, incorporation, diversification, hedging, and insurance. Risk transfer is most likely ideal for a risk with a low expected frequency and a high potential severity.

Robinson-Patman Act
The Robinson-Patman Act of 1936 further addresses the issue of price discrimination established in the Clayton Act. It prohibits sellers from offering a discriminatory price where the effect of discrimination may limit competition or create a monopoly. There is also a provision that prohibits purchasers from inducing a discriminatory price. While a seller may legally lower price as a concession during negotiations, the purchaser should not mislead or trick the seller, thus resulting in a price that is discriminatory to other buyers in the market.

Scenario analysis
Scenario analysis is a risk analysis technique in which "bad" and "good" sets of financial circumstances are compared with a most likely, or base case, situation.

Scenario building
Scenario building involves identifying crucial variables and determining their effects on different cases or approaches.

Scenario planning
Scenario planning is a strategic planning process that generates multiple stories about possible future conditions, allowing an organization to look at the potential impact on them and different ways they could respond.

Scenario writing
Scenario writing is a qualitative forecasting method that consists of developing a conceptual scenario of the future based on a well-defined set of assumptions.

Sensitivity analysis
Sensitivity analysis refers to the study of how changes in the probability assessments for the states of nature and/or changes in the payoffs affect the recommended decision alternative. It involves using a model to determine the extent to which a change in a factor affects an outcome. The analysis is done by repeating if-then calculations. Sensitivity analysis is a means of incorporating risk in financial outcomes that involves varying key inputs, one at a time, and observing the effect on the decision variable(s). For example, the analyst might vary the sales level and observe the effect on the company's cash forecast. It is also called what-if analysis.

Sherman Antitrust Act
The Sherman Antitrust Act of 1890 prohibits actions that are "in constraint of trade" or actions that attempt to monopolize a market or create a monopoly. Legal actions under this act typically involve price fixing or other forms of collusion among sellers. However, the law also prohibits reciprocity or reciprocal purchase agreements.

Speculative risk
Speculative risk exists when there is uncertainty about an event that could produce either a profit or a loss. It involves the chance of loss or gain (e.g., hedging, options, and derivatives).
A spot market is a financial market where buying and selling of foreign exchange takes place or where currencies are traded for current delivery on the spot.

Spread
Spread is the difference between selling and buying rates of a foreign exchange. It is a financial market risk.

Static risk

Static risk, which can be either pure or speculative, stems from an unchanging society that is in stable equilibrium. Examples of pure static risk include the uncertainties due to such random events as lightning, windstorms, and death. Business undertakings in a stable economy illustrate the concept of speculative static risk.

Strategic alliance

A strategic alliance is a firm's collaboration with companies in other countries to share rights and responsibilities as well as revenues and expenses as defined in a written agreement. Some common types of strategic alliances are research collaboration, a licensing program, and a copromotion deal. A strategic alliance is two or more companies that band together to attain efficiency. *See* Joint venture. A strategic alliance is a form of strategic partnership.

Strategic risk

Strategic risk is a high-level and corporate-wide risk, which includes strategy, political, economic, regulatory, reputation, global, leadership, customer, and market brand management risk. It is also related to failure of strategy and changing customer needs and business conditions.

Striking price

A striking price is the price at which currency can be bought or sold in a financial market.

Subjective risk

"Subjective risk" refers to the mental state of an individual who experiences doubt or worry as to the outcome of a given event. In addition to being subjective, a particular risk may be either pure or speculative and either static or dynamic.

Transaction

A transaction is a logical unit of work for an end user. Also, the term is used to define a program or a dialog in a computer system.

Vertical analysis

Vertical analysis is an analysis that compares each item in a current statement with a total amount within the same statements. It is a tool that converts financial statement numbers to percentages so that they are easy to understand and analyze.

Vertical market

A vertical market is a market in which the goods of one business are used as raw materials or components in the production or sale process of another business.

What-if analysis

What-if analysis is a trial-and-error approach to learning about the range of possible outputs for a model. Trial values are chosen for the model inputs (these are the what-ifs) and the value of the output(s) is computed. It is an analysis that is conducted to test the degree to which one variable affects another. It is also called sensitivity analysis.

Worst-case scenario

A worst-case scenario is an analysis in which all of the input variables are set at their worst reasonably forecasted values.

- *Sources*: U.S. GAO's Financial Audit Manual Glossary. www.gao.gov.
- The Institute of Internal Auditors (IIA) Glossary. www.theiia.org.

About the Author

S. RAO VALLABHANENI is an educator, author, publisher, consultant, and practitioner in business with more than 30 years of management and teaching experience in auditing, accounting, manufacturing, and IT consulting in both public and private sectors. He is the author of more than 60 trade books, study guides, review books, monographs, audit guides, and articles on auditing and IT, mostly to prepare candidates for professional certification exams in business. He holds 24 professional certifications in business management in the general management, accounting, auditing, finance, information technology (IT), manufacturing, quality, and human resource fields. He taught several undergraduate and graduate courses in business administration and management programs at the university level for many years. He earned four master's degrees in management, accounting, industrial engineering, and chemical engineering.

Index